NP 27

CHANNEL PILOT

Isles of Scilly and south coast of England,
from Cape Cornwall to Bognor Regis,
and
north-west and north coasts of France,
from Pointe de Penmarc'h to Cap d'Antifer

SEVENTH EDITION
2008

PUBLISHED BY THE UNITED KINGDOM HYDROGRAPHIC OFFICE

Previous editions of Admiralty Pilots
covering the same area:

PREFACE

The Seventh Edition of the *Channel Pilot* has been prepared by Captain M. Waight, Master Mariner based on the fully revised Sixth Edition (2005) compiled by Mr S. C. Mason, Captain R. S. Coles, Master Mariner and Captain M. Waight, Master Mariner. The United Kingdom Hydrographic Office has used all reasonable endeavours to ensure that this Pilot contains all the appropriate information obtained by and assessed by it at the date shown below. Information received or assessed after that date will be included in *Admiralty Notices to Mariners* where appropriate. If in doubt, see *The Mariner's Handbook* for details of what *Admiralty Notices to Mariners* are and how to use them.

This edition supersedes the Sixth Edition (2005), which is cancelled.

Information on climate and currents has been based on data provided by the Met Office, Exeter.

The following sources of information, other than UKHO Publications and Ministry of Defence papers, have been consulted:

British
> *Ports of the World 2007*
> *Port Handbooks produced by Port Authorities*
> *Lloyd's Register Fairplay, Ports and Terminals Guide 2006-2007*
> *Whitaker's Almanack 2008*
> *The Statesman's Year Book 2008*

French
> *Instructions Nautiques C2A France (Côtes Nord et Ouest) 2005 with corrections to March 2008*

General
> *Port websites produced by Port Authorities*

Mr M S Robinson
Chief Executive of the United Kingdom Hydrographic Office

The United Kingdom Hydrographic Office
Admiralty Way
Taunton
Somerset TA1 2DN
England
1st May 2008

CONTENTS

CHAPTER 1

CHAPTER 2

CHAPTER 3

CHAPTER 4

CHAPTER 5

CHAPTER 6

EXPLANATORY NOTES

Admiralty Sailing Directions are intended for use by vessels of 150 gt or more. They amplify charted detail and contain information needed for safe navigation which is not available from Admiralty charts, or other hydrographic publications. They are intended to be read in conjunction with the charts quoted in the text.

This volume of Sailing Directions will be kept up-to-date by the issue of a new edition at intervals of approximately 3 years, without the use of supplements. In addition important amendments which cannot await the new edition are published in Section IV of the weekly editions of *Admiralty Notices to Mariners*. A list of such amendments and notices in force is published quarterly. Those still in force at the end of the year are reprinted in the *Annual Summary of Admiralty Notices to Mariners*.

This volume should not be used without reference to Section IV of the weekly editions of Admiralty Notices to Mariners.

References to United Kingdom Hydrographic Office publications and *The International Code of Signals*

The Mariner's Handbook gives general information affecting navigation and is complementary to this volume of Sailing Directions.

Ocean Passages for the World and *Routeing Charts* contain ocean routeing information and should be consulted for other than coastal passages.

Admiralty List of Lights or *Admiralty Digital List of Lights* should be consulted for details of lights, lanbys and fog signals, as these are not fully described in this volume of Sailing Directions.

Admiralty List of Radio Signals should be consulted for information relating to coast radio stations, pilotage services, vessel traffic services, port operations, radar beacons and radio direction finding stations, meteorological services, radio aids to navigation, Global Maritime Distress and Safety System (GMDSS) and Differential Global Positioning System (DGPS) stations, as these are only briefly referred to in this volume of Sailing Directions.

Admiralty Digital Radio Signals Volume 6 may also be consulted for information relating to pilotage services, vessel traffic services, port operations and ship reporting systems.

Annual Summary of Admiralty Notices to Mariners contains, in addition to the temporary and preliminary notices, and amendments and notices affecting Sailing Directions, a number of notices giving information of a permanent nature covering radio messages and navigational warnings, distress and rescue at sea and exercise areas.

The International Code of Signals should be consulted for details of distress and life-saving signals, international ice-breaker signals as well as international flag signals.

Remarks on subject matter

Buoys are generally described in detail only when they have special navigational significance, or where the scale of the chart is too small to show all the details clearly.

Chapter index diagrams in this volume show only those Admiralty charts of a suitable scale to give good coverage of the area. Mariners should consult NP 131 *Catalogue of Admiralty Charts and Publications* for details of larger scale charts.

Chart references in the text normally refer to the largest scale Admiralty chart but occasionally a smaller scale chart may be quoted where its use is more appropriate.

Firing, practice and exercise areas. Submarine exercise areas are mentioned in Sailing Directions. Other firing, practice and exercise areas may be mentioned with limited details. Signals and buoys used in connection with these areas may be mentioned if significant for navigation. Attention is invited to the Annual Notice to Mariners on this subject.

Names have been taken from the most authoritative source. When an obsolete name still appears on the chart, it is given in brackets following the proper name at the principal description of the feature in the text and where the name is first mentioned.

Port plans in this book are intended to assist the mariner in orientation and they are not to be used for navigation. The appropriate scale of chart should always be used.

Tidal information relating the daily vertical movements of the water is not given. For this information *Admiralty Tide Tables* or *Admiralty Total Tide* should be consulted. Changes in water level of an abnormal nature are mentioned.
Time difference used in the text when applied to the time of High Water found from the *Admiralty Tide Tables*, gives the time of the event being described in the Standard Time kept in the area of that event. Due allowance must be made for any seasonal daylight saving time which may be kept.

Wreck information is included where drying or below-water wrecks are relatively permanent features having significance for navigation or anchoring.

Units and terminology used in this volume

Latitude and Longitude given in brackets are approximate and are taken from the chart quoted.

Bearings and directions are referred to the true compass and when given in degrees are reckoned clockwise from 000° (North) to 359°
Bearings used for positioning are given from the reference object.
Bearings of objects, alignments and light sectors are given as seen from the vessel.
Courses always refer to the course to be made good over the ground.

Winds are described by the direction from which they blow.

Tidal streams and currents are described by the direction towards which they flow.

Distances are expressed in sea miles of 60 to a degree of latitude and sub-divided into cables of one tenth of a sea mile.

Depths are given below chart datum, except where otherwise stated.

Heights of objects refer to the height of the object above the ground and are invariably expressed as "... m in height".

Elevations, as distinct from heights, are given above Mean High Water Springs or Mean Higher High Water whichever is quoted in *Admiralty Tide Tables*, and expressed as, "an elevation of ... m". However the elevation of natural features such as hills may alternatively be expressed as "... m high" since in this case there can be no confusion between elevation and height.

Metric units are used for all measurements of depths, heights and short distances, but where feet/fathoms charts are referred to, these latter units are given in brackets after the metric values for depths and heights shown on the chart.

Time is expressed in the four-figure notation beginning at midnight and is given in local time unless otherwise stated. Details of local time kept will be found in *Admiralty List of Radio Signals Volume 2*.

Bands is the word used to indicate horizontal marking.

Stripes is the word used to indicate markings which are vertical, unless stated to be diagonal.

Conspicuous objects are natural and artificial marks which are outstanding, easily identifiable and clearly visible to the mariner over a large area of sea in varying conditions of light. If the scale is large enough they will normally be shown on the chart in bold capitals and may be marked "conspic".

Prominent objects are those which are easily identifiable, but do not justify being classified as conspicuous.

Principal marks are marks which qualify for inclusion and are outstanding and clearly visible throughout most of the waterway (or 15 to 20 miles of the waterway for particularly long waterways) as marks by day or lights by night; thereby being associated with the waterway as a whole, rather than being confined to any single set of Directions with it. In particular:
Landmarks comprise buildings and structures (including lighthouses, whether major lights or not), daymarks and natural features. They may be on the coast or farther inland, provided they are distinctly visible from seaward.
Offshore marks include light vessels, light floats, lanbys, buoyant beacons, and oil production platforms.
Major lights is used in Sailing Directions to refer to all lights with a range of 15 miles or over.

ABBREVIATIONS

The following abbreviations are used in the text:

AIS	Automatic Identification System	IALA	International Association of Lighthouse Authorities
ALC	Articulated loading column	IHO	International Hydrographic Organization
ALP	Articulated loading platform	IMDG	International Maritime Dangerous Goods
AMVER	Automated Mutual Assistance Vessel Rescue System	IMO	International Maritime Organization
ASL	Archipelagic Sea Lane	ITCZ	Intertropical Convergence Zone
ATBA	Area To Be Avoided		
		JRCC	Joint Rescue Co-ordination Centre
°C	degrees Celsius		
CALM	Catenary anchor leg mooring	kHz	kilohertz
CBM	Conventional buoy mooring	km	kilometre(s)
CHA	Competent Harbour Authority	kn	knot(s)
cm	centimetre(s)	kW	kilowatt(s)
CDC	Certain Dangerous Cargo		
CVTS	Co-operative Vessel Traffic System	LANBY	Large Automatic Navigation Buoy
		LASH	Lighter Aboard Ship
DF	direction finding	LAT	Lowest Astronomical Tide
DG	degaussing	LF	low frequency
DGPS	Differential Global Positioning System	LHG	Liquefied Hazardous Gas
DW	Deep Water	LMT	Local Mean Time
DSC	Digital Selective Calling	LNG	Liquefied Natural Gas
dwt	deadweight tonnage	LOA	Length overall
DZ	danger zone	LPG	Liquefied Petroleum Gas
		LW	Low Water
E	east (easterly, eastward, eastern, easternmost)	m	metre(s)
EEZ	exclusive economic zone	mb	millibar(s)
ELSBM	Exposed location single buoy mooring	MCTS	Marine Communications and Traffic Services Centres
ENE	east-north-east	MF	medium frequency
EPIRB	Emergency Position Indicating Radio Beacon	MHz	megahertz
ESE	east-south-east	MHHW	Mean Higher High Water
ETA	estimated time of arrival	MHLW	Mean Higher Low Water
ETD	estimated time of departure	MHW	Mean High Water
EU	European Union	MHWN	Mean High Water Neaps
		MHWS	Mean High Water Springs
feu	forty foot equivalent unit	MLHW	Mean Lower High Water
fm	fathom(s)	MLLW	Mean Lower Low Water
FPSO	Floating production storage and offloading vessel	MLW	Mean Low Water
FPU	Floating production unit	MLWN	Mean Low Water Neaps
FSO	Floating storage and offloading vessel	MLWS	Mean Low Water Springs
ft	foot (feet)	mm	millimetre(s)
		MMSI	Maritime Mobile Service Identity
g/cm³	gram per cubic centimetre	MRCC	Maritime Rescue Co-ordination Centre
GMDSS	Global Maritime Distress and Safety System	MRSC	Maritime Rescue Sub-Centre
GPS	Global Positioning System	MSI	Marine Safety Information
GRP	glass reinforced plastic	MSL	Mean Sea Level
grt	gross register tonnage (obsolete)	MV	Motor Vessel
gt	gross tonnage	MW	megawatt(s)
		MY	Motor Yacht
HAT	Highest Astronomical Tide	N	north (northerly, northward, northern, northernmost)
HF	high frequency		
hm	hectometre	NATO	North Atlantic Treaty Organization
HMS	Her (His) Majesty's Ship	Navtex	Navigational Telex System
hp	horse power	NE	north-east
hPa	hectopascal	NNE	north-north-east
HSC	High Speed Craft	NNW	north-north-west
HW	High Water	No	number
		nrt	net register tonnage (obsolete)

nt	net tonnage
NW	north-west
ODAS	Ocean Data Acquisition System
PEC	Pilotage Exemption Certificate
PEL	Port Entry Light
PLEM	Pipe line end manifold
PMSC	Port Marine Safety Code
POL	Petrol, Oil & Lubricants
PSSA	Particularly Sensitive Sea Areas
PWC	Personal watercraft
RCC	Rescue Co-ordination Centre
RMS	Royal Mail Ship
RN	Royal Navy
RoRo	Roll-on, Roll-off
RT	radio telephony
S	south (southerly, southward, southern, southernmost)
SALM	Single anchor leg mooring system
SALS	Single anchored leg storage system
SAR	Search and Rescue
Satnav	Satellite navigation
SBM	Single buoy mooring
SE	south-east
SHA	Statutory Harbour Authority
SPM	Single point mooring
sq	square
SRR	Search and Rescue Region
SS	Steamship
SSCC	Ship Sanitation Control Certificate

SSE	south-south-east
SSCEC	Ship Sanitation Control Exemption Certificate
SSW	south-south-west
STS	ship to ship
SW	south-west
SWATH	small waterplane area twin hull ship
teu	twenty foot equivalent unit
TSS	Traffic Separation Scheme
UHF	ultra high frequency
UKC	under keel clearance
UKHO	United Kingdom Hydrographic Office
ULCC	Ultra Large Crude Carrier
UN	United Nations
UT	Universal Time
UTC	Co-ordinated Universal Time
VDR	Voyage Data Recorder
VHF	very high frequency
VLCC	Very Large Crude Carrier
VMRS	Vessel Movement Reporting System
VTC	Vessel Traffic Centre
VTMS	Vessel Traffic Management System
VTS	Vessel Traffic Services
W	west (westerly, westward, western, westernmost)
WGS	World Geodetic System
WMO	World Meteorological Organization
WNW	west-north-west
WSW	west-south-west
WT	radio (wireless) telegraphy

GLOSSARY

Terms occasionally found on the charts and in the sailing directions, and to assist the mariner in the use of French charts and publications.

FRENCH

French	English
abri, abrité	shelter, sheltered
aigu, -e	pointed, sharp
aiguille	needle
amer	landmark, beacon
amont	upstream, landward
appontement	landing stage
anse	bay, cove
argile	clay
arrière-port	inner port
asséchant	drying
aval	downstream, seaward
avant-port	outer port
azur	blue
baie	bay
balise	beacon
baliser	to mark
banc	bank
barre	bar
bas,-se	low
basse	shoal
basse mer	low water
bassin	basin, dock
bassin à flot	wet basin
batterie	battery
blanc, -he	white
bleu, -e	blue
bois	woods
bouche	mouth of a river
boue	mud
bouée	buoy
brisant, brisants	shoal, breakers
brise-lames	breakwater
brouillard	fog
brume	mist
butte	knoll, mound
caboteur	coaster
cale	ramp, slip
canal	canal, channel
cap	cape, headland
carré, -e	square
chaîne	chain, range of mountains
champ-de-tir	firing range
chantier	dockyard
château	castle
château d'eau	water tower
chausée	bank, causeway
chenal	channel
clocher	steeple, belfry
col	neck, mountain pass
colline	hill
côte	coast
courant	current, stream
couvent	convent
crête	ridge, crest
crique	creek
croix	cross
darse	basin
débarcadère	wharf, landing place
découvrant	uncovering, drying
détroit	strait, narrow
déversoir	weir
digue	mole, breakwater
douane	customs
droit	right (side)

French	English
duc d'albe	dolphin
dur, -e	hard
échouage	beaching
écluse	lock of a canal or basin, sluice
écueil	rock, reef
église	church
épave	wreck
épi	short mole, spur
est	east
estuaire	estuary
étale	slack water
étier	a creek which can receive small vessels
falaise	cliff
flèche	spire
fleuve	river, stream
flot	flood tide
forêt	forest
fosse	ditch, a deep
gabare	lighter
galets	shingle
gauche	left (side)
golfe	gulf
goulet	inlet, narrow entrance
grand, -e	great
gravier	gravel
grève	sandy beach
gris, -e	grey
gros, -se	coarse, large
guérite	watch-tower, turret
guet	lookout
haut, -e	high, tall
haut-fond	a shoal
hauturier	deep-sea
havre	haven
île	island, isle
îlot	islet
jaune	yellow
jetée	jetty
jusant	ebb tide
lac	lake
lamanage	inshore pilotage
large	broad, wide
maison	house
marais	swamp, marsh
marée	tide
menhir	a large raised stone
mer	sea
méridional, -e	southern
milieu	middle
môle	mole, pier
mont, montagne	mount, mountain
morte-eau	neap tide
mouillage	anchorage
moulin	mill
mur	wall
musoir	mole, pierhead
neuf, -ve	new
nez	nose, promontory

FRENCH (continued)

noeud	knot
noir, -e	black
nord	north
nouveau, -el, -elle	new
occidental, -e	western
oriental, -e	eastern
ouest	west
passe	passage, pass
pertuis	opening or strait
petit, -e	small
phare	lighthouse
pic	peak
pierre	stone
pignon	gable
pin	pine or fir tree
plage	shore, beach
plaine	plain
plat, -e	flat, level
plateau	table land, or flat below water
pleine mer	high water
pointe	point
pont	bridge, deck
port	port, harbour
presqu'île	peninsula
quai	quay, wharf
rade	road, roadstead
raz	race, violent tidal stream
récif	reef
redoute	redoubt, fort
ressac	surf

rivage	shore
rive	bank of river
rivière	river
roche	rock
rocher	rock generally above water
rond, -e	round
rouge	red
roux, rousse	reddish
ruisseau	rivulet
sable	sand
sablon	fine sand
saline	salt water lagoon, salt works
septentrional, -e	northern
sommet	summit
sud	south
tenue	holding ground
terre-plein	levelled ground, platform
tertre	hillock, knoll
tête	head
torrent	stream, torrent
tour	tower
tourelle	small tower, turret
traverse	shallow ridge across channel or river
val	narrow valley
vallée	valley
vasière	mudbank
vert, -e	green
vieil, vieille, vieux	old, ancient
village	village
ville	town
vive-eau	spring tide

BRETON

Breton	*English*
aber	haven, river mouth
ar	the, on
arvor	coast
aven	river, stream
barr	top, summit, rocky shoal
baz	shoal
beg	point, summit
benven, bosven	rock which never covers
bian, bihan	little, small
braz, bras	great
carn	cairn
doun, don	deep
du	black
enez, inis	island
er	the
garo	rugged, hard
glas	green
gwenn	white
hir	long
karreg	reef, rock
kleiz	north
koad, goad	wood, forest
kornog	shoal
koz	old
kréac'h, krech	hillock, knoll
kreiz	middle
krenn	round, massive

Breton	*English*
laez	high
lann	monastery
léach, lec'h	flat rock
ledan	wide, broad
lemm	pointed, sharp
lost	tail, projection
men, mein (pl.)	stone
melen	yellow
menez	mountain
meur	great
mor, vor	sea
nevez	new
pell	far off
penn	head
porzig, porz	port, harbour
poul	roadstead
poull	lake, hole, pool
raz	strait, strong tidal stream
reter	east
roc'h	rock
run(iou)	hill
ruz	red
ster	river
stiv, stiff	fountain, spring
toull	hole, pass, low
traoñ, traou	low, west, valley
trez	sandy beach, sand
uhel	high

*BRETON GEOGRAPHICAL NAMES

The language of Brittany, or Armorica, belongs to the Brythonic or southern Keltic group; it is akin to that of the Welsh and Old Cornish, by whom it was introduced in the fifth and sixth centuries. Breton (Brezoneg) is spoken westward of a line from Baie de Saint Brieuc to the mouth of La Vilaine.

The orthography of Breton names is much gallicised: e.g., k often becomes c or qu; g before e or i becomes gu; em, en, become French nasal im, in, etc.: e.g., Kemper becomes Quimper. There are four main dialects; that of Vannes is the most distinct, particularly in keeping the stress on the final, instead of on the penultimate, syllable.

Initial consonants are subject to "Mutations", but there is no nasal form as in Welsh, though Breton is full of nasal sounds. The consonants g, b, d, are also subject, when medial, to "Provections", i.e., after certain words they become k, p, t.

The following is the Table of Mutations and Provection:—

Radical Form	Middle Mutation	Weak Mutation	Provection
k	g	c'h	
p	b	f	
t	d	z	
g	c'h		k
b	v		p
d	z		t
m	v		
s	z		
gw	w		kw

Alphabets of Foreign Languages, 2nd Edition, published by The Royal Geographical Society, London, 1933.

Examples:— Karrek Greis (kreis), Roc'h Zu (du), Lizen Ven (men).

The definite article is ar, which becomes al before I and an before d, n, t, or a vowel; it is not much used in place-names.

The letters a, b, d, e, f, g, h, i, k, 1, m, n, o, p, r, s, t, v, w, y, z, in Breton are identical with the corresponding letters in R.G.S. II, except that b and d are explosive as in Gaelic, and n has both hard, liquid, and nasal sounds.

The following are different:–

Breton	R.G.S. II	
ch	sh	Welsh si; rare.
c'h	kh	Penmarc'h. (The French mispronounce c'h, either as k or mute)
j	zh	As French j.
lh	Iy, I'	
ou	u	Welsh vowel w; Douarnenez
u	u, w	As French u, but sometimes written for w: Guengamp for Gwengamp (French — Guingamp).

Chapter Index Diagram

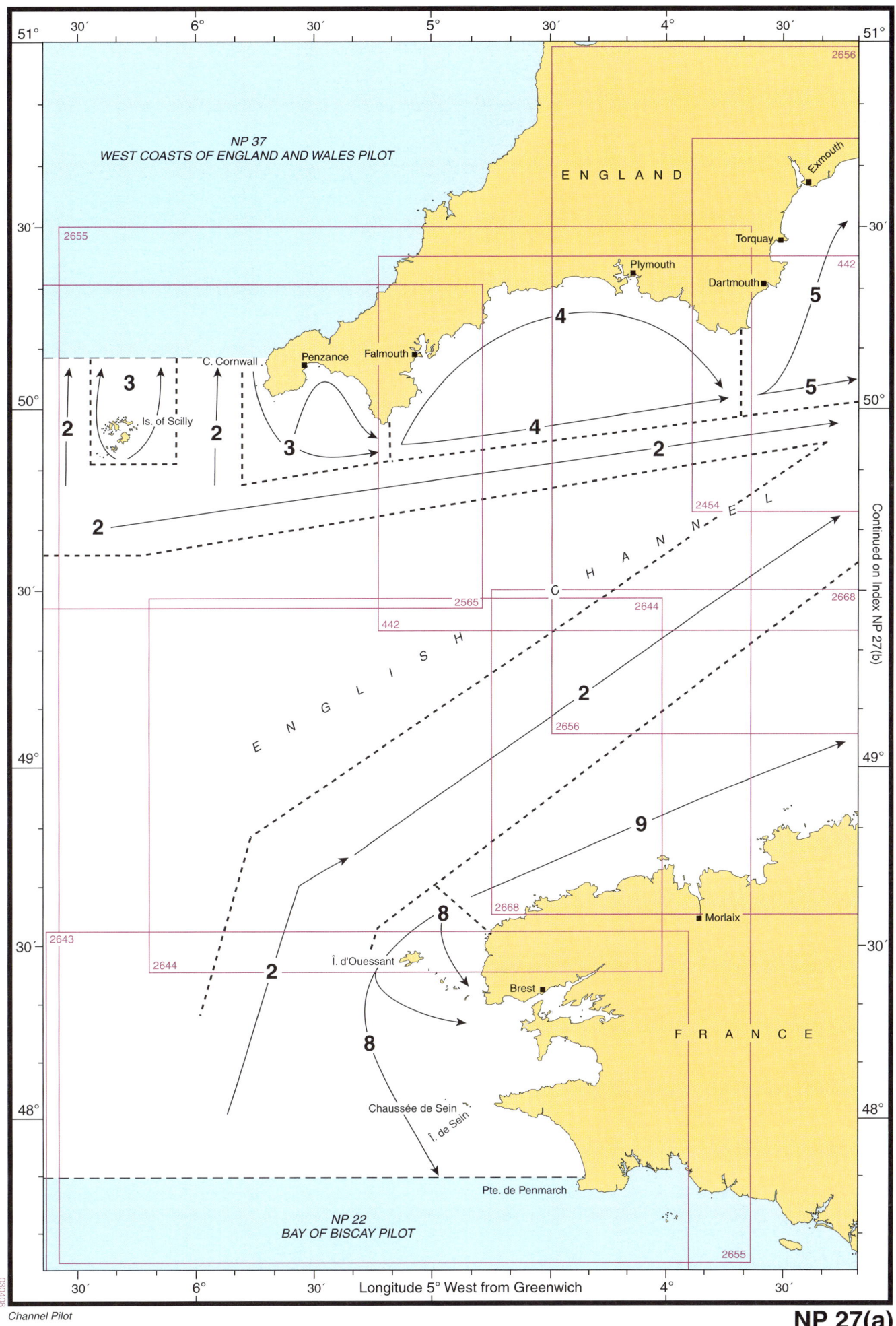

Chapter Index Diagram

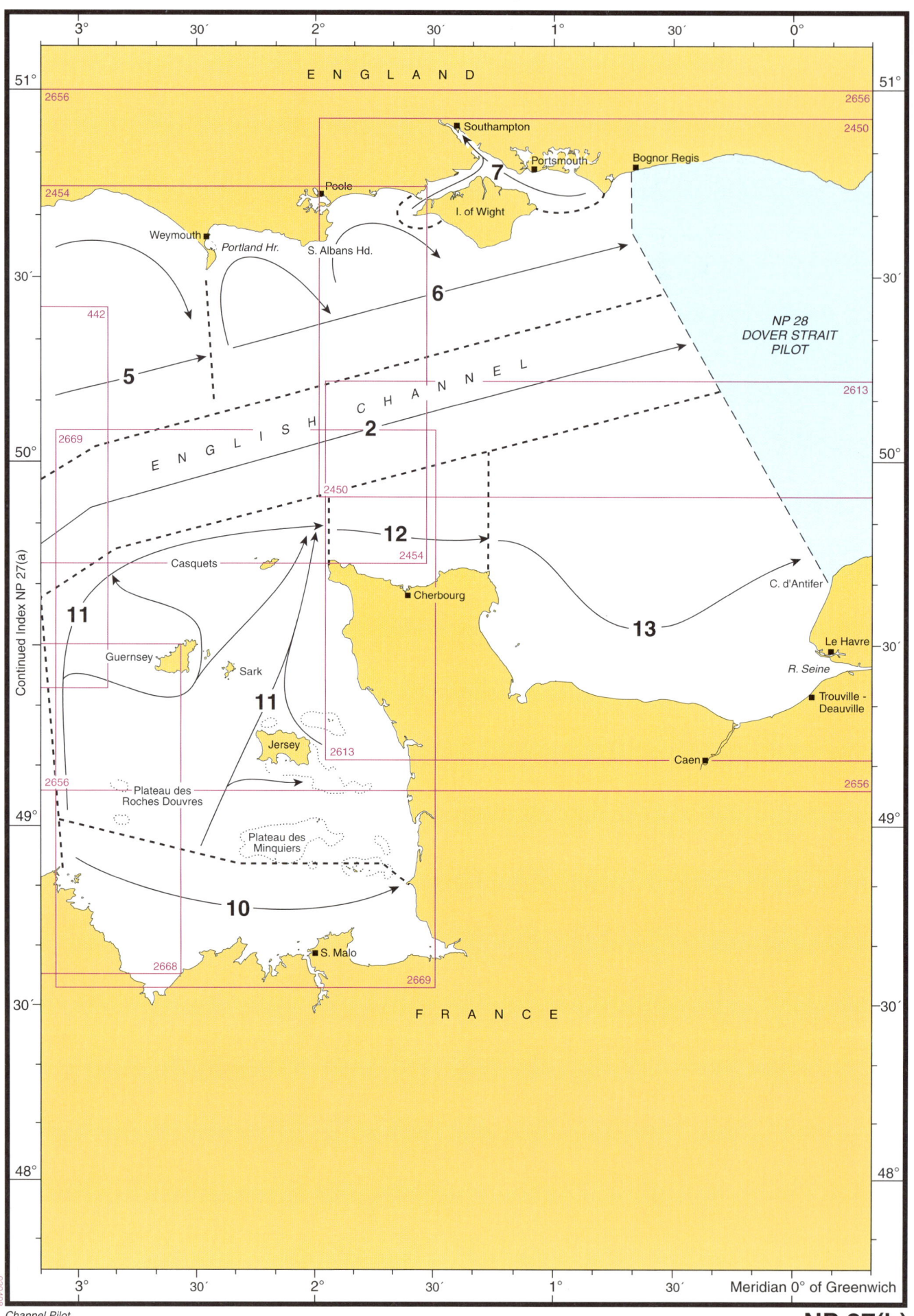

NP 27(b)

Channel Pilot

ENGLAND

Southampton

Portsmouth

Bognor Regis

Poole

Weymouth

Portland Hr.

S. Albans Hd.

I. of Wight

7

6

5

2

NP 28 DOVER STRAIT PILOT

Casquets

12

Cherbourg

11

Guernsey

Sark

11

Jersey

13

C. d'Antifer

Le Havre

R. Seine

Trouville - Deauville

Plateau des Roches Douvres

Plateau des Minquiers

Caen

10

S. Malo

FRANCE

ENGLISH CHANNEL

Continued Index NP 27(a)

Meridian 0° of Greenwich

2656 2450 2454 442 2669 2613 2656 2668 2669

CHANNEL PILOT

CHAPTER 1
NAVIGATION AND REGULATIONS
COUNTRIES AND PORTS
NATURAL CONDITIONS

NAVIGATION AND REGULATIONS

LIMITS OF THE BOOK

Charts 2649, 2656, 2675, 4103

Area covered

1.1

1   This volume contains sailing directions for the English Channel and its W approaches.

The seaward limits of the volume extend W from Cape Cornwall and Pointe de la Torche along the parallels of latitude of 50°08′N and 47°50′N, respectively, to the meridian of 20°W. It covers Isles of Scilly (49°55′N 6°20′W) with the dangers lying between them and Land's End and the S coast of England from Cape Cornwall (50°08′N 5°43′W) to Bognor Regis (50°47′N 0°40′W), including Isle of Wight. It also covers the NW and N coasts of France between Pointe de la Torche (47°50′N 4°21′W), situated 2½ miles NNE of Pointe de Penmarc'h, and Cap d'Antifer (49°41′N 0°10′E) and the Channel Islands.

2   The water separating the coast of England from that of France is known in England as the English Channel, and in France as La Manche. The English Channel is entered between Île Vierge (48°38′N 4°34′W) and Land's End (50°04′N 5°43′W); the sea area W and SW of the English Channel to the edge of the continental shelf forms part of Celtic Sea (*West Coasts of England and Wales Pilot*).

NAVIGATIONAL DANGERS AND HAZARDS

Coastal conditions

General information

1.2

1   **Navigational notes.** The Continental Shelf which is approximately delineated by the 200 m line lies more than 200 miles W and 150 miles SW of the SW coast of England. It may generally be recognised in calm weather by the numerous ripplings in its vicinity, and in boisterous weather by a turbulent sea and the sudden alteration in the colour of the water from a dark blue to green. Within the 200 m line, the shoaling is irregular on account of the banks and ridges described at 1.142; however in general the soundings shoal gradually E, the depth on a line joining Île d'Ouessant (48°28′N 5°05′W), known in England as Ushant, and Bishop Rock (49°52′N 6°27′W) being almost uniformly about 100 m decreasing a little within 20 miles of Isles of Scilly.

2   Approaching the English Channel from W, it is essential to use every opportunity to ascertain the vessels position until a landfall is made. Although soundings will be of service, they give no exact determination of position as the inequalities in depths are generally too slight, with the exception of Hurd Deep (1.143).

3   Careful consideration should be given to the effects of wind, currents and tidal streams to ensure keeping well S of Isles of Scilly; recently prevailing S and SW winds combined with the influence of surface drift and tidal stream is almost certainly to result in a N set. In low visibility mariners should not close Isles of Scilly within a depth of 100 m unless certain of position.

4   In navigating the English Channel it is important that the mariner should be acquainted with the general system of winds in it, as well as with the incidence of poor visibility. To this must be added the caution that the wind has considerable effect on the strength and direction of the tidal stream, as well as on the range of the tides.

5   The tidal streams are strong in the central part of the English Channel especially at spring tides in the area between Portland, Isle of Wight and Cotentin Peninsula; strong winds opposing the tidal streams raise steep seas which can be hazardous for small vessels, see also 1.152.

1.3

1   **Fairway.** The W and SW approaches to the English Channel pass through deep water and there are no navigational hazards.

The fairway of the English Channel, when E of Isles of Scilly or when well N of Île d'Ouessant, may be defined as far E as The Owers (50°37′N 0°41′W) (6.179), as lying between 12 and 40 miles from the headlands of the English coast.

In low visibility Hurd Deep (1.143) will indicate the approach to Casquets (49°43′N 2°22′W) from NW and N.

1.4

1   **Local topography.** The coasts on opposite sides of the English Channel have widely different characteristics; off the English coast the depths are mostly regular and the coast, except in the vicinity of Isles of Scilly, may be approached with confidence, while off the French coast the shore is rocky and uneven and numerous dangers exist.

Safe harbours and anchorages

1.5

1   **Shelter.** Numerous ports and anchorages where the mariner may seek shelter are to be found on both the English and French coasts; however, apart from the harbours of Dartmouth (5.23) and Tor Bay (5.64), there is little shelter during strong SW winds between Start Point (50°13′N 3°38′W) and Bill of Portland, 50 miles ENE.

Dangers and hazards

Dangers

1.6

1   **General information.** The principal navigational dangers to be borne in mind when approaching the coasts which lie within the area covered by this volume are:

> The shoals in the vicinity of Isles of Scilly (49°55′N 6°20′W) and off-lying dangers between Isles of Scilly and Land's End, 25 miles ENE.
>
> Chaussée de Sein, a chain of rocky shoals extending about 14 miles W from Pointe du Raz (48°02′N 4°44′W).

2
> The dangers extending up to 1½ miles offshore and surrounding Île d'Ouessant (48°28′N 5°05′W).
>
> The numerous dangers lying up to 3 miles off the NW coast of Guernsey (49°27′N 2°35′W).
>
> Casquets (49°43′N 2°22′W) and the dangers extending E to Alderney.

Hazards

1.7

1   **Crossing traffic** in parts of the English Channel and Dover Strait increases the risk of collision in these areas. Mariners are reminded that when risk of collision is deemed to exist *International Regulations for Preventing Collisions at Sea (1972)* fully apply and in particular the Rules of Part B, Sections II and III, of which Rules 15 and 19(d) are of specific relevance in the crossing situation.

2   **High Speed Ferries** operate in the area covered by this volume. Mariners are advised to keep a good lookout. Some high speed craft may generate large waves, which can have a serious impact on small craft and their moorings close to the shoreline and on shallow off-lying banks. For further details see *Annual Summary of Admiralty Notice to Mariners No 23.*

Cargo transhipment. Transhipment of liquid cargo between tankers takes place in Lyme Bay (5.124) and in the NW part of Baie de Seine (13.2). Vessels engaged in these operations may be at anchor, or otherwise unable to

manoeuvre, and should be given a wide berth. For details see 5.5 and 13.4.

3   **Former mined area.** An area off the N coast of France, which remains dangerous due to mines laid during the war of 1939–1945. Due to the lapse of time the risk to surface navigation is now considered to be no more dangerous than the ordinary risks of navigation, but a very real risk still exists with regard to anchoring, fishing or any form of submarine or seabed activity. Details of the affected areas are given at 9.42, and 10.149 and in Appendix IV.

For further information, see *Annual Summary of Admiralty Notices to Mariners.*

4   **Dumping grounds.** Disused dumping grounds for explosives are situated at the W and E ends of Hurd Deep (1.143). For details of disused dumping grounds off Channel Islands, see 11.15.

Temporary explosives dumping grounds (Zones de Dépôt d'Explosifs). In French waters fishing vessels with suspected explosive devices on board, or caught in nets should, if possible, make for the nearest temporary explosives dump to jettison the device. For locations, see Appendix V.

TRAFFIC AND OPERATIONS

Regulation of vessel traffic

Routeing

1.8

1   **General information.** The main through routes from Bay of Biscay and the North Atlantic Ocean to, and through, the English Channel all lie within TSS and recommended directions of traffic flow. The routes are given in outline below and directions for these routes are given in Chapter 2.

See IMO Publication *Ships Routeing* for general provisions on ships routeing.

2   Within the area covered by this volume TSS have been established in the following focal areas:

> To the W and S of Isles of Scilly (49°55′N 6°20′W), and between those islands and the English coast.
>
> To the NW of Île d'Ouessant (48°28′N 5°05′W).
>
> To the N of Casquets (49°43′N 2°22′W).

3   All these schemes are IMO adopted and Rule 10 of *International Regulations for Preventing Collisions at Sea (1972)* applies.

Special provisions have been adopted by IMO for use in the scheme NW of Île d'Ouessant, for details see 2.32.

4   **Mariners' Routeing Guide** (chart 5500) contains Passage Planning Charts which show the routes through the English Channel, Dover Strait and the Southern North Sea as far as the entrance to Europoort, for details see 2.2.

Traffic Separation Schemes

1.9

1   **General information.** In principle TSS consist of two traffic lanes lying either side of a separation zone. Traffic in each lane is one-way, so that opposing traffic is kept apart by the separation zone. These lanes are shown on the charts with arrows which indicate the general direction of the traffic flow. The full width of the lane is available for navigation, subject to compliance with Rule 10(b) of *International Regulations for Preventing Collisions at Sea (1972)*, which requires vessels to proceed in the general direction of the traffic flow and in so far as is practicable keep clear of the separation zone.

1.10

1   **Rule 10** of *International Regulations for Preventing Collisions at Sea (1972)* does not in any way alter the overriding requirement for vessels to comply with the other Steering and Sailing rules. In particular, vessels do not, by virtue of using the traffic lanes in the general direction of the traffic flow, enjoy any privilege that they would not have elsewhere. In addition, vessels using the TSS are not relieved of the requirement to proceed at a safe speed, especially in conditions of restricted visibility.

2   Rule 10 (b) (iii) states that:

A vessel using a TSS shall "normally join or leave a traffic lane at the termination of the lane, but when joining or leaving from either side shall do so at as small an angle to the general direction of traffic flow as practicable."

3   Rule 10 (c) states that:

"A vessel shall, so far as practicable, avoid crossing traffic lanes but if obliged to do so shall cross on a heading as nearly as practicable at right angles to the general direction of traffic flow."

4   To follow this advice low powered vessels and sailing vessels should therefore not make allowance for the tidal stream while crossing, if by doing so they will not have a heading nearly at right angles to the traffic flow.

Rule 10 (j) states that:

"A vessel of less than 20 m in length or a sailing vessel shall not impede the safe passage of a power-driven vessel following a traffic lane."

Inshore traffic zones
1.11

1   Regulations for the use of inshore traffic zones are given in Rule 10(d) of *International Regulations for Preventing Collisions at Sea (1972)* which states that:

2   (d)(i) "A vessel shall not use an inshore traffic zone when she can safely use the appropriate traffic lane within the adjacent traffic separation scheme. However, vessels of less than 20 m in length, sailing vessels and vessels engaged in fishing may use the inshore traffic zone.

3   (d)(ii) Notwithstanding sub-paragraph (d)(i), a vessel may use an inshore traffic zone when en route to or from a port, offshore installation or structure, pilot station or any other place situated within the inshore traffic zone, or to avoid immediate danger."

4   A vessel outbound from a port or pilot station within an inshore traffic zone is recommended to join the adjacent traffic lane as soon as possible, as described in Rule 10 (b)(iii).

5   The United Kingdom Department of Transport view is that, if a vessel, other than one of less than 20 m in length, a sailing vessel or a vessel engaged in fishing, commences its voyage from a location beyond one limit of the inshore traffic zone and proceeds to a location beyond its furthest limit, and is not calling at a port, pilot station, destination or sheltered anchorage within the inshore traffic zone, then that vessel should, if it can safely do so, use the appropriate lane in the adjacent TSS unless some abnormal circumstances exist in that lane. In that context reduced visibility in the area or the density of traffic using the lane does not in itself justify use of the inshore traffic zone. However it should be noted that national regulations apply in the inshore traffic zone of the Off Ushant TSS; these regulations are given at 8.5.

Deep-water routes
1.12

1   **Deep-water route to Port du Havre-Antifer.** A deep-water route entered 36 miles WNW of Cap d'Antifer (49°41′N 0°10′E) leads to Port du Havre-Antifer (49°40′N 0°08′E) (13.213), a deep-water port for VLCC's which lies 10 miles N of Le Havre. This deep-water route is a continuation of the buoyed fairway leading from Port du Havre-Antifer harbour.

For details see 13.228.

2   **Deep-draught route through Dover Strait to Europoort.** Deep-draught routes follow the NE-going and SW-going traffic lanes through Dover Strait except that they run through specific points, known as waypoints; they are outside the area covered by this volume.

3   The Netherlands authorities have selected a route within the NE-going traffic lane of Dover Strait and Noord Hinder South TSS as being the most favourable for vessels with draughts of 20·7 m or more. The route is described in detail in a Deep Draught Planning Guide (HP8), published by the Netherlands Hydrographer, which should be consulted when the route is used by mariners in vessels of these draughts. There is no official deep-draught guide for a SW-bound passage. Neither route is endorsed by the British authorities in every detail. Both routes are shown on chart 5500.

For further details, see *Dover Strait Pilot.*

Vessels constrained by their draught
1.13

1   Mariners are reminded that in certain critical areas vessels constrained by their draught may not be able to alter course without the danger of running aground. A good lookout must be kept for vessels exhibiting the signals laid down in Rule 28 of *International Regulations for Preventing Collisions at Sea (1972).*

Vessels may only exhibit these signals when actually so constrained.

2   **Local regulations** are in force for such vessels within the limits of the Dockyard Port of Portsmouth and Port of Southampton, for details see 7.19.

Ship Movement Report Systems
1.14

1   **Off Ushant TSS.** A mandatory Ship Reporting System (OUESSREP) covers the Off Ushant TSS and the adjacent inshore traffic zone. The limit of the reporting area is the arc of a circle 40 miles in radius centred on Le Stiff radar tower (48°29′N 5°03′W). The system applies to vessels over 300 gt.

For further details see *Admiralty List of Radio Signals Volume 6(1)* and 1.69

1.15

1   **Off Casquets TSS.** A mandatory Ship Reporting System (MANCHEREP) covers the Off Casquets TSS and the adjacent inshore traffic zone. The limits of the reporting area are:

50°10′N 2°58′W.
50°10′N 2°00′W.
49°20′N 2°00′W.
49°20′N 2°58′W.

2   The system applies to the following vessels:

Vessels of 300 gt and over.
Vessels not under command.
Vessels at anchor in the TSS or the Inshore Traffic Zone

Vessels restricted in their ability to manoeuvre.

Vessels with defective navigation aids.

For further details see *Admiralty List of Radio Signals Volume 6(1)* and 1.69.

1.16

1   **Reporting format.** A common reporting format for OUESSREP and MANCHEREP exists (2007), in accordance with IMO requirements. CALDOVREP, details of which may be found in the *Dover Strait Pilot*, uses the same format.

1.17

1   **MAREP.** A voluntary Ship Movement Report System (MAREP) is in operation for the area between, in the W, a line joining Bishop Rock Lighthouse (49°52′N 6°27′W) and Ouessant SW Lanby (48°30′N 5°45′W), and to the NE, by a line joining North Foreland (51°23′N 1°27′E) through Mid Falls Light-buoy (51°19′N 1°47′E) (*Dover Strait Pilot*) to the Belgian coast.

2   The system applies to the following vessels:

All merchant vessels of 300 gt and over.

Any vessel "not under command" or at anchor in a TSS or an Inshore Traffic Zone.

Any vessel restricted in her ability to manoeuvre.

Any vessel with defective navigation aids.

3   IMO recommend that all merchant ships of 300 gt and over participate in the scheme.

It is further recommended that ships of less than 300 gt should make reports under MAREP when they:

Are "not under command" or at anchor in a TSS or associated Inshore Traffic Zone.

4   Are restricted in their ability to manoeuvre.

Have defects with their navigational equipment.

Further details may be found in *Admiralty List of Radio Signals Volume 6(1)*, and on chart 5500.

Channel Navigation Information Service

1.18

1   The Channel Navigation Information Service provides navigational information and assistance to mariners on passage through Dover Strait, for details, see 2.9.

General information on traffic

Density of traffic

1.19

1   **Risk of collision.** Owing to the density of traffic, one of the greatest hazards to safe navigation in the English Channel and its approaches lies in the risk of collision, especially in poor visibility. In addition to shipping in the fairways, as well as fleets of fishing vessels and numerous yachts in the summer months, it should be remembered that there are fast cross-channel vessels plying regularly between English and French ports, principally between Plymouth and Roscoff, between Weymouth and Channel Islands and Cherbourg, between Poole and Cherbourg and from The Solent to Saint-Malo, Cherbourg, Caen-Ouistreham and Le Havre.

2   There is a focal point about 20 miles N of Cherbourg where several cross channel routes cross the general flow of traffic up and down channel. See 1.7.

International Maritime Organisation recommendations

1.20

1   **Recommendations on navigation through the English Channel and Dover Strait.** The following recommendations on navigation through the English Channel and Dover Strait have been promulgated by IMO:

All ships of 300 gt and over should be fitted with electronic position fixing equipment suitable for the area in order to improve navigation in the routeing system.

2   Masters of deep-draught vessels should ensure that there will be an adequate under-keel clearance at the time of passage. In order to get this clearance the static under-keel allowance should not be less than 4 m, which includes an allowance for squat for a speed not exceeding 12 kn. The static under-keel allowance is the difference between the calculated depth of water and the ship's draught when stopped.

3   Subject to any factors that may adversely affect safe navigation, IMO strongly recommends that ships proceeding from the W part of the English Channel to Dover Strait or vice versa should use Off Casquets TSS.

4   Vessels proceeding from Off Casquets TSS to the TSS In the Strait of Dover and adjacent waters, or vice versa, are recommended to leave the mid-channel areas to be avoided to port, proceeding parallel to a line connecting the centres of those areas.

5   Ships crossing or leaving or joining the E or W flow of traffic between Off TSS Casquets and In the Strait of Dover and adjacent waters should cross as nearly as practicable at right angles or join or leave at as small an angle as practicable to the recommended directions of traffic flow.

6   Ships having defects affecting operational safety, in addition to reporting such defects by participating in the MAREP scheme, should take appropriate measures to overcome these defects before entering Dover Strait.

Fishing

General

1.21

1   Throughout the area covered by this volume fishing vessels of varying sizes, from small open boats to much larger vessels, and of different nationalities, may be encountered.

Mariners are reminded that fishing vessels in addition to being hampered may need to make immediate and unannounced manoeuvres. Every care should be taken therefore when approaching vessels engaged in fishing.

Methods of fishing employed

1.22

1   The principal methods of fishing in the area covered by this volume are trawling, scallop dredging, potting, handlining and skin-diving.

For a general description of the methods of fishing employed see *The Mariner's Handbook*.

Principal fisheries

1.23

1   **English waters.** Trawlers may be encountered throughout the year between Isles of Scilly and Bill of

Portland, and between Selsey Bill and Dover Strait, usually between 3 and 12 miles offshore. Many boats will be working twin beam trawls, and the larger beam trawlers will be found more than 12 miles offshore.

Vessels towing dredges for scallops may be encountered from the coast to mid-Channel off Cornwall and Devon, and to the E of Selsey Bill.

2   Mid-water trawling inshore for sprats takes place in Lyme Bay, in Poole Bay and along the Sussex and Kent coast from October to March, where bass and bream are caught in summer. Mid-winter single and pair trawling plus purse-seining for mackerel, scad and pilchard takes place from October to March, E from Mounts Bay to S of the Isle of Wight.

3   **Fixed fishing gear.** Mariners are warned that concentrations of fixed fishing gear may be encountered generally off the S coast of England; in particular up to 6 miles offshore E of Selsey Bill and off the Dorset coast between Anvil Point and Portland, and up to 30 miles offshore and sometimes beyond, in Lyme Bay, off Start Point, Eddystone Rocks, the Lizard and Isles of Scilly. Fishing is furthest from the shore during neap tides throughout the year. Moored shellfish tangle nets or pots are to be found in large numbers in the summer months from Land's End to Trevose Head.

4   Potting for crabs, lobster and whelks by inshore fishing boats of up to about 10 m in length takes place all along the S coast of England up to 10 miles offshore between March and November, with larger boats setting crab pots in mid-Channel S of Start Point, N of Channel Islands and between Cherbourg Peninsula and Dorset, mainly between June and November.

5   Large concentrations of small boats handlining for mackerel may be found off the coast of Cornwall and S Devon, up to 15 miles from the land in winter, and for bass closer inshore in the same area and off Dorset, Hampshire and Sussex between April and October.

Skin-divers may be encountered by day around the wrecks and on any part of the coast, particularly at weekends.

1.24

1   **Mid-channel.** Concentrations of fixed fishing gear may be found NW and N of Channel Islands in the following areas:

     Mid August to end December. An area bounded by latitudes 49°27′N and 49°58′N and longitudes 3°05′W and 3°45′W.

2   All year round. An area bounded by a line joining:
     49°33′N   2°49′W.
     49°43′N   2°57′W.
     50°11′N   2°18′W.
     50°04′N   2°00′W.

1.25

1   **Channel Islands.** Fishing activities in the vicinity of Jersey, Les Écrehou and Plateau des Minquiers consist mainly of lobster potting; trots of about 40 pots, 18 m apart and marked by unlit dan buoys, are laid near the rocks.

Crab potting boats occasionally work on the edge of Hurd Deep, N of Alderney.

1.26

1   **French waters.** Concentrations of inshore fishing vessels trawling or setting lines, pots or nets may be encountered anywhere along the French coast.

Trawlers and dredgers operate throughout the Channel in the same areas fished by the larger UK vessels.

The principal fishing ports are, in book order, Brest, Camaret-sur-Mer, Douarnenez, Paimpol, Saint-Brieuc, Cherbourg, Caen-Ouistreham and Le Havre.

1.27

1   **Oyster fisheries** are situated in many of the estuaries and harbours to the W of Selsey Bill, the largest number of small boats being found towing dredges in The Solent between November and April, whilst there are numerous shellfish beds in the vicinity of the French coast. The beds are normally marked by poles or perches, while off the French coast they may be marked by buoys. Mariners should avoid navigating outside the channels, where they exist, and should not anchor or ground in these areas. Claims arising from damage to oyster beds can be heavy.

2   Shellfish beds, where they are known to exist, are mentioned in the appropriate geographical chapters and are usually shown on the chart.

Fishery limits
1.28

1   British limits are given at 1.121, French limits at 1.131.

Marine farms
1.29

1   The farming of marine species is carried out in the area covered by this book; marine farms are added and removed on a continuous basis. Such farms include aquaculture areas, shellfish beds and fish havens. Marine farms, which may be fixed or floating structures sometimes moored to the seabed by a spread of anchors, are marked by yellow buoys or beacons which may be lit by yellow flashing lights. The position of anchors when used may be marked by a different type and colour of buoy. The charted positions of the farms are approximate and the area covered by individual farms and associated moorings can be extensive.

2   Within French waters it is forbidden to anchor, take the bottom, engage in fishing by any method or carry out diving operations within the areas occupied by marine farms.

Mariners are cautioned to avoid areas of marine farms, and to note that their presence has rendered many hitherto accepted anchorages either unsuitable or limited in swinging space.

Exercise areas

Naval exercises and firing practices
1.30

1   **British waters.** Practice exercise area (PEXA) charts Q6401, Q6402, and Q6407 give details of British exercise areas covered by this volume. Such areas are also shown on all new and new edition navigation charts. Details of the warning signals and firing practices for all British warships, submarines and aircraft are given in *Annual Summary of Admiralty Notices to Mariners* for the current year.

2   **Subfacts.** Information relating to the activity of both surfaced and dived submarines off the S coast of England is broadcast by Brixham Coastguard and Falmouth Coastguard (Subfacts - South Coast). See *Admiralty List of Radio Signals Volume 3(1)* for details. In submarine exercise areas mariners may encounter submarines on the surface; a good lookout is essential when transiting these areas.

3   **Gunfacts.** Information relating to gunnery and missile firings of 20 mm calibre and above, and controlled underwater explosions in the South Coast Exercise Areas, is broadcast by Brixham Coastguard and Falmouth

Coastguard (Gunfacts - South Coast). See *Admiralty List of Radio Signals Volume 3(1)* for details. There are no restrictions placed on mariners transiting a firing practice area at any time. Such areas operate a clear range procedure, ensuring that firing will only take place when the area is clear of all shipping.

For vessels requiring special consideration see *The Mariner's Handbook*.

1.31

1   **French waters.** Exercises and practices may take place anywhere off the coast of France, but in particular in the following areas:

    Île d'Ouessant.
    L'Iroise.
    Off Brest.
    Baie de Douarnenez.
    Baie de Seine.

2   French warships carrying out firing practices will hoist a red flag by day and exhibit a red all-round light at night.

    Coastal batteries. Firing practices take place from French coastal batteries in the following areas:

    In Avant-Goulet de Brest (48°18′N 4°40′W) (Secteur de Toulbroc'h).
    In Anse de Camaret (Secteur de Camaret-sur-Mer) (48°18′N 4°34W).

3   In Anse de Vauville (Secteur de Biville) (49°36′N 1°51′W).
    Off Cherbourg (Zone de Querqueville) (49°40′N 1°42′W).
    In Baie de Seine (Zone de Baie de Seine) (49°35′N 0°45′W).

4   In daylight hours the firing battery displays a red flag from 1 hour before until the practice is completed. Target tugs and range craft also display a red flag.

    At night the firing battery displays two horizontally disposed red lights and signal stations in the vicinity display a single red light. Target tugs display three red lights vertically disposed and range craft one red light at the masthead; in both cases these lights are in addition to usual navigation lights.

5   Times when firings are to take place are promulgated in French notices to mariners and broadcast by Avurnav, for details see *Admiralty List of Radio Signals Volume 3(1)*.

Minelaying and mineclearance exercises
1.32

1   British minelaying and mineclearance vessels exercise periodically in the areas listed in *Annual Summary of Admiralty Notices to Mariners* for the current year.

    In addition French vessels are frequently engaged in hydrographic sweeping and mine clearance off French ports. They generally operate under similar conditions to those given in *Annual Summary of Admiralty Notices to Mariners*.

Submarine exercises
1.33

1   **British and French submarines** exercise frequently in the English Channel and in its W approaches. Submarine exercise areas are indicated on the charts and described in the appropriate part of this volume. French submarines may be met anywhere in French waters, but are more likely to be encountered in Bay of Biscay, off Brest, off the entrance to Baie de Douarnenez and off Cherbourg.

Annual Summary of Admiralty Notices to Mariners for the current year gives details concerning British submarines and the warning signals used by them; see also 1.30. French submarines conform in general with these signals.

Marine exploitation

General
1.34

1   **Continental Shelf Boundaries,** agreed between France and the United Kingdom and shown on the relevant charts, define the area in which the two countries may exploit the natural resources of the seabed and its sub-soil.

Surveys
1.35

1   Seismic and other survey vessels surveying in connection with oil and gas fields are liable to be encountered throughout the Channel. Seismic survey methods are outlined in *The Mariner's Handbook*.

Aggregate dredging
1.36

1   Aggregate dredging is carried out in the waters of the English Channel, particularly E of the meridian of 2°00′W. Such areas are usually charted and mariners are advised to exercise caution in their vicinity.

Drilling rigs
1.37

1   Drilling rigs may operate in the Channel throughout the year. Buoys, lighters and other equipment associated with drilling rigs are often moored or laid near the rigs; wires may extend up to 1½ miles from the rigs, which should be given a wide berth.

    Methods of search and production, together with a full description of the structures, safety zones, their identification markings, visual signals in use and other equipments associated with them are given in *The Mariner's Handbook*.

2   Drilling rigs are not charted. Their positions are announced, when known, by NAVAREA I navigational warnings and are listed in Section III of each weekly edition of *Admiralty Notices to Mariners*.

Trinity House vessels engaged in surveying and wreck marking
1.38

1   Trinity House vessels engaged in searching for wrecks or surveying, when they proceed at slow speed on various headings, or when marking wrecks prior to laying buoys, exhibit the lights and shapes prescribed by Rule 27(b) of *International Regulations for Preventing Collisions at Sea (1972)* for vessels restricted in their ability to manoeuvre.

2   When wreck marking, Trinity House vessels show additional signals prescribed by Rule 27(d) of *International Regulations for Preventing Collisions at Sea (1972)* to show the clear and disengaged side of the vessel. They may also use a racon (agile frequency, X and S bands, code D, range 10 miles). If a vessel appears to be passing dangerously close, the Trinity House vessel may fire detonating signals and may institute reporting procedures against the offender. Other vessels should reduce speed and keep clear.

CHARTS

General information

British Admiralty Charts
1.39
1   **Source data.** British Admiralty charts of British waters are compiled from the latest surveys in the United Kingdom Hydrographic Office.

Those of French waters are compiled from, or are adopted versions of, French government charts.

Foreign charts
1.40
1   **France.** French charts of their own coastline are, in many cases, on a larger scale than British Admiralty charts of the same area.

French charts may be obtained from the French hydrographic authority and are corrected by French Notices to Mariners; the address is given in the *Catalogue of Admiralty Charts and Publications*. These charts are not issued by the Hydrographic Office nor are they corrected by *Admiralty Notices to Mariners*.

Datums

Horizontal datum for British charts
1.41
1   Within the area of this volume charts of English waters and Channel Islands are referred to a WGS 84 compatible datum. Charts of French waters are normally referred to the European Datum (1950), although certain charts are now on WGS 84 datum.

Satellite derived positions are normally referred to World Geodetic System (1984) Datum and the difference between this and the horizontal datum of the published chart is given on the chart.

Vertical datum
1.42
1   The vertical datum used by the UK Hydrographic Office for the reduction of soundings equates approximately to the level of the LAT. Most French charts now use LAT. For an explanation of LAT and other datums see *Admiralty Tide Tables*.

When predicting offshore tidal heights use should be made of the Co-Tidal Charts.

Under-keel allowance and clearance

General information
1.43
1   Under-keel allowance and clearance are defined in *The Mariner's Handbook*.

Masters of ships, when planning their passage through Dover Strait and its approaches, should ensure that there is an adequate under-keel clearance at the time of passage. To achieve this, allowance must be made for the effects of squat at the passage speed, for uncertainties in charted depths and tide levels, and for the effects of waves and swell resulting from local and distant storms.

2   General guidance on under-keel allowance and clearance for Dover Strait and approaches is given in *Dover Strait Pilot*. See also 1.20.

AIDS TO NAVIGATION

Buoyage-General information
1.44
1   **The IALA Maritime Buoyage System** (Region A) is in force in the waters surrounding the British Isles, and in French waters, and is described in *IALA Maritime Buoyage System* and *The Mariner's Handbook*.

Only the principal buoys are described in this volume. Radar reflectors are not mentioned in the directions as they are fitted to the majority of the important buoys.

Oceanographical Data Buoys
1.45
1   Oceanographical data light buoys and buoys (special), including Ocean Data Acquisition Systems (ODAS) Light Buoys, which gather oceanographic and meteorological data for environmental research purposes, and which may vary considerably in size, may be encountered anywhere in the area. Many are laid temporarily only and not charted.

2   Oceanographical data buoys are described in *The Mariner's Handbook*; those that are permanent are shown on the charts, those temporary are given in *Admiralty Notices to Mariners*.

As the buoys have no navigational significance and as they are liable to be removed at short notice they are not normally mentioned in the text of this pilot. All data gathering buoys should be given a wide berth.

British Isles buoyage
1.46
1   **Authority.** Trinity House is the authority responsible for lights and buoys around the coasts of England, Wales and Channel Islands.

Firing practice areas are marked by buoys (special). Some buoys have the letters DZ and an identifying number painted on the side.

2   **Light vessels** are charted as light floats, or Lanbys, which are described in the *Admiralty List of Lights Volume A*. The smaller buoys are shown on the charts, but are not described in the *Admiralty List of Lights*.

French buoyage
1.47
1   Details of light buoys off the coast of France are published in the French Lists of Lights.

Firing practice areas may still be marked by white buoys, with a blue cross as seen from above and have the letters ZD painted on the side.

Landmarks
1.48
1   Care is necessary when evaluating the descriptions given in this volume concerning landmarks, such as trees, the colour and shape of buildings and other marks. New buildings may have been erected and old trees or houses destroyed, so that the marks, which may at one time have been conspicuous on account of their isolation, shape or colour, may no longer exist or may now be difficult to identify.

PILOTAGE

General information

Information and signals
1.49
1   **Information on pilotage** relevant to entry is given under the port concerned. *Admiralty List of Radio Signals Volume 6(1)* should be consulted for full details of pilotage at each port.

Signals to be made by a vessel requiring a pilot are laid down in *The International Code of Signals*:

By day: Flag G.

2 By night: Morse letter G (— — •) by light.

In low visibility: Morse letter P (• — — •) by sound.

Pilot vessels may respond by sounding H (• • • •).

The sound signals are in addition to the normal signals prescribed by Rule 35 of *International Regulations for Preventing Collisions at Sea (1972)*.

Deep-sea pilotage

General information
1.50

1 **Qualified pilots.** Mariners passing through the English Channel and Dover Strait should take into account the possibility of availing themselves of the services of a deep-sea pilot in connection with the requirements of safe navigation. Masters of ships approaching from the W are advised to embark their deep-sea pilot as far W in the English Channel as practicable and make an early decision either to request helicopter delivery or to approach a pilot station.

2 Licensed deep-sea pilots for ports in NW Europe, including the British Isles and The Baltic, should be requested through the various pilotage agencies based in the British Isles or other European countries. These pilots may be embarked before reaching the complex traffic schemes in Dover Strait and the S part of the North Sea, in which case embarkation normally takes place off Brixham (50°24′N 3°30′W) or Cherbourg (49°38′N 1°38′W). For details, see 5.95 and 12.34.

3 Arrangements can also be made through the pilotage agencies to embark deep-sea pilots by helicopter in the English Channel and Dover Strait area, for details see 12.34.

4 Deep-sea pilots often have to travel long distances to their point of embarkation and as much notice as possible should be given to the pilotage agency of the requirement for a pilot. Similar arrangements can be made for outward bound vessels and those coasting from port to port in the area.

For further details see *Admiralty List of Radio Signals Volume 6(1)* under the heading "Deep Sea Pilots". See also chart 5500.

Pilotage in British ports

General
1.51

1 **Licensed pilots.** Every port of consequence on the British side of the English Channel, and in Channel Islands, is designated a Competent Harbour Authority under the *Pilotage Act 1987*. It is their duty to provide licensed pilots if required and decide whether pilotage should be compulsory.

Passage plans
1.52

1 Every British port is able to use its powers of direction under the Port Marine Safety Code to require that all vessels arriving, departing or transiting the waters of the port use an agreed pilotage passage plan, whether a pilot is embarked or not. Such requirements are generally incorporated in the General Directions for Navigation for the port.

Pilot vessels
1.53

1 **Description.** Most British pilot vessels are black-hulled with the letter "P" or PILOT painted on the bow or side. A pilot flag, upper horizontal half white, lower horizontal half red, is flown when pilots are embarked.

Pilotage in French ports

General
1.54

1 Pilotage is determined by the tonnage or length of a vessel and is laid down for each French port and given in the text of this volume.

French pilots are licensed by the state; in naval ports pilotage is undertaken by naval pilots. On boarding they should be informed of the vessel's draught, speed and any special conditions affecting handling.

Pilot vessels
1.55

1 **Description.** Most French pilot vessels have a black hull with a narrow white band and an anchor painted on the funnel, if the latter is fitted. The station letters, in white, are painted forward and aft on the bulwarks.

RADIO FACILITIES

Electronic position fixing systems
1.56

1 **General information.** Full details of the electronic position fixing systems are given in *Admiralty List of Radio Signals Volume 2*; comments on the use of systems within the area are given below.

Loran C. The North-West European Loran C System (NELS) provides positional information in the area covered by this book.

2 **Differential GPS** corrections are transmitted from:

Lizard Light (49°58′N 5°12′W).

Saint Catherine's Point Light (50°35′N 1°18′W).

Saint-Mathieu Light (48°20′N 4°46′W).

La Hague (49°34′N 1°46′W).

3 **Irregularities** in the operation of any of these systems are broadcast as navigation warnings by the appropriate coast radio station or may be sent by NAVTEX, see 1.59.

Sylédis, a close range hyperbolic navigation system, is available in some French coastal waters. For details consult the French Hydrographic Service:

L'Établissement Principal du Service Hydrographique et Océanographique de la Marine, 13 rue du Chatellier, BP30316–29603 BREST-CEDEX.

Radio aids to navigation
1.57

1 **Racons** are fitted to many lighthouses, light floats and buoys.

Automatic Identification System (AIS). For further details see 1.71 and *Admiralty List of Radio Signals Volume 6(1)*. General information about AIS may be found in *The Mariner's Handbook*. Mariners should note that AIS is also being fitted to offshore oil platforms, lighthouses and selected navigational buoys around the coast in order to enhance navigational safety.

VHF direction-finding service, for emergency use only is operated by Her Majesty's Coastguard for UK waters and CROSS for French waters, see 1.105 and 1.111.

Full details of all radio aids to navigation are given in *Admiralty List of Radio Signals Volume 2*, see also chart 5500.

Port operations
1.58

1   All the ports within the area have VHF radio communications and the larger ports have local radar surveillance. They provide navigational information and assistance. For details see *Admiralty List of Radio Signals Volume 6(1)*.

Radio navigational warnings
1.59

1   **Long range navigational warnings.** The Channel lies within NAVAREA I of the World-wide Navigational Warnings Service broadcast by Inmarsat-C Safety NET. The French coast, S of Latitude 48°27′S, to the limit of this volume at Pointe de la Torche (47°50′N 4°21′W), is covered by NAVAREA II warnings also broadcast by Inmarsat-C Safety NET.

2   **NAVTEX,** a navigational telex service, broadcasting maritime safety information is also available in the area.

    Coastal navigation warnings are broadcast at scheduled times by Coastguard radio stations.

    See *Admiralty Lists of Radio Signals Volume 3(1)* and *Annual Summary of Admiralty Notices to Mariners* for details.

Maritime Safety Information (MSI)
1.60

1   **Maritime Safety Information**. All MRCCs broadcast Maritime Safety Information including navigational warnings, gale warnings, shipping forecasts, local inshore forecasts and storm tide warnings. For further details see *Admiralty List of Radio Signals Volume 3(1)*.

Medical aid procedure
1.61

1   **Medical aid procedure.** HMCG has responsibility for handling Medical Link Calls and PAN PAN MEDICO calls for vessels requiring medical advice or assistance. For further details see *Admiralty List of Radio Signals Volume 1(1)*.

2   **Note.** Medical advice and if necessary, assistance, may also be obtained by GMDSS communications; for details see *Admiralty List of Radio Signals Volume 1(1)*.

Radio weather forecasts
1.62

1   Details of meteorological services for shipping, including broadcasts by BBC Radio 4 and radio-facsimilie weather charts, are given in *Admiralty List of Radio Signals Volume 3(1) and Annual Summary of Admiralty Notices to Mariners*.

    The Meteorological Office transmits routine forecasts, gale warnings and strong coastal wind forecasts by internet, telephone and facsimilie. See www.metoffice.gov.uk.

2   Weather bulletins, including gale warnings are also broadcast in English by Coastguard radio stations in the United Kingdom.

    French CROSS stations broadcast weather bulletins in French and English.

3   Requests for weather reports can also be made to CROSS radio stations as well as local authorities.

Global Maritime Distress and Safety System
1.63

1   Full details of GMDSS are given in *Admiralty List of Radio Signals Volume 5*.

REGULATIONS

International regulations
Submarine cables and pipelines
1.64

1   **General information.** A number of submarine cables cross the English Channel and the S part of North Sea. They are shown on the charts and, in the case of pipelines, are marked with the appropriate legend (oil or gas).

    Regulations to prevent damage to submarine cables and pipelines are contained in *International Convention for the Protection of Submarine Cables, 1884*, as extended by the *Convention on the High Seas, 1958*. See *The Mariner's Handbook* for details.

2   **Caution.** Gas from a damaged oil or gas pipeline could cause an explosion or some other serious hazard. Pipelines are not always buried and their presence may effectively reduce the charted depth by as much as 2 m. Where pipelines are close together, only one may be charted. Mariners should not anchor or trawl in the vicinity of a pipeline; they may risk prosecution if damage is caused.

    See *The Mariner's Handbook* for a full description of pipelines.

Pollution of the sea
Marpol 73/78
1.65

1   *The Mariner's Handbook* gives a summary of The International Convention for the Prevention of Pollution from Ships 1973, as modified by the Protocol of 1978, and known as MARPOL 73/78.

    Pollution reports. Under the Convention, a Master has a duty to report pollution incidents or damage and breakdowns affecting the safety of his vessel. For further details see *Admiralty List of Radio Signals Volume 1*.

2   **Special areas.** Under MARPOL 73/78 designated Special Areas, owing to their sensitive oceanographic and ecological conditions and to their maritime traffic, are provided with a higher level of protection and regulation than other areas of the sea. The North Sea region is regarded as a Special Area in respect of Annexes I (Oil) and V (Garbage from Ships) and, in respect of Annex VI (Air Pollution), it is a special SOx (sulphur oxide) Emission Control Area.

Combating oil pollution
1.66

1   All the countries which border the North Sea have agreed to co-operate in combating oil pollution by means of surveillance and in the pooling of resources in an emergency incident. Other European Union measures contributing to the subject include Port State Control Inspections (Directive 95/21/EEC), Expanded Inspection Notification (Directive 2001/106/EC), Port Reception Facilities for Ship-Generated Waste and Cargo Residues (Directive 2000/59/EC) and the phasing out of Single-Hull Tankers (Directive 417/2002/EEC).

Western European Tanker Reporting System and Particularly Sensitive Sea Areas.
1.67

1   The Western European Tanker Reporting System (WETREP) is a mandatory reporting system covering the Western European Particularly Sensitive Sea Area (PSSA). The objectives of the system are to initiate SAR and measures to prevent pollution.

    The system applies to every kind of oil tanker of more than 600 dwt carrying a cargo of:

2   Heavy crude oil.
Heavy fuel oils.
Bitumen and tar and their emulsions.

3   For limits of the area and further details see *Admiralty List of Radio Signals Volume 6(1)*.

European Union regulations

Directive 2002/59/EC
1.68

1   **General information.** This Directive establishes a common vessel traffic monitoring and information system throughout European Union waters. The principal provisions are described below. They apply in general to all commercial vessels over 300 gt but the rules concerning the notification of carriage of dangerous and polluting goods applies to all vessels regardless of size.

Caution. These extracts are for reference purposes only and are not to be regarded as a statement of the applicable law. The full text of the regulations is the sole authoritative statement of the applicable law and should be consulted. The regulations to which the following refers is *Directive 2002/59/EC* or the appropriate enabling legislation drafted by individual member states, which in the United Kingdom is *The Merchant Shipping (Traffic Monitoring and Reporting Requirements) Regulations 2004,* a copy of which can be obtained from Her Majesty's Stationery Office (www.hmso.gov.uk).

1.69

1   **Ship reports.** All vessels bound for a port within the EC must report to the port authority at least 24 hours prior arrival, or, if the voyage is less than 24 hours, no later than the time of departure from the previous port. The report shall include the following information:

Name, call sign, IMO or MMSI number.
Port of destination.
ETA and ETD at port of destination.
Total number of persons onboard.

2   Upon receipt of a ship's report, the port authority will notify the national coastguard authority by the quickest means possible. This information will then be pooled in the European-wide telematic network called SafeSeaNet.

Any amendments to the initial ship report must be notified immediately.

Mandatory ship reporting systems. All vessels shall report to the coastguard authority on entering an IMO adopted mandatory ship reporting system, the report being made in the recognised format, see *Admiralty List of Radio Signals Volume 6(1)*. The coastguard authority is to be informed of any changes to the initial report.

1.70

1   **Vessel Traffic Service.** All vessels are to participate in and comply with VTS operated by EU member states and also those systems operated by member states in conjunction with co-operating non-member states. This includes those systems operated by member states outside their territorial waters but which are operated in accordance with IMO guidelines.

Routeing Schemes. All vessels must comply with IMO recommended TSS and Deep Water route regulations, see IMO publication *Ships' Routeing Guide.*

1.71

1   **Auotmatic Identification System and Voyage Data Recorder**. All vessels are to be equipped with AIS and VDR. The systems shall be in operation at all times.

Coastguard stations throughout the EU are able to receive AIS information and to relay it to all other coastguard stations within the EU.

1.72

1   **Notification of dangerous and polluting goods.** All vessels leaving an EU port are to report dangerous and polluting goods as specified within the Directive to the harbour authority. Vessels arriving from outside EU waters must transmit a report to their first EU port or anchorage upon departure from their port of loading. If, at the time of departure, the port of destination in the EC is not known, the report must be forwarded immediately such information becomes known. Where practical, this report is to be made electronically and must include the information described in Annex 1(3) of the Directive.

2   When a harbour authority receives a dangerous or polluting cargo report, it shall retain the report for use in the event of an incident or accident at sea, forwarding it whenever requested by the national coastguard authority.

1.73

1   **Reporting of Incidents and Accidents.** Whenever a vessel is involved with one of the following, the coastguard authority of the EU coastal state is to be informed immediately;

(a) any incident or accident affecting the safety of the ship;

(b) any incident or accident which compromises shipping safety, such as a failure likely to affect a ship's manoeuverability or seaworthiness;

(c) any event liable to pollute the waters or shores of the coastal state;

(d) The sighting of a slick of polluting material or drifting containers and packages.

The owner of a vessel, who has been informed by the Master that one of the above has occured, must inform the coastguard and render any assistance that may be required.

1.74

1   **Measures to be taken in the event of exceptionally bad weather or sea conditions.** If, on the advice of the national meteorological office, the coastguard authority deems a threat of pollution or a risk to human life exists due to impending severe weather, the coastguard authority will attempt to inform the Master of every vessel about to enter or leave port as to the nature of the weather and the dangers it may cause.

2   Without prejudice to measures taken to give assistance to vessels in distress, the coastguard may take such measures as it considers appropriate to avoid a threat of pollution or a risk to human life. The measures may include:

(a) a recommendation or a prohibition on entry or departure from a port;

(b) a recommendation limiting, or, if necessary, prohibiting the bunkering of ships in territorial waters.

3   The Master is to inform his owners of any measures or recommendations initiated by the coastguard. If, as a result of his professional judgement, the Master decides not to act in accordance with measures taken by the coastguard, he shall inform the coastguard of his reasons for not doing so.

1.75

1   **Measures relating to incidents or accidents at sea.** The coastguard authority will take measures to ensure the safety of shipping and of persons and to protect the marine and coastal environment. Measures available to EU states include;

(a) a restriction on the movement of a ship or an instruction to follow a specific course.

(b) a notification to put an end to the threat to the environment or maritime safety;

2   (c) send an evaluation team aboard a ship to assess the degree of risk and to help the Master remedy the situation;

(d) instruct the Master to put in at a place of refuge in the event of imminent peril, or, cause the ship to be piloted or towed.

The owner of the ship and the owner of the dangerous or polluting goods onboard must cooperate with the coastguard authority when requested to do so.

1.76

1   **Places of refuge.** EU states are required to designate places of refuge where a vessel which has undergone an accident or is in distress can receive rapid and effective assistance to avoid environmental pollution.

1.77

1   For further details of signals required by the above regulations and detailed format, see *Admiralty List of Radio Signals Volume 6(1)*.

Directive 2002/417EC
1.78

1   **Single-hull petroleum tankers.** This regulation establishes a timetable for the phasing out of all single-hull petroleum tankers of more than 5000 dwt in European waters. Ultimately only double-hull tankers or tankers of equivalent design will be permitted to visit European ports and offshore terminals.

The timetable is based upon a vessel's date of build, its design and the types of petroleum carried. The schedule for Category 1 and 2 tankers completed in 2007. Completion for Category 3 tankers will be in 2015.

Measures to enhance maritime security

Security information
1.79

1   In compliance with Regulation 725/2004/EC, all vessels are required to provide security information, as required by SOLAS XI-2 and the ISPS Code, to the appropriate national authority 24 hours prior to arrival.

French regulations

French regulations regarding single-hulled tankers in French Exclusive Economic Zone.
1.80

1   Single-hulled tankers more than 15 years old and carrying heavy fuel oil, tar, asphaltic bitumen, or heavy crude oil and intending to enter the French Exclusive Economic Zone must give 24 hours notice to the relevant French MRCC/CROSS, see 1.110. Such access is strictly controlled by the French authorities.

2   Additionally, all single-hulled tankers of whatever age, irrespective of their flag, transporting heavy petroleum products in areas under French jurisdiction are not authorised to enter, depart from or anchor adjacent to any French port or sea terminal without permission to do so.

Joint Prefectural Order 2002/99 Brest. 2002/58 Cherbourg: Regulations for tankers and vessels carrying dangerous and polluting goods off the North and West coasts of France (SURNAV).
1.81

1   **General.** Tankers and vessels carrying dangerous or polluting cargoes, which are over 1600 gt must keep at least 7 miles from the French coast in the area covered by this volume, unless within:

The access channels to Douarnenez, Brest, Cherbourg, Saint-Brieuc, Caen-Ouistreham, Saint-Malo, Roscoff, Rouen, Le Havre, and Port du Havre-Antifer.

1.82

1   **Reports.** Tankers and vessels carrying dangerous or polluting cargoes which intend to enter French territorial waters, or sail from a French port or anchorage, must inform the appropriate Centre Régional Opérationnel de Surveillance et de Sauvetage (CROSS). The message must be prefixed SURNAV-FRANCE and sent 6 hours before entering French territorial waters, or getting underway if already in territorial waters. Amendments must be reported immediately. Full details are given in *Admiralty List of Radio Signals Volume 6(2)*.

1.83

1   **Reporting maritime incidents, accidents, defects and assistance.** All vessels of 300 gt or more, on commercial passage within the French Economic Zone and within 50 miles of the French coast must report in the SURNAV format any such occurrence to CROSS (Griz-Nez, Jobourg, Corsen or Étel). Additionally, any vessel sighting pollution, oil slicks, containers or packages afloat in the area must report same to the aforementioned CROSS.

2   The same regulations apply to all vessels of 300 gt or more whilst navigating within a Marine Nature Reserve. In this instance the report must be made to CROSS La Garde.

A vessel going to the assistance of a damaged vessel within 50 miles of the French coast is also required to report to the same authorities.

For further details of signals required by the above regulations and detailed format, see *Admiralty List of Radio Signals Vol 6(1)*.

3   Vessels with defects affecting their ability to manoeuvre or navigate safely, whilst within French territorial waters, are required to take such action as the Préfet Maritime may require to ensure the safety of navigation and avoid pollution.

Closure of French ports
1.84

1   Normally only International Port Traffic Signals (see *The Mariner's Handbook*) are used to control vessel traffic in and out of a port. In small ports these signals may be replaced by a simplified system, which consists of a red flag by day or a red light by night to indicate that entry is not permitted and a green flag by day or a green light by night to indicate that vessels may not exit the port. If both signals are shown then the port is closed in both directions, see 1.84.

French ports – simplified entry control signals (1.84)

Quarantine

General
1.85

1   Vessels arriving at any port in the United Kingdom or France are subject to the national quarantine regulations.

For information concerning pratique see *Admiralty List of Radio Signals Volume 1(1)*, which also lists the authorities to whom notification should be addressed.

Quarantine and Customs regulations in British ports
1.86

1   Vessels arriving at any ports or harbours in the United Kingdom are subject to British Quarantine regulations and Customs regulations.

In British Territorial Waters, no person is permitted to leave a vessel coming from a foreign place, except in the case of an emergency, until pratique has been granted by the local authority.

2   The Master of a foreign-going vessel, is required to inform the Port Health Authority if any person onboard is suffering from an infectious disease or has symptoms which may be indicative of an infectious disease, or if there are any circumstances requiring the attention of the Port Medical Officer. This information should be passed not more than 12 hours and not less than 4 hours before arrival. See *Admiralty List of Radio Signals Volume 1(1)*.

Regulations to prevent the spread of rabies
1.87

1   Stringent regulations are in force to prevent the spread of rabies into the British Islands.

The following is an extract from Article 12 of *The Rabies (Importation of Dogs, Cats and Other Mammals) Order 1974* (as amended 1977). This extract is applicable to any animal which has, within the preceding 6 months, been in a place outside Great Britain, Northern Ireland, the Republic of Ireland, the Channel Islands and the Isle of Man, except one for which an import licence has been issued.

2   "It shall be the duty of a person having charge or control of a vessel in harbour in Great Britain to ensure that an animal which is onboard that vessel:
(a) is at all times restrained, and kept securely confined within a totally enclosed part of the vessel from which it cannot escape;
(b) does not come into contact with any other animal or any contact animal (other than an animal or contact animal with which it has been transported to Great Britain); and
(c) is in no circumstances permitted to land."

3   If an animal to which the above extract applies is lost from a vessel in harbour the person having charge or control of that vessel must immediately inform the Local Animal Health Officer from the State Vetinary Service, an agency of the Department for the Environment, Food and Rural Affairs, or the Police, or an officer from HM Revenue and Customs.

4   No "native" animals or contact animals are permitted to go on board the vessel on which there is an animal from abroad. This does not apply to dogs belonging to the Police, HM Customs and Excise or the Armed Forces and under the constant control of a trained handler, or to animals being loaded for export.

5   A "contact animal" is any one of 25 species, listed in an Appendix to the Order, which are not normally subject to quarantine for Rabies unless they have been in contact with an animal which is subject to quarantine; for example, a horse, listed as a "contact animal", could become subject to quarantine if it came into contact with a dog or other animal which is subject to quarantine.

6   Other than in exceptional circumstances, only certain ports are authorised for the landing of animals for which an import licence has been issued; within the limits of this volume Southampton is an authorised port.

Similar regulations are in force in Channel Islands.

7   *The Pet Travel Scheme (Pilot Arrangements) (England) Order 1999* amends the above mentioned Order in respect of certain pet animals (cats and dogs only) which may be brought into the United Kingdom without being subject to quarantine provided a number of conditions are fulfilled. The scheme is limited to pets coming from certain designated countries and territories, and operates only on certain sea, air and rail routes to England by designated carriers. Pets may not be brought into the United Kingdom in any private vessel. The scheme is administered by the Department for the Environment, Food and Rural Affairs, from whom advice is available (www.defra.gov.uk).

Quarantine regulations in French ports
1.88

1   In normal conditions, vessels, irrespective of flag, proceeding from one port to another within the European Union, need not ask for pratique.

Vessels entering French waters from a port outside the European Union should hoist, by day, Flag "Q" International Code and by night, but only within port limits, a red light over a white light.

2   The Master of a foreign-going vessel is required to inform the Port Health Authority by radio of any case of illness suspected to be of an infectious nature, see *Admiralty List of Radio Signals Volume 1(1)*.

Protected sites and features

Historic wrecks in British waters
1.89

1   **General information.** Wrecks that are considered of historic, archaeological or artistic importance, or of their potentially dangerous condition, are protected under *The Protection of Wrecks Act 1973*. Within a given area this act prohibits unauthorised interference with the wrecks, tampering with, damaging them or removing any part. Diving or depositing anything on the seabed, for example anchoring, is also prohibited, without a special licence.

2   Entry into the area is prohibited when the wrecks are declared to be in a potentially dangerous condition.

Historic wrecks within the area covered by this volume are mentioned in the text; see also *Annual Summary of Admiralty Notices to Mariners*.

Military wrecks
1.90

1   To prevent the disturbance of the dead, certain wrecks, less than 200 years old, are protected from interference by the *Protection of Military Remains Act 1986*. See *Annual Summary of Admiralty Notices to Mariners*.

Nature reserves
1.91

1   **General information.** Until 1991 the main government body responsible for nature conservation was the Nature Conservancy Council (NCC). Since 1992 the NCC has been replaced by three separate councils; in England by

English Nature, in Scotland by Scottish Natural Heritage and in Wales by the Countryside Council for Wales.

2 These conservation bodies give advice on nature conservation to government and to all those whose activities affect wildlife and wild places. They are also responsible for establishing, maintaining and managing a series of national nature reserves and marine reserves and identifying and notifying Sites of Special Scientific Interest. The work is based on detailed ecological research and survey.

Information concerning bye-laws, codes of conduct, descriptions and positions of nature reserves and sites of special interest can be obtained from the above Councils.

3 **National Nature Reserves.** There are about 400 National Nature Reserves in the United Kingdom of Great Britain and Northern Ireland; only those which can be found on or near the coastlines and river estuaries contained in this volume, which may be of direct interest to the mariner, are mentioned in the text. Reserves are shown on certain charts of the British Isles.

4 **Marine Nature Reserves** provide protection for marine flora and fauna and geological and physiographical features on land covered by tidal waters up to and including the limit of territorial waters; they are shown on the charts. They also provide opportunities for study and research.

5 **Local Nature Reserves.** Local authorities in England and Wales and district councils in Scotland are able to acquire and manage local nature reserves in consultation with the conservation councils. Conservation Trusts can also manage non-statutory local nature reserves.

SIGNALS

International signals

Distress signals
1.92

1 For details of distress signals made by ships and aircraft see *Annual Summary of Admiralty Notices to Mariners.*

International Port Traffic Signals
1.93

1 International Port Traffic Signals, which are given in *The Mariner's Handbook*, are in use by most of the ports covered in this volume.

Certain small French ports use a simplified system set out in Diagram 1.84.

National signals

Special signals by naval vessels
1.94

1 *The Mariner's Handbook* should be consulted concerning the characteristics and special signals shown by naval vessels.

There is also information on submarines and minelaying and mine countermeasure in *Annual Summary of Admiralty Notices to Mariners.*

Storm warnings and signals
1.95

1 **British waters.** Visual storm warnings are no longer displayed. See 1.62 for broadcast warnings.

French waters. The International System of Visual Storm Warning Signals (see *The Mariner's Handbook*) are displayed from French signal stations listed at 1.110.

At some points on the coast small craft are warned when winds above force 6 are expected. A quick flashing light indicates that such winds may be expected within 3 hours and an interrupted quick flashing light that such winds may be expected within 6 hours.

Tidal and water level signals
1.96

1 These signals are only in general use in French waters. They are given in the French publication *Signalisation Maritime.*

French police vessels
1.97

1 **Signals.** French vessels operated by the police show the following signals:

By day. White and blue triangular flag with a blue letter "P" on the white part of the flag.

At night. Flashing violet light visible all round.

Marking of breakwaters, jetties and bridges in French waters
1.98

1 **French waters.** In some French ports the extremities of breakwaters, jetties and certain port installations are sometimes painted in distinctive colours, either to make them more visible, in which case they are painted white or pale yellow, or to indicate the side on which they should be left, in which case they are painted:

Red rectangle on white background — leave to port.

Black, or dark green triangle on white background — leave to starboard.

2 Bridges under which navigation is practicable are similarly marked, either on the piles of the bridge if the navigable channel extends over the whole width of the arch, or under the arch of the bridge at the limits of the navigable channel. At night the panels are illuminated or the channel indicated by lights, green on the starboard hand, red on the port hand; in addition a white light (isophase or flashing) may be exhibited on the arch to indicate the best part of the channel.

DISTRESS AND RESCUE

General information

Search and Rescue
1.99

1 **General arrangements** for SAR, together with details of distress signals made by ships and aircraft, are given in *Admiralty List of Radio Signals Volume 5* and *Annual Summary of Admiralty Notices to Mariners.*

Global Maritime Distress and Safety System, see 1.63.

British waters

General information
1.100

1 Her Majesty's Coastguard Service (HMCG) (see below) is part of the Maritime Operations Directorate of the Maritime and Coastguard Agency (MCA) and is the authority responsible for initiating and co-ordinating all civil maritime SAR operations in the United Kingdom Search and Rescue Region (UK SRR).

The RN provides ships and helicopters to assist casualties.

2　　The Royal Air Force is responsible for co-ordinating and controlling rescue on behalf of military and civil aviation in the UK SSR and provides SAR fixed wing aircraft and helicopters, controlled through the Aeronautical Rescue Co-ordination Centre at Kinloss.

The Royal National Lifeboat Institution (RNLI) (1.113) provides all-weather and inshore lifeboats around the coast for saving life at sea.

Her Majesty's Coastguard Service
1.101

1　　**General information.** The primary role of the Coastguard Service is the initiation and co-ordination of civil maritime SAR within the UK SRR. This includes the mobilisation, organisation and tasking of adequate resources to respond to persons either in distress at sea, or to persons at risk of injury or death on the cliffs or shoreline of the United Kingdom.

2　　In a maritime emergency the Coastguard Service calls on and co-ordinates the appropriate facilities such as RNLI lifeboats, RN and Royal Air Force rotary and fixed wing aircraft and ships, as well as merchant ships and commercial aircraft. Close liaison is maintained with adjacent foreign SAR organisations.

3　　HMCG also maintains over 400 Initial Response and Coastal Rescue Teams at strategic locations around the UK coast.

1.102

1　　**Coastguard network.** The UK SRR is bounded by latitudes 45°N and 61°N, by longitude 30°W and to the E by the adjacent European Search and Rescue Regions. The Coastguard maintains close liaison with all countries with adjoining SRR boundaries.

2　　HMCG is organised into three Search and Rescue Regions (SRR). The sea area within the limits of this book lies within the Wales and West of England Region (MRCC Falmouth) and the East of England Region, Southern Sector (MRCC Solent and MRCC Portland). For further details see *Admiralty List of Radio Signals Volume 5.*

All MRCCs keep a constant VHF radio, Digital Selective Calling (DSC), telephone and telex watch and have a VHF DF capability.

1.103

1　　**Coastguard communications.** MRCCs, Coastguard boats and Initial Response and Coastal Rescue Teams are fitted with VHF radio.

2　　**Note.** Radio and telephone traffic to and from Maritime Rescue Co-ordination Centres is recorded for the purposes of public safety, preventing and detecting crime and to maintain the operational standards of HM Coastguard.

1.104
1.105

1　　**VHF Direction-finding service for use in emergency.** The Coastguard operate a VHF DF service for SAR purposes at 48 stations around the United Kingdom. Triangulation from adjacent MRCCs can be used to establish the position of a vessel in distress. For further information see *Admiralty List of Radio Signals Volume 2.*

1.106

1　　**National Coastwatch Institution** is a voluntary organisation which maintains a visual lookout from coastal vantage points and monitors the VHF radio distress frequency, reporting incidents to the Coastguard. In addition, stations monitor local weather conditions and provide information to mariners on request. Some stations are equipped with radar. There are stations at:

2　　Gwennap Head (3.88)
Cape Cornwall (3.88)
Bass Point (3.103)
Porthscatho (4.85)
Charlestown (4.86)

3　　Prawle Point (4.273)
Exmouth (5.102)
Bill of Portland (5.127)
Saint Albans (6.85)
Peveril Point (6.85)

Channel Islands waters
1.107

1　　**General information.** Channel Islands area is within the sector of MRCC CROSS Joburg and is split in two zones for the purpose of SAR. MRSCs are situated at the Harbour Authorities of Guernsey and Jersey which are responsible for the N and S areas respectively. In the N area, in addition to Guernsey, there is a Sub-Station at Alderney.

The area is recognised as extending up to 12 miles from Channel Islands coastline or the median line whichever is the nearer.

Search and Rescue Aircraft
1.108

1　　**SAR Helicopters** chartered by the Coastguard are based at Lee-on-Solent (50°49′N 1°12′W) and Portland (50°33′N 2°27′W) (0900–2100 only).

Aeroplanes. A search aircraft is based at Guernsey (49°26′N 2°36′W).

Emergency Towing Vessel (ETV)
1.109

1　　An ETV, one of four positioned around the UK, is stationed off the SW coast of England throughout the year; it is equipped for fire-fighting, salvage and towing.

French waters

Centre Régionaux Opérationnels de Surveillance et de Sauvetage
1.110

1　　**Coastguard.** France has four Regional Surveillance and Rescue Operations Centres (CROSS) situated on the Atlantic coast. The centres applicable to this volume are located at: Jobourg (49°41′N 1°54′W); Corsen (48°24′N 4°47′W) and Étel (47°39′N 3°12′W).

2　　SAR operations in French waters are conducted by CROSS centres which provide a permanent, full time, all weather operational presence along the coast of France and cooperates with foreign MRCC's and MRSC's as required. Their main duties are surveillance of maritime traffic including policing IMO agreed TSS's and Inshore Traffic Zones, particularly inside the 12 mile limit, SAR, surveillance of fisheries out to 200 miles and monitoring of pollution, including tracking vessels carrying dangerous substances.

3　　Within each CROSS region, signal stations and naval lookout stations are established at prominent positions on the coast. These stations are manned by the French Navy and operate continuously (Vigie) or by day (Sémaphore). They pass urgent signals concerning the safety of ships, communicating mainly by VHF radio, but they are also able to communicate by light and flags, if required. The stations also display storm signals (1.95) and inform and direct lifeboats.

4　The stations applicable to this volume are established, in book order, at: Le Stiff Radar Tower; Créac'h; Pointe de Saint-Mathieu; Toulinguet; Cap de la Chèvre; Pointe du Raz; Brignogan; Île de Batz; Ploumanc'h; Île de Bréhat; Saint-Quay-Portrieux; Saint-Cast; Le Roc, Granville; Barneville-Carteret; Cap de la Hague; Homet, Cherbourg; Barfleur; Saint-Vaast-la-Hougue; Port-en-Bessin; Villerville; La Hève.

For details see *Admiralty List of Radio Signals Volume 5*.

1.111

1　**VHF Direction-finding service for use in emergency.** Each VHF direction-finding station is remotely controlled by either a CROSS centre, signal station or naval lookout station, details of which are given above. In addition, VHF direction-finding facilities are operated from CROSS Jobourg and a CROSS controlled station at Roches-Douvres.

2　VHF DF triangulation can, from adjacent stations, be used to establish the position of a vessel in distress.

Full details of these services are given in *Admiralty List of Radio Signals Volume 2*.

Rescue tugs

1.112

1　**Emergency ocean-going tugs** are stationed at Brest (48°23′N 4°29′W) and Cherbourg (49°39′N 1°38′W) and are equipped for fire-fighting, salvage and towage.

Lifeboats in British waters

Royal National Lifeboat Institution

1.113

1　**General information.** The Royal National Lifeboat Institution (RNLI) maintains a fleet of over 250 lifeboats of various types at stations around the coast of the United Kingdom. It is a privately run organisation supported entirely by voluntary contributions; its headquarters are at Poole, Dorset.

2　There are approximately 211 lifeboat stations around the coasts of the United Kingdom and the Republic of Ireland. A great number operate all-weather lifeboats, often supported by inshore lifeboats, and others operate only inshore lifeboats; about one half of the inshore lifeboats are permanently on station, while the remainder are on station only during the summer.

1.114

1　**All-weather lifeboat characteristics:**
　　Length between 12 and 17 m.
　　Speed 13 kn or more.
　　Radius of action about 100 miles.
　　Equipment: radar; DF on 2182 kHz and VHF; communications on MF (2182 kHz) and VHF(FM) multi-channel RT; Electronic Navigator.

2　Blue quick flashing light exhibited at night, when on service.

Inshore lifeboat characteristics:
　　Inflatable or rigid inflatable construction.
　　Outboard motor(s).
　　Speed 20 to 30 kn.
　　VHF(FM) multi-channel RT.

1.115

1　**Lifeboat stations.** Within the limit of this volume all-weather lifeboats are permanently stationed at the following locations:
　　Saint Mary's (3.9), Isles of Scilly.
　　Sennen Cove* (3.87).

　　Penlee* (3.101).
　　The Lizard (Church Cove) (4.19).
2　Falmouth* (4.69).
　　Fowey* (4.147).
　　Plymouth (4.247).
　　Salcombe (4.254).
　　Torbay* (5.71).
　　Exmouth* (5.102).
　　Weymouth* (6.17).
3　Swanage* (6.100).
　　Poole* (6.152).
　　Selsey* (6.182).
　　Yarmouth (7.43).
　　Bembridge* (7.92).
　　Calshot* (7.271).
　　Saint Peter Port (11.31), Guernsey.
4　Braye Harbour* (11.150), Alderney.
　　Saint Helier (11.184), Jersey.
　　*Supported by an inshore lifeboat
Inshore lifeboats are also stationed at:
　　Looe (4.153).
　　Teignmouth (5.102).
5　Lyme Regis (5.127).
　　Mudeford (6.100).
　　Lymington (7.43).
　　Southsea (7.92) (Portsmouth).
　　Hayling Island (7.92).
　　Saint Catherine Bay (11.275), Jersey.

1.116

1　The general arrangements for SAR are given in *Annual Summary of Admiralty Notices to Mariners.*

Lifeboats in French waters

General information

1.117

1　**La Société Nationale de Sauvetage en Mer (SNSM)** is responsible for providing lifeboats.

All-weather lifeboats. Within the limits of this volume all-weather lifeboats are stationed at:
　　Île d'Òuessant (Lampaul) (8.21).
　　Île Molène (8.41).
　　Île de Sein (8.196).
　　Audierne* (8.221).
2　Portsall (9.14).
　　Àber-Wrac'h* (9.14).
　　Ile de Batz (9.43).
　　Ploumanac'h-Perros-Guirec (9.128)
　　Saint-Malo* (10.181).
　　Granville (10.191).
　　Goury (11.324).
　　Barfleur (13.14).
　　Ouistreham (13.14).
　　*Supported by an inshore lifeboat.

3　**Inshore lifeboats.** Lighter boats, some of which may be inflatables, are also stationed at:
　　Port de Conquet (8.41)
　　Camaret-sur-Mer (8.76).
　　Douarnenez (8.167).
　　Argenton (9.14).
　　Brignogan-Plouescat (9.43)
　　Plouguerneau (9.43).
　　Roscoff (9.78).
　　Primel-Trégastel (9.90).
4　Locquirec (9.90).
　　Trébeurden (9.90).
　　Loguivy-de-la-Mer (10.14).

5

Saint-Quay-Portrieux (10.65).
Erquy (10.65).
Saint-Cast (10.127).
Lancieux (10.127).
Saint-Briac-sur-Mer (10.127).
Dinard (10.181).
Cancale (10.191).
Barneville-Carteret (11.275).

Saint-Vaast-la-Hougue (13.14).
Grandcamp-Maisy (13.14).
Port-en-Bessin (13.14).
Courseulles-sur-Mer (13.14).
Cabourg-Dives-sur-Mer (13.14).
Honfleur (13.113).
Le Havre (13.113).
Trouville-Deauville (13.113).

COUNTRIES AND PORTS

UNITED KINGDOM AND CHANNEL ISLANDS

General description
1.118

1   The United Kingdom of Great Britain and Northern Ireland is a constitutional monarchy comprising England, Scotland, Wales and Northern Ireland, but does not include Isle of Man or Channel Islands, which are Dependencies of the Crown. The Sovereign is also Head of the Commonwealth.

2   The estimated population of the United Kingdom (2006) was 60 533 000.

Definitions
1.119

1   **Great Britain:** England, including the Isles of Scilly, Wales and Scotland; the Shetland and Orkney Islands are part of Scotland

The United Kingdom of Great Britain and Northern Island: Great Britain, as above, and Northern Island.

British Isles: Great Britain, The Isle of Man and Ireland both the Republic and the North.

British Islands: British Isles, as above, and Channel Islands.

National limits
1.120

1   **Territorial waters.** The breadth of the Territorial Sea adjacent to the United Kingdom and the Isle of Man extends for a distance of 12 miles as defined by the Territorial Sea Act 1987, given in Appendix III. The breadth of the Territorial Sea adjacent to the Channel Islands is 3 miles.

2   Baselines to be used for measuring the breadth of the territorial waters adjacent to the United Kingdom, the Channel Islands and the Isle of Man are defined in the Territorial Waters Order in Council 1964 as amended by the Territorial Sea (Amendment) Order 1998, given in Appendix III. This 12 mile Territorial Sea limit is depicted on selected Admiralty charts.

See also *Annual Summary of Admiralty Notices to Mariners.*

1.121

1   **Fishery limits.** The exclusive fishing limits of the United Kingdom extend up to 6 miles from the baselines of the Territorial Sea and for the next 6 miles fishing is limited to countries with established rights in accordance with the European Union's Common Fisheries Policy. These 6 mile and 12 mile limits are depicted on selected Admiralty charts. Foreign fishing rights in these waters are depicted on Admiralty chart Q6385. The Fishery Limits Act 1976 extended British fishery limits to 200 miles measured from the baselines of the Territorial Sea, or to such limits as may be specified. This limit is depicted on Admiralty chart Q6353 and is administered in accordance with the European Union's Common Fisheries Policy.

2   **Channel Islands.** Fishery zones extend for 3 miles outside the baselines in the waters around the Bailiwick of Jersey and there are additional restrictions in the Jersey and French 3-6 mile limits in accordance with the Granville Bay Agreement. The Bailiwick of Guernsey maintains a 12 mile fisheries zone.

History
1.122

1   During the first four centuries AD, Britain was a province of the Roman Empire, which withdrew its protection in 429. The country then fell into the power of the Saxon invaders from the continent of Europe. There followed a period of rivalry for leadership between various Anglo-Saxon kings and invasion by the Vikings from Scandinavia. The various kingdoms were joined into one in the early tenth century and ruled by Saxon kings until the land was conquered by the Danes in 1016. The Saxon house was restored 26 years later.

2   Meanwhile in Europe in the tenth century, a Viking settlement in Normandy, was becoming a feudatory in France. It was from this Duchy that the future rulers of England were to come. In 1066, Duke William of Normandy laid claim to the English throne, invaded and conquered the country, and founded the Norman dynasty. The monarchial system of rulers continued by descent, though not without dispute, for nearly 600 years until 1649 when it was overthrown by Oliver Cromwell, who created the Protectorate. With his death in 1658, a reaction against the Protectorate and strife over his successor resulted in the restoration of the monarchy in 1660, which has continued uninterrupted to the present day.

3   The eighteenth century was marked by the gradual increase in the power of Parliament, rise of political parties, advances in colonisation and trade, and progress of Britain as a sea power.

In the twentieth century self-government was handed over to the majority of the former colonies, most of which joined the British Commonwealth of Nations as independent sovereign states.

In 1973 Great Britain joined the European Economic Community, now the EU.

Government
1.123

1   The supreme legislative power is vested in Parliament, which is divided into two Houses of Legislature, the House of Lords and the House of Commons, and in its present form dates from the middle of the fourteenth century, although in 1999 the House of Lords was reformed to exclude the majority of hereditary peers and peeresses.

2   The House of Lords is non-elected and consists of life peers and peeresses, Law Lords, two archbishops and twenty four bishops of the established Church of England, and as an interim measure, 92 hereditary peers and peeresses. The House of Lords has judicial powers as the ultimate Court of Appeal for courts in Great Britain and Northern Ireland, except for criminal cases in Scotland.

3   The House of Commons consists of members representing county and borough constituencies. Every constituency returns a single member. In 2004 there was a total of 659 members, 529 from England, 72 from Scotland, 40 from Wales and 18 from Northern Ireland. Suffrage is limited to men and women of 18 years and above.

4 Executive government is vested nominally in the Crown, but is exercised in practice by the Cabinet, a committee of ministers, which is dependent on the support of the majority in the House of Commons. The Prime Minister presides over the Cabinet and dispenses the greater portion of the patronage of the Crown.

Parliament can be dissolved by the will of the Sovereign, or by proclamation during its recess or by lapse of the statutory duration of five years.

5 In Scotland, where the judiciary and certain other areas of government still differ significantly from those of the remainder of the United Kingdom, the Scottish Parliament, first elected in 1999, has legislative power over all matters not reserved to the United Kingdom Parliament in Westminster, or otherwise outside its powers.

International relations
1.124

1 The United Kingdom is a permanent member of the Security Council of the United Nations, and a member of the Commonwealth, the EU, the Western European Union, the Council of Europe, the Organisation for Economic Co-operation and Development and NATO.

Coastal features and rivers
1.125

1 The S coast of England, between Land's End and Start Point, consists mainly of bold granite cliffs and igneous rock; farther E the coast becomes more gently sloping and is formed of clay, sandstone and limestone interspersed in places with bluff chalk cliffs.

2 There are numerous rivers which flow in to the sea on the S coast, the principal ones being the rivers Fal, Fowey, Tamar, Dart, Exe, Frome, Trent, Stour, Avon, Test and Itchen. The estuaries of these rivers contain ports of varying size, described in the text of this volume, but the rivers themselves are not generally navigable by sea-going vessels above the ports.

The principal islands off the English coast are Isles of Scilly and Isle of Wight.

Industry and trade
1.126

1 Britain is more dependent than most countries on its industries and trades world-wide.

2 Major industries are iron and steel, heavy engineering, and the processing of imported goods such as wool, cotton and tobacco. In recent years with the decline of some of the traditional industries, Britain has had to rely on technical skill and scientific inventiveness and a new range of industries has developed including motor vehicles, aircraft, nuclear power equipment, instruments, man-made fibres and chemical products as well as electrical goods and machines. Considerable quantities of crude oil are imported to be refined into petroleum products.

3 The production of oil and gas from offshore fields plays an important part in the country's industry and technology.

The country is intensively farmed, mainly for home consumption but an important export trade in agricultural products has been established. A considerable fishing fleet is maintained.

The Channel Islands

General information
1.127

1 The Channel Islands lie to the S of the English Channel in the bight formed by the N coast of Britanny and the W coast of Normandy. They consist of the four main islands of Jersey, Guernsey, Alderney and Sark, with innumerable islets and rocks which, with a few sparsely populated exceptions, are uninhabited. They are Dependencies of the Crown (of the United Kingdom).

2 Plateau des Minquiers, which at LW exposes an area as large as the island of Jersey, and Les Écrehou form part of The Channel Islands.

National limits, see 1.120.
Fishing limits, see 1.121.

History
1.128

1 The skeletons of mammoths, rhinoceroses and primitive man, dating back to 100 000 years BC or earlier, have been discovered. Iberian settlers left flint instruments everywhere in the islands and great burial chambers in Jersey, Guernsey and Alderney, dating back to about 2000 years BC. In later years the islands were occupied by the Gauls and subsequently by the Romans. More fully recorded history began when Rollo the Viking established the Duchy of Normandy, and during successive centuries the islands were constantly raided and plundered. It was not until the nineteenth century that a measure of prosperity was enjoyed from seaborne trade. Later the intensive cultivation for exports to British and other markets created an unprecedented development to which the encouragement of the tourist trade was also a contributing factor.

2 **Language.** The English language is in general use although a Norman-French *patois* is often heard in the country districts of Jersey and Guernsey, and in Sark.

3 **Constitution.** Jersey has its own legislature consisting of a Lieutenant-Governor, the Crown representative, and a Bailiff who is also appointed by the Crown and is President of the locally elected Assembly (The States) and also of the Royal Court. The legislature of Guernsey is on similar lines but the Bailiwick includes the islands of Alderney, Sark, Herm and Jethou, within which Alderney and Sark retain a considerable measure of self-government.

Industry and trade
1.129

1 The basic industry has always been agriculture; Jersey growers concentrating mainly on early potatoes and tomatoes, and those of Guernsey on tomatoes, flowers and grapes. Both islands are famous for their cattle.

Banking and finance are the principal activities in Jersey and Guernsey and all the islands maintain a busy tourism industry, their ports and anchorages being visited by numerous yachts and pleasure craft in the summer months.

FRANCE

General description
1.130

1 France is the largest country in Western Europe and lies on the W coast of that continent between the parallels of 43°20′N and 51°05′N.

In June 2005 the estimated population was 60 656 178. It includes nearly 4 million resident foreigners, the largest groups being Algerian, Portugese and Moroccans.

National limits
1.131

1   **Territorial waters** of France extend for a distance of 12 miles from the baselines, which are formed by straight lines along some parts of the coast.

    Fisheries jurisdiction extends to 200 miles from the baselines.

    For further information see *The Mariner's Handbook* and *Annual Summary of Admiralty Notices to Mariners*.

History
1.132

1   France, descended from the Roman province of Gaul, may be said to have come into being in 987 when Hugh Capet, ruler of the western Franks first became King of France.

    Medieval France was a feudal monarchy which grew in strength, reaching its apogee in the reign of Louis XIV (1643–1715).

2   The French monarchy was overthrown by the Revolution of 1789–1792, and the First Republic came into being, lasting until 1804. The period had a notable achievement in the production of the Metric system of weights and measures, since adopted by many countries.

3   In 1804, Napoleon Bonaparte became Emperor, and for the next 10 years continued his career of conquest, which at one time made him master of most of Europe. After the Napoleonic wars, the monarchy was restored in 1815 and lasted until the revolution of 1848, when it gave way to the Second Republic. Louis Napoleon, nephew of Napoleon Bonaparte, was elected President, later ruled as Napoleon II until the Franco-Prussian war of 1870, a period known as the Second Empire.

4   The Third Republic, which came into existence in 1871 and lasted until 1940, was a period of comparative calm and prosperity marred only by World War I 1914–18. During the German occupation, World War II 1940–44, Marshal Petain ruled France as a dictator.

    After the liberation of Paris in 1944 a provisional government was formed under General de Gaulle.

5   The Fourth Republic, following a referendum, was set up in 1944. Its constitution, however, favoured political instability and France had 26 governments in 14 years. In 1958 General de Gaulle was temporarily invested with dictatorial powers and invited to reform the Constitution, introducing the Fifth Republic.

Government
1.133

1   Under the constitution of the Fifth Republic France is governed by a President elected by universal suffrage for a period of 5 years. He may assume special powers in an emergency, dissolve Parliament and submit disputed legislation to a referendum.

    The Prime Minister is appointed by the President and is responsible to Parliament, consisting of a Senate and a National Assembly.

2   There is a constitutional Council which supervises elections and referenda, and which must be consulted before the President assumes emergency powers.

    For administrative purposes the country is divided into 96 Departments, in each of which the Government is represented by a resident Préfet. The Departments are divided into Arrondissements (sous-préfectures) or Municipal Wards, and further sub-divided into Cantons, which contain a number of Communes or parishes with local administrative authority. Each Commune is presided over by an elected mayor or municipal council.

3   The Departments are also grouped into 22 Economic Regions, each under a Regional Préfet, the coastal regions and their headquarters within the area covered by this volume are: Haute-Normandie (Rouen); Basse-Normandie (Caen) and Bretagne (Rennes).

    For administrative purposes the N and W coasts of France are divided into two maritime regions, Préfet Maritime de la Manche with headquarters in Cherbourg and Préfet Maritime de l' Atlantique with headquarters in Brest. Préfet Maritime de la Manche is responsible for an area extending from the North Sea adjacent the Belgian border to a line across the English Channel between Land's End (50°02′N 5°40′W) and Baie du Mont Saint-Michel (48°38′N 1°34′W). Préfet Maritime de l'Atlantique is responsible for an area extending W from the limits mentioned above, and S as far as the Spanish border.

    The policing of coastal waters, pilotage and fisheries come under the jurisdiction of the Préfets Maritimes.

4   **Languages.** The principal and official language of the country is French, which has numerous regional dialects. Breton, a language closely allied to Welsh, is spoken by about a million people in W Brittany.

International relations
1.134

1   France is a permanent member of the Security Council of the United Nations, and a member of the EU, the Western European Union, the Council of Europe, the Organisation for Economic Co-operation and Development and NATO. It is also the focus of the French Community which formally links it with its former colonies in Africa.

Coastal features and navigable rivers
1.135

1   The NE part of the N coast of France consists of chalk cliffs and sandy beaches; farther SW the coasts of Contentin Peninsula and Brittany are rocky and uneven.

    The only river on the N coast of France navigable by large vessels is La Seine. Of less importance are the smaller rivers of L'Élorn, L'Aulne, Le Morlaix, Le Léguer, Le Tréguier, Le Trieux, La Rance, L'Orne and La Dives.

    The principal islands off the French coast are Île de Seine, Île d'Ouessant, Île de Batz, Île de Bréhat, Îles Chausey and Channel Islands.

Industry and trade
1.136

1   France is nearly self-sufficient in agriculture, producing chiefly dairy products, cereals, potatoes, sugar-beet, early vegetables, fruit and hops. The wine industry is among the largest in the world and forestry is also important.

    The fisheries meet the country's needs.

2   Coal, iron ore, bauxite, uranium, potash and sulphur are mined but not in sufficient quantities to meet the requirement for these materials. Natural gas is an important provider of energy, but there are only small quantities of hydro-carbons. Electricity is produced by a mix of thermal and nuclear powered stations, with a few hydro-electric power stations.

3   Imports are mainly of the basic materials, but also of machine tools and other manufactured products. Exports are of agricultural products, luxury goods and manufactured products. Because of her comparative self-sufficiency France is less dependent on foreign trade than her neighbours.

PRINCIPAL PORTS HARBOURS AND ANCHORAGES

1.137

Place and position	*Remarks*

ENGLAND

Isles of Scilly

Place and position	*Remarks*
Saint Mary's Road (3.65) (49°55′N 6°20′W)	Open anchorage

England - south coast

Newlyn (3.119) (50°06′N 5°33′W)	Important fishing port
Penzance (3.126) (50°07′N 5°32′W)	Small commercial port
Falmouth (4.35) (50°09′N 5°03′W) Carrick Roads Docks	Anchorage within river estuary Commercial and repair port
Fowey (4.114) (50°20′N 4°38′W)	Small commercial port and yachting centre
Plymouth (4.168) (50°22′N 4°11′W) Sound HM Dockyard (Devonport) Millbay Docks Sutton Harbour Cattewater	Large protected anchorage Major naval dockyard port Commercial harbour Commercial and fishing harbour Commercial harbour
Salcombe Harbour (4.260) (50°14′N 3°46′W)	Sheltered yachting centre
Dartmouth (5.23) (50°21′N 3°35′W)	Sheltered harbour and yachting centre
Tor Bay Harbour (5.64) (50°26′N 3°08′W) Brixham Torquay	Large open anchorage and off–limits service area Important fishing harbour Small commercial harbour and yachting port
Teignmouth (5.106) (50°33′N 3°30′W)	Small commercial port
Portland Harbour (6.28) (50°35′N 2°26′W)	Protected anchorage and commercial port
Weymouth (6.61) (50°36′N 2°27′W)	Commercial and ferry port; yachting centre
Poole Harbour (6.112) (50°43′N 1°59′W)	Extensive natural harbour Commercial and ferry port Yachting centre
Portsmouth (7.130) (50°48′N 1°05′W) HM Dockyard Commercial harbours	Major naval dockyard port Commercial port and yachting centre
Cowes (7.214) (50°46′N 1°18′W)	Commercial port and yachting centre
Southampton (7.227) (50°54′N 1°24′W) Esso Marine Terminal BP Hamble Terminal Docks	Major oil refining complex Oil terminal Major commercial port

Place and position	*Remarks*

CHANNEL ISLANDS

Saint Peter Port, Guernsey (11.102) (49°28′N 2°32′W)	Commercial port, yachting centre
Alderney Harbour (11.169) (49°44′N 2°12′W)	Small commercial port and yacht harbour
Saint Helier, Jersey (11.246) (49°11′N 2°07′W)	Commercial port, yachting centre

FRANCE

Brest (8.108) (48°23′N 4°29′W)	Major French naval base, important commercial, repair and fishing port, yachting centre
Douarnenez (8.178) (48°06′N 4°20′W)	Important fishing port and yachting centre
Port de Roscoff-Bloscon (9.48) (48°43′N 3°58′W)	Ferry port
Baie de Morlaix (9.99) (48°43′N 3°53′W)	Open anchorage
Le Légué (10.74) (48°32′N 2°44′W)	Small commercial port for Saint-Brieuc
Saint-Malo (10.159) (48°39′N 2°01′W)	Commercial, ferry and fishing port, yachting centre
Granville (10.207) (48°50′N 1°36′W)	Commercial and ferry port, yachting centre
Cherbourg (12.21) (49°39′N 1°38′W)	Major naval, commercial, and fishing port, yachting centre
Caen-Ouistreham (13.67) (49°17′N 0°15′W)	Ferry port at Ouistreham with access by canal to commercial port of Caen, yacht harbours
Le Havre (13.115) (49°29′N 0°07′E)	Major commercial and oil port, fishing and yacht harbours
Honfleur (13.182) (49°25′N 0°14′E)	Commercial and fishing port
Rouen (13.193) (49°27′N 1°05′E)	Important commercial river port, yachting centre
Havre-Antifer (13.213) (49°40′N 0°08′E)	Oil terminal for deep-draught tankers

PORT SERVICES — SUMMARY

Docking facilities

1.138

1   Ports with docking facilities and, where available, the dimensions of the largest vessel that can be accommodated are given below. Details of dock sizes are given at the reference.

    England:

        Penzance. Dry dock for vessels up to 1600 dwt (3.132).

        Falmouth. Three dry docks for vessels up to 100 000 dwt (4.64).

2   Fowey. Patent slip lifting capacity 600 tonnes (4.143).

        Plymouth. Dry docks available at Devonport for naval vessels (4.242).

Dartmouth. Patent slip for vessels up to 500 dwt (5.50).

Poole. Slipway for vessels up to 700 tonnes (6.148).

3   Portsmouth. Naval base, dry docks for naval vessels; Porchester mechanical lift dock capacity 877 tonnes (7.182).

Cowes. Patent slip lifting capacity 600 tonnes (7.225).

Channel Islands:

Guernsey, Saint Sampson. Patent slip lifting capacity 400 tonnes (11.93).

4   **France:**

Camaret-sur-Mer. Slipway for vessels up to 350 tonnes (8.106).

Brest. Three commercial dry docks for vessels up to 550 000 dwt (8.142).

Douarnenez. Slipway for vessels up to 420 tonnes (8.186).

5   Saint-Malo. Dry dock for vessels up to 120 m in length (10.181).

Granville. Dry dock (10.215).

Cherbourg. Several government dry docks some of which can be used by commercial vessels (12.65).

6   Port-en-Bessin. Slipways for vessels up to 200 dwt (13.59).

Le Havre. Several dry docks for vessels up to 80 000 dwt; floating dock with a lifting capacity of 50 000 tonnes for vessels up to 220 000 dwt (13.153).

Rouen. Floating dock with a lifting capacity of 14 000 tonnes (13.201).

Other facilities

Compass adjustment
1.139

1   Facilities for compass adjustment usually exist at ports where major repairs or shipbuilding are carried out.

Suitable marks for compass adjustment exist at Plymouth (4.243) and Portsmouth (7.183).

Ship sanitation control certificates
1.140

1   In accordance with the International Health Regulations ship sanitation control certificates or ship sanitation control exemption certificates are issued at the following ports:

British waters. Falmouth (4.65); Fowey (4.144); Plymouth (4.243); Teignmouth (5.113); Weymouth (6.79); Poole (6.149); Portland (6.60); Portsmouth (7.183); Southampton (7.268); Saint Helier, Jersey (11.271).

France. Brest (8.143); Roscoff (9.78) Cherbourg (12.66); Caen-Ouistreham (13.92); Le Havre (13.154); Rouen (13.202).

Measured distances
1.141

1   **British waters.** Measured distances are established at:

West Looe (4.152).

Anvil Point (6.84).

Southampton Water (7.245).

Trawling and fishing on the alignment of a measured distance are prohibited.

21

NATURAL CONDITIONS

MARITIME TOPOGRAPHY

Seabed

Charts 2649, 2655, 2675, 4103
Approaches to the English Channel
1.142

1   To the W and SW of Isles of Scilly (49°55′N 6°20′W), within the continental shelf (1.2), are a series of ridges, some of considerable length but of no great breadth, all of which lie in a NE/SW direction. The geographical positions given in the following paragraphs indicate the approximate positions of the least depth on the named banks. Other shoaler depths of less than 90 m exist in this incompletely surveyed area.

2   Great Sole Bank (100 m) (49°51′N 9°46′W) lies about 30 miles within the W edge of the continental shelf and 140 miles W of Isles of Scilly. Cockburn Bank (93 m) (50°01′N 8°45′W) and Jones Bank (71 m) (49°53′N 7°58′W) lie between Great Sole Bank and Isles of Scilly. Another depth of 73 m lies 35 miles WSW of Jones Bank. Melville Knoll (104 m) (49°27′N 8°09′W) lies almost 27 miles SSW of Jones Bank.

3   Between Île d'Ouessant (48°28′N 5°05′W) and the edge of the continental shelf about 180 miles W are situated Little Sole Bank (115 m) (48°27′N 8°53′W), Shamrock Knoll (111 m) (48°31′N 7°19′W) and Parsons Bank (99 m) (48°22′N 6°34′W) which lies 58 miles W of Île d'Ouessant. Kaiser-i-hind Bank (117 m) (48°06′N 6°34′W) lies about 16 miles S of Parsons Bank.

   Between Parsons Bank and Île d'Ouessant, the bottom is more even and there are depths of not less than 77 m to within about 3½ miles of the W danger of Île d'Ouessant.

   La Fosse d'Ouessant, a remarkable deep about 1 mile wide with depths of more than 100 m lies about 5 miles NW of Île d'Ouessant.

4   The bottom of the W approaches to the English Channel appears mainly to consist of fine or coarse sand, a great deal of broken shell, occasional patches of pebbles, gravel, small stones, and now and then, mud. The sand is mostly white though in many places it is yellow, and with black specks. The black specks are often found mixed both with the white and yellow sand; they are very fine, resembling fine cinder dust. The greater proportion of yellow sand lies S of the parallel of 49°30′N, and that of black specks N of that line. This distribution is very marked, especially between the meridians of 9°40′W and 7°30′W.

English Channel
1.143

1   Hurd Deep, with general depths of more than 100 m, and from 2 to 3 miles wide, extends about 80 miles NE from a position 38 miles N of Île de Batz (48°45′N 4°01′W). In its NE part, about 9 miles NNE of Casquets, the depths increase to 174 m. Although there exist in various parts of the English Channel sudden variations in depths, there is none so marked as that afforded by Hurd Deep.

2   Generally, in the entrance to the English Channel, the bottom on the S side is coarser, the stones larger, and the specimens of a paler colour than on the N side of the Channel; this latter is an invariable feature when S of the fairway.

3   Between Isle of Wight and Cherbourg the general quality of the bottom S of the fairway is loose, or rocky, the stones being generally covered with reddish encrustations; within 15 miles of the English coast the bottom becomes finer being mainly sand mixed with fine gravel.
1.144

1   **Sandwaves.** Several fields of sandwaves exist in the W part of the English Channel in deep water; the waves tend to run in a N to S direction.

2   Between Eddystone Rocks (50°11′N 4°16′W) and Hurd Deep there are two such fields, centred about 17 miles and 33 miles SE of Eddystone Rocks. Each field is about 15 miles in extent in a N to S direction and 10 miles in an E to W direction. Average amplitudes are from 1 to 2 m, with a maximum amplitude of 5 m, and average wavelengths are between 100 and 300 m. A third field is centred about 30 miles SE of Start Point (50°13′N 3°38′W) and is about 10 miles in extent in a N to S direction and 12 miles in an E to W direction. Average amplitudes are from 5 to 15 m, with occasional sandwaves exceeding heights of 20 m; average wavelengths are between 250 and 1500 m.

CURRENTS AND TIDAL STREAMS

Currents

Currents diagram
1.145

1   In Diagram 1.145 arrows indicate the predominant direction, average rate and constancy, which are defined as follows:

   Predominant direction. The mean direction within a continuous 90° sector containing the highest proportion of observations from all sectors.

2   Average rate, to the nearest ¼ kn, of the highest 50% in the predominant sectors as indicated by the figures on the diagram. It is emphasised that rates above and below those shown may be experienced.

   Constancy, as indicated by the thickness of the arrows, is a measure of its persistence, eg low constancy implies marked variability in rate and, particularly, in direction.

North Atlantic Current
1.146

1   In the North Atlantic Ocean, E of about 46°W, the Gulf Stream ceases to be a well defined current, becoming weaker as it fans out up the E side of Grand Banks of Newfoundland. The resulting wide NE and E flow is directed across the ocean towards the British Isles, and the adjacent European coasts, and is known as the North Atlantic Current.

Open ocean
1.147

1   In the W half of the area covered by this volume, from about 10° to 20°W, the current sets in a predominantly E to ENE direction. The constancy of the predominant E to ENE set lies between 50 and 60% over the greater part of the area but decreases to less than 50% in the extreme SE. The mean rate of all currents in the area is around ½ kn. Around 95% of observed currents are less than 1 kn and of the remainder only a very small percentage exceed 2 kn.

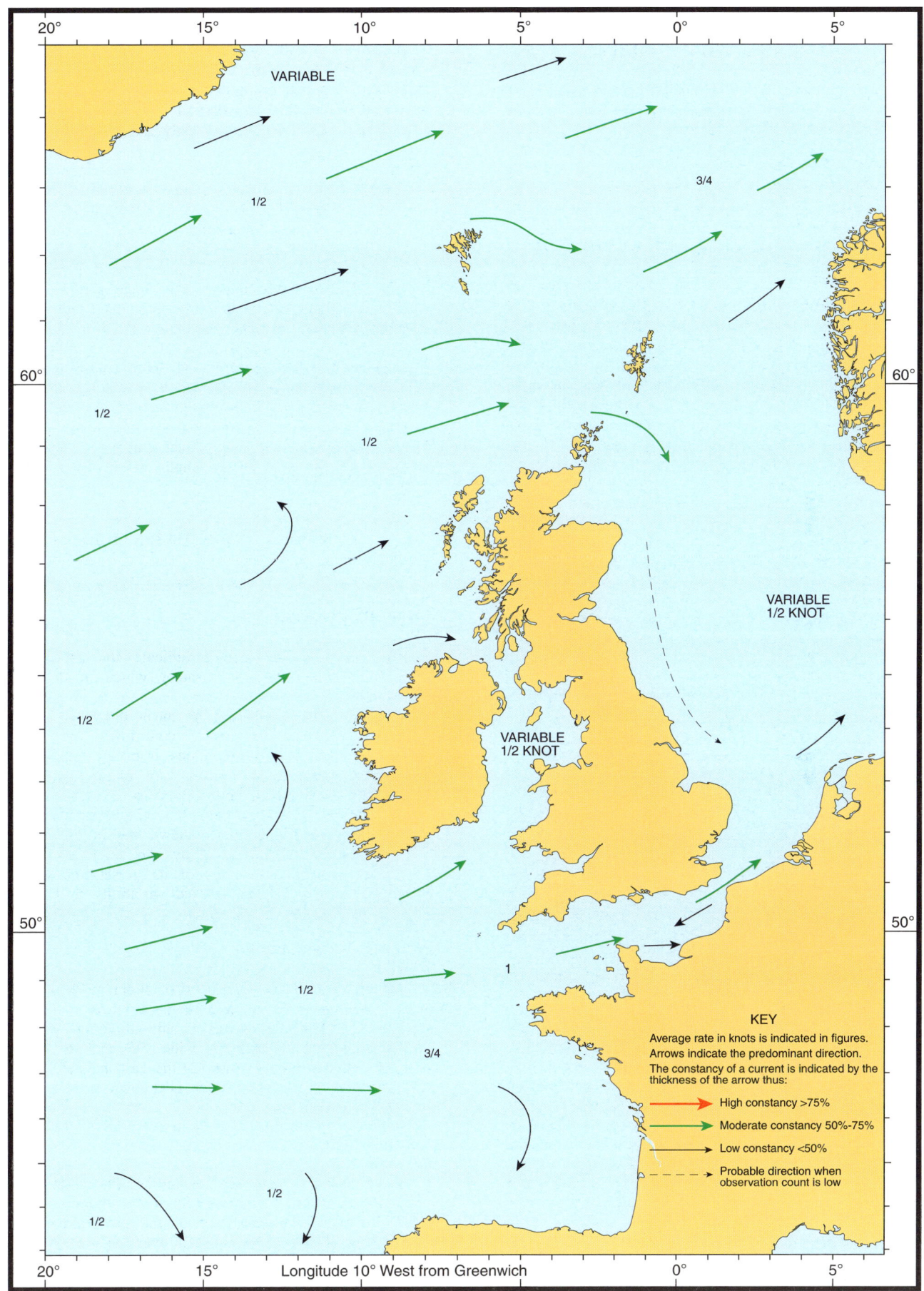

VARIABLE

1/2

3/4

1/2

1/2

1/2

1/2

VARIABLE
1/2 KNOT

VARIABLE
1/2 KNOT

1/2

1

3/4

KEY

Average rate in knots is indicated in figures.
Arrows indicate the predominant direction.
The constancy of a current is indicated by the
thickness of the arrow thus:

→ High constancy >75%

→ Moderate constancy 50%-75%

→ Low constancy <50%

--→ Probable direction when
observation count is low

1/2

1/2

Longitude 10° West from Greenwich

Predominant surface currents JANUARY to DECEMBER (1.145)

English Channel
1.148

1 Within the 200 m depth contour, E of about 11°W, tidal streams generally predominate. However, with tidal effects removed there is usually a residual ENE set in the English Channel which steadily strengthens near the approaches to Dover Strait.

2 Near the Brest peninsula the currents can be very variable in both direction and rate. In winter, the ENE set usually divides as it approaches the Brest peninsula with one branch turning ESE towards Bay of Biscay and the other continuing ENE towards the English Channel. By early summer, both branches frequently set more to the S in the area between Brest and about 10°W.

Effects of strong winds
1.149

1 Strong and persistent winds from any quarter can induce a surface current which may accentuate or retard the average current indicated in the diagram. Over the area covered by this volume the rate of the surface current due to the wind may be estimated as about one fortieth of the speed of the wind, and its direction as about 30° to the right of the direction to which the wind is blowing. There is usually a lag of some hours between the setting in of the wind and the full establishment of its associated current, which if strong, is likely to persist for a day or more after the wind has ceased.

2 In the area covered by this volume, these effects are particularly apparent. The predominant E to ENE set is likely to be enhanced after prolonged W to SW gales, and within the 200 m depth contour the effect of wind upon tidal streams is even more marked.

Tidal streams

General
1.150

1 The following brief general account is intended only to describe the principal features of the tidal streams in the W approach and fairway of the English Channel.
Data for predictions should be obtained from information on the charts and in *Admiralty Tide Tables* and the following *Admiralty Tidal Stream Atlases:*

2 The English Channel.
Falmouth to Padstow, including Isles of Scilly.
The West Country: Falmouth to Teignmouth.
Plymouth Harbour and approaches.
Lyme Bay.
Approaches to Portland.
The Solent and adjacent waters.
Portsmouth Harbour and approaches.
The Channel Islands and adjacent coasts of France.

3 Time references in the tidal stream information in this volume are given in four-figure groups, where the first two figures are hours and the second two figures minutes. References preceded by a minus (–) sign are intervals before HW and those preceded by a plus (+) sign are intervals after HW.

West approaches to the English Channel
1.151

1 Over the continental shelf extending W and SW from the Brittany coast there are almost certainly streams, probably rotary and barely perceptible near the edge of the shelf, but increasing in velocity and becoming more and more nearly rectilinear as the land is approached.

2 Information regarding the streams over the shelf S of 48°30′N is lacking.

2 In the W approach to the English Channel the streams are more or less rotatory clockwise. Variations in direction and rate at different positions are not great; taking averages over the whole area the streams run as follows:

Approx interval from HW Dover	Direction	Spring rate kn	Stream
+0400/+0500	NE/ENE	1	Strongest inwards
–0500	SE	¾	Weakest inwards
–0100	WSW	1	Strongest outwards
+0100/+0200	WNW/NW	¾	Weakest outwards

3 Near the W limit of the W approach, the greatest and least rates are attained rather earlier, and the rates are rather less, than the averages; near the E limit, the greatest and least rates are attained rather later, and the rates are considerably greater, than the averages.

Fairway of the English Channel
1.152

1 As the English Channel is entered, and the fairway narrows, the rotatory streams of the approach become gradually more and more rectilinear.

2 The rates of the streams in the fairway vary with the width and are greatest in the narrowest parts. In the middle of the fairway, between Bill of Portland (50°31′N 2°27′W) to Saint Catherine's Point (50°35′N 1°18′W), on the English coast, and Cap de la Hague (49°44′N 1°56′W) to Pointe de Barfleur (49°52′N 1°16′W), on the French coast, spring rates up to about 3½ kn occur. In the widest parts spring rates of from 2 to 2½ kn are seldom exceeded.

South coast of England
1.153

1 Between Durlston Head (50°36′N 1°57′W) and Selsey Bill (50°43′N 0°47′W) the streams are much affected by shallow water; the effects are most apparent in Poole Harbour, Southampton Water, the E part of The Solent and Portsmouth Harbour. In Poole Harbour the flood stream runs for about 5 hours only, the ebb stream runs in two periods, separated by an interval of slack water, or even of weak flood stream, and has a total duration of about 7½ hours. In Southampton Water, the E part of The Solent and Portsmouth Harbour these circumstances are reversed; the flood stream runs in two periods, separated by an interval of slack, or nearly slack, water, and has a total duration of about 7½ hours; the ebb stream runs for about 5¼ hours only. In Southampton Water and off the entrance to Portsmouth Harbour, though the durations of the streams are not affected, the ebb stream also runs in two periods, though less evidently than the flood stream.

2 The streams run directly through The Solent and cannot well be referred to as in-going and out-going, or as flood and ebb, for the in-going stream in the W part of The Solent is the out-going stream in the E part of The Solent, and the flood stream, which is actually the E-going stream, runs in a direction away from Portsmouth Harbour. The Solent streams are therefore called E-going and W-going, but these directions are general only. The E-going stream, for instance, runs NE in Needles Channel, but SE in the E approach to The Solent and Portsmouth Harbour. The streams running into and out of Southampton Water and

Portsmouth Harbour, which must be distinguished from The Solent streams, are called the flood and ebb streams.

3   The streams of The Solent, including the entrances to Southampton Water and Portsmouth Harbour, and off the S coast of the Isle of Wight, are shown in *Admiralty Tidal Stream Atlas for The Solent and adjacent waters*.

North coast of France
1.154

1   The time of HW changes rapidly along the French coast and is about 6 hours later at Le Havre than at Île d'Ouessant. Furthermore, the time at which the stream turns usually differs considerably from the time of local HW. The streams, therefore, cannot be described as flood and ebb and are usually called E-going and W-going but it must be understood that the E-going stream is merely that which runs up the Channel from the Atlantic towards Dover Strait, and the W-going stream that which runs down the Channel from Dover Strait towards the Atlantic.

2   The actual directions of the streams may differ considerably from E or W and, when this occurs, the directions are stated. In the estuaries and rivers, streams are usually called the in-going and out-going, but may also be called flood and ebb.

3   **Differences.** The streams near the N coast of France differ materially from those in the main fairway of the English Channel, especially off the W part of the coast between Île d'Ouessant and Île de Bréhat. In this locality, the time at which the stream turns, only about 5 miles outside the islands and rocks which fringe the coast, may be as much as 3 hours later than inside them. Among Channel Islands, also, the times and directions of the stream differ greatly from those in the fairway of the English Channel. Great care is therefore required when approaching the above localities.

SEA LEVEL AND TIDES

Sea level

Predicted and actual tidal levels
1.155

1   Meteorological conditions which differ from the average will cause differences between the predicted and actual tidal levels. Variations in tidal heights are mainly caused by strong or prolonged winds, and by unusually high or low barometric pressure, causing positive or negative surges which raise or lower sea level.

2   Differences between predicted and actual times of high and low waters are caused mainly by the wind. A strong wind blowing with the tidal stream will tend to increase the height of tide and prolong the flood stream, while a wind blowing with the ebb stream will have the opposite effect. Winds blowing against the stream will have the opposite effect to those blowing with the stream. Currents are also markedly affected.

3   Seiches, which are short period oscillations in sea level, may be caused by abrupt changes in meteorological conditions, such as the passage of an intense depression. Small seiches occur from time to time around the coasts of the British Isles, especially during the winter months.

For further information see *The Mariner's Handbook* and *Admiralty Tide Tables*.

Tides

Tidal ranges
1.156

1   In the area covered by this volume the tide is predominately semi-diurnal off the S coast of England and the NW coast of France; off the latter the tidal range is very large.

The mean spring range is greatest, 11·5 m, in Baie du Mont Saint-Michel (48°40′N 1°35′W), and least 1·5 m, at Swanage (50°37′N 1°57′W).

Approximate tidal time differences
1.157

1   The approximate tidal time differences between Dover and some of standard ports situated within the area covered by this volume are as follows:

Dover	Devonport	Portsmouth	Saint Helier
−0600	−0020	−0535	−0110
−0500	+0040	−0435	−0010
−0400	+0140	−0335	+0050
−0300	+0240	−0235	+0150
−0200	+0340	−0135	+0250
−0100	+0440	−0035	+0350
HW	+0540	+0025	+0450
+0100	−0545	+0125	+0550
+0200	−0445	+0225	−0535
+0300	−0345	+0325	−0435
+0400	−0245	+0425	−0335
+0500	−0145	+0525	−0235
+0600	−0045	+0625	−0135

2   Time differences used in the text, when applied to the time of HW found from *Admiralty Tide Tables* give the time of the event being described in the Standard Time kept in the area of that event. Due allowance must be made for any seasonal Daylight Saving Time which may be kept.

SEA AND SWELL

General information
1.158

1   For general information on sea and swell, and the terminology used in describing their characteristics, see *The Mariner's Handbook*.

Sea conditions
1.159

1   The whole of the area covered by this volume is frequently affected by E-moving depressions from the North Atlantic Ocean. The highest frequency of rough to high seas over the open ocean, to the W of about 5°W, are associated with winds from between S and NNW. In January, about 27% of observations over the W part of the area record sea waves of 4 m and over, reducing to about 20% between Cape Cornwall (50°08′N 5°43′W) and Brest. By July, the percentage is generally less than 5% over the whole of the area.

2   In general, rough seas may be expected in the English Channel on about 6 to 7 days a month in winter and on about 2 to 3 days a month in summer.

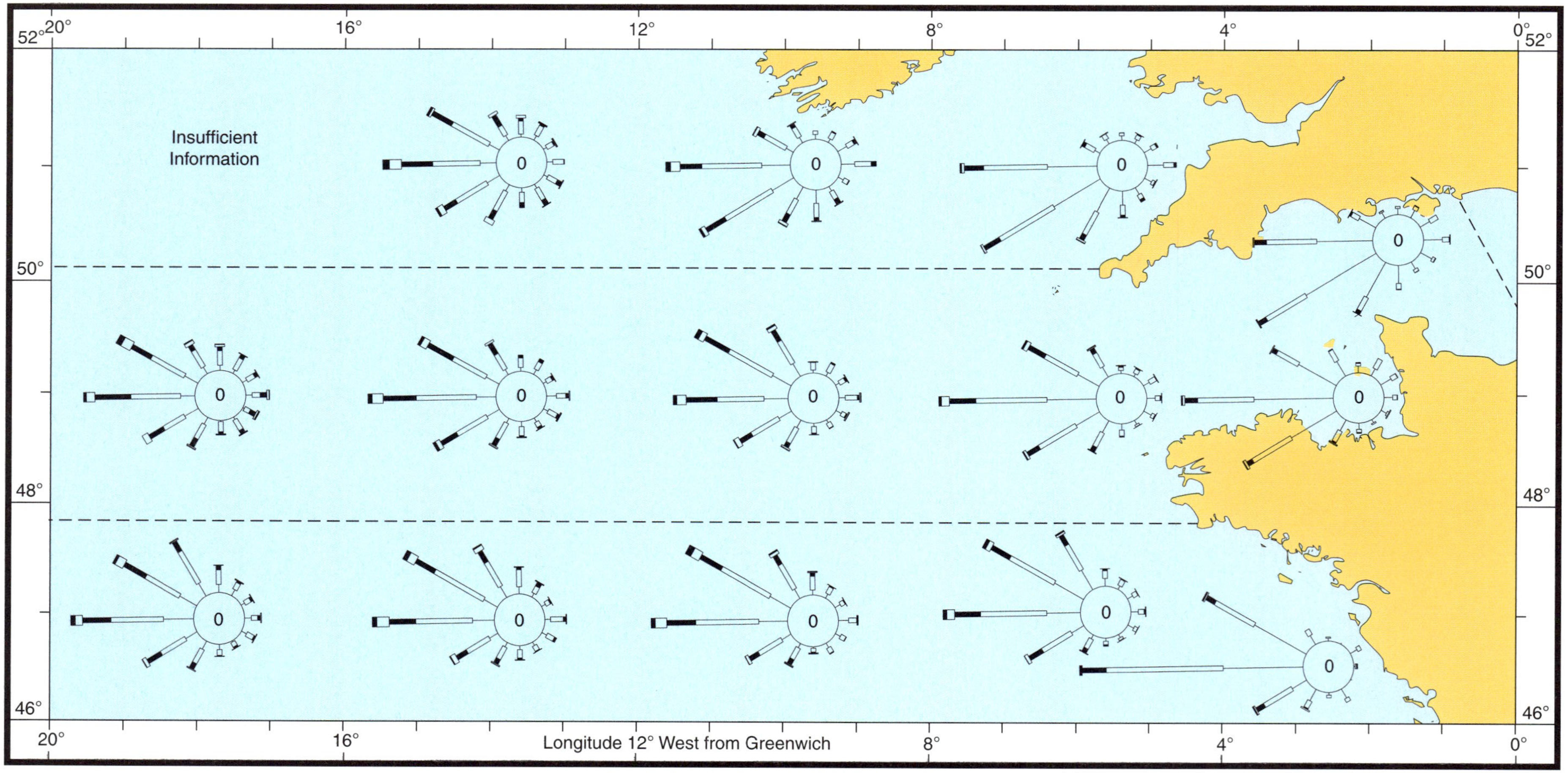
52°
20°
16°
12°
8°
4°
0°
52°
50°
48°
46°
50°
48°
46°
Insufficient
Information
0
Longitude 12° West from Greenwich

Swell distribution JANUARY (1.160.1)

EXPLANATION. The frequency of swell from any direction is given according to the scale:

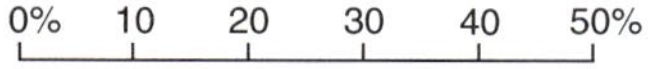
0%
10
20
30
40
50%

This scale is further subdivided to indicate the frequency of swell of different heights (in metres) according to the legend:

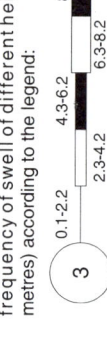

3
0.1-2.2
2.3-4.2
4.3-6.2
6.3-8.2
8.3+

Swell direction is towards the circle centre. The figure within the circle gives the percentage of calms.

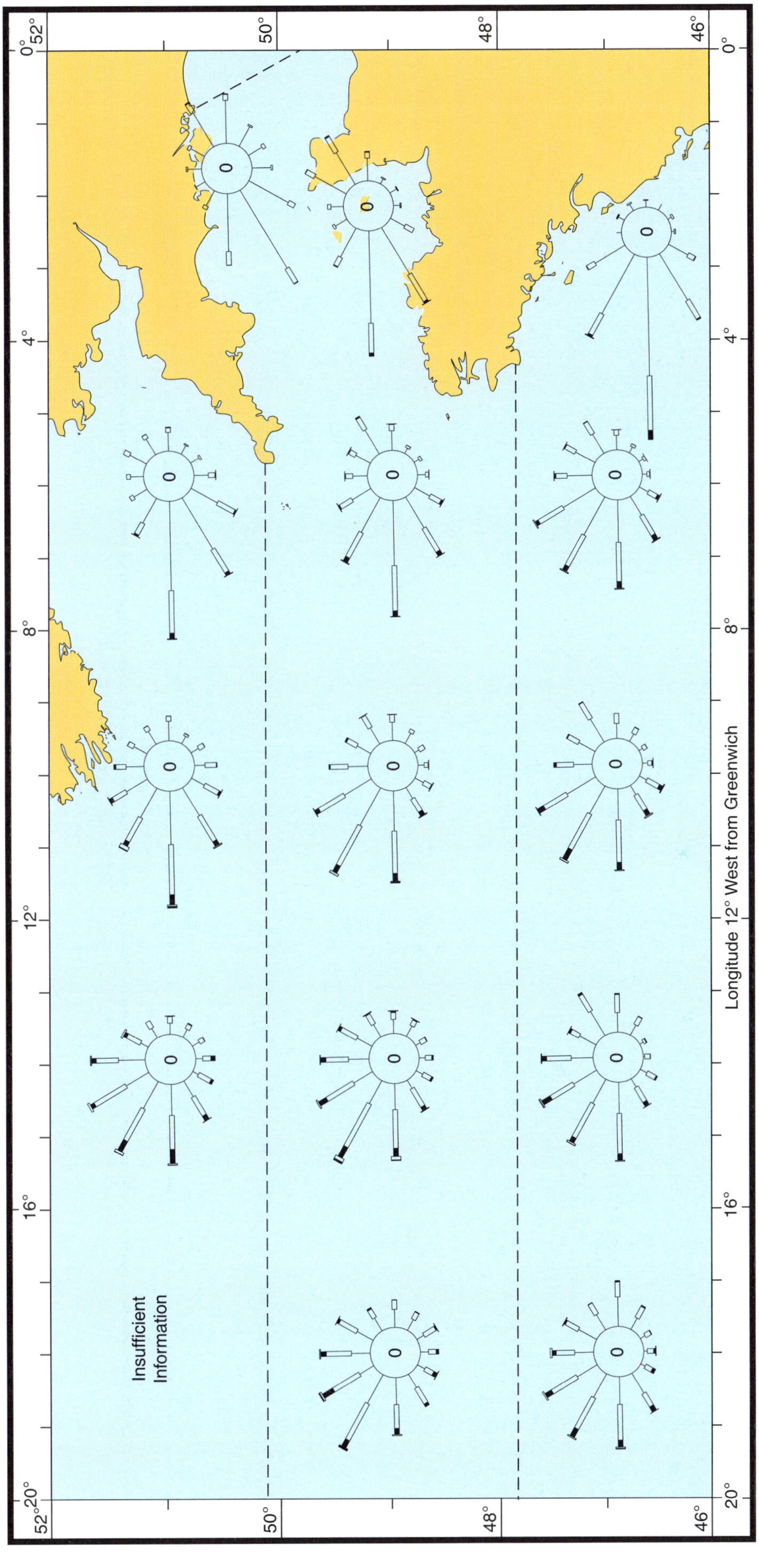

Swell distribution APRIL (1.160.2)

Longitude 12° West from Greenwich

Insufficient
Information

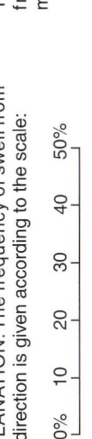

EXPLANATION. The frequency of swell from any direction is given according to the scale:

0% 10 20 30 40 50%

This scale is further subdivided to indicate the frequency of swell of different heights (in metres) according to the legend:

0.1-2.2   2.3-4.2   4.3-6.2   6.3-8.2   8.3+

3

Swell direction is towards the circle centre. The figure within the circle gives the percentage of calms.

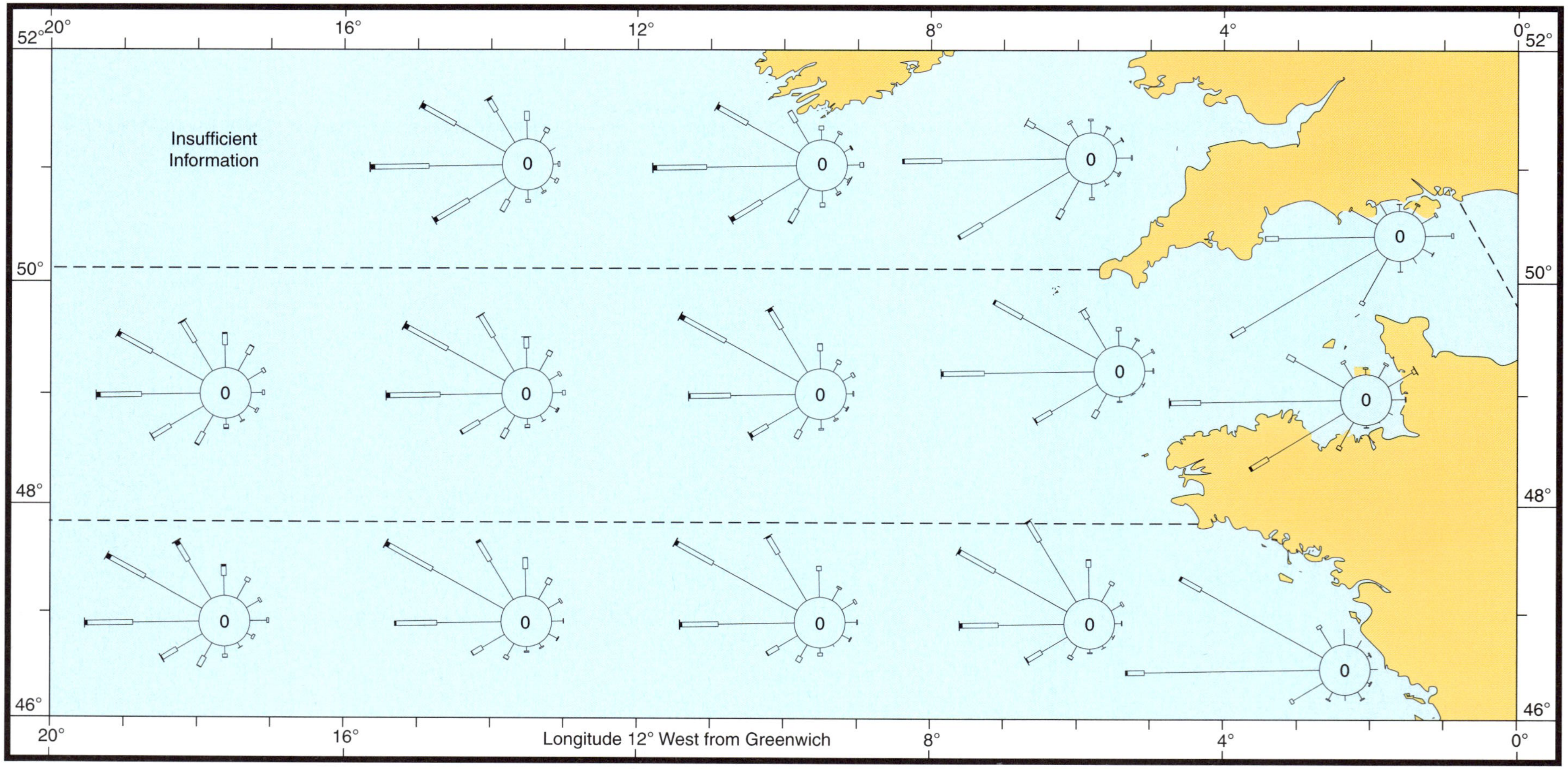

Swell distribution JULY (1.160.3)

Longitude 12° West from Greenwich

Insufficient
Information

EXPLANATION. The frequency of swell from
any direction is given according to the scale:

0% 10 20 30 40 50%

This scale is further subdivided to indicate the
frequency of swell of different heights (in
metres) according to the legend:

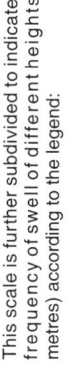

0.1-2.2   2.3-4.2   4.3-6.2   6.3-8.2   8.3+

Swell direction is towards the circle centre. The
figure within the circle gives the percentage of
calms.

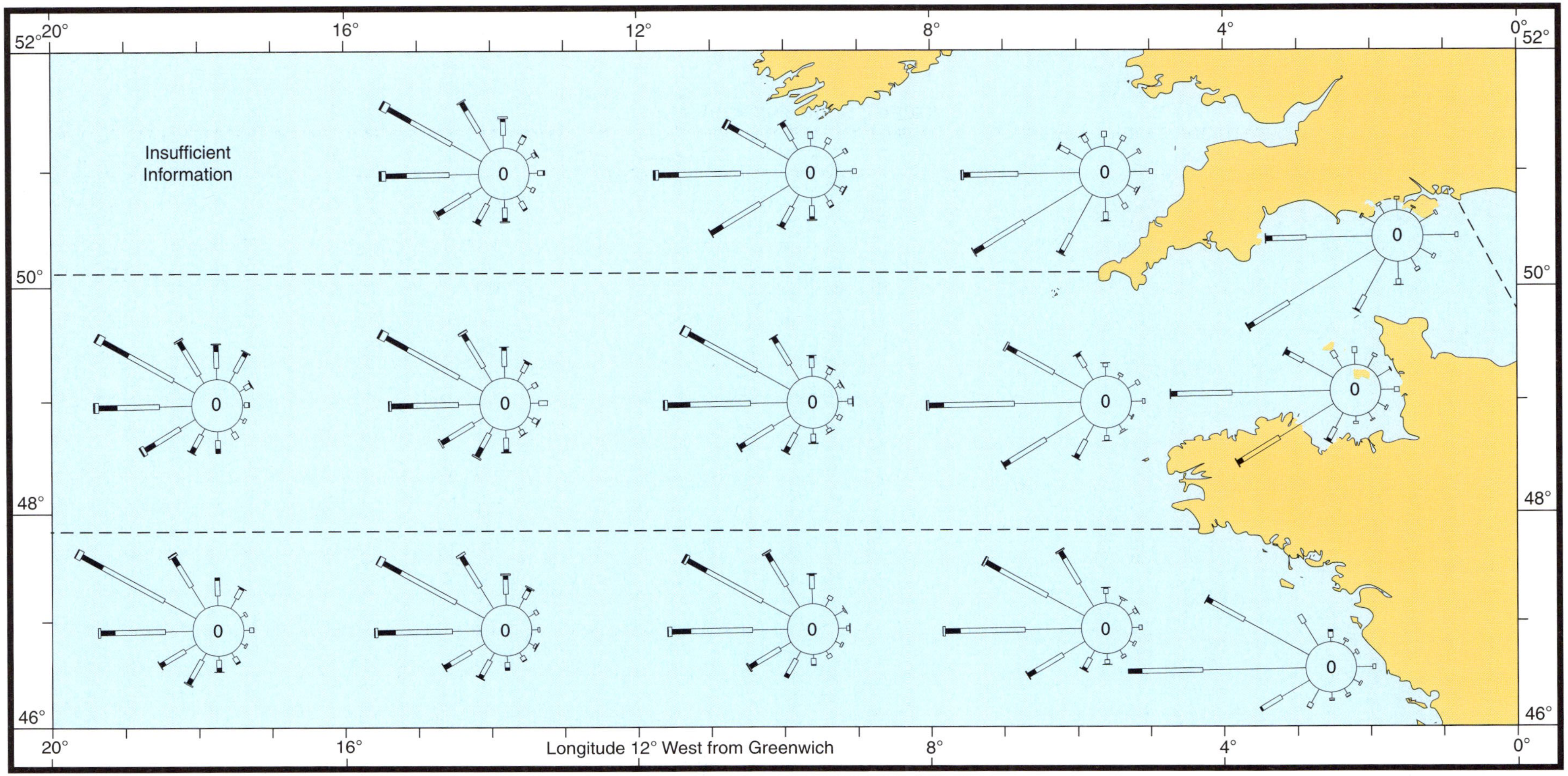

Swell distribution OCTOBER (1.160.4)

Longitude 12° West from Greenwich

Insufficient
Information

EXPLANATION. The frequency of swell from
any direction is given according to the scale:

0%   10   20   30   40   50%

This scale is further subdivided to indicate the
frequency of swell of different heights (in
metres) according to the legend:

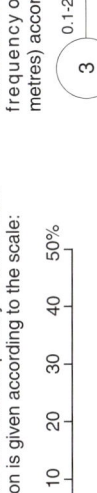

0.1-2.2   2.3-4.2   4.3-6.2   6.3-8.2   8.3+

Swell direction is towards the circle centre. The
figure within the circle gives the percentage of
calms.

Swell conditions
1.160

1   Diagrams 1.160.1 to 1.160.4 give swell roses for several areas for January, April, July and October. The roses show the percentages of observations recording swell waves for each sector and for several ranges of wave height.

2   Swell waves over the W half of the area covered by this volume are predominantly from between WSW and NW. In this area in winter, about 30% of observations record a swell of 4 m and over, reducing to around 20% between Cape Cornwall and Brest. In summer, the percentage reduces to less than 5% across the area.

3   In the English Channel the predominant direction of the swell is from between WSW and W but with a small increase in the frequency of swells from the ENE in late winter and spring. In winter, about 10% of observations record swells greater than 4 m, but this reduces to less than 2% in summer.

SEA WATER CHARACTERISTICS

Salinity
1.161

1   For an explanation of salinity as applied to sea water, see *The Mariner's Handbook*.

The salinity of seawater for the area covered by this volume remains relatively constant during the year but varies across the area. In the W approaches to the area the value is between 35·30 and 35·50. In the English Channel values between 35·00 and 35·20 will be found in mid-Channel. Off the N coast of France the value is less than 34·00 and the values off the S coast of England are between 34·75 and 35·00.

Density
1.162

1   For an explanation of density as applied to sea water, see *The Mariner's Handbook*.

The density in the area covered by this volume varies seasonally. In winter (February) the area has a general value of 1·02725 g/cm^3 reducing to 1·02700 g/cm^3 off the N coast of France. The area has a general value of 1·02575 g/cm^3 in summer (August) rising to 1·02600 g/cm^3 off the SW coast of England and in the W approaches to the area covered by this volume.

2   Ports within the area covered by this volume have varying values of density as follows:

Locality	Density g/cm^3
Falmouth	1·02220
Fowey	1·01920
Plymouth	1·02820–1·02620
Exmouth	1·02220
Exeter Canal	1·02320
Exeter	1·00320
Weymouth	1·02520–1·02420
Poole	1·02320
Portsmouth	1·02720–1·02620
Southampton	1·02520–1·02120
Cherbourg	1·02620
Le Havre	1·02720–1·02520

Sea surface temperature
1.163

1   Diagrams 1.163.1 to 1.163.4 shows the average sea surface temperature of the waters surrounding the British Isles for the months of February, May, August and November.

Sea surface temperatures are generally at their lowest in late February and highest in August. In winter, the mean sea surface temperature ranges from about 7·5°C in the E of the area to around 12°C in the extreme SW. In summer the temperature increases to around 16·5°C in the N and E of the area, and to about 17·5°C in the extreme SW.

2   In winter, the sea is warmer than the over-laying air by about 2°C, and in summer the reverse tends to be true, although the difference is generally small.

Variability
1.164

1   Mean sea surface temperature variations tend to be smaller in winter than in summer, and are unlikely to exceed 2°C except in shallow coastal waters in summer.

CLIMATE AND WEATHER
General

General information
1.165

1   The following information on climate and weather should be read in conjunction with the information contained in *The Mariner's Handbook* which explains in more detail many aspects of meteorology and climatology of importance to the mariner.

Weather reports and forecasts, that cover the area, are regularly broadcast in a number of different languages; for details see *Admiralty List of Radio Signals Volume 3(1)*.

Weather pattern
1.166

1   The region covered by this volume is affected by the numerous E moving mobile depressions that transit the British Isles, and by the Azores and Asiatic anticyclones. The depressions giving rise to periods of unsettled weather with strong winds and rough seas, and the anticyclones to generally more settled conditions. Gales can occur in any month but are most frequent in the winter months with winds reaching storm strength on occasions.

2   Rainfall is plentiful and frequent, and is well distributed throughout the year with generally the driest months from April to July. It is frequently cloudy in all seasons but marginally less so in the summer months.

The region generally enjoys a mild maritime climate, although an E airflow in winter can bring exceptionally cold conditions which, on occasions, may persist for several weeks.

Fog is rare over the open sea in winter but more common in summer with moist SW winds.

Pressure

Average distribution
1.167

1   The average pressure distribution at mean sea level in January, April, July and October is shown in Diagrams 1.167.1 to 1.167.4.

The dominant features of the pressure field are the Azores anticyclone, which is situated to the SW of the area covered by this volume, and the semi-permanent Icelandic low pressure area to the NW. The latter resulting from the many mobile depressions that affect this area, especially in winter.

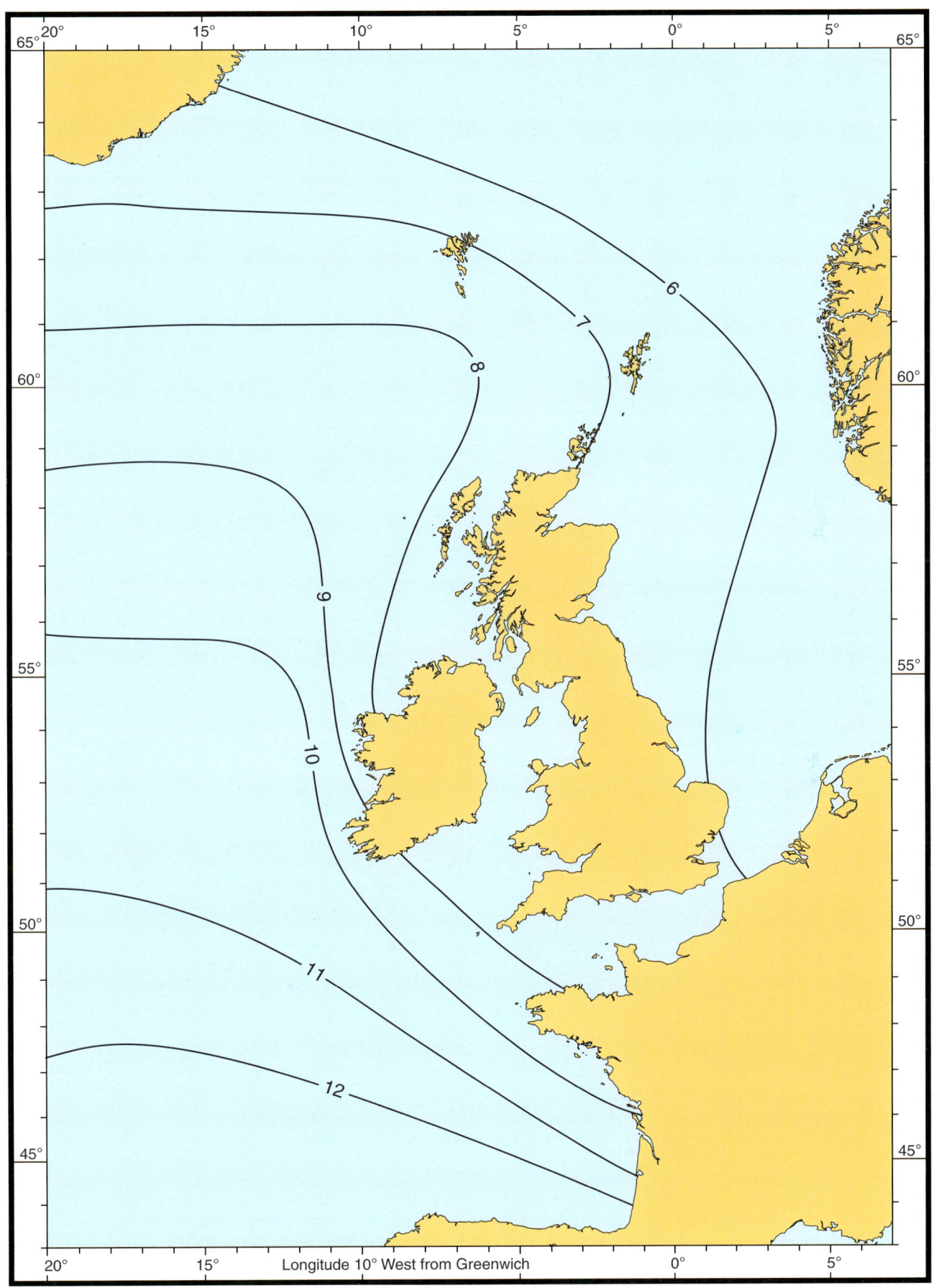

Mean sea temperature (°C) - FEBRUARY (1.163.1)

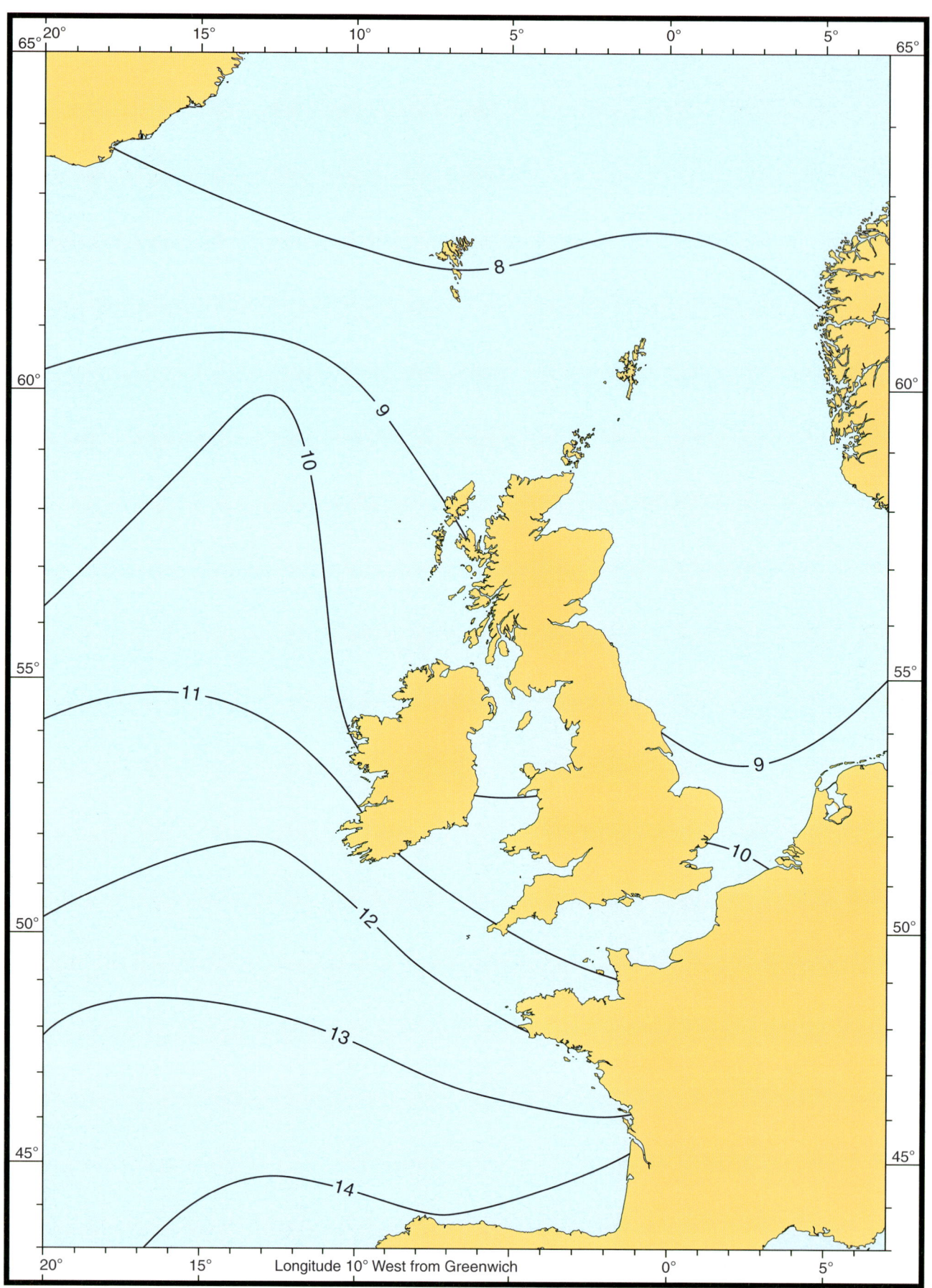

Mean sea temperature (°C) - MAY (1.163.2)

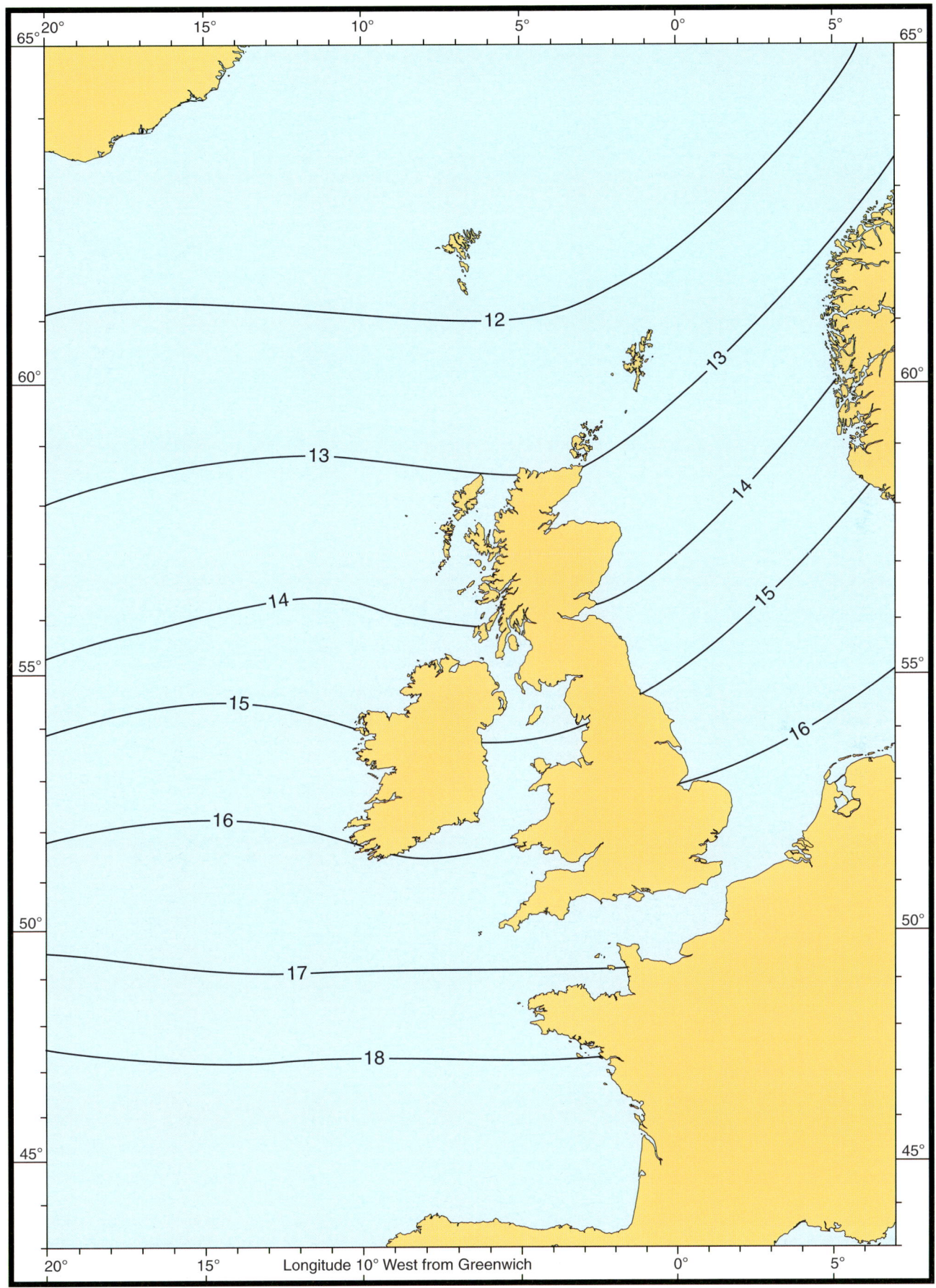

Mean sea temperature (°C) - AUGUST (1.163.3)

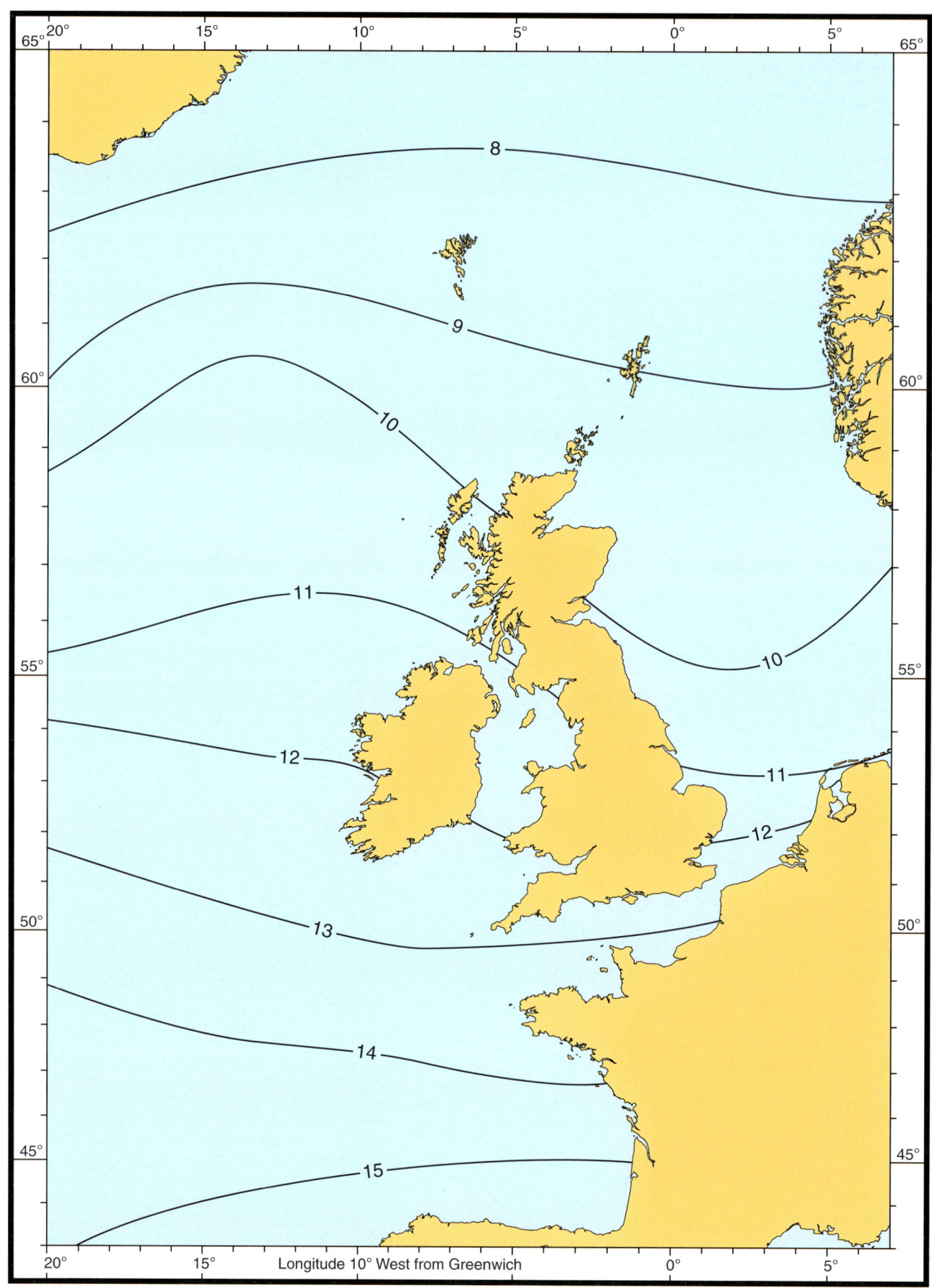

Mean sea temperature (°C) - NOVEMBER (1.163.4)

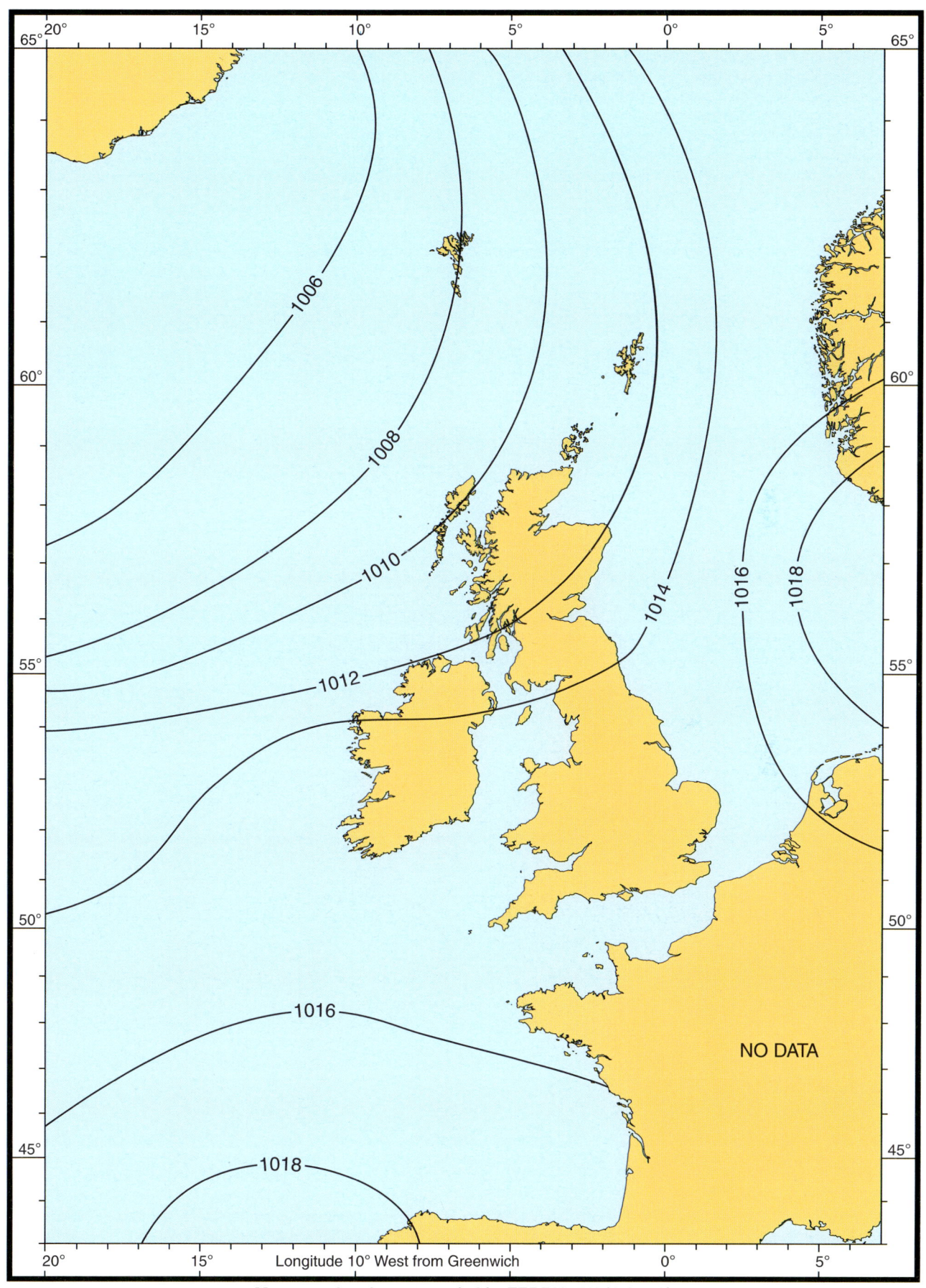

Mean sea level pressure (mb) - FEBRUARY (1.167.1)

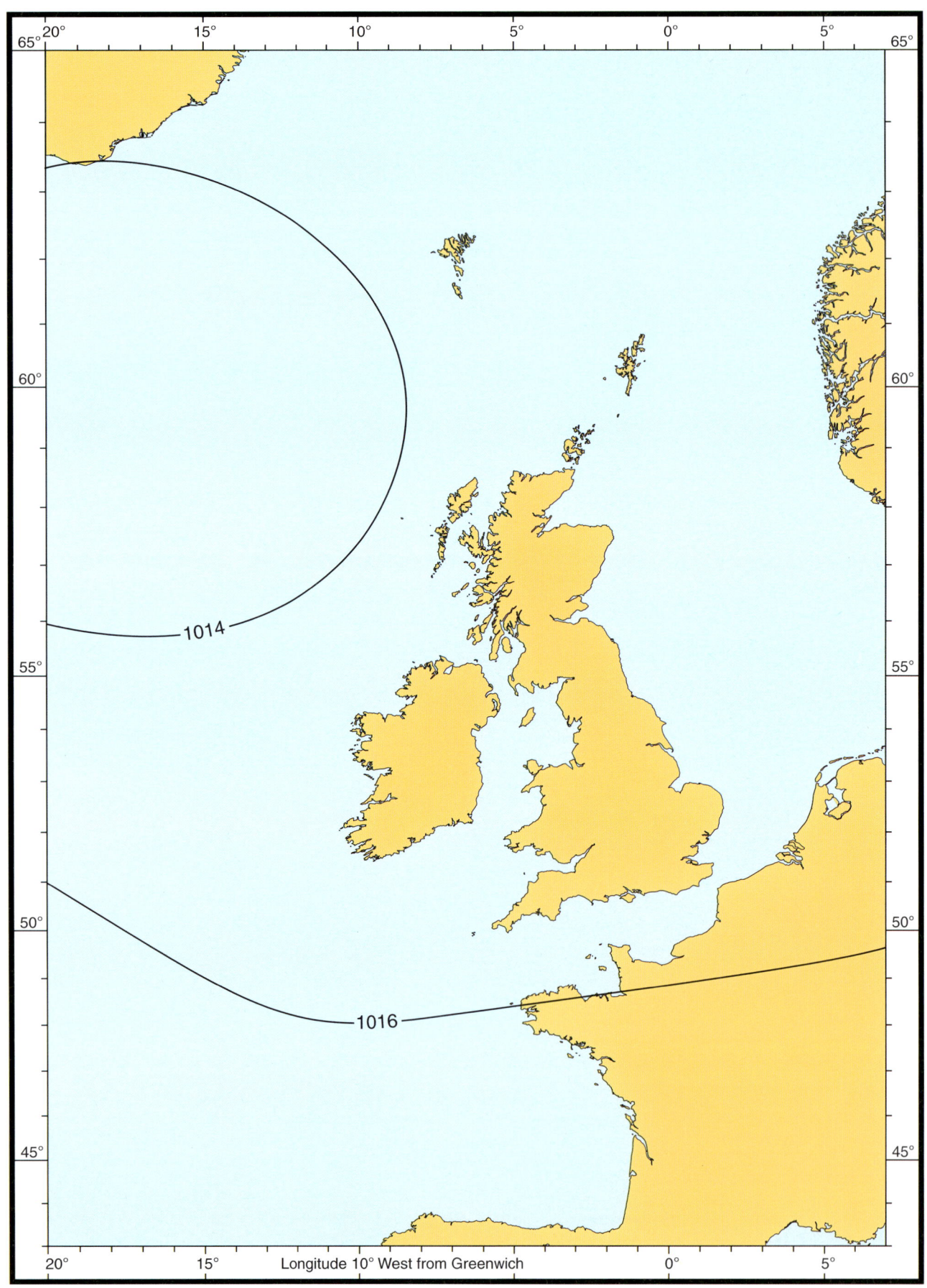

Mean sea level pressure (mb) - MAY (1.167.2)

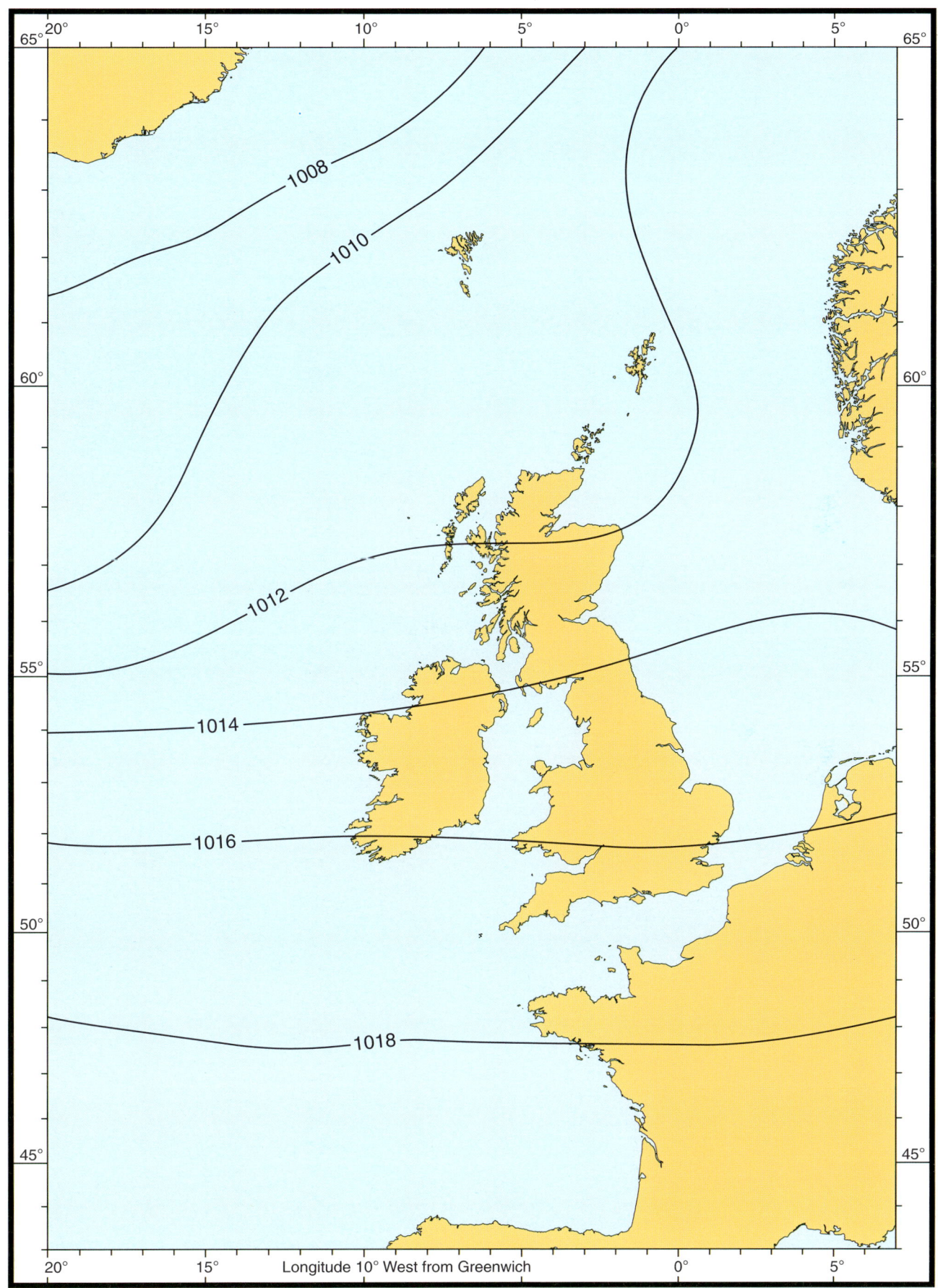

Mean sea level pressure (mb) - AUGUST (1.167.3)

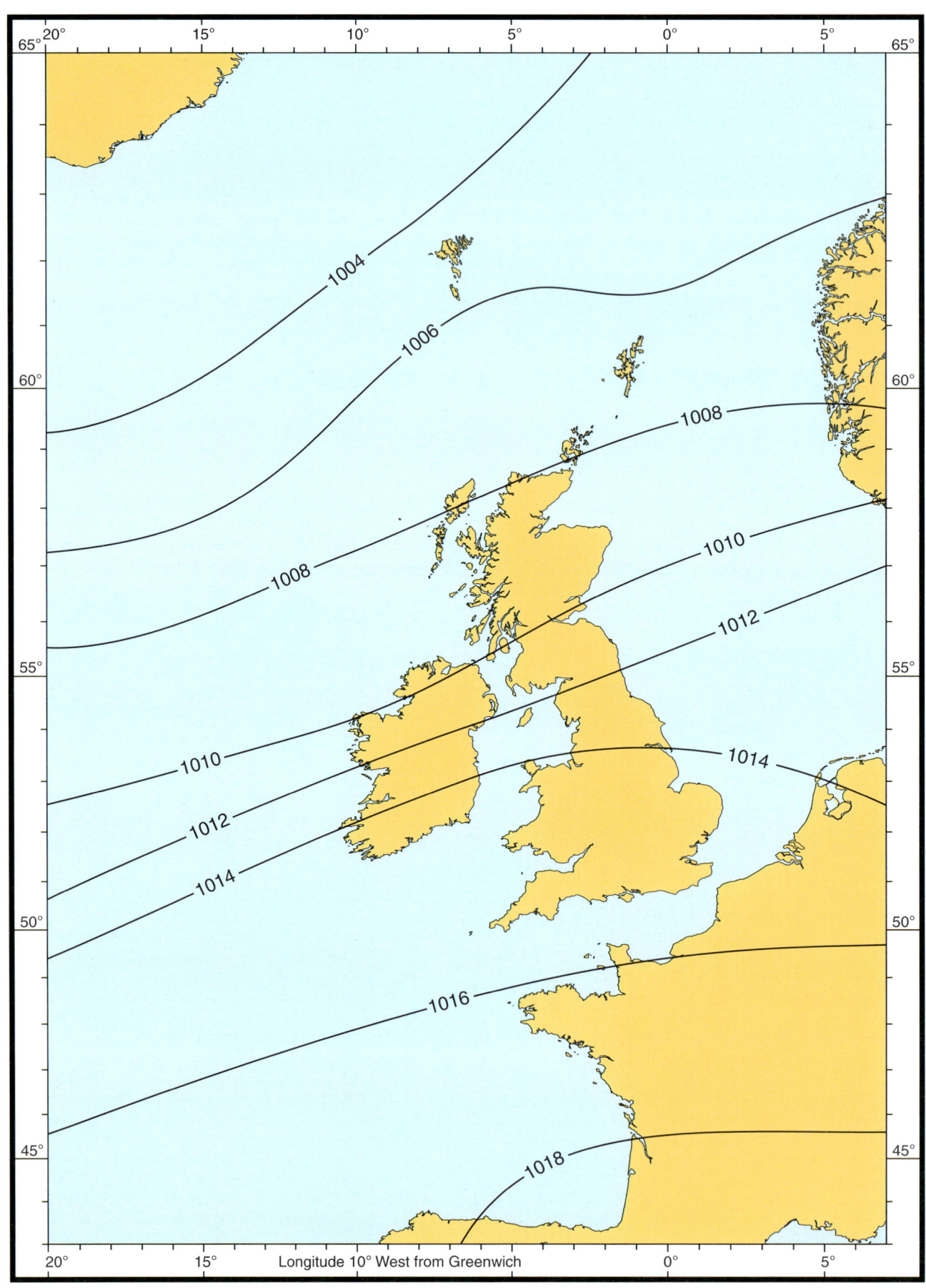

Mean sea level (mb) - NOVEMBER (1.167.4)

Variability
1.168
1   The actual pressure pattern can be significantly different from the mean for long periods, due to the numerous depressions that can affect the area. When intense depressions affect the area, pressure changes of about 35 to 40 hPa in 24 hours are possible. On other occasions, especially in winter, when a high pressure cell becomes established over NW Europe, the mean pressure distribution may be reversed with high pressure to the N and relatively low pressure to the S.

Diurnal variation
1.169
1   The diurnal variation is small, about 0·4 to 0·7 hPa amplitude, and is nearly always masked by larger pressure changes due to E-moving mobile depressions.

Anticyclones

The Azores anticyclone
1.170
1   This anticyclone tends to be the dominating feature in the area in summer, especially when a ridge of high pressure extends NE from its centre towards France and central Europe. The ridge usually gives rise to settled weather conditions in the area covered by this volume, whilst forcing E-moving mobile depressions further N.

The Asiatic anticyclone
1.171
1   The Asiatic Anticyclone develops in winter over Siberia and, on occasions, a ridge of high pressure may extend W to NW Europe. When this occurs, a very cold dry E wind can affect the area and may last for several weeks. During this period, mobile depressions are prevented from approaching the area until the ridge recedes.

Depressions

Atlantic depressions
1.172
1   Depressions, that form over the W North Atlantic, frequently move NE towards the Icelandic area with secondary depressions forming to their rear. These secondary depressions, often in a family of three to five, frequently move E with increasingly S tracks to affect the area covered by this volume. The intervals between depressions can be as long as 2 to 3 days or as short as 24 hours and often give rise to gale or storm force winds, especially in winter. When depressions are small, and in their development stage, their E movement can be very rapid.

Polar depressions
1.173
1   Polar depressions generally develop in cold N airstreams in the Norwegian Sea area and can, on occasions, bring snow or frequent wintry showers to the area as they move S in winter.

Hurricanes
1.174
1   During the hurricane season in the W North Atlantic, July to early October, spent hurricanes can, on rare occasions, recurve NE towards the area and re-intensify with winds of force 10 or more.

Fronts

Polar front
1.175
1   The polar front is the most important front in the region and plays a dominant role in the weather throughout the year. It marks the boundary between the cold air to the N and the warm moist air in the S. In winter its mean position, in the E North Atlantic, is 40°N 40°W to the S coast of England, but moves N in summer to lie 45°N 40°W to the N coast of Wales. The majority of mobile depressions that affect the area originate within the polar frontal zone in the W North Atlantic.

Warm and cold fronts
1.176
1   Warm and cold fronts are generally very active in the area and are responsible for much of the bad weather, see *The Mariner's Handbook* for a full description of warm and cold fronts. Even depressions passing well to the N of the area may have associated warm and cold fronts which extend S into the region covered by this volume.

2   Warm fronts, frequently associated with low cloud and rain, usually approach the area from between SSE and NW, in summer, and SW and W, in winter. Cold fronts, however, generally move into the area from between N and SW and may bring a sudden shift of wind together with strong winds and squally conditions but with often good visibility to the rear of the front.

Winds

Average distribution
1.177
1   Winds roses showing the frequency of winds from various directions and for different speeds are given in Diagrams 1.177.1 to 1.177.4.

Variability
1.178
1   The winds in the area are to a large extent controlled by the E-moving mobile depressions, and associated fronts, and are therefore very variable in both speed and direction. Steady winds are unusual, although E to NE winds can persist, on occasions, for up to several weeks when a high pressure cell becomes established over NW Europe in winter and spring.

Open sea
1.179
1   In the area covered by this volume, the winds are variable but predominantly from between SSW and NW. There is an increase in the frequency of NE winds in late winter and spring, especially in the English Channel. The strongest winds are reported during the autumn and winter with winds of force 5 and over being reported, in December, on around 65% of occasions in the W and 50% in the E. By July the frequency falls to around 25% in the W and 15% in the E.

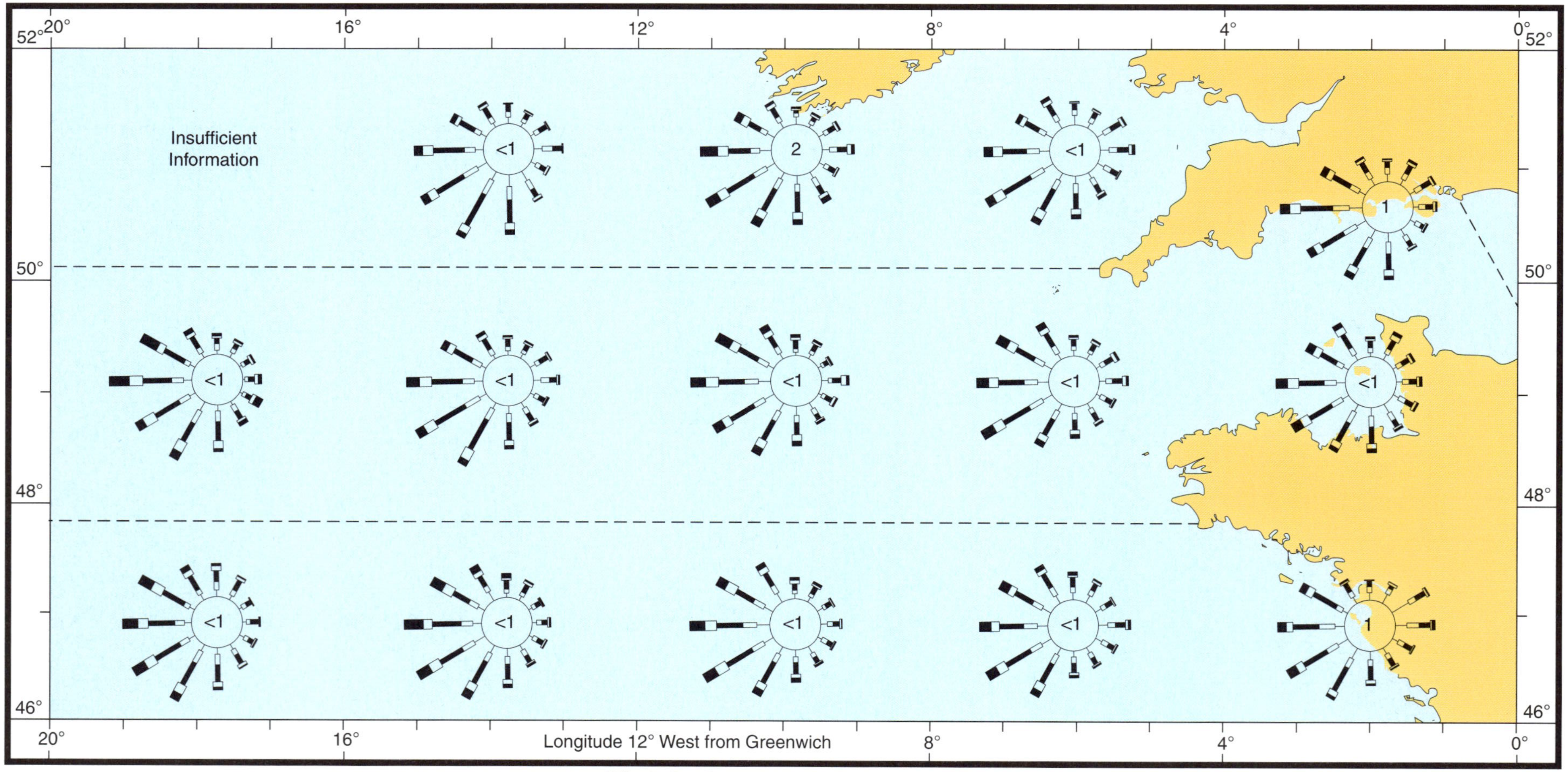

Wind distribution JANUARY (1.177.1)

Longitude 12° West from Greenwich

Insufficient
Information

EXPLANATION. The frequency of wind from
any direction is given according to the scale:

0%   10   20   30   40   50%

This scale is further subdivided to indicate the
frequency of winds of different Beaufort force
according to the legend:

1-3   4   5-6   7   8-12

Wind direction is towards the circle centre. The
figure within the circle gives the percentage of
calms.

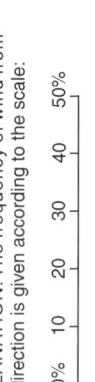

4

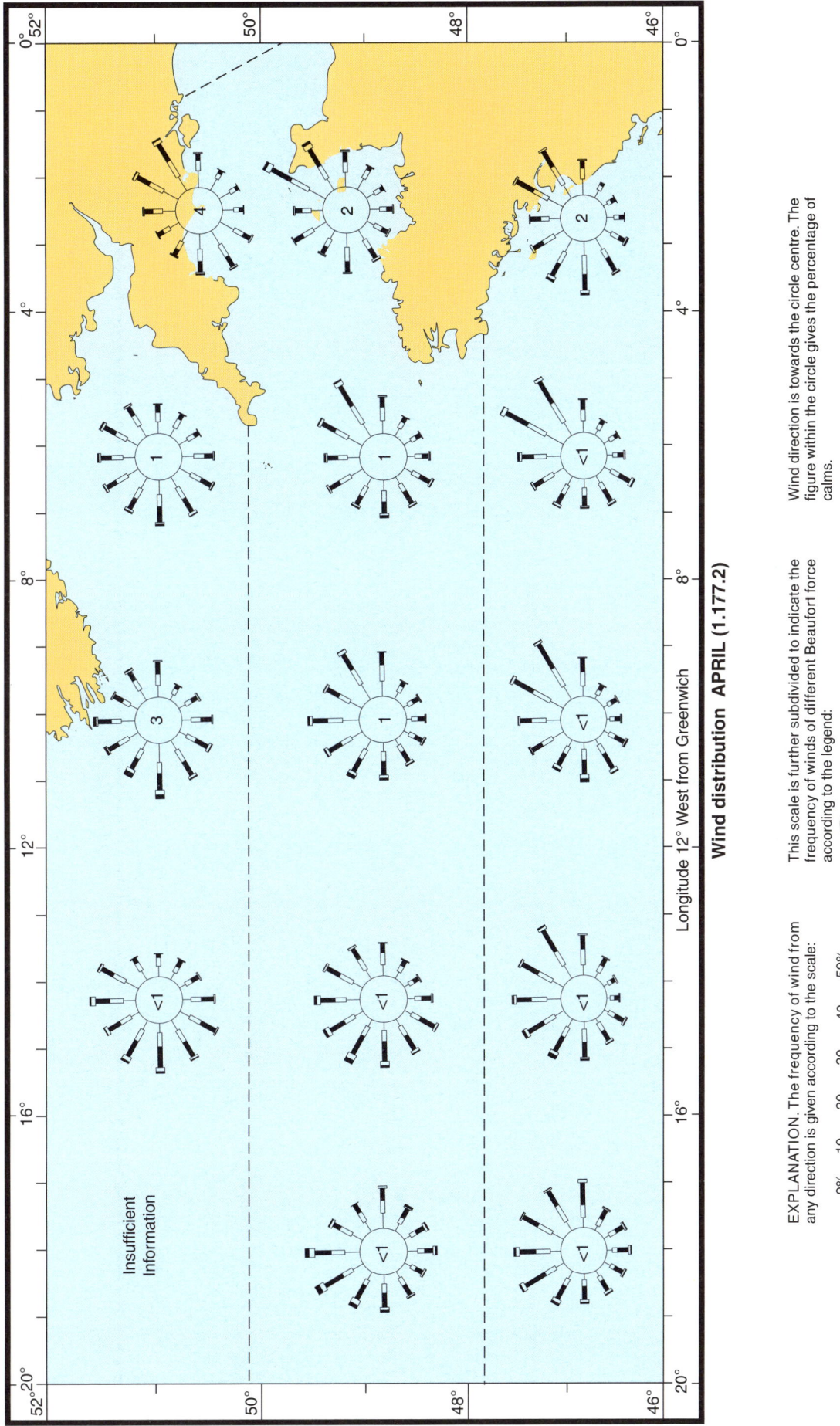

Wind distribution APRIL (1.177.2)

Longitude 12° West from Greenwich

EXPLANATION. The frequency of wind from any direction is given according to the scale:

0% 10 20 30 40 50%

This scale is further subdivided to indicate the frequency of winds of different Beaufort force according to the legend:

0.1-2.2   4.3-6.2   8.3+
2.3-4.2   6.3-8.2

Wind direction is towards the circle centre. The figure within the circle gives the percentage of calms.

Insufficient Information

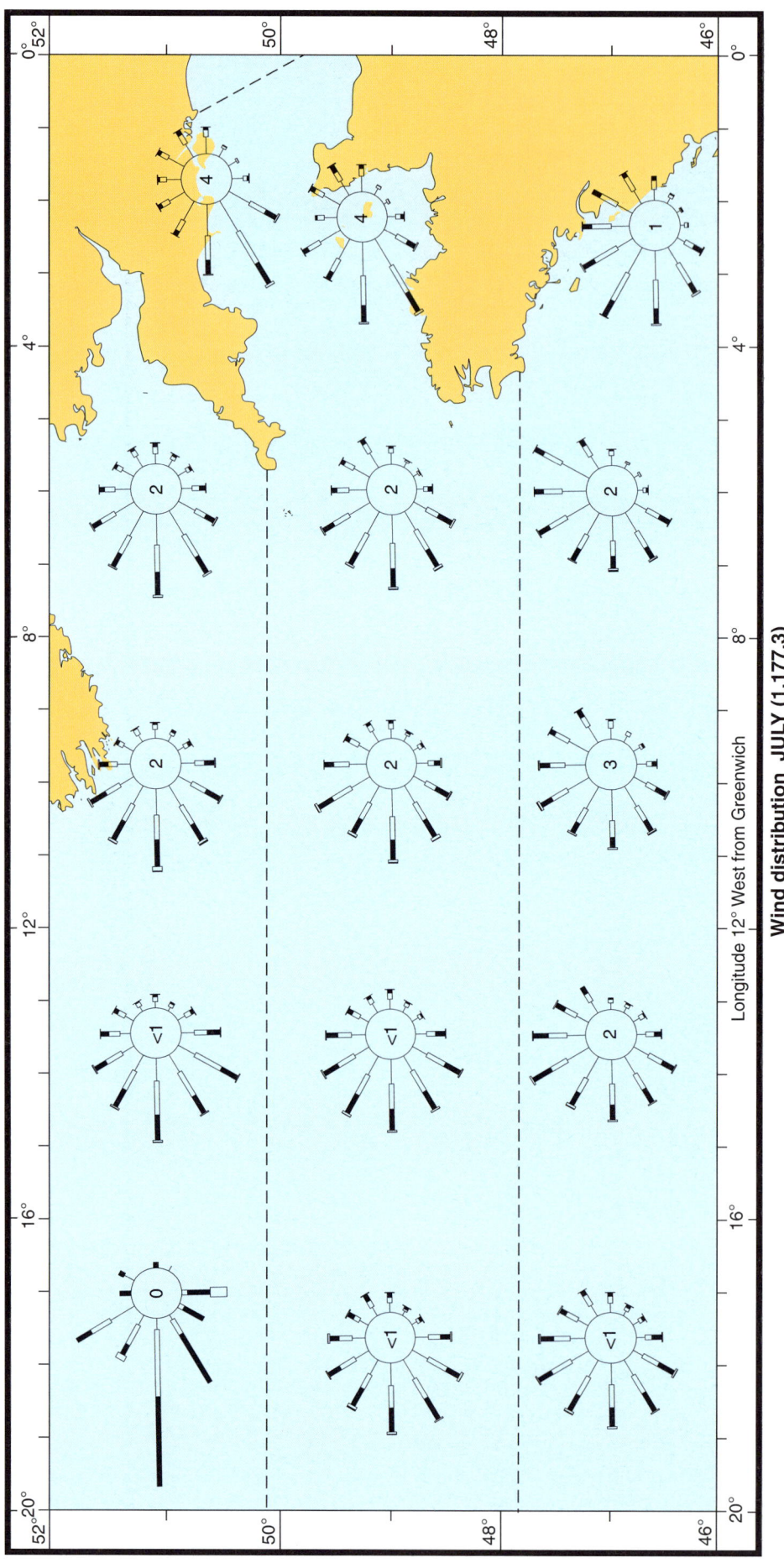

Wind distribution JULY (1.177.3)

Longitude 12° West from Greenwich

EXPLANATION. The frequency of wind from any direction is given according to the scale:

0% 10 20 30 40 50%

This scale is further subdivided to indicate the frequency of winds of different Beaufort force according to the legend:

1-3 4 5-6 7 8-12

Wind direction is towards the circle centre. The figure within the circle gives the percentage of calms.

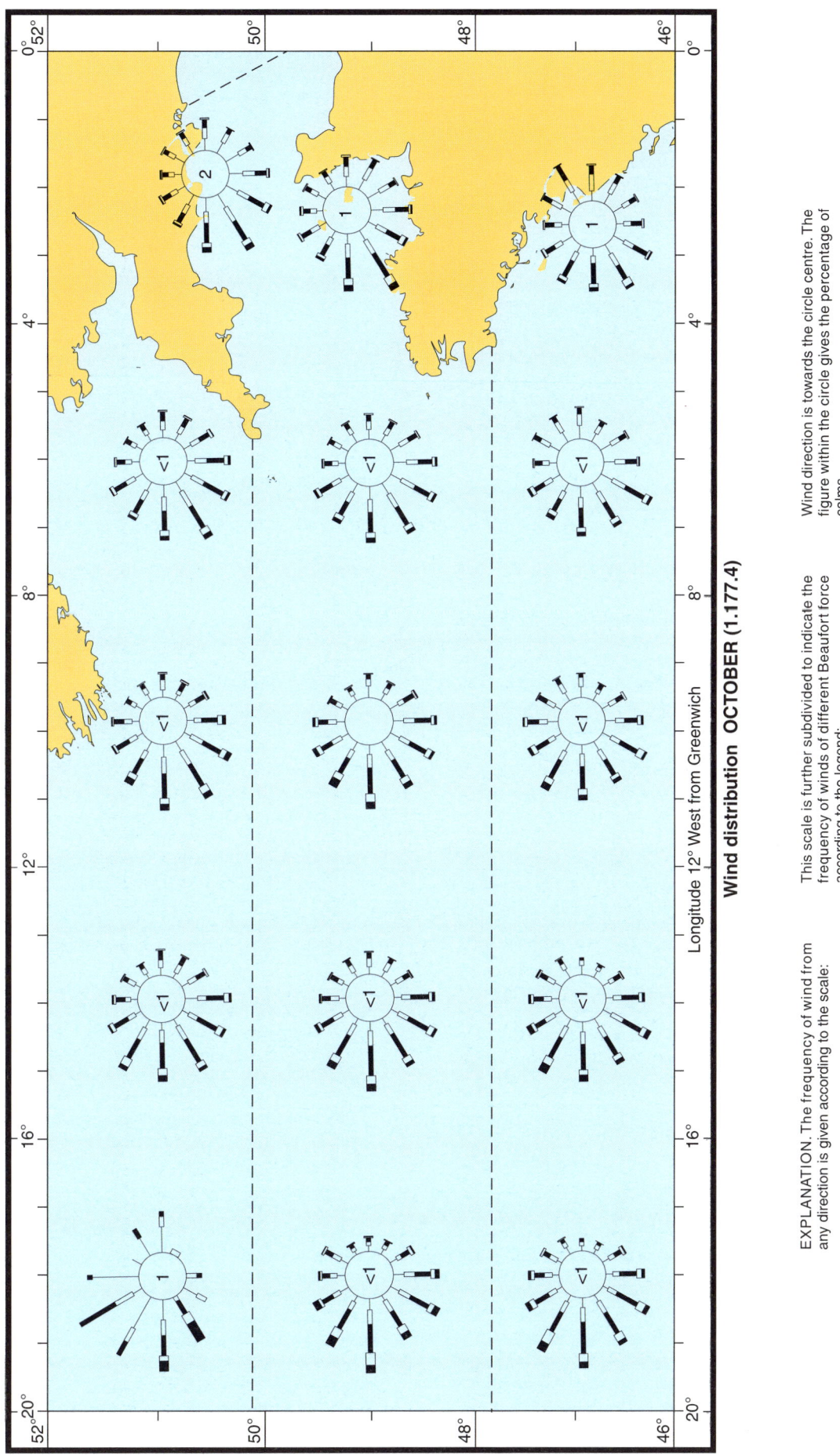

Wind distribution OCTOBER (1.177.4)

Longitude 12° West from Greenwich

EXPLANATION. The frequency of wind from any direction is given according to the scale:

0% 10 20 30 40 50%

This scale is further subdivided to indicate the frequency of winds of different Beaufort force according to the legend:

1-3 4 5-6 7 8-12

Wind direction is towards the circle centre. The figure within the circle gives the percentage of calms.

Coastal areas
1.180

1   Within 20 miles of the coast there are frequently local modifications to both the wind speed and direction and these may be caused by topography, "funnelling" and land and sea breezes; see *The Mariner's Handbook* for further details. Winds in the vicinity of headlands, e.g. Saint Alban's Head with winds between E and SE, are often in excess of those well offshore due to the deflection of the winds near high ground bordering the coast.

2   The climate information pages at the end of this chapter give wind information for a number of coastal stations within the area covered by this volume.

Land and sea breezes
1.181

1   Sea breezes are most evident with calm or light wind conditions from late spring to early autumn, however, land breezes tend to be more common on calm winter nights. Depending on the direction of the prevailing wind, these breezes may reinforce or moderate the wind speed.

Sea breezes are particularly noticeable on both the French and English coasts bordering the English Channel. These breezes tend to set in around midday and die away by about 1900 in summer.

Gales
1.182

1   Diagram 1.182 gives the percentage frequency of winds of force 7 and over in January and July. Gales, force 8 and over, are reported, in winter, on about 15% of occasions in the extreme W of the area and around 8% in the E. The most common direction for gales is between SSW and NNW although gales from any direction are possible, especially from the NE in late winter and spring in the E of the area. The S coast of England is somewhat sheltered from N gales, as is the N coast of France from S gales.

Cloud

Cloud cover
1.183

1   The average cloud amount over the whole of the area is around 6 oktas in winter and reduces in the E of the area in summer to between 4 and 5 oktas. However, on any particular day the actual cloud amount can be very different from the mean. Overcast skies are most common with moist SW winds, especially in winter. Clear skies are possible with E or SE winds from the continent, and near the S coast of England with N winds.

Precipitation

General
1.184

1   The climate information pages after 1.195 give the average amounts of precipitation for each month at several coastal stations and the mean number of days in each month when significant precipitation is recorded.

Rain
1.185

1   At sea in winter, rain can be expected on about 22 days a month in the W of the area and on around 15 days in the E and, in summer, on about 13 and 9 days, respectively. However, amounts and duration can vary significantly from one day to another.

2   At coastal stations, rainfall amounts vary according to their exposure to the prevailing winds and the proximity of high ground. The average rainfall is around 840 mm with the E part of the English Channel being generally drier that the W part. April to July are usually the driest months with October to January the wettest.

Thunderstorms
1.186

1   Thunderstorms are infrequent over the open ocean in the W of the area. In the E of the area, thunderstorms are rare between January and March but are recorded on around one day per month between April and December with a slightly higher incidence in summer.

Snow
1.187

1   The majority of snow, in coastal areas, falls at irregular intervals between November and April, and with the greatest incidence during the period January to March. Snow generally lies for 1 to 2 days a year in W coastal areas and around 5 days in the E. Snow over the open ocean in the W of the area, and over NW France, is infrequent, occurring on about 3 days a year compared with 10 to 12 days a year on the coasts of Hampshire and Sussex.

Fog and visibility

General information
1.188

1   Fog, visibility less than 1 km, and poor visibility is most likely in the late spring and summer when warm moist W to SW winds blow over a relatively cool sea. The frequency of occurrence of fog is between 3 and 4% in June compared with less then 2% in January; see *The Mariner's Handbook* for details on Sea and Radiation fogs. Although fog is rare in winter, the visibility may fall to near fog limits in precipitation near fronts.

Fog is most likely to form near the S coast of England with a SW wind in summer but may extend to the Channel Islands and the N coast of France should the wind veer to the W.

2   The sea area in the vicinity of Brest and Île d'Ouessant has a high incidence of fog during the summer due to cool water in the area. During the winter months, coastal areas to the E of Brest and Le Havre are affected by radiation fogs which form over land and are liable to spread to coastal sea areas by dawn.

The climate information pages after 1.195 give, for several coastal stations, the average number of days for which fog is recorded.

Air temperature

General information
1.189

1   In general the coldest time of the year is January and February and the warmest is July and August. Because of the numerous mobile depressions that affect the area, with frequent changes in airstream, the air temperature can be extremely variable, particularly in winter. High pressure over NW Europe can give rise to exceptionally cold spells in winter and warm spells in summer.

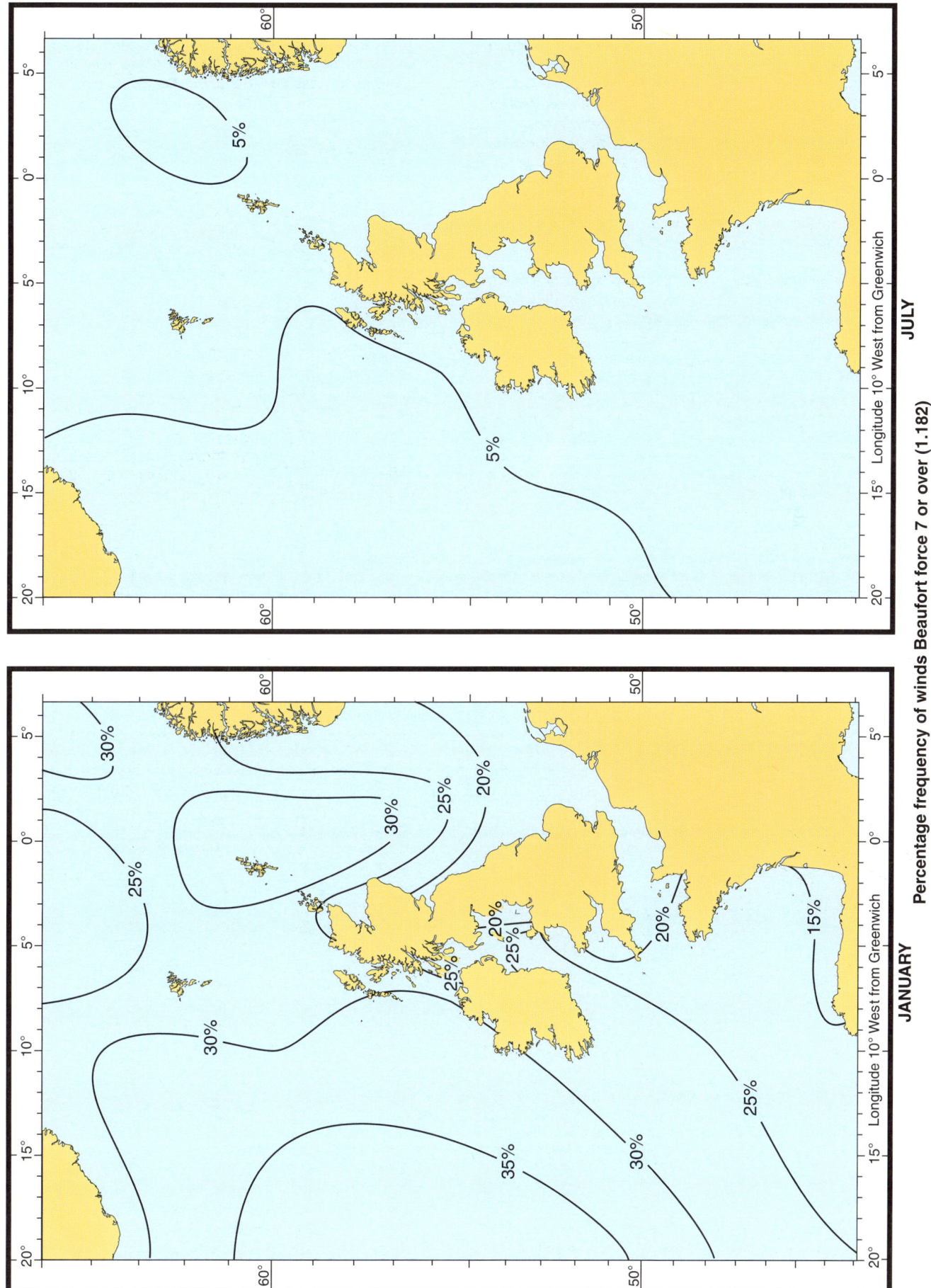

JULY

JANUARY

Longitude 10° West from Greenwich

Percentage frequency of winds Beaufort force 7 or over (1.182)

Open sea
1.190

1   In the W of the area the mean air temperature is about 10·5°C in January and around 16°C in July, and in the E about 8° and 16°C, respectively. On average the air is sightly colder than the sea from October to March in the W of the area but similar in the E. During the summer, the mean air temperature is close to the mean sea surface temperature.

Coastal areas
1.191

1   Air temperatures along the coasts of S England and N France are generally much more variable than over the open sea to the W. In summer, the warmest spells are frequently associated with winds from between S and E and with air temperatures, on occasions, of over 30°C. Cold spells, in winter, are frequently associated with winds between N and E and with air temperatures around −2°C in the E of the area.

2   Air frosts are reported, mainly between December and March, on about 2 days a year in the extreme W of the area and around 30 to 35 days a year on the coasts of Hampshire and Sussex.

Humidity

General information
1.192

1   Humidity is closely related to air temperature and generally decreases as the temperature rises. During the early morning, when the air temperature is normally at its lowest, the humidity is generally at a maximum, and falls to a minimum when the temperature is at its highest during the early afternoon.

Open sea
1.193

1   In winter, the mean humidity is generally between 79 and 81% and, in summer, increases to around 83% with comparatively small variations from one month to the next.

Coastal areas
1.194

1   Relatively large fluctuations in humidity are possible in coastal areas depending on the exposure of the site to the prevailing wind and its distance from the open sea. In general, areas exposed to W to SW winds will have a higher humidity than those in the lee of high ground. Particularly in winter, relatively dry E winds can give rise to significant falls in humidity along the N and S coasts of the English Channel.

CLIMATE INFORMATION
1.195

1   Stations for which climate information pages are included in the following pages are shown in Diagram 1.189.

    It is emphasised that these data are average conditions and refer to the specific location of the observing station and therefore may not be representative of the conditions to be expected over the open sea or in the approaches to ports in their vicinity. The following comments briefly list some of the differences to be expected between conditions over the open sea and those at the nearest reporting station:

2   Wind speeds tend to be higher at sea with more frequent gales than on land, although funnelling in narrow inlets can result in an increase in wind strength.

    Precipitation on wind facing high ground sites can be considerably higher than at sea to windward. Similarly, precipitation in the lee of high ground is generally less.

3   Air temperature over the open sea is less variable than over the land.

    Topography has a marked affect on local conditions. See *The Mariner's Handbook* for further details.

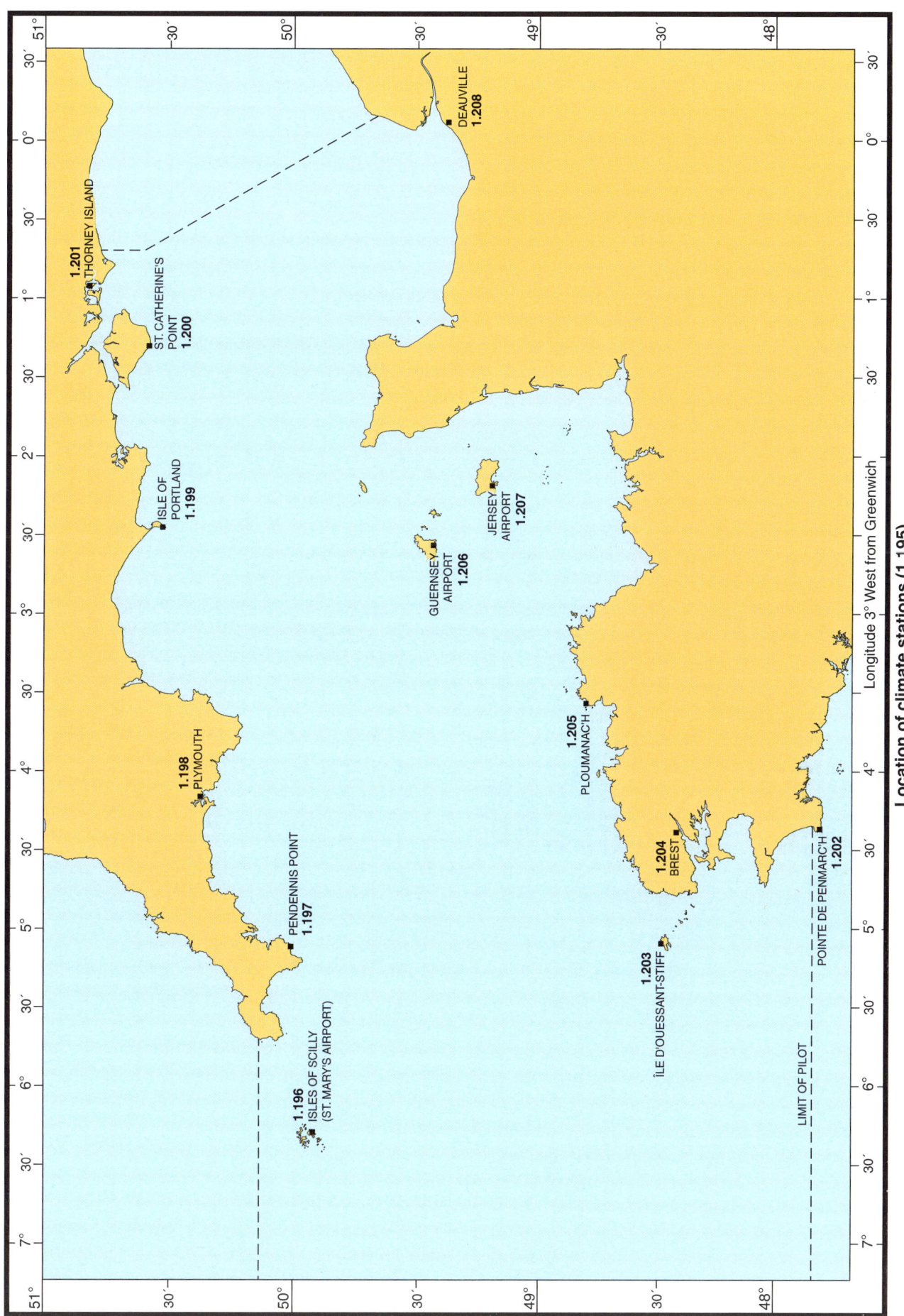

THORNEY ISLAND
1.201

ST. CATHERINE'S
POINT
1.200

DEAUVILLE
1.208

ISLE OF
PORTLAND
1.199

JERSEY
AIRPORT
1.207

GUERNSEY
AIRPORT
1.206

PLOUMANAC'H
1.205

1.198 PLYMOUTH

PENDENNIS POINT
1.197

1.204
BREST

POINTE DE PENMARC'H
1.202

1.203
ÎLE D'OUESSANT-STIFF

LIMIT OF PILOT

1.196
ISLES OF SCILLY
(ST. MARY'S AIRPORT)

Longitude 3° West from Greenwich

Location of climate stations (1.195)

WMO No 03803 ISLES OF SCILLY (ST MARY'S AIRPORT)

49°55'N 06°18'W.   Height above MSL - 30 m Climate Information for period 1997 - 2007

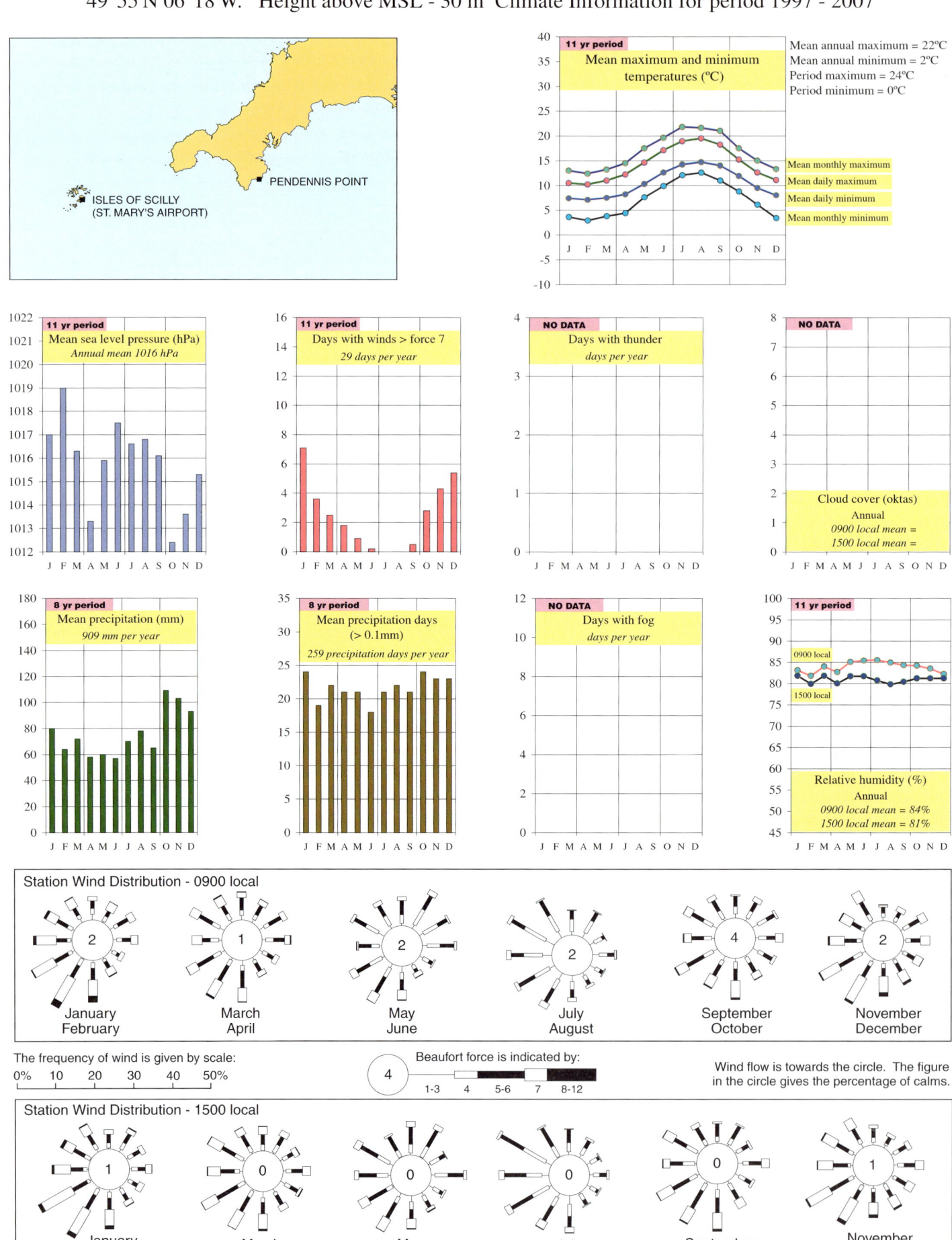

Mean maximum and minimum temperatures (°C) *(11 yr period)*

Mean annual maximum = 22°C
Mean annual minimum = 2°C
Period maximum = 24°C
Period minimum = 0°C

Mean monthly maximum
Mean daily maximum
Mean daily minimum
Mean monthly minimum

Mean sea level pressure (hPa) *(11 yr period)* — *Annual mean 1016 hPa*

Days with winds > force 7 *(11 yr period)* — *29 days per year*

Days with thunder *(NO DATA)* — *days per year*

Cloud cover (oktas) *(NO DATA)* — Annual; 0900 local mean = ; 1500 local mean =

Mean precipitation (mm) *(8 yr period)* — *909 mm per year*

Mean precipitation days (> 0.1mm) *(8 yr period)* — *259 precipitation days per year*

Days with fog *(NO DATA)* — *days per year*

Relative humidity (%) *(11 yr period)* — Annual; 0900 local mean = 84%; 1500 local mean = 81%
0900 local
1500 local

Station Wind Distribution - 0900 local

January February (2) · March April (1) · May June (2) · July August (2) · September October (4) · November December (2)

The frequency of wind is given by scale:
0% 10 20 30 40 50%

Beaufort force is indicated by: (4) — 1-3, 4, 5-6, 7, 8-12

Wind flow is towards the circle. The figure in the circle gives the percentage of calms.

Station Wind Distribution - 1500 local

January February (1) · March April (0) · May June (0) · July August (0) · September October (0) · November December (1)

ISLES OF SCILLY (ST. MARY'S AIRPORT)
PENDENNIS POINT

WMO No 03810 PENDENNIS POINT

50°09'N 05°04'W.   Height above MSL - 42 m Climate Information for period 1997 - 2007

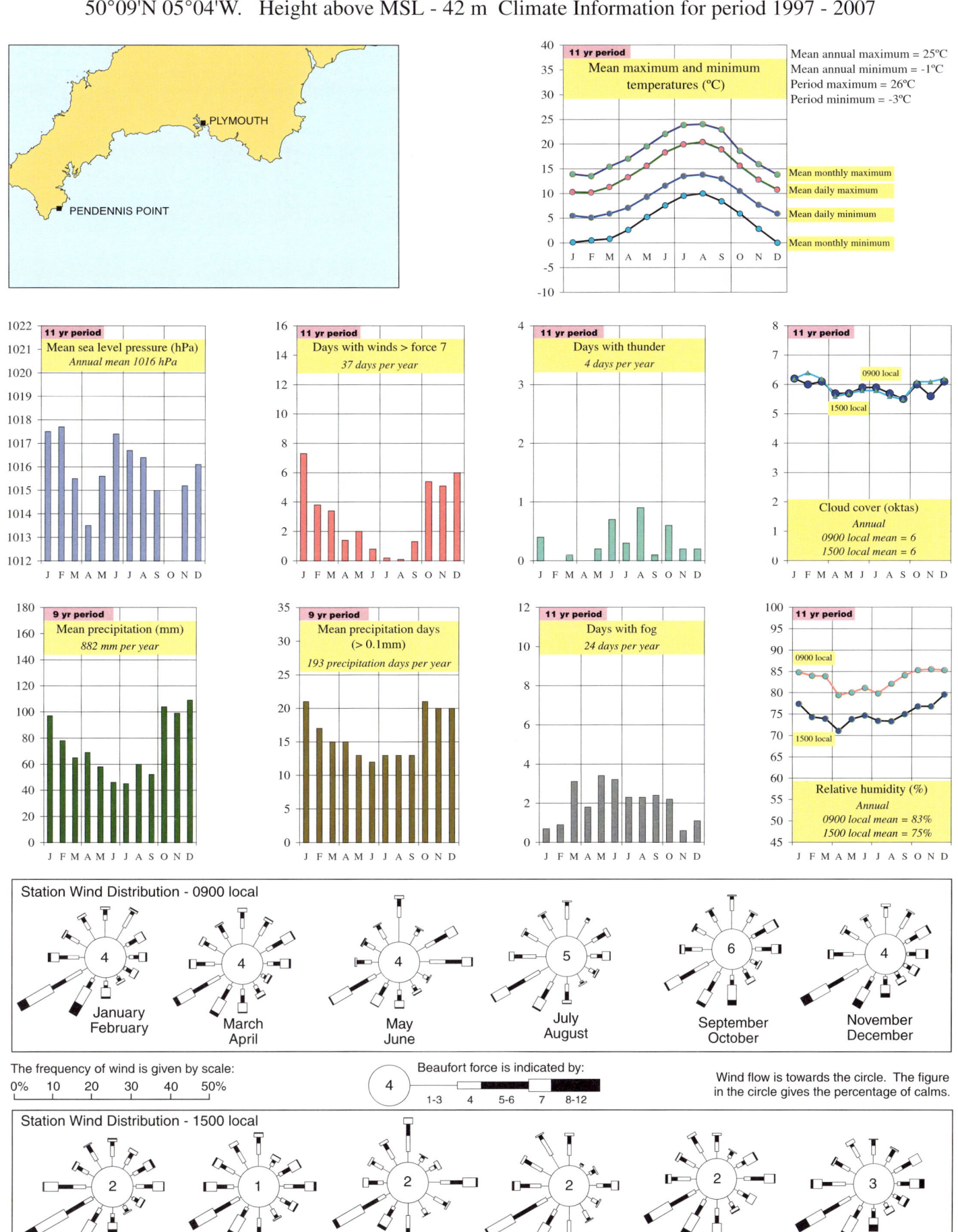

WMO No 03827 PLYMOUTH

50°21'N 04°07'W. Height above MSL - 50 m Climate Information for period 1997 - 2007

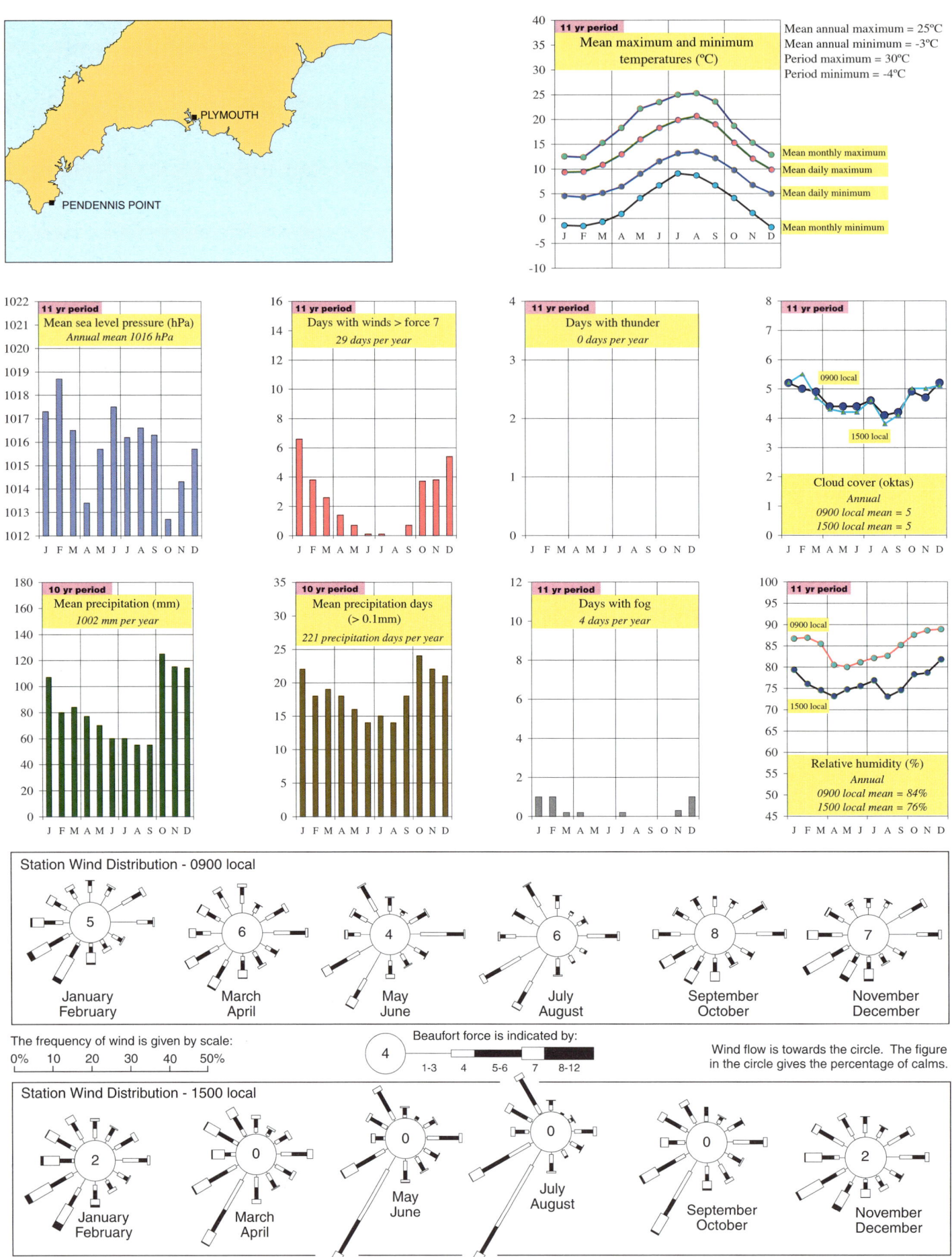

Mean annual maximum = 25°C
Mean annual minimum = -3°C
Period maximum = 30°C
Period minimum = -4°C

WMO No 03857 ISLE OF PORTLAND

50°31'N 02°27'W.   Height above MSL - 52 m Climate Information for period 1997 - 2007

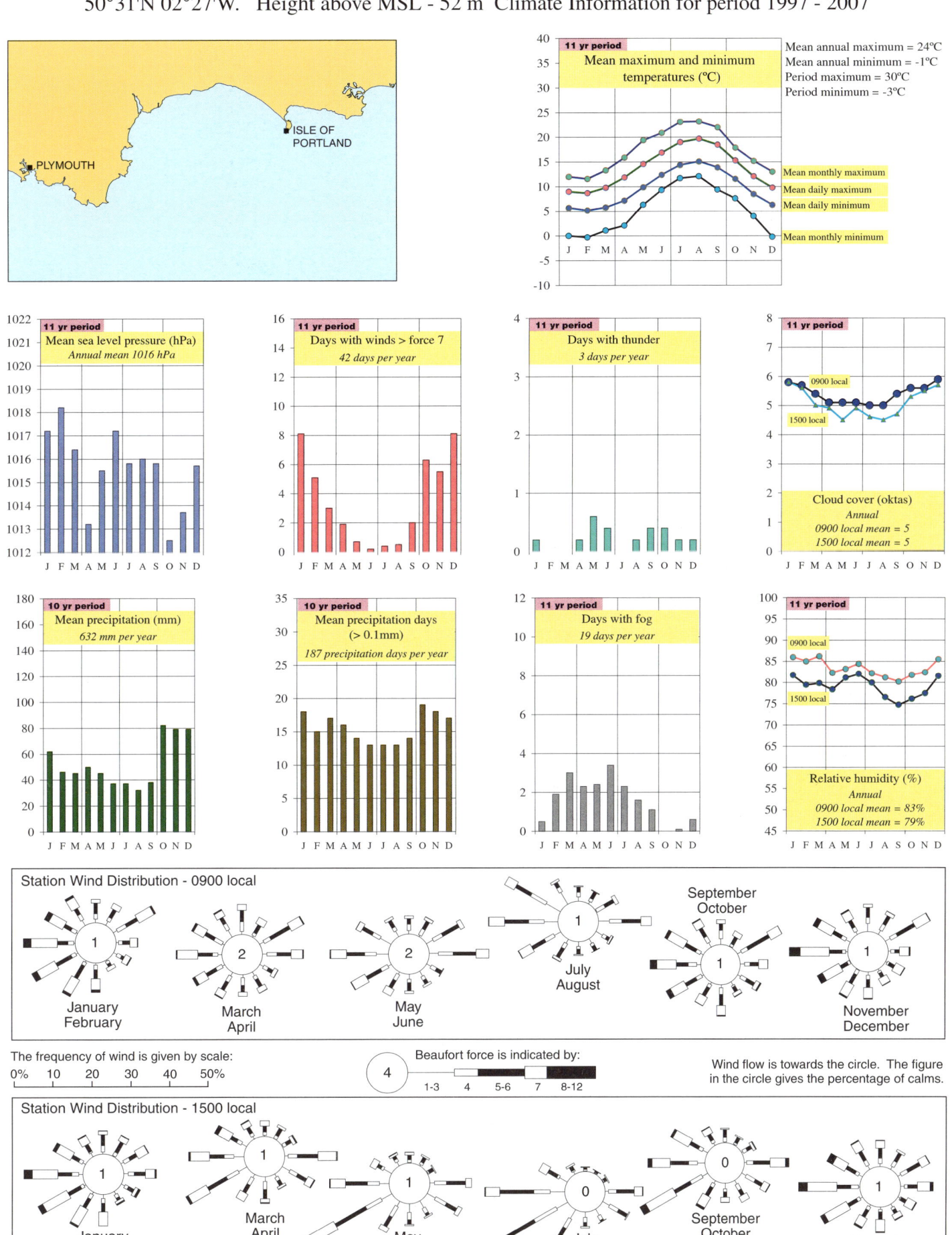

Mean maximum and minimum temperatures (°C) — 11 yr period
Mean annual maximum = 24°C
Mean annual minimum = -1°C
Period maximum = 30°C
Period minimum = -3°C
Mean monthly maximum
Mean daily maximum
Mean daily minimum
Mean monthly minimum

Mean sea level pressure (hPa) — 11 yr period
Annual mean 1016 hPa

Days with winds > force 7 — 11 yr period
42 days per year

Days with thunder — 11 yr period
3 days per year

Cloud cover (oktas) — 11 yr period
0900 local
1500 local
Annual
0900 local mean = 5
1500 local mean = 5

Mean precipitation (mm) — 10 yr period
632 mm per year

Mean precipitation days (> 0.1mm) — 10 yr period
187 precipitation days per year

Days with fog — 11 yr period
19 days per year

Relative humidity (%) — 11 yr period
0900 local
1500 local
Annual
0900 local mean = 83%
1500 local mean = 79%

Station Wind Distribution - 0900 local

January February — 1
March April — 2
May June — 2
July August — 1
September October — 1
November December — 1

The frequency of wind is given by scale:
0% 10 20 30 40 50%

Beaufort force is indicated by:
4
1-3 4 5-6 7 8-12

Wind flow is towards the circle. The figure in the circle gives the percentage of calms.

Station Wind Distribution - 1500 local

January February — 1
March April — 1
May June — 1
July August — 0
September October — 0
November December — 1

WMO No 03866 ST CATHERINE'S POINT

50°35'N 01°18'W.   Height above MSL - 24 m Climate Information for period 1997 - 2007

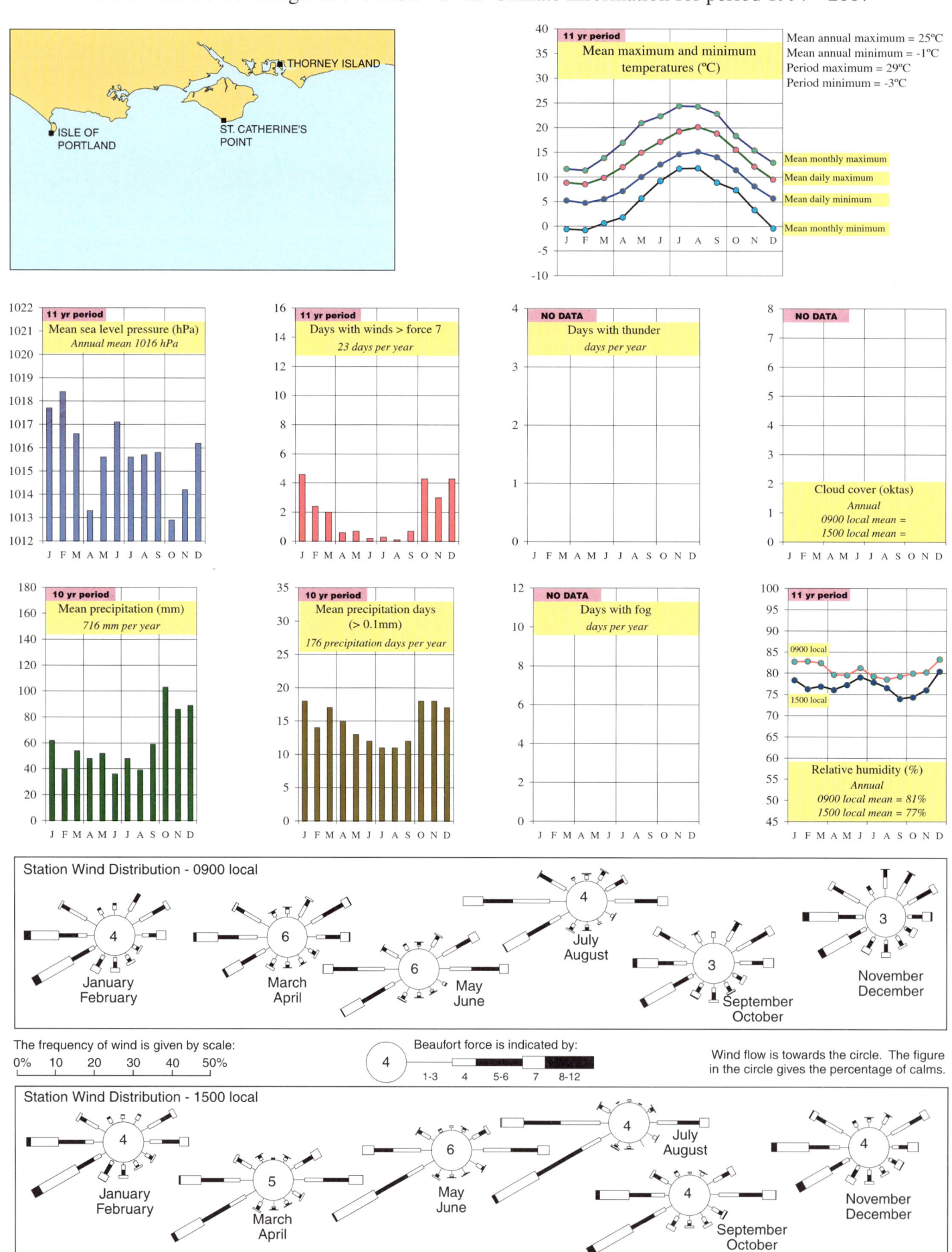

Mean annual maximum = 25°C
Mean annual minimum = -1°C
Period maximum = 29°C
Period minimum = -3°C

Mean maximum and minimum temperatures (°C)

11 yr period

Mean monthly maximum
Mean daily maximum
Mean daily minimum
Mean monthly minimum

Mean sea level pressure (hPa)
Annual mean 1016 hPa
11 yr period

Days with winds > force 7
23 days per year
11 yr period

Days with thunder
days per year
NO DATA

Cloud cover (oktas)
Annual
0900 local mean =
1500 local mean =
NO DATA

Mean precipitation (mm)
716 mm per year
10 yr period

Mean precipitation days (> 0.1mm)
176 precipitation days per year
10 yr period

Days with fog
days per year
NO DATA

Relative humidity (%)
Annual
0900 local mean = 81%
1500 local mean = 77%
11 yr period
0900 local
1500 local

Station Wind Distribution - 0900 local

January February — 4
March April — 6
May June — 6
July August — 4
September October — 3
November December — 3

The frequency of wind is given by scale:
0% 10 20 30 40 50%

Beaufort force is indicated by:
1-3   4   5-6   7   8-12

Wind flow is towards the circle. The figure in the circle gives the percentage of calms.

Station Wind Distribution - 1500 local

January February — 4
March April — 5
May June — 6
July August — 4
September October — 4
November December — 4

WMO No 03872 THORNEY ISLAND

50°49'N 00°55'W.   Height above MSL - 3 m Climate Information for period 1997 - 2007

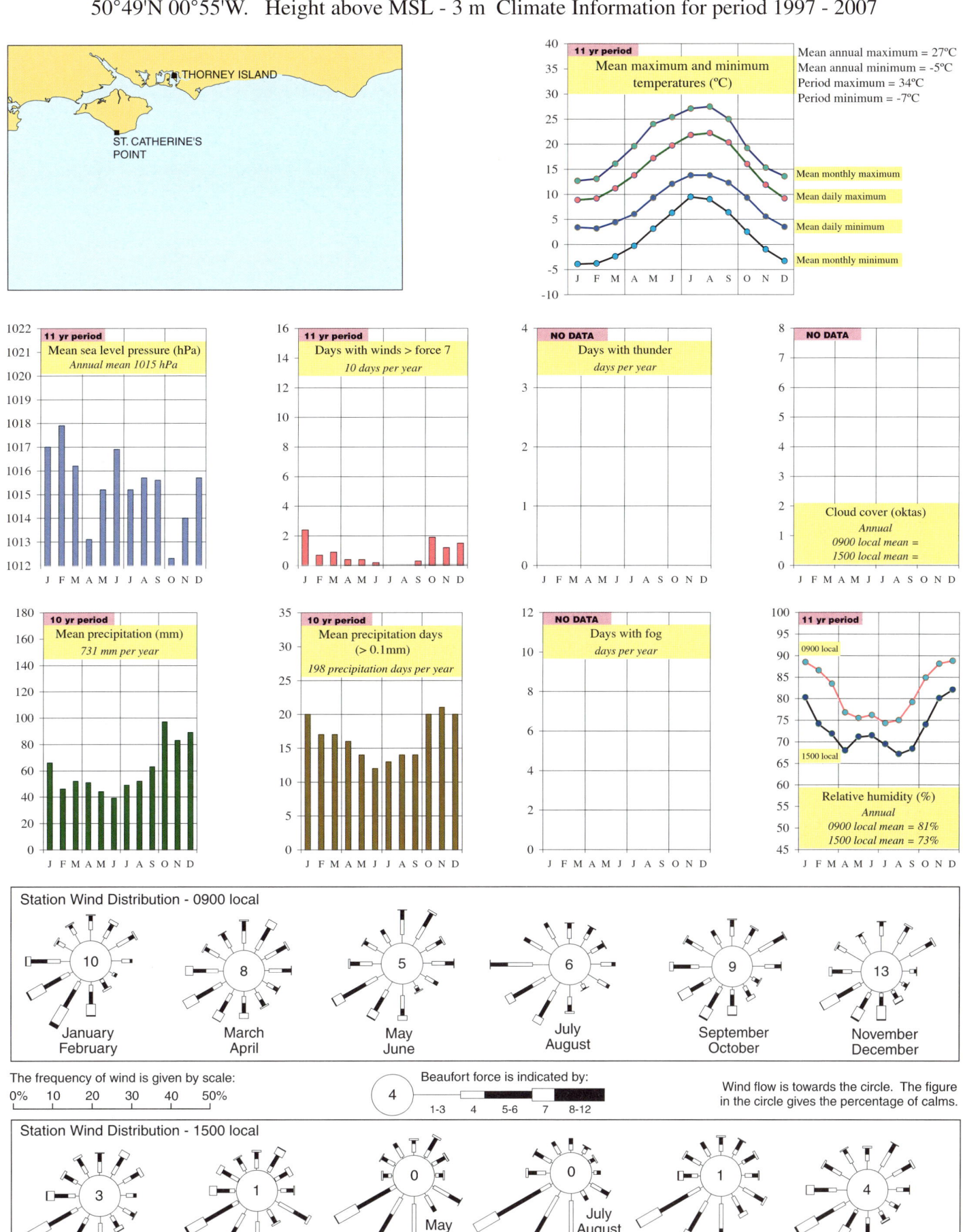

11 yr period
Mean maximum and minimum temperatures (ºC)

Mean annual maximum = 27ºC
Mean annual minimum = -5ºC
Period maximum = 34ºC
Period minimum = -7ºC

Mean monthly maximum
Mean daily maximum
Mean daily minimum
Mean monthly minimum

11 yr period
Mean sea level pressure (hPa)
Annual mean 1015 hPa

11 yr period
Days with winds > force 7
10 days per year

NO DATA
Days with thunder
days per year

NO DATA
Cloud cover (oktas)
Annual
0900 local mean =
1500 local mean =

10 yr period
Mean precipitation (mm)
731 mm per year

10 yr period
Mean precipitation days
(> 0.1mm)
198 precipitation days per year

NO DATA
Days with fog
days per year

11 yr period
0900 local
1500 local
Relative humidity (%)
Annual
0900 local mean = 81%
1500 local mean = 73%

Station Wind Distribution - 0900 local

January February — 10
March April — 8
May June — 5
July August — 6
September October — 9
November December — 13

The frequency of wind is given by scale:
0% 10 20 30 40 50%

Beaufort force is indicated by:
4
1-3 4 5-6 7 8-12

Wind flow is towards the circle. The figure in the circle gives the percentage of calms.

Station Wind Distribution - 1500 local

January February — 3
March April — 1
May June — 0
July August — 0
September October — 1
November December — 4

47°48'N 04°23'W.   Height above MSL - 19 m Climate Information for period 1984 - 2007

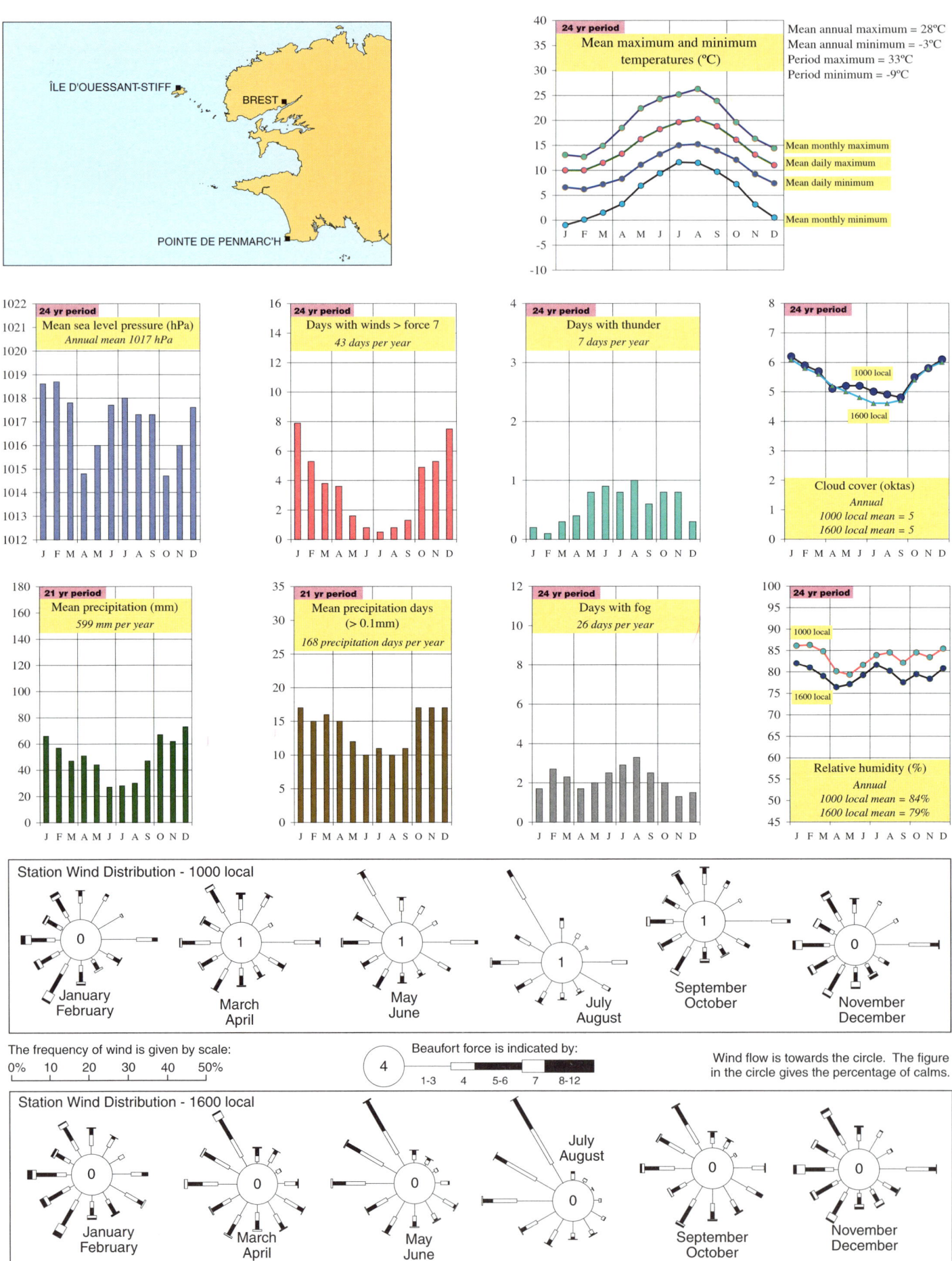

WMO No 07100 ÎLE D'OUESSANT-STIFF

48°29'N 05°03'W. Height above MSL - 68 m Climate Information for period 1984 - 2007

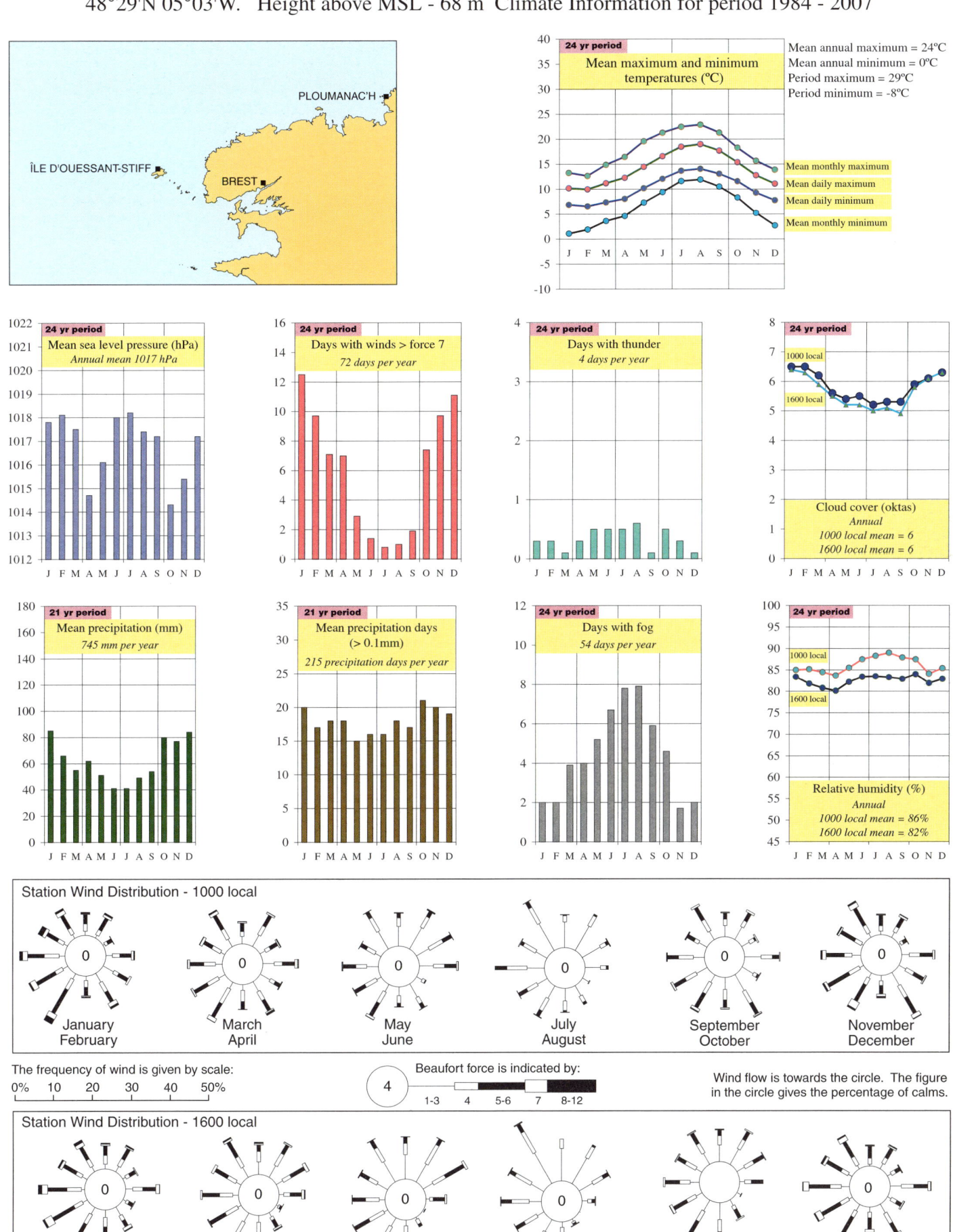

WMO No 07110 BREST

48°27'N 04°25'W.   Height above MSL - 95 m Climate Information for period 1974 - 2007

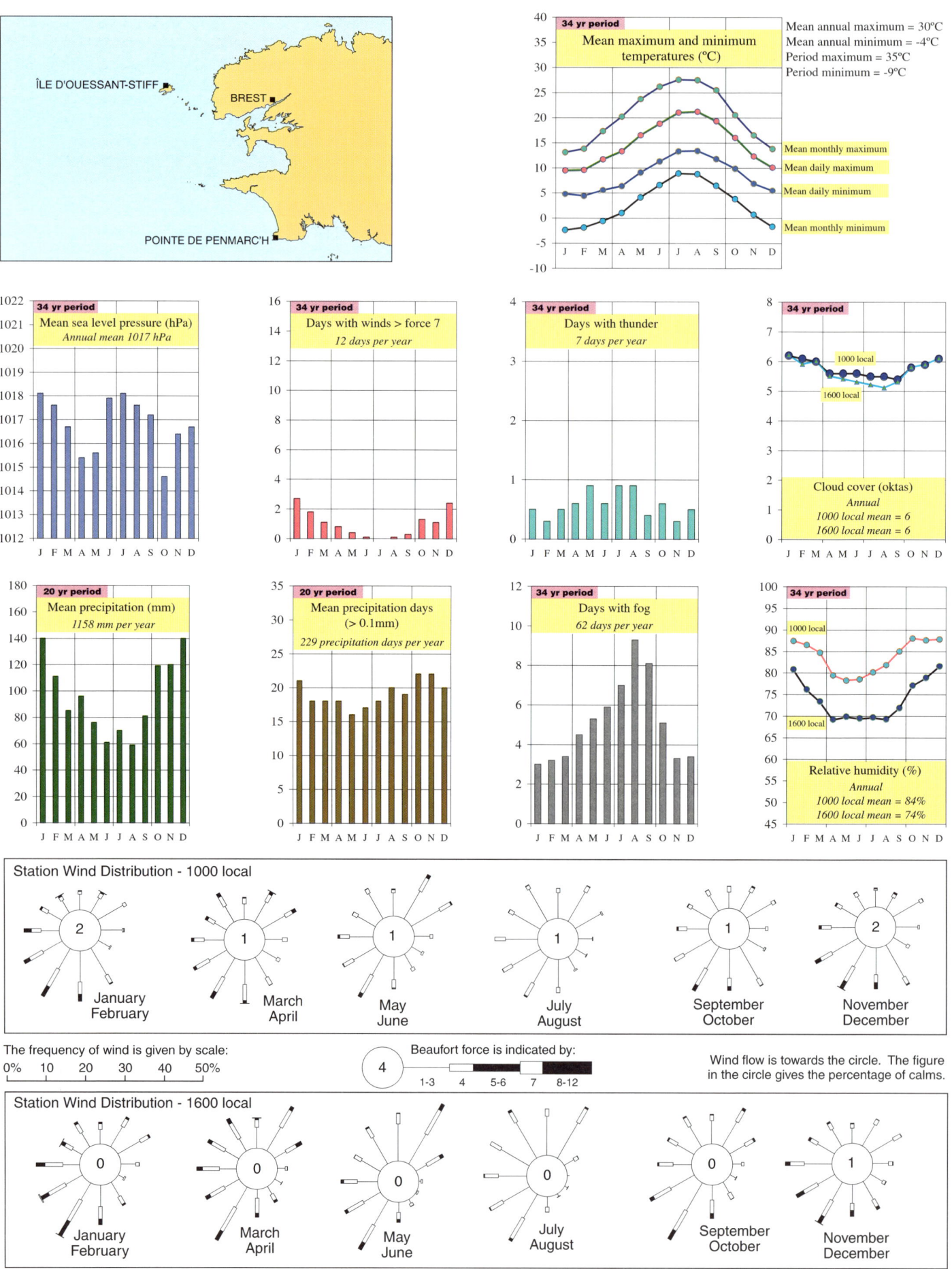

WMO No 07117 PLOUMANAC'H

48°50'N 03°28'W.   Height above MSL - 58 m Climate Information for period 1998 - 2007

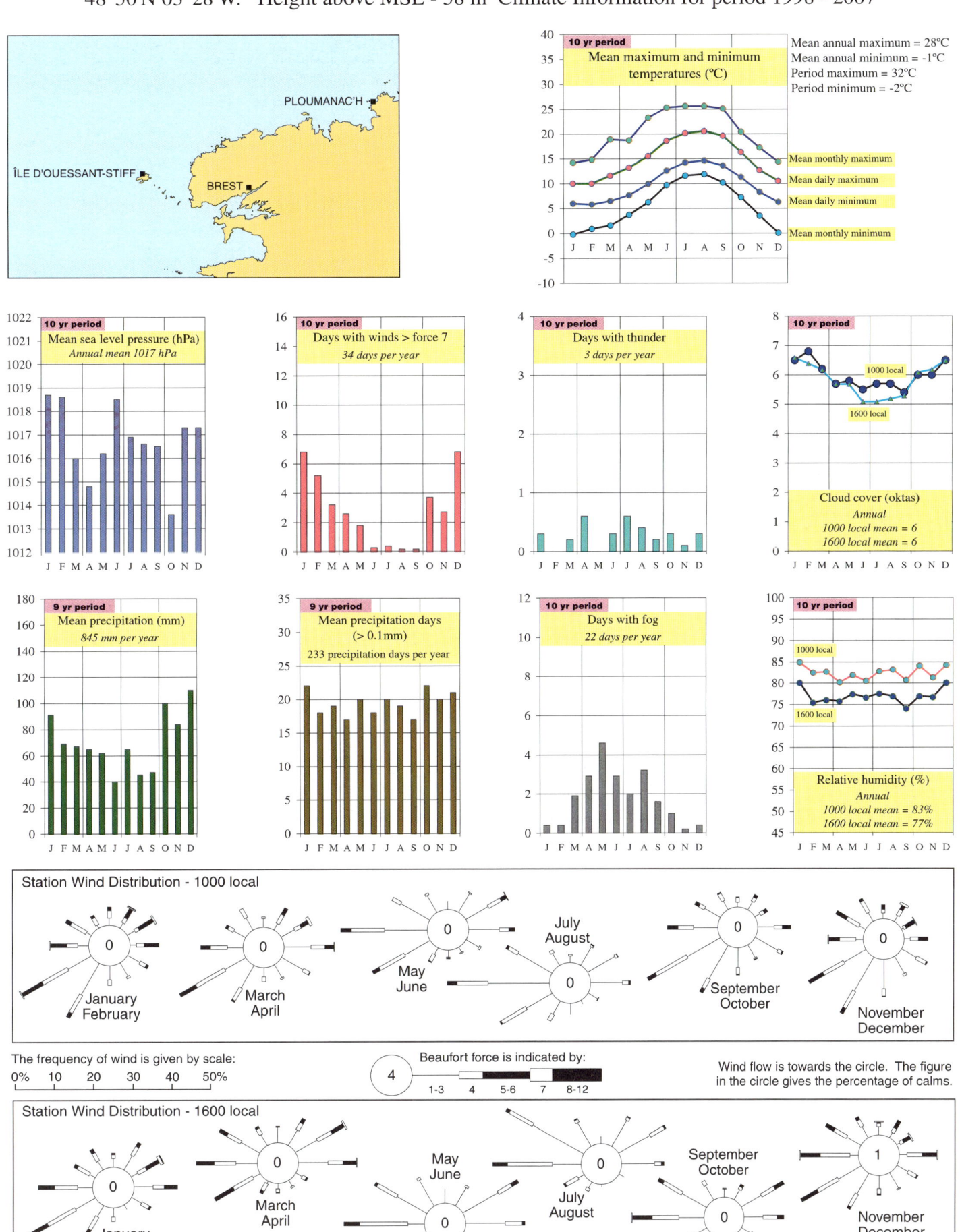

Mean maximum and minimum temperatures (°C) — 10 yr period

Mean annual maximum = 28°C
Mean annual minimum = -1°C
Period maximum = 32°C
Period minimum = -2°C

Mean monthly maximum
Mean daily maximum
Mean daily minimum
Mean monthly minimum

Mean sea level pressure (hPa) — 10 yr period
Annual mean 1017 hPa

Days with winds > force 7 — 10 yr period
34 days per year

Days with thunder — 10 yr period
3 days per year

Cloud cover (oktas) — 10 yr period
Annual
1000 local mean = 6
1600 local mean = 6
1000 local
1600 local

Mean precipitation (mm) — 9 yr period
845 mm per year

Mean precipitation days (> 0.1mm) — 9 yr period
233 precipitation days per year

Days with fog — 10 yr period
22 days per year

Relative humidity (%) — 10 yr period
Annual
1000 local mean = 83%
1600 local mean = 77%
1000 local
1600 local

Station Wind Distribution - 1000 local

January February — 0
March April — 0
May June — 0
July August — 0
September October — 0
November December — 0

The frequency of wind is given by scale:
0% 10 20 30 40 50%

Beaufort force is indicated by:
4
1-3 4 5-6 7 8-12

Wind flow is towards the circle. The figure in the circle gives the percentage of calms.

Station Wind Distribution - 1600 local

January February — 0
March April — 0
May June — 0
July August — 0
September October — 0
November December — 1

WMO No 03894 GUERNSEY AIRPORT

49°26'N 02°36'W. Height above MSL - 101 m Climate Information for period 1997 - 2007

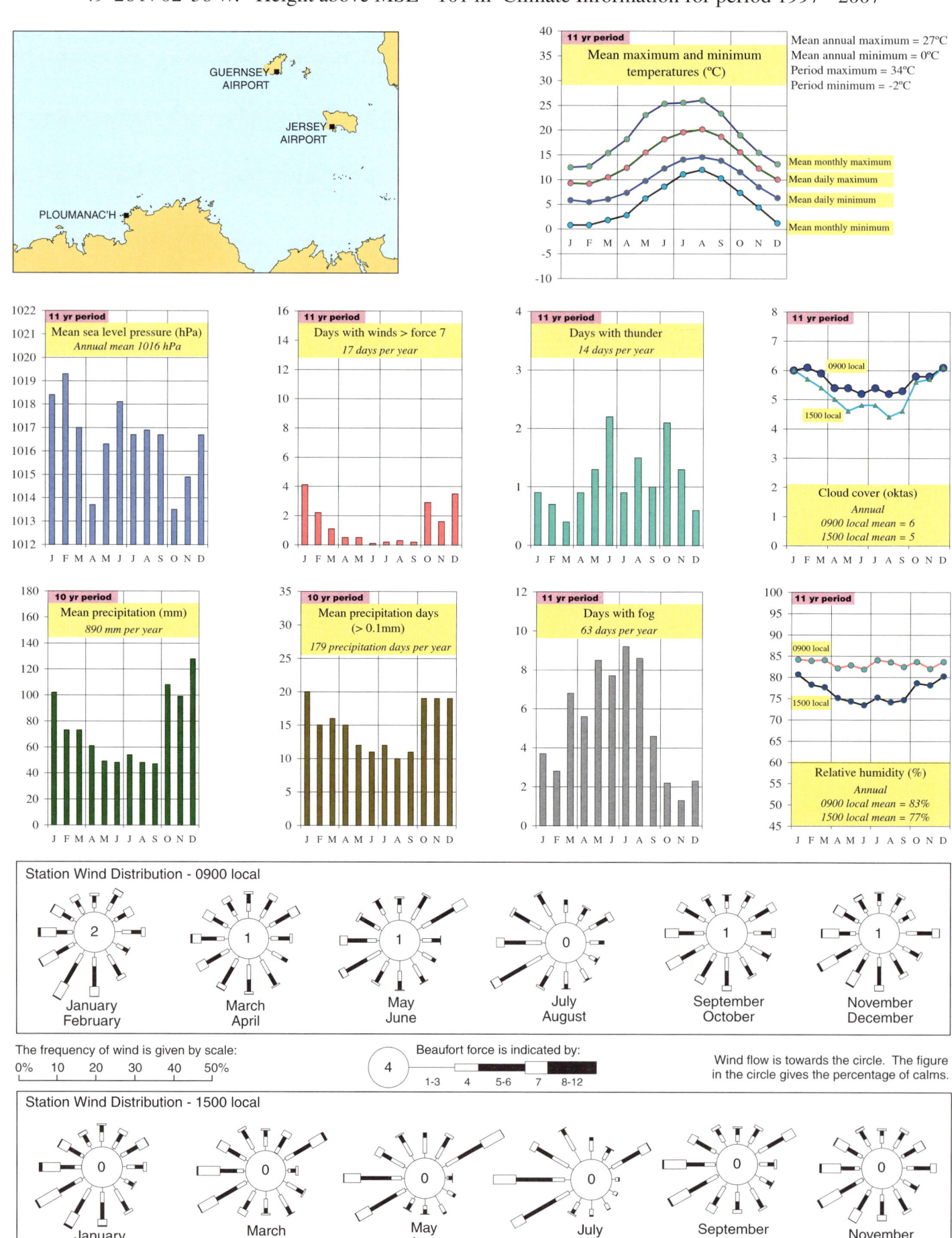

Mean annual maximum = 27°C
Mean annual minimum = 0°C
Period maximum = 34°C
Period minimum = -2°C

WMO No 03895 JERSEY AIRPORT

49°13'N 02°12'W.   Height above MSL - 48 m Climate Information for period 1997 - 2007

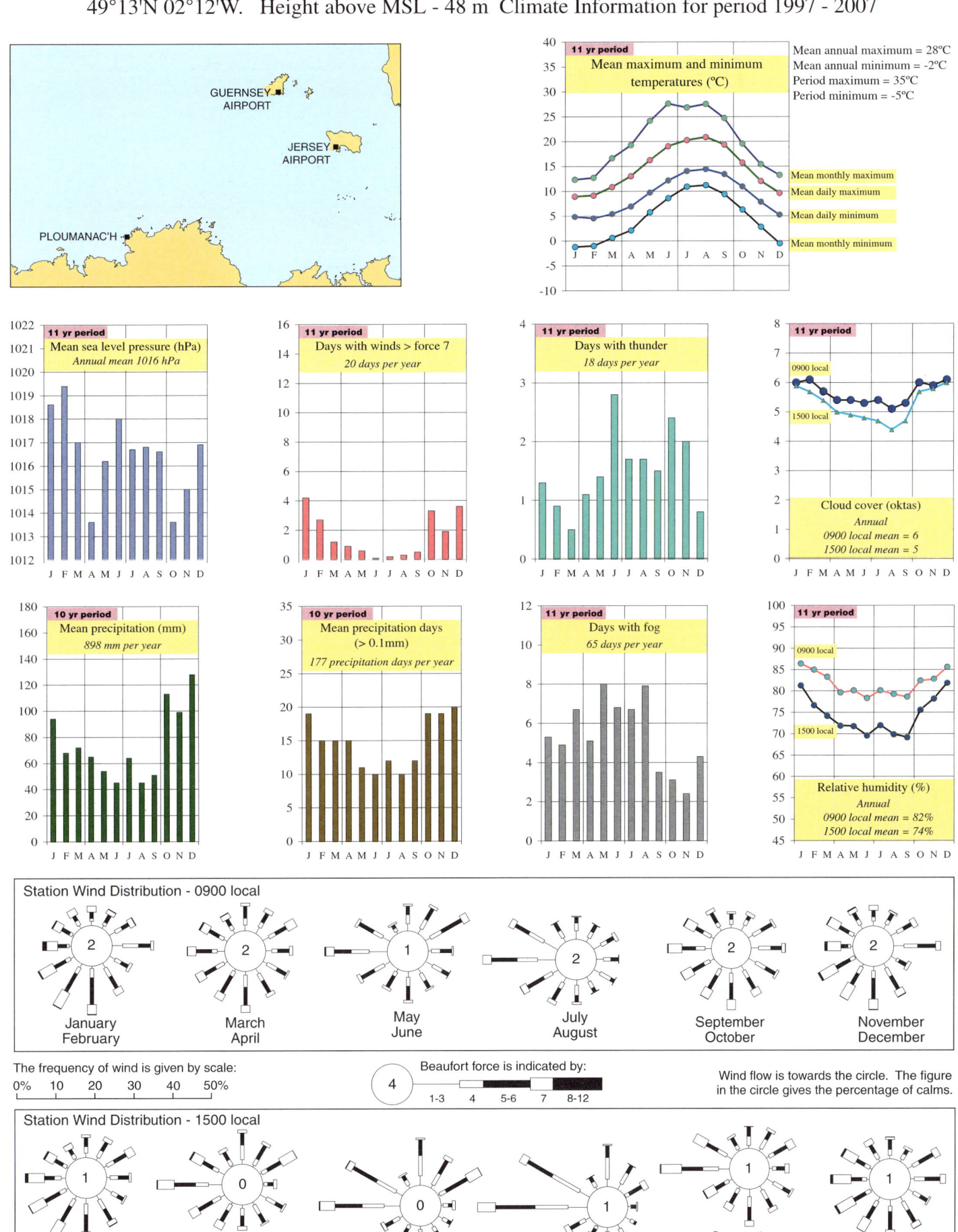

WMO No 07031 DEAUVILLE

49°22'N 00°10'E.   Height above MSL - 147 m Climate Information for period 1983 - 1991

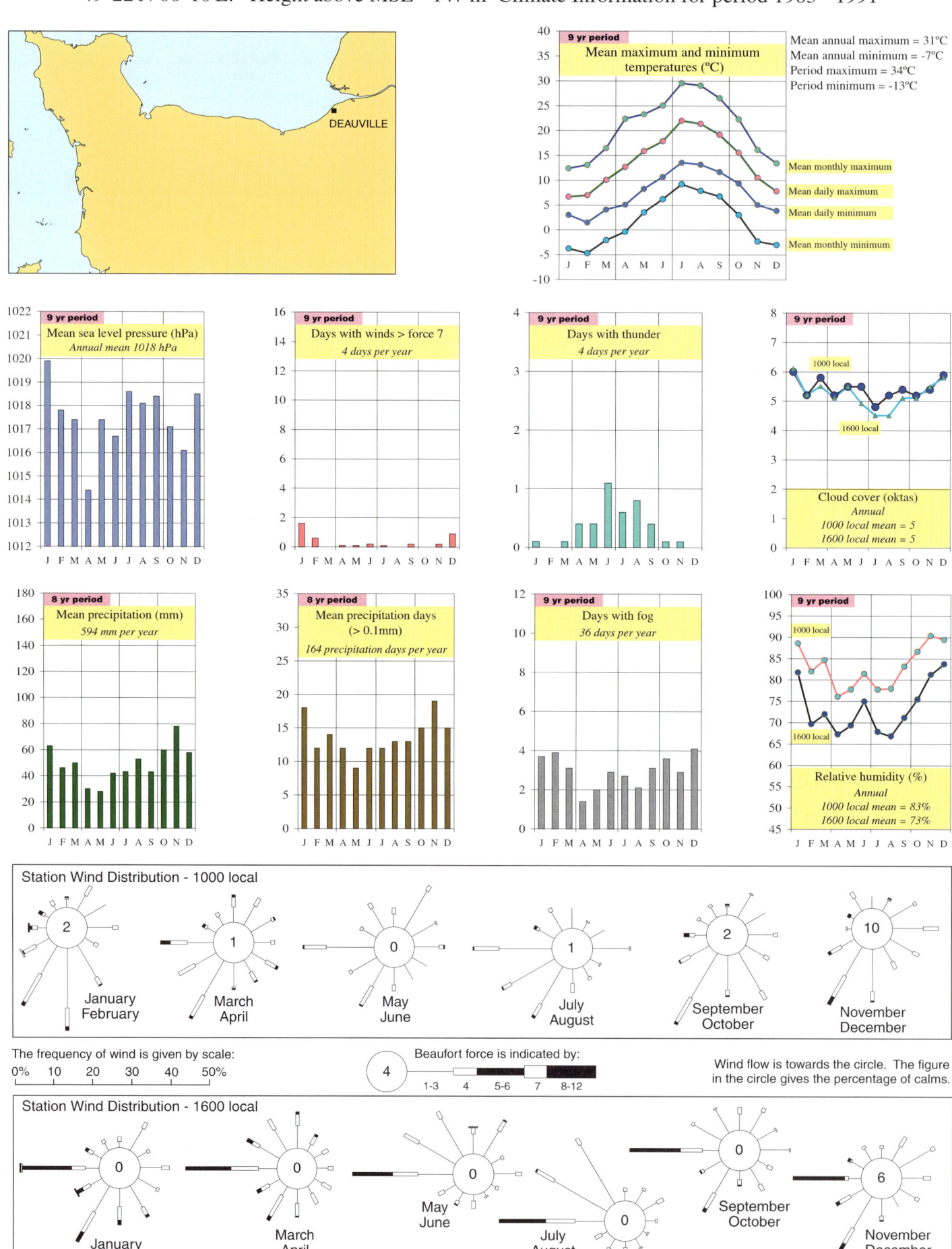

Mean annual maximum = 31°C
Mean annual minimum = -7°C
Period maximum = 34°C
Period minimum = -13°C

Mean maximum and minimum temperatures (°C)

9 yr period

Mean monthly maximum
Mean daily maximum
Mean daily minimum
Mean monthly minimum

Mean sea level pressure (hPa)
Annual mean 1018 hPa
9 yr period

Days with winds > force 7
4 days per year
9 yr period

Days with thunder
4 days per year
9 yr period

Cloud cover (oktas)
Annual
1000 local mean = 5
1600 local mean = 5
9 yr period
1000 local
1600 local

Mean precipitation (mm)
594 mm per year
8 yr period

Mean precipitation days
(> 0.1mm)
164 precipitation days per year
8 yr period

Days with fog
36 days per year
9 yr period

Relative humidity (%)
Annual
1000 local mean = 83%
1600 local mean = 73%
9 yr period
1000 local
1600 local

Station Wind Distribution - 1000 local

2 — January February
1 — March April
0 — May June
1 — July August
2 — September October
10 — November December

The frequency of wind is given by scale:
0% 10 20 30 40 50%

Beaufort force is indicated by:
4
1-3 4 5-6 7 8-12

Wind flow is towards the circle. The figure in the circle gives the percentage of calms.

Station Wind Distribution - 1600 local

0 — January February
0 — March April
0 — May June
0 — July August
0 — September October
6 — November December

60

1.209

METEOROLOGICAL CONVERSION TABLE AND SCALES

Fahrenheit to Celsius
°Fahrenheit

	0	1	2	3	4	5	6	7	8	9
°F					Degrees Celsius					
-100	-73·3	-73·9	-74·4	-75·0	-75·6	-76·1	-76·7	-77·2	-77·8	-78·3
-90	-67·8	-68·3	-68·9	-69·4	-70·0	-70·6	-71·1	-71·7	-72·2	-72·8
-80	-62·2	-62·8	-63·3	-63·9	-64·4	-65·0	-65·6	-66·1	-66·7	-67·2
-70	-56·7	-57·2	-57·8	-58·3	-58·9	-59·4	-60·0	-60·6	-61·1	-61·7
-60	-51·1	-51·7	-52·2	-52·8	-53·3	-53·9	-54·4	-55·0	-55·6	-56·1
-50	-45·6	-46·1	-46·7	-47·2	-47·8	-48·3	-48·9	-49·4	-50·0	-50·6
-40	-40·0	-40·6	-41·1	-41·7	-42·2	-42·8	-43·3	-43·9	-44·4	-45·0
-30	-34·4	-35·0	-35·6	-36·1	-36·7	-37·2	-37·8	-38·3	-38·9	-39·4
-20	-28·9	-29·4	-30·0	-30·6	-31·1	-31·7	-32·2	-32·8	-33·3	-33·9
-10	-23·3	-23·9	-24·4	-25·0	-25·6	-26·1	-26·7	-27·2	-27·8	-28·3
-0	-17·8	-18·3	-18·9	-19·4	-20·0	-20·6	-21·1	-21·7	-22·2	-22·8
+0	-17·8	-17·2	-16·7	-16·1	-15·6	-15·0	-14·4	-13·9	-13·3	-12·8
10	-12·2	-11·7	-11·1	-10·6	-10·0	-9·4	-8·9	-8·3	-7·8	-7·2
20	-6·7	-6·1	-5·6	-5·0	-4·4	-3·9	-3·3	-2·8	-2·2	-1·7
30	-1·1	-0·6	0	+0·6	+1·1	+1·7	+2·2	+2·8	+3·3	+3·9
40	+4·4	+5·0	+5·6	6·1	6·7	7·2	7·8	8·3	8·9	9·4
50	10·0	10·6	11·1	11·7	12·2	12·8	13·3	13·9	14·4	15·0
60	15·6	16·1	16·7	17·2	17·8	18·3	18·9	19·4	20·0	20·6
70	21·1	21·7	22·2	22·8	23·3	23·9	24·4	25·0	25·6	26·1
80	26·7	27·2	27·8	28·3	28·9	29·4	30·0	30·6	31·1	31·7
90	32·2	32·8	33·3	33·9	34·4	35·0	35·6	36·1	36·7	37·2
100	37·8	38·3	38·9	39·4	40·0	40·6	41·1	41·7	42·2	42·8
110	43·3	43·9	44·4	45·0	45·6	46·1	46·7	47·2	47·8	48·3
120	48·9	49·4	50·0	50·6	51·1	51·7	52·2	52·8	53·3	53·9

Celsius to Fahrenheit
°Celsius

	0	1	2	3	4	5	6	7	8	9
°C					Degrees Fahrenheit					
-70	-94·0	-95·8	-97·6	-99·4	-101·2	-103·0	-104·8	-106·6	-108·4	-110·2
-60	-76·0	-77·8	-79·6	-81·4	-83·2	-85·0	-86·8	-88·6	-90·4	-92·2
-50	-58·0	-59·8	-61·6	-63·4	-65·2	-67·0	-68·8	-70·6	-72·4	-74·2
-40	-40·0	-41·8	-43·6	-45·4	-47·2	-49·0	-50·8	-52·6	-54·4	-56·2
-30	-22·0	-23·8	-25·6	-27·4	-29·2	-31·0	-32·8	-34·6	-36·4	-38·2
-20	-4·0	-5·8	-7·6	-9·4	-11·2	-13·0	-14·8	-16·6	18·4	-20·2
-10	+14·0	+12·2	+10·4	+8·6	+6·8	+5·0	+3·2	+1·4	-0·4	-2·2
-0	32·0	30·2	28·4	26·6	24·8	23·0	21·2	19·4	+17·6	+15·8
+0	32·0	33·8	35·6	37·4	39·2	41·0	42·8	44·6	46·4	48·2
10	50·0	51·8	53·6	55·4	57·2	59·0	60·8	62·6	64·4	66·2
20	68·0	69·8	71·6	73·4	75·2	77·0	78·8	80·6	82·4	84·2
30	86·0	87·8	89·6	91·4	93·2	95·0	96·8	98·6	100·4	102·2
40	104·0	105·8	107·6	109·4	111·2	113·0	114·8	116·6	118·4	120·2
50	122·0	123·8	125·6	127·4	129·2	131·0	132·8	134·6	136·4	138·2

HECTOPASCALS TO INCHES

HECTOPASCALS

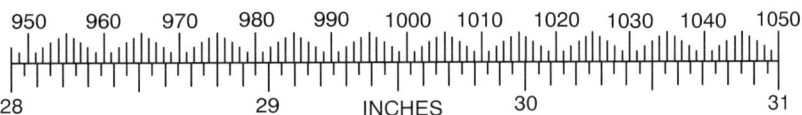

MILLIMETRES TO INCHES

(1) (for small values)
millimetres

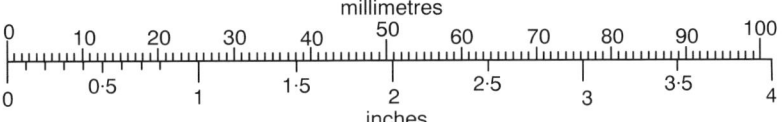

(2) (for large values)
millimetres

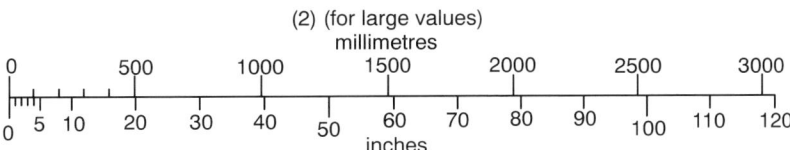

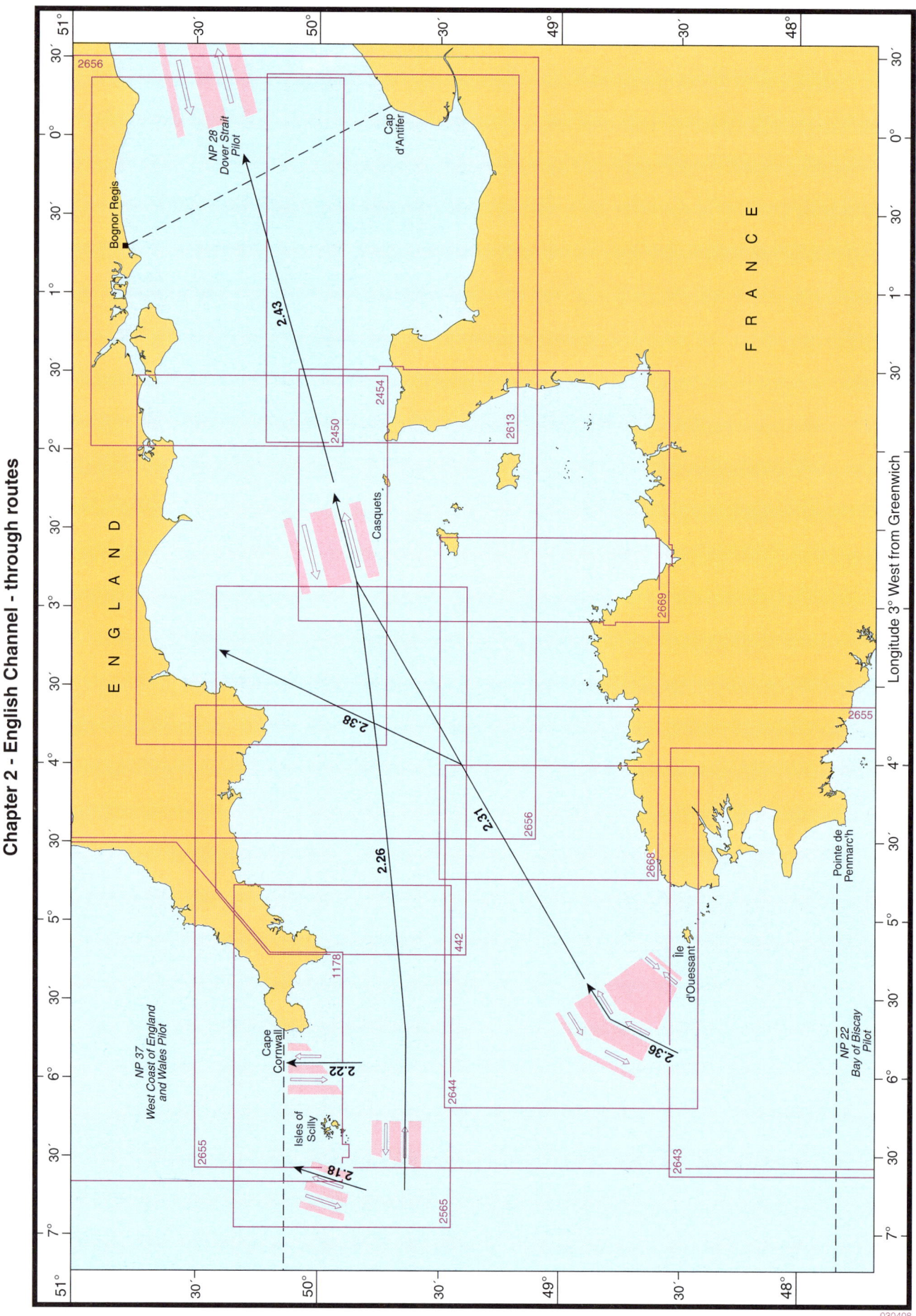

030408

CHAPTER 2

ENGLISH CHANNEL — THROUGH ROUTEING

GENERAL INFORMATION

Charts 2675, 4103, 5500
Scope of chapter
2.1

1   The scope and purpose of this chapter is to provide general information and directions for mariners in traffic proceeding through the approaches to the English Channel and the channel itself.

Routes
2.2

1   **Ocean routes** leading to the English Channel from the North Atlantic Ocean are described in *Ocean Passages for the World.*

2   **Mariners' Routeing Guide** (chart 5500) contains Passage Planning Charts which show the routes through the English Channel, Dover Strait and the Southern North Sea as far as the entrance to Europoort. These charts also refer to tables on the guide which give further information on routeing, regulations, pilotage and maritime radio services. The routes to be followed in accordance with the traffic regulatory measures, which are approved by IMO, are outlined in 2.3 and detailed in the directions contained in this chapter.

3   The *Mariners' Routeing Guide* is maintained in date by *Admiralty Notices to Mariners.*

    The IMO has adopted a recommendation that all vessels navigating in the English Channel and Dover Strait should carry the latest edition of chart 5500 or other equivalent guide.
2.3

1   **Traffic Separation Schemes.** Within the area covered by this book TSS have been established in the following focal areas:

        To the W and S of the Isles of Scilly (49°55′N 6°20′W), and between those islands and the English coast.

        To the NW of Île d'Ouessant (48°28′N 5°05′W) known in English as Ushant.

        To the N of Casquets (49°43′N 2°22′W).

2   All these schemes are IMO-adopted and Rule 10 of *International Regulations for Preventing Collisions at Sea (1972)* applies.

    Special provisions have been adopted by IMO for use in the scheme NW of Île d'Ouessant, for details see 2.32.

3   **Amending circumstances.** Mariners may pass between the TSS S of the Isles of Scilly and the TSS NW of Île d'Ouessant if considered safer to do so in the prevailing circumstances.
2.4

1   **Recommended direction of traffic flow.** Two recommended directions of traffic flow, leading generally NE and ENE, link the TSS NW of Île d'Ouessant with the TSS N of Casquets, and thence with the TSS in Dover Strait and adjacent waters.
2.5

1   **The Inshore Traffic Zones** which lie W and S of Isles of Scilly and between those islands and the English coast, NW of Île d'Ouessant, and N of Casquets are described in the appropriate geographical chapters.

    French national regulations govern navigation in the Inshore Traffic Zone off Île d'Ouessant and certain channels off the NW coast of Bretagne, for details see 8.5.

2   For further information on routeing and traffic measures see 1.8 to 1.17, *Annual Summary of Admiralty Notices to Mariners* and *The Mariner's Handbook.*
2.6

1   **Recommendations on navigation through the English Channel and Dover Strait,** see 1.20.

    Ship Movement Report System (MANCHEREP), see 1.14.

Exercise areas
2.7

1   Detailed information concerning these areas, which are found in the waters of this chapter, may be found on Practice Exercise Area (PEXA) charts. Such areas are also shown on all new, and new edition navigation charts. For further details see 1.30 and *Annual Summary of Admiralty Notices to Mariners Nos 5 and 8.*

Deep-sea pilotage
2.8

1   The services of a licensed deep-sea pilot may be obtained from a number of pilotage authorities bordering the English Channel. See 1.50 for details.

Channel Navigation Information Service
2.9

1   The Channel Navigation Information Service (CNIS) is operated by Dover Strait Coastguard and Cap Gris-Nez Traffic (CROSS) and comprises navigational and traffic information of immediate interest to mariners on passage through the Dover Strait together with the movements of vessels which appear to be acting in contravention of the rules governing the scheme.

2   For details of this service, which falls just outside the area covered by this volume, see *Dover Strait Pilot* and *Admiralty List of Radio Signals Volume 6(1).*

DIRECTIONS

GENERAL INFORMATION
2.10

1   The general information pertinent to all routes is given in the first section of this chapter and only information specific to a given route, such as principal marks, is given prior to the directions themselves.

2   For general navigational notes approaching the English Channel from the Atlantic Ocean and Bay of Biscay, see 1.2.

    The directions are divided as follows:

3

North-north-east going traffic lane of the TSS West of Isles of Scilly (49°55′N 6°20′W).

North-going traffic lane of the TSS Off Land's End between Isles of Scilly and the English coast.

East-going traffic lane of the TSS South of Isles of Scilly to the Off Casquets TSS (49°43′N 2°22′W).

North-east going traffic lane and two-way traffic lane of the Off Ushant TSS (48°28′N 5°05′W) and the recommended NE direction of traffic flow to the Off Casquets TSS.

4

East-north-east going traffic lane of the Off Casquets TSS and the recommended ENE direction of traffic flow to the NE-going traffic lane of the TSS in Dover Strait and adjacent waters at the Greenwich meridian.

ISLES OF SCILLY TO CASQUETS INCLUDING TRAFFIC SEPARATION SCHEMES WEST AND EAST OF THE ISLES

General information

Charts 2565, 2675
Traffic Separation Scheme
2.11

1   A TSS is established as shown on the charts W, S and E of Isles of Scilly (49°55′N 6°20′W) including the area between Seven Stones (50°02′N 6°07′W) and Longships, 14 miles E. This scheme is IMO adopted and Rule 10 of *International Regulations for Preventing Collisions at Sea (1972)* applies.

2   **IMO recommendation.** A recommendation has been adopted by IMO that laden tankers over 10 000 gt using the TSS Off Land's End between Longships and Seven Stones should keep at least 3 miles to seaward of Wolf Rock (49°57′N 5°48′W) and should not use the scheme in restricted visibility or other adverse weather. Mariners in laden tankers should report to Falmouth Coastguard at least 1 hour before ETA and on final departure from the TSS, for details see *Admiralty List of Radio Signals Volume 6(1)*. Falmouth Coastguard accepts reports by AIS (1.71).

Topography
2.12

1   Bishop Rock (49°52′N 6°27′W) (3.13) is the SW-most danger of Isles of Scilly. Bishop Rock Lighthouse (3.16), a conspicuous lighthouse situated on the rock, will be the first landmark seen by mariners approaching Isles of Scilly from the SW. There are numerous other landmarks in Isles of Scilly which are described in Chapter 3.

2   On approaching the English coast Land's End (50°04′N 5°43′W) (3.89) may be seen in clear weather from a distance of approximately 25 miles.

Farther E, Lizard Point (49°58′N 5°13′W) (3.112), from which a powerful light is exhibited, is used as a point of departure for mariners outward bound from the English Channel, and as a landfall for mariners inward bound.

Submarine exercise areas
2.13

1   Submarines, both surfaced and dived, exercise frequently in the SW approaches and in an area which extends up to approximately 40 miles S from the English coast to longitude 7°W. A good lookout for submarines must be kept when passing through these waters; for details see 1.33 and *Annual Notice to Mariners No 8*.

Low visibility
2.14

1   In low visibility, unless certain of their position, mariners are recommended not to approach the Isles of Scilly within depths of 100 m on account of the rocky ledges which extend SW from the islands. This depth contour lies approximately 11 miles W and 12 miles S of Bishop Rock.

Traffic
2.15

1   Mariners using the TSS W or E of Isles of Scilly should be aware of vessels using the TSS S of Isles of Scilly which crosses close S to the S ends of the W and E schemes.

Submarine cables
2.16

1   For details of submarine cables, including a submarine power cable, see 3.4.

Offshore tidal streams
2.17

1   The offshore tidal streams are shown by means of information on the chart and in *Admiralty Tidal Stream Atlas of the English Channel*.

For further details, see also 1.151.

West of Isles of Scilly

Chart 2565
General information
2.18

1   **Route.** From a landfall W of Bishop Rock (49°52′N 6°27′W) the through route passes through the TSS W of the Isles of Scilly to the parallel of 50°08′N, W of Cape Cornwall, a distance of about 16 miles.

Directions
(continued from the open ocean)
2.19

1   **Landmarks:**
Bishop Rock Lighthouse (49°52′N 6°27′W) (3.16).
Round Island Lighthouse (49°59′N 6°19′W) (3.16).
Major lights:
Bishop Rock Light — as above.
Round Island Light — as above.
2.20

1   **Other aids to navigation — racon:** Bishop Rock Light (49°52′N 6°27′W), Round Island Light (49°59′N 6°19′W) (3.16).

For details see *Admiralty List of Radio Signals Volume 2*.
2.21

1   From the S end of the TSS W of Isles of Scilly (49°55′N 6°20′W) the route leads through the NNE-bound traffic lane, which is 3 miles wide and shown on the chart, passing:
WNW of Bishop Rock (49°52′N 6°27′W) (3.13); thence:
WNW of Round Island (49°59′N 6°19′W) (3.13); thence:

2   WNW of Seven Stones (50°02′N 6°07′W) (3.34) to a position W of Cape Cornwall (3.84) on the parallel of 50°08′N.
Useful mark:
Seven Stones Light Float (50°04′N 6°04′W) (3.30).
(Directions continue in West Coasts of England and Wales Pilot)

East of Isles of Scilly

Charts 1148, 2565
General information
2.22

1   **Route.** From a landfall WSW of Wolf Rock (49°57′N 5°48′W) the through route passes through the TSS Off Land's End passing between Seven Stones (50°02′N 6°07′W) and Longships, 14 miles E, to W of Cape Cornwall (50°08′N 5°43′W) a distance of about 13 miles.

2   The recommended channel for large vessels between Seven Stones and Longships is approximately 12 miles wide, with a least depth of 34 m, and the passage is perfectly simple by day as well as by night in clear weather. However this part of the coast is subject to sudden changes of weather and a mariner's position should be determined at frequent intervals even in the clearest weather.

3   **IMO recommendation for mariners in laden tankers,** see 2.11.

Submarine power cable, see 3.4.

Directions
(continued from the open ocean)
2.23

1   **Landmark:**
Land's End (50°04′N 5°43′W) (3.89).

Major lights:
Peninnis Head Light (49°54′N 6°18′W) (3.30).
Wolf Rock Light (49°57′N 5°48′W) (3.89).
Longships Light (50°04′N 5°45′W) (3.89).
Seven Stones Light Float (50°04′N 6°04′W) (3.30).

2.24

1   **Other aids to navigation — racons:**
Wolf Rock Light (49°57′N 5°48′W).
Seven Stones Light Float (50°04′N 6°04′W).

For details see *Admiralty List of Radio Signals Volume 2.*
2.25

1   From the S end of the TSS Off Land's End the route leads through the N–bound traffic lane, which is 3 miles wide and shown on the chart, passing (with positions given from Wolf Rock):
E of Isles of Scilly (17 miles W) (3.6); and:
W of Wolf Rock; thence:
W of Carn Base (5½ miles NNE) (3.92); thence:

2   E of Seven Stones (13 miles WNW) (3.34). Seven Stones Light Float (3.30) is moored 2 miles ENE. Thence:
W of Longships (8 miles NNE) (3.92); thence:
W of Cape Cornwall (12 miles NNE) (3.84).

3   In thick weather it should be borne in mind that Seven Stones and Wolf Rock are steep-to on all sides and Longships from NW and W. Soundings should not be relied on to give warnings of the proximity of these dangers. It should be noted however that there are differences in interval and frequency between the fog signals at Wolf Rock, Seven Stones and Longships, which, if heard and carefully attended to, will enable a mariner to avoid these dangers.

4   **Useful marks:**
Tater-du Light (50°03′N 5°35′W) (3.112).
Bishop Rock Light (49°52′N 6°27′W) (3.16).
Round Island Light (49°59′N 6°19′W) (3.16).
Pendeen Light (50°10′N 5°40′W) (*West Coasts of England and Wales Pilot*).
(Directions continue in West Coasts of England and Wales Pilot)

Isles of Scilly to Casquets

Charts 2565, 442, 2656, 2675
General information
2.26

1   **Route.** From a landfall SSW of Bishop Rock (49°52′N 6°27′W) the through route passes through the TSS S of Isles of Scilly to S of Saint Mary's (49°55′N 6°18′W), a distance of about 10 miles, and then continues generally E, about 135 miles, to the Off Casquets TSS (49°43′N 2°22′W).

Directions
(continued from the open ocean)
2.27

1   **Landmark:**
Bishop Rock Lighthouse (49°52′N 6°27′W) (3.16).
Major lights:
Bishop Rock Light (49°52′N 6°27′W) (3.16).
Peninnis Head Light (49°54′N 6°18′W) (3.30).
Round Island Light (49°59′N 6°19′W) (3.16).

2   Wolf Rock Light (49°57′N 5°48′W) (3.89).
Tater-du Light (50°03′N 5°35′W) (3.112).
Lizard Light (49°58′N 5°12′W) (3.112).
Start Point Light (50°13′N 3°38′W) (5.18).
Channel Light Float (49°54′N 2°54′W) (2.40).

2.28

1   **Other aids to navigation — racons:**
Bishop Rock Light (49°52′N 6°27′W).
Channel Light Float (49°54′N 2°54′W).

For details see *Admiralty List of Radio Signals Volume 2.*
2.29

1   **Traffic Separation Scheme south of Isles of Scilly.**
From the W end of the TSS S of Isles of Scilly (49°55′N 6°20′W) the route leads through the E-bound traffic lane, which is 3 miles wide and shown on the chart, passing:
S of Bishop Rock (49°52′N 6°27′W) (3.13) noting The Pol Bank (3.32) which lies 3 miles SSW of Bishop Rock; thence:
S of Isles of Scilly (49°55′N 6°20′W) (3.6).

2.30

1   **Traffic Separation Scheme south of Isles of Scilly to Off Casquets Traffic Separation Scheme.**
From a position S of Saint Mary's (49°55′N 6°18′W) (3.51), at the E end of the E-bound traffic lane of the TSS S of Isles of Scilly, the route leads generally E, about 135 miles, passing:

2   S of Lizard Point (49°58′N 5°13′W) (3.112); thence:
S of Prawle Point (50°12′N 3°43′W) (4.252); thence:
To a position SSE of Channel Light Float (49°54′N 2°54′W) (2.40).
(Directions continue at 2.40)

USHANT TO CASQUETS

General information

Charts 2655, 2675
Navigational notes
2.31

1   Approaching Île d'Ouessant (48°28′N 5°05′W) which is surrounded by dangers, guard against the danger of being set E; caution is also needed when rounding it as the tidal streams are strong and the extent of their influence seaward undetermined. In thick weather, which is not uncommon, no dependence can be placed on seeing the lights nor upon hearing the fog signals; in such conditions, unless certain of position, Île d'Ouessant should be given a wide berth, see 2.3.

2 In clear weather, mariners in small vessels with permission (8.5) to use the inshore channels, proceeding from Bay of Biscay ports to the English Channel, may pass through Raz de Seine (8.202) and Chenal du Four (8.45) after having first sighted Pointe de Penmarc'h (47°48′N 4°22′W) (*Bay of Biscay Pilot*); Raz de Sein should be avoided when the tidal stream is opposed to a strong wind, see 8.202.

3 Approaching from W, mariners can avoid the dangers off Casquets (49°43′N 2°22′W), Alderney and Cap de la Hague by paying attention to the soundings in Hurd Deep (1.143).

Traffic Separation Scheme
2.32

1 The Off Ushant TSS is situated NW of Île d'Ouessant (48°28′N 5°05′W). The scheme is IMO-adopted and Rule 10 of *International Regulations for Preventing Collisions at Sea (1972)* applies. In addition IMO have adopted the following special provisions for this scheme.

2 1) The two-way traffic lane, 2 miles wide, may only be used by passenger ships operating regular schedules to or from a Channel port situated W of meridian 1°W, and by ships sailing between ports situated between Cap de la Hague and Cabo Finisterre. This lane must not be used by:

3 a) Ships carrying oils listed in Appendix I of Annex I of *The International Convention for the Prevention of Pollution from Ships, 1973*, as modified by the *Protocol of 1978* (MARPOL 73/78), and:
b) Ships carrying in bulk the substances listed in categories X and Y listed in Appendix I of Annex II of that Convention.

4 2) Such vessels, when proceeding in the NE-bound lane, 5 miles wide, must as far as possible, navigate in the outer part of that lane.

IMO state, however, that navigation within the Inshore Traffic Zone of the Ushant TSS is subject to national regulations; for details see 8.5.
2.33

1 **Mandatory Vessel Traffic Management System.** For vessels in the NE-bound traffic lane and the two-way traffic lane, see 8.6.

Ship Movement Report System (MANCHEREP), see 1.14.

Directions
(continued from directions given in Bay of Biscay Pilot)

Principal marks
2.34

1 **Landmarks:**
Créac'h Lighthouse (48°28′N 5°08′W) (8.25).
Le Stiff Lighthouse (48°29′N 5°03′W) (8.25).
Radar Tower (48°29′N 5°03′W) on Île d'Ouessant.
Major lights:
Ouessant SW Lanby (48°30′N 5°45′W) (2.36).
La Jument Light (48°25′N 5°08′W) (8.25).
Créac'h Light (48°28′N 5°08′W) (8.25).

2 Le Stiff Light (48°29′N 5°03′W) (8.25)
Le Four Light (48°31′N 4°48′W) (8.43).

Île Vierge Light (48°38′N 4°34′W) (9.16).
Channel Light Float (49°54′N 2°54′W) (2.40).

Other aids to navigation
2.35

1 **Racons:**
Ouessant SW Lanby (48°30′N 5°45′W).
Créac'h Light (48°28′N 5°08′W).
Ouessant NE Light Buoy (48°59′N 5°24′W).
Channel Light Float (49°54′N 2°54′W).

2 For details see *Admiralty List of Radio Signals Volume 2*.

Charts 2644, 442, 2656
Off Ushant Traffic Separation Scheme
2.36

1 **North-east going traffic lane.** From a position WNW of Ouessant SW Lanby (safe water) (48°30′N 5°45′W) moored 25 miles WNW of Créac'h Light, at the SW end of the Off Ushant TSS, the route follows the NE-bound traffic lane, which is 5 miles wide and leads NNE thence NE about 30 miles, as shown on the chart, to a position SE of Ouessant NE Light Buoy (safe water) (48°59′N 5°24′W) moored 34 miles NNW of Créac'h Light.

2 **Caution:** An obstruction (position doubtful) lies in position 48°48′·5N 5°23′·5W, close SE of the NE exit of the NE lane.

North-east going recommended direction of traffic flow
2.37

1 From a position SE of Ouessant NE Light Buoy the recommended direction of traffic flow leads in a general ENE direction for about 111 miles, to a position SSE of Channel Light Float (49°54′N 2°54′W) (2.41) moored at the W end of the Off Casquets TSS.
(Directions continue at 2.40)

Lyme Bay
2.38

1 From a position SE of Ouessant NE Light Buoy (safe water) (48°59′N 5°24′W) mariners in vessels bound for Lyme Bay (5.124) are advised to follow the NE-going recommended direction of traffic flow for about 56 miles to a position in the vicinity of meridian 4°W when a general NNE track can be followed for about 69 miles to the Deep-Sea Pilot Boarding place off Tor Bay.

For details regarding Deep-Sea Pilots off Tor Bay, see 5.95.

CASQUETS TO GREENWICH MERIDIAN

General information

Chart 2656
Route
2.39

1 **Traffic Separation Scheme.** From SSE of Channel Light Float (49°54′N 2°54′W), moored at the W end of the Off Casquets TSS, the route follows the ENE-bound traffic lane to a position N of Casquets (49°43′N 2°22′W).

2 **Recommended direction of traffic flow between the Traffic Separation Scheme NW of Casquets and the Greenwich meridian.** All ships should follow the recommended direction of traffic flow between Off

Casquets TSS and Dover Strait TSS, as shown on the charts.

Directions
(continued from 2.30 and 2.37)

Principal marks
2.40

1 **Landmarks — French coast:**
Chimney (49°41′N 1°53′W) (12.9) on the summit of the high land S of Cap de la Hague.
Cap de la Hague Lighthouse (49°43′N 1°57′W) (12.9).

Major lights — in the waterway:
Channel Light Float (red hull light tower amidships) (49°54′N 2°54′W).

2 Casquets Light (49°43′N 2°23′W) (11.151).
Alderney Light (49°44′N 2°10′W) (11.151).
Greenwich Light Float (50°25′N 0°00′) (*Dover Strait Pilot*).

Major lights — French coast:
Cap de la Hague Light (49°43′N 1°57′W) (12.9).
Cap Lévi Light (49°42′N 1°28′W) (12.9).
Pointe de Barfleur-Gatteville Light (49°42′N 1°16′W) (12.9).

3 **Major lights — English coast:**
Portland Light (50°31′N 2°27′W) (6.21).
Anvil Point Light (50°36′N 1°58′W) (6.87).
Saint Catherine's Point Light (50°35′N 1°18′W) (6.167).

Other aids to navigation
2.41

1 **Racons:**
Channel Light Float (49°54′N 2°54′W).
East Channel Light Buoy (49°59′N 2°29′W).

Casquets Light (49°43′N 2°23′W).
Greenwich Light Float (50°25′N 0°00′).
For details see *Admiralty List of Radio Signals Volume 2.*

Charts 2669, 2454, 2450, 2656

East–north–east going traffic lane
2.42

1 From a position SSE of Channel Light Float (49°54′N 2°54′W) at the W end of the Off Casquets TSS, the route follows the ENE-going traffic lane, which is 5 miles wide and shown on the charts, for about 20 miles passing:
Between East Channel Light Buoy (special) (49°59′N 2°29′W), which is moored 3 miles WSW of the E end of the TSS, and Casquets (49°43′N 2°22′W) (11.140) to a position SE of the light buoy.

East–north–east going recommended direction of traffic flow
2.43

1 **IMO recommendations:** see 1.20.
From a position SE of East Channel Light Buoy (49°59′N 2°29′W), moored near the E end of the Off Casquets TSS, the route follows the ENE-going recommended direction of traffic flow, which is shown on the charts, for about 95 miles passing:
NNW of Alderney (49°43′N 2°12′W) (11.142) and associated dangers; thence:

2 NNW of Cap de la Hague (49°44′N 1°56′W) (12.9); thence:
To a position S of Greenwich Light Float (50°25′N 0°00′) (*Dover Strait Pilot*), moored at the W end of the TSS in Dover Strait and adjacent waters.
(Directions for the TSS in Dover Strait and adjacent waters continue in Dover Strait Pilot.
Directions for the deep-water route to Port du Havre-Antifer are given at 13.226)

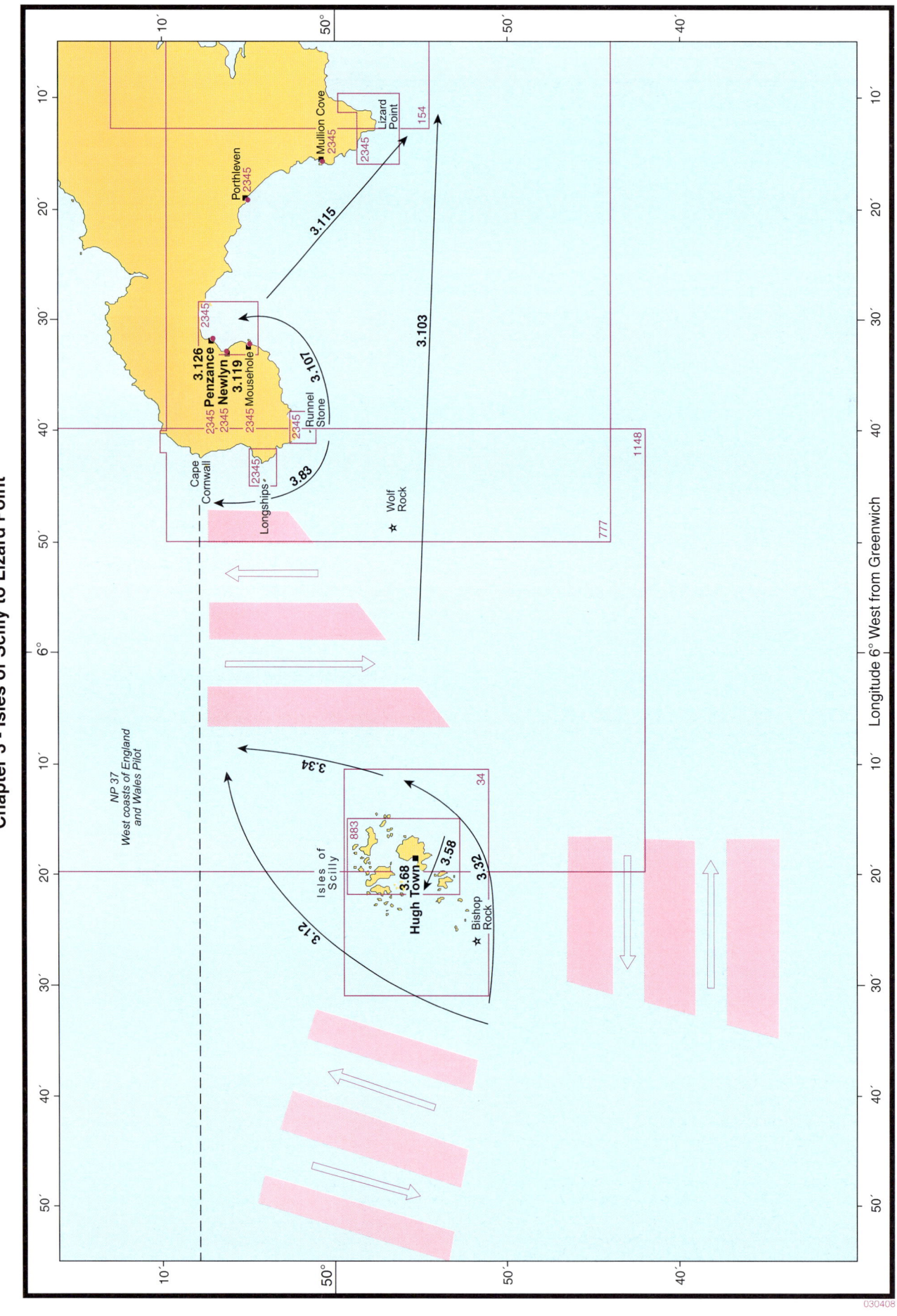

CHAPTER 3

ISLES OF SCILLY TO LIZARD POINT

GENERAL INFORMATION

Charts 2565, 2649
Scope of chapter
3.1

1   This chapter covers Isles of Scilly and the S coast of England from Cape Cornwall (50°08′N 5°43′W) to Lizard Point, 22 miles ESE.

Ports. The ports of Hugh Town Saint Mary's (3.68), Newlyn (3.119) and Penzance (3.126) are covered by this chapter.

Traffic separation scheme
3.2

1   A TSS is established as shown on the charts W, S and E of Isles of Scilly (49°55′N 6°20′W) including the area between Seven Stones (50°02′N 6°07′W) and Longships, 14 miles E. This scheme is IMO adopted and Rule 10 of *International Regulations for Preventing Collisions at Sea* (1972) applies; for details, see 1.8 to 1.14.

2   **IMO recommendation for laden tankers;** see 2.11.

Through routes. Details and directions for the through routes using the TSS surrounding Isles of Scilly are given in Chapter 2.

Firing practice and exercise areas
3.3
Exercise areas

1   Detailed information concerning these areas, which are found in the waters of this chapter, may be found on Practice Exercise Area (PEXA) charts. Such areas are also shown on all new, and new edition navigation charts. For further details see 1.30 and *Annual Summary of Admiralty Notices to Mariners Nos 5* and *8.*

2   Submarines, both surfaced and dived, exercise frequently in the SW approaches in an area which extends up to approximately 40 miles S from the English coast to longitude 7°W. A good lookout for submarines must be kept when passing through these waters; for details see 1.33 and *Annual Notice to Mariners No 8.*

Submarine cables
3.4

1   Submarine cables are laid W of Isles of Scilly, from Sennen Cove (50°05′N 5°42′W) NW through the Celtic Sea, and from the vicinity of Land's End extending S and SW passing SE of Isles of Scilly.

A submarine power cable is laid between Isles of Scilly and the mainland from Porth Cressa, Saint Mary's to a point in Whitesand Bay, 1½ miles NE of Land's End.

For further information regarding submarine cables, see 1.64.

Offshore tidal streams
3.5

1   The offshore tidal streams are shown by means of information on the chart and in *Admiralty Tidal Stream Atlas of the English Channel.*

For further details, see also 1.151.

ISLES OF SCILLY

GENERAL INFORMATION

Charts 34, 1148, 2565
Isles of Scilly
3.6

1   Isles of Scilly (49°55′N 6°20′W), a group of islands, islets and rocks, lie from 21 to 31 miles WSW of Land's End, the W extremity of the English coast. The isles comprise 48 islands, five of which are inhabited, namely Saint Mary's, which contains the principal town and harbour and the majority of the population, Saint Agnes, Saint Martin's, Tresco and Bryher.

Harbours and anchorages
3.7

1   The principal harbour in the islands is at Hugh Town, Saint Mary's (49°55′N 6°19′W); there are many other harbours for vessels capable of taking the ground. There are two anchorages for vessels of relatively deep draught at Saint Mary's Road (3.65) and Crow Sound (3.36), but the bottom among these islands being generally of loose sand, where not rocky, is not good holding ground.

2   The best harbours for small craft are at Tresco (49°57′N 6°20′W) in Old Grimsby Sound (3.23) and New Grimsby Sound (3.20), of which the latter is the better. Berthing space within these harbours is not available for visiting craft.

Traffic regulations
3.8

1   **Inshore traffic zones** are established W, S and E of Isles of Scilly inshore of the adjacent TSS (2.11) and Rule 10 of *International Regulations for Preventing Collisions at Sea (1972)* applies.

Rescue
3.9

1   **Coastguard rescue teams** operate from:
Saint Mary's (49°56′N 6°18′W).
Saint Agnes (49°53′N 6°21′W).
Saint Martin's (49°58′N 6°17′W).
Tresco (49°57′N 6°20′W).
Bryher (49°57′N 6°21′W).

2   **All-weather lifeboat.** Saint Mary's all-weather lifeboat is stationed at Hugh Town (49°55′N 6°19′W).

For details of coastguard stations, see 1.100 and for lifeboats 1.113.

VHF Direction-finding station, for emergency use only, operates from the coastguard signal station (49°56′N 6°18′W) on Saint Mary's, for details see *Admiralty List of Radio Signals Volume 2* and 1.105.

Climate information
3.10

1   See 1.195 and 1.196

Tidal streams
3.11

1   **Offshore streams** are rotary in a clockwise direction and run towards the isles from a different direction at each hour of the day and, in passing round and between them, are much affected by the trend of the land and channels, and by shallow water. These effects vary with the direction of the approaching stream so that the streams near and between the islands are subject to great irregularities and apparent inconsistencies.

2   Though the streams round the isles are not of any great strength, their rates increase off salient points, and over and near rocks and shoals, where overfalls and races may occur.

The streams E of the isles are strongest in about the directions and at about the times of the weakest streams elsewhere round the isles.

3   For greater detail see the tidal information on the appropriate charts and *Admiralty Tidal Stream Atlas of the English Channel and Falmouth to Padstow including Isles of Scilly*.

Inshore streams. Hourly tidal stream diagrams for the waters among the islands are shown on chart 34.

INSHORE PASSAGE NORTH WEST OF ISLES OF SCILLY

General information

Charts 34, 2565
Route
3.12

1   From W of Bishop Rock (49°52′N 6°27′W), off the entrance to Broad Sound, the coastal passage NW of Isles of Scilly through the inshore traffic zone to Seven Stones leads N, then NE, about 20 miles.

Topography
3.13

1   Bishop Rock the highest of a group of rocks, some of which dry, is the SW danger of Isles of Scilly, a

conspicuous lighthouse (3.16) stands on the rock. Crim Rocks, a group of above and below-water rocks the most prominent being Peaked Rock, lie 1½ miles NNW of Bishop Rock.

2   Maiden Bower (49°57′N 6°24′W) is the outermost islet of a chain of islets and dangerous rocks which extend 1¼ miles E to Bryher.

Tresco (49°57′N 6°20′W) lies close E of Bryher and separates Old Grimsby Sound and New Grimsby Sound, both of which afford anchorage to small craft.

3   Between Tresco and Saint Martin's (49°58′N 6°17′W) there are numerous small islands, islets and rocky shoal ground much of which dries. Saint Helen's lies near the N end of this shoal ground with Round Island, the N-most island of this group on which stands a conspicuous lighthouse (3.16), lying 2½ cables farther N. Men-a-vaur (3.45) a group of three islets is a useful mark and lies the same distance NW of Saint Helen's.

Traffic regulations
3.14

1   **Experimental area.** Mariners are cautioned against anchoring or fishing in an experimental area, approximately 1 mile square, situated 1 mile NW of Bryher (49°57′N 6°21′W), see information on chart 34.

Inshore traffic zone: for details, see 3.8.

Tidal streams
3.15

1   For details of tidal streams see 3.11 and information on the charts.

Directions
(Directions for Broad Sound are given at 3.60 and for the inshore passage SE of Isles of Scilly at 3.30)

Principal marks
3.16

1   **Landmarks:**

Bishop Rock Lighthouse (grey round granite tower, 49 m in height) (49°52′N 6°27′W) partially and totally obscured from N from 204° to 259°.

Round Island and Lighthouse (3.16)

(Photograph - Richard Coles)   *(Original dated 2007)*

Round Island Lighthouse (white round tower, 19 m in height) (49°59′N 6°19′W) visible 021° to 288°, obscured from ESE through S to SSW of the light.

2 **Major lights:**

Bishop Rock Light — as above.

Round Island Light — as above, shown throughout 24 hours.

Other aids to navigation
3.17

1 **Racons:**

Bishop Rock Light (3.16).

Round Island Light (3.16).

Seven Stones Light Float (50°04′N 6°04′W).

For details see *Admiralty List of Radio Signals Volume 2.*

Bishop Rock to Seven Stones
3.18

1 From a position W of Bishop Rock off the entrance to Broad Sound the route leads initially N passing (with positions given from Bishop Rock):

W of Crim Rocks (1½ miles NNW) (3.13) noting the 7·6 m isolated rocky patch lying 5 cables S of the rocks; thence:

2 W of North Rock (1¾ miles N) the N-most danger off Crim Rocks.

Useful mark:

Peninnis Head Light (49°54′N 6°18′W) (3.30).

3.19

1 The passage then leads NE passing (with positions given from Maiden Bower (49°57′N 6°24′W)):

NW of North Rock (3½ miles SW) (3.18); thence:

NW of Carntop (2¼ miles SSW) and associated dangers; thence:

Across the entrance to North West Passage (North Channel) (1¼ miles SSW) (3.49); thence:

2 NW of Westward Ledge (1½ cables NW) with a rock awash close WSW, the outermost dangers NW of Maiden Bower (3.13); thence:

NW of Northern Rocks of which Scilly Rock (8 cables NE), two islets, is the largest, noting Westward Ledge lying 1 cable NW, the outermost danger off Scilly Rock; thence:

3 NW of Shipman Head (1¾ miles NE) the N extremity of Bryher; thence:

NW of Kettle Bottom (2 miles NE) a drying rocky ledge between the entrance to Old and New Grimsby Sounds, the outermost danger NW of Tresco; thence:

4 NW of Golden Ball (2½ miles NE) a small islet near the NW extremity of a drying ledge and foul ground which extends W from Saint Helen's; thence:

5 NW of Men-a-vaur (3 miles NE) (3.45); thence:

NW of Round Island (3¼ miles NE) (3.13) noting Deep Ledges and Lion Rock, with a dangerous wreck close N, which lie 4 and 8 cables ENE, respectively, the N-most dangers of the Isles of Scilly; thence:

NW of Seven Stones (50°02′N 6°07′W) (3.34).

6 **Useful marks:**

Pendeen Light (50°10′N 5°40′W) (*West Coasts of England and Wales Pilot*).

Seven Stones Light Float (50°04′N 6°04′W) (3.30).

(Directions continue in West Coasts of England and Wales Pilot)

Anchorages

Charts 883, 34
New Grimsby Sound
3.20

1 **General information.** New Grimsby Sound between Bryher (49°57′N 6°21′W) and the NW side of Tresco, although only ½ cable wide, is better than Old Grimsby Sound as it is easier of access than the latter, less encumbered with shoals and open only to NW winds. The sound affords secure anchorage to mariners in small craft and there are 22 deep-water moorings for visiting craft.

Kettle Point   Hangman Island   Bryher Island

Tresco Island   Shipman Head

New Grimsby Sound from NW (3.20)

(Original dated 2001)

(Photograph - Air Images)

3.21

1 **Directions.** See View B on chart 34. From a position NNW of Tresco the alignment (157°) of the W side of Hangman Isle (49°57′·6N 6°21′·0W), a small islet with a distinctively steep cone-shaped summit, with Star Castle Hotel, 3 miles SSE, leads about 1 mile SSE into the entrance of the sound passing between Shipman Head and Kettle Bottom (3.19) to anchorage as convenient.

2 **Useful marks:**

Kettle (49°58′·2N 6°21′·1W) a small islet off the NW extremity of Tresco.

Cromwell's Castle (49°57′·7N 6°21′·0W) a prominent square building.

3.22

1 **Secure anchorage** can obtained between Hangman Isle and Cromwell's Castle, as indicated on the chart, in depths of 8 to 11 m, also about 1½ cables SE of Hangman Isle in depths of 2 to 4 m.

For details of a small craft channel between New Grimsby Sound and Saint Mary's Road, see 3.63.

2 **Caution.** Submarine cables, including power cables, are laid across New Grimsby Sound between New Grimsby Harbour and Bryher.

Facilities: several slipways and a quay in New Grimsby Harbour, which dries; quay which dries on the E side of Bryher.

Cromwell's Castle *Hangman Island*

New Grimsby Sound from S (3.20)
(Original dated 2007)

(Photograph – Richard Coles)

Little Kettle

Gimble Point

Entrance to North Grimsby Sound from S (3.20)
(Original dated 2007)

(Photograph – Richard Coles)

Saint Martin's   Block House Point   Ruin

Old Grimsby Harbour from E (3.23)

(Original dated 2007)

(Photograph - Richard Coles)

Old Grimsby Sound
3.23

1   Old Grimsby Sound, on the NE side of Tresco, affords anchorage for mariners in small craft in depths of 7 to 8 m, or less, sheltered from all but W winds. There are six deep-water moorings for visiting craft. The harbour is not easy of access as it is encumbered with shoals. The cove fronting Old Grimsby Harbour, where there is a quay, dries.

Local knowledge is required.

INSHORE PASSAGE SOUTH EAST OF ISLES OF SCILLY

General information

Charts 34, 2565
Route
3.24

1   From W of Bishop Rock (49°52′N 6°27′W), off the entrance to Broad Sound, the inshore passage through the inshore traffic zones to Seven Stones passing SE of Isles of Scilly leads SE, then E, then generally NE.

Topography
3.25

1   Western Rocks consist of a chain of islets with Gorregan (49°52′N 6°23′W) at their SE end, Pednathise Head at their SW end and Great Crebawethan at their N end. Together with Gilstone Ledges (3.26) they are the S-most danger of Isles of Scilly.

2   Saint Agnes (49°53′N 6°21′W) (3.66) lies SW of Saint Mary's from which it is separated by Saint Mary's Sound. A conspicuous old lighthouse (3.30) stands on the summit of Saint Agnes.

Saint Martin's (49°58′N 6°17′W) lies 1½ miles N of Saint Mary's and a conspicuous daymark (3.30) stands at the E, and highest, end of the island.

3   Eastern Isles, a group of islets extend 1¼ miles SE from Saint Martin's. Great Ganilly, the largest and a useful mark, lies near the centre of the group, with Menawethan, another useful mark, at their SE end.

Historic wrecks
3.26

1   **Restricted areas,** 200 m radius, centred on position 49°52′·2N 6°26′·5W, close E of Tearing Ledge, contains the historic wreck of HMS *Eagle* lost in 1707. For details of restrictions, see 1.89.

It was upon Gilstone Ledges (49°52′N 6°24′W) that Admiral Sir Cloudesley Shovell's squadron, including his flagship HMS *Association*, foundered in 1707 with great loss of life.

Traffic regulations
3.27

1   **Inshore traffic zones,** for details see 3.8.

Submarine power cable
3.28

1   For details of a submarine power cable, see 3.4.

Tidal streams
3.29

1   For details of tidal streams see 3.11 and information on the charts.

Directions
(Directions for Broad Sound are given at 3.60 and for the inshore passage NW of Isles of Scilly at 3.16)

Principal marks
3.30

1   **Landmarks:**

Saint Agnes Old Lighthouse (white tower) (49°53′·5N 6°20′·7W).

Peninnis Head Lighthouse (white round metal tower on black metal framework tower, black cupola, 14 m in height) (49°54′N 6°18′W).

Saint Agnes Old Lighthouse (3.30)
(Original dated 1985)

(Photograph - Dr. M. P. Bender)

2   Coastguard Signal Station (disused) (old telegraph tower surmounted by a flagstaff) (49°55′·7N 6°18′·2W) on Saint Mary's.

Television Tower (elevation 119 m) (49°55′·9N 6°18′·3W).

Saint Martin's Daymark (red and white bands) (49°58′·0N 6°16′·0W). See sketch on chart 883.

Television Tower on Saint Mary's (3.30)

(Original dated 1996)

(Photograph - R. G. Maddock)

Peninnis Head Lighthouse from S (3.30)

(Original dated 1998)

(Photograph - R. G. Maddock)

3 **Major lights:**

Peninnis Head Light — as above.

Wolf Rock Light (49°57′N 5°48′W) (3.89).

Seven Stones Light Float (red hull, light tower amidships, name in white letters on each side) (50°04′N 6°04′W).

Other aids to navigation
3.31

1 **Racons:**

Bishop Rock Light (49°52′N 6°27′W).

Round Island Light (49°59′N 6°19′W).

Seven Stones Light Float (50°04′N 6°04′W).

2 For details see† *Admiralty List of Radio Signals Volume 2.*

Bishop Rock to Hard Lewis Rocks
3.32

1 From a position W of Bishop Rock, off the entrance to Broad Sound, the passage leads initially SE passing (with positions given from Gorregan (49°52′N 6°23′W)):

SW of Crebinicks (2 miles W) a drying rocky ledge and Tearing Ledge (3.26) which lies between Bishop Rock and Crebinicks; thence:

2 SW of a 9·9 m rocky patch (2 miles WSW) which lies 1½ cables S of Bishop Ridge; and:

Clear of The Pol Bank (4 miles SW) in rough weather there are overfalls over the bank which make it dangerous to open boats; thence:

To a position S of Bishop Ridge.

3 The passage then leads E passing:

S of a 9·6 m shoal (1¼ miles W) lying 2 cables WSW of Isaacs Ledge; thence:

S of Gilstone Ledges (8 cables WSW) (3.26); thence:

S of Pednathise Head (6 cables WSW) (3.25); thence:

4 S of Trenemene which lies close S of Gorregan (3.25); thence:

S of Melledgan (8 cables ENE) and associated dangers; thence:

S of Saint Agnes (1¾ miles NE) (3.66) at the entrance to Smith Sound (3.50).

Charts 34, 1148, 2565
3.33

1 The passage then leads NE passing (with positions given from Peninnis Head Light (49°54′N 6°18′W)):

SE of Great Wingletang (2 miles SW) noting Wingletang Ledges and a 9·8 m wreck which lies close SSW; thence:

2 SE of The Hoe (1½ miles SW); thence:

SE of Little Ledge (8 cables SW); thence:

Across the entrance to Saint Mary's Sound (3.47); thence:

SE of Gilstone (4 cables E) a drying rock the SE-most danger off the SE side of Saint Mary's; thence:

3 SE of Newfoundland Point (1 mile ENE); thence:

Across the entrance to Crow Sound (3.36); thence:

SE of Trinity Rock (2¾ miles NE); thence:

SE of Menawethan (3¼ miles NE) (3.25); thence:

SE of Hard Lewis Rocks (49°58′N 6°15′W) the NE-most danger of the Isles of Scilly.

4 **Clearing marks:**

Menawethan well open E of Newfoundland Point clears SE of Gilstone.

The alignment (241½°) of the S extremity of The Hoe (49°53′·3N 6°19·7W) with the summit of Pidney Brow, 6 cables WSW, clears SSE of Gilstone.

5   The alignment (282½°) of the S end of White Island (49°59′N 6°17′W) with Round Island Light, 1¼ miles W, clears N of Hard Lewis Rocks.

    The alignment (190¼°) of Hanjague (49°57′·5N 6°14′·6W), a remarkable conical rock, with the summit of Menawethan, 7½ cables S, clears close E of Hard Lewis Rocks.

6   **Useful mark:**

    Radio Mast (49°54′·7N 6°17′·5W) marked by a red obstruction light at the airport 2½ cables E of Old Town, Saint Mary's.

Charts 1148, 2565

Hard Lewis Rocks to Seven Stones

3.34

1   From a position SE of Hard Lewis Rocks (49°58′N 6°15′W) the passage leads generally N passing:

    W of Seven Stones (50°02′N 6°07′W) a group of rocks many of which dry. The rocks are mainly steep-to with depths of more than 50 m outside a distance of 1 mile except on their SW side where there are depths of less than 25 m within 1½ miles. In rough weather the breakers upon them may be seen from a considerable distance. Seven Stones Light Float (3.30) is moored 2 miles ENE of the group. Mariners should not pass between Seven Stones and the light float.

2   **Clearing marks:**

    By day, the line of bearing 234° of the coastguard signal station (3.30) on Saint Mary's seen between the hills of Great Ganilly (3.25), 2¼ miles NE, and open SE of Hanjague clears 7½ cables SE of Seven Stones.

3   By night, the line of bearing 235° of Bishop Rock Light (3.16) seen between Saint Mary's and Saint Martin's, clears 7½ cables SE of Seven Stones.

    The alignment (218°) of the SE extremity of Saint Martin's (49°58′N 6°17′W) with the coastguard signal station on Saint Mary's, 2½ miles SE, clears 1 mile NW of Seven Stones.

Useful marks

3.35

1   Bishop Rock Light (49°52′N 6°27′W) (3.16) visible from N only between 233° to 236° when it shows between Saint Mary's and Saint Martins.

    Round Island Light (49°59′N 6°19′W) (3.16).

    Longships Light (50°04′N 5°45′W) (3.89).

    Pendeen Light (50°10′N 5°40′W) (*West Coasts of England and Wales Pilot*).

*   (Directions continue in West Coasts of England and Wales Pilot)*

Crow Sound

Charts 883, 34

General information

3.36

1   **Description.** Crow Sound (49°56′N 6°16′W) lies between Saint Mary's and Eastern Isles and affords good anchorage for vessels of relatively deep draught with winds between SW to NE through N.

2   **Local weather.** Strong E winds render the anchorage untenable.

Saint Mary's   Innisidgen

Tolls Island

Crow Sound from ESE (3.36)

(Original dated 2001)

(Photograph – Air Images)

Historic wreck

3.37

1   **Restricted area.** A site of historic interest, 75 m radius lies in position 49°56′·5N 6°16′·4W, in the N part of Crow Sound. The site is protected from unauthorized interference. For details of restrictions see 1.89.

Directions

3.38

1   From a position E of Saint Mary's the alignment (315°) of Deason's Cap, a large boulder on the summit of Guther's Island (49°57′N 6°18′W) with the SW extremity of Saint Helen's, 1¾ miles NW, leads clear of danger through the middle of Crow Sound passing (with positions given from Innisidgen (49°56′S 6°17′W)):

2   SW of Trinity Rock (1½ miles E); thence:

    SW of Ridge Lower Corner (1 mile E); thence:

    NE of Vinegar Ledge (6 cables SE) the NE-most danger off Toll's Island.

3   The alignment (284½°) of the NE extremity of Innisidgen with the summit of Samson Hill (2½ miles WNW), near the S extremity of Bryher, then leads towards the anchorage passing:

    Between Trenear's Rock (5 cables SE) and Little Ganinick (7 cables NE).

Anchorage

3.39

1   Crow Sound affords good anchorage in depths of approximately 14 m. The bottom is sand and the holding ground is fairly good, but it is better near Saint Mary's than farther NE. This anchorage affords considerable protection from large swells during SW and W gales, when it is preferable to Saint Mary's Road (3.65).

2   Mariners should not anchor on Ridge Lower Corner, nor on the ground S of it, as the bottom is rocky and uneven.

    Recommended berth lies 3½ cables E of Innisidgen in a depth of 12 m, as shown on the chart, 1¼ cables W of a 7·9 m patch.

    For details of a small craft anchorage see 3.43.

Crow Bar

Chart 883
General information
3.40

1 **Description.** Crow Bar separates Crow Sound from Saint Mary's Road and is usable only by mariners in vessels of shallow draught near HW.

Controlling depth. There is a least depth of 0·8 m over a width of ¾ cable across the bar S of Queen's Ledge (49°56'·4N 6°17'·8W).

2 **Submarine cables,** including power cables, are laid across Crow Bar between the SE part of Tresco and the N end of Saint Mary's.

Directions
3.41

1 From Crow Sound the line of bearing 289° of the summit of Green Island (49°56'·6N 6°19'·1W), ahead, leads in the approach passing (with positions given from Green Island):

Close SSW of Hats Light Buoy (S cardinal) (1¼ miles ESE) which is moored off the S extremity of Hats, a group of rocky shoals. A boiler drying 0·6 m lies near the centre of these shoals. Thence:

2 Close NNE of the foul ground and shoal water extending 1 cable ENE from Innisidgen (1 mile ESE); thence:

Between Bar Point (8 cables ESE) and Queen's Ledge (8 cables E).

3 The alignment (254°) of Crow Rock Light Beacon (isolated danger) (5 cables SE) with South Hill (1½ miles WSW) then leads over Crow Bar towards Crow Rock. Crow Rock may be passed on either side; the recommended route passes N of the rock.

When S of Crow Rock the line of bearing 050° of Crow Rock Light Beacon, astern, then leads into Saint Mary's Road passing between The Pots (5 cables SSW) and Creeb (7 cables SSE).

4 **Clearing marks.** The alignment (066°) of Crow Rock Light Beacon (5 cable SE) with the summit of Little Ganilly (1¾ miles E) clears SE of The Pots.

Anchorages

Porth Hellick
3.42

1 **General information.** Mariners in small craft intending to anchor in the approaches to Porth Hellick are cautioned that the area inshore of the dangerous wreck charted close S of Porth Hellick Point (49°54'·9N 6°16'·7W) has been reported (1992) to be foul due to the spread of wreckage W into the bay.

Anchorage west of Hats'
3.43

1 **Approach.** From Crow Sound the approach to the anchorage W of Hats (49°56'N 6°17'W) (3.41) is along the alignment (322°) of Landing Carn (49°58'·2N 6°19'·6W) with the centre islet of Men-a-vaur, 4 cables NW (3.45).

Submarine cables, including power cables, are laid between the S point of Saint Martin's and Bar Point.

Anchorage can be obtained between Hats and Crow Bar, about 2½ cables W of Hats, in depths of 5 to 7 m.

Men-a-vaur in line with Landing Carn bearing 322° (3.43)

(Original dated 1998)

(Photograph - R. G. Maddock)

Saint Helen's Pool
3.44

1 **General information.** Saint Helen's Pool (49°58'N 6°19'W), an anchorage for small craft S of Saint Helen's, is reported to be sheltered from all directions and can be approached from Crow Sound by mariners in small craft near HW.

Local knowledge is required.

2 **Submarine cables,** including power cables, are laid between the E side of Tresco and the SW side of Saint Martin's.

3.45

1 **Directions.** From the anchorage W of Hats the alignment (322°) of Landing Carn with the centre islet of Men-a-vaur indicates a passage which can be used by mariners in small craft near HW leading to Saint Helen's Pool. It should be noted that the centre islet of Men-a-vaur, a group of three, is considerably lower than the two adjacent islets and becomes obscured by Landing Carn on approaching Saint Helen's.

2 Saint Helen's Pool can also be entered from N through Saint Helen's Gap, between Saint Helen's and Tean Islands. Leading lines for the approach, passing between Round Island and Deep Ledges, 3½ cables NE, are shown on the large scale chart.

3 **Anchorage** can be obtained in Saint Helen's Pool, in the NW and SE parts as indicated on the chart, in depths of approximately 4 m.

SAINT MARY'S ROAD AND APPROACH CHANNELS

General information

Charts 883, 34
Description
3.46

1 Saint Mary's Road (49°55'N 6°20'W) (3.65) has five channels leading to it. Saint Mary's Sound, Broad Sound and North West Passage (North Channel) are buoyed and are the easiest to navigate. Smith Sound (3.50) is narrow and not buoyed and there is no advantage in using it. Crow Sound (3.36) is easy of access from E but the channel over Crow Bar is only usable by mariners in vessels of shallow draught near HW.

3.47

1 **Saint Mary's Sound** (49°54'N 6°19'W) between Saint Mary's and Gugh is the easiest entrance for mariners approaching from E or S.

Least depth, exactly on the leading line, is 9·9 m situated 1¾ cables WSW of Woolpack Rock (49°54'·4N 6°19'·4W).

3.48

1 **Broad Sound,** the SW approach to Saint Mary's Road, is entered between Bishop Rock (49°52'N 6°27'W) and Flemming's Ledge, 7½ cables N. The channel is straight and is approximately 2½ cables wide at its narrowest point.

Least depth on its centre line is 14·9 m.

3.49

1 **North West Passage (North Channel)** (49°55'N 6°24'W), the NW approach to Saint Mary's Road is entered between Steeple Rock and Carnbase. The channel is approximately 7½ cables wide.

Least depth is 12·3 m over two banks which lie in the middle of the fairway midway between Jeffrey Rock (49°54'·3N 6°23'·5W) and Spencers Ledge, 1 mile NE. There is a heavy sea over these banks during gales.

3.50

1 **Smith Sound,** between Saint Agnes and Annet (49°54'N 6°22'W), is deep in the fairway but bounded on either side by rocks and ledges and is only 1½ cables wide.

Local knowledge is essential.

Topography

3.51

1 Saint Mary's (49°55'N 6°18'W) the largest of Isles of Scilly has its summit in its N part. Hugh Town, the capital containing the principal harbour, lies on the neck of a peninsula at the SW end of the island. Star Castle Hotel, a prominent building, lies near the N end of this peninsula.

Historic wrecks

3.52

1 **Restricted areas.** Two sites of historic wrecks, in positions 49°54'·4N 6°19'·9W and 49°55'·5N 6°20'·5W, are protected from unauthorized interference, the former is

marked by Barthlomew Ledges Light Beacon (port hand). For details of restrictions, see 1.89.

Pilotage

3.53

1 **Compulsory Pilotage Area** is defined as being anywhere within a distance of 6 miles from the S point of Samson (49°56'N 6°21'W).

Pilotage is compulsory for all vessels within the Compulsory Pilotage Area with the following exceptions:

> HM vessels.
> Trawlers under 47·5 m in length.
> Yachts under 30 m.

2 ETA should be sent to the Harbour Master at least 24 hours in advance of arrival at the outer limits of the Compulsory Pilotage Area. For details see *Admiralty List of Radio Signals Volume 6(1)*. There is a dedicated pilot vessel at Saint Mary's.

Boarding place. Pilot boards 1½ miles SSE of Peninnis Head (49°54'N 6°18'W) or 1¾ miles miles E of Gap Point (49°55'N 6°17'W), as shown on the chart.

Submarine cables

3.54

1 Submarine cables, including power cables, cross the entrance to Saint Mary's Sound from Porth Cressa to The Cove, Saint Agnes.

Natural conditions

3.55

1 **Tidal streams:** see 3.11.

Sea and swell. Saint Mary's Road anchorage is exposed to winds from between NW and SW. Winds from SW bring in a heavy sea and render the anchorage unsafe. Even in calm weather a heavy swell often rolls in from the Atlantic.

For an alternative anchorage, see 3.39.

Little Carn

Saint Mary's –Porth Cressa Anchorage from S (3.54)

(Original dated 2007)

(Photograph - Richard Coles)

Directions

(Directions for passage SE of Isles of Scilly are given at 3.30 and for passage NW of the isles at 3.16)

Principal marks

3.56

1   **Landmarks:**

Tresco Abbey (tower with flagstaff on its SE corner) (49°56′·8N 6°19′·8W).

Bishop Rock Lighthouse (49°52′N 6°27′W) (3.16).

Saint Agnes Old Lighthouse (49°53′·5N 6°20′·7W) (3.30).

Peninnis Head Lighthouse (49°54′N 6°18′W) (3.30).

2   Coastguard Signal Station (49°55′·7N 6°18′·2W) (3.30).

Saint Martin's Daymark (49°58′·0N 6°16′·0W) (3.30).

Conspicuous Television Tower (49°55′·9N 6°18′·3W) (3.30).

Major lights:

Bishop Rock Light (49°52′N 6°27′W) (3.16).

Peninnis Head Light (49°54′N 6°18′W) (3.30).

Other aids to navigation

3.57

1   **Racon:** Bishop Rock Light (49°52′N 6°27′W).

For details see *Admiralty List of Radio Signals Volume 2.*

Saint Mary's Sound

3.58

1   From a position SE of the entrance to Saint Mary's Sound the alignment (307°) of the W extremity of Great Minalto (49°55′·4N 6°21′·7W) with North Carn of Mincarlo, 1¼ miles NW, leads through Saint Mary's Sound. Approaching from E, Great Minalto and Mincarlo can be identified as they are in transit with Woolpack Beacon bearing about 304°. The route passes (with positions given from Woolpack Point (49°54′·5N 6°19′·3W)):

2   SW of Gilstone (1¼ miles ESE) (3.33); thence:

SW of Outer Head (8 cables ESE) the S-most point of Peninnis Head, noting Pollard, a rock which covers and uncovers, which lies 1 cable W of Outer Head; thence:

3   NE of Spanish Ledges (6 cables SSE); Spanish Ledge Light Buoy (E cardinal) is moored 1 cable E of the shallowest head of the ledges very close SW of the leading line. Thence:

SW of Woolpack (1 cable S), marked by a beacon (S cardinal), noting the rock with a least depth of 7·6 m over it which lies ¾ cable SW of the beacon and closer to the track; thence:

4   NE of Bartholomew Ledges (3½ cables WSW). marked by Barthlomew Ledges Light Beacon (port hand). With a W swell there is a heavy sea in the vicinity of these shoals and mariners in boats should keep clear of them. Thence:

5   Between North Bartholomew (4 cables W) marked by North Bartholomew Light Buoy (port hand) and Serica Rock (3 cables WNW).

Caution. This leading line is good and distinct, except in poor visibility, and must be followed accurately.

6   On the leading line at the intersection of the clearing marks (3.60) for Woodcock Ledge the track then leads generally N to Saint Mary's Road passing between Southward Well (1¼ miles NW) and Woodcock Ledge (6 cables NNW), noting Trisky close SW.

7   **Clearing marks:**

The line of bearing 267° of Haycocks (49°54′·0N 6°22′·5W), three small islets lying close off the N end of Annet, the S islet 18 m high and the N islet 9 m high, open of Peninnis Head, 2¾ miles E, clears S of Gilstone.

3.59

1   **Saint Mary's Sound alternative route.** There is a channel with a least depth of 4·9 m for vessels of suitable draught between the rocky ledges NE of Gugh (49°54′N 6°20′W) and Spanish and Bartholomew Ledges on the NE. **Local knowledge** is required.

Directions. The alignment (344°) of Steval (49°54′·7N 6°19′·7W) with Hangman Isle, 3 miles NNW, leads in the approach passing (with positions given from The Bow (49°53′·8N 6°19′·7W)):

2   ENE of Cuckold's Ledge (4½ cables S); thence:

Between Brow Ledge (2 cables SE) and Little Ledge (4 cables ESE); thence:

Between Round Rock (2 cables ESE) and Spanish Ledges (4 cables E) (3.58); thence:

ENE of The Bow, distant 2 cables, noting Bow Ledges close ESE.

3   The passage then leads generally WNW passing:

NNE of the coastal bank with depths of less than 5 m extending 1 cable N from The Bow; thence:

SSW of Bartholomew Ledges (5 cables NNW) (3.58); thence:

Clear of Perconger Ledge (5 cables WNW) noting Little Perconger, 1½ cables SSW.

4   **Clearing line:**

The line of bearing 108° of The Bow open N of Kittern Rock (3 cables WNW) clears NNE of Bristolman, Little Bristolman and Teneers Ledge, but noting the 3·4 m patch which lies to the N of the clearing line, ½ cable NNE of Little Bristolman.

Broad Sound

3.60

1   From a position W of Bishop Rock the line of bearing 059° of the N summit of Great Ganilly (49°57′N 6°15′W) (3.25), and just open N of the slope of Bant's Carn at the NW end of Saint Mary's, leads through Broad Sound passing (with positions given from Great Smith (49°54′·1N 6°21′·7W)):

2   NNW of Bishop Rock (49°52′N 6°27′W) (3.13) numerous shoal heads with depths of less than 6 m over them lie within 3½ cables NE of Bishop Rock. Heavy tide-rips occur over these heads during spring tides. Thence:

SSE of Flemming's Ledge (3¼ miles WSW); thence:

3   NNW of Round Rock (2½ miles WSW), the NW-most danger off Western Rocks (3.25), marked on its N side by Round Rock Buoy (N cardinal); thence:

SSE of Gunners Ledge (2¼ miles W), marked on its S side by Gunner Buoy (S cardinal), noting Gunners, a group of rocks, some of which dry, at the N end of Gunners Ledge and a 7·9 m rocky patch 2 cables ESE of the ledge; and:

4   NNW of an 8·8 m rocky patch (2 miles WSW) which lies 2 cables NNW of North Tinks; thence:

NNW of George Peters Ledge (1 mile WSW); thence:

SSE of Jeffrey Rock (1 mile W); and:

NNW of Flat Ledge (7½ cables WSW) noting the depths of less than 8 m which lie on the SSE side of the fairway between Flat Ledge and George Peters Ledge; thence:

5   NNW of Old Wreck Rock (7 cables W) marked on its
N side by Old Wreck Light-Buoy (N cardinal);
thence:

NNW of Great Smith, rocks 8 m high, the NW-most
danger off Saint Agnes; thence:

6   Between Spencers Ledge (8 cables NNW), with a
9·1 m patch 1 cable SE, at the extremity of shoal
rocky ground extending 1 mile SW from the S end
of Samson and a 9·4 m patch (4 cables N); the S
edge of the shoal area is marked by Spencers
Ledge Light Buoy (S cardinal). Thence:

7   Between Southward Well (1¼ miles NNE) and
Woodcock Ledge (1¾ miles NE) (3.58) into Saint
Mary's Road.

Clearing marks:

The alignment (040½°) of Creeb (49°55'·9N
6°18'·7W) with Saint Martin's Daymark (3.30),
2¾ miles NE, clears ½ cable NW of Woodcock
Ledge.

8   **Caution.** The leading line is only distinct in very clear
visibility. If Great Ganilly is not discernible the line of
bearing 066° of the N islet of Haycocks (5 cables W)
(3.58) in line with Star Castle Hotel (1¾ miles ENE) leads
between Flemming's Ledge and the shoal heads NE of
Bishop Rock, the track then leads 059° as directed above.
Do not mistake the N islet of Haycocks for Ruddy
(6 cables W) lying 1 cable NW, which under certain
atmospheric conditions looms up largely.

North West Passage
3.61

1   From a position W of Maiden Bower (49°57'N 6°24'W)
the alignment (127°) of the stone obelisk (white with black
stripe) on Tins Walbert (49°53'·8N 6°21'·3W) with the old
lighthouse on Saint Agnes (5 cables SE) leads through the
centre of North West Passage passing (with positions given
from Great Smith) (49°54'·1N 6°'21'·7W):

Saint Agnes Old Lighthouse in line with gap in
Great Smith bearing 130° (3.61)

(Original dated 1998)

(Photograph - R. G. Maddock)

2   Between Steeple Rock (2 miles NW), marked by
Steeple Rock Light Buoy and Carnbase (2 miles
WNW); thence:

Between Baccabu (1¼ miles NW) and an 8·2 m shoal
(1¼ miles WNW); thence:

3   Between the shoal rocky ground extending 1 mile SW
from Samson, of which Spencers Ledge (8 cables
NNW) (3.60) is the SW-most danger, and Jeffrey
Rock (1 mile W).

The track then leads ENE to join the Broad Sound
approach route (3.60) on the line of bearing 059° of Great
Ganilly (49°57'N 6°15'W) which leads into Saint Mary's
Road.

4   **Caution.** Mariners should guard against the set of the
tidal stream when using North West Passage.

Useful mark:

Monument (49°56'·9N 6°20'·2W) on Abbey Hill,
Tresco, conspicuous from N through W to S.

Smith Sound
3.62

1   From a position S of Saint Agnes the alignment (350½°)
of the gap between the summits of Great Smith (49°54'·1N
6°21'·8W) (3.60) with the summit of Castle Bryher, a rocky
islet 2½ miles N, leads in the S part of Smith Sound
passing (with positions given from Great Smith):

Annet   *Saint Agnes*

Smith Sound from S (3.62)   *Long Point*

(Original dated 2001)

(Photograph - Air Images)

E of Melledgan (1¾ miles S); thence:

2   W of Lethegus Rocks (1¼ miles SSE) which extend
nearly 5 cables S from Long Point on the E side
of the fairway; and:

E of Menpingrim (11 cables S) and Buccabu (9 cables
S), two drying ledges, distant ½ cable. Castle
Bryher can be opened a little E when near these
dangers.

3   On the alignment (091°) of Penny Ledges (6 cables SSE)
with the old lighthouse on Saint Agnes (9 cables SE), open
Castle Bryher W of Great Smith to give a greater clearance
to Pascoe Rock (5 cables SSE) on the E side of the
fairway.

When past this rock the line of bearing 182° of the E
extremity of Annet (6 cables SSW), astern, then leads in
the fairway passing:

4   W of Quoins (1 cable S); thence:

Between Great Smith, distant ½ cable, and Annet
Head (4 cables WSW).

The track then leads NE to Saint Mary's Road.

5   **Clearing line:**

Carn Irish (6 cables SW), on the W extremity of
Annet, open NW of Great Smith clears NW of
Bristolman (2 cables ENE) and adjacent shoals
lying NW of Saint Agnes.

6   **Useful mark:**

Tins Walbert Beacon (black and white tower)
(49°53'8N 6°21'·3W).

(Directions continue at 3.76)

Side channels
General information
3.63

1   There is a passage over Tresco Flats (49°57'N 6°20'W)
between Saint Mary's Road and New Grimsby Sound
(3.20) which can be used by mariners in small craft

between 2 hours on either side of HW, but there are several rocky ledges between Crow Point (49°56′N 6°20′W) and Samson, 7 cables WSW.

2 **Directions.** From close W of Hulman, a rock marked by a beacon (platform and balustrade topmark) (49°56′·3N 6°20′·3W), the recommended track, leading and clearing lines, are shown on the large scale chart.

Landing. There is a landing at Carn Near, a slipway close E of Crow Point. The end of the slipway dries and care is necessary when approaching it as there is a quay which covers near the outer end of the slipway.

Tresco Flats to North West Passage
3.64

1 **Directions.** The alignment (058°) astern of Yellow Rock (49°56′N 6°21′W) with Abbey Hill monument, 8 cables NE, leads about 2 miles SW passing between Samson and Mincarlo (49°56′N 6°23′W) to join North West Passage SE of Steeple Rock.

Local knowledge is required.

Saint Mary's Road anchorage

General information
3.65

1 Saint Mary's Road the most spacious anchorage in the Isles of Scilly lies between Saint Mary's and Samson (49°56′N 6°21′W), 1½ miles E, where there are depths of 16 m at the SW end of the anchorage decreasing gradually to Crow Bar (3.40) at the NE end.

2 **Holding ground.** The holding ground of sand is fairly good S of a line joining Nut Rock (49°56′N 6°20′W) and the coastguard signal station (disused) on Saint Mary's, but

N of this line the sand is loose and the holding ground insecure. In general the holding ground is better in depths of over 10 m, but towards Saint Agnes and Annet this ground becomes rocky and mariners should not anchor within 4 cables of these islands.

3 **Recommended berth,** indicated on the chart, lies 6¾ cables ESE of Southward Well Point, at the S end of Samson, in depths of 10 to 12 m.

Saint Agnes

General information
3.66

1 **Description.** Saint Agnes (49°53′N 6°21′W) is connected with Gugh an island close off its E side by a narrow spit of boulders and sand, which dries 4·6 m, named The Bar. Small craft can obtain anchorage in Porth Conger, N of The Bar, and in The Cove, S of The Bar.

Both anchorages are open to onshore winds and swell.

2 **Tidal stream.** It has been reported (1992) that at, or near, HW a strong S-going tidal stream runs across The Bar into The Cove, where it sometimes becomes a rotary stream circulating anti-clockwise around the anchorage.
3.67

1 **Anchorages and landing.** Anchorage, as indicated on the chart, can be obtained in Porth Conger which is approached between The Cow, a small islet off the NE side of Gugh, and Round Rock a drying ledge, 1½ cables W, but mariners should keep clear of a jetty and slipway on Black Point, on the NE side of Saint Agnes. Landing can be obtained at the jetty and slipway; the end of the slipway has a depth of 0·3 m alongside and is marked by a beacon.

2 Anchorage can also be obtained in the E part of The Cove, as indicated on the chart. This anchorage is deeper

Gugh *Saint Agnes Lighthouse* *Pidney Brow*

Browarth Point *Burnt Island* *Long Point*

Saint Agnes Island from NW (3.66)
(Original dated 2001)

(Photograph – Air Images)

and has more room than off Porth Conger. The Cove is entered between Hakestone, a small islet off the SW side of Gugh, and Little Hakestone, a rock which covers and uncovers, 1¼ cables SW.

Caution. Submarine cables, including power cables, extend SSE through the centre of The Cove.

SAINT MARY'S HARBOUR

General information

Chart 883
Position
3.68

1   Saint Mary's Harbour (49°55′N 6°19′W) lies on the N side of Hugh Town (3.51).

Function
3.69

1   Saint Mary's Harbour is the principal harbour in the Isles of Scilly. The harbour is used by visiting yachts.

Harbour limits
3.70

1   The harbour limits, as shown on the chart, extend ENE from Newman (49°55′N 6°19′W) to Newford Island, 4 cables ENE.

Approach and entry
3.71

1   The harbour is approached from Saint Mary's Road and entered through one of three passages leading through Saint Mary's Pool, a bay which is entered between Rat Island and Taylor's Island, 4 cables NNE.

Port Authority
3.72

1   The Port Authority is The Duchy of Cornwall represented by a Harbour Master.

Limiting conditions
3.73

1   **Deepest and longest berth** is situated alongside the pierhead (3.81).

Maximum size of vessel handled. The largest vessel which can be handled is one of 80 m length and 4 m maximum draught.

Tidal levels. Mean spring range 5.0 m; mean neap range 2·3 m. For further information see *Admiralty Tide Tables.*

Arrival information
3.74

1   **Port radio** station, with limited hours, operates from the Harbour Master's office. For details see *Admiralty List of Radio Signals Volume 6(1).*

Pilotage. For details see 3.53.

Tugs are not available.

2   **Traffic regulations.**

Bye-laws are in force for the control of traffic and berthing in the harbour, and for vessels carrying dangerous substances; copies may be obtained from the Harbour Master.

Ferry turning area. Mariners should anchor clear of the ferry turning area, indicated on the chart, N of the pierhead.

Harbour
3.75

1   **General layout.** The harbour lies on the N side of Hugh Town and is protected from W winds by Rat Island, artificially connected with the land S. A short pier extends N from the N end of Rat Island.

Channels. There are three passages, a S, middle and N, leading from Saint Mary's Road to Saint Mary's Pool. The S passage, which is the best, is marked by leading lights on Mount Flagon.

Swell. With a heavy swell from W the sea sometimes breaks across the middle passage.

Mount Flagon   Lifeboat slipway   Peninnis Head

Rat Island   Hugh Town

Saint Mary's Harbour from NW (3.74)

(Original dated 2001)

(Photograph - Air Images)

Directions for entering harbour
(continued from 3.62)

Landmarks
3.76

1   Chimney (elevation 48 m) (49°54'·8N 6°18'·6W).
Coastguard Signal Station (disused) (49°55'·7N 6°18'·2W) (3.30).
Conspicuous Television Tower (49°55'·9N 6°18'·3W) (3.30).
Tresco Abbey (49°56'·9N 6°19'·8W) (3.56).

South passage
3.77

1   **Mount Flagon Leading Lights:**
Front light (white beacon orange triangle topmark) (49°55'·1N 6°18'·5W).
Rear light (white beacon orange X topmark) (110 m E of the front light).
From Saint Mary's Road the alignment (097¼°) of these lights leads through the passage passing (with positions given from Star Castle Hotel (49°54'·9N 6°19'·3W)):

2   N of Woodcock Ledge (3 cables WNW) (3.58); thence:
S of The Ridge (4½ cables NNW); thence:
N of Newman (2 cables NNW); thence:
S of Bacon Ledge (3½ cables N) marked by a light buoy (port hand); thence:

3   N of the drying ledges extending from Rat Island (2 cables NE); thence:
To the berth as convenient.
Caution. The Bodnic, a rock awash, lies NW of Carn Thomas (3.80).

Middle passage
3.78

1   **Leading marks:**
Front mark Shelter (white stripes on each end and in the centre of its roof) (49°54'·9N 6°18'·8W).
Rear mark Tower (37 m) on Buzza Hill (1½ cables SSE of the front mark).
From Saint Mary's Road the alignment (151°) of these marks leads through the passage passing (with positions given from Star Castle Hotel):

2   WSW of a 4·9 m patch (7 cables NNE) the outermost danger off Carn Morval Point; thence:

ENE of The Ridge (4½ cables NNW); thence:
Between The Cow (5 cables NNE) and Bacon Ledge (3½ cables NNE); thence:
Between Rat Island (2 cables NE) and Newford Island (5 cables NE); thence:
To the berth as convenient.

North passage
3.79

1   The N passage between The Cow (49°55'·4N 6°19'·0W) and The Calf, 1 cable ENE, should only be taken in fine weather.
Local knowledge is required.

Useful marks
3.80

1   Carn Thomas (49°55'·0N 6°18'·7W) a distinctive mound with a flagstaff on its W side. A lifeboat slip extends NW from the carn.
Sector light (49°55'·1N 6°19'·0W) on pierhead.

Berths
3.81

1   **Anchorage.** Limited anchorage can be obtained 1 cable N of Rat Island pierhead on the line of bearing 106° of the rear leading beacon on Mount Flagon, in a depth of about 5 m. This anchorage is exposed to W winds.
Alongside berths. A short pier (49°55'·1N 6°19'·0W) extends N from the N end of Rat Island where there are depths of 2 m alongside its head, decreasing gradually towards the shore. There are berths alongside, 45 and 65 m in length, for small coasting vessels which can take the ground.

Port services
3.82

1   **Minor repairs** can be undertaken. There is a grid for craft of up to 15 m in length.
Hospital services are available.
Facilities for small craft.
Supplies: provisions; fresh water; diesel oil and petrol in small quantities.
Communications: airport 8 cables E of Hugh Town.
Rescue, see 3.9.

GWENNAP HEAD TO CAPE CORNWALL

General information

Charts 1148, 777
Route
3.83

1   From S of Gwennap Head (50°02'N 5°41'W) the inshore route using the inshore traffic zone to Cape Cornwall, 5¾ miles NNW, leads WNW, then N, about 10 miles passing W of Longships.

Topography
3.84

1   From Gwennap Head to Land's End, 2½ miles NW, the cliffs are continuous at an elevation of approximately 60 m.
Cape Cornwall (50°08'N 5°43'W), 60 m high, has the chimney of a disused mine shaft situated on its summit.

The cliffs between Cape Cornwall and Aire Point, 2 miles S, rise to a height of 90 m.

Traffic regulations
3.85

1   **Traffic separation scheme** is established between Longships (50°04'N 5°45'W) and Seven Stones, 14 miles W; for details and directions for this TSS see 2.11 and 2.25.
IMO recommendation for laden tankers, see 2.11.
Inshore traffic zone is situated between the adjacent TSS and the coast and Rule 10 of *International Regulations for Preventing Collisions at Sea (1972)* applies.
Mariners are recommended to use the TSS.

Submarine cables
3.86
1   For details of submarine cables, see 3.4.

Rescue
3.87
1   **Coastguard rescue teams** operate from:
> Saint Just Auxiliary Station on Cape Cornwall (50°08′N 5°43′W).
> Lands End Auxiliary Station (50°04′N 5°43′W).

Lifeboats. An all-weather lifeboat and an inshore lifeboat are stationed at Sennen Cove (50°05′N 5°42′W) (3.97).

2   **National Coastwatch Institution** (NCI) stations are situated at:
> Gwennap Head (50°02′·2N 5°40′·8W)
> Cape Cornwall (50°07′·6N 5°42′·2W)

For details of coastguard stations see 1.101, for lifeboats see 1.113 and for NCI see 1.106.

3   **VHF Direction-finding station,** for emergency use only, operates from Pendeen (50°08′N 5°38′W) (*West Coasts of England and Wales Pilot*), for details see *Admiralty List of Radio Signals Volume 2* and 1.105.

For details of a VHF Direction-finding station on Scilly Isles, see 3.9.

Tidal streams
3.88
1   Tidal streams W of Longships are shown by means of information on the charts.

Off Runnel Stone (50°01′N 5°40′W) the streams are probably fairly strong, but are also probably subject to considerable variation; they begin as follows:

Interval from HW Devonport (Dover)	Direction	Remarks
−0020(−0600)	E	Runs for 3 hours only.
+0240 (−0300)	NW	Runs for 9½ hours.

Directions
(Directions for the TSS between Isles of Scilly and Land's End are given at 2.23.
Directions for the inshore passage ENE from Gwennap Head are given at 3.112)

Principal marks
3.89
1   **Landmarks:**
> Land's End (50°04′N 5°43′W), the SW extremity of England, approximately 60 m high; when first seen from S or SW it has the appearance of two detached hummocks.
> Sennen Church (tower) (50°04′N 5°42′W).
> Television Mast (50°08′N 5°40′W) (*West Coasts of England and Wales Pilot*).

2   **Major lights:**
> Wolf Rock Light (grey round granite tower black lantern, 41 m in height) (49°57′N 5°48′W) shown throughout 24 hours.
> Longships Light (grey round granite tower, 35 m in height) (50°04′N 5°45′W) shown throughout 24 hours.
> Round Island Light (49°59′N 6°19′W) (3.16).
> Seven Stones Light Float (50°04′N 6°04′W) (3.30).

Wolf Rock Lighthouse from SW (3.89)
(Original dated 2000-02)

(Photograph - Jean Guichard)

Other aids to navigation
3.90
1   **Racons:**
> Wolf Rock Light (49°57′N 5°48′W).
> Seven Stones Light Float (50°04′N 6°04′W).

For details see *Admiralty List of Radio Signals Volume 2.*

Inshore passage
3.91
1   **Runnel Stone position beacons:**
> Front beacon (red conical, cone topmark) (50°02′·2N 5°40′·6W).
> Rear beacon (black and white stone base, conical topmark) (60 m N of the front beacon).

2   The above beacons, situated close E of Gwennap Head, in line (352°) indicate the position of Runnel Stone, a rock which dries, marked on its S side by a light buoy (S cardinal). No reliance should be placed on this buoy as it is liable to drift or break away from its moorings. Poldew, a steep-to rocky ledge, lies 3 cables W. Runnel Stone and the dangers in its vicinity are covered by the red sector (060°–074°) of Tater-du auxiliary Light, shown from the

same tower, 3 m below the main light, and the red sector (307°–327°) of Longships Light.

3.92

1 Initial position S of Runnel Stone with Tater-du Light (50°03′N 5°35′W) (3.112) bearing less than 060° and Longships Light bearing more than 327°; by night the same bearings are used to avoid crossing into the overlapping red sector (060°–074°) of Tater-du auxiliary Light and the red sector (307°–327°) of Longships Light, both of which cover Runnel Stone.

2 From this position the route then leads generally WNW passing (with positions given from Land's End):

NNE of Wolf Rock (8¼ miles SSW); thence:

Clear of Carn Base (2¾ miles SW), rocky patches near the W edge of a bank which extends 2½ miles W from the coast between Gwennap Head and Land's End, marked on its W side by a light buoy (W cardinal), and over which there are irregular depths. A heavy confused sea breaks on this bank during W gales against the tidal streams.

3 The route then leads N passing:

W of Longships (1 mile W), a group of detached rocks, distant at least 1 mile; thence:

W of an 11 m patch (2¼ miles N), over which the sea breaks, which lies 5 cables SW of Inner Greeb; thence:

W of The Brisons (3 miles N) (3.96); thence:

W of The Vyneck (3¾ miles N), detached rocks awash lying 3½ cables NW of Cape Cornwall.

4 **Local knowledge** is essential for the passage between Runnel Stone and the mainland, which is not described in this book.

3.93

1 **Clearing bearings:**

The line of bearing 058° of Carn-du (50°04′N 5°33′W) open N of Godolphin Hill, 8½ miles NE, clears 5 cables SE of Runnel Stone.

The Brisons (3.96) in line clears W of the coastal dangers SW of Gribba Point (50°07′N 5°42′W).

The coastal dangers between The Vyneck and Longships are covered by the intensified red sector (189°–208°) of Longships Light.

3.94

1 **Useful marks:**

Lizard Light (49°58′N 5°12′W) (3.112).

Radio Mast (red obstruction light) (50°07′N 5°39′W) obscured from S by high land when close to the coast.

Pendeen Light (50°10′N 5°40′W) (*West Coasts of England and Wales Pilot*).

(Directions continue in West Coasts of England and Wales Pilot)

Side channel

Charts 2345 plan of Longships, 1148

Channel east of Longships

3.95

1 **General information.** There is a channel for vessels of suitable draught E of Longships between Kettle's Bottom

(50°04′N 5°44′W) and Peal Rocks, 5 cables E, with a least depth of 9 m.

Local knowledge is required.

3.96

1 **Directions.** The line of bearing 001° of the highest part of the N islet of The Brisons (50°07′N 5°43′W), two rocky islets of which the N islet is the larger and higher of the two, open W of the highest part of the S islet leads in the channel passing (with positions given from Armed Knight (50°04′N 5°43′W)):

2 W of the reef and coastal bank with depths of less than 10 m extending 2 cables W from Armed Knight; thence:

Between Kettle's Bottom (7 cables WNW) and Peal Rocks (4 cables N) close NW of The Peal; thence:

Between Shark's Fin (11 cables NW) and Cowloe (11 cables NNE) noting Little Bo and Bo Cowloe, drying patches, close NW.

Whitesand Bay

General information

3.97

1 Whitesand Bay is entered between Aire Point (50°06′N 5°42′W) and Pedn-mên-du, 1¼ miles SW. Sennen Cove lies at the S end of the bay. It is protected by a stone breakwater, 1 cable long, the outer end of which dries, and by Cowloe.

Sennen Cove from N (3.97)

(Original dated 2001)

(Photograph – Air Images)

Submarine power cable (3.4) from the Scilly Isles is landed at Whitesand Bay, 4 cables SE of Aire Point; its position is marked by a yellow beacon on the shore.

2 **Approach.** The alignment (150°) of beacons on the cliffs at Sennen Cove leads WSW of Bounder, situated 4 cables SW of Aire Point, and ENE of the dangers NW of Cowloe.

Lifeboats, see 3.87.

GWENNAP HEAD TO LIZARD POINT

GENERAL INFORMATION

Mounts Bay

Chart 777
Description
3.98

1   Mounts Bay is entered between Runnel Stone (50°01′N 5°40′W), which lies 7 cables SSE of Gwennap Head, and Lizard Point, 18 miles ESE. Penzance Bay lies at its head and contains the two tidal harbours of Newlyn (3.119) and Penzance (3.126). There are three other small tidal harbours in Mounts Bay, namely at Mousehole (3.136), at Saint Michael's Mount (3.137) and at Porthleven (3.138).

Depths
3.99

1   The depths in the bay decrease regularly, the bottom consisting chiefly of coarse sand and shell, but there are several patches of shoal ground extending up to 2½ miles from the middle of the N shore of the bay. The outermost shoal patches in the bay are Pollack Ground and The Boa (3.115).

Anchorage
3.100

1   Anchorage can be obtained in several places in Mounts Bay except during winter months when it may be obtained temporarily while waiting to enter harbour. The best anchorages (3.121) are in Penzance Bay.

Rescue
3.101

1   **Coastguard rescue teams** operate from:
   Penzance Auxiliary Station (50°07′N 5°32′W).
   Porthleven Auxiliary Station (50°05′N 5°19′W).
   Mullion Auxiliary Station at Porth Mellin (50°01′N 5°15′W).
   Lizard Auxiliary Station (49°58′N 5°11′W).
   Lifeboats. Penlee all-weather lifeboat and an inshore lifeboat are stationed in Newlyn Harbour (50°06′N 5°33′W) (3.119).

2   **National Coastwatch Institution** (NCI) stations are situated at:
   Gwennap Head (50°02′·2N 5°40′·8W)
   Bass Point (49°57′·8N 5°11′·2W)
   For details regarding coastguard see 1.101, for lifeboats see 1.113 and for NCI see 1.106.

Natural conditions
3.102

1   **Tidal streams** in the middle of the entrance to Mounts Bay are shown by means of information on the chart. Elsewhere in the bay they are weak and irregular.
   Tidal streams are fairly strong and nearly rectilinear near the coast off Lizard Point where they begin as follows:

Interval from HW Devonport (Dover)	Direction
−0500 (+0145)	E
+0155 (−0345)	W

2   The maximum in-going and out-going spring rates are 2 kn and 3 kn respectively.

Approximately 5 miles S of Lizard Point the streams tend to become slightly rotary in a clockwise direction, for details see information on the chart.
   Race. For details of a race off Lizard Point, see 3.115.
3   **Flow.** A sub-surface current, direction not stated, is said to run in Mounts Bay during strong onshore winds.
   Swell. With the exception of Newlyn no attempt should be made to enter the harbours in Mounts Bay when there is a ground swell running or with strong onshore winds. Under such conditions Newlyn is best entered between 2 hours on either side of HW. See also *Admiralty Tidal Stream Atlas; Falmouth to Padstow including Isles of Scilly.*

OFFSHORE PASSAGE

General information

Charts 777, 1148
Route
3.103

   From WSW of Gwennap Head (50°02′N 5°41′W), S of the TSS off Land's End, the offshore passage across Mounts Bay leads E, about 30 miles, to S of Lizard Point (49°58′N 5°13′W).

Directions
(Directions for the TSS between Isles of Scilly and Land's End are given at 2.23)

Principal marks
3.104

1   **Landmark:**
   Lizard Point (49°58′N 5°13′W) (3.112).
   Major lights:
   Wolf Rock Light (49°57′N 5°48′W) (3.89).
   Tater-du Light (50°03′N 5°35′W) (3.112).
   Lizard Light (49°58′N 5°12′W) (3.112).

Other aids to navigation
3.105

1   **Racon:** Wolf Rock Light (49°57′N 5°48′W).
   For details see *Admiralty List of Radio Signals Volume 2.*
3.106

1   From a position WSW of Gwennap Head (50°02′N 5°41′W), S of the TSS off Land's End, the offshore passage to Lizard Point leads E passing:
   Clear of Wolf Rock (49°57′N 5°48′W); thence:
   Clear of Epson Shoal (49°58′N 5°39′W), a pinnacle rock; the sea is reported to break over it when gales occur at springs. Thence:
   S of The Boa (49°58′N 5°17′W) (3.115); thence:
   S of Lizard Point (49°58′N 5°13′W) (3.115).
2   **Useful marks:**
   Land's End (50°04′N 5°43′W) (3.89).
   Saint Michael's Mount (50°07′N 5°29′W) (3.112).
   Seven Stones Light Float (50°04′N 6°04′W) (3.30).
   Longships Light (50°04′N 5°45′W) (3.89).
   Round Island Light (49°59′N 6°19′W) (3.16).
   Penzance South Pier Light (50°07′N 5°32′W) (3.112).
   (Directions continue at 4.11)

INSHORE PASSAGE

General information

Chart 777
Route
3.107

1   From a position S of Gwennap Head (50°02′N 5°41′W) the passage through Mounts Bay leads ENE then N to Penzance Bay, a distance of about 9 miles, thence SE and ESE from Penzance Bay to Lizard Point, a distance of about 16 miles.

Topography
3.108

1   **West side of Mounts Bay.** Between Castle Treveen Point (50°02′N 5°38′W), 1¾ miles ENE of Gwennap Head, and Tater-du, a point 2½ miles ENE, the cliffs are from 30 to 45 m high except in Boskenna Bay. The land behind Tater-du rises abruptly.

At Penzer Point (50°04′N 5°33′W) the cliffs are approximately 25 m high with the land rising abruptly behind, thence to Mousehole, 7½ cables N, the cliffs decrease to half that height. From Mousehole to Penlee Point, 4 cables N, the cliffs increase in height to 18 m near the latter with the land behind rising steeply to approximately 70 m.

2   **East side of Mounts Bay.** From Cudden Point (50°06′N 5°26′W) the cliffs are high, precipitous and regular until near The Enys, a rock 7½ cables E, whence they recede N to form Prussia Cove and gradually decrease in height for a short distance, then rise again to a height of 20 m as far as Hoe Point, 5 cables E, where they terminate.

3   Near Rinsey Head, 2¼ miles E, the cliffs rise again to a height of 25 m and continue with little variation 5 cables farther SE to Trewavas Head thence to Porthleven, 1½ miles ESE, where the cliffs rise to a height of 45 m.

From Porthleven the coast is low as far as Loe Bar, a bar of shingle 1 mile SE, thence to Lizard Point, 8 miles SSE, the coast consists of cliffs which rise from 15 to 75 m.

Historic wrecks
3.109

1   Restricted areas surround sites of historic wrecks in the following positions:

      50°03′·8N 5°17′·4W, radius 250 m.
      50°03′·4N 5°17′·1W, radius 75 m.
      50°03′·3N 5°16′·9W radius 150 m.
      50°02′·3N 5°16′·5W, radius 75 m.
      49°58′·5N 5°14′·4W, radius 100 m.
      49°57′·5N 5°12′·9W, radius 200 m.

For details of restrictions see 1.89

Submarine cables
3.110

1   Submarine cables, as shown on the chart, extend S from Porth Curno (50°02′N 5°39′W) on the W side of Mounts Bay and WSW thence SSW from Poldhu Cove (50°02′N 5°16′W) on the E side of Mounts Bay.

Nature reserve
3.111

1   A coastal nature reserve extends between Mullion Island (50°01′N 5°16′W) and Kynance Cove, 3 miles SSE. For details see 1.91.

Directions
(Directions for the inshore passage N from Gwennap Head are given at 3.89)

Principal marks
3.112

1   **Landmarks:**
    Saint Buryan Church (tower) (50°04′N 5°37′W).
    Building (50°04′N 5°33′W) at Penzer Point.
    Hotel (50°05′N 5°32′W) situated 3½ cables SW of Saint Clement's Isle.
    Church (tower) (50°05′N 5°33′W) at Paul.
    Saint Mary's Church (tower) (50°07′·0N 5°32′·0W) at Penzance.

2   Dome (50°07′·1N 5°32′·2W) on Penzance Market House.
    Saint Michael's Mount (conical in shape with a castellated building on the summit) (50°07′N 5°29′W) bears a striking resemblance, though smaller, to Mont Saint-Michel off the N coast of France.

Harbour
Saint Michael's Mount from W (3.112)
(Original dated 2000)
(Photograph - HMSML Gleaner)

3   Church (tower) (50°07′N 5°27′W) at Perranuthnoe.
    Saint Hilary Water Tower (50°07′N 5°26′W).
    Hotel (50°01′·4N 5°15′·2W) on the cliffs above Polurrian Cove.
    Tower (water tank) (50°01′·1N 5°15′·3W).
    Lizard Point (bold precipitous promontory) (49°58′N 5°13′W) easily identified by two white octagonal towers 5 cables E of the point.

4   **Major lights:**
    Wolf Rock Light (49°57′N 5°48′W) (3.89).
    Tater-du Light (white round tower, 15 m in height) (50°03′N 5°35′W).
    Penzance South Pier Light (white round tower, black base, 9 m in height) (50°07′N 5°32′W).
    Lizard Light (white 8-sided tower at E end of building, 19 m in height) (49°58′N 5°12′W) obscured from N until WNW of the point.

Other aid to navigation
3.113

1   **Racon:** Wolf Rock — as above.
For details see *Admiralty List of Radio Signals Volume 2.*

Charts 777, 2345 with plan of Penzance Bay
Gwennap Head to Penzance Bay
3.114

1   From a position well clear S of Runnel Stone (50°01′N 5°40′W) (3.91) the passage leads initially ENE passing

Lizard Point

Rill Point

Polbream Cove

Lizard Lighthouse

Lizard from SE (3.112)

(Original dated 2000-02)

(Photograph - Jean Guichard)

(with positions given from Saint Clement's Isle (50°05′N 5°32′W)):

> SSE of the detached rocks extending 1 cable S from Castle Treveen Point (4¾ miles WSW) (3.108); thence:
>
> SSE of a 1·2 m shoal lying 2½ cables SE of Boscawen Point (3 miles SW); thence:

2

> SSE of The Bucks (2½ miles SW), drying rocks lying 2 cables ESE of Tater-du; thence:
>
> SSE of The Stannock (2 miles SW); thence:
>
> SSE of Carn-du (1½ miles SW), noting Kemyel Rock which dries 1·4 m close NE; thence:
>
> SSE of Penzer Point (7 cables SSW) (3.108), noting the dangerous wreck (position approximate) which lies 3 cables NNE; thence:

3

> SSE of Saint Clement's Isle (3.136).

The track then leads N. By day, keep Penzance South Pier Light-structure (2 miles N) bearing less than 351° and well open E of The Gear Beacon (1¾ miles N) (3.123). By night, keep in the white sector of Penzance South Pier Light which changes from red to white on the line of bearing 344½°, passing:

4

> W of Pollack Ground (2¾ miles SE) (3.115); thence:
>
> E of Saint Clement's Isle; thence:
>
> E of Low Lee (7 cables NNE), a steep-to rock marked on its NE side by Low Lee Light Buoy (E cardinal); thence:

5

> As convenient for anchoring in Penzance Bay (3.126) or for entering Newlyn (3.119) or Penzance harbours (3.126) having regard to the dangers in the approaches to these harbours.

Clearing line:

> Saint Michael's Mount (3 miles NE) bearing less than 041° and open SE of Carn-du clears SE of The Bucks.

Charts 777, 2345 plan of Penzance Bay, plan of Lizard Point
Penzance Bay to Lizard Point
3.115

1

From Penzance Bay the line of bearing 325° of Penzance South Pier Light, astern, leads SE through Mounts Bay, passing (with positions given from Cudden Point (50°06′N 5°26′W)):

> Between Saint Michael's Mount (2¼ miles WNW) and Low Lee (3¾ miles W) (3.114), noting a waverider light buoy (special) moored 1½ miles NE of Low Lee; thence:
>
> Between Iron Gates (2 miles S) (3.117) and Pollack Ground (3 miles SW); thence:

2

> SW of The Boa (9½ miles SE), a rocky shoal over which the sea breaks heavily during SW gales, noting the 12·4 m shoal and the dangerous wreck which lie 7½ cables SSE and 1 mile ESE, respectively.

The track then leads ESE passing:

3

> SSW of Lizard Point (49°58′N 5°13′W), distant at least 1 mile, noting the 5 m shoal which lies 7 cables SSE of the point. A race extends up to 2 or 3 miles from the outer rocks during the strength of the stream in both directions. There may also be a race SE of the point. With a strong W wind the sea in this area is short and heavy. In low

visibility it is advisable to keep in depths of more than 50 m.

4 **Clearing line:**

The line of bearing 340° of the tower on Saint Michael's Mount clears WSW of Iron Gates and the dangers inshore.

Useful mark
3.116

1 Light (white round metal tower, red base and cupola, 10 m in height) (50°06′·2N 5°32′·6W) on Newlyn South Pierhead.

(Directions continue at 4.21)

Side channel

Chart 777
General information
3.117

1 **Description.** Between Cudden Point (50°06′N 5°26′W) and Rinsey Head, 2¼ miles E, a bank with depths of less than 20 m, on which there are numerous dangers, extends 2½ miles S from the coast. There is a clear channel, 7½ cables wide, between Iron Gates (50°04′N 5°26′W), a rocky patch near the outer edge of this bank, and Mountamopus, 1 mile N.

Directions
3.118

1 The alignment (327¾°) astern of the tower on Saint Michael's Mount with Rogers Tower on Castle an Dinas, 3¼ miles NW, leads in the fairway passing (with positions given from the tower on Saint Michael's Mount):

Very close SW of a light buoy (S cardinal) marking Mountamopus (2½ miles SE); thence:

2 Between Carn Mallows (3 miles SE) and Iron Gates (3½ miles SSE); thence:

SW of Great Row (4½ miles SE).

In bad weather with winds between SE and W the sea breaks heavily over these dangers.

Newlyn Harbour

Chart 2345 plans of Penzance Bay and of Newlyn Harbour
General information
3.119

1 **Position and function.** Newlyn Harbour (50°06′N 5°33′W) lies at the head of Gwavas Lake, an indentation in the NW corner of Penzance Bay, and is used principally by fishing vessels. The harbour is one of the most important in England for the landing of high quality demersal fish. The port is also used by small commercial vessels and leisure craft.

2 **Approach and entry.** The harbour is approached through Penzance Bay, which is entered between Carn-du (50°04′N 5°31′W) and Cudden Point, 5 miles ENE. The harbour is entered between two piers.

Harbour Authority. Newlyn Pier and Harbour Commissioners, Harbour Office, Newlyn, Penzance, Cornwall.

Limiting conditions
3.120

1 **Tidal levels.** Mean spring range about 4·8 m; mean neap range about 2·4 m. For further information see *Admiralty Tide Tables.*

Maximum size of vessels handled. Vessels of up to 5·5 m draught can be accepted at MHWS and 5·2 m draught at MHWN.

Local weather and sea state. South-east winds bring a heavy swell into the harbour.

Arrival information
3.121

1 **Port radio**, with limited hours, operates from the harbour office on Newlyn North Pier. For details see *Admiralty List of Radio Signals Volume 6(1).*

Outer anchorages. Anchorage, as shown on the chart, for vessels waiting to enter Newlyn Harbour can be obtained (positioned from Newlyn South Pier (50°06′N 5°33′W):

3 cables SE in a depth of 7 m.

2 6½ cables E in a depth of 15 m.

8½ cables ENE in a depth of 12 to 13 m.

Undertow. Anchorage in Penzance Bay is sheltered from all winds except those between SSW and SE. Winds from this exposed quarter send in a heavy sea against which few vessels could ride at anchor were it not for the powerful undertow which increases with the strength and duration of the wind and enables ships to ride more easily.

Pilotage. The Harbour Office can provide information on vessel movements and a boat service can be arranged at all states of the tide as necessary. For further details see *Admiralty List of Radio Signals Volume 6(1).*

Speed limit. There is a speed limit of 3 kn within the harbour.

Harbour
3.122

1 Newlyn Harbour is protected by two piers, North Pier and South Pier; the entrance faces NE. Approximately one third of the harbour dries, mostly to the S and SW of Mary Williams Pier, but small craft can enter at all states of the tide.

Mary Williams Pier, which extends SE from the NW end of the harbour, has berths on both sides, South Pier has berths throughout its length whilst North Pier affords good berths for vessels to ground.

Directions for entering harbour
3.123

1 From Penzance Bay the route leads generally W passing (with positions given from Saint Mary's Church (50°07′N 5°32′W)):

S of The Gear (4½ cables SE), a drying rock marked by a light beacon (isolated danger, 7 m in height), noting the 4·4 m patch lying 1½ cables SSW; and:

N of Carn Base (1¼ miles S), noting a rock with a depth of 4·9 m, lying 3½ cables NNW; thence:

2 S of a rock with a depth of 2 m (6½ cables SSW) which lies 1 cable S of Dog Rock, noting the 3·2 and 4·9 m patches which lie 2 cables ENE and 1 cable SSW, respectively, of the 2 m rock; thence:

Between the pierheads to the berth as convenient.

Useful marks:

Light (green metal post on pedestal) (50°06′·2N 5°32′·6W) on Newlyn North Pierhead.

3 Light (white round metal tower, red base and cupola, 10 m in height) (50°06′·2N 5°32′·6W) on Newlyn South Pierhead.

Light (grey metal column, 4 m in height) (50°06′·2N 5°32′·7W) on Mary Williams Pierhead.

Albert Pier

West Dock   *Ferry Berth*

Penzance Harbour from S (3.126)

(Original dated 2001)

(Photograph - Air Images)

Light (red lantern on column, 2 m in height) (50°06'·2N 5°32'·8W) on Old Quay Head.

Berths
3.124

1   Mary Williams Pier (50°06'·2N 5°32'·8W) has a length of 340 m with a maximum depth alongside of 2·4 m. A quay, 104 m in length, at the root of Mary Williams Pier on its N side has a maximum depth of 1·9 m.

Finger pontoons to accommodate small craft lie to the W of Mary Williams Pier in depths of up to 2 m.

North Pier (50°06'·2N 5°32'·7W), 500 m in length, has a depth of 2·4 m at its head. The outer part affords good berths for vessels to ground on a bottom of sand, or on sand and gravel farther in.

2   South Pier (50°06'·1N 5°32'·6W), 120 m in length, with a depth of 2·7 m at its outer end is available for berthing throughout its length.

Old Quay (50°06'·1N 5°32'·8W) on the SW side of the harbour affords good shelter for numerous small fishing boats.

Port services
3.125

1   **Repairs:** slipways for vessels up to 33 m in length, 7 m beam, and a draught up to 3·7 m; diver.

Supplies: diesel fuel piped to all berths at North Pier S of the custom's house, petrol; fresh water laid on to all berths; provisions.

2   **Landing.** Steps at the outer end of South Pier provide the best landing. Those at the inner end cannot be used at LW without difficulty.

Penzance Harbour

Chart 2345 plans of Penzance Bay and of Penzance Harbour
General information
3.126

1   **Position, function and approach.** Penzance Harbour (50°07'N 5°32'W), the mainland terminal of the ferry which plies between Penzance and the Isles of Scilly, is also used by vessels requiring repair. The harbour is approached through Penzance Bay.

2   **Yacht race marker buoys.** Buoys (special), used for yacht racing marks are moored in Penzance Bay and the approaches to Penzance between April and September. The buoys are shown on the chart.

Harbour Authority. Penwith District Council, Harbour Office, North Arm, Wharf Road, Penzance, Cornwall TR18 4AH.

Limiting conditions
3.127

1   **Tidal levels.** Mean spring range about 4·8 m; mean neap range about 2·4 m. For further information see *Admiralty Tide Tables.*

Maximum size of vessel handled. The harbour can accommodate vessels of up to 92 m in length with a maximum draught of 5·6 m at MHWS, and of 4·2 m at MHWN.

Arrival information
3.128

1   **Port operations.** Entrance gates to the Wet Dock are usually opened from 2 hours before HW until 1 hour after HW, unless requested otherwise.

Port radio, with limited hours, operates from the harbour office on North Arm. For details see *Admiralty List of Radio Signals Volume 6(1)*.

Outer anchorages: for details see 3.121.

2   **Pilotage** is not available although the Harbour Master can provide a passage plan if required.

Tugs. Work boats are available for use as small tugs.

Harbour
3.129

1   Penzance Harbour, formed by Albert Pier and South Pier, contains a wet dock and a tidal dock. The greater part of the latter dries. The entrance between the piers is ¾ cable wide but is restricted by drying ledges.

Docking signals (Diagram 3.129) are shown from the flagstaff at the head of North Arm.

Signal	*Meaning*
🔴🔴🔴	Dock gates are closed
🟢🟢🟢	Dock gates are open

Penzance – docking signals (3.129)

Directions for entering harbour
3.130

1   From Penzance Bay the approach leads generally NW passing (with positions given from Saint Mary's Church (50°07′N 5°32′W)):

   SW of Ryeman Rocks (11 cables ENE), marked on their S side by a beacon (S cardinal), noting the 2·7 m patch which lies at the end of a spit extending 4½ cables SW from the beacon; thence:

2   Between The Gear (4½ cables SE) (3.123) and Western Cressar (6 cables ENE), marked by a beacon (S cardinal).

The approach then leads generally W passing between the two pierheads noting that drying ledges extend ½ cable ESE from Albert Pierhead (1½ cables NE).

3   **Clearing line:**

   The sector limit (268°) of Penzance South Pier Light changing from white to red passes S of Ryeman Rocks and Western Cressar.

   Useful marks:

   Monument (50°06′·9N 5°31′·9W) on Battery Rocks Bathing Pool.

4   Light (grey metal column, 6 m in height) (50°07′·1N 5°31′·8W) on Albert Pierhead.

   Light (column, 4 m in height) (50°07′·1N 5°31′·8W) on the knuckle of Wet Dock North Arm.

Berths
3.131

1   Tidal Harbour (50°07′·1N 5°31′·9W) which dries up to 2·5 m with the exception of four alongside berths with a maximum length of 137 m. At MHWS there is a depth of 7·6 m at the ferry terminal at the head of South Pier and of 4·6 m at the head of Albert Pier.

Wet Dock (50°07′·0N 5°31′·8W), entered through gates 15·3 m wide, is enclosed by the inner end of South Pier and by North Arm; there is usually a depth of 4·3 m, with a depth of 5·3 m at MHWS.

Port services
3.132

1   **Repairs:** dry dock; length 75 m, breadth 11·85 m, for vessels up to 74·5 m LOA, 11·5 m beam, 3·5 m draught and 1600 dwt; slipway.

Supplies: marine diesel oil; fresh water laid to all quays; provisions.

Other facilities: Ship sanitation certificates issued and extended; hospital.

2   **Communications:** heliport at the E end of the town; airport for light aircraft at Saint Just, 5 miles W, airport (naval) at Culdrose, 10 miles E.

Rescue, see 3.101.

Landing. Boats can land at all stages of the tide at steps at the outer end of South Pier, and at most times at those at the inner end.

Anchorages and minor harbours

Chart 777

Baulk Head anchorage
3.133

1   Anchorage can be obtained 5 cables W of Baulk Head (50°03′N 5°17′W) in a depth of 12 m, fine white sand.

Penberth Cove
3.134

1   **General information.** Penberth Cove (50°03′N 5°38′W), a fishing village, lies 5 cables NE of Castle Treveen Point.

Dangers in the vicinity. There are detached rocks within 1 cable of Castle Treveen Point and Seghys Rock lies close E of the point. Rocks extend 1 cable off Merthen Point which lies 8 cables W of the cove.

Slipway, formed of large flat stones, used by local fishing boats, is situated at the head of the cove.

Lamorna Cove
3.135

1   **General information.** Carn-du (50°04′N 5°33′W) is the E entrance point of Lamorna Cove at the head of which there is a small stone pier.

Dangers in the vicinity. Gull Rock, 24 m high and precipitous, lies close off Carn-du, with Little Heaver, a rock which dries 1 m, lying ½ cable SW. Kemyel Rock (3.114) lies 1¾ cables ENE of Gull Rock.

Chart 2345 plan of Mousehole Harbour

Mousehole harbour
3.136

1   **General information.** Mousehole (50°05′N 5°32′W) has a small tidal harbour formed by two piers with an entrance about 10 m wide. The harbour dries out to a bottom of gravel or rocky ground, but has a depth of 2·7 m at MHWS, and of 1·8 m at MHWN. The harbour is closed from November until March during which time baulks of timber are placed across the harbour entrance. Saint Clement's Isle lies 1½ cables E of the entrance to Mousehole harbour and affords protection to it from SE winds.

2   **Traffic signals.** Two green lights, vertically disposed, are exhibited from a grey metal mast, 3 m in height, on the N pierhead when the harbour is open. Three red lights exhibited from the same position indicate that the harbour is closed.

Harbour   Mousehole

Saint Clement's Isle

Mousehole and Saint Clement's Isle from SE (3.136)

(Original dated 2001)

(Photograph – Air Images)

3 **Marine farm.** A mussel bed marked by buoys lies about 2 cables ENE from Mousehole S Pierhead.

Directions. The S approach to Mousehole harbour is about 1½ cables wide and there are no dangers outside a distance of approximately ½ cable from the mainland shore and the W shore of Saint Clement's Isle.

Mousehole Harbour from E (3.136)

(Original dated 2001)

(Photograph – Air Images)

4 The N approach, which is narrower, lies between drying rocky ledges extending from the mainland and The Drigg Maen, an isolated drying rock which lies close NW of Saint Clement's Isle. It has a least depth in the fairway of 1 m.

Anchorage is available 1¼ cables SE of Mousehole S Pierhead in depths of approximately 8 m as shown on the plan.

Chart 2345 plan of Penzance Bay
Saint Michael's Mount harbour
3.137

1 **General information.** Saint Michael's Mount harbour (50°07′N 5°29′W) (3.112) is connected with Marazion, a small town 2 miles E of Penzance, by a causeway which uncovers at LW lying on a drying rocky ledge which extends S from the coast.

Saint Michael's Mount and Harbour from SW (3.137)

(Original dated 2001)

(Photograph – Air Images)

Pilotage is available for mariners in small craft.

Harbour at Saint Michael's Mount lies on its N side and is formed by two piers; the entrance is 37 m wide. The harbour dries but has depths of 3·0 m at MHWS and 2·0 m at MHWN.

2 **Swell.** The harbour, although protected from winds from S, should only be considered as a fine weather berth. In heavy weather the backwash of swell from the mainland can produce a surge in the harbour hazardous to small craft lying aground.

3 **Directions.** The line of bearing 084° of the pierheads leads towards the harbour entrance passing very close S of Outer Penzeath Rock and N of an obstruction (2·4 m) which lie 5 cables W and 1½ cables SW, respectively, of the pierheads in a least depth of 3·0 m, noting Guthen Rock which lies 2¾ cables SW of the pierheads, leaving the pierhead not more than ½ cable to the S to avoid Great Hogus, 1 cable NW.

4 **Clearing marks:**
  The alignment (281°) of Penzance South Pier Light with the dome of Penzance Market House, 3½ cables W, leads clear S of the dangers on the S side of the mount keeping clear of the charted obstruction close SE on the 2 m contour.

5 **Anchorage** can be obtained ¾ cable W of the pierhead, as shown on the plan, in depths of 2 to 3 m, sand, good holding ground avoiding the obstruction which lies close SE.

Charts 777, 2345 plan of Porthleven
Porthleven harbour
3.138

1 **General information.** Porthleven (50°05′N 5°19′W), a small fishing harbour consisting of an inner and outer harbour, is situated 6½ miles ESE of Saint Michael's Mount. The harbour is used by a few small fishing boats and is rarely visited by mariners in small craft.

Inner Harbour

Little Trigg Rocks
Porthleven from S (3.138)

(Original dated 2001)

(Photograph - Air Images)

Outer anchorage. In offshore winds anchorage can be obtained approximately 5 cables WSW of Porthleven.

2   **Local knowledge** is advisable; pilotage is not compulsory but can be arranged by the harbour authority, the Porthleven Harbour and Dock Company.

Harbour. A pier extends ½ cable SW from the SE entrance point; it is fringed on its NW side by drying rocks. The entrance is open SW and in bad weather baulks of timber are placed across it for protection. There are depths in the entrance of 1·8 m but from abreast the root of the pier the harbour dries. At the entrance to the inner part of the harbour there are depths of 3·7 m at MHWS and 2·4 m at MHWN.

3   **Docking signals.** By day, a red or black ball is displayed on a mast by the clock tower at the root of the pier when the harbour is closed, when the harbour is open to shipping nothing is displayed on the mast. By night, two green lights are exhibited, one from a green metal column, 6 m in height, 30 m from the head of the pier, the other set into a stone wall 1½ cables NE, when the harbour is open to shipping.

4   **Directions.** The line of bearing of 013° of Trewavas Head (50°05′N 5°22′W) clears E of Great Row and the dangers (3.117) extending S from the coast. Approach the harbour on a track parallel to the outer end of the pier, about 20 m NW of it, passing between Great Trigg Rocks and Little Trigg Rocks which extend from the NW and SE entrance points.

5   **Port services:** repairs to small craft, ramp for craft up to 9 m in length; fresh water and provisions; small quantities of fuel; airport at Culdrose (naval) 2 miles E.

Rescue, see 3.101.

Charts 777, 2345 plan of Mullion Cove
Mullion Cove
3.139

1   **General information.** Porth Mellin (50°01′N 5°15′W), a small harbour which dries out, is formed by two piers at the head of Mullion Cove and is owned by the National Trust. The harbour is exposed to the winds and swell. Mullion Island, precipitous on its W side, lies close off Mullion Cove; landing on the island is prohibited. For details of a nature reserve, see 3.111.

2   **Anchorages:**

For shelter from E winds; N of Mullion Island (50°01′N 5°16′W) in depths of 14 to 16 m. A recommended berth is 7½ cables NNW of the island, but mariners should be prepared to weigh instantly if the winds shift W.

3   Midway between the N end of Mullion Island and the S end of the W pier, as shown on the plan, in depths of about 7 m; smaller craft can anchor closer inshore ¾ cable SW of the harbour entrance in 4 m, sand, good holding.

Rescue, see 3.101.

Charts 777, 2345 plan of Lizard Point
Kynance Cove
3.140

1   Kynance Cove (49°58′N 5°14′W) with a sandy shore is entered between Asparagus Island and Gull Rock on its W side, and Lion Rock on its E side,

Anchorage as shown on the plan can be obtained in the cove in depths of about 5 m.

NOTES

93

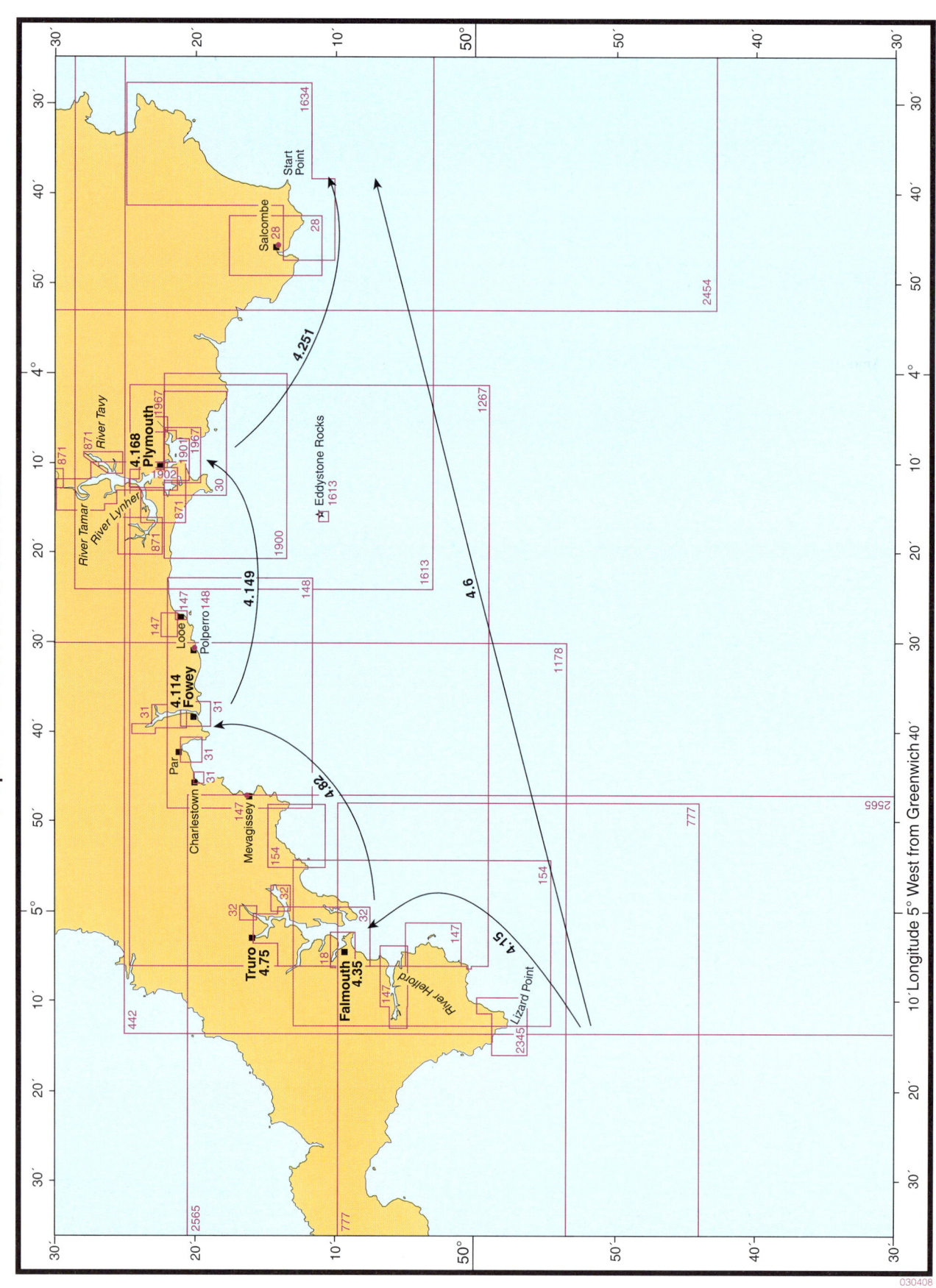

030408

CHAPTER 4

LIZARD POINT TO START POINT

GENERAL INFORMATION

Chart 442
Scope of chapter
4.1

1 This chapter covers the S coast of England from Lizard Point (49°58′N 5°13′W) to Start Point, about 62 miles ENE and is arranged in the following sections:

> Offshore passage (4.6)
> Lizard Point to Plymouth (4.14)
> Plymouth to Start Point (4.167)

Ports. Among the ports and harbours covered by this chapter are the larger ports of Falmouth (4.35), Fowey (4.114) and Plymouth (4.168).

Exercise areas
4.2

1 Detailed information concerning these areas, which are found in the waters of this chapter, may be found on Practice Exercise Area (PEXA) charts. Such areas are also shown on all new, and new edition navigation charts. For further details see 1.30 and *Annual Summary of Admiralty Notices to Mariners Nos 5 and 8.*

Submarine cables
4.3

1 Submarine cables, comprising the main submarine cables

between the United Kingdom and Spain and Portugal extend SE from Kennack Cove (50°00′N 5°10′W). A beacon at the head of the cove marks the inshore ends of the cables.

Racing marker buoys
4.4

1 Yacht racing marker buoys (special) may be encountered up to 5 miles offshore throughout the waters of this chapter, between April and October

Tidal streams
4.5

1 Off Lizard Point and Start Point the tidal streams are shown by means of information on the chart; they are nearly rectilinear outside a line joining the two points.

In the bight between these two points there is a slight indraught, and the streams follow the direction of the coast, turning rather earlier near the land than in the fairway of the English Channel. They are also weaker, with a tendency to become rotary in a clockwise direction, but their rates increase off salient points and over rocks and shoals where overfalls may occur. See *Admiralty Tidal Stream Atlas of The English Channel and Falmouth to Padstow including Isles of Scilly.*

OFFSHORE PASSAGE

General information

Chart 442
Route
4.6

1 From S of Lizard Point (49°58′N 5°13′W) the offshore passage leads ENE, about 62 miles, to S of Start Point.

Topography
4.7

1 Between Lizard Point and Start Point the coast recedes to a depth of 15 miles and is moderately high, backed by higher ground farther inland. It contains several deep openings which from a distance seem to break the continuity of the coastline.

Exercise areas
4.8

1 For details of exercise areas see 4.2 and information on the chart.

Submarine cables
4.9

1 For details of submarine cables, see 4.3.

Tidal streams
4.10

1 For details of tidal streams, see 4.5.

Directions
(continued from 3.106)

Principal marks
4.11

1 **Landmarks:**
> Lizard Point (49°58′N 5°13′W) (3.112).
> Dish-shaped Aerials (50°03′N 5°11′W) (4.21).

Major lights:
> Lizard Light (49°58′N 5°12′W) (3.112).
> Eddystone Light (50°11′N 4°16′W) (4.215).
> Start Point Light (50°13′N 3°38′W) (5.18).

Other aid to navigation
4.12

1 **Racon:** Eddystone Light (50°11′N 4°16′W).
For details see *Admiralty List of Radio Signals Volume 2.*

Directions
4.13

1 From a position S of Lizard Point (49°58′N 5°13′W) the route leads ENE passing:

> SSE of Black Head (50°00′N 5°06′W) (4.16); thence:

SSE of Hand Deeps (50°13′N 4°20′W) (4.159). A light buoy (special) is charted 8½ miles SW of the deeps. Thence:

2   SSE of Eddystone Rocks (50°11′N 4°16′W) (4.218). In low visibility by keeping in depths of not less than 70 m these rocks will be avoided. A group of ODAS light buoys (special) (uncharted) is centered on a position 10 miles SSW of the rocks. Thence:

SSE of Prawle Point (50°12′N 3°43′W) (4.252); thence:

To a position S of Start Point (50°13′N 3°38′W) (4.252).

3   **Useful marks:**
    Dodman Point (50°13′N 4°48′W) (4.87).
    Daymark Beacon (50°19′N 4°40′W) (4.87).
    Rame Head (50°19′N 4°13′W) (4.215).
    Bolt Head (50°13′N 3°47′W) (4.252).
    Bolt Tail (50°14′N 3°52′W) (4.252).
    Radio Masts (50°14′N 3°40′W) (5.18).

(Directions continue at 5.12)

LIZARD POINT TO PLYMOUTH

GENERAL INFORMATION

Chart 442

Area covered
4.14

1   This section covers the coast from Lizard Point to Plymouth, a distance of about 43 miles and is arranged as follows:
    Lizard Point to Falmouth (4.15).
    Falmouth and approaches and the port of Truro (4.35).
    Falmouth to Fowey (4.82).
    Fowey Harbour and approaches (4.114).
    Fowey to Plymouth (4.149).

LIZARD POINT TO FALMOUTH

General information

Charts 154, 777
Route
4.15

1   From S of Lizard Point (49°58′N 5°13′W) the route leads ENE, about 8 miles, to SSE of Lowland Point, the route then leads N, about 7 miles, to E of Nare Point.

Topography
4.16

1   Between Lizard Point and Black Head, 5 miles NE, the cliffs rise to a height of 60 m with a low gap at Kennack Cove (4.3). Between Black Head (50°00′N 5°06′W) and Chynhalls Point, 8 cables NNE, the cliffs continue at a height of over 60 m, thence to Nare Point, 4 miles farther N, the cliffs are lower but the land rises abruptly behind them.

Exercise areas
4.17

1   For details of exercise areas, see 4.2 and information on the charts.

Submarine cables
4.18

1   For details of submarine cables, see 4.3.

Rescue
4.19

1   **Coastguard rescue teams** operate from:
    Lizard Auxiliary Station on Bass Point (49°58′N 5°11′W).

Porthoustock Auxiliary Station on Manacle Point (50°03′N 5°03′W).

    Lifeboat. Lizard lifeboat is stationed at Kilcobben Cove (49°58′N 5°11′W).

2   **National Coastwatch Institution** (NCI) station is situated at:
    Bass Point (49°57′·8N 5°11′·2W)

For details of coastguard stations see 1.101, for lifeboats see 1.113 and for NCI see 1.106.

Tidal streams
4.20

1   At a position 2½ miles E of The Manacles (50°03′N 5°03′W) the stream is nearly rectilinear. Near The Manacles the rate increases but the direction remains rectilinear. Farther E the stream weakens and becomes rotary in a clockwise direction. For details see information on the chart and *Admiralty Tidal Stream Atlas Falmouth to Padstow including Isles of Scilly.*

Directions
(continued from 3.116)

Principal marks
4.21

1   **Landmarks:**
    Hotel (50°01′N 5°06′W) near Chynhalls Point.
    Dish-shaped aerials (50°03′N 5°11′W) on Goonhilly Downs.
    Church (spire) (50°03′N 5°05′W) at Saint Keverne.
    Radio Mast (401 m) (50°13′N 5°14′W) marked by red obstruction lights (chart 442).

Saint Anthony Head Light from SW (4.21)
(Original dated 1985)

(Photograph - Dr. M. P. Bender)

2   **Major lights:**
    Lizard Light (49°58′N 5°12′W) (3.112).
    Saint Anthony Head Light (white octagonal tower, 19 m in height) (50°08′N 5°01′W) shown throughout 24 hours.

Lizard Point to Lowland Point
4.22

1   From a position S of Lizard Light (49°58′N 5°12′W) (3.112) the passage to Lowland Point leads ENE passing (with positions given from Black Head (50°00′N 5°06′W)):
> SSE of Vrogue Rock (4 miles SW) (4.23); thence:
> SSE of Spernan Shoals (3½ miles SW); thence:
> SSE of Black Head (4.16); thence:
> SSE of Lowland Point (2¼ miles NE) (4.27).

4.23
Marking transits:

1   A mark (red and white stripes) and a beacon (red and white stripes, 3 m in height) in line (292°) on Bass Point together with a white patch on Hot Point (49°58′N 5°11′W) in line (325½°) with Balk Beacon (red and white mast, white diamond topmark), 4 cables NNW at the head of Parn Voose Cove, mark Vrogue Rock.

Clearing line:

2   Lizard Light in sight, which is obscured on a bearing less than 250°, and open S of Bass Point, 6 cables ENE, clears SSE of Black Head.

Lowland Point to Nare Point
4.24

1   When Saint Anthony Head Light bears less than 004°, and at night when in the white sector of that light which changes from red to white on the bearing of 004°, the passage leads N passing (with positions given from Manacle Point (50°03′N 5°03′W)):
> E of Lowland Point (1 mile SSW); thence:

2   E of The Manacles (8 cables E), a group of dangerous rocks many of which dry, marked by Manacle Light Buoy (E cardinal). These dangers are covered by the red sector (004°–022°) of Saint Anthony Head Light. Thence:
> E of The Wrigglers (1½ miles NE); thence:
> E of Nare Point (2 miles NNW); and:

Useful mark:

> Pendennis Castle (50°09′N 5°03′W) (4.56).

(Directions continue at 4.56 and for Fowey at 4.87)

Anchorages, moorings and harbours

Chart 2345 plan of Lizard Point
Housel Bay
4.25

1   **Anchorage** can be obtained in Housel Bay (49°58′N 5°12′W) as shown on the chart. A conspicuous hotel stands at the head of the bay.

Charts 2345 plan of Lizard Point, 154
North of Bass Point
4.26

1   **General information.** Anchorage in offshore winds can be obtained in the bight between Bass Point (49°58′N 5°11′W) and Black Head, 4 miles NE, clear of the submarine cables (4.3) and dangers listed below.

Dangers in the bight with positions given from Bass Point:
> Spernan Shoals (6 cables E).
> Voge Rock (5 cables N).

2   Craggan Rocks (1 mile NNE).
> Shoal (8 m) (1¾ miles NNE).
> Shoal (9·4 m) (4 miles ENE).

Caution. A submarine pipeline extends 3 cables E from the coast passing N of Voge Rock; its outer end is marked by a buoy (special).

Anchorage. Recommended berth indicated on the chart lies 3 cables E of Balk Beacon (49°58′·4N 5°11′·4W) in a depth of 10 m. Smaller craft can anchor farther inshore in depths of 3 to 5 m.

Chart 147
Coverack Cove
4.27

1   **General information.** Coverack Cove is entered between Chynhalls Point (50°01′N 5°05′W) and Lowland Point, 1½ miles NE, and affords anchorage to small coasting vessels in offshore winds.

Dolor Point
Coverack Cove from E (4.27)
(Original dated 2001)

(Photograph - Air Images)

2   **Dangers.** Chynhalls Point, on the S side of the cove, is fringed by a drying rocky ledge which extends over 1 cable from the shore. The Guthens and a rock drying 1·6 m lie close off the NE and E end of this ledge. Pedn-myin, a group of drying rocks, extend nearly 2 cables offshore between Dolor Point (50°01′N 5°06′W), on which the village of Coverack stands, and Lowland Point and thence E to Lowland Point there are rocks which extend up to 2 cables offshore. Lowland Point is surrounded by a drying rocky ledge outside of which there are numerous detached rocks, some of which dry, which lie up to 4 cables offshore; their positions can best be seen from the chart.
4.28

1   **Anchorage.** A recommended berth, as shown on the chart, is 2 cables ENE of Dolor Point in a depth of 9 m.

A pier extends NW from Dolor Point and affords shelter for boats which can take the ground. There are depths of 3·7 m within the pier at MHWS and of 2·4 m at MHWN. A recommended anchorage berth for small craft is 1½ cables NNE of the pier in depths of 2 to 5 m.

Lowland Point
4.29

1   **General information.** There is a small jetty, 3 cables N of Lowland Point (50°02′N 5°04′W), which is used by coasting vessels up to 1500 tons for loading stone from Dean Quarries nearby.

The jetty dries at LW and its outer end is marked by a green beacon; a similar beacon is situated on a building 1 cable WNW. The beacons are indistinct but the jetty can be identified by the gantries on it and by the buildings behind it.

2   Maen Land, with two rocks awash close S, lies 2 cables ESE of the head of the jetty.

Blasting. It is reported (1993) that the quarry operators monitor VHF radio channels 16 and 19 whenever blasting is due to take place in order to give warning to shipping close inshore.

Porthkerris Point

4.30

1   A mooring buoy (black) (uncharted), which is liable to be moved, is situated 4 cables N of Porthkerris Point (50°04′N 5°04′W).

Landing. There is a landing place cut into the rock at Porthkerris Point.

Charts 147 plan of Helford River, 154

Helford River

4.31

1   **General information.** Helford River is entered between Nare Point (50°05′N 5°05′W) and Rosemullion Head, 1½ miles N. Its sheltered waters are used by yachts and pleasure craft.

Helford
Point   Pedn Billy

Bosham   Helford
Point   Helford River from E (4.31)   Passage
              (Original dated 2001)

(Photograph - Air Images)

River authority. Helford River Moorings Office.
    Website: www.helfordrivermoorings.co.uk
    Email: moorings@helford-river.com

Limiting conditions. The river is navigable by mariners in small craft at HW to Gweek, 4½ miles within the entrance, some silting has occurred (1995) and mariners taking this route should do so with caution.

2   E winds cause a heavy sea in the river between Mawnan Shear (50°06′N 5°06′W) and Bosahan Point, 1 mile W.

Tidal levels. Mean spring range about 4·7 m; mean neap range about 2·3 m. For further information see *Admiralty Tide Tables.*

4.32

1   **Anchorages:**
        Mariners in vessels of deeper draught may anchor 5 cables NNE of Nare Point, sheltered from SW winds, in a depth of 12 m.

Between Mawnan Shear (50°06′N 5°06′W) and Bosahan Point, 1 mile WSW, in depths of 3 to 7 m, see 4.31. The best anchorage for larger vessels is E of Bosahan Point, in the centre of the river between Durgan (50°06′·2N 5°06′·9W) on the N coast and The Voose Buoy (N cardinal) (50°05′·8N 5°07′·0W) on the S coast, clear of the moorings and eelgrass

2   The Pool, N and W of Bosahan Point, is also available for anchorage, clear of small craft moorings and a submarine cable, in depths between 5 and 15 m. .

3   **Local pilot** is available from Porth Navas for mariners in small craft proceeding to Gweek.

Speed limit. Between the months of April and October inclusive there is a speed limit of 6 kn in Helford River and its adjacent creeks.

4.33

1   **Harbour.** The river contains several creeks which branch out from either side. Moorings are available for visiting yachts in Helford River.

Hazards. Oyster beds lie in the river and creeks W of The Pool; they are not always marked in the traditional fashion by stakes, and therefore anchoring is prohibited W of the moorings in The Pool. Eelgrass beds, marked by buoys, lie up to 250 m offshore between Durgan (50°06′·2N 5°06′·9W) and Toll Point (6 cables ESE); mariners are advised not to anchor inshore of the marker buoys.

2   A passenger ferry, seasonal, crosses The Pool between Helford Point and Helford Passage. A submarine cable, marked at each end by a beacon, crosses the river close W of Bosahan Point and a submarine power cable crosses the river 2 miles above Pedn Billy (50°06′·0N 5°08′·3W).

4.34

1   **Directions for entering harbour.** The line of bearing 270° of the N extremity of an un named point 2½ cables WNW of Helford Point (50°05′·7N 5°08′·0W) just open of Bosahan Point leads into the middle of the entrance to the river passing (with positions given from Bosahan Point (50°05′·7N 5°07′·4W)):

2   Between Nare Point (2 miles ESE) and August Rock or The Gedges (1½ miles ENE) marked by a buoy (starboard hand) (position approximate; seasonal) on its SE side. There is deeper water on the S side of the approach approximately 3 cables N of Nare Point (2 miles ESE). Thence:
        Between Mawnan Shear (1 mile ENE) and The Gew (8 cables E).

3   The track then leads generally W in mid-channel passing:
        N of The Voose (3½ cables E), a drying rocky ledge marked by a buoy (N cardinal; position approximate) to The Pool which lies W of Bosahan Point. Bar Buoy (starboard hand; position approximate) (2 cables WNW) marks the S side of the drying mudbanks on the N side of The Pool.

4   **Caution.** In 1973 it was reported that the N bank had extended E and that there was less water than charted off Helford Passage situated on the N side of The Pool. A considerable spit extends to mid channel from the buttress of land E of the cable landing beacon (yellow pole) (50°06′·0N 5°07′·5W) and W of Polgwidden Cove (50°06′N 5°07′W). Care is necessary in this vicinity at low water. It was also reported that the shore bank in the vicinity of Bosahan Point was silting up.

Clearing line. Bosahan Point bearing more than 259° and open S of Mawnan Shear clears S of August Rock.

Black Rock Beacon   *Castle Point*

Falmouth – Approaches from S (4.35)

(Original dated 2004)

(Photograph - HMS Gleaner)

FALMOUTH AND APPROACHES AND THE PORT OF TRURO

General information

Charts 154, 32, 18

Position
4.35

1 Port of Falmouth (50°09′N 5°03′W) lies at the mouth of River Fal.

Function
4.36

1 The port handles cruise liners, cargo vessels and fishing vessels. It is also an important centre for ship repairs and for bunkering vessels alongside and at anchor.

Topography
4.37

1 Falmouth Bay is entered between Rosemullion Head (50°07′N 5°05′W) and Pendennis Point, 2½ miles NE. Between Rosemullion Head and Pennance Point, 1½ miles N, the coast consists of cliffs up to 15 m in height. From Pennance Point to Pendennis Point, 1¼ miles ENE, the coast is fringed by drying rocks which extend up to 1 cable from the shore.

2 Saint Anthony Head (50°08′N 5°01′W), the SW extremity of a headland forming the E entrance point to the Port of Falmouth, may be identified by the light (4.21) which stands upon it.

Port limits
4.38

1 The S limit of the port is bounded by a line extending SE and then SW from Zone Point (50°08′N 5°01′W) to a position about 5 miles S of Saint Anthony Head thence NW to Rosemullion Head (50°07′N 5°05′W) as shown on the chart. The N limit is a line joining a pillar on Penarrow Point (50°10′N 5°03′W) and two pillars on Messack Point, 1 mile NE, and the W limit is a line joining the W end of Boyer's Cellars (50°09′·9N 5°04′·9W) to the W side of Sailor's Creek, 2 cables NNE.

Approach and entry
4.39

1 Port of Falmouth is approached E of Falmouth Bay and entered between Pendennis Point and Saint Anthony Head.

Traffic
4.40

1 In 2006 the harbour was used by 763 vessels totalling 23 684 353 dwt.

Port Authority
4.41

1 Falmouth Harbour Commissioners, 44 Arwenack Street, Falmouth, TR11 3JQ.

Docks Authority: A & P (Falmouth) Ltd., The Docks, Falmouth, TR11 4NR. Website: www.falmouthport.co.uk

Limiting conditions

Controlling depths
4.42

1 The E channel (4.57) between Black Rock (50°09′N 5°02′W) and Saint Anthony Head, the principal entrance channel, has a least depth of 11·3 m close to the outer leading line and is usable by deep-draught vessels at all times.

The W channel (4.59) between Black Rock and Pendennis Point has a least depth of 5·4 m.

The channel (4.61) to Falmouth Inner Harbour: 5·5 m, noting a 5·0 m patch at the NE extremity of the channel.

Deepest and longest berths
4.43

1 **Alongside berths:**
Falmouth Docks (10°09′N 5°03′W) (4.62).

Saint Anthony Head Light

Saint-Mawes Castle

(Black Rock Beacon)

(Pendennis Castle)

Falmouth – Approaches from S (4.37)

(Original dated 2004)

(Photograph – HMS Gleaner)

Tidal levels
4.44
1 Mean spring range about 4·6 m; mean neap range about 2·2 m. For further information see *Admiralty Tide Tables*.

Maximum size of vessel handled
4.45
1 Vessels of up to 280 m in length have been accommodated in Falmouth Docks.

In Falmouth Bay the size of vessel is unlimited; the largest vessel handled in the bay was 413 012 dwt, 366 m LOA and 25 m draught.

Arrival information

Notice of ETA required
4.46
1 Vessels should send ETA 72, 48, 24 and 12 hours in advance, with amendments up to 2 hours before original ETA. For details see *Admiralty List of Radio Signals Volume 6(1)*.

Outer anchorage
4.47
1 Anchorage can be obtained off Falmouth Bay about 1¼ miles SW of Saint Anthony Head (50°08′N 5°01′W) in depths of approximately 17 m.

Caution. There are several wrecks in this vicinity; the positions of the wrecks can best be seen from the chart.

Prohibited anchorage. Anchoring is prohibited in the approach channel to Falmouth Docks and in the vicinity of the docks themselves. See 4.68, harbour regulations.

Pilotage
4.48
1 **Falmouth Pilotage Area** is divided into four zones inside a line from Black Head (50°00′N 5°06′W) to Dodman Point, 19 miles NE.

2 **Pilotage** is available 24 hours and is compulsory for the following vessels when under way:
> All vessels over 180 m LOA navigating N of a line between Black Head and Dodman Point (Zone A).
> All commercial vessels over 30 m LOA navigating W of a line between Rosemullion Head and 50°03′·35N 5°01′·60W (Zone B).

3
> All vessels over 75 m LOA navigating N of a line between Zone Point and Rosemullion Head and S of a line between Messack Point and Penarrow Point (Zone C), or elsewhere in the Pilotage Area within 1 mile of the shore.
> All vessels over 60 m LOA navigating N of a line between Messack Point and Penarrow Point (Zone D) or in Penryn River W of a line between Prince of Wales Pier and Flushing New Quay.

4
> All vessels carrying dangerous or polluting goods.
> All commercial vessels not equipped with corrected Admiralty Charts numbers 154, 32 and 18 (or equivalent) as necessary for their entire passage.
> All vessels over 50 m LOA entering or leaving a dry dock.
> All manned vessels over 50 m LOA using the services of a harbour tug.

5
> Vessels of any size when so directed by the Harbour Master or Dock Master in the interests of safety of the vessel, other vessels, persons, the port or its infrastructure.

These regulations apply to tugs and tows as if the combined length of the tug and tow is the length overall of a single vessel.

6 **Exceptions** to compulsory pilotage:
> a) HM Ships and foreign warships.
> b) Vessels less than 20 m LOA.
> c) Registered fishing vessels less than 47·5 m LOA.

7 **Boarding place.** For vessels over 180 m LOA, the pilots board in position 50°05′N 5°01′W. Smaller vessels should give their ETA for this boarding place but may be given a position closer inshore depending on weather conditions.

For further details see *Admiralty List of Radio Signals Volume 6(1)*.

Tugs
4.49
1 Three tugs are available; one is fitted for deep-sea towage and firefighting.

Regulations concerning entry
4.50
1 **Dangerous and polluting goods.** All vessels carrying dangerous and polluting goods as classified in the International Maritime Dangerous Goods (IMDG) Code should comply with *The Merchant Shipping (Reporting Requirements for vessels carrying dangerous or polluting goods) Regulations 1995*.

For details see *Admiralty List of Radio Signals Volume 6(1)* and 1.68 to 1.76.

2 All vessels carrying explosives must, immediately prior to arrival at the port, request an anchorage position from the Harbour Master. Anchor positions will be dependent on the amount of explosives carried and whether or not the explosives are to be worked at the port, or in transit.

Quarantine information, see 1.85.

Harbour

General layout
4.51
1 Port of Falmouth includes Falmouth Bay, Falmouth Harbour with the capacious anchorages at Carrick Roads and Cross Road, Falmouth Inner Harbour, excluding the area surrounding Falmouth Docks, and Penryn River as far as Boyer's Cellars. Falmouth Docks Basin, which is formed by Eastern Breakwater and the complex of jetties 2½ cables to the W. Falmouth Docks are primarily a shiprepair yard although various cargoes can be handled.

2 **Channels.** The entrance to the harbour is divided into two channels by Black Rock, a drying rock, which is situated 3½ cables E of Pendennis Point; the E channel is the principal entrance channel.

Anchorages. Deep-draught vessel anchorages lie within River Fal at Carrick Roads (50°10′N 5°02′W) (4.63) with, farther N, the anchorage at Cross Road (4.63).

Anchorages for smaller vessels are available inside the harbour entrance, at Saint Just Pool (4.63) and on Falmouth Bank.

3 Small craft are accommodated in Falmouth Inner Harbour, and Penryn River, and at Saint Mawes Harbour and Saint Just Creek on the E side of the port.

Development
4.52
1 Works are in progress (2008) to demolish Empire and King's Jetties and construct a marina.

Hazards

4.53

1   **Ferries** for passengers run regularly from Prince of Wales Pier (50°09′N 5°04′W) to Saint Mawes (4.73), Town Quay at Flushing and Town Quay at Truro (seasonal). In summer there is also a ferry from Custom House Quay to Saint Mawes.

    Buoys of various shapes and colours, used for yacht racing marks, are moored in Port of Falmouth from March to September annually.

Signals

4.54

1   Dredgers and other vessels conducting operations which restrict their manoeuvrability display the lights and shapes as described in *International Regulations for Preventing Collisions at Sea (1972)*.

Natural conditions

4.55

1   **Tidal streams** at the entrance to the E channel are shown by information on the chart. The streams run generally in the direction of the channel, and in the narrows they attain a spring rate of 1½ kn, but less over the banks. During freshets the out-going stream runs for a longer period and its rate increases to a maximum of 2 kn, with a corresponding reduction in the duration and rate of the in-going stream.

2   Tidal streams in the approach channel to Inner Harbour are shown by information on the chart.

    Climate information. See 1.195 and 13.234

Directions for entering harbour

(continued from 4.24)

Principal marks

4.56

1   **Landmarks:**
    Coastguard Station (radio mast) (50°08′·7N 5°02′·7W).
    Pendennis Castle (turret) (50°08′·8N 5°02′·8W).
    Falmouth Hotel (50°08′·9N 5°03′·5W).
    Old Observatory Tower (50°09′·1N 5°04′·2W).
2   Water Tower (50°10′·1N 5°00′·9W).
  Major light:
    Saint Anthony Head Light (50°08′·4N 5°00′·9W) (4.21).

Approaches — east channel

4.57

1   **From south.** The line of bearing 004° of the E extremity of Saint Mawes Castle situated on Castle Point (50°09′N 5°01′W) leads in the approach to the E channel passing (with positions given from Pendennis Castle):
    E of Rosemullion Head (2½ miles SSW); thence:
2   W of Old Wall (2¼ miles SE), several rocky heads lying 1¼ miles S of Zone Point; the ground between is uneven and overfalls occur in this area especially with SE winds and a rising tide; thence:
    E of Pennance Point (1¼ miles SW), noting an obstruction with 11·3 m over it in position 50°08′·0N 5°01′·4W; thence:
3   Between Pendennis Point (2 cables SE) and Saint Anthony Head (1¼ miles ESE) (4.37). Shag Rock marked by a post (3 m) lies close under the head. Thence:

St. Mawes Light-buoy
(S cardinal)

Falmouth – Saint-Mawes Castle and Point from S (4.57)
(Original dated 2004)

(Photograph - HMS Gleaner)

Turret

Falmouth Approaches – Pendennis Point and Castle from SSE (4.57)

(Original dated 2004)

E of a 10·5 m depth (8 cables ESE) which lies close W of the recommended track; thence:

4   E of a light buoy (E cardinal) (7 cables E) marking patches of less than 5 m which lie E and S of Black Rock (5 cables E), noting the 10·5 m depth which lies 1¼ cables ENE of the light buoy. Black Rock Light Beacon (isolated danger) marks the rock.

Caution. In low visibility give Saint Anthony Head and the land N a clearance of 2½ cables.

4.58

1   **From east.** Give a clearance of at least 2 miles to Saint Anthony Head and in low visibility keep in depths of more than 65 m until the ship's position has been accurately determined, noting Old Wall (4.57) which lies 1¼ miles

SSE of the head. Then proceed through the E channel, as above.

Approaches — west channel
4.59

1   From S of Pendennis Point the track leads N through the W channel passing (with positions given from Pendennis Castle):

      W of Old Wall (2¼ miles SE) (4.57); thence:
      E of Pennance Point (1¼ miles SW); thence:
      Midway between Pendennis Point (2 cables SE) and Black Rock (5 cables E) (4.57).

2   On the alignment (111°) of Black Rock Light Beacon with Saint Anthony Head (1¼ miles ESE) the track then

Saint-Mawes   *Carricknath Point*   *Saint Anthony Head and Light*

Falmouth Approaches – Saint Anthony Head and Light from SSW (4.57)

(Original dated 2004)

turns NE using Saint Mawes Castle (1 mile ENE) as a headmark to join the main fairway (4.60) SW of the castle.

Harbour entry
4.60

1   From E of Black Rock, distant 3½ cables, the track leads NNW in the deepest part of the fairway between Saint Mawes Bank, which borders the E shore of the harbour, and a bank extending from the W shore between Pendennis Point and Penarrow Point, 2 miles N, passing (with positions given from Penarrow Point):

2   Close WSW of Castle Light Buoy (starboard hand) (1¾ miles SSE) marking the SW side of Saint Mawes Bank; thence:

         ENE of The Governor Light Buoy (E cardinal) (1½ miles S) marking the E edge of the S part of the coastal bank fronting the W shore; thence:

3   Between West Narrows and East Narrows Light Buoys (port and starboard hand) (1¼ miles SSE) marking the W and E sides of the fairway; thence:

         WSW of The Vilt Light Buoy (starboard hand) (6 cables SSE) marking the NW side of Saint Mawes Bank.

4   The track then turns sharply and leads generally NE in mid-channel passing:

         SE of Northbank Light Buoy (port hand) (3¼ cables ESE); and:

         Clear of Cross Roads Lighted Mooring Buoy (special) (5 cables ESE) to Saint Just Pool.

5   **Caution.** In low visibility do not approach Saint Mawes Bank within a depth of 14 m as the edge of the bank is steep-to.

Charts 18, 32
Falmouth Inner Harbour
4.61

1   Inner Harbour is approached from the main fairway abreast of West Narrows Light Buoy (port hand) (50°09'·4N 5°02'·0W) through a channel (4.42) across the S part of Falmouth Bank. A turn inside West Narrows Light Buoy is recommended for entering and leaving at all states of tide.

2   **Useful marks:**

         Light (tower, 2 m in height) (50°09'·4N 5°03'·2W) on Northern Arm E Head.

         Lights (50°09'·3N 5°02'·9W) on Eastern Breakwater Head; white floodlights illuminate the breakwater.

         Lights (metal pole) (50°09'·4N 5° 03'·5W) on W end of Queen's Jetty.

Basins and berths

Falmouth Docks
4.62

1   The longest and deepest berths in Falmouth Docks (50°09'·3N 5°03'·3W) are as follows:

         Eastern Breakwater: length 291 m with depths alongside ranging from about 2 m to 7·6 m.

         Duchy Wharf: length 235 m; least depth 8·0 m.

2   **Mooring buoys.** Caldy and Frigate Mooring Buoys (50°09'·5N 5°03'·6W) are situated 2½ cables NW of

Dry docks   *The Western*   *Queen's Jetty*

Eastern Breakwater   Falmouth Docks from NE (4.62)   *Northern Arm*

(Original dated 2001)

(Photograph - Air Images)

Falmouth Docks Basin. The maximum size of vessel normally permissible on either of these buoys, except by special arrangement with the Harbour Master, is 61 m LOA, 3·5 m draught. Larger vessels can moor between the buoys.

Cross Roads Lighted Mooring Buoy (special) (50°10'·3N 5°02'·0W) is suitable for vessels up to 183 m LOA.

Anchorages
4.63

1 **Carrick Roads** (50°09'·8N 5°02'·3W) between Falmouth Bank and Saint Mawes Bank affords anchorage for vessels, up to 170 m in length with a maximum draught of 10 m. Normally two anchors are employed in the form of a running moor.

Cross Road (50°10'·2N 5°02'·1W) can accept vessels up to 200 m LOA lying to two anchors in the form of a running moor. Additionally, there is a swinging buoy available (4.62) moored in a depth of 22 m for vessels up to 183 m.

2 Carrick and Cross Roads are generally well sheltered but are exposed to S gales.

Saint Just Pool lies 4 cables farther upriver and provides anchorage for smaller vessels.

Port services

Repairs
4.64

1 **Major repairs** can be undertaken; divers and an underwater hull cleaning service are available.

Dry docks. There are three dry docks available operated by A & P (Falmouth) Ltd; the largest, Queen Elizabeth Dock, can take vessels up to 100 000 dwt and has the following dimensions: extreme length 259 m; extreme breadth 39·62 m; depth on the sill at MHWS 10·88 m and can accommodate vessels up to 250 m LOA and 38 m beam.

Other facilities
4.65

1 **Customs Office** in Falmouth.

Ship sanitation control and ship sanitation control exemption certificates are issued and extended at Falmouth. Truro and Penryn are also covered.

Hospital in Falmouth.

Oily waste disposal facilities and a tank cleaning service are available.

Supplies
4.66

1 **Fuel.** A full range of fuel is available on a 24 hour basis either by barge or alongside at Eastern Breakwater jetty.

Fresh water: available by barge or laid on to the wharves and jetties.

Provisions: numerous ship chandlers.

Communications
4.67

1 **Local airport:** at Newquay, 45 km distant, with connecting flights to London.

Helicopter pad at Falmouth Docks.

Harbour regulations
4.68

1 **Immobilizing.** Mariners in commercial vessels should not immobilize main engines whilst at anchor in Cross or Carrick Roads or Falmouth Bay without permission of the Harbour Office and in compliance with certain directions made by the Harbour Master. Vessels must also maintain an anchor watch with a continuous listening watch on VHF.

2 **Security.** Vessels not engaged in authorized activities within the port, must not enter the waters of the prohibited anchorage area (4.47) or approach within 10 m of vessels alongside County Wharf or moored N of Queen's Jetty and Northern Arm.

Rescue
4.69

1 **Coastguard.** Falmouth MRCC is situated on Pendennis Point, with a Rescue Team at Falmouth.

Lifeboats. An all-weather lifeboat and an inshore lifeboat are stationed at Falmouth.

For details of coastguard stations see 1.101 and for lifeboats 1.113.

2 **VHF Direction-finding station**, for emergency use only, operates from Falmouth MRCC For details see *Admiralty List of Radio Signals Volume 2* and 1.105.

Rescue tug. See 1.109

Minor harbours
Falmouth Inner Harbour
4.70

1 **General information.** Falmouth Inner Harbour lies at the mouth of Penryn River which flows into the River Fal close within its W entrance point. The town of Falmouth and Falmouth Docks lie on the S side of the harbour.

The town is fronted by quays and there are a number of landing steps where small craft may go alongside to load and unload. There are numerous moorings for small craft off the quays and pontoons for visiting craft connected to North Quay; for depth information at the visitor berths consult the Harbour Master.

2 **Ferries** for details, see 4.53.

Directions. For Directions for Inner Harbour, see 4.61.

Buoyage. The navigable channel in Penryn River is subject to change; the buoys are moved accordingly.

| Prince of Wales Pier | Greenbank Quay | New Quay |

Penryn River from SE (4.70)

(Original dated 2001)

(Photograph – Air Images)

4.71

1 **Berths and landings.** Boyer's Cellars, a wharf, lies at the N end of Falmouth and is approached from Inner Harbour through a buoyed channel in Penryn River which has a least charted depth of 2·1 m. The wharf has a depth of 2·6 m off the wharf.

Landing can be made at Custom House Quay, at Prince of Wales Pier, at Royal Cornwall Yacht Club and at

Greenbank Quay on the S side of Inner Harbour, and at Flushing on the N side of Inner Harbour.

Penryn

4.72

1   **General information.** Penryn (50°10′N 5°06′W), a small port, lies approximately 1 mile W of Falmouth on Penryn River (4.70) and is used by fishing vessels and recreational craft. The channel to Exchequer Quay is marked by buoys and the quay has depths of about 4·8 m at MHWS. There are a number of local boatyards and slipways for craft of up to 50 tonnes.

2   **Submarine pipeline** (disused) extends WSW from Boyer's Cellars through Falmouth Yacht Marina across Turnpike Creek.

Chart 32
Saint Mawes Harbour

4.73

1   **General information.** Saint Mawes Harbour (50°09′N 5°01′W) lies at the entrance to Percuil River on the E side of Falmouth Harbour and provides a sheltered anchorage for yachts. The harbour is entered between Carricknath Point and Castle Point, 5 cables N.

Hazards: oyster beds on both banks of the river above Saint Mawes; submarine power cable at Percuil. See information on the chart.

2   **Dangers.** Lugo Rock lies in the entrance to the harbour, 1½ cables S of Castle Point, and is marked on its S side by Saint Mawes Light Buoy (S cardinal).

Berths. A quay which dries lies on the N side of the harbour; a light is occasionally shown from its head.

Polvarth   Amsterdam
Point   Point

S.Mawes Castle
Saint Mawes Harbour from SW (4.73)
(Original dated 2001)

(Photograph – Air Images)

Saint Just Creek

4.74

1   Saint Just Creek, 1½ miles N of Saint Mawes, is entered close S of Messack Point (50°11′N 5°01′W) and provides sheltered anchorage for yachts. The creek dries 1½ cables within the entrance.

Overhead cable. An overhead power cable, with a safe vertical clearance of 24 m, crosses the head of the creek.

Port of Truro

Chart 32
General information

4.75

1   **Position and function.** Port of Truro embraces that part of River Fal N of Port of Falmouth, together with Penryn Harbour (4.72), the several creeks which indent the river and its estuary, and includes the small port at the city of Truro which lies on Truro River, 4½ miles above Turnaware Point (50°12′N 5°02′W).

Lighterage Quay   Sunny Corner

Truro River from SE (4.75)
(Original dated 2001)

(Photograph – Air Images)

2   Deep-water moorings, for laid-up vessels, are available on the W side of River Fal by King Harry Passage (50°13′N 5°02′W). Oil rigs can also be accommodated.

Port limit. The S limit of the port is contiguous with the N limit of Port of Falmouth, for details see 4.38.

3   **Traffic.** In 2006 the port was visited by 16 vessels totalling 27 760 dwt.

Port Authority. Carrick District Council, Harbour Office, Town Quay, Truro, Cornwall TR1 2HJ.

Limiting conditions

4.76

1   **Largest vessels handled:** Lighterage Quay (4.80) can handle vessels up to 2000 dwt, 85 m LOA and 4·4 m draught at HW.

The moorings at King Harry Passage can handle vessels up to 219 m LOA in a least depth of about 10 m.

Arrival information

4.77

1   **Pilotage** is compulsory for vessels over 60 m in length; pilots are available from Falmouth.

Harbour

4.78

1   The only commercial quay in Port of Truro is Lighterage Quay (4.80) which is situated 7 cables downriver from the city of Truro.

2   A tidal barrage consisting of a single pair of mitre gates is situated at the N end of Lighterage Quay; lights (port and starboard hand) are exhibited from the upstream and down stream ends of the structure. A waiting pontoon and walkway are situated at the down stream end of the barrage. The gates are sometimes closed for periods of up to 2 hours 20 minutes either side of HW depending upon

Ruan Creek   *Carrick Road*

Port of Truro from N (4.78)

(Original dated 1997)

(Photograph – Port of Truro Harbour Master)

the river level. Three flashing red lights on the barrage indicate the barrage is closed.

3   **Hazards.** Buoys of pyramidal shape and various colours, used for yacht racing, are moored in the port from March to September, annually. A vehicle ferry crosses River Fal at King Harry Passage, 8 cables NNE of Turnaware Point.

Submarine cables, one of which is a power cable, cross the river close N and S of the ferry crossing and are marked by beacons.

Regulations. For details of regulations in force, see 4.50.

Directions
4.79
1   **Channel.** River Fal starts at Messack Point (4.38) and ends at Ruan Creek about 2¾ miles N. The channel of River Fal, N of Saint Just Pool, has an average width of 1 cable as far as Turnaware Point, 1½ miles N, at which point the river narrows. The E side of the channel is marked by light buoys (starboard hand) between Messack Point and Turnaware Point. Concrete mooring clumps, which dry, lie near the W bank of the river 3 cables S and ½ cable N of the ferry crossing at King Harry Passage and constitute a danger to navigation; the clumps are marked by a yellow post. Truro River joins River Fal at Ruan Creek,

about 7 cables NE of King Harry Passage. At Maggoty Bank, 5 cables N of Ruan Creek, the E side of the channel of Truro River is marked by a light buoy (starboard hand). At Malpas Point (50°14′·7N 5°01′·2W), 5 cables farther N, Tresillian River forks E and dries; Truro River forks NW and continues for a farther 1½ miles to Truro the channel being marked by buoys, light buoys and beacons.

Berths
4.80
1   **Alongside berth.** Lighterage Quay has a length of 350 m. Vessels take bottom at LW. See 4.76.

Deep-water moorings. The moorings at King Harry Passage are generally used for lay-up. A maximum of 15 vessels can be accepted. See 4.76.

Port services
4.81
1   **Facilities and supplies.** Fuel can be obtained by road tanker or by bunker barge in Falmouth Bay or Carrick Roads. Small quantities of stores and provisions are available, and there is fresh water at Lighterage Quay. There are hospitals in Truro. The nearest airport is at Newquay, 24 km distant.

FALMOUTH TO FOWEY

General information

Chart 1267
Route
4.82

1 From S of Saint Anthony Head (50°08′N 5°01′W) the passage to Fowey leads ENE to abreast Dodman Point, thence NNE to Fowey, a total distance of about 20 miles.

Topography
4.83

1 Nare Head (50°12′N 4°55′W), a bold headland 79 m high, is the N entrance point to Gerrans Bay and lies 5 miles NE of Saint Anthony Head. Dodman Point (50°13′N 4°48′W) (4.87) stands out boldly and Black Head (50°18′N 4°45′W), 5 miles NNE, is a bold steep-to headland and separates Mevagissey Bay to the S from Saint Austell Bay to the N.

Exercise areas
4.84

1 For details of exercise areas, see 4.2 and information on the chart.

Rescue
4.85

1 **Coastguard rescue teams** operate from:
   Porthscatho Auxiliary Station at Pednvaden (50°11′N 4°58′W).
   Mevagissey Auxiliary Station (50°16′N 4°47′W).
   Saint Austell Auxiliary Station (50°20′N 4°45′W).
2 **National Coastwatch Institution (NCI)** stations are situated at:
   Porthscatho (50°11′·1N 4°58′·1W).
   Landrion Point (50°19′·9N 4°44′·7W).
   For details of coastguard stations see 1.101 and for NCI see 1.106.

Tidal streams
4.86

1 Tidal streams 4 miles to seaward of Gerrans Bay and Veryan Bay (50°13′N 4°51′W) are nearly rectilinear and are shown by information on the chart.

Directions
(continued from 4.24)

Principal marks
4.87

1 **Landmarks:**
   Dodman Point (50°13′N 4°48′W), a precipitous bluff with a steep E face and a gradually sloping W face with a stone cross standing on the summit of its SW extremity.
2 Daymark Beacon (stone tower, red and white bands, 26 m in height) (50°19′N 4°40′W) on Gribbin Head.
   Major light:
   Eddystone Light (50°11′N 4°16′W) (4.215).

Charts 148, 154, 1267
Falmouth to Dodman Point
4.88

1 From S of Saint Anthony Head, distant at least 2 miles, the passage leads ENE passing (with positions given from Nare Head (50°12′N 4°55′W)):
   SSE of Old Wall (5½ miles SW) (4.57); thence:

SSE of Porthmellin Head (3¾ miles SW); thence:
2 SSE of The Bizzies (2½ miles SSW), a group of rocky patches at the extremity of a spit extending 1 mile ESE from Greeb Point. Overfalls occur on, or near, these patches. Thence:
SSE of The Whelps (6 cables ESE), detached drying rocks lying 3 cables SW of Gull Rock (4.92); thence:
3 SSE of The Bellows and The Field, two rocks lying 9 cables S and 8 cables SSE, respectively, of Dodman Point (5 miles ENE). The depths for over 1 mile S of Dodman Point are irregular and there are heavy overfalls in this vicinity. In bad weather and under these conditions it is advisable to give Dodman Point a clearance of 2 miles. Special light buoys A, B and C are moored respectively 4¾ miles SSE, 3½ miles SE and 2¾ miles S, of the point in support of naval gunfire training.

4.89

1 **Useful marks:**
   Gerrans Church (spire) (50°10′·7N 4°58′·9W) distinctive from seaward.
   Carne Beacon (50°12′·6N 4°55′·6W), a mound 6 m high surmounted by a hut, stands on a hill with an elevation of 102 m; readily identified from SW.
   Saint Anthony Head Light (50°08′N 5°01′W) (4.21).

Dodman Point to Fowey
4.90

1 From a position SSE of Dodman Point (50°13′N 4°48′W) the passage then leads NNE passing (with positions given from Black Head (50°18′N 4°45′W)):
   ESE of Curran Vean (4 miles SSW), a group of drying rocks extending nearly 2 cables offshore close S of Pen-a-maen (4.111); thence:
2 ESE of Gwineas (3¼ miles S), noting Yaw Rock and depths of less than 10 m which lie up to 4 cables E of Gwineas. A light buoy (E cardinal) is moored 3 cables SE of Gwineas. Thence:
ESE of Black Head (4.83); thence:
To a position S of Gribbin Head (3¼ miles ENE) (4.87).

4.91

1 **Useful marks:**
   Mevagissey Victoria Pierhead Light (white metal tower, black base 8 m in height) (50°16′·1N 4°46′·9W).
   Fowey Light (white octagonal tower, red lantern, 6 m in height) (50°19′·6N 4°38′·8W).
   Whitehouse Point Light (red metal column, 4 m in height) (50°20′·0N 4°38′·2W).
   (Directions continue at 4.137 and for Plymouth at 4.155)

Side channels

Chart 154
South-east of Nare Head
4.92

1 **General information.** Between Gull Rock and the coast NE of Nare Head (50°12′N 4°55′W) there is a clear passage with a least depth of 6·1 m which leads from Gerrans Bay to Veryan Bay.

Chart 148
Between Gwineas and the shore
4.93

1 **General information.** The passage between Gwineas (50°15′N 4°46′W) (4.90) and the shore has a depth of

Gribbin Head and daymark from S (4.90)
(Original dated 2001)

(Photograph - Air Images)

10·7 m but its width is reduced to approximately 3 cables by a 3·4 m patch about 4½ cables SSW of Chapel Point.

Charlestown Harbour

Chart 31 plan of Charlestown Harbour
General information
4.94

1   **Position and function.** Charlestown Harbour (50°20′N 4°45′W) lies in the NW part of Saint Austell Bay. It is no longer a commercial port but is used by sailing vessels and leisure craft.

    Port Authority: Square Sail Limited, Charlestown Harbour, Charlestown, Saint Austell, Cornwall PL25 3NJ.

Limiting conditions
4.95

1   **Maximum size of vessel handled.** Vessels of up to 1050 dwt, length 56 m at 10 m beam and 58 m at 9 m beam and 3·7 m draught can be accommodated in the inner basin.

Arrival information
4.96

1   **Port radio** station operates from Charlestown which keeps watch from 2 hours before to 1 hour after HW, but only when a vessel is expected.

    Notice of ETA required: 24 hours in advance with amendments not less than 6 hours before original ETA.

Anchorage is available off the harbour in depths of 2 to 6 m, in good holding ground of firm sand.

Charlestown Harbour from SE (4.96)
(Original dated 2001)

(Photograph - Air Images)

Pilotage is compulsory for vessels over 37·5 m in length and is available from 2 hours before to 1 hour after HW.

2 **Pilot boarding place.** Charlestown is serviced by cutter from Fowey (4.131). Pilots will board vessels at a position arranged between pilots and masters of vessels. During periods of poor weather boarding may take place off Fowey (4.114), anywhere in St Austell Bay (4.108) and inside the harbour entrance.

3 **Pilotage Authority:** Fowey Harbour Commissioners.

For details of procedure see 4.131 and *Admiralty List of Radio Signals Volume 6(1).*

Harbour
4.97

1 **General layout.** The harbour consists of an inner wet basin and an outer tidal basin. The outer basin is formed by two piers and a light is exhibited on each side of the entrance. The inner wet basin is entered through lock gates. A mooring buoy is moored 2 cables SSE of the harbour entrance.

Docking signal. A red light is exhibited from a flagstaff, 10 m in height, at the N entrance when the port is closed; the signal is supplemented by notice on VHF.

Basins and berths
4.98

1 **Outer Basin** has a width of 13·7 m between the two piers and a depth of 4·3 m at MHWS, and of 3·0 m at MHWN in the entrance. The outer basin dries out at MLWS for over ½ cable beyond the entrance.

Inner Basin is entered between lock gates 10·7 m wide, with depths over the sill similar to those at the entrance to the outer basin. The lock gates are opened only when a vessel is expected. There are three berths in the inner basin.

2 **Moorings.** Holding moorings, for craft up to 15 tons, are available at LW about 2 cables S of the harbour wall; at HW craft wait in the outer harbour.

Port services
4.99

1 **Facilities.** Minor repairs can be carried out.
Supplies: fuel by road tanker; water; provisions.
Rescue, see 4.85.

Par Harbour

Chart 31 plan of Par Harbour
General information
4.100

1 **Position and function.** Par Harbour (50°21′N 4°42′W), situated at the N end of Tywardreath Bay, can be identified by several conspicuous chimneys close W of the harbour entrance. The harbour is used mainly for the export of china clay and aggregate, and for the import of some oil and timber.

2 **Traffic.** In 2006 the port handled 125 vessels totalling 253 005dwt.

Port Authority: Imerys Port Operations, Harbour Office, Par, Cornwall, PL24 2BP.

Limiting conditions
4.101

1 The harbour is tidal and vessels lie aground at LW.
Tidal levels. Mean spring range about 4·5 m; mean neap range about 2·2 m. For further information see *Admiralty Tide Tables.*

Maximum size of vessel handled. Vessels with a maximum length of 125 m, beam 13·5 m and draught of 3·4 m (5·2 m at spring tides) can be accommodated.

Arrival information
4.102

1 **Port operations.** Par Port monitors VHF radio during normal working hours and the pilots set watch from 2 hours before until 2 hours after HW. It is important that mariners should maintain contact with the radio station for purposes of amending movements, berthing or sailing instructions in light of unforeseen circumstances. Mariners may be directed at short notice to Fowey (4.114) for loading.

Notice of ETA required: 24 hours in advance with amendments as soon as possible and not less than 6 hours before arrival.

2 **Outer anchorage.** Mariners waiting to enter harbour may anchor in a convenient depth S of the harbour entrance on a sandy bottom, but should avoid anchoring inside the 10 m depth contour W of a line drawn 180° from Spit Point, 3 cables SW of the harbour entrance, where the bottom is rocky. A recommended berth, indicated on the chart, is 7½ cables SSE of the harbour entrance in depths of about 6 m. See also 4.108.

Pilotage is compulsory for all vessels over 37·5 m in length and is available from 2 hours before to 2 hours after HW.

3 **Pilot boarding place.** Par is serviced by a cutter from Fowey (4.131). Pilots will board vessels at a position arranged between pilots and masters of vessels. During periods of poor weather boarding may take place off Fowey (4.114), anywhere in St Austell Bay (4.108) and inside the harbour entrance.

4 **Pilotage authority:** Fowey Harbour Commissioners.

For procedure, see 4.131 and *Admiralty List of Radio Signals Volume 6(1).*

Tugs are not available but the pilot boat provides berthing and towage assistance.

Long Arm

Par Harbour from SE (4.102)
(Original dated 2001)

(Photograph – Air Images)

Harbour
4.103

1 **General layout.** The harbour is protected from S winds by a breakwater which extends 1¾ cables NE from a position 1 cable NE of Spit Point (50°20′·4N 4°42′·4W).

Inside the harbour there are three quays; Long Arm, on the N side, has three working berths; Short Arm and West Arm each have two working berths; Oil Berth opposite West Arm is used only for the discharge of oil and the loading of clay in slurry.

2 **Traffic signals** are shown from a mast near the SE end of Long Arm as follows:

> A red flag by day, or a red light at night, indicates that the harbour is closed, or that entry is prohibited owing to an outward movement. Mariners may only enter the harbour when neither of these signals is shown.

Directions
4.104

1 Puckey's Ground (4.108) lies in the approach to the harbour nearly 1 mile SW of the entrance which is approached from S over Par Sands. These sands lie E of the harbour and dry out as far as Killyvarder Rock (50°20'·3N 4°41'·7W) which is marked by a beacon (starboard hand). The approach passes between that rock and Bream Rocks 4 cables W.

Berths
4.105

1 **Berths.** The entrance between the head of the breakwater and the N side of the harbour is 38 m wide. An area, maintained at a level of 0·2 m above chart datum, extends from close within the harbour entrance to the head of Short Arm across the harbour to Oil Berth including Middle Dock and West Arm. West Arm Berth can accommodate vessels up to 90 m in length and Long Arm can accommodate vessels up to 125 m in length.

Port services
4.106

1 **Supplies and facilities:** marine diesel fuel, 24 hours notice required; fresh water; provisions; minor repair facilities.

Ship sanitation control and ship sanitation control exemption certificates are issued and extended at Par.

Communications: airport at Newquay, 30 km distant, with connecting flights to London.

Harbour regulations, including those affecting the loading turn of vessels are in force; copies should be obtained from the Port Authority.

Anchorages and minor harbours

Chart 148
Mevagissey Bay
4.107

1 **General information.** Mevagissey Bay is entered between Chapel Point (50°15'N 4°46'W), a low point, and Black Head, 2½ miles N, and affords good shelter from SW gales.

2 Portmellon, a sandy cove, and Mevagissey Harbour (4.112) lie in the SW corner of the bay S of Penare Point which projects into the middle of the bay. The coast NE of Pentewan, a small seaside village fronted by a sandy beach N of Penare Point, becomes craggy and precipitous and rises to Black Head (4.83).

Anchorage can be obtained in the bay in depths of 10 to 20 m, sand.

Saint Austell Bay
4.108

1 **General information.** Saint Austell Bay with Tywardreath Bay in its NE portion is entered between Black Head (50°18'N 4°45'W) and Gribbin Head, 3¼ miles ENE, and affords temporary anchorage from E or W winds.

Topography. A conspicuous building (50°20'N 4°44'W), with a conspicuous hotel 3 cables WSW, stand in the NW part of the bay.

2 **Offshore danger.** Puckey's Ground, a rocky patch, lies in the middle of Tywardreath Bay approximately 1¼ miles NW of Little Gribbin (50°19'N 4°41'W). A buoy (special) marking a diffuser at the end of an outfall is moored 3 cables SW of Puckey's Ground.

3 **Temporary anchorage** can be obtained in the W part of Saint Austell Bay approximately 7½ cables N of Black Head in a depth of 11 m, stiff clay, sheltered from W winds but noting a mussel farm, marked by light buoys (special) centred on position 50°18'·6N 4°44'·9W,, or in the E part of Tywardreath Bay N of Little Gribbin in depths of 5 to 10 m, sand, sheltered from E gales, or off Par Harbour (4.100).

Charts 154, 1267
Porthscatho
4.109

1 **General information.** Gerrans Bay is entered between Greeb Point (50°10'N 4°58'W) and Nare Head, 2¾ miles NE. From Greeb Point to the E end of Pendower Beach, at the head of the bay, the cliffs are from 6 to 12 m high, thence they rise gradually to Nare Head (4.83). Drying rocks extend 1 cable from the shores of the bay.

2 **Harbour.** Porthscatho (50°10'·7N 4°58'·3W), a fishing village on the W side of Gerrans Bay, lies in the SW corner of a small indentation which is entered between Pencabe and Pednvaden.

Berth and facilities: steep slip and a jetty which affords shelter for small craft.

Rescue, see 4.85.

Portloe
4.110

1 **General information.** Veryan Bay is entered between Nare Head (50°12'N 4°55'W) and Dodman Point, 5 miles NE. The shores of the bay are precipitous, from 6 to 60 m high, and are indented by several small coves. Rocky ledges extend up to 2 cables offshore in places.

Harbour. Portloe, a small fishing village, lies 1¾ miles NE of Nare Head.

2 **Offshore dangers.** Shag Rock lies 2 cables offshore, 5 cables NE of Portloe, and Lath Rock lies 1 mile SE of the same harbour.

Clearing bearing:
> The line of bearing 248° of Gerrans Church (4.89) midway between Nare Head and Gull Rock clears very close SSE of Lath Rock.

Chart 148
Gorran Haven
4.111

1 **General information.** Pen-a-maen (50°14'N 4°47'W) projects from the coast 1½ miles NE of Dodman Point and Chapel Point lies 1¼ miles NE.

Harbour. Gorran Haven lies 3 cables NW of Pen-a-maen at the SW end of a bay with a sandy shore and high sloping cliffs; it has a granite L-shaped pier which shelters a small boat harbour that dries. At or near HW it is possible to berth alongside the inside of the pier.

Anchorage: ENE of the pier in 2 m or more, sand.

Charts 147 plan of Mevagissey Harbour, 148
Mevagissey Harbour
4.112

1 **General information.** Mevagissey Harbour (50°16′N 4°47′W), consisting of an inner and outer harbour, is situated in the SW corner of Mevagissey Bay (4.107) and is used mainly by fishing vessels and pleasure craft. The harbour affords good shelter except in strong E winds.

Port radio station, with limited hours, operates from the port; for details see *Admiralty List of Radio Signals Volume 6(1)*.

West Quay   East Quay

Victoria Pier   North Pier

Mevagissey Harbour from E (4.112)

(Original dated 2001)

(Photograph - Air Images)

2 **Harbour.** Outer Harbour is formed by North Pier and South Pier, the entrance between the outer piers is approximately 50 m wide with a depth of 2·1 m. Rocky ledges extend from the S side of the harbour and a short distance from both sides of North Pier; the base of the seaward end of North Pier, which dries at LW, extends about 2 m from the structure. The depths in the outer harbour are from 0·3 to 2 m.

3 Inner Harbour is formed by East Quay and West Quay and has a quay frontage of more than 200 m. The harbour dries out completely to a bottom of mud on which craft can lie aground. At MHWS there is a depth of 4·3 m and at MHWN of 3·0 m in the centre of the harbour.

4 **Anchoring** is not permitted in the inner or outer harbours. Safe anchorage may be found in offshore winds ½ cable ESE of South Pier Head in depths of 4 m; larger vessels should not anchor closer than 2 cables.

5 **Supplies and facilities:** fuel; water; provisions; boatyard with slipway; landing steps.

Rescue, see 4.85.

Charts 31 plan of Par Harbour, 148
Polkerris Harbour
4.113

1 **General information.** Polkerris Harbour (50°20′N 4°41′W) lies in the NE corner of Tywardreath Bay (4.100). It is very small, and open W, but the S end of the harbour is sheltered from that direction by a pier, ½ cable long, which curves N from the S side. The harbour dries out to a bottom of sand for ¼ cable outside the pier. At MHWS the depth in the harbour is approximately 4·3 m, and at MHWN 3·0 m. The length of the quay frontage is approximately 65 m.

FOWEY HARBOUR AND APPROACHES

General information

Charts 31 plan of Fowey Harbour, 148
Position
4.114

1 Fowey Harbour (50°20′N 4°38′W) is situated at the mouth of River Fowey.

Fowey   Polruan Pool

Saint Catherine's Point   Fowey Harbour entrance from S (4.114)

(Original dated 2001)

(Photograph - Air Images)

112

Above Fowey Harbour, River Fowey is navigable by mariners in small craft at HW for 5½ miles up to the town of Lostwithiel.

Function
4.115
1   Fowey is a commercial port used mainly for the export of china clay. The port is also a yachting centre.

Topography
4.116
1   The entrance to Fowey Harbour may be identified by high land on either side. The tower and flag staff of Saint Fimbarrus Church (50°20'·1N 4°38'·2W) are prominent from the outer approaches. On the E side of the entrance the ruined tower of Saint Saviour's Church is prominent.

Port limits
4.117
1   The S limit of the port is a line joining Saint Catherine's Point (50°19'·7N 4°38'·7W) and Punch Cross Rocks, 1½ cables ESE.

Approach and entry
4.118
1   The port is approached from clear water S or E of Gribbin Head (50°19'N 4°40'W) and entered between Saint Catherine's Point and Punch Cross Rocks.

Traffic
4.119
1   In 2006 339 vessels used the port.

Port Authority
4.120
1   Fowey Harbour Commissioners, Harbour Office, Albert Quay, Fowey, Cornwall PL23 IAJ.

        Email: fhc@foweyharbour.co.uk
        Website: www.fhc@foweyharbour.co.uk

Limiting conditions

Controlling depth
4.121
1   The fairway from the entrance to Wiseman's Point, 1½ miles up the river, has a least charted depth of 6·0m. Mariners in vessels of less than 6·0 m draught can enter the harbour at any time, otherwise according to the height of tide.

Deepest and longest berth
4.122
1   Deepest No 8 Quay (50°20'·8N 4°38'·2W). Longest Nos 5 and 6 Quays

Tidal levels
4.123
1   See information in *Admiralty Tide Tables*. Mean spring range about 4·8 m; mean neap range about 2·3 m.

Density of water
4.124
1   Density: 1·025 g/cm^3.

Maximum size of vessel handled
4.125
1   A vessel of 17 000 dwt, 164 m LOA, and 8·5 m draught has used the port. A cruise vessel of 28 000 gt has berthed on buoys in the lower harbour.

Arrival information

Vessel traffic service
4.126
1   A vessel traffic and information service is operated throughout 24 hours.

Port radio
4.127
1   A port radio station, with limited hours, operates from the port. There is also a pilotage radio station which operates from 2 hours before to 1 hour after the vessel's ETA. For further details see *Admiralty List of Radio Signals Volume 6(1)*.

Notice of ETA required
4.128
1   ETA: 24 hours in advance to the agents or direct to the pilots, with amendments as soon as possible and not later than 6 hours before arrival; for details see *Admiralty List of Radio Signals Volume 6(1)*.

Outer anchorage
4.129
1   Anchorage may be obtained about 5 cables S of Saint Catherine's Point (50°19'·7N 4°38'·7W) in depths of 15 m, as indicated on the chart.

Submarine cables
4.130
    Submarine cables, including a power cable, of which the landward ends are marked on each shore by yellow diamond–shaped marks bearing the legend "SUBMARINE CABLES", whose positions can best be seen from the chart, are laid in the river entrance between Fowey and Polruan.

Pilotage and tugs
4.131
1   **Pilotage** is compulsory for all vessels over 37·5 m in length except HM ships, foreign warships and those exempt by law, and is available throughout 24 hours.

    Pilot boarding place. In normal weather conditions pilots will board vessels up to one mile from the harbour entrance. During poor weather conditions the boarding position may be varied, and include inside the harbour entrance.

2   **Pilot launch:** black hull, orange upperworks.

    Tugs are available and are compulsory for vessels over 92 m in length.

    Harbour Directions require that ships over 92 m in length swing in the lower harbour using one tug, and are then towed stern first and dragging an anchor to a loading berth. Vessels over 102 m in length use two tugs for swinging. Tugs meet the ship off the harbour entrance.

Traffic regulations
4.132
1   The following regulations are extracts from the Fowey Harbour Byelaws:

        The master of any vessel exceeding 30·48 m (100 ft) registered length (or overall length in the case of a hovercraft) shall not navigate his vessel north of a line between Prime Cellars and Pottery Corner without having first obtained the permission of the harbour master to do so.

2   A vessel entering, leaving, using or navigating within the harbour shall not without the express permission of the harbour master be navigated at a speed exceeding 6 kn over the ground.

A vessel exceeding 30·48 m (100 ft) registered length and proceeding in the same direction as another vessel shall not overtake and pass that other vessel by night.

3   No vessel exceeding 30·48 m (100 ft) registered length shall at any time be moved from any moorings to any other moorings, or to any commercial berth or vice-versa, or between commercial berths, or from any berth to proceed to sea, unless the master or his agent shall have previously notified the harbour master of such proposed movement or sailing.

4   Vessels of less than 20 m, vessels crossing the channel, and sailing vessels, must not impede the passage of large commercial vessels.

Any vessel or craft not fitted with navigation lights must display a light during the hours of darkness and during periods of reduced visibility.

Regulations concerning entry
4.133
1   **Dangerous and polluting goods.** See 1.68 and 1.76.

Harbour

General layout
4.134
1   Fowey Harbour is a river port lying with its facilities within and along the river banks. The main berthing areas are located between Town Quay (50°20'·1N 4°38'·0W) and Wiseman's Point (50°20'·8N 4°38'·2W), 8 cables farther N. The alongside berths (4.142) are along the W bank. There are buoy berths (4.142) close N of the alongside berths. The remaining buoy berths lie off the E bank; vessels lie stern-to at these moorings, with anchors down, heading either up or down river, depending upon their length and or draught.

Inch's Quay   *Penleath Point*

Town Quay   *Brawn Point*

Fowey Harbour from S (4.134)

(Original dated 2001)

(Photograph - Air Images)

Hazards
4.135
1   **Ferries** cross the fairway:
Between Whitehouse Point (50°20'·0N 4°38'·3W) and Polruan, 2½ cables SSE, in summer and between Fowey Town Quay (50°20'·1N 4°38'·0W) and Polruan in winter.

Between Lower Carn Point (50°20'·4N 4°38'·0W) and Bodinnick, 1¼ cables ESE.

2   **Salmon fishing** takes place between Wiseman's Reach (50°20'·9N 4°38'·2W) and Golant, 7 cables N, as indicated on the chart. Anchoring in this area is prohibited during the fishing season (April to December) when the area is marked by buoys.

Tidal streams
4.136
1   Tidal streams in the harbour entrance begin as follows:

Interval from HW Devonport (Dover)	*Direction*
+0610 (+0030)	In-going
−0015 (−0555)	Out-going

The maximum in-going and out-going spring rates are 1 kn and 1½ kn respectively.

Directions for entering harbour
(continued from 4.91)

Landmarks
4.137
1   Daymark Beacon (50°19'·0N 4°40'·4W) (4.87).
White House (50°19'·6N 4°38'·0W) at Polruan.
Castle (ruins) on Saint Catherine's Point (50°19'·7N 4°38'·7W).

Approaches
4.138
1   **From south-west.** From a position S of Gribbin Head, by day the line of bearing 026° of Saint Fimbarrus Church (tower and flagstaff) (50°20'·1N 4°38'·2W) just open SE of Whitehouse Point Light (4.91), 1½ cables SSW, or by night, the line of bearing 025° of Whitehouse Point Light, which shows white between the bearings of 022° to 032°, leads in the approach passing (with positions given from Saint Catherine's Point (50°19'·7N 4°38'·7W)):

2   ESE of Cannis Rock (1¼ miles SW), the SE-most danger off Gribbin Head. The rocks are marked on their S side by a light buoy (S cardinal). Thence:
ESE of a wreck with a depth of 7 m over it (8 cables SSW); thence:

3   ESE of a 4·6 m patch (4 cables SSW) at the outer end of a spit extending E from the coast; thence:
ESE of Fowey Light (4.91); thence:
Between Saint Catherine's Point and Punch Cross Rocks (1¾ cables ESE), a beacon (white, cross topmark) marks the outer rock.

4.139
1   **From east.** By day, keep parallel with the coast and 1 mile offshore until Saint Fimbarrus Church comes open of the E entrance point of the harbour. The track then leads N thence NNE to join the approach from SW (as above) on the line of bearing 026° of Saint Fimbarrus Church.

2   By night, alter course N when in the green sector (017°–022°) of Whitehouse Point Light to join the approach from SW on the line of bearing 025° of Whitehouse Point Light.
    Useful mark:
    Fowey Light (50°19'·6N 4°38'·8W) (4.91).

Side channel
4.140
1   **Gribbin Head** (50°19'N 4°40'W) (4.87) is bordered by rocks on which the sea breaks heavily in bad weather and Cannis Rock (4.138) lies 2½ cables SE of the head. There is a narrow passage between this rock and the coast.

Directions. From S of Gribbin Head the alignment (048½°) of the ruins of a castle on Polruan Point (50°19'·8N 4°38'·3W) with the monument (4.141) on Penleath Point, 5 cables NE, leads through the passage in a least depth of about 3·0 m.

River
4.141

1 From a position in mid-channel between Saint Catherine's Point and Punch Cross Rocks the track continues NNE passing (with positions given from Saint Catherine's Point):

Between Mundy Rocks (¾ cable N) and Lamp Rock (1½ cables E) marked by a beacon (starboard hand); thence:

WNW of Polruan Point (2½ cables ENE).

2 The track then continues generally NE thence N in mid-channel, to the berth or buoys, as convenient.

Caution. Mariners are warned not to pass E of ships laid up on the E side of the fairway between Penleath Point (50°20'·1N 4°37'·8W) and Bodinnick, 3 cables N, as they may be connected to the shore by breast lines.

3 **Useful marks:**
Castle (ruins) (50°19'·8N 4°38'·3W) on Polruan Point.
Tower (50°20'·2N 4°38'·2W) on Place House.
Monument (50°20'·1N 4°37'·7W) on Penleath Point.
Light (lamp box) (50°19'·7N 4°38'·7W) on the NE side of Saint Catherine's Point, visible only from inside the harbour.

4 Light (lamp box) (50°19'·7N 4°38'·4W) on the coast close E of Lamp Rock; visible only from inside the harbour.
Lights (50°19'·8N 4°38'·1W) on Polruan Town Quay.
Lights (red post, 2 m in height) (50°20'·0N 4°38'·2W) on N Pier Head.
Lights (50°20'·1N 4°38'·0W) on Fowey Town Quay.

Berths

General layout
4.142

1 **No 1 Swing Buoy** (50°20'·0N 4°38'·0W), moored 1½ cables SW of Penleath Point, has swinging ground in the vicinity with a least charted depth of 5·6 m. The buoy is primarily used as a mooring for vessels up to 149 m in length, with two anchors down, heading upstream.

2 **Mooring buoys.** No 2 Buoy and No 3 Buoy (50°20'·2N 4°37'·8W), 1½ cables N of Penleath Point, for vessels up to 137 m in length and 6·1 m draught, heading up river (ebb tide berth); vessels of up to 200 m in length and 8·0 m draught can be accommodated stern-to with anchors down to seaward (flood tide berth).

No 5 Buoy (50°20'·5N 4°37'·8W) in Lew Roads is not used for mooring, being attached to the pontoon close NE, which is used for small commercial and leisure craft.

No 8 Buoy (50°20'·8N 4°38'·3W), ½ cable W of Wiseman's Point, for vessels up to 165 m in length, stern-to with anchors down to seaward; deep-draught vessels are required to run breast lines to No 8 Jetty.

3 **Alongside berths.** There are five berths on the W bank of the river, four of which are in use. The longest No 5/6 Quay (50°20'·7N 4°37'·9W) with a length of 168 m has a least charted depth of 6·0 m alongside. No 9 Buoy on the W bank of the river close off Upper Carne Point is for use by vessels lying at No 5/6 Quay.

No 8 Quay (50°20'·8N 4°38'·2W) can accept vessels up to 164 m length with a draught of 8·5 m.

Lower Carn Point   Upper Carn Point   Polmort Point

Lew Roads from S (4.142)

(Original dated 2001)

(Photograph - Air Images)

Port services

Repairs
4.143

1 **Slipway** at Polruan (4.135) operated by Fowey Harbour Commissioners: length 216·4 m; lifting capacity 600 tonnes; for vessels up to 4 m draught.
Boatyards: several.
Repairs: limited facilities.

Other facilities
4.144

1 **Ship sanitation control and ship sanitation control exemption certificates** are issued and extended at Fowey.
Hospital in Fowey.
Compass adjustment can be arranged.
Refuse barge: moored (April to October) off Pont Pill (50°20'·0N 4°37'·6W).

Supplies
4.145

1 **Fuel.** Diesel can be obtained at Polruan Town Quay for vessels up to 20 m and bunkers can be delivered by road.
Fresh water is laid on to the quays.
Provisions and stores can be obtained.

Communications
4.146

1 **Local airport** at Newquay, distant 40 km, with connecting flights to London, The Scilly Isles and The Continent.

Rescue
4.147

1 **Coastguard Rescue Team:** Polruan Rescue Team (50°20'N 4°38'W).
For details of coastguard stations see 1.100 and for lifeboats 1.113.
Lifeboats. An all weather lifeboat and an inshore lifeboat are stationed in Fowey Harbour.
National Coast Watch Institute keep a visual watch and a listening watch on VHF 16 from the Polruan CG look-out (50°19'·6N 4°38'·1W) from 0800 to dusk during the winter and 0800 to 2030 during the summer.

Polridmouth

General information
4.148

1   Polridmouth (50°19′N 4°40′W), a small cove situated about 1 mile WSW of the entrance to Fowey Harbour, affords anchorage to mariners in small craft in N winds; the cove is not sheltered from the prevailing winds when a heavy swell then sweeps into the cove. Anchorage can be obtained about 3½ cables ENE of the Daymark Beacon on Gribbin Head.

FOWEY TO PLYMOUTH

General information

Chart 1267
Route
4.149

1   From S of Gribbin Head (50°19′N 4°40′W) the passage to Plymouth leads E, about 17 miles, passing N of Eddystone Rocks (50°11′N 4°16′W).

Topography
4.150

1   Pencarrow Head (50°19′N 4°36′W), 80 m high, lies 1¾ miles E of the entrance to Fowey Harbour and separates Lantic Bay, on its W side, from Lantivet Bay on its E side. The cliffs forming this part of the coast vary in height from 15 to 90 m and are fronted by drying rocks which extend up to 1 cable offshore. Nealand Point, identifiable by its overhanging cliff, lies 2 miles E of Pencarrow Head.

Exercise areas
4.151

1   For details of exercise areas, see 4.2 and 4.161, also information on the chart.

Measured distance
4.152

1   Between Talland Bay (50°20′N 4°30′W) and Looe Island, 1½ miles E, there is a measured distance in one section.

    West limit marks. Two beacons (white with black stripe, 11 and 15 m in height) (50°20′·3N 4°29′·3W) situated close E of Talland church, in line 356°.

2   East limit marks. Two beacons (white with black stripe, approximately 11 m in height) (50°20′·9N 4°27′·8W) situated 5 cables NW of Hannafore Point, in line 356°.

    Distance: 1852·9 m.
    Running track: 086°–266°.

Rescue
4.153

1   **Coastguard.** Rescue Team at Looe is situated on Hannafore Point (50°21′N 4°27′W).

    Lifeboat. An inshore lifeboat is stationed at Looe (50°21′N 4°27′W).

    For details of coastguard stations, see 1.101 and for lifeboats 1.113.

2   **VHF Direction finding station**, for emergency use only, operates from Rame Head (50°19′N 4°13′W), for details see 1.105 and *Admiralty List of Radio Signals Volume 2.*

Tidal streams
4.154

1   At a position 3 miles S of Looe Island (50°20′N 4°27′W) the streams are rotary in a clockwise direction; for details see information on the chart.

Directions
(continued from 4.91)

Principal marks
4.155

1   **Landmarks:**
    Daymark Beacon (50°19′N 4°40′W) (4.87) on Gribbin Head.
    Rame Head (50°19′N 4°13′W) (4.215).
    Major light:
    Eddystone Light (50°11′N 4°16′W) (4.215).
    Banjo Pier Light (red metal column, 6 m in height) (50°21′N 4°27′W).

Other aids to navigation
4.156

1   **Racon:** Eddystone Light (50°11′N 4°16′W).
    For details see *Admiralty List of Radio Signals Volume 2.*

Charts 148, 1267
Fowey to Looe Island
4.157

1   From a position SSW of the entrance to Fowey Harbour (50°20′N 4°38′W) the passage leads E passing (with positions given from Nealand Point (50°19′N 4°32′W)):
    S of Blackbottle Rock (3 miles W); thence:
    S of Pencarrow Head (2 miles W) (4.150); thence:
    S of Udder Rock (1 mile WSW), marked on its S side by a light buoy (S cardinal); and:

2   N of Owen Rock (3 miles SSW); thence:
    S of Larrick Rock (2 cables W); and:
    N of Middle Rocks (4½ miles S); thence:
    S of Downend Shoals (1½ miles E); thence:

3   S of Hore Stone (2½ miles ENE); the coastal bank, with depths of less than 10 m, extends nearly 4 cables SSE from Hore Stone; thence:
    S of Ranneys Light Buoy (S cardinal) (4 miles E), marking The Ranneys, rocks which dries 4·6 m and extend 2½ cables SE from Looe Island. A depth of 9·4 m lies 6 cables SSE of The Ranneys and closer to the track.

4.158

1   **Positioning and clearing marks:**
    The alignment (020°) of Shag Rock (white mark) (50°19′·6N 4°33′·5W) with a beacon (white stone, 5 m in height), close NNE, indicates the approximate position of Udder Rock.
    The line of bearing 283° of a white mark (20°19′·6N 4°36′·9W) on the W side of Lantic Bay just open of Pencarrow Head, 6 cables ESE, indicates the position of Udder Rock.

2   The red sector of Fowey Light (50°20′N 4°39′W) (4.91) between the bearings of 284° and 295° clears S of Udder Rock.
    The line of bearing 266° of Daymark Beacon (4.87) on Gribbin Head (50°19′N 4°40′W) open S of Nealand Point, 5 miles E, clears S of The Ranneys.

3   **Useful marks:**
    Light (white concrete pillar, 3 m in height) (50°20′N 4°31′W) on Spy House Point.
    Monument (50°20′N 4°30′W) on Downend Point.

Charts 148, 1900, 1267, 1613
Looe Island to Plymouth
4.159

1   From a position S of Looe Island (50°20′N 4°27′W) the passage continues E passing (with positions given from Rame Head (50°19′N 4°13′W)):

S of Knight Errant Patch (6 miles WNW) at the SE end of the coastal bank extending 2 miles offshore from Seaton Beach; a 5 m patch lies near the SW end of the bank. And:

2   N of Hand Deeps (7½ miles SW) marked by a light buoy (W cardinal); thence:

N of Eddystone Rocks (8 miles S) (4.218), noting two data buoys (special) moored in position 50°15′N 4°13′W.; thence:

To a position S of Rame Head, distant 1 mile.

4.160

1   **Clearing bearings:**

The alignment (093°) of Rame Head (50°19′N 4°13′W) with Great Mew Stone, 4½ miles E, clears S of all dangers between Polperro and Rame Head.

Hand Deeps are covered by the red auxiliary light (110·5°-130·5°), which is shown from a window on the NW side of Eddystone Lighthouse, below the main light.

2   **Useful marks:**

Banjo Pier Light (4.155).

Beacon (elevation 128 m, diamond topmark) (50°20′N 4°14′W).

Radio Mast (50°19′N 4°13′W), 23 m in height standing at an elevation of 102 m and marked by a red obstruction light, 4 cables NE of Rame Head.

(Directions continue at 4.215
and for Start Point at 4.256)

Whitsand Bay

Charts 1900, 1267
General information
4.161

1   **Description.** Whitsand Bay lies between The Long Stone (50°22′N 4°20′W) and Rame Head, 5 miles ESE. The shores of the bay are rugged, with cliffs of from 30 to 75 m high.

Portwrinkle (50°22′N 4°18′W), 1 mile E of The Long Stone, is a small harbour, protected by a pier, which dries out; it is used by small fishing vessels. The entrance to the harbour is marked by a small stone beacon.

2   **Firing range.** Tregantle Rifle Ranges lie 1¾ mile E of Portwrinkle (50°22′N 4°18′W). The limits of the ranges are marked by beacons (black and white bands, conical topmarks). When firing is in progress red flags are displayed by day, and red lights are exhibited at night, from flagstaffs in the vicinity of the range. See also 4.2 for details of general exercise area.

Anchorage
4.162

1   Anchorage for small vessels, sheltered from offshore winds, can be obtained off Polhawn Cove in the SE part of Whitsand Bay.

Recommended berth: Queener Point (50°19′N 4°14′W) in line with the W edge of Rame Head, 4 cables S, in depths of 6 m, sand.

2   **Dangers.** A wreck with a depth of 3·2 m over it lies 8¼ cables NW of Queener Point and a dangerous wreck

lies 1¼ miles NW of the same point. Both wrecks are marked by a light buoy (port hand) moored 1 mile WNW of Queener Point. A rock with a depth of 4·7 m over it and Peader Rock lie 4 cables NNW and 1 cable WSW, respectively, of the same point. Coastal shipping is advised to keep outside the 10 m depth contour of Whitsand Bay.

3   **Spoil ground and explosives dumping ground (disused)** lies 1½ miles W of Rame Head.

Minor harbours

Chart 148 plan of Polperro Harbour
Polperro
4.163

1   **General information.** Polperro (50°20′N 4°31′W), a small tidal harbour used by yachts and small fishing vessels, lies at the head of a narrow inlet which is about ¼ cable wide between the drying rocky ledges which project from either side.

West Pier

Peak Rock   *East Pier*

Polperro Harbour from SE (4.163)

(Original dated 2001)

(Photograph - Air Images)

2   The harbour is formed by two piers, with a width of 9·8 m between the pierheads; a light (post, 3 m in height) is exhibited from the head of West Pier. East Pier projects a short distance from the N shore outside the inner piers and gives protection to the entrance. The harbour dries, but has depths of 3·4 m at MHWS and of 1·5 m at MHWN.

3   The approach is dangerous in strong SE or S winds or with a ground swell; under these conditions the harbour is closed by a storm gate between West Pier and the pier close NE. This gate does not impound the water and the harbour will dry at LW.

Harbour signals. A black ball displayed by day on West Pier denotes that the harbour is closed for navigation. At night, when the harbour is closed, the light on West Pier shows red.

4   **Directions.** The alignment (310°) of the S face of East Pier with the E face of West Pier leads through the outer part of the inlet passing between the drying ledges extending from Spy House Point (50°19′·8N 4°30′·7W) (4.158) from which a light is exhibited and The Polca, a rock at the entrance of the inlet, ½ cable SW, in a least depth of 1·8 m.

Anchorage is available outside the piers; the holding is poor.

Charts 148, 147 plan of Looe Harbour

Looe Harbour

4.164

1   **General information.** Looe Harbour (50°21′N 4°27′W) lies at the mouth of River Looe and is used by fishing vessels and pleasure craft. The town is divided into two parts, East Looe and West Looe, lying on either side of the river mouth. The river is spanned by a stone bridge 4 cables within the entrance. The Harbour Authority is Looe Harbour Commissioners; harbour offices are situated on East Quay. The roadstead in Looe Bay affords good shelter from W winds.

2   **Limiting conditions.** The harbour is tidal and dries and can accommodate vessels up to 16 m in length and 2·9 m draught.

    Tidal levels. Mean spring range about 4·8 m; mean neap range about 2·2 m. For further information see *Admiralty Tide Tables.*

3   **Arrival information.** Anchorage can be obtained on the line of bearing 308° of Saint Mary's Church tower at East Looe, 8½ cables SE of the pier head, as indicated on the chart, in depths of 12 m, mud. Smaller craft can anchor nearer the harbour entrance on approximately the same line of bearing, and 2¾ cables SE of the pier head in the red sector of the pier head light, in lesser depths, sand. Pilots are not available. The harbour speed limit is 5 kn.

4   **Harbour.** Banjo Pier extends ¾ cable ESE from the N entrance point of the harbour; pleasure vessels sometimes lie alongside its end. Stone quays extend along both sides of the river fronting the two sides of the town. Off the E quay there are depths of 3·8 to 4·3 m at MHWS and of 2·6 to 3·1 m at MHWN, with approximately 0·3 m less alongside the quay. The lower quay wall at East Looe, W of Saint Mary's Church, has a concrete toe-beam at the base of the wall which extends about 3·7 m into the river; this toe-beam may be exposed at LW. Alongside the W quay there are depths of 2·6 to 3·5 m at MHWS and of 1·4 m to 2·3 m at MHWN. The bed of the harbour is mainly shingle, which dries up to 2·8 m, and in the centre there is a drying sandy bank extending 2 cables S from the bridge to abreast Saint Nicholas Church on the W side of the harbour. A narrow stream, 15 m wide, and from 0·3 to 0·6 m deep, flows close off the E quay when the remainder of the harbour is dry.

5   A submarine power cable and pipeline cross the river abreast Saint Nicholas Church and a gas pipeline crosses the river above the bridge, see 1.64 for details of caution.

    A red flag is displayed from the root of the pier when conditions outside the harbour are unsuitable for boats, or when the tide has started to fall.

    Tidal streams in the harbour can attain a rate of 5 kn at springs on both the in-going and out-going streams.

4.165

1   **Directions.** Approaching from W the track passes 1 mile S of Looe Island (50°20′N 4°27′W). When on the alignment (323°) of Saint Mary's Church tower with Banjo Pier Light (4.160), the track leads N for the roadstead and thence NW for the harbour entrance.

    At night approach the harbour from E on the line of bearing 275° of Banjo Pier Light.

2   **Useful marks:**
      Mid Main Light Beacon (E cardinal) (50°20′·5N 4°26′·9W).
      White Rock Light Beacon (red post) (50°21′·0N 4°27′·0E).

3   **Facilities:** 11 m boat grid.

    Supplies: marine diesel oil and petrol; fresh water; provisions.

    Rescue, see 4.153.

4.166

1   **Boat passage.** There is a boat passage between Looe Island (50°20′N 4°27′W) and the mainland from Portnadler Bay to Looe Bay but this can only be used near HW. Local knowledge is required.

Banjo Pier

Looe Harbour from SE (4.164)

(Original dated 2001)

(Photograph – Air Images)

PLYMOUTH TO START POINT

GENERAL INFORMATION

Chart 1613
Area covered
4.167

1   This section covers the coast from Plymouth to Start Point, a distance of about 19 miles and is arranged as follows:

> Plymouth and approaches (4.168)
> Plymouth to Start Point (4.251)

PLYMOUTH AND APPROACHES

General information

Charts 30, 1967, 1901, 1902, 871
Position
4.168

1   The Dockyard Port of Plymouth (50°22′N 4°11′W) lies at the mouth of River Tamar and River Plym, and embraces the commercial harbours of Millbay Docks, the Cattewater and Sutton Harbour, together with HM Naval Base Devonport.

The city of Plymouth lies on the N side of Plymouth Sound.

Function
4.169

1   The port is a major naval dockyard, a ferry port and an important port of call for cruise liners and cargo ships, including refined oil products. Plymouth Sound and its environs provide a centre for numerous sailing and other leisure boat activities.

Topography
4.170

1   **West side.** Rame Head (50°19′N 4°13′W) (4.215) a prominent headland, serves to identify the entrance to Plymouth Sound. Penlee Point, 1½ miles ENE, is high, dark and rocky. On Picklecombe Point (50°20′·6N 4°10′·3W), the NE entrance point to Cawsand Bay, there is an old fort which has been modernised and converted into flats.

Redding Point

Plymouth Sound – Picklecombe Point
and Fort Picklecombe from SSE (4.170)

(Original dated 2005)

(Photograph - HMS Scott)

2   Drakes's Island or Saint Nicholas's Island (50°21′·3N 4°09′·2W), a prominent cliffy island surrounded by drying rocky ledges, lies in the NW part of Plymouth Sound.

North side. On the N side of Plymouth Sound there are numerous conspicuous or prominent landmarks, see 4.216.

3   **East side.** Great Mew Stone (50°18′N 4°06′W) (4.215) on the E side of the entrance is a conspicuous mark.

The coast N of Staddon Point (50°20′·2N 4°07′·6W) consists of high steep cliffs.

Historic wrecks and historical notes
4.171

1   **Historic wrecks** The sites of historic and military wrecks are protected from unauthorised interference; for further details see *Annual Summary of Admiralty Notices to Mariners.*

Restricted areas. Historic and military wrecks, the positions of which can be seen on the chart, lie within the Port of Plymouth and its approaches. They are situated with reference to the following salient points:

2   Penlee Point (50°19′N 4°11′W):

> 4¼ miles W.
> 2 cables WSW.
> 6½ cables SW; (HMS *Coronation*).

Mount Batten Tower (50°21′·6N 4°07′·8W):

> 1½ cables NNE; (dated about 1520).

4.172

1   **Historical note.** Smeaton Tower (50°22′N 4°08′W) (4.216) was originally erected on Eddystone Rocks by John Smeaton in 1759. Constructed of granite it was the first traditionally shaped lighthouse to be designed. The rock foundation was found to be unsafe and in 1882 the tower was moved to its present position on The Hoe, where, no longer used as a lighthouse, it stands as a monument of historic interest.

Port limits
4.173

1   The limits of the port are given in Appendix I and are shown on the chart. The outer limits extend from Rame Head (50°19′N 4°13′W) to Shag Stone, nearly 4 miles E.

Approach and entry
4.174

1   The port is approached from clear water and entered between Penlee Point (50°19′N 4°11′W) and Great Mew Stone, 3¼ miles ESE, passing either side of Plymouth Breakwater (50°20′N 4°09′W). The recommended track passes W of the breakwater.

Traffic
4.175

1   In 2006 1054 vessels totalling 4 712 463 dwt visited the port.

Port Authority
4.176

1   **The Dockyard Port of Plymouth** is a naval port, under the control of the Queen's Harbour Master (QHM), and is subject to the rules and regulations set out in *The Dockyard Port of Plymouth Order* 1999 given in Appendix I.

QHM's Office is situated adjacent to Longroom Port Control Station (50°21′·8N 4°09′·4W), near the W entrance to Millbay Docks.

Address. Queen's Harbour Master Plymouth, Longroom House, Stonehouse Barracks, Plymouth, PL1 3RT.

4.177

1   **Commercial harbours:**

Millbay Docks, Associated British Ports, Port Office, Millbay Docks, Plymouth PL1 3EF.

Cattewater Harbour, Cattewater Harbour Commissioners, 2 The Barbican, Plymouth, PL1 2LR.

Limiting conditions

Controlling depths
4.178

1   **Western Channel.** The least dredged depth in Western Channel (4.204) as far as C Mooring Buoy (50°20'·3N 4°08'·9W) is 11·0 m (2006).

Plymouth Sound. The least dredged depth on the recommended track through Plymouth Sound is 8·6 m (2006).

2   **Eastern Channel.** The least charted depth in the approach to Eastern Channel (4.204) is 5·6 m in position 50°19'·6N 4°08'·1W. This depth is close E of the 354½° alignment (4.224) but outside the white sector of the light on the E head of Plymouth Breakwater. It is advisable to allow 2 m for scend and for the inequalities of the rocky bottom, for details see 4.184.

3   **Cobbler Channel** (50°22'N 4°08'W) (4.210), the approach to Cattewater, has a dredged depth of 5·5 m (2006).

Cattewater. The channel through Cattewater is dredged to 5·0 m (1995-2006) apart from a number of shoaler patches between 4·0 to 4·7 m whose positions can best be seen on the chart. Dredging takes place to reduce siltation.

Vertical clearances
4.179

1   **Bridges.** Minimum vertical clearances under Royal Albert Bridge and Tamar Bridge, at the N end of Hamoaze, at Saltash (50°24'·5N 4°12'·5W) are 30 m and 35 m, respectively.

Deepest and longest berths
4.180

1   **HM Naval Base.** The deepest and longest berths in HM Naval Base, Devonport are:

South Yard (50°22'N 4°11'W); Rubble Jetty and No 1 Jetty (4.236).

North Yard (50°23'N 4°11'W); sea wall S of No 5 basin and Weston Mill Lake Jetty (4.237).

Hamoaze; Yonderberry Point Oil Jetty (50°23'·0N 4°11'·7W) (4.238).

River Tamar; Ernesettle Pier (50°24'·7N 4°12'·1W) (4.238).

4.181

1   **Commercial harbours.** The deepest and longest commercial berths in Millbay Docks and Cattewater are:

Millbay Docks; West Wharf (50°21'·8N 4°09'·4W) (4.239).

Cattewater; Cattedown Wharves (50°21'·7N 4°07'·0W) and Victoria Wharves (50°21'·9N 4°07'·5W) (4.241).

Tidal levels.
4.182

1   Mean spring range about 4·7 m; mean neap range about 2·2 m. For further information see *Admiralty Tide Tables*.

Maximum size of vessels handled
4.183

1   **Millbay Docks:** 8·5 m draught; 200 m LOA at West Wharf.

2   **Cattewater:** Vessels of up to 150 m in length at Cattedown Wharves.

Sea state
4.184

1   **Scend** is occasionally experienced in Eastern Channel with S winds.

Arrival information

Vessel traffic service
4.185

1   **Vessel traffic service** is in operation throughout 24 hours from Longroom Port Control (4.176), near the entrance to Millbay Docks, and is mandatory for vessels over 20 m in length. The positions of reporting points are shown on the charts. For full details see *Admiralty List of Radio Signals Volume 6(1)*.

Notice of ETA required
4.186

1   **ETA:** 24 hours in advance, or on leaving the previous port if later.

Vessels carrying dangerous and polluting goods. ETA 24 hours in advance, including description of cargo, substance identification number, quantity or weight, and the appropriate classification in accordance with current legislation. See 1.72 and *Admiralty List of Radio Signals Volume 6(1)*

Outer anchorages
4.187

1   **South of Plymouth Breakwater** (50°20'N 4°09'W) there are three numbered anchorage berths, 21, 22 and 23, as shown on the chart, situated 6 and 9 cables and 1¼ miles SSW, respectively, from Plymouth Breakwater Fort.

2   **Cawsand Bay** (50°20'N 4°12'W). Anchorage can be obtained sheltered from all except SE winds. Mariners should anchor clear of the recommended track for deep-draught vessels and of the DG range. Numbered anchorage berths are shown on the chart.

Pilotage
4.188

1   Pilotage is compulsory for:

All vessels over 50 m LOA proceeding to or from an alongside, or buoy berth in the port

All vessels over 50 m LOA not carrying navigational charts of Plymouth of a scale of 1:12,500 or larger and which show all numbered anchorages.

All vessels over 100 m LOA proceeding within the area N of a line joining Maker Point Lighthouse, Plymouth Breakwater and Staddon Point.

2   All vessels over 125 m LOA proceeding to an anchorage in Cawsand Bay.

All vessels over 150 m LOA proceeding N of a line from Penlee point to Shag Stone.

All vessels carrying hazardous, noxious or polluting cargoes, including those vessels not gas-freed from a previous cargo proceeding to or from a berth in the port.

3   At QHM's discretion, the following vessels may be exempted from compulsory pilotage:

HM Ships.

Government owned ships and foreign warships and auxiliaries taking up or leaving a Ministry of Defence anchorage or berth.

Any vessel proceeding between the Sound and a Ministry of Defence berth.

4   **Availability.** Pilots are available throughout 24 hours.

Location. Plymouth Pilots, for commercial vessels, are located at Cattewater Harbour (4.201). Ministry of Defence Pilots, for Naval berths or buoys, are located at Longroom Port Control adjacent to Millbay Docks.

5   **Boarding place.** For vessels over 150 m LOA the pilot boards 7·5 cables SE of Penlee Point and for vessels under 150 m LOA, the pilot boards 7·5 cables SW of the W end of Plymouth Breakwater, as shown on the charts, having first established direct communication with the vessel requiring pilotage service.

Pilot vessel is a dark blue boat with white upperworks and yellow top, with the word PILOT in black on both sides of the wheelhouse. The pilot vessel for military vessels is a black boat with white upperworks.

Tugs
4.189
1   Tugs are available for the commercial harbours.

Ministry of Defence tugs may also be made available through the operating company or through QHM.

Local knowledge
4.190
1   Local knowledge, or the assistance of a pilot, is advisable for mariners proceeding through the Cattewater.

Traffic regulations
4.191
1   **Speed limits** exist in certain areas N of Plymouth Breakwater (50°20′N 4°09′W), for details see Appendix I.

Prohibited anchorages. Anchorage is prohibited in those areas shown on current Admiralty charts. For details, see Appendix I.

Prohibited area. Entry to Weston Mill Lake (50°23′·5N 4°11′·4W) is prohibited to commercial and recreational craft.

2   **Traffic rules and regulations.** Plymouth Local Notices to Mariners modify and amplify certain traffic rules and regulations in *The Dockyard Port of Plymouth Order 1999* as given in Appendix I; copies of these local Notices to Mariners can be obtained from QHM or viewed online at www.qhmplymouth.org.uk.

4.192
1   **Cattewater Harbour.** The whole of the Cattewater comprises a "narrow channel" for the purposes of Rule 9 of *International Regulations for Preventing Collisions at Sea (1972)*. Large vessels requiring a clear channel are to sound at least five short and rapid blasts.

2   Outbound vessels over 20 m LOA have right-of-way over inbound vessels and vessels crossing or joining the fairway. Inbound vessels over 20 m LOA have right-of-way over vessels crossing or joining the fairway.

Quarantine
4.193
1   **Quarantine anchorage** is situated in the S part of Jennycliff Bay, entered between Ramscliff Point (50°20′·6N 4°07′·7W) and Dunstone Point, 7 cables N, E of a line drawn 351° from Bovisand Pierhead.

For full details regarding quarantine see 1.85.

Notice of medical requirements
4.194
1   No advanced notice required.

Harbour
General layout
4.195
1   **Plymouth Sound** is entered between Penlee Point (50°19′N 4°11′W) and Great Mew Stone, 3¼ miles ESE,

Breakwater Fort

Plymouth Breakwater East End Light Beacon from E (4.195)

(Original dated 2007)

(Photograph - Chris Howlett)

Drake's Island   *Plymouth*   *Cattewater*

Breakwater Fort
Plymouth Sound from S (4.195)

(Photograph - Air Images)   *(Original dated 2001)*

and includes the outer part of the Dockyard Port of Plymouth, as far N as the entrance to Millbay Docks.

2   **Plymouth Breakwater**, 8½ cables long, lies within the entrance to Plymouth Sound and affords protection to the N part of the Sound. A light (4.215) is exhibited from the W end of the breakwater and a light beacon (4.224) stands on the E end of the breakwater; the structure and base is a refuge in case of shipwreck and can accommodate six persons within. Four stone shelters are also situated at intervals along the breakwater and there is a landing pier midway along its N side. Access to the breakwater is by permission of QHM. Breakwater Fort is situated ¼ cable N of the centre of the breakwater.

4.196

1   **Hamoaze** is that part of the lower reach of River Tamar bounded at its S end by a line joining Devil's Point (50°21'·6N 4°10'·0W) and Wilderness Point, 2 cables WSW, and at its N end by Royal Albert Bridge (50°24'·4N 4°12'·2W). Its entrance is somewhat contracted and circuitous but it is well sheltered from wind and sea and contains numerous berths for naval vessels.

2   The E side of Hamoaze between Mutton Cove (50°21'·9N 4°10'·6W) and Weston Mill Lake, 1½ miles N, is mainly occupied by HM Naval Base, Devonport (4.198). Bull Point (50°23'·9N 4°12'·3W) lies on the E side of Hamoaze 6 cables NW from Weston Mill Lake and is fronted by a small basin which dries.

3   Saint John's Lake and Millbrook Lake, two large inlets which are fronted by West Mud, the whole of which dries, extend W from Hamoaze opposite South Yard. Torpoint lies on the W side of Hamoaze, N of Saint John's Lake, and at Yonderberry Point, 5 cables farther N, an L-shaped jetty extends 260 m from the shore.

4.197

1   **Royal William Yard** occupies the land N of Devil's Point and consists of a quadrangular group of buildings and quays, fronted by a sea wall on which there are jetties on the W and N sides. A boat basin is entered at the centre of the wall on the N side of the yard. The yard, now in the public domain, is being developed for industry, tourist and leisure facilities.

4.198

1   **HM Naval Base, Devonport** consist of two main portions, namely North Yard, and South Yard with Morice

Yard at its N end. The two portions are separated by the chain ferry landings at the old Pottery Quay, Tamar Canal, Tamar Quay, and Moon Cove, occupying a water frontage of 1½ cables, which lie midway between, but outside, the limits of the N and S portions of the Naval Base which are connected by tunnel and overhead roadway.

2   South Yard extends N in a circular sweep from Mutton Cove to Morice Yard. A camber and boat pond nearly divide it into two parts, in the S part of which are several building slips and Slip and Rubble Jetties. In the N part of South Yard are Nos 1 to 4 Dry Docks and No 1 Ship Basin; the caissons of No 2 and No 3 Dry Docks have to be closed at least 1 hour before HW. Morice Yard lies at the N end of South Yard; a landing stage is situated at its S end.

3   North Yard lies between Moon Cove and Weston Mill Lake; bordering on the latter is HMS *Drake*, a naval shore establishment. The sea wall of North Yard has, for convenience in berthing ships, been divided into a number of wharves on its W and N fronts. North Yard contains four ship basins, one boat basin, and a number of docks. Nos 2, 3 and 5 ship basins are non-tidal and can only be opened from 2 hours before to 1 hour before HW. Weston Mill Lake Jetty lies on the N side of Weston Mill Lake.

4.199

1   **River Tamar.** Royal Albert Bridge (50°24'·4N 4°12'·2W), a railway bridge, and Tamar Bridge close N, a road bridge, span the river at Saltash; the piers of both bridges are conspicuous. Ernesettle Pier, which is L-shaped, projects 1 cable from the E bank of River Tamar, 1½ cables N of Tamar Bridge. From Tamar Bridge to Skinham Point, on the W bank of the river 1 mile upstream, depths shoal from about 10 to 2 m. Above Looking Glass Point there are a number of mooring trots on both sides of the river. Above Skinham Point the river is suitable only for small craft. For general information on the river see 4.249.

4.200

1   **Millbay Docks**, at the head of Plymouth Sound, are entered between Millbay Pier (50°21'·8N 4°09'·2W) and Eastern King Point, 1¾ cables WSW. The docks comprise a tidal basin with a RoRo terminal operating continental vehicle and passenger ferry services; the docks also handle cruise liner traffic. West Wharf with the RoRo Terminal and linkspan No 2 is the main deep-water berth. Close NE

lies a former RoRo terminal, retaining linkspan No 1 for the transfer of passengers from cruise liners anchored in Plymouth Sound. The area on the E side of the harbour between Millbay Pier and Trinity Pier, ¾ cable N, is occupied by Millbay Marina village complex. Trinity Pier and the marina are fronted to the W by three dolphins, the central dolphin being connected to the S head of Trinity Pier; lights are exhibited on the N and S dolphins. The N side of Trinity Pier offers a wide range of cargo operations. A small boat basin exists at the S end of West Wharf between the wharf and Camber Jetty. The Inner Basin, N of the main basin, is currently closed to navigation. Works are in progress (2008) for refurbishment of the lock between the two basins.

4.201

1 **The Cattewater** (50°22′N 4°07′W) lies at the mouth of River Plym and is entered through Cobbler Channel (4.205). The harbour is well sheltered; the bottom is mainly mud and sand with patches of rock around the drying line. The principal wharves situated on the N side are Victoria Wharves and Cattedown Wharves, and at Turnchapel Point on the S side of the Cattewater, opposite Cattedown Wharves, there are the Turnchapel Wharves, which are Admiralty property. Pomphlett Jetty, a dolphin berth, connected to the shore NE by a movable conveyor system, lies on the E side of Cattewater opposite Corporation Wharf. Laira Bridge, a road bridge, crosses the N end of the Cattewater 6 cables NNE of Turnchapel Point and a disused railway bridge crosses the river close NE of Laira Bridge.

4.202

1 **Sutton Harbour** (50°22′N 4°08′W), a non-tidal basin, is approached between Fisher's Nose and the breakwater protecting Queen Anne's Battery Marina, which occupies the E side of the approach. The entrance to the harbour, through a tidal defence barrier lock at the harbour entrance is 12 m wide; an emergency stop log gate situated immediately W of the lock also has a minimum width of 12 m. Traffic signals are displayed from the lock entrance. The harbour is used by fishing vessels. Sutton Harbour Marina is situated in the N part of the harbour.

2 The approach to the harbour is dredged to 3·0 m reducing to 2·0 m (1995); within the harbour the depth is maintained at 3·5 m.

Outside the pier, on the W side of the approach to the harbour, Baltic Wharf lies close N of Fisher's Nose with Phoenix Wharf and Commercial Wharf, which both dry out to a bottom of mud, between Baltic Wharf and West Pier.

Main anchorages and moorings

4.203

1 **Plymouth Sound.** The greater part of the Sound, clear of the channels, is occupied by anchorages and buoy berths, the positions of which can best be seen from the chart. Details of these berths are given at 4.232 and 4.233.

Submarine cables (disused) are laid SSE from The Bridge (4.204) to Plymouth Breakwater Fort.

Channels

4.204

1 **Western Channel**, the principal entrance to Plymouth Sound, lies W of Knap and Panther Shoals (50°19′·8N 4°09′·6W) thence between the W end of Plymouth Breakwater and Queen's Grounds, 5 cables NW, thence passing S of New Grounds, 5 cables NNE. The recommended track for deep-draught vessels through Western Channel is shown on the charts.

2 **Eastern Channel** lies between the E end of Plymouth Breakwater and Staddon Point, 4 cables ENE. Its use by small craft in strong W winds is not recommended on account of a dangerous sea and the proximity of a lee shore.

4.205

1 **Channels from Plymouth Sound.** Two channels, Smeaton Pass and Asia Pass, lead NW from Plymouth Sound between the shoals which lie between Drake's Island (50°21′N 4°09′W) and Mount Batten, 8 cables ENE, and lead to the Hamoaze or Millbay Docks. A third channel, Cobbler Channel, leads NNE into the commercial harbours on the E side of the port.

2 **Smeaton Pass**, the channel for deep-draught vessels, lies between Winter Shoal (50°21′·5N 4°08′·6W) and Mallard Shoal, 1½ cables ENE. The centre line of the channel is indicated by West Hoe Direction Light Beacon (50°21′·8N 4°08′·8W) (4.225).

Asia Pass lies between Winter Shoal and Asia Knoll, 1½ cables W. The fairway is indicated by Millbay Direction Light Beacon (50°21′·8N 4°09′·0W) (4.226).

3 **Cobbler Channel** lies between Mount Batten Breakwater (50°21′·6N 4°08′·1W) and Fisher's Nose, 2½ cables N, and leads to the Cattewater or Sutton Harbour. The fairway into, and through, the Cattewater is indicated by leading lights, leading marks, leading beacons and direction lights.

4 **Drake Channel**, forming the deep water approach to Hamoaze, leads NW of Drake's Island (50°21′N 4°09′W) and is approached from either Smeaton Pass or Asia Pass. The channel is marked by light buoys and is indicated by Ravenness Direction Light Beacon (50°21′·1N 4°10′·1W) (4.228), for inward bound vessels, and by Millbay Direction Light Beacon (50°21′·8N 4°09′·0W) (4.226), for outward bound vessels. Recommended tracks for inward and outward bound vessels are shown on the chart.

Drake's Island from ESE (4.205)
(Original dated 1998)

(Photograph - T R J Popplewell)

5 **The Narrows**, the S entrance to Hamoaze, lies between Devil's Point (50°21′·6N 4°10′·0W) and Cremyll Shoal, 2 cables WNW. The channel is marked by light buoys and light beacons and is indicated by Mount Wise Direction Light Beacon (50°22′·0N 4°10′·3W) (4.228). At the N end of The Narrows the channel turns sharply W and the inward and outward bound tracks for deep-draught vessels diverge. Recommended tracks for deep-draught vessels are shown on the chart.

Torpoint

Wilderness Point   *Devil's Point*

The Narrows from SE (4.205)

(Original dated 2001)

(Photograph - Air Images)

6   **The Bridge** (50°21′·0N 4°09′·6W), a narrow rocky ridge, connects Drake's Island with the W shore of Plymouth Sound between Redding Point (50°20′·8N 4°10′·0W) and Ravenness Point, 3½ cables N. Heaps of rocks or stones, awash and unmarked, lie on The Bridge. A narrow passage, clearly marked by four beacons (lateral), with a depth of 1·3 m, lies midway along The Bridge but it is suitable only for mariners in small craft.

The Bridge from SE (4.205)

(Original dated 1998)

(Photograph - T R J Popplewell)

Hazards
4.206

1   **Operational Sea Training.** Warships and auxiliaries engaged in operational sea training may be encountered both in the approaches to Plymouth Sound and N of the breakwater. Their movements may not follow customary traffic patterns.

A pilotage training route for such warships and auxiliaries has been established between Rame Head (4.215) and Gara Point (4.252).

2   Warships frequently enter harbour by either Western or Eastern Channel to transfer personnel to and from support craft, usually in the vicinity of C, D and E mooring buoys. Up to date information may be sought from Longroom Port Control on VHF.
4.207

1   **Submarines.** The main berths in Plymouth Sound for submarines are D and E Buoys. Mariners are warned that submarines at night may well be indistinct especially when viewed from seaward. In addition to normal anchor lights they may exhibit a very quick-flashing yellow light as described in *The Mariner's Handbook* together with enhanced upper deck lighting.

Submarines operate regularly in Plymouth Sound and its approaches with equipment deployed near the surface extending up to 800 m astern. Other vessels must not pass within 200 m of any submarine or within 800 m astern when the submarines are underway. A clearance of 100 m is required when submarines are occupying berths D and E.

Nuclear submarines are constrained by draught and can only navigate within the principal deep-water channels of the port. They will be accompanied by tugs that will display the signals described in *International Regulations for Preventing Collisions at Sea (1972)* for a vessel constrained by draught.
4.208

1   **Harbour ferries** cross the channels in the following places, their routes are shown on the charts:

Between Cremyll (50°21′·6N 4°10′·5W) and Stonehouse Pool.

Between Torpoint (50°22'·5N 4°11'·6W) and an area N of Morice Yard. These latter ferries are floating bridges and are confined to fixed tracks.

For regulations regarding ferries and floating bridges, and for signals to be shown by the latter, see Appendix I.

4.209

1 **Diving operations** are carried out N and S of Bovisand Pier (50°20'·3N 4°07'·7W). Mariners in the vicinity of the diving areas, as shown on the chart, should proceed at slow speed whilst diving signals are displayed on the pier or on Breakwater Fort (50°20'·1N 4°08'·9W).

2 A diving training area is established in the SW corner of No 1 Basin (50°22'·1N 4°11'·0W) South Yard, for details see information on the chart.

Diving training operations are also carried out in Weston Mill Lake (50°23'·5N 4°11'·4W) (4.196). Care is necessary when these operations are taking place; special rules are in force for vessels in this lake.

4.210

1 **Submarine cables**, including power cables, and pipelines are laid in many places within the port, their positions can best be seen from the charts.

2 **Yachts** may be encountered manoeuvring off the starting lines extending into Cobbler Channel off the Royal Plymouth Corinthian Yacht Club (50°21'·8N 4°08'·1W) and off Fisher's Nose, 1½ cables E.

3 **Small boat training** for the RN is conducted in an area, marked by buoys (special), on the SW side of Hamoaze NE of Inswork Point (50°21'·6N 4°11'·8W) at speeds in excess of 10 kn. See information on the chart.

Degaussing ranges
4.211

1 Degaussing ranges, indicated on the chart, lie in the vicinity of Penlee Point (50°19'N 4°11'W) and 2¼ cables ESE of Eastern King Point (50°21'·7N 4°09'·4W).

Natural conditions
4.212

1 **Tidal streams** in the approaches off Penlee Point are rotary in a clockwise direction, but off Great Mew Stone they are rectilinear.

Between the W end of Plymouth Breakwater and Queen's Grounds, tidal streams are nearly rectilinear. In Eastern Channel, NE of the E end of the breakwater, they are rotary in a clockwise direction.

2 Streams (4.213) in the passes and channels can be subject to considerable irregularities.

Strong N winds prolong the out-going stream and retard the in-going stream by up to 15 minutes.

Strong S winds prolong the in-going stream and retard the out-going stream by up to 15 minutes.

Freshets after heavy rain have the same effect as a strong N wind and long summer droughts can prolong the in-going stream for up to 30 minutes.

3 In Plymouth Sound the in-going and out-going streams run between Western Channel and Asia Pass, and between Eastern Channel and Smeaton Pass.

There is a large triangular area N of the breakwater in which the streams, especially the in-going stream, are less regular than those on the direct lines between the entrances and the passes. About 3 cables N of Breakwater Fort the stream is irregular and may, at any time, run in any direction at a rate not exceeding ½ kn at springs.

4 Across The Bridge (50°21'·0N 4°09'·5W) (4.205) the streams run strongly NNW and SSE, and vessels in the NW part of the sound may experience a set accordingly.

In Asia Pass, Drake Channel, The Narrows and The Hamoaze, the streams begin as in the sound and run generally in the direction of the channel, but there is a tendency for them to set across the channel in the following places:

Pass or channel	Spring rate (kn)	Direction of set
Asia Pass	1	The in-going stream sets towards the shoal extending NE from Drake's Island. The out-going stream sets towards Winter Shoal
Vanguard Bank	2	S of Vanguard Bank the in-going stream sets towards Barn Pool. The out-going stream sets across the bank SE towards The Bridge
The Narrows	2¾	At the S end the in-going stream sets strongly NE out of Barn Pool and the out-going stream towards Vanguard Bank. At the N end the in-going stream sets towards Mount Wise and the out-going stream towards Devil's Point
The Hamoaze	1¾	S of Rubble Bank the out-going stream sets towards Millbrook Lake

5 Details of tidal streams are shown by information on the charts and by *Admiralty Tidal Stream Atlas of Plymouth Harbour and Approaches*.

4.213

1 **Period for safe navigation** in Drake Channel (50°21'·5N 4°09'·5W) (4.205) and the Hamoaze (4.196) depends upon various conditions, as freshets (4.212) in River Tamar alter the turn of the tidal stream considerably, as well as increasing the strength of the out-going stream. It must be remembered that near half in-going stream the tide runs with considerable strength, so that great caution is necessary, and, if it can be avoided, it is not desirable to move a vessel during the strength of the stream. In The Narrows (4.205) it is at its maximum and runs in swirls, so that close attention is always required.

2 The best times for vessels to leave Plymouth Sound for the Hamoaze at springs are from 1 hour to 40 minutes before HW, and at neaps 1¼ hours to 40 minutes before HW, and 1¼ hours to ¾ of an hour before LW. Vessels of an appropriate length and draught can enter and depart The Hamoaze at any state of the tide; the Chief Admiralty Pilot can advise.

3 Vessels leave the Hamoaze for the Sound, at springs, ¾ of an hour before HW or ¼ of an hour before LW, and at neaps from 1¼ to ¾ of an hour before HW or ¾ to ¼ of an hour before LW.

Vessels of about 2000 tonnes or less, can, normally, be taken in or out of the Hamoaze at any state of the tide.

4 Navigating cross tide to enter or leave Weston Mill Lake (50°23'·5N 4°11'·4W) is hazardous. Navigation is subject to approval by QHM and to tidal range constraints when movements may be restricted, as follows:

Range	Closed period
Less than 3·0 m	No restrictions
3·1 m – 3·5 m	HW +2½ to HW +3½
3·6 m – 4·0 m	HW +2 to HW +4
Greater than 4·0 m	HW +1½ to HW +4½

4.214

1   **Eddies.** During the out-going tidal stream eddies run W along the shore of Firestone Bay (50°21′·6N 4°09′·6W), round Western King Point to Devil's Point where it is strong, and W along the dockyard wall from Slip Jetty to No 1 Jetty.

During the in-going tidal stream there is a strong eddy off Devil's Point.

Sandwaves. For details of sandwaves in the approaches to Plymouth, see 4.255.

Climate information. See 1.195 and 13.235

Directions for entering harbour
(continued from 4.160)

Principal marks
4.215

1   **Landmarks - approaches to Plymouth Sound:**

Rame Head (50°19′N 4°13′W), a prominent headland conical in shape with a ruined chapel on its summit, serves to identify the entrance to Plymouth Sound.

Great Mew Stone (50°18′N 4°06′W), a precipitous rocky islet rising to a sharp apex.

2   Radio Mast (elevation 175 m) (50°20′·8N 4°06′·8W) marked by a red obstruction light on Staddon Heights near the summit of which there is a high

Chapel   *Mast*

Rame Head from SE (4.215)
(Original dated 2004)

(Photograph - HMS Scott)

wall. A second smaller conspicuous mast stands close SSW.

Plymouth Breakwater W Head Light (white round granite tower, 23 m in height) (50°20′·1N 4°09′·5W).

Breakwater Fort   *Great Mew Stone*

Plymouth Breakwater W Head Light from NW (4.215)
(Original dated 1986)

(Photograph - Dr. M. P. Bender)

Eddystone Light from NE (4.215)
(Original dated 2007)

(Photograph - Chris Howlett)

3 **Major light:**
Eddystone Light (grey granite tower, red lantern, 49 m in height) (50°11′N 4°16′W) with a helicopter landing platform above the lantern.

4.216

1 **Landmarks – Plymouth Sound inner part:**
Naval War Memorial (stone column, 30 m in height, surmounted by a copper sphere) (50°21′·9N 4°08′·5W).
Smeaton Tower (red and white bands, red lantern, 28 m in height) (50°21′·9N 4°08′·5W) standing on The Hoe (see 4.172 for historical note).

2 Civic Centre (red lights) (50°22′·2N 4°08′·6W).
Hotel (50°22′·0N 4°08′·5W).
Hotel (50°21′·9N 4°08′·9W).

Other aids to navigation

4.217

1 **Racon:** Eddystone Light (50°11′N 4°16′W). For details see *Admiralty List of Radio Signals Volume 2.*

Direction lights. Navigation is facilitated by a number of direction lights exhibited from structures displaying daymarks and described in the directions for entering harbour. The direction lights are exhibited by day as well as at night.

2 An orange flashing light is exhibited on all main direction lights when mains power supplies in Plymouth are interrupted.

Fog lights. Special high intensity fog lights are exhibited, on request to Longroom Port Control Station, from West Hoe, Raveness, Mount Wise and Ocean Court Direction Light Beacons and at Mallard Shoal, Eastern King, Devil's Point, Cremyll Shoal and North-west Corner Light Beacons, and also at Slip Jetty E and No 1 Jetty S.

3 **Light** (50°19′·0N 4°06′·6W) for DF calibrations is exhibited (occasionally) from a building on the headland at Wembury Point.

Compass adjustment. The following distant marks will be found useful for compass adjustment by mariners lying in Plymouth Sound and Hamoaze.

4 Plymouth Sound:
Eddystone Light (50°11′N 4°16′W), see information on charts 30 and 1967.
Hamoaze:
Saint Macra's Church (tower and flagstaff) (50°20′·8N 4°11′·1W), see information on chart 1902.
Tamar Bridge East Tower (50°24′·5N 4°12′·1W), see information on chart 1902.

Charts 30, 1900, 1613, 1267

Approaches to Plymouth Sound

4.218

1 **From south.** From a position about 4 miles E of Eddystone Light (50°11′N 4°16′W) the line of bearing 000° of Plymouth Breakwater W Head Light (50°20′N 4°10′W) (4.215) leads in the approach passing (with positions given from Penlee Point (50°19′N 4°11′W)):
E of Eddystone Rocks (8¾ miles SSW) thence:

2 W of West Rutts (6½ miles SE) (4.255).

The line of bearing 350° of Maker Light (white concrete tower, red stripe, 5 m in height) (1½ miles NNE) situated on Hooe Lake Point, or at night within its white sector (330°–004°), then leads towards the entrance to Western Channel passing:

3 W of OSR South Light Buoy (special) (8 cables ESE); OSR North Light Buoy (special) lies nearly 2 cables farther NE. And:

White Building

Penlee Point from ENE (4.218)

(Original dated 2004)

(Photograph – HMS Scott)

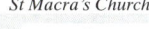
St Macra's Church

Maker Light from SE (4.218)
(Original dated 1998)

(Photograph – Dr. M. P. Bender)

E of Draystone (1 cable SE) a reef. Draystone Light Buoy (port hand) is moored 1½ cables SSE of the reef closer to the recommended track. Thence:

4 W of Knap (1 mile ENE), a shoal marked on its SW side by Knap Light Buoy (starboard hand); thence:
To the pilot boarding place (4.188).

4.219

1 **From west.** From a position about 1 mile S of Rame Head (50°19′N 4°13′W) (4.215) the line of bearing 080° of the summit of Great Mew Stone (4.215), 4½ miles E, leads in the approach passing (with positions given from Penlee Point (50°19′N 4°11′W)):
S of Penlee Point (4.170).

2 On the line of bearing 020° of Plymouth Breakwater W Light (1½ miles NE) (4.215) the track then leads NNE thence N to join the recommended track from S (4.218) on the line of bearing 350° of Maker Light (1½ miles NNE).

4.220

1 **From east.** From a position about 1¼ miles SSW of Great Mew Stone (50°18′N 4°06′W) the line of bearing 290° of the summit of Rame Head, 4½ miles W, leads in the approach passing SSW of Mewstone Ledge, which extends 2 cables SW from Great Mew Stone, to join the recommended track from S (4.218) on the line of bearing 350° of Maker Light.

Saint Macra's Church

Maker Light aligned with Hooe
Lake Cottage (340°) (4.219)

(Original dated 2004)

(Photograph - HMS Scott)

4.221

1　**Clearing bearings.** The sector limit (004°) of Maker Light, which changes from red to white, clears E of Draystone.

The sector light, which shows white between the bearings of 033°–037° and is shown from a window in the tower below the main light of Plymouth Breakwater W Light, covers the W part of Knap.

Charts 1967, 1901, 1902
Plymouth Sound to Hamoaze
4.222

1　**General information.** Recommended tracks for deep-draught vessels both inward-bound and outward-bound are shown on the charts.

4.223

1　**Western Channel.** From a position near the pilot boarding place on the line of bearing 350° of Maker Light (50°20'·5N 4°10'·9W) (4.218) the line of bearing 044° of Mount Batten (tower) (50°21'·6N 4°07'·8W), which from the offing appears as an island, leads in the fairway passing (with positions given from Plymouth Breakwater Fort (50°20'·1N 4°08'·9W)):

Mountbatten Tower from SW (4.223)

(Original dated 1998)

(Photograph - Dr. M. P. Bender)

2　SE of Queen's Grounds (8 cables WNW) marked on their S side by Queens Ground Light Buoy (port hand).

Round the W end of Plymouth Breakwater at a distance of 1¾ cables. The line of bearing 070° of Withyhedge Direction Light Beacon (white triangle point down, orange stripe on column) (1¼ miles NE), or at night within its white sector (069°–071°), then leads in the fairway passing:

Withyhedge Direction Light-beacon bearing 070° (4.223)

(Original dated 2000)

(Photograph - HMS Scott)

3　SSE of New Grounds (5 cables NNW) marked at their SW edge by New Ground Light Buoy (port hand); thence:

NNW of C Mooring Buoy (2 cables N); thence:

Between D and E Mooring Buoys (3½ cables NE and 5½ cables NNE).

4　The track then leads to anchorage (4.203) if required, or NE thence N passing W of F Mooring Buoy (9 cables NE) towards Smeaton Pass (4.225) or Asia Pass (4.226).

Useful marks:

Ramscliff Point Beacons (white columns) (50°20'·6N 4°07'·7W)

4.224

1　**Eastern Channel.** From a position about 1 mile W of Great Mew Stone (50°18'N 4°06'W) (4.215) the alignment (354½°) of Plymouth Breakwater E Head Light Beacon (grey, conical cage structure with spherical topmark) (50°20'·0N 4°08'·2W) with Smeaton Tower (4.216), 1¾ miles N, or at night in the white sector (353°–001°) of the breakwater E end light, leads in the approach passing (with positions given from Plymouth Breakwater Fort (50°20'·1N 4°08'·9W)):

2　W of Mewstone Ledge which extends 2 cables SW from Great Mew Stone, noting an isolated 5 m patch (2 miles SSE); thence:

W of a ledge with a depth of 6·7 m at its extremity which extends 1 cable WSW from Shag Stone (1¼ miles SE) marked by a beacon; thence:

3　Between Tinker (9 cables SSE), a shoal marked by E Tinker Light Buoy (E cardinal), and an isolated 4·1 m patch (1 mile SSE). Several isolated patches on the E side of the fairway, with depths of less than 5 m over them, extend 1¾ cables NNE from the 4·1 m patch.

4　When W of Whidbey Light Beacon (orange and white metal column) (1¼ miles ESE) the line of bearing 044° of Staddon Point Light Beacon (white concrete structure red bands, 6 m in height) (9 cables E) or at night in its white sector (038°–050°) leads in the fairway passing:

Between Andurn Point (11 cables ESE) and Plymouth Breakwater E Head (4½ cables E).

Bovisand Pier   *Staddon Point Light Beacon*

Staddon Point from SW (4.224)

(Original dated 2007)

(Photograph – Chris Howlett)

5   The line of bearing 320° of Devil's Point Light Beacon (50°21'·6N 4°10'·0W) (4.228), or at night in the white sector (137½°–139½°) of Whidbey Light Beacon, astern, then leads in the fairway passing:

    Between the ledge N of Plymouth Breakwater and Beaufort Rock (6½ cables ENE). West Staddon Light Beacon (W cardinal) marks a 1·8 m patch 1 cable ESE of the rock. Thence:

6   Between D Mooring Buoy (3½ cables NE) and Duke Rock (5½ cables ENE) marked by Duke Rock Light Buoy (W cardinal).

    The track then leads as appropriate to the anchorages (4.203) or for Smeaton Pass (4.225) or Asia Pass (4.226).

7   **Cautions.** Due to the nature of the holding ground the position of the light buoys marking Tinker cannot be relied upon after periods of heavy weather.

Useful mark:

    Bovisand Pier Light (white metal column) (50°20'·3N 4°07'·7W).

4.225

1   **Smeaton Pass** leading marks:

    Front mark. Mallard Shoal Light Beacon (white triangle point up on white column, orange bands) (50°21'·6N 4°08'·3W).

    Rear mark. Hoe Light Beacon (white triangle point down, orange stripe on column) (2 cables N).

2   The alignment (349°) of these leading lights leads in the approach to Smeaton Pass passing (with positions given from the summit of Drake's Island (50°21'·3N 4°09'·2W)):

    Between Melampus Light Buoy (port hand) (3½ cables ESE) (4.226) and Dunstone Rock Buoy (special) (8½ cables E); thence:

Royal Citadel

Smeaton Tower   *Hoe Light Beacon*   *Mallard Shoal Beacon*

Smeaton Pass from SW (4.225)

(Photograph – T R J Popplewell)   *(Original dated 1998)*

Mallard Shoal Light–beacon (4.225)

(Original dated 2004)

Hoe Light-beacon

Mallard Shoal Light-beacon
Smeaton Pass Leading Marks from SSE (4.225)

(Original dated 2000)

(Photograph - HMS Scott)

West Hoe Direction Light Beacon from SE (4.225)

(Original dated 2007)

(Photograph - Christopher Hewson)

(314°–317°), leads through the centre of the channel passing:

> SW of S Mallard Light Buoy (S cardinal) (6 cables ENE) which marks the S end of the flat extending W from Mount Batten; thence:

4   Between NE Winter Light Buoy (port hand) (5 cables ENE) and W Mallard Light Buoy (starboard hand) (5¾ cables ENE).

The route then leads W on the recommended track for Drake Channel passing N of NW Winter Light Buoy (W cardinal) (4 cables NE) or as required for entering Millbay Docks.

4.226

1   **Asia Pass.** From a position ESE of Drake's Island (50°21′·3N 4°09′·2W) the line of bearing (325½°) of Millbay Direction Light Beacon (white concrete tower, red

3   E of S Winter Light Buoy (S cardinal) (4 cables ENE) which marks the S side of Winter Shoal.

The line of bearing 315½° of West Hoe Direction Light Beacon (orange triangle, point down on white painted wall) (5½ cables NNE), or at night within its white sector

bands, 11 m in height) (50°21'·8N 4°09'·0W), or at night within its white sector between the bearings 321½° to 329½°, leads in the fairway passing (with positions given from the summit of Drake's Island):

Millbay Direction Light Beacon from ESE (4.226)

(Original dated 2007)

(Photograph - Christopher Hewson)

2   NE of Pilot Shoal (2½ cables SE); Melampus Light Buoy (port hand) is moored close E of the shoal; thence:
SW of S Winter Light Buoy (4 cables ENE); thence:
Between Winter Shoal (4 cables ENE) and Drake's Island; thence:

3   Between NW Winter Light Buoy (W cardinal) (4 cables NE) and Asia Knoll (3 cables NE) marked on its S side by Asia Light Buoy (port hand).

The route then leads W on the recommended track for Drake Channel or as required for entering Millbay Docks.

4.227

1   **Approach to Drake Channel.** From a position N of Winter Shoal (50°21'·5N 4°08'·6W) the line of bearing 270° of Western King Direction Light Beacon (white triangle point down, orange stripe on column) (50°21'·6N 4°09'·8W), or at night within its white sector (270°–272°), leads towards Drake Channel passing (with positions given from the summit of Drake's Island (50°21'·3N 4°09'·2W)):

Western King Direction Light-beacon bearing 270° (4.227)

(Original dated 2000)

(Photograph - HMS Scott)

2   S of Ash Light Buoy (starboard hand) (4¼ cables NE); thence:
Between Drake's Island and Millbay Pier (4½ cables N) from where a light (concrete column, 8 m in height) is exhibited, thence;
N of St. Nicholas Light Buoy (port hand) (2½ cables N).

The track then leads SW towards Drake Channel.

3   Outward–bound vessels should follow these directions in reverse, and when in the channel N of Drake's Island, keep in the white sector (087°–099°) of Mallard Shoal Light Beacon (6 cables ENE) (4.225).

4.228

1   **Drake Channel.** From a position S of Millbay Pier (50°21'·7N 4°09'·2W) the line of bearing 225° of Ravenness Direction Light Beacon (white triangle point down, orange stripe on column) (50°21'·2N 4°10'·1W), and at night within its white sector (224°–226°), leads in the fairway passing (with positions given from Devil's Point (50°21'·6N 4°10'·0W)):

Ravenness Direction Light-beacon bearing 225° (4.228)

(Original dated 2000)

(Photograph - HMS Scott)

     SE of Eastern King Point (4 cables ENE); thence:

2   NW of N Drakes Island Light Buoy (port hand) (4¼ cables E); thence:
Between NW Drakes Island Light Buoy (port hand) (3½ cables ESE) and East Vanguard Light Buoy (starboard hand) (2½ cables ESE), noting the 8·7 m patch close SSE of the light buoy.

3   The track then alters gradually NW rounding S of Vanguard Bank (2 cables SSE) which extends nearly 2 cables S from Western King Point. The line of bearing 343° of Mount Wise Direction Light Beacon (white triangle point down, orange stripe, on white hut) (4 cables NNW), and at night within its white sector (342°–344°), then leads through The Narrows passing:
WSW of West Vanguard Light Buoy (starboard hand) (1 cable SSE); thence:

4   Between Battery Light Buoy (port hand) (1¼ cables WSW), which is moored close off Wilderness Point, and Devil's Point. A light Beacon (orange and white concrete column) is situated on Devil's Point. Thence:
ENE of Cremyll Shoal Light Beacon (white) (2 cables WNW) standing on Cremyll Shoal inshore of its E edge.

Mount Wise Light-beacon

Ocean Court

Wilderness Point

The Narrows from SSE (4.228)

Devil's Point

(Original dated 2000)

(Photograph - Naval Party 1016)

Mountwise Direction Light-beacon bearing 343° (4.228)

(Original dated 2000)

(Photograph - HMS Scott)

Ocean Court Direction Light-beacon bearing 085° (4.228)

(Original dated 2000)

(Photograph - HMS Scott)

5   **Hamoaze.** The recommended track then alters gradually W when the line of bearing 265° of Sango Point Light

Beacon (50°21′·7N 4°12′·4W) then leads in the fairway passing:

N of Cremyll Light Buoy (port hand) (3 cables WNW); thence:

6   S of South Rubble Light Buoy (starboard hand) (7¼ cables WNW), which is moored close within the S edge of Rubble Bank, and at night keeping within the white sector (080°–090°), astern, of Ocean Court Direction Light (orange triangle point down on white structure, 3 m in height) (2½ cables NNW) until rounding Rubble Bank.

7   Mariners approaching Slip Jetty (5½ cables NW) should be careful to avoid the projecting aprons from No 1 and No 3 building slips which project into the fairway on each side of Slip Jetty.

The recommended track then proceeds generally N in mid–channel through Hamoaze noting West Mud Light Buoy (port hand) (9 cables WNW) on the port side of the fairway and also noting an isolated 7·6 m patch (8½ cables WNW). The chart is the best guide.

8   **No 5 Basin** (50°23′·3N 4°11′·3W) approach leading marks:

Front mark. Beacon (white with triangle point up topmark) (50°23′·17N 4°12′·05W).

Rear mark. Beacon (white with triangle point down topmark) (350 m WSW of front mark).

The alignment (252°), astern, of these marks leads through the entrance of No 5 Basin.

No 5 Basin leading marks (4.228)

(Original dated 2001)

(Photograph - HMSML Gleaner)

Plymouth – Carew Point Light Beacon from NNE (4.229)

(Original dated 2008)

(Photograph - CPO (SR) Birch, Port Surveyor to QHM Plymouth)

4.229

1   **Useful marks:**

Mast (40 m in height) (50° 22'·0 N 4° 10'·4W).

Millbrook Light Beacon (white triangle point up, orange stripe on column) (50°21'·3N 4°11'·4W).

Lights on the E and W end of Rubble Jetty (50°21'·9N 4°10'·9W).

Lights on Yonderberry Point Oil Jetty (50°22'·9N 4°11'·6W).

2   North–west Corner Light Beacon (50°23'·4N 4°11'·6W).

Plymouth – Henn Point Light Beacon from SSE (4.229)

(Original dated 2008)

(Photograph - CPO (SR) Birch, Port Surveyor to QHM Plymouth)

Light (50°23'·5N 4°11'·7W) on the W end of Weston Mill Lake Jetty.

Radio Tower (50°23'·6N 4°11'·5W).

3   Carew Point Light Beacon (white metal pile, 4 m in height) (50°23'·6N 4°12'·7W).

Henn Point Light Beacon (white metal pile, 4 m in height) (50°23'·9N 4°12'·7W).

4.230

1   **Outward–bound** vessels should, in general, follow these directions in reverse, but should approach the turn off Rubble Bank on the line of bearing 183° of Millbrook Light Beacon (4.228), and at night just within its white sector. After rounding Rubble Bank the line of bearing 085° of Ocean Court Direction Light Beacon (4.228), and at night within its white sector on this bearing, leads in the fairway. Then pass through The Narrows on the line of

Cattedown

Mount Batten   *Plymouth Yacht Haven*

Cattewater from WSW (4.230)

(Original dated 2001)

(Photograph - Air Images)

bearing 163° of Bridge Light Beacon (white triangle point down, orange stripe, on column) (50°21'·0N 4°09'·8W). After rounding Vanguard Bank the line of bearing 048½° of Millbay Direction Light Beacon (4.226), and at night within its white sector on this bearing, leads through Drake Channel. Thence proceed as previously directed for Asia Pass or Smeaton Pass.

Chart 1967

Plymouth Sound to the Cattewater and Sutton Harbour

4.231

1 **Cobbler Channel leading marks:**
    Front mark. Fisher's Nose Light (metal column, 4 m in height) (50°21'·8N 4°08'·0W).
    Rear mark. Saint John's Church (spire) (4½ cables NNE of the front mark).

2 **Leading lights:**
    Front light. Fisher's Nose Light (metal column, 4 m in height) (50°21'·8N 4°08'·0W).
    Rear light. (mounted on S side of building) (400 m NNE of front light)

From a position S of Mallard Shoal (50°21'·6N 4°08'·3W) the alignment (026½°) by day of the above leading marks, or by night the above leading lights, leads in the approach passing (with positions given from Mount Batten Tower (50°21'·6N 4°07'·8W)):

3 ESE of S Mallard Light Buoy (S cardinal) (3½ cables W); thence:
    Between Mallard Shoal (3¼ cables W) and Mount Batten Breakwater. Mallard Shoal Light Beacon (4.225) is exhibited on the W part of the shoal and a light (metal column) is exhibited on the breakwater head.

4 Leading lights:
    Front light. Beacon (red circle on white beacon with red bands) (2½ cables N) standing on the S knuckle of the breakwater protecting Queen Anne's Battery Marina.
    Rear light. Queen Anne's Battery Light (white tower on red roofed building) (¾ cable NE of the front mark).

5 The alignment (048½°) of these lights leads in the fairway passing:

Between Fisher's Nose (2¾ cables NW), the W approach point to Sutton Harbour (4.202), and the coastal bank extending N from Mount Batten.

6 The line of bearing 102° of Cattedown Approach Direction Light Beacon (red and white column), or at night the white sector (100¾°–103¼°) of the direction light beacon, leads in the fairway passing SSW of Victoria Pier (4.241) from where a light (metal column, 5 m in height) is exhibited, noting No 2 Light Buoy (port hand) ¾ cable WSW of the pierhead and No 3 Light Buoy (starboard hand) 1 cable SSW of the pierhead.

7 The line of bearing (128½°) of Turnchapel Approach Direction Light Beacon (red and white tower), or at night within the white sector (127¾°–129¼°) of the direction light beacon, leads in the fairway.

The alignment (198°) of leading light beacons (50°21'·5N 4°07'·4W) at the marina dock in Plymouth Yacht Haven provides a reference line for vessels manoeuvring in the turning area 2 cables NNE.

8 The route then leads generally E to Cattedown or Turnchapel wharves, thence generally NNE through Oreston Channel, which is dredged to a depth of 2 m (1995-2006) and marked by light buoys, to Pomphlett Jetty; the chart is the best guide.
    Useful mark:
    Gasholder (50°21'·9N 4°07'·4W) at Cattedown.

Basins and berths

Charts 1967, 1901, 1902

Anchorages and moorings

4.232

1 **Anchorages,** indicated on the chart, are situated as follows (with positions given from Plymouth Breakwater Fort (50°20'N 4°09'W)):
    Anchorages for vessels over 7·5 m draught are No 1 (11 cables NNE), No 2 (9¼ cables NNE), No 6 (7¼ cables NNE) and No 7 (5 cables N).

2 Anchorage areas for vessels of less than 7·5 m draught are situated SE of The Bridge (50°21'·0N 4°09'·6W) and in Jennycliff Bay, (8 cables NNW and 1¼ miles NE).

All anchorages except those in Jennycliff Bay are numbered.

Mount Batten and Mount Batten Breakwater from SE (4.231)
(Original dated 2007)

(Photograph - Christopher Hewson)

4.233

1 **Plymouth Sound.** Mooring buoys, shown on the charts, are situated in Plymouth Sound (with positions given from Plymouth Breakwater Fort):

C Mooring Buoy (2 cables N): dredged depth 12·0 m (2006).

D Mooring Buoy (3½ cables NE): dredged depth 11·6 m (2006).

2 E Mooring Buoy (5½ cables NNE): dredged depth 9·7 m (2006).

F Mooring Buoy (9 cables NE): dredged depth 8·6 m (2006).

Lights (special) are exhibited from these buoys.

4.234

1 **Hamoaze.** Mooring buoys are situated on the W side of Hamoaze between South Yard and Weston Mill Lake, thence between Weston Mill Lake and Saltash there are numerous mooring buoys on both sides of the fairway. The positions and depths are best seen from the chart.

4.235

1 **Cattewater.** Three mooring buoys lie close N of Plymouth Yacht Haven (50°21'·5N 4°07'·3W) and four mooring buoys, one with a light (special), lie 1¾ cables NNW of Mount Batten. Small craft moorings lie N and NE of Mount Batten.

Alongside berths

4.236

HM Naval Base – South Yard. The deepest and longest berths in South Yard are:

Rubble Jetty (50°21'·9N 4°10'·9W): length 130 m; dredged depth alongside 10·0 m (2007), with a dredged depth of 8·5 m (2007) in the approach.

No 1 Jetty (50°22'·1N 4°11'·1W): length 145 m; dredged depth 9·8 m (2007) alongside.

4.237

1 **HM Naval Base – North Yard.** The longest and deepest berths are on the sea wall S of No 5 Basin entrance (50°23'·3N 4°11'·4W) and comprise No 5 Wharf, No 6 Wharf, No 7 Wharf South and No 7 Wharf North. Each berth is 127 m in length with a dredged depth alongside of 11·9 m (2007). There is a dredged depth of 9·1 m (2007) in the approach to these berths. To the N of No 5 Basin entrance No 8 Wharf South and No 8 Wharf North are situated; each berth about 100 m in length and dredged to 11·0 m (2007). There are dredged depths of 9·1 and 8·5 m (2007) in the approach to these berths.

2 Weston Mill Lake (50°23'·5N 4°11'·4W) at the N end of North Yard has three berths on the S side with dredged depths of 9·2 m (2007) alongside, and three berths on the N side with a dredged depth of 8·5 m (2007) alongside.

The largest and deepest basin is No 5 Basin with a maintained depth of 9 m, as shown on the chart; a small area in the SW corner is maintained to 10·7 m.

4.238

1 **Hamoaze and River Tamar.** Yonderberry Point Oil Jetty (50°22'·9N 4°11'·8W) has a berthing head 61 m in length with a dredged depth of 11·6 m (2007) alongside. Mooring dolphins and buoys N and S of jetty extend the length of the berth.

Ernesettle Pier (50°24'·7N 4°12'·1W) has a berthing face 100 m long with a dredged depth of 6·1 m (2007) alongside. A mid–channel shoal, with a least depth of 2·7 m, lies 3 cables N of the pier.

Yorderberry Jetty   *No 5 Basin*

Torpoint Ferry   *South Yard*
HM Naval Base

Hamoaze from S (4.238)

(Original dated 2001)

(Photograph – Air Images)

4.239

1 **Millbay Docks.** West Wharf (50°21'·8N 4°09'·4W) the main deep-water berth for ferries, cruise ships and cargo vessels is also the RoRo Terminal: length 170 m; maximum depth 9·0 m at MLWS; for vessels up to 200 m LOA and 8·5 m draught. Three mooring dolphins, used by large RoRo vessels, lie to the W of Trinity Pier and the Millbay marina complex. Lights are exhibited from the N and S dolphins.

Trinity Pier (50°21'·9N 4°09'·2W), on the N side of Trinity Wharf, offers a wide range of cargo operations for vessels up to 100 m in length, with maximum draught of 5·0 m.

4.240

1 **Sutton Harbour.** Bayly's Wharf (50°22'·0N 4°07'·9W) the site of the fish quay: length 180 m; maintained depth 3·5 m.

4.241

1 **Cattewater.** Cattedown Wharves (50°21'·7N 4°07'·0W): length 216 m; W part (oil tanker berth) dredged to 7·6 m (2003), E part (dry cargo berth) dredged to 6·3 m (2003), except for a 4·9 m shoal patch midway along the berth. The area W of the wharves is liable to silting.

2 **Victoria Wharves**, (50°21'·9N 4°07'·5W): dredged to 6 m below datum; vessels up to 140 m LOA can be accepted.

Howard's Quay (50°21'·9N 4°06'·7W): length 183 m; dries along its full length; used occasionally.

3 **Turnchapel Wharves** (50°21'·6N 4°07'·0W) The W jetty is dredged to 6·1 m (1995); it has a dolphin for mooring lines close SW. The E jetty dredged to 5·5 m (1995) except for a 4·6 m shoal patch very close N of the W end of the jetty and a 4·8 m patch close N of the E end of the jetty. A jet float pontoon extension extends about 20 m from the E jetty and a wreck, with a depth of 2·5 m over it, lies close NE of the extension.

Millbay Docks – Millbay Pier from ESE (4.239)
(Original dated 2007)

Millbay Direction Light Beacon

(Photograph – Christopher Hewson)

Pomphlett Jetty (50°22′·0N 4°06′·6W) a cement and aggregates berth: length about 95 m; dredged depth 2·9 m (1995–2006).

Port Services

Repairs
4.242
1   **Dockyard Port of Plymouth.** Major repairs to vessels up to 12 000 tonnes can be carried out by Devonport Management Limited who operate the repair facilities in the former Royal Dockyard.
2   Dry docks. The largest dry dock in HM Naval Base, Devonport is No 10 Dock: length 242·14 m, can be increased by 12·19 m by placing caisson in outer stop; extreme breadth 43·59 m; entered from No 5 Basin with 37·74 m dock entrance width at MHWS; depth on sill 14·73 m at MHWS.
    Divers are available.

Other facilities
4.243
1   **Customs Office** in Plymouth.
    Degaussing facilities are available.
    Ship sanitation control and ship sanitation control exemption certificates are issued and extended at the ports of Plymouth.
    Compass adjustment is available, see 4.217.
    Hospitals are situated in the city; no advance notice required.

Supplies
4.244
1   **Fuel.** Large stocks of fuel oil and diesel are maintained and are available at most berths or can be supplied by road tanker or barge to vessels alongside or at anchor.
    Water is available to all vessels both alongside or at anchor.

Provisions and stores are plentiful and are available both alongside and at anchor.

Communications
4.245
1   **Local Airport:** Roborough, 8 km N of the city, with connecting flights to international airports.
    Helicopter landing sites.

Harbour regulations
4.246
1   **Regulations:** for full details, see Appendix I.
    Dangerous and polluting goods. See *Admiralty List of Radio Signals Volume 6(1)* and 1.68 to 1.76.
    Propellers. Ships with protruding propellers are required to display a notice indicating the position of the propellers.

Rescue
4.247
1   **Coastguard.** Rescue Teams are situated at Rame, Plymouth and Tamar; for details see 1.100.
    Lifeboat. Plymouth all-weather lifeboat and an inshore lifeboat are stationed at Millbay Marina, see 1.113.

Rivers and minor harbours
Charts 1902, 871
Saint Germans River
4.248
1   Saint Germans, or Lynher River flows into Hamoaze between Carew Point (50°23′·5N 4°12′·6W) and Henn Point, 4 cables N. Wearde Quay, built of stone, lies 2 cables SW of Henn Point; the quay dries but mariners should not dry out alongside the quay as the bottom consists of large boulders. There are moorings for small craft off the quay.
2   Entrance to the river is N of Lynher Light Buoy (port hand) which is moored on the S side of the fairway, 3 cables NNW of Carew Point. The fairway, with depths of

from 5 to 7 m as far as Jupiter Point (50°23′·4N 4°13′·8W), is marked by Beggar Island Light Buoy (port hand) and Sandacre Point Light Buoy (starboard hand).

3 There are some small craft moorings, for naval use only, situated off two jetties which project 120 m NE from Jupiter Point. Security fences extend from the shore into the river N and S of the jetties, 10 and 30 m, respectively; the outer fence posts are marked with yellow triangles, point up, and warning signs are exhibited on the shore.
Tidal information, see chart.

4 The river is tidal as far as Tideford, situated on River Tiddy 6¾ miles within the entrance, which can be reached at MHWS by mariners in craft with a draught of 2 m. The river is navigable by mariners in yachts as far as Saint Germans Quay, 4 miles above the entrance. Mariners in small craft can reach Tideford, with some difficulty at HW; they can also reach Notter Bridge on River Lynher, about the same distance above the entrance under similar conditions.

5 Anchorages for small craft in the river below Saint Germans Quay are shown on the chart. In 1992 foul ground was reported 1 cable ENE of Sand Acre Point (50°23′·7N 4°13′·5W) and mariners are advised not to anchor in this position.
A power cable with a safe overhead clearance of 27 m spans the river 2 cables NW of Redshank Point (50°22′·6N 4°16′·6W).

6 A submarine power cable is laid across the river NW from Jupiter Point and a second power cable is laid from the point to the seamanship training barge *Ajax* moored to a buoy about 1 cable N of the point. A gas pipeline is laid ESE across the river from Shillingham Point, 4 cables W. The landing places of the cables and pipeline are marked by beacons and notice boards. See 1.64 for caution regarding gas pipelines.

River Tamar
4.249

1 River Tamar rises in the moors of the NE part of Cornwall and, after following a S direction for approximately 60 miles, flows into the sea through Hamoaze and Plymouth Sound. The river estuary forms a nature reserve.

2 From Skinham Point (50°25′·5N 4°12′·5W), on the W bank about 1 mile upstream from Tamar Bridge, to the head of navigation at Gunnislake, 12½ miles above Tamar Bridge, depths are generally less than 2 m, although there are a number of areas, which can best be seen from the chart, where there are depths from 3 to 6 m. In general the channel keeps to the outside of all bends in the river. At LW care should be exercised due to the amount of debris caught in the river bed.

3 Two power cables, suspended between conspicuous pylons, with safe overhead clearances of 21 m and 16 m, respectively, span the river 4 cables below and 1¼ miles above Cargreen, a village on the W bank 2¼ miles N of Tamar Bridge. At Calstock, on the W bank 6½ miles above Cargreen, the river is spanned by a railway viaduct with a vertical clearance of 24 m.

4 Vessels up to 3 m draught can reach Calstock at MHWS; it can be reached by smaller craft at MLWS. Weirhead at Gunnislake (50°31′N 4°12′W), 4 miles above Calstock, is the limit of tidal waters; this head, or barrier, is a solid wall 5 m wide at the top and 30 m in length, and partly dries when the river is very low. Small craft of up to 1·5 m draught can navigate to within 2½ cables of Weirhead at MHWS.

Tamar Bridges from S (4.249)

(Original dated 2001)

(Photograph - Air Images)

5 Extensive anchorages and moorings are situated in the river; their positions may best be seen from the chart.
A submarine gas pipeline is laid across the river W from Thorn Point (50°26′·7N 4°11′·9W), the landing places are marked by beacons. See 1.64 for caution regarding gas pipelines.

River Tavy
4.250

1 River Tavy, the largest tributary of River Tamar, joins the latter between Warleigh Point and Lime Point 1½ miles above Tamar Bridge. The river is tidal for 2½ miles as far as a dam which can be reached at MHWS by small craft drawing up to 1·5 m.

PLYMOUTH TO START POINT

General information

Chart 1613
Route
4.251

1 From Plymouth the passage to Start Point leads initially ESE, about 16 miles across Bigbury Bay and the entrance to Salcombe Harbour to Prawle Point, thence E, about 4 miles, to S of Start Point.

Topography
4.252

1 Wembury Bay is entered between Great Mew Stone (50°18′N 4°06′W) and Gara Point, a low point 1¼ miles E, at the SW extremity of Yealm Head. Between Gara Point and Stoke Point, 2 miles E, the coast is very indented, with cliffs of moderate height and higher ground behind.

2 Bigbury Bay is entered between Stoke Point (50°18′N 4°01′W) and Bolt Tail, a prominent headland 6½ miles ESE. Between Bolt Tail and Thurlestone Rock, a perforated rock resembling the hull of a stranded vessel 1 mile N, the coast is high, precipitous and rocky. From a distance the coast appears as a line of even topped hills backed by the craggy mountainous outline of the Dartmoor hills which rise to a height of over 500 m, 10 miles or more inland.

Start Point and Lighthouse from S (4.252)
(Original dated 2001)

(Photograph - Air Images)

3   Bolt Head (50°13′N 3°47′W), a prominent headland, lies 3¾ miles ESE of Bolt Tail and these two features are connected by a high ridge faced by abrupt, dark rugged cliffs.

Prawle Point (50°12′N 3°43′W) is a prominent rock headland with craggy gneiss rock features. Start Point, 3¼ miles ENE, lies at the E end of a headland on which there are five hillocks, each approximately 60 m high, which have the appearance of a cock's comb. A light (5.18) is exhibited from Start Point.

Exercise areas
4.253

1   For details see 4.2 and information on the chart.

Rescue
4.254

1   **Coastguard rescue teams**operate from:
    Yealm at Hilsea Point (50°18′N 4°03′W).
    Bigbury-on-Sea (50°17′N 3°53′W).
    Hope Cove (50°14′N 3°52′W) on Bolt Tail.
    Prawle (50°12′N 3°42′W).

2   **Lifeboats**: An all-weather and an inshore lifeboat are stationed at Salcombe Harbour (50°14′N 3°46′W).

National Coastwatch Institution (NCI) station is situated at:
    Prawle Point (50°12′·4N 3°43′·1W)

For details of coastguard stations see 1.101, for lifeboats see 1.113, and for NCI see 1.106.

Natural conditions
4.255

1   **Tidal streams** within Bigbury Bay are weak, but SE of Bolt Tail the rates increase considerably. For details of the streams 7 miles seaward of Bigbury Bay and in the vicinity of Start Point see information on the chart.

Race. With strong winds a race may extend up to 1 mile SE from Start Point.

2   **Sandwaves.** There is a continuous area of sandwaves extending from 4½ to 16½ miles S of East Rutts (50°13′N 3°59′W), W to a line extending S from West Rutts (50°14′N 4°05′W) and E to a line extending S from Bolt Tail. The sand waves in this area have an average height of 2 to 3 m, with isolated peaks of 5 m. The distance between consecutive crests varies from 100 to 300 m. The waves lie mainly in a N to S direction, and at the W end of the area they tend to form a more ragged pattern, terminating in spurs extending up to 3 miles from the main body.

Directions
(continued from 4.160)

Principal marks
4.256

1   **Landmarks:**
    Rame Head (50°19′N 4°13′W) (4.215).
    Great Mew Stone (50°18′N 4°06′W) (4.215).
    Conspicuous building (50°18′N 4°03′W) situated
      2½ cables E of Hilsea Point.
    Bigbury Church (spire) (50°18′N 3°52′W).

Major lights:

Eddystone Light (50°11′N 4°16′W) (4.215).

Start Point Light (50°13′N 3°38′W). (5.18).

Other aid to navigation
4.257

1   **Racon:** Eddystone Light (50°11′N 4°16′W). For details see *Admiralty List of Radio Signals Volume 6(1)*.

Charts 1634, 1900, 1613
Plymouth to Prawle Point
4.258

1   From a position about 1¼ miles SSW of Great Mew Stone (50°18′N 4°06′W) the passage leads ESE passing (with positions given from Bolt Tail (50°14′N 3°52′W)):

SSW of Ebb Rocks (8¾ miles WNW) which lie near the W end of a shallow ledge which extends nearly 3 cables SW from Gara Point (4.252); thence:

2   SSW of a 3 m patch (8 miles WNW), the outer-most danger off Blackstone Point; thence:

SSW of Hilsea Point Rock (7½ miles WNW); thence:

3   Clear of East Rutts (4½ miles WSW) (4.255); thence:

SSW of Graystone Ledge (7½ cables SSE) which extends 2½ cables from the coast SE of Bolt Tail; thence:

4   SSW of Ham Stone (2 miles SE), a rugged black rock; thence:

SSW of Gregory Rocks (2½ miles SE); thence:

SSW of Bolt Head (3¾ miles ESE) (4.252). Mariners are advised to keep at least 5 cables offshore between Bolt Tail and Bolt Head on account of the numerous rocky heads inshore of this distance. Thence:

SSW of Prawle Point (6¼ miles ESE) (4.252).

5   **Clearing marks:**

The alignment (306¾°) of Plymouth Breakwater W Light (50°20′N 4°10′W) (4.215) with Saint Macra's Church Tower, 1¼ miles NW, and seen between Great Mewstone and Wembury Point, clears 2 cables SW of Eastern Ebb Rocks.

6   **Useful marks:**

Saint Anchorite's Rock (50°18′N 3°59′W).

Prawle Point to Start Point
4.259

1   From a position SSW of Prawle Point (50°12′N 3°43′W) the passage leads E passing (with positions given from Prawle Point):

S of Langerstone Point (5 cables ENE); a drying ledge and depths of less than 6 m extend 5 cables ESE from the point. Thence:

S of a 1·5 m patch (2½ miles ENE) with a drying rock close NE which lies at the S extremity of a spit extending 2 cables S from Great Sleaden Rock; thence:

2   S of Black Stone (3¼ miles ENE) at the N end of Cherrick Rocks, which dry and extend 1 cable farther S, at the extremity of foul ground extending S from Start Point, noting the depths of less than 10 m which lie within 3½ cables S and E of the point. For details of a race off Start Point, see 4.255.

3   **Useful mark:**

Radio masts (50°14′N 3°40′W) (5.18).

(Directions continued at 5.18)

Salcombe

Charts 28, 1634
General information
4.260

1   **Position and function.** Salcombe Harbour (50°14′N 3°46′W) entered between Splatcove Point and Limebury Point is well sheltered and is predominantly a large yachting centre capable of handling vessels of up to 30 m in length and 5·5 m draught, with moorings for visiting yachts up to 100 tons.

Topography. At Bolt Head (50°13′N 3°47′W) (4.252) the coast turns sharply N towards the entrance to Salcombe Harbour, maintaining the same high elevation but rising less abruptly than W of the headland.

2   **Port limits.** The seaward limit, a line from Great Eelstone (50°12′·9N 3°46′·9W) drawn ENE to a point in the Parish of East Portlemouth, as shown on the chart.

Historic wrecks. Two restricted areas (50°12′·7N 3°44′·6W) each with a radius of 300 m, centred 4½ and 6½ cables NW of Gammon Head, contain historic wreck sites. For protection regulations see 1.89.

3   **Approach and entry.** The harbour is approached E of Bolt Head on Sandhill Point Direction Light (50°13′·8N 3°46′·7W) (4.264), passing over a bar, thence entered on leading lights situated close N of Scoble Point, 1 mile NE, which lead NE through the harbour to abreast of Batson Creek.

Harbour Authority: South Hams District Council, Harbour Office, Whitestrand, Salcombe, TQ8 8BU.

Limiting conditions.
4.261

1   **Controlling depth.** The Bar (50°13′·2N 3°46′·6W), consisting of sand with a least depth of 1 m extends NE across the harbour entrance from a position 6 cables S of Sandhill Point to Limebury Point, the E entrance point of the harbour. The deepest water over The Bar is towards the W shore; within The Bar the depths increase.

2   **Tidal levels**. Mean spring range about 4·6 m; mean neap range about 2·0 m. For further information see *Admiralty Tide Tables*.

Swell. The Bar is dangerous with onshore winds between E and S, particulary during the out-going tide, see also information on the chart regarding dangerous breakers. Should there be any swell running a crossing should not be attempted until there is a considerable rise in the tide.

Arrival information
4.262

1   **Vessel traffic scheme.** Berthing instructions, local weather and tidal information are available on request.

Port radio and notice of ETA required. A port radio station with limited hours operates from the port; send ETA during working hours.

2   **Outer anchorages.** Anchorage may be obtained in Starehole Bay entered between Mew Stone (50°12′·6N 3°47′·1W) and Great Eelstone, a high overhanging rock 3½ cables N, about mid-way between the entrance points. Anchorage may also be obtained on The Range (50°13′N 3°46′W) about 5½ cables S of Limebury Point in depths of up to approximately 11 m, sand and shell. The anchorages are indicated on the chart.

Batson Creek   *Snapes Point*   *Southpool Creek*

Sandhill Point   *Biddlehead Point*

Salcombe Harbour from SW (4.262)

(Photograph – Air Images)   *(Original dated 2001)*

3   **Pilotage.** Pilots may be obtained from Plymouth.
Speed limit within the harbour is 8 kn.

Harbour
4.263
1   **General layout.** The town of Salcombe is built along the W side of the harbour between Sandhill Point and Batson Creek, 7 cables NE.
Ferry crosses the harbour between Salcombe and Portlemouth, on the E side of the harbour.
2   **Shellfish cages** marked by coloured fish dans are laid 2 cables S of Snapes Point (50°14′·4N 3°45′·5W)
Oyster beds are found throughout Frogmore Creek from about 2 cables W, to 7½ cables NE of Wareham Point (50°15′·3N 3°45′·4W).
3   **Yacht race marker buoys** are laid on The Range between May and September; their positions can best be seen from the chart.
Tidal streams set fairly in and out of the harbour; those off the town are shown by information on the chart. Rates of up to 3 kn may be experienced during springs.

Directions for entering harbour
4.264
1   **Landmarks:**
House (50°13′·3N 3°46′·9W).
Radio Mast (50°13′·5N 3°47′·9W).
2   **Leading marks:**
Front mark. Pound Stone Beacon (red and white, red cage topmark) (50°13′·6N 3°46′·7W).
Rear mark. Sandhill Point Direction Light (red and white diamond on white mast, 12 m in height) (1 cable N of the front mark).
The alignment (000°) of these marks, and at night in the white sector (357½°–002½°) of the direction light, leads in

the approach passing (with positions given from Sandhill Point):
3   E of Mew Stone and Little Mew Stone, two conical rocks (1¼ miles SSW); thence:
E of Cadmus Rocks (8½ cables S); thence:
E of Little Eelstone (8 cables S); and:
W of Rickham Rock (9 cables SSE) on the SW side of Chapple Rocks; thence:
Over The Bar (5 cables S) (4.261); thence:
4   Between Bass Rock (2½ cables SSW), marked on its SE side by a buoy (port hand), and Wolf Rock (2 cables SSE) marked at its SW side by a light buoy (starboard hand).
4.265
1   **Leading lights:**
Front light (mast) (50°14′·5N 3°45′·3W).
Rear light (stone column 2 m in height) (1 cable NE of the front light).
The alignment (042½°) of these lights leads through the harbour to the anchorages (4.266) passing:
2   Between Pound Stone marked by a beacon (1 cable S) (4.264) and Black Stone (2 cables SE) marked at its W extremity by a light beacon (green and white); thence:
SE of Old Harry (1 cable SE), the extremity of rocky ledges which fringe Sandhill Point, marked by a beacon (red and white), noting Castle Beacon (red and white) which marks the E extremity of the same ledges.
3   The track then passes S and E of Middle Ground (9 cables NE); farther N the chart is the best guide.
Clearing bearing:
The line of bearing 218° of Black Stone Light Beacon clears NW of the shoal water on the SE side of the fairway.

Useful mark:

Light (white metal column, 3 m in height) (50°14′·2N 3°46′·0W) on Salcombe Landing Stage.

Berths
4.266

1   **Anchorage** can be obtained, with reference to Snapes Point (50°14′·4N 3°45′·5W):

In Sunny Cove (9 cables SW).

Off Small's Cove (5¼ cables SSW).

Clear of the fairway off the entrance to Batson Creek (3¼ cables SW) in depths of 5 to 8 m.

Batson Creek from SE (4.266)

(Original dated 2001)

(Photograph - Air Images)

In The Bag (1¼ cables N) clear of the small craft moorings.

West and NW of Halwell Point (5¾ cables N).

Several of the above anchorages are shown on the chart.

2   **Prohibited anchorage.** Anchorage is prohibited, as indicated on the chart, between Biddlehead Point (50°13′·7N 3°46′·3W) and Small's Cove, 3 cables NE, and in the fairway SE of the entrance to Batson Creek.

Submarine cables, marked by notice boards, are laid across the N end of the former area.

Port services
4.267

1   **Repairs:** boatyards at Salcombe, Kingsbridge and Frogmore for repairs to hull and machinery to craft up to 21 m in length.

Other facilities: refuse barge moored off Whitestrand Quay from April to October; slips and landings as indicated on the chart.

2   **Supplies:** fuelling barge moored on Middle Ground; water as indicated on the chart; provisions and ship chandlery available.

Rescue: see 4.254.

Minor bays and rivers

Chart 30
Wembury Bay and River Yealm
4.268

1   **General information.** Wembury Bay, entered between Great Mew Stone (50°18′N 4°06′W) and Gara Point, 1¼ miles E, has irregular depths of less than 15 m with a bottom of rock, sand and gravel, and is used mainly as an anchorage in fair weather for small craft bound for River Yealm.

2   River Yealm is entered between Mouthstone Point (50°18′·5N 4°04′·3W) the NW extremity of Yealm Head and Season Point a steep cliffy head with a black rock lying close off it, 2 cables NE. The river estuary is used predominantly as a yachting centre. Newton Creek branches E from the river opposite Warren Point (50°18′·7N 4°03′·2W); it dries but has a depth of approximately 3·5 m at HW.

3   **Local knowledge** is essential.

Harbour Authority: River Yealm Harbour Authority.

Tidal streams in Wembury Bay are weak, the out-going stream from River Yealm sets W along the coast and then NW between Great Mew Stone and Wembury Point. In River Yealm they begin as follows:

Interval from HW Devonport (Dover)	Direction
–0545 (+0100)	In-going
+0015 (–0525)	Out-going

The maximum in-going and out-going spring rates are 1½ kn and 2 kn.

4   **Freshets.** During freshets the out-going stream attains a rate of up to 4 kn off Warren Point.

Channel. The Sand Bar is a drying spit which extends S and E from Season Point and is subject to frequent alteration in extent and depth. The spit extends S of the leading marks which clear the Mouthstone Ledge and the tip turns E towards Cellar Bay. The Sand Bar Light Buoy marks the S extremity of the spit and the fairway is 40 m wide with a least depth of 1·5 m at this point.

5   Between the sandspit and Misery Point, 2¼ cables NE, there is a depth of 0·8 m. Thence N of Misery Point the channel deepens to 3·0 m, inclining towards the N side of the river, and then shoals again to 2·2 m up to Yealm Pool abreast Warren Point. Above Yealm Pool the river turns N and has depths of up to 2 m almost as far as Steer Point, 1 mile N. At this point the river divides into two branches and ceases to be navigable at LW even by boats.

4.269

1   **Directions.** No attempt should be made to enter during strong SW winds when not only does a line of breakers extend across the mouth of Wembury Bay but the sea also breaks heavily on the irregular ground within.

The line of bearing 023° of Saint Werburgh's Church (square tower) (50°19′·1N 4°04′·9W) leads in the approach passing (with positions given from Mouthstone Point (50°18′·5N 4°04′·3W)):

2   ESE of Outer and Inner Slimers (11 cables W), and:

WNW of Western Ebb Rocks (5 cables SW).

The alignment (088¾°) of beacons (white with black stripe, triangle topmarks) (3 cables E) then leads in the fairway passing:

S of Porchopen Shoal (5 cables W); thence:

N of Mouthstone Ledge (1 cable W).

3   The track then leads generally ESE thence ENE passing:

S of Sand Bar Light Buoy (port hand) (1¼ cables ENE); thence:

SE of the Inner Bar Buoy (port hand, seasonal) (1½ cables ENE).

4   The track then leads generally NE using a beacon (white with red stripe) (5 cables NE) as a headmark until the deeper water on the N side of the river is reached. Thence continue round Misery Point (4 cables ENE) and into Yealm Pool passing SE of Spit Buoy (port hand) (7 cables E) marking the drying spit extending SE from Warren Point.

5   **Clearing bearing:**

The line of bearing 002° of Saint Werburgh's Church clears ¼ cable W of Western Ebb Rocks.

4.270

1   **Anchorage** is possible in Cellar Bay (50°18′·6N 4°03′·9W), as indicated on the chart. Once E of Misery Point anchoring is not recommended, as there are extensive small craft moorings which are continuous to Madge Point. Mooring buoys and pontoon berths are available for visiting vessels. Vessels over 17 m LOA exceeding 2·2 m draught should seek guidance from harbour staff before entry. Larger vessels proceeding beyond Misery Point may find difficulty in turning.

2   **Prohibited anchorage.** Anchorage is prohibited in an area NE of Madge Point (50°19′·1N 4°03′·2W), see information on the chart.

Submarine cables, including power cables, cross the river in three places between Warren Point and Steer Point and across Newton Creek at Newton Ferrers, as indicated on the chart; their landing places are indicated by beacons.

Chart 1613

River Erme

4.271

1   **General information.** The mouth of River Erme, entered between Battisborough Island (50°18′N 3°58′W) and Fernycombe Point, 7 cables E, can be identified by the clumps of trees just within the W entrance point and a small ruined house on the E shore just within Muxham Point. From the offing, at HW, the river appears to be of some importance, but the greater part dries. At HW, with a smooth sea, mariners in boats can navigate for about 7½ cables up river.

2   **Historic wrecks.** Restricted areas, radius 250 m and 100 m, centred 4 cables NW and W of Fernycombe Point (50°18′·1N 3°56′·8W) contain historic wreck sites, for protection regulations see 1.89.

Entrance to the river is obstructed by a reef extending 4½ cables W from Fernycombe Point. West Mary's Rock and East Mary's Rock lie on the reef with Edward's Rock about 2 cables SSW of West Mary's Rock.

3   **Anchorage** can be obtained inside the reef in a basin about 1½ cables in extent, in depths of 5 to 7 m, sand and rock. The anchorage affords poor shelter except with N winds.

Local knowledge is required as the river is liable to change its course.

River Avon

4.272

1   **General information.** Burgh Island (50°17′N 3°54′W), with a small ruined chapel on its summit, is connected to the coast at Bigbury-on-Sea, a seaside resort, by a sandy neck which dries. River Avon, entered between Bigbury-on-Sea and a high, dark cliffy point 5 cables SE, is navigable at HW by mariners in small craft.

2   **Channel.** Drying rocks lie on each side of the entrance 2 and 4 cables, respectively, ESE of Burgh Island, and a beacon marks the end of a reef extending 1 cable E from the same island. Close within the E entrance point a sandy tongue of land, prolonged by a drying spit, extends N towards the N bank of the river which here makes a sharp turn S and becomes narrower thus causing an acceleration of the tidal stream.

3   **Vertical clearance.** There is a power cable with a safe overhead clearance of 5·6 m at Aveton Gifford, 4 miles within the entrance.

Local knowledge is essential. In 1985 it was reported that there were depths of less than 3 m on the bar at HW springs and that the river to Aveton Gifford had silted.

Hope Cove

4.273

1   **General information.** Hope Cove, with a village and boat slip at its head, lies on the N side of Bolt Tail (50°14′N 3°52′W) and is frequently used as an anchorage but the holding ground is not good and it is only safe with offshore winds.

Caution. A rock drying 2·5 m lies ½ cable offshore approximately 3 cables ENE of Bolt Tail.

NOTES

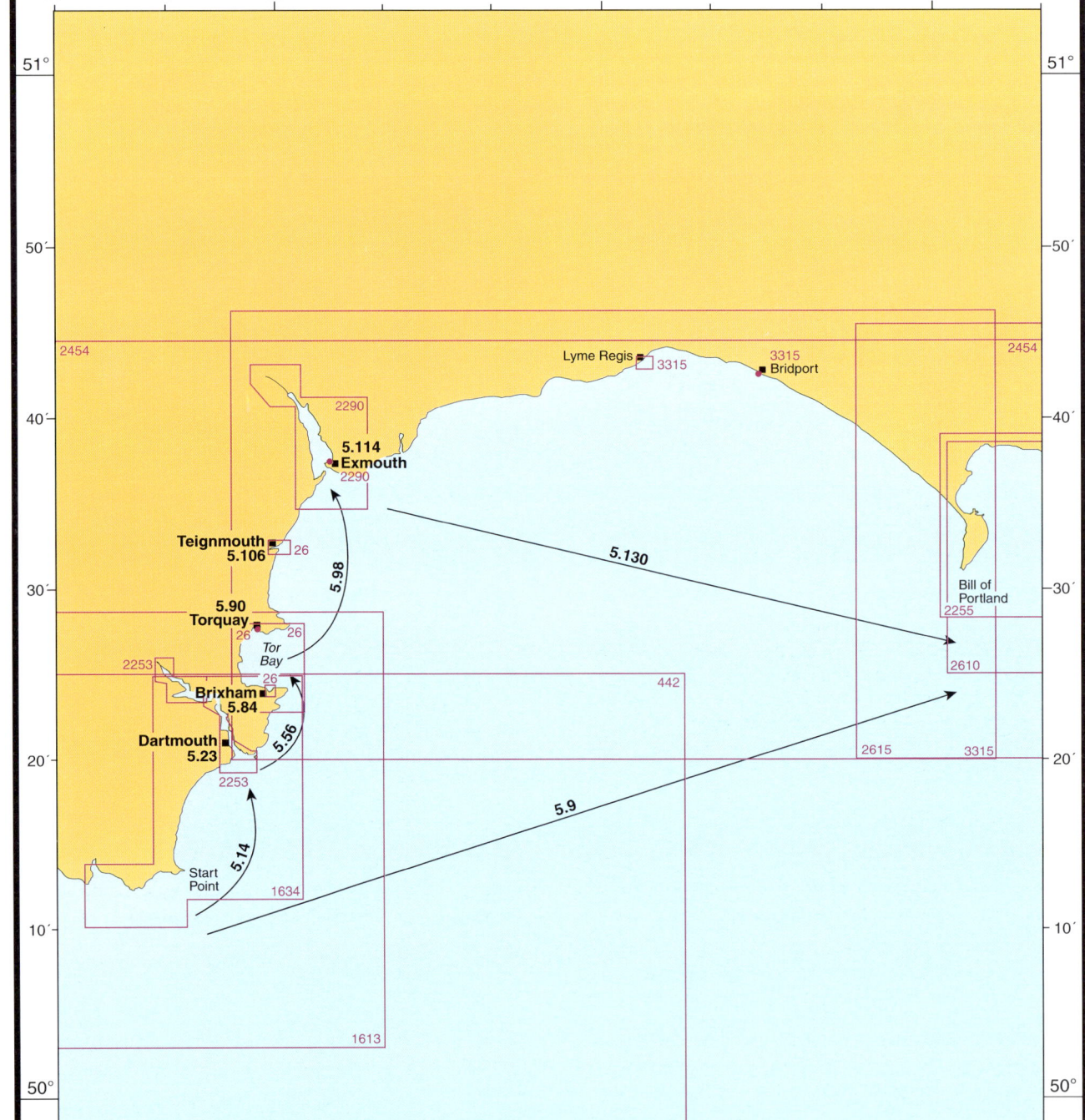

CHAPTER 5

START POINT TO BILL OF PORTLAND

GENERAL INFORMATION

Chart 2454
Scope of chapter
5.1

1   This chapter covers the S coast of England from Start Point (50°13′N 3°38′W) to the Bill of Portland, 50 miles ENE.

Ports. The ports of Dartmouth (5.23), Tor Bay Harbour (5.64) including Brixham and Torquay harbours, Teignmouth (5.106) and Exmouth (5.114) are covered by this chapter.

Topography
5.2

1   From Start Point to the Bill of Portland the coast curves inward in a broad sweep, in the N part of which is Lyme Bay (5.124).

Coast radio
5.3

1   Start Point coast radio station, remotely controlled, operates on VHF from position 50°21′N 3°43′W. For details, see *Admiralty List of Radio Signals Volume 1(1)*.

Exercise areas
5.4

1   Detailed information concerning these areas, which are found in the waters of this chapter, may be found on Practice Exercise Area (PEXA) charts. Such areas are also shown on all new, and new edition navigation charts. For further details see 1.30 and *Annual Summary of Admiralty Notices to Mariners Nos 5 and 8*.

Cargo transhipment
5.5

1   Cargo transhipment takes place approximately 5 miles offshore in Lyme Bay, E of Tor Bay, S of Beer Head, S of Bridport and off Chesil Beach. For details, see 1.7.

Deep-draught vessel anchorage
5.6

1   An anchorage, about 2 miles square (chart 3315) for vessels of deep-draught, sheltered from SW winds, is situated E of Tor Bay, outside of harbour limits, centred about 4 miles NE of Berry Head (50°24′N 3°29′W); vessels are normally anchored under pilot's advice.

For details of deep-sea pilot boarding arrangements and other facilities provided outside of Tor Bay Harbour limits from Brixham and Torbay harbours, see 5.95.

Shelter
5.7

1   In S and SE gales it should be borne in mind that there is no shelter except in the harbours of Dartmouth, Brixham and Torquay, since under these conditions the sea breaks across the entrances to the small harbours of Teignmouth, Exmouth, Lyme Regis and Bridport rendering them unapproachable.

Tidal streams
5.8

1   Tidal streams are fairly strong off Start Point, and very strong off Bill of Portland. In the W part of the bay between these points the stream is weak but becomes stronger in the E part towards Isle of Portland; midway between the two points it attains a maximum rate of approximately 1½ kn at springs.

2   The streams in the bays both E and W of Isle of Portland, and off Bill of Portland, provide outstanding examples of eddies from a salient point; their effects, namely a set N into these bays, and a set S, S of Bill of Portland, are noticeable as much as 8 to 10 miles W and E, and 5 to 6 miles S of Bill of Portland. Mariners bound up or down the Channel are advised to keep well S of Bill of Portland in order to avoid them. For details of Portland Race, see 6.20.

See also *Admiralty Tidal Stream Atlas for the English Channel and The West Country - Falmouth to Teignmouth*.

OFFSHORE PASSAGE

General information

Chart 2454
Route
5.9

1   From S of Start Point (50°13′N 3°38′W) the offshore passage leads ENE, about 50 miles, to S of Bill of Portland.

Exercise areas
5.10

1   For details of exercise areas see 5.4 and information on the charts.

Tidal streams
5.11

1   For details of tidal streams, see 5.8 and information on the charts.

Directions
(continued from 4.13)
Principal marks
5.12

1   **Landmarks:**
        Conspicuous Radio Masts (50°14′N 3°40′W) (5.18).
        Isle of Portland (50°34′N 2°26′W) (6.13).
        Portland Lighthouse (50°31′N 2°27′W) (6.21).
    Major lights:
        Start Point Light (50°13′N 3°38′W) (5.18).

Portland Light (50°31′N 2°27′W) (6.21).
Channel Light Float (49°54′N 2°54′W) (2.40).

Start Point to Bill of Portland
5.13

1 From a position S of Start Point (50°13′N 3°38′W) (4.252) the route leads ENE passing:

SSE of Skerries Bank (50°14′N 3°37′W) (5.19); thence:

To a position S of Bill of Portland (50°31′N 2°27′W) (6.13).

Clearing marks: for details of clearing marks for Skerries Bank, see 5.20.

(Directions continue at 6.9)

START POINT TO BILL OF PORTLAND

START POINT TO DARTMOUTH HARBOUR

General information

Charts 1634, 1613
Route
5.14

1 From a position S of Start Point (50°13′N 3°38′W) the passage to Dartmouth leads initially NE, about 3 miles, thence NNE, about 6 miles, passing E of Skerries Bank.

Topography
5.15

1 Start Bay (5.22) is entered between Start Point (50°13′N 3°38′W) and Combe Point, 7 miles NNE. The shore for 7½ cables NW of Start Point is fringed by a rocky ledge, thence to Strete Head, 5 miles N of Start Point, it is bordered, respectively, by Hall Sands, Bee Sands and Slapton Sands together forming an almost continuous beach interrupted only for a short distance by Limpet Rocks (50°16′N 3°39′W) at Torcross.

Hazards
5.16

1 **Exercise areas,** for information regarding same, see 5.4.
Yacht race marker buoys. For details of yacht race marker buoys in the approaches to Dartmouth, see 5.37.

Tidal streams
5.17

1 Tidal streams in Start Bay are rectilinear; for details see information on the charts.
An eddy forms close N of Start Point during the NNE-going stream.

Directions
(continued from 4.259)

Principal marks
5.18

1 **Landmarks:**
Radio masts (50°14′N 3°40′W) 1 mile WNW of Start Point.
Church (square tower) (50°19′N 3°36′W) at Stoke Fleming.
Berry Head (50°24′N 3°29′W) (5.81).

2 **Major light:**
Start Point Light (white round granite tower, 28 m in height) (50°13′N 3°38′W).

Start Point Lighthouse (5.18)
(Original dated 2006)

(Photograph - P. McManaway)

5.19

1 From a position S of Start Point (50°13′N 3°38′W) the passage leads initially NE passing:

SE of Skerries Bank which extends approximately 3½ miles NE from a position 6 cables NE of Start Point. The shoalest parts of the bank are at its SW and NE ends with the shoalest part (2·1 m) (50°13′·8N 3°37′·2W) at its SW end. In bad weather the sea breaks heavily on all parts of the bank, especially on its SW end.

2 When Berry Head (50°24′N 3°29′W) bears less than 021° the passage then leads NNE passing:

ESE of Skerries Bank Buoy (port hand) (50°16′N 3°34′W) which marks the NE end of Skerries Bank; thence:
ESE of Earlstones (50°19′N 3°35′W) (5.42); thence:
ESE of Outer Combe Rocks which lie 1 cable S of Combe Point (50°20′N 3°34′W).

5.20

1 **Clearing bearings:**
The line of bearing 250° of Prawle Point (50°12′N 3°43′W) (4.252) open S of Start Point, 3¼ miles ENE, clears S of Skerries Bank.

Skerries Bank is covered by Start Point red auxiliary light between the bearings of 210°–255°.

2   The line of bearing 021° of Berry Head (50°24′N 3°29′W) (5.81) seen midway between Scabbacombe Head (50°21′N 3°31′W) and Eastern Blackstone (5.61), 1 mile S, clears SE of Skerries Bank.

The alignment (033°) of Old Combe Rock (50°19′·5N 3°34′·3W) with Western Blackstone, 6½ cables NNE, clears ESE of Earlstones.

3   **Useful marks:**

Mew Stone (50°20′N 3°32′W) (5.40).

Day Beacon (50°21′N 3°33′W) (5.40).

(Directions continue at 5.40 and for Tor Bay at 5.60)

Side channel

Between Start Point and Skerries Bank.
5.21

1   There is a passage between Start Point (50°13′N 3°38′W) and the SW end of Skerries Bank, 6 cables NE. The line of bearing 318½° of a conspicuous house (50°15′·8N 3°40′·7W) on the skyline with the SE-most house at Beesands, 1¼ miles SE, clears SW of Skerries Bank. In 1981 the house on the skyline was pink, and the house at Beesands white.

Anchorage

Start Bay
5.22

1   **General information.** Start Bay is entered between Start Point (50°13′N 3°38′W) and Combe Point, 7 miles NNE. The whole of Start Bay inside of Skerries Bank (5.19) affords good anchorage in depths 12 to 14 m, sand and gravel, except within 5 cables of Start Point, where the ground is rocky, and except during SE gales. In strong E winds there is no shelter between the bank and the land as broken waters extend to the coast.

2   **Recommended berth** is charted 1 mile NNW of Start Point.

Anchorage for small craft, shown on the chart, 1 mile NW of Start Point is available at Hallsands, about 1 cable offshore in a depth of 3 m. Wilson's Rock and Long Rock lie close inshore N and S of this anchorage.

Submarine cables are laid from the centre of Blackpool Sands (50°19′N 3°36′W) SE to deep water; their positions can best be seen from the chart.

3   **Clearing bearings:**

The line of bearing 038° of Mew Stone (50°20′N 3°32′W) (5.40) just open of the high land on Scabbacombe Head, 1 mile NE, clears NW of Skerries Bank.

Skerries Bank is covered by Start Point red auxiliary light, for details see 5.20.

DARTMOUTH HARBOUR AND APPROACHES

General information

Chart 2253

Position
5.23

1   Dartmouth Harbour, situated at the mouth of River Dart, lies between Combe Point (50°19′·6N 3°34′·2W) and Inner Froward Point, 1 mile ENE.

Function
5.24

1   Dartmouth does not now generally operate as a commercial port except for cruise liners up to 3000 dwt using mainstream buoys and small vessels up to about 800 dwt en route to Totnes (5.47), although the harbour is suitable for vessels up to 10 000 tons displacement. It is used mainly by yachts and pleasure craft.

2   The harbour is well known as the home of Britannia Royal Naval College which stands on high ground on the N side of Dartmouth.

Port limits
5.25

1   The outer port limits are indicated on the chart by a line joining Combe Point and Inner Froward Point and the inner limits by River Dart as far as a weir at Totnes.

Approach and entry
5.26

1   The harbour is approached between Earlstones (50°19′N 3°35′W) and Mew Stone, 2 miles ENE, and entered between a narrow channel, approximately 1 cable wide, between Castle Point (50°20′·5N 3°33′·9W) and Kettle Point. Buoys (special), used for yacht racing marks, are moored in the approaches to Dartmouth on a seasonal basis; their positions and dates on station can be seen on chart 1634.

Port Authority
5.27

1   Dart Harbour and Navigation Authority, Dart House, Oxford Street, Dartmouth, TQ6 9AL.

Limiting conditions
5.28

1   **Controlling depth** in the entrance (50°20′·0N 3°33′·3W) is 7·9 m on The Range.

Deepest and longest berths. Mooring buoys (5.45) in River Dart.

Tidal levels. Mean spring range about 4·3 m; mean neap range about 1·8 m. For further information see *Admiralty Tide Tables.*

2   **Density of water:** normally 1·025 g/cm^3.

Maximum size of vessel handled. The harbour is suitable for vessels up to 183 m LOA and 8·3 m draught; the mooring buoys are rated for vessels of up to 10 000 tons displacement.

Arrival information

Port radio
5.29

1   Limited hours for details see *Admiralty List of Radio Signals Volume 6(1).*

Notice of ETA required
5.30

1   ETA should be sent one working day in advance for vessels requiring a pilot, with confirmation 30 minutes before arrival. Vessels not requiring a pilot should notify the Harbour Office before entering the port limits (5.25).

Outer anchorages
5.31

1   **Anchorage** is available in the vicinity of the pilot boarding place near Castle Ledge Light Buoy (50°20′N 3°33′W).

Quarantine anchorage. Mariners in vessels with infectious diseases onboard are required to anchor in The Range (50°20′N 3°33′W) until granted pratique.

Explosives anchorage: in The Range.

2   **Submarine cables**, abandoned, extend SE from Compass Cove between Combe Point and Blackstone Point.

Pilotage
5.32

1   The limits of the pilotage area are the same as the port limits (5.25). The area is divided into an Outer Zone, S of Anchor Stone (50°22′·8N 3°35′·2W), and an Inner Zone, N of Anchor Stone.

In the Outer Zone pilotage is compulsory for the following:

2   Vessels over 20 m carrying passengers or dangerous goods in bulk (including non-gas free tankers).

Towing vessels and tows of 50 m and over in combined length where the towing vessel or one or more of the vessels in the tow is 20 m in length or over.

All other vessels of 50 m and over in length.

3   In the Inner Zone pilotage is compulsory for the following:

Fishing vessels with a registered length of 47·5 m or over.

Towing vessels and tows of 20 m and over in combined length where the towing vessel or one or more of the vessels in the tow is 20 m in length or over.

4   Other vessels of 20 m and over in length either carrying dangerous and polluting goods in bulk (including non-gas free tankers), or carrying passengers, or having a draught exceeding 1·5 m.

All other vessels of 30 m and over in length.

HM Ships are exempt compulsory pilotage.

5   Pilots board near Castle Ledge Light Buoy (50°20′N 3°33′W).

Requests for pilots should be made through the local agent or the Harbour Office.

See *Admiralty List of Radio Signals Volume 6(1)* for further details.

Tugs
5.33

1   **Tugs** are available from Brixham (5.84) or from Teignmouth (5.106). Requests should be made through the Harbour Office.

Local knowledge
5.34

1   Local knowledge is advisable for entry at night.

Traffic regulations
5.35

1   No vessel within the harbour shall exceed a maximum speed of 6 kn unless consent in writing has been previously obtained from the harbour master.

2   All vessels arriving are to secure to mooring buoys or, if swinging room permits, anchor on the E side of the harbour, E of the fairway mooring buoys. The space on the W side of the buoys abutting on the town of Dartmouth being reserved as a fairway, no vessel is permitted to moor therein, except such as require to communicate with the wharves to discharge or receive cargo or passengers, or for other temporary purposes.

3   **Sound signals.** Mariners entering harbour should sound one prolonged blast before making the N turn off Kingswear.

Harbour
General layout
5.36

1   Dartmouth Harbour lies between the town of Dartmouth on the W bank of River Dart, 5 cables within the entrance, and the smaller town of Kingswear, on the E side. Mooring buoys are laid in the harbour between Kingswear and Sandquay; the fairway lies to the W of these mooring buoys. The N part of Sandquay, about 4 cables upstream from Dartmouth on the W bank, comprises Ministry of Defence property. Sandquay Jetty, of open construction which serves Britannia Royal Naval College, extends from the shore. Opposite Lower Noss Point (50°21′·9N 3°34′·6W), about 7½ cables above Dartmouth, there is a bar across the river with depths of just less than 5 m over it in the fairway to the E of the small boat mooring trots. River Dart (5.47) above Dartmouth is navigable by small vessels as far as Totnes, 10 miles upstream.

Dartmouth   Kingswear

Deadman's Cove   Dartmouth Castle   Kingswear Castle

Dartmouth Harbour Entrance from SW (5.35)

(Original dated 2001)

(Photograph - Air Images)

Hazards
5.37

1 **Vehicle and passenger ferries** ply between Dartmouth and Kingswear; their routes are shown on the chart.

Floating bridge. A floating bridge operates in the N part of the harbour, abreast Sandquay, under its own power along guide wires.

Yacht race marker buoys. In spring and summer yacht race marker buoys are laid in the approaches to the harbour; their positions can best be seen from the chart.

Tidal streams
5.38

1 **Coastal stream,** outside a line drawn between Combe Point and Mew Stone, is weak; it begins as follows:

Interval from HW Devonport (Dover)	Direction
–0105 (+0540)	NE
+0440 (–0100)	SW

The maximum spring rates are 1½ kn.
5.39

1 **Harbour streams.** The tidal streams in the approaches to the harbour are shown by information on the chart.

Rising stream. For the first 5 hours of the rising stream into the harbour the coastal stream is SW-going; for the last 1½ hours the rising stream in the approaches and the coastal stream run in the same direction.

2 At the beginning of the in-going stream, –0550 Devonport (+0055 Dover), the SW-going coastal stream turns N off Homestone (50°19′·6N 3°33′·7W), then NNE towards Wash Point (50°20′·3N 3°33′·1W) and Kingswear Castle, and NW into the harbour; a branch of this stream also forms an eddy, running NE from Homestone across the harbour entrance, at a rate of about 1 kn, towards Inner Froward Point and Castle Ledge, where it turns E past The Verticals and Mew Stone, and rejoins the SW-going coastal stream. The eddy stream from Homestone across the harbour entrance continues till the SW-going coastal stream ends, –0115 Devonport (+0540 Dover), after which, and till the end of the in-going stream, +0025 Devonport (–0515 Dover), a branch of the NE-going coastal stream runs directly into the harbour.

3 The rising stream is weak along the W shore off the entrance, and does not exceed about 1 kn in mid-channel; its rate increases as the channel narrows, to a maximum of about 1¼ kn off Battery Point (50°20′·5N 3°33′·9W), decreasing inside as the channel widens. The rising stream runs generally in the direction of the channel; close inshore on the E side of the entrance, a weak eddy runs SSE between Brookhill House (50°20′·8N 3°33′·8W) and Kettle Point. Inside the entrance an eddy runs strongly S and E along the shore from Bayard's Cove Castle (50°20′·8N 3°34′·6W) to One Gun Point, beginning –0400 Devonport (+0245 Dover).

4 **Effect of set during rising stream.** Outside a line drawn between Homestone and Mew Stone mariners entering or leaving harbour may experience a SW set during the rising stream, except near its end. Inside this line, whilst the eddy is still running, mariners may expect a NE set.

Falling stream. For the first 4 hours of the falling tide the coastal stream is NE-going; for the last 2 hours falling tide, the coastal and falling streams run in the same direction.

5 The falling stream runs obliquely across the channel from off Kingswear towards Warfleet Point (50°20′·6N 3°34′·3W), and thence outwards in the direction of the channel. Outside the entrance it, at first, meets the NE-going coastal stream about on the line Homestone to Mew Stone, and turns NE, but it runs directly outwards when the coastal stream slackens, and turns SW with the coastal stream after +0440 Devonport (–0100 Dover). The falling stream attains a rate up to 1½ kn in the narrowest part of the channel, decreasing to about 1 kn outside. During the falling stream a weak eddy runs W close inshore between Castle Point and One Gun Point, and, on the opposite side, an eddy runs strongly W between Brookhill House and Kingswear.

6 **Effect of set during falling stream.** Outside a line drawn between Homestone and Mew Stone mariners entering or leaving harbour may experience a NE set during the falling stream, except near its end when the set turns SW. Inside this line the falling stream from the entrance runs mainly in the direction of the fairway and consequently little set is to be expected. After heavy rain freshets may advance the time of commencement of the falling stream.

7 **Caution.** In April 1978 a falling stream of 2½ kn and a strong eddy were reported in the vicinity of Sandquay.

Directions for entering harbour
(continued from 5.20)

Principal marks
5.40

1 **Landmarks:**

White Cottages (50°20′·2N 3°34′·1W), old coastguard cottages.

White cottages

White Cottages (old Coastguard cottages)
and Blackstone Point from E (5.40)

(Original dated 2002)

(Photograph - Crown Copyright)

Dartmouth Castle from N (5.40)

(Original dated 2002)

Kingswear Light from SSE (5.41)

(Original dated 2002)

Dartmouth Castle (50°20′·5N 3°34′·0W) with Saint Petrox Church adjoining, situated on Castle Point. Water Tower (50°20′·6N 3°35′·2W).

2   Mew Stone (50°20′N 3°32′W) a conical rocky islet. Day Beacon (truncated pyramid) (50°20′·5N 3°32′·5W). Kingswear Castle (square tower) (50°20′·5N 3°33′·6W).

Approaches
5.41

1   The best time for entering harbour is on the last of the rising tide.

From a position ESE of Combe Point the track leads NW keeping in the white sector (325°–331°) of Kingswear Light (white round GRP tower) (50°20′·8N 3°34′·1W) passing (with positions given from Western Blackstone (50°20′·0N 3°33′·7W)):

2   SW of West Rock Light Buoy (S cardinal) (8 cables ESE) marking the line of rocks extending WSW from Mew Stone (5.40), thence:

NE of The Pin (4½ cables SE), a shoal lying 2½ cables E of Homestone Ledge; the ledge is marked on its SE side by Homestone Light Buoy (port hand); and:

3   SW of Smellstone (4½ cables ESE), a rocky shoal; thence:

Between Scottstone (2½ cables SSE) and Castle Ledge (4 cables E) marked on its S side by Castle Ledge Light Buoy (starboard hand); thence:

NE of Western Blackstone, the outermost danger off Blackstone Point (5.42); and:

4   SW of Wash Point (4 cables NE), noting The Brat and a 4·6 m patch lying 1 cable WNW of the point; thence:

Between Kitten Rock (4 cables N) with Checkstone close within, near the outer edge of Western Ledge marked at their outer end by Checkstone Light Buoy (port hand), and Kingswear Castle (5 cables N); thence:

5   Between Battery Point (5 cables NNW) and Kettle Point (5 cables N) noting Kettle Rock and Point Rock which lie close off Kettle Point.

Clearing marks:

The line of bearing 314° of the W edge (50°20′·9N 3°34′·4W) of the point at Kingswear well open E of Battery Point clears NE of Kitten Rock and associated dangers.

West of Homestone
5.42

1   There is a channel between Homestone (50°19′·6N 3°33′·8W) and Outer Combe Rocks, 3 cables WSW, with a least charted depth of 7·9 m.

The line of bearing 014° of Kingswear Castle (5.40) seen midway between Blackstone Point (50°20′·1N 3°33′·8W), with two flagstaffs on it, and Western Blackstone, 1 cable SE, leads in the channel passing (with positions given from Blackstone Point):

2   ESE of Earlstones (50°19′·2N 3°34′·8W) rocky patches; thence:

ESE of Outer Combe Rocks (6½ cables SSW); thence:

Between Homestone (5 cables S) and a patch drying 0·6 m (6 cables SSW) which lies close off Combe Point; thence:

ESE of Meg Rocks (4 cables SSW).

3   The track then leads NE clear of Scottstone (4 cables SSE) to join the track as described above.

Clearing marks:

For details of clearing marks for Earlstones, see 5.20.

North of Mew Stone
5.43

1   There is a narrow channel between Mew Stone and Outer Froward Point, on the coast 1½ cables N, Local

knowledge is essential but because of the irregular nature of the ground and of the SE set of the rising stream it is prudent to give this locality a wide berth.

Harbour.
5.44
1 Mariners in deep-draught vessels should keep on the W edge of the white sector on the line of bearing 331° of Kingswear Light (5.41) passing (with positions given from Castle Point (50°20′·5N 3°33′·9W)):

Between Castle Point and a 7·8 m depth (¾ cable ENE); thence:

SW of a 6·7 m depth (¾ cable NNE).

Britannia Royal Naval College *Dart Marina* *Higher Noss Point*

Darthaven Marina

Dartmouth Harbour from S (5.44)

(Original dated 2001)

(Photograph - Air Images)

2 **Inward bound.** The line of bearing 293° of Bayard's Cove Castle Light (white stripe on rock) (5 cables WNW), and at night in its white sector (289°–297°), then leads in the fairway passing:

NNE of One Gun Point (1¼ cables WNW) and Halftide Rock (2½ cables WNW) marked by a beacon (port hand); and:

SSW of the shoal bank on the N side of the fairway.

3 When the outer end of Kingswear Railway Pontoon (5 cables NW) bears 010° the track then leads N for the harbour.

Outward bound. This part of the fairway is indicated by a light (red lantern) (1¼ cables NE) which shows white between the bearings 102° to 107°.

Moorings and berths

Moorings
5.45
1 **Mooring buoys** and lay-up facilities are available for vessels up to 10 000 tons displacement; the positions of the mooring buoys can best be seen from the chart.

Caution. Mariners are cautioned not to anchor in the vicinity of Warfleet Point (50°20′·6N 3°34′·3W), on account of the groundwork of swamped moorings which extend to the shore on each side of the channel, nor in the fairway W of the mooring buoys off Dartmouth, nor within 1 cable of the floating bridge.

2 **Submarine cables,** including a power cable, cross the river in the area between Kingswear and Sandquay; their positions can best be seen from the chart.

Alongside berth
5.46
1 Sandquay Jetty (50°21′·5N 3°34′·6W) with a maintained depth of 7·5 m alongside can accommodate vessels of approximately 100 m in length. The training vessel *Hindostan* is permanently moored to the NW of the jetty; a mooring buoy is laid close ahead of the vessel.

River Dart

General information
5.47
1 **Description.** River Dart above Dartmouth is navigable as far as Totnes, a market town 10 miles upstream. At spring tides the river almost dries for 2 miles below Totnes, but small craft drawing no more than 1 m can proceed there 1½ hours after LW. Above the bar (5.36) across the River Dart at Lower Noss Point (50°21′·9N 3°34′·6W) the river deepens and the channel, which hugs the E bank, has a least charted depth of 10·8 m in the centre of the fairway as far as Dittisham, on the W bank, 2½ miles above Dartmouth. Above Greenway Quay (50°22′·9N 3°35′·5W) the river opens out into a basin about 5 cables in diameter, known locally as Dittisham Lake. There are two navigable channels through this basin, separated by Flat Owers; the W channel is the preferred channel. Above Dittisham Lake the channel contracts and becomes winding and intricate. It is marked by buoys and beacons as far as Totnes.

Dart Marina *Higher Noss Point*

River Dart from SE (5.47)

(Original dated 2001)

(Photograph - Air Images)

2 **Local knowledge** is essential.

Controlling dimensions. Vessels of up to 75 m in length and with draught of up to 3·6 m at MHWS and 2·5 m at MHWN can reach Baltic Wharf on the W bank of the river, 4 cables below the bridge at Totnes. A ship turning bay has been cut opposite this wharf.

Unless prepared to take the ground, mariners should not linger at Totnes after HW as the tide falls quickly; facilities for drying out are poor.

3 **Ferry** plies between a floating pontoon at Dittisham and Greenway Quay on the E bank. Care should be taken when going alongside the pontoon at half out-going stream when an eddy setting NW at up to 2 kn may be experienced.

4 **Tidal streams.** The strength and duration of the out-going stream varies according to the amount of surface water running off Dartmoor. The duration of the out-going stream increases progressively up river until, at Totnes, during neap tides and with much water running off

Dartmoor, there is no in-going stream at all. Between Higher Noss Point and Anchor Stone (50°22'·8N 3°35'·3W) streams run parallel to the river banks. In the vicinity of Anchor Stone strong eddies occur, particularly at half out-going stream. In Dittisham Lake streams follow the line of the channels except at half out-going stream when a pronounced set to the E occurs in the E channel due to water running off Flat Owers as it uncovers. Pronounced eddies of up to 2 kn also occur in the SW part of Dittisham Lake in the vicinity of the pier and floating pontoon. Streams between Dittisham Lake and Totnes run in the direction of the navigable channels.

5   **Speed.** There is a speed limit of 6 kn in River Dart as far as the S end of Home Reach, about 1 mile below Totnes; thence mariners should proceed at dead slow speed. The passage from Dartmouth to Totnes takes about 1½ hours and should be made on a rising tide so as to arrive at Totnes at the top of HW.

Directions
5.48

1   Between Lower Noss Point and Dittisham mariners should keep in the deep water close to the E bank of the river passing E of Anchor Stone (50°22'·8N 3°35'·3W) marked by a light beacon (port hand) to abreast Greenway Quay, distant ½ cable.

2   Directions continue, with positions given from the N extremity of Blackness Point (50°23'·3N 3°36'·5W):
    The line of bearing 020° of Waddeton Boat House (9 cables ENE) then leads in the channel W of Flat Owers to abreast No 1 Buoy (port hand) (7½ cables E).

3   The line of bearing 310° of Sandridge Boat House (5 cables NE) then leads in the channel. When ½ cable from the boat house with Dittisham Mill Creek open of Higher Gurrow Point (3 cables ENE) the channel leads SW passing:

4   NW of Higher Gurrow Point, distant ½ cable, Sandridge Boat House, astern, is a useful mark on this leg. Thence:
        To a position close N of Blackness Point Beacon (port hand) (¾ cable ENE).
    The channel then continues W thence generally NW passing:

5   Close SW of Pighole Point (3 cables NNW); thence:
        Through Long Stream (4 cables NW) to close S of Mill Point (8 cables NW).
    The channel then leads W passing close N of White Rock (9½ cables WNW).
    The channel then leads WNW towards Langham Wood Point (13 cables WNW) keeping to the S side of the river passing:

6   Between No 2 Buoy (port hand) (12½ cables WNW) marking the entrance to Bow Creek and No 3 Buoy (starboard hand) marking the drying bank extending S and SW from Stoke Point (11 cables NW).
    The channel then leads NE through Duncannon Reach (13 cables NW) with the houses at Duncannon as a headmark passing:

7   NW of small craft moorings and E of No 4 Buoy (port hand) marking the drying bank extending E from Ashprington Point (14 cables NW).
    From Duncannon Reach to Home Reach, 2½ miles upstream, the deepest water will be found on the outside of all bends. From Home Reach to Totnes mariners should keep in mid-channel, where the deepest water is to be found.

8   **Caution.** Occasional sunken waterlogged trees, whose branches may reach the surface of the river, obstruct the seabed between Duncannon and Fleet Mill Quay, about 2 miles downstream from Totnes and could prove hazardous to small craft.

Berths
5.49

1   **Baltic Wharf:** (50°25'·5N 3°40'·7W) on the W bank of the river; length 250 m for three ships of 75 m in length.
    Steamer Quay: (50°25'·7N 3°40'·9W) on the E bank of the river; for passenger vessels.

Port services
Repairs
5.50

1   Repairs can be carried out.
    Slip: extreme length 120 m; extreme breadth 13 m; for vessels up to 55 m LOA, 10 m breadth, maximum draught 4 m and 500 tonnes deadweight.

Other facilities
5.51

1   **Hospital** in Dartmouth.
    Compass adjustment can be carried out.

Supplies
5.52

1   **Fuel.** Diesel oil is available by barge.
    Fresh water is available at South Embarkment.
    Stores are available for small craft.

Communications
5.53

1   **Airport:** Exeter or Plymouth, distant about 50 km, with internal flights to international airports.
    Helicopter landing site.

Harbour regulations
5.54

1   It is forbidden to throw ashes, ballast, rubbish etc., or pump oily water, into the harbour.

Rescue
5.55

1   There is a Coastguard Rescue Team at Dartmouth, for details see 1.100.

DARTMOUTH TO TOR BAY

General information

Charts 26, 1634, 1613
Route
5.56

1   From ESE of Combe Point (50°20'N 3°34'W), off the entrance to Dartmouth Harbour, the passage to Tor Bay leads NNE, about 6 miles.

Topography
5.57

1   Between Inner Froward Point (50°20'N 3°33'W) and Berry Head, 4½ miles NNE, the coast is rugged with cliffs of up to 120 m high, and high undulating land behind; it is fringed by steep-to above and below-water rocks lying up to 5 cables offshore.

Exercise areas
5.58
1　For information regarding exercises, see 5.4.

Area of Special Protection
5.59
1　The area within Berry Head (50°24′N 3°29′W) and Mew Stone, 4 cables SSW, is an Area of Special Protection and certain regulations with regard to wildlife are in force. For details, see 1.91.

<h1 style="text-align:center">Directions</h1>
(continued from 5.20)

Principal marks
5.60
1　**Landmarks:**
　　Berry Head (50°24′N 3°29′W) (5.81).
　　Mew Stone (50°20′N 3°32′W) (5.40).
　Major light:
　　Start Point Light (50°13′N 3°38′W) (5.18).
5.61
1　From a position ESE of Combe Point (50°20′N 3°34′W) the passage leads NNE passing (with positions given from Sharkham Point (50°23′N 3°30′W))·
　　ESE of Mew Stone (3¼ miles SSW) (5.40), marked by Mew Stone Light Buoy (S cardinal) 1½ cables SSE of it; thence:
　　ESE of Eastern Blackstone (3 miles SSW) noting New Ridge 7 cables E; thence:
2　　ESE of Boatfield Rock (2½ miles SSW); thence:
　　ESE of Nimble Rock (2 miles SSW) and clear of The Bull (2¼ miles SSE); thence:
　　ESE of Druids Mare (1¼ miles SSW), a group of drying rocks; thence:
3　　ESE of a wreck (1·9 m) (8 cables SSW), the outermost danger off Crabrock Point; thence:
　　ESE of Mudstone Ledge (5 cables E), the outermost danger off Sharkham Point; thence:
　　ESE of Cod Rock (9 cables NNE); thence:
　　ESE then E of Berry Head (1¼ miles NNE) (5.81).
5.62
1　**Clearing bearings:**
　　The line of bearing 214¾° of Start Point Light open E of Eastern Blackstone clears E of Nimble Rock.
　　Hope's Nose (50°28′N 3°29′W) (5.64) bearing less than 359° and open E of Berry Head clears E of all dangers S of Berry Head.
2　**Positioning marks:**
　　The line of bearing 330½° of the right hand edge of Scabbacombe Head (50°21′N 3°31′W) in line with the cliff summit, 5 cables NW, marks the position of Nimble Rock.
(Directions continue at 5.81 and for Exmouth at 5.104)

Side passage
5.63
1　Bastard Rocks, drying 2·8 m, lie on a rocky reef extending ½ cable W from Cod Rock (50°23′·6N 3°29′·0W); there is a narrow passage, with depths of up to 6·4 m, between these rocks and Mew Stone, which lies ¾ cable SE of Oxley Head.
　Local knowledge is required.

<h1 style="text-align:center">TOR BAY AND HARBOUR AREA</h1>

<h2 style="text-align:center">General information</h2>

Charts 26, 1613, 3315
Position
5.64
1　Tor Bay, a well sheltered bay open E, lies between Berry Head (50°24′N 3°29′W) and Hope's Nose, 3¾ miles N.

Function
5.65
1　Tor Bay affords good anchorage, sheltered from W winds. Torbay Harbours provides numerous off–port services from Brixham and Torquay harbours to vessels at anchor or underway, for details see 5.95.

Topography
5.66
1　Paignton, a large seaside resort, occupies much of the W side of the bay which is bordered by sandy beaches. The cliffs at Roundham Head, in the centre of the W side, and those of Livermead Head and Corbyn's Head in the NW corner of the bay, are all composed of red sandstone and are similar in appearance; care should be taken not to confuse one with the others. The edges of the cliffs at Roundham Head can be easily seen, while those at Livermead Head are not easily distinguishable. Roundham Head is not easily identified on the radar screen. Paignton Pier (50°26′·2N 3°33′·4W), a promenade pier, is readily identified on the radar screen.
2　Torquay, a large seaside resort and yachting centre, stands on the N shore of Tor Bay at the meeting of two deep valleys; it contains several conspicuous buildings, the positions of which can best be seen from the chart. The town forms part of the Torbay Borough.

Port limits
5.67
1　Port limits are enclosed by a line, as shown on the chart, from Sharkham Point (50°23′N 3°30′W) to a point on the coast about 3½ miles NNW of Hope's Nose.

Approach and entry
5.68
1　Tor Bay is approached from deep water to the E and entered between Berry Head and Ore Stone, which lies 5 cables SE of Hope's Nose.

Traffic
5.69
1　In 2006 Tor Bay harbours were used by 91 vessels totalling 756 902 dwt.

Port Authority
5.70
1　The overall Harbour Authority for Tor Bay is Torbay Borough Council, Town Hall, Castle Circus, Torquay, TQ1 3DR.
　Brixham (5.84), Torquay (5.90) and Paignton Harbours (5.97) are municipal harbours under the one Harbour Authority of Torbay Borough Council and are enclosed harbours within Torbay Harbours.

Rescue
5.71
1　**Coastguard.** Brixham MRSC is situated at Kings Quay, Brixham (50°24′N 3°31′W) with Rescue Teams situated at Berry Head and Torbay.

Lifeboat. Torbay all-weather lifeboat and an inshore lifeboat are stationed at Brixham.

2 For details of coastguard stations see 1.100 and for lifeboats 1.113.

VHF Direction-finding station, for emergency use only, operates from Berry Head (50°24′N 3°29′W), for details see *Admiralty List of Radio Signals Volume 2* and 1.105.

Limiting conditions

Local weather
5.72

1 Strong E or SE winds send a heavy sea into Tor Bay.

Arrival information

Port radio
5.73

1 A radio station operates from Brixham pilot station throughout 24 hours. The station also accepts requests for deep-sea pilots for English Channel, North Sea and the Skagerrak and river/district pilots.

Torbay Harbours radio station, with limited hours, operates from the harbours of Brixham, Paignton and Torquay, see *Admiralty List of Radio Signals Volume 6(1)* and 5.95.

Notice of ETA required
5.74

1 **ETA**: Vessels should send ETA 48 hours in advance to BrixhamPilots and contact the pilot on VHF 2 hours before arrival; see *Admiralty List of Radio Signals Volume 6(1)*.

Outer anchorages
5.75

1 **Deep-draught vessel anchorage.** For details of an anchorage for deep-draught vessels, E of Tor Bay outside of harbour limits, see 5.6.

2 **Tor Bay.** Nearly the whole of Tor Bay affords good anchorage in depths of about 11 m, mud and clay, sheltered from W winds, but mariners should avoid anchoring in the vicinity of The Ridge (50°25′N 3°32′W), a patch of rock, in the SW corner of the bay. Several designated anchorage areas exist within the harbour limits, as shown on the chart.

3 **Brixham Roads** (50°25′N 3°30′W) affords anchorage N or E of Victoria Breakwater in depths of 8 or 9 m. During E gales there is an under-set to windward which strengthens with the wind and affords easy riding. Brixham Roads is reported (1997) to be fouled with old wires up to 1 mile NE of the breakwater. A recommended berth, shown on the chart, is 3¼ cables NNE of the head of Victoria Breakwater; in 1995 this anchorage was reported to be fouled with old wires. A confirmed foul area lies 5¼ cables NNE of the head of Victoria Breakwater.

4 **Paignton Roads** (50°26′N 3°32′W) off the W side of the bay affords anchorage in depths of 5 to 10 m, sand.

Torquay Roads (50°27′N 3°32′W) in the NW part of the bay affords anchorage in depths of about 10 m; it is the anchorage generally used by HM ships.

Pilotage and tugs
5.76

1 **Harbour pilots.** Pilotage is available throughout 24 hours and is compulsory for all vessels within the Tor Bay Harbour Area with the following exceptions:

Ships of the Royal Navy and Royal Fleet Auxiliary.

Foreign warships proceeding to, or leaving, a designated anchorage.

2 Vessels less than 36 m LOA not carrying dangerous and polluting goods.

Vessels under tow where the combined length of tug and tow is less than 36 m.

Fishing vessels of less than 47·5 m LOA.

3 Vessels proceeding to, or leaving, a designated anchorage where stress of weather has obliged the vessel to seek sheltered anchorage.

Boarding area: 2¼ miles ENE of Berry Head (50°24′N 3°29′W) as shown on the chart.

For details see *Admiralty List of Radio Signals Volume 6(1)*. For details regarding deep-sea pilots, see 5.95.

4 **Local knowledge** is necessary for entering Brixham Harbour (5.84) at night.

Tugs are available.

Traffic regulations
5.77

1 Vessels and craft under way in Tor Bay and intending to pass vessels at anchor shall do so at slow speed and at a distance of not less than 200 m.

Regulations concerning entry
5.78

1 **Dangerous and polluting goods.** For details see *Admiralty List of Radio Signals Volume 6(1)* and 1.68 to 1.76.

Marine farm
5.79

1 A marine farm lies 6 cables WNW of Brixham Harbour entrance. It is marked by a light buoy (special) moored at the NE corner of the farm and a buoy (special) to the NW. Mariners are advised to avoid the area.

Harbour

General layout
5.80

1 Torbay Harbours area encloses the whole of Tor Bay, and the small harbours of Brixham (5.84) and Torquay (5.90) are situated in the S and NW parts of the bay, respectively.

Controlled areas charted around the coast of Tor Bay are mainly for the use of swimmers, and are in use between May and September. Within these areas, and in the enclosed harbours, mariners should proceed with caution and must not exceed 5 kn. Water ski approach lanes have been established at Elberry Cove (50°24′·2N 3°32′·6W) and Livermead Sands (50°27′·4N 3°32′·6W).

2 **Canoeists.** Mariners are advised that canoeists, in groups or singly, may frequently be encountered in Tor Bay Harbour Area. A good lookout is advised and a wide berth requested.

Special operations. Vessels anchored in Tor Bay are frequently engaged in special operations including diving and stores/personnel transfer. Other vessels should keep at least 200 m clear, and proceed at slow speed, when passing vessels displaying special operations or diving signals.

3 **Tidal streams** in Tor Bay are very weak.

Directions for entering Tor Bay
(continued from 5.62)

Landmarks
5.81

1 Berry Head (50°24′N 3°29′W), a nearly perpendicular cliff with a flat summit, readily identified on the

radar display. A light (white tower, 5 m in height) is exhibited on the head.

Ore Stone (50°27′N 3°28′W), a conspicuous rock.

Thatcher Rock (50°27′·3N 3°29′·4W).

2   East Shag (50°27′·3N 3°30′·5W), a conspicuous rock.

Building (50°27′·6N 3°29′·9W), large white block of flats on the N side of Tor Bay.

Hotel (50°27′·5N 3°30′·6W) on the N side of Tor Bay.

Two Radio Masts (red lights) (50°27′N 3°37′W) (chart 1613).

5.82

1   **From south.** From a position E of Berry Head (50°24′N 3°29′W) the route leads generally NW, about 1 mile, to the harbour pilot boarding place (5.76) and then as required for anchoring (5.75) or entering Brixham (5.84) or Torquay (5.90) harbours. Berry Head is steep-to and may be rounded at any safe distance, as convenient, avoiding Penny Rock and The Rows, two rocky patches which lie 3 and 4 cables NW of Berry Head. For details of clearing marks for the dangers S of Berry Head, see 5.62.

2   **From east.** Two conspicuous radio masts (50°27′N 3°37′W) (5.81) between the bearings 270° to 295° leads in the approach to Tor Bay from E, then as required to the harbour pilot boarding place or for anchoring or entering the harbours.

3   **From north.** From a position E of Hope's Nose (50°28′N 3°29′W) with the W extremity of Cod Rock (50°23′·6N 3°29′·0W) bearing more than 195° and open E of Berry Head, 3 cables N, the track leads SSW passing (with positions given from Hope's Nose):

4   ESE of Tucker Rock (7½ cables ESE); thence:

ESE of Bream Rock (8 cables SE), the outermost danger SE of Ore Stone (5.81); thence:

ESE of Outer Livermeads (8 cables SSE); thence:

To the pilot boarding place or as required for anchoring or entering the harbours.

Caution. A bank (50°26′N 3°30′W) with a least depth of 9·9 m lies in the centre of Tor Bay.

5.83

1   **Useful marks:**

Victoria Breakwater Light (white tower, 6 m in height) (50°24′·3N 3°30′·8W).

Lights (metal columns, 7 m in height) (50°27′·4N 3°31′·7W) on Princess and Haldon pierheads, Torquay. The light-structures are difficult to identify by day but the piers are readily identified on the radar display.

Brixham Harbour

Chart 26 plan of Brixham Harbour

General information

5.84

1   **Position and function.** Brixham Harbour (50°24′N 3°31′W), on the S side of Tor Bay, is used principally by fishing vessels and yachts of up to 30 m in length.

The harbour is no longer used by commercial shipping.

Enclosed harbour limits are defined by a line, as shown on the chart, between the head of Victoria Breakwater (50°24′·3N 3°30′·8W) and a point on the W side of the harbour, 3 cables WSW.

Prince William Marina   *Inner Harbour*

Victoria Breakwater

Brixham Harbour from N (5.86)

(Original dated 2001)

(Photograph – Air Images)

2   **Approach and entry.** The harbour is approached from Tor Bay and entered by Main Fairway, W of Victoria Breakwater.

Harbour Authority: see 5.70.

Limiting conditions
5.85

1   **Deepest berth:** W side of Eastern Pier, MFV Basin. **Density of water:** 1·025 g/cm^3.

Harbour
5.86

1   **General layout.** Brixham Harbour consists of an outer and inner harbour. The outer harbour is protected from seaward by Victoria Breakwater which extends 5 cables NW from the shore, 1 mile W of Berry Head. Main Fairway leads SSE through outer harbour to MFV Basin and Prince William Marina at the head of outer harbour. Lights are exhibited from the heads of Fish Quay Pier, Eastern Pier and New Pier, on the W side of the fairway, and from the ends of Brixham Marina wave screen and from the head of a special events pontoon, on the E side of the fairway. A disused jetty, from which lights are exhibited, is situated inside the head of Victoria Breakwater. There are numerous moorings for fishing craft and yachts in the outer harbour on each side of Main Fairway and on account of these there is no space for vessels to anchor.

2   Inner harbour, in the SW corner of the port behind MFV Basin, mostly dries.

3   **Development.** Construction of a new fish quay is taking place (2008).

Controlled areas. For details of controlled areas, mainly for the use of swimmers, see 5.80.

Directions for entering harbour
5.87

1   Mariners should approach the Main Fairway from a position about 1½ cables NW of Victoria Breakwater head. The line of bearing 159° of a direction light (lantern box on metal column, 3 m in height) (50°23′·8N 3°30′·6W) leads through the Main Fairway, which is marked by numbered light buoys (port and starboard hand).

Basins and berths
5.88

1   **Anchorage:** 2 cables WSW of Victoria Breakwater head, as shown on the chart.

2   **MFV Basin** (50°23′·9N 3°30′·7W), with depths of 3·3 m, can accommodate vessels of up to 43 m in length. The basin is enclosed by Fish Quay, Southern Quay, New Pier and Eastern Pier and provides facilities for the fishing industry. The longest berth, Fish Quay, is 147 m in length with a depth of 3 m at its N end.

3   **Marina.** There is a marina in SE part of the harbour.

Port services
5.89

1   For facilities and services available from Brixham outside of Torbay Harbours limits, see 5.95.

Repairs: minor facilities for small vessels; slipway for vessels up to 80 tonnes.

Divers are available.

Compass adjustment can be carried out.

2   **Supplies:** fuel by arrangement; water at the jetty, MFV Basin and New Pier; stores and provisions.

Rescue, see 5.71.

Communications: nearest airports Plymouth and Exeter, distant 48 and 56 km, with connecting flights to international airports.

Torquay Harbour
Chart 26 plan of Torquay Harbour
General information
5.90

1   **Position and function.** Torquay Harbour (50°27′N 3°32′W) is situated in the NW corner of Tor Bay. The port is a yachting centre during the summer months. Visits of cargo vessels are occasional and mainly during the winter months.

Approach and entry. The harbour is approached in clear water through Tor Bay and entered between two piers.

Harbour Authority: see 5.70.

Limiting conditions
5.91

1   **Controlling depth.** 4·7 m at the entrance; for alongside berths the Harbour Master should be consulted in advance.

Tidal levels. Mean spring range about 4·1 m; mean neap range about 1·7 m. For further information see *Admiralty Tide Tables.*

2   **Maximum size of vessel handled.** Vessels over 36 m are accepted after consultation with the Harbour Master.

Harbour
5.92

1   **General layout.** The harbour consists of an outer and an inner harbour protected by piers; the entrance between the piers is approximately 50 m wide.

2   **Development.** Works are taking place (2008) in the E part of the outer harbour for the construction of a piled pontoon mooring system.

Outer harbour is formed by Haldon Pier, extending W from the SE side of the harbour, and by Princess Pier, extending S and SE from the NW side; vessels can also lie alongside the outer arm of Princess Pier. Entrance Light Buoy (starboard hand) (50°27′·4N 3°31′·8W) is moored 0·3 cables W of the head of Haldon Pier during the summer months. A marina is situated in the NW part of outer harbour with Beacon Quay on the E side of outer harbour.

Signal	Meaning
● ● ● (orange)	Vessels shall not proceed - sill gates raised and/or bridge operating.
● ● ○ (green, green, white)	Vessel may proceed - sill gates lowered, two way traffic is subject to air-draft restrictions. Bridge lifted on request.

Torquay Harbour – Inner harbour traffic signals (5.92)

3   **Inner Harbour**, or Old Harbour, is entered between South Pier, which extends W from the N end of Beacon Quay, and Old Fish Quay. Lights are exhibited from the head of South Pier. Connecting the pier heads is a bridge, beneath the centre span of which, there are a pair of hydraulic sill gates, 11·5 m wide, over which entry and exit are effected; a fixed sill exists under the N and S spans and navigation is not permitted beneath them. At half tide a depth of 2·2 m is available over the sill.

4   During operating hours, the sill gates are opened from approximately 3½ hours before HW to 3 hours after HW, at which times the bridge will be opened as required for vessels which cannot safely pass beneath the bridge. When the sill gates are raised, the bridge will remain closed. The signals (Diagram 5.92) are displayed from both sides of the bridge to control traffic.

5   **Controlled areas.** For details of controlled areas see 5.80. Swimming is strictly prohibited within the inner and outer harbours.

6   **Landmarks:**
         Imperial Hotel (50°27'·4N 3°31'·3W).
         Building (50°27'·8N 3°31'·8W).
         Hotel (50°27'·6N 3°32'·5W).

Berths
5.93
1   Princess Pier (50°27'·5N 3°31'·8W) has berths on both sides; charted depths 2·2 to 3·1 m on its N side and 2·3 to 4·1 m on its S side.

Haldon Pier (50°27'·4N 3°31'·6W), with charted depths between 1·8 and 2·5 m alongside its N side, is used occasionally for cargo operations and generally accepts vessels up to 36 m LOA; longer vessels may be accepted after consultation with the Harbour Master. A slip extends WSW from the root of the pier on its N side for about 70 m.

Port services
5.94
1   **Repairs:** limited facilities.
         Divers are available.
         Supplies: fuel by road tanker; limited quantities of marine diesel oil and petrol at South Pier; water at Haldon Pier; provisions.
         Communications: nearest airport Exeter, distant 35 km, with connecting flights to international airports.

Off-port services

Charts 1613, 3315
Deep-sea pilots
5.95
1   Brixham (Torbay) pilots provide boarding facilities for deep-sea pilots for English Channel, North Sea and Skagerrak and river/district pilots, and are available throughout 24 hours.

Prior arrangements for deep-sea pilots should be made with one of the various agencies, for details see 1.50.

2   **Boarding area:** 2½ miles ENE of Berry Head (50°24'N 3°29'W), or, for vessels with draughts greater than 18 m, 4 miles E of Berry Head, as shown on the charts.

ETA required. Send ETA for required boarding position 48 hours in advance and contact Brixham Pilots 2 hours in advance.

Pilot launch: black hull, orange wheelhouse with PILOT in black letters on wheelhouse.

Other facilities
5.96
1   Facilities are available from Brixham and Torquay harbours to provide superintendents, technicians, service engineers, repair squads, surveyors, chemists, spares, stores and provisions.

Divers and underwater inspections and cleaning operations are available.

2   **Compass adjustment** can be carried out.
         Medical facilities are available.
         Crew changes and full repatriation services are available.

Vessels are serviced underway or at the deep-draught vessels anchorage (5.6) centred 3¾ miles NE of Berry Head.

Paignton Harbour

Chart 26
General information
5.97
1   **Controlled areas.** For details of controlled areas, mainly for the use of swimmers, see 5.80.

Paignton Harbour, used by pleasure craft, is formed by two jetties on the N side of Roundham Head (50°26'N 3°33'W). A light (red metal column, 5 m in height) is exhibited from the E jettyhead; the light-structure is difficult to identify by day. The harbour dries 1·3 m but has depths of approximately 3 m at MHWS. A light beacon (E cardinal) marking the end of an outfall stands close to the E edge of Black Rock, a rocky ledge 1 cable E of the harbour entrance.

TOR BAY TO EXMOUTH

General information

Chart 3315
Route
5.98
1   From Tor Bay (50°26'N 3°28'W) the passage to Exmouth leads NNE, about 9 miles, passing E of Teignmouth.

Topography
5.99
1   Long Quarry Point (50°28'N 3°30'W), which is distinguished by the quarry scars on the cliffs, lies 1 mile NW of Hope's Nose, the N entrance point to Tor Bay, with Black Head midway between. From Long Quarry Point to The Ness (5.104), 4 miles N, the coast is cliffy, backed by high ground, with no offshore dangers.

2   Between The Point (50°32'N 3°30'W) (5.109), at the N entrance to River Teign, and The Parson and Clerk, a point 1¾ miles NE on which stands a white tower, there are numerous rocks lying up to 1 cable offshore. Dawlish a seaside resort lies in a valley about 1 mile N of The Parson and Clerk.

Historic wreck
5.100
1   **Restricted area,** 200 m square, in position 50°32'·9N 3°39'·2W contains an historic wreck, for further details see 1.89.

Exercise areas
5.101
1   For information regarding exercises, see 5.4.

Rescue
5.102
1   **Coastguard Rescue Teams** are situated at:
         Teignmouth Auxiliary Station (50°33'N 3°30'W).
         Dawlish Auxiliary Station (50°35'N 3°28'W)

Exmouth Auxiliary Station (50°37′N 3°23′W).

Lifeboats. An inshore lifeboat is stationed at Teignmouth (5.106) and an all-weather and an inshore lifeboat are stationed at Exmouth (5.114).

2 **National Coastwatch Institution** (NCI) station is situated at:

Exmouth (50°36′·6N 3°25′·8W).

For details of coastguard stations see 1.101, for lifeboats see 1.113 and for NCI see 1.106.

Tidal streams
5.103

1 For details of tidal streams about 4 miles E of Hope's Nose, see information on the chart.

Coastal stream seaward of Pole Sand (50°36′N 3°25′W) (5.109) is weak and rotary in a clockwise direction; it begins as follows:

Interval from HW Devonport (Dover)	Direction
−0200 (+0445)	NE–E
+0540 (HW)	WSW–N

The maximum rates are 1 kn.

Directions
(continued from 5.62)

Landmarks
5.104

1 Berry Head (50°24′N 3°29′W) (5.81).
Ore Stone (50°27′N 3°28′W) (5.81).
The Ness (50°32′N 3°30′W), a bold headland of red sandstone covered with vegetation.

5.105

1 From a position off the entrance to Tor Bay E of Hope's Nose (50°28′N 3°29′W) the passage leads NNE passing (with positions given from The Ness):

ESE of Long Quarry Point (4 miles S) (5.99); thence:
ESE of The Ness, the S entrance point to River Teign (5.106); thence:

2 ESE of Shag Rock which lies close off The Parson and Clerk (2 miles NNE) (5.99), noting a wreck (9·8 m) which lies 1¼ miles ESE; thence:
ESE of Dawlish Rock (3 miles NE); thence:
ESE of Langstone Point (4 miles NNE) (5.114); thence:

3 To a position about 5 cables S of Straight Point (7 miles NE). A light (metal mast, 7 m in height) is exhibited from the point; the structure is not easily seen from a distance. Do not approach on a line of bearing more than 022° of Straight Point Light.

4 **Useful marks:**
Church (spire) (50°29′N 3°31′W).
Teignmouth Harbour front positioning light (50°33′N 3°30′W) (5.111).
(Directions continue at 5.118 and for Lyme Bay at 5.129)

Teignmouth and approaches

Charts 26 plan of Teignmouth Harbour, 3315
General information
5.106

1 **Position and function.** Teignmouth (50°33′N 3°30′W) on the N side of the entrance to River Teign is a tourist

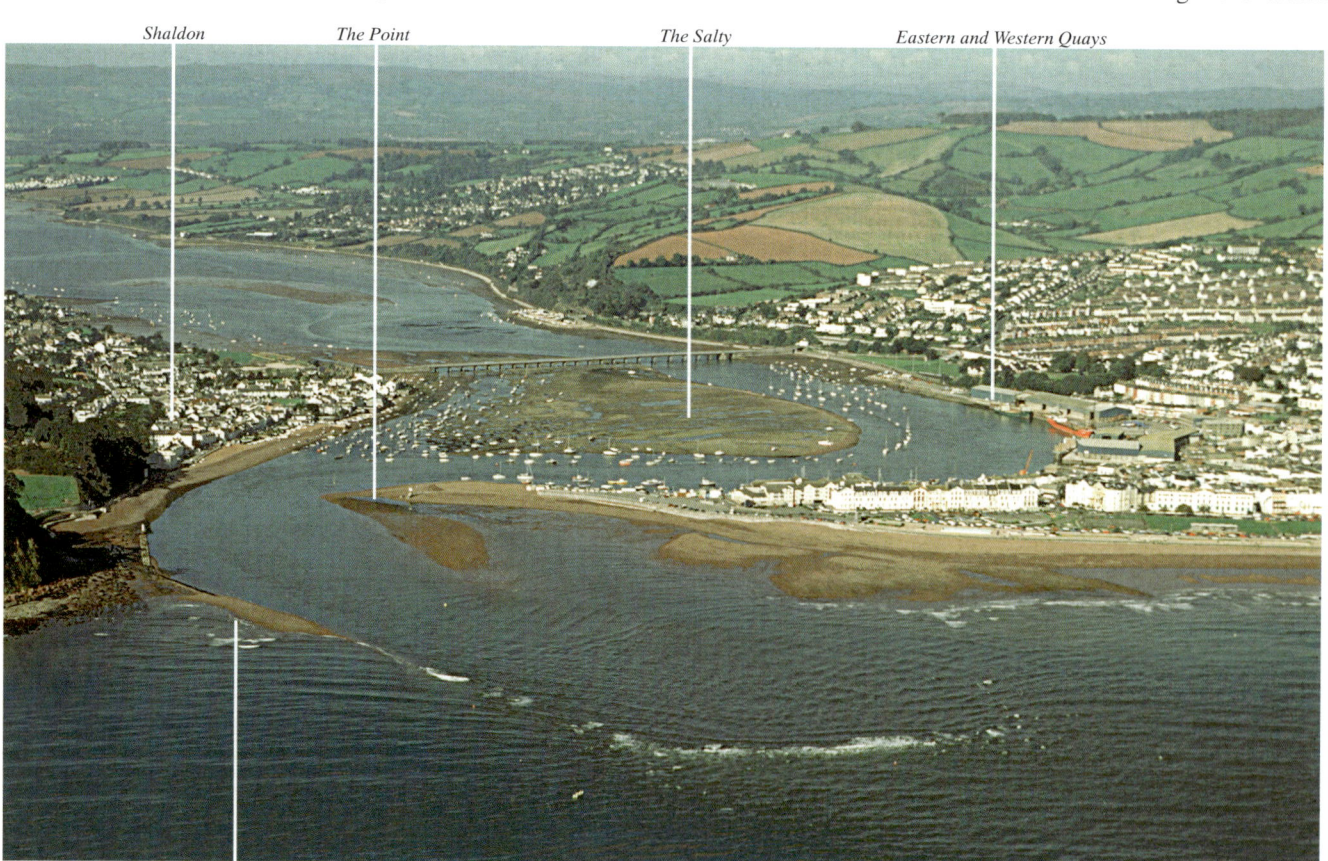

Shaldon   The Point   The Salty   Eastern and Western Quays

Pole Sand

Teignmouth from SE (5.106)
(Original dated 1997)

(Photograph - PRPA/Patrick Roach)

centre which attracts marine leisure craft. Ball clay, cereals and stone for sea defences are exported, and imports include building materials, timber, coal, animal feeds and fertilizer.

2 **Harbour limit**: as shown on the chart.

Traffic. In 2006 the port handled 358 vessels totalling 861 411 dwt.

Port Authority: Teignmouth Harbour Commissioners, 2–3 Orchard Gardens, Teignmouth, Devon, TQ14 8DR. Website: www.teignmouth-harbour.com

Limiting conditions
5.107

1 **Maximum dimensions.** In fair weather vessels of up to 124 m in length and 5·2 m draught can enter the port at MHWS, but as heights of tide can vary with strong winds, ship's owners are strongly advised to contact the local shipping agents prior to making arrangements for any vessel which has a draught approaching that given above.

2 **Tidal levels** (Approaches). Mean spring range about 3·9 m; mean neap range about 1·6 m. For further information see *Admiralty Tide Tables*.

Maximum size of vessel handled: 126 m LOA with draught of 5 m at Springs and 4 m at Neaps.

Local weather. In E and SE gales the harbour may be inaccessible.

Arrival information
5.108

1 **Port radio** station, with limited hours and when a vessel is expected, operates from the port.

Notice of ETA required for a pilot should be sent at least 12 hours in advance, stating length and precise draught; amendments may be made up to 2 hours before arrival.

2 **Outer anchorage:** about 1 mile E or SE of The Ness, silt over clay, good holding. Mariners should avoid anchoring near an obstruction (6·7 m) about 6 cables ENE of The Ness.

3 **Submarine pipeline.** An outfall with diffusers at its head, marked at its seaward end by a light buoy (special), extends 1¼ miles ESE from The Ness.

4 Anchorage is possible for small craft, in settled weather and with offshore winds, outside the harbour 1 to 2 cables SE of Teignmouth Pier or 1 cable SE of The Ness.

Pilotage is compulsory for vessels of 30 m LOA or more; pilot boards 1 mile SE of The Ness, as indicated on the chart, from a vessel with a black hull and white superstructure, see *Admiralty List of Radio Signals Volume 6(1)*.

5 **Local knowledge** is essential.

Tug is available; mooring boat, with limited towing facilities, by arrangement.

Speed limit of 6 kn is in force in the port.

Regulations concerning entry. See 1.68 to 1.76 and *Admiralty List of Radio Signals Volume 6(1)* for vessels carrying dangerous or polluting goods

Harbour
5.109

1 **General layout.** The entrance to River Teign lies between The Ness (50°32′N 3°30′W) and The Point, 2½ cables NW. A low tongue of loose sand, which is subject to constant change, extends SW from The Point and is marked near its SW extremity by a light beacon. A beacon marks the end of a masonry groyne situated on The Point. Spratt Sand, which dries and whose shape is liable to constant change, extends up to 4 cables E of The Point.

2 Pole Sand, which dries, extends 1½ cables E from The Ness. East Pole Sand, which also dries, lies about 2½ cables E of The Ness. It is sometimes joined to Pole Sand by the action of E winds, but there is normally a narrow channel between them. Shoal water extends E from East Pole Sand.

3 The Bar (50°32′·4N 3°29′·5W), which has been known to dry, lies between East Pole Sand and the SE edge of Spratt Sand; it is subject to constant change.

Teignmouth Harbour, fronts the W side of the town within the river entrance; it contains working berths at Eastern Quay and Western Quay. The berths are owned by Associated British Ports (ABP) Holdings Plc.

4 **Approach channels.** Sand tends to build up on The Point as a result of NE and E gales until it extends from the light beacon to the seaward end of the masonry groyne. The sand is subsequently eroded by the strong out-going tidal streams and is deposited on the sandbanks described above. Spring tides cut channels through the sandbanks. These channels are marked by buoys (special); these buoys have no navigational significance other than for the guidance of the pilots. The position of the best channel moves constantly and may be over The Bar, between Pole Sand and East Pole Sand, or close SE of the pier. See information on the chart.

5 **Entrance channel.** The channel into the river is approximately ½ cable wide between the drying sandbanks on each side and tends to be deepest on the S side abreast the training wall. Shaldon Pool, with depths of up to 7 m, lies SW of The Point, thence the channel turns sharply N and is bordered on its W side by The Salty, a hard bank of gravel and sand. The Salty is marked on its E side by buoys which are moved as the channel, which is confined to the E and N sides of the estuary, is dredged. From The Point almost as far as Shaldon Bridge, which spans the river 4 cables W, the channel has depths from 2 to 4 m.

5.110

1 **Tidal streams.** Outside The Bar the coastal stream begins as follows:

Interval from HW Devonport (Dover)	Direction
−0135 (+0510)	NNE
+0510 (−0030)	SSW

2 At the harbour entrance the in-going and out-going stream begin as follows:

Interval from HW Devonport (Dover)	Direction
−0535 (+0110)	in-going
+0040 (−0550)	out-going

3 **In-going stream.** On the Bar the in-going stream runs in the direction of the channel, at a rate of ¾ to 1½ kn until the banks are covered. As the banks cover the S-going coastal stream runs inward across Spratt Sand and later, when the N-going coastal stream begins, the stream runs in across Pole Sand.

4 Inside The Bar the in-going stream, which attains a rate of 4 to 5 kn off The Point, at first turns N and runs in the channel at a rate of 2 to 3 kn, but later as the tide rises, it runs across The Salty in a NW and N direction, giving rise to an eddy on the town side of the main channel which extends from New Quay to The Point.

5 **Out-going stream.** The out-going stream runs at first from Shaldon Bridge, across The Salty, towards The Point; later, as the tide falls, it is more and more confined to the channel. After passing The Point the stream at first runs

ENE across Spratt Sand, but, as the tide falls it sets more directly in the channel. The last of the out-going stream, after +0510 Devonport (–0030 Dover), runs from the outer end of Pole Sand, S with the S-going coastal stream.

6 Inside The Point the out-going stream is weak at first, but increases as The Salty uncovers, and attains a rate of about 1½ kn at Shaldon Bridge, 3 kn in the channel off the town, increasing to 5 kn off The Point and then decreasing to from 1 to 2½ kn on The Bar.

Eddies and overfalls occur in the confined water off The Point when the rate of stream exceeds about 3 kn.

Directions for entering harbour
5.111

1 Since the depths over the sandbanks fronting the entrance to River Teign and their positions are subject to constant change directions for anything but local craft or small visiting craft is misleading. Mariners will be advised of the best channel when the pilot boards.

2 **Positioning marks.** The alignment (334°) of the following lights on the S end of The Den indicate the approximate E limit of Pole Sand:

Front light (grey round stone tower, 6 m in height) (50°32'·5N 3°29'·8W).

Rear light (black column, 6 m in height) (62 m NNW of the front light).

Caution. These lights should not be used as leading lights.

3 Having found the best channel to the river entrance mariners should alter course W for the entrance keeping approximately ¼ cable S of a light buoy (starboard hand) (52°32'·4N 3°29'·8W), moored on the S extremity of Spratt Sand, and approximately ¼ cable N of Philip Lucette Light

Beacon (port hand) situated on the middle of the training wall 1¼ cables WNW of The Ness, thence the track leads round The Point, marked near its SW extremity by a light beacon (starboard hand), and NNE through the channel, marked by light buoys (port and starboard hand) as shown on the chart, passing E of The Salty (5.109). Pilots will advise mariners of the best route to take to their berth.

4 **Useful mark:**
Saint Michael's Church (tower and flagstaff) (50°32'·8N 3°29'·5W).

Berths
5.112

1 Eastern Quay, riverside (50°32'·7N 3°30'·0W), 119 m total length, maintained depth alongside 2·6 m.

Western Quay, riverside (50°32'·8N 3°30'·2W), 300 m total length, maintained depth alongside 2·6 m.

2 Four berths in total; three on Western Quay and one on Eastern Quay. Vessels up to 126 m LOA handled with draught of 5 m at Springs and 4 m at Neaps. Heavy lift facilities are available. A RoRo berth is available but has not been used for some time (2007).

The maximum depth alongside Teignmouth Quays at MHWS is 7·2 m.

Port services
5.113

1 **Repairs:** limited facilities; divers available.

Other facilities: hospital in Teignmouth; ship sanitation control and ship sanitation control exemption certificates are issued at Teignmouth.

Supplies: fuel by road tanker; water available at quays; provisions.

Warren Point   *Exmouth*

Pole Sand   River Exe and Approaches from SE (5.113)
(Original dated 2001)

(Photograph - Air Images)

Hazards
5.126
1   **Cargo transhipment** takes place in Lyme Bay, for details see 5.5.

Firing practice areas are situated E of Straight Point and SW of Chickerell (50°35′N 2°31′W); red flags are displayed when the ranges are in use. The former range is marked by DZ light buoys. See information on the chart and *Annual Summary of Admiralty Notices to Mariners*.

For information regarding exercises throughout Lyme Bay, see 5.4.

2   **Cable area.** An area in which mariners are warned against anchoring, sweeping and trawling, owing to the existence of cables, buoys and obstructions, is indicated on the chart and extends 3 miles SSW from the shore, 4 miles SE of Bridport.

Rescue
5.127
1   **Coastguard Rescue Teams** are situated at:
    Sidmouth (50°41′N 3°14′W).
    Beer (50°42′N 3°05′W).
    Lyme Regis (50°43′N 2°56′W).
    West Bay, Bridport (50°43′N 2°46′W).
    Wyke Regis (50°36′N 2°30′W).
Inshore lifeboat is stationed at Lyme Regis (5.140).

2   **National Coastwatch Institution** (NCI) station is situated at:
    Portland (50°30′·6N 2°27′·5W).
For details of coastguard stations see 1.101, for lifeboat see 1.113 and for NCI see 1.106.

Tidal streams
5.128
1   The inshore streams between Straight Point and the W end of Chesil Beach are weak; they run generally in the direction of the coast with a maximum spring rate of less than 1 kn.

In West Bay (50°33′N 2°29′W) the E-going stream near the coast runs SE along the coast, and S off the W side of Portland, changing to ESE clear of the land. During the W-going stream a clockwise eddy forms and fills the whole bay.

2   For details of Portland Race, see 6.20.

The offshore streams are shown by means of information on the chart, see also 5.8 and *Admiralty Tidal Stream Atlas Lyme Bay*.

Directions
(continued from 5.105)

Principal marks
5.129
1   **Landmarks:**
    Beer Head (50°41′N 3°06′W), a precipitous cliff readily identified on the radar display.
    Isle of Portland (50°34′N 2°26′W) (6.13).
    White Building (50°32′N 2°27′W) on the W side of Isle of Portland.
    Portland Lighthouse (50°31′N 2°27′W) (6.21).
    Major light:
    Portland Light (50°31′N 2°27′W) (6.21).

Straight Point to Bill of Portland
5.130
1   From a position about 5 cables S of Straight Point (50°36′N 3°22′W), from which a light (5.105) is exhibited, the route leads ESE passing:

    SSW of DZS Light Buoy (special) (50°36′N 3°19′W) (5.126) noting DZN Light Buoy which lies 7 cables N; thence:

2   SSW of Otterton Ledge (50°38′N 3°18′W), noting Foot Clout Rock, 3 cables WSW, the outermost dangers off Otterton Point (5.125); thence:

    SSW of Beer Head (50°41′N 3°06′W) (5.129); thence:

3   SSW then S of Bill of Portland (50°31′N 2°27′W) keeping outside of Portland Race (6.20). Mariners in coastal traffic are advised to pass approximately 5 miles S of Bill of Portland.

Useful mark:
    Saint George's Church (cupola) (50°32′·8N 2°26′·7W) on the W side of Isle of Portland.
(Directions continue at 6.21)

Anchorage

West Bay
5.131
1   **Anchorage** may be obtained in West Bay (50°33′N 2°29′W), sheltered from E winds, in depths of 25 to 30 m, loose coarse gravel and shells, but the holding ground is not good. Small vessels can anchor in Chesil Cove in the E part of West Bay, approximately 3 cables offshore, as shown on the chart, in depths of 15 m.

If a sudden, but not uncommon, shift of wind takes place the sea quickly rises.

2   **Outfall** extends 8 cables S from the coast; its seaward end is marked by a light buoy (special) moored 3¼ miles NNW of Portland Light.

Caution. A dangerous wreck (50°32′·8N 2°27′·5W), the position of which is approximate, lies about 2 cables offshore in the S part of West Bay 3 cables N of Blacknor Point.

Bridport Harbour

Chart 3315 plan of Bridport Harbour
General information
5.132
1   **Position and function.** Bridport Harbour (50°43′N 2°46′W), locally known as West Bay, lies 3 miles ESE of Golden Cap (5.125).

Port Authority: West Dorset District Council, 58–60 High West Street, Dorchester, Dorset DT1 1UZ.
    Website: www.westdorset-dc.gov.uk/westbay
    Email: j.radcliff@westdorset-dc.gov.uk

Limiting conditions
5.133
1   **Sill** ½ cable N of East Pier head, 0·2 m below chart datum, beyond which the basin dries at MLWS. The harbour can accommodate vessels of up to 50 m in length and of up to 3·2 m draught.

In S gales the sea breaks heavily at the entrance and may, on particularly severe occasions, render the harbour unapproachable. Under such circumstances port entry information should be sought from the Harbour Master before entry is attempted.

2   **Silting.** The outer harbour is prone to silting following periods of heavy rain. Further information should be obtained from the Harbour Master prior to arrival.

3   **Tidal levels.** Mean spring range about 3·5 m; mean neap range about 1·4 m. For further information see *Admiralty Tide Tables*.

Bridport – West Bay Harbour from E (5.132)
(Original dated 2004)

(Photograph – A. Grattan-Cooper)

Arrival information
5.134

1 **Anchorage** can be obtained approximately 4 cables S of the harbour entrance in depths of 6 m, fine sand. Farther offshore the ground is foul but there is good holding ground outside the 10 m depth contour. A sewer outfall, marked at its outer end by a light buoy (special) extends 7 cables SW from the shore close E of the harbour entrance.

2 **Historic wreck** which is not considered dangerous to navigation lies 6¼ cables WSW of the harbour entrance. Historic wrecks are protected from unauthorized interference; for details see 1.89 and *Annual Summary of Admiralty Notices to Mariners.*

Harbour
5.135

1 **General layout.** Bridport Harbour is protected by two piers, East Pier and West Pier; both pier heads are extended and surrounded by rock-armouring, on which lights are exhibited; the entrance faces SSE. The inner basin is reached via a cut, width 22 m, between the root of the old W pier and the root of East Pier; lights are exhibited on both sides of the cut.

2 A sill at the cut prevents silt from exiting the basin. The basin, 160 m long and 42 m wide, dries out, except for a relatively deep area in its centre extending to the sluice gates at the middle of the N side. The sluice gates are opened near LW releasing water from the River Brit which has sufficient scour to keep the entrance clear.

3 **Docking signals.** When all is clear for entering a red flag with a white Saint Andrew's cross is displayed, by day, on the flagstaff on the harbour master's office at the root of West Pier; at night a green light is exhibited from the E Pierhead and a red light from the W pierhead. If the entrance is not clear a black ball is displayed on the flagstaff. These signals are only shown when a vessel is about to enter.

Directions for entering harbour
5.136

1 The line of bearing 336°, or by night the white sector of the directional light (50°42′·6N 2°45′·9W) (steel column 5 m in height) exhibited from the root of West Pier, leads in the approach passing (with positions given from the directional light:

Close NE of The Ram (6½ cables SSE) a 4·6 m patch thence:

2 E of a 3·7 m patch (4 cables SW), thence:

Close NE of West Pier head, noting rock-armour extending 35 m SSE on which a light (red steel column 5 m in height) is exhibited, thence:

Close SW of East Pier head, noting rock-armour extending 45 m SSE on which a light (green steel column 5 m in height) is exhibited.

3 **Clearing mark:**

The line of bearing 099° of The Knoll (50°41′·3N 2°39′·6W), a conical hill, clears S of the foul ground off Bridport Harbour.

4 **Useful marks:**

Lights (50°42′·5N 2°45′·8W) on the E and W pierhead rock-armour extensions.

Bridport Church (tower and flagstaff) (1¼ miles N of direction light).

Berths
5.137

1 There are two berths in the basin. The N most berth on W side of the Quay has depths of up to 2·0 m alongside; the remaining berth dries.

Port services
5.138

1 **Repairs:** slipway for craft up to 12 m in length; minor repair facilities.

Supplies: small quantities of marine diesel oil by road tanker; water; provisions.

Rescue, see 5.127.

Anchorage and minor harbour

Chart 3315
Beer Roads
5.139

1   **Anchorage** sheltered from N winds may be obtained in Beer Roads, a small anchorage fronting the village of Beer, which is situated 7½ cables N of Beer Head (50°41′N 3°06′W) (5.129). A recommended berth, shown on the chart, lies 4 cables SE of the village in a depth of 8 m, sand.

2   A prominent water tower stands 2 miles N of Beer Head and a light (metal column, 5 m in height) is exhibited near the church at Beer; the light-structure is difficult to identify.

    Crab pots are laid off Seaton Bay, from 2 to 4 miles offshore, E of Beer Head.

    Landing. The beach at Beer is composed of steep-to shingle from which small craft can be launched.

Chart 3315 plan of Lyme Regis Harbour
Lyme Regis
5.140

1   **Position and function.** Lyme Regis (50°43′N 2°56′W) situated 6½ miles E of Beer Head has a small tidal harbour which is used principally by pleasure craft.

    Caution. It is reported (2007) that sandbars build up outside the entrance which may affect craft with draughts of more than 1 m.

    Local knowledge is advisable for entry at night.

    Depths. At MHWS there are depths of approximately 4 m in the entrance and of 2·7 to 4·3 m inside the harbour.

2   **Limiting dimensions.** Pleasure craft of up to 9 m in length and small fishing vessels up to 11 m in length with draughts of up to 1·9 m can be accommodated.

Port radio station, with limited hours, operates from the port.

    Anchorage: about 5 cables SE of the harbour entrance; the quality of the bottom varies with the position. A light buoy (S cardinal) is moored 500 m E of the harbour entrance and marks the seaward end of a sewage outfall.

3   **Harbour.** The harbour is protected from SW gales by The Cobb, a substantial stone pier, extended an additional 70 m E by rocks. Victoria Pier, an inner pier, curves N and E from The Cobb and forms the S entrance to the harbour. North Wall projects S from the shore and protects the harbour from SE gales. In strong S winds the sea breaks heavily round the piers.

4   **Leading lights:**

        Front light (blue metal column, 5 m in height) (50°43′·2N 2°56′·2W) on Victoria Pierhead.

        Rear light (Harbour Master's building) (280 m WNW of the front light).

    The alignment (284°) of the above lights leads in the approach to the harbour passing about 40 m NNE of the E end of The Cobb.

5   **Berths:** The harbour dries at LW and is suitable for bilge keel craft; fin keel craft may lie against the stone quays at Victoria Pier.

6   **Repairs:** A slipway 65 m in length with large apron, is available on a shared basis with the RNLI; basic engine repairs; boat hoist for vessels up to 9 m or 6½ tonnes, except fin keeled craft.

    Other facilities: medical centre.

    Supplies: marine diesel oil and petrol by arrangement; water at Victoria Pier; provisions and small quantities of stores.

    Rescue, see 5.127.

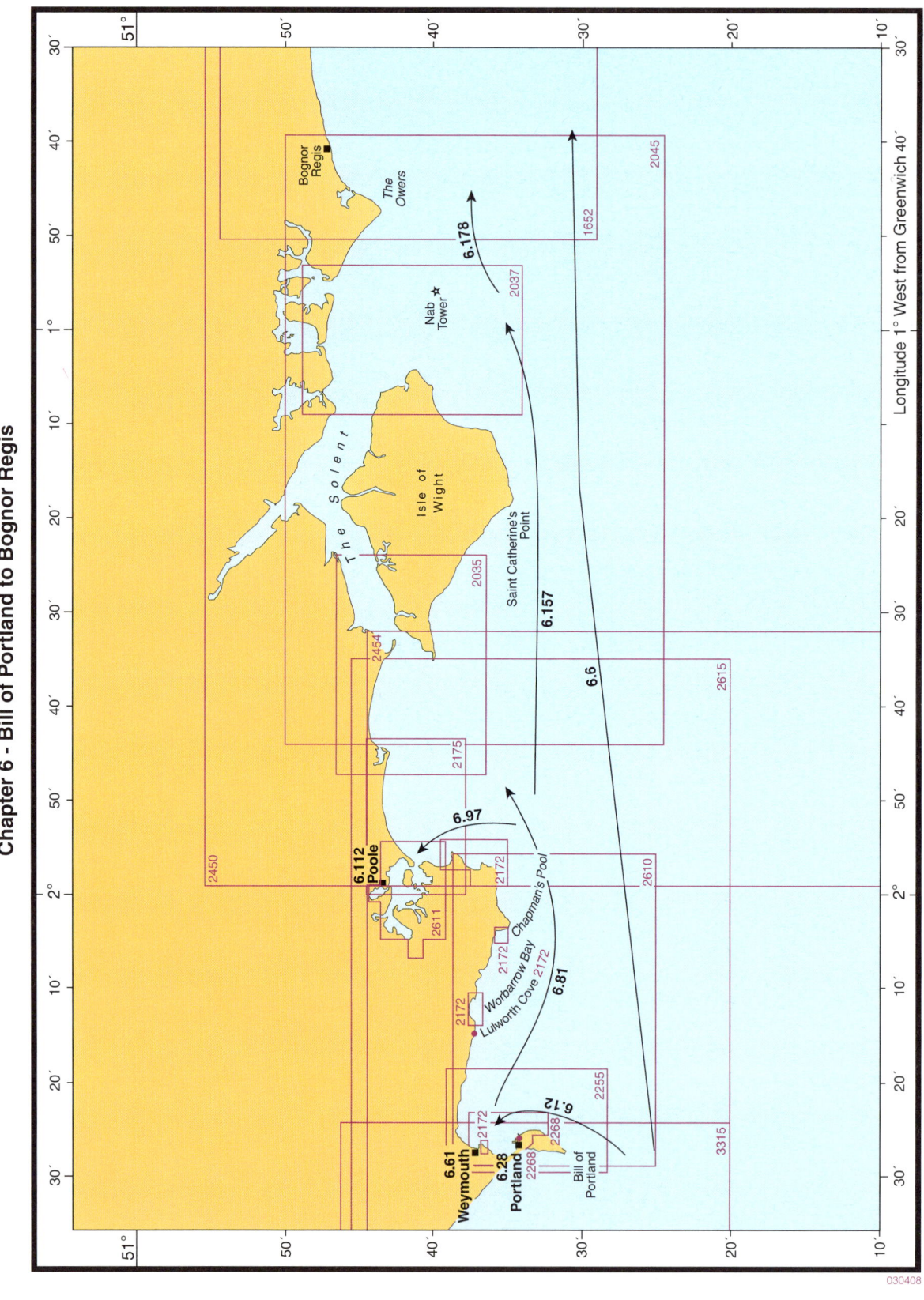

CHAPTER 6

BILL OF PORTLAND TO BOGNOR REGIS

GENERAL INFORMATION

Chart 2656
Scope of chapter
6.1

1   This chapter covers the S coast of England from Bill of Portland (50°31′N 2°27′W) to Bognor Regis (50°47′N 0°40′W) and The Owers and includes the S coast of Isle of Wight. The N coast of Isle of Wight, together with The Solent and approaches, Portsmouth and the port of Southampton, are covered in Chapter 7.

2   **Ports.** Portland Harbour (6.28) and the ports of Weymouth (6.61) and Poole (6.112) are covered by this chapter.

Offshore section. This chapter also contains an offshore section from Bill of Portland to Saint Catherine's Point, the S extremity of Isle of Wight, for mariners ENE-bound through the Channel and not calling at intermediate ports.

Topography
6.2

1   Between Bill of Portland and Saint Catherine's Point, 45 miles ENE, the coast is divided into two bays by Isle of Purbeck, a peninsula at the SE of which lie Saint Alban's Head and Durlston Head, 15 and 20 miles ENE, respectively, of Bill of Portland.

Portland Harbour and Weymouth Bay lie at the NW end of the bay W of Saint Alban's Head. Poole Harbour and Poole Bay lie N and NE of Durlston Head; Christchurch Bay lies E of Poole Bay with Needles Channel, leading to the W part of The Solent and Southampton Water, situated at its E end and NW of Isle of Wight.

2   Isle of Portland is easily recognised and there are numerous landmarks on the peninsula. The white chalk cliffs at Needles Point, the W extremity of Isle of Wight, are conspicuous from the offing.

The E approach to Spithead and thence to Portsmouth, or through The Solent to Southampton, lies between Foreland, the E extremity of Isle of Wight, and Selsey Bill, 11 miles ENE.

Exercise areas
6.3

1   Detailed information concerning these areas, which are found in the waters of this chapter, may be found on Practice Exercise Area (PEXA) charts. Such areas are also shown on all new, and new edition navigation charts. For further details see 1.30 and *Annual Summary of Admiralty Notices to Mariners Nos 5 and 8.*

Fishing
6.4

1   Fishing vessels at anchor may be encountered within the area between Saint Alban's Head and Saint Catherine's Point, bounded by the parallels of 50°30′N and 50°45′N and the meridians of 1°58′W and 1°15′W. Anchor lines may be on or near the surface extending 250 m. For further details regarding fishing, see 1.23 and *The Mariner's Handbook.*

Tidal streams
6.5

1   Tidal streams are shown by means of information on the charts. In the vicinity of Bill of Portland they are strong and there are strong onshore sets; their effect can be experienced a considerable distance offshore. For further details, see 6.18.

OFFSHORE PASSAGE

General information

Charts 2454, 2450, 2656
Route
6.6

1   From a position S of Bill of Portland (50°31′N 2°27′W) the offshore passage leads ENE, about 45 miles, to S of Saint Catherine's Point, the S extremity of Isle of Wight, where it combines with the coastal route for traffic proceeding to the E Solent, or continuing E passing S of The Owers (6.186) and entering the English Inshore Traffic Zone.

Off-lying dangers
6.7

1   The Shambles (6.23), a bank with several shoal heads, lies 3 miles E of Bill of Portland (50°31′N 2°27′W); it is marked by light buoys. Saint Alban's Ledge (6.89) extends 4 miles SW from Saint Alban's Head (50°35′N 2°03′W). There are no dangers outside these between Bill of Portland and Saint Catherine's Point but there are numerous wrecks with less depths over them than the general depths of the seabed.

Hazards
6.8

1   **Exercise areas.** For details of exercise areas, see 6.3 and information on the chart. See 2.7.

Yacht Ocean Safety buoys. Two light buoys (special) are moored SW and SE of the Isle of Wight.

Directions
(continued from 5.13)

Principal marks
6.9

1   **Landmarks:**
    Isle of Portland (50°34′N 2°26′W) (6.13).
    Saint Alban's Head (50°35′N 2°03′W) (6.87).
    Needles Point (50°40′N 1°35′W) (6.158).
    Saint Catherine's Point (50°35′N 1°18′W) (6.158).
Major Lights:
    Portland Light (50°31′N 2°27′W) (6.21).
2   Portland Harbour A Head Light (50°35′N 2°25′W) (6.21).
    Anvil Point Light (50°36′N 1°58′W) (6.87).
    Needles Light (50°40′N 1°35′W) (6.167).

Saint Catherine's Point Light (50°35′N 1°18′W) (6.167).

Charts 2615, 2454, 2045
Isle of Portland to Saint Catherine's Point
6.10

1   **General information.** Approaching and passing Saint Catherine's Point (50°35′N 1°18′W) (6.158) caution is necessary as the bottom is uneven and the deepest water lies near the shore. Should the depth increase rapidly from 33 or 37 m to 55 m or more, haul to the S as the vessel will almost certainly be entering Saint Catherine's Deep, which lies parallel with the SE coast of Isle of Wight and about 1 mile from it and extends up to 5 miles SW of the point, and be very close to the shore.

2   From a position S of Isle of Portland (50°34′N 2°26′W) the offshore passage leads ENE passing:

SSE of The Shambles (50°30′N 2°23′W) (6.23) keeping in depths of more than 35 m until clear of this bank; thence:

SSE of Saint Alban's Ledge (50°32′N 2°07′W) (6.89); thence:

3   SSE of Anvil Point (50°35′N 1°58′W) (6.82); thence:

SSE of Needles Point (50°40′N 1°35′W) (6.158); thence:

To a position S of Saint Catherine's Point where the offshore route combines with the coastal route and continues generally E to S of Nab Tower (50°40′N 0°57′W).

Clearing marks. For details of clearing marks for The Shambles and the dangers on the SW coast of Isle of Wight, see 6.25 and 6.170.

(Directions continue at 6.171)

BILL OF PORTLAND TO NEEDLES CHANNEL APPROACHES

GENERAL INFORMATION

Chart 2615
Area covered
6.11

1   The section is arranged as follows:
Approaches to Portland and Weymouth (6.12).
Portland Harbour (6.28).
Weymouth (6.61).
Weymouth to Needles Channel Approaches (6.81).

APPROACHES TO PORTLAND AND WEYMOUTH

General information

Charts 2610, 2615
Route
6.12

1   From a position S of Bill of Portland (50°31′N 2°27′W) the passage leads between Bill of Portland and The Shambles, 3 miles E, or E of The Shambles, thence generally N to the pilot boarding place for Portland (6.41) or Weymouth (6.71).

Bill of Portland from S (6.12)
(Original dated 2001)

(Photograph –Air Images)

Topography
6.13

1   Isle of Portland, a peninsula, contains large quantities of freestone from which many famous buildings in England have been built, and its quarries are extensively worked. It is being constantly eroded by the encroachment of the sea, and the greater part of the E side is said to be losing an average of 0·3 m annually; portions of the cliffs and land, being undermined, have fallen into the sea. The Verne (50°34′N 2°26′W), near the N end of the peninsula, is conspicuous; its N face is precipitous, thence the land slopes gradually S terminating in Bill of Portland, the whole presenting a wedge-shaped appearance which is easily recognisable.

Exercise areas
6.14

1   **General exercise areas.** See 6.3.

Vessel traffic service
6.15

1   A compulsory reporting system is in operation for all vessels over 50 m in length and for vessels over 20 m in length carrying dangerous and polluting goods, inward bound or outward bound from Portland and Weymouth. All vessels are required to make reports on the appropriate channel to Portland Harbour Radio, when passing through the various Reporting Points; the positions of Reporting Points are shown on the charts. In addition it is mandatory that a listening watch is kept on the appropriate channel when within 3 miles of A Head (50°35′N 2°25′W). Mariners bound for Weymouth should establish contact with Weymouth Harbour Control 3 miles from A Head and switch to Weymouth working channel at the Weymouth pilot boarding place.

See *Admiralty List of Radio Signals Volume 6(1)* and information on the charts.

Traffic regulations
6.16

1   **Authorized vessels.** Mariners in authorized commercial fishing vessels and recreational craft may enter Portland Harbour with prior approval.

Prohibited anchorages. For details of prohibited anchorage areas in the approaches to Portland and Weymouth, see 6.45.

Rescue
6.17

1   **Coastguard.** Portland MRSC is situated at Custom House Quay, Weymouth (50°36′N 2°27′W) with a Rescue Team at Wyke Regis (50°36′N 2°29′W).

Lifeboats. An all-weather and an inshore lifeboat are stationed at Weymouth (50°36′N 2°27′W) (6.61).

National Coastwatch Institution (NCI) station is situated at:

2   Portland (50°30′·6N 2°27′·5W).

For details of coastguard stations see 1.101, for lifeboats see 1.113 and for NCI see 1.106.

VHF Direction-finding service, for emergency use only, operates from Grove Point (50°33′N 2°25′W). For details see 1.105 and *Admiralty List of Radio Signals Volume 2.*

3   **Helicopter.** An SAR helicopter operates from Osprey Quay (50°34′N 2°27′W) adjacent to Portland Port.

Natural conditions
6.18

1   **Tidal streams.** The streams run very strongly off Bill of Portland and eddies of great extent form in the bays on each side; off both sides of Isle of Portland the streams run nearly continuously S and there is violent turbulence off the Bill where these streams meet the E and W-going coastal streams.

2   The following general account of the streams in the locality refer to conditions at springs. The eddies are much smaller at neaps, at which time, though the general features of the streams are probably about as described, the streams may run in directions differing appreciably from those given, and the duration of the S-going streams on both sides of Isle of Portland may be considerably shorter than stated. The streams at times other than at springs should therefore be predicted in the usual manner but used with caution.

6.19

1   **Anti-clockwise eddy, east-going stream.** The E-going stream begins about –0100 Devonport and runs for about 6 hours. Soon after the stream begins an anti-clockwise eddy forms E of Bill of Portland, and about 2 hours later its centre is situated about 2 miles E of the Bill; from this time till the end of the E-going stream the eddy increases in size, and towards the end of the stream it fills the whole of the bay E of Portland with its centre situated about 5½ miles E of Bill of Portland, the eddy extending 5 to 6 miles further E.

2   When the E-going stream ends the W-going stream N of the eddy, and the S-going stream W of it, continue as the W-going stream. Thus, on the E side of Isle of Portland, close to the land, the S-going stream runs for about 10¼ hours.

3   During the whole of the E-going stream the stream in West Bay (50°34′N 2°30′W) runs, near the land, about SE in the direction of the coast and S off the W side of Isle of Portland, changing gradually to about ESE seaward of Bill of Portland.

4   **Clockwise eddy, west-going stream.** The W-going stream begins about +0530 Devonport and runs for about 6 hours. Soon after the stream begins a clockwise eddy forms W of Bill of Portland, and, though smaller, weaker and less symmetrical then the eddy in the bay E of Portland, resembles that eddy in its general features. At its greatest, shortly before the end of the W-going stream, the centre of the eddy is about 3 miles, and its W edge about 8 miles, W of Bill of Portland, but the stream runs NW towards the coast for several miles farther W.

5   During the whole of the W-going stream the stream near the land E of Portland runs in the direction of the coast and S off the E side of Isle of Portland, changing gradually to about W seaward of Bill of Portland.

6.20

1   **Portland Race** is caused by the very strong S-going streams from both sides of the Bill meeting the E and W-going streams off Bill of Portland, and its violence is increased by the sudden decrease in depths and inequalities of the bottom on Portland Ledge.

2   The race is very variable in both position and extent but usually extends SE during the E-going stream and SW during the W-going stream; it extends farthest from Bill of Portland, up to about 2 miles, with strong N winds. Though the streams run very strongly in the immediate vicinity of the race, they are not specially strong in the race itself, which, in fact, consists of an area of overfalls and steep heavy breaking seas in which the streams are subject to great and sudden changes in both direction and rate.

3   **Caution.** The race is most violent, and dangerous, to boats and even small vessels, in heavy weather at the times when the streams are strongest, especially with a gale blowing against the direction of the stream; with an E gale and a strong E-going stream the whole area from The Shambles to about 1½ miles S of Bill of Portland, and, as far N as Grove Point (50°33′N 2°25′W), may be covered by overfalls and heavy breaking seas.

4   **Tidal streams in the vicinity of Portland Race.** The streams in the vicinity of the race run strongly and are subject to rapid changes. There is a strong S set at a position about 1¼ miles SSE from Portland Light. Streams stronger than those given in the tables on the charts, possibly up to as much as 10 kn, may be found in the immediate vicinity of, but not necessarily in, the race.

For more detailed information, *Admiralty Tidal Stream Atlas for Approaches to Portland* and tidal information on the charts should be consulted.

Directions
(continued from 5.130)

Principal marks
6.21

1   **Landmarks:**

Portland Lighthouse (white round tower, red band, 41 m in height) (50°30′·9N 2°27′·4W).

Portland Lighthouse from SW (6.21)
(Original dated 1997)

(Photograph - Dr M P Bender)

Old Low Lighthouse (50°31′·2N 2°27′·1W).
Old Coastguard Station (50°32′·9N 2°25′·2W) on the Grove.
Radio Mast (elevation 158 m) (50°33′·5N 2°25′·9W).

Portland – Verne – Radome from NE (6.21)

(Original dated 2005)

(Photograph - RMAS Newton)

Radome (red light) (50°33'·8N 2°26'·1W) on The Verne.

2 **Major lights:**
Portland Light — as above.
A Head Light (white metal tower, 22 m in height) (50°35'·2N 2°25'·1W) on the SE end of North-eastern Breakwater.

Charts 2255, 2610

Between Isle of Portland and The Shambles
6.22

1 **General information.** The channel between Bill of Portland (50°31'N 2°27'W) and The Shambles, 3 miles E, may be used at all times, but as previously mentioned, the strong tidal streams may cause heavy seas. Portland is safe to approach on all sides but depths are irregular, particulary near the Bill where a large mass of rock and loose stones extend at least ¼ cable from the point. A white stone beacon (elevation 18 m) stands at the S end of the Bill as a warning of this danger.

2 **Approach from west.** Mariners are recommended to keep outside Portland Race (6.20) until reaching the alignment of the leading marks.
Approach from east or south. Give a wide berth to The Shambles (6.23) and at night keep well S of the red sector of Portland Auxiliary Light (6.25).

6.23

1 **Leading marks:**
Front mark. Grove Point (50°33'N 2°25'W), the E extremity of Isle of Portland.
Rear mark. A Head Light (2¼ miles N of the front mark) (6.21).
From a position S of Bill of Portland (50°31'N 2°27'W), clear of Portland Race, the alignment (358°) of the above marks leads in the channel in a least depth of 15·9 m passing (with positions given from Grove Point):

2 Between Portland Ledge (3 miles SSW) and W Shambles Light Buoy (W cardinal) (3¼ miles S) moored off the W end of The Shambles.
When Portland Light (6.21) bears less than 270°, or at night when N of its red sector (6.25), the track then leads NE passing:

3 Between The Ledge (1½ miles S), a narrow shelf with depths of less than 20 m over it which extends E from God Nore, and The Shambles (2¾ miles SSE) a bank of sand and broken shell over 2 miles in extent; depths over this bank are irregular, the least depth is near its centre. Except at slack water the bank is clearly indicated by a ripple or overfall on the N or S side according to the direction of the tidal stream, noting E Shambles Light Buoy (E cardinal) (3¾ miles SE) moored about 3 cables E of the bank.

4 From a position SE of Grove Point, on which stands a beacon (special) marking the shore end of a submarine cable and clear of The Shambles, the track then leads N passing:
Between Grove Point, noting the rock awash which lies ½ cable off the point, and Adamant Shoal (50°33'N 2°17'W) (6.24); thence:
E of a four light buoys (special) (9 cables NNE) marking a noise range (6.50); thence:

5 E of Portland Outer Breakwater (1¼ miles N) allowing ample room to make the turn W for the approach to Portland or Weymouth; thence:
To the inner pilot boarding place for Portland (3 miles N) or the pilot boarding place for Weymouth (4 miles NNE) as required (6.41 and 6.71).

East of The Shambles
6.24

1 From a position well clear of E Shambles Light Buoy (E cardinal) (50°31'N 2°20'W) moored about 3 cables E of The Shambles (6.23) the route leads NNW passing:
WSW of Adamant Shoal (50°33'N 2°17'W); thence:
To a position between Grove Point (6.23) and Adamant Shoal where the track continues generally NNW to join that given at 6.23 leading N to the pilot boarding places.

Clearing mark
6.25

1 The Shambles are covered by the red auxiliary light (271°–291°) exhibited from Portland Light below the main light.

Useful marks
6.26

1 D Head Light (framework tower on concrete hut, 8 m in height) (50°34'·2N 2°25'·2W) on the S end of Outer Breakwater.
Fort Head Light (metal framework tower, 2 m in height) (50°35'·1N 2°24'·9W) on the N end of Outer Breakwater.

2 B Head Light (grey metal column, 2 m in height) (50°35'·7N 2°25'·9W) on the NW end of North-eastern Breakwater.
C Head Light (grey metal column, 2 m in height) (50°35'·8N 2°25'·9W) on the SE end of Northern Arm.
Training vessel *Tristram* (50°34'·3N 2°25'·2W) (6.51).

3 Weymouth South Pier Light (white mast on grey metal platform, 8 m in height) (50°36'·6N 2°26'·5W).
Weymouth North Pier Light (green column) (50°36'·6N 2°26'·6W).

(Directions continue for Portland Harbour at 6.53
for Weymouth at 6.76
and for Needles Channel approaches at 6.87)

B Head *C Head*

Portland – North Ship Channel Entrance from NNE (6.31)

(Original dated 2005)

(Photograph – RMAS Newton)

Side channel

General information
6.27

1   There is usually an area of relatively smooth water, from 5 to 7½ cables wide, between Bill of Portland (50°31′N 2°27′W) and Portland Race (6.20) with depths of from 5 to 16 m, which is very useful to mariners in small vessels. The passage should be made at slack water and never attempted on spring tides.

2   **Local knowledge** is required and fishing buoys in the inshore passage render night transit through this route hazardous at all times.

PORTLAND HARBOUR

General information

Charts 2268, 2255
Position
6.28

1   Portland Harbour (50°35′N 2°26′W), which is privately owned, is situated at the N end of Isle of Portland.

Function
6.29

1   The harbour is a deep-water commercial port and is well sheltered from the prevailing SW winds. Main traffic includes cruise ships, cable ships, general cargo vessels and vessels calling for bunkers.

Weymouth and Portland Sailing Academy operates from Osprey Quay. Sailing events and training take place all year round both inside and outside the breakwaters.

Port limits
6.30

1   The limits of the port are enclosed by lines, as shown on the chart, between The Nothe (50°36′N 2°27′W) and Church Ope Cove, about 4 miles SSE. For further information, see Appendix II.

Approach and entry
6.31

1   The port is approached from S or E and entered through East Ship Channel or North Ship Channel (6.49).

Traffic
6.32

1   In 2007 the port was used by 350 vessels.

Port Authority
6.33

1   **Port operators:** Portland Port Limited, Castletown, Portland, Dorset DT5 1PP.
  Website: www.portland-port.co.uk
  E-mail: marine@portland-port.co.uk

Limiting conditions

Controlling depths
6.34

1   **East Ship Channel:** 13·8 m decreasing to 12·5 m about 1 cable within the entrance.
  North Ship Channel: 12·4 m.
  General depths over a large part of the Inner Harbour are from 10 to 15 m.

Deepest and longest berth
6.35

1   **Alongside berths:** Deep Water Berth (6.57) and Outer Coaling Pier are capable of accepting vessels up to 250 m in length.

Tidal levels
6.36

1   Mean spring range about 2·0 m; mean neap range about 0·6 m. For further information see *Admiralty Tide Tables*.

Local weather and sea state
6.37

1   With strong W or SW winds a long S ground swell runs across Outer Harbour.

In Inner Harbour strong W to SW, or E winds can cause moderate waves or swell, which can be dangerous for boats.

Arrival information

Vessel Traffic Service
6.38

1   Vessel Traffic Service operates throughout 24 hours. For details see 6.15 and *Admiralty List of Radio Signals Volume 6(1).*

Notice of ETA required
6.39

Notice of ETA and request for pilotage should be sent 24 hours in advance and confirmed 6 hours and 2 hours before arrival.

For details see *Admiralty List of Radio Signals Volume 6(1).*

Outer anchorages
6.40

1   Anchorage may be obtained at specified berths, as shown on the chart, NE and E of North-eastern Breakwater (50°35′N 2°25′W) in depths of 12 to 19 m. It should be noted that G4 anchorage may only be used when the DG range is not in use. G3 and G6 anchorages are reserved for vessels carrying hazardous cargoes.

Refuge anchorage for vessels seeking shelter in adverse weather is situated 2 miles NE of the North-eastern Breakwater, as shown on the chart.

Prohibited anchorage. For details see 6.45 and information on the charts.

Pilotage
6.41

1   **Pilotage** is compulsory for the following vessels:
 Vessels of 50 m or more LOA.
 Vessels of 20 m or more LOA carrying dangerous cargo.
 Vessels of 20 m or more LOA carrying more than 12 passengers.
Certain categories of vessels are exempt from compulsory pilotage. For details see *Admiralty List of Radio Signals Volume 6(1).*

2   **Pilotage area.** West of a line joining Grove Point (50°33′N 2°25′W) and White Nothe, 5¾ miles NE.

Boarding places. Pilots board in positions:
 50°36′·0N 2°24′·0W (Inner), for vessels less than 180 m in length.
 50°35′·0N 2°22′·3W (Outer), for vessels greater than 180 m in length.

3   In adverse weather the the above boarding positions may be varied; VTS will advise vessels accordingly.
For details see *Admiralty List of Radio Signals Volume 6(1).*

Tugs
6.42

1   Tugs are available by arrangement with Portland Port Limited. A minimum of 6 hours notice is required.

Local knowledge
6.43

1   Local knowledge, or the use of a pilot, is recommended as there are many local regulations requiring strict compliance.

Traffic regulations
6.44

1   **Anchoring and fishing prohibited.** Owing to the presence of submarine cables and buoys mariners are warned to navigate with caution and not to anchor, fish or

sweep in areas, indicated on the chart, extending up to 1 mile E of Portland Harbour, E and SE of The Nothe (50°36′N 2°27′W), see information on the chart.

2   **Unauthorised navigation prohibited.** Vessels are prohibited from entering or navigating within an area enclosing Portland Port, as shown on the charts, except with prior permission of the Harbour Authority.

Speed limit. There are two speed limits within the port, 6 kn and 12 kn, depending on area. For further details, see Appendix II.

Regulations concerning entry
6.45

1   **Dangerous and polluting goods.** For details see *Admiralty List of Radio Signals Volume 6(1)* and 1.68 to 1.76.

2   **Escort towage.** Most vessels of 180 m LOA or more are required to have an escort tug secured when entering or leaving the port. When entering in normal weather conditions, the tug will meet a vessel at the pilot boarding station.

Marine farms
6.46

1   Marine farms exist in the Inner Harbour.
 Close W of Outer Breakwater centred on 50°34′·6N 2°25′·0W.
 Close SW of Northern Arm centred on 50°35′·9N 2°26′·5W. The SE extremity of the farm is marked by buoys (special).

Harbour

General layout
6.47

1   Portland Harbour is divided into Outer Harbour and Inner Harbour by breakwaters. Inner Harbour is protected by the breakwaters which are 4 m above HW. Inner Breakwater extends ENE from the NE end of Isle of Portland. The detached Outer Breakwater, separated from Inner Breakwater by South Ship Channel curves in a N direction for approximately 1 mile. Northern Arm extends ESE from the N part of harbour. The detached North-eastern Breakwater, 7½ cables long, lies between Outer Breakwater and Northern Arm. Apart from Fort Head, the N end of Outer Breakwater, the heads of the remaining breakwaters are designated with letters, which may be seen from the chart, for convenience of reference.

2   Portland Port (6.57) is situated in the S part of the harbour fronting the N side of Isle of Portland.

In the N part of the harbour between Small Mouth (50°35′N 2°28′W) and Bincleaves, 1 mile NE, there are cliffs from 15 to 18 m high. The ruins of Sandsfoot Castle stand on the cliffs, on a point fringed by rocky ledges, 7½ cables NE of Small Mouth. Castle Cove, close N of Sandsfoot Castle, has a pier for small craft which projects from the premises of a sailing club. The seaward ends of submarine outfalls extending from Castle Cove Pier and from the shore at Bincleaves, 3 cables NE, are marked by beacons.

Development
6.48

1   Berthing facilites for leisure craft are under construction (2008) to the N of Osprey Quay (50°34′N 2°27′W).

6.49

1   **Harbour entrances.** There are two usable entrances to the Inner Harbour; East Ship Channel, between Fort Head

Portland – C Head from ENE (6.49)

(Original dated 2005)

(Photograph – RMAS Newton)

Portland – North–Eastern Breakwater – B Head from NNE (6.49)

(Original dated 2005)

(Photograph – RMAS Newton)

and A Head, and North Ship Channel, between B Head and C Head.

South Ship Channel, between D Head and Inner Breakwater, is closed by a sunken vessel and overhead cables.

Cables
6.50

1 **Submarine power cables** are laid in North Ship Channel.

Cable area extends 1 mile E from Newton's Cove (50°36′N 2°27′W), within the area is a degaussing range marked by a light buoy and 2 buoys (special). For further details, see 6.44, and information on the chart.

2 **Noise range,** indicated on the chart and marked by four light buoys, lies 1½ miles SSE of A Head. For further details, see 6.23.

Training facility
6.51

1 The training vessel *Tristram*, 136 m in length, 18 m breadth, is permanently moored in the SE part of the Inner Harbour, centred on position 50°34′·3N 2°25′·2W, close NNE of South Ship Channel entrance. Anchors extend about 80 m NE and SE from the stern and NW and SW from the bow. The vessel is surrounded by a 50 m exclusion zone. Mariners should keep well clear.

Natural conditions
6.52

1 **Tidal streams.** In the entrance channels the streams are irregular; they attain a maximum spring rate of approximately 1 kn and extend for only very short distances into and out of the harbour. There are eddies off the heads of the breakwaters, see information on the chart.

2 In the approach to East Ship Channel predicted tidal streams can be modified significantly by the wind. With a W wind a set onto Fort Head can be experienced out to

2 cables NE of the breakwater. Normally this set can be observed visually coming off A Head and setting clockwise around Fort Head.

3 When the predicted tidal stream is N and wind is from the E the set is onto A Head.

Inside the harbour the streams are imperceptible.

Climate information. See 1.195 and 13.236

Directions for entering harbour
(continued from 6.26)

Principal marks
6.53

1 **Landmarks:**
Buildings (50°36′·0N 2°26′·9W) on Torpedo Pier.
Aluminium Chimney (50°36′N 2°27′W) near the root of Northern Arm.
Television Mast (red lights) (50°35′·9N 2°28′·6W).
Crane (50°34′·1N 2°25′·6W) on Inner Breakwater.
Major light:
A Head Light (50°35′·2N 2°25′·1W) (6.21).

East Ship Channel
6.54

1 **Initial position** In the vicinity of Portland pilot boarding place (50°36′N 2°24′W).
Leading lights:
Front light (mounted on stone quay wall) (50°34′·1N 2°25′·9W), on NW corner of Storehouse Jetty.
Rear light (mounted on white building) (120 m SSW of front light).

2 The alignment (210°) of these lights leads through East Ship Channel entrance passing midway between A Head and Fort Head. Lights (6.21 and 6.26) are exhibited from the breakwater heads. Guard against the eddies which generally exist close to the breakwater heads, see also information on the chart.

Portland – Outer Breakwater – Fort Head from N (6.54)

(Original dated 2005)

(Photograph – RMAS Newton)

Portland North–Eastern Breakwater
A Head from N (6.54)

(Original dated 2005)

(Photograph - RMAS Newton)

South Ship   *Isle of*
Channel   *Portland*   *Portland Port*

Fort Head   *"A Head"*   *NE breakwater*

Portland – East Ship Channel from N (6.54)

(Original dated 2001)

(Photograph –Air Images)

Portland – East Ship Channel Leading Lights 210°
from NNE (6.54)

(Original dated 2005)

(Photograph - RMAS Newton)

North Ship Channel
6.55

1   From the vicinity of Portland pilot boarding place (50°36′N 2°24′W) the line of bearing 250¼° of Wellworthy Light Beacon (white square on metal pile) (50°35′·3N 2°27′·8W) leads through North Ship Channel entrance passing between B Head and C Heads. Lights (6.26) are exhibited from the breakwater heads.

2   Small craft are advised to enter Inner Harbour via the North Ship Channel due to the increase of commercial traffic. For the latest information regarding regulations in force mariners should refer to local Notices to Mariners issued by the Harbour Authority

Useful marks
6.56

1   Beacon E (5 m in height) (50°34′·8N 2°24′·9W) on Outer Breakwater.

Lights (metal framework towers, 3 m in height) on Q Pierhead (50°34′·3N 2°26′·3W) and elbow.

Inner Breakwater   *New Quay*

Coaling Pier   *Q Pier*   *Phoenix Pier*

Portland Port from NW (6.56)

(Photograph –Air Images)   *(Original dated 2001)*

Berths

Alongside berths
6.57

1   There are numerous berths at piers and jetties at Portland Port, the designations of which and the depths to which they have been dredged, are shown on the berthing plan which is inset on the chart.

2   Coaling Pier (50°34'·2N 2°26'·0W), with berths on its S side, extends ENE from a position 4 cables W of the root of Inner Breakwater.

Deep Water Berth, a jetty 150 m in length extended to 250 m by a dolphin, is situated parallel with and about 30 m off the E end of the N side of Coaling Pier; maintained depth 11·6 m.

3   Q Pier, to the W of Coaling Pier, has six main berths, three on each side of the pier.

Bunker Berth, N side of Inner Breakwater; jetty and dolphins with total length 750 m and depth 13 m; lights are exhibited from the dolphins.

4   Other main berths in the port are Crane Berth and Oiling Jetty.

Various other minor piers are situated to the S of Coaling Pier.

Anchorage berths
6.58

1   There are numerous lettered and numbered anchor berths inside the harbour which are indicated on the chart and in which mariners may anchor, sheltered from swell, with a good holding ground of blue slimy mud. Ships usually ride at single anchor with a good scope of cable. Mariners should note that a submerged wreck with 9 m over it lies in the SE section of M 9 anchorage position.

Small vessels should anchor in the W part of the harbour, clear of the prohibited anchorage.

2   M 1 and M 2 anchorages (50°35'·1N 2°25'·8W) are designated for vessels carrying hazardous cargo.

6.59

1   **Prohibited anchorages.** Anchorage is prohibited in a sector, shown on the chart, in the SW part of the harbour extending 2¼ cables NE from the SAR air station due to low flying aircraft.

Anchoring and trawling are prohibited in the vicinity of the marine farm which lies close W of the centre of Outer Breakwater.

Port services
6.60

1   **Repairs:** facilities available.

Other facilities: Oily waste and waste reception; Ship sanitation control and ship sanitation control exemption certificates issued.

Supplies: fresh water and fuel available at all berths and anchorages.

Communications: Hurn Airport, Bournemouth, distant 60 km, with international flights.

2   **Harbour regulations.** Restrictions to fishing, diving and underwater swimming in the harbour are shown on the chart, and full details are given at Appendix II. A permit, issued by the Harbour Authority, is required before diving, underwater swimming or commercial fishing within 100 m of the breakwaters.

No person may at any time land upon any of the breakwaters save with prior approval, in writing, from the Harbour Authority.

Rescue, see 6.17.

WEYMOUTH

General information

Charts 2172 plan of Weymouth Harbour, 2268, 2255
Position
6.61

1   Weymouth Harbour (50°36'N 2°27'W) lies at the mouth of River Wey which flows into the sea at the SW end of Weymouth Bay.

Function
6.62

1   The port is principally used by passenger and vehicle ferries and contains a RoRo ferry terminal.

Topography
6.63

1   Weymouth Bay lies between The Nothe (50°36'N 2°27'W), a bluff headland with a fort at its E end, and Redcliff Point, 2 miles NE; the seaside resort of Weymouth fronts the W side of the bay.

Port limits
6.64

1   The E port limits are enclosed by a line drawn from the NE corner of the N limit of Portland Harbour to the W side of Redcliff Point (50°38'N 2°25'W), as shown on the chart.

Approach and entry
6.65

1   The port is approached from Weymouth Bay and entered on leading lights (6.77) between two piers.

Port Authority
6.66

1   Weymouth and Portland Borough Council, Environmental Services, Municipal Offices, North Quay, Weymouth, Dorset DT4 8TA.

Limiting conditions
6.67

1   **Controlling depth** for the port is an isolated 4·6 m patch ½ cable E of North Pier Head and 2·9 m in mid channel S of No 5 berth.

Deepest and longest berths are No 1 and Nos 3 to 4 berths (6.78).

Maximum size of vessel handled. A vessel of 135 m LOA, 28 m beam and 5·2 m draught has used the port.

Arrival information

Vessel traffic service
6.68

1   A reporting system, operated by the Harbour Master, Portland, is in operation in the approaches, for details see 6.15 and *Admiralty List of Radio Signals Volume 6(1).*

Notice of ETA required
6.69

1   Notice of ETA and request for a pilot for should be sent 24 hours in advance and confirmed 2 hours in advance.

Weymouth Harbour from E (6.61)

(Original dated 1999)

(Photograph –Weymouth and Portland Borough Council)

Nothe Fort

South Pier Head

North Pier Head

Weymouth Harbour entrance from NNE (6.73)

(Original dated 2004)

(Photograph – Dennis George, Weymouth Port Authority)

Outer anchorages
6.70

1   Anchorage can be obtained in Weymouth Road (50°37'N 2°25'W), fronting Weymouth Bay, in specified berths in depths of 9 to 18 m. The holding ground is best at the W side of the bay; E of Redcliff Point the holding ground is poor due to clay and swell.

    A bad weather refuge anchorage area centred on position 50°37'N 2°23'W lies outside the port limits of Portland and Weymouth.

2   Anchorage, for mariners waiting to enter Weymouth, can also be obtained 6 cables ENE of South Pier in depths of 11 m.

    Caution. A wreck, with a depth of 4·6 m over it, lies 5 cables SSE of Redcliff Point (50°38'N 2°25'W) and a large domed rock, with a depth of 4·1 m over it, lies 3 cables SE of the same point.

Pilotage and tugs
6.71

1   **Pilotage** is compulsory for all vessels of 50 m in length and over; for vessels of over 36·6 m with dangerous cargoes; and for vessels carrying 12 or more passengers. Regular ferries and those plying only within the pilotage area, HM Ships, Foreign and Commonwealth Naval Vessels and those vessels exempted by law are excluded.

2   **Boarding place.** Pilots board in position 50°36'·7N 2°23'·0W, about 2 miles E of the harbour entrance.

    See *Admiralty List of Radio Signals Volume 6(1)* for further details.

    Tugs are available by arrangement with Portland Towage Ltd. Weymouth pilot boat is available to assist vessels inside the harbour.

Regulations concerning entry
6.72

1   **Dangerous and polluting goods.** See *Admiralty List of Radio Signals Volume 6(1)* and 1.68 to 1.76.

2   **Main channel.** Within the harbour, and the harbour limits, mariners in boats, whether under oars, sail or power, are to keep clear of the main channel and are not to impede vessels entering or leaving the harbour.

Harbour

General layout
6.73

1   Weymouth Harbour, a long narrow harbour, is entered between two piers of stone construction, North Pier and South Pier. The harbour entrance is 137 m wide between the piers with a channel width of 76 m. A RoRo ferry terminal is situated on berth No 3 just inside the harbour entrance. There are a total of six berths on the N side of the harbour with a quay length of 610 m.

2   Shoaling has taken place on the S side of the harbour.

Traffic signals
6.74

1   Traffic signals (Diagram 6.74), disposed vertically, are exhibited from a mast situated 1 cable SW of the head of South Pier.

    When no signal is shown the entrance is clear for either entry or departure, but mariners in approaching vessels must be prepared for the signal to be put against them. See also 6.15.

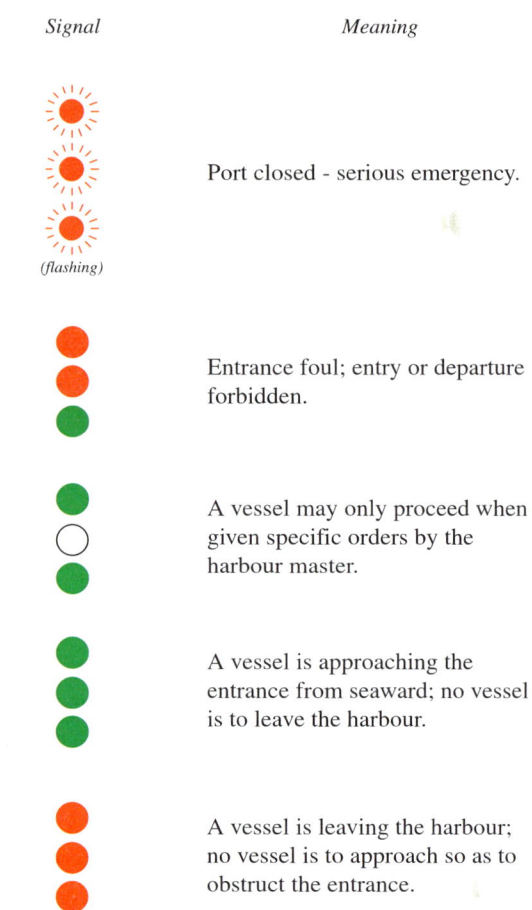

Signal	Meaning
	Port closed - serious emergency.
(flashing)	
	Entrance foul; entry or departure forbidden.
	A vessel may only proceed when given specific orders by the harbour master.
	A vessel is approaching the entrance from seaward; no vessel is to leave the harbour.
	A vessel is leaving the harbour; no vessel is to approach so as to obstruct the entrance.

Weymouth – traffic signals (6.74)

Tidal streams
6.75

1   The streams in Weymouth Bay are weak. They are affected by the eddy which forms E of Portland and are nearly always W-going; there may be a barely perceptible SE-going stream between about +0030 and +0230 Devonport (–0510 and –0310 Dover), but the stream is W-going, spring rate ½ kn, at all other times.

2   In the vicinity of the harbour tidal streams are weak. The rise and fall of the tide within the harbour is considerably affected by winds.

    Tidal heights, see information on chart 2172.

Directions for entering harbour
(continued from 6.26)

Principal marks
6.76

1   **Landmarks:**
      Hotel (white tower) (50°38'·2N 2°25'·1W).
      Saint John's Church (spire) (50°37'·1N 2°27'·0W).
    Major light:
      A Head Light (50°35'·2N 2°25'·1W) (6.21).
6.77

1   From the vicinity of Weymouth pilot boarding place (6.41), South Pier Light (50°36'·6N 2°26'·5W) (6.26) bearing less than 280° leads in the approach until about 1 mile from the light.

The track then leads NW to open the harbour entrance.

Leading lights:

2   Front light (red diamond on white post, 3 m in height) (50°36′·5N 2°26′·9W) on Ballast Quay.

Rear light (red diamond on white mast, 5 m in height) (17 m WSW of the front light).

Weymouth - Leading Marks from NE (6.77)

(Original dated 2005)

(Photograph - RMAS Newton)

The alignment (239¾°) of these lights then leads into the harbour passing between South Pier and North Pier until abreast the SE corner of the Ferry Terminal; thence keep in mid-channel.

3   **Clearing mark:**

The line of bearing 300°, or less, of Saint John's Church passes NNE of all buoyage (6.50) E of the harbour.

Berths

Alongside berths
6.78

1   No 1 Berth (50°36′·5N 2°26′·7W) is 100 m long with a least depth of 4·3 m, for vessels up to 115 m in length, and is a multi–user berth for bulk cargo operations and Ro-Ro side operations.

No 3 and No 4 Berths (50°36′·5N 2°26′·8W) are 260 m long, in total, with a least depth of 3·5 m at No 3 and 4·4 m at No 4; a linkspan and Ro-Ro facilities are available at No 3 Berth.

2   Nos 5 and 6 Berths are fitted with pontoons in summer and used as yacht berths.

No 7 Berth is a designated Fish Landing Area; its use by visiting yachts is prohibited.

Port services
6.79

1   **Repairs.** Hull and machinery repairs can be carried out afloat. Divers are available.

Other facilities.

Medical. Full accident and emergency facilities are available at Dorchester (13 km N) and there is a minor injuries unit at Weymouth Community Hospital. Both have helicopter landing sites.

2   **Ship sanitation control and ship sanitation control exemption certificates** issued at Weymouth.

Customs office in Poole.

Supplies.

Fuel can be supplied to all berths by road tanker, with prior arrangement. Diesel fuel is available from a pontoon on the S side of the harbour.

3   **Fresh water** is available at all berths.

Provisions and stores are available.

Communications: Hurn Airport, Bournemouth, distant 56 km, and; Exeter airport, distant 101 km, both with international flights.

Rescue. For details of rescue facilities available, see 6.17.

Westham Bridge

North Quay

Weymouth Inner Harbour from S (6.79)

(Original dated 2001)

(Photograph –Air Images)

Inner Harbour

General information
6.80

1   Town Bridge, a double bascule bridge with a passage through 24·4 m wide, spans the harbour 5 cables within the entrance and leads to Inner Harbour (The Backwater) a large pool in which are situated Weymouth Marina and Weymouth Harbour Marina. Pontoons are provided on each side of the bridge for use by craft waiting for the bridge to be opened. The bridge is opened every 2 hours between 0800 and 1800, with the last lift between 1930 and 2130 depending upon the time of year. Between October and March 1 hours notice is required. Bookings for bridge lifts can be arranged through Weymouth Harbour radio; mariners requiring bridge lifts should be within sight of the bridge operator by the scheduled opening time.

Traffic signals (Diagram 6.80) are shown from each side of the S bastion of the bridge when it is open.

Signal	Meaning
🟢🟢🟢	Vessels may proceed through the bridge cut.
🔴🔴🔴	Vessels may not proceed through the bridge cut.

Weymouth - Town Bridge traffic signals (6.80)

WEYMOUTH TO NEEDLES CHANNEL APPROACHES

General information

Charts 2610, 2615

Route
6.81

1 From Weymouth the passage to Needles Channel (50°39′N 1°37′W) approaches leads generally E passing clear or over Saint Alban's Ledge, which extends 4 miles SW from Saint Alban's Head (50°35′N 2°03′W), and S of Anvil Point (50°35′N 1°58′W) to a position S of Poole Bay, SW of the approaches to Needles Channel.

Topography
6.82

1 From Redcliff Point (50°38′N 2°25′W) to White Nothe, 3½ miles E, the cliffs, intersected by steep ravines, gradually rise to an elevation of 168 m with high ground inland. Between White Nothe (50°37′N 2°19′W) and Worbarrow Tout, identifiable by a small conical hill on its summit 5¼ miles E, the coast is generally bold. The entrance to Lulworth Cove (50°37′N 2°15′W) (6.93), about 3 miles E of White Nothe, is not easily distinguishable. Worbarrow Bay (50°37′N 2°12′W) (6.94) has high cliffy shores divided in the centre by Arish Mell Gap, with its white sandy beach which is a clear and prominent landmark, especially in sunny weather.

2 Brandy Bay and Kimmeridge Bay lie between Worbarrow Tout and Saint Alban's Head but neither afford safe anchorage. Between the latter bay and Saint Alban's Head the coast consists of dark cliffs fringed by flat ledges of hard clay some of which extend more than 5 cables offshore.

3 Saint Alban's Head (50°35′N 2°03′W) (6.87) is a bold headland; it is readily identified on the radar display. Between the head and Anvil Point, 3¾ miles E, the coast is bold and is composed of dark limestone cliffs where quarries are extensively worked. A light (6.87) is exhibited from the point.

Hazards
6.83

1 **Firing danger areas.** Firing practice from sea and shore is carried out periodically between Lulworth Cove (50°37′N 2°15′W) and Saint Alban's Head; the danger areas extends up to 12 miles offshore. When the danger areas are in use, red flags are displayed and red lights are exhibited, night and day, from Bindon Hill near Lulworth Cove and from above the coastguard station on Saint Alban's Head.

2 Mariners may pass through the areas but should endeavour to comply with advice from range safety vessels. The DZ buoys near Saint Alban's Ledge are targets for naval gunnery and, for safety, mariners are advised to keep at least 1 mile clear of them.

Exercise areas. For details of exercise areas, see 6.3 and information on the chart.

3 **Fishing.** In summer crab pots are laid within about 5 cables of the shore between Saint Alban's Head and Studland Bay (6.108), and on Whitehouse Grounds; they are frequently inconspicuously marked. See also 6.4.

Measured distance
6.84

1 Between Anvil Point and a position about 1 mile W there is a measured distance in one section:
  W limit marks. Beacons (50°35′·5N 1°59′·0W).
  E limit marks. Beacons (50°35′·6N 1°57′·5W) close E of the lighthouse.
  Distance: 1848·9 m.
  Running track: 083½° or 263½°.

Rescue
6.85

1 **Coastguard Rescue Team** is situated at:
  Saint Alban's Head Auxiliary Station (50°35′N 2°03′W).

National Coastwatch Institute (NCI) stations are situated at:
  Saint Albans (50°34′·6N 2°03′·5W).
  Peveril Point (50°36′·3N 1°56′·8W).

For details of coastguard stations see 1.101 and for NCI see 1.106.

Natural conditions
6.86

1 **Tidal streams.** At a position about 1 mile S of Saint Alban's Head the stream begins as follows:

Interval from HW Devonport (Dover)	Direction
−0100 (+0545)	ESE
+0525 (−0015)	W-WNW

The maximum spring rates are 4¾ kn.

2 Tidal streams E and W of Saint Alban's Ledge are shown by means of information on the chart.

At a position about 1 mile ESE of Durlston Head (50°36′N 1°57′W) the streams begin as follows:

Interval from HW Devonport (Dover)	Direction
−0115 (+0530)	NE
+0510 (−0030)	SW

The maximum spring rates are 3kn.

At times there is a considerable race over Peveril Ledge (50°36′N 1°56′W) especially during the W-going stream; the latter sets well S of Durlston Head and Anvil Point.

3 **Eddies** similar to those off Isle of Portland form off Saint Alban's Head, but the eddies are smaller, and, on account of the shape of the coast, only the eddy on the W side is of any importance. Along the W side of Saint Alban's Head the stream runs nearly continuously SE and a race forms off the head. The area of overfalls on the W-going stream extends about 2½ miles farther SW than on the E-going stream, and they are considerably more dangerous to small craft. At spring tides the period during

which Saint Alban's Ledge is free from overfalls and rips rarely exceeds half an hour at the turn of the stream.

Directions
(continued from 6.26)

Principal marks
6.87

1   **Landmarks:**
Isle of Portland (50°34′N 2°26′W) (6.13).
Saint Alban's Head or Saint Aldhelm's Head (50°35′N 2°03′W), a bold headland on which stands a chapel and a coastguard station.
Major lights:
2   Portland Light (50°31′N 2°27′W) (6.21).
A Head Light (50°35′N 2°25′W) (6.21).
Anvil Point Light (white round tower and dwelling, 12 m in height) (50°35′·5N 1°57′·6W) shown throughout 24 hours.
Needles Light (50°40′N 1°35′W) (6.167).
Saint Catherine's Point Light (50°35′N 1°18′W) (6.167) (chart 2656).

Other aid to navigation
6.88

1   **Racon:** Bridge Light Buoy (50°39′·6N 1°36′·9W).
For details see *Admiralty List of Radio Signals Volume 2.*

Charts 2255, 2610
Weymouth Bay to Saint Alban's Head
6.89

1   From the vicinity of Weymouth pilot boarding place (50°37′N 2°23′W) (6.71) the route leads generally E passing (with positions given from Worbarrow Tout (50°37′N 2°11′W)):
S of Ringstead Ledge (50°38′N 2°22′W), the outermost danger off Bran Point; thence:
S of White Nothe (50°37′N 2°19′W) (6.82); thence:
Clear or over, according to draught, of Lulworth Banks (3½ miles WSW), noting Adamant Shoal which lies 3 miles S; thence:
2   Clear of a light buoy (special) (2 miles S) (6.94); thence:
S of Broad Bench Point (1½ miles ESE); thence:
S of Kimmeridge Ledges (3 miles ESE); thence:
S of a dangerous wreck (4¼ miles ESE); and:
3   S or over, according to draught, of Saint Alban's Ledge which extends 4 miles SW from Saint Alban's Head (5½ miles ESE), its least depth (8·5 m) is situated 8 cables S of the headland. DZ light buoys (special) (6.83), the positions of which can best be seen from the chart, are moored NW and SE of the ledge. Thence:
S of Saint Alban's Head (6.87).
6.90

1   **Useful marks:**
Saint John's Church (50°37′·1N 2°27′·1W) (6.76).
Tower (50°36′N 2°08′W) on the E side of Kimmeridge Bay.
In addition to the marks above, all those listed at 6.26.

Charts 2610, 2615
Saint Alban's Head to Needles Channel approaches
6.91

1   From a position S of Saint Alban's Head (50°35′N 2°03′W) the route leads generally E passing (with positions given from Anvil Point (50°35′N 1°58′W)):

S of Anvil Point (6.82); thence:
S of Durlston Head (5 cables NE) (6.103); thence:
S of Whitehouse Grounds (2 miles ENE), a rocky ledge; thence:
To a position S of Poole Bay, SW of the approaches to Needles Channel (50°39′N 1°37′W).
6.92

1   **Useful marks:**
Radar scanner (50°37′·3N 2°14′·5W).
Hurst Point Leading Light (50°42′N 1°33′W) (7.45).
*(Directions continue,
for Approaches to Poole Harbour at 6.103,
for Nab Tower approaches at 6.167
and for Needles Channel at 7.45)*

Anchorages
Chart 2172 plan of Lulworth Cove
Lulworth Cove
6.93

1   Lulworth Cove (50°37′N 2°15′W) is a small circular basin encompassed by high cliffs of chalk and sand. The cove affords shelter to small craft except during S winds when a heavy swell rolls in.

Lulworth Cove from SW (6.93)

(Original dated 2001)

(Photograph -Air Images)

Entrance, not easily distinguishable, is ½ cable wide between ledges of rocks which dry, extending from each side of the entrance, the longest ledge being on the W side; when entering mariners should keep closer to the E cliff.
2   **Anchorage** can be obtained in the NE corner of the cove, as indicated on the chart, in a depth of 3 m, good holding ground of clay, sand and weed.
Mooring buoy, for Ministry of Defence vessels, is situated in the NE part of the cove; small craft moorings are available in the W part.
Landing can be obtained on the W side of the cove.

Charts 2172 plan of Worbarrow Bay, 2610,
Worbarrow Bay
6.94

1   Worbarrow Bay is entered between Mupe Rocks (50°37′N 2°13′W) and Worbarrow Tout (6.82), 1¼ miles E. The bay affords shelter except with S winds.
Leading marks:
Front mark. Beacon (white post, orange triangle) (50°37′·3N 2°11′·3W).
Rear mark. Beacon (white post, orange diamond) (1½ cables NE of the front mark).

| Mupe Ledges | Arish Mell | Worbarrow Tout |

Worbarrow Bay from S (6.94)

(Photograph –HMSML Gleaner)   *(Original dated 1992)*

2   The alignment (042½°) of these marks, standing on the NE side of the bay, leads into the bay to the recommended anchorage passing close NW of a spit, with depths of less than 10 m over it, which extends 4 cables W from Worbarrow Tout.

3   **Anchorage** can be obtained in the E half of the bay, as indicated on the chart, in depths of about 11 m, fine sand. Anchoring is only permitted when Lulworth Gunnery Ranges are not in use. For advance information, contact the Range Safety Officer. For details regarding firing danger areas, see 6.83 and information on the chart.

Small craft can obtain anchorage in Mupe Bay, on the W side of the bay close N of Mupe Rocks in depths of 3 to 10 m, and in a cove on the E side of the bay 1½ cables NNE of Worbarrow Tout, in depths of 2 to 5 m, as indicated on the chart.

4   **Submarine pipeline** extends 2 miles SSE from Arish Mell Gap (6.82); its inner end is marked by a beacon (black and yellow) and a light buoy (special) is moored 3 cables S of its seaward end.

Chart 2172 plan of Chapman's Pool
Chapman's Pool
6.95

1   **General information.** Chapman's Pool (50°35′·5N 2°03′·9W), situated 1 mile N of Saint Alban's Head, provides an anchorage for yachts near the centre of the pool in depths of about 2 m.

Depths close inshore are liable to change due to cliff falls.

Swell. The anchorage is open from S to W and swell rolls into the pool.

Chapman's Pool from SW (6.95)
(Original dated 2001)

(Photograph –Air Images)

NEEDLES CHANNEL APPROACHES TO BOGNOR REGIS AND THE OWERS

GENERAL INFORMATION

Chart 2450
Area covered
6.96

1   The section is arranged as follows:
Approaches to Poole Harbour (6.97)
Poole Harbour (6.112)
Needles Channel Approaches to Nab Tower Approaches (6.157)
Nab Tower Approaches to Bognor Regis and The Owers (6.178)

APPROACHES TO POOLE HARBOUR

General information

Charts 2175, 2035, 2615
Route
6.97

1   From a position S of Poole Bay, SW of the approaches to Needles Channel (50°39′N 1°37′W), the passage to Poole Harbour leads generally N.

Topography
6.98

1   **Durlston Head to Poole Harbour.** Durlston Bay lies between Durlston Head (50°36′N 1°57′W) and Peveril

Point, a low cliffy point, 8 cables NNE. Swanage Bay (6.107) is entered between Peveril Point and Ballard Point, 1½ miles NNE. Swanage, a seaside resort, occupies the S half of the bay. The N shore of the bay consists of coloured cliffs of clay and sand which extend to the N corner where they join the steep chalk cliffs below Ballard Down.

2 From Ballard Point (50°38′N 1°56′W) to Handfast Point (6.103), a conspicuous point 8 cables NNE, the coast consists of perpendicular chalk cliffs close off which there are two pinnacle rocks, 37 m and 21 m high, neither of which is prominent when viewed from E.

3 Studland Bay (6.108), in the SW part of Poole Bay, lies between Handfast Point (50°38′N 1°55′W) and the entrance to Poole Harbour, approximately 2 miles NNW. The shore of the bay consists of low sand dunes covered with scrub and spartina grass. The Yards, three remarkable projections on the chalk cliff, are situated close W of Handfast Point.

6.99

1 **Poole Harbour to Hurst Point.** Between the entrance to Poole Harbour and Hurst Point, 15 miles E, the coast is indented by Poole Bay and Christchurch Bay, the shores of which consist of a succession of earthy cliffs intersected by deep ravines, known as chines, worn by the action of small streams. The sea is encroaching on the whole of this part of the coast causing frequent landslips.

2 The shore of Poole Bay (6.109) is almost entirely occupied by the seaside town of Bournemouth, with its suburbs of Boscombe and Southbourne. There are numerous conspicuous buildings, the positions of which can best be seen from the chart, within 5 cables W and 8 cables E of Bournemouth Pier. Works are in progress (2008) close SE of Boscombe Pier to construct an artificial reef for the benefit of leisure activities; the site is marked by a light buoy (S cardinal) and 12 light buoys (special).

3 The land bordering Christchurch Bay (6.110) is low. Hengistbury Head its W entrance point, is of dark reddish ironstone and is being steadily eroded, though more slowly than the coast farther W. A stone groyne extends 1 cable S from the head, its extremity is marked by a beacon. At the E end of the bay Hurst Beach, a narrow low-lying neck of land extends SE from Milford-on-Sea (50°43′N 1°35′W) to Hurst Point, 1¼ miles SE. North Channel, which leads between the N end of Shingles and Hurst Beach, is described at 7.54.

Rescue
6.100

1 **Coastguard Rescue Teams** are situated at:
Swanage on Peveril Point (50°36′N 1°57′W).
Poole (50°43′N 1°58′W).
Southbourne on Warren Hill (50°43′N 1°46′W).
Lifeboats. An all-weather lifeboat and an inshore lifeboat are stationed at Swanage (50°36′N 1°57′W) (6.107) and an inshore lifeboat is stationed at Mudeford (50°44′N 1°44′W) (6.111).

2 For details of coastguard stations see 1.100 and for lifeboats 1.113.
VHF Direction-finding service, for emergency use only, operates from Southbourne coastguard station situated WNW of Hengistbury Head. For details see 1.105 and *Admiralty List of Radio Signals Volume 2.*

Marine Research Area
6.101

1 A Marine Research Area extends from Anvil Point to Peveril Point, 1 mile NE, and is designated a Voluntary

Marine Nature Reserve. A hydrophone, marked by a buoy (special), is situated in Durlston Bay 4 cables NE of Durlston Head. See also 1.91.

Natural conditions
6.102

1 **Tidal streams.** Between Durlston Head and the entrance to Needles Channel (50°39′N 1°37′W) the stream is nearly rectilinear, for details see information on the chart.
In Swanage Bay the streams are weak and run round the bay, in general in a NNE direction on the E-going stream and in a SSW direction on the W-going stream. There may be eddies near Peveril Point and Ballard Point.

2 Within Poole Bay and Christchurch Bay the streams are weak, running generally in the direction of the land, but they run with some strength across Christchurch Ledge (50°41′N 1°42′W); they begin as follows:

Interval from HW Portsmouth (Dover)	Direction
+0445 (+0510)	E
−0130 (−0105)	W

3 The maximum rates at springs are 1kn and at neaps ½ kn.
Race extends E from Handfast Point during the W-going stream, which in this vicinity runs S. There may be eddies near the point.

Directions
(continued from 6.92)

Principal marks
6.103

1 **Landmarks:**
Castle (50°36′N 1°57′W) on Durlston Head.
Handfast Point (50°38′N 1°55′W). Old Harry, a column of chalk with a flat grassy top, lies close off the point.
Water Tower (elevation 52 m) (50°43′N 1°48′W) at Southbourne.

2 Coastguard Station (50°43′N 1°46′W) on Warren Hill.
Major lights:
Needles Light (50°40′N 1°35′W) (6.167).
Saint Catherine's Point Light (50°35′N 1°18′W) (6.167).
Anvil Point Light (50°36′N 1°58′W) (6.87).

Other aid to navigation
6.104

1 **Racon:** Bridge Light Buoy (50°39′·6N 1°36′·9W).
For details see *Admiralty List of Radio Signals Volume 2.*

Charts 2172 plan of Swanage and Studland Bays, 2175, 2035 2615
6.105

1 From a position S of Poole Bay, SW of the approaches to Needles Channel (50°39′N 1°37′W), the route leads generally N passing (with positions given from Handfast Point (50°38′N 1°55′W)):
W of Dolphin Sand, which fronts the approach to Christchurch Bay and the SE approach to Poole Bay, and has a least depth (9·6 m) (50°39′N 1°46′W) approximately 3¼ miles SSW of Hengistbury Head. And:

2 Over or clear, according to draught, of Whitehouse Grounds (50°36′N 1°55′W) (6.91); thence:
E of Peveril Ledge which extends 3 cables E from Peveril Point (50°36′N 1°57′W) (6.98). A light

3 E of Evans Rock (1¾ miles SSW); thence:

E of Ballard Point (7½ cables SSW); thence:

E of Handfast Point (6.103), distant at least 3 cables, to avoid the rocks which lie close offshore between Ballard and Handfast Points; thence:

To a position ½ mile NE of Handfast Point.

4 **Caution.** The E-going tidal stream sets towards Christchurch Ledge (50°41′N 1°42′W) (6.110) and when crossing the entrance to Poole Bay a set N must be expected. The W-going stream sets well S of Durlston Head. For times of the tidal streams ESE of Durlston Head, see 6.86.

6.106

1 **Useful marks:**

Methodist Church (spire) (50°36′·5N 1°57′·7W) at Swanage.

Rock scree (50°36′·1N 1°57′·2W).

Christchurch Priory (tower) (50°43′·9N 1°46′·5W) conspicuous except from E.

(Directions continue at 6.140)

Swanage Bay

Chart 2172 plan of Swanage and Studland Bays
General information
6.107

1 **Description.** Swanage Bay is entered between Peveril Point (50°36′N 1°57′W) and Ballard Point, 1½ miles NNE, and provides good shelter from W winds.

Swanage Pier, in the S part of the bay, has depths of approximately 2 to 3 m at its head; a light is exhibited at the pierhead. Berthing on the pier is restricted, and anchoring in the area close to the pier is prohibited, as shown on the chart.

Peveril Point and Swanage Pier from E (6.107)
(Original dated 2001)

(Photograph –Air Images)

2 **Directions.** Approaching Swanage Bay from SW do not let Durlston Head (6.103) bear less than 230°, astern, and do not approach within 5 cables of Peveril Point until the Methodist church (6.106) at Swanage is well open of the N side of Peveril Point. At night keep Anvil Point Light

(6.87) in sight, open SE of Durlston Head, until well clear N of Peveril Point.

3 **Anchorage** can be obtained 7½ cables N of Peveril Point in a depth of 8 m, clay and sand, good holding ground.

Mariners should avoid anchoring on Potters Shoal, lying 9 cables NNE of Peveril Point, during the months of February to April on account of the prawn fishing ground on the shoal.

Rescue, see 6.100.

Studland Bay

Charts 2172 plan of Swanage and Studland Bays, 2175
General information
6.108

1 Studland Bay, in the SW part of Poole Bay, lies between Handfast Point (50°38′N 1°55′W) (6.103) and the entrance to Poole Harbour, approximately 2 miles NNW, and affords good shelter to small vessels of suitable draught.

Anchorage can be obtained 3¼ cables NW of Handfast Point in *After Paragraph 6.108 2 line 2 Add:*

Aggleston
small h **Marine nature reserve.** A marine nature reserve is centred on position 50°38′·64N 1°56′·30W and marked *2* **Caut** by buoys (special) at the corners and centre. The close o reserve is designated as a voluntary prohibited **Yach** anchorage area and mariners are requested not to is moor anchor within the buoyed limits.

Addition

Poole Bay

Chart 2175
General information
6.109

1 **Description.** Poole Bay is entered between Handfast Point (50°38′N 1°55′W) (6.103) and Hengistbury Head, 8 miles ENE.

2 Bournemouth Pier, a promenade pier, extends about 1¼ cables S from the shore at Bournemouth; the outer part has a width of 37 m. There are landing stages on its E and W sides used by pleasure steamers and small boats; there are depths of from 2·7 to 3·4 m at the outer part of the landing stages, shoaling immediately inshore of the wide portion to 1·2 m.

3 Boscombe Pier (50°43′·1N 1°50′·6W), a promenade pier, extends about 1 cable S from the shore at Boscombe; there is a depth of 2·7 m at its outer end.

Anchorage can be obtained in the bay, as convenient, sheltered from all but E winds, in good holding ground.

4 **Dangers.** Within approximately 7½ cables of the shore there are two areas of foul ground, indicated on the chart, which lie parallel with the shore between Poole Head (50°42′N 1°56′W) and Hengistbury Head; numerous sewer outfalls, marked by buoys, extend up to 3 cables from the shore. Outside these areas of foul ground there are several relevant dangers positioned as follows from Bournemouth Pierhead (50°42′·8N 1°52′·5W):

5 Middle Poole Patch or Lobster Rock (2 miles SSW).

Poole Rocks (1¾ miles SSW).

Outer Poole Patch (1½ miles S).

Dolphin Sand (50°39′N 1°46′W) (6.105) fronts the SE approach to the bay.

Yacht race buoys. Five scattered buoys (special) used for yacht races are moored in the W part of the bay as shown on the chart.

Christchurch Bay

Charts 2035, 2172

General information

6.110

1   **Description.** Christchurch Bay lies between Hengistbury Head (50°43′N 1°45′W) (6.99) and Hurst Point, 7½ miles E; the land bordering the bay is low.

2   **Bathing area,** marked by yellow buoys and shown on the chart, fronts the coast between Hengistbury Head and Chewton Bunny, 1½ miles NE, and is in use from April to October. Within this area mariners are not to exceed 8 kn and are to proceed with extreme caution, giving way to swimmers.

3   **Yacht racing buoys** (special, spherical) are laid throughout Christchurch Bay between April and October up to 2½ miles from the coast as shown on the chart.

   Directions. The anchorage should be approached S and E of Christchurch Ledge, a narrow rocky ledge which extends 2¾ miles SE from Hengistbury Head, passing between Christchurch Ledge and Dolphin Bank, 2 miles SE, noting Dolphin Sand (50°39′N 1°46′W) (6.105) which fronts the approach to the bay. A buoy (special, seasonal) is moored close NE of the outer end of the ledge.

4   **Clearing marks:**

     The line of bearing 333° of Christchurch Priory (50°43′·9N 1°46′·5W) (6.106) open SW of the coastguard station (6.103) on Warren Hill, 1¼ miles SSE, clears SW of Christchurch Ledge.

   Anchorage can be obtained 1½ miles E of Hengistbury Head, as shown on the chart, in depths of 6 to 7 m, good holding ground. Small craft can anchor closer inshore.

Charts 2172 plan of Christchurch Harbour, 2035

Christchurch Harbour

6.111

1   **Description.** Christchurch Harbour, situated N of Hengistbury Head, mostly dries and is only suitable for small craft of up to 20 m in length and 1·6 m draught.

Mudeford Quay

Christchurch Harbour entrance (The Run) from NE (6.111)

(Original dated 2001)

(Photograph –Air Images)

2   **Channel.** A narrow spit of shingle and sand extends about 8 cables NNE from Hengistbury Head and the entrance to the harbour lies between this spit and the coast N. The Run, the inner part of the entrance channel, leads in a SW direction nearly parallel with the shore. The entrance channel is marked by beacons (lateral) and is buoyed in summer. The town of Christchurch stands a little above the junction of River Avon and River Stour, about 1½ miles NW of the harbour entrance; the channel between The Run and Christchurch is marked by buoys (port and starboard).

3   **Tidal streams** in The Run are very strong with an average rate of 3 to 5 kn; the outgoing stream may attain a rate of 7 kn. See also diagram on chart 2172.

   Local knowledge is essential as the position of the entrance channel and depths over the bar frequently change and the buoys are moved accordingly. Fishermen may sometimes offer their services as pilots.

4   **Approach.** The line of bearing 282° of Christchurch Priory leads in the approach to the vicinity of the channel entrance. Entry later than ½ hour after the second HW is inadvisable.

   Anchorage. There is no designated anchorage within the harbour and swinging room is limited on account of the large number of moorings. The quay and moorings superintendent at Mudeford will give guidance as to space available during summer months.

5   **Berths.** Mudeford Quay, on the sea wall which fronts Haven House on the N side at the inner end of The Run, has a depths of less than 1 m alongside. A light (metal mast, 5 m in height) is exhibited from the quay. Town Quay, Christchurch, has a depth of 0·6 m alongside.

   Rescue, see 6.100.

POOLE HARBOUR

General information

Charts 2611, 2175

Position

6.112

1   Poole Harbour is an extensive natural harbour with a port fronting the town of Poole (50°43′N 1°59′W), which lies on its N side.

Function

6.113

1   The port is used by commercial vessels and operates ferry services, with RoRo facilities, to Channel Islands and a daily freight and a passenger and freight ferry service to the N coast of France. The harbour is an important yachting centre.

Topography

6.114

1   Poole Harbour is a spacious estuary which at HW resembles an inland lake. At LW large expanses of mudflats uncover and these are intersected by numerous creeks and channels. The bottom of the harbour is mainly composed of sand over clay and gravel but it varies extensively; in places there is soft mud, locally known as quags, which is dangerous.

2   The entrance to the harbour lies between South Haven Point (50°40′·8N 1°57′·0W), a low sandy point with a few low buildings on it situated at the N end of sand-dunes bordering Studland Bay, and the S end of Sandbanks, a peninsula which extends 1 mile SW from Poole Head (50°41′·7N 1°55′·7W); the peninsula is built up along its length.

3   There are five main islands in Poole Harbour. Brownsea Island, the largest and thickly wooded, lies close within the harbour entrance, together with Furzey Island, Green Island,

Round Island and Long Island. The area between these islands and the S side of the harbour is intersected by numerous small channels and creeks.

Port limits
6.115
1 Poole Harbour limits are as shown on the chart.

Approach and entry
6.116
1 The port is approached through the SW part of Poole Bay through Swash Channel (6.141) and entered between South Haven Point and the S end of Sandbanks, 2 cables NNE.

Traffic
6.117
1 In 2006 the port was used by 320 vessels, not including ferry traffic, totalling 719 973 dwt.

Port Authority
6.118
1 Poole Harbour Commissioners, Harbour Office, 20 New Quay Road, Poole, Dorset, BH15 4AF.
Internet: www.phc.co.uk
Email: harbourmaster@phc.co.uk

Limiting conditions
Controlling depths
6.119
1 The controlling depth for the port is 7·5 m and is the maintained depth in Swash Channel (6.141), Middle Ship Channel (6.142) and in the turning basin off the Continental Freight Ferry Terminal (50°42'·5N 1°59'·5W). Little Channel dredged to 6·0 m (2006).

Harbour control should be consulted for the most recent depth information in the channels and alongside berths.

Density of water
6.120
1 Density: 1·021 g/cm^3.

Deepest and longest berths
6.121
1 The deepest berths are at the Continental Freight Ferry Terminal (6.146); the longest berth is Poole Town Quay (6.146).

Tidal levels
6.122
1 **General information.** Within the harbour the tidal cycle is abnormal as described at 1.153 and results in the phenomenon of a double HW with the tide standing at or near HW for approximately 6 or 7 hours. The rise and fall of the tide at the harbour entrance is shown on chart 2175; the tide at Poole RoRo Terminal is shown by diagram on chart 2611.

2 Neap tides however are very irregular and may produce a second HW which is higher than the first. Barometric pressure and strong winds can alter the tidal cycle significantly.

3 **Poole Harbour** (RoRo Terminal). Mean spring range about 1·6 m; mean neap range about 0·5 m. For further information see *Admiralty Tide Tables*.

Maximum size of vessel handled
6.123
1 A vessel of 20 133 gt, 158 m LOA and 5·4 m draught regularly uses the port.

Local weather and sea state
6.124
1 Strong S winds raise a heavy sea on The Bar and strong E winds are liable to alter the depth over The Bar.

Arrival information
6.125
Vessel traffic service
1 A VTS is in operation and reporting points are shown on the chart. Vessels of 25 m LOA, or more, transitting the harbour should report to Poole Harbour Control, for details see *Admiralty List of Radio Signals Volume 6(1)*.

Port radio
6.126
1 Operates from the harbour office, 24 hours, for details see *Admiralty List of Radio Signals Volume 6(1)*.

Notice of ETA required
6.127
1 ETA: 24 hours in advance to Poole Harbour Control and the port agents, indicating requirement for a pilot when appropriate, for details see *Admiralty List of Radio Signals Volume 6(1)*.

Outer anchorages
6.128
1 Anchorage can be obtained in Poole Bay (6.109) as convenient. A recommended berth is 5 cables E of No 1 Bar Light Buoy (50°39'·3N 1°55'·1W); the anchorage is exposed and can become very uncomfortable in prolonged S or SE gales.

2 A berth, with reasonable shelter from W winds, can be obtained approximately 5 cables E of Handfast Point (50°38'N 1°56'W) (6.103) in a depth of 12 m, sand and gravel.

Alternatively anchorage can be obtained in Studland Bay (6.108), as convenient, in lesser depths.

3 **Prohibited anchorage.** Anchoring is prohibited in the vicinity of submarine cables laid between Brownsea Island and North Haven Point, approximately 3 cables E; its landing place is marked by beacons.

Pilotage and tugs
6.129
1 **Pilotage** is compulsory for all vessels over 50 m LOA and for vessels of 30 m or more in length, or 10 m or more in beam, capable of carrying more than 12 passengers, except for those exempt by law. It is available throughout 24 hours.

2 **Boarding place**: in the vicinity of No 1 Bar Light Buoy (50°39'·3N 1°55'·2W), as shown on the chart.

Notification for a pilot should be confirmed at least 1½ hours before arrival.

Tug. A tug, 17 tonnes bollard pull, is available.

Traffic regulations
6.130
1 **Speed limits.** There is a speed limit of 10 kn within an area extending 1 400 m seaward of South Haven Point (50°40'·8N 1°57'·0W) to the point where the Rivers Frome and Piddle enter Poole Harbour in the W, except in those areas in which the 6 kn speed limit below applies. During the period 1st October to 30th April each year, this 10 kn speed limit will be relaxed and will not apply within Middle Ship Channel, North Channel and Wareham Channel from Brownsea Road to the W limit.

2 There is a speed limit of 6 kn in Little Channel, between No 29 Stakes Light Buoy (50°42'·4N 1°59'·0W) (S cardinal) to, and within Holes Bay (6.155).

Movements within the port. Vessels proposing to shift berth must obtain prior permission from harbour control.

Fog routine. In reduced visibility, normally less than 500 m, the Harbour Control Officer will order a fog routine. Whilst in force the following precautions are to be observed:

3
    a. Vessels over 20 m must seek permission before moving in the harbour.
    b. Small craft are to keep clear of the main shipping channels.
    d. Vessels are not to pass in the channel except with the agreement of both masters, who should be in radio contact.
    e. Vessels are not to exit Little Channel until any other vessel using the Middle Ship Channel or Turning Basin is clear.
    f. Vessels are not to overtake in the channels.

4
Restricted areas. Two restricted areas surrounding historic wrecks exist in the approaches to Poole. One, marked by a light buoy (special) is centred on position 50°39′·7N 1°54′·9W; the other is centred on position 50°39′·9N 1°55′·5W close E of the dredged entrance channel. For protection details see 1.89.

Chain ferry. See 6.135

5
Boat channels exist for use by recreational craft and fishing vessels with a draught of up to 3·0 m on the W side of Swash Channel, and by recreational craft and fishing vessels with a draught of up to 1·5 m on the S side of Middle Ship Channel. The S limits of these channels are marked by beacons and buoys (port hand) in Swash Channel and by beacons (port hand) in Middle Ship Channel. Mariners in recreational craft and fishing vessels are to use these boat channels whenever possible. See information on the chart.

6
Mariners in yachts and small craft are required to keep clear of all large commercial vessels in the shipping channels and when manoeuvring between the quays at Poole; such vessels will sound the appropriate sound signals. RoRo vessels sound one prolonged blast before leaving the terminal to warn craft of their departure.

7
Water skiing, personal watercraft and wind surfing areas are established within the Poole Harbour area and are shown on the chart. Such activities must take place within the designated areas.

8
Kite surfing is only permitted at Whitley Lake (50°41′·7N 1°56′·3W) and off Hamworthy Park (50°42′·7N 2°00′·4W).

Regulations concerning entry
6.131

1
Dangerous and polluting goods. Vessels carrying dangerous and polluting goods bound for Poole are required to complete a checklist of information, for details see *Admiralty List of Radio Signals Volume 6(1)*. See also 1.68 to 1.76.

Port Marine Safety Code. The Standard Pilotage Passage Plan is to be used by commercial vessels using Poole. Copies are available from the Harbour Master and pilots.

Marine farms
6.132

1
There are concentrations of shellfish beds throughout Poole Harbour; their positions are best seen from the chart. Anchoring and taking the bottom in these areas are prohibited.

Marine nature reserves
6.133

1
Marine nature reserves exist in the Poole Harbour area; their positions are best seen from the chart.

Harbour

General layout
6.134

1
Main berthing areas. Continental Freight Ferry Terminal (50°42′·5N 1°59′·5W), a RoRo freight and passenger terminal with a turning basin on its S side, lies at the inner end of Middle Ship Channel. BP Marine Base, a small basin for offshore support of oil exploration drilling operations, is situated close W of the terminal.

2
Conventional berths lie along the E and N sides of the Continental Freight Ferry Terminal and are used for general cargo and petroleum products. Poole Town Quay fronts the S side of the town of Poole below Poole Bridge and is used by pleasure craft.

3
Approach channel. Swash Channel (6.141), with a maintained depth, leads about 2 miles NW through a shallow coastal bank to the harbour entrance. The channel is marked by light buoys.

4
Channels inside Poole Harbour. There are two channels from Brownsea Road, which lies off the E side of Brownsea Island (50°41′·5N 1°58′·0W), leading to the Continental Freight Ferry Terminal, Middle Ship Channel (6.142) and North Channel (6.143), which converge W of Parkstone Shoal (50°42′N 1°57′W).

5
Little Channel (6.144), branching N from the inner end of Middle Ship Channel, passes E of the Continental Freight Ferry Terminal and is the approach channel leading to Poole quays.

Hazards
6.135

1
Chain ferry. A chain ferry plies between South Haven Point and Sandbanks and the following regulations concerning the ferry are in force:
    The chain ferry will give way to vessels subject to compulsory pilotage proceeding in or out through the harbour entrance.
    All vessels navigating in the harbour which are not subject to compulsory pilotage shall give way to the chain ferry.
    All vessels and craft of less than 50 m in length will be obliged to give way to the chain ferry.

2
The chain ferry when underway, shall:
    Display a white strobe light, and in addition by day, display a black ball, to indicate the direction of travel.
    In fog, sound on its whistle, at intervals of not more than 2 minutes, one prolonged blast followed by two short blasts.

3
Should the chain ferry become stationary in the fairway, it shall:
    By day exhibit a red flag in place of the black ball.
    At night, exhibit a fixed all-round white light.
    In fog, ring a bell rapidly for about 5 seconds at intervals of not more than 1 minute.

High speed craft operate between Poole and N France; see 1.7.

Harbour entrance warning signals
6.136

1
A yellow flashing light is exhibited from a mast at South Haven Point (50°40′·8N 1°57′·0W) when a large

Continental Ferry Terminal   Poole Old Town   Parkstone Bay   Blue Lagoon

Brownsea Island   North Haven Point   Haven Hotel

Poole Harbour from SSE (6.131)

(Original dated 2001)

(Photograph -Kitchenham Ltd. Bournemouth)

vessel is about to enter that part of the channel situated between No 6 Light Buoy (50°40′·1N 1°55′·9W) and No 22 Aunt Betty Light Buoy (2 miles NNW). The light is displayed for vessels that are both inward bound and outward bound.

2   When the light is flashing small craft should take special care in navigating the harbour entrance, and not impede the passage of the large vessel.

Bridge traffic signals
6.137

1   Poole Bridge (50°42′·8N 1°59′·6W), a bascule bridge with an opening 18·4 m wide, connects the SW end of the town with Lower Hamworthy, a suburb on the W side of the port. Bridge traffic signal lights, visible by day and night, are exhibited from the towers of the bridge (Diagram 6.137). A digital clearance display screen is installed at the bridge indicating the height between the water level and the transverse beams under the lifting spans.

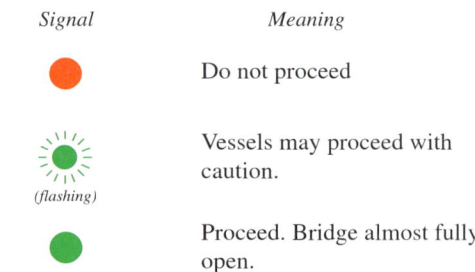

Signal	Meaning
🔴	Do not proceed
🟢 *(flashing)*	Vessels may proceed with caution.
🟢	Proceed. Bridge almost fully open.

Poole Bridge – traffic signals (6.137)

2   **Opening times.** The bridge will be opened once during a period of 15 minutes at times as shown on the chart. In addition the bridge will be opened at any time for commercial vessels; mariners should contact Poole Harbour Control or Poole Bridge on VHF.

Tidal streams
6.138

1   **Coastal stream** outside The Bar is shown by means of information on chart 2175.

2   **Harbour entrance.** The streams between South Haven Point and Sandbanks begin as follows:

Interval from LW Poole Harbour	Direction
+0055	In-going
−0645	Out-going

3   The maximum spring rates are 3 kn for the in-going stream and 4¾ kn for the out-going stream, which is weak for the first 3 hours. At neaps the streams are weak and uncertain.

Strong tide rips occur on the NE side of the entrance, both on the in-going and out-going streams.

6.139

1   **Poole Harbour.** The following description refers to the tidal streams in Poole Harbour, between Brownsea Road and the port of Poole, at springs; at neaps the streams are weak and uncertain.

In Brownsea Road, the in-going stream, spring rate 3 to 3½ kn, begins +0055 Poole Harbour; the out-going begins −0615 Poole Harbour but is weak until -0230 Poole Harbour after which it runs strongly and attains a rate of 3 kn at springs.

2   From Brownsea Road, the in-going stream runs at first in the buoyed channels; later as the mudflats cover, it runs across them towards Poole. In the channels the in-going stream begins +0040 Poole Harbour and attains a rate of 2½ to 3 kn at springs, but its rate decreases when the mudflats cover. The out-going stream begins about −0630 Poole Harbour but is weak until -0230 Poole Harbour after which it increases and attains a rate of 2½ to 3 kn at springs.

3   In North Channel the in-going stream begins +0055 Poole Harbour and attains a rate of 2½ kn at springs. The out-going stream begins about −0630 Poole Harbour but is weak until about -0215 Poole Harbour after which it increases and attains a rate of 3 kn at springs.

4   In Little Channel and off Poole Quay the in-going stream begins +0055 Poole Harbour and runs at first in the direction of Little Channel; off the quay it splits and, while the main stream continues W, a weak stream also runs E along the E part of the quay. As the mudflats cover the in-going stream runs across them, diagonally across Little Channel and W along the whole length of the quay. The in-going stream attains its greatest rate, 2 to 3 kn at springs, quickly but about 2 hours later, as the mudflats cover, it decreases to 1½ to 2 kn at springs.

5   The out-going stream begins −0645 Poole Harbour and at first runs, from the bridge, E along the quay and SE across Little Channel; later, as the mudflats dry, it runs more and more in Little Channel and the stream along the

E part of the quay decreases. At first the out-going stream is weak but after about -0230 Poole Harbour it increases and attains a rate of 3 kn at springs in the river and 2½ to 3 kn along the E part of the quay and across Little Channel. As the mudflats dry the stream in Little Channel attains a rate of 3 kn.

6   Tidal observations taken in 1977 in Brownsea Road and in Little Channel give mean spring rates ¼ to 1 kn less than those quoted above; the quoted rates are approximately maximum spring rates. Full details of the 1977 observations are given on chart 2611.

Directions for entering harbour
(continued from 6.106)

Landmarks
6.140

1   **Outside the entrance:**
Haven Hotel (50°41′·0N 1°56′·8W).
Within the entrance:
Brownsea Castle (tower and flagstaff) (50°41′·3N 1°57′·5W).

Entrance to Poole Hbr - Brownsea Castle (6.140)
(Original dated 2002)

(Photograph - D.M. Ives)

Tall Buildings (50°42′·4N 1°57′·0W) at Salterns Marina.

2   Saint Mary's Church (spire) (50°43′·4N 1°58′·3W).
Chimney (50°43′·4N 1°58′·5W) at Poole General Hospital.
White Building (elevation 47 m) (50°43′·2N 1°58′·8W).

Swash Channel
6.141

1   **Cautions – Aids to navigation.** The buoys and stakes in Poole Harbour and approaches may be moved to meet changes in the channels. Wooden stakes are frequently replaced, and may then be slightly repositioned.

Brownsea Castle   Haven Hotel

South Haven   North Haven
Point   Point

Poole Harbour Entrance from SE (6.141)
(Original dated 2002)

(Photograph - D.M. Ives)

Entrance. The harbour entrance is a high risk area, particularly for small craft during busy summer weekends. Sailing craft are advised to use their engines where fitted.

2   **Directions.** From a position 6 cables NNE of Handfast Point (50°38'·5N 1°55'·5W) the fairway leads generally NW through Swash Channel to the harbour entrance. Swash Channel which leads to the harbour entrance, lies between Hook Sand and The Bar, on its E side, and a rubble training bank, which covers at half tide, retaining Milkmaid Bank and Bar Sand on its W side. The fairway is 130 m wide. There are no leading marks for the initial stages of entering the harbour and the buoyed channel should be followed passing (with positions given from South Haven Point (50°40'·8N 1°57'·0W)):

     Between No 1 Bar Light Buoy (starboard hand) and No 2 Light Buoy (port hand) (both 2 miles SE) which mark the entrance to Swash Channel; thence:

     Between No 10 Light Buoy (port hand) (¾ cable ENE) and No 9 Swash Light Buoy (W cardinal) (2 cables ENE).

3   The line of bearing 299° of a light beacon (port hand) (50°41'·2N 1°57'·7W), or the very narrow white sector of the light, activated for commercial vessels only, leads through the harbour entrance, passing:

     Between No 12 Light Buoy (port hand) (1¾ cables NW) and Chapmans Peak (2¼ cables N), an isolated 4·7 m patch.

4   Course should then be shaped NNW, thence N, passing:

     ENE of No 14 Light Buoy (port hand) (3 cables NW), thence:

     Between a light beacon (W cardinal) (3½ cables NNW) which marks the E edge of the channel off North Haven Point, and Brownsea Light Buoy (E cardinal) (4 cables NW) which marks the shoal water close SE of Brownsea Island.

The track then leads generally N to Brownsea Road (6 cables NNW).

5   **Useful marks:**

     Lights (50°40'·8N 1°57'·0W) at each corner of the ferry landing ramp at South Haven Point.

     Lights (50°41'·0N 1°56'·9W) at each corner of the N side ferry landing ramp.

Middle Ship Channel
6.142

1   Middle Ship Channel, 80 m wide at its narrowest point, is the main channel for commercial vessels and lies S and W of Middle Ground and Parkstone Shoal (50°42'N 1°57'W). The channel is marked by light buoys.

2   From Brownsea Road (50°41'·4N 1°57'·2W) the fairway leads generally N then WNW through Middle Ship Channel passing between light buoys (lateral and cardinal), the positions of which can best be seen from the chart, to S of No 29 Stakes Light Buoy (S cardinal) (50°42'·4N 1°59'·0W). The track then leads as required to the appropriate berth at Continental Freight Ferry Terminal or N through Little Channel (6.144) to Poole quays.

3   **Positioning lights:**

     Front light. East Transit Light Beacon (X on yellow metal beacon) (50°42'·4N 2°00'·1W).

     Rear light. West Transit Light Beacon (as above) (2½ cables W of the front light).

The alignment (270½°) of the above lights marks the centre line of the turning basin off the S side of Continental Freight Ferry Terminal; the basin is marked by light buoys and buoys around its S and W sides.

North Channel
6.143

1   North Channel, marked by light buoys, lies E and N of Middle Ground and Parkstone Shoal (50°42'N 1°57'W), between these shoals and the mudflats which extend from the E and N side of the harbour.

2   From Brownsea Road (50°41'·4N 1°57'·2W) the fairway leads generally N, NW then W through North Channel passing between light buoys (port and starboard hand), the positions of which can best be seen from the chart, to No 25 Diver Light Buoy (W cardinal) (50°42'·3N 1°58'·4W) when the track then continues generally W to join Middle Ship Channel.

3   North Channel is not maintained by dredging and is only used by commercial traffic in emergencies. For controlling depth see 6.119.

   Useful marks:

     Bullpit Light Beacon (W cardinal) (50°41'·7N 1°56'·7W).

     Salterns Marina Breakwater Lights (50°42'·2N 1°57'·1W).

     Light (hut on dolphin) (50°42'·4N 1°58'·1W) on Parkstone Yacht Club starting platform.

Little Channel
6.144

1   From a position in the fairway at the W end of Middle Ship Channel S of No 29 Stakes Light Buoy (S cardinal) (50°42'·4N 1°59'·0W) the track leads generally N through Little Channel passing:

     E of Oil Jetty and New Quay, which lie on the E side of Continental Freight and Ferry Terminal; thence:

2   W of Oyster Bank Light Beacon (starboard hand) (50°42'·6N 1°59'·1W); thence:

     To the appropriate berth at Poole quays or above Poole Bridge (6.137) as requisite.

Caution. Between the quays the in-going stream runs strongly and mariners waiting to pass through the bridge should guard against being carried onto it.

Side channel
6.145

1   **East Looe Channel,** a channel for light-draught craft, runs parallel to the shore close to the S side of Sandbanks (50°41'N 1°57'W) (6.114).

Directions. From a position 1 mile ENE of South Haven Point the route leads W across Hook Sand with a least depth of 1·1 m, then SW in depths of up to 5 m, passing (with positions given from South Haven Point (50°40'·8N 1°57'·0W)):

2   Between EL1 Light Buoy (starboard hand) and EL2 Light Buoy (port hand), (both 8 cables ENE), thence:

     Between EL3 Light Buoy (starboard hand) and EL4 Light Buoy (port hand), (both 6¼ cables ENE), thence:

     NW of North Hook Light Buoy (port hand) (4 cables NE); thence:

3   SE of a Light Beacon (starboard hand) (3 cables ENE), thence:

     Between Swash Light Buoy (W cardinal) (2 cables ENE) and a light beacon (starboard hand) (2 cables NE).

The route then joins the Swash Channel (6.141).

Caution. Continuous strong E winds are liable to alter the shape of Hook Sand.

Berths

Alongside berths
6.146

1 **Continental Freight Ferry Terminal,** with three linkspan berths for RoRo vessels, longest and deepest berth:

Continental Freight Ferry Terminal from S (6.146)

(Original dated 2001)

(Photograph –Air Images)

> No 3 berth (50°42′·4N 1°59′·5W), length 130 m with a depth of 6·0 m alongside for vessels up to 165 m LOA.

2 **Poole Quays,** longest and deepest berths:
> Poole Town Quay (50°42′·7N 1°59′·2W), length 400 m, depth alongside 3·3 to 4·5 m, for pleasure craft.
> New Quay (50°42′·6N 1°59′·2W), length 158 m, depth alongside 5·0 m, for general and bulk cargoes, and containers.

3 Oil Jetty (50°42′·5N 1°59′·2W), length 82 m, depth alongside 5·0 m, for petroleum products.
> Bulwark Quay (50°42′·7N 1°59′·2W), length 89 m, depth alongside 6·0 m, for general and bulk cargoes.

4 Ballast Quay (50°42′·7N 1°59′·3W), length 77 m, depth alongside 6·0 m, for general and bulk cargoes.

There are a number of marinas at Poole.

Anchorage berths
6.147

1 There are no anchorage berths inside the harbour for commercial vessels.

Port services

Repairs
6.148

1 Limited repair facilities for commercial vessels and full facilities for pleasure craft are available.
Divers are available.

Other facilities
6.149

1 **Customs office** in Poole.
Ship sanitation control certificates are issued at Poole.
2 **Medical.** There is a hospital in the town.
Compass adjustment can be carried out.

Supplies
6.150

1 **Fuel.** Fuel oil and diesel oil are available.
Fresh water: available.
Provisions and stores: available.

Poole Harbour commercial berths from SE (6.146)

(Original dated 2001)

(Photograph –Air Images)

Communications

6.151

1   **Local airport:** Hurn Airport, Bournemouth, distant 16 km, with international flights.

Helicopter landing site close NE of Parkstone Bay (50°43′N 1°58′W).

Rescue

6.152

1   **Coastguard.** Poole Sector Office is situated at the Old Harbour Office, The Quay, Poole with an Auxiliary Station at Poole.

Lifeboats. An all-weather lifeboat and an inshore lifeboat are stationed at Poole. The headquarters of the Royal National Lifeboat Institution is situated at Poole.

For details of coastguard stations see 1.100 and for lifeboats 1.113.

Poole Harbour channels

South Deep

6.153

1   **General information.** South Deep, leading S and W of Brownsea, Furzey and Green Islands, is marked by light beacons and beacons (port and starboard hand).

Leading lights. The alignment (305°) of leading lights (50°40′·9N 1°59′·0W) on the SE side of Furzey Island, privately owned, leads from South Deep to a slip on Furzey Island in a least depth of 1·5 m.

2   **Submarine cables,** including a power cable, are laid between Furzey Island and the mainland. Anchoring is prohibited in the vicinity of the cables as shown on the chart.

Wych Channel

6.154

1   **General information.** Wych Channel leading N and W of Brownsea Island is marked by beacons (port and starboard hand).

Cables, including a power cable, are laid NW and S from Round Island (50°41′·2N 2°01′·0W) to the mainland, and an overhead power cable, with a vertical clearance of 7·2 m, crosses Wych Lake 1 mile SW of Round Island.

Backwater Channel

6.155

1   Backwater Channel leading from Poole Bridge (50°42′·8N 1°59′·6W) into Holes Bay is marked by a beacon (port hand) and light buoys (port hand). It divides into two branches E of Cobb's Quay Marina. Upton Lake, the W branch, leads into the marina and Creekmoor Lake forms the E branch. A railway crosses the N end of the bay.

2   **Cables.** Overhead cables, the vertical clearances of which can be seen from the chart, cross the SW side of Holes Bay close S of Cobb's Quay Marina and a submarine power cable crosses the S side of the bay.

Anchoring is prohibited in the vicinity of the submarine power cable as shown on the chart.

Wareham and approaches

6.156

1   **General information.** The town of Wareham (50°41′N 2°06′W) stands about 5 miles W of Poole, between Rivers Trent and Frome, which unite about 1 mile below the town and are tidal as far as the town. The channel through River Frome is navigable to Wareham for small craft of 20 to 30 tons, but is liable to silting.

2   **Approach channel.** Wareham Channel, a continuation W from Middle Ship Channel, is marked on each side by light buoys and buoys as far as the entrance to Rockley Channel which is marked by a beacon (E cardinal) (50°42′·8N 2°01′·9W). Thence the channel is marked by buoys for 1½ miles, thence by beacons on each side to Turner's Cove, about 1 mile below Wareham.

3   **Depths** in the channel decrease gradually to 0·1 m close E of Wareham.

Anchoring is prohibited in the salmon holes in River Frome, as shown on the chart.

NEEDLES CHANNEL APPROACHES TO NAB TOWER APPROACHES

General information

Charts 2045, 2450

Route

6.157

1   From a position S of Poole Bay, SW of the approaches to Needles Channel (50°39′N 1°37′W), the route leads generally E along the S coast of Isle of Wight to S of Nab Tower (50°40′N 0°57′W).

Topography

6.158

1   **South-west coast of Isle of Wight.** High and precipitous white chalk cliffs extend E from Needles Point (50°40′N 1°35′W) to within 1 mile of Hanover Point (6.170), about 5 miles E, whence they merge into a shore of clay and sand; there is a break in the cliffs at Freshwater Bay (6.175), midway between these points. These cliffs, rising perpendicularly from the sea for more than 120 m, are conspicuous in contrast with the dark ground behind. Needles Light (6.167) is situated on the outer of the three Needles Rocks which extend 2 cables W from the point. Steep clay cliffs, intersected by chines and backed by high downs, extend almost to Saint Catherine's Point, the S extremity of Isle of Wight, which is a low rounded point. A light (6.167) is exhibited on the point. The land within the point rises gradually towards Saint Catherine's Hill, about 1 mile N of the point; this hill is the highest in the island.

2   **South-east coast of Isle of Wight.** Between Saint Catherine's Point (50°35′N 1°18′W) and Dunnose, 5 miles ENE, the coast consists of a low cliff with large masses of rock, named The Undercliff, rising behind. This is backed by a precipitous rocky wall rising to an elevation of nearly 150 m with downs rising still higher behind. Rocks extend up to 2½ cables from the coast. Ventnor, a seaside resort, lies W of Dunnose in a sheltered position under Saint Boniface Down. The town, with its lights at night, is conspicuous and there are several conspicuous and prominent radio masts and radar scanners, the positions of which can best be seen on the chart, on the down.

3   The shore of Sandown Bay, entered between Dunnose and Culver Cliff, 5 miles NE, dips N of Dunnose but rises again towards Culver Cliff, which can easily be identified by the marked contrast between its white chalk cliff and the land in its vicinity, especially a cliff of red clay close

W of it. Shanklin, a seaside resort, lies 1¾ miles N of Dunnose.

4   Foreland, the low E extremity of Isle of Wight, lies 1½ miles NE of Culver Cliff and is fronted by a continuous rocky ledge which extends up to 3 cables offshore.

Hazards
6.159

1   **Exercise areas.** For details of submarine and firing practice exercise areas, see 6.3 and information on the chart.

Fishing. For information regarding local fishing vessels, see 6.4.

Ground swell. Some ground swell may be felt in the area between Saint Catherine's Point and Owers Light Buoy (50°37′N 0°41′W).

2   Mariners in vessels drawing 13 m or more should exercise extreme caution when approaching the pilot station (6.160) S of Nab Tower (50°40′N 0°57′W) and should not proceed N of the latitude of Owers Light Buoy at LW springs.

3   **Deep-draught vessels approach area.** A deep-draught vessels approach area, shown on the chart, lies 4 miles S of Nab Tower. Deep-draught vessels manoeuvre in this area to board pilots and enter Nab Channel (7.86).

Mariners in other vessels are advised not to anchor within this approach area or to impede the safe approach of deep-draught vessels.

Shoal depths, see 7.88.

4   **Dredging areas.** Vessels engaged in dredging for ballast are frequently at work in the E and W approaches to The Solent; to the SSE, S and SSW of Nab Tower and to the SSE, SSW and SW of the Needles Light; the areas are charted.

Explosives Dumping Ground (disused) lies centred about 3½ miles E of Saint Catherine's Point.

Pilotage
6.160

1   For details of pilotage information for Port of Southampton compulsory pilotage area, see 7.10 and *Admiralty List of Radio Signals Volume 6(1).*

Local knowledge
6.161

1   The coast between Hanover Point and Saint Catherine's Point is fronted by dangerous reefs which extend up to 1½ miles offshore. Mariners without local knowledge are advised to keep at least 2 miles off the coast in this vicinity on account of these dangers and of the onshore set of the E-going tidal stream.

Traffic regulations
6.162

1   **Movement reporting.** Mariners inward-bound into Port of Southampton compulsory pilotage area when approaching The Needles or The Nab should establish contact with Southampton Vessel Traffic Service. For details see 7.6 and *Admiralty List of Radio Signals Volume 6(1).*

Rescue
6.163

1   **Coastguard Rescue Teams** are situated at:
    Needles (50°40′N 1°35′W) in Scratchell's Bay.
    Ventnor at Woody Point (50°35′N 1°14′W).
For details see 1.100.

2   **VHF Direction-finding station,** for emergency use only, operates from South Boniface Down (50°36′N 1°12′W), for details see 1.105 and *Admiralty List of Radio Signals Volume 2.*

Natural conditions
6.164

1   **Offshore tidal streams.** At a position approximately 5 miles SSW of Needles Point the offshore stream is nearly rectilinear.

Caution. The E-going offshore tidal stream starts in a direction NE but changes very quickly to E by N and runs strongly towards the SW coast of Isle of Wight.

2   Between Saint Catherine's Point and Foreland the E-going offshore stream does not turn appreciably into the E entrance to The Solent, but meets the E-going Solent stream, combines with it, and runs ENE past The Owers. Similarly, the W-going stream from off Selsey Bill divides, and runs NW towards The Solent and WSW past Isle of Wight.

For details see information on the chart.

6.165

1   **Inshore tidal streams.** In the bight between Needles Point and Hanover Point the stream is weak close inshore but gains strength E; the E-going stream sets towards Brook Ledges, and the W-going stream towards Needles Point. The E-going inshore stream, E of Hanover Point, gains strength and runs strongly across Atherfield Ledges and Chale Rock. The W-going stream also runs across the rock and ledges, but less strongly.

2   Along the coast between Saint Catherine's Point and Dunnose the streams are strong, they begin as follows:

Interval from HW Portsmouth (Dover)	Direction
+0500 (+0525)	E
HW (+0025)	W

The maximum spring rates are 5 kn in both directions.

3   With the main E-going stream of The Solent, the stream in Sandown Bay sets NE following the coast and meets a SSE-going stream N of Foreland. At certain times the main W-going stream runs from near Nab Tower towards Foreland where it divides and runs NNW and SSW following the coast round Sandown Bay. Off the centre of Sandown Bay and off Foreland they run more strongly; the streams near the land are weak.

For details see information on the chart.

6.166

1   **Race** occurs off Saint Catherine's Point and may be violent when the stream is strong and a strong wind is blowing in the opposite direction. The race is specially violent SE of the point in W gales at springs, during the W-going stream. A race also occurs along the coast between Saint Catherine's Point and Dunnose, in this vicinity there are probably many eddies near the land when the stream is strong.

2   **Eddies** occur near the land W of Saint Catherine's Point during the W-going stream, and between the point and Dunnose when the streams are strong.

Overfalls. Violent overfalls are encountered in SW and W gales 13½ miles SSE of Nab Tower particularly when gales are veering.

Climate information. See 1.195 and 13.237

Isle of Wight – The Needles Lighthouse from SW (6.167)

(Original dated 2005)

(Photograph – Studio 8, Bournemouth)

Saint Catherine's Point Lighthouse from S (6.167)

(Original dated 2005)

(Photograph – Studio 8, Bournemouth)

Nab Tower from SE (6.167)

(Original dated 2003)

(Photograph – Crown Copyright)

Directions
(continued from 6.92)

Principal marks
6.167

1 **Landmarks:**

Needles Lighthouse (round granite tower, red band, red lantern, 31 m in height) (50°40′N 1°35′W).

Saint Catherine's Point Lighthouse (white octagonal castellated tower and dwelling, 26 m in height) (50°35′N 1°18′W) stands out boldly when viewed from E or W.

2 Nab Tower (red lantern on concrete and metal tower, 28 m in height) (50°40′N 0°57′W). Its submerged portion projects about 18 m and vessels over 2·7 m draught should not lie alongside at LW springs.

Major lights:

Anvil Point Light (50°35′N 1°58′W) (6.87).

Needles Light — as above.

3 Saint Catherine's Point Light — as above. Various experimental light transmissions may be made from this position; they have no navigational significance.

Nab Light — as above.

Other aids to navigation
6.168
1   **Racon:**

Nab Light — as above.

Bridge Light Buoy (50°39'·6N 1°36'·9W).

For details see *Admiralty List of Radio Signals Volume 2*.

Needles Point to Saint Catherine's Point
6.169
1   From a position S of Poole Bay, SW of the approaches to Needles Channel (50°39'N 1°37'W), the track leads generally E passing (with positions given from Saint Catherine's Point (50°35'N 1°18'W)):

S of Needles Point (50°40'N 1°35'W) (6.158); thence:

S of an 8·6 m patch (9 miles WNW), the outermost danger off Compton Bay; thence:

2   S of Brook Ledges (7 miles NW) (6.177); thence:

S of a 9·8 m patch (3½ miles WNW) the outermost danger off Atherfield Ledges (6.177); thence:

S of Chale Rock (1¾ miles WNW); thence:

3   S of Saint Catherine's Point (6.158). Coastal traffic is recommended to pass about 5 miles S of Saint Catherine's Point, where the tidal streams are nearly rectilinear, so as to avoid the indraught of the tidal stream between Isle of Wight and The Owers.

Caution. For details of strong tidal streams off Saint Catherine's Point, see 6.164. For details of dangerous reefs between Hanover Point and Saint Catherine's Point see 6.161.

6.170
1   **Clearing bearings:**

The alignment (315°) of Hanover Point (50°39'N 1°28'W) with the highest part of the chalk cliff, 1½ miles NW, on the E side of Freshwater Bay clears SW of Atherfield Ledges. A beacon stands on the rocky ledge close off the point.

2   The line of bearing 099° of the S limit to the red sector of Saint Catherine's Point Auxiliary Light changing from red to white clears S of the dangers on the SW side of Isle of Wight, but passes very close to Chale Rock.

3   **Useful marks:**

Hurst Point Light (50°42'N 1°33'W) (7.45).

Television Mast (red lights) (50°40'·6N 1°22'·1W) at Rowridge.

Television Mast (red lights) (50°39'·0N 1°19'·7W) on Chillerton Down.

Tennyson's Cross (50°40'·0N 1°32'·5W).

4   Hotel (50°40'·2N 1°30'·7W) in Freshwater Bay.

House (grey mansion) (50°39'·5N 1°26'·4W).

Houses (terrace of five houses) (50°38'·3N 1°25'·3W) at Chilton Chine.

Houses (red) (50°36'·8N 1°21'·7W) a former coastguard station at Atherfield Point.

Hoy's Monument (50°36'·5N 1°18'·0W).

5   Old Lighthouse (tower) (50°35'·5N 1°18'·2W) on Saint Catherine's Hill.

Saint Catherine's Point to Nab Tower approaches
6.171
1   From a position S of Saint Catherine's Point (50°35'N 1°18'W) the track leads generally E passing (with positions given from Dunnose (50°36'N 1°11'W)):

S of a rocky ridge with a least depth of 14·7 m (4 miles WSW); thence:

2   S of a bank with a least depth of 14 m (2½ miles SSW) which lies seaward of Saint Catherine's Deep (6.10); thence:

S of Dunnose (6.158); thence:

S of Culver Spit (6 miles NE) which extends 2½ miles ESE from Culver Cliff (6.158); thence:

To a position S of Nab Tower (9½ miles ENE).

3   **Caution.** In the S part of the approach, about 7 miles SSE of Nab Tower, there are depths of less than 20 m the positions of which can best be seen from the chart. Heavy overfalls have been observed in this area. There are many wrecks charted in this area.

6.172
1   **Useful marks:**

Yarborough Monument (50°40'·0N 1°06'·3W) close within Culver Cliff.

Isle of Wight – Earl of Yarborough's
Monument from S (6.172)

(Original dated 2005)

(Photograph - Studio 8, Bournemouth)

Ashey Down Tower (black and white stone obelisk, 9 m in height) (50°41'N 1°11'W).

Bembridge Lifeboat House Pier (50°41'·4N 1°04'·2W) close N of Foreland; conspicuous when viewed clear of the land.

(Directions continue at 6.184 and for
East Solent at 7.94)

Side channel

Charts 2022 plan of Sandown Bay, 2037
Coastal channel
6.173
1   **General information.** There is a coastal channel, 2½ cables wide, between Princessa Shoal (50°40'N 1°03'W), marked on its W side by W Princessa Light Buoy (W cardinal), and Long Ledge, a continuous rocky ledge which extends up to 3 cables offshore fronting Foreland, 8 cables NW, in a least depth of 6·7 m.

2   The channel may be used by mariners in vessels of suitable draught proceeding to Saint Helen's Road (7.103).

Lobster pots are laid on Princessa Shoal, particularly over the W end, between April and October annually.

Anchorages and landings

Chart 2037
Nab anchorage
6.174

1   For vessels requiring to anchor, and specifically for deep-draught vessels, the Nab anchorage area lies between 2½ and 6½ miles SW of Nab Tower (50°40′N 0°57′W). Mariners using this anchorage are required to report to Southampton Vessel Traffic Service and must also report to Queen's Harbour Master, Portsmouth. For details see 7.6, 7.9 and *Admiralty List of Radio Signals Volume 6(1)*.

2   **Spoil ground,** shown on the chart and centred 4½ miles S of Nab Tower, is situated close E of the deep-draught vessels anchorage area.

Charts 2021 plan of Freshwater Bay, 2035, 2045
Freshwater Bay
6.175

1   **General information.** Freshwater Bay (50°40′·1N 1°30′·6W) is a small cove at the head of the bight between Needles Point and Hanover Point, 5 miles E, with Compton Bay on the E part of the bight.

Anchorage, with offshore winds, may be obtained approximately 2 cables S of the entrance, as shown on the chart, in depths of 10 m, sand.

2   **Landing.** Drying rocky ledges project approximately ¾ cable from each side of the entrance and a detached ledge, drying 0·1 m, lies close NE of the ledge on the W side. Except at MLWS or with strong S winds, mariners in boats can land in the lee of the ledge on the W side even with a moderate swell. There are slipways at the head of the bay.

Charts 2037 2045
Whitecliff Bay
6.176

1   Whitecliff Bay (50°40′N 1°05′W) lies on the N side of Culver Cliff (6.158). Black Rock, where the cliff is 27 m high, stands at the N end of the bay. There is a limited extent of clear ground in the bay, which, with offshore winds affords shelter, out of the tidal streams, for vessels of suitable draught in depths of 2 to 7 m.

Chart 2045
Landings
6.177

1   **Chilton Chine.** Brook Ledges, dangerous reefs, extend nearly 1 mile offshore between Hanover Point (50°39′N 1°28′W) and Chilton Chine, 2 miles SE. There is a landing place, practicable only in fine weather, at Chilton Chine.

2   **Atherfield Point.** Chale Bay is entered between Atherfield Point (50°37′N 1°22′W) and Blackgang Chine, 2 miles SE. Atherfield Ledges extend nearly 1 mile offshore from Atherfield Point and a reef extends 1¼ miles offshore from Blackgang Chine. There is a landing place, practicable only in fine weather, on the E side of Atherfield Point.

Puckaster Cove lies 1 mile E of Saint Catherine's Point (50°35′N 1°18′W); there is a landing place in this cove.

3   **Ventnor Harbour** (50°35′·5N 1°12′·3W) comprises a small basin enclosed by substantial W and E breakwaters. The harbour entrance opens E and is marked by light beacons located at the heads of the breakwaters. The channel in the close approach and within the entrance is marked by buoys (special) and yellow piles. At LW depth in the entrance is about 1·5 m and the harbour partially dries.

Chart 2022 plan of Sandown Bay
4   **Sandown Pier** (50°39′·1N 1°09′·2W), with a pavilion at its head, extends 2 cables SE from the shore in the centre of Sandown Bay and has depths of 1·8 m alongside its head. Lights are exhibited from the pierhead.

NAB TOWER APPROACHES TO BOGNOR REGIS AND THE OWERS

General information

Charts 2045, 1652
Route
6.178

1   From S of Nab Tower (50°40′N 0°57′W) the route leads generally E, about 10 miles, to S of The Owers.

Topography
6.179

1   The coast between Selsey Bill (50°43′N 0°47′W), which appears from E or W as a low sharp point, and Bognor Regis, 5 miles NE, is fronted mostly by a shingle beach, broken by the entrance to Pagham Harbour (6.193) midway between. Towards Bognor Regis, a coastal town which is conspicuous from seaward and the glare of the town lights at night rendering it obvious, the coast gradually changes its character to a low earthy bank which is being constantly

Isle of Wight – Whitecliff Bay from SE (6.176)

(Original dated 2005)

(Photograph - Studio 8, Bournemouth)

eroded by the sea. Inland the country is flat and highly cultivated.

2   The Owers is the collective name for the foul ground and extensive rocky patches which lie within the 10 m depth contour 3 miles S 6 miles SE and 4 miles E of Selsey Bill (50°43′N 0°47′W).

Hazards
6.180
1   For information on ground swell with recommendations for mariners in deep-draught vessels, a deep-draught vessels approach area to Nab Channel, and dredging areas, see 6.159.

2   **Fishing.** An offshore scallop fishing ground extends from S of Selsey Bill (50°43′N 0°47′W) to a line S of Rye, 60 miles further E, in a band 15 miles wide. Fishing vessels may be encountered anywhere within this area, which includes the entire W portion of the SW-going traffic lane of Dover Strait TSS (*Dover Strait Pilot*) and the waters close W of it. See also 1.23.

Traffic regulations
6.181
1   Mariners bound E towards Dover Strait should take note of the instructions for TSS in Strait of Dover and adjacent waters and for the English Inshore Traffic Zone as detailed in *Dover Strait Pilot*.

Rescue
6.182
1   **Coastguard Rescue Team** at Selsey (50°44′N 0°48′W), is situated NW of Selsey Bill.
   Lifeboats. An all-weather lifeboat (50°44′N 0°46′W) and an inshore lifeboat are stationed at Selsey.
   For details of coastguard stations see 1.100 and for lifeboats 1.113.

2   **VHF Direction-finding station**, for emergency use only, operates from Selsey coastguard station. For details see 1.105 and *Admiralty List of Radio Signals Volume 2*.

Tidal streams
6.183
1   Tidal streams 1 mile W and 3 miles S of Outer Owers (50°40′N 0°39′W) are rectilinear; for details see information on the chart.

Directions
(continued from 6.172)

Principal marks
6.184
1   **Landmarks:**
   Nab Tower (50°40′N 0°57′W) (6.167).
   Tower (coastguard station) (50°44′N 0°48′W) near Selsey Bill.
   Building (block of flats) (50°47′N 0°41′W) at Bognor Regis.
2   Water Tower (50°48′N 0°40′W) at Bognor Regis.
   Major lights:
   Saint Catherine's Point Light (50°35′N 1°18′W) (6.167).
   Nab Light (50°40′N 0°57′W) (6.167).

Other aids to navigation
6.185
1   **Racons:**
   Nab Light (50°40′N 0°57′W).
   Owers Light Buoy (50°37′N 0°41′W).
   For details see *Admiralty List of Radio Signals Volume 2*.

6.186
1   From a position S of Nab Tower (50°40′N 0°57′W) the track leads generally E passing (with positions given from Selsey Bill):
   S of Pullar Bank (3 miles SSW) which together with Boulder Bank (2½ miles SW) and Middle Ground (3 miles SSE) are an almost continuous shoal forming the S side of The Looe (6.189). Pullar Light Buoy (W cardinal) is moored off the SW edge of Boulder Bank; thence:
   S of South Pullar Light Buoy (S cardinal) (4½ miles SSW); thence:
2   S of Outer Owers (5 miles SE), the SE-most of the shoals off Selsey Bill. Its off-lying position, combined with strong tidal streams, and the heavy seas caused by S gales, renders it one of the most dangerous shoals in the English Channel. Shoal of the Lead is situated on the E edge of the shoal. Elbow, the S spit of Outer Owers, is steep-to with depths of over 50 m within ½ cable of its S end and great caution must be observed when approaching it; on the W-going stream it is marked by a well defined tide rip. Owers Light Buoy (S cardinal) (50°39′N 0°41′W) is moored 7 cables SE of Elbow. At night, the bearing of Owers Light Buoy and careful soundings are the best safeguards when approaching The Owers. An extensive rocky bank, with depths of from 11 to 20 m over it, lies SW of The Owers, with greater depths between it and Pullar Bank. By close attention to the soundings this bank gives the mariner warning of his approach to The Owers. Thence:
3   S of Hooe Bank (7 miles SE), which is clearly marked in windy weather by overfalls due to the tidal streams which cause a heavy broken sea when running to windward. Coastal traffic is recommended to pass about 5 miles S of Owers Light Buoy so as to avoid the indraught of the tidal stream between Isle of Wight and The Owers, and in thick weather mariners unsure of their position should make use of soundings to ensure passing well S of The Owers.
4   **Caution.** With an E-going tidal stream there is a strong set towards The Owers, specially after a SW gale.
6.187
1   **Clearing bearing:**
   The line of bearing 289° of Nab Tower clears about 2 miles S of Pullar Bank, and S of Hooe Bank.
   (Directions continue in Dover Strait Pilot)

The Park

Anchorage
6.188
1   **General information.** The Park is an anchorage lying between Outer Owers (50°40′N 0°39′W) (6.186) and the foul ground fronting the entrance to Pagham Harbour, approximately 5 miles NW. It is well sheltered from W and SW winds, but is most unsafe in winds from E to S. There is excellent holding ground of stiff clay under a thin layer of gravel, but the anchorage cannot be recommended for large vessels owing to the frequent and sudden shifts of wind and the rapidity with which the sea gets up, especially during the winter months.
2   **Tidal streams** in The Park are rotary anti-clockwise, for details see information on the chart.

The Looe

General information
6.189

1   **Description.** The Looe (50°41′N 0°46′W) lies between Boulder Bank, Pullar Bank and Middle Ground, on the S, and a chain of banks running generally E, with depths of from 4·5 to 5·0 m, on the N. It is about 1¼ miles wide with general depths from 5 to 7 m and is suitable only for small vessels.

2   **Entrances.** The Looe is entered from W through a narrow entrance, marked by light buoys, between Brake Ledge and Boulder Bank, or from S through The Swashway, a passage about 5 cables wide with a depth of 8·1 m, between the E end of Middle Ground and West Head. This latter entrance is not recommended.

    Tidal streams in The Looe are rectilinear, for details see information on the chart. There are overfalls in the W entrance.

Directions
6.190

1   **General information.** Passage through The Looe should only be attempted in daylight and good visibility and it should be borne in mind that the buoys cannot be relied on implicitly, and they may give a poor radar response.
6.191

1   **West entrance.** From a position S of Medmery Bank (50°42′N 0°51′W) the track leads E passing (with positions given from Selsey Bill (50°43′N 0°47′W)):

    Between Brake Ledge or Cross Ledge (1¾ miles SW), a rocky bar extending SW from The Dries (1¼ miles SSW), its S extremity is marked by Street Light Buoy (port hand), and Boulder Bank (2¼ miles SW) marked on its N extremity by Boulder Light Buoy (starboard hand); thence:

2   S of The Mixon (1½ miles SE), a group of rocks which dry. A light beacon (port hand) stands on the E, and highest part, of The Mixon; the beacon is readily identified on radar. And:

    N of Pullar Bank (3 miles SSW) (6.186).

On the alignment (358°) of The Mixon Light Beacon with Chichester Cathedral Spire (7 miles N) the track then alters ENE passing:

3   SSE of the chain of banks (6.189) on the N side of The Looe and:

    NNW of Middle Ground (3 miles SSE); thence:

    NNW of West Head (4 miles SE); thence:

    NNW of East Borough Head (4½ miles ESE); thence:

    NNW of East Bank (5 miles ESE).

4   **Clearing bearing:**

    The line of bearing 314° of the conspicuous hotel (50°47′·2N 0°59′·4W) on Hayling Island clears SW of the shoalest part of Medmery Bank, 7¼ miles SE.

    Useful mark:

    Light (occasional) (Selsey Bill Lifeboat Station) (50°43′·6N 0°46′·8W) prominent when viewed from SW.
6.192

1   **South entrance — leading marks:**

    Front mark. The Mixon Light Beacon (50°42′·4N 0°46′·3W).

    Rear Mark. Selsey Radio Direction finding station tower, 2 miles NW of the front mark.

The alignment (320°) of these marks leads through The Swashway passing:

CG tower

Mixon Beacon from SE (6.192)

(Original dated 2002)

(Photograph - Crown Copyright)

2   SW of Outer Owers (50°40′N 1°41′W) (6.186); thence:

    Between Middle Ground and West Head.

    Caution. These leading marks are distant and not easily identified.

Minor harbour, anchorage and landing
Pagham Harbour
6.193

1   **General information.** Pagham Harbour, an area of saltings, intersected with drying creeks, lies 2½ miles NE of Selsey Bill (50°43′N 0°47′W).

    Nature reserve. Most of the harbour is a nature reserve where anchoring and landing are not permitted. For further details see 1.91.

    Tidal streams in the harbour entrance are very strong.

2   **Entrance.** There are no navigational aids and the harbour entrance is fronted by an area of foul ground in which there are numerous above and below-water obstructions, one of which, in the N corner of the area, is marked by a beacon. Navigation within this area which extends 2½ miles offshore, and is indicated on the chart, is not recommended.

Bognor Regis
6.194

1   **General information.** Bognor Regis (50°47′N 0°40′W) is a coastal town and the remains of iron pier extend from the centre of the esplanade fronting the town; lights are exhibited from the head of the pier.

2   **Offshore dangers.** Bognor Rocks extend 1¾ miles E from a position 7½ cables W of the pier; the rocks are steep-to on their seaward side. Bognor Spit, with depths of less than 2 m over it, extends 5 cables E from Bognor Rocks and another spit, with a least depth of 3·1 m, extends 8 cables S from the end of Bognor Spit.

3   **Anchorage,** usable by mariners in craft of light draught in offshore winds, can be obtained on the NE side of Bognor Rocks, between them and the shore. SE winds bring in a heavy sea.

    Outfall, marked at its seaward end by a buoy (special), extends 3½ cables offshore 7 cables E of the pier.

4   **Approach.** The line of bearing 328° of the conspicuous water tower leads to the anchorage between Bognor Spit

and the dangers E which are described in *Dover Strait Pilot*.

Bye-laws, applying to the operation of pleasure craft, are in force at Bognor Regis.

5   **Yacht-racing and warning buoys** are moored up to 5 cables offshore, between March and September. each year. The warning buoys mark restricted speed areas.

Landing
6.195

1   Between Selsey Bill (50°43′N 0°47′W) and Bognor Regis, 5 miles NE, there are shoal flats, with depths of less than 5 m, which extend up to 2 miles offshore, and, except near Selsey Bill, no landing can be made anywhere along this stretch of coast at LW.

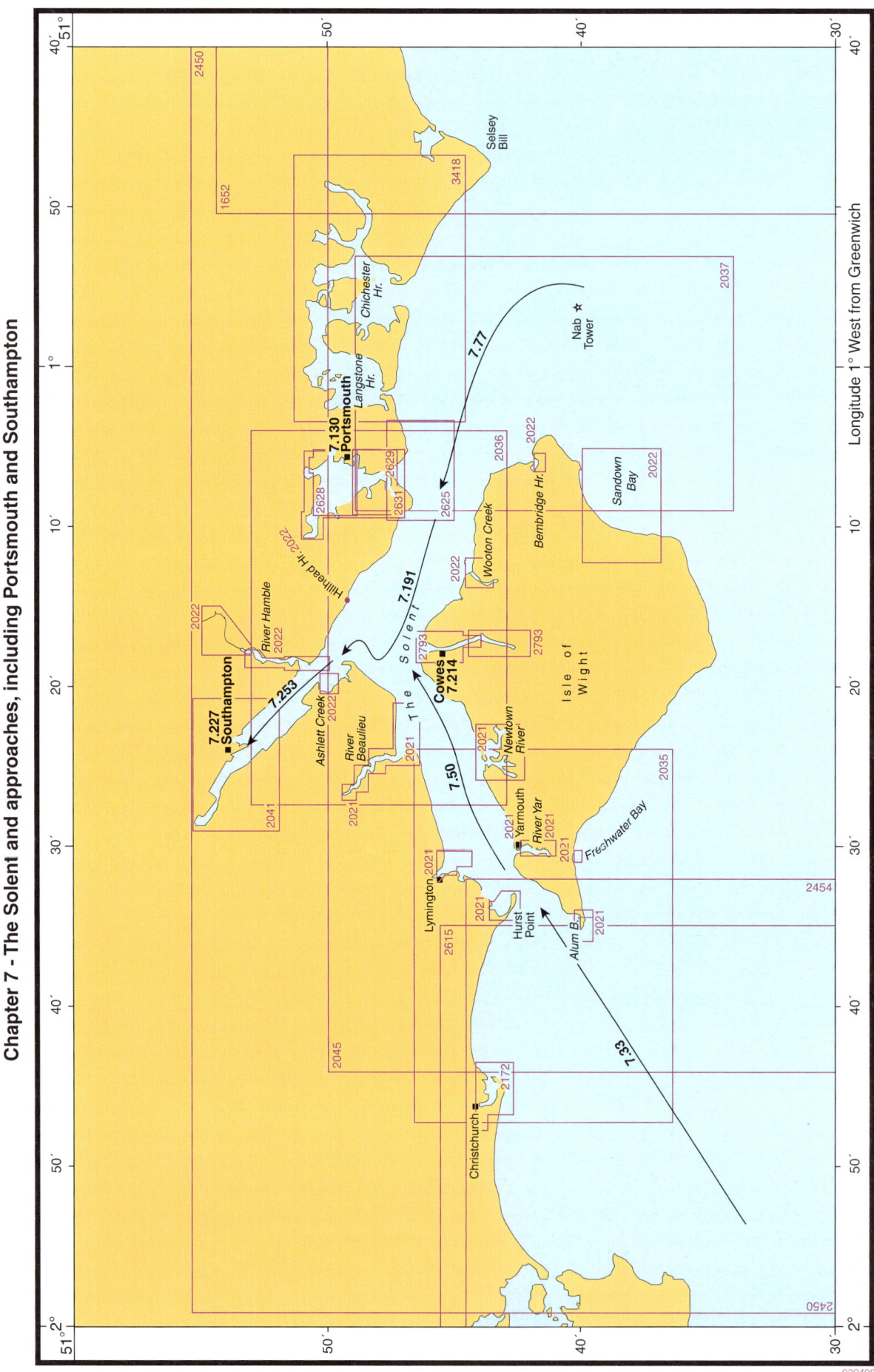

030408

CHAPTER 7

THE SOLENT AND APPROACHES INCLUDING PORTSMOUTH AND PORT OF SOUTHAMPTON

GENERAL INFORMATION

Introduction

Chart 2045
Scope of the chapter
7.1

1   The chapter covers The Solent and approaches, including the N coast of Isle of Wight, and the mainland coast from Hurst Point (50°42′N 1°33′W) to Selsey Bill, 29 miles E.

    Ports. The Dockyard Port of Portsmouth (7.130), Port of Southampton (7.227) and the small port of Cowes (7.214) are covered by this chapter.

Exercise areas
7.2

1   Detailed information concerning these areas, which are found in the waters of this chapter, may be found on Practice Exercise Area (PEXA) charts. Such areas are also shown on all new, and new edition navigation charts. For further details see 1.30 and *Annual Summary of Admiralty Notices to Mariners Nos 5 and 8.*

Description

The Solent
7.3

1   The Solent is the name given to the waters separating the mainland and Isle of Wight. It forms the approach to Portsmouth and Port of Southampton, and can be entered either from W, via Needles Channel, or from E, via channels in the vicinity of Nab Tower, including Nab Channel.

2   A mariner bound for Spithead, NE of Isle of Wight, from W saves about 10 miles by using Needles Channel instead of passing S and E of Isle of Wight. For limiting conditions for this channel and traffic recommendation, see 7.36.

Port limits

Port of Southampton
7.4

1   The seaward limit of Port of Southampton is shown on the chart. It is bounded by a line joining Stansore Point (50°47′N 1°20′W) and Egypt Point, 1½ miles SE, thence along the N limit of Cowes Harbour (7.214) and thence by a line joining Old Castle Point (50°46′N 1°16′W) and a position on the mainland at Hillhead (50°49′N 1°15′W).

2   The N limits lie at Woodmill (50°56′N 1°22′W) on River Itchen, and at Redbridge (50°55′N 1°28′W) on River Test, but excluding River Hamble (7.273).

Dockyard Port of Portsmouth.
7.5

1   The limits of the Dockyard Port of Portsmouth are shown on the chart. The limits extend, on the E, from the vicinity of Shanklin (50°38′N 1°10′W) on Isle of Wight, E thence N, thence WNW to Eastney Point (50°47′N 1°02′W)

on the mainland, and on the W with the E limits of Port of Southampton, with which it is contiguous. For further details, see Appendix I.

Port operations

Southampton Vessel Traffic Service
7.6

1   A VTS embracing VHF communications, pilotage, navigational and radar advisory services, traffic information, closed circuit television, data collection and evaluation is situated at Berth 37, Eastern Docks, Southampton, for the co-ordination of movement of all vessels of 20 m LOA or over in The Solent and Southampton Water, excluding the Port of Portsmouth N of a line joining Gilkicker Point and Horse Sand Fort Light.

2   **Procedure.** The following procedures are mandatory for all vessels over 20 m in length:

    Inward-bound vessels should report to Southampton VTS Centre when 10 miles from the Nab or when approaching The Needles. Vessels must request clearance from VTS prior to entering Nab Channel.

    Within the area vessels should maintain a continuous listening watch on VHF and should report when passing the appropriate reporting points and at other times, as designated in *Admiralty List of Radio Signals Volume 6(1).*

3   Vessels proceeding to an anchorage in The Solent must report to Southampton VTS when anchored and maintain a listening watch whilst anchored. On departure, such vessels must report at least 30 minutes before getting under way.

    Vessels outward-bound from. or shifting berth in, Port of Southampton should report to Southampton VTS at least 30 minutes before leaving the berth and obtain permission before letting go.

4   Vessels outward-bound from Portsmouth Harbour should report to Southampton VTS on passing Southsea War Memorial. Such vessels are additionally required to report to Queen's Harbour Master, see 7.142.

    The requirement to maintain contact with Southampton VTS Centre cannot be over-emphasised, particularly in the event of unforeseen circumstances developing within the limits of the port.

    Reporting points. Positions of reporting points are shown on the chart.

5   **Southampton Patrol.** The duty VTS officer is assisted by a duty patrol officer, who maintains continuous patrol within the Port area of jurisdiction in a launch fitted with radio, callsign Southampton Patrol, and which exhibits, in addition to normal steaming lights, a blue fixed light visible all round, and by day the Associated British Ports harbour master flag.

    For further details, frequencies and a list of reporting points, see *Admiralty List of Radio Signals Volume 6(1).*

7.7

1 **Radar assistance** is available on request to Southampton VTS Centre. Mariners can be supplied with continuous information about their progress relative to navigational marks, other vessels, channel margins and West Bramble and Calshot turns. Positions are given from the stem of the vessel concerned.

2 Radar coverage extends from almost as far as Solent Bank (50°45′N 1°26′W) in the W Solent, to S of Nab Tower in the E, with a service area from East Lepe Light Buoy (50°46′·1N 1°20′·9W), W Solent, to Nab Tower, E Solent.

For further details see *Admiralty List of Radio Signals Volume 6(1)* and information on the charts.

Portsmouth Vessel Traffic Service
7.8

1 The Queen's Harbour Master (QHM) Portsmouth operates a VTS Centre embracing VHF communications, pilotage, navigational and radar advisory services, traffic information, data collection and evaluation from Semaphore Tower, HM Naval Base, for the co-ordination of movement of vessels of 20 m LOA and over entering or leaving Portsmouth Harbour.

For further details, see 7.142 and *Admiralty List of Radio Signals Volume 6(1).*

2 **QHM Harbour Patrol** is a launch controlled by QHM, exhhibiting a blue light and operating on VHF channel 11 (call sign Harbour Patrol Launch). Its primary tasks are to educate and assist recreational mariners in the small boat channel at the harbour entrance during busy periods and to enforce Dockyard Port of Portsmouth regulations. In addition, the launch will patrol various areas throughout the Dockyard Port of Portsmouth.

Outer anchorages

Nab Anchorages
7.9

1 Twelve designated anchoring positions, as shown on the chart, are situated between 2½ and 6½ miles SW of Nab Tower (50°40′N 0°57′W) in depths of between 15 and 27 m, mixed bottom. Anchoring is prohibited within 1 cable of Nab Tower.

It should be noted that wrecks lie within anchoring positions 9, 10 and 11.

Southampton Pilotage
7.10

1 **Pilotage area.** Port of Southampton Compulsory Pilotage Area covers Port of Southampton, Southampton Water and The Solent and has a boundary joining the following positions.

Western limit:
Stansore Point (50°47′N 1°20′W).
Egypt Point (50°46′N 1°19′W), Isle of Wight.

2 **Southern limit, Isle of Wight:**
Egypt Point.
Old Castle Point (50°46′N 1°16′W).

Eastern Outer limit:
Culver Cliff (50°40′N 1°06′W), Isle of Wight.
Nab Tower (50°40′N 0°57′W).
1·1 miles S of Selsey Bill (50°43′N 0°47′W).

3 0·1 miles S of Selsey Bill.
Chichester Bar Beacon (50°46′N 0°56′W).
Horse Sand Fort Light (50°45′N 1°04′W).
Outer Spit Light Buoy (50°46′N 1°05′W).
Gilkicker Point Light (50°46′N 1°08′W).

Eastern Inner limit:
Gilkicker Point Light.
West end of Ryde Pier (50°44′N 1°10′W), Isle of Wight.

7.11

1 **Pilotage is compulsory** for the following categories of vessel:
All vessels over 61 m in length, including fishing vessels and vessels under tow, where the length from the bow of the towing vessel to the stern of the last vessel towed is more than 61 m.
All vessels of 20 m or more in length carrying more than 12 passengers.

2 The following categories of vessel are exempt from compulsory pilotage by Port of Southampton Competent Harbour Authority:
Ministry of Defence (MOD) owned or operated vessels and HM vessels.
Naval vessels of foreign or Commonwealth countries.

7.12

1 **Notice of ETA required.** Mariners inward-bound, who require the services of a pilot, should send ETA at least 12 hours in advance to Southampton VTS Centre and confirm 3 hours before arrival at the pilot boarding place. VHF contact should be maintained if it is necessary to vary the ETA.

2 Mariners requiring a pilot for Portsmouth, Cowes Harbour or River Medina only, should contact the appropriate Competent Harbour Authority, see 7.15 and 7.217.

The pilots only put to sea when required and it is therefore essential that advance notice for their services is given.
7.13

1 **Boarding place Western Approach — Solent — Western Limit:**
For all vessels subject to compulsory pilotage; those exceeding 61 m LOA, or 20 m LOA if carrying more than 12 passengers, in the vicinity of West Lepe Light Buoy (50°45′·2N 1°24′·1W).

2 **Boarding places Eastern Approach — Spithead — Eastern Outer Limit:**
For deep-draught VLCCs, 4 miles S of Nab Tower (50°40′N 0°57′W) in the vicinity of the position shown on the chart.
All other vessels of 150 m LOA or more, either Nab East or Nab West boarding areas as advised by the pilots.
For vessels of less than 150 m LOA, when carrying dangerous and polluting goods, in the vicinity of St Helen's Buoy (50°43′·5N 1°02′·4W) Boarding Area, as shown on the charts.

3 **Note.** Vessels having carried cargo referred to above and which have not been rendered gas-free or the cargo spaces rendered completely inert will be subject to the same conditions as specified above.

Eastern Inner Limit:
4 For vessels of 61 m or more but less than 150 m LOA, and for vessels 20 m LOA if carrying more than 12 passengers, in the vicinity of North Sturbridge Light Buoy (50°45′·4N 1°08′·2W). In the event of visibility falling below one mile or the presence of heavy traffic in the vicinity of North Sturbridge Light Buoy, then the pilot boarding place for the E inner limit may be temporarily relocated to the St Helen's boarding area or as

specified by Southampton VTS Centre. Mariners requiring a pilot for the Eastern Inner Limit in these conditions will be advised by Southampton VTS Centre.

5   **Note.**The pilots should always be consulted for confirmation of boarding position.

7.14

1   **Voluntary/optional pilotage.** For the E Solent from Nab Tower to the Eastern Inner Limit a facility is available, by prior arrangement, to engage a pilot on a voluntary/optional basis for those vessels under 150 m LOA to the Inner Compulsory Pilotage Limit in the E Solent.

It is recommended that if voluntary/optional pilotage is required in a non-compulsory area, advance notification of 24 hours is desirable to ensure that a pilot will be available at the appropriate pilot boarding place.

Portsmouth Pilots

7.15

1   **Pilotage area.** Portsmouth Harbour and approaches Compulsory Pilotage Area has a boundary joining the following positions:

Gilkicker Point Light (50°46′N 1°08′W).

Western end of Ryde Pier (50°44′N 1°10′W), Isle of Wight then along the coast to.

Culver Cliff (50°40′N 1°06′W), Isle of Wight.

Nab Tower (50°40′N 0°57′W).

2   1·1 miles S of Selsey Bill (50°43′N 0°47′W).

0·1 miles S of Selsey Bill.

Chichester Bar Light Beacon (50°46′N 0°56′W).

Cambrian Wreck Buoy (50°44′N 1°03′W) then due N to the shore (50°47′N 1°03′W) and all tidal water within Portsmouth Harbour.

7.16

1   **Pilotage is compulsory** for:

A vessel of 48 m or more LOA.

A vessel of 20 m or more LOA carrying more than 12 passengers.

Exemptions. The following categories of vessel are exempted from compulsory pilotage by the Portsmouth Competent Harbour Authority:

a. A vessel in Government service except when berthing or unberthing at any non-MOD facility.

2   b. A vessel with an Admiralty Pilot embarked while proceeding to or from any MOD facility. Such a vessel proceeding between a MOD facility and a commercial facility is not exempt compulsory pilotage for the berthing or unberthing operation at the commercial facility.

3   c. Vessels in transit through The Solent on passage to or from any position W of the line joining the following positions:

i) Gilkicker Point Light.

ii) Western Point end of Ryde Pier; such vessels should keep S of a line joining the following positions:

i) Gilkicker Point Light.

ii) Horse Sand Fort Light (50°45′N 1°04′W).

ii) Cambrian Wreck Buoy (7.15).

4   d. Vessels of less than 150 m proceeding to or from any position W of the line joining Gilkicker Point to Ryde Pier and/or going to an anchorage in Saint Helen's Roads.

5   e. Vessels of LOA not greater than 150 m while to the SE of a line joining the following positions:

i) Nettlestone Point (50°43′·3N 1°06′·6W) to

ii) Warner Light Buoy (50°43′·8N 1°04′·4W), thence to

iii) Cambrian Wreck Buoy (7.15) thence

iv) Due N to the shore.

7.17

1   **Boarding places:**

For vessels from W Solent, pilot boards 6¼ cables SSW of Gilkicker Point (50°46′·4N 1°08′·5W).

For vessels from E, pilot boards 1 mile W of Nab Tower, or for vessels less than 150 m in length in the vicinity of Saint Helens Light Buoy (port hand), in an area centred on position 50°43′·3N 1°01′·8W as shown on the charts.

2   In adverse weather these boarding places may be altered and up to date information can be obtained from Portsmouth Pilots on VHF.

7.18

1   **Notice of ETA required.** Mariners inward-bound should send ETA at least 24 hours in advance to Portsmouth Pilots and confirm ETA at pilot boarding place 8 hours before arrival. ETA should also be confirmed 2 hours before arrival at the Nab boarding area or 1½ hours before arrival at the Saint Helens and North Sturbridge boarding areas. Mariners at anchor requiring a pilot should also follow the inward-bound procedure.

Pilot boats: black hull; orange wheelhouse with Portsmouth Pilots in black letters.

2   **Signals for a pilot.** Mariners requiring a pilot should show the usual signals, for details, see 1.49.

For further details regarding pilotage, including details of pilotage information for outward-bound vessels, see *Admiralty List of Radio Signals Volume 6(1)*.

Traffic regulations

Special regulations

7.19

1   **Special regulations concerning vessels constrained by their draught and vessels restricted in their ability to manoeuvre** are in force within the limits of the Dockyard Port of Portsmouth and Port of Southampton.

2   Any vessel other than a "vessel not under command"* or a "vessel restricted in her ability to manoeuvre"* should, if the circumstances admit, avoid impeding the safe passage of a vessel which is displaying the shape or lights for a "vessel constrained by her draught" and should allow such vessel freedom to alter course and speed as necessary to maintain her planned track.

3   A vessel "not under command" and a vessel "restricted in her ability to manoeuvre" should exhibit the appropriate shapes and lights and in restricted visibility should make the appropriate sound signals. Dredgers are an exception.

4   A vessel showing the signal for a "vessel constrained by her draught" when inward-bound from Nab Tower to Southampton is at particular risk from outward-bound vessels when:

Off the entrance channel to Portsmouth.

Off North Sturbridge Light Buoy and shaping a course to pass S of Ryde Middle shoal.

5   It follows that vessels proceeding seaward from Portsmouth, and from Southampton N of Ryde Middle shoal, should take every precaution to avoid embarrassing an inward-bound vessel showing the shape or lights for a "vessel constrained by her draught", and in particular should avoid presenting her with a crossing situation.

6   A vessel "constrained by her draught" and a "vessel restricted in her ability to manoeuvre" must have

permission from Queen's Harbour Master, Portsmouth or the Harbour Master, Southampton, before navigating in the Dockyard Port of Portsmouth or Port of Southampton respectively.

7   All vessels navigating within Port of Southampton shall ensure that a vessel greater than 220 m (722 ft) in length shall be given a "clear channel" when within the Precautionary Area between Hook Light Buoy (50°50′N, 1°18′W) and Prince Consort Light Buoy at the E end of the area. Such a vessel requires a clear and unimpeded passage ahead when transiting the area. For details of passing regulations, see 7.242.

*As defined in *International Regulations for Preventing Collisions at Sea (1972)*.

Precautionary area
7.20

1   **Moving prohibited zone.** A precautionary area has been established in Thorn Channel as shown on the chart. All vessels of over 150 m LOA whilst navigating within this precautionary area will be given a moving prohibited zone around the vessel of 1000 m ahead and 100 m either side of the vessel. Small vessels of under 20 m in length are prohibited from entering the moving prohibited zone.

2   All vessels of over 150 m LOA when navigating in the precautionary area are required to display, where it can best be seen, by day a black cylinder, by night three all round red lights in a vertical line, as defined by Rule 28 of *International Regulations for Preventing Collisions at Sea (1972)* to indicate visually the presence of the moving prohibited zone ahead and either side of the vessel. When operationally possible such vessels will be preceded by the Southampton Harbour patrol launch.

3   Between April and October Southampton VTS Centre makes hourly broadcasts on VHF channel 14 giving information on moving prohibited zones in operation in the precautionary area.

Dangerous and polluting goods
7.21

1   For vessels carrying dangerous and polluting goods see *Admiralty List of Radio Signals Volume 6(1)*, and 1.68 to 1.76. For detailed local requirements, prior contact should be made with QHM Portsmouth or VTS Southampton.

Special regulations concerning tankers
7.22

Tankers of 60 000 dwt or more, whether fully or partially laden and bound to or from Southampton Water oil terminals, are required to have escort towage. Under normal conditions such towage will commence S of Nab Tower for inbound vessels and when leaving the berth for outbound vessels.

1   **Traffic recommendations for tankers using W Solent,** see 7.36.

2   **Gas tankers.** Special regulations to ensure the safe navigation of gas tankers are also in force within Port of Southampton Compulsory Pilotage Area.

All gas tankers loaded, partly loaded or not gas-free, navigating between Warner (50°43′·9N 1°04′·0W) and N Sturbridge Light Buoys should contact Queen's Harbour Master, Portsmouth, for traffic information.

3   Gas tankers in transit within The Solent may not enter an area in which the visibility is less than 5 cables.

Gas tankers when navigating between Hook Light Buoy (50°49′·5N 1°18′·3W) and W Bramble Light Buoy in Thorn Channel and between East Bramble Buoy (50°47′·2N

1°13′·6W) and Calshot Light Buoy in North Channel shall be given the sole occupancy of these channels.

4   No vessel may anchor closer to a gas tanker than twice their combined length and at no time will more than three gas tankers be permitted to anchor within the designated small vessels controlled anchorage (7.239) in Southampton Water.

5   Further details of the regulations applicable to gas tankers may be obtained from the Harbour Master, Southampton or Queen's Harbour Master, Portsmouth.

Speed off Ryde
7.23

1   All vessels transiting the Solent, whether inbound or outbound, in the area between a line running N/S passing through Motherbank Light Buoy (port hand) (50°45′·5N 1°11′·2W) and a line running N/S passing through No Man's Land Fort (50°44′·4N 1°05′·7W) must take all reasonable measures to minimize the effects of their wash on ferries berthed at Ryde Pier.

Speed off Cowes
7.24

1   As considerable damage is caused to boats and embankments at Cowes (50°46′N 1°18′W), as well as danger to life, by vessels proceeding at high speed past the entrance to the harbour, mariners should proceed at a moderate speed when passing through the area enclosed between a line extending N from Isle of Wight, 5 cables E of Old Castle Point (50°46′N 1°17′W) and a line extending N from the island, 5 cables W of Egypt Point (50°46′N 1°19′W).

Accident procedures
Damaged vessels
7.25

1   Vessels damaged outside the limits of Port of Southampton or the Dockyard Port of Portsmouth, whose seaworthiness is likely to be affected, or from which oil or dangerous or inflammable substances are likely to escape, must notify the Harbour Master, Southampton or Queen's Harbour Master, Portsmouth as appropriate, and remain outside the seaward limit of the port until permission is given for them to enter.

Contingency plans
7.26

1   **Solent and Southampton Water Marine Emergency Plan — "Solfire".** "Solfire" is a contingency plan developed to deal with any marine accident or emergency within the ports of Portsmouth or Southampton, Southampton Water, The Solent and coastal waters S of Isle of Wight.

2   Assistance for a vessel involved in such an incident should be requested by its master, owner or agent. In a grave emergency endangering navigation, assistance will be requested on its behalf by the appropriate Marine Response Centre as follows:

Incident in Port of Southampton; Southampton VTS Centre, "Solfire West".

Incident in Portsmouth or E Solent; Queen's Harbour Master, Portsmouth, "Solfire East".

Incident in W Solent or S of Isle of Wight; HM Coastguard, Lee-on-Solent, "Solfire South".

3   Details of the emergency "Emergency Solfire" will be broadcast by Southampton VTS Centre or Queen's Harbour Master, Portsmouth, as appropriate. Actions to be taken by

vessels in the event of Solfire will be broadcast by VTS Centre or QHM Portsmouth. The end of the emergency will be indicated by "Cancel Solfire (East/West/South)".

For details of radio frequencies, see *Admiralty List of Radio Signals Volume 6(1)*.

Incident reports
7.27

1   Vessels involved in an incident or accident should immediately report to Southampton VTS Centre, stating whether assistance is required, and whether vessels, navigational marks or shore facilities have been damaged, navigational marks moved or a close quarter situation has resulted.

2   All sightings of significant patches of oil pollution should be reported to Southampton VTS Centre or Queen's Harbour Master, Portsmouth, as appropriate.

Reports from small craft should be made to HM Coastguard.

For details of radio frequencies, see *Admiralty List of Radio Signals Volume 6(1)*.

Buoyage

General direction of buoyage
7.28

1   In The Solent the general direction of buoyage changes off Egypt Point (50°46'N 1°19'W), see information on the chart.

Yacht racing marks
7.29

1   Buoys of various shapes and colours, mainly spherical yellow or orange, most of which exhibit a yellow light, used for yacht racing marks, are moored in The Solent and approaches, Port of Southampton, the Dockyard Port of Portsmouth and Cowes Harbour, on a seasonal basis; their positions and dates can best be seen from the chart.

Fishing gear marks
7.30

1   Seasonal light buoys (special), with radar reflectors and flags may be encountered in the following areas of Southampton Water between mid-March and mid-June:

NW of Thorn Channel (7.252) in Stanswood Bay between Stansore Point and Calshot Spit (7.252).
NE of Calshot Reach (7.252) and North Channel (7.205) between Coronation Light Buoy (special) (50°49'·5N 1°17'·6W) and Hillhead Harbour (7.193).

Signals

Indication to small craft
7.31

1   Mariners in yachts and other small craft in The Solent are sometimes confused as to whether a vessel, outward-bound from Southampton and approaching West Bramble Light Buoy, is proceeding towards The Nab or The Needles.

Outward-bound vessels are therefore requested to display the flags of the International Code shown in Diagram 7.31 during daylight hours:

Signal	*Meaning*

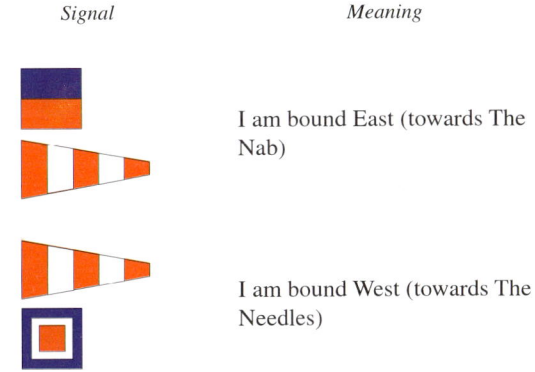

I am bound East (towards The Nab)

I am bound West (towards The Needles)

Solent - small craft signals (7.31)

Dredgers
7.32

1   Dredgers at work within the port area show signals prescribed in Rule 27 of *International Regulations for Preventing Collisions at Sea (1972)*. Mariners should reduce speed and navigate with caution when passing a dredger at work.

THE SOLENT WEST PART AND WESTERN APPROACHES

General information

Charts 2045, 2450
Route
7.33

1   From a position S of Poole Bay, SW of the approaches to Needles Channel (50°39'N 1°37'W), the route leads generally NE through Needles Channel, thence ENE through the W Solent to Egypt Point (50°46'N 1°19'W), at the W port limit of Port of Southampton.

Description
7.34

1   Needles Channel (50°39'N 1°37'W) forms the W approach to The Solent. It is buoyed and there are leading marks and lights. The entrance to the channel is 1½ cables wide at its narrowest point which lies between the two light buoys marking the SW end of Shingles and the W end of The Bridge.

2   The fairway of the W part of The Solent lies between the mudflats and coastal bank on the N shore and the banks off the NW side of Isle of Wight, and is clear of dangers.

Topography
7.35

1   **Isle of Wight north-west coast.** Alum Bay is entered between Needles Point (50°40'N 1°35'W) and Hatherwood Point, 8½ cables NE; it may be identified by the high white cliffs on its S side and the cliffs of variegated colours on its E side. The junction of these two different types of cliffs is a conspicuous feature.

2   Between Sconce Point (50°42'N 1°31'W), the NW extremity of Isle of Wight, and Egypt Point, 9 miles ENE, the NW coast of Isle of Wight forms the SE side of the W part of The Solent.

Mainland coast. Between Hurst Point (50°42'N 1°33'W) and Stansore Point, 9 miles ENE, the N shore of the W part of The Solent is fronted by marshes and broad mudflats intersected by narrow creeks, the principal of which lead into Lymington River and Beaulieu River.

Charts 2035
Controlling depth and draught
7.36

1   Needles Channel has a least depth of 10 m and may be used at any time but should not be attempted by mariners in vessels exceeding 9·5 m draught, especially at LW, if there is any scend.

Traffic recommendation. Needles Channel is subject to strong tidal streams and its width is liable to change. IMO have adopted a recommendation that laden tankers over 10 000 gt should avoid this channel.

For a prohibition on gas tankers, see 7.22.

Hazards
7.37

1   **Dredging areas.** Vessels engaged in dredging for ballast are frequently at work in the vicinity of Pot Bank (50°39′N 1°37′W) and Shingles (50°41′N 1°35′W).

Vessels depositing dredged material may also be encountered in the N part of Needles Channel during the first 4 hours of the ebb stream.

2   **Exercise area.** The use of the firing practice area on Newtown Rifle Range (50°44′N 1°23′W) is indicated by the display of red flags, for details, see 1.30.

The range is also used for military exercises during which times the red flags may not be shown but landing is forbidden.

Large vessels turning, see 7.244.

Yacht racing marks, see 7.29.

Pilotage
7.38

1   For details of pilotage, see 7.10.

Buoyage
7.39

1   For details of the general direction of buoyage, see 7.28.

Traffic regulations
7.40

1   **VTS scheme,** see 7.6.

Speed off Cowes, see 7.24.

Accident procedures, see 7.26.

Restricted areas. An area of 200 m radius (50°39′·7N 1°35′·5W) centred close W of Needles Light contains the historic wreck of HMS *Assurance* lost in 1753.

2   An area of 50 m radius (50°42·6N 1°29′·7W) situated 2 cables ENE from Yarmouth Pierhead and marked by a buoy (special) contains an historic wreck.

For protection details, see 1.89.

7.41

1   **Anchoring and trawling prohibited — obstructions.** Mariners are warned not to anchor, sweep or trawl in the area, indicated on the chart, which crosses The Solent close W of Solent Bank (50°44′·5N 1°26′·0W) owing to the existence of obstructions on the seabed. Passage inshore of the light structure on the N bank, situated 3½ cables SSW of Durns Point, should not be attempted.

7.42

1   **Cable and pipeline area.** Between Egypt Point (50°46′N 1°19′W) and Stansore Point, 1½ miles NW, there is a large area, indicated on the chart, extending from 1½ to 2 miles W in which submarine cables, including power cables, water pipelines and gas pipelines, cross The Solent,

some of which lie close to the E and W limits of the area. Mariners are warned not to anchor, dredge, trawl or engage in any other activity which may damage the telephone and high voltage cables and gas pipelines within this area on account of the serious interference which would result from damage to these pipelines and cables, and in some cases serious risk to life. For details regarding caution see information on the chart and 1.64.

Rescue
7.43

1   **Coastguard.** A Rescue Team is situated at Lymington (50°45′N 1°32′W).

Lifeboats. An all-weather lifeboat is stationed at Yarmouth (50°42′N 1°30′W), and an inshore lifeboat is stationed at Lymington (50°45′N 1°32′W)

For details of coastguard, see 1.100 and for lifeboats 1.113.

Tidal streams
7.44

1   The NE-going stream, which runs across the entrance to Poole Bay, divides as it approaches Needles Channel and runs ENE across Shingles, NE into Needles Channel, and E along the SW coast of Isle of Wight. The streams from the opposite direction meet off Needles Channel and run SW towards Durlston Head (50°36′N 1°57′W). The streams in both directions run strongly across Shingles.

2   At the entrance to Needles Channel the stream is nearly rectilinear; it runs mainly in the direction of the channel, attaining its greatest rate of up to 4½ kn at springs off Hurst Point.

On the W side of Needles Channel a set may be experienced away from, or towards, Shingles according to the direction of the stream. On the SE side of the channel the NE-going stream runs strongly. At the S end of the channel the stream runs strongly across The Bridge.

3   In the W part of The Solent the streams run in about the direction of the channel; near the land or shoals at the side of the channel they do not differ appreciably from those in mid-channel. The W-going stream is stronger than the E-going stream, but the rates differ considerably in different parts of the channel; they attain a maximum rate of 3½ kn off Lepe Middle (50°46′N 1°23′W).

4   Tidal streams in North Channel (7.54) are strong and run mainly in the direction of the channel; they gain and loose strength quickly. The streams from North Channel and Needles Channel meet and separate SE and S of Hurst Point where there may be turbulence when they are strong, especially during the NE-going stream. During the W-going stream a strong eddy runs E along the land S of Hurst Point.

For details see information on the charts and *Admiralty Tidal Stream Atlas for The Solent and adjacent waters.*

Directions
(continued from 6.92)

Principal marks
7.45

1   **Landmarks:**

Anvil Point Light (50°35′N 1°58′W) (6.87).

Needles Light (50°39′·7N 1°35′·5W) (6.167).

Hurst Point Lighthouse (white round tower, 26 m in height) (50°42′·5N 1°33′·0W).

Chimney (50°49′·0N 1°19′·8W) (7.250).

Saint Catherine's Point Light (50°35′N 1°18′W) (6.167).

Other aid to navigation
7.46

1   **Racon:** Bridge Light Buoy (50°39′·6N 1°36′·9W), for details see *Admiralty List of Radio Signals Volume 2.*

Charts 2035, 2036, 2038, 2045

Needles Channel and approaches
7.47

1   From a position S of Poole Bay, SW of the approaches to Needles Channel (50°39′N 1°37′W), the track leads NE passing (with positions given from Needles Light (50°40′N 1°35′W))

   SE of Dolphin Sand (50°39′N 1°46′W) (6.105), noting two light buoys (special) moored in position 50°38′·0N 1°43′·0W, thence:

   Clear of Fairway Light Buoy (safe water) (50°38′·2N 1°39′·0W).

2   The line of bearing 041° of Hurst Point Light (7.45), or at night within a narrow white sector (040¾°–041¾°) of the light, leads through the channel passing:

3   Between SW Shingles Light Buoy (port hand) (1¼ miles WSW), marking the SW end of Shingles, and Bridge Light Buoy (W cardinal) (9 cables W) marking the W extremity of The Bridge, a reef which extends about 11 cables from Needles Point; the bottom in this vicinity is very uneven. The reef is distinctly marked by overfalls on the W-going tidal stream in rough weather, and by ripples in calm weather. During S gales it is marked by a well defined line of broken water and, with much ground swell, the sea breaks heavily some distance from Needles Light.

4   On passing Bridge Light Buoy, and at night when Needles Light has changed from white to red bearing 083°, the track leads NE, keeping in the middle of the buoyed channel, passing:

5   Along the SE side of Shingles (1 mile N) a bank of sand, shingle and gravel which forms the NW side of Needles Channel. The SE side of the bank, bordering the channel, is steep-to and is marked by light buoys (port hand). The bank is subject to great changes of form from the wash of the sea and the scour of the tidal streams particulary in S gales. After long periods of moderate weather banks may be heaped up which are not wholly covered at HW, but these usually disappear after SW gales. There is a tendency for the bank to extend SW. There are overfalls on the SE side of the bank on the flood stream and a ripple on the N edge during the ebb stream. Care is necessary in approaching either side of Shingles owing to the strong tidal streams and the violence which with the sea breaks, with the least swell, over its shoal heads. And:

   NW of a 9 m patch (7 cables NNE).

7.48

1   The track continues NE in the fairway passing (with positions given from Hurst Point Light (50° 42′ N 1° 33′ W)):

   NW of Warden Light Buoy (starboard hand) (1 mile SSW), distant about ¾ cable, which marks the NW side of Warden Bank; thence:

Needles Lighthouse

The Needles from SW (7.47)
(Original dated 2000)

(Photograph – Naval Party 1016)

Hurst Castle bearing 041° (7.49)

(Original dated 2000)

(Photograph - Naval Party 1016)

2 Between NE Shingles Light Buoy (E cardinal) (6 cables SW), which marks the NE end of Shingles, and Warden Ledge (9 cables S), noting How Ledge 2¾ cables farther NE; thence:

3 Midway between Hurst Point (1 cable SE) and Cliff End (7.49), 6 cables SE of the point; thence: NW of Sconce Light Buoy (N cardinal) (1 mile E) moored 1½ cables NNW of Sconce Point.

4 **Cautions.** Needles Channel in the vicinity of The Bridge (7.34) may be subject to dangerous overfalls in heavy weather at all states of the tide. In strong SW winds small craft may find the North Channel (7.54) a safer route when entering and leaving The Solent, as Shingles may give some protection to the SW.

An eddy forms off Hurst Point during the NE-going stream and an indraught into North Channel during the SW-going stream.

7.49

1 **Useful marks:**

Needles Rocks (50°39′·7N 1°35′·4W), three in number.

Needles Point (50°40′N 1°35′W) (6.158).

Fort Albert (50°42′N 1°32′W) at Cliff End.

Hurst Castle (50°42′·4N 1°33′·1W), standing at sea level on Hurst Point.

Fort Victoria

Sconce Point from WSW (7.50)

(Original dated 2000)

(Photograph - Naval Party 1016)

Fort Albert from WSW (7.49)

(Original dated 2000)

(Photograph - Naval Party 1016)

Sconce Point to Egypt Point

7.50

1 From a position NW of Sconce Point the line of bearing 251°, astern, of Hurst Point Light (50°42′·5N 1°33′·0W) (7.45), and at night on the S limit (250°) of the red sector of that light, leads in the fairway passing (with positions given from Hamstead Point (50°43′·6N 1°25′·5W)):

2 NNW of Black Rock Light Buoy (starboard hand) (3½ miles WSW) moored 1 cable N of Black Rock. With a strong wind against the tidal stream care should be taken to avoid the relatively deep hole in the vicinity of Black Rock Buoy because of great overfalls and a dangerous sea known locally as Fiddlers Race. Thence:

3 SSE of Lymington Banks (3 miles W) (7.58) marked at the SW end by Lymington Bank Light Buoy (port hand); thence:

Between Hamstead Ledge (4 cables WNW), marked on its N side by a Hamstead Ledge Light Buoy (starboard hand), and Solent Bank (1 mile NNW), marked on its SW side by Solent Bank Light Buoy

208

Hamstead Cliff

Hamstead Point inc. Hamstead Ledge Light Buoy from NW (7.50)

(Original dated 2006)

(port hand), which just lies in the red sector (244°–250°) of Hurst Point Light; thence:
NNW of Newtown Gravel Banks (6 cables ENE).

7.51

1   From a position E of Solent Bank course should be adjusted to bring the line of bearing 247°, astern, of Hurst Point Light, or at night in the middle of its red sector (244°–250°), which leads in the fairway passing (with positions given from Gurnard Head (50°45′·0N 1°20′·7W)):

2   NNW of Salt Mead Ledges (1¾ miles WSW) marked on their N side by Salt Mead Light Buoy (starboard hand); and:
SSE of a 9·4 m patch (1¼ miles WNW) which lies off Lepe Middle, a coastal bank with depths of less than 5 m over it extending 1 mile offshore. West Lepe Light Buoy (port hand) (2 miles W) marks the S side of the bank. Thence:

Stansore Point from SE (7.51)

(Original dated 2006)

3   NNW of Quarry Ledge (2 cables W); thence:

     NNW of Gurnard Ledge (4 cables NNE); Gurnard Ledge Light Buoy (starboard hand) is moored off the NW side of the ledge.

     SSE of East Lepe Light Buoy (port hand) (9 cables N).

4   The track then leads NE in mid-channel passing between Stansore Point (2¼ miles N) and Egypt Point (1½ miles NE). A drying bank extends up to 3 cables offshore between Stansore Point and the entrance to Beaulieu River (7.73). Lepe Spit Light Buoy (S cardinal) (1¾ miles N) marks the SE edge of the bank.

7.52

1   **Caution.** Several rocky ledges and banks fringe the NW coast of Isle of Wight between Sconce Point and Egypt Point for distances of up to 4 cables offshore. Mariners in small vessels hugging the coast to avoid the tidal stream must be aware of these dangers.

7.53

1   **Useful marks:**

     Lights (column) (50°42′·5N 1°31′·2W) on Victoria Pierhead.

     Column (white with a broad red band, 7 m in height) (50°46′·0N 1°18′·9W) on Egypt Point.

     (Directions for Southampton continue at 7.250.

     Directions for the E Solent are given at 7.200)

Side channel

Chart 2035
North Channel
7.54

1   **General information.** North Channel (50°43′N 1°36′W) leading between Hurst Beach (6.99) and North Head, the N part of Shingles (7.47), has a least charted depth of 5·8 m in the fairway.

   Local knowledge is required.

   Tidal streams, see 7.44.

7.55

1   **Directions.** From a position W of Shingles the route leads NE passing (with positions given from Hurst Castle (50°42′·4N 1°33′·1W)):

     Clear of a dangerous wreck (position approximate) (4 miles WSW), thence:

     Between North Head Light Buoy (starboard hand) (1½ miles W), which marks the NW side of North Head, and The Mineway (1¾ miles WNW), a shoal, noting a light buoy (special) 1¼ miles W,, until nearly 2 cables from Hurst Beach (1 mile WNW).

2   The route then leads generally SE maintaining a distance of about 1½ cables from Hurst Beach passing:

     NNE of NE Shingles Light Buoy (E cardinal) (4¾ cables SSW), thence:

     Over the bar (2¾ cables SSW), least depth 6·8 m, marked by heavy overfalls, noting The Trap (1 cable S), a small ridge of sand and gravel at the N extremity of the bar.

Lymington

Charts 2035, 2021 plan of Lymington River
General information
7.56

1   **Position and function.** Lymington (50°45′N 1°32′W) lies on the W side of Lymington River and is an important yachting centre with two large yacht marinas. There is a vehicular ferry service between Lymington and Yarmouth (7.63) in the Isle of Wight.

   Harbour Authority: The Lymington Harbour Commissioners, Harbour Office, Bath Road, Lymington, Hampshire, SO41 3SE.

     Email: harbouroffice@lymingtonharbour.co.uk

Egypt Point Beacon

Egypt Point from W (7.53)

(Original dated 2006)

Lymington Marina

Lymington Yacht Haven   *Wave Screens*

Lymington River from SE (7.56)

(Original dated 2001)

(Photograph – Air Images)

Limiting conditions
7.57

1 **Controlling depth.** The river has a least charted depth of 2·6 m in Long Reach (50°44′·4N 1°30′·6W).

Deepest and longest berth. Car Ferry Terminal (7.61) on the E bank.

Tidal levels. Mean spring range about 2·3 m; mean neap range about 1·2 m. For further information see *Admiralty Tide Tables*.

Arrival information
7.58

1 **Outer anchorage.** Anchorage can be obtained on Lymington Banks on the line of bearing 326° of Jack in the Basket Light Beacon (50°44′·3N 1°30′·6W) (7.60), distant about 8 cables, in about 7 m, sand and mud.

Prohibited anchorage. Anchorage is prohibited in Lymington River.

Traffic regulations. All craft must give way to ferries.

2 Vessels navigating within the harbour shall proceed at such speed as to avoid setting up excessive wash and shall be navigated at all times with a due regard to the safety and comfort of other vessels navigating or moored in the river. Water ski-ing, aqua-planing and board-sailing are forbidden.

There is a speed limit of 6 kn within Lymington River.

Harbour
7.59

1 **General layout.** Lymington River flows through the saltmarsh on the N side of The Solent, W of Nash Point. There are two marinas on the W side of the river, and a Car Ferry Terminal on the E side. The harbour contains several pontoons and moorings for small craft.

Directions for entering harbour
7.60

1 **Leading lights:**

Front light (metal column, 11 m in height) (50°45′·2N 1°31′·6W) on the outer edge of the river wall at Waterford.

Rear light (metal column, 17 m in height) (2 cables NW of the front light).

2 From a position in the vicinity of Lymington Spit about 6 cables SE of Jack in the Basket Light Beacon (red sphere and rectangle on post, 12 m in height) (50°44′·3N 1°30′·6W), a large structure situated on the E side of the entrance channel 1 mile S of Nash Point, the alignment

(319½°) of these leading lights leads in the fairway through the entrance of the river and through Long Reach passing between light beacons (port and starboard hand), the positions of which can best be seen from the chart, to a position about ½ cable SE of Seymour's Post Light Beacon (port hand) (50°44′·8N 1°31′·1W) where the channel then turns N.

3 **Leading lights:**

Inward-bound. Light beacons (black beacon white bands) (50°45′·0N 1°31′·1W).

Outward-bound. Light beacons (red beacon white bands) (50°44′·8N 1°31′·2W).

4 The alignment (007½°/187½°) of these two sets of directional leading light beacons leads in the fairway of this part of the channel on the inward-bound and outward-bound legs, respectively, passing between light beacons and beacons (port and starboard hand).

5 These leading lights are primarily used as guides to ferries when passing.

The route then continues generally NW in mid-channel between light beacons and beacons. The river above the Car Ferry Terminal has silted and there is a least depth of 1·1 m as far as Town Quay, fronting the town of Lymington. The quay is approximately 50 m long with depths of 0·9 m alongside.

6 **Useful mark:**

Platform (white mast, black and white diamond topmark) (50°44′·4N 1°30′·4W). A small orange buoy is situated close S of the platform. These marks in line indicate Royal Lymington Yacht Club starting line.

Berth
7.61

1 Car Ferry Terminal (50°45′·4N 1°31′·7W): maximum depth 2·6 m alongside.

Port services
7.62

1 **Supplies:** fuel is available.

Rescue: see 7.43.

Yarmouth

Charts 2035, 2021 plan of Yarmouth Harbour

General information
7.63

1 **Position and function.** Yarmouth (50°42′N 1°30′W) lies on the NW coast of Isle of Wight on the E side of the mouth of River Yar and is the terminus of the vehicular ferry from Lymington (7.56). The harbour is well protected and much used by mariners in yachts and pleasure craft.

Harbour Authority: Yarmouth Harbour Commissioners, The Quay, Yarmouth, IOW, PO41 0NT.

Email: info@yarmouth-harbour.co.uk

Limiting conditions
7.64

1 **Controlling depth:** 2·0 m maintained depth.

Tidal levels. Mean spring range about 2·0 m; mean neap range about 1·0 m. For further information see *Admiralty Tide Tables*.

Arrival information
7.65

1 **Outer anchorage.** Yarmouth Road affords good shelter except with winds between NE and ESE. There is anchorage about 1 cable NW of Yarmouth Pierhead in depths of about 11 m, reasonable holding ground. Larger

vessels can anchor farther out in depths of 15 m, but here the tidal streams run strongly at springs. Foul area, radius 213 m, the remains of ground tackle, exists about 3 cables NW of the pierhead as shown on the chart.

2   Trots of unlit mooring buoys for small craft are laid within the anchorage area between April and September.

Mariners intending to approach the anchorage area from W should note that a waterskiing area lies W of the anchorage, between Norton Spit and Black Rock.

3   Anchorage is also available E of the pier, clear of the historic wreck (7.40).

Better anchorage with less tidal stream can be obtained on Lymington Banks (7.58) on the opposite coast.

Speed restriction of 6 kn exists throughout the small craft moorings and anchorage to the N and W of the harbour. Inward of the entrance dolphins, the speed limit is 4 kn.

Harbour
7.66

1   **General layout.** Yarmouth Pier, a wooden pier, extends 1 cable N from the town, on the E side of the entrance. The entrance to the harbour lies between a jetty, on the E side, and a breakwater extending E from the W bank of River Yar, on the W side. At the root of the jetty there is a Car Ferry Terminal and linkspan for the vehicular ferry to Lymington. Town Quay and South Quay front the E and S sides, respectively, of the harbour, S of the Car Ferry Terminal. The harbour contains several rows of mooring piles and various pontoons.

2   **Propeller wash.** The vehicular ferry from Lymington causes a strong wash in the narrow entrance when berthing and unberthing.

3   **Traffic signals.** When the harbour is full a red flag is displayed from the signal stations on the pierhead and on the Car Ferry Terminal jetty head. In addition, two red lights, vertically disposed, and an illuminated "HARBOUR FULL" sign are displayed at Car Ferry Terminal jetty head signal station and a similar illuminated sign is also exhibited from the dolphin on the W side of the harbour entrance.

4   Passage through the River Yar swing bridge is controlled by traffic lights.

Directions for entering harbour
7.67

1   **Landmark:**

Saint James' Church (square tower and flagstaff) (50°42'·3N 1°30'·0W).

Other aids to navigation. Tide gauges, the positions of which can best be seen from the chart, indicate the depth in the entrance.

2   **Leading lights:**

Front light (white diamond black band on white metal post) (50°42'·4N 1°30'·1W).

Rear light (white diamond black band on white mast) (63 m S of the front light).

The alignment (187½°) of these lights leads in the approach passing:

3   W of East Fairway Light Buoy (port hand) (50°42'·6N 1°29'·9W); thence:

Between Yarmouth Pier and a conical light buoy (special), moored 1 cable W of the pierhead, to the requisite berth.

4   **Useful marks:**

Lights (green metal column) (50°42'·5N 1°30'·0W) on the centre of Yarmouth Pierhead. In fog a high

intensity light is shown from the same position. A berthing light is occasionally exhibited at each corner.

5   Light (white wooden mast) (50°42'·4N 1°23'·0W) on the jetty head signal station. In fog a high intensity light is shown from the same position.

Light (dolphin) (50°42'·4N 1°30'·0W) on the W side of the Car Ferry Terminal.

Light (dolphin) (50°42'·4N 1°30'·1W) close off the breakwater head.

Berths
7.68

1   **Ferry Terminal:** jetty (50°42'·4N 1°30'·0W), 50 m in length, with a charted depths of between 2·3 and 2·8 m alongside.

2   **South Quay.** 100 m in length, maintained depth 2·0 m.

Pontoons. Numerous pontoon berths throughout the harbour for small and leisure craft.

Port services
7.69

1   **Supplies.** Fuel, gas, provisions, stores and waste disposal facilities are available.

Rescue: see 7.43.

Minor bays, rivers and anchorages

Chart 2035
Needles Point to Sconce Point
7.70

1   **General information.** Totland Bay lies between Hatherwood Point (50°40'N 1°34'W) (7.35) and Warden Point, 1½ miles NE, and affords good shelter in E winds to small craft which can lie close inshore out of the strength of the tidal streams. A pier, from which lights are exhibited, projects from the coast 3 cables S of Warden Point.

Tidal streams. The NE-going stream runs strongly round Alum Bay, Totland Bay and Colwell Bay, but there is little stream in these bays during the SW-going stream.

2   **Directions.** Mariners in small craft are advised to give Needles Light (50°40'N 1°35'W) a berth of at least 1 cable to avoid Goose Rock and a dangerous wreck (awash) lying close W of the light. Between Needles Point and Sconce Point, 3½ miles NE, the bottom is mostly foul and mariners, even in vessels of light draught, should exercise caution when navigating between Needles Channel and the coast. When N of Warden Point (50°41'N 1°32'W) the line of bearing 065° of Sconce Point, and open NW of Round Tower Point, 4 cables WSW, clears NNW of the dangers off Colwell Bay and the shoal bank extending up to 1 cable offshore between Cliff End and Sconce Point.

3   **Anchorage,** for small vessels, can be obtained 5¼ cables W of the pier in Totland Bay, as indicated on the chart, in a depth of about 6 m, in which position the ebb stream is moderate and the greatest strength of the flood stream is avoided. Holding ground is uncertain and plenty of room should be allowed to tideward of dangers. Tinker Shoal, a rocky ledge, extends 4 cables WNW from the pier.

Hurst Road
7.71

1   Hurst Road on the NE side of Hurst Point (50°42'N 1°33'W) affords bad anchorage in E and SE winds, and is seldom used because of uncertain eddies which make it almost impossible to keep a clear anchor. Mariners in small craft which can get close enough inshore to be out of the tidal stream sometimes anchor here during offshore winds.

2   **Useful marks:**
NB Beacon (port hand) (50°43′·5N 1°31′·9W) marking the seaward end of a submarine pipeline 1½ miles NNE of Hurst Point; the inshore end is marked by a similar beacon 4 cables NW.

Charts 2021 plan of approaches to Keyhaven, 2035
Keyhaven Lake
7.72

1   **General information.** Keyhaven Lake is a small creek leading NW from Hurst Road to Keyhaven (50°43′·3N 1°34′·2W).

2   **Channel.** The alignment (283°) of leading beacons situated 5 cables NNW of Hurst Point (50°42′N 1°33′W) leads in the channel to N of North Point (50°42′·8N 1°33′·3W) passing between buoys (port and starboard hand) in a least depth of 0·3 m. Within the entrance the channel is marked by buoys (starboard hand) for about 2½ cables. Short Reach, drying 0·1 m, is marked by buoys (starboard hand) at the N and S ends.

3   **Depths.** The channel within has depths of 6·2 to 2·6 m; these depths gradually decrease until off the quay at Keyhaven where it dries.
Anchorage: close inside the entrance, in a position shown on the chart.

4   **Submarine cable** is laid along part of the channel between Hurst Point and Keyhaven.

Charts 2036, 2021 plan of Beaulieu River
Beaulieu River
7.73

1   **General information.** Beaulieu River is entered close around the E end of Beaulieu Spit a drying mudflat which extends 1¼ miles E from Needs Ore Point (50°47′N 1°23′W). Within the bar the channel turns abruptly WSW along the N side of Beaulieu Spit to Needs Ore Point, thence NW for about 7 cables to Gins Farm where the channel turns N past Exbury Point to Gilbury Hard and Bucklers Hard about 1 mile farther N.

Beaulieu River Leading Marks from SE (7.73)
(Original dated 1996)

(Photograph - HMSML Gleaner)

2   **Bird sanctuary.** North Solent Nature Reserve bird sanctuary lies between 1 mile WSW and 1 mile ENE of Needs Ore Point. Landing on Gull Island, which is joined by a causeway to Needs Ore Point, is prohibited. See 1.91.
River Authority. The sole authority for the river is the owner of the Beaulieu Estate, Lord Montagu of Beaulieu; the river is managed by Beaulieu Enterprises Limited, John Montagu Building, Beaulieu, Brockenhurst, Hampshire SO42 7ZN.
E-mail: river@beaulieu.co.uk.

3   **Limiting conditions.** The entrance is dangerous from 2 hours before to 2 hours after LW, depending on prevailing weather and tidal conditions.
Speed limit. Mariners are prohibited from exceeding a speed of 5 kn above Needs Ore Point.
Directions. Leading marks:
Front mark. No 2 Beacon (port hand) (50°46′·9N 1°21′·8W).
Rear mark. Lepe House (2½ cables NW of the front mark) on the shore N of the entrance.

4   From a position 2 cables NNE of East Lepe Light Buoy (port hand) (50°45′·9N 1°21′·1W) the alignment (324°) of these leading marks leads in the approach to the river entrance in a least depth of 0·9 m to a position ½ cable ESE of Beaulieu Spit Dolphin (red dolphin white band) from which a light is exhibited, which stands near the SE extremity of the spit.

5   Direction light beacon (white round tower with lantern, 8 m in height) (50°47′·1N 1°21′·9W).
The line of bearing (334°) by day, or at night in the white sector, of the direction light leads between numbered beacons (starboard and port hand) to a position close W of No 5 Light Beacon. Thence the channel, which leads generally WSW, is marked by beacons (port and starboard hand) as far as Needs Ore Point. For night navigation some of the beacons exhibit lights; the port hand beacons carry red reflectors and the starboard hand beacons green reflectors. Thence in mid-channel to the required berth.

6   **Anchorage** is permitted only in the channel N of Beaulieu Spit, between Inchmery House (50°47′·2N 1°22′·7W) and Needs Ore Point.
Mariners are warned not to anchor, dredge or trawl within the area marked SE of Inchmery House, for details see information on the chart and 7.42.
Landing can be obtained at positions shown on the chart.

Charts 2021 plan of Newtown River
Newtown River
7.74

1   **General information.** The approach to Newtown River lies between Newtown Gravel Banks (50°43′·9N 1°24′·7W) and Hamstead Ledge, about 8 cables WSW.
Exercise area, see 7.37.
Bird sanctuary. Fishhouse Point (50°43′·5N 1°24′·6W) is a bird sanctuary; landing is not permitted. The area to the E of the point has been designated a Marine Archaeological Site; anchoring and fishing are prohibited. For further details, see 1.91.

2   **Channel.** Within the entrance the river divides into two main channels. The one to the E is Clamerkin Lake and the other which continues S is Newtown River, which again opens into four branches, Western Haven, Corf Lake, Causeway Lake and the river itself which continues through Shalfleet Lake to Shalfleet.

3   The entrance to Clamerkin Lake is marked by a beacon (preferred channel to starboard). Thereafter the channel is marked by beacons (lateral) and stakes. The N extremity of the ruined sea wall to the S of the channel is marked by a stake (N cardinal).
The channel through Newtown River is marked by beacons (lateral). A stake (N cardinal) marks the point where Shalfleet Lake and Western Haven meet.

4   **Directions.** Leading marks:
Front mark. Wooden beacon (red and white stripes, Y shaped topmark).

Rowridge TV Mast

Outer Port Hand Light Buoy
Newtown Bay Approach and Entrance from NNW (7.74)
(Original dated 2006)

Fishhouse Point
Newtown River from N (7.74)
(Original dated 2001)

(Photograph - Air Images)

Rear mark. Wooden beacon (red post 6 m in height, topmark red circle with white centre).

5   The alignment (130°) of these marks situated on Fishhouse Point, the E entrance point of the river, leads

over the bar in a least depth of 1·1 m passing SW of a light buoy (port hand) moored 2¼ cables NW of the leading beacons. Within the entrance the channels are marked by beacons, both lateral and cardinal.

6   **Anchorage:** in Clamerkin Lake and in the channel between the junction with Clamerkin Lake and Newtown River, as shown on the chart, in depths of about 2 m.

Anchoring is prohibited in the upper reaches of Clamerkin Lake and in Western Haven due to the existence of oyster beds, see information on the chart.

Anchoring is also forbidden between or alongside the mooring buoys in the Newtown River.

Chart 2036
Thorness Bay
7.75

1   **General information.** Thorness Bay (50°44′N 1°21′W) lies between Salt Mead Ledges and Gurnard Head and is a site of Special Scientific Interest, for details see 1.91.

There are drying rocks in the bay about 2 cables offshore and a sewer outfall extends nearly 2 cables NNW from the shore about 8½ cables SW of Gurnard Head; a beacon (starboard hand) marks the seaward end of the sewer.

THE SOLENT EAST PART AND EASTERN APPROACHES

GENERAL INFORMATION

Chart 2045

Area covered
7.76

1　The section is arranged as follows:
> Eastern approach to Portsmouth and Solent (7.85)
> Portsmouth Harbour and approaches including Spithead (7.130)
> Spithead to Southampton (7.191)
> Port of Southampton (7.227)

Description
7.77

1　The E approach to Spithead and thence to Portsmouth, or through The Solent to Southampton, lies between Foreland (50°41′N 1°04′W), the E extremity of Isle of Wight, and Selsey Bill, 11 miles ENE. It is well lighted and buoyed and is regularly used by mariners in VLCCs.

Topography
7.78

1　The SE coast of Isle of Wight, between Saint Catherine's Point (50°35′N 1°18′W) and Dunnose, 5 miles ENE, rises to a height of more than 200 m about 1½ miles inland; there are several conspicuous features on this stretch of coast which are described in Chapter 6.

　The mainland coast NW of Selsey Bill (50°43′N 0°47′W) is mainly low-lying, and is described at 7.87.

Dangers
7.79

1　The principal dangers on the SW side of the outer part of the approach to Spithead are Princessa Shoal (50°40′N 1°03′W) (6.173) and New Grounds (7.99), about 6 cables NE. The principal dangers on the E and NE sides of the approach are The Owers (6.186) and Bullock Patch (50°42′N 0°55′W) (7.101).

Large vessels navigating in the east Solent
7.80

1　Mariners entering Portsmouth or navigating in the E Solent should do so with extreme caution as large vessels, deep-draught vessels with limited manoeuvrability and other crossing traffic may be encountered.

High speed craft
7.81

1　Mariners should be aware that high speed craft operate throughout the Dockyard Port of Portsmouth area. See 1.7.

Cross Channel ferries
7.82

1　Mariners should be aware that cross Channel ferries, inbound or outbound, may be encountered on passage through Saint Helen's Road, W of New Grounds.

Exercise areas
7.83

1　There are firing practice areas to the S of Nab Tower, distant about 4 miles, the limits of which are charted. See 1.30 and 7.2 for details.

Submarine cables
7.84

1　A cable area in which numerous cables cross the E Solent between Southsea (50°47′N 1°05′W) and Nettlestone Point on Isle of Wight, 3½ miles SSW, is shown on the chart.

　Anchoring and fishing is prohibited in the cable area.

EASTERN APPROACH TO PORTSMOUTH AND THE SOLENT

General information

Charts 2037, 2036, 2045
Route
7.85

1　From a position S of Nab Tower (50°40′N 0°57′W) the route leads N, thence generally NW passing across the entrance to Portsmouth Harbour to N of Sturbridge Shoal, at Spithead (50°45′N 1°07′W).

Nab Channel
7.86

1　Nab Channel (50°40′N 0°57′W), about 5 miles in length extends from 1¾ miles S, to 2¾ miles NNW of Nab Tower (50°40′N 0°57′W), as shown on the chart. This channel is intended for deeply-laden inward-bound tankers and also for large container vessels and other vessels constrained by their draught. Accordingly, vessels of lesser draught should keep clear of this channel.

Topography
7.87

1　Between Foreland (50°41′N 1°04′W) and Nettlestone Point, 2½ miles NW, on which the town of Seaview stands, the NE coast of Isle of Wight is fronted by several shoal areas lying on the SW side of the E approach to Spithead and The Solent. From Nettlestone Point the coast runs WNW for about 2 miles to Ryde. On Puckpool Point, midway between them, stands a beacon (white diamond, black stripe, 8 m in height).

2　The coast between Bognor Regis (50°47′N 0°40′W) and Portsmouth, 16 miles W, is low; it is backed by South Downs a range of chalk hills, approximately 10 miles inland. Between Selsey Bill (50°43′N 0°47′W) (6.179) and Portsmouth, 10 miles WNW, there is an extensive inlet which is occupied by Thorney Island, Hayling Island and Portsea Island, and which is intersected by Chichester and Langstone Harbours. Bracklesham Bay (50°45′N 0°53′W) lies between Selsey Bill and the entrance to Chichester Harbour, 6 miles NW. The coast fronting the bay consists of a low earthy bank with the towns of West Wittering and East Wittering lying near its NW end. Groynes, some of which are marked by beacons, extend from the shore in the NW part of the bay.

Controlling depths and draught
7.88

1　**Maintained depth.** The maintained depth in Nab Channel is 13·3 m.

　Maximum draught. Nab Channel is intended for deeply-laden inward-bound tankers with draughts up to 14·9 m.

2　**Shoal depths.** A rock or gravel ridge, with depths of less than 15 m over it, extends WNW-ESE across the deep-draught vessels approach area to Nab Channel with a least depth of 13·3 m lying 2¼ miles SSE of Nab Tower; lesser depths lie farther WNW, outside the deep-draught vessels approach area. See information on the chart.

Hazards
7.89

1 **Deep-draught vessels approach area,** see 6.159 and information on the chart.
Large vessels navigating in the east Solent, see 7.80.
High speed craft, see 7.81.
Dredging areas, see 6.159 and information on the chart.
Yacht racing marks, see 7.29.

Pilotage
7.90

1 For information regarding pilotage, see 7.10.

Traffic regulations
7.91

1 **VTS scheme,** see 7.6.
Accident procedures, see 7.26.
Special regulations. For details of special regulations concerning vessels constrained by their draught and vessels restricted in their ability to manoeuvre, see 7.19.
Prohibited anchorage and areas, see 7.146.
Submarine cables, see 7.84.

2 **Restricted areas.** In Bracklesham Bay two historic wrecks are surrounded by restricted areas; 500 m radius for the wreck in position 50°44'·6N 0°55'·3W and 100 m radius for the wreck in position 50°45'·1N 0°51'·6W. Additionally, a 100 m radius area surrounds the wreckss on the N side of Horse Tail in position 50°44'·4N 1°02'·3W. For details of restrictions see 1.89.

3 **Prohibited entry area,** radius 50 m, containing a wreck with a depth of 5·2 m over it (50°43'·0N 0°59'·5W), marked on its N side by a light buoy (N cardinal) and on its S side by Dean Tail S Light Buoy (S cardinal) lies 3½ miles NNW of Nab Tower; diving, anchoring, fishing or passage of any vessel through the area is prohibited.

Rescue
7.92

1 **Coastguard Rescue Teams** are situated at:
Portsmouth (50°48'N 1°05'W).
Selsey (50°44'N 0°48'W) situated 8 cables NW of Selsey Bill.
Hayling Island (50°48'N 0°58'W).
Havant (50°51'N 0°59'W).
Bembridge (50°41'N 1°04'W).

2 **Lifeboats** are stationed as follows:
Hayling Island; two inshore lifeboats (50°47'N 0°56'W) at Chichester Harbour.
Portsmouth; two inshore lifeboats in Langstone Harbour (50°48'N 1°02'W) at Eastney.
An all-weather lifeboat and an inshore lifeboat at Bembridge (50°41'N 1°04'W).

3 For details of Selsey lifeboats, see 6.182.
For details of coastguard stations see 1.100 and for lifeboats 1.113.
VHF Direction-finding service, for emergency use only, operates from Selsey coastguard station. For details see *Admiralty List of Radio Signals Volume 2* and 1.105.

Tidal streams
7.93

1 For detailed information concerning the tidal streams in the approach to Spithead, *Admiralty Tidal Stream Atlas for*

The Solent and adjacent waters and the tidal information on the charts should be consulted. The following tidal information is given in the broadest terms.
At a position about 3½ miles S of Nab Tower the stream is more or less rotary in an anti-clockwise direction.

2 At a position close E of Nab Tower the stream is more or less rotary in an anti-clockwise direction and there is no slack water.
Off the E side of Warner Shoal (50°44'N 1°04'W) the E-going stream changes direction irregularly in an anti-clockwise direction; its rate is also irregular. At the end of the W-going stream, the stream changes in a clockwise direction.

3 Off Bracklesham Bay (50°45'N 0°53'W) the E-going stream is nearly rectilinear, but the W-going stream is slightly rotary anti-clockwise.
Off Hayling Bay (50°47'N 0°59'W) the streams are rotary anti-clockwise, but rather irregular.

Directions
(continued from 6.172)

Principal marks
7.94

1 **Landmarks:**
Saint Helen's Fort (large round stone structure) (50°42'·3N 1°05'·1W) from which a light is exhibited.
No Man's Land Fort (large round stone structure) (50°44'·4N 1°05'·7W), from which a light is exhibited, near the N extremity of No Man's Land.

2 Horse Sand Fort (large round stone structure) (50°45'·0N 1°04'·3W) from which a light is exhibited.
Spinnaker Tower (50°47'·7N 1°06'·5W) (7.169) from which aircraft warning lights are exhibited.
Offshore mark:
Nab Tower (50°40'N 0°57'W) (6.167).
Major light:
Nab Light (50°40'N 0°57'W) (6.167).

Other aids to navigation
7.95

1 **Racons:**
Owers Light Buoy (50°37'N 0°41'W).
Nab Light (50°40'N 0°57'W).
For details see *Admiralty List of Radio Signals Volume 2*.

Charts 2037, 2045
Nab Tower approach to Spithead - deep-draught vessels
7.96

1 From a position S of Nab Tower (50°40'N 0°57'W) in the deep-draught vessels approach area the track leads N passing (with positions given from Nab Tower):
Between Outer Nab No 1 Light Buoy (W cardinal) (2 miles SSE) and Outer Nab No 2 Light Buoy (E cardinal) (1¾ miles SSW), noting the precautionary area at the S end of the channel and also noting a depth of 13·5 m, 2 cables ESE of Outer Nab No 1 Light Buoy (W cardinal), thence:

2 E of Nab Tower (6.167), and dependent upon draught, clear of the 12·9 m and 12·7 m depths, (respectively 6½ cables and 8 cables ENE), thence:
Between N2 Light Buoy (special) (1 mile NNE) and N1 Light Buoy (special) (1¼ miles NNE).

3 The track then leads NNW through Nab Channel passing:

ENE of New Grounds Light Buoy (E cardinal)
(2 miles NNW).

From a position WSW of N7 Light Buoy (special)
(2¼ miles N). near the N end of Nab Channel and the
precautionary area, the track leads NW thence WNW
passing:

Between Dean Tail Light Buoy (starboard hand)
(3¼ miles NNW) and Nab End Light Buoy (port
hand) (3 miles NNW); thence:

4   SSW of Dean Tail S Light Buoy (S cardinal)
(50°43′·0N 0°59′·6W) which marks the S end of a
prohibited entry area (7.91). A wreck, with a swept
depth of 13·1 m over it, lies in the middle of the
fairway about 2½ cables S of the prohibited area.

Chart 2037
7.97

1   The track continues WNW passing (with positions given
from Saint Helen's Fort (50°42′·3N 1°05′·0W)):

Between Horse Tail Light Buoy (starboard hand)
(50°43′·2N 1°00′·1W) and Nab East Light Buoy
(port hand) (2¾ miles ENE), marking the N limit
of New Grounds (7.99); thence:

2   Between Dean Elbow Light Buoy (starboard hand)
(2½ miles ENE), marking the S side of Horse Tail,
the SE part of Horse and Dean Sand (7.164), and
Saint Helens Light Buoy (port hand) (2 miles
ENE).

The track then leads generally NW passing:

3   Between Warner Light Buoy (port hand) (1¾ miles
NNE), which marks the NE side of Warner Shoal,
steep-to on its NE side, and Horse Elbow Light
Buoy (starboard hand) (2 miles NNE) which marks
Horse Elbow, the steep-to SW side of Horse and
Dean Sand, noting Cambrian Wreck Buoy (S
cardinal) which marks a foul area lying 3½ cables
ENE of the light buoy.

4   The line of bearing 310° of Fort Gilkicker (50°46′·4N
1°08′·4W) (7.166), or of its light at night, leads in the
fairway passing:

Between No Man's Land Fort (2 miles NNW) and
Horse Sand Fort (2¾ miles N) (7.94).

The track then continues WNW in mid-channel across
the entrance channel (2½ miles N) to Portsmouth passing:

5   NNE of a mine laying practice area (charted as a
firing practice area) (3 miles NNW) (7.146);
thence:

To a position N of N Sturbridge Light Buoy (N
cardinal) (50°45′·3N 1°08′·2W) marking the N
edge of a small detached shoal lying 1 cable NE of
Sturbridge Shoal.

Chart 2037
Nab Tower approach to Spithead – non deep-draught vessels
7.98

1   Vessels not constrained by draught may use an
alternative route parallel to, and W of, the Nab Channel
passing (with positions given from Nab Tower):
Clear of Nab Tower.

The track then leads NNW passing:

2   WSW of N2 Light Buoy (special) (1 mile NNE)
keeping clear of Nab Channel; thence:

Between New Grounds Light Buoy (E cardinal)
(2 miles NNW) and N7 Light Buoy (special)
(2¼ miles N).

The track then leads WNW to join the main route from
Nab Channel between Nab End LightBuoy (port hand)
(3 miles NNW) and Dean Tail S Light Buoy (S cardinal) as
given above.

Alternative channel over New Grounds
7.99

1   Vessels not constrained by draught may use an
alternative route over the NE part of New Grounds, in a
least charted depth of 8·3 m, passing (with positions given
from Nab Tower):
Clear of Nab Tower.

The line of bearing 138°, astern, of Nab Tower then
leads over the NE end of New Grounds passing:

NE of Outer Nab Rock (2¼ miles WNW): and;

2   SW of New Grounds Light Buoy (E cardinal)
(2 miles NNW); thence:

Over New Grounds, a large shoal which extends
3½ miles E from Foreland (50°41′N 1°04′W),
noting the 6·4 m wreck (2¼ miles WNW), and SW
of Nab End Light Buoy (port hand) (3 miles
NNW), distant 6 cables, noting depths of 8·0 and
8·1 m which lie 1½ cables SE and NW of the
track, respectively; thence:

3   SW of a 6·2 m wreck lying close SW of Nab East
Light Buoy (port hand) (50°42′·8N 1°00′·8W) to
join the main route from Nab Channel.

Charts 2037, 2045
Approach from east
7.100

1   From a position S of Owers Light Buoy (50°37′N
0°41′W) (6.186) the line of bearing 289° of Nab Tower
(50°40′N 0°57′W) leads in the approach, for mariners in
vessels of suitable draught, passing SSW of an 11·2 m
wreck (50°39′N 0°49′W) lying about 1½ miles SW of
Pullar Bank (6.186) and marked by South Pullar Light
Buoy (S cardinal) moored close SE, to join the routes,
appropriate to draught, as described above.
7.101

1   **Alternative approach from east.** The line of bearing
300° of Fort Gilkicker (50°46′·4N 1°08′·5W) (7.166) open
SW of Horse Sand Fort, 3 miles SE (7.94), leads in a least
depth of 10 m passing (with positions given from Nab
Tower):

Between an 11·2 m wreck (5 miles ESE) (7.100) and
Pullar Bank (5 miles E) (6.186) noting the wreck
with 10·7 m over it on the line of bearing; thence:

2   Between N5 Light Buoy (special) (2 miles N) and N7
Light Buoy (special) (2¼ miles N).

The track then continues generally WNW to join the
main channel (7.96) between Dean Tail S Light Buoy (S
cardinal) (48°43′·0N 0°59′·6W) and Nab End Light Buoy
(port hand) (3 miles NNW).

For information regarding use of Nab Channel, see 7.86
and information on the chart.

Useful marks
7.102

1   Tower (coastguard station) (50°44′N 0°48′W) near
Selsey Bill.

Chichester Cathedral (spire) (50°50′N 0°47′W) visible
many miles from seaward.

(Directions for Portsmouth continue at 7.162
and for the E Solent at 7.200)

Saint Helen's Road

Chart 2037
General information
7.103

1   **Description.** Saint Helen's Road (50°43′N 1°03′W) lies E of Saint Helen's Fort and is bounded on its E side by New Grounds (7.99) and on its S side by Nab Shoal. The roadstead is well sheltered from all but SE winds and has good holding ground of mud and stiff blue clay in depths of 7 to 14 m.

   Yacht racing marks, see 7.29.

2   **Tidal streams** in Saint Helen's Road are, in general, weak; they begin as follows:

Interval from HW Portsmouth (Dover)	Direction
+0200 (+0225)	S–SE–S
−0300 (−0235)	NW–W–WSW

   The maximum S–going and N–going spring rates are 1 kn and ½ kn respectively.

Directions
7.104

1   **From south.** The line of bearing 301° of Saint Helen's Seamark (white brick structure) (50°42′·1N 1°06′·0W), and just open N of the land, leads in the approach passing (with positions given from Foreland (50°41′N 1°04′W)):

     SSW of Outer Nab Rock (2¼ miles E) at the S end of New Grounds; thence:

2   Over the NE edge of Princessa Shoal (1 mile SE) (6.173).

   The line of bearing 344° of Saint Jude's Church (50°47′·2N 1°05′·3W) (7.162), at Southsea, open E of Horse Sand Fort, 2¼ miles SSE (7.94), then leads in the fairway passing:

3   Between Bembridge Ledge, marked on its E side by Bembridge Ledge Light Buoy (E cardinal) (9 cables E), and Nab Rock (1½ miles ENE); a 5·3 m wreck lies 2 cables NW of the rock and closer to the track. Thence:

     For vessels of suitable draught, over Nab Shoal (1 mile NE), noting Long Rock (1 mile NNE), and to the required anchorage.

7.105

1   **From north.** Mariners are recommended to pass E of Warner Light Buoy (port hand) (50°43′·9N 1°04′·0W) on the line of bearing 344°, astern, of Saint Jude's Church passing:

     ENE of Warner Shoal (2¾ miles N) (7.97); thence:

     ENE of Saint Helen's Patch (2 miles N) to the required anchorage.

Side channel
7.106

1   There is a side channel, about 4 cables wide with a least charted depth of 5 m, between the W side of Warner Shoal and the shore. The line of bearing 336° of Haslar Water Tower (50°47′N 1°07′W) (7.166) just open E of No Man's Land Fort, 3 miles SSW, leads in this channel.

Anchorage.
7.107

1   **Recommended berths** lie ENE from Saint Helen's Fort, centred on position 50°42′·6N 1°03′·7W, as indicated on the chart, in a depth of about 11 m.

   Mariners in smaller vessels can anchor close inshore but should not bring Haslar Water Tower (50°47′N 1°07′W) W of No Man's Land Fort.

2   **Anchoring is prohibited** within 1 cable of Saint Helen's Fort.

   Obstruction, with a depth of 12·3 m over it, lies about 1½ miles NE of Saint Helen's Fort.

   Foul ground, radius 1 cable as shown on the chart, lies centred 8½ cables E of Saint Helen's Fort. A foul patch, the remains of a wreck no longer dangerous to surface navigation, lies 1½ miles ENE of the fort in position 50°42′·7N 1°03′·2W.

Chichester Harbour and approaches

Chart 3418
General information
7.108

1   **Position and function.** Chichester Harbour, a large area of low-lying land, marsh and drying banks, with 17 miles of navigable channels, lies between the E side of Hayling Island (50°48′N 0°58′W) and the mainland farther E.

   The harbour is an important yachting centre and conservation area. During the summer more than 5000 yachts and pleasure craft are moored in its various branches and in the marinas and yacht harbours. Mariners in visiting yachts requiring moorings are advised to make prior arrangements.

2   **Approach and entry.** The harbour is approached from The Solent over a bar between West Pole and Middle Pole, two drying sandbanks, and entered through a narrow channel E of Eastoke Point (50°47′N 0°56′W).

   Port Authority. Chichester Harbour Conservancy, The Harbour Office, Itchenor, Chichester, PO20 7AW.

     Email: harbourmaster@conservancy.co.uk

Limiting conditions
7.109

1   **Controlling depth.** Chichester Bar (50°46′N 0°56′W) is crossed between West Pole and Middle Pole. The bar is normally dredged to 1·5 m, but shoaling may occur after strong winds. Depths over the bar can vary by as much as 0·8 m as a result of gales. The Port Authority should be consulted for the latest minimum depths.

2   **Tidal levels** (Harbour entrance). Mean spring range about 4·0 m; mean neap range about 2·1 m. For further information see *Admiralty Tide Tables.*

   Maximum size of vessel. The harbour is suitable for vessels of up to 30 m in length and 2·7 m draught.

   Local weather and sea state. The banks fronting the entrance are subject to change, and when there is any swell the sea breaks heavily on them, and even across the entrance.

3   With an ebb tide and strong winds from a southerly direction a dangerous sea may be encountered. In these circumstances caution should be exercised and it is advisable to cross the bar beween 3 hours before and 1 hour after HW.

Arrival information
7.110

1   **Port radio** station, with limited hours, operates on VHF. A port information service covering an area within a radius of 5 miles of the harbour entrance is operated from the Harbour Master's office at Itchenor (50°48′N 0°52′W).

   Pilotage. Formal pilotage services are not available though masters of larger vessels may obtain advice from the Harbour Master's office.

Thorney Island

Black Point Chichester Harbour Entrance from S (7.108) *The Spit*

(Original dated 2001)

(Photograph - Air Images)

2   **Local knowledge.** The approach is dangerous in poor visibility, particularly with strong winds against an ebb tide. In these conditions local knowledge is advisable.

    Traffic regulations. There is a speed limit of 8 kn in the whole of Chichester Harbour. Mariners wishing to carry out speed trials in excess of 8 kn must obtain written permission from the Harbour Master.

3   Vessels navigating in areas of moored craft shall reduce speed to avoid excessive wash, avoid overtaking and whenever possible avoid passing between lines of moorings. Sails should be furled well before the moorings are reached.

    Sailing vessels navigating under sail and power are to display the daymark described in Rule 25 (e) of *International Regulations for Preventing Collisions at Sea (1972).*

Harbour
7.111
1   **General layout.** The approach to the harbour lies between West Pole, a drying spit which extends 9 cables SSW from Eastoke Point (50°47′N 0°56′W), the W entrance point to the harbour, and Middle Pole, a drying sandbank lying about 5 cables SSE of the same point. East Pole Sands, which dry, extend about 1½ miles S from the E entrance of the harbour. The entrance channel, about ¾ cable wide, lies close to the W shore at Eastoke Point. The E side of the entrance channel is formed by the W edge of The Winner, a drying bank of shingle which extends 6½ cables N from The Spit on the E side of the entrance.

2   Thorney Island (50°49′N 0°56′W), in reality a peninsula, together with two other peninsulas farther E, extend about 2 miles S into the harbour from its N side. Pilsey Sands and Stocker's Sands, which dry, extend nearly 1 mile from the S side of Thorney Island.

7.112
1   **Channels within the harbour.** Within the entrance the channel divides into two main branches, Chichester Channel (7.118) and Emsworth Channel (7.119). These channels are well marked by beacons and buoys, some of which are lighted. The junction of these two channels is marked by Fishery Light Buoy (S cardinal) moored

2 cables NE of Black Point (50°47′N 0°56′W), the N end of a small peninsula which extends 6 cables N from Eastoke Point.

7.113
1   **Hazards — yacht racing marks and moorings.** In the summer many yacht racing marks and moorings are laid within the harbour. For details of yacht racing marks in The Solent, see 7.29.

    Ferry, summer only, crosses Itchenor Reach between Itchenor (50°48′N 0°52′W) and the N shore.

7.114
1   **Tidal streams** in the entrance to Chichester Harbour run strongly; at springs the out-going stream attains a maximum rate of 6½ kn and the in-going stream a maximum of 2¾ kn.

2   In the various branches of the harbour tidal streams change at times of local HW and LW; the maximum rates occur about 2½ hours before and about 4 hours after local HW. The in-going stream runs for about 7¼ hours and the out-going stream for about 5¼ hours. The streams set fairly with the channels.

    For further details, see information on the chart.

Directions for entering harbour
7.115
1   **Landmarks:**
      Cakeham Tower (brick ruins) (50°46′·4N 0°53′·3W) surrounded by trees.
      Club House (50°47′·2N 0°56′·2W) of Hayling Island Sailing Club.

7.116
1   **Other aids to navigation.** Some of the light beacons in Chichester Harbour and approaches are fitted with depth or tide gauges, as shown on the chart; the information provided is not displayed on the beacons but may be requested from the harbour office.

7.117
1   **Approaches. From south or south-east** make for a position 1 mile S of West Pole Light Beacon (port hand) (50°45′·7N 0°56′·5W) in order to keep well clear of West Pole and East Pole Sands.

    The track then leads N, and at night keeping in the white sector (321°–081°) of West Pole Light Beacon, passing (with positions given from Eastoke Point (50°47′N 0°56′W)):

2   W of East Pole Sands; a stranded wreck, used as a target, displaying a beacon (S cardinal) (1½ miles SE) lies on the S edge of the sands. Another stranded wreck, also used as a target, lies in the middle of the sands and is marked on its NE side by a beacon (N cardinal) (1¼ miles SE). Thence:

3   E of West Pole Light Beacon (port hand) (9 cables S) which marks the SE edge of West Pole, thence:

E of Chichester Bar Light Beacon (port hand) (7 cables S), and:

W of Middle Pole (6 cables SSE); thence:

4   Midway between Eastoke Light Beacon (port hand), which is exhibited from the SE-most groyne off Eastoke Point, and W Winner Light Beacon (starboard hand) (3 cables NE); thence:

Between Black Point (6 cables N) (7.112) and NW Winner Light Buoy (starboard hand) (6 cables NNE), noting the 1·9 m patch in position 50°47′·3N 0°55′·9W.

5   **From south-west — leading marks:**

Front mark. Stranded wreck target beacon (N cardinal) (50°45′·8N 0°54′·9W) on East Pole Sands.

Rear mark. Cakeham Tower (1 mile ENE of the front mark) (7.115).

6   The alignment (064°) of these marks leads in the approach passing:

S of West Pole (4 cables SSW).

When Eastoke Light Beacon (port hand) is open E of West Pole Light Beacon (port hand) (9 cables S) the track then leads 013° for the harbour entrance, as indicated on the chart, and as directed above.

7.118

1   **Chichester Channel** leads N of The Winner and S of Pilsey Sands and Stocker's Sands, thence through Itchenor Reach to Chichester Lake. It is joined by Thorney Channel and Bosham Channel about 1½ and 3 miles, respectively, within the entrance. The channel is navigable by mariners in vessels of up to 2·7 m draught as far as Itchenor, and thence by small craft as far as Dell Quay on the E side of the channel 2 miles farther NE. The channel is entered between N Winner Light Buoy (starboard hand) (50°47′·3N 1°55′·8W) and Fishery Light Buoy (S cardinal), 1½ cables NW. The depths in the entrance to the channel are subject to change and the buoys are moved accordingly. In the outer part of the channel S of Stocker's Sands the depths vary from about 2·5 m to 7·5 m. In this part of the channel, after The Winner is covered on a rising tide, a weak stream sets NE across the channel.

2   Thorney Channel, on the W side of Chichester Channel, is entered W of Camber Light Beacon (S cardinal) which stands 2½ cables SE of Pilsey Island (50°48′·0N 0°54′·5W). The channel lies between Pilsey Island Light Beacon (port hand) and a beacon (starboard hand), ¾ cable farther NE. Broken piles extend NE from the beacon to the shore and care is necessary when navigating in this vicinity. Two cables farther N the channel leads between a beacon (port hand) and Thorney Light Beacon (starboard hand) marking a gap between broken piles E of Longmere Point (50°48′·2N 0°54′·7W). The channel then continues N along the E side of Thorney Island, where, after about 1½ miles it leads to Prinsted and Nutbourne Channels, both of which dry.

3   Bosham Channel, with a depth of about 3 m in its entrance, is entered from Chichester Channel between a

line of yacht moorings and Deep End Beacon (S cardinal) which marks the entrance to the channel. There is a quay at Bosham (50°50′N 0°51′W) with a depth of 3 m alongside at HW.

4   **Leading marks:**

Front mark. Roman Transit Beacon (port hand) (50°48′·6N 0°53′·3W).

Rear mark. Main Channel Beacon (white, rectangular topmark) (2½ cables NNE of the front mark.

5   The alignment (033°) of these marks standing on the N side of the channel near Cobnor Point leads in the centre line of the section of Chichester Channel NE of East Head (50°47′·3N 0°54′·7W), marked on its NW side by East Head Light Buoy (starboard hand), as far as Chalkdock Light Beacon (starboard hand) which marks the S side of a bend in the channel S of Roman Transit Beacon.

6   Fairway Light Buoy (starboard hand) (50°48′·6N 0°52′·4W) is moored at the W end of Itchenor Reach 1 cables SE of Cobnor Point; this reach extends about 1 mile ESE before turning NE into Chichester Lake. Above CM Light Beacon (starboard hand), which marks the W end of the approach channel to Chichester Marina, the channel dries at MLWS. Mariners can berth alongside Dell Quay in 2 m at HW.

7.119

1   **Emsworth Channel,** between Hayling Island and Thorney Island, extends N for more than 3 miles from the harbour entrance. The channel has a least charted depth of 2·7 m in the fairway as far as its junction with Sweare Deep (50°49′·6N 0°56′·8W) which leads N of Hayling Island to North Lake (7.126) in Langstone Harbour. The following creeks and channels lead W off Emsworth Channel: Mengham Rithe; Mill Rithe; Sweare Deep.

2   Mariners proceeding to Emsworth pass E of Emsworth Light Beacon (S cardinal) (50°49′·6N 0°56′·7W).

Useful marks:

Verner Light Beacon (port hand) (50°48′·2N 0°56′·6W).

Marker Light Beacon (starboard hand) (50°48′·9N 0°56′·7W).

North-east Hayling Light Beacon (port hand) (50°49′·6N 0°56′·8W)

Berths

7.120

1   **Anchorages** exist, as shown on the chart:

North of East Head (50°47′·3N 0°54′·7W).

In Thorney Channel, NE of Pilsey Island (50°48′·0N 0°54′·5W).

South of a line from Chalkdock Light Beacon (50°48′·5N 0°53′·3W) to Fairway Light Buoy, 6 cables E.

Vessels are to avoid anchoring in the middle of a fairway; when at anchor they are to display the lights and shapes for a vessel at anchor described in *International Regulations for Preventing Collisions at Sea (1972).*

2   **Prohibited anchorages.** Anchoring is prohibited in Itchenor Reach and Bosham Channel E and N of Fairway Light Buoy (50°48′·6N 0°52′·4W) and in Emsworth Channel N of Emsworth Light Beacon (50°49′·7N 0°56′·8W) because of the many moorings. Moorings also occupy extensive parts of all the sheltered channels and drying channels within the harbour. Mariners are warned not to anchor in any established mooring area owing to the existence of ground tackle.

Southsea Marina   *Farlington Marshes*

Chimney   *Gunner Point*

Langstone Harbour entrance from S (7.121)

(Original dated 2001)

(Photograph – Air Images)

Langstone Harbour and approaches

General information
7.121

1   **Position and function.** Langstone Harbour (50°49′N 1°01′W) lies between Portsea Island and Hayling Island and is intersected by several channels and creeks. There is a connection with Chichester Harbour by a shallow channel at its NE end, but there is no navigable channel leading NW to Portsmouth Harbour, except for dinghies. Farlington Marshes (50°50′N 1°02′W) is a nature reserve and the cluster of islets close E of the marshes is a bird sanctuary. The harbour is used extensively by yachts and has two commercial berths.

2   **Approach and entry.** The harbour is approached over Langstone Bar (50°46′N 1°01′W) between West Winner, a gravel bank, and East Winner, a sandbank, both of which dry, and entered between Eastney Point (50°47′·2N 1°01′·9W) and Gunner Point, about 3 cables E.

3   **Harbour Authority:** Langstone Harbour Board, Harbour Office, Ferry Road, Hayling Island, Hants PO11 0DG.
    E-mail: harbourmaster@langstoneharbour.org.uk
    Website: www.langstoneharbour.org.uk.

Limiting conditions
7.122

1   **Controlling depth:** Langstone Bar 1·2 m.
    Vertical clearance in North Lake (7.126) is 1·7 m.
    Maximum size of vessel: 80 m LOA with a draught of 4·4 m at MHWS. See 7.128.
    Sea state. No attempt should be made to enter the harbour during strong onshore winds as the seas break on the bar. The breakers are particularly hazardous when a strong ebb tide is flowing.

Arrival information
7.123

1   **Port radio** station, with limited hours, operates from the harbour office at Ferry Point.

2   **Submarine cables,** marked by beacons at each end, cross the harbour entrance close S of the Harbour Master's office.
    Pilotage is compulsory for vessels of 48 m LOA and over and vessels of 20 m LOA and over carrying more than 12 passengers. The pilot boarding service is provided by the Portsmouth Pilotage Service (7.15) on behalf of Langstone Harbour Board. ETA at the pilot station (1½ miles S of Langstone Fairway Light Beacon) and requests for pilotage should be sent to Langstone Harbour Master 24 hours in advance.
    For details see *Admiralty List of Radio Signals Volume 6(1).*

3   **Local knowledge** is advisable.
    Traffic regulations. Bye-laws are in force for the navigation and general use of the harbour. Special sound signals are also in use.
    Vessels over 30 m LOA should notify their arrival in advance to the harbour master.
    Mariners must not exceed a speed of 10 kn in Langstone Harbour, or 5 kn in Southsea Marina Channel.

4   **Visibilty.** In reduced visibility vessels over 20 m in length must contact the harbour office prior to crossing Langstone Bar (50°46′N 1°01′W) and entering Langstone Fairway.

5   **Waterskiing.** A designated area for waterskiing between 1 April and 31 October, is provided by the harbour authority in the S and central parts of Langstone Harbour to the E of Sword Point. The area, which is charted, is marked by buoys (special).

6   **Jet-skiing and PWC.** An area set aside for jet-skiing and personal watercraft is situated about 6 cables SSW of

Eastney Point (50°47'·2N 1°01'·2W). The area is marked by six small buoys (special)

7   **Swimming area.** A designated area for swimmers lies off Eastney Beach (50°46'·8N 1°03'·5W) and is marked by yellow floats (special) moored up to 100 m offshore. Mariners in the vicinity should keep well to seaward of this area.

Harbour
7.124
1   **General layout.** Sword Sands, which occupy the central part of Langstone Harbour, dry up to 4·2 m, Sword Point (50°48'·4N 1°01'·6W), their SW extremity, is situated about 1¼ miles NNE of Eastney Point; the sands and Sword Point are continually on the move. At Sword Point the channel divides into two branches, Langstone Channel, leading generally NE to Bedhampton Quay or to Chichester Harbour (7.108) and the other, Broom Channel, leading NNW.

2   **Dredgers.** In the approaches to Langstone Harbour, between Langstone Fairway Light Beacon and the pilot boarding position (1½ miles S of the fairway beacon), loaded dredgers with restricted manoeuvrability may be encountered and should not be impeded.
Yacht racing marks, see 7.29.

3   **Tidal streams** in the harbour entrance are strong, attaining a maximum spring rate of 3½ kn, for details see information on the chart.

Directions
7.125
1   **Principal marks:**
Chimney (50°47'·4N 1°01'·8W).
Lattice Towers (50°47'·2N 1°02'·2W) on Eastney Point.
Radar Tower (column) (50°47'·3N 1°01'·8W)
Water Tower (50°47'·1N 1°03'·4W) (7.162).
Saint James' Hospital (chimney) (50°47'·9N 1°03'·0W).
Barnard Tower (conspicuous building) (50°47'·8N 1°02'·5W).

2   **Approaches.** From a position S of Langstone Fairway Light Beacon (safe water) (50°46'·3N 1°01'·4W) and W of Winner Buoy (S cardinal), 1½ miles SE, moored off the S side of East Winner and Hayling Shoal, the track leads N passing (with positions given from Eastney Point (50°47'N 1°02'W)):

3   Over Langstone Bar (1¼ miles S) noting Roway Wreck Light Beacon (isolated danger) (1 mile SSW) and an obstruction with a depth of 2·1 m over it which lies 3½ cables S of the wreck; thence:
Clear of Langstone Fairway Light Beacon (safe water) (1 mile SSE); thence:

4   Between West Winner (6 cables S) and East Winner (1½ miles SE). The W side of East Winner is steep-to and can usually be distinguished by broken water. These two banks, known locally as The Woolseners frequently shift and are subject to alteration in height after gales. In rough weather, if there is any swell, there is generally one sheet of broken water over them, with heavy rollers. Thence:

5   Between Eastney Point and Gunner Point (3 cables E).

Clearing marks:
The alignment (353°) of Eastney Point Outfall Light Beacon (port hand) (50°47'·2N 1°01'·7W), on a concrete dolphin at the end of an outfall, with the edge of the land, 4 cables N, clears E of West Winner.

6   **Useful marks:**
East side of entrance. Lights (dolphin) (50°47'·8N 1°01'·5W) on Hayling Island Ferry Landing Stage. A useful headmark as these two lights, vertically disposed, are easily distinguishable against the background lights.

7   West side of entrance. Light (50°47'·3N 1°01'·7W) on a jetty head.
Light (pile) (50°47'·7N 1°01'·7W) on water intake.
Lights (dolphins) (50°47'·8N 1°01'·8W) on the N and S ends of Eastney landing Stage.

7.126
1   **Langstone Channel** is entered S of Sword Point. This channel, with general depths from 2 to 4 m, extends NE and N for about 2 miles from Sword Point and is marked by buoys and beacons, some of which are lit, and by perches. At the N end of Langstone Channel, abreast the S end of Long Island (50°49'·9N 1°00'·3W), the channel forks; North Lake leads into Sweare Deep and thence into Chichester Harbour (7.108), and Broad Lake, the NNW fork, leads to Bedhampton Quay. North Lake dries but has a depth of 3·7 m at MHWS. It is spanned by a road bridge connecting Hayling Island with the mainland; the passage through the bridge is 9 m wide. The pile of the bridge on the N side of the passage is painted white with a red square, that on the S side is painted white with a green triangle; the channel is marked by buoys (starboard hand).

2   From Eastney Point the track continues N passing (with positions given from Eastney Point):
W of a concrete structure (4·2 m high) (7½ cables NNE) noting the 0·3 m shoal which lies close NW; thence:
Between E Milton Light Buoy and NW Sinah Light Buoy (port and starboard hand) (1 mile N).

3   The track then leads NE into Langstone Channel passing:
SE of a stranded wreck marked by a pile (isolated danger) (1¼ miles NNE).
The track then continues generally NE thence NNE through the marked channel to the entrance to Broad Lake (2½ miles NNE).

4   The alignment (343°) of leading marks (beacons) (50°50'·4N 1°00'·3W) leads through a channel marked on its W side by beacons (port hand), through Broad Lake, to near the front leading beacon where the channel then leads 018° to Bedhampton Quay.

5   **Useful marks:**
South Lake Light Beacon (starboard hand) (50°49'·5N 0°59'·9W).
Binness Light Beacon (port hand) (50°49'·6N 0°59'·9W).

7.127
1   **Broom Channel** is marked at its entrance by buoys (port and starboard hand) moored at the SW extremity of Sword Sands. Russells Lake branches NE from Broom Channel about 3 cables N of Sword Point. A light buoy (port hand) is moored SSE of the entrance to Salterns Lake, a rivulet through the drying flats on the W side of Broom Channel about 5 cables NNW of Sword Point, and marks the bend in Broom Channel. North of Salterns Lake, Broom Channel is marked by buoys and light buoys, and

becomes very narrow, with depths of less than 1 m at its N end, ending at Kendall's Wharf, situated on the W side of the channel about 8 cables NNW of Great Salterns Lake.

Berths
7.128
1 **Alongside berths:** Bedhampton Quay (50°50'·7N 1°00'·0W) has a jetty with a length of 73 m and can accept vessels up to 72 m LOA and draught 4·3 m at MHWS.

Kendall's Wharf (50°49'·5N 1°02'·5W) has a jetty with a length of 105 m and can accept vessels up to 80 m LOA and draught 4·4 m at MHWS.

In 2004 the bottom at Kendall's Wharf was irregular and vessels were advised not to take bottom at LW unless they were satisfied that it was safe to do so.

Anchorages. Anchorage for small commercial craft can be obtained in Langstone Channel. Pleasure craft can also anchor in Russells Lake and in other minor creeks. Elsewhere the channels are occupied by numerous moorings. There is a marina 3 cables NNW of Eastney Point.

Anchoring is not permitted without the prior permission of the harbour authority.

Elsewhere the channels are occupied by numerous moorings.

Bembridge Harbour

Chart 2022 plan of Bembridge Harbour
General information
7.129
1 **Position.** Bembridge Harbour lies close W of Bembridge Point (50°41'·7N 1°05'·6W) and is nearly land-locked. Bembridge, on the E side of the harbour, is a yachting centre.

Harbour Authority: Bembridge Harbour, Harbour Office, The Duver, St Helens, Ryde, Isle of Wight PO33 1YB.

Pilots. Mariners requiring a pilot should make arrangements through the Harbour Office.

2 **Approach.** The harbour is approached from Saint Helen's Road by a buoyed channel through the drying coastal bank. The buoyed entrance channel is entered W of Saint Helen's Fort and trends SW until about 2 cables E of Saint Helen's seamark, thence S to the harbour entrance whence it turns W.

3 **Harbour.** The harbour is protected by two groynes; one extends about ½ cable N from the E entrance point the other extends about ½ cable E from the W entrance point. There are quays and pontoons along the S side of the harbour. Within the entrance the harbour mostly dries.

4 **Useful marks:**
Bembridge Approach Light Beacon (X on yellow pile) (50°42'·5N 1°05'·0W). A tide gauge indicating the depth of water in the shallowest part of the channel is mounted on the beacon.

5 **Regulations.** Anchoring is not permitted in the approach channel. Mariners are required to navigate the harbour with caution and at such a speed of less than 6 kn as will not endanger or cause damage to other vessels, boats, quays, premises, or works therein. No ballast, earth, ashes, stones or rubbish are on any account to be allowed to be discharged into any part of the harbour.

PORTSMOUTH HARBOUR AND APPROACHES INCLUDING SPITHEAD

General information

Charts 2631, 2625, 2036
Position
7.130
1 The city of Portsmouth (50°48'N 1°05'W) with its suburbs and the town of Southsea occupy the whole of Portsea Island. on the E side of Portsmouth Harbour. The town of Gosport occupies a large part of the frontage on the W side of the harbour.

Function
7.131
1 The port is a major naval base, which occupies a large part of the frontage on the E side of the harbour, and an important continental ferry terminal. The harbour also contains a small commercial harbour at Old Portsmouth, commercial wharves N of HM Naval Base, and several yacht marinas.

Topography
7.132
1 From Eastney Point (50°47'N 1°02'W) to Southsea Castle, 2¼ miles WSW, the coastline is fronted by the S part of the town of Southsea. South Parade Pier, a promenade pier, extends for nearly 1 cable from the coast 5 cables E of the castle; lights (posts, 3 m in height) are exhibited at each end of the pierhead. There are numerous groynes, some of which have beacons at their outer ends, extending from the beach NW of Southsea Castle. Round Tower, the E entrance point of Portsmouth Harbour, lies 1 mile NW of Southsea Castle.

2 Fort Blockhouse (50°47'·4N 1°06'·8W) stands at the W entrance to the harbour. Most of the intervening coastline between Fort Blockhouse and Gilkicker Point, 1½ miles SW, is fronted by sea-wall.

Port limits
7.133
1 For details regarding port limits, see 7.5.

Approach and entry
7.134
1 Portsmouth Harbour is approached from the E or W Solent between Spit Sand (50°46'N 1°06'W) and Horse and Dean Sand, farther E, and entered between Fort Blockhouse, at the W entrance, and Round Tower, about 1 cable ENE.

Traffic
7.135
1 In 2006 1802 vessels, not including ferries, used the port, totalling 7 255 898 dwt.

Port Authority
7.136
1 **Naval harbour authority.** The Queen's Harbour Master, Semaphore Tower, HMS Nelson, HM Naval Base, Portsmouth, PO1 3LT.
Email: dnbsqhm@a.dii.mod.uk

Civil harbour authority. Portsmouth Commercial Port, Harbour Offices, Continental Ferry Port, George Byng Way, Portsmouth, PO2 8SP.
Email: info@portsmouth-port.co.uk

Limiting conditions

Controlling depth
7.137

1   The main approach channel to the harbour is maintained at a depth of 9·5 m. Within the entrance this depth is maintained for 9 cables farther N to abreast North Corner (50°48'·4N 1°06'·7W).

Deepest and longest berths
7.138

1   For details of the deepest and longest berths, see 7.172 to 7.175.

Tidal levels
7.139

1   Mean spring range about 3·9 m; mean neap range about 1·9 m. For further information see *Admiralty Tide Tables*.

Density of water
7.140

1   Density: 1·025 g/cm³.

Maximum size of vessels handled
7.141

1   **Commercial vessels:** a cruise vessel of 198·6 m LOA and 28 437 gt has used Albert Johnson Quay; Superferries of up to 37 500 gt have used Continental Ferry Port.

Arrival information

Port operations
7.142

1   **Vessel Traffic Service.** Portsmouth Harbour Control, through Queen's Harbour Master (QHM), Portsmouth, co-ordinates all traffic movements entering or leaving harbour N of a line joining Gilkicker Point (50°46'·4N 1°08'·5W) and Horse Sand Fort, 3 miles ESE. For details of a reporting scheme, see 7.152.

2   **Radio reporting.** All vessels of more than 20 m in length when underway in Portsmouth Harbour and approach channels, N of a line joining Gilkicker Point and Horse Sand Fort, are to maintain continuous listening watch on VHF and should report to Portsmouth Harbour Control (callsign QHM) when passing the designated reporting points. In addition inward-bound vessels should report before weighing anchor at Spithead.

3   The positions of Reporting Points are shown on the chart. For details see *Admiralty List of Radio Signals Volume 6(1)*.

      For details regarding VTS in The Solent and Southampton Water, see 7.6.

Port radio
7.143

1   There are port radio stations at Portsmouth operated by QHM at Harbour Control in Semaphore Tower, and by Portsmouth Harbour Radio at Continental Ferry Terminal, for details see *Admiralty List of Radio Signals Volume 6(1)*.

Notice of ETA required
7.144

1   For details of ETA requirements, see 7.18.

Outer anchorage — Spithead
7.145

1   **General information.** Spithead (50°45'N 1°07'W) is bounded on its S side by Ryde Sand (7.211) and No Man's Land (7.94), and on its N side by Spit Sand and Horse and Dean Sand (7.164) and affords anchorage to many vessels.
      Regulations. Merchant vessels may only anchor in Man-of-War Anchorage (Warship Anchorage) at Spithead with the consent of QHM Portsmouth.

2   For regulations respecting the anchorage of merchant and other private vessels at Spithead, for rules to be observed when a fleet or squadron is assembled there, and for directions to ships approaching vessels displaying the royal or any other standard, see Appendix I.

3   **Tidal streams.** In the N part of Man-of-War Anchorage (Warship Anchorage) at Spithead the rate of the E-going stream is irregular during its first 4 hours. There is no slack water between the end of the W-going stream and the beginning of the E going stream, but at this time the direction changes rapidly from SW to ESE in the space of half an hour, continuing at a rate of ½ kn at springs and ¼ kn at neaps. For details see *Admiralty Tidal Stream Atlas for The Solent and adjacent waters*, and information on the chart.

7.146

1   **Anchorage.** Man-of-War Anchorage (Warship Anchorage) at Spithead, with depths of 5 to 24 m, lies S of Spit Sand; the limits of the anchorage, together with numbered anchor berths within it, are shown on the chart. Warner Shoal (50°44'N 1°04'W) and No Man's Land afford protection to the anchorage in S gales, and Horse and Dean Sand affords protection in SE gales.

2   **Prohibited anchorage and areas.** Mariners are prohibited from anchoring or fishing in an area, used as a minelaying practice area the limits of which are shown on the chart, situated ESE of Sturbridge Shoal (50°45'N 1°08'W).

3   Anchoring and trawling is also prohibited in an area, indicated on the chart, covering the approach to Portsmouth Harbour, and within 1 cable of any of the forts at Spithead or its approaches.
      Submarine cables, see 7.84.

7.147

1   **Restricted area.** An area (50°45'·8N 1°06'·3W) of 300 m radius marks the previous position of the historic wreck of King Henry VIII's great ship *Mary Rose* sunk in 1545 and raised in 1982. The area is marked by Mary Rose Light Buoy (special). Following disturbances on the seabed charted depths on the site should be treated with caution. For protection details, see 1.89.

Pilotage and tugs
7.148

1   **Pilotage.** For details of Portsmouth pilots, see 7.15.
      Tugs are available for commercial vessels at commercial berths. In addition Ministry of Defence tugs may be made available by arrangement with QHM Portsmouth.

Traffic regulations
7.149

1   **Regulations.** The information given below is taken from The Dockyard Port of Portsmouth Order (2005), extracts of which may be found at Appendix I. Local notices to mariners issued by QHM from time to time provide more detailed information. QHM should always be consulted prior to any planned arrivals and departures being undertaken.

2   **Main channel.** The main approach channel to Portsmouth Harbour is considered to be a narrow channel for the purposes of applying Rule 9 of *International Regulations for Preventing Collisions at Sea (1972)*. The main approach channel from Outer Spit Light Buoy (50°45′·6N 1°05′·5W) to the harbour entrance is bounded by the channel buoys; within the harbour it is bounded on both sides by the 10 m depth contour.

Regulations for RoRo ferries over 20 000 dwt when moving in Portsmouth Harbour are in force, for details see Local Notices to Mariners.

3   **Boat channel.** A boat channel the use of which is mandatory for vessels under 20 m in length and PWC entering or leaving the port is established W of the main approach channel. The boat channel is 50 m wide and extends from No 4 Bar Light Buoy (50°47′·0N 1°06′·3W) to Ballast Light Beacon 7 cables NNW. In practical terms mariners in yachts and small vessels using this channel should keep W of the W limit of the dredged channel S of the entrance, and W of a line drawn from the NW corner of the dredged area to Ballast Light Beacon N of the entrance. At night mariners should keep in the red sector of Harbour Entrance Direction Light (50°47′·9N 1°07′·0W) (7.165). By using this channel mariners in vessels under 20 m in length entering Portsmouth Harbour and bound for the berths on the Gosport side do not need to cross the main channel twice in order to comply with Rule 9(a) of *International Regulations for Preventing Collisions at Sea (1972)*.

4   Vessels may only enter or leave the boat channel at either end or to the W. The effect of this regulation is to create two separate channels in which *International Regulations for Preventing Collisions at Sea (1972)* apply to the two individual traffic streams.

Normal traffic rules apply in Haslar Creek.

5   Pile BC4 (port hand) situated on the W side of the boat channel abreast Fort Blockhouse carries a depth gauge to indicate the depth of water at the pile for the benefit of mariners using the boat channel.

Vessels under 20 m in length bound for Gunwharf Quays and Town Camber are to enter and leave Portsmouth Harbour via the boat channel, crossing the main approach channel N of the Ballast Light Beacon (50°47′·6N 1°06′·8W) having first obtained permission from QHM.

6   Commercial vessels under 20 m in length and vessels belonging to other recognised groups based in Town Camber, which are specifically registered for this purpose with QHM, may enter and leave the harbour close inshore on the easten side.

Certain vessels under 20 m in length such as pilot boats, police launches, customs launches are authorized to use the main approach channel when their duties so require.

7   All sailing vessels fitted with engines are to proceed under power entering and leaving harbour between the parallel of Southsea War Memorial and Ballast Light Beacon, 7 cables NNW.

7.150

1   **Restrictions — harbour fog routine.** Harbour fog routine will be ordered and promulgated by QHM when visibility is so low that shipping movements would be dangerous. While this routine is in force no movements of naval or merchant vessels over 20 m in length are to take place in the harbour or its approach channel without prior permission of QHM. Cross-harbour ferries may continue to

operate unless otherwise directed. Mariners in small boat and yacht traffic may continue at their discretion.

2   **Speed limits** within the Dockyard Port of Portsmouth are:

> Within Portsmouth Harbour; 10 kn.
> Within 1000 yards of the shore in any part of the Dockyard of Portsmouth; 10 kn.
> Within Wootton Creek (7.213) to the W of 1°12′·8W, the meridian of the mouth of the creek; 5 kn.

The limit in each case to be taken as speed through the water. Any vessel requiring to exceed the above limits for specific reasons should apply to QHM for a licence.

3   Exemptions:

> The above speed limits do not apply within the designated water skiing areas off Lee-on-Solent (7.193) and Wootton (7.213) if exceeded for the purpose of towing a water skier.
> Jet-skis or PWC (7.151) may only exceed the speed limit within the area designated for their use off Lee-on-Solent (7.193) and to the W of Langstone Harbour entrance (7.123).
> Fast Military Craft will also be exempt on specific occasions for operational training reasons.

4   **Static fishing.** The use of static fishing equipment is prohibited in the following areas:

> Fareham Creek, as far as Town Quay.
> Portchester Lake.
> The approaches to Port Solent.

5

> Tipner Lake.
> Haslar Creek.
> Weevil Lake.
> Brick Kiln Lake.
> Wootton Creek, Isle of Wight.

In areas S of the harbour entrance, where fishing is permitted, static fishing equipment must be clearly marked.

6   **Distance from HM Ships and HM Naval Base.** No merchant vessel or other private vessel shall navigate:

> Within 50 m of any of Her Majesty's vessels (save submarines) or foreign warships or auxiliaries alongside any Crown Establishment or at anchor, secured to a buoy or mooring within the Dockyard Port of Portsmouth. To identify and physically indicate the 50 m exclusion zone requirement, a lighted buoy (special) has been established 70 m SSW from SW corner of South Railway Jetty. A boom, with numerous high visibility orange floats connects the buoy to South Railway Jetty.

7

> Within 50 m of the walls, slip ways and boundaries of any Crown Establishments.
> Within 100 m of any submarine alongside in any Crown Establishment or at anchor, secured to a buoy or mooring within the Dockyard Port of Portsmouth.

7.151

1   **Exclusion zones for warships underway** in the Dockyard Port of Portsmouth may be activated by QHM. When in force, they will exist for 250 m round the subject vessel, or to the limits of navigable water if this is less. During such activation, all vessels underway, except those involved in the escort or specifically authorized by the escort commander, are to remain clear of the zone.

2   An exclusion zone will be activated by direction from QHM on VHF channels 11 or 13. It will be terminated on the subject vessel departing the Dockyard Port of Portsmouth boundary, or when notified by QHM on VHF channel 11 or Southampton VTS on VHF channel 12.

3   During activation Southampton VTS, on behalf of QHM, will direct traffic within the Dockyard Port of Portsmouth to remain at least 250 m clear of the subject vessel. Where this is not possible, commercial traffic will be held until the warship is clear. During the harbour entry or exit phase, all small craft traffic is to cease through the harbour entrance.

4   The warship for which an exclusion zone is activated will display two diamond shapes vertically disposed by day, or two flashing red lights horizontally disposed at the masthead by night. All escorting vessels will show a blue flashing light by day and night.

Mariners are cautioned that vessels in contravention of the exclusion zone, after being warned by at least two of the following methods; radio, flashing light or voice, will be deemed to have the intention of committing a hostile act against the warship being escorted.

5   **Exclusion zones for warships alongside** in the Dockyard Port of Portsmouth. A temporary exclusion zone of up to 150 m for warships alongside whilst carrying out X-ray surveys on their hulls and other surveys and trials, will be activated by QHM. Local navigation warnings will be promulgated by QHM in advance.

6   **Personal watercraft** are prohibited from using the Inner and Outer Camber in the vicinity of Town Quay (50°47′N 1°06′W).

Regulations concerning entry
7.152
1   **Dangerous and polluting goods,** for details see 7.21 and Appendix I. Local notices to mariners may also apply; QHM should be consulted.

    Accident procedures, see 7.26.

    Regulations for the Dockyard Port of Portsmouth, see Appendix I.

Harbour

General layout
7.153
1   **Approach channel.** The outer part of the main approach channel to Portsmouth Harbour lies between Spit Sand and Horse and Dean Sand (7.164), the inner part of the channel lies between Spit Sand and East Sand (7.164) the narrow coastal bank fronting the coast NW of Southsea Castle. The channel is well marked by leading marks and light buoys.
7.154
1   **Harbour area.** The entrance to Portsmouth Harbour is about 1¼ cables wide between Fort Blockhouse (50°47′·4N 1°06′·7W) and Round Tower. Farther N the harbour widens out and merges into Fareham Lake and Porchester Lake, off which branch several smaller lakes; at HW the mud banks bordering these lakes are covered to form one large expanse of water. There are a number of mooring buoys for HM ships in the harbour.

2   Portsmouth Naval Base occupies a large part of the frontage on the E side of the harbour. Fort Blockhouse is situated at the W entrance point to the harbour. Royal Clarence Yard and Priddy's Hard lie on the W side of the harbour opposite the Naval Base.

3   Fountain Lake (7.170), between the N end of HM Naval Base and Whale Island, 2 cables NNE, is the main commercial area of the port. There is a small commercial harbour, which includes Isle of Wight Car Ferry Terminal

in Outer Camber, at Old Portsmouth, at the E entrance to the harbour.

Hazards
7.155
1   **Traffic congestion.** There is usually much congestion of traffic near the harbour entrance, especially during the summer months. Special care should be taken when in the vicinity of Fort Blockhouse. The Gosport ferry crosses the harbour at frequent intervals; its track can best be seen from the chart.

2   **Firing practice.** Tipner Small Arms Firing Range, the limits of which are marked by piles and notice boards, extends 1¼ miles WNW from the butts, situated about 3 cables NNW of the N extremity of Whale Island. When firing is taking place red flags are displayed, and at night a red light is exhibited from the W-most flagstaff at Tipner Range, and all vessels are warned to keep clear. Mariners navigating the channel through Porchester Lake are advised not to linger in the firing area and to transit the channel without delay.

3   **Large vessels navigating in the east Solent,** see 7.80. **High speed craft,** see 7.81.
    Yacht racing marks, see 7.29.

Signals
7.156
1   **Traffic signals.** Instructions from QHM will be passed on appropriate VHF channels, for details see *Admiralty List of Radio Signals Volume 6(1)*. The signals shown in Diagram 7.156 may be displayed as indicated.

2   **Sound signals.** Mariners approaching North Corner (50°48′·4N 1°06′·7W) and North West Wall, 3 cables NE, may sound one prolonged blast as a warning to mariners in vessels leaving Fountain Lake.

Natural conditions
7.157
1   **Tidal streams — channel.** On the leading line of the channel E of Spit Refuge Light Buoy, 3 cables E of Spit Sand Fort (50°46′·2N 1°05′·9W), the stream is irregular; between +0100 and +0230 Portsmouth (+0125 and +0255 Dover) the stream changes direction quickly from W to S.

At a position about 1 cable N of Spit Refuge Light Buoy the stream is less irregular and more or less rotary in an anti-clockwise direction. The SE-going stream tends to set on to the W part of Horse and Dean Sand.

2   **Caution.** There is a sudden increase and decrease in the rate of the stream, which occurs at both the above positions about +0330 Portsmouth (+0355 Dover), and the differences in the direction of the strongest streams (162° on the leading line E of Spit Refuge Light Buoy, and 142° 1 cable farther N) should be specially noted. This sudden increase does not occur at neaps, when, at the N position, the stream runs in about the same direction as at springs, but its rate does not exceed about ½ kn.
7.158
1   **Channel — inner part.** In the inner part of the channel the streams are more regular and are forced to the line of the channel by the banks at the sides and by the strength of the streams running into and out of the harbour. The streams begin earlier as the harbour entrance is approached.

2   The flood stream runs in two periods everywhere in the channel and is weak until about −0400 Portsmouth (−0335 Dover); it then increases, and attains its greatest rate, 1¼ kn at springs and ½ kn at neaps, WSW of Southsea

	Signal			
Day		*Night*	*Meaning*	*Shown from*

Clear channel - Signal flown by privileged vessel. Vessels flying this signal are to be given a clear passage in accordance with the "Clear Channel" instructions, which will be promulgated on the Daily Movements signal and also passed to vessels by VHF as appropriate.

Vessels and tugs in whose favour a "Clear Channel" is in force.

Diving.
Vessels conducting diving operations.
Note: Diving tenders, operating close to and under the control of a vessel showing appropriate diving lights, will only show a white all round light by night.

Vessel concerned.

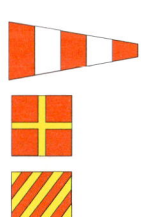

Potentially Hazardous Operations.
You should proceed at slow speed when passing me.

Vessel concerned.

Portsmouth Harbour - traffic signals (7.156)

castle, 3½ kn at springs and 1½ kn at neaps W of Victoria Pier, about −0130 Portsmouth (−0105 Dover).

The ebb stream WSW of Southsea Castle runs continuously, and attains a maximum rate of 2½ kn at springs, ½ kn at neaps, +0330 Portsmouth (+0355 Dover).

3   Farther in, W of Victoria Pier, at springs the ebb runs at a rate of about 1 kn until +0130 Portsmouth (+0155 Dover). It then increases, and from +0300 to +0330 Portsmouth (+0325 to +0355 Dover) runs at about 4 kn, after which it decreases, to become slack at +0530 Portsmouth (+0555 Dover). At neaps the maximum rate, 2 kn, occurs from +0230 to +0300 Portsmouth (+0255 to +0325 Dover).

4   **Caution.** At all times between +0330 and +0530 Portsmouth (+0355 and +0555 Dover) and between −0200 and +0015 Portsmouth (−0135 and +0040 Dover) the harbour entrance and Spithead streams run in more or less opposite directions. Under these circumstances the streams over Spit Sand and the W part of Horse and Dean Sand are confused and irregular.

7.159

1   **Harbour entrance.** In mid-channel close outside the harbour entrance there are significant quarter-diurnal variations in the streams; the most significant is an increase in the rate of the flood stream from 2¾ kn to 3½ kn at springs at −0130 Portsmouth (−0105 Dover), decreasing half an hour later to 2¾ kn.

2   **Caution.** The direction of the out-going stream in the entrance to the harbour is towards Hamilton Bank; the direction of the in-going stream off Victoria Pier is towards Fort Blockhouse. Allowance must be made for these sets.

7.160

1   **Within the harbour.** In the narrowest part of the entrance to Portsmouth Harbour the flood stream runs in two periods, in the second of which the greatest rate is attained. The ebb stream, unlike the stream close outside the entrance, runs in one period only, the rate in the first hour increasing rather slowly after which it increases rapidly and is stronger than the flood stream. The stream runs as follows:

Interval from HW Portsmouth (Dover)	*Direction*	*Max rate kn*
+0515 (+0540)	Flood stream begins	–
−0500 (−0435)	Flood	1
−0400 (−0335)	Flood	½
−0130 (−0105)	Flood	3¼
+0025 (+0050)	Ebb stream begins	–
+0300 (+0325)	Ebb	5+

2   Between the entrance and The Point, 1½ cables N, the streams do not change appreciably, though there is some small decrease in the rates, especially that of the ebb stream.

Above The Point the times at which the streams begin become gradually, but very slightly, later, and the rates decrease considerably; farther N the rate of the ebb stream decreases more rapidly than the rate of the flood stream, and N of Portsmouth Harbour Railway Jetty the rate of the flood stream is a little greater than the rate of the ebb stream.

3   The flood stream runs NW, and the ebb stream SE, across the entrance to Haslar Lake. There is little stream in

Haslar Lake, except near Haslar Bridge, or in Cold Harbour, and in Weevil Lake.

Eddies are to be expected on both sides of the harbour entrance, and off the piers and jetties on both sides of the harbour, when the streams are running strongly. There is a strong anti-clockwise SE-going eddy across the entrance of Haslar Lake at all stages of the flood except at −0400 Portsmouth (−0335 Dover).

4   There are dangerous clockwise eddies off South Railway Jetty, with a set on to the jetty, between −0300 to HW Portsmouth (−0235 to +0025 Dover).

Above North Corner Jetty the flood stream divides and runs into Fountain Lake, Portchester Lake and Fareham Lake. The flood streams in Portchester Lake and Fareham Lake also divide and run up the various subsidiary channels. The ebb streams from all the channels meet in the main channel above North Corner Jetty, that from Portchester Lake being particularly marked.

5   The streams are very weak in Fountain Lake and do not exceed about ½ kn at springs in a mid-channel position N of North Corner Jetty, or ¼ kn at springs between North Wall and Whale Island.

The rates of the streams decrease rapidly as the Portchester Lake and Fareham Lake are ascended. The ebb stream begins off Portchester Castle about +0035 Portsmouth (+0100 Dover) and off the town at Fareham about +0025 Portsmouth (+0050 Dover); the ebb stream ceases at both places about +0500 Portsmouth (+0525 Dover) after which the stream is probably slack for some 3 hours or more before the flood stream begins.

7.161

1   **Caution.** Tidal stream rates within Portsmouth Harbour are believed to have changed in recent years (2002) as a direct result of numerous dredging/construction works.

For further details of tidal streams, see information on the charts, 1.153 and *Admiralty Tidal Stream Atlas for Portsmouth Harbour and Approaches.*

Directions for entering harbour
(continued from 7.102)

Principal marks
7.162

1   **Landmarks — approaches Portsmouth side:**
Water Tower (illuminated clock) (50°47'·1N 1°03'·4W) at Eastney.
Buildings (50°46'·8N 1°04'·8W).
Saint Jude's Church (spire) (50°47'·2N 1°05'·3W).
Naval War Memorial (50°46'·9N 1°05'·7W).
Building (tower block) (50°47'·1N 1°05'·5W).

Naval War Memorial from SW (7.162)
(Original dated 1996)

(Photograph - HMSML Gleaner)

Pall Europe Building (elevation 63 m) (50°47'·9N 1°06'·4W).
Spinnaker Tower (elevation 167 m) (50°47'·7N 1°06'·5W) (7.169) from which aircraft warning lights are exhibited.

2   **Landmarks — approaches Gosport side:**
Spit Sand Fort (large round stone structure) (50°46'·2N 1°05'·9W) from where a light is exhibited.
White Tower (elevation 43 m) (50°47'·2N 1°07'·0W).

White Tower from SE (7.162)
(Original dated 1998)

(Photograph - HMS Birmingham)

Buildings (4 blocks of flats) (50°47'·6N 1°07'·0W).
Holy Trinity Church (tower) (50°47'·6N 1°07'·2W).

Holy Trinity Church Tower,
Building (48) and Building (51) from SE (7.162)
(Original dated 1998)

(Photograph - HMS Birmingham)

3   **Landmarks — harbour.**
Semaphore Tower (octagonal white stone tower) (50°48'·0N 1°06'·6W) the harbour control station on Watering Island.
Chimney (elevation 36 m) (50°48'·2N 1°06'·6W).
Spinnaker Tower (elevation 167 m) (50°47'·7N 1°06'·5W) (7.169).

General information
7.163

1   The usual times for taking vessels into or out of Portsmouth Harbour are during the first 3 or 4 hours of the flood tide, and during the 1st, 2nd and 5th hours of the ebb tide, including the LW slack. At neap tides the tidal streams are sufficiently weak to allow safe navigation into or out of the harbour at all states of the tide. The flood stream is strong between the 4th and 5th hour of the flood tide, but strongest between the 5th and 7th hours; the ebb stream is strongest between the 3rd and 4th hours of the ebb tide. Mariners should avoid entering at these times on account of the eddies.

2   The best time for mariners in large vessels to enter is as soon after LW as to give sufficient depth on the outer bar, or to pass Outer Spit Light Buoy between half an hour and 1 hour after HW, dependent on the berth to be taken up; if going to South Railway Jetty or Pitch House Jetty, the time should be 1 hour after HW. Mariners in vessels of very deep draught should only enter the harbour at this latter flood.

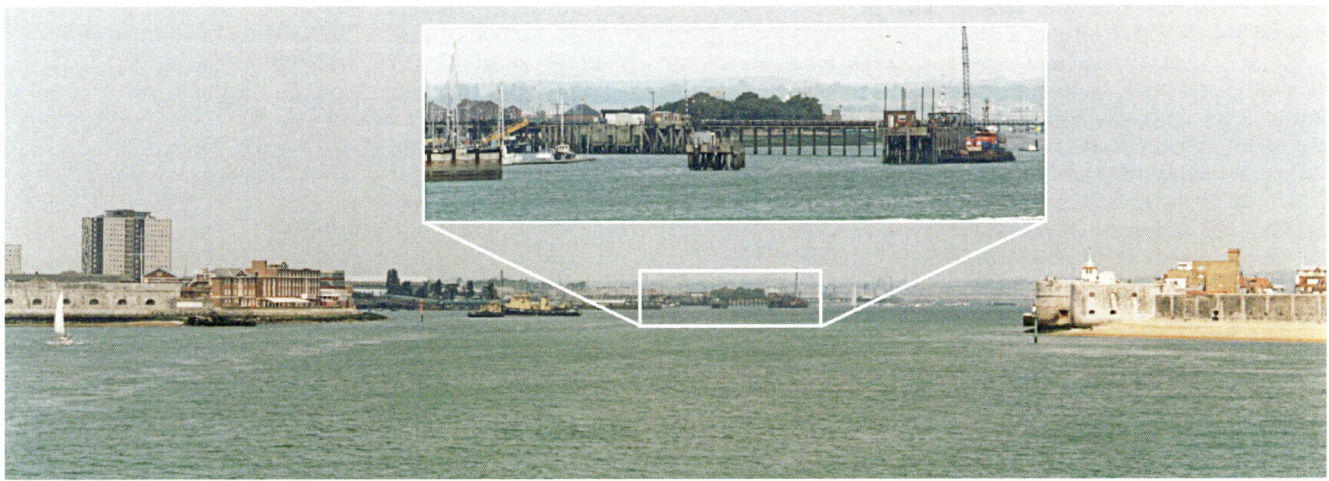

Fort Blockhouse
Direction Light

Harbour Entrance
Direction Light

Round Tower

Portsmouth Harbour Entrance from SSE (7.163)

(Original dated 1998)

(Photograph - HMS Birmingham)

3   HM ships proceed to the moorings in the harbour as directed by QHM.

Mariners in merchant ships wishing to berth in Portsmouth Harbour should consult the First Schedule of the Order-in-Council with reference to the Dockyard Port of Portsmouth, see Appendix I.

Charts 2625, 2036, 2037
Approaches
7.164

1   Horse and Dean Sand, which extends from 2 to 3 miles from the coast between Southsea Castle and Eastney Point, has depths of less than 5 m over it. Horse Elbow and Horse Tail (7.97) form the SW and SE part of this sand respectively. Horse Sand Fort (7.94) is situated close within the steep-to SW edge of the sand. The fort is connected with the shore N by a submerged barrier (7.189) of concrete blocks, partially uncovered at LW. East Sand, with depths of less than 5 m over it, extends 1 cable offshore between Round Tower (50°47'·4N 1°06'·5W) and a position 2 cables SSE of Clarence Esplanade Pier, 4 cables SE. The SW side of East Sand and the narrow coastal bank which fronts the coast NW of Southsea Castle is marked by light buoys (starboard hand), which also mark the NE side of the main entrance channel to Portsmouth.

2   Spit Sand extends about 1½ miles SE from the coast between Fort Blockhouse (50°47'·4N 1°06'·7W) (7.171) and Gilkicker Point, 1½ miles SW; its E and NE sides are marked by light buoys which also mark the W side of the main approach to Portsmouth.

7.165

1   **Leading marks:**
> Front mark. Southsea Castle Direction Light (white stone tower black band, 10 m in height) (50°46'·7N 1°05'·3W) shown throughout 24 hours.
> Rear mark. Saint Jude's Church (5 cables N of the front mark) (7.162).

2   From a position W of Horse Sand Fort (50°45'·0N 1°04'·3W) (7.94) the alignment (003°) of these marks, or at night in the centre of the white sector (000°–003°) of Southsea Castle Direction Light leads in the outer part of the dredged channel passing (with positions given from the front mark):

3   W of Saddle Light Buoy (starboard hand) (1½ miles S); thence:
> Between Outer Spit Light Buoy (S cardinal) (1 mile S) and Horse Sand Light Buoy (starboard hand) (1¼ miles S) which mark the entrance to the main approach channel; thence:
> Between Spit Refuge Light Buoy and Boyne Light Buoy (port and starboard hand) (5½ cables S).

4   **Leading marks:**
> Front mark. Fort Blockhouse Direction Light (base of mast) (50°47'·4N 1°06'·7W) shown throughout 24 hours.
> Rear mark. Centre of block of Flats (3 cables NW of the front mark).

Fort Blockhouse Direction Light and Leading Marks
bearing 320° (7.165)
(Original dated 1996)

(Photograph - HMSML Gleaner)

The alignment (320°) of these marks, or at night in the centre of the white sector (318½°–321½°) of Fort Blockhouse Direction Light, leads in the fairway passing:

5   Between Castle NB Light Buoy (starboard hand) (2½ cables S) and Ridge Light Buoy (port hand) (3¼ cables SW); thence:
> Between No 1 NB Light Buoy (starboard hand) (3 cables WNW) and No 2 Light Buoy (port hand) (4 cables W); thence:
> Between No 3 and No 4 NB Light Buoys (starboard and port hand) (7 cables WNW).

6   **Leading mark:**
The line of bearing 333¾° of Harbour Entrance Direction Light (concrete dolphin, 4 m in height) (50°47'·8N 1°07'·0W) at Cold Harbour, or at night in the

centre of its white sector (332½°–335°), then leads in the fairway through the harbour entrance.

For details of a boat channel for mariners in small craft entering Portsmouth, see 7.149

7.166

1   **Useful marks:**

No Man's Land Fort Light (50°44'·4N 1°05'·7W) (7.94).

No Man's Land Fort (7.166)

(Original dated 2004)

(Photograph - Drew Given, MV Doulos)

Horse Sand Fort Light (50°45'·0N 1°04'·3W) (7.94).

Fort Gilkicker Light (signal and radar mast) (50°46'·4N 1°08'·5W).

2   Water Tower (50°47'·2N 1°07'·6W) standing in the complex of Royal Hospital, Haslar.

Victoria Light Beacon (starboard hand) (50°47'·3N 1°06'·4W) about ½ cable W of Victoria Pier, from which lights (metal columns) are exhibited.

3   Lights (20 m E of Fort Blockhouse Direction Light) on the W side of the harbour entrance.

Lights (50°47'·4N 1°06'·5W) on Round Tower at the E entrance point.

Saint Thomas Cathedral (white cupola) (50°47'·4N 1°06'·2W).

Saint Thomas Cathedral from SW (7.166)

(Original dated 1996)

(Photograph - HMSML Gleaner)

Charts 2629, 2631

Harbour

7.167

1   From the harbour entrance keep within the maintained depth areas indicated on the chart, noting Ballast Light Beacon (port hand) (50°47'·6N 1°06'·8W) which marks the E extremity of Ballast Bank, and proceed to the required berth.

7.168

1   **Useful marks:**

The Point Light Beacon (starboard hand) (50°47'·6N 1°06'·6W).

Lights (masts, 5 m in height) (50°47'·7N 1°07'·0W) on the N and S ends of Gosport ferry landing stage.

2   Light (50°48'·6N 1°06'·2W) on Fountain Lake Corner.

Continental Ferry Port Light Beacon (W cardinal) (50°48'·7N 1°05'·8W) at the head of No 3 and 4 berths. Fog lights are displayed from the jetty head in low visibility.

3   **Transit marks:**

Front mark. No 97 Beacon (orange X) (50°48'·6N 1°06'·8W).

Rear mark. No 91 Light Beacon (starboard hand) (5 cables N of the front mark).

The alignment (002°) of these marks, situated near the W edge of the drying flat extending W from Whale Island, indicate a transit line through the N part of the harbour.

Basins and berths

Main berthing areas

7.169

1   **East side of harbour.** The E side of the harbour entrance fronting Old Portsmouth is formed by a peninsula terminating N in The Point (50°47'·6N 1°06'·5W), Outer and Inner Town Cambers lie within this peninsula. Gunwharf Quays lie 1½ cables N of The Point.

Inner Camber   *Round Tower*

Outer Camber   *The Point*

Old Portsmouth Town Quays from NW (7.169)

(Original dated 2001)

(Photograph - DLO Photo Unit, Bath)

2   Harbour Railway Jetty containing Portsmouth Harbour Station, from which ferries ply to Gosport and Isle of Wight, lies 2½ cables N of The Point. Wightlink Hulk Moorings, two barges secured end to end, are permanently moored to buoys ¾ cable W and parallel to the jetty. Spinnaker Tower, at an elevation of 167 m, stands at the S end of Harbour Railway Jetty. Common Hard runs parallel with and N of the railway station; the berth for HMS *Warrior* (1860) lies close to the N side of the hard.

3   The W frontage of Portsmouth Naval Base extends N from the S point (50°47'·9N 1°06'·7W) of Watering Island for about 5 cables to North Corner Jetty, thence NE across the Tidal Basin and E into Fountain Lake and is bounded on its N side by Fountain Lake Jetty. It has numerous jetties suitable for berthing vessels of deep draught. The designation of jetties, dry docks, locks, basins and berths, and their positions and depths, can best be seen on the chart.

North Corner Jetty   Fountain Lake

Victoria Jetty   South Railway Jetty

W side of HM Naval Base from SW (7.169)

(Original dated 2001)

(Photograph - Air Images)

7.170

1   **North side of harbour.** Fountain Lake, between the N end of HM Naval Base and Whale Island (50°49′N,1°06′W), is the main commercial area of the port

and contains Continental Ferry Port, a RoRo terminal for passenger and vehicle ferries, and berths for refrigerated, container, dry-bulk and tanker traffic, amongst others. The S portion of the lake is maintained at a depth of 8·0 m and the approach to the quays E has a maintained depth of 7·0 m. Depths 0·3 m shoaler than charted exist (2007) in an area 1 cable NNE of Fountain Lake Corner (50°48′·6N 1°06′·2W). The outer part of Rudmore Channel between the NW side of Continental Ferry Port and Whale Island has a dredged depth of 6·5 m (2003). The inner part of the channel adjacent to North Quay has a dredged depth of 3·5 m (2003) with a dredged depth of 2·7 m (2003) on the NW side; the channel is marked by light beacons.

2   Whale Island, occupied by a naval establishment, is connected to the shore E by a causeway; HMS *Bristol*, a training vessel, is moored to a jetty at the SW end of the island. Whale Island Marina complex, for service personnel, extends S from the centre of the S side of the island.

7.171

1   **West side of harbour.** Haslar Lake lies between Fort Blockhouse (50°47′·4N 1°06′·7W) and the SE side of the town of Gosport. Fort Blockhouse is situated at the E end of a small peninsula. The SE part of the lake has a maintained depth of 6·0 m decreasing to 5·0 m maintained depth at the S end of the lake. A sailing centre is situated in the SW part of the lake and Haslar Marina is situated on the NW side of the lake.

2   Weevil Lake is entered between Oil Fuel Jetty and a drying flat, close N, on which stands Burrow Island (50°48′·2N 1°07′·2W). The lake runs N for about

Whale Island

Continental
Ferry Port

Fountain
Lake Jetty   No 3 Basin

N side of HM Naval Base from W (7.170)

(Original dated 2001)

(Photograph - Air Images)

2½ cables, then turns W into Forton Lake, which dries. Royal Clarence Yard is separated from Priddy's Hard by Forton Lake, but connected by a footbridge. East Jetty lies close N of the root of Oil Fuel Jetty. For a distance of 1 cable N of East Jetty an area has been dredged to 5 m (2002); on the N side of the area there are pontoon berths for boats and on the W side, landing pontoons.

3   Shell Pier (disused), on which there is a radar scannner (lattice tower, 9 m in height), extends ENE from Priddy's Hard across the mudflats, with Powder Jetty, Vosper's Jetty and Sultan Landing, 2, 4½ and 5 cables NW, respectively, of Shell Pier.

HM Dockyard berths
7.172
1   **Deepest berth:**
     Middle Slip Jetty (50°48'·3N 1°06'·7W); length 275 m; maintained depth 12·0 m.
     Longest berth:
     Fountain Lake Jetty (50°48'·6N 1°06'·0W); length 650 m; maintained depths 6 and 8 m.
2   **Largest and deepest basins:**
     Basin No 3 (50°48'·4N 1°05'·9W) maintained depth 5·7 m but 7·5 m in circular area of 80 m diameter centred on position 50°48'·5N 1°05'·9W, entered through locks A, B, C or D.
     Tidal Basin (50°48'·4N 1°06'·3W), entrance to Basin No 2 and No 9 Dry Dock; maintained depth 8·0 m. There is a depth of 3·3 m close W of the inner S corner of the entrance to Basin No 2.

Haslar Lake berths
7.173
1   **Deepest and longest berths:**
     No 1 Jetty (50°47'·4N 1°06'·9W) on the NW side of Fort Blockhouse fronted by a reserved area; maintained depth 6·0 m.
     No 2 Jetty (50°47'·3N 1°07'·0W) on the S side of the lake; maintained depth 5·0 m.

Oil Fuel Jetty
7.174
1   **Deepest berth:**
     South-east berth (50°47'·9N 1°07'·0W); maintained depth 12·0 m.
     Longest berth:
     Gosport Fuel Jetty (50°48'·0N 1°07'·2W); maintained depth 9·0 m.

Fountain Lake berths
7.175
1   **Continental Ferry Port** (50°48'·7N 1°05'·6W) RoRo terminal with five berths. Longest and deepest berths No 2, 3 and 4 each 180 m in length; depth alongside about 7 m.
     Flathouse Quay (50°48'·5N 1°05'·5W) for refrigerated products, maintained depth 7 m; for vessels up to 156 m LOA.
2   **Albert Johnson Quay** (50°48'·6N 1°05'·5W) for general and container traffic, and refrigerated products, maintained depth 7 m; length 245 m; for vessels up to 173 m in length.
     North Quay (50°48'·8N 1°05'·6W) for small coastal tankers and bunkering barges, length 125 m; depth alongside 3·5 m.

Gunwharf Quays
7.176
1   Depths between 3 and 6 m. Lay-by berth 80 m in length and numerous quays and jetties for small craft.

Camber berths
7.177
1   **Outer Camber** (50°47'·5N 1°06'·5W) for Isle of Wight ferries, fishing vessels and the occasional commercial vessel; entrance 45 m wide; commercial berth 80 m in length; depth about 3·0 m; maximum depth at berths for fishing vessels 2·0 m.

Moorings
7.178
1   **Buoys:**
     No 3 Mooring Buoy (50°48'·5N 1°07'·0W) situated about 2 cables WNW of North Corner; maintained depth 8·0 m.
     Dolphins:
     Fareham Lake dolphins (50°49'·0N 1°07'·7W) the upper harbour ammunitioning facility; maintained depth 10 m.

Prohibited anchorages
7.179
1   **Anchorage is prohibited** in many areas indicated on the chart on account of numerous submarine and disused submarine cables which cross the harbour; some of the latter are marked by beacons and dolphins and notice boards.
     Magnetic measurement range crosses the harbour entrance between The Point and Fort Blockhouse.

Portchester Lake
Charts 2628, 2631
General information
7.180
1   Portchester Lake (50°49'N 1°07'W) extends NE and N from the N part of the harbour for about 2¼ miles to Paulsgrove Lake and Port Solent Marina, its N limit. The channel is marked by numbered beacons, some of which exhibit lights. There are mooring buoys and yacht moorings in the channel.

Vosper Thorneycroft Shipyard   *Port Solent Marina*

Portchester Castle
Paulsgrove Lake from SW (7.180)
(Original dated 2001)
(Photograph – Air Images)

2   Horsea Island, on the E side of the lake, lies about 6½ cables N of Whale Island. It is effectively isolated from the shore E by a bridge carrying a motorway over Tipner Lake; the bridge has a vertical clearance of 6·2 m and the width in the channel under the bridge is 20 m at HW. Anchoring is prohibited, in an area shown on the chart about 2 cables W of the bridge, due to submarine power

cables. Horsea Island is connected to the shore N at Paulsgrove.

3 **Firing practice area,** see 7.155.

Depths. The channel has depths of from 4 to 9 m at its entrance, shoaling gradually to less than 3 m about 5 cables SSE of Portchester Castle (50°50′N 1°07′W). From Portchester Castle to Port Solent Marina the channel is dredged (2001) to a depth of 1·5 m.

4 There is a wet dock and a shiplift at the boat building yard 5 cables N of Portchester Castle; the dock is approached through a channel branching NNW from the main channel close N of No 73 beacon.

Fareham Lake

General information
7.181

1 Fareham Lake leads NW from the N part of the harbour for about 3 miles to the town of Fareham (50°50′N 1°11′W); the channel in Fareham Lake is marked by numbered beacons (port and starboard hand) some of which are lighted.

Hardway Sailing Club is situated on the W side of Fareham Lake, close W of Sultan Landing (50°48′·8N 1°07′·9W), with numerous yacht moorings in the vicinity.

2 Bombketch Lake and Spider Lake open from the E side of Fareham Lake about 6½ cables N of Sultan Landing; Pewit Island lies on the mudflat between Spider Lake and Fareham Lake.

Frater Lake, which dries, is a narrow creek opening from the W side of Fareham Lake about 4 cables above the entrance to Spider Lake; there is a wharf on its N bank.

3 Bedenham Pier (50°50′·1N 1°09′·0W), from which lights are exhibited, lies about 4 cables above Frater Lake, another pier from which lights are exhibited with a depth of 1·0 m alongside, is situated at Foxbury Point, at the E end of Heavy Reach, about 4 cables WNW of Bedenham Pier. There are numerous piles and pontoons for small craft on both sides of Fareham Lake to the N of Bedenham Pier.

4 **Depths.** The channel in Fareham Lake has depths of from 10 m at its entrance to 6 m off the entrance to Bombketch Lake, thence the width decreases and there is a maintained depth of 5 m in the fairway as far as Bedenham Pier. Above this pier the channel shoals considerably, and about 2 cables below Fareham it dries out completely.

5 **Berth.** Bedenham Pier and its approach channel has a maintained depth of 5·0 m. Mariners are prohibited from approaching within 12 m of the pier without authority.

Port services

Charts 2629, 2625
Repairs
7.182

1 **Portsmouth Naval Base — dry docks.** There are several dry docks, the two largest "C" and "D" Locks each have an extreme length of 259 m and extreme breadth of 33·5 m.

Commercial facilities. Major deck and engine repairs to commercial vessels can be carried out.

Mechanical lift dock at Porchester: extreme length 56 m; extreme breadth 14 m; lifting capacity 877 tonnes.

Other facilities
7.183

1 **Customs office** at Portsmouth.

Compass adjustment. Nelson's Monument (50°51′·6N 1°07′·8W), a conspicuous obelisk about 5 miles N of Gilkicker Point, may be used as a distant object for ascertaining the error of the compass; the true bearings of this object from different parts of the anchorage at Spithead, and in the harbour, are given on the charts.

2 **Medical:** there are hospitals in the city.

Ship sanitation control and ship sanitation control exemption certificates are issued at Portsmouth.

Supplies
7.184

1 **Fuel:** available by road tanker or by bunker barge from Southampton.

Fresh water: available.

Provisions: available.

Harbour regulations
7.185

Water skiing and, jet-skiing. Water skiing is prohibited inside Portsmouth Harbour north of Fort Blockhouse and half a nautical mile from any shore within the Dockyard Port (E Solent) area, except in designated areas (7.150). Jet-skiing is only allowed in designated areas (7.150). The designated areas are charted.

1 **Underwater swimming and diving.** For details see Appendix I.

Parascending and similar activities. For details see Appendix I.

Side channels – Portsmouth Harbour and approaches

Chart 2625
Boat channel
7.186

1 For details of a boat channel for entering Portsmouth Harbour, see 7.149.

Passages over Spit Sand
7.187

1 **General information.** Spit Sand (50°46′·5N 1°06′·5W) (7.164) may be crossed by mariners in small craft of suitable draught.

7.188

1 **Swashway — leading marks:**

Front mark. Naval War Memorial (50°46′·9N 1°05′·7W).

Rear mark. SE edge of Conspicuous Building (2 cables NE of the front mark).

Swashway Leading Marks bearing 049½° (7.188)

(Original dated 1996)

(Photograph - HMSML Gleaner)

The alignment (049½°) of these marks leads through Swashway in a least depth of 2·3 m passing between Spit Bank and Hamilton Bank lying 6 cables SW and 5 cables W, respectively, of the front mark, into the main approach channel for Portsmouth.

2 **Caution.** Mariners attention is drawn to the high level of vessel traffic which may be encountered when navigating in the vicinity of Swashway, including

hovercraft and high-speed ferries enroute to and from Isle of Wight. Mariners in yachts and slow-moving craft are advised to maintain a careful all-round lookout, particularly before making an alteration of course.

3 **Tidal streams.** On the leading line the stream is more or less rotary anti-clockwise, but the direction and rate are irregular, for details see information on the chart.

4 **Inner Swashway** between Fort Blockhouse and the N tip of a drying patch about 1¾ cables S, has a least depth of 0·3 m. Mariners in craft of 20 m or over in length must not use Inner Swashway.

Passages north of Horse Sand Fort
7.189

1 **General information.** Horse Sand Fort (50°45′N 1°04′W) (7.94) is connected with the shore N at the former Lumps Fort site by a submerged barrier of concrete blocks, partially uncovered at LW. The barrier is irregular in size and shape and should not be approached within 30 m on either side and is marked by yellow beacons with yellow topmarks.

2 **Passages.** There are two passages through the submerged barrier. Main Passage, situated 1 mile N of Horse Sand Fort, is 55 m wide and is marked on its N side by a beacon (starboard hand) and on its S side by a light (dolphin) (port hand). A boat passage, 12 m wide with a depth of 0·6 m in it, lies 1 cable from the shore at the N end of the barrier. The N side of the passage is marked by a beacon (starboard hand) and the S side by a buoy (port hand).

3 **Tidal streams.** In Main Passage, 1 mile N of Horse Sand Fort, the E-going stream slackens rapidly 3 hours after it begins, and then increases again to its maximum rate about 2 hours later.

Chart 2629
Haslar Lake
7.190

1 Haslar Jetty (50°47′·3N 1°07′·1W), on the W side Haslar Lake (7.171), is situated close W of No 2 Jetty, and serves Royal Hospital Haslar. HMS *Alliance*, part of the submarine museum, is permanently moored on the W side of Haslar Jetty; the jetty is usable at all states of the tide. Haslar Bridge, with a vertical clearance of 2·2 m, connects Haslar with Gosport.

Haslar Lake from S (7.190)
(Original dated 2001)

(Photograph - DLO Photo Unit, Bath)

2 Joint Services Sailing Centre, a marina for service personnel, with depths of 2 to 3 m, is situated between Haslar Jetty and Haslar Bridge.

SPITHEAD TO SOUTHAMPTON
General information

Chart 2036, 2038
Route
7.191

1 From N of Sturbridge Shoal (50°45′N 1°08′W), at Spithead, the route leads generally W through the E Solent, about 6 miles, to S of Bramble Bank (50°47′N 1°17′W) at the entrance to Thorn Channel.

Description
7.192

1 The E part of The Solent, which forms the E approach to Southampton and the W approach to Spithead and Portsmouth, is well lighted and buoyed and can be used by mariners in all classes of vessels of suitable draught by day and night. It lies between the N coast of Isle of Wight and the mainland coast, E of Southampton Water.

2 **Fairways.** The principal fairway lies S of Ryde Middle (50°46′N 1°14′W), a bank of mud, gravel, sand and shells, which lies with its E extremity approximately 2½ miles W of Gilkicker Point, and N of Mother Bank and Peel Bank which front the N coast of Isle of Wight.

There is an equally good fairway, with a depth of about 13 m, N of Ryde Middle, between it and the coastal bank fronting the mainland coast.

Topography
7.193

1 **Isle of Wight.** Between Ryde (50°44′N 1°09′W) and Old Castle Point, 5 miles WNW, the coast is fronted by a drying bank extending up to 3 cables offshore, on which there are occasional patches of rock. Mother Bank and Peel Bank extend N from bank.

2 **Mainland coast.** Stokes Bay, a slight indentation on the coast, lies between Gilkicker Point (50°46′N 1°08′W) and Browndown Point, 1¾ mile WNW; foul ground exists in this bay. Lee-on-Solent (50°48′N 1°12′W), a seaside town, fronts the coast NW of Lee Point. Hillhead (50°49′N 1°14′W) a seaside town lies at the mouth of River Meon, near which there is a coastal nature reserve. Hillhead Harbour, a small boat harbour which dries, lies at the mouth of the river.

Hazards
7.194

1 **Large vessels navigating in the E Solent,** see 7.80.
Large vessels turning, see 7.244.
High speed craft, see 7.81.
Moving Prohibited Zone, see 7.20.
Yacht racing marks, see 7.29.

Pilotage
7.195

1 For details of pilotage, see 7.10.

Buoyage
7.196

1 For details of the general direction of buoyage in The Solent, see 7.28.

Traffic regulations
7.197

1 **Vessel Traffic Service,** see 7.6.
Accident procedures, see 7.26.
Special regulations. For details of special regulations concerning vessels constrained by their draught and vessels restricted in their ability to manoeuvre, see 7.19.

Calshot Castle and Radar Tower from NE (7.200)
(Original dated 2004)

(Photograph - H.M.S. Gleaner)

Tankers. For details of regulations applying to tankers, see 7.22.

Speed off Cowes, see 7.24.

Rescue
7.198

1   **Coastguard Rescue Teams** are situated at:
> Ryde (50°44′N 1°09′W).
> Newport (50°42′N 1°17′W).
> For details see 1.100.

Tidal streams
7.199

1   In the E part of The Solent, between Ryde (50°44′N 1°09′W) and Egypt Point, 6 miles WNW, the streams run generally in the direction of the channel, both N and S of Ryde Middle. On average they begin in the centre of this area as follows:

Interval from HW Portsmouth (Dover)	Direction
+0420 (+0445)	ESE
–0130 (–0105)	WNW

The maximum E-going spring and neap rates are 2 kn and 1 kn and the maximum WNW-going rates are 2½ kn and 1¼ kn, respectively.

2   The time at which the stream begins becomes progressively later from E to W; at the E end about 20 minutes should be subtracted, and at the W end about 20 minutes should be added to these times.

The W-going stream is everywhere stronger than the E-going; the rates off Gilkicker Point are about ¼ kn weaker than those given above; off Cowes they are about 1 kn stronger; off Egypt Point the rates are about the same as those given above.

3   Tidal streams over the banks which fringe the coast between Ryde and Old Castle Point are variable. Near HW, or during the first half of the W-going stream, the stream runs nearly the same as in the channel N of Peel Bank, though its rate is less. Near LW, or towards the end of the W-going stream and during the first part of the E-going stream, the streams are irregular and uncertain, with many eddies.

Directions
(continued from 7.102)

Landmarks
7.200

1   No Man's Land Fort (50°44′·4N 1°05′·7W) (7.94).
   Horse Sand Fort (50°45′·0N 1°04′·3W) (7.94).
   Spinnaker Tower (50°47′·7N 1°06′·5W) (7.169).
   Alverstoke Church (square tower and flagstaff) (50°47′·1N 1°08′·9W) on the mainland coast.
2   Quarr Abbey (turret) (50°43′·9N 1°12′·2W) on Isle of Wight.
   Osborne House (tower and flagstaff) (50°45′·1N 1°16′·2W) on Isle of Wight.
   Chimney (50°49′·0N 1°19′·7W) (7.250).
   Calshot Castle (50°49′·2N 1°18′·5W) (7.250).

Other aids to navigation
7.201

1   **Racon:** W Bramble Light Buoy (50°47′·2N 1°18′·6W), for details see *Admiralty List of Radio Signals Volume 2.*

South of Ryde Middle
7.202

1   From Spithead the route leads initially W passing (with positions given from Wootton Point (50°44′N 1°13′W)):
> N of Mother Bank Spit (2 miles ENE); thence:
> Between Mother Bank Light Buoy (port hand) (1½ miles NE), which marks the N edge of Mother Bank (7.192), and SE Ryde Middle Light Buoy (S cardinal) (1¾ miles NNE) marking the SE edge of Ryde Middle (7.192); thence:
2 > Between Peel Bank Light Buoy (port hand) (1¼ miles NNW) marking the N edge of Peel Bank (7.192), noting an obstruction drying 1·4 m (reported 1986) (1¼ miles N), and S Ryde Middle Light Buoy (starboard hand) (2 miles NNW).
3   When Osborne House (2¼ miles WNW) (7.200) bears 235° the route then leads WNW passing:
> Between Norris Light Buoy (port hand) (2½ miles NW) and W Ryde Middle Light Buoy (W cardinal) (3 miles NW); thence:

SE Ryde Middle Light-buoy (S. Cardinal)
Egypt Point just open of Old Castle Point-bearing 272° (7.202)
(Original dated 2004)

(Photograph - Drew Given, MV Doulos)

4 NNE, then N, of Prince Consort Light Buoy (N cardinal) (50°46'·4N 1°17'·5W), distant about 2 cables, moored off the NE end of Prince Consort Shoal (7.223); and:
S of South Bramble Light Buoy (starboard hand) which marks the S side of Bramble Bank (50°47'N 1°17'W) (7.252).

5 **Clearing bearing:**
The line of bearing 272° of Egypt Point (50°46'N 1°19'W) just open of Old Castle Point, 1½ miles E, clears S of Ryde Middle.

North of Ryde Middle

7.203

1 From Spithead, Horse Sand Fort Light (50°45'N 1°04'W), astern, between the bearings 105° to 107°, leads in the fairway passing (with positions given from Browndown Point (50°47'N 1°11'W)):
NNE of Mother Bank Spit (2 miles SSE); and:
SSW of an obstruction (5·3 m) (1 mile SE); thence:

2 SSW of Browndown Light Buoy (starboard hand) (7 cables S) which marks the seaward end of a sewer outfall; sewage is discharged on the falling tidal stream when close approach is not recommended. Thence:

3 NNE of NE Ryde Middle Light Buoy (port hand) (1¼ miles SSW) marking the NE side of Ryde Middle (7.192).
The line of bearing 096°, astern, of Spit Sand Fort (50°46'·2N 1°05'·9W) (7.162) and open its own breadth S of Fort Gilkicker, 1½ miles W, or its light at night, leads in the fairway passing:

4 S of East Bramble Light Buoy (E cardinal) (1¾ miles W) noting a depth of 11·9 m 4¼ cables SSW of the buoy; thence:
N of N Ryde Middle Light Buoy (port hand) (2¼ miles WSW)
The line of bearing 085°, astern, of Haslar Water Tower (2¼ miles E) then leads in the fairway passing:

N of W Ryde Middle Light Buoy (W cardinal) (50°46'·5N 1°15'·7W), distant 2 cables; thence:

5 N of Prince Consort Light Buoy (N cardinal) (50°46'·4N 1°17'·5W), distant about 2 cables; and:
S of South Bramble Light Buoy (starboard hand) which marks the S side of Bramble Bank (50°47'N 1°17'W) (7.252).

Useful marks

7.204

1 No Man's Land Fort Light (50°44'·4N 1°05'·7W) (7.94).
Horse Sand Fort Light (50°45'·0N 1°04'·4W) (7.94).
Bramble Beacon (special) (tide gauge) (50°47'·4N 1°17'·1W) standing about 2 cables SE of the shoalest part of Bramble Bank.
(Directions for Southampton continue at 7.250. Directions for the W Solent are given at 7.45)

Side channel

North Channel

7.205

1 **General information.** North Channel leads from Spithead across the coastal bank NE of Bramble Bank (50°47'N 1°17'W) (7.252) into Southampton Water.
Depths. There are least depths of 3·4 m in the channel.
Hazards. There is a landing stage and a hovercraft slipway at Lee-on-Solent (50°48'N 1°12'W); the approach to the latter is marked by buoys. For information concerning Hovercraft characteristics, see *The Mariner's Handbook.*

2 A water-ski area and a jet-ski area, buoyed and shown on the chart, are situated about 1½ miles and 1 mile NW, respectively, of Lee Point (50°47'·5N 1°11'·5W).
Fishing gear marks may be encountered to the N of North Channel, for details see 7.30.
Tidal streams, see information on the chart.

7.206

1 **Directions.** From a position S of Browndown Point (50°47'N 1°11'W) the line of bearing 299° of the S end of

Ryde Leisure Harbour

Ryde Pier from ENE (7.210)

(Original dated 1996)

(Photograph – Patrick Eden)

the activities centre (large white building) close S of Calshot Castle (50°49′N 1°18′W) leads in the fairway passing (with positions given from Calshot Castle):

NNE of E Bramble Light Buoy (E cardinal) (50°47′·2N 1°13′·6W), distant about 2 cables; thence:

2   NNE of Hill Head Light Buoy (port hand) (2 miles SE), distant 1 cable; thence:

NNE of Calshot Light Buoy (N cardinal) (1¼ miles SE) into Calshot Reach (7.252).

Anchorages

Spithead
7.207

1   Anchorage is available at Spithead (50°45′N 1°07′W) but mariners in merchant vessels may only anchor in the Man of War Anchorage with the consent of QHM Portsmouth. For details, see 7.145.

North of Ryde Middle
7.208

1   **General information.** Lettered anchor berths, for use by large merchant vessels, are situated N and E of Ryde Middle (50°46′·3N 2°14′·0W). Smaller vessels should anchor to the W of A Anchorage. Permission to anchor should be obtained from QHM Portsmouth or Southampton VTS. Mariners in other vessels anchoring in Stokes Bay should do so W of the meridian of the lettered anchor berths. Mariners are recommended to buoy their anchors.

Unexploded mortar bombs may lie on the seabed up to 1 mile WSW of Browndown Point.

Cowes Roads.
7.209

1   For anchorage details in Cowes Roads, see 7.216.

Ryde

General information
7.210

1   **Position and function.** Ryde (50°44′N 1°09′W) is a coastal town and terminus of the passenger ferry from Portsmouth. Ryde Pier, with a railway on it, extends 4 cables N from the town. A hovercraft terminal is situated close E of the root of the pier. Information concerning hovercraft characteristics and lights is given in *The Mariner's Handbook.*

Rescue, see 7.198.

Tidal streams. The streams run regularly, and fairly strongly, through the channel between Ryde Pier and Inner Spit, about 3 cables N, but there are eddies off the pier.

2   The streams over Ryde Sand (7.211) and the shoals between the Sand and Nettlestone Point (50°43′N 1°07′W) and No Man's Land Fort, are uncertain and vary with the height of the tide. Near HW springs, when Ryde Sand is well covered, the streams run almost uninterruptedly NW from Saint Helen's Road, and W, between Nettlestone Point and the fort, and across Ryde Sand. Near LW springs, however, when the whole area of Ryde Sand is dry, the E-going stream runs along the N side of the sand, E towards the fort, and SE between the fort and Nettlestone Point; at this time there are many eddies between the sand, Nettlestone Point and No Man's Land Fort. As the tide rises the stream runs more and more across the sand. At neaps conditions are different, for there is never enough water for the stream to run uninterruptedly across Ryde Sand, and the sand is not entirely dry at LW.

Directions
7.211

1   **Landmarks:**

Holy Trinity Church (spire) (50°43′·7N 1°09′·4W).

All Saints Church (spire) (50°43′·6N 1°09′·9W).

2   Mariners approaching or leaving Ryde Pier must keep within the channels of approach indicated on the chart. The N edge of Ryde Sand, which extends approximately 1 mile

offshore between Nettlestone Point and Ryde Pier, is steep-to and must be approached with caution.

3 **Clearing bearing:**

The line of bearing 252° of Quarr Abbey (50°43'·8N 1°12'·2W) (7.200) open N of the head of Ryde Pier, 1¾ miles ENE, clears NNW of Ryde Sand.

Useful marks:

Several lights are exhibited from Ryde Pierhead (50°44'·4N 1°09'·6W); in fog a special light is exhibited from the N corner.

4 Ryde Sands Light Beacon (port hand) (50°44'·5N 1°07'·2W) marking NE edge of Ryde Sand.

Anchorage and berth
7.212

1 **Anchorage.** Ryde Roads lie parallel to the coast between Inner Spit, the E extension of Mother Bank (7.192), and Ryde Pierhead. The roads are about 1½ miles long but only about 1 cables wide, with depths of 5 to 9 m.

2 **Prohibited anchorage.** Anchorage is prohibited in the approach channels to Ryde Pier as shown on the chart.

Anchoring and fishing is also prohibited in the approaches to Ryde Pier in the mine laying practice area (7.146) SE of Sturbridge Shoal (50°45'N 1°08'W) and in the hovercraft manoeuvring area E of Ryde Pier, as indicated on the chart.

3 **Outfall** extends about 1¾ miles NNW from Ryde Rowing Club (50°43'·7N 1°08'·6W). Diffusers lie in a depth of 18·9 m at the head of the outfall.

Berth. Ryde Pierhead has a depth of 2·7 to 3·7 m at its head; a short distance inshore the sands dry.

Wootton Creek

Charts 2022 plan of Wootton Creek, 2036
General information
7.213

1 **Description.** Wootton Creek (50°44'N 1°13'W) on Isle of Wight, the terminal of the vehicle ferries which run by day and night to and from Portsmouth, is principally a yachting centre which is entered from The Solent close E of Wootton Point.

Harbour Authority: Wightlink, Wightlink House, 70 Broad Street, Portsmouth PO1 2LB.

2 **Controlling depth.** The dredged approach channel has a maintained depth of 3·0 m as far as the Car Ferry Terminal and then depths of less than 2 m as far as Fishbourne.

Water-skiing area inshore of Peel Bank (7.192), buoyed and indicated on the chart, is situated about 7½ cables NNW of Wootton Point. Two dangerous wrecks, the positions of which are best seen from the chart, lie inside the area.

3 **Harbour.** The entrance to the dredged channel lies 5 cables NE of Wootton Point and is marked on its NW side by Wootton Light Beacon (N cardinal) (50°44'·5N 1°12'·1W). The channel is then marked on its SE and NW sides by light beacons (port and starboard hand). Fishbourne lies on the S side of the entrance to Wootton Creek. There is a Car Ferry Terminal with a jetty and linkspan at Fishbourne. Between Fishbourne and Wootton Bridge, 5½ cables SW, the channel dries 2·1 m.

4 **Caution.** Mariners are warned that ferries may operate outside the confines of the approach channel and may conduct starboard to starboard passing manoeuvres within the channel.

5 **Speed limit.** There is a speed limit of 5 kn within Wootton Creek.

Static fishing. The use of static fishing equipment is prohibited within Wootton Creek.

Sector light is exhibited near the Car Ferry Terminal. The white sector (224¼°–225¾°) of this light indicates the dredged channel.

Cowes and Newport

Charts 2793 plan of Cowes Harbour and River Medina, 2036, 2038
General information
7.214

1 **Position.** Cowes (50°46'N 1°18'W), at the mouth of River Medina, stands on both sides of the entrance to the river and is divided into two parts, East Cowes and West Cowes.

2 **Function.** Cowes is the principal port in Isle of Wight; it is a considerable yachting centre as well as a commercial port. It is the headquarters of the Royal Yacht Squadron, as well as several other yacht clubs of importance.There are several marinas, boatyards and four commercial wharfs.

3 **Port limits.** The seaward limits of the harbour are shown on the chart; they are bounded approximately by lines joining Egypt Point (50°46'N 1°19'W), Prince Consort Light Buoy, and a position about 2 cables NNE of Old Castle Point. The S limit is at Folly Point (50°44'N 1°17'W).

4 **Approach and entry.** The harbour is approached from the E or W Solent and entered through the fairway of River Medina.

Traffic. In 2006 the port was used by 58 vessels, excluding ferries, totalling 124 952 dwt.

5 **Port Authority:** Cowes Harbour Commissioners, Harbour Office, Town Quay, Cowes, Isle of Wight, PO31 7AS.

Website: www.cowes.co.uk
Email: chc@cowes.co.uk

Limiting conditions
7.215

1 **Controlling depth.** General depths in the fairway are between 1·5 and 5 m, with a least charted depth of 1·5 m m in position 50°45'·3N 1°17'·6W.

Deepest and longest berths. The deepest commercial berth is Kingston Quay in East Cowes, and the longest, Medina Wharf in West Cowes (7.224).

Tidal levels. Mean spring range about 3·4 m; mean neap range about 1·7 m. For further information see *Admiralty Tide Tables.*

2 **Maximum size of vessel.** The largest vessel which can normally be accommodated at Cowes is 100 m LOA, 13·5 m beam and a draught of 5·4 m at springs and of 4·7 m at neaps. Vessels of greater length/beam will be considered on an individual basis after consultation with the Harbour Master.

River Medina is navigable to Newport by vessels of 60 m length with a maximum draught of 2·9 m at MHWS, and of 2·1 m at MHWN.

Arrival information
7.216

1 **Port radio** station operates from the Harbour Office during office hours.

Notice of ETA required. Send ETA at the pilot boarding point to Harbour Office or Agents at least 12 hours in advance.

2   **VHF.** All commercial vessels, and private or recreational vessels of 30 m LOA and above, operating within the jurisdiction of the Harbour Authority should maintain a continuous watch on VHF. In addition all such vessels must transmit a CQ call on VHF stating identification and giving notice of entry or departure from the harbour. This call is supplementary to that required for the chain ferry. For details see *Admiralty List of Radio Signals Volume 6(1)*.

3   **Outer anchorage — Cowes Roads.** Cowes Roads off the entrance to River Medina, is bounded on its NW side by Prince Consort Shoal (7.223) and affords an anchorage in depths of 9 to 17 m; mariners should anchor SE of Prince Consort Light Buoy (50°46'·4N 1°17'·5W). Tidal streams run strongly in the outer part of the roads but less strongly inshore, for details see information on the chart.

4   **Mooring groundwork.** Several buoys (special, seasonal) are moored during the winter season SE of the permanent Trinity House mooring light buoy (50°46'·3N 1°17'·7W) and mark the E limits of the mooring ground chains in this vicinity. A second, seasonal, Trinity House unlit mooring buoy is normally laid about 2 cables E of the permanent mooring buoy between April and September.

   Prohibited anchorages. Anchoring is prohibited within the fairway and in the area of small craft moorings to the E of the fairway, as shown on the chart.

5   An outfall extends 3½ cables N from the coast close W of Old Castle Point; diffusers lie in a depth of 21 m at the head of the outfall. Anchoring is prohibited in an area, shown on the chart, surrounding the diffusers.

6   Anchoring is prohibited inside the submarine cable area in the vicinity of the chain ferry (50°45'·5N 1°17'·4W), and in the submarine power cable area in the vicinity of the power station, about 7 cables S, as shown on the chart.

   Marker buoy. Should it be necessary to let go an anchor in the fairway or roads then a marker buoy is to be attached to indicate its position.

7.217

1   **Pilotage and tugs — area.** Cowes Harbour Compulsory Pilotage Area is bounded on its N side by the port limits, and includes River Medina and Newport Harbour.

   Pilotage is compulsory within the Cowes Pilotage Area for the following vessels:

      Passenger ferries and passenger vessels of 20 m LOA and above whilst carrying more than 12 passengers.

2   All vessels of 48 m LOA and above.
      Sub-standard commercial vessels as initially determined by Master's or pilot's report or Department for Transport survey and those vessels which lack the proper amended charts and equipment.
      For vessels carrying dangerous and polluting goods. See see *Admiralty List of Radio Signals Volume 6(1)* and 1.68 to 1.76.

3   All vessels engaged in towing where the overall length from bow of towing vessel to stern of towed vessel is 48 m or more.
      All vessels whose beam or aggregate beam exceeds 15 m.
   The following categories of vessels are exempt from compulsory pilotage:

4   MOD owned or operated vessels and HM vessels. Naval vessels of foreign and Commonwealth countries.

      Vessels exempted by law.
   The following arrangements have been agreed with the Southampton Competent Harbour Authority (CHA):

5   Vessels of 61 m or more LOA on passage to or from Cowes Harbour or Cowes Harbour anchorage are subject to compulsory pilotage within the W limit and E inner limit of Southampton Pilotage Area (7.10).

6   On application, Cowes Pilotage Authority will provide an Authorized Cowes Pilot to conduct the vessel to Cowes from the W limit or the E inner limit, or outer limit, of the Southampton CHA Area, providing that the vessel is not on route to other locations in the Southampton CHA area, N of the line 50°46'·9N passing through South Bramble Light Buoy.

7   **Boarding places:**
      Vessels of 61 m LOA and above, using the W approach, 7 cables W of Gurnard Ledge Light-buoy (50°45'·5N 1°20'·6W).
      Vessels over 61 m LOA using the E approach, 7½ cables NW of North Sturbridge Light Buoy (50°45'·3N 1°08'·2W).

8   Vessels over 61 m LOA using the E approach, and carrying dangerous and polluting cargoes, in the boarding area in the vicinity of Saint Helen's Light Buoy (port hand). Vessels may also embark a pilot on a voluntary basis in the vicinity of New Grounds Light Buoy (E cardinal) (50°41'·8N 0°58'·5W).
      Vessels of less than 61 m LOA in the vicinity of Prince Consort Light Buoy (50°46'·4N 1°17'·5W). This position is rarely used and is not shown on the chart.

   For further details, see *Admiralty List of Radio Signals Volum 6(1)*.

   Tugs. A tug and tow-boat launches are available.

7.218

1   **Traffic regulations.** The use of a whistle or siren in the harbour or roads, except for the legitimate purposes of navigation, is prohibited.

   For details of dangerous substances, see 7.21.

   Within the harbour there is a maximum speed limit of 6 kn over the ground.

2   Power driven vessels are required to navigate the harbour with caution, and at slow speed which will not endanger or cause damage to other vessels, boats or property. Damage to vessels, navigational marks, harbour structures or shore facilities are to be reported immediately to the Harbour Master, preferably by VHF.

   Masters of vessels leaving a marina or mooring within the harbour are required to give way to vessels navigating within the fairway of the harbour or roads.

Harbour
7.219

1   **General layout.** Shrape Breakwater, from the head of which a light (50°45'·9N 1°17'·5W) is exhibited, extends about 1¾ cables NW over The Shrape Mud from East Cowes Point, the E entrance point to the river. A bank with depths of less than 1 m, bordering the E side of the channel, extends from The Shrape Mud to within ¾ cable of the bank of the river at West Cowes.

   The channel into the harbour lies near the West Cowes bank of the river. The fairway is shown on the chart and the channel into the harbour is marked by light buoys.

Ferry Terminal

Cowes Yacht Haven

Cowes Harbour from N (7.219)

(Original dated 2001)

(Photograph - Air Images)

2   There is a Ferry Terminal at East Cowes Ferry Pontoon and there are numerous wharves, including, amongst others, Venture Quays, Trinity Wharf, Medina Wharf, Kingston Quay North, Kingston Quay South, and National Power Jetty, pontoons and slipways, on both sides of the river as far as Folly Point (50°44′·0N 1°16′·8W), some marked by lights. Numerous pile and pontoon moorings lie on each side of the fairway and there are buoy moorings for visiting yachts, the positions of which can be seen from the chart. Unlit small craft day class moorings lie N and NE of the Shrape Breakwater.

7.220

1   **Hazards — High speed craft.** All mariners entering and leaving Cowes Harbour by the fairway and fairway approaches must keep a good lookout for high speed craft on regular services between Cowes and Southampton. These vessels may enter and leave the fairway at speeds in excess of 6 kn; such vessels will exhibit a quick flashing yellow light.

2   **Chain ferry.** A floating bridge chain ferry crosses the river close S of Trinity Wharf (50°45′·5N 1°17′·4W). The ferry chains are suspended above the bottom in a catenary and depths over them vary with the state of the tide and the position of the ferry; at times the chains may rise to the surface. The maximum depth over the chains exists in the middle of the fairway when the ferry is berthed. At such times the least navigable depth of water is approximately 1·7 m below chart datum and mariners are advised this is the safest time to pass over the chains. In addition, strong tidal flows in excess of 3 kn exist in this area and mariners are advised to navigate with extreme caution in the vicinity. The following regulations are in force. The ferry shall:

3   Give way to all traffic.

        Show by day and by night, when underway, a fixed amber light visible all round the horizon.

        In fog, or low visibility, sound two prolonged blasts at intervals of 1 minute.

All commercial vessels, and private or recreational vessels of 30 m LOA and above, are required to advise the chain ferry of their intention to pass through the ferry area; the ferry will acknowledge the call. For details see *Admiralty List of Radio Signals Volume 6(1)*.

4   **Submarine pipelines.** Submarine gas pipelines cross the river about 1 mile S of chain ferry and are marked by notice-boards on each side of the river. For details of caution, see 1.64.

    Yacht racing marks, see 7.29.

7.221

1   **Tidal streams** in River Medina begin as follows:

Interval from HW Portsmouth (Dover)	Directions
+0530 (+0555)	Flood
+0015 (+0040)	Ebb

2   Both streams are strong, especially the ebb. Strong tidal streams are likely to be experienced in the entrance to Cowes Harbour with rates of at least 3 kn during outgoing spring tides, about 1½ hours after HW Cowes.

    In the vicinity of No 1 Light Buoy a W going stream may be experienced during the E going flood tide. It should be noted that the tidal flow may change direction within a relatively short distance.

3   In the vicinity of the chain ferry (7.220) the out-going stream is particularly strong on the E side of the river, where it may exceed 3 kn.

Directions for entering harbour

7.222

1   **Landmarks:**

    Osborne Court (white block of flats) (50°45′·9N 1°18′·0W) at the W entrance point of the river.

    Conspicuous crane (50°45′·4N 1°17′·6W) at West Cowes about 6 cables within the entrance to the river.

Norris Castle Turret

Isle of Wight – Old Castle Point from ESE (7.223)

(Original dated 2004)

(Photograph - H.M.S. Gleaner)

Cowes Power Station (two conspicuous chimneys) (50°44'·8N 1°17'·2W) on the E bank of the river.

7.223

1 Mariners entering the harbour between 1st March and 30th November annually, must keep within the fairway as shown on the chart.

From a position 4 cables N of Osborne Court (7.222) the fairway leads SSE, passing (with positions from Osborne Court):

2 WSW of Prince Consort Light Buoy (N cardinal) (6 cables NE); thence:

WSW of Prince Consort Shoal (3½ cables NNE) which is subject to change in extent, depth and position. Trinity House lighted mooring buoy is moored off the NE end of the shoal. Thence:

3 Between No 1 Light Buoy (starboard hand) (1½ cables N) and No 2 Light Buoy (port hand) (1½ cables NNE) which mark the W and E sides, respectively, of the fairway at the entrance to the river, noting the bank with depths of less than 2 m (7.215) which extends into the fairway about ¼ cable NE of No 1 Light Buoy.

4 The track then continues generally SSE in the middle of the fairway to the required berth.

Outside the above period, mariners approaching from E should pass at least 2½ cables N of Old Castle Point (50°46'·0N 1°16'·5W), keeping in depths of more than 11 m passing:

5 N of Trinity House lighted mooring buoy (4 cables NNE); thence:

To join the fairway approach N of No 2 Light Buoy (port hand) (1½ cables NNE).

Useful marks:

Royal Yacht Squadron club house (50°46'N 1°18'W) at the W entrance point of the river.

6 Lights (columns) on the N and S sides of Jubilee Pontoon (50°45'·8N 1°17'·8W). In fog a flashing light is exhibited on the N side.

Lights (50°45'·6N 1°17'·5W) off the outer end of East Cowes Ferry Pontoon. Lights (metal post) are exhibited off the N end of Trinity Wharf which lies close S.

Berths

7.224

1 **Alongside berths:**

Trinity Landing (50°46'·0N 1°17'·9W), dredged depth 3·0 m (2006) on the NE side and between 1·8 m and 2·0 m (2006) on the SW side. The landing is suitable for vessels, including large sailing vessels of up to 600 tonnes displacement.

Venture Quays (50°45'·6N 1°17'·5W), with berths for leisure craft; charted depths between 2·7 and 5·6 m.

East Cowes Ferry Pontoon (50°45'·6N 1°17'·5W) has a depth of 3·8 m alongside.

2 Jubilee Pontoon (50°45'·8N 1°17'·8W) has depths of between 1·5 and 7·0 m alongside.

Trinity Wharf (50°45'·5N 1°17'·4W), close S of East Cowes Ferry Pontoon, has a least charted depth of 3·6 m alongside; the wharf is not for commercial use.

3 Medina Wharf (50°44'·9N 1°17'·6W), on the W side of the river, is used for bulk cargoes and has a maintained depth of 1·4 m. The wharf is 160 m in length and can accommodate vessels up to 2500 tonnes and 100 m LOA.

Kingston Quay North used for bulk oils, and Kingston Quay South (50°44'·8N 1°17'·3W), both on the E side of the river and both 60 m in length have a maintained depth of 1·4 m.

4 Numerous marinas, for which the chart is the best guide, on both sides of the River Medina, from the entrance in the vicinity of Osbourne Court to Newport.

Port services

7.225

1 **Repairs.** Hull and engine repairs for commercial vessels are available. There are building and repair facilities for every type of yacht at Cowes and numerous slipways.

Cowes Harbour from SE (7.224)
(Original dated 1998)

(Photograph – Patrick Eden)

Other facilities: medical facilities available.

Supplies: fuel available by road tanker at commercial berths; fresh water available at commercial berths; provisions and stores plentiful.

2   **Harbour regulations.** Water-skiing and aqua-planing are prohibited.

Exhibiting searchlights, floodlights and other bright lights, except in an emergency, in such a way as to interfere with safe navigation, is prohibited.

Vessels at anchor in the port are required to have a competent person on board at all times to maintain the anchor position, ensure that correct signals are displayed and, when so fitted, maintain listening watch on VHF radio.

3   Every boat or vessel fitted with or propelled by an internal combustion engine must have its exhaust adequately silenced so as to prevent a nuisance or annoyance arising therefrom.

No ballast, earth, ashes, stones or rubbish are on any account to be thrown or be allowed to fall into the harbour.

Chart 2793 plan of Folly Point to Newport
Newport
7.226

1   **General information.** Newport (50°42′N 1°17′W) is a port, a market town and the capital of the island. Formerly known as Medina it received its first charter in 1180; its buildings include Carisbrooke Castle, dated 1170, and the church of Thomas à Becket, dated 1857 and built on the site of an earlier church dated 1175. Pioneer Wharf, with Cement Mills Wharf close S, lie on the W side of the river, about 7 cables SSW of Folly Point (50°44′·0N 1°16′·8W); lights are exhibited from the S end of each wharf.

2   **Rescue,** see 7.198.

Port Authority: Isle of Wight Council, County Hall, High Street, Newport, Isle of Wight, PO30 1UD.

Depths in the river from Kingston Quay North (7.224) to South Folly Light Beacon (starboard hand), 1 mile SSE,

Newport from S (7.226)
(Original dated 1996)

(Photograph – Patrick Eden)

are from 3·2 m to 0·4 m; S of the light beacon the river dries.

3   **Maximum size of vessel,** see 7.215.

Vertical clearance. Power cable, with a safe overhead clearance of 33 m, spans the river midway between Cement Mills Wharf and Medina Valley Centre, about 3 cables SSW; lights (starboard hand) are exhibited from a pontoon pier at Medina Valley Centre.

4   **Leading lights.** The alignment (192¼°) of light beacons (white diamond on beacons) (50°42′·4N 1°17′·4W) at Newport indicate the fairway in the approaches to Newport.

Useful mark:

South Folly Light Beacon (starboard hand) (50°43′·8N 1°16′·9W).

5   **Berths.** There are two commercial berths at Newport, the longest Seaclose Quay No 2, has a length of 81 m.

PORT OF SOUTHAMPTON

General Information

Charts 2041, 2036, 2038

Position
7.227

1   Southampton Docks (50°54′N 1°24′W) lie at the head of Southampton Water at the confluence of River Itchen and River Test.

Function
7.228

1   Port of Southampton is a free port and is one of the principal ports of the United Kingdom. The docks system comprises 14 km of deep-water quays supported by a wide range of terminal facilities catering for ocean-going vessels, ferry passengers and vehicles, containerised, conventional and RoRo freight traffic.

2   Within the port there are numerous waterside industries including a very large oil refining complex and adjacent petrochemical installations.

Port limits
7.229

1   For details of port limits, see 7.4.

Approach and entry
7.230

1   The port is approached from W Solent or E Solent and entered through Thorn Channel (7.252).

It can also be entered from E Solent through North Channel (7.205), a side channel for light-draught vessels.

Traffic
7.231

1   In 2006 3429 vessels used the port of Southampton, with an additional 2496 vessels using the tanker terminals in Southampton Water.

Port Authority
7.232

1   Associated British Ports, Ocean Gate, Atlantic Way, Southampton SO14 3QN.

Website 1: www.abports.co.uk
Website 2: www.southamptonvts.co.uk
Email: hmsouthampton@abports.co.uk

Limiting conditions

Controlling depths
7.233

1   **Thorn Channel** (50°47′N 1°19′W) (7.252) is from 1¾ to 4 cables wide and is maintained by dredging at a depth of 12·6 m.

Southampton Water. From Calshot Reach (50°49′N 1°18′W) the channel through Southampton Water (7.253) to Southampton Docks is dredged to a maintained depth of 12·6 m, with a maximum width of about 3 cables, as far as Esso Marine Terminal (50°50′N 1°20′W); thence the channel has a width of about 1¼ cables.

2   **Southampton Docks.** The approach to all berths fronting River Test is dredged to a maintained depth of 12·6 m; the SW limit of the dredged area is indicated on the chart and marked by light buoys (port hand). The approach to the majority of berths in Eastern Docks fronting River Itchen is dredged to a depth of 9·1 m.

Deepest and longest berths
7.234

1   **Tankers:** Esso Marine Terminal at Fawley, No 5 Berth (7.256).

Passenger liners, ferries and others: Western Docks (7.260).

Containers vessels: Southampton Container Terminals (7.260).

Tidal levels
7.235

1   Mean spring range about 4·0 m; mean neap range about 1·9 m. For further information see *Admiralty Tide Tables*.

Maximum size of vessel handled
7.236

1   Vessels of up to 14·9 m draught can be accepted in Thorn Channel but those of this maximum draught are only permitted to enter during the HW period.

Arrival information

Vessel traffic service
7.237

1   For details of VTS and radar assistance, see 7.6 and 7.7.

Notice of ETA required
7.238

1   For details of notice of ETA required, see 7.12.

Anchorage
7.239

1   **Controlled anchorage** N of Hook Light Buoy (50°49′·5N 1°18′·3N. With prior permission from the Harbour Master, vessels of 91·4 m LOA or more, and small coastal tankers may use berths 1, 2 and 3; vessels of less than 91·4 m LOA and coastal vessels of all types, other than tankers, may use the anchorage area centred on 50°49′·8N 1°18′·2W.

2   Such vessels must anchor so as to be clear of vessels leaving or berthing at adjacent jetties, and also clear of the main channel.

No vessel in the anchorage shall be voluntarily immobilized without permission from the Harbour Master, who shall be informed immediately should a vessel be unable to move.
7.240

1   **Prohibited anchorage.** A submarine pipeline, indicated on the chart, crosses Southampton Water about 1½ cables NW of the Esso Marine Terminal, Fawley. Anchoring and fishing are prohibited in an area extending 1 cable either side of the pipeline. A Direction Light (50°51′·3N 1°19′·7W), situated at the N shore end of the pipeline, using the moiré pattern indicates the centreline (032¾°) of the prohibited area.

Pilotage and tugs
7.241

1   **Pilotage.** For details of pilotage information for Port of Southampton, see 7.10.

Tugs are available, some of which are sea-going. Fire-fighting and anti-pollutant tugs are permanently stationed at Esso Marine Terminal, Fawley.

Traffic regulations
7.242

1   **Special regulations.** For details of special regulations concerning vessels constrained by their draught and vessels restricted in their ability to manoeuvre, see 7.19.

    Precautionary area. For details of the entry restrictions to moving prohibited zones within the precautionary area in Thorn Channel, see 7.20.

2   **Tanker regulations.** For details of regulations applying to tankers, see 7.22.

    Dangerous and polluting goods. For details of dangerous substances and dangerous and polluting goods reports, see 7.21.

3   **Tanker Safety - Escort towage requirements.** Tankers of 60 000 dwt or more, arriving or departing from Southampton Water oil terminals in a loaded or part-loaded condition, are to be accompanied by an escort tug between a position S of Nab Tower and the berth. Under normal conditions a tow wire will be attached.

    Buoyage. For information regarding the general direction of buoyage in The Solent, see 7.28.

    Accident procedure contingency plans. For details of accident procedure contingency plans, see 7.26. and 1.73.

4   **Reporting of damage, incidents or potential risks.** Incidents and accidents involving the risk of, or actual damage to, vessels, movements or damage to navigational marks, damage to shore facilities, close quarter situations and other "near miss" incidents must be reported to VTS Southampton.

    Passing regulations. No two vessels, each having a length of 180 m (590 ft) or more, are to pass or overtake each other while within the precautionary area between Hook Light Buoy (50°50′N 1°18′W) and Prince Consort Light Buoy at the E end of the area.

    For regulations concerning vessels constrained by their draught and for gas tankers, see 7.19 and 7.22.

5   **Speed regulations.** Special care should be exercised within the port area and speed should be reduced consistent with safe navigation so as not to endanger lives of persons ashore and afloat, or cause damage to vessels alongside and at moorings, or to seawalls and other works. A speed limit of 6 kn applies to personal water craft being operated within 200 m of MHWS on either side of Southampton Water.

6   Attention is drawn to the fact that in the summer months there may be numerous holiday-makers on the beaches in the vicinity of Calshot. Mariners should therefore reduce speed in order not to endanger lives by excessive wash over Calshot Spit which might otherwise be caused by passing vessels.

7   Consistent with safe navigation, mariners in vessels drawing 6·0 m or over must not exceed a speed over the ground of 7 kn when approaching or passing Esso Marine Terminal at Fawley. Mariners in other vessels should not pass the terminal at excessive speed.

    There is a speed limit of 6 kn in the area N of a line joining Hythe Pier (50°52′·4N 1°23′·5W) and Weston Shelf Light Buoy, 3 cables NE.

8   **Speed off Cowes,** see 7.24.

    Marine farms. Oyster beds lie between Calshot Spit and Stansore Point in Stanswood Bay (50°48′N 1°20′W), see 7.244.

9   **Leisure activities and associated craft.** Water skiing, aquaplaning, power boat racing, paragliding, parakiting, parachute towing, sail boarding or any similar activity may only be carried out with written permission from the Harbour Master. Such activities must be carried out in accordance with the relevant Bye-laws. More detailed information is available from Southampton VTS.

Harbour

General layout
7.243

1   **Channels.** Thorn Channel (50°47′N 1°19′W) (7.252) leading into Calshot Reach forms the main approach to Southampton Water (7.253) which extends NW for about 5 miles to Southampton Docks.

    Oil terminals. Esso Marine Terminal (7.256) at Fawley lies on the SW side of Southampton Water, about 1½ miles NW of Calshot Castle, with BP Hamble Terminal (7.257) on the NE side of Southampton Water opposite Fawley.

2   **Southampton Docks** (7.254) lie at the head of Southampton Water at the confluence of River Itchen and River Test; there are three basins, two of which are used for ocean-going vessels, and extensive river quays. Eastern Docks lie at the junction of the rivers with a frontage to both. Western Docks, fronting River Test, are formed by a straight quay wall, at the W end of which lie the Vehicle Handling Terminal and Southampton Container Terminals. Town Quay and Royal Pier lie between Eastern and Western Docks. Both Eastern and Western Docks are used by ocean-going shipping whilst Town Quay caters principally for local ferry traffic.

3   Marchwood Sea Mounting Centre (7.263) and Marchwood Basin (7.264) lie on the SW side of the River Test, opposite Western Docks.

    Ministry of Defence mooring buoys are situated on the NE side of Southampton Water close NE of Netley Shoal (50°52′·3N 1°22′·5W). The shoal is marked by NW Netley Light Buoy (starboard hand) which also marks the NE side of the main channel.

4   **Redbridge and Eling Channels** are entered W of Southampton Container Terminals. Redbridge Channel leads to Redbridge Wharf, where the river is spanned by a railway bridge. Eling Channel which dries leads to Eling Wharf.

Hazards
7.244

1   **Large vessels.** Large and deeply laden tankers may be encountered turning into Thorn Channel from E about 5 cables NNW of Egypt Point (50°46′N 1°19′W); smaller vessels and pleasure craft should keep well clear of such vessels. For details of a moving prohibited zone around such vessels, see 7.20.

2   **High speed craft** operate throughout the Port of Southampton area particularly in areas immediately adjacent to the main channels as shown on the chart. See 1.7.

3   **Hovercraft testing area**, shown on the charts, is established in Southampton Water, off Netley (50°52′N 1°21′W), NE of the main channel. The area limits are marked by buoys and light beacons; Netley Light Buoy (starboard hand) marks the SW limit of the area.

    The hovercraft are at all times in communication with Southampton VTS Centre.

    Dredgers. For information regarding dredgers, see 7.32.

4   **Oyster fishery.** Numerous oyster dredgers may be encountered at certain times of the year working off Stanswood Bay (50°48′N 1°19′W), W of Thorn Channel.

    Fishing gear marks. For details of marks indicating submarine fishing gear, see 7.30.

    Yacht racing marks. For details of yacht racing marks, see 7.29.

VTS Centre   Grain Silos and   Itchen Bridge
                    berths 34,35 & 36
Confluence of Rivers Test and Itchen from SSE (7.243)
(Original dated 2004)

(Photograph - Drew Given, MV Doulos)

Measured distance

7.245

1 On the SW side of Southampton Water, below Hythe, there is a measured distance in two equal sections.

> South-east limit marks. Two beacons (yellow X topmark) (50°50′·9N 1°21′·4W).
>
> Middle marks. Two beacons (yellow X topmark) (50°51′·1N 1°22′·1W) in line with Lains Lake Beacon (yellow topmark, yellow X, 10 m in height), close SW.

2
> North-west limit marks. Two beacons (yellow X topmark) (50°51′·4N 1°22′·7W) in line with Bird Pile Beacon, 3 cables NE.
>
> Distance: each section 926·6 m.
>
> Running track: 132¾°.

Signals

7.246

1 **Traffic signals** are displayed from the N entrance point to Ocean Village Marina and control vessels entering and leaving the marina.

> **Vessels constrained by draught,** see 7.19.
>
> **Indication to small craft.** For details of flag signals for vessels outward-bound approaching W Bramble Light Buoy (50°47′·2N 1°18′·6W), see 7.31.

Natural conditions

7.247

1 **Thorn Channel.** In The Solent and approaches to Southampton Water the tidal streams run in general E and W directions, but are subject to considerable irregularities, both because of the shoals and because the flood and ebb streams to and from Southampton Water meet with and separate from the streams in The Solent. The flood (NW-going) stream in Southampton Water corresponds approximately with the E-going stream in The Solent, and vice-versa.

2 From a position about 1 mile SE of Calshot Castle, the streams run generally in the direction of the channel and change to the special Southampton Water streams soon after passing Calshot.

Approximate Interval from HW Portsmouth (HW Dover)	Remarks
+0500 (+0525)	E-going stream in The Solent begins and runs at first ENE in Thorn Channel where it meets the last of the ebb from Southampton Water and is deflected E across Bramble Bank and in North Channel.
+0600 (+0625)	Flood stream in Southampton Water begins; the NE-going stream from Thorn Channel turns NW into Southampton Water; the streams over Bramble Bank and in North Channel continue to run E.
−0400 (−0335)	Flood stream in Southampton Water continues, but the NE-going stream in Thorn Channel turns E off Calshot and joins the E-going stream in The Solent.
−0200 (−0135)	The last of the NE-going stream in the W part of The Solent continues to run NE in Thorn Channel and turns NW into Southampton Water; it runs E round the S part of Bramble Bank and then begins to run NW in North Channel.
−0100 (−0035)	W-going stream begins in The Solent.
−0015 (+0010)	Flood stream in Southampton Water ends, and as the ebb stream gains strength the streams in North Channel, across Bramble Bank and in Thorn Channel turn S and SW to join the W-going stream in The Solent.

7.248

1   **Southampton Water.** In Southampton Water the unusual phenomenon of double HW occurs. The flood stream and HW period has a duration of 9 hours, and the ebb stream a duration of 3½ hours. The short duration of the ebb stream creates a greater velocity of flow. A stand of the tide, locally known as the "Young Flood Stand", starts about 2 hours after LW at Southampton and is particularly pronounced during spring tides. This lasts for about 2 hours, during which time the stream slackens considerably before the final accelerated rise to first HW.

2   These important quarter-diurnal variations in streams are given for each half hour of the tide, at various positions, in a tidal stream table on chart 2041.

The tidal streams in mid-channel off Hythe Pier may be summarised as follows, the times refer to first HW at Southampton:

Max rate (kn)

Stream begins	Direction	Sp	Np
+0545	First Flood	½	¼
−0200	Second Flood	1	½
+0015	Ebb	Very	weak
+0215	Main Ebb	1¾	1

3   The flood stream divides a little S of the S arm of Southampton Docks and runs up the dredged channels in Rivers Test and Itchen; the ebb streams from the rivers meet S of the same point. There may be some turbulence off this point when the streams, especially the ebb, are strong.

4   During and after long periods of heavy rain, the outgoing current from the rivers, which runs only from the surface down to a depth of from 1 to 2 m, may decrease the duration of the flood stream and decrease its rate by about ½ kn, and correspondingly increase both the duration and rate of the ebb stream.

7.249

1   **Tidal information.** For further tidal details, see information on the chart, 1.153 and *Admiralty Tidal Stream Atlas for The Solent and adjacent waters.*

Tide gauges exist at various beacons and places in the port area; their positions are best seen from the chart.

Water level. During strong SW gales, especially at neaps, the following features may occur in Southampton Water:

2   A phenomenal rise immediately after LW followed by a drastic fall in level about 1½ hours later.

A fall of about 0·3 m immediately after the time of first HW without further rise at the predicted time of second HW.

Climate information. See 1.195 and 13.238

Directions for entering harbour
(continued from 7.53 and 7.204)

Principal marks
7.250

1   **Thorn Channel:**

Luttrell Tower (flagstaff) (50°48′·4N 1°19′·5W).

Calshot Castle (radar tower) (50°49′·2N 1°18′·5W) on the low W entrance point of Southampton Water.

Chimney (elevation 198 m) (50°49′·1N 1°19′·8W), marked by obstruction lights, at Fawley Power Station.

2   House (red roof) (50°49′·7N 1°16′·0W).

Southampton – Calshot Castle, Calshot radar tower and Fawley power station chimney from E (7.250)

(Original dated 2004)

(Photograph - Drew Given, MV Doulos)

Southampton Water:
> Admiralty Jetty (radar scanner) (50°52'·1N 1°23'·2W). Lights are exhibited from dolphins extending up to 1 cable NE.
> Netley Great Dome (50°52'·0N 1°20'·5W).

Netley Great Dome (7.250)
(Original dated 2004)

(Photograph - H.M.S. Gleaner)

3   Building (elevation 70 m, red lights) (50°53'·0N 1°21'·8W) with five smaller conspicuous blocks of flats close NW.
> Southampton Vessel Traffic Services Centre (framework mast) (50°53'·0N 1°23'·7W) at the head of the S arm of Eastern Docks. A conspicuous silo stands close E of the VTS Centre Dome and chimneys at Marchwood Energy Recovery Facility (50°54'·0N 1°26'·3W).

Other aids to navigation
7.251

1   **Racon:** W Bramble Light Buoy (50°47'·2N 1°18'·6W), for details see *Admiralty List of Radio Signals Volume 2.*
> **Tidal and weather information** are available from Southampton VTS Centre on request. For details of other information available from this centre, see 7.6.

Thorn Channel and approaches
7.252

1   **Description.** Thorn Channel (50°47'N 1°19'W), leading into Calshot Reach, forms the main approach to Southampton Water. The channel is bounded on its W side by Calshot Spit, and on its E side by Bramble Bank which lies at the SW end of the coastal bank which fronts the coast on the N side of the approaches to Southampton Water; Thorn Knoll, a spur, extends from the NW side of Bramble Bank. The entrance to the channel is marked by NE Gurnard Light Buoy (port hand) and W Bramble Light Buoy (W cardinal), moored 7 cables and 1¼ miles, respectively, E of Stansore Point (50°47'·1N 1°20'·6W) (7.51) and is marked on either side by light buoys.
> For limiting conditions in the channel, see 7.233.

2   **From west.** From a position between Stansore Point and Egypt Point, 1½ miles SE, the track leads NE in mid-channel to enter Thorn Channel between NE Gurnard Light Buoy (port hand) and W Bramble Light Buoy (W cardinal).

From east. From a position between South Bramble Light Buoy (starboard hand) (50°47'·0N 1°17'·6W) and Prince Consort Light Buoy (N cardinal), 6 cables S, the track leads in mid-channel to enter Thorn Channel between NE Gurnard Light Buoy (port hand) and W Bramble Light Buoy (W cardinal).

3   **Precautionary area.** See 7.20. When making the turn from E into Thorn Channel, large commercial vessels may alter course to port N of Prince Consort Light Buoy to pass about 1¼ cables N of Gurnard Light Buoy (N cardinal) (50°46'·2N 1°18'·8W) before altering course to starboard to enter Thorn Channel WNW of W Bramble Light Buoy (W cardinal). Such vessels may be encountered anywhere in the precautionary area and, depending on the state of tide and other prevailing conditions, will endeavour to follow the tracks indicated in the precautionary area diagram on the chart.

4   **Thorn Channel.** The track leads NE in mid-channel passing E of Calshot Spit Light Float (red hull, light-tower amidships) (50°48'·4N 1°17'·6W) which marks the E extremity of Calshot Spit at the NW edge of Thorn Channel. The track then leads N thence NW into Calshot Reach passing between Calshot Castle and Hook Light Buoy (starboard hand), 3½ cables NNE.

5   **Useful marks:**
> Bourne Gap Beacon (orange diamond on orange pole) (50°48'·0N 1°19'·8W).
> Lights (metal column on square concrete structure) (50°48'·3N 1°18'·8W) on the end of an outfall.
> Calshot Beacon (orange pole) (50°48'·6N 1°18'·7W).

Southampton Water
7.253

1   **Southampton Water** is entered through Calshot Reach between Calshot Castle and the shore on the N side at Hook. It extends NW for about 5 miles to Southampton Docks and is marked on each side by light buoys. Banks of soft mud, which dry, extend from both sides on which there are numerous sewer outfalls marked by beacons. Southampton Water is nearly landlocked and thus no sea of any consequence can arise. For limiting conditions in Southampton Water, see 7.233.

2   From Calshot Reach the track leads NW through the buoyed channel to abreast Admiralty Jetty at Hythe, thence follow the buoyed channel to Southampton Docks.
> Special attention is drawn to the presence of vessels loading and discharging at Esso Marine Terminal at Fawley, at BP Hamble Terminal and at Marchwood, and at anchorages in Southampton Water, also to the presence of craft moored or alongside the jetties at Calshot and Admiralty Jetty at Hythe.

3   Mariners in all vessels passing the Esso Marine Terminal and the BP Hamble Terminal should not navigate closer than 130 m from the face of the jetties in order to protect vessels alongside, to guard against the interaction between vessels and to prevent the risk of naked lights within these areas.
> For details of a speed limit in Southampton Water, see 7.242.

4   **Useful marks:**
> Lights at the SE end and NW end of Esso Marine Terminal (50°50'N 1°20'W).
> Lights (mast, 9 m in height) (50°52'·5N 1°23'·6W) on Hythe Pierhead.
> Hook Shore Beacon (red beacon) (50°49'·7N 1°16'·4W).

Radar scanner

Deans Elbow Light-buoy
(Port hand)

Hythe – Admiralty Jetty from E (7.253)

(Original dated 2004)

(Photograph - Drew Given, Doulos)

Southampton Docks
7.254

1   **General information.** Navigation to and from Southampton Docks is possible both by day and by night and at all stages of the tide.

    Eastern Docks. The approach to Empress Dock and the E side of Eastern Docks lies through the entrance to River Itchen. The E side of this channel is formed by Weston Shelf, a mudflat which extends from Weston Point (50°53′·4N 1°23′·0W); it is marked by light buoys and light beacons (starboard hand).

2   **Foul areas.** The shoal area along the SW side of River Test between Hythe Pier (50°52′·4N 1°23′·7W) and Marchwood Sea Mounting Centre, 1½ miles NW, is foul. Part of this shoal area abreast of Town Quay is known as The Gymp. The seaward limit of foul ground on The Gymp is marked by Upper and Lower Foul Ground Light Beacons (port hand), see information on the chart.

3   **Swinging grounds.** There are four swinging grounds off the berths fronting the River Test.

    Lower Swinging Ground is situated off the S arm of Eastern Docks, and is marked by a pair of transit light beacons:

       Front mark. Light beacon (white triangle point up, green border, on metal framework tower) (50°53′·5N 1°24′·3W).

4   Rear mark. Light beacon (white diamond, red border on metal framework tower, 23 m in height) (2 cables NNW of the front mark).

    The alignment (329°) of these marks, the topmarks of which are illuminated in outline when required, situated at the head of Town Quay and the centre of Royal Pier indicate the transit for Lower Swinging Ground.

5   **Middle Swinging Ground** is situated off the E end of Western Docks and is marked by light beacons in transit.

6   **Upper Swinging Ground** is situated off the W end of Western Docks and is marked by a pair of transit lights:

       Front light (black triangle point up on yellow mast with black and red bands) (50°54′·5N 1°26′·3W).

       Rear light (black X, on yellow mast with black and red bands) (100 m N of the front light).

    The alignment (011°) of these lights standing at the W end of the quay wall indicate the transit for Upper Swinging Ground.

7   **Bury Swinging Ground** is situated off the SW side of Southampton Container Terminals. The limits are marked by four light buoys (port hand).Depths within the swinging ground range from 7·5 to 4·7 m (2004).

8   **West transit marks:**

       Front mark. A Light Beacon (orange triangle point up on grey framework tower) (50°54′·5N 1°28′·4W).

       Rear mark. B Light Beacon (orange diamond on grey framework tower) (1¾ cables WNW of the front mark).

    The alignment (287°) of these marks indicate the transit for the swinging ground.

7.255

1   **Useful marks:**

       Lights (framework tower, 16 m in height) (50°53′·0N 1°23′·7W) at the S end of Queen Elizabeth II Terminal.

2   Lights (yellow triangle, point up, on grey metal framework tower) and (red triangle, point down, on grey framework tower) (50°53′·3N 1°23′·6W) on the N and S sides of the entrance to Empress Dock.

       Lights (metal column, 8 m in height) (50°53′·7N 1°24′·6W) on the SE head of Royal Pier.

Berths

Esso Marine Terminal
7.256

    Esso Marine Terminal (50°50′N 1°20′W), about 7½ cables in length, lies on the SW side of Southampton

Southampton – ESSO marine terminal from SE (7.256)

(Original dated 2004)

(Photograph – Drew Given, MV Doulos)

Water, about 1½ miles NW of Calshot Castle; two piers connect it with the shore and a floating pontoon mooring for tugs is situated at the SE end of the terminal. There are a number of tall chimneys, some of which emit flares, in the Esso Petroleum Company's oil refinery W of the terminal; their positions and heights can best be seen from the chart.

1   There are five main ocean berths on the outer face of the terminal and four coastal berths on the inner face; the berth numbers and limits of the dredged areas can best be seen from the chart. The terminal can accept part laden VLCC's of up to 14·9 m draught. There are facilities for handling liquified gas and chemicals.

2   **Deepest berth.** No 5 Berth dredged to a depth of 14·9 m for vessels up to 14·9 m draught and 244 000 tonnes displacement. This draught is subject to change and latest values should be checked with the terminal operator to ensure that arrival draught will not interfere with berthing prospects.

BP Hamble Terminal
7.257

1   **BP Hamble Terminal** (50°50'·9N 1°19'·6W) extends from the shore 5 cables WNW of the entrance to River Hamble. The terminal consists of a jetty head connected to the shore by a 450 m long ramp which supports a walkway,

Netley Great Dome

Southampton – BP Hamble Terminal from S (7.257)

(Original dated 2004)

(Photograph – Drew Given, MV Doulos)

light rail track and pipework; there is one berth. The terminal can accept vessels of up to 110 000 dwt in ballast and depart the berth with a load limit of 70 000 tons of crude oil.

Berth: 13·6 m depth for vessels up to 260 m LOA and 13·1 m draught.

Eastern Docks
7.258
1 **Eastern Docks** (50°53'·6N 1°23'·7W) comprise two basins, Empress Dock and Ocean Dock, and Itchen and Test Quays, and handle, amongst others, RoRo, passenger, bulk, vehicle carrying and general cargo vessels. Ocean Dock and Queen Elizabeth II Terminal lie in the W part of Eastern Docks, facing River Test. There are also single-user specialized facilities for handling grain products at Berth No 36 on Itchen Quays.

2 **Deepest and longest berths:**
Itchen Quays. Berths 34 to 36: length 484 m; depth 9·9 m.
Empress Dock entrance 48·5 m wide, maintained depth 7·8 m, Berths 20 to 21: length 258 m; depth 7·5 m.

3 Test Quays. Queen Elizabeth II Terminal Berths 38 to 39: length 360 m; depth 10·5 m; for passenger vessels.
Ocean Dock entrance 121·9 m wide, Berths 43 and 44: length 450 m; depth 11·7 m.

Town Quay and Royal Pier
7.259
1 **Town Quay** (50°53'·7N 1°24'·4W) lies W of Ocean Dock. A high speed ferry terminal is situated on the E side of the quay. Vehicular, passenger and cargo vessels connecting with Isle of Wight use facilities adjacent to Town Quay. Town Quay Marina lies at the root of the quay.

2 **Royal Pier**, close W of Town Quay, is disused; on the NW side of the pier is a foul area and a beacon (starboard hand) off the W corner of the pier marks a foul patch. There are dolphins and piles between the pier and Town Quay from which high speed ferries are operated.

Western Docks
7.260
1 **Western Docks**, fronting River Test, are formed by a quay wall nearly 1¼ miles in length (Berths 101 — 109) with City Cruise Terminal (Berth 101), Mayflower Cruise Terminal (Berth 105) at its centre and a vehicle handling terminal (Berths 201 - 202), branching S from its W end. Berth 203 lies on its S side with Southampton Container Terminals Ltd. (Berths 204 — 207), which can accept the largest container ships, farther W.

2 The former King George V dry dock, between berths 109 and 110 is now fully tidal. Currently (2008) the E side is in use as short-sea container feeder vessel berth.

3 The docks comprise specialized terminals for RoRo, container, cruise liner, fruit and vegetables, animal feed and fertilizer, and bulk products, together with general purpose berths.

Deepest and longest berths:
4 Mayflower Cruise Terminal, Berths 105 and 106 with a link span and RoRo Terminal at the E end: length 525 m; maintained depth 11·7 m.

Southampton - Ocean Dock from S (7.258)
(Original dated 2004)

(Photograph - Drew Given, MV Doulos)

Grain elevator   *Berths 38-40*

Southampton – Eastern Docks–Queen Elizabeth II Terminal from SSE (7.258)
(Original dated 2004)

(Photograph - Drew Given, MV Doulos)

Pier Head Light-buoy
(Starboard hand)

Southampton – Western Docks–Berths 101 and 102 from SSE (7.260)
(Original dated 2004)

(Photograph - Drew Given, MV Doulos)

Berth 201   *Berth 103*

Cracknore Light-buoy
(Port hand)

Southampton – Western Docks–Berths 103 to 201 from SE (7.260)

(Original dated 2004)

(Photograph - Drew Given, MV Doulos)

Southampton
Container Terminal

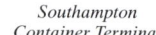

Vehicle Handling
Terminal

Southampton Docks (Berths 110-207) from SE (7.260)

(Original dated 2001)

(Photograph - Air Images)

Ocean Village
Mooring   *Itchen Bridge*

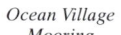

Ferry Terminal   *Weston Jetty*

Southampton Docks and River Itchen from S (7.261)

(Original dated 2001)

(Photograph - Air Images)

Berth 201 with a linkspan at its N end; length 280 m; maintained depth 10·2 m. Berth No 202; length 274 m; depth 12·2 m.

Southampton Container Terminals, Berths 204 to 207: length 1350 m; depths 12·8 m at Berths 204 and 205, 13·6 m at Berth 206 and 15·0 m alongside Berth 207.

River Itchen
7.261

1 **General information.** Woolston lies on the E side of the entrance to River Itchen, N of Weston Point (50°53′·4N 1°23′·0W) (7.254). Weston Jetty extends from the vicinity of Weston Point to the edge of the channel and has a maintained depth of 2·3 m.

2 **Berth.** Woolston Berth, currently disused (2008), extends for about 250 m along a quay on the E side of River Itchen opposite the entrance to Ocean Village Marina.

River Itchen above Woolston is described at 7.272

Admiralty Jetty
7.262

1 **General information.** Admiralty Jetty (50°52′·1N 1°23′·3W), with a conspicuous radar scanner (7.250) at its head, extends NE from the shore Three connected dolphins are situated 100 m NE of the head of the jetty. One trot of mooring buoys is laid in a NW to SE line off the head of the jetty and SW of the main dredged channel. Another trot of mooring buoys is laid close NW of the jetty. Numerous buoys (special) are moored in the approaches to, and vicinity of, the jetty; these buoys mark submerged mooring systems and limit lines. Close SE of the jetty there is a

U.S. Base – Admiralty Jetty–Radar Scanner from NE (7.262)
(Original dated 2004)

(Photograph - H.M.S. Gleaner)

slipway with dolphins on either side of its outer end and a linkspan RoRo berth with breasting dolphins.

Marchwood Sea Mounting Centre
7.263

1   **General information.** Marchwood Sea Mounting Centre (50°53'·6N 1°25'·3W) lies on the SW side of River Test about 5 cables W of Royal Pier. There are six berths situated on three piers, Mulberry Wharf, Falkland Wharf and Gunwharf, extending NE from the shore. There are RoRo facilities at Mulberry and Falkland Wharves.

2   **Depths.** The approach area from the main channel has a maintained depth of 8·0 m.

Deepest and longest berth: Falkland Wharf maintained depth 8·0 m.

Marchwood Basin
7.264

1   **General information.** Marchwood Channel (50°54'·0N 1°25'·6W) leading to Marchwood Basin is entered between Swinging Ground No 2 Light Buoy and Cracknore Light Buoy and leads to Husbands Jetty and Marchwood Wharf,

Gun Wharf   *Falkland Wharf*   *Mulberry Wharf*

Marchwood Military Port from NE (7.263)
(Original dated 2004)

(Photograph - Drew Given, MV Doulos)

a bulk cargo handling terminal dredged to 4 m (1993) that can accommodate vessels up to 6000 dwt.

Husbands Jetty (50°23'·9N 1°25'·7W), with a T-shaped head, extends N across the mudflats at the E end of Marchwood Wharf.

2   **Depths** in the basin are from 1·4 m to 3·0 m and it is bounded on its SW side by Marchwood Wharf, at each end of which there are shoal areas.

Lights are exhibited from Marchwood Wharf at the NW and SE limit of the deepest water alongside. Lights (mast) are also exhibited at Husbands Jetty Elbow and from the outermost dolphin situated SE of the jettyhead.

7.265

1   **Directions.** From a position between Swinging Ground No 2 Light Buoy (port hand) and Cracknore Light Buoy (port hand), Marchwood Channel leads WNW in the middle of the channel in a least depth of 2·2 m passing between a beacon (port hand), marking a drying shoal on the N side of the channel, and Marchwood Light Buoy (special) moored on the S side of the channel at its junction with Marchwood Basin. When about 1 cable WNW of Marchwood Light Buoy course may be shaped for Marchwood Wharf or Husbands Jetty as required.

2   **Caution.** At the SE entrance to Marchwood Channel between −0200 and −0100 first HW Southampton (−0215 and −0115 Dover) the tidal stream sets W across the entrance at a rate of about ½ kn at springs. At other times in the entrance and at all times in the remainder of the channel the stream runs in the direction of the channel. Owing to the sheltering effect of the shallow bank which extends NW from Cracknore Light Buoy this W-setting stream has the greatest effect on the stern of a vessel entering the channel and may cause her to swing towards this bank.

Bury Creek

7.266

1   **General information.** Bury Creek (50°54'N 1°27'W) lies on the S side of Bury Reach, S of Southampton Container Terminals, and leads to Slowhill Copse Jetty, for the use of sludge disposal vessels. The NW side of the dredged area is marked by two beacons (starboard hand).

Depths. The entrance to the creek was dredged (1997) to a depth of 2·5 m.

Port services

Repairs

7.267

1   Limited repair facilities are available.

Other facilities

7.268

1   **Customs office** at Southampton.

Ship sanitation control and ship sanitation control exemption certificates are issued at Southampton.

Hospitals are available.

Oily waste reception facilities are available.

Supplies

7.269

1   **Fuel.** Fuel oil and marine diesel oil are available by lighter or alongside Esso Marine Terminal.

Fresh water is available at all berths, or can be supplied by barge.

Provisions: available.

Harbour regulations

7.270

1   Regulations and bye-laws are in force; a copy of these regulations should be obtained from Associated British Ports.

Rescue

7.271

1   **Coastguard Stations.** Solent MRSC is situated on Marine Parade West, at Lee-on-Solent (50°48'N 1°12'W) with Rescue Teams at Southampton at Marsh Parade, Hythe (50°52'N 1°24'W) and Hillhead (50°49'N 1°18'W). For details see 1.100.

2   **Lifeboats.** Calshot all-weather lifeboat and an inshore lifeboat are stationed at Calshot (50°49'N 1°18'W), for details see 1.113.

Helicopters. A SAR helicopter operates from Lee-on-Solent (50°48'N 1°12'W).

River Itchen above Woolston

General information

7.272

1   Itchen Bridge (50°53'·9N 1°23'·1W) spans the river close N of Woolston Berth. Lights are exhibited, on each side of the bridge, from the centre of the navigable arch and from each pier of the navigable arch.

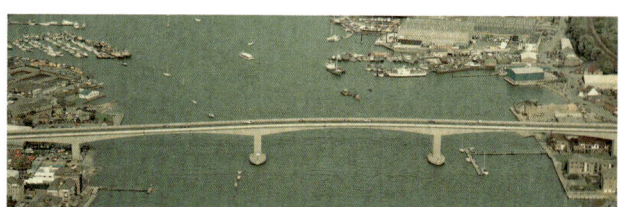

Itchen Bridge from S (7.272)

(Original dated 2001)

(Photograph – Air Images)

2   Crosshouse Light Beacon (port hand) and Chapel Light Beacon (starboard hand) mark the W and E sides of the channel, respectively, 1 and 2 cables N of the bridge. The river N of Crosshouse Light Beacon curves NE to Millstone Point (50°54'·6N 1°22'·6W), where it turns W, the channel at this bend being marked by light beacons (starboard hand) on its E side and by No 6 Light Beacon (port hand) and No 8 Beacon (port hand) on its W side. Millstone Point Jetty extends 100 m E from Millstone Point and is connected to a floating pontoon berth. An oil spillage response base is situated at the jetty. Lights (dolphins) are exhibited from the N and S extremities of the jetty and a fixed red light marks a tower crane on the jetty. Lights (metal column) are also exhibited from a jetty head 1¼ cables NNW.

3   Between Millstone Point and Woodmill, approximately 2 miles farther up the river, the river is crossed by Northam Bridge, Railway Bridge and Cobden Bridge.

Above Northam Bridge the river turns NE and close above Saint Denys Railway Bridge it turns N. Above Cobden Bridge the width of the river narrows to ½ cable.

4   **Depths** in the river between Millstone Point and Northam Bridge are from 0·6 to 2·6 m; above this bridge the depths are less than 1 m, but are greatly affected by the amount of fresh water in the river.

Vertical clearances: 23·0 m under Itchen Bridge and 4·2 m under Northam Bridge.

5   **Prohibited anchorage.** Anchorage is prohibited in a submarine pipeline and cable area between lines, shown on the chart, about 1½ cables N to ¾ cable S of Itchen Bridge. The submarine pipeline is marked on the W bank by two beacons (yellow topmarks, red border, on black columns); the alignment (256°) of which indicates the submarine pipeline.

6   **Tidal streams.** Above Northam Bridge the stream begins as follows:

Interval from 1st HW Southampton	Direction
–0600	Flood
+0030	Ebb

The maximum flood and ebb spring and neap rates are 1 and 1½ kn, and ½ and 1 kn, respectively.

River Hamble

Charts 2022 plan of entrance to River Hamble, 2038
General information
7.273

1   **Position and function.** River Hamble (50°51′N 1°18′W) flows into the NE side of Southampton Water about 1 mile N of Calshot Castle. The river is a yachting centre of considerable importance.

Hamble Point Marina   Warsash

Warsash Jetty

Hamble River entrance from SSW (7.273)

(Original dated 2001)

(Photograph – Air Images)

River Authority. The jurisdiction of the river, within the limits shown on the chart, lies with the Hampshire County Council, Harbour Master's Office, Shore Road, Warsash, SO3 9FR.

2   **Historic wreck.** A restricted area (50°53′·5N 1°17′·3W), radius 75 m marked by a beacon (special) lies in the centre of the river 3 cables above the M27 bridge and contains the historic wreck of the *Grace Dieu*, burnt out in 1439. For protection details, see 1.89.

Limiting conditions
7.274

1   **Controlling depth:** 2·2 m in position 50°50′·4N 1°18′·7W.

Charted depths in the river from Warsash Jetty as far as Bursledon Bridge are from 1·2 to 5·7 m.

Vertical clearance: 4 m under Bursledon Road Bridge.

2   **Tidal levels.** Warsash mean spring range about 3·7 m; mean neap range about 1·9 m. Bursledon mean spring range about 3·9 m; mean neap range about 1·8 m. For further information see *Admiralty Tide Tables*.

Maximum size of vessel. The river is navigable by small craft as far as Botley, 6 miles above the entrance.

Arrival information
7.275

1   **Radio reporting.** Mariners in vessels of 20 m LOA and over, vessels engaged in towing and vessels restricted by their draught, are required to contact Hamble Harbour Radio on VHF before entering the river or getting underway.

All vessels and small craft whilst underway within the limits of the River Hamble Harbour Authority are advised to monitor Hamble Harbour Radio on VHF.

2   **Prohibited anchorage.** Anchoring is not permitted between No 1 Light Beacon (50°50′·3N 1°18′·6W) and the M27 bridge, 3 miles upriver. See information on the chart.

Speed restriction. In the interests of safety and of protecting small craft, moored vessels and river banks from excessive wash, a speed limit of 6 kn through the water exists throughout the Hamble Harbour area.

3   **Oyster dredging** takes place on annual basis between November and February. Detailed information is available from the Harbour Master.

Quarantine. A quarantine buoy is moored 1 cable SSW of the head of Warsash Jetty.

Directions for entering harbour
7.276

1   **Landmark:**

Harbour Master's Office (tower, white with black bands, flagstaff) (50°51′·2N 1°18′·4W) at Warsash.

2   The channel into the river lies between drying mudbanks and is marked by light beacons (port and starboard hand), the positions of which can best be seen from the chart.

From the vicinity of Hook Light Buoy (starboard hand) (50°49′·5N 1°18′·3W) the line of bearing, 352°, in the white sector (351°–353°) of Hamble Common Light Beacon (50°51′·0N 1°18′·9W), leads in the approach passing:

3   Close WSW of Hamble Point Light Buoy (S cardinal) (50°50′·2N 1°18′·7W), and;

Between Nos 1 and 2 Light Beacons (starboard hand and E cardinal), thence;

W of No 5 Light Beacon (starboard hand).

From abreast No 6 Light Beacon (port hand) the line of bearing, 028°, in the white sector (027°–029°) of Warsash Light Beacon (50°51′·1N 1°18′·3W) leads in the fairway to abreast Warsash Jetty.

4   Above Warsash Jetty there are numerous pile moorings on each side of the fairway, and pontoons; their positions can best be seen from the chart.

Useful marks:

Lights (port hand) on the N and S ends of mid-stream pontoons abreast Hamble Point Marina (50°51′·2N 1°18′·7W).

Warsash Jetty head

Hamble Point Light-buoy
(S. Cardinal)

Southampton - Entrance to River Hamble from S (7.275)

(Original dated 2004)

(Photograph - Drew Given, MV Doulos)

Lights are exhibited from the jetty heads of the various marinas and from some of the pile moorings and pontoons; their positions can best be seen from the chart.

Berths
7.277

1 Warsash Jetty (50°50′·9N 1°18′·4W) projects from the E entrance point of the river. A pierhead with a brow linking up to a pontoon on its N side is situated at the head of the jetty. Lights are exhibited from the SW face of the jetty and from the N end of the pontoon.

2 Hamble Point Quay is situated at the W entrance point of the river, 1½ cables NW of Warsash Jetty. A pontoon jetty extends into the river from the quay; lights are exhibited at the N and S ends of the jetty. Buoys (special) (uncharted) for securing an oil boom, if required, are moored ½ cable E and 1½ cables S, respectively, of Hamble Point Quay.

NOTES

257

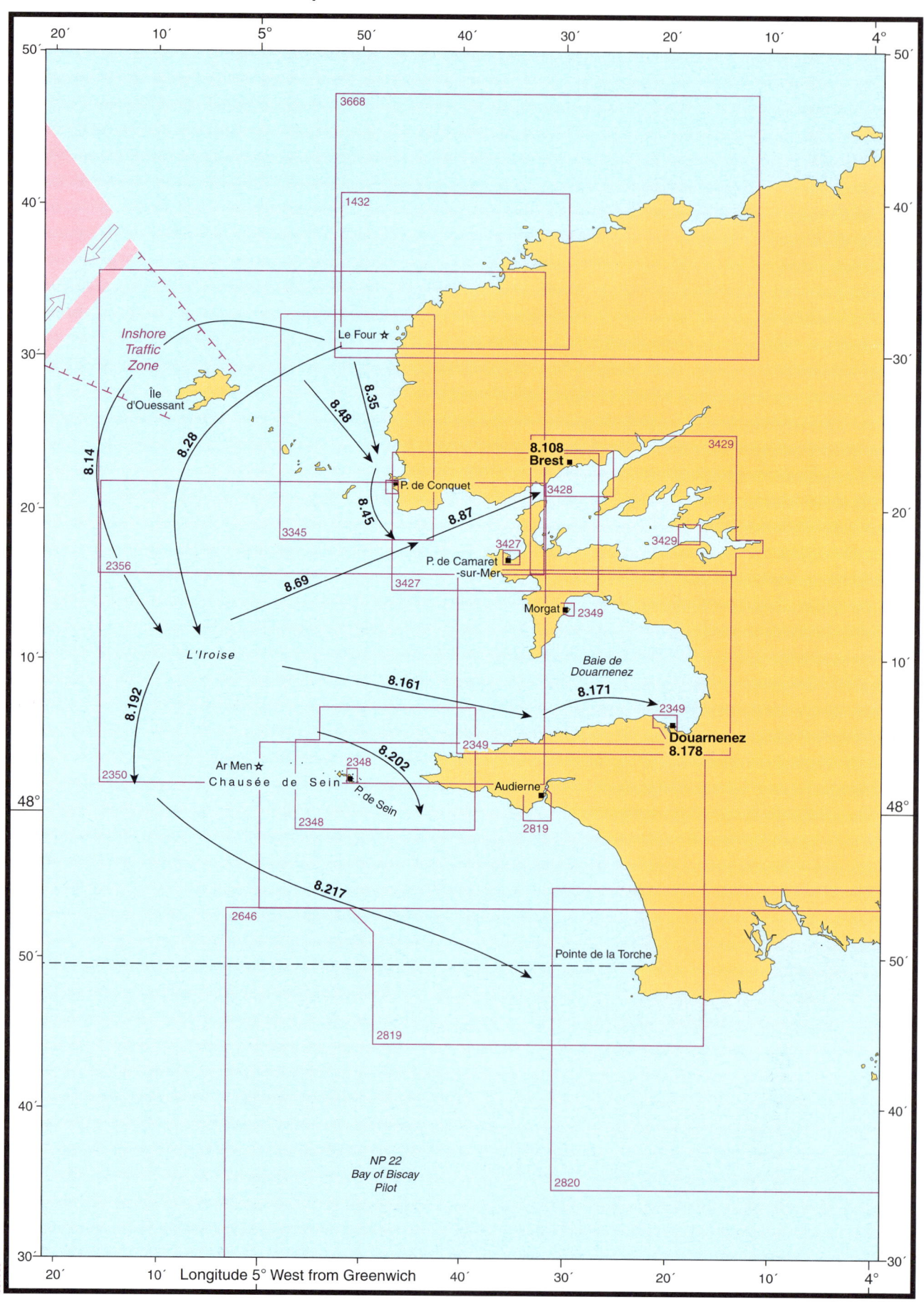

20′   10′   5°   50′   40′   30′   20′   10′   4°

50′   50′

3668

1432

40′   40′

Inshore Traffic Zone

Le Four ★

30′   30′

Île d'Ouessant

8.35

8.48

8.28

8.14

8.108
Brest ■

3429

P. de Conquet ■

3428

8.45

8.87

20′   20′

3345

3427

3429

2356

P. de Camaret
-sur-Mer ■

8.69

3427

Morgat ■ 2349

Baie de Douarnenez

8.161

8.171

L'Iroise

8.192

2349

10′   10′

2349

Douarnenez ■

8.178

2350

Ar Men ★

2348

8.202

Chausée de Sein

P. de Sein ■

48°   48°

2348

Audierne ■

2819

8.217

2646

Pointe de la Torche

50′   50′

2819

40′   40′

*NP 22
Bay of Biscay
Pilot*

2820

30′   30′

20′   10′   Longitude 5° West from Greenwich   40′   30′   20′   10′   4°

030408

CHAPTER 8

NORTH-WEST COAST OF FRANCE — LE FOUR TO POINTE DE LA TORCHE

GENERAL INFORMATION

Charts 2643, 2644
Scope of the chapter
8.1

1 This chapter covers the NW coast of France between Le Four (48°31′N 4°48′W) and Pointe de La Torche, about 45 miles SSE. It includes Île d'Ouessant (48°28′N 5°05′W), the Inshore Traffic Zone close NW of the island, and the channels between that island and the mainland SE.

2 L'Iroise (8.62) with the port of Brest (8.108), Baie de Douarnenez (8.161), Chaussée de Sein (8.193) and the passage from Chaussée de Sein to Pointe de La Torche are also covered by this chapter.

Description
8.2

1 The NW coast of Brittany, which comprises the NW part of France, is encumbered with dangers. In the N part lies Île d'Ouessant, 10 miles offshore, with numerous islands and dangers extending SE to the mainland, and in the S part Chaussée de Sein, a dangerous reef, which extends approximately 14 miles offshore.

2 Between these two dangers lies L'Iroise, the wide expanse of sea fronting the W approaches to the port of Brest and Baie de Douarnenez, both of which deeply indent the coast.

Safe anchorage, sheltered from all weather, for all classes of vessels can be obtained in Rade de Brest.

Regulations concerning vessels carrying hydrocarbons or other dangerous and polluting goods
8.3

1 For regulations concerning tankers laden with hydrocarbons and other vessels carrying dangerous and polluting goods navigating in the approaches to the N and W coasts of France, see 1.68 to 1.76

Traffic separation scheme
8.4

1 The Off Ushant (Ouessant) TSS NW of Île d'Ouessant is IMO adopted and Rule 10 of *International Regulations for Preventing Collisions at Sea (1972)* applies. For details see 2.32 and 1.70

8.5

1 **Inshore Traffic Zone and inner channels.** IMO state, however, that navigation within the Inshore Traffic Zone, shown on the chart SE of the TSS, is subject to French national regulations. These state that traffic movements are to be in accordance with Rule 10(d) of *International Regulations for Preventing Collisions at Sea (1972)*.

2 (1) Navigation within Chenal du Four, Chenal de la Helle, Passage du Fromveur and in Raz de Sein is authorized only for the following categories of vessel:
  French state vessels.
  Rescue craft and those giving assistance to others.
  Passenger craft employed on local services between the mainland and the islands.
  Fishing vessels whose length is less than 35 m.
  Pleasure craft.

3 Exceptions are possible under certain circumstances for other categories of vessel, notably vessels under 1600 gt not carrying passengers or dangerous goods, who may be permitted to transit by day only.

Exception in special circumstances may also be given to vessels over 1600 gt but these must not be carrying any cargo.

4 All transits of the Inshore Traffic Zone and the above channels must be preceded by radio contact with Cross Corsen at least 2 hours before commencement of passage. For further details see 8.6.

Mandatory Vessel Traffic Management System
8.6

1 **Vessel Traffic Service.** The Off Ushant (Ouessant) TSS reporting system, with full radar surveillance, is maintained for the control of shipping. The system covers a circular area of 40 miles radius, centred on Le Stiff Radar Tower (48°28′·7N 5°03′·4W) on Île d'Ouessant. Participation in the scheme is mandatory for all vessels of 300 gt or over.

2 Vessels entering the area should make a report (OUESSREP) on VHF to Ushant Traffic (Ouessant Trafic), similar in style to the MAREP POSREP reports.

For further details see *Admiralty List of Radio Signals Volume 6(1).* and 1.69

Ship Movement Report System (MAREP), see 1.14.

Pilotage area
8.7

1 **Limits.** The Compulsory Pilotage Area limits of the port of Brest are:
  North; the parallel of Le Four Light 48°31′N.
  West; the meridian of longitude 5°15′W.
  South; the parallel of Pointe de Lervily 48°00′N.

2 The area also includes L'Elorn up to Landerneau and L'Aulne up to Châteaulin.

For details of pilot boarding places and notice required, see 8.67.

Explosives dumping grounds
8.8

1 **Dumping grounds** for explosives, shown on the chart, lie about 15 miles SSW and 4 miles NW of Île d'Ouessant.

Prohibited area, radius 1 mile, is centred in position 48°17′N 5°40′W, about 24 miles SW of Créac'h Light.

Marine farms
8.9

1 Marine farms may be encountered in the waters of this chapter and should be avoided. Farms in proximity to shipping routes are generally marked by buoys. Other farms are marked by beacons (X topmark) and some are fitted with radar reflectors. Lights, when fitted, show flashing yellow. See 1.29.

Fishing vessels
8.10

1 For information regarding fishing vessels in French waters, see 1.26.

Thick weather

8.11

1 In thick weather, when S of Île d'Ouessant, it is

essential to guard against being set towards the dangers SE of the island on the rising stream or towards Chaussée de Sein on the falling stream.

LE FOUR TO POINTE DE SAINT-MATHIEU AND OUESSANT

GENERAL INFORMATION

Chart 2356
Area covered

8.12

1 This section is arranged as follows:
Île d'Ouessant (8.14) and Passage du Fromveur (8.28)
Le Four (8.35) to Pointe de Saint-Mathieu and the islands and dangers between Île d'Ouessant and the mainland.

Topography

8.13

1 The area between Île d'Ouessant (48°28′N 5°05′W) and the mainland SE is encumbered by islands, reefs and shoals. The principal islands, which are low and rocky with white beaches, are, from the NW, Île de Bannec (48°26′N 5°01′W) and Île de Balanec, Île Molène (8.61), the highest island, 23 m high, Île de Trielen, Île de Quéménès and Île de Béniguet. These islands lie between 2½ and 10 miles SE of Île d'Ouessant.

2 Passage du Fromveur (8.28) is the channel between Île d'Ouessant and these dangers, and Chenal du Four (8.45) and Chenal de la Helle (8.48) are the channels between these dangers and the mainland; there are numerous dangers between these two latter channels.

ÎLE D'OUESSANT AND PASSAGE DU FROMVEUR

General information

Chart 2356
Route

8.14

1 From a position W of Le Four (48°31′N 4°48′W) the route leads generally SW passing either NW of Île d'Ouessant (48°28′N 5°05′W) through the Inshore Traffic Zone, or SE of the island through Passage du Fromveur.

Topography

8.15

1 Île d'Ouessant, also known in English as Ushant, lies about 10 miles W of the NW extremity of the coast of France. Viewed from N or NW the E and NE coasts appear as high steep cliffs declining in a gentle slope towards the W and SW coasts. It is surrounded by dangers which extend 1½ miles offshore. Île de Keller lies close off the NW coast from which it is separated by a narrow shallow passage. The S coast of the island is indented by several bays.

2 Île d'Ouessant is readily identified on the radar display from SW by the two headlands, which have the appearance of the open claw of a lobster, extending SW from the SW end of the island.

Adverse sea and swell

8.16

1 In Passage du Fromveur the sea is liable to be very high and turbulent when the wind is against the tidal stream and in such conditions mariners in small vessels should avoid this channel.

Traffic regulations

8.17

1 **Inshore Traffic Zone.** The area lies within Ushant Inshore Traffic Zone, for details see 8.5.
Mandatory Vessel Traffic Management System, see 8.6.

2 **Restricted access.** Vessels over 1600 gt are prohibited from using Passage du Fromveur (8.28). Smaller vessels proceeding to or from French ports on the Atlantic, Channel or North Sea coasts may use these channels provided they are not carrying cargoes listed in the annexes to MARPOL 1973, and have permission from the Maritime Prefect for the Atlantic.

Pilotage

8.18

1 Pilots are available from Brest; they will board at the port of departure or disembark at the port of arrival.
For details of the compulsory pilotage area, see 8.8.
Local knowledge is desirable.

Explosives dumping ground

8.19

1 For details of an explosives dumping ground, see 8.7.

Marine nature reserves

8.20

1 Marine nature reserves are established on and around the coasts of the following islands and islets:
île d'Ouessant at Roc'h Mell and Enez Bougeviou (49°29′N 5°04′W).

2 Île de Bannec and île de Balanec (48°25′N 5°00′W).
Île de Trielen (48°22′N 4°56′W).
Rocher Aigu (48°19′N 4°52′W).
The sites at île d'Ouessant, Île de Trielen and Rocher Aigu are subject to general French regulations regarding marine nature reserves. Access to the sites at Île de Bannec and Île de Balanec is prohibited.

Rescue

8.21

1 **All-weather lifeboat.** Île d'Ouessant lifeboat is stationed at Porz-Pol (48°27′N 5°06′W) in Baie de Lampaul, see 1.117.
Signal stations are situated at:
Le Stiff Radar Tower (Vigie) (48°29′N 5°03′W) (8.25).

2 Close W of Créac'h Light (Sémaphore) (48°28′N 5°08′W).
For details see 1.95 and 1.110.
VHF Direction-finding service, for emergency use only, operates from Créac'h Light (48°28′N 5°08′W), for details see *Admiralty List of Radio Signals Volume 2.*

Natural conditions
8.22
1   **Tidal streams** in general run as follows:

Position	Rising stream	Falling stream
North of Île d'Ouessant	NE	SW
West of Long 5°10′W	mainly NNE	mainly SSW
South of Île d'Ouessant	ENE	S

For details, see information on the chart.

2   The streams W and NW of Île d'Ouessant are considerably affected by the current due to the prevailing wind, for details see 1.148.

8.23
1   **Tidal streams near Île d'Ouessant.** Tidal streams at the positions indicated begin as shown in the following table:

Interval from HW Brest	Direction
Off Baie du Stiff:	
+0400	NW
–0200	SE

2   The maximum in-going and out-going spring rates are 2¾ kn.

Off NW coast of Île d'Ouessant:	
–0550	NE
–0245	SW

3   The maximum in-going and out-going spring rates are 3½ kn.

At Baz Veur (5 cables W of Pointe de Pern):	
–0550	NE
+0045	SW

4   The maximum in-going and out-going spring rates are 5½ kn.

At La Jument:	
+0435	NW
–0045	S

5   The maximum in-going and out-going spring rates are 4½ kn.

About 1½ miles SW of La Jument:	
–0545	NW
+0015	S

6   The maximum in-going and out-going spring rates are 3½ kn.

Off S coast of Île d'Ouessant:	
+0340	ENE
–0245	WSW

The maximum in-going and out-going spring rates are 2 kn.

8.24
1   **Tidal streams in Passage du Fromveur.** In the narrow part of the channel between Île d'Ouessant and Kéréon Light, 1¼ miles SE, the streams begin as follows:

Interval from HW Brest	Direction
–0515	NE
+0045	SW

2   The maximum rates are 8 to 9 kn on the NE-going stream and 7 to 8 kn on the SW-going stream.

Near Kéréon the streams run NNE and SSW at about the same rate, but they commence about 1¼ hours earlier.

Between Kéréon and Ar Staon Vraz, 1 mile S, a counter current setting NNE forms on the falling stream with a rate of about 4 kn.

3   Near the SE coast of Île d'Ouessant there is a weak counter current running opposite to that in Passage du Fromveur.

Climate information, see 1.195, 13.239 and 13.240

Directions
(continued from 9.16 where directions for the passage NE along the N coast of France are given)

Principal marks
8.25
1   **Landmarks:**
Radar Tower and Signal Station (48°28′·6N 5°03′·1W).
Le Stiff Lighthouse (two adjoining white towers, 32 m in height) (48°29′N 5°03′W) situated near Pointe du Stiff.

Kéréon Lighthouse from E (8.25)

(Original dated 2000-02)

(Photograph - Jean Guichard)

Créac'h Lighthouse (white tower black bands, 55 m in height) (48°28′N 5°08′W) situated on Pointe de Créac'h.

2 **Major lights:**

Le Four Light (48°31′N 4°48′W) (8.43).

Le Stiff Light — as above.

Créac'h Light — as above; exhibited in fog during the day.

La Jument Light (grey octagonal tower red top, 48 m in height) (48°25′N 5°08′W).

Kéréon Light (grey tower, 41 m in height) (48°26′N 5°01′W).

Other aids to navigation
8.26

1 **Racon:** Créac'h Light (48°28′N 5°08′W) and can only be received when passing NW of the island.

For details see *Admiralty List of Radio Signals Volume 2.*

2 **Radar assistance.** On request, Ouessant Traffic provides mariners with radar information relative to their position in an area which extends up to 40 miles SSW through W to ENE of Le Stiff Radar Tower (48°29′N 5°03′W). For details see *Admiralty List of Radio Signals Volume 6(1).*

Inshore Traffic Zone
8.27

1 From a position W of Le Four (48°31′N 4°48′W) the route leads generally SW passing (with positions given from the summit of Île de Keller (48°29′N 5°06′W)):

NW of Roc'h Mell (1 mile ENE); a drying rock (existence doubtful) is charted close N. Thence:

NW of Chaussée de Keller, a rocky reef which extends 1 mile W from Île de Keller terminating in Baz Kalet; thence:

2 NW of Baz Veur (3 miles WSW).

The track then rounds Île d'Ouessant at a safe distance and then leads generally S passing:

W of Leur Vaz (3¼ miles SW), the outermost danger SW of the Pointe de Pern, the W extremity of Île d'Ouessant. Nividic Lighted Beacon Tower (grey octagonal tower 36 m in height) stands on a reef of the same name 2 cables N. Thence:

3 W of Ar Vridig (3¾ miles SSW), the outermost danger extending SW from the S entrance point of Baie de Lampaul (8.32). La Jument Light (8.25) stands 6 cables SE on a rock of the same name. Thence:

To L'Iroise (8.62).

Passage du Fromveur
8.28

1 **Channel.** Passage du Fromveur lies between the S side of Île d'Ouessant and the dangers in the vicinity of Kéréon. The channel is straight and easy to follow and is advantageous to take in good weather with a favourable tidal stream which runs strongly in both directions. For information regarding adverse sea and swell conditions, see 8.16.

8.29

1 **Route.** From a position W of Le Four (48°31′N 4°48′W) the route leads generally SW passing (with positions given from the N summit of Île de Bannec (48°26′N 5°01′W)):

2 SW of Men Korn (2¼ miles NNW), marked by a lighted beacon tower (E cardinal, 29 m in height), the outermost danger off the S entrance point to Baie du Stiff (8.31), noting Basse du Fromveur (position doubtful) charted 3 cables SSE and closer to the track; and:

3 NW of Baz Penn Glok (1 mile NE); thence:

Between Kéréon (7 cables NW), from where a light (8.25) is exhibited, and a 3·3 m shoal (1¾ miles NW) lying 1½ cables SE of Men Darland; thence:

SW of Men ar Froud (2 miles WNW), marked by a beacon tower (S cardinal), noting rocky ground 3 cables NE.

4 The track continues generally SW along the NW side of Chaussée des Pierres Vertes, a group of drying and below-water rocks which extend up to 3 miles SSW from Île de Bannec; Pierres Vertes Light Buoy (W cardinal) (4½ miles SW) is moored near the SW end of these dangers. The track passes:

5 SW of Roc'h Agou (3¼ miles W), the outermost danger off Penn ar Roc'h, the W entrance point to Baie de Penn ar Roc'h (8.33), noting Men Krenn close NE; thence:

SW of Poullou Doun (3¾ miles W); thence:

6 SW of Pen ar C'heinigou (4¼ miles W); thence:

Between La Jument (5 miles W) (8.27), from where a light (8.25) is exhibited, and Pierres Vertes Light Buoy (W cardinal) (4½ miles SW) to L'Iroise (8.62).

7 **Clearing lines.** The islands and dangers between Île d'Ouessant and the mainland lie within the red sector (248°–019°) of Kéréon Light (48°26′N 5°01′W) (8.25).

Clearing marks
8.30

1 Front mark. Pyramide des Runiou (white pyramidal beacon) (48°26′·2N 5°06′·5W).

Rear mark. Créac'h Light (1½ miles NNW of the front mark) (8.25).

The alignment (327¾°) of these marks clears WSW of Chaussée de Pierres Vertes.

Caution for mariners in deep-draught vessels, see 8.84.

(Directions continue at 8.80;
for Baie de Douarnenez at 8.169
and for Chaussée de Sein at 8.199)

Minor bays and harbours
Baie du Stiff
8.31

1 **General information.** Baie du Stiff (48°28′N 5°03′W) lies S of the point on which Le Stiff Light (8.25) stands and affords shelter to mariners from winds between S and NW; the holding ground is not good. In bad weather the W swell runs along the coast and renders the anchorage untenable.

Local knowledge is necessary.

2 **Leading marks:**

Front mark. Port du Stiff Direction Light (white tower green top, 6 m in height) (48°28′N 5°03′W), exhibited from the head of Digue Jarland, the E mole.

Rear mark. Créac'h Light (3 miles W of the front mark) (8.25).

3 The alignment (259½°) of these marks, or at night in the white sector (254°–264°) of the direction light, leads in the approach passing N of Baz Legounek and S of Gorle Vihan Beacon Tower (isolated danger, 4 m in height) lying 1·1 miles E and 5 cables ENE, respectively, of the direction light.

4 **Clearing marks:**

Front mark. Gorle Vihan Beacon Tower.

Rear mark. Coastguard Station (mast) (5 cables W of the front mark.

The alignment (277°) of these marks clears N of the dangers NW of Men Korn.

5   **Harbour:** slip protected by a jetty 60 m in length at the head of Baie du Stiff; Digue Jarland, a mole extending S from the coast 90 m E of the jetty.

Longest berth: Digue Jarland length 95 m; depth alongside 3 to 12 m.

Landing, at any stage of the tide, at the outer end of the slip.

Baie de Lampaul
8.32

1   **General information.** Baie de Lampaul (48°26′N 5°09′W), the largest bay in the island, is entered between Pointe de Pern and a point about 1 mile SE and affords anchorage in good weather conditions. With W winds the sea is very high and breaks heavily in the entrance, especially during the rising stream.

2   **Anchorage** can be obtained in Baie de Lampaul in depths of 8 to 13 m, sand and mud, good holding ground, but the anchorage should only be used in good weather. Tidal streams are not felt at the head of the bay.

3   **Directions.** The alignment (054½°) of the NW side of Youc'h Korz (48°27′N 5°07′W), an islet in the middle of the bay, with Le Stiff Light (8.25), 3 miles NE, leads into the bay clear of the dangers on either side (8.27) thence pass either 100 m N of Youc'h Korz, or 30 m S of it. If proceeding into the harbour pass between Men ar Blank and Men ar Groas Beacon towers (port and starboard hand) situated 7½ cables NE of Youc'h Korz noting Ar Gern, a rock drying 0·6 m, lying 2½ cables NE of the same islet.

4   **Harbour:** Porz Pol a small harbour at the head of the bay protected by two moles; dries up to 3·5 m. Transverse chains assist anchors in holding.

Landing at the lifeboat slip when the harbour is dry or at the outer end of the new quay, depth 0·5 m.

Supplies: fresh water; provisions.

Baie de Penn ar Roc'h
8.33

1   **General information.** Baie de Penn ar Roc'h (48°27′N 5°04′W) a wide bay in the centre of the S coast is entered between Pen ar Roc'h, the W entrance point, and Men ar Froud (8.29), 1¼ miles ENE. It is only frequented by vessels plying between the island and the mainland when the weather is too bad to enter Baie du Stiff.

Local knowledge is necessary as the bay contains numerous drying rocks and shoal patches.

2   **Berths:** anchorage, not recommended for overnight stay, NE of Pen ar Roc'h in depths of 10 to 12 m. A marine farm lies close N of Roc'h Nel.

Landing available at a slip on S side of Pointe de Penn Arouez situated 2½ cables N of Pen ar Roc'h.

Porz Darland
8.34

1   **General information.** Porz Darland (48°27′·5N 5°02′·9W), a small harbour, lies at the head of a cove near the E end of the S coast. The harbour provides good shelter from N winds, but there is usually a swell in the cove, particularly between HW and 3 hours after.

2   **Local knowledge** is required as there are numerous islets and rocks in the approaches.

Harbour: jetty 80 m long, drying 1·5 m at its head.

Berths: mooring buoy off the entrance in a depth of 6 m; landing slip on the N side of the root of the jetty.

LE FOUR TO POINTE DE SAINT-MATHIEU AND THE ISLANDS AND DANGERS BETWEEN ÎLE D'OUESSANT AND THE MAINLAND

General information

Charts 3345, 2356

Route
8.35

1   Chenal du Four (8.45) and Chenal de la Helle (8.48) lie between the dangers fronting the coast between Presqu'île Saint-Laurent (48°31′N 4°47′W) and Pointe de Saint-Mathieu, 11 miles S, and the dangers which lie SE of Île d'Ouessant (48°28′N 5°05′W).

2   **Shelter.** Between these two points there are some small harbours only suitable for small craft and fishing vessels; the only anchorage in this part of the coast offering any security is that at Anse des Blancs-Sablons (48°22′N 4°46′W) (8.52).

The channels are more sheltered than the open sea W of Île d'Ouessant.

Topography
8.36

1   **Mainland coast.** Between Presqu'île Saint-Laurent and Pointe de Saint-Mathieu the coast is composed of moderately high cliffs interspersed with sandy beaches, and is bordered by islets, rocks, and shoals which extend in places over 2 miles offshore.

2   Pointe de Corsen (48°25′N 4°48′W) is prominent, especially when viewed from S; a direction light (8.46) is exhibited from the point.

Pointe de Kermorvan (48°22′N 4°47′W) from which a light (8.43) is exhibited lies at the W extremity of a peninsula of the same name which lies at the N entrance point of Port du Conquet.

3   **Prominent offshore features.** It would be imprudent to rely upon fixing the vessel's position by bearings of the rocks, as only pilots and those with local knowledge can identify them with certainty at all states of the tide, and in varying conditions of visibility. There are however several identifiable features and fixed navigational aids in the area.

4   The most prominent rocks off the coast are Les Liniou (48°30′N 4°48′W) of which Grand Liniou, the principal rock of the group, is sheer on its W side and enables the reef to be easily identified, also those on Plateau des Fourches (48°27′N 4°48′W) of which Grande Fourche has two summits. Farther seaward the only marks which can be easily distinguished at HW are La Helle Rock (8.50) and Les Plâtresses (8.45) and Le Faix (8.48) Lighted Beacon Towers; the two towers are excellent marks.

5   From N, the entrance to Chenal du Four is readily identified on the radar display.

Controlling depths
8.37

1   **Chenal du Four.** The N part of Chenal du Four has been swept to a depth of 5 m and the S part to a depth of 7 m. The least charted depth in the channel is a rocky shoal (8.45) lying 2½ miles NW of Pointe de Corsen (48°25′N 4°48′W), noting Basse Saint-Paul (8.45) lying 9 cables W of Pointe de Corsen, on the E limit of the direction light at Pointe de Saint-Mathieu (8.43).

2   **Maximum draught.** Mariners in vessels of more than 7·9 m draught should avoid this channel except at HW which is also the time of slack water.

Chenal de la Helle. The channel has been swept to a depth of 7 m.

Hazards
8.38

1   **Visibility.** From July to September the visibility in Chenal du Four is sometimes poor while the weather outside it is clear.

Heavy weather. In heavy weather the sea breaks heavily on the shore between Presqu'île Saint-Laurent and Pointe de Saint-Mathieu. During these conditions Chenal de la Helle is preferable to Chenal du Four.

2   **Temporary explosives dumping grounds** (Zones de Dépôts d'Explosifs) are situated NE of Île Molène (48°24′N 4°57′W) and NNW of Le Conquet (48°22′N 4°47′W), for details see 1.7 and Appendix V.

Pilotage
8.39

1   Pilots for Chenal du Four are available from Brest; they will board at the port of departure or disembark at the port of arrival.

For details of Brest Compulsory Pilotage Area, see 8.8.

Local knowledge is desirable.

Traffic regulations
8.40

1   **Restricted access.** Vessels over 1600 gt are prohibited from using Chenal de la Helle (8.48) and Chenal du Four (8.45). Smaller vessels proceeding to or from French ports on the Atlantic, Channel or North Sea coasts may use these channels provided they are not carrying hydrocarbons, dangerous goods or passengers, and have permission from the Maritime Prefect for the Atlantic.

2   **Inshore Traffic Zone.** The area lies within Ushant Inshore Traffic Zone, for details see 8.4.

Fishing is restricted in the S part of Chenal du Four, as shown on the chart.

Rescue
8.41

1   **All-weather lifeboats** are stationed as follows:
At Port du Conquet (48°22′N 4°47′W).
At Île Molène (48°24′N 4°57′W).
For details see 1.117.

Signal station, (Vigie) is situated on Pointe de Saint-Mathieu (48°20′N 4°46′W) (8.43), for details see 1.95 and 1.110.

2   **VHF Direction-finding service,** for emergency use only, operates from Pointe de Saint-Mathieu, for details see *Admiralty List of Radio Signals Volume 2.*

Tidal streams
8.42

1   **Chenal de la Helle and Chenal du Four.** In general the streams set obliquely across Chenal de la Helle and the N part of Chenal du Four; they become more nearly in the line of the fairway S of Basse Saint-Paul (48°25′N 4°49′W). They are influenced by the direction of the wind; the N-going (rising) stream is prolonged by S winds and vice-versa.

2   The following table shows the directions of the tidal streams, their rates at springs, and the times at which they begin, at positions in Chenal du Four and in Chenal de la Helle.

Interval from HW Brest	*Direction*
Off Basse Saint Louis (48°28′N 4°53′W):	
−0600	070°
−0100	220°

3   The maximum spring rates are 1½ kn.

1 mile N of Les Plâtresses (48°27′N 4°51′W):	
+0600	020°
−0100	170°

4   The maximum spring rates are 1 kn.

Close S of La Valbelle (48°26′N 4°50′W):	
+0600	010°
−0100	200°

5   The maximum spring rates on the N and S-going stream are 1½ and 1¾ kn, respectively.

Basse de la Maison Blanche (48°26′N 4°52′W):	
−0600	350°–280°
HW	230°–190°

6   The maximum spring rates on the N and S-going streams are 1 and 1½ kn, respectively.

Basse Saint-Paul (48°25′N 4°49′W):	
+0600	340°
HW	170°

7   The maximum spring rates on the N and S-going streams are 2½ and 2 kn, respectively.

Basse Saint-Pierre (48°23′N 4°49′W):	
−0600	358°
+0100	160°

8   The maximum spring rates on the N and S-going streams are 2¼ and 2½ kn, respectively.

Close E of Grande Vinotière (48°22′N 4°48′W):	
−0600	345°
HW	185°

9   The maximum spring rates on the N and S-going streams are 5¼ and 5 kn, respectively.

Roche du Tournant (48°21′N 4°48′W):	
+0600	000°
HW	185°

10   The maximum spring rates on the N and S-going streams are 3 and 3¼ kn, respectively.

Roche de la Fourmi (48°19′N 4°48′W):	
−0600	000°
HW	180°

The maximum spring rates on the N and S-going streams are 2½ and 3 kn, respectively.

Directions

*(continued from 9.16 where directions for the
passage NE along the N coast of France are given)*

Principal marks
8.43

1   **Landmarks:**

Le Four (grey truncated conical tower, 28 m in
height) (48°31′N 4°48′W) on a reef of the same
name.

Radar Tower (48°28′·6N 5°03′·1W) (8.25).

Le Stiff Lighthouse (48°29′N 5°03′W) (8.25).

2   Cross Corsen Radar Surveillance Station (pylon)
(48°24′·8N 4°47′·3W) from which red obstruction
lights are exhibited.

Trézien Lighthouse (grey truncated conical tower,
white on S side, 37 m in height) (48°25′N
4°47′W).

Kermorvan Lighthouse (white square tower, 20 m in
height) (48°22′N 4°47′W).

3   Saint-Mathieu Lighthouse (white truncated conical
tower red top, 37 m in height) (48°20′N 4°46′W);
a direction light is exhibited below the main light.
Saint-Mathieu Auxiliary Light (white turret, 6 m in
height) is situated ¼ cable WNW of the main
light. A signal station (grey square tower, white
dwelling and flagstaff) and abbey ruins stand
nearby on Pointe de Saint-Mathieu.

4   **Major lights:**

Le Stiff Light (48°29′N 5°03′W) (8.25).

Kéréon Light (48°26′N 5°01′W) (8.25).

Le Four Light — as above.

Kermorvan Light — as above.

Saint-Mathieu Light — as above.

Channels
8.44

1   Chenal du Four passes E of Les Plâtresses (48°26′N
4°51′W) (8.45), a group of reefs and drying rocks, and
Chenal de la Helle passes W of these dangers before
joining Chenal du Four. Both channels are well marked by
buoys, direction lights and leading lines.

2   In order to make the best use of the swept depths in
avoiding the dangers which border the channels the
alignments, indicated on the chart, should be closely
followed. Great care is necessary, particularly when altering
course, as the tidal streams set obliquely across the fairway
in places. The best time for using the channels is between
3 hours on either side of HW.

Chenal du Four
8.45

1   **Leading lights:**

Front light Kermorvan Light (48°22′N 4°47′W)
(8.43).

Rear light Saint-Mathieu Light (2 miles SSE of the
front light) (8.43).

2   From a position W of Le Four (48°31′N 4°48′W) the
alignment (158½°) of these lights, or at night on the same
alignment in the centre of Saint-Mathieu Direction Light
which shows white between the bearings 157½° to 159½°,
leads in the fairway passing (with positions given from
Pointe de Corsen (48°25′N 4°48′W)):

3   Over, or clear, of Banc du Four (48°32′N 4°53′W) on
which there is a high sea in bad weather; thence:

WSW of Basse Veur (48°29′·7N 4°51′·2W); thence:

ENE of Basse Saint-Louis (48°27′·7N 4°52′·5W);
thence:

Pointe Saint Mathieu Lighthouse (8.43)

(Original dated 2002)

(Photograph - Mr. C. Nelson)

4   ENE of Basse Talarmin (3½ miles NW); thence:

ENE of Plâtress Nord Light Buoy (starboard hand)
(2¾ miles NW), thence:

Very close WSW of a 6·3 m rocky shoal (2½ miles
NW) the least charted depth for the passage;
thence:

5   Between Les Plâtresses (2½ miles NW) a group of
reefs and drying rocks, noting the dangerous wreck
(position doubtful) (2½ miles NW), and La
Valbelle (2¼ miles NW), marked on its W side by
Valbelle Light Buoy (port hand). The buoy is
liable to drift. Thence:

6   ENE of Basse du Lipari (2¼ miles NW), noting
Plâtresses SE Light Buoy (starboard hand) marking
Roche du SE which lies 4 cables SW and farther
from the track; thence:

ENE of Basse du Moulin (2 miles WNW); thence:

7   WSW of Le Tendoc (1½ miles NW), marked on its
W side by a buoy (port hand), noting a 7·9 m
rocky patch 3 cables WNW and closer to the track;
thence:

WSW of Basse Saint-Paul (9 cables W) marked on
its NNW side by Saint-Paul Light Buoy (port
hand), noting an 8·3 m rocky patch 4½ cables SE
and farther from the track; thence:

8   WSW of a 0·6 m wreck (position doubtful) (1 mile SSW), marked on its W side by Taboga Buoy (isolated danger).

Caution. During the N-going tidal stream Saint-Mathieu Light should be kept slightly open W of Kermorvan Light to avoid Saint-Paul Light Buoy.

Useful mark:
> White Tower (48°30'·3N 4°46'·3W) marked by red obstruction lights.

8.46

1   The line of bearing 012°, astern, of the W side of Pointe de Corsen, or at night in the white sector (012°–015°) on the line of bearing 013°, astern, of Corsen Direction Light (white hut, 3 m in height) (48°25'N 4°48'W) leads in the fairway passing (with positions given from Pointe de Kermorvan (48°22'N 4°47'W)):

2   Midway between Grande Vinotière (7 cables WNW), marked by a lighted beacon tower (red octagonal tower, 24 m in height), and Rouget Light Buoy (starboard hand) (1 mile WNW), noting a dangerous wreck (position doubtful), Roche du Lieu and Roche du Rouget lying 7 cables NW, 4½ cables WNW and 5½ cables WSW, respectively, of Grande Vinotière; thence:

3   Between a 7·9 m rocky patch (7 cables WSW) and a 7·6 m rocky patch (11 cables WSW) which lie close E and W of the track.

4   From a position on the track on the alignment (079°) of La Louve Beacon Tower (port hand) (1½ cables SE) with the N end of Le Conquet E Mole (5 cables E), or at night on the line of bearing 028°, astern, of Grande Vinotière Lighted Beacon Tower, the route leads 174°, about 7½ cables, in the red sector (116°–134°) of Saint-Mathieu Auxiliary Light (2 miles SSE) (8.43) passing:

5   Between a 5·8 m rocky patch (8 cables WSW) and a 6·9 m depth (1¼ miles WSW).

Leading marks:
> Front mark. Grande Courleau Beacon Tower (N cardinal) (48°22'·4N 4°50'·5W).
> Rear mark. Le Faix Lighted Beacon Tower (4 miles NW of the front mark) (8.48).

6   The alignment (325½°), astern, of these marks, on the alignment (009°) of Grande Vinotière Lighted Beacon Tower (7 cables WNW) with Pointe de Corsen (3 miles N), or at night on the alignment of Grande Vinotière Lighted Beacon Tower with Corsen Light, leads, passing:

7   Close SW of a 7·8 m rocky patch (1½ miles SSW) which lies 2 cables W of Roche du Tournant, marked on its N side by Tournant et Lochrist Light Buoy (port hand); thence:
> SW of a dangerous wreck (position doubtful) charted 2 cables SW of Basse de Penzer (1¾ miles S).

8.47

1   **By day,** the track continues 145½° passing (with positions given from Pointe de Kermorvan (48°22'N 4°47'W)):
> SW of Les Vieux Moines (2½ miles SSE) from where a light (red octagonal tower, 19 m in height) is exhibited.

2   **Leading marks:**
> Front mark. Bozmen Oriental (3 miles SSW).
> Rear mark. Bozmen Occidental (5 cables W of the front mark).

The alignment (275°), astern, of these marks leads in the approach to Avant-Goulet de Brest passing:
> S of Roche de la Dorade (2½ miles SSE) towards the pilot boarding place (8.67).

3   **By day and by night.** From a position 2 miles S of Kermorvan Light (8.43) the alignment (007°), astern, of that light with Trézien Light (8.43), 3¾ miles N, or at night on the same alignment in the centre of the white sector (003°–011°) of Trézien Direction Light on the line of bearing 085° of Saint-Mathieu Auxiliary Light which shows green between the bearing 085° to 107°, leads, passing:

4   E of Roche de la Fourmi (2½ miles SSW) marked on its E side by La Fourmi Buoy (starboard hand), noting Basse du Chenal 3 cables SW and farther from the track, to the waiting area (8.63) or towards the pilot boarding place (8.67) as required.

Chenal de la Helle
8.48

1   **Channel.** Chenal de la Helle leads between Plateau de la Helle (48°26'N 4°54'W), a large area of shoal rocky ground forming the NE side of the dangers situated 3 miles NE of Île Molène (8.61), and shoals which extend WNW from Les Plâtresses (8.45). It joins Chenal du Four either 1 mile WSW of Pointe de Corsen (48°25'N 4°48'W) or 1·1 miles NW of Pointe de Kermorvan (48°22'N 4°47'W).

2   **Leading lights:**
> Front. Kermorvan Light (48°22'N 4°47'W) (8.43).
> Rear. Lochrist Direction Light (white octagonal tower red top, 17 m in height) (1·6 miles SE of the front light); not easily distinguished by day.

3   From a position between Le Four (48°31'N 4°48'W) and Île d'Ouessant, 10 miles WSW, the alignment (138°) of these lights, and by night on the same line of bearing in the white sector (135°–140°) of Lochrist Direction Light, leads in the fairway passing (with positions given from Pointe de Corsen (48°25'N 4°48'W)):

4   Between Basse Luronne (48°26'·6N 4°53'·3W), marked by Luronne Buoy (W cardinal), and a 7 m rocky patch (48°26'·4N 4°54'·5W); thence:
> Between Basses de la Maison Blanche (3½ miles WNW) and Le Faix, a drying rock marked by a lighted beacon tower (N cardinal, 21 m in height) (48°26'N 4°54'W); thence:

5   NE of Le Chevreau (3½ miles W) at the E end of Les Chèvres.

Leading lights:
> Front. Le Faix Lighted Beacon Tower — as above.
> Rear. Le Stiff Light (7 miles WNW of the front mark) (8.25).

6   The alignment (293½°), astern, of the above lights then leads in the fairway passing:
> Between Basse du Moulin (2 miles WNW) and Roche NE de la Chaussée des Pourceaux (2½ miles WSW) (8.49); thence:

7   SSW of Basse Saint-Paul (9 cables W) (8.45) to join Chenal du Four 1 mile WSW of Pointe de Corsen on the alignment (158½°) of Kermorvan and Saint-Mathieu Lights; this latter alignment must be followed at night.

8.49

1   **Alternative track by day — leading marks.**
> Front mark. Kermorvan Light (48°22'N 4°47'W) (8.43).
> Rear mark. Les Pignons de Kéravel (two white gables 2 miles SE of the front mark).

From a position on the 113½° track an alternative track, by day, on the alignment (142½°) of the above marks leads in the fairway passing (with positions given from Pointe de Kermorvan (48°22'N 4°47'W)):

2 NE of Roche NE de la Chaussée des Pourceaux (48°24′·1N 4°51′·4W), marked on its NE side by Pourceaux Light Buoy (N cardinal), noting a 4·4 m rocky patch which lies 2 cables SE; thence:

NE of Basse Occidentale du Courleau (2½ miles NW); thence:

3 NE of Basse Saint-Pierre (1¾ miles NW), distant 1 cable, marked on its NE side by Saint-Pierre Buoy (starboard hand); thence:

NE of Basse Orientale du Courleau (1½ miles NW) to join Chenal du Four 1·1 miles NW of Pointe de Kermorvan on the line of bearing 012°, astern, of the W side of Pointe de Corsen.

Useful marks
8.50

1 La Helle (isolated rock) (48°25′·7N 4°54′·7W).

Les Trois-Pierres Light (white column, 16 m in height) (48°25′N 4°57′W).

Men Korn Lighted Beacon Tower (48°28′N 5°01′W) (8.29).

(Directions continue at 8.80;
for Baie de Douarnenez at 8.169
and for Chaussée de Sein at 8.199)

Side channel

Chenal du Four
8.51

1 There is also a direct route on a track of 172°–352° passing 1¾ cables W of Grande Vinotière Lighted Beacon Tower (48°22′N 4°48′W) (8.46). It can be used between the parallel of L'Aber Ildut (48°28′N) and the white sector (107°–116°) of Saint-Mathieu Auxiliary Light, and has the advantage of running with the axis of the tidal streams, but the disadvantage that small parts lie outside the areas swept to a depth of 5 m (8.37) as follows:

2 Between the bearings 070° and 020°of Le Tendoc Rock (48°25′·8N 4°49′·2W).

In the sector between Basse Saint-Pierre (48°23′·1N 4°49′·1W) bearing 290° and Basse Occidentale du Courleau, 3 cables S, bearing 300°.

Anchorage

Chart 3345
Anse des Blancs-Sablons
8.52

1 **General information.** Anse des Blancs-Sablons (48°22′N 4°46′W) is the only anchorage in this vicinity affording any security. It is sheltered from E winds, and the tidal streams are weak here, but the protection from a W swell is mediocre. At the S end of the anchorage Presqu'île de Kermorvan gives good shelter from SW winds.

2 **Anchorage** may be obtained in depths of 6 to 12 m, sand and shells; the holding ground is good. A recommended anchorage is shown on the chart. Disused submarine cables are laid NNW across the bay from the peninsula.

Marine farms are established in the bay.

L'Aber Ildut

General information
8.53

1 **Position and function.** The entrance to Chenal de L'Aber Ildut, the narrow fairway leading to the tidal harbour of L'Aber Ildut (48°28′N 4°45′W) lies

approximately 1½ miles S of Les Liniou (8.36). The harbour is used mostly by fishing vessels, small coasting vessels and yachts.

2 **Limiting conditions.** Most of the harbour is tidal and its entrance is fronted by a rocky bar over which there is a depth of 2 m.

Tidal levels. Mean spring range about 6·3 m; mean neap range about 3·1 m. For further information see *Admiralty Tide Tables.*

3 **Outer anchorage.** A long narrow channel in the centre of the estuary has been dredged to a maximum depth of 6 m in which vessels can lie afloat at all states of the tide.

Tidal streams. The rising stream sets E and the falling stream sets NW; they attain a rate of 3 kn.

Directions for entering harbour
8.54

1 **Leading marks:**

Front mark. Lanildut Church (spire) (48°28′·4N 4°44′·7W).

Rear mark. Brélès Church (spire) (1¼ miles ENE of the front mark).

2 The alignment (078½°) of these marks, which are not always easily seen, or at night in the white sector (081°–085°) of L'Aber-Ildut Direction Light (white building, 5 m in height) (48°28′·3N 4°45′·5W) at the N entrance point to the harbour, leads in the fairway to the harbour entrance passing (with positions given from the front mark):

3 NNW of Basse Grilhed (2½ miles WSW) distant ¾ cable, the outermost danger; thence:

NNW of Pierre de l'Aber (1¾ miles WSW) marked by a beacon (starboard hand); thence:

Between Basse ar Ganol and Basse Madame (1½ miles WSW) passing very close NNW of the former; thence:

4 SSE of Le Lieu Beacon Tower (port hand, 5 m in height) (1¼ miles W) to the harbour entrance.

Within the bar the channel is marked by beacons (port and starboard hand); the harbour is encumbered by shoals.

Useful mark:

Water Tower (48°28′·9N 4°45′·5W).

Berths
8.55

1 **Harbour.** Mariners with local knowledge, in small craft, can lie aground.

Facilities: slipways, each about 40 m long, all of which dry.

Port du Conquet

General information
8.56

1 Port du Conquet (48°22′N 4°47′W), an estuary 1 mile long and about 1 cable wide, is entered between Pointe de Kermorvan and Pointe Sainte-Barbe, about 4 cables SE.

Port radio station, with limited hours, operates from the port, for details see *Admiralty List of Radio Signals Volume 6(2).*

2 **Dangers.** Les Renards, a drying reef extends 2¼ cables WSW from Pointe des Renards, and is marked by a beacon tower (port hand). Basse des Renards lies 2 cables WSW of the beacon tower and is marked by a buoy (isolated danger) at the SW side of the shoal; a dangerous wreck (dries 0·2 m, position doubtful) is charted 1 cable WSW of the buoy.

3   **Anchorage.** The roadstead off the entrance to the port is sheltered from E winds, but is untenable with winds from other directions.

Tidal streams. At the anchorage the N-going rising stream begins 6 hours before HW Brest and causes eddies, running at a rate of 3 to 5 kn, sometimes towards the entrance to the port and at other times towards Pointe de Kermorvan; the falling stream is imperceptible.

4   **Harbour.** The port fronts the town of Le Conquet, situated on the S side of the estuary, and is entered between a mole extending 1 cable NW from Pointe Sainte-Barbe and La Basse du Filet; a light (green mast, 4 m in height) is exhibited from the end of the mole. Quai Aviso Vauquois lies E of Môle Sainte-Barbe and Môle Saint-Christophe extends ½ cable NNW from the shore close E of the E end of the quay. The area between the entrance and the W part of the quay is dredged to 3 m and the area E is dredged to 2 m.

5   **Berth:** Quai Aviso Vauquois; length 170 m; depth alongside 2 to 3 m; reserved for fishing vessels at its NE end and commercial vessels at its SW end.

Landing place: Môle Sainte-Barbe E head; depth alongside 2·7 m.

Supplies: marine diesel oil and petrol; fresh water; provisions.

Lifeboat, see 8.41.

Minor harbour, channels and anchorage

Charts 3345, 2694
Minor channels
8.57

1   There are several channels between the islands and dangers which should never be attempted without local knowledge. The principal are:

Chenal Nord-Ouest de Molène, the NW channel of Île Molène (48°24′N 4°57′W) (8.61).

Chenal des Laz (48°24′N 4°54′W) (8.61) between the dangers extending about 1½ miles N from Île de Quéménès and the S edge of Plateau de la Helle.

2   Passe de la Chimère (48°22′N 4°56′W) between Île Molène and Île de Trielen to W and Île de Quéménès to E.

Passe du Morgol (48°22′N 4°52′W), Passe du Petit Courleau (48°22′N 4°51′W) and Passe du Grand Courleau (48°22′N 4°51′W) between Île de Quéménès to W and Île de Béniguet to E.

8.58

1   **Tidal streams** at the positions indicated begin as shown in the following table:

Interval from HW Brest	*Direction*
Between Île de Balance and Île de Bannec:	
+0550	NE
–0030	SW

2   The maximum NE-going and SW-going spring rates are 7½ and 6½ kn, respectively.

Near Les Pierres Vertes:	
–0615	NNE
HW	SSW

3   The maximum spring rates are 3½ kn.

Interval from HW Brest	*Direction*
In NW channel of Île Molène (W part):	
–0615	NNE
–0015	SSW

4   The maximum spring rates are 4 kn.

In NW channel of Île Molène (E part):	
–0615	ENE
–0015	WSW

5   The maximum spring rates are 6 kn.

In Chenal des Laz:	
–0600	N
–0215	S

6   The maximum N-going and S-going spring rates are 3 and 2 kn, respectively.

In Passe de la Chimère:	
–0615	N
–0015	S

7   The maximum N-going and S-going spring rates are 3 and 4 kn, respectively.

In Passe du Grand Courleau:	
–0615	NE
–0015	SW

8   The maximum spring rates are 4 kn.

About 1 mile ESE of Les Pierres Noires Light:	
–0615	N
–0015	S

9   The maximum spring rates are 3 kn.

Porspaul
8.59

1   **General information.** Porspaul (48°27′N 4°47′W), a small sandy haven which dries from 4 to 5 m and used mainly by fishing vessels and lighters, is entered between Beg ar Vir, the N entrance point of the haven, and Basse de Porspaul Beacon Tower (starboard hand) standing on the N edge of drying reefs which extend 2½ cables N from Île Ségal lying close to the coast on the S side of the entrance.

The harbour is encumbered by transverse chains to assist anchors in holding. There are two slipways.

Anse de Porsmoguer
8.60

1   Anse de Porsmoguer (48°24′N 4°47′W), a small anchorage, affords good shelter from winds between NE and E; the bottom is sand and mud with good holding ground.

Dangers. Basse Jaune lies 2 cables NW of Pointe de Brenterc'h in the S approach to the anchorage.

Île Molène
8.61

1   **General information.** Île Molène (48°24′N 4°57′W) contains a small harbour which is encumbered by transverse chains used by fishing craft as an aid to mooring.

Local knowledge is essential for the two approaches to the harbour.

2   **Directions north approach.** By day, the alignment (190°) of white marks on the old mole with Moulin Sud, a prominent mill, (white) on the S part of the island, or at night in the white sector (190°–192°) of Molène Direction Light (column on a hut, 5 m in height) (48°23′·9N 4°57′·2W) situated on the old molehead, leads in the N approach passing W of Les Trois Pierres Light (48°25′N 4°57′W) (8.50) thence between Men Réal Beacon Tower (E cardinal) and Roche Goulin Light Buoy (W cardinal) situated 7 cables N of the direction light.

3   **East approach leading marks:**

Front mark. Beacon (white truncated tower surmounted with red daymark reflector) (48°24′·0N 4°56′·9W) on Lédénez Vraz.

Rear mark. Moulin Nord (red and white tower) (4 cables W of the front mark) on the N part of the island.

4   The alignment (264°) of these marks, or at night in the centre of the white sector (259½°–262½°) of Molène Direction Light, on the line of bearing 261°, leads through Chenal des Laz.

When N of the W end of Île de Quéménès, lying 2 miles SE of the front mark, the track then leads NW passing NE of Les Trois Pierres Lighted Beacon Tower to join the N approach as given above.

5   **Useful marks:**

Disused Signal Station (yellow square tower, white dwelling black flagstaff) (48°23′·8N 4°57′·4W).

Men ar Roued Beacon Tower (S cardinal) (48°23′·7N 4°53′·8W).

6   **Anchorage.** There is poor temporary anchorage between Men Réal and the dangers off the N coast of the island in depths of 3 to 4 m, rock.

7   **Harbour,** on the E side of the island is formed of two moles, the new mole and the old mole with levelled ground between, sheltered by Môle du Bon Retour, lying about 2 cables N, and to the S by a slipway. There is a landing slip which dries about 1·5 m on the S side of the old mole and another slip on the S side of Môle du Bon Retour, which dries at its head. A lifeboat (8.41) with slipway lies about 2½ cables S of the two moles.

L'IROISE WITH BREST AND BAIE DE DOUARNENEZ

GENERAL INFORMATION

Charts 3427, 2350, 2349, 2643

Description

8.62

1   L'Iroise comprises the waters bounded N by Île d'Ouessant (48°28′N 5°05′W) and Les Pierres Noires, 10 miles SE, and S by Chaussée de Sein (48°03′N 5°00′W); it forms the W approach to Avant-Goulet de Brest (8.70) and Baie de Douarnenez (8.161).

Approach channels

8.63

1   An approach channel, marked on the chart, leads from L'Iroise to a waiting area, radius 1·4 miles, situated 2½ miles S of Pointe de Saint-Mathieu (48°20′N 4°46′W) in the approach to Brest.

Another approach channel, 2 miles wide and marked on the chart, leads from L'Iroise to the meridian of Basse Vieille Light Buoy (48°08′N 4°36′W) at the entrance to Baie de Douarnenez.

2   The use of these approach channels, and the waiting area, is compulsory for vessels exceeding 1600gt laden with hydrocarbons or with dangerous substances, for details see 1.68.

Traffic information

8.64

1   **Movements Reporting System.** The system is compulsory for vessels of 25 m LOA, or over, and provides surveillance and regulation of maritime traffic in Goulet de Brest, Rade de Brest and Baie de Douarnenez.

Shore stations. The Control Centre (Maritime Prefecture of the Atlantic) operates from the following coastguard stations:

2   Pointe de Saint-Mathieu (Vigie) (48°20′N 4°46′W).

Pointe du Portzic (Vigie) (48°22′N 4°32′W) the control station for the port.

Tour César (48°23′N 4°30′W) the control station for Rade de Brest.

Cap de La Chèvre (Sémaphore) (48°10′N 4°33′W).

Pointe du Raz (Vigie) (48°02′N 4°44′W).

8.65

1   **Procedure — vessels inward-bound to Goulet de Brest and Rade de Brest:**

2   All vessels over 1600 gt carrying hydrocarbons or dangerous substances must inform Brest Harbour Master of their entry into the approach channel either directly through RT or through one of the coastguard stations listed above; the vessel must also maintain a continuous listening watch on VHF and contact Brest Port.

3   At least 1 hour in advance of the ETA of crossing the line between Pointe du Toulinguet (48°17′N 4°38′W) and Charles-Martel Light Buoy, 3½ miles NW, vessels should contact Brest Port stating reason for entry, whether the cargo comprises hydrocarbons, gas, dangerous substances or is contaminated. Vessels should remain W of the above line until authority has been given to enter. Brest Port will inform the vessel which route, N or S of Roche Mengam in Goulet de Brest, is to be taken.

4   Vessels with a risk of grounding, pollution or accident because of damage or other difficulties, must wait outside Goulet de Brest in an area designated by the Control Centre.

A vessel should contact the Control Centre in order to obtain a mooring place within Rade de Brest, Anse de Camaret (48°17′N 4°35′W) and Anse de Bertheaume (48°21′N 4°41′W).

5   On arrival in Rade de Brest vessels should contact PC Rade on VHF.

Vessels within Goulet de Brest and Rade de Brest:

Vessels should maintain a listening watch on VHF and follow the instructions from Pointe du Portzic Port Control Station (Brest Port) or the Poste de Commandment de la Rade at Tour César Control Station (PC Rade).

6   **Baie de Douarnenez:**

Vessels inward-bound to Baie de Douarnenez should contact the control centre, either from one of the coastguard stations listed above or through Ouessant Traffic (8.6), in order to obtain a mooring place within Baie de Douarnenez because of bad weather, damage or in the case of force majeure.

7   All vessels over 1600 gt carrying hydrocarbons or dangerous and polluting goods bound for the port of Douarnenez should advise the Harbour Master at Douarnenez of the vessels entry into the approach channel. See also 1.72.

Foreign vessels within Baie de Douarnenez should maintain a listening watch on VHF with Cap de La Chèvre or Pointe du Raz coastguard stations.

8   **Information.** Brest Port and PC Rade will provide information on the meteorological conditions, tidal heights and vessels movements on request.

For further details and for instructions for vessels outward bound from Brest and Baie de Douarnenez, see *Admiralty List of Radio Signals Volume 6(2)*.

9   **Small vessels.** Vessels less than 25 m long not bound by these regulations may pass through Goulet de Brest by the pass of their choice unless ordered otherwise by Brest Port Control Station or by a patrol boat. These vessels must keep to starboard in the passes and must not obstruct the free passage of submarines or large vessels.

Hazards
8.66

1   **Exercise areas,** see 1.31.
Submarine exercises, see 8.128 and 8.163.
Minesweepers frequently carry out exercises in Avant-Goulet de Brest and Rade de Brest; details are broadcast by Pointe du Portzic Control Station for the former area and by Tour César Control Station for the latter area.

For mine countermeasures exercises, see 1.32.

Pilotage
8.67

1   **Area.** For details of Brest Compulsory Pilotage Area limits see 8.8.
Pilotage is compulsory for the following:
Vessels of 50 m in length or more in the Grande Rade and in the port.
Vessels of 35 m in length or more in L'Elorn and L'Aulne rivers up to Landerneau and Châteaulin.

2   All vessels carrying hydrocarbons, gas or dangerous substances.
Towed vessels whose overall length exceeds the lengths mentioned above.
Commercial vessels on entry and on departure from the port areas reserved for the Military (Navy).
Pilotage is also compulsory for vessels entering Baie de Douarnenez (8.161) from the end of the approach channel at L'Iroise roadstead.

3   **Notification for a pilot.** Send initial request for a pilot 48 hours in advance of ETA at Charles-Martel Light Buoy (48°19′N 4°42′W) through the agent. Thereafter send request for a pilot 12 hours and 3 hours in advance of ETA at the Waiting Area S of Saint Mathieu by VHF to Vigie de Saint Mathieu.

Mariners should call the pilot vessel direct on VHF before arrival at Pointe de Saint-Mathieu.

4   **Boarding places.** Pilot boards as follows:
In good weather NW of Pointe du Toulinguet in position 48°18′·3N 4°40′·8W as shown on the chart.

In bad weather the pilot vessel positions itself in front of the vessel, guiding it to Rade de Brest where the pilot boards.

5   The pilot can also board as follows:
At the entrance to Anse de Camaret (48°17′N 4°35′W).
Between Pointe du Portzic (48°22′N 4°32′W) and La Cormorandière, about 8 cables S.

6   If the pilot vessel is not available, mariners should obtain authority to enter Rade de Brest and anchor 5 cables SW of Passe Sud Light (48°22′N 4°29′W) at the entrance to Rade-Abri.

For further details see *Admiralty List of Radio Signals Volume 6(2)*.

Prohibition on jettisoning
8.68

1   No objects of any form or substance exceeding 10 m³ in capacity may be jettisoned in L'Iroise and in Rade de Brest in the area enclosed by the following limits.
The N limit, formed by lines joining:
Position 48°17′N 4°55′W.
Les Vieux Moines Lighted Beacon Tower (48°19′N 4°47′W).

2   Pointe du Petit Minou (48°20′N 4°37′W).
The light tower at the head of Jetée Est of Rade-Abri.
The E limit, formed by lines joining:
The light tower at the head of Jetée Est of Rade-Abri.
Pointe de l'Armorique (48°20′N 4°27′W).
Pointe de Lanvéoc (48°18′N 4°28′W).

3   The S limit, formed by lines joining:
The coast from Pointe de Lanvéoc to Pointe du Toulinguet (48°17′N 4°38′W).
Position 48°14′·5N 4°50′·0W.

4   The W limit, formed by lines joining:
Position 48°17′N 4°55′W.
Position 48°14′·5N 4°50′·0W.

APPROACHES TO BREST

General information

Charts 3427, 2350
Route
8.69

1   The approach to Rade de Brest lies through L'Iroise, Avant-Goulet de Brest and Goulet de Brest.

Topography
8.70

1   Avant-Goulet de Brest is entered between Pointe de Saint-Mathieu (48°20′N 4°46′W) (8.43) and Pointe de Pen-Hir (8.92), about 7½ miles SE, and extends NE to a line joining Pointe du Petit Minou (48°20′N 4°37′W) and Pointe des Capucins, about 1½ miles SE.

Between Pointe de Saint-Mathieu and Pointe du Petit Minou, 6 miles E, the N coast is cliffy.

2   The S coast between Pointe de Pen-Hir (48°15′N 4°37′W) and Pointe des Capucins, 4 miles NNE, appears as a cliff interrupted by the declivity at Anse de Camaret, midway between. Presqu'île de Quélern, with a wooded summit 71 m high, is situated ENE of Pointe des Capucins the W extremity of the peninsula.

Swept depths
8.71

1   **South approach to waiting area** (8.85) passing W of La Vandrée (48°15′N 4°47′W): 13 m swept depth.

Alternative south approach to waiting area (8.86) passing between Le Goëmant and La Parquette (48°16′N 4°44′W): 13 m swept depth.

Passe Nord: (8.82) 11 m swept depth.
Passe Sud: (8.82) 12 m swept depth.

Hazards
8.72

1   **Exercise areas.** Secteur de Toulbroc'h and Secteur de Camaret-sur-Mer exercise areas lie in the approach to Brest, see 1.31.

Minesweeping exercise areas, see 8.66.

Submarine exercises, see 8.128 and information on the chart.

2   **Explosives dumping ground,** see 8.7.

Temporary explosives dumping grounds (Zones de Dépôts d'Explosifs) are situated in the N part of Anse de Camaret (8.103), S of Pointe des Capucins (48°19′N 4°35′W) and in Anse de Dinan (48°14′N 4°35′W) (8.105), for details see 1.7 and Appendix V.

Pilotage
8.73

1   For details of pilotage, see 8.67.

Traffic regulations
8.74

1   For details of traffic regulations, see 8.64 to 8.65.
8.75

1   **Prohibition of anchoring and fishing.** Mariners are prohibited from anchoring and fishing in the areas of Goulet de Brest and Avant-Goulet de Brest, shown on the charts, from S of Point de Saint-Mathieu to the entrance to Rade-Abri at Brest.

Mariners who have anchored in these areas from force of circumstance will be obliged to slip their cable after having buoyed it.

2   There are, however, a number of anchor berths within these prohibited areas which are described at 8.101.

Site of historic interest. Anchoring, trawling and dredging are prohibited in a W semi-circle of 500 m radius centred on Basse Goudron Light Buoy (48°20′·1N 4°34′·8W).

Rescue
8.76

1   **Inshore lifeboat** is stationed at Camaret-sur-Mer (48°17′N 4°35′W), see 1.117.

Signal stations are situated on:
   Pointe de Saint-Mathieu (Vigie) (48°20′N 4°46′W) (8.43).
   Pointe du Toulinguet (Sémaphore) (48°17′N 4°38′W).
   Pointe du Portzic (Vigie) (48°22′N 4°32′W).
For details, see 1.95 and 1.110.

2   **VHF Direction-finding service,** for emergency use only, operates from:
   Pointe de Saint-Mathieu (48°20′N 4°46′W).
   Pointe du Toulinguet (48°17′N 4°38′W).
For details see *Admiralty List of Radio Signals Volume 2.*

Tidal streams
8.77

1   **L'Iroise.** In the middle of L'Iroise, about 13 miles SW of Pointe de Saint-Mathieu, the tidal streams are strong and are rotary in a clockwise direction; they are greatly influenced by the wind. For details, see information on the chart.

2   In the vicinity of La Vandrée, La Parquette and Basse du Lis (48°13′N 4°44′W) they run as follows, beginning at the times stated:

Interval from HW Brest	*Direction*
−0535	N
+0030	S

The maximum spring rates are 2¾ kn.

3   Between Pointe de Dinan (48°14′N 4°34′W) and Cap de la Chèvre, about 4 miles S, the stream runs nearly continuously S at a rate of about 1 kn at springs; only between −0550 and −0445 Brest is there a weak N-going stream. There is no appreciable stream in Anse de Dinan and Anse de Pen-Hir.

4   It appears probable that the rising NE-going stream divides on Les Tas de Pois and Pen-Hir, one part running N towards Pointe du Toulinguet, and the other running E towards Anse de Dinan and then S to Cap de la Chèvre.
8.78

1   **Avant-Goulet de Brest.** Tidal streams off the middle of the entrance to Anse de Bertheaume (48°20′N 4°40′W) begin as follows:

Interval from HW Brest	*Direction*
+0535	E
−0045	W

The maximum spring rates are 2 kn.

In the E part of Anse de Bertheaume an eddy runs ESE from +0230 to −0430 Brest at a rate not exceeding 1 kn.
8.79

1   **Goulet de Brest.** Tidal streams in Goulet de Brest run as follows, beginning at the times indicated:

Interval from HW Brest	*Direction*
In Passe Nord:	
−0535	ENE
+0030	WSW

2   The maximum in-going and out-going spring rates are 4 and 4½ kn, respectively.

In Passe Sud:	
−0605	ENE
HW	WSW

The maximum in-going and out-going spring rates are 4 and 3 kn, respectively.

3   Near the N shore of Goulet de Brest, between Pointe du Petit-Minou and Anse du Dellec, the E-going stream runs for 9 hours from +0300 to HW Brest; the WSW-going stream only runs for 3 hours. In contrast, the stream off Anse de Sainte Anne runs E for only 2 hours from −0600 to −0400 Brest, at a rate of 2 kn, and then WSW for the remainder of the time.

4   Near the S shore of Goulet de Brest, between Pointe des Capucins and Pointe des Espagnols an eddy, extending about 100 m offshore, runs ENE during the falling SW-going stream. The streams off Pointe des Espagnols run very strongly, up to a rate of about 5 kn, between −0330 and +0300 Brest.

Lighthouse   *Coastguard*   *Pointe de Pern*

Le Créac'h Lighthouse from N (8.80)

(Original dated 2000-02)

(Photograph - Jean Guichard)

Les Pierres Noires Lighthouse (8.80)

(Original dated 2000-02)

(Photograph - Jean Guichard)

Directions
(continued from 8.30 and 8.50)

Principal marks
8.80

1 **Landmark:**
Saint–Mathieu Lighthouse (48°20′N 4°46′W) (8.43).
Major lights:
Le Stiff Light (48°29′N 5°03′W) (8.25).

Créac'h Light (48°28′N 5°08′W) (8.25).
La Jument Light (48°25′N 5°08′W) (8.25).

2 Les Pierres Noires Light (white truncated conical tower red top, 28 m in height) (48°19′N 4°55′W).
Kermorvan Light (48°22′N 4°47′W) (8.43).
Saint–Mathieu Light (48°20′N 4°46′W) (8.43).
Pointe du Toulinguet Light (white square tower on building, 14 m in height) (48°17′N 4°38′W).

3 Pointe du Petit Minou Light (48°20′N 4°37′W) (8.83).
Pointe du Portzic Light (48°22′N 4°32′W) (8.83).
Ar Men Light (48°03′N 5°00′W) (8.199).
Île de Sein Main Light (48°03′N 4°52′W) (8.199).

Channels
8.81

1 **Avant–Goulet de Brest.** An approach channel, marked on the chart, leads from L'Iroise to a waiting area in Avant–Goulet de Brest situated 2½ miles S of Pointe de Saint–Mathieu (40°20′N 4°46′W), for details see 8.63.
8.82

1 **Goulet de Brest** is entered from the E end of Avant–Goulet de Brest and extends NE to a line joining Pointe du Portzic (48°22′N 4°32′W) and Pointe des Espagnols, about 1 mile S.

2 A rocky bank, approximately 1 mile in length, lies in the centre of Goulet de Brest, parallel with its axis. Plateau des Fillettes and Roche Mengam (8.89) lie at the SW and NE ends, respectively, of this bank. Passe Nord, the usual entrance, leads N of these dangers and Passe Sud, leads S of them.

Sea to waiting area
8.83

1 **Leading lights:**
Front light. Pointe du Petit Minou Light (grey round tower white on the SW side red top, 26 m in height) (48°20′N 4°37′W) a smaller tower (white with black base) (8.87) stands close SW.
Rear light. Pointe du Portzic Light (grey octagonal tower, 35 m in height) (3½ miles ENE of the front light).

2　From a position in L'Iroise the alignment (068°) of the above lights, or at night on the same alignment of their direction lights which are exhibited from the same structures as their main lights, the main lights being obscured on this alignment, leads in the approach channel to the waiting area passing (with positions given from Pointe de Saint-Mathieu (48°20′N 4°46′W)):

3　　SSE of Basse Occidentale des Pierres Noires (7½ miles W), marked at its SW side by Pierres Noires Buoy (S cardinal), the W-most danger of Chaussée des Pierres Noires, and noting two light buoys (special) 1½ miles S of Basses Occidentale des Pierres Noires; thence:

　　SSE of Les Pierres Noires (5¾ miles W), a group of rocks and dangers from where a light (8.80) is exhibited, lying close within the S end of Chaussée des Pierres Noires; thence:

4　　SSE of Roche du Varech (4 miles WSW); thence:

　　Between Basse Royal (3 miles SW), the SE-most danger of Chaussée des Pierres Noires, marked on its SE side by a light buoy (S cardinal), and La Vandrée (4¾ miles S). Vandrée Light Buoy (W cardinal) is moored 7 cables WNW; thence:

5　　NNW of L'Astrolabe and La Boussole (4 miles S), two rocks lying close together; thence:

　　To the waiting area passing between Les Vieux Moines (5 cables SSW), from where a light (8.47) is exhibited, and La Parquette (4 miles SSE) on which stands a Lighted Beacon Tower (white octagonal tower black diagonal stripes, 25 m in height).

8.84

1　**Clearing marks:**
　　Front mark. La Parquette Lighted Beacon Tower (48°16′N 4°44′W) (8.83).
　　Rear mark. W rock of Les Tas de Pois (4¼ miles ESE of the front mark) (8.92).

The alignment (104°) of these marks clears SSW of the dangers between Île d'Ouessant and the mainland.

2　**Caution.** Mariners in deep-draught vessels should note a wreck with a depth of 15·4 m over it (position doubtful) (48°19′N 5°01′W) charted about 2½ miles W of the W side of Les Pierres Noires; such mariners should pass at least 1½ miles SW of the clearing marks described at 8.30.

3　**Useful marks:**
　　Le Diamant (prominent rock) (48°18′·6N 4°55′·0W) situated on Les Pierres Noires close to the Lighted Beacon Tower.
　　Kéréon Light (48°26′N 5°01′W) (8.25) (chart 2694).

South approach to waiting area
8.85

1　**Leading lights:**
　　Front light. Kermorvan Light (48°22′N 4°47′W) (8.43).
　　Rear light. Trézien Light (3¾ miles N of the front light) (8.43) (chart 2694).

The alignment (007°) of these lights leads in the S approach to the waiting area passing (with positions given from Pointe de Saint-Mathieu (48°20′N 4°46′W)):

2　　Between Basse du Laborieux (48°12′N 4°50′W) and Basse de l'Iroise (7½ miles S); the sea breaks heavily on these rocks in bad weather. Thence:
　　W of La Vandrée (4¾ miles S) (8.83); thence:
　　To the waiting area on the alignment (068°) of Petit Minou and Portzic Leading Lights as given above.

Alternative south approach to waiting area
8.86

1　**Leading lights:**
　　Front light. Les Vieux Moines Lighted Beacon Tower (48°19′N 4°47′W) (8.47).
　　Rear light. Kermorvan Light (2½ miles NNW of the front light) (8.43).

The alignment (348°) of these lights leads in the alternative S approach to the waiting area passing (with positions given from Point de Saint-Mathieu (48°20′N 4°46′W)):

2　　WSW of Basse du Lis (6¾ miles SSE), marked on its SW side by a light buoy (S cardinal), passing close to the buoy; and:
　　ENE of Basse de l'Iroise (7½ miles S) (8.85); thence:

3　　ENE of Le Goëmant (4¾ miles S), marked on its NE side by a buoy (E cardinal); thence:
　　Between L'Astrolabe (4 miles S) (8.83) and La Parquette Lighted Beacon Tower (4 miles SSE) (8.83) to the waiting area.

Waiting area to Brest
8.87

1　**Leading lights:**
　　Front light. Petit Minou Light (48°20′N 4°37′W).
　　Rear light. Portzic Light (3½ miles ENE of the front light).

From a position in the waiting area between Pointe de Saint-Mathieu (48°20′N 4°46′W) and Basse de la Parquette, 4 miles SSE, the alignment (068°) of the above leading lights (8.83) continues to lead in the fairway passing (with positions given from Pointe du Toulinguet (48°17′N 4°38′W)):

2　　SSE of Le Coq (48°19′·2N 4°43′·9W) marked on its S side by Coq Iroise Buoy (port hand); thence:
　　NNW of Le Trépied (2½ miles W) marked on its N side by a buoy (starboard hand); thence:
　　Close SSE of Charles-Martel Light Buoy (port hand) (3½ miles NW) which marks the S side of Roche du Charles-Martel, noting Basse Beuzec marked on its SE side by a buoy (port hand) close ENE.

3　**Poor visibility.** Mariners using this alignment in poor visibility should not confuse the smaller tower, situated close SW of Pointe du Petit Minou Light, with Pointe du Portzic Light, as under these circumstances these two towers could present the appearance of the real alignment.

4　**Clearing bearing.** The line of bearing 090° of Pointe du Toulinguet Light (48°17′N 4°38′W) (8.80) changing from red to white clears N of the dangers extending WSW from Pointe du Toulinguet.

8.88

1　**Alternative track.** The line of bearing 060° of Pointe du Portzic Light (48°22′N 4°32′W) (8.83) leads from the waiting area through Avant-Goulet de Brest into Passe Nord, passing close NNW of Basse Hermine (48°19′·3N 4°37′·4W), to join the route NW of Plateau des Fillettes (8.89).

Clearing bearing — as above.

8.89

1　**Passe Nord — leading marks:**
　　Front mark. Roche Mengam Lighted Beacon Tower (isolated danger, 15 m in height) (48°20′N 4°35′W).
　　Rear mark. Plougastel Water Tower (8½ miles ENE of the front mark).

2　From a position about 4 miles from the front mark the alignment (074½°) of these marks, or at night on the line of bearing 075° of Roche Mengam light, then leads in the approach to Passe Nord passing (with positions given from Pointe du Toulinguet (48°17'N 4°38'W)):

3

SSE of a 9·9 m rocky patch (3¼ miles NNW); thence:

NNW of Swansea Vale Light Buoy (isolated danger) (1½ miles NNW); thence:

SSE of a charted 11·5 m depth (3 miles WNW); thence:

NNW of Basse Hermine (2½ miles N); thence:

Between the coastal bank fronting Pointe du Petite Minou (3½ miles N) and Roche Pollux (3 miles NNE), noting a 10·1 m rocky patch 3 cables W; thence:

4

NNW of Plateau des Fillettes (3¼ miles NNE) marked on its W side by Fillettes Light Buoy (W cardinal) and on its E side by Kerviniou Light Buoy (port hand).

The line of bearing 060° of Pointe du Portzic Light (48°22'N 4°32'W) (8.83) then leads in the fairway passing:

5

NNW of Basse Goudron (3¾ miles NNE) marked on its NE side by a light buoy (port hand); thence:

NNW of Roche Mengam (4¼ miles NNE), distant 2 cables, marked by a lighted beacon tower.

6

The line of bearing 256°, astern, of Petit Minou Light (3½ miles NNE) or at night in the centre of the white section (252°–260°), astern, of this light leads in the fairway into Rade de Brest.

8.90

1

Passe Sud. From a position in Avant-Goulet de Brest between Point du Toulinguet (48°17'N 4°38'W) and Swansea Vale Light Buoy (isolated danger), 1½ miles NNW, the line of bearing 045° of Saint Martin Church (pointed spire) (48°23'·8N 4°28'·7W) at Brest just open W of Pointe du Portzic Light (8.83), or at night in the centre of the intensified white sector (045°–050°) of Pointe du Portzic Direction Light, leads through Passe Sud passing (with positions given from Pointe du Toulinguet):

2

NW of Roche du Crabe (3 cables NNE); thence:

NW of a dangerous wreck (position doubtful) (charted 9 cables NE); and:

SE of a dangerous wreck (12 cables N); thence:

NW of Roche Castor (2½ miles NE); thence:

3

Between Plateau des Fillettes (3¼ miles NNE) and associated dangers on the NW side (8.89) and the NW coast of Presqu'île de Quélern (4 miles NE) (8.70) on the SE side.

On the alignment (265°), astern, of Roche Mengam Lighted Beacon Tower (4¼ miles NE) with Petit Minou Light (3½ miles N) the track then leads ENE into Rade de Brest.

8.91

1

Clearing marks:

Plateau des Fillettes and Basse Goudron are covered by the red sector (034°–054°) of Roche Mengam Light.

Plateau des Fillettes, Basse Goudron and Roche Mengam are covered by the red sector of Petit Minou Light between the bearings of 260° to 307°.

8.92

1

Useful marks:

Fort de Bertheaume (old fort) (48°20'·3N 4°41'·8W) standing on a large rock.

Water Tower (48°21'·6N 4°33'·4W) marked by a red obstruction light.

Îlot des Capucins (fort) (48°19'·2N 4°34'·9W) joined by an arch to Point des Capucins.

2

Monument (48°15'·6N 4°37'·4W) standing 4 cables N of Pointe de Pen-Hir, formed of steep black cliffs,

erected in memory of the Free French Naval Forces.

Les Tas de Pois (five prominent detached rocks) (48°15'N 4°38'W).

(Directions continue at 8.135 and 8.147)

Side channels

General information

8.93

1

Passages. The S side of Avant Goulet de Brest is formed by the rocky chain between Pointe du Toulinguet (48°17'N 4°38'W) and La Vandrée, 6½ miles WSW. There are several channels leading into Avant-Goulet de Brest passing either W of, or between the shoals extending W from Pointe du Toulinguet which may be used by mariners approaching from S, especially from Raz de Sein (8.202).

2

The alignments of the leading marks of these channels must be closely followed in order to avoid the isolated dangers which exist in their vicinity.

Some of these channels are described below.

8.94

1

Tidal streams at the following positions begin at the times shown:

Interval from HW Brest	Direction
At Le Trépied Buoy (48°17'N 4°41'W):	
−0535	ENE
+0030	WSW
In Chenal du Petit Léac'h:	
−0550	NE
+0015	SW
In Chenal du Toulinguet:	
−0550	N
+0015	S

2

The maximum in-going and out-going spring rates at each of the above positions are 2¾ kn.

See also tidal information on the chart. For tidal streams in the vicinity of La Vandrée, see 8.77.

Chenal du Petit Léac'h

8.95

1

General information. The narrow part of Chenal du Petit Léac'h is bounded on its NW side by Petit Léac'h (48°16'N 4°40'W) and on its SE side by the dangers extending SW from Rochers du Toulinguet, 7 cables E.

Swept depth: 12 m.

8.96

1

Directions. The line of bearing 043½° of Saint Martin Church (48°23'·8N 4°28'·7W) (8.90) open SE of Pointe du Portzic, 3 miles SW, leads in the approach and through Chenal du Petit Léac'h passing (with positions given from Pointe du Toulinguet (48°17'N 4°38'W)):

2

SE of Basse de L'Iroise (8 miles WSW) (8.85); thence:

Between Basse du Lis (5½ miles SW) (8.86) and a 10·3 m rocky patch (4¾ miles SW) passing close SE of the former shoal; thence:

NW of Basse Rozen (4¼ miles SW); thence:

3

NW of Basse Ménéhom (3¾ miles SW); thence:

NW of Basse Poulmalcote (2¾ miles SSW); thence:

Between Petit Léac'h and Basse Mendufa (1¼ miles WSW) marked by a beacon (S cardinal) and a buoy (N cardinal), respectively, noting Pelen, a drying rock marked by a beacon (S cardinal), and Basse du Sud extending 5½ cables SSW from Basse Mendufa; thence:

4 NW of Rochers du Toulinguet (6 cables SW); thence:
NW of La Louvre, marked by a beacon tower (W cardinal, 4 m in height), standing 1 cable W of Pointe du Toulinguet.

The track then continues NE to join the route (8.90) through Passe Sud.

Chenal du Toulinguet
8.97

1 **General information.** Chenal du Toulinguet lies about 5 cables W of the coast between Pointe de Pen-Hir and Pointe du Toulinguet (48°17′N 4°38′W).
Swept depth: 8·5 m.
Local knowledge is required.
8.98

1 **Directions.** From a position W of Cap de la Chèvre (48°10′N 4°33′W) (8.169) the line of bearing 011° of Pointe du Petit Minou Light (48°20′N 4°37′W) (8.83) just open W of Pointe du Toulinguet, 3½ miles S, leads in the approach passing (with positions given from Pointe du Toulinguet (48°17′N 4°38′W)):

W of Basse du Bouc (5½ miles S), a bank lying 1 mile W of Le Bouc, a drying rock marked by a light buoy (W cardinal); thence:

2 W of La Queue du Bouc (5 miles S); thence:
E of La Queue de Chevreau (4½ miles SSW); thence:
W of Basse du Chevreau (4 miles S); thence:
E of Basse Poulmalcote (2¾ miles SSW); thence:
W of Les Tas de Pois (2 miles S) (8.92) distant about 2½ cables.

3 The line of bearing 156½°, astern, of L'Aiguille de Pen-Hir just open W of Pointe de Pen-Hir (1¾ miles SSE) then leads through Chenal du Toulinguet passing:

ENE of Le Pohen (4½ cables SW) distant ½ cable, the N-most rock of Rochers du Toulinguet; and:
WSW of a 5·5 m depth at the SW end of Le Louveteau (2½ cables WSW), noting Banc de La Louvre close SSE.

4 The track then joins Chenal du Petit Léac'h (8.95) on the line of bearing 043½° of Saint Martin Church.

Alternative leading mark. The line of bearing 026½° of the W rock of Les Tas de Pois (48°15′N 4°38′W) (8.92) leads WNW of the dangers offlying the coast W of Cap de la Chèvre to join the above route 1 mile SSW of Les Tas de Pois on the line of bearing 011° of Pointe du Petit Minou Light.

Chenal du Grand Léac'h
8.99

1 **General information.** Chenal du Grand Léac'h (48°16′N 4°39′W) forks NW from the channel of approach to Chenal du Toulinguet NW of Le Tas de Pois and then passes between Basse Mendufa and Rochers du Toulinguet.
Swept depth: 11 m.
8.100

1 **Directions.** The line of bearing (148°), astern, of the W extremity of Cap de la Chèvre (48°10′N 4°33′W) (8.169) open E of the drying rock NE of Le Tas de Pois Ouest, 5½ miles NNW, leads through Chenal du Grand Léac'h passing (with positions given from Pointe du Toulinguet (48°17′N 4°38′W)):

2 Between a 10 m patch (1¼ miles SW), lying 2 cables E of Basse Mendufa and associated dangers (8.96),

and a depth of 7·4 m (1 mile SW) at the SW end of a bank extending SW from Rochers du Toulinguet.

The track then joins Chenal du Petit Léac'h (8.95) on the line of bearing 043½° of Saint Martin Church.

Anchorages

Chart 3427
Avant-Goulet de Brest
8.101

1 Two anchor berths are situated 3 miles WNW of Pointe du Toulinguet (48°17′N 4°38′W) in the prohibited anchorage area (8.75). Another anchorage berth, within which lies a dangerous wreck, is situated on the edge of the prohibited anchorage area, 1¼ miles N of Pointe du Toulinguet.

The positions of the berths are shown on the chart.

Anse de Bertheaume
8.102

1 **General information.** Anse de Bertheaume is entered between Pointe de Créac'h Meur (48°20′N 4°42′W) and Pointe du Grand Minou, about 3 miles E. The head of the bay is bordered by a bank with depths of less than 5 m over it, which, in places, extends 4 cables offshore.
Tidal streams, see 8.78.

2 **Anchorage.** A designated anchorage area with numbered berths lies at the W side of the cove, as shown on the chart. There is indifferent anchorage, sheltered from N winds, in depths of 10 to 15 m, sand. The holding ground is bad and the W swell penetrates to the head of the bay. An anchorage, rather more sheltered from W winds, lies 3 cables NNE of Fort de Bertheaume (48°20′·3N 4°41′·8W) (8.92) in depths of 5 to 7 m, sand.

3 **Caution.** Roche Plate and Roche du Pêcheur lie on the W side of the entrance 8 cables ENE and 1¼ miles NE, respectively, of Pointe de Créac'h Meur. Pen Hir Buoy (isolated danger) marks a 13·1 m wreck in the centre of the entrance about 2 miles E of the same point.

Anse de Camaret
8.103

1 **General information.** Anse de Camaret is entered between Pointe du Grand Gouin (48°17′N 4°36′W) and Pointe Trémet, 1¼ miles NE. The roadstead affords shelter from winds from W through S to E, but is dangerous with NW and N winds. There is no appreciable tidal stream.

2 Camaret-sur-Mer (8.106), a harbour for small craft, is situated in the SW part of the bay.
Anchorage A designated anchorage area with numbered berths is shown on the chart. Anchorage can be obtained in the middle of the bay in depths of 10 to 14 m, gravel and coral, with good holding ground, or farther S in depths of 3 to 10 m, sand and mud.

3 **Caution.** A rocky shoal with a depth of 8·5 m over it lies in the middle of the bay 7½ cables E of Pointe du Grand Gouin. Fish farms are situated in the E and SE parts of the bay 9 cables SE of the same point.

Minor bays and harbour

Chart 2349
Anse de Pen-Hir
8.104

1 **General information.** Anse de Pen-Hir (48°16′N 4°37′W) is entered between Pointe de Pen-Hir and Pointe de la Tavelle, 1 mile E, and affords shelter to mariners in small craft from winds from N and W.

2   **Anchorage** can be obtained at the N end of the bay.

   Caution. Basse de Dinan lies in the centre of the entrance to the bay 1 mile WSW of Pointe de la Tavelle and a bank on which there are some drying rocks extends 3 cables S from the same point.

Anse de Dinan
8.105

1   Anse de Dinan is entered between Pointe de Portzen (48°15′N 4°35′W) and Pointe de Dinan, 1 mile S, and has depths of 6 to 9 m with a fine sandy bottom. A wide sandy beach dries out up to 3 cables offshore.

2   **Caution.** Le Chevreau, a drying rock, marked by a buoy (W cardinal) and Le Chevreau Beacon (W cardinal) with La Chèvre, a small rock, lie 1¾ and 1¼ miles WSW, respectively, of Pointe de Dinan in the S approach to the bay.

3   **Temporary explosives dumping ground** is situated 8 cables NW of Pointe de Dinan. For details see 1.7 and Appendix V.

Chart 3427 plan of Port de Camaret-sur-Mer
Camaret-sur-Mer
8.106

1   **General information.** Camaret-sur-Mer (48°17′N 4°36′W), a small harbour used principally by fishing vessels and pleasure craft, is situated on the SW side of Anse de Camaret. Several marine farms exist in the approach and within the harbour itself as shown on the chart.

2   **Port radio** station, with limited hours, operates from the port, for details see *Admiralty List of Radio Signals Volume 6(1)*.

   Harbour. The harbour is protected on its N side by a long breakwater, prolonged ENE by a mole which branches S at its E extremity to enclose a marina. On the S side the harbour is protected by a mole extending NNW from the shore. A light is exhibited from the head of each mole.

3   **Depths.** The harbour dries with the exception of an area close within the entrance which has been dredged to 1·5 m; an area close S of this which is dredged to 2 m for mariners anchoring and manoeuvring for access to berths. Unauthorized anchoring is not permitted in these dredged areas.

4   **Berths:** quays and landing slips on the W side of the harbour for drying out; wharf and stone-faced quay on the S side of the harbour for fishing vessels and an anchorage in the centre of the harbour in depths up to 2 m.

5   **Facilities:** repair facilities available; slipways for vessels up to 350 tonnes; fresh water; fuel; provisions.

Chart 3427
Anse de Sainte-Anne
8.107

1   **General information.** Anse de Sainte-Anne (48°21′·5N 4°32′·8W) is entered W of Pointe du Portzic; Roches de la Drague lie in the entrance of the bay.

   Entry is prohibited in an area, shown on the chart, S and SW of the jetty.

   Berth: stone jetty on the NW side of the bay; landing stage on its N side.

BREST AND RADE DE BREST
General information

Charts 3428, 3427, 3429
Position
8.108

1   The town of Brest (48°23′N 4°29′W) is situated on the N side of Rade de Brest.

Function
8.109

1   Brest is a major French naval base as well as an important commercial, repair and fishing port.

   Rade de Brest affords good shelter with excellent holding ground and is accessible at all times. Grande Rade de Brest is the NW part of the roadstead bounded SE by a line drawn from Île Ronde (48°19′N 4°28′W) to Pointe de l'Île Longue, 1¾ miles SW.

Approach and entry
8.110

1   Rade de Brest is approached through Avant-Goulet and Goulet de Brest and is entered from Goulet de Brest between Pointe du Portzic (48°22′N 4°32′W) and Pointe des Espagnols, about 1 mile S.

2   Rade-Abri and Port Militaire are entered from Rade de Brest through Passe Sud.

   Port de Commerce, the commercial harbour, is entered from the E side of Rade-Abri through Passe de l'Ouest the usual passage, or from Rade de Brest through Passe de l'Est, at the E end of Port de Commerce.

Traffic
8.111

1   In 2006 the port was used by 639 vessels totalling 6 559 310 dwt.

Port Authority
8.112

1   Port de Brest, Direction Departementale de l'Equipement, 2 Rue Alderic Lecomte, 29200 Brest Cedex, France.

Limiting conditions
Controlling depths
8.113

1   **Rade-Abri.** With the exception of the NE part, the greater part of Rade-Abri is maintained by dredging at a depth of from 10 to 11 m.

   Port du Commerce. The general depths in Basins No 1 to 5, between Jetée Ouest and Quai Est No 5, are from 6 to 7 m with a maximum depth of 9·5 m at Quai Est.

2   Depths in the entrances are:

      Passe du l'Ouest 7 m.

      Passe de l'Est 6 m.

   The maximum depth in No 6 Basin lying close E of No 5 Basin is 12·7 m at Quai Sud No 6.

Vertical clearances
8.114

1   **La Penfeld:**

      Pont de Recouvrance (8.135) 18·8 m closed; 43·4 to 45·4 m open (see also note chart 3428).

      Pont de l'Harteloire (48°23′·6N 4°30′·0W) 41 m.

Deepest and longest berths
8.115

1   **Rade-Abri:** No 4 Berth (8.140).

Port du Commerce: Quai Est No 5. (8.141).
Bassin No 6: Quai Sud No 6 (8.141).

Tidal levels
8.116

1 Mean spring range about 5·9 m; mean neap range about 2·8 m. For further information see *Admiralty Tide Tables*.

Maximum size of vessel handled
8.117

1 **Port du Commerce.** Entry to the port is dependant upon draught and height of tide; vessels of up to 320 m LOA and 10·6 m draught can use the port, subject to tide. A vessel of 255 m LOA has used Bassin No 6.

2 The length of vessels which can be accommodated between the moles in Port de Commerce is limited by the difficulty of manoeuvring them. Vessels of 220 m in length can cross this part of the port to enter No 1 Dry Dock in its NE corner, but with fresh winds the berthing of vessels in excess of 150 m in length is difficult.

Arrival information

Vessel Traffic Service
8.118

1 A VTMS is in operation in the approaches to Brest and in Rade de Brest, for details see 8.64 to 8.65.

Tour César (49°22'·9N 4°29'·6W), the port control station, stands on top of Château de Brest situated on the E side of the mouth of La Penfeld.

Port radio
8.119

1 There are port radio stations at Brest, for details see *Admiralty List of Radio Signals Volume 6(1)*.

Notice of ETA required
8.120

1 For details of notice of ETA required, see 8.67.

Outer anchorages
8.121

1 **Grande Rade de Brest.** Mariners may anchor anywhere in Grande Rade clear of the prohibited areas (8.125). Anchor berths are assigned by PC Rade and shown on the chart.

Spoil ground, shown on the chart, is situated S of Pointe des Espagnols (48°20'·5N 4°31'·9W).

2 Anchorage is not recommended within an area of 500 m radius, formerly used as a spoil ground, in which the holding ground is poor, situated in position 137° distant 3900 m from Pointe du Portzic Light.

Waiting anchorage. An anchorage, radius 360 m, shown on the chart in a prohibited anchorage area (8.125), for mariners awaiting a pilot to berth, is situated 5 cables SW of the head of Jetée Sud.

3 **Caution.** Banc du Corbeau, which extends up to 1½ miles from the shore on the NE side of Grande Rade, Banc du Caro, Basse de l'Armorique and a dangerous rock lie on the E side of the roadstead 1¾ miles N 8 cables NNE, 3 cables NW and 2 cables SW, respectively, of Île Ronde (48°19'·5N 4°27'·7W). Basse du Renard marked on its W side by Basse du Renard Light Buoy (W cardinal) lies near the centre of the roadstead 8½ cables NW of the same isle.

8.122

1 **Baie de Roscanvel** (40°19'N 4°32'W) offers good shelter in W winds; there is anchorage in depths from 12 to 22 m in the entrance to the bay clear of the prohibited areas (8.125), and the holding ground of sand and mud is good.

A mooring buoy is situated at the entrance to the bay 5 cables N of Île Longue.

2 **Tidal stream** during the first three hours of the rising tide runs from Pointe des Espagnols towards Île Longue thence towards Île Trébéron; thereafter until LW the stream runs N.

Caution. Basse Fortunée lies near the S entrance to the bay 6 cables NW of Pointe de l'Île Longue.

8.123

1 **Anse du Fret** is entered between Île Longue (48°19'N 4°30'W) (8.135) and Pointe de Lanvéoc, 1¾ miles ESE. It is completely sheltered from SW winds but exposed to E winds, which make the anchorage dangerous.

2 **Tidal streams.** There is little stream in the bay at any time. During the rising stream there may be a weak eddy running from Pointe de Lanvéoc towards Pointe de l'. During the falling tide there may be a very weak stream running WSW into the bay, and NNE along the coast of , but the greater part of the stream runs from Pointe de Lanvéoc towards Pointe de l'Île Longue.

3 **Anchorage,** for mariners permitted to anchor in the prohibited areas (8.125), is available in depths of 5 to 9 m, good holding ground, mud.

Pilotage and tugs
8.124

1 **Pilotage,** see 8.67.
Tugs are available.

Traffic regulations
8.125

1 **Entry is prohibited** to the following areas:
Within an area up to a distance of 2½ cables of the coast surrounding the naval port at Île Longue.
In the vicinity of an oil jetty situated 4 cables E of Pointe de Lanvéoc (48°18'N 4°28'W).

2 Along the W side of Anse du Poulmic from Pen-ar-Vir (48°18'N 4°25'W) to a point 1¼ miles SSE encompassing the naval school.
Within the occasional area centred on position 48°18'·2N 4°24'·3W.

3 **Entry is restricted** in the occasional areas of the following DG ranges when the permanent areas of the same ranges are in use:
In the DG range extending up to 1¼ miles N and E from Pointe de l'Ile Longue (48°19'N 4°30'W).
In the DG range in the entrance to Anse de Fret situated WNW of Pointe de Lanvéoc.

4 In the DG range surrounding the jetty close W of Pointe de Lanvéoc.
For details see 8.130.

Anchoring and fishing are prohibited in the following areas:
An area, about 1 mile wide, extending from Goulet de Brest to the S entrance to Rade–Abri.

5 In the permanent areas of the DG ranges off Pointe de l'Ile Longue and Pointe de Lanvéoc mentioned above.

Anchoring is prohibited in an area surrounding Pointe de l'Ile Longue including Ile Trébéron, Ile Longue and Anse du Fret.

The above areas where entry, anchoring, diving, dredging and fishing are prohibited are shown on the charts.

6   **Shellfish beds.** Numerous mussel and oyster beds exist close to the shore in L'Élorn, Baie de Roscanvel, Baie de Daoulas and L'Aulne. Vessels should not anchor or ground in these areas.

8.126

1   **Rade-Abri.** Navigation in Rade-Abri is regulated, the following are extracts from the regulations:

> That part of Rade-Abri which lies W of a line joining the head of Jetée Sud and Terre-plein du Château is reserved for the use of the French navy; all merchant vessels, fishing boats and pleasure craft are prohibited, without authorisation, from entering this area.

2   All vessels authorized to navigate in Rade-Abri must not exceed a speed of 10 kn.

> Except in cases of emergency, anchorage is prohibited.

Harbour

General layout
8.127

1   **Main berthing areas.** Rade-Abri and Port Militaire, together with Port de Commerce close E, lie on the N side of Rade de Brest; the harbours are protected by breakwaters. Saint-Marc Industrial Estate, with repair quays and dry docks, lies on the E side of No 6 Basin. Port du Moulin-Blanc (48°23′N 4°26′W), a marina with extensive facilities for yachts, is situated in the NE part of the port.

2   L'Elorn (8.148) and L'Aulne (8.150), two rivers, flow into the NE and SE corners, respectively, of Rade de Brest.

Channels. Rade-Abri is protected on its S side by Jetée Sud and on its E side by Jetée Est. Passe Sud, the entrance, lies between the head of each jetty.

3   There are two passages into Port de Commerce which is protected to the S by Jetée du Sud, which extends E from the N end of Jetée Est. The usual passage is Passe de l'Ouest which, together with the alternative Passe de l'Est, are described at 8.138.

Submarine exercise area
8.128

1   When the appropriate flags of *The International Code of Signals* are displayed from a vessel escorting submerged submarines, mariners in all vessels navigating in Rade de Brest should avoid entering the area defined below. This is the only part of the road in which submarines are permitted to exercise submerged.

2   The area is bounded N by a line drawn 068° from Roche Mengam (48°20′N 4°34′W); W by a line drawn from Pointe des Espagnols to the E extremity of Île Tréberon; thence by the alignment of Pointe de l'Île Longue and Le Grénoc Beacon Tower, 3½ cables WNW, projected NW to meet the line just described; by a line joining Pointe de l'Île Longue, Pointe de Lanvéoc, and Pointe Doubidy (48°20′N 4°25′W); and by the alignment of the W extremity of Île Ronde and Pointe des Espagnols, projected SE to meet the line joining Pointe de Lanvéoc and Pointe Doubidy; by a line joining the W extremity of Île Ronde and Saint Martin Church (48°23′·8N 4°28′·7W); and by the alignment of Saint Pierre Church (48°22′·8N 4°32′·0W) and the head of Jetée Sud of Rade-Abri projected E to meet the line joining the lines previously mentioned.

3   See 1.33 and *The Mariner's Handbook*.

Temporary explosives dumping ground
8.129

1   A temporary explosives dumping ground (Zones de Dépôts d'Explosifs) is situated on Banc de Corbeau (48°21′N 4°27′W), for details see 1.7 and Appendix V. GPD Atlantic Light buoy (special) is moored in the centre of the dumping ground.

Ranges
8.130

1   **Magnetic and acoustic ranges** are situated in the N part of Anse de Fret and marked by light buoys and buoys. When these areas are in use signals are displayed from the control post of Fort Lanvéoc (48°17′·7N 4°27′·7W).

Natural conditions
8.131

1   **Tidal streams - Rade de Brest.** The tidal streams in Rade de Brest and adjacent estuaries run as follows; the times refer to HW Brest.

2   **In-going stream.** This begins in Goulet de Brest at −0545 Brest and after passing Pointe du Portzic it spreads out with diminishing rate and divides into two principal branches W of Banc du Corbeau; E of this bank the stream is weak and direction variable but between −0400 Brest and HW it is mainly S. The N branch of the stream passes N of the bank towards L'Élorn (8.148) attaining a maximum rate of 1½ kn at −0300 Brest in the vicinity of Pont Albert-Louppe (48°23′N 4°24′W); a W-going eddy runs along the N shore, E of Port de Commerce, from −0500 to −0200 Brest. The S branch of the stream passes W of Banc du Corbeau in a SE direction and again divides into two branches on the parallel of Île Ronde, one branch running SW towards Baie de Roscanvel and Anse du Fret, and the other SE towards the estuary of L'Aulne (8.150); the rates in general do not exceed 1½ kn except in the vicinity of Île Ronde, and between Pointe de l'Armorique (48°20′N 4°27′W) and Pointe de Lanvéoc, where they are up to 1 kn greater.

3   **Out-going stream.** The out-going stream in Grande Rade is dominated by the amount of water flowing from L'Aulne which is much greater than that from L'Élorn.

4   In the estuary of L'Aulne, between Pointe de l'Armorique and Pointe de Lanvéoc, the W-going stream begins at −0010 Brest, and from +0100 Brest an E-going eddy runs along the coast between Pen ar Vir and Pointe de Lanvéoc. The out-going stream in L'Élorn begins at −0030 Brest in the vicinity of Pont Albert-Louppe, and from HW Brest until +0500 a weak S or SW stream is perceptible E of a line joining Rade-Abri and Pointe de l'Armorique; at the latter point it meets the W-going stream from L'Aulne, and they run together NW towards Goulet de Brest. The existence of this S stream in the NE part of the roads and of a N stream in the NW part induces a weak clockwise rotary stream in Grande Rade which continues during the whole of the falling stream, becoming stronger S of a position about 1 mile S of the entrance to Rade-Abri. However, between +0100 and +0500 Brest a strong out-going stream runs close to the coast in the vicinity of La Cormorandière (48°20′·7N 4°31′·7W), attaining a rate of 4 kn or more.

5   Thus there are important dissimilarities between the out-going and the in-going streams in an area about 1 mile S of the entrance to Rade-Abri, where, during the falling tide, the stream is weak and at neaps with W winds it sometimes never becomes established, whereas during the rising tide the stream here runs strongly.

The out-going stream runs strongly between Pointe de l'Armorique and Île Ronde.

For hourly details see information on the charts.

8.132

1 **Tidal streams - Passe Sud.** Tidal streams in Passe Sud leading to Rade-Abri run as follows:

Interval from HW Brest	Direction
From –0600 to HW	N
From HW to +0500	S

The maximum spring rates are 1¼ kn.

2 At –0330 Brest an eddy begins to run SW off the SW corner of Jetée Sud and gradually extends NW until, at –0200 Brest, the stream along the whole length of Jetée Sud from Passe Sud runs WSW at a rate of about 1½ kn at springs, whilst about 2½ cables from Jetée Sud it is running ENE; this eddy continues to run during the remainder of the rising stream.

3 It can happen that the rising stream in Grande Rade de Brest, S of Passe Sud to Rade-Abri, is running E, while the stream inside Rade-Abri is running W; the best indication of this is given by the direction in which ships are swung to their moorings in Rade-Abri.

4 Tidal streams at the entrance to La Penfeld run directly inwards and outwards as follows:

Interval from HW Brest	Direction
–0500	Rising stream begins
–0230	Inward
–0030	Falling stream begins
+0400	Outward

The maximum in-going and out-going spring rates are ½ kn and ¾ kn respectively.

8.133

1 **Tidal streams - Port de Commerce.** Tidal streams in Port de Commerce, on the line between the two entrances, begin as follows:

Interval from HW Brest	Direction
–0500	E
–0100	W

The maximum spring rates are ¾ kn.

Climate information
8.134

1 See 1.195 and 13.241.

Directions for entering harbour
(continued from 8.92)

Principal marks
8.135

1 **Landmarks:**
Radio Mast (elevation 166 m) (48°22′·4N 4°31′·2W) marked by a red obstruction light.
Pont de Recouvrance (conspicuous towers) (48°23′·1N 4°29′·7W), a lifting bridge across La Penfeld.

2 Pont Albert-Louppe (48°23′N 4°24′W) (8.148).
Water Tower (48°21′·2N 4°24′·0W).
Television Mast (48°21′·4N 4°25′·5W) marked by a red obstruction light.
Water Tower (48°17′·0N 4°27′·0W).

3 Île Longue (48°19′N 4°30′W), a peninsula with square building on the summit and site of a naval port.

Île Trébéron (48°18′·4N 4°31′·7W), the quarantine station.
Île des Morts (48°18′·3N 4°32′·1W).
Major light:
Pointe du Portzic Light (48°22′N 4°32′W) (8.83).

Grande Rade de Brest
8.136

1 From a position between Pointe du Portzic (48°21′N 4°32′W) and Pointe des Espagnols, about 1 mile S, on the line of bearing 256°, astern, of Pointe du Petit Minou Light (8.83) the track continues ENE passing (with positions given from Pointe du Portzic):
NNW of La Cormorandière (8 cables SSE) marked by a white beacon; thence:

2 SSE of Banc de Saint-Pierre, an extensive bank lying S of Jetée Sud. Basse Pennou Pell (1 mile E) and Basse Saint-Pierre, 2 cables farther E, lie on this bank; the former shoal is marked on its S side by Pénoupèle Light Buoy (port hand). Thence:
To a position S of the entrance (2 miles ENE) to Rade-Abri, noting Basse Kler (2¼ miles E).

3 **Clearing bearing.** The line of bearing 338° of Pointe du Portzic Light changing from red to white clears E of La Cormorandière and associated dangers.

Rade-Abri
8.137

1 **Pass Sud.** The best time to enter Rade-Abri is 1 hour before HW Brest.
Leading lights:
Front light (white round tower) (48°22′·9N 4°29′·5W).
Rear light (intensified direction light on Le Château ramparts) (118 m NNW of the front mark).

2 The alignment (344°) of these marks, together with the E tower of Pont de Recouvrance (8.135) which stands on the same alignment, or at night in the white sector (342°–346°) of the front light, leads through Passe Sud passing between the head of Jetée Sud and the S end of Jetée Est into Rade-Abri. Below-water foundations extend about 15 m from the head of each jetty leaving a navigable width of about 1¼ cables.

3 **La Penfeld.** The alignment (314°) of leading lights (48°22′·9N 4°29′·9W) situated on Quay Jean Bart leads through the S reach of La Penfeld.
Front Light (white pylon red top, 8 m in height).
Rear Light (three-storey building, 15 m high) (17 m NW of the front light).

Port de Commerce
8.138

1 **Passe de l'Ouest,** the usual passage, is entered from Rade-Abri between the head of Jetée Ouest and the W end of Jetée du Sud, from both of which below-water foundations project; the passage is 140 m wide.

2 **Passe de l'Est,** 120 m wide, lies between the E end of Jetée du Sud and the head of Quai Est No 5 and is approached through a channel marked by light buoys (port hand and S cardinal) entered about 8 cables E of the entrance to Rade-Abri. Passe de l'Est is sometimes obstructed by large vessels, and their hawsers, lying at berths at the S end of Quai Est.

Useful marks
8.139

1 Light (white tower red top, 9 m in height) (48°22′·2N 4°29′·4W) on the head of Jetée Sud.
Light (white tower green top, 10 m in height) (48°22′·2N 4°29′·1W) on the head of Jetée Est.

2   Light (white column red top, 11 m in height) (48°22′·7N 4°29′·0W) on the head of Jetée Ouest.

Light (white column green top, 10 m in height) (48°22′·7N 4°29′·0W) on the W head of Jetée du Sud.

3   Light (white pylon green top, 9 m in height) (48°22′·8N 4°28′·4W) on the head of Quai Est No 5.

Light (white pylon red top, 7 m in height) (48°22′·8N 4°28′·4W) on the E head of Jetée du Sud.

Basins and berths

Rade–Abri and Port Militaire
8.140

1   Port Militaire extends along both banks of La Penfeld and in Rade–Abri, W of a line drawn on the chart from the head of Jetée Sud to Jetée Ouest. Works in progress (2006) between Jetée Ouest and the entrance to La Rivière Penfeld. Quai d'Armement and Quai des Flottilles, with the submarine shelters at its SW end, front the N side of Rade–Abri. Pontoons, constructed of wood and concrete with rubber fenders, are moored at right-angles to Quai des Flottilles; Epi de la Grande Rivière is the NE-most of these berths. Two parallel jetties, No 3 and No 4 with berths for large vessels, extend NE from the N side of Jetée Sud, near its W end, Quai des Petroliers, an oil berth is situated at the W end of Port Militaire. Mooring buoys, the positions of which can best be seen from the chart, are laid in Port Militaire.

2   There are numerous obstructions within Port Militaire for which the chart is the best guide.

3   La Rivière Penfeld flows into the NE corner of Rade–Abri; berths in La Penfeld are normally reserved for naval vessels in reserve or refitting.

There are dry docks in Rade–Abri, W of the entrance to La Penfeld.

Largest and deepest berths: No 3 and No 4 (48°22′·0N 4°30′·5W) on Jetée Sud.

Port de Commerce
8.141

1   Port de Commerce is situated close E of Port Militaire. It consists of five basins divided by spurs. Bassins Nos 1, 2, 3 and 5 lie between Jetée Ouest and Quai Est No 5; Bassin No 6 lies E of Bassin No 5.

Saint-Marc Industrial Estate, with repair quays and dry docks, lies E of Basin No 6.

2   **Longest and deepest berths:**
Quai Est, Bassin No 5, for petroleum, cereal and refrigerated products; length 440 m; depth alongside 9·3 to 9·5 m.
Quai Est, Bassin No 6, for cereal and bulk cargoes; length 175 m; depth alongside 8·0 m.
Quai Sud for containers and agricultural products; length 230 m; depth alongside 12·7 m.

Port services

Repairs
8.142

1   **Naval dockyard.** The naval dockyard in Rade–Abri has full facilities for the docking and repair of all naval vessels. There are several dry docks, the largest No 9 has extreme bottom dimensions of length 321·6 m and breadth 35·2 m; when not in use by warships the dock may be used by merchant vessels in case of urgency on special application to Government Authorities.

2   **Port de Commerce.** Repairs of all kinds can be carried out. There are three commercial dry docks and five repair berths capable of accommodating vessels up to 550 000 dwt. There is also a gas freeing plant and tank cleaning station for similar sized tankers.

Largest dry dock:

3   No 3 dry dock for tankers up to 550 000 dwt; length 420 m; width 80 m; depth on the sill 15·5 m (MHWS).

Deepest and longest repair berths:
No 2 and No 3 repair quays for vessels up to 550 000 dwt, combined length 608 m; depth alongside 8 to 10·5 m.

Other facilities
8.143

1   **Ship sanitation control and ship sanitation control exemption certificates** issued at Brest.

Medical. Naval and civil hospitals are available.

Compass adjustment can be carried out.

Hydrographic Office. The French Hydrographic Office (Service Hydrographique et Océanographique de la Marine) is situated at Brest.

Supplies
8.144

1   **Fuel,** all grades available, supplied by pipeline depending upon berth, lighter or road tanker.

Fresh water available at all berths and by lighter to vessels in Rade de Brest.

Fresh provisions and stores: available.

Communications
8.145

1   There is an airport at Guipavas, 10 km from the port.

Île Longue

General information
8.146

1   There is a naval port, formed of a basin protected by two breakwaters, at the NE end of Île Longue (48°19′N 4°30′W) (8.135); the port lies within a prohibited area (8.125).

Directions
(continued from 8.92)
8.147

1   From a position 6 cables NE of Pointe des Espagnols (48°20′·5N 4°31′·9W) on the line of bearing 315°, astern, of Pointe du Portzic Light (8.83), the track leads SE in the fairway, passing (with positions from Pointe des Espagnols):

2   NE of La Cormorandière (1½ cables NE); thence:
SW of Basse du Renard (2 miles ESE) (8.121); thence:
NE of Lanvéoc 1 Light Buoy (starboard hand) (2 miles ESE), marking the NW edge of a degaussing range; thence:
SW of Île Ronde (3 miles ESE).

3   The route then turns S and W.

Leading lights:
Front light (48°18′·5N 4°30′·0W).
Rear light (about 100 m from front light).
The alignment (281°) of these lights leads in the fairway, passing:

4   S of Lanvéoc 5 Light Buoy (starboard hand) (3 miles SE); thence:
S of a group of four buoys (2¾ miles SE) in a degaussing range; thence:

N of Île Longue E Light Buoy (port hand) (2¾ miles SSE); thence:

Between the breakwater heads (2½ miles SSE) into the basin. Lights are exhibited from the breakwater heads.

L'Élorn

General information
8.148

1 **Description.** L'Élorn or Rivière de Landerneau flows into the NE part of Rade de Brest between Pointe Sainte-Barbe (48°23′N 4°24′W) and Pointe de Keraliou, 5 cables SSW, and gives access to the pyrotechnical works at Saint-Nicolas (48°24′N 4°22′W) and Port de Landerneau, situated 11 miles above Port de Commerce.

2 **Channel.** Approach to the river lies between R1 and R2 Light Buoys (starboard and port hand) moored about 5 cables ESE of the entrance to Rade-Abri; thence the channel to Saint-Nicolas is marked by light buoys and a water intake (2 cables S of Saint Marc Industrial Estate) from which a light is exhibited. A submarine pipeline and a submarine power cable connect the water intake to the shore at the SW extremity of Port du Moulin Blanc (8.155).

3 Pont Albert-Louppe (48°23′N 4°24′W), a conspicuous bridge with three arches, crosses the river at Pointe Sainte-Barbe, the N arch of which spans the river. Pont de l'Iroise, a second bridge, spans the river close NE. Lights are exhibited from the arches of the bridges.

4 A direction light (masonry hut) (48°24′·6N 4°21′·7W) is exhibited on the N side of the channel 5 cables NE of the quay at Saint-Nicolas and a beacon tower (port hand) stands 8 cables E of the direction light and marks the N side of the channel; a tide gauge is fitted to the beacon tower. Above this the channel between the mudflats, which dries 3·5 m, is very narrow.

5 **Vertical clearances:**

 Pont Albert-Louppe 28 m on the N arch; Pont de l'Iroise 25 m.

Anchorage is prohibited within 50 m above and below the bridges, as shown on the chart. Navigation, stopping, anchoring and fishing in the buoyed area in the vicinity of pyrotechnical works at Saint-Nicolas is also prohibited.

Local knowledge is essential above Saint-Nicolas.

Pilotage, see 8.67.

6 **Tidal streams** in L'Élorn, above the bridge, run in the direction of the channel, beginning as follows:

Interval from HW Brest	*Direction*
−0545	In-going
+0015	Out-going

The maximum spring rates are 3 kn.

SW and NE winds influence the height of the tide by as much as 0·3 m.

7 **Berth.** Saint-Nicolas lies on the N side of the river 1½ miles above the bridge. There is a quay about 250 m long alongside which the bottom is foul; it dries 0·5 m at the S end and 2 m at the N end. A light (red mast) is exhibited from the quay.

8.149

1 **Port de Landerneau** is situated 7 miles above Pont Albert-Louppe and can accommodate vessels of up to 4 m draught and less than 57 m in length. This port is formed by quays on the right bank of the river, which dry between 3 and 4 m, and is limited E by the bridge which crosses the river at Landerneau. Vessels alongside the quays lie on the mud; the best berths, which dry about 3·4 m, are at the N quay.

Port services: fresh water; provisions; hospital.

L'Aulne

General information
8.150

1 **Description.** L'Aulne, or Rivière de Châteaulin, flows into the SE part of Rade de Brest between Pointe Doubidy (48°20′N 4°25′W) and Pen-ar-Vir, about 2 miles S, and is accessible by vessels as far as Landévennec (48°17′·5N 4°16′·0W), by small coasting vessels as far as Port-Launay, and by small craft as far as Châteaulin.

2 **Buoyage.** The channel is buoyed in accordance with the IALA Maritime Buoyage System (Region A), except that the port hand buoys are conical.

Controlling depths: 3·7 m as far as Landévennec; thence as far as Écluse de Guily-Glas it dries 1·8 m in places.

3 **Vertical clearance:** 27 m at Pont de Térénez.

Pilotage, see 8.67.

Restricted area, see 8.125.

Tidal streams in L'Aulne run in the direction of the channel, at a spring rate of about 2¾ kn, beginning as follows:

Interval from HW Brest		*Direction*
At Landévennec	−0505	In-going
	+0015	Out-going
At Écluse de Guily-Glas	−0245	In-going
	+0030	Out-going

4 South-west and NE winds influence the height of the tide by as much as 0·3 m. For a general description of tidal streams in Rade de Brest and adjacent estuaries see 8.131.

Landévennec: naval establishment; landing place; anchorage for yachts 3 cables N of Île de Térénez

Minor rivers, bays and harbours
8.151

1 **Anse du Poulmic,** obstructed by a shallow shelf, is entered between Pen-ar-Vir (48°18′N 4°25′W) and Pointe de Lomergat, 2½ miles E.

Prohibited area. Entry is prohibited in the W part of Anse de Poulmic, both in an area fronting the naval school which stands 8 cables S of Pen-ar-Vir and in a rectangular area, used occasionally, centred on position 48°18′·1N 4°24′·3W.

2 **Channel.** A light buoy (N cardinal) is moored 1 cable NE of Pen-ar-Vir and marks the entrance of the channel leading to the harbour of the naval school at Poulmic; the harbour lies within the prohibited area. Approaching the harbour pass close W of a line of mooring buoys which are moored on a N to S line parallel to the W side of the bay.

Harbour: mole at the N end with depths of 2 m on its S side.

8.152

1 **Rivière de Daoulas** flows into the N side of the estuary of L'Aulne between Pointe Pen a Lan (48°20′N 4°22′W) and Pointe du Bindy, about 1¾ miles E, through Baie de Daoulas, which is obstructed with mudbanks. Vessels of 3 m draught can, in exceptionally favourable conditions, reach Daoulas, about 4½ miles within the entrance, where there is a landing place which dries 5 m.

2 **Anchorage:** S of Pointe de Ker Santon (48°21′N 4°18′W) near the S bank of the river.

Drying-out berths: Anse de Saint-Jean (48°20′N 4°19′W).

Harbour: Port de Tinduff close N of Pointe Pen a Lan; quay 100 m long; landing slip; slipway 35 m long, 8 m wide.

8.153

1 **Rivière de l'Hôpital-Camfrout** flows into the N side of the estuary of L'Aulne W of Pointe de Hanvec (48°19′N 4°17′W). The channel leading to Port de l'Hôpital-Camfrout dries 5 m and lies midway between the entrance points and thence midway between the banks.

Anchorage: on the N bank of the river within the entrance near a landing place; the anchorage dries.

Harbour: slips drying 5m; drying-out berths on mud and gravel.

8.154

1 **Rivière du Faou** flows into L'Aulne between Île de Tibidy (48°18′N 4°15′W) and Île d'Arun, 5 cables SE. The channel is marked by buoys. Vessels up to 3 m draught can, at spring tides, proceed about 3¼ miles up this river to Faou where a bridge crosses it. There are two quays on the N side of the river which dry from 4·0 to 4·5 m. This small haven is however silting up rapidly.

8.155

1 **Anse du Moulin-Blanc** entered between the SE end (48°23′N 4°26′W) of Saint-Marc Industrial Estate and Pointe Sainte-Barbe, about 1½ miles ENE, is obstructed with drying banks of mud and weed.

8.156

1 **Anse du Caro** (48°20′·5N 4°26′·5W), a small bay which dries, has a slipway on its S side which dries 1·5 m at its extremity.

8.157

1 **Roscanvel** (48°19′N 4°33′W), a small harbour on the W side of Baie de Roscanvel, has a stone jetty which dries 0·4 m at its head, and a slipway which dries 3 m. Another slipway, marked by a beacon (starboard hand), with a depth of 1·6 m at its extremity is situated at Kervian, about 5 cables S.

8.158

1 **Le Fret** (48°17′N 4°30′W), in the SW corner of Anse du Fret, is small harbour. Plateau des Roches Noires, a drying rocky reef, extends about 1 cable NE from the harbour, a slipway with a depth of 1·1 m at its extremity, marked at its outer end by a beacon (starboard hand), lies close W of the reef.

Berth: wharf which dries.

Repairs: slipway and landing place which dry; small shipyard.

8.159

1 **Lanvéoc** (48°18′N 4°28′W) has a small harbour, which lies within a prohibited area (8.125), on the W side of Pointe de Lanvéoc. A landing slip is situated 1 cables SE of the point; a beacon (starboard hand) marks the extremity of the slip which dries 1 m. The slip is sheltered from W winds but with a strong E wind landing is impracticable. A jetty, 2 cables E of the landing slip, extends 500 m N; the jetty lies within a prohibited area (8.125).

8.160

1 **Anse de l'Auberlac'h** is entered between Pointe de l'Armorique (48°20′N 4°27′W) and Pointe Doubidy, 1½ miles E. Shell-fish beds lie along the shores of the bay and a marine farm is situated 8 cables ESE of Pointe de l'Armorique.

2 **Anchorage:** at the head of the bay, clear of the prohibited area (8.125), midway between its sides in depths of 3 to 4 m, good holding.

Harbour: jetty, drying 1·8 m on the N side of the bay.

Repairs: slipway drying 3·2 m.

BAIE DE DOUARNENEZ AND APPROACHES

General information

Chart 2349, 2350

Description

8.161

1 Baie de Douarnenez is entered between Cap de La Chèvre (48°10′N 4°33′W) (8.169) and Pointe du Van, 9 miles SW, and is bordered by cliffs.

Topography

8.162

1 The cliffs forming the NW shore of the bay are bold and cleft by fissures.

The E shore of the bay is composed of cliffs interspersed with wide sandy beaches. On the skyline behind, and about 3 miles inland, is the elongated Sommet du Ménez-Hom (48°13′N 4°14′W) which attains a height of 327 m at its N end.

2 Pointe du Van (48°04′N 4°43′W), the S entrance point, is a high sheer cliff, thence E the S shore of the bay is formed by high cliffs.

Exercise areas

8.163

1 **Submarine exercise area,** swept to a depth of 28 m, is situated in the approaches to the bay. The approximate limits of the area lie between the meridians of 4°23′W and 4°40′W, and between the latitude of Basse Vieille Light Buoy (48°08′N 4°36′W) and the coast S.

2 For further details see 1.33 and *The Mariner's Handbook*.

Pilotage

8.164

1 Pilotage is compulsory from the end of the approach channel to Douarnenez, for details see 8.67

For details of Brest Compulsory Pilotage Area, see 8.8.

Traffic regulations

8.165

1 **Approach channel,** see 8.63.

Reporting system, see 8.64 to 8.65.

Temporary explosives dumping ground

8.166

1 A temporary explosives dumping ground (Zones de Dépôts d'Explosifs) is situated in the NE part of the bay WNW of Pointe de Tal ar Grip (48°10′N 4°18′W), for details see 1.7 and Appendix V.

Rescue

8.167

1 **Inshore lifeboat** is stationed at Douarnenez (48°06′N 4°20′W), see 1.117.

Signal station (Sémaphore) is situated on Cap de la Chèvre (48°10′N 4°33′W) (8.169) for details see 1.110.

VHF Direction-finding service, for emergency use only, operates from Cap de la Chèvre, for details see *Admiralty List of Radio Signals Volume 2.*

Natural conditions

8.168

1 **Tidal streams** within Baie de Douarnenez are generally weak, and rates do not exceed 1 kn at springs. They are much influenced by the wind.

The streams begin as follows:

Interval from HW Brest	Direction
Approach to Baie de Douarnenez (48°08′N 4°40′W):	
−0520	E
+0045	W
Near Basse Vieille (48°07′N 4°36′W):	
−0550	ENE
+0015	WSW

2 Along the S shore of the bay the streams run E and W beginning approximately at the times of LW and HW Brest, respectively. The rates increase from virtually nil off Pointe de Leydé (48°07′N 4°22′W) to about 1 kn off Pointe du Van.

3 **Swell.** With W winds a swell penetrates as far as the anchorages off Morgat and Douarnenez.

Directions
(continued from 8.30 and 8.50)

Principal marks
8.169
1 **Landmarks:**
 Cap de la Chèvre (conspicuous signal station with flagstaff and radar aerial) (48°10′N 4°33′W) can be identified by a large white fissure in the cliffs.
 Major lights:
 Ar Men Light (48°03′N 5°00′W) (8.199).
 Île de Sein Main Light (48°03′N 4°52′W) (8.199).
 Pointe du Milier Light (white house, 8 m in height) (48°06′N 4°28′W).

Other aid to navigation
8.170
1 **Racon:**
 Chaussée de Sein Light Buoy (48°04′N 5°08′W).
 For details see *Admiralty List of Radio Signals Volume 2.*

L'Iroise to Cap de la Chèvre
8.171
1 From a position in L'Iroise (8.62) the line of bearing 100° of Pointe du Milier Light (48°06′N 4°28′W) (8.169) leads along the N side of Chaussée de Sein (8.193) through the approach channel marked on the chart passing (with positions given from Tévennec (48°04′N 4°48′W)):
 S of Basse du Laborieux (7¾ miles NNW); thence:
2 S of Basse de L'Iroise (8¼ miles N) (8.85); and:
 N of Basse Triton lying 5 cables N of Tévennec from where a light (8.203) is exhibited; thence:
 Between a 12 m rocky patch (7 miles NE) and Basse Jaune (3¾ miles E) marked on its SW side by a buoy (isolated danger); thence:
3 S of Basse Vieille (48°08′·5N 4°35′·5W), the SW-most danger off Cap de la Chèvre, marked on its SW side by a light buoy (isolated danger). The heavy swell which often runs in this vicinity breaks heavily on these rocks. And:
 N of Duellou (8 miles E) noting Forhic a drying rock close E.

8.172
1 **Approaching from south through Raz de Sein.** At night when approaching Baie de Douarnenez from S through Raz de Sein (8.202) it is advisable to remain in the white sector (158°–205°) of La Vieille Light (48°03′N

4°45′W) (8.199) until reaching the white sector (087°–113°) of Pointe du Milier Light (48°06′N 4°28′W) (8.169).

8.173
1 **Clearing marks:**
 The line of bearing 351° of Rochers du Toulinguet (48°16′·5N 4°38′·4W) open W of Les Tas de Pois Ouest, 1½ miles S, (8.92) clears W of Basse Vieille.
 Basse Vieille is covered by the red sector (113°–120°) of Pointe du Milier Light (48°06′N 4°28′W).
 Useful marks:
2 Créac'h Light (48°28′N 5°08′W) (8.25) (chart 2643).
 La Jument Light (48°25′N 5°08′W) (8.25) (chart 2643).
 Les Pierres Noires Light (48°19′N 4°55′W) (8.80).
 Saint-Mathieu Light (48°20′N 4°46′W) (8.43).
 Pointe du Toulinguet Light (48°17′N 4°38′W) (8.80).
 La Vieille Light (48°03′N 4°45′W) (8.199).

Cap de la Chèvre to Douarnenez
8.174
1 From a position S of Cap de la Chèvre the route continues generally E along the S coast of Baie de Douarnenez passing (with positions given from Pointe du Milier (48°06′N 4°28′W)):
 S of La Corne SE de la Chèvre (5 miles WNW); thence:
 S of Roche du Sud (4½ miles NW) noting Roche du Dolmen 5 cables NE; thence:
 N of Basse Veur (4¾ miles E) to Douarnenez (8.178).

8.175
1 **Clearing bearing:**
 The line of bearing 250°, and less, of Pointe du Milier Light (48°06′N 4°28′W) (8.169) and at night in its white sector (148°–251°) clears N of Basse Veur.
 Useful marks:
2 Church (spire) (48°04′·6N 4°30′·7W) at Beuzec-Cap-Sizun.
 Water Tower (48°04′·8N 4°25′·6W) at Poullan-sur-Mer.
 House on Pointe de Tal ar Grip (48°10′N 4°18′W).
 House on Pointe du Bellec (48°12′N 4°22′W).
3 **Major light:**
 Pointe de Morgat Light (white square tower, red top, white dwelling, 15 m in height) (48°13′N 4°30′W); visible only inside the bay.

Anchorages

Anse de Saint Nicolas
8.176
1 **General information.** Anse de Saint-Nicolas (48°11′N 4°32′W), close NE of Cap de la Chèvre, affords temporary shelter from NW winds; the swell is little felt here.
 Anchorage is available in the bay in depths from 7 to 11 m, sand.

Designated berths
8.177
1 **General information.** Designated anchorage berths are shown on the chart. A number of berths lie off Pointe de Morgat (48°13′N 4°30′W) and Douarnenez port (48°06′N 4°20′W). Other designated berths lie off Pointe de la Jument (48°06′N 4°25′W). Vessels wishing to anchor in Baie de Douarnenez must request permission from VTS Ouessant; they will be directed to one of the designated anchorage berths (see above).

Anse de Morgat, a bold headland, affords good shelter during winds from between W and NE; there is a swell during onshore winds.

2   **Caution.** La Pierre Profonde and Le Taureau, with Les Verrès 4 cables farther E, are three dangers lying in the approach to Anse de Morgat about 2 miles ESE of Pointe de Morgat; they are covered by the green sector (281°–301°) of Pointe de Morgat Light.

Douarnenez

Chart 2349 with plan of Port de Douarnenez
General information
8.178
1   **Position and function.** Douarnenez (48°06′N 4°20′W) lies at the mouth of Rivière de Pouldavid and has four harbours. It is an important fishing port.

Port limits are shown on the chart.

Approach and entry. Port Neuf and Port de Rosmeur are approached from E of Île Tristan (48°06′N 4°20′W) (8.181) and entered between breakwaters. Port Tréboul and Port Rhu, small craft harbours, are approached from either side of Île Tristan, and entered through Rivière Pouldavid.

Limiting conditions
8.179
1   **Controlling draught.** The port is accessible by vessels up to 5 m draught.

Arrival information
8.180
1   **Outer anchorage.** Anchorage in depths of up to 15 m, sand and shells, may be obtained in the numbered anchorage positions NE of the port. The area is sheltered from winds between E and W through S, but with SW winds a swell penetrates into the anchorage.
2   **Restricted area** where fishing and anchoring are prohibited lies N of the root of Môle Est–Ouest and close

SW of No 11 anchorage position. The area surrounds an outfall pipeline.

Cautions. A marine farm lies about 1½ cable SSE of the head of Môle du Rosmeur.

Harbour
8.181
1   **General layout.** The port is divided into four small harbours. Port Neuf, NE of the town, is enclosed by breakwaters. Port de Rosmeur, immediately S of Port Neuf is protected from N by the S mole of Port Neuf and from E by a jetty projecting 1 cable S from the mole.

Ports de Tréboul and Rhu, for small craft, lie on the W side of Rivière de Pouldavid opposite Île Saint-Michel and on the E bank of the river at Douarnenez, respectively.

Directions for entering harbour
8.182
1   **Landmarks:**

Rocher le Coulinec (48°06′·5N 4°21′·2W).

Île Tristan (48°06′N 4°20′W), from where a light (grey tower white band black top, 11 m in height) is exhibited.

Rocher de l'Ermitage (48°06′·1N 4°19′·6W) at the NW corner of Port Neuf.

Water Tower (48°05′N 4°21′W).

Water Tower (48°05′N 4°18′W).

2   **Port Neuf and Port de Rosmeur.** From a position N of Basse Veur (48°07′N 4°21′W) the track leads generally SE passing (with positions given from Île Tristan Light):

NE of Basse Veur (8 cables NW); thence:

NE of Basse Neuve (5 cables NW); thence:

NE of Île Tristan; thence:

To the harbour entrances; a buoy (starboard hand) is moored off the E end of Môle Est–Ouest.

8.183
1   **Clearing marks:**

The line of bearing 150° of Ploaré Church (pointed belfry) (48°05′·2N 4°19′·2W) open E of Île Tristan, 1 mile NNW, clears ENE of Basse Veur and Basse Neuve.

Church Spire   *Tréboul*   *Ile Tristan*

Slips   *Port de Rosmeur*   *Port Neuf*

Douarnenez from ESE (8.178)

(Original dated 1997)

(Photograph - Service Hydrographique et Océanographique de la Marine)

The red sector (138°–153°) of Île Tristan Light covers Basse Veur and Basse Neuve.

2   **Useful marks:**

Light (white and green pylon, 8 m in height) on the head of Môle Est-Ouest.

Light (white and red pylon, 5 m in height) on the head of Môle Nord-Sud.

Light (white pylon green top, 6 m in height) on the elbow of Môle de Rosmeur.

Basins and berths
8.184

1   Port Neuf is dredged to a depth of 5 m. Môle Est-Ouest, the N breakwater, extends 2¼ cables E from Rocher de l'Ermitage; Môle Men Léon, the W breakwater, extends SW from the same point to the shore. Môle de Rosmeur forms the S side of the harbour and Môle Nord-Sud, the E breakwater, extends 1¼ cables N from the head of Môle de Rosmeur. The harbour is entered from E between the heads of Môle Est-Ouest and Môle Nord-Sud; the entrance is 80 m wide.

2   **Anchorage.** Two berths in depths of between 2 and 3 m are situated in Rade de Guet, respectively 2 and 3½ cables SE of Île Tristan Light.

3   **Alongside berths.** There are berths alongside the quays on the SW side of the harbour; with W or NW winds a swell can be felt alongside the quays.

8.185

1   **Port de Rosmeur,** used mainly by fishing vessels, lies S of Môle de Rosmeur. A jetty projects 1 cable S from the mole, ¾ cable within its head; the E side of the jetty is dredged to 4·4 m.

The W side of the harbour is quayed and there are two stone slipways; between the quay and the jetty the harbour nearly dries.

Port services
8.186

1   **Repairs** to small vessels can be carried out. Slipways are available, one of which, with a lifting capacity of 420 tonnes, can accommodate vessels up to 47 m LOA and 8·5 m beam.

Fuel: available.

Fresh water and stores: available.

Hospital at Douarnenez.

Lifeboat, see 8.167.

Rivière de Pouldavid
8.187

1   **Rivière de Pouldavid,** leading to Port de Tréboul and Port Rhu, has two entrance channels separated by Île Tristan.

2   **Grande Passe,** the usual channel, lies between Île Tristan and the head of a mole projecting NE from Pointe Biron, at the W side of the river entrance, and has depths of 1·8 m. The line of bearing 157° of Port Rhu Direction Light (lantern on bridge) leads through Grande Passe; the pass is marked on its E side by two beacons (port hand). Mariners waiting for the tide in order to proceed to Tréboul and Port Rhu usually berth alongside the mole at Pointe Biron.

3   **Useful mark:**

Light (white column green top, 7 m in height) (48°06'·1N 4°20'·5W) at the head of Pointe Biron mole.

Passe du Guet lies between the causeway extending SSE from Île Saint-Michel, situated on the reef which extends S from Île Tristan, and Pointe du Guet, the NW extremity of the town of Douarnenez. This channel, which dries 2 m, is preferable with winds between E and S. A submarine power cable is laid across the channel.

8.188

1   **Port de Tréboul,** for fishing vessels and pleasure craft, lies on the W side of the river opposite Île Saint-Michel and has depths of 1·0 m; close within its N entrance is a quay used by fishing craft. The remainder of the harbour is reserved for small craft.

2   **Port-Rhu** is a wet basin on Rivière Pouldavid in the centre of Douarnenez. It is approached through a drying channel and entered through a gate, 10 m wide, with a submersible sill and has quays on its E side as far as the bridge which crosses the river. Lights are exhibited from each side of the entrance.

Minor bay and harbour

Chart 2350, 2349
Baie de Brézellec
8.189

1   **General information.** Baie de Brézellec (48°04'N 4°40'W) E of the point of the same name affords anchorage; there is a landing place at the head of the bay.

Chart 2349 plan of Port de Morgat
Morgat
8.190

1   **General information.** A mole extends about 1 cable N from the N side of Pointe de Morgat (48°13'N 4°30'W) sheltering the old harbour, which dries. A new mole lies parallel with the old mole and about 200 m SE of it. The yacht harbour lies E of the old harbour and is sheltered from E by a breakwater, with rough stone underwater foundations built on an arc 2½ cables long, forming a breakwater; wave reducing pontoons extend 1 cable WNW from the head of the breakwater sheltering the yacht harbour from NE.

2   **Port radio** station, with limited hours, operates from the port for details see *Admiralty List of Radio Signals Volume 6(1).*

Access. The port is approached from NE, passing NW of a light buoy (port hand) (48°13'·6N 4°29'·6W) and close NW of a light beacon (port hand) (48°13'·6N 4°29'·7W), thence entering the harbour between the breakwater to the E and the wave reducing pontoons to the W.

Anchorage: off the entrance, 1¼ cables NNW of the breakwater head as shown on the chart.

3   **Berths.** A drying quay, about 100 m long extends W from the root of the old mole. Vessels lie along the W side of this mole on sand and mud. The end of the new mole, which is about 100 m long, is reserved for fishing vessels and there is a slipway, 30 m wide, on its W side. A quay projects SE from the root of the new mole.

Supplies: fuel; fresh water.

L'IROISE TO POINTE DE LA TORCHE

GENERAL INFORMATION

Chart 2643
Area covered
8.191

1   The section is arranged as follows:
Chaussée and Raz de Sein (8.193).
Point du Raz to Pointe de la Torche (8.217).

Route
8.192

1   Chaussée de Sein (48°03′N 5°00′W) (8.193), with its navigable channel Raz de Sein (8.202), extends 13½ miles W of Pointe du Raz (48°02′N 4°44′W). Mariners bound from L'Iroise (8.62) to Pointe de Penmarc'h (47°48′N 4°22′W), 2½ miles SSW of Pointe de la Torche, and beyond, usually pass W of Chaussée de Sein.

2   Mariners bound to ports on the W coast of France, who are permitted to use the Inshore Traffic Zone (8.202), may shorten their route by passing through Raz de Sein, and, in favourable conditions, there is less sea in it than there is W of Chaussée de Sein, but, it is never free from danger when conditions are unfavourable.

CHAUSSÉE AND RAZ DE SEIN

General information

Chart 2350, 2819
Description
8.193

1   Chaussée de Sein consists of a chain of islands, dangerous rocks and shoals, 12 miles in length, with its W extremity lying 13½ miles W of Pointe du Raz (48°02′N 4°44′W) on the mainland.
Passe d'Ar Men, a narrow passage with depths of about 9 m, divides Chaussée de Sein into two parts; Basse Froide is the W part and Pont de Sein, the E part.

2   **Channel.** Raz de Sein (8.202) is the navigable channel which lies between the E end of Chaussée de Sein and the dangers extending 7½ cables W from Pointe du Raz.

Topography
8.194

1   Île de Sein (48°03′N 4°52′W) (8.209) is a low narrow island situated near the E end of Chaussée de Sein; it contains a small harbour (8.209) suitable only for mariners in small craft. The island is readily identified on the radar display.
The beacons marking the outer dangers of Chaussée de Sein are liable to be washed away in heavy weather.

Temporary explosives dumping ground
8.195

1   A temporary explosives dumping ground (Zones de Dépôts d'Explosifs) is situated NE of Île de Sein, for details see 1.7 and Appendix V.

Rescue
8.196

1   **All-weather lifeboat** is stationed at Île de Sein (48°03′N 4°52′W), see 1.117.
Signal station, (Vigie) is situated on Pointe du Raz (8.199), for details see 1.110 and 1.95.
VHF Direction-finding station, for emergency use only, operates from Pointe du Raz (48°02′N 4°44′W), for details see *Admiralty List of Radio Signals Volume 6(1).*

Tidal streams
8.197

1   Tidal streams about 1¼ miles N or S of Chaussée de Sein tend to flow along the reef. At a distance of less than 1 mile the streams set strongly on to the rocks to the N and to the S, and flow through them; locally they may exceed a rate of 4 kn.
About 10 miles W of Ar Men the streams are more or less rotary clockwise; for details see information on the chart.

2   The streams, at the positions shown, run as follows, beginning at the times indicated:

Interval from HW Brest	*Direction*
About 1¼ miles N or S of Chaussée de Sein:	
−0600	E (Rising)
HW	W (Falling)
About 1½ miles S of Chaussée de Sein:	
−0605	E
HW	W

3   The maximum spring rates at the above positions are 2 kn.

Vicinity of Chaussée de Sein Light Buoy (48°04′N 5°08′W):	
−0505	N
+0010	S

The maximum N-going and S-going spring rates are 3¾ kn and 2¾ kn, respectively.
8.198

1   Tidal streams in Raz de Sein, at the positions shown, run as follows, beginning at the times indicated:

Interval from HW Brest	*Direction*
Between Île de Sein and Plateau de Tévennec:	
+0550	NNW
−0030	SSE

2   The maximum spring rates are 3 kn.

Off Pointe du Van:	
+0605	NE
−0130	SW

3   The maximum NE-going and SW-going spring rates are 2¾ kn and 1½ kn, respectively.

Interval from HW Brest	*Direction*
Off La Vieille (48°02′N 4°45′W):	
−0045	SSE
In the middle of Raz de Sein:	
+0540	NNE
−0045	SW
In the S part of Raz de Sein:	
+0540	NW
−0045	SE

4   The maximum N-going and S-going spring rates at the above positions are 6 and 5¼ kn, respectively.

There are eddies near La Vieille during both the rising and falling streams. During the whole of the rising stream an eddy runs S between La Vieille and a position about 5 cables farther N; during the whole of the falling stream an eddy runs N between La Vieille and a position about 2½ cables SE of La Plate.

5   In the middle of Raz de Sein the stream is weak for a period of about 30 minutes between the end of the rising stream and the beginning of the falling stream.

To the N of Plateau de Tévennec an eddy runs S during the rising stream.

Between La Vieille and Pointe de Raz the rising stream runs WNW towards the S side of the rocks; the falling streams run S.

Ar Men Lighthouse (8.199)
(Original dated 2000-02)

(Photograph - Jean Guichard)

La Vieille Lighthouse (8.199)
(Original dated 2000-02)

(Photograph - Jean Guichard)

Directions
(continued from 8.30 and 8.50)

Principal marks
8.199

1   **Landmarks:**

Ar Men Lighthouse (white tower black top dark base, 37 m in height) (48°03′N 5°00′W).

Île de Sein Main Lighthouse (white tower black top, 51 m in height) (48°03′N 4°52′W).

Le Chat Lighted Beacon Tower (S cardinal, 31 m in height) (48°02′N 4°49′W).

Pointe du Raz Signal Station (8.199)
(Original dated 2002)

(Photograph - Mr. C. Nelson)

2   La Plate Lighted Beacon Tower (48°02′·4N 4°45′·5W) (8.203).

La Vieille Lighthouse (grey tower black top, 27 m in height) (48°02′·5N 4°45′·3W).

Signal Station (square tower white dwelling) (48°02′N 4°44′W) on Pointe du Raz a high steep cliff.

3   **Major lights:**

Ar Men Light — as above.

Île de Sein Main Light — as above.

La Vieille Light — as above.

Other aid to navigation
8.200

1   **Racon:** Chaussée de Sein Light Buoy (48°04′N 5°08′W).

For details see *Admiralty List of Radio Signals Volume 2.*

West of Chaussée de Sein
8.201

1   From a position in L'Iroise (8.62) the route leads generally S passing W of Chaussée de Sein (8.193). Chaussée de Sein Light Buoy (W cardinal) (48°04′N 5°08′W) is moored 1½ miles WNW of the W end of this rocky chain.

Tévennec Lighthouse (8.201)

(Original dated 2000-02)

(Photograph - Jean Guichard)

Clearing marks:

Chaussée de Sein is covered by the red sector (090°–345°) of Tévennec Light (48°04′N 4°48′W) (8.203) and by the green sector (035°–105°) of La Vieille Light (48°03′N 4°45′W) (8.199).

(Directions continue at 8.223)

Raz de Sein

Charts 2350, 2348
General information
8.202

1   **Route.** In the N part of Raz de Sein mariners can pass on either side of Plateau de Tévennec (48°04′N 4°48′W). In the S part of Raz de Sein there is a passage either between Masklou Greiz (48°01′N 4°46′W) and the dangers S and SE of Pointe du Raz or between Masklou Greiz and Kornog Braz (Kornog Bras), 7½ cables W. The preferred route lies to the W of the plateau and thence between Masklou Greiz and the dangers S and SE of Pointe du Raz.

Controlling depths: 17 m between Masklou Greiz and Pointe du Raz or 11 m between Masklou Greiz and Kornog Braz.

2   **Local weather.** As a general rule mariners should always avoid Raz de Sein during bad weather when the wind is against the tidal stream. In these conditions a steep breaking sea is caused. Raz de Sein should also be avoided during strong W winds while the rising or falling streams are running, for at these times similar sea conditions prevail either N or S of this passage.

3   The best time to make the passage is during slack water, whatever the direction of the wind, but it can be made during the N-going stream with fresh winds between S and SW, or during the S-going stream with fresh winds between NW and NE.

4   **Pilots** for Raz de Sein are available from Brest; they will board at the port of departure and disembark at the port of arrival.

For details of Brest Compulsory Pilotage Area, see 8.8.

Inshore Traffic Zone. Raz de Sein is part of the Ouessant TSS, for details see 8.5.

Vessel Traffic Service, see 8.6.

Directions
8.203

1   **West of Plateau de Tévennec by day — leading marks:**

Front mark. Kermorvan Light (48°22′N 4°47′W) (8.43).

Rear mark. Trézien Light (48°25′N 4°47′W) (8.43) (chart 2643).

From a position in L'Iroise (8.62) the alignment (007°), astern, of the above marks leads in the approach passing (with positions given from Tévennec (48°04′N 4°48′W)):

2   W of Basse Moudénou (6 cables W), the W-most danger off Plateau de Tévennec, a group of rocky islets and dangerous shoals which extend 7½ cables from Tévennec, a prominent island from where a light (white tower and dwelling, 15 m in height) is exhibited.

3   **Leading marks:**

Front mark. La Vieille Light (48°03′N 4°45′W) (8.199).

Rear mark. Rocher Koummoudog (black conical rock, 16 m in height) (1¼ miles ESE of the front mark).

The alignment (112°) of these marks then leads in the fairway passing:

4   Between Chaussée de Sein (2 miles SW) (8.193) and Ar Vaz (5 cables SW), the SW-most danger off Plateau de Tévennec, to a position about 5 cables from La Plate Lighted Beacon Tower (W cardinal, 26 m in height) (2½ miles SE), which marks the W extremity of the dangers extending W from Pointe du Raz (8.199).

5   The line of bearing 328°, astern, of Tévennec Light and well open SW of La Plate Lighted Beacon Tower (2½ miles SE) then leads in the fairway passing:

Between Roche Moulleg (4 miles SE), noting an 8·6 m depth 4 cables NW, and Masklou Greiz (3¼ miles SSE), a group of rocky patches; thence:

6   ENE of a dangerous wreck (position doubtful) (4¼ miles SSE); thence:

WSW of Basse ar C'harn (5 miles SE); thence:

WSW of An Hinkinou (6 miles SE); thence:

WSW of Basses Piriou (48°08′N 4°39′W).

8.204

1   **West of Plateau de Tévennec — at night.** The line of bearing 187° of Men Brial Light (green and white tower, 14 m in height) (48°02′N 4°51′W) on Île de Sein, and in its white sector (186°–192°), leads in the approach passing W of Plateau de Tévennec.

The line of bearing 112° of La Vieille Light, and in its white sector (105°–123°), then leads in the fairway passing:

2   Between Plateau de Tévennec and Chaussée de Sein until within the intensified white sector (324°–332°) of Tévennec Direction Light, which is exhibited from the same structure as Tévennec Light, when the track leads SE on the line of bearing 328°, astern, of Tévennec Direction Light as directed above.

8.205

1   **East of Plateau de Tévennec — by day.** From a position in L'Iroise (8.62) the line of bearing 180° of La Vieille Light (48°03′N 4°45′W) (8.199) leads in the approach passing (with positions given from Tévennec (48°04′N 4°48′W)):

Between Plateau de Tévennec and Basse du Nord-Ouest (2¼ miles ESE), the W-most danger off Pointe du Van (8.162).

2   When La Vieille Light bears 180°, distant about 1 mile, the track leads SW passing:

NW of La Plate Lighted Beacon Tower (2½ miles SE) (8.203), distant about 5 cables.

The track then rounds La Plate Lighted Beacon Tower at a distance of about 5 cables.

Leading marks:

3   Front mark. Gorle Greiz (48°02′·5N 4°44′·7W), a remarkable ragged rock.

Rear mark. Pointe du Van (2 miles NE of the front mark) (8.162).

From a position SW of La Plate Lighted Beacon Tower the alignment (041°), astern, of these leading marks leads in the fairway passing:

Between Masklou Greiz (3¼ miles SSE) and Kornog Braz (Kornog Bras) (3 miles S).

8.206

1   **East of Plateau de Tévennec — at night.** The line of bearing 180° of La Vieille light, or in its white sector (158°–205°) leads in the approach.

The line of bearing 225° of Le Chat Lighted Beacon Tower (3 miles SSW) (8.199) and in its white sector (215°–230°) then leads in the fairway until within the intensified white sector (8.204) of Tévennec Direction Light

when the line of bearing 328°, astern, of the centre of this white sector then leads SE in the fairway for about 1 mile.

2   The track then leads SSW in the white sector (017°–035°) of La Vieille Light, astern, passing between Masklou Greiz and Kornog Braz noting that the 017° boundary crosses Masklou Greiz.

8.207

1   **Clearing bearings:**

The dangers on the ENE side of the fairway between Pointe du Raz and Anse du Loc'h, 4½ miles ESE, are covered by the red sector (298°–325°) of La Vieille Light.

2   The line of bearing 355° of La Vieille Light changing from green to white clears E of Masklou Greiz.

The line of bearing 345° of Tévennec Light changing from red to white clears E of Kornog Braz.

The line of bearing 035° of La Vieille Light changing from green to white clears E of Kornog Braz.

3   **Useful marks:**

Water Tower (48°02′N 4°41′W).

Plogoff Church (spire) (48°02′N 4°40′W).

Chapel (48°02′N 4°39′W).

Anchorage

Baie des Trépassés

8.208

1   **Anchorage** can be obtained in Baie des Trépassés (48°03′N 4°43′W) where the tidal streams are weak, sheltered from E and S winds; the bottom is sand.

Caution. There are numerous dangers on the N side of the approach to the bay, for which the chart is the best guide, within 1 mile W and SW of Pointe du Van, the N entrance point of the bay.

Île de Sein

General information

8.209

1   **Description.** Île de Sein (48°03′N 4°52′W) contains a small harbour which offers shelter in bad weather to mariners in small craft which can take the ground; it is much frequented by fishing vessels.

Approach channels. There are three approach channels which lead through the shoals and dangers which extend about 1¼ miles from the NE side of the island.

2   **Tidal streams** along the shoals N of Île de Sein and N of An Nerroth begin as follows:

Interval from HW Brest	Direction
−0600	NNW–W
−0130	S

See also 8.198.

3   **Harbour.** The small harbour, which partly dries, is protected by breakwaters. It is entered close SE of Men Brial Light. Between April and October, small craft moorings and buoys are laid in a NNW–SSE line close E of the N breakwater

Directions for entering harbour

8.210

Landmarks:

Men Brial Light (48°02′N 4°51′W) (8.204).

An Nerroth (48°02′·5N 4°50′·7W), an islet composed of three large rocks marked at both its N and S ends by white beacon towers.

289

1   **Chenal d'An Ezodi,** the N approach, is the recommended channel except in heavy weather from N or during the rising stream.

      Leading marks:

          Front mark. Men Brial Light.

          Rear mark. Third house from the left (white with black stripe) (close S of the front mark).

2   The alignment (187°) of these marks, or at night in the white sector (186°–192°) of Men Brial Light, leads through the channel passing (with positions given from Men Brial Light):

          Close E of Kornog-an-ar-Braden (9 cables N) marked on its N side by Cornoc-An-Ar-Braden Light Buoy (starboard hand), thence:

          Close E of a mooring buoy (3½ cables N), thence:

3   When abreast the N end of An Nerroth (2 cables NE) the track continues generally S passing:

          Between An Nerroth and Guernic Beacon Tower (starboard hand) (2 cables N).

   When well past Guernic Beacon Tower the track leads generally SW to the harbour.

8.211

1   **Chenal d'Ar Vas Du,** the NE approach, is usable by day and night except in heavy weather.

      Leading marks:

          Front mark. An Nerroth S Beacon Tower.

          Rear mark. Men Brial Light.

2   The alignment (224½°) of these marks, or at night in the centre of the white sector (221°–227°) of Men Brial Light, leads in the channel passing (with positions given from Men Brial Light):

          NW of Ar Vas Du (1 miles NE), distant 1½ cables.

3   When about 1½ cables E of An Nerroth N Beacon Tower the track leads generally WNW passing about ½ cable N of the same beacon tower to join Chenal d'An Ezodi; thence as given above.

8.212

1   **Chenal Oriental** the E approach is usable with S or SW winds by day or night.

      Leading marks:

          Front mark. An Nerroth N Beacon Tower.

          Rear mark. Plas ar Scoul Pyramid (white tower with retro-reflective orange cladding on its upper section) (1 mile W of the front mark).

2   **Directional light:**

          Île de Sein Main Light (8.199).

   The alignment (265°) of the above marks by day and the white sector (269–271°) of Île de Sein Main Light by night, leads through the channel passing (with positions given from Men Brial Light):

          N of Cornoc-ar-Vaz-Nevez (1 mile ENE) marked by a beacon tower (port hand), distant about ½ cable; thence:

3   To a position about 1½ cables E of An Nerroth N Beacon Tower to join Chenal d'Ar Vas Du as given above.

   Caution. It is reported that these leading marks are difficult to identify, and that the line of bearing 270° of Île de Sein Main Light leads in the approach until N of Cornoc-ar-Vaz-Nevez.

Berths
8.213

1   **Anchorage** can be obtained 3 cables N of Men Brial Light in depths of 4 to 6 m, sand and rock; the anchorage is indifferent.

   Alongside berths. Môle du Guernic extends NE from the shore, close N of Men Brial Light, and is usable by mariners in small craft at all states of the tide; it has a depth of 2 m at its extremity.

   Môle du Rohic lies 1 cable S of the light; it is about 85 m in length and at its extremity there are rocks, which dry 2·6 m, extending to a distance of 10 m.

2   Cale de la Poste lies S of Môle du Rohic; its extremity dries 1·5 m.

   The berths alongside the quay between Môle du Rohic and Cale de la Poste are not recommended on account of the swell which arises in bad weather; in addition these berths are not good for drying out alongside.

3   **Other berths.** Mooring buoys, reserved for the lifeboat (8.196) and ferry boats, are situated close to Môle du Guernic. There are transverse chains in the harbour, oriented in an E-W direction, to assist anchors in holding.

Port services
8.214

1   **Supplies:** small quantities of diesel oil and petrol; limited quantities of fresh water.

Side channel and landings
Reported passage
8.215

1   It is reported that mariners in fishing boats and small craft occasionally pass through the dangers extending W from Pointe du Raz (48°02'N 4°05'W) out to La Vieille. Passage through this area is extremely dangerous; the tidal streams are very strong and no attempt should be made without expert local knowledge.

   French sailing directions do not mention this passage.

Landing places
8.216

1   For details of landing places for small craft ESE of Pointe du Raz, inshore of An Hinkinou (8.203) and the other offshore dangers on the NE side of the channel on the S side of Raz de Sein, see 8.239.

POINTE DU RAZ TO POINTE DE LA TORCHE

General information
Chart 2643, 2819
Route
8.217

1   From W of Chaussée de Sein (8.193) the route leads generally ESE, about 33 miles, passing S of Chaussée and Raz de Sein to a position NW of Pointe de Penmarc'h (47°48'N 4°22'W) situated 2½ miles SSW of Pointe de la Torche.

Topography
8.218

1   From Pointe du Raz (48°02'N 4°44'W) to Anse du Loc'h, 4½ miles ESE, the coast is composed of high cliffs, thence to Pointe de Lervily, 3 miles farther ESE, it becomes lower. The sandy beach at the head of Anse du Cabestan is prominent.

2   Baie d'Audierne lies between Pointe de Lervily and Pointe de la Torche (47°50'N 4°21'W). The coast SE of Port d'Audierne (8.227) slopes gently and is covered with houses, windmills and cultivation; it is fronted by a long sandy beach between Penhors (47°56′N 4°24′W) and Pointe de la Torche, 6½ miles SSE.

Temporary explosives dumping ground
8.219

1 A temporary explosives dumping ground (Zones de Dépôts d'Explosifs) is situated S of Port d'Audierne, for details see 1.7 and Appendix V.

Restricted areas
8.220

1 A restricted area, shown on the chart, in which fishing for shellfish is prohibited extends 2½ miles S of the coast between Pointe ar C'hastell (48°01′·1N 4°37′·3W) and Pointe de Lervily (2½ miles ESE). Another restricted area, also shown on the chart, in which anchoring, dredging and trawling are prohibited extends up to 4 miles W of Pointe de la Torche (47°50′·3N 4°21′·3W). A second restricted area, in which anchoring and dredging are prohibited, adjacent to this area extends up to 11 miles W of the same point. For details, see the *Bay of Biscay Pilot*.

Rescue
8.221

1 **All-weather lifeboat** is stationed at Audierne (48°01′N 4°32′W), see 1.117.

VHF Direction-finding service, for emergency use only, operates from:

Pointe du Raz (48°02′N 4°44′W)

Pointe de Penmarc'h (47°48′N 4°22′W).

For details see *Admiralty List of Radio Signals Volume 2*.

Tidal streams
8.222

1 Between Raz de Sein and Pointe de Lervily, the streams run E and W along the coast at a rate of about 2 kn at springs, the W-going stream beginning at +0335 Brest. It is probable that the streams in this locality are affected by eddies due to the strong streams in Raz de Sein.

2 Off the middle of Baie d'Audierne they begin as follows:

Interval from HW Brest	Direction
−0540	NNW
+0025	SE

The maximum spring rates are ¾ kn.

Directions
(continued from 8.201)

Principal marks
8.223

1 **Landmark:**

Signal Station (48°02′N 4°44′W) (8.199) on Pointe du Raz.

Major lights:

In addition to those given at 8.199:

Eckmühl Light (47°48′N 4°22′W) on Pointe de Penmarc'h (see *Bay of Biscay Pilot*).

Other aid to navigation
8.224

1 **Racon:**

Chaussée de Sein Light Buoy (48°04′N 5°08′W).

For details see *Admiralty List of Radio Signals Volume 2*.

Chaussée de Sein to Pointe de La Torche
8.225

1 From a position W of Chaussée de Sein Light Buoy (48°04′N 5°08′W) (W cardinal) the route leads generally ESE along the S side of Chaussée de Sein (8.193) and across the S entrance to Raz de Sein (8.202) to a position about 5 miles NW of Pointe de Penmarc'h, and W of Pointe de La Torch (48°50′N 4°21′W). The chart is the best guide.

8.226

1 **Clearing marks,** see 8.201.

Useful marks:

An Amouig Beacon Tower (white) (48°03′N 4°57′W) near the centre of Chaussée de Sein.

Ar Guéveur Beacon Tower (white conical topmark, 17 m in height) (48°02′N 4°51′W) on the S side of Île de Sein.

2 Pointe de Lervily Light (white round tower red top, 12 m in height) (48°00′N 4°34′W).

Kergadec Direction Light (48°01′N 4°33′W) (8.231).

Pors-Poulhan Light (white square tower red top, 6 m in height) (47°59′N 4°28′W).

(Directions continue in Bay of Biscay Pilot)

Port d'Audierne

Chart 2819 plan of Audierne

General information
8.227

1 **Position and function.** Port d'Audierne (48°01′N 4°32′W) is situated on the W side of Le Goyen Rivière; it is an important centre of the fishing industry.

There is an outer port outside and W of the river entrance, at Sainte-Évette, off which there is a roadstead where anchorage can be obtained.

2 **Approach and entry.** The port is approached either E or W of La Gamelle (48°00′N 4°32′W), a rocky flat which dries, lying about 1 mile S of the river entrance. The best approach is by Passe de l'Ouest, which leads W of it. The inner harbour is entered through Le Goyen Rivière.

Limiting conditions
8.228

1 **Controlling depths.** The river is subject to silting. Local authorities should be consulted for latest information on depths in the access channel between Raoulic jetty and the Port of Audierne.

Maximum size of vessels handled. The largest vessel to enter the port was one of 230 tonnes with a draught of 3·4 m.

Local weather. The inner harbour is well sheltered but the entrance is dangerous in fresh winds from between SE and SW when the sea breaks across the entrance and sometimes renders it inaccessible.

Arrival information
8.229

1 **Outer anchorage.** Anchorage can be obtained in the roadstead between La Gamelle, which gives only slight protection to the roadstead, and Jetée de Raoulic, about 7 cables N. The bottom is sandy and the holding ground poor.

There is also anchorage in the outer harbour of Sainte-Évette in depths of about 2 to 3 m, but this is not safe with SE winds, and with SW winds the sea sometimes breaks over the breakwater.

2   **Local knowledge** is desirable for entering the port as the depths in the entrance are subject to frequent variation especially after strong winds.

Harbour

8.230

1   **General layout.** Sainte-Évette, the outer harbour, is formed by a breakwater which extends 2 cables E into Anse de Sainte-Évette on the W side of the roadstead.

The inner harbour lies on the W bank of the river, 5 cables within its mouth. The smaller port of Poulgoazec lies on the opposite side of the river.

2   **Tidal streams.** In the approach to the port the streams in Passe de l'Ouest begin as follows:

Interval from HW Brest	Direction
−0505	NE
+0025	SW

The maximum spring rates are ½ kn.

3   In the river the streams run strongly and at the narrowest part in the bend off Poulgoazec they can attain a maximum spring rate of 5 kn.

Directions for entering harbour

8.231

1   **Passe de l'Ouest — leading marks:**

Front mark. Trescadec Old Lighthouse (white stone tower grey top, 10 m in height) (48°00′·8N 4°32′·7W).

Rear mark. Kergadec Direction Light (white octagonal tower red top, 15 m in height) (2 cables N of the front mark).

2   The alignment (006°) of the above marks, or at night in the centre of the narrow white sector (005¼°–006¾°) of the direction light, leads through Passe de l'Ouest passing (with positions given from Kergadec Light):

W of Gamelle Ouest Light Buoy (W cardinal) (1½ miles S) which is moored off the SW side of La Gamelle (8.227); thence:

3   Between Basse Barzig (1 mile S) and Basse Poull-Du (1 mile SSW).

The track then leads as required to the inner or outer harbours.

Caution. The front leading mark stands in a gap between some houses and is not easily seen.

4   **Clearing marks:**

Front mark. Jetée de Raoulic Light (white round tower, 11 m in height) (48°00′·6N 4°32′·5W).

Rear mark. Pyramide des Capucins (white beacon) (5½ cables NNE of the front mark.

The alignment (016°) of these marks clears WNW of the W extremity of La Gamelle.

8.232

1   **Passe de l'Est — leading lights**

Front mark. Jetée de Raoulic Light — as above.

Rear mark. Kergadec Direction Light (4½ cables NNW of the front light).

The alignment (331°) of these lights leads through Passe de l'Est passing (with positions given from Kergadec Light):

2   ENE of Gamelle Est Buoy (S cardinal) (1½ miles SSE) moored off the SE side of La Gamelle; thence:

WSW of Le Quével Beacon Tower (W cardinal) (1 mile SE); thence:

WSW of Le Corbeau Beacon Tower (W cardinal) (6 cables SE) to the inner harbour entrance.

3   **Clearing mark:**

La Gamelle is covered by the red sector (269°–294°) of Pointe de Lervily Light (48°00′N 4°34′W) (8.226).

8.233

1   **Le Goyen Rivière entrance - leading marks:**

Front mark (48°00′·8N 4°32′·4W).

Rear mark (70 m N of front mark).

2   The alignment (359°) of these marks leads into the river passing (with positions from the front mark):

E of the head of Jetée du Raoulic (2½ cables S), thence:

E of a beacon (port hand) (1¾ cables S), thence:

To a position ½ cable S of the front mark.

8.234

1   **Le Goyen Rivière - leading marks:**

Front mark (48°00′·7N 4°32′·5W).

Rear mark (120 m SW of front mark).

The alignment (223°) astern of these marks, leads NE to Poulgoazec. The track then leads NW for the quays at Audierne, passing close to them.

8.235

1   **Useful marks:**

Jetée de Sainte-Évette Light (red lantern) (48°00′·4N 4°33′·0W).

La Petite Gamelle Beacon Tower (S cardinal) (48°00′·6N 4°32′·8W).

Berths

8.236

1   **Inner harbour.** There are quays on the W bank of the river abreast of the town. At Poulgoazec on the E bank there is a quay, 136 m in length with depths of 2 m alongside, and a slipway utilizing the dredged channel. This quay is used solely by fishing vessels.

2   **Outer harbour.** The breakwater at Sainte-Évette, on the W side of the roadstead, extends 2 cables E and is surrounded by stone blocks which extend up to a distance of 10 m from it. There is a shallow patch extending up to 30 m from the N side of the breakwater close within its head. A jetty, with berths on each side, lies 100 m N of the breakwater and parallel with it; it is 225 m in length and has a depth of 1·7 m at its head, mostly covered at HW, which is marked by a beacon (E cardinal). The lifeboat slipway lies midway between the breakwater and the jetty; mariners are not allowed to moor alongside this slipway. There are small craft moorings in the outer harbour.

Port services

8.237

1   **Repairs.** Small repairs can be effected and there is a grid on the E bank of the river below the bridge.

Supplies: diesel oil and petrol; fresh water; provisions.

Lifeboat see 8.221.

Minor harbour and landings

Chart 2819

Pors-Poulhan

8.238

1   **Description.** Pors-Poulhan (47°59′N 4°28′W) a small haven is situated 4 miles ESE of Pointe de Lervily; a light (8.226) is exhibited at the W side of the entrance. Two small breakwaters give protection from the prevailing winds, but access to this small haven is not practicable in bad weather.

Facilities are available for hauling up small craft.

Landing places
8.239

1   Port–Bestrées (48°02′·0N 4°43′·1W) (chart 2348), situated 1 mile ESE of Pointe du Raz, has a small jetty sheltered from SW winds.

Anse de Feunten Aod (48°02′N 4°42′W) (chart 2348), entered E of a point of the same name, provides a landing place in fair weather.

2   Porz Loubous (48°02′N 4°40′W) (chart 2348), a small cove situated 3¼ miles E of Pointe du Raz, affords partial shelter to boats and has a landing place.

Anse du Loc'h (48°02′N 4°38′W), situated 4 miles E of Pointe du Raz, is bordered by a rocky reef; Basse du Loc'h lies on the E side of the approach about 3 cables offshore. A mole, which protects a landing slip, extends from the S side of the village at the head of the cove.

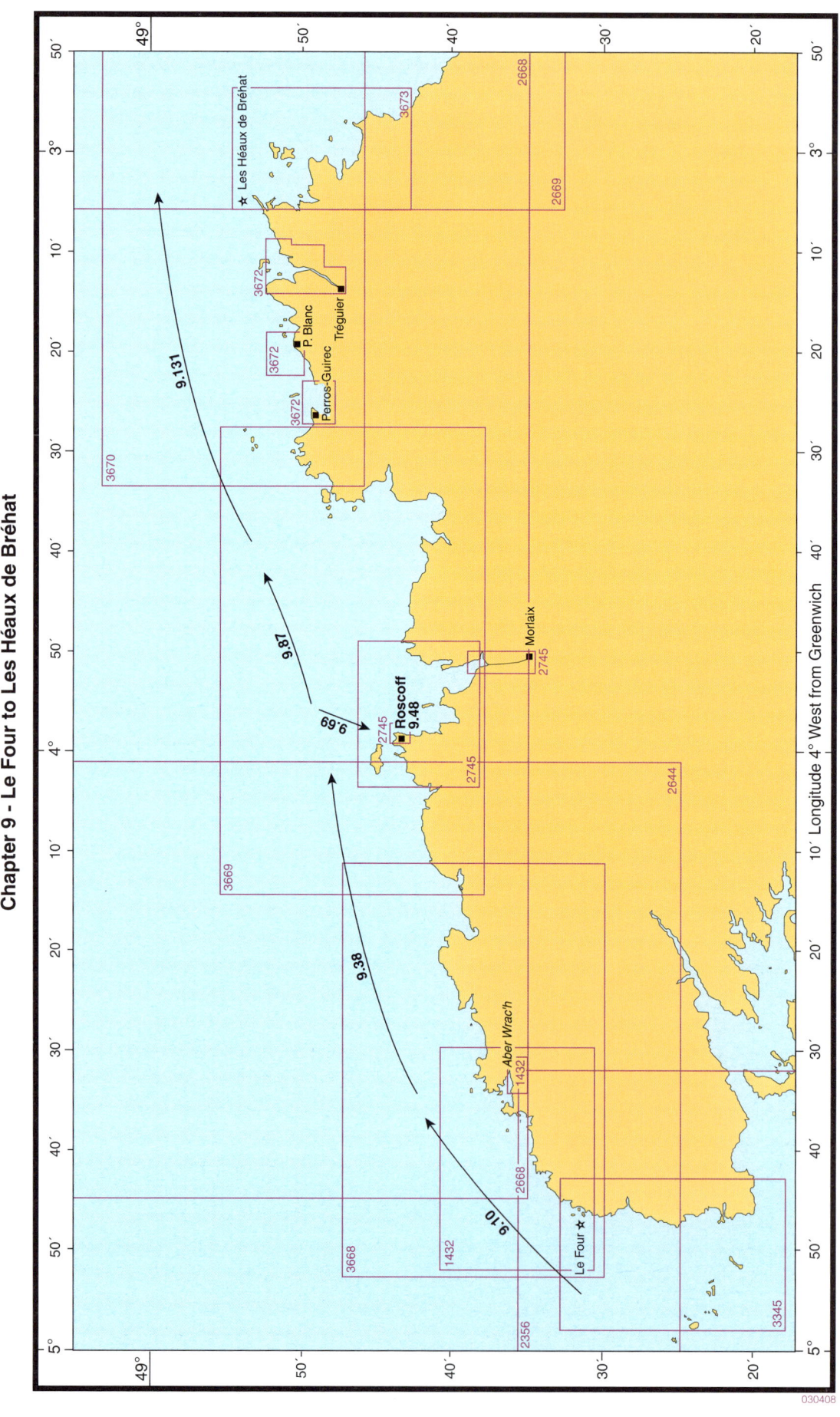

030408

CHAPTER 9

NORTH-WEST COAST OF FRANCE — LE FOUR TO LES HÉAUX DE BRÉHAT

GENERAL INFORMATION

Charts 2644, 2668, 2675
Scope of the chapter
9.1

1   This chapter covers the NW coast of France from Le Four (48°31′N 4°48′W) to Les Héaux de Bréhat, about 72 miles ENE.

    Port. The only port of note on this coast is Roscoff-Bloscon (9.48) which is a ferry port with a RoRo terminal.

Topography
9.2

1   Between Le Four and Île de Batz (9.50), about 33 miles ENE, the coast is moderately high and is bordered by reefs and shoals, on which are many above-water rocks, lying in places, 3 miles offshore. Two large bays indent the coast between Île de Batz and Île Grande, 16 miles ENE. Plateau des Triagoz (48°52′N 3°39′W) (9.93), a group of rocks, and Les Sept-Îles (48°53′N 3°29′W) (9.122), an archipelago, lie off the coast about 16 miles and 21 miles ENE, respectively, of Île de Batz. Les Héaux (48°55′N 3°05′W) (9.131), a drying reef, together with several above-water rocks, stand about 2½ miles offshore at the E end of the area, about 16 miles E of Les Sept Îles.

Regulations concerning vessels carrying dangerous and polluting goods
9.3

1   For regulations concerning tankers laden with hydrocarbons and other vessels carrying dangerous and polluting goods navigating in the approaches to the N and W coasts of France, see 1.68 to 1.76

Submarine cables
9.4

1   A submarine cable runs from an offshore position (48°55′·5N 3°55′·3W) to a landfall on the W side of Baie de Lannion (48°44′·8N 3°32′·9W). Anchoring, dredging and trawling are prohibited within 5 cables either side of the cable, for most of its length. Also see 9.115. The chart is the best guide.

2   Anchoring, dredging and trawling should be avoided in the vicinity of all submarine cables. See *Annual Notices to Mariners No 24* and *The Mariners Handbook*.

Marine farms
9.5

1   Marine farms, also charted as marine culture exploitation areas, but mostly in the form of shellfish beds, are situated throughout the waters of this chapter; most are charted and should be avoided. Some areas are subject to local regulations. Farms in proximity to shipping routes are generally marked by buoys. Other farms are marked by beacons (X topmark) and some are fitted with radar reflectors. Lights, when fitted, show flashing yellow. See 1.29.

Marks
9.6

1   The rocks, islets and church towers, of which there are many along this coast, are difficult to identify with certainty; caution is therefore necessary when using bearings of such objects to obtain a position.

Dangers
9.7

1   Between Le Four and Pointe de Pontusval, about 21 miles ENE, the outermost dangers are marked by light buoys. In general, mariners should, unless it is absolutely necessary to approach closer, give a clearance of 5 or 6 miles to this part of the coast, especially at night when it should not be approached within depths of 85 m.

Anchorages and harbours
9.8

1   On this coast between Le Four and as far E as Les Héaux de Bréhat (48°55′N 3°05′W) there are no anchorages or harbours suitable for large vessels, but small craft and yachts can find shelter in many of the small ports or creeks, although access to many of them is difficult without local knowledge.

Tidal information
9.9

1   **Tidal streams** offshore, in general, run parallel with the coast and attain a maximum spring rate of 3 to 4 kn, see tidal information on the charts and *Admiralty Tidal Stream Atlas of the English Channel*.

    Range. The tidal range is large. At Roscoff (9.48) the mean spring range is about 7·5 m.

LE FOUR TO ÎLE VIERGE

General information

Charts 3668, 2644, 1432
Route
9.10

1   From W of Le Four (48°31′N 4°48′W) the route leads NE along the NW coast of France to NW of Île Vierge, a distance of about 15 miles.

Topography
9.11

1   The coast between Presqu'île Saint-Laurent (48°31′N 4°47′W) and Pointe Koun, 4 miles NE, is bordered by Roches d'Argenton and Roches de Portsall (9.18).

    Between Pointe Koun and Île Vierge (48°38′N 4°34′W) the coast recedes and is indented by the estuaries of Aber Benoît (9.26) and Aber Wrac'h (9.30) which are separated by Presqu'île Sainte-Marguerite (48°36′N 4°36′W).

Traffic regulations
9.12

1   For details of the Off Ushant (Ouessant) TSS NW of Île d'Ouessant (48°28′N 5°05′W), the mandatory VTMS, the limits of which are shown on the chart and the Inshore

Traffic Zone, SE of the TSS, which lie adjacent to this chapter see 2.32, 8.5 and 8.6.

Fishing is regulated in an area, as shown on the chart, in the vicinity of Roches de Portsall (48°35′N 4°44′W).

Temporary explosives dumping grounds
9.13

1 Temporary explosives dumping grounds (Zones de Dépôts d'Explosifs) are situated:
> In the approaches to Portsall (48°33′N 4°45′W) (9.19).
> At the entrance to l'Aber Benoît (48°35′N 4°41′W) (9.26).
> At the entrance to l'Aber Wrac'h (48°38′N 4°37′W) (9.30).

For details see 1.7 and Appendix V.

Rescue
9.14

1 **All-weather lifeboats** are maintained at:
> Portsall (48°33′N 4°42′W) (9.19).
> Port de L'Aber Wrac'h (48°36′N 4°34′W) (9.35).

Inshore lifeboats are maintained at:
> Argenton (48°31′N 4°46′W) (9.25).
> Aber Wrac'h.

For details of lifeboats, see 1.117.

Tidal streams
9.15

1 Tidal streams at the positions indicated begin as shown in the following table:

Interval from HW Brest	Position	Direction
−0545	One mile W of Le Four Light (48°31′N 4°48′W)	NNE
+0100		SSW

2 The maximum N-going and S-going spring rates are 3½ and 2¼ kn respectively.

−0505	At Basse Paupian Buoy (48°35′N 4°46′W)	E
+0100		SW

3 The maximum spring rate in each direction is 3¾ kn.

−0430	At Grande Basse Portsall Light Buoy (48°37′N 4°46′W)	NE
+0200		WSW

4 The maximum E-going and W-going spring rates are 3¾ and 3½ kn respectively.

−0500	Off Le Libenter (48°38′N 4°37′W)	E
+0110		W

5 The maximum spring rate in each direction is 2½ kn.

−0300	Five miles seaward of Le Libenter	E
+0310		SW

The maximum spring rate in each direction is 2¾ kn. See also information on the chart.

Directions
(continued from 8.25 and 8.43 where directions for the Inshore Traffic Zone of Île d'Ouessant and Chenal du Four are given)

Principal marks
9.16

1 **Landmarks:**
> Le Four Lighthouse (48°31′N 4°48′W) (8.43).
> White Tower (red lights) (48°30′·3N 4°46′·2W).
> Corn Carhai Lighthouse (white octagonal tower black top, 20 m in height) (48°35′N 4°44′W).
2
> Water Tower (48°33′·1N 4°43′·4W) standing 5 cables SW of Beg ar Galéti.
> Water Tower (glass rotunda) (48°31′·8N 4°39′·6W) standing 8 cables S of Ploudalmézeau Church.
> Île Vierge Lighthouse (grey tower, 82 m in height) (48°38′N 4°34′W), an old disused shorter light tower stands close NNW.

New Lighthouse   *Old Lighthouse*

Ile Vierge from ENE (9.16)
(Original dated 2000-02)

(Photograph - Jean Guichard)

3 **Major lights:**
> Creac'h Light (48°28′N 5°08′W) (8.25).
> Le Stiff Light (48°29′N 5°03′W) (8.25).
> Kéréon Light (48°26′N 5°01′W) (8.25).
> Le Four Light (48°31′N 4°48′W) (8.43).
> Île Vierge Light — as above.

Presqu'île Saint-Laurent to Île Vierge
9.17
1   **Dangers,** see 9.7.
9.18
1   **Route.** From a position W of Le Four (48°31′N 4°48′W), NE of Île d'Ouessant (8.15), the route leads generally NE passing (with positions given from Pointe Koun (48°34′N 4°42′W)):

    NW of Le Four (48°31′N 4°48′W) from where a light (8.43) is exhibited; thence:

2   NW of Roches d'Argenton (3½ miles SW), a chain of rocks some of which are above water. The rocks, which are covered by the green sector (058°–084°) of Portsall Light (48°34′N 4°42′W) (9.22), lie about 1 mile offshore and extend about 3 miles NE from Le Four Light. Thence:

3   NW of Grande Basse de Portsall (3 miles NW), marked on its NW side by Grande Basse Portsall Light Buoy (W cardinal). It is the NW extremity of Roches de Portsall, numerous above-water, drying and below-water rocks which extend 3 miles NW from Pointe Koun. Basse Paupian Buoy (W cardinal) (9.22) is moored 1½ miles S of the light buoy. Corn Carhai Lighthouse (1½ miles NW) (9.16) stands in the middle of Roches de Portsall; in thick weather it can be distinguished from Le Four Lighthouse by the fact that no rocks can be seen W of Le Four. Thence:

4   NW of Basses Occidentales du Libenter (4½ miles NE) and Brisant Septentrional du Libenter (5½ miles NE), shoals lying within 1 mile N and W of Le Libenter, a rocky shoal, marked on its W side by a light buoy (W cardinal); thence:

    To a position NW of Basse de l'Île Vierge (7 miles NE), the NW-most danger off Île Vierge.

5   **Caution.** The sea breaks heavily on all these offshore rocks. It is prudent to give Grande Basse Portsall Light Buoy (W cardinal) a wide clearance to the N and W.

    Useful marks:
    Radar Tower (48°28′·6N 5°03′·1W).
    Kéréon Light (48°26′N 5°01′W) (8.25).
    (Directions continue at 9.45)

Portsall and approaches

Charts 1432, 3668
General information
9.19
1   **Position and function.** Portsall (48°33′N 4°42′W), a drying harbour, lies on the E side of Anse de Portsall; the harbour is used mainly by fishing vessels.

    The villages of Trémazan and Kersaint lie close SW of Beg ar Galéti and at the S end of Anse de Portsall.

2   **Approach and entry.** The port is approached from W by Chenal de Men Glas (9.22), which is the best approach, from SW through Chenal Méridional de Portsall (9.23), from N through Chenal de Bosven Amont or from NE through Chenal du Relec. Anse de Portsall is entered between Pointe Koun (48°34′·2N 4°42′·3W) and Beg ar Galéti, 7 cables SSW.

Arrival information
9.20
1   **Outer anchorage.** Anchorage can be obtained W of La Pendante Beacon Tower (48°33′·7N 4°42′·8W) (9.22), in a position shown on the chart, in depths of 10 to 12 m.

    Requirement for local knowledge. The leading line for Chenal de Men Glas is difficult to follow on account of the strong tidal streams; local knowledge is recommended for this channel and for Chenal Méridional de Portsall.

    Local knowledge is essential for the N and NE approaches which should only be used, by day, and at or near HW.

Harbour
9.21
1   The harbour is formed by a creek filled by a drying sand flat on which there are some above-water and drying rocks.

    Tidal streams, see 9.15.

Directions for entering harbour
9.22
1   **Caution.** The charted beacon tower (white and yellow) in position 48°33′·3N 4°43′·0W is not visible on, and is not part of, the alignment described below.

2   **Chenal de Men Glas — leading marks:**
    Front mark. Le Yurc'h (rock with pronounced V-shaped cleft) (48°33′·5N 4°44′·0W).
    Rear mark. Ploudalmézeau Church (spire) (3¼ miles ESE of the front mark).

    From a position SSW of Basse Paupian Buoy (W cardinal) (48°35′·3N 4°46′·3W) the alignment (109°) of these marks leads through Chenal de Men Glas a deep channel which lies S of Roches de Portsall (9.18), passing (with positions given from the front mark):

3   NNE of Basse Corn ar C'hleus (1½ miles WNW), noting a shallower 6 m patch which lies 1½ cables ENE of the bank and closer to the track; thence:

    Between the S side of Roches de Portsall and Basse ar Martro (1¼ miles WNW) with Basse Névez lying 5 cables ESE.

    Leading marks:
4   Front mark. Beacon (white rectangular) (1¼ miles ENE) near Portsall Light.
    Rear mark. Beacon (red and white) on a wall (1½ miles ENE).

    The alignment (085°) of these marks, which are not easily distinguishable, or at night in the white sector (084°–088°) of Portsall Light (white column red top, 7 m in height) (1¼ miles ENE) leads in the approach to the anchorage passing (with positions given from Le Yurc'h):

5   S of Bosven Aval (3½ cables NNW), an islet marked by a beacon tower (white); thence:
    N of a dangerous wreck (position approximate) (2 cables N) charted close NW of Men ar Pic, marked by a beacon tower (starboard hand); thence:

6   Between Basse Idi (3 cables NE) and the drying rocky area on which Île Verte (5 cables NE) lies; thence:
    N of the anchorage (5 cables ENE) (9.20). Two beacon towers (white) mark the drying rocks N of the leading line and the anchorage.

7   The track then leads generally E to the harbour entrance passing between La Pendante Beacon Tower (N cardinal) (8 cables ENE) and Besquel Beacon Tower (isolated danger) about 1 cable farther NE passing close N of this former beacon.
9.23
1   **Chenal Méridional de Portsall.** From a position SE of Le Four Light (48°31′N 4°48′W) (8.43) the alignment (049°) of the following marks leads in Chenal Méridional de Portsall, a deep but narrow passage which lies between

297

Roches d'Argenton (9.18) and the reefs and islets which border the coast from Presqu'île Saint-Laurent to Pointe de Landunvez (48°32'·6N 4°45'·2W); a beacon tower (red and white) stands close within the point.

2   **Leading marks:**

Front mark. Le Yurc'h (48°33'·5N 4°44'·0W) (9.22). Rear mark. Grand Men Louet Beacon Tower (squat tower white on its SW side) (6 cables NE of the front mark).

    Useful marks:

3   Le Taureau Beacon Tower (W cardinal) (48°31'·5N 4°47'·3W).

Water Tower (48°31'·3N 4°44'·8W) standing 5 cables E of Argenton.

    Leading marks:

Front mark. Bosven Aval Beacon Tower (white) (48°33'·8N 4°44'·3W) (9.22).

4   Rear mark. Bosven Kreiz Beacon Tower (white) (5 cables NE of the front mark) standing on an islet of the same name.

The alignment (036°) of these marks then leads in the channel from Pointe de Landunvez to join Chenal de Men Glas.

Berths
9.24

1   At Portsall there is a small jetty, quay and slipways all of which dry up to 4·5 m.

    Facilities are very limited.

    Rescue, see 9.14.

Argenton
9.25

1   **General information.** Argenton (48°31'N 4°46'W) contains a small harbour, which dries, situated on the E side of Île Dolvez. A short breakwater extends N from Île Dolvez and gives some shelter from W winds, but the harbour is not recommended in threatening weather as strong W winds bring in a heavy surf.

2   **Directions.** From a position at the entrance to Chenal Méridional de Portsall the alignment (084½°) of two beacons on Île Dolvez leads in the approach passing N of Melgorn Bihan, a prominent rock lying at the end of a reef which extends 4 cables W from Presqu'île Saint-Laurent, and S of Le Bélier, Brividic and Les Trois Pierres, rocks which are each marked by beacon towers (port hand).

3   **Anchorage:** on the leading line near Île Dolvez, or NW of this island in depths of about 2 m at MLWS.

    Berth: short jetty on the W side of the harbour; yachts can dry out to a sandy bottom on the S side.

    Rescue, see 9.14.

Aber Benoît

General information
9.26

1   **Description.** The estuary of Aber Benoît (48°35'N 4°37'W) is frequented by fishing boats and other small craft.

    Limiting conditions. The approach to Aber Benoît should only be made by day, and preferably at or near LW when all the dangers may be easily seen.

    Marine farms mainly in the form of marine culture exploitation areas, shown on the chart, lie in the entrance to Aber Benoît.

2   **Tidal streams** N of Île Guénioc (48°36'N 4°38'W) run transversely across the approach to Aber Benoît; S of Île Guénioc they run inward and outward to and from the estuary. They begin as follows:

Interval from HW Brest	Position	Direction
−0515	La Petite Fourche (48°37'N 4°39'W)	ENE
+0055		W

3   The maximum spring rate in each direction is 2¾ kn.

−0500	S of Île Guénioc	SE
+0100		NW

4   The maximum spring rate in each direction is 2½ kn.

−0445	In Aber Benoît	In-going
+0100		Out-going

The maximum in-going and out-going spring rates are 3 kn.

Directions
9.27

1   **Approach from north.** From a position W of Libenter Light Buoy (W cardinal) (48°37'·5N 3°38'·5W) the track leads generally SSE passing (with positions given from La Jument (48°35'·1N 4°37'·2W)):

WSW of La Petite Fourche (2 miles NNW) marked by a buoy (W cardinal). A dangerous wreck (position approximate) is charted about 1½ cables NW of the buoy and closer to the track. Thence:

2   WSW of Trouskennou, consisting of a number of dangerous rocks and drying patches, of which La Grande Fourche (1¾ miles NNW) and Basse Brisante (1½ miles NNW) are the W-most dangers; and:

3   ENE of Ruzven Est Buoy (starboard hand) (1½ miles NNW), which marks the E side of Plateau de Ruzwenn on which there are a number of drying and below-water rocks.

The alignment (142°) of the E extremity of La Jument with Le Chien Beacon Tower (isolated danger) (5 cables SE) then leads in the fairway passing:

4   Between Basse du Chenal, marked by Basse du Chenal Buoy (starboard hand), and a beacon (port hand) (1 mile NW respectively) standing S of Île Guénioc.

The track then continues generally SE passing:

Between Karreg ar Poul Doun (6 cables NNW), marked on its S side by a beacon (port hand), and Men Renead (5 cables NW) marked on its SE side by a buoy (starboard hand); thence:

5   SW of La Jument marked on its W side by a beacon (port hand); thence:

NE of Ar Gazel Buoy (starboard hand) (2 cables SSE); thence:

6   Clear of Le Chien (5 cables SW), marked by a beacon tower (isolated danger), the recommended track passing W. Thence the alignment, astern, of the beacon tower with the W edge of Île Garo (1½ cables E) leads into the estuary passing NE of Kervigorn Buoy (starboard hand) (6 cables SSE).

7   **Clearing bearing:**

The line of bearing 183° of Ploudalmézeau Church (spire) (48°32'·5N 4°39'·5W) open W of Lampaul-Ploudalmézeau Church (spire), 1¼ miles N, passes W of Basses Occidentales du Libenter (9.18) passing very close E of a dangerous wreck (position doubtful) charted 4 cables W of the shoal.

9.28

1 **Approach from north west.** From a position between Plateau de Ruzwenn (9.27), marked on its SW side by a Ruzven Ouest Buoy (W cardinal), and Plateau de Trévors (48°35′N 4°39′W), a chain of islets and rocks which extends 1¼ miles offshore on the W side of the channel leading to Aber Benoît, the line of bearing 130° of Le Chien Beacon Tower (isolated danger) (48°34′·7N 4°36′·9W) leads in the fairway passing between Plateau de Trévors and associated dangers and Poul Orvil, close E, marked on its W side by a buoy (W cardinal) to join the N approach SW of La Jument.

2 **Caution.** Numerous unmarked dangers, the positions of which can be seen from the chart, lie close to the leading line N of Île Trévors.

3 **Useful marks:**
> Penven (48°35′·6N 4°38′·9W), a prominent rock standing near the N end of Plateau de Trévors.
> Water Tower (48°34′N 4°37′W) at Ruellou.

Anchorage and harbours
9.29

1 **Port du Vill** (48°34′·5N 3°36′·5W) on the N bank at the entrance to the estuary: quay 35 m in length drying 1·2 m; slip.

Stellac'h on the S bank 6 cables ESE of Port du Vill: quay 50 m in length drying 2 m; slip.

Anchorage: in the middle of the estuary SSE of Port du Vill, as shown on the chart, in a least depth of 2 m.

Aber Wrac'h

General information
9.30

1 **Description.** The estuary of Aber Wrac'h (48°37′N 4°36′W) contains sheltered anchorages, three small ports which dry, and a large yacht harbour.

Route. The estuary is approached by one of three channels; from W by Grand Chenal (9.31) the principal approach, from NW by Chenal de la Pendante (9.32) and from N by Chenal de la Malouine (9.33).

2 **Marine farms** mainly in the form of marine culture exploitation areas, shown on the chart, lie in the entrance to Aber Wrac'h.

Local knowledge. The channel between Port de l'Aber Wrac'h (48°35′·9N 4°33′·7W) and Port de Paluden, 2 miles ESE, should not be attempted without local knowledge.

3 **Tidal streams** at the entrance to Grand Chenal run transversely across the approach. Farther inshore they tend to run in the direction of the channel, and off Île Cézon (48°36′·5N 4°35′·1W) they begin as follows:

Interval from HW Brest	Direction
–0515	SE
+0055	NW

The maximum spring rates are 1½ kn.

4 In Chenal de la Pendante tidal streams N of the parallel of 48°38′N run transversely across the approach to the channel beginning as follows:

Interval from HW Brest	Direction
–0500	NE
+0100	WSW

The maximum spring rate is 2½ kn.

5 The streams E of Le Libenter (48°38′N 4°37′W) also run transversely but begin about 15 minutes earlier.

At the N entrance to Chenal de la Malouine the tidal streams run transversely across it at a maximum spring rate of about 3 kn; but S of La Malouine (48°37′·6N 4°36′·0W) they run in the direction of the channel at a maximum rate of about 2½ to 3 kn.

Directions
9.31

1 **Grand Chenal** has least depths of 5·2 m in its outer part and of 4·1 m in its inner part; it is navigable by day and night and is the principal approach.

Leading lights:
> Front light. Île Wrac'h Light (white square tower, orange top, dwelling, 15 m in height) (48°37′N 4°34′W).

2 > Rear light. Lanvaon Light (white square tower, orange triangle point up on top, 27 m in height) (1½ miles E of the front mark).

The alignment (100°) of these lights, together with Plouguerneau Belfry (spire), 1¼ miles farther E, which stands on the same alignment, leads in Grand Chenal passing (with positions given from the front light):

3 > S of Libenter Light Buoy (W cardinal) (2¾ miles WNW); thence:
> Between Trepied Buoy (port hand) (2 miles W), which marks the S side of Le Libenter (9.18), and Basse du Chenal (2¼ miles W), the NE most danger off Trouskennou (9.27); thence:

4 > Between Basse Névez (1½ miles W) and Grand Pot de Beurre (1¼ miles WNW), marked by a beacon (port hand); thence:
> Between Petit Pot de Beurre Beacon Tower (E cardinal, 5 m in height) (1 mile WNW) and Îles de la Croix (1¼ miles W).

5 **Leading marks:**
> Front mark. La Palue Beacon Tower (white round tower, red top, orange dome, 8 m in height) (48°35′·8N 4°33′·6W).
> Rear mark. Saint-Antoine Beacon Tower (white round tower, red top, orange dome, 6 m in height) (2 cables SE of the front mark).

6 The alignment (128°) of these marks, or at night in the white sector (127¼°–128¾°) on the same line of bearing of Aber Wrac'h Breakwater Direction Light (white structure, 4 m in height) (48°36′N 4°34′W), leads in the channel passing:

7 > NE of Basse de la Croix (1 mile W) marked by a light buoy (starboard hand); thence:
> NE of Bréac'h Ver Lighted Beacon Tower (starboard hand) (6 cables WSW); thence:
> SW of a light buoy (port hand) (7 cables S) marking the N side of the channel; thence:

8 > NE of Roche aux Moines (9 cables SSE), marked on its NE side by a beacon tower (starboard hand); another beacon tower (white) stands on its SW side.

The track then leads generally ESE then E to the river entrance passing between the N end of the W mole (1 mile SSE), distant about ½ cable, and S of Touris Beacon Tower (port hand) (1 mile SE).

9.32

1 **Chenal de la Pendante** has a least depth of about 0·3 m; it should only be used by day and in fine weather.

Leading marks:
> Front mark. Disc (white with black edge) (48°36′·4N 4°35′·2W) on the fort on Île Cézon.

Rear mark. Amer de la Pendante (black tower vertical white line surmounted by orange triangle) (1¼ miles SE of the front mark).

2   From a position about 2½ miles W of Île Vierge (48°38′N 4°34′W) the alignment (135¾°) of these marks leads in the channel passing (with positions given from Île Cézon fort):

Close NE of Men C'hoz (2 miles NW) at the N end of Le Libenter (9.18); thence:

SW of La Pendante (1½ miles NW), a white rock.

3   When about 1½ cables N of Grand Pot de Beurre Beacon (1¼ miles NW) the line of bearing 110° of Île Wrac'h Light (6 cables NE) leads in the channel for about 2 cables.

The track then reverts SE passing:

SW of Barr ar Bleiz marked by a buoy (port hand) (1 mile NW); thence:

4   Between Plate Aber Wrac'h (9½ cables NW), marked on its SW side by a buoy (port hand), and Petit Pot de Beurre Beacon Tower (E cardinal) (1 mile NW) to join the alignment (128°) of La Palue and Saint-Antoine Beacon Towers as directed for Grand Chenal (9.31).

Caution. The leading marks for Chenal de la Pendante should be followed exactly; the rear mark is not easily distinguishable.

9.33

1   **Chenal de la Malouine** has a least depth of about 1 m and a least width of ½ cable; it should only be used by day and in fine weather.

Leading marks:

Front mark. Petit Pot de Beurre Beacon Tower (48°37′·1N 4°36′·2W) (E cardinal) (9.31).

Rear mark. Beacon Tower (white) (4 cables S of the front mark) standing on Petite Île.

2   From a position about 1½ miles W of Île Vierge (48°38′N 4°34′W) the alignment (176¼°) of these marks leads in the channel passing (with positions given from the front mark):

Very close E of the rocks extending up to 3½ cables NNE of La Pendante (5 cables NNW) (9.32); and:

3   Close W of La Malouine (4½ cables N), a rock standing on the W edge of a drying reef; thence:

Between Karreg Bazil Beacon Tower (port hand) (3½ cables N) and Reun (3 cables NNW); thence:

To a position abreast Barr ar Bleiz (1½ cables NNE) (9.32) when directions for Chenal de la Pendante (9.32) and Grand Chenal (9.31) should be followed.

4   **Useful marks:**

Landéda Church (spire) (48°35′·2N 4°34′·4W).

Water Tower (48°35′·3N 4°34′·0W) at Landéda.

Anchorages

9.34

1   Anchorage can be obtained SE of Île Cézon (48°36′·4N 4°35′·2W), as shown on the chart, in depths of 7 to 12 m, sand and shell, good holding ground.

Karreg Du anchorage lies between Roches aux Moines (48°36′·0N 4°34′·2W) and the slipway at the entrance to the river about 3 cables SE; the anchorage is about ¾ cable wide between steep banks of mud on which there are oyster beds.

2   Between L'Aber Wrac'h and Pointe Cameuleut, 8 cables E, the channel passes close S of Touris Beacon Tower and lies close to the N side of the river, between mudbanks on which there are oyster beds marked by stakes; after

rounding Pointe Cameuleut the fairway lies in mid-channel and affords sheltered anchorage in depths of up to 3 m, mud.

Harbours

9.35

1   **L'Aber Wrac'h** (48°35′·9N 4°33′·7W) lies on the S side of the entrance to the river. It is protected to the W by a mole leading NNE which extends to a breakwater leading ENE; a light is exhibited from the head of the breakwater. To the E the harbour is protected by a breakwater leading NNE, then NW; a light is exhibited from the head of the breakwater. The W part of the harbour is used by leisure craft and contains the lifeboat slipway. The E part of the harbour, which is separated from the E part by a central pier, is used by fishing vessels. There are good drying-out berths alongside the E side of the mole. A quay at right angles to the E side of the mole dries 5 m. A mooring buoy, for use of French naval authorities, lies 1 cable NW of the end of the lifeboat slipway.

2   **Facilities:** fuel; fresh water; provisions.

Rescue, see 9.14.

9.36

1   **Perros** (48°36′·3N 4°33′·0W) on the N bank of the river 5 cables NE of L'Aber Wrac'h is entered through a buoyed approach channel. There are several well protected alongside berths, which dry up to 3 m, for small craft. Local vessels are moored afloat in the approach. Nearby oyster beds are marked with perches.

9.37

1   **Port de Paluden** (48°35′·3N 4°31′·3W) is situated about 2 miles above L'Aber Wrac'h at the point where navigation ceases; there are depths of 2·7 m in the channel between these two places.

2   At Paluden there are small quays on each side of the river, each of which dries 2·5 m; that on the E bank dries out to a concrete bed and that on the W bank to a bottom of mud and shingle. Each quay has a landing slip, extending down river, which dries 1 m. Port de Paludin is used by small commercial vessels.

ILE VIERGE TO ROSCOFF

General information

Charts 3668, 3669, 2668

Route

9.38

1   From NW of Île Vierge (48°38′N 4°34′W) the route leads ENE along the NW coast of France to NNW of Île de Batz, a distance of about 25 miles.

Topography

9.39

1   Between Île Vierge and Île de Batz the coast slopes gently, is bordered by sandy beaches and contains some small havens. The coast is fronted by dangerous rocks, reefs and shoals which extend nearly 3 miles offshore.

Fishery

9.40

1   **Fishing** is regulated in an area, as shown on the chart, NW of Pointe de Beg Pol (48°41′N 4°21′W).

Temporary explosive dumping grounds

9.41

1   Temporary explosive dumping gounds, for occasional use, are situated NW of Port de Kerlouan (48°40′N 4°23′W) (9.82) and WNW of Île de Batz (48°45′N 4°03′W), for details see 1.7 and Appendix V.

Former mined areas
9.42

1 The minor harbours of Corréjou (9.79) and Port de Tréssény (9.81) lie within a former mined area. For information concerning former mined areas see Appendix IV and *Annual Summary of Admiralty Notices to Mariners.* It is dangerous to anchor, trawl or dredge in these areas.

Rescue
9.43

1 **All-weather lifeboat.** Île de Batz all-weather lifeboat is stationed at Keffen (48°45′N 4°01′W) (9.86) on the S side of the island.

Inshore lifeboats:
Plouguerneau inshore lifeboat is stationed at Corréjou (48°38′N 4°31′W) (9.79).
Brignogan-Plouescat (9.83).

Signal Stations situated at:
Brignogan (Vigie) (48°41′N 4°20′W).
Île de Batz (Sémaphore) (48°45′N 4°01′W) (9.45).

2 For details regarding lifeboats, see 1.117 and for signal stations 1.95 and 1.110.

VHF Direction-finding services, for emergency use only, operate from:
Brignogan (48°41′N 4°20′W).
Île de Batz (48°45′N 4°01′W).

For details see *Admiralty List of Radio Signals Volume 2.*

Tidal streams
9.44

1 Tidal streams about 3 miles N of Pointe de Pontusval (48°41′N 4°19′W) begin as follows:

Interval from HW Brest	Direction
−0400	E
+0200	W

The maximum spring rate is about 2¾ kn, see also information on the chart.

Directions
(continued from 9.18)

Principal marks
9.45

1 **Landmarks:**
Île Vierge Lighthouse (48°38′N 4°34′W) (9.16).
Water Tower (48°39′N 4°22′W) at Kerlouan.
Water Tower (48°37′N 4°12′W).
Plouescat church belfry (48°40′N 4°10′W).
Île de Batz Lighthouse (grey tower black lantern, 43 m in height) (48°45′N 4°02′W).

2 Coastguard Signal Station (grey square tower and flagstaff) (48°44′·8N 4°00′·6W) on an old fort in the middle of Île de Batz.

Major lights:
Île Vierge Light (48°38′N 4°34′W) (9.16).
Île de Batz Light — as above.

Île Vierge to Île de Batz
9.46

1 **Dangers,** see 9.7.
Route. From a position NW of Île Vierge (48°38′N 4°34′W) the route leads ENE passing (with positions given from Pointe de Beg Pol (48°41′N 4°21′W)):
NNW of Plateau de Lizenn Wenn, marked near its NW extremity by Lizen Ven Ouest Light Buoy (W cardinal) (48°41′N 4°34′W); thence:
NNW of Plateau d'ar Guern (6 miles W); thence:

2 NNW of Plateau d'Amann ar Rouz; Aman ar Ross Light Buoy (N cardinal) (4¼ miles WNW) is moored about 1 mile NNE of its N extremity; thence:
NNW of Pointe de Beg Pol. Pontusval Light (white tower black top white dwelling, 15 m in height) is exhibited from the point. Thence:

3 NNW of Qeyn-Cos (4 miles ENE), a detached rocky bank; thence:
To a position NNW of Grande Basse (48°46′N 4°02′W), the outer-most danger N of Île de Batz. The dangers surrounding Île de Batz are covered by the red sector (073°–197°) of Men Guen Bras Lighted Beacon Tower (48°44′N 3°58′W) (9.69).

9.47

1 **Clearing bearing:**
The line of bearing 096° of Pontusval Light (48°41′N 4°21′W) changing from red to white clears N of the dangers which extend nearly 3 miles offshore between Île Vierge and Basses Saint Egarec, 7 miles ENE.

2 **Useful marks:**
Creac'h Light (48°28′N 5°08′W) (8.25).
Water Tower (48°40′N 4°20′W) at Brignogan-Plages.
Church (belfry) (48°40′N 4°10′W) at Plouescat.
Water Tower (48°40′N 4°04′W) at Sibiril.
(Directions for Roscoff continue at 9.68 and for the passage continuing ENE at 9.92)

ROSCOFF AND APPROACHES

General information

Charts 2745, 3669
Position
9.48

1 The ferry port of Port de Roscoff-Bloscon lies about 5 cables SE of Pointe de Bloscon (48°44′N 3°58′W). The smaller port of Roscoff, a drying harbour, lies W of the same point.

Function
9.49

1 Port de Roscoff-Bloscon is the terminal for the RoRo ferries which operate regularly between Roscoff and Plymouth and Roscoff and Cork; it is also used by coasting and fishing vessels.
Port de Roscoff (48°43′N 3°59′W) is used mainly by coasting and fishing vessels, yachts and other small craft.

Topography
9.50

1 Île de Batz (48°45′N 4°01′W), a low–lying island surrounded on all side by dangerous rocks and shoals, lies about 1 mile off the coast between Île Siec and Roscoff, 3½ miles ENE. The conspicuous lighthouse and signal station (9.45) help to identify the island.

Approach and entry
9.51

1 Port de Roscoff-Bloscon is approached from NE of Île de Batz through a controlled approach channel (9.69) and entered between Môle Pierre Lemaire and a light buoy moored 2 cables S. The port can also be approached from Baie de Morlaix (9.99) passing between Plateau des Duons (48°44′N 3°55′W) and Bazenn ar Menk (9.69).

2 Port de Roscoff is approached either through the controlled approach channel, from Baie de Morlaix, or through Canal de l'Île de Batz (9.63) and entered by Passe de Benven or Passe du Rannic.

Traffic
9.52

1 In 2006 a total of 231 vessels totalling 862 449 dwt, excluding ferries, used Port de Roscoff-Bloscon.

Port Authority
9.53

1 Chambre de Commerce, Port de Roscoff-Bloscon, F29680, Roscoff.

Limiting conditions

Controlling depths
9.54

1 The controlling depth for Port de Roscoff-Bloscon is 6 m on an isolated patch 1¼ cables NNE of the breakwater head in the white approach sector of Bloscon Light (48°43′N 3°58′W) (9.72).

The port of Roscoff (9.77) dries.

Tidal levels
9.55

1 Mean spring range about 7·5 m; mean neap range about 3·6 m, see *Admiralty Tide Tables*.

2 It has been reported (2006) that breaking seas caused by the tidal stream in opposition to the wind direction can present a danger to small craft for a distance up to two miles offshore.

Arrival information

Notice of ETA required
9.56

1 At least 24 hours in advance, reporting any amendment of more than 3 hours, for details see *Admiralty List of Radio Signals Volume 6(1)*.

Outer anchorages
9.57

1 **Waiting anchorages.** Anchorage for mariners waiting to enter Port de Roscoff-Bloscon, can be obtained NE of the entrance to the port in an area sheltered from SE and NW winds bounded on the W by Basse de Bloscon (48°44′N 3°58′W) and on the E by Plateau des Duons and Bazenn ar Menk.

2 One of the best anchorages, principally used by mariners proceeding to Roscoff, is NE of Men Guen Bras Lighted Beacon Tower (48°44′N 3°58′W), as shown on the chart, in depths of about 14 m, sand and shells, good holding ground.

Caution. A rock with a depth of 2·5 m over it lies 3 cables ENE of the lighted beacon tower.
9.58

1 **Canal de l'Île de Batz.** In E winds mariners can anchor in the W part of Canal de l'Île de Batz, W of the meridian of Malvoch Beacon Tower (48°44′·3N 4°00′·6W).

Mariners in smaller vessels can anchor in Mouillage de Tisaoson, W of Ar Chaden Lighted Beacon Tower (48°44′N 3°58′W) in depths of 3 to 5 m, sand and gravel, but the holding ground is bad and the swinging room restricted.

For a requirement for local knowledge, see 9.60.

2 **Prohibited anchorage.** Submarine power cables cross the channel between Penn ar Cleguer, the SE point of Île de Batz, and Roscoff. Anchoring and fishing are prohibited in an area, shown on the chart, on either side of the cables.

Pilotage and tugs
9.59

1 **Area.** Roscoff-Morlaix Compulsory Pilotage Area limits are bounded as follows:

  North limit. Île de Batz, Les Trépieds (48°45′N 3°50′W) and La Méloine (48°47′N 3°48′W).

  West limit. A line through Plougoulm Bell Tower (48°40′·0N 4°02′·6W) joining the E end of Île de Siec, 2¼ miles NNW.

2 East limit. A line joining Chapelle Sainte Rose en Guimaec (48°41′·7N 3°42′·4W) to Pointe de Beg an Fry, 7 cables NNW.

The area also includes Rivière de Morlaix (9.107) up to the port of Morlaix.

Pilotage is compulsory in the above area for all vessels over 50 m LOA, or 45 m LOA for Morlaix, except those exempt by law.

3 **Boarding places:** in position 48°44′·5N 3°56′·9W, about 1 mile NE of Men Guen Bras Lighted Beacon Tower, as shown on the chart.

During strong E winds pilots will board in the vicinity of Basse Plate (48°44′·3N 4°02′·4W), near the W entrance to Canal de l'Île de Batz as shown on the chart, passing W and N of Île de Batz before joining the approach channel SE of Basse Astan (48°45′N 3°58′W) (9.69).

4 For details of pilot boarding places for Baie de Morlaix, see 9.99.

For further details see *Admiralty List of Radio Signals Volume 6(1)*.

Tugs are not available.

Local knowledge
9.60

1 Local knowledge is required for the E approach to Port de Roscoff-Bloscon from Baie de Morlaix, for Chenal de l'Île de Batz, and for Passe de Benven and Passe du Rannic, the two approaches to Port de Roscoff.

Regulations concerning entry
9.61

1 The use of the approach channel (9.69) is compulsory for vessels over 1600 gt laden with dangerous and polluting goods, see 1.68 to 1.76.

Such vessels should contact Île de Batz Signal Station, which is designated for communication between vessels using the channel and the port authority, and inform them of their entry into the approach channel and should maintain a continuous watch on VHF.

Harbour

General layout
9.62

1 **Port de Roscoff-Bloscon** is sheltered from N and NE by Môle Pierre Lemaire, an angled mole extending about 2½ cables from the coast; a RoRo terminal lies on the inner side of the mole. A quay with berths for commercial vessels, fronting a large open plan freight storage area, lies on the W side of the port.

Roscoff & Ile de Batz from E (9.62)

(Original dated 2005)

(Photograph – PRPA/Patrick Roach)

2   **The port of Roscoff,** a drying harbour, lies on the E side of the town and is protected on the N side by Nouveau Môle which extends about 2½ cables E from the N part of the town, and on the E by Jetée Penn ar Vil; it is divided into N and S basins by Vieux Môle, which lies 1 cable S of and nearly parallel with Nouveau Môle. The area between these basins and the jetty E is known as Vieux Port.

9.63

1   **An approach channel,** in which navigation is controlled and which is 1 mile wide, leads from a position 9½ miles NNE of the head of Port de Roscoff–Bloscon breakwater to a position 1 mile NE of Pointe de Bloscon (48°44′N 3°58′W).

   Canal de l'Île de Batz is the channel which separates Île de Batz from the mainland and gives access to Roscoff (9.77) and Porz Kernok (9.86). The channel, which is marked by beacons, is encumbered with rocks and shoals.

Temporary explosive dumping ground
9.64

1   A temporary explosive dumping ground, for occasional use, is situated E of Île de Batz (48°45′N 4°01′W) for details see 1.7 and Appendix V.

Natural conditions
9.65

1   **Tidal streams** at the positions indicated begin as shown in the following table:

Interval from HW Brest	Position	Direction
–0400	2 miles N of Île de Batz	E
+0200		W
–0435	1 mile NE of Île de Batz	SE
+0105		NW

The maximum spring rates in each direction are 3¾ kn.

9.66

1   **Canal de l'Île de Batz.** In the W approach to Canal d'Île de Batz the streams run as follows, the W-going stream running for only 4 hours:

Interval from HW Brest	Direction	Spring rate kn
About 5 cables W of Men Aodi (48°45′N 4°03′W)		
–0455	N	1
–0155	NE	3
–0055	ENE	3
+0105	E	1½
+0205	SE	½
+0305	SW	1
+0405	W	3
+0505	WNW	½
+0605	NW	½

Interval from HW Brest	Direction	Spring rate kn
About 5 cables W of Basse Plate (48°44'N 4°02'W)		
−0455	NE	1½
−0355 to		
+0010	NE	2½
+0105	ENE	1
+0205	E	1½
+0305	SSW	1½
+0405	SW	3
+0505	W	1½
+0605	NW	1½

2   Off the E entrance to the channel the stream runs N and S, and in the channel they run E and W beginning as follows:

Interval from HW Brest	Direction	Max spring rate kn
Between Le Menk and the coast west (48°43'N 3°57'W)		
−0525	S	1
HW	N	1
In Canal de l'Île de Batz		
−0435	E	3¾
+0110	W	3¾

3   Tidal streams run transversely across the approach to Roscoff; slack water occurs at −0005 Brest, which is 1 hour before local HW.

In Passe de Benven the W-going stream (falling) begins about 1½ hours before local HW and runs for about 9 hours.

See also information on the chart.

9.67

1   **Sea state.** With strong NE winds conditions in Port de Roscoff-Bloscon are uncomfortable for small craft.

In heavy weather from N and NE there is a scend in Roscoff harbours; the effect is much less in the S Basin.

Directions for entering harbour
(continued from 9.47)

Principal marks
9.68

1   **Landmarks:**
     Île de Batz Lighthouse (48°45'N 4°02'W) (9.45).
     Coast Guard Signal Station (48°44'·8N 4°00'·6W) (9.45).

    Major lights:
     Île de Batz Light (48°45'N 4°02'W) (9.45).
     La Lande Light (48°38'N 3°53'W) (9.101).

Roscoff Approach Channel
9.69

1   From a position about 9 miles NE of Île de Batz Light (48°45'N 4°02'W), at the entrance to the approach channel, the route leads SSW to the pilot boarding place (9.59) through the approach channel which is shown on the chart passing between Astan (48°44'·8N 3°57'·7W), marked on

its NE side by a light buoy (E cardinal), and Plateau des Duons, consisting of numerous above-water, drying and below-water rocks. Duon Beacon Tower (white stone tower, 10 m in height) (48°43'·7N 3°55'·3W), in which there is a small refuge, stands on the highest rock of the W part of the plateau.

2   **Clearing marks:**
     Front mark. Chapel (spire) (48°41'·6N 3°55'·4W) on Île Callot.
     Rear mark. Carantec Belfry (spire) (1½ miles SSE of the front mark) on the summit of a hill on the S side of Baie de Morlaix.

The alignment (163°) of these marks clears ENE of Astan.

3   **Useful marks:**
     Cathedral (twin spires, 86 m) (48°41'·2N 3°59'·1W) at Saint Pol de Léon.
     Kreisker Church (spire, 105 m) (48°41'·0N 3°59'·1W).

4   Men Guen Bras or Braz Lighted Beacon Tower (N cardinal, 20 m in height) (48°43'·8N 4°58'·0W).
     Port de Roscoff Rear Leading Light (grey square tower white on NE side, 24 m in height) (48°43'·4N 3°58'·8W).
     Le Menk Lighted Beacon Tower (48°43'·3N 3°56'·6W) (9.70).

From Baie de Morlaix
9.70

1   **Leading marks:**
     Front mark. Île Pigued Beacon (white pyramid) (48°44'·0N 3°58'·2W).
     Rear mark. Notre-Dame de Bon Secours Church (spire) (1¾ miles WNW of the front mark) standing on Île de Batz.

2   From a position in Baie de Morlaix N of Vieille Beacon Tower (starboard hand) (48°42'·7N 3°54'·0W) the alignment (293¼°) of these marks, or at night in the white sector (289½°–293°) of Ar Chaden Lighted Beacon Tower (S cardinal, 22 m in height) standing close S of Île Pigued, leads in the E approach passing (with positions given from Île Pigued):

3   NNE of Les Cochons Noirs (2½ miles ESE); thence:
     Between Plateau des Duons (2 miles E) (9.69) and Bazenn ar Menk and associated dangers passing close N of the dangers extending E from the shoal; Le Menk Lighted Beacon Tower (W cardinal, 11 m in height) (1¼ miles ESE) stands on the W part of the shoal. Thence:
     To the white sector of Bloscon Light (9.72).

Canal de l'Île de Batz
9.71

1   **West approach — leading marks:**
     Front mark. Le Loup (white rock) (48°43'·9N 4°00'·1W).
     Rear mark. Sainte-Barbe Pyramid (white) (1¼ miles ESE of the front mark).

From a position W of Île de Batz the alignment (106¼°) of these marks, which are not easily seen, leads in the W approach passing (with positions given from the front mark):

2   SSW of Men Aodi (2¼ miles WNW), the W-most danger off Ar C'hein the W extremity of Île de Batz; thence:
     NNW of Basse Plate (1½ miles WNW) on which stands a beacon tower (N cardinal); thence:

3   Between L'Oignon (8 cables WNW), distant ½ cable, marked by a beacon (N cardinal) and Basse La

Croix (1·2 m) (8 cables WNW) which lies near mid-channel ¾ cable SW of Roche La Croix, a drying rock marked by a beacon (S cardinal).

The line of bearing 083° of Penn ar Cleguer (5 cables NE), the SE point of Île de Batz, then leads in the channel passing:

4   S of Bazenn Blenkaod (7 cables WNW); thence:

Very close S of a rock (1·1 m) (5 cables WNW) which lies 1 cable NNW of Tec'hit Bihan, marked by a beacon (N cardinal); thence:

S of Bazenn Malvog (4 cables NW); Malvoch Beacon Tower (S cardinal) (9.86) stands close N of the bank. Thence:

5   Over La Traverse (3 cables NNW), a bank with less than 2 m over it, passing between two drying rocks (2½ and 3½ cables NNE).

The alignment (about 100°) of Run Oan Beacon (S cardinal) (6½ cables ENE) with the white pyramid (1¼ miles E) on Île Pigued then leads in the channel passing:

6   Between Perroch (4 cables NE), on which stands a beacon tower (N cardinal), and Penn ar Cleguer (5 cables NE).

The track then continues generally E passing:

S of Run Oan (6½ cables ENE), distant about ½ cable; thence:

7   Between the landing stage (8½ cables E) (9.77), marked by a light beacon (white and purple column, 14 m in height) on the jettyhead, and a beacon (S cardinal) (9 cables E) standing close SSE of An Dreuz Lenn Beacon Tower (white).

8   The line of bearing 090° of Ar Chaden Lighted Beacon Tower (S cardinal) (1¼ miles E) then leads in the channel passing:

N of Roc'h Zu (1 mile E) marked by a beacon (N cardinal), distant ½ cable; thence:

Close S of Le Trépied (0·4 m) (1¼ miles E).

9   The alignment (282°), astern, of An Dreuz Lenn Beacon Tower (9 cables E) with Malvoch Beacon Tower (5 cables NW) then leads in the channel passing:

Between Ar Chaden Lighted Beacon Tower (S cardinal) (1¼ miles E) and Banc de Pêche (drying 1 m) (1¼ miles E); thence:

N of Men Guen Bras (1½ miles E) marked by a lighted beacon tower (9.69).

10   The alignment (293¼°), astern, of the leading marks (1¼ miles E) (9.70) for the E approach to Port de Roscoff-Bloscon from Baie de Morlaix, or at night in the white sector of Ar Chaden Light (1¼ miles E) (9.70) then leads in the fairway passing between Basse de Bloscon Light Buoy (N cardinal) (48°43'·8N 3°57'·5W) and a rock with a depth of 2·5 m over it, lying 2¼ cables NNW, to a position in the white sector of Bloscon Light (9.72).

Port de Roscoff-Bloscon
9.72

1   From the vicinity of the pilot boarding place the line of bearing 215° of Bloscon Light (white turret green top, 5 m in height) (48°43'N 3°58'W) or by night in its white sector (200°–210°) leads in the approach passing (with positions given from Bloscon Light):

Between Basse de Bloscon (4¾ cables NNE), marked on its N side by a light buoy (N cardinal), distant about 2 cables, and Bazenn ar Menk (7 cables E) on which stands a lighted beacon tower (9.70).

2   The track then continues generally SSW passing E of the breakwater, rounding the latter to enter harbour passing

between the breakwater head and Ar Pourven Light Buoy (N cardinal) (2 cables S).

Caution. A 4·4 m rocky patch lies 2 cables NNE of the breakwater head near the W limit of the white sector of Bloscon Light and a 5·6 m rocky patch lies 1¼ cables ENE of the breakwater head with a 6 m rocky patch, the controlling depth for the port (9.54), midway between.

Roscoff
9.73

1   **General information.** There are two channels of approach to the port of Roscoff. Passe de Benven, which can be used by day or night, leads direct from Mouillage de Tisaoson (9.58) and is indicated by leading lights, and Passe du Rannic which is approached from a position close N of Basse de Bloscon Light Buoy (48°43'·8N 3°57'·5W).

9.74

1   **Passe de Benven — leading lights:**

Front mark. Nouveau Môle Light (white column green top, 7 m in height) (48°43'·6N 3°58'·6W).

Rear mark. Roscoff Light (2½ cables SSW of the front mark) (9.69).

The alignment (209°) of these lights leads in the channel from Mouillage de Tisaoson passing (with positions given from the front mark):

2   Close WNW of Roc'h C'hlaz (2½ cables NNE); thence:

ESE of Ar Benven Braz (2¼ cables N) marked by a beacon (concrete cross); thence:

Close WNW of Toull Ranig (1½ cables NNE) to the harbour entrance.

9.75

1   **Passe du Rannic — leading marks:**

Front mark. Rannic Beacon Tower (N cardinal) (48°43'·7N 3°58'·2W).

Rear mark. Roscoff Belfry (5½ cables WSW of the front mark).

From a position close NNW of Basse de Bloscon Light Buoy (N cardinal) the alignment (261°) of these marks leads in the approach passing (with positions given from the front mark):

2   SSE of Men Guen Bras Lighted Beacon Tower (N cardinal, 20 m in height) (2 cables ENE).

The track then continues generally WSW passing:

NNW of Rannic Beacon Tower, distant about 30 m.

The track then leads SW, or at night in the white sector (068°–073°) of Men Guen Bras Light, astern, through Passe du Rannic.

The track then leads generally SSW to the harbour entrance.

Harbours and berths

Chart 2745 plan of Roscoff

Port de Roscoff-Bloscon
9.76

1   **Controlled anchorage.** Anchorage is controlled, in an area shown on the chart extending SE from Bloscon Light (48°43'N 3°58'W), for the port of Roscoff-Bloscon; anchorage berths are assigned by the harbour authority.

Alongside berths:

Pierre Lemaire RoRo Terminal (48°43'·3N 3°57'·7W), length about 240 m, charted depths of 6·7 and 6·8 m at Berth No 1.

2   Nos 3 and 4 berths (48°43'·3N 3°57'·8W), length 120 m, maximum depth 5 m.

Fishing vessel quay, dredged to 4·0 m on its S side lies close S of No 4 berth.

Roscoff
9.77

1   **Bassin Nord** (48°43′·6N 3°58′·7W), used mainly by fishing vessels, is quayed on the W and NW sides and has berths on the S side of Nouveau Môle; the berths alongside the mole and the quays dry 3 to 4 m. A promenade pier extends 3½ cables NNW from the root of Nouveau Môle to Canal de l'Île de Batz; it can be used in an emergency by light vehicles.

2   **Bassin Sud,** used by a variety of small craft, is quayed on its W and SW sides and has berths on the S side of Vieux Môle; the berths alongside the mole and the quays dry 5 m and 6 m, respectively.

Port services
9.78

1   **Repairs.** Ship-building and repair facilities are available at Roscoff.

Ship sanitation control and ship sanitation control exemption certificates are issued at Roscoff.

Supplies: fresh water; fuel; provisions.

Communications: airports at Morlaix and Brest, distant 8 and 22 km respectively, with flights to London and Paris.

Rescue. Roscoff inshore lifeboat is stationed at Port de Roscoff-Bloscon.

Minor anchorages and harbours

Charts 1432, 3668
Corréjou
9.79

1   Corréjou (48°38′N 4°31′W) is a small drying harbour within a former mined area (see 9.42) and is used by fishing boats and other small craft. The harbour is approached from W through Chenal Occidental du Corréjou or from N through Chenal Oriental du Corréjou. Local knowledge is required as the approaches are difficult. A 60 m long mole provides a berthing area.

Harbour

Chart 3669
Moguériec
9.80

1   Moguériec (48°41′N 4°05′W), a small drying harbour provides precarious shelter for fishing boats and other small craft. A jetty extending E from the coast gives some shelter.

Chart 3668
Port de Trésseny
9.81

1   Port de Tresseny (48°39′N 4°26′W), a small drying harbour within a former mined area (see 9.42) which is used by fishing boats and leisure craft. Local knowledge is required as there are numerous dangers in the approach.

Port de Kerlouan
9.82

1   Port de Kerlouan (48°40′N 4°23′W) is a small harbour which dries up to 6 m; it is well sheltered and is used by fishing boats and leisure craft. Local knowledge is required as the access to the harbour is difficult.

Brignogan
9.83

1   Brignogan (48°40′N 4°19′W), or Port de Pontusval, is a small drying port encumbered with rocks and used by local fishing boats and pleasure craft. Entry requires local knowledge.

Charts 3668, 3669
Anse de Kernic
9.84

1   Anse de Kernic (48°39′N 4°13′W), known also as Port de Plouescat, is a small drying harbour used by local fishing boats and other small craft. The entrance to the harbour is encumbered by rocks and shoals and the approaches are not buoyed.

Porz Guen (48°40′N 4°13′W), a small haven protected by a breakwater, lies close N of the entrance to Anse de Kernic; it dries up to 5·5 m and is used by local fishing boats.

Chart 3669
Kerfissien
9.85

1   Kerfissien (48°41′·5N 4°09′·5W) is a small haven protected by a breakwater; it dries up to 5·7 m and is used as a shelter for fishing boats. Approach is from the NW.

Chart 2745
Porz Kernok
9.86

1   Porz Kernok (48°45′N 4°01′W), a small sheltered harbour which dries completely, lies in the centre of the S coast of Île de Batz; it is used by local fishing boats. The harbour is protected from SW by a breakwater which extends ESE from the shore. There is a landing stage at the end of a 1¾ cable long jetty at the E end of the harbour and two slips in the N part.

ROSCOFF TO ÎLE GRANDE

General information

Charts 3669, 2668
Route
9.87

1   From NNW of Île de Batz (48°45′N 4°01′W) the route leads ENE to NNW of Île Grande (48°48′N 3°34′W), a distance of about 16 miles, passing seaward of Plateau des Triagoz (48°52′N 3°39′W).

Topography
9.88

1   The coast between Île de Batz and Île Grande is indented by Baie de Morlaix (9.99) and Baie de Lannion (9.115), two large bays separated by Pointe de Primel (48°43′N 3°49′W).

Plateau de la Méloine (48°47′N 3°47′W) (9.93) is situated about 4 miles offshore midway between Île de Batz and Île Grande, with Plateau des Triagoz (9.93) lying offshore, 5 miles NW of the latter island.

Temporary explosive dumping ground
9.89

1   A temporary explosive dumping ground, for occasional use, for vessels bound to Baie de Lannion, is situated on the E side of the bay SSW of Île Grande; for details see 1.7 and Appendix V.

Rescue
9.90

1   **Inshore lifeboats** are stationed at:
Primel-Trégastel (48°43′N 3°49′W) (9.114).

Locquirec (48°42′N 3°39′W) (9.120).
Trébeurden (48°46′N 3°35′W) (9.120).
For details see 1.117.

Tidal streams
9.91

1 Tidal streams seaward of Plateau de la Méloine attain a maximum spring rate of about 2½ kn and are mainly rectilinear, ENE and WSW.

Tidal streams close N of Plateau des Triagoz begin as follows:

Interval from HW Brest	Direction
−0325	ENE
+0245	WSW

The maximum spring rate in each direction is 3¾ kn. See also information on the chart.

Directions
(continued from 9.47)

Principal marks
9.92

1 **Landmarks:**
For marks in the vicinity of Roscoff, see 9.68.
Les Triagoz Lighthouse (grey square stone tower red lantern, 30 m in height) (48°52′N 3°39′W).
Major lights:
Île de Batz Light (48°45′N 4°02′W) (9.45).
La Lande Light (48°32′N 3°53′W) (9.101).
Les Sept-Îles Light (48°53′N 3°29′W) (9.130).

Île de Batz to Plateau des Triagoz
9.93

1 From a position NNW of Île de Batz the route continues ENE passing:
NNW of Plateau de la Méloine (48°47′N 3°47′W), an area of numerous above-water, drying and below-water rocks about 5 miles in length orientated in a NE to SW direction. Grande Roche is the highest rock and is situated in the middle of the plateau. Thence:

2 NNW of Plateau des Triagoz about 4 miles in length consisting of a group of high rocks in its E part and of numerous other isolated rocks farther W. Les Triagoz Light (48°52′N 3°39′W) (9.92) stands on Guen Braz, an above-water rock on the SE part of the plateau. La Fouillie, an under-water rock, lies at the W end of the plateau and Basse Le Méré at its NE end.

3 **Caution.** The sea breaks heavily up to 3 miles W of the light and the plateau should be given a wide berth in bad weather.

(Directions continue at 9.130)

Side channels

Charts 2745, 3669
Toull Tan Braz
9.94

1 **General information.** Toull Tan Braz, a deep channel about 1½ miles wide, is the NE approach to Baie de Morlaix allowing mariners to proceed directly from either Grand Chenal (9.101) or Chenal de Tréguier (9.103) to Canal des Sept-Îles (9.132) and lies between Plateau de la Méloine (48°47′N 3°47′W) and Les Chaises de Primel, about 2½ miles S.

The channel should only be used in good visibility.

2 **Topography.** Plateau de la Méloine (48°47′N 3°47′W) (9.93) is situated about 4 miles offshore midway between Île de Batz and Île Grande.

Pointe de Primel, on the S side of the channel about 4 miles SSW of Grande Roche, is a prominent point with a watch house on its conical summit.

9.95

1 **Directions — leading marks:**
Front mark. N end of Le Vezoul (48°42′·4N 3°54′·2W).
Rear mark. Kreisker Spire (3½ miles WSW of the front mark).

From a position in Baie de Morlaix N of Stolvezen (48°43′N 3°53′W) (9.101) the alignment (245°), astern, of these marks leads in the channel passing (with positions given from Pointe de Primel (48°43′N 3°49′W)):

2 SSE of Ar Rater (2¼ miles WNW); thence:
NNW of Pointe de Primel; thence:
SSE of Basse Brien (1½ miles N); thence:
NNW of Les Chaises de Primel, a rocky plateau which extends 2 miles ENE from Pointe de Primel.

3 The line of bearing 230°, astern, of Carantec Belfry (48°40′N 3°55′W) (9.69) open NW of Pointe de Primel then leads in the channel along the SE side of Plateau de la Méloine (3¾ miles NNE) (9.93) passing:
NW of Haut-fond du Chenal (4¼ miles NE); thence:
SE of Karreg an Hir (5½ miles NE), the NE-most danger of Plateau de la Méloine; thence:

4 NW of Basse Blanche (7 miles ENE) with Le Crapaud, a rocky reef, 6 cables ENE, dangers marked on their W side by Le Crapaud Light Buoy (W cardinal). Ar Goumonenn lies 9 cables N of the reef and closer to the track; thence:

5 Between Bar ar Gall (48°50′N 3°36′W), the NW-most danger off Île Grande, and Plateau des Triagoz (48°52′N 3°39′W) (9.93) from where a light is exhibited. A light buoy (W cardinal) is moored 2 cables W of Bar ar Gall.

Chart 3669
Between Plateau de la Méloine and Plateau des Triagoz
9.96

1 **General information.** A side channel leads E from N of Baie de Morlaix passing between Plateau de la Méloine (48°47′N 3°47′W) (9.93) and Plateau des Triagoz, about 5 miles NE, which if continued E, leads to Canal des Sept-Îles (9.132).
9.97

1 **Directions.** From a position N of Baie de Morlaix (9.99) the route leads E passing (with positions given from Grande Roche (48°47′N 3°47′W)):
N of Les Trépieds (2½ miles WSW) (9.103); thence:
N of Karreg an Hir (2 miles ENE) the NE-most danger of Plateau de la Méloine, noting an 8·5 m rocky patch which lies 1 mile NW and closer to the track; thence:

2 S of La Petite Fouillie (7 miles NNE), the W-most danger of Plateau des Triagoz (9.93); thence:
S of Plateau des Triagoz, from where a light (48°52′N 3°39′W) (9.92) is exhibited, noting Men Plat, the S-most danger, which lies 6 cables WSW of the light; thence:
N of Bar ar Gall (48°50′N 3°36′W) (9.95), the NW-most danger off Île Grande.

Useful mark
9.98

1 La Fourchie (48°52′·6N 3°38′·0W), a rock with two well-separated summits on Plateau des Triagoz.

Baie de Morlaix

Chart 2745
General information
9.99

1 **Description.** Baie de Morlaix is entered between Pointe de Bloscon (48°44′N 3°58′W) and Pointe de Primel, about 5¾ miles E.

Rivière de Morlaix (9.107), leading to the port of Morlaix, and La Penzé Rivière (9.109), flows into the head of the bay.

2 **Route.** Baie de Morlaix can be approached from N between Plateau des Duons and Plateau de la Méloine and thence by Grand Chenal or Chenal de Tréguier, or alternatively from NE between Plateau de la Méloine and Pointe de Primel, through Toull Tan Braz (9.94), to join either of these channels.

3 **Controlling depths:**
 Grand Chenal (9.101) 2·0 m.
 Chenal Ouest de Ricard (9.102) 5·8 m.
 Chenal de Tréguier (9.103) dries 0·9 m.

Tidal levels, see information in *Admiralty Tide Tables.* Mean spring range about 7·6 m; mean neap range about 3·7 m.

4 **Pilotage** is compulsory for vessels over 45 m in length. For details of pilotage information for Roscoff-Morlaix Compulsory Pilotage Area see 9.59 and *Admiralty List of Radio Signals Volume 6(1).*

Boarding places: in fine weather the pilot vessel will be on station, when a vessel is expected, in the vicinity of Pot de Fer Buoy (48°44′N 3°54′W) for mariners proceeding by Grand Chenal or in the vicinity of Méloine Buoy (48°46′N 3°51′W) for mariners proceeding by Chenal de Tréguier.

5 **Marine farms,** in the form of marine culture exploitation areas and shellfish beds, the limits of which can be seen on the chart, are situated on the S side of the bay.

6 **Local knowledge.** The bay is encumbered with islets, rocks and shoals and access is difficult; local knowledge is recommended before attempting any of the approach channels.

Local knowledge is essential for Rivière de Morlaix and La Penzé Rivière should not be attempted without a pilot.
9.100

1 **Tidal streams** in Baie de Morlaix at the positions indicated begin as shown in the following table:

Interval from HW Brest	Position	Direction
−0505	Near Plateau des Duons (48°44′N 3°55′W)	E-SSE
+0140		SSW-NNW

2 The maximum spring rate in each direction is 2¾ kn.

−0450	Near Roches Jaunes (48°42′N 3°51′W)	NE
−0220		SW

3 The maximum N and S-going spring rates are 2 and 2½ kn, respectively.

−0450	In Grand Chenal and Chenal de Tréguier	In-going
+0105		Out-going

The maximum spring rate in each direction is 2½ kn.

4 On the parallel of Plateau des Duons the streams are rotary in a clockwise direction.

An eddy runs along the land between Roches Jaunes and Pointe de Primel during the E-going offshore stream.

In Grand Chenal, NW of Ar Beg Lem (48°42′N 3°53′W), the stream runs SE and NW across the channel; farther S they run in the direction of the channel.

5 In Chenal Ouest de Ricard, NW of Île Ricard (48°41′N 3°54′W), the stream sets diagonally across the channel, but SW of that island they run in the direction of the channel at a spring rate of up to 2¾ kn; farther SE the in-going stream sets towards Château du Taureau (48°41′N 3°53′W), and the out-going stream sets towards Le Corbeau, 2 cables NW.

6 In Chenal de Tréguier the maximum spring rate is about 2 kn in each direction. At the S end of the channel, in the vicinity of Château du Taureau, the in-going stream sets SSW, while the out-going stream sets NW; this is caused by the fact that the in-flow to the river is dominated by the stream flowing through Chenal de Tréguier, and the out-flow is directed NW towards Chenal Ouest de Ricard.

Directions
9.101

1 **Grand Chenal — leading marks:**
 Front mark. Île Louet Light (white square tower black top, 12 m in height) (48°40′·5N 3°53′·3W).
 Rear mark. La Lande Light (white square tower black top, 19 m in height) (2¼ miles S of the front mark).

From a position E of Plateau des Duons (9.69) the alignment (176½°) of these lights leads in the channel passing (with positions given from the front mark):

2 Between Basse NE du Pot de Fer, the NE-most danger of Plateau des Duons, marked on its NE side by Pot de Fer Buoy (E cardinal) (48°44′·3N 3°53′·9W), and Ar Rater, a rock which lies 1 mile farther E. A dangerous wreck, position approximate, is charted 4 cables SW of the rock and closer to the track. Thence:

3 Between La Vieille Beacon Tower (starboard hand) (2¼ miles NNW) and Stolvezen (2¼ miles N) marked on its NW side by a buoy (port hand); thence:

 Over Rocher de l'Equinoxe (1½ miles N), the controlling depth (9.99) for the channel.

The alignment then continues through a narrow channel passing:

4 Between Île Ricard (1 mile N), distant 1 cable, and the W end of a rocky drying area on which Ar Beg Lemm (1¼ miles N) stands. Ricard Beacon Tower (starboard hand) stands on a drying rock extending NE from Île Ricard and marks the W side of the channel. Thence:

5 Between Île aux Dames (8 cables NNE) and La Morlouine (9 cables N) marked by a beacon (starboard hand) which marks the W side of the channel; thence:

 Between Île de Sable (5 cables NNE) and Calhic Beacon Tower (6 cables NNW). A dangerous wreck (9.102) and a rock drying 1·6 m lie closer to the track W and E, respectively, of the alignment.

6   The track then leads 160°, as shown on the chart, passing:

> Between Corbeau Beacon Tower (starboard hand) (2¼ cables N) and Taureau Beacon Tower (port hand) (2¼ cables NNE); thence:
>
> Between Château du Taureau (large square building) (2 cables NE) standing on an islet and Ile Louet, which is conical in shape, into Rade de Morlaix (9.104).

9.102

1   **Chenal Ouest de Ricard,** marked on its W side by beacons, is a branch of Grand Chenal which leads W of Île Ricard (48°41'·5N 3°53'·5W) before rejoining it farther S; it passes close to several dangers and the tidal streams set transversely across the fairway. It should not be used at night.

Leading marks:

2
> Front mark. Pierres de Carantec (white rocks) (48°40'·5N 3°54'·1W).
>
> Rear mark. White Wall Mark (3 cables S of the front mark) at Kergrist.

From a position in Grand Chenal about 5 cables NNW of Stolvezen (48°42'·7N 3°53'·2W) the alignment (188¾°) of these marks leads in the channel passing (with positions given from Île Louet (48°41'N 3°53'W)):

3
> Between La Vieille Beacon Tower (starboard hand) (2¼ miles NNW) and Stolvezen (2¼ miles N) marked on its NW side by a buoy (port hand); thence:
>
> E of La Fourche (1¾ miles NNW), marked by a beacon (starboard hand); thence:

4
> Between Petit Ricard (1¼ miles NNW) and La Noire (1¼ miles NNW), marked by a beacon (starboard hand). A 1·4 m rocky patch lies 2 cables NNE of the beacon and closer to the track.

The alignment (161°) of Calhic Beacon Tower (6 cables NNW) with Île Louet Light then leads in the channel passing:

5
> ENE of Ar Courguic (1¼ miles NNW), marked by a beacon (starboard hand); and:
>
> WSW of Île Ricard (1 mile NNW).

The line of bearing 148° of Château du Taureau (2 cables NE) open NE of Taureau Beacon Tower (2¼ cables NNE) then leads in the channel passing:

6
> Between Bezhinennou (8½ cables NNW), marked by a beacon (starboard hand), and a 3·3 m rocky patch lying 1 cable NE of the beacon, to join Grand Chenal (9.101) between Calhic Beacon Tower (6 cables NNW) and Île de Sable (5 cables NNE), avoiding a dangerous wreck (position approximate) charted 1 cable E of the beacon tower.

9.103

1   **Chenal de Tréguier** passes over some patches which dry; it should not be used at night unless the visibility allows all beacons and marks to be clearly identified.

Leading marks:

> Front mark. Île Noire Light (white square tower red lantern, 13 m in height) (48°40'·4N 3°52'·5W).
>
> Rear mark. La Lande Light (2¼ miles S of the front mark) (9.101).

2   From a position W of Les Trépieds (48°45'N 3°50'W) which lie at the SW side of Plateau de la Méloine (9.93), marked on their NW side by Méloine Buoy (W cardinal),

the alignment (190½°) of these lights leads in the channel passing (with positions given from the front mark):

3
> E of Ar Rater (48°44'·2N 3°52'·5W) (9.101); thence:
>
> E of La Pierre Noire (2¼ miles N), marked by a beacon (starboard hand); thence:
>
> Between Baz Garo (2 miles N) and Jaune du Large (2 miles NNE), a drying rock painted white, standing near the NW end of Roches Jaunes; thence:

4   The alignment then leads over a rocky area with some drying patches (9.99) passing E of An Dourgi (1¼ miles N), marked by a beacon (starboard hand), and between Grand Aremen Beacon Tower (starboard hand) (7 cables N) and Petit Aremen Beacon Tower (port hand) (7½ cables NNE).

5   The track then leads generally S, as shown on the chart, passing:

> Between La Chambre Beacon Tower (starboard hand) (4 cables N) and Île Blanche Beacon Tower (port hand) (3 cables NNE).

6   The alignment (027°), astern, of Petit Aremen Beacon Tower (7½ cables NNE) with Grande Jaune (1¾ miles NNE) then leads in the channel passing between Île Noire, a low flat islet, and Château du Taureau, 4 cables NW, into Rade de Morlaix.

9.104

1   **Rade de Morlaix** (48°40'N 3°53'W) lies S of Château du Taureau and extends about 1½ miles SSE from La Barre de Flot (48°40'·2N 3°52'·9W), marked by No 1 Buoy (starboard hand), to the anchorage off Kerarmel. There are drying soft mudbanks on each side of the river, on which there are oyster beds marked by stakes, as far as the entrance to Rivière de Morlaix. The fairway between La Barre de Flot and the river entrance is marked by numbered light buoys (port and starboard hand).

2   **Leading marks.** The alignment (336°), astern, of the E side of Château du Taureau with the W side of Île Ricard, or the alignment (334°), astern, of Le Taureau Beacon Tower with Tour de Duons (48°43'·7N 3°55'·3W) (9.69) lead in the fairway between the light buoys to the entrance to Rivière de Morlaix.

Anchorages
9.105

1   **Outer anchorage.** The outer anchorage in Baie de Morlaix is bounded on the NW and N by Plateau de Duons (48°44'N 3°55'W) (9.69), Le Pot de Fer and Ar Rater, which lie 1 and 2 miles ENE, respectively, and on the S by La Vieille (48°43'N 3°54'W), Stolvezen and La Pierre Noire, which lie 5 cables and 1¼ miles E, respectively. The anchorage affords shelter during offshore winds in depths of 15 to 20 m, sand and shells, in fairly good holding ground clear of the prohibited entry area (9.99).

2   Recommended anchorages, shown on the chart, lie on either side of the leading marks for Grand Chenal, or on the E side of the leading marks for Chenal de Tréguier.

9.106

1   **Anchorage,** sheltered from winds from all directions, can be obtained in Rade de Morlaix with good holding ground of mud and sand, but the tidal streams are fairly strong. There are chains laid on the bottom of the E side of the fairway extending 5½ cables in a direction 150° from a position 4¾ cables S of Île Noire Light.

2   Anchorage can also be obtained in Mouillage des Herbiers, a creek about 5 cables S of La Barre de Flot (48°40'·2N 3°52'·9W), which is separated from Rade de

Morlaix by a drying mudbank; a recommended anchorage is shown on the chart.

3   Occasional anchorage can be obtained between La Barre de Flot and Penn al Lann, the point 3 cables W, where landing can be made from small boats near its NE corner.

Prohibited anchorage. A submarine cable is laid SSW from Île Louet to the shore; anchoring and fishing is prohibited in the area.

Rivière de Morlaix
9.107

1   **General information.** Rivière de Morlaix is entered between Locquénolé (48°37'·5N 3°51'·5W), a small drying harbour used by fishing boats, on the W side, and its confluence with Le Dourduff Rivière, which is impounded, on its E side.

2   **Limiting conditions.** The river is navigable by mariners in vessels of up to 63 m in length, with draughts of up to 3·5 m at springs and 1·5 m at neaps, as far as the port of Morlaix, about 3 miles above Locquénolé. The channel is tortuous and contains some bends which, for vessels exceeding 50 m in length, can present some difficulty in negotiating. The river dries 3·6 m and is marked by buoys (port and starboard hand) and by beacons and leading marks.

3   **Vertical clearance:** 30 m under a bridge spanning the river 1 cable seaward of the lock at Morlaix.

Tidal levels (Chateau du Taureau). Mean spring range about 7·6 m; mean neap range about 3·7 m. For further information see *Admiralty Tide Tables*.

Regulations. Anchorage is prohibited in the channel between the S end of Rade de Morlaix and the port of Morlaix.

4   Navigation in Rivière de Morlaix is not permitted at night except by vessels fitted with a searchlight having an effective beam of not less than 1 cable.

Tidal streams. Between the anchorage off Kerarmel (48°39'N 3°51'W) and Toul Mahot bend, about 6 cables above Locquénolé, the rate of the in-going stream does not exceed 2 kn at springs; above this bend the in-going stream is only felt at springs when there is not a freshet in the river. See also information on the chart.

9.108

1   **Morlaix** (48°35'N 3°50'W) consists of an Avant-port and a wet dock; the latter is formed by a barrage, which acts as a weir, across the river. The lock leading to the wet dock is situated at the W end of the barrage. The port is used mainly by coasting vessels and other small craft.

2   **Basins and berths.** Avant-port is 53 m wide with quays on both sides of the river. The E quay extends 130 m from the weir and dries 3 m. On the W side there is a quay 180 m in length, only usable alongside its down-stream half, which dries 3 m to a hard bottom; at the N end of this quay there is a gridiron, N of which there is another low quay, 150 m in length, which dries up to 6 m to a bottom of very soft mud.

3   The wet dock, with depths of from 3 to 4 m and quays on both sides, is 1100 m in length with a width of 65 m at its outer end and 25 m at its inner end is entered from Avant-port through the lock which has a usable length of 63 m, width 16 m; the outer and inner sills of the lock are 2·2 and 3·1 m respectively above chart datum. The lock is normally operated from 1½ hours before until 1 hour after HW, but exceptionally outside these times if there is more than 2·5 m of water over the sill as indicated by the tide-gauge situated close outside the lock entrance.

La Penzé Rivière
9.109

1   **General information.** La Penzé Rivière flows into the SW corner of Baie de Morlaix; it is narrow and tortuous and the approach, which is encumbered with numerous dangers, is difficult at LW.

Approach. The river is approached from E passing S of Plateau des Duons (48°44'N 3°55'W) (9.69); the approach then leads SW passing between Bazenn ar Menk (48°43'N 3°57'W) and Les Bizeyer, about 6 cables SE.

2   **Limiting conditions.** The channel is marked by beacons and has depths of 1·5 m as far as Mouillage de Carantec; there are oyster beds marked by stakes on the drying mudbanks on each side.

Vertical clearance: 10 m under Pont de la Corde (48°38'·8N 3°57'·0W).

3   **Tidal streams** begin at about the same time as those at the entrance to Rivière de Morlaix (9.100); the spring rate does not exceed about 2½kn.

Ploumanac'h (48°50'N 3°29'W) (9.153).
9.110

1   **Directions.** The inner leading marks are not easily distinguishable, and as there are some unmarked dangers close to the leading line it is recommended that entry should be made about half-flood. For requirement for local knowledge, see 9.99.
9.111

1   **Anchorages.** Anchorage can be obtained in the channel about 1¼ miles E of Pempoul (48°41'N 3°58'W) in depths of more than 10 m, sand and gravel, in poor holding ground. With N or NE winds there is a swell at this anchorage when the rocks in the offing are covered, and the tidal streams are fairly strong. Coasting vessels seldom go further upstream.

2   Anchorage, marked on the chart, is also available in Mouillage de Carantec, S of Le Figuier Beacon (isolated danger) (48°40'·5N 3°56'·1W), in depths of about 4 m, sand, but the swinging room is restricted. Farther upstream the river becomes narrower and shallower.
9.112

1   **Harbours.** Port de Pempoul (48°41'N 3°58'W), or Saint-Pol-de-Leon, is a small port on the W side of the estuary of La Penzé Rivière, with some small quays which dry from 4·9 to 6·1 m; it is protected from NE by a breakwater which extends NW from Île Sainte Anne to the shore.

2   Port de Carantec (48°40'N 3°55'W), which dries, is situated on the E side of the river S of Île Callot and can be reached by small craft of 3 m draught at HW. The harbour comprises a slip and anchorage berths.

Port de Penzé is situated 3 miles upstream of Pont de la Corde (48°39'N 3°57'W); the channel dries 5 m in places. The port has a two quays, the longest 80 m on the left bank, and about a dozen moorings in the river.

Minor bays
9.113

1   **Anse de Térénez** (48°40'N 3°51'W) which dries completely lies on the E side of the estuary of Rivière de Morlaix. A landing slip, marked at its extremity by a beacon (port hand), is situated on the SE side of Pointe de Térénez.
9.114

1   **Anse de Primel** is entered close W of Pointe de Primel (48°43'N 3°49'W) (9.94); it is a small harbour which provides good anchorage for small craft. The sea often

breaks across the entrance which is narrow but well marked by beacons.

Rescue. Inshore lifeboat stationed at Primel-Trégastel.

Baie de Lannion

Chart 3669
General information
9.115

1 **Description.** Baie de Lannion is entered between Pointe de Primel (48°43′N 3°49′W) (9.94) and Île Grande, about 10½ miles ENE.

Topography. The S side of the bay between Pointe de Primel and Pointe du Château, 7 miles ESE, is cliffy; the latter, with its conical summit, is easily identifiable. Les Chaises de Primel (9.95) extend NE from Pointe de Primel; thence E as far as the entrance to Rivière de Lannion (9.119) there are several dangerous rocks which lie within about 1 mile of the shore.

2 The SE corner of the bay and Île Grande are low-lying; on approaching the coast on the SE side of the bay a Radome (48°47′·2N 3°31′·4W) (9.134) will probably be the first object sighted.

On the E side of the bay numerous islets and rocky reefs extend 1½ miles offshore and the W-most offlying danger is Basse Blanche (48°47′N 3°40′W) (9.95).

3 **Submarine Cable.** From its landing 4 cables N of Beg Léguer Light (48°44′·4N 3°32′·8W) (9.116), a submarine cable is laid W across Baie de Lannion and thence NW between Le Crapaud (48°47′N 3°39′W) and Plateau de Méloine (48°47′N 3°47′W) as shown on the chart.

Mariners should note that anchoring, dredging and trawling are prohibited in the designated areas shown on the chart.

4 **Pilotage.** Unofficial local pilots for Mouillage de Bihit (9.118) or the port of Lannion (9.119) are stationed at Le Yaudet (48°44′N 3°31′W); their vessels are motor fishing boats. The pilot for Lannion boards about 6 cables S of Pointe de Bihit (48°45′N 3°35′W). Mariners should send advance notice of their ETA to the Bureau du Port de Lannion.

5 **Marine farms,** in the form of marine culture exploitation areas and shellfish beds, the limits of which can be seen on the chart, are situated on the E side of the bay.

Local knowledge is essential for Rivière de Lannion, for details see 9.119.

6 **Tidal streams** in Baie de Lannion begin as follows:

Interval from HW Brest	Position	Direction
–0345	In centre of bay	S-E-S
+0145		S-W-S

7 The maximum E-going and W-going spring rates are 1 and 1½ kn, respectively.

–0405	At Le Crapaud Light Buoy (48°47′N 3°40′W)	SE-E
+0220		SW-W

The maximum spring rate in each direction is 2 kn.

–0355	About 5 cables W of Île Losket (48°48′N 3°36′W)	N
+0200		S

8 The maximum spring rate in each direction is 2 kn.

In the approaches to the entrance to Rivière de Lannion, the effect of the tidal streams is perceptible within a line joining Pointe de Dourvenn (48°44′N 3°34′W) and An Taro Braz, 2 miles WNW. The rising stream, N of An Taro Braz, sets SE or E, and ENE or NE when S of it; it then follows the contour of the coastline E of Pointe de Bihit. The falling stream sets in the opposite directions.

9 At the river entrance the streams begin as follows:

Interval from HW Les Héaux-de-Bréhat	Direction
–0600	In-going
–0045	Out-going

The maximum spring rate on the in-going stream is 2 kn, and on the out-going stream 2½ kn.

10 The effect of the in-going stream is felt at Lannion 2 hours after its commencement at the river entrance. The out-going stream, which lasts for about 7 hours, attains its greatest rate at Le Yaudet.

Directions
9.116

1 **Locquémeau Leading Lights:**
Front light (white pylon red top, 19 m in height) (48°43′·5N 3°34′·4W).
Rear light (white gabled building red lantern, 6 m in height) (2¾ cables ESE of the front light).

2 From a position S of Le Crapaud (48°47′N 3°39′W) (9.95) and the dangerous rocks to the S of the shoal, the alignment (121°) of these lights leads in the approach passing (with positions given from the front light):
SSW of Le Four (2¾ miles NW); thence:
SSW of An Taro Braz (2 miles NW).

3 The line of bearing 090° of Beg Léguer Light (west face of white house red lantern, 8 m in height) (1½ miles NE), which is not easily seen by day against the background of the land, especially in hazy visibility, or at night in its white sector (084°–098°) leads in the approach to Rivière de Lannion passing N of Kinierbel (1 mile NW), marked by a buoy (starboard hand), lying 1½ miles W of Beg Léguer Light.

9.117

1 **Clearing bearings:**
The line of bearing 010° of Plateau de Triagoz Light (48°52′N 3°39′W) changing from red to white clears W of the dangers extending W from the E entrance to the bay.
The line of bearing 098° of Beg Léguer Light changing from red to white clears S of the dangers extending W from the E entrance to the bay.

2 **Useful marks:**
Île Milliau (48°46′N 3°36′W) with two summits, on the N of which stands a white house with a flat roof.
Trébeurden Belfry (spire) (48°46′N 3°34′W).

Mouillage de Bihit
9.118

1 **General information.** Mouillage de Bihit is situated in the bay which lies between Pointe de Bihit (48°45′N 3°35′W) and the N entrance point to Rivière de Lannion, 2 miles SE. The anchorage is bounded on its NW side by the reef which extends SW from Pointe de Bihit towards An Taro Braz, and on its S side by Kinierbel (9.116) lying 1¼ miles S of the same point.

2 **Anchorage,** sheltered from E winds and out of the tidal streams, can be obtained in the bay in depths of 5 to 13 m,

with good holding ground, sand and shells. A recommended anchorage is shown on the chart 5 cables S of Pointe de Bihit.

Landing can be obtained on the SE side of Pointe de Bihit NW of Roc'h Mignon.

Rivière de Lannion
9.119

1   **General information.** Rivière de Lannion, sometimes known as Le Léguer, flows into Baie de Lannion between Pointe Servel (48°44′N 3°33′W) and Pointe de Dourvenn, 6 cables WSW.

2   **Limiting conditions.** A bar extends 2 cables N from Pointe de Dourvenn; with NW winds the sea breaks on this bar preventing entry into the river. The river dries 2·6 m as far as Le Yaudet, a village on the S side of the river about 1 mile within the entrance, and thence it dries 5 m as far as Lannion 5 miles within the entrance, which is accessible by vessels of up to 50 m in length with a draught of up to 4 m at springs and 2·2 m at neaps.

A bridge spans the river at Lannion with a vertical clearance of 3 m.

Local knowledge is essential as the river is narrow and tortuous and navigation is difficult on account of the sharp bends. For pilotage information, see 9.115.

3   **Passage directions.** Mariners are recommended to proceed to the port at Lannion on a single tide if possible, as the drying-out berths everywhere, except at Le Yaudet, are rather dangerous. The S side of the channel, close within the entrance, is marked by two beacon towers (starboard hand) thence the channel is marked by beacons.

4   **Berths.** At Le Yaudet, drying out berths lie close E of the point on which the village is situated; landing can be made at one or the other of the landing slips at Le Yaudet, or at the point on the opposite side of the river.

At Lannion there are quays on both sides of the river with berths drying alongside up to about 5 m.

5   **Facilities:** repair facilities for small craft; fuel; fresh water; stores.

Communications: airport at Lannion-Serval 10 km E of the port.

Minor harbours
9.120

1   **Anse de Locquirec**, into which flows Le Douron River, lies on the S side of Baie de Lannion. It is entered between Pointe du Château (48°42′N 3°39′W) and Pointe de Plestin, 1 mile SE. Within the entrance the creek dries completely.

2   Port de Locquirec, close within the W entrance to the creek, is a small harbour formed by a jetty, bordered by rocks on its outer side, within which it dries from 5 to 6 m. The surf in the harbour is considerable with N and E winds.

3   **Port Trébeurden** (48°46′·3N 3°35′·0W), a marina protected by a breakwater and enclosed by a sill which dries 4 m, is situated on the mainland E of Île Milliau. .

ÎLE GRANDE TO LES HÉAUX DE BRÉHAT

General information

Chart 2668
Route
9.121

1   From NNW of Île Grande (48°48′N 3°34′W) the route leads ENE, about 20 miles, passing seaward of Plateau des Triagoz and Les Sept-Îles, to a position NNW of Les Héaux de Bréhat (48°55′N 3°05′W).

Topography
9.122

1   Between Île Grande and Les Héaux de Bréhat the coast is rocky, cut through by Le Jaudy Rivière (9.141) and formed by a number of bays, Anse de Perros (9.135) being the most important. It is bordered by many rocks and islands.

2   Les Sept-Îles (48°53′N 3°29′W), an archipelago about 4 miles in length consisting of four principal islands and numerous islets and rocks orientated in an ENE to WSW direction, lies offshore about 2½ miles N of Pointe de Mean Ruz (9.133) on the mainland coast, from which they are separated by Canal des Sept-Îles (9.132).

Unsurveyed areas
9.123

1   Four charted (charts 3669 and 3670) unsurveyed areas are centred on:
    48°53′·0N   3°44′·3W,
    48°54′·6N   3°39′·1W,
    48°55′·0N   3°35′·0W,
    48°55′·1N   3°31′·3W,

2   Caution should be exercised when navigating close to these areas.

Offshore bank
9.124

1   Banc des Langoustiers (49°17′N 3°22′W) lies about 25 miles offshore; it has depths of less than 30 m over it amidst surrounding depths of more than 65 m. Soundings can give a useful indication of a mariner's position.

Prohibited areas
9.125

1   Vessels are prohibited from entering an area, shown on the chart, which surrounds Les Sept Îles (48°53′N 3°28′W). Fishing is prohibited in an area E of Île Tomé (48°50′N 3°24′W).

Temporary explosives dumping grounds
9.126

1   Temporary explosives dumping grounds for occasional use, are situated on the S side of Canal des Sept-Îles N of Île Tomé (48°50′N 3°24′W) and W of Les Héaux de Bréhat (48°55′N 3°05′W). The areas are shown on chart 3670..

For details see 1.7 and Appendix V.

Marine farms
9.127

1   Marine farms, in the form of marine culture exploitation areas and shellfish beds, lie within the outer part of Rivière de Tréguier (9.141).

Rescue
9.128

1   **All-weather lifeboat** is stationed at:
    Ploumanac'h (48°50′N 3°29′W) (9.153).
    Signal station. Ploumanac'h Signal Station (Vigie) is situated on Pointe de Mean Ruz (48°50′N 3°29′W).
    For details of lifeboats see 1.117 and for signal stations 1.95 and 1.110.

2   **VHF Direction-finding service,** for emergency use only, operates from Ploumanac'h Signal Station; for details see *Admiralty List of Radio Signals Volume 2.*

Natural conditions
9.129
1   **Tidal streams** at the positions indicated begin as shown in the following table:

Interval from HW Brest	Position	Direction
–0325	Close N of Plateau des Triagoz	ENE
+0245		WSW

2   The maximum spring rates are 3¾ kn in each direction.

–0150	7 miles N of Les Sept-Îles	ENE
+0415		WSW

3   The maximum spring rates are 2¾ kn in each direction.

–0235	4 miles N of Île Rouzic (48°54′N 3°26′W)	ENE
+0345		WSW

The maximum spring rates are 2¾ kn in each direction.

4   **Climate information:** See 1.195 and 13.242

Directions
(continued from 9.93)

Principal marks
9.130
1   **Landmarks:**
      Les Triagoz Lighthouse (48°52′N 3°39′W) (9.92).
      Les Sept-Îles Lighthouse (grey tower and dwelling, 20 m in height) (48°53′N 3°29′W).
      Plougrescant church spire (48°51′N 3°14′W)
      Les Héaux de Bréhat Lighthouse (grey round tower, 57 m in height) (48°55′N 3°05′W).

2   **Major lights:**
      Les Sept-Îles Light — as above.
      Kerprigent Light (48°47′N 3°28′W) (9.137).
      Les Héaux de Bréhat Light — as above.
      Roches Douvres Light (49°06′N 2°49′W) (10.16).
      Rosédo Light (48°52′N 3°00′W) (10.16).

Plateau des Triagoz to Les Héaux de Bréhat
9.131
1   From a position NNW of Plateau des Triagoz (48°52′N 3°39′W) (9.93) the route continues ENE passing:
      NNW of Les Sept-Îles (48°53′N 3°29′W) (9.122). Les Sept-Îles Light (9.130) is exhibited on the E end of Île aux Moines, the S-most island of the archipelago, and an old fort lies at the W end of the same island. Île Bono, the largest island of the group, lies 2 cables NE of Île aux Moines; Île de Malban, with a conical summit, and Île Rouzic lie 6 cables and 1¾ miles, respectively, NE of Île Bono. There are numerous dangers within 1 mile NW of a line joining the four principal islands of the group; none of these dangers are marked. Thence:
2   NNW of Barr an Traou (48°55′N 3°22′W), the NE-most off-lying bank off Les Sept-Îles; thence:
      NNW of La Jument des Héaux Light Buoy (N cardinal) (48°55′N 3°08′W), which marks the N side of La Jument and Petite Jument, the

Les Héaux de Bréhat Lighthouse (9.130)
(Original dated 2000-02)

(Photograph - Jean Guichard)

NW-most dangers off Les Héaux de Bréhat. A light (9.130) is exhibited from Les Héaux, a drying reef; several above-water rocks extend 3 cables NW and SE, and 7 cables W from the light.
(Directions continue, for Baie de Saint-Brieuc at 10.16 and for Guernsey W coast at 11.19)

Canal des Sept-Îles

Charts 3669, 3670
General information
9.132

1   **Description.** Canal des Sept-Îles, a side channel, is the channel between Les Sept-Îles (48°53′N 3°29′W) (9.122) and the mainland, 2½ miles S.

    Topography. Between Île Grande (48°48′N 3°34′W) and Pointe de Mean Ruz, 4 miles NE, the coast is mostly high and fronted by piled up blocks of reddish coloured rocks. Between Pointe de Mean Ruz and Pointe du Château, 10½ miles ENE the coast recedes.

2   **Natural conditions.** Tidal streams between Île Grande and Mer Lang begin as follows:

Interval from HW Brest	Direction
−0335	ENE
+0230	WSW

The maximum spring rate is 3¾ kn.

3   In Canal des Sept-Îles tidal streams begin as follows at the positions indicated:

Interval from HW Brest	Position	Direction
−0435	One mile SW of Île aux Moines (48°53′N 3°29′W)	SE
+0130		NW

4   The maximum spring rates are 4¾ kn in each direction.

Interval from HW Brest	Position	Direction
−0320	Middle of Canal des Sept-Îles	ENE
+0250		WSW

5   The maximum spring rates are 3¾ kn in each direction.

−0435	One mile S of Île Rouzic (48°54′N 3°26′W)	SE
+0130		NW

The maximum spring rates are 2¾ kn in each direction. The sea in Canal des Sept-Îles and vicinity is very high with wind against the tidal stream.

Directions
9.133

1   From a position N of Île Grande (48°48′N 3°34′W) the route leads initially E passing (with positions given from Les Sept-Îles Light (48°53′N 3°29′W)):

    N of Marlank (4 miles SW), distant about 1 mile, the NW-most offshore danger of the numerous islets and shoals which extend up to 2 miles offshore on the S side of the W entrance to the channel; thence:

2   S of Plas ar Marc'h, a 10 m patch (2¼ miles WSW); thence:

    S of Plas Nevez, a 20 m patch (2 miles SW), thence:

    N of Le Taureau (2¾ miles SSW), marked by a beacon (starboard hand); thence:

    Between Basse Meur (8 cables SSW) and Pointe de Mean Ruz (2½ miles S), from where a light (pink square tower, 15 m in height) is exhibited.

3   The line of bearing 234°, astern, of Mean Ruz Light, or at night in its white sector (226°–242°), with Kerjean Directional Light (6¼ miles SE) (9.136) bearing 143½°, leads in the channel passing:

    Between Les Dervinis (1¼ miles E), the SE-most danger of Les Sept-Îles, marked on their S side by a buoy (S cardinal), and Les Couillons de Tomé (3¼ miles SE), marked on their NW side by a buoy (W cardinal); thence:

4   Between Basse du Chenal (2½ miles ESE) and Toull Carr (3½ miles ESE), passing very close SE of the former shoal; thence:

    Between Pradio Glas (3¾ miles ENE) and Basse Kerlaut (4¾ miles ESE); thence:

5   Between Barr an Traou (5¼ miles ENE) and Basse Gourlet Bihan (48°52′·3N 3°17′·4W) noting Plasou Nevez which lies 2 cables NE; thence:

    NW of Barr Laerez (48°52′·9N 3°15′·8W).

    Caution. There are numerous islets, rocks and shoals within 3 miles of the coast between Pointe de Mean Ruz and Pointe du Château, 10½ miles ENE, the positions of which can best be seen from the chart.
9.134

1   **Useful marks:**

    Radome (aluminium) (48°47′·2N 3°31′·3W) standing 8 cables NNW of Pleumeur-Bodou.

    Trégastel Water Tower (48°48′·6N 3°29′·8W).

    Le Corbeau (black rock square top) (48°48′·8N 3°34′·4W).

2   La Pierre Pendue (overhanging whitened rock) (48°50′·4N 3°30′·9W).

    Château Coastaérès (prominent towers) (48°50′·2N 3°29′·5W) on Île Coastaérès.

    Television Mast (48°49′·2N 3°26′·2W).

    Plougrescant Church (tall slim spire) (48°50′·7N 3°13′·9W).

Anse de Perros

Charts 3672 plan of Perros-Guirec, 3670
General information
9.135

1   **Description.** Anse de Perros is entered between Castell-Perros (48°49′N 3°26′W) and the drying reefs which extend from the coast 2 miles E. It affords good shelter from S and W winds and the S part of the bay provides good drying out berths on mud and weed.

2   **Route.** There are two approaches to Anse de Perros, both of which are indicated by direction lights, passing either E or W of Île Tomé, a high rugged rocky island lying in the approaches to the bay. The island is surrounded by numerous dangers some of which extend up to nearly 7½ cables from its shores.

3   **Least charted depths:**

    Passe de l'Ouest (9.136) 1 m.

    Passe de l'Est (9.137) 0·4 m.

    Pilotage. Pilots can be ordered from the Bureau du Port de Lannion, for details see 9.115.

    Tidal streams in Passe de l'Ouest begin as follows:

Interval from HW Brest	Direction
−0435	SE
+0250	NW

4   The maximum spring rate in each direction is 2¾ kn.

Off Les Couillons de Tomé the streams run E and W, beginning at the same times, but the E-going stream attains a maximum spring rate of 3¾ kn.

In Passe de l'Est tidal streams begin as follows:

Interval from HW Brest	Direction
−0435	ENE
+0250	WSW

The maximum spring rate in each direction is 3 kn.

Directions
9.136
1   **Passe de l'Ouest — leading marks:**
Front mark. Nantouar Old Lighthouse (48°48′·1N 3°23′·6W).
Rear mark. Kerjean Direction Light (white tower black top, 16 m in height) (4 cables SE of the front mark).

2   From a position in Canal des Sept-Îles about 1½ miles NE of Pointe de Mean Ruz (48°50′N 3°29′W) the alignment (142¾°) of these marks, or by night in the narrow white sector (143¼°–143¾°) of Kerjean Direction Light, leads in the channel passing (with positions given from Kerjean Direction Light):

3   SW of Les Couillons de Tomé (3¼ miles NNW) (9.133); thence:
SW of Bilzic (2¾ miles NNW), marked by a beacon tower (port hand), thence:

4   NE of La Fronde (2¾ miles NW), marked on its N side by a buoy (starboard hand); thence:
NE of Roche Bernard (2 miles NW), marked on its N side by a beacon tower (starboard hand); thence:

5   SW of Pierre du Chenal (1¾ miles NNW), marked by a beacon tower (isolated danger), noting a rock awash lying 2 cables WNW of the beacon tower NE of the track, to the anchorage off Castell Perros (9.139).
(Directions for Perros-Guirec continue at 9.140)

9.137
1   **Passe de l'Est — leading lights:**
Front mark. Le Colombier Direction Light (white house, 7 m in height) (48°47′·9N 3°26′·6W).
Rear mark. Kerprigent Direction Light (white tower, 14 m in height) (1½ miles SW of the front mark).

2   The alignment (224¾°) of these lights, the structures of which are not easily distinguishable particularly in the afternoon light but which are intensified near their alignment, leads in the channel passing (with positions given from the front light):

3   NW of Basse Guazer (5¼ miles NE), marked on its NW side by a buoy (port hand); thence:
NW of Roche Morville (3¼ miles NE); thence:
Close SE of Pierre á Jean Rouzic (2¼ miles NE), marked on its E side by a buoy (starboard hand); thence:

4   Between Pierre du Chenal (2 miles NE) (9.136) and Cribineyer (1¾ miles NE), a group of drying rocks marked on their NW side by a buoy (port hand); thence:
NW of Roc'h Hu de Perros (1½ miles NE), marked by a beacon tower (port hand), to the anchorage off Castell-Perros (9.139).
(Directions for Perros-Guirec continue at 9.140)

Anchorages
9.138
1   **East of Île Tomé.** Anchorage can be obtained E of Île Tomé (48°50′N 3°24′W), sheltered from W winds in depths of 6 to 16 m, sand and shells, in good holding ground; a recommended berth is shown on the chart.
Caution. Platier de Tomé, a rock, lies about 2 cables from the middle of the E side of the island.
9.139
1   **Mouillage de Castell-Perros,** about 5 cables ESE of Castell-Perros and sheltered from the S and SW, has depths of about 2 m, sand and mud, in good holding ground. The anchorage is shown on the chart.
Landing can be made from a small boat on the rocks W of the anchorage.

Perros-Guirec
9.140
1   **General information.** Perros-Guirec, a small port, lies in the SW corner of Anse de Perros and is well sheltered from W winds. The port can accept vessels up to 40 m in length with a draught of 3·5 to 4 m at HW springs and 3 m at neaps.

2   **Harbour.** Jetée du Linkin extends S from the N side of the harbour and gives protection from E winds. A short mole with a landing slip extends E from the W side of the harbour. The N part of the port comprises a marina within a basin enclosed by a sea-wall about 7 m in height above chart datum; the sea wall covers at HW and is marked at intervals by posts. The basin is entered through a dock gate with a usable width of 6 m situated near the E end of the sea-wall. The gate is opened from 1½ hours either side of HW; the dock gate cannot be worked at weak neap tides. A tide-gauge near the dock gate indicates the depth over the sill.

3   **Directions** *(continued from 9.136 and 9.137)*. From the anchorage (9.139) the route leads SW for 1¼ miles with Passe de l'Est leading marks (9.137) in line, passing (with positions given from the light at the head of Jetée du Linkin (48°48′·2N 3°26′·2W)):
NW of Roc'h Hu de Perros (1 mile NE), marked by a beacon tower (port hand), noting an obstruction 3 cables WNW of the beacon; thence:

4   SE of Banc du C'hraou (3 cables NNE), marked by Lost ar C'hraou beacon (starboard hand); thence:
NW of Gommonénou de Perros (3 cables E), marked by Gommonénou Lighted Beacon Tower (port hand); thence:
SE of the head of Jetée du Linkin from where a light (white pile, green top; 4 m in height) is exhibited.

5   The route then leads N into the harbour.
Berths. Jetée du Linkin dries from 3 to 4 m to a hard bottom and can be used by vessels of up to 40 m in length with a draught of 4 m at springs and 3 m at neaps.
Facilities: small repair facilities; fuel; fresh water; stores.
Communications: airport at Lannion-Servel 10 km from port.
Rescue, see 9.128.

Tréguier and approaches
Charts 3672 plan of Rivière de Tréguier, 3670
General information
9.141
1   **Position.** Le Jaudy or Rivière de Tréguier flows into the sea about 2½ miles E of Pointe du Château (48°52′N 3°13′W). Port de Tréguier, about 5 miles within the

entrance to the river, is situated at the confluence of the rivers Jaudy and Guindy.

2 **Approach.** There are three approach channels leading to the entrance of Rivière de Tréguier, Grande Passe (9.145), Passe du Nord-Est (9.147) and Passe de la Gaine (9.148); of these Grande Passe is the deepest and easiest to navigate both by day and also at night, provided the visibility is clear enough to distinguish the buoys and beacons in the channel. Other approach passages exist but these are encumbered by uncharted rocks and shoals and should not be used.

3 **Caution.** All approach channels may be encumbered by fish traps and associated equipment on the seabed.

Limiting conditions
9.142

1 **Controlling depths — approach channels:**
  Grande Passe 4·4 m.
  Passe du Nord-Est 1·9 m.
  Passe de la Gaine 0·3 m.
  Controlling depths — Rivière de Tréguier:
  To Mouillage de Taureau (48°51′·0N 3°11′·5W); least depth 3·2 m.
2 To Mouillage de Palamos (48°49′·0N 3°12′·1W); least depth 2·6 m.
  To Port de Tréguier; least depth level of chart datum.
  Tidal levels, see information in *Admiralty Tide Tables.* Mean spring range about 8·6 m; mean neap range about 4·1 m. It is reported (2008) that HW is consistently 0·2 m below predicted levels.

3 **Local weather and sea state.** Passe du Nord-Est is only practicable in good weather; with W winds the sea breaks right across the channel.
  Passe de la Gaine and Passe du Nord-Est are only practicable by day in good visibility; it should not be attempted at night.
  Maximum size of vessel. By day only, Port de Tréguier is accessible by vessels of up to 110 m in length with draughts of up to 6 m at springs and of up to 3·7 m at neaps.

Arrival information
9.143

1 **Notice of ETA required.** At least 48 hours.
  Pilotage is compulsory for vessels of more than 45 m in length; pilots are supplied by Le Légué pilot station (10.63). The pilotage zone is limited to the N by the parallel of 48°55′N and to the E and W by the meridians of 3°05′W and 3°15′W, respectively. The pilot boards in the vicinity of Basse Crublent Light Buoy (48°54′N 3°11′W) as shown on the chart.
  Local knowledge is recommended for Passe de la Gaine.

Harbour
9.144

1 **General layout.** The port has quays fronting the W bank of Le Jaudy river where commercial vessels berth.
  A marina, approached through a buoyed channel, is situated upstream of the commercial berths.

2 **Tidal streams.** Owing to the strength of the current it is recommended that river transits and berthing operations are not undertaken at mid-tide, especially during spring tides.

3 In Grande Passe at the positions indicated begin as shown in the following table:

Interval from HW Brest	Position	Direction
−0535	N of Chaussée des Renauds (48°54′N 3°12′W)	E
+0135		W

4 The maximum spring rate in each direction is 3¾ kn.

−0435	N of La Corne (48°51′N 3°11′W)	SW
+0135		NE

The maximum spring rate in each direction is 2¾ kn.

5 In Passe du Nord-Est tidal streams in the vicinity of La Jument des Héaux Light Buoy (48°55′N 3°08′W) begin as follows:

Interval from HW Brest	Direction
−0350	E
+0220	W

The maximum spring rate in each direction is 3¾ kn.

6 In Passe de la Gaine tidal streams between Les Héaux (48°55′N 3°05′W) and the mainland begin as follows:

Interval from HW Brest	Direction
−0450	ENE
−0025	WSW

The maximum spring rate in each direction is 2½ kn.

7 In the river tidal streams begin as follows:

Interval from HW Brest	Direction
−0425	In-going
+0130	Out-going

The maximum spring rate is 2½ kn.

Directions for entering harbour
9.145

1 **Grande Passe — leading lights:**
  Front light. Port la Chaîne Light (white house, 5 m in height) (48°51′·6N 3°07′·8W).
  Rear light. Saint-Antoine Light (red and white house, 6 m in height) (7½ cables SE of the front light).

2 From a position about 2½ miles NNE of Pointe du Château (48°52′N 3°13′W) the alignment (137°) of these lights, the rear of which is intensified 3° on either side of the alignment, leads in the outer part of the channel passing (with positions given from the front light):

3 Between Basse Crublent (3¼ miles NW), marked on its NW side by a light buoy (port hand), and Chaussée des Renauds (3¼ miles NW), a chain of drying and below-water rocks; thence:

4 Between Le Corbeau (2¼ miles NW), marked on its W side by a light buoy (port hand), and Pierre à l'Anglais (2½ miles NW), marked on its E side by a light buoy (starboard hand); thence:
  Over Basses du Corbeau (2¼ miles NW), the least depth (9.142) in the channel; thence:

5 NE of Pen ar Guézec (1¾ miles NW), a drying reef the NE and SE extremities of which are marked by a beacon tower (starboard hand) and a beacon (starboard hand) respectively; thence:
  Close NE of a light buoy (starboard hand) (1½ miles NW) marking Petit Pen ar Guézec, a group of rocks which dry.

9.146

1 **Leading marks:**

Front mark. left hand edge of La Corne Light (white tower red base, 23 m in height) (48°51′·4N 3°10′·5W).

Rear mark. Roc'h Skeiviec Beacon Tower (white) (4 cables SW of the front mark).

2 On passing Petit Pen ar Guézec light buoy the track then alters sharply SW when the alignment (215½°) of the above marks, or at night in the white sector (213°–220°) of La Corne Light leads in the channel passing (with positions given from Roc'h Skeiviec):

3 NW of Basse du Port Béni (1 mile NE); thence:

Between Banc de la Pie (7 cables NNE) which extends from the W side of the channel, passing very close to the bank, and Les Trois Pierres (6½ cables NE), marked by a beacon tower (N cardinal), to join the last part of Passe du Nord-Est (9.147) S of Banc de la Pie, which leads to the river entrance.

9.147

1 **Passe du Nord-Est.** From a position close W of La Jument des Héaux Light Buoy (N cardinal) (48°55′·4N 3°08′·0W) the line of bearing 205° of Tréguier Cathedral (spire) (48°47′·3N 3°13′·8W) seen midway between the two beacon towers of Pen ar Guézec (9.145), 6 miles NNE, leads in the approach passing (with positions given from Roc'h Skeiviec (48°51′·0N 3°10′·9W)):

2 WNW of Petite Jument (4½ miles NNE), noting La Jument (9.131) close SE and farther from the track; thence:

Close ESE of a dangerous rock, existence doubtful, (4¼ miles NNE); thence:

WNW of Paro Sud (drying 6·8 m) (4¼ miles NNE), the S-most of two drying rocks lying on Les Epées de Tréguier.

3 The line of bearing, 158°, of the Old Signal Station (white facade) on Créac'h Maout (3 miles ENE) a rounded knob on the coast, in line with the central part of Les Duono (3¼ miles NE), a chain of above-water and drying rocks, then leads in the channel for about 3 cables.

4 **Leading marks:**

Rear mark. Tréguier Cathedral — as above.

Front mark. Roc'h Skeiviec Beacon Tower (9.146).

The alignment (207°) of these marks then leads in the channel passing:

5 Over Basses de Roc'h Hir (2¾ miles NNE), an area of shoal ground with some drying rocks, the controlling depth (9.142) for this channel; thence:

Between Petit Pen ar Guézec and Pen ar Guézec (1¾ miles NNE respectively) (9.145), passing close WNW of the shallow bank extending W from the former; thence:

Over Banc de la Pie (7 cables NNE) to the river entrance.

9.148

1 **Passe de la Gaine,** the E approach to Rivière de Tréguier, lies between Les Héaux de Bréhat (48°55′N 3°05′W) and the coastal reef surrounding Sillon de Talbert, a natural dyke of shingle, which extends NE from the mainland coast and terminates at Rocher du Sark (48°54′N 3°03′W). There are several dangerous rocks in the E approach and in the E entrance to the channel; the E-most shoal is Roch ar Bel (10.17) which lies 2½ miles NE of Rocher du Sark.

2 **Leading marks:**

Front mark. Men Noblance Tower (white tower black band) (48°52′·0N 3°10′·7W) standing on the SE end of Île d'Er.

Rear mark. Plougrescant Daymark (white, black stripe) (1¾ miles WSW of the front mark).

3 From a position about 1 mile E of Les Héaux de Bréhat Light (9.130) the alignment (241¾°) of these marks, which must be closely followed, together with a large house which stands on the same alignment 2 miles WSW of the front mark, leads in the channel passing (with positions given from the front mark):

4 NNW of Basse de la Gaine (4¾ miles ENE); thence:

SSE of Roc'h ar Hanaf (4½ miles ENE); thence:

Very close NNW of a rock awash (3¾ miles ENE); thence:

Very close NNW of a dangerous rock (3¼ miles ENE); thence:

5 Over Pont de la Gaine (2½ miles ENE), a shallow rocky shelf, the controlling depth (9.142) for the channel, at the SE end of Les Duono (9.147) noting Le Colombier, an above-water rock on the N side of the channel. The channel over Pont de la Gaine is marked on its S and N sides by a beacon (port and starboard hand, respectively) and the N side of the channel between Roc'h ar Hanaf and Le Colombier is marked by beacons (starboard hand). Thence:

6 Very close SSE of Basse du Colombier (2¼ miles ENE); thence:

Close SSE of the buoy (starboard hand) moored NE of Petit Pen ar Guézec (1 mile ENE) (9.145) to join the inner part of Grande Passe.

9.149

1 **Rivière de Tréguier** From a position at the river entrance between Banc de la Pie and Les Trois Pierres the track leads generally SW to join the alignment (206¾°) of Roc'h Skeiviec (48°51′·0N 3°10′·9W) with Tréguier Cathedral (9.147) which leads through the river entrance passing (with positions given from Roc'h Skeiviec):

2 Between Le Petit Taureau Beacon Tower (starboard hand) (5½ cables NNE) and La Corne Light (4½ cables NE); thence:

ESE of a light buoy (starboard hand) (3 cables NNE) marking the SE extremity of Banc du Taureau, a drying bank which extends from the W side of the river.

3 The alignment (051°), astern, of La Corne Light with Trois Pierres Beacon Tower (6½ cables NE), or at night in the white sector (052°–059°) of La Corne Light then leads in the river to Mouillage du Taureau. Thereafter the route leads generally SSW through the channel, marked by light buoys and beacons (lateral), to Tréguier.

4 **Useful mark:**

Saint Gonéry Church (spire) (48°50′·7N 3°13′·8W) at Plougrescant.

Anchorages
9.150

1 Mariners may anchor anywhere in the river, well clear of the channel. The usual anchorages are in Mouillage du Taureau and Mouillage de Palamos, which are shown on the chart.

Mouillage du Taureau, (48°51′·0N 3°11′·5W) is situated SW of Banc du Taureau, in depths of 7 to 12 m, mud, with very good holding ground. It is sheltered from all winds except those from N when the banks are covered, and there is swinging room of 1½ cables in depths of more than 5 m.

2   **Mouillage de Palamos,** (48°49'·0N 3°12'·1W) is situated about 2½ miles SSW of La Corne Light, in depths of about 7 m with good holding ground of mud, but the swinging room is more restricted.

Caution. Areas of oyster beds and fish cages are established at the entrance and in the river.

Port de Tréguier
9.151

1   **General information.** Port de Tréguier (48°47'N 3°13'W) has about 350 m of quayage mainly fronting the W bank of Le Jaudy river below a bridge which spans the river. Berths; quay, 75m in length, dredged to 2·5 m; quay, 75 m in length, drying 1·5 m; quay 250 m in length drying between 3 and 4 m. Mouillage de la Fosse (48°47'·4N 5°13'·5W), depth about 1·0 m, on which mariners can anchor in very soft mud, lies abreast the NW portion of these quays.

Facilities: minor repair facilities; fuel; fresh water; provisions; hospital.

Minor harbours and landing

Chart 3670
Trégastel
9.152

1   Trégastel (48°50'N 3°31'W) affords anchorage for mariners in small craft, sheltered from all except onshore winds, and the small port of Coz Porz provides two slips where landing is safe and sheltered.

Ploumanac'h
9.153

1   Ploumanac'h (48°50'N 3°29'W), a small harbour which dries completely, is situated on the E side of the bay which lies between Pointe de Mean Ruz and Île Renote, about 6 cables W. The harbour is frequented by local fishing boats.

Anse de Trestraou
9.154

1   Anse de Trestraou (48°49'N 3°27'W), about 1¼ miles W of Castell-Perros, has a landing slip at its W end.

Charts 3672 plan of Port Blanc, 3670
Port Blanc
9.155

1   Port Blanc (48°50'N 3°18'W) is a small port used by local fishing vessels and other small craft; it is exposed to N winds. It is entered by following the alignment (150½°) indicated on the chart or by night in the white sector of Le Voleur Direction Light (white tower, 12 m in height) (48°50'·3N 3°18'·4W).

2   Anchorage is available as shown on the chart and landing can be made at Port des Bateaux slipway about 1¼ cables ESE of Le Voleur Light.

Chart 3670
Buguélès
9.156

1   Buguélès (48°50'·6N 3°16'·4W), a small port which dries, is used by small fishing craft. Access to the harbour is difficult and by day only.

NOTES

319

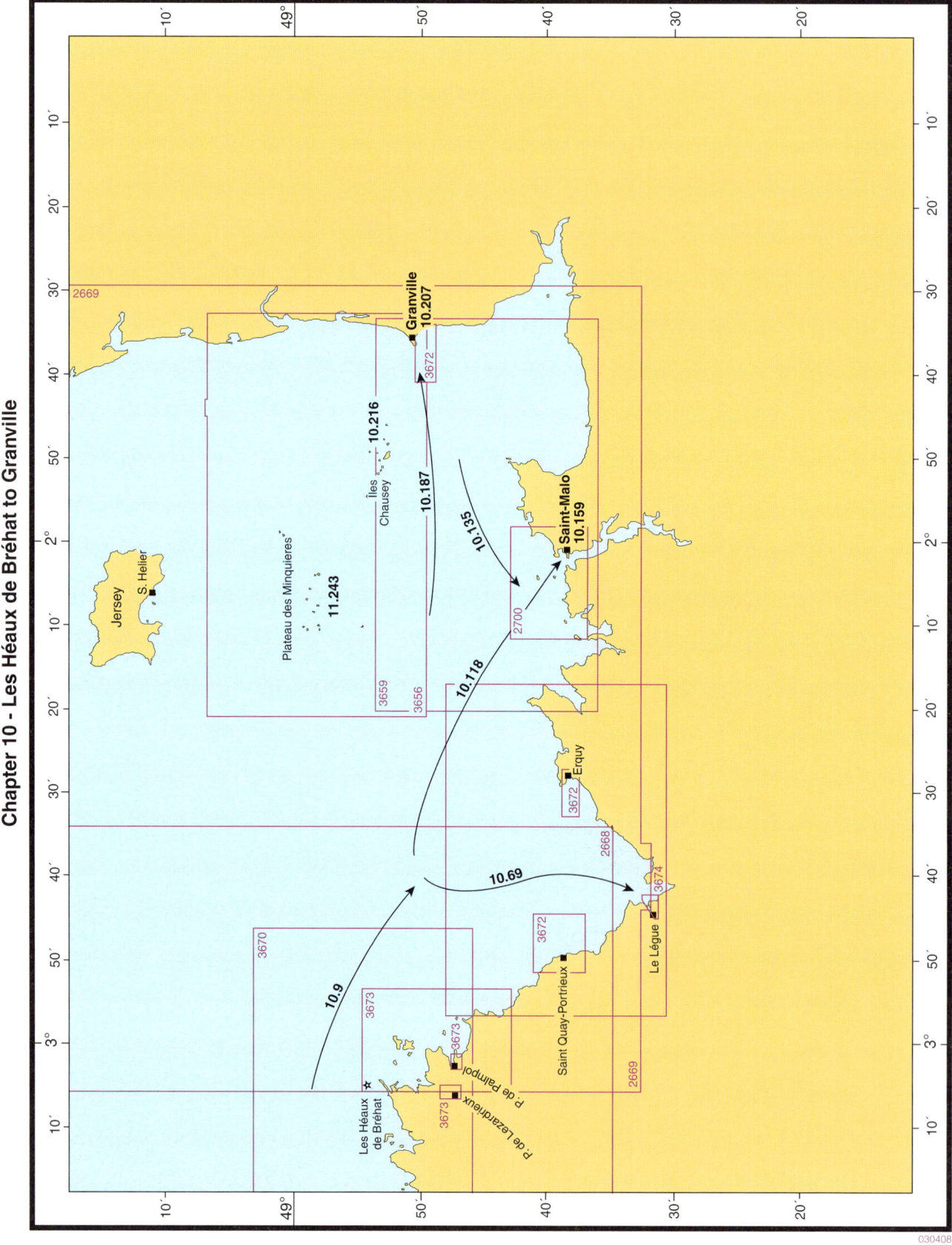

030408

CHAPTER 10

NORTH COAST OF FRANCE — LES HÉAUX DE BRÉHAT TO GRANVILLE

GENERAL INFORMATION

Chart 2669
Scope of chapter
10.1

1   This chapter covers the N coast of France from Les Héaux de Bréhat (48°55′N 3°05′W) to Granville, about 59 miles E.
   Ports. The important port of Saint-Malo (10.159) and the port of Granville (10.207), together with other smaller ports, are covered by this chapter.
2   **Anchorages.** There is anchorage (10.144) off Saint-Malo but it is not very well sheltered. Off Granville during W gales mariners can find shelter in Grande Rade de Cancale (10.200), and in N gales anchorage is available under the lee of Îles Chausey (10.217).

Route
10.2

1   From N, and bound for Saint-Malo or Granville it is usual to pass W of Jersey (49°13′N 2°08′W) (11.181) and W of Plateau des Minquiers (48°58′N 2°04′W) (11.243).
   Passage de la Déroute (11.290) and Déroute de Terre (11.289), two passages which lead from Race of Alderney (11.318) to the S of Plateau des Minquiers and Îles Chausey (48°53′N 1°49′W) (10.216) passing E of Jersey, are little used.

Topography
10.3

1   Between Les Héaux de Bréhat and Cap Fréhel, about 33 miles SE, the coast, consisting of cliffs, interspersed with sandy beaches and backed by high ground, recedes S to form the large Baie de Saint-Brieuc (10.58). Large rocky reefs border the coast for distances of up to 6 miles, but a wide passage gives access to the head of the bay.
2   From Cap Fréhel (48°41′N 2°19′W) to Pointe du Grouin, 19 miles E, the coast is formed by many bays with sandy beaches, and by inlets separated by rocky headlands. Nearly midway between these points the coast recedes to form Baie de Saint-Malo, containing the important port of the same name.
3   Between Pointe du Grouin (48°43′N 1°51′W) and Pointe de Champeaux, 11 miles farther E, the coast again recedes to form Baie du Mont Saint-Michel (10.199), a large part of which dries.
   Le Roc (48°50′N 1°36′W) (10.188), the peninsula which protects Granville, lies about 5 miles N of Pointe de Champeaux.

Outlying dangers
10.4

1   North of the entrance to Baie de Saint-Brieuc, Plateau des Roches Douvres (49°06′N 2°49′W) (11.17) and Plateau de Barnouic (49°02′N 2°48′W) (11.17), the outermost dangers fronting this part of the coast, lie about 17 and 13 miles, respectively, offshore.
2   Plateau des Minquiers (48°58′N 2°04′W) (11.243) and Îles Chausey (48°53′N 1°49′W) (10.216), two large expanses of rocky shoals, lie parallel with the coast between Cap Fréhel and Pointe de Champeaux, and

between 9 and 15 miles N of it. Between the coast and Les Minquiers there are a number of unmarked isolated shoals. There are also numerous other dangers within 4 miles of the coast.

Submarine cables
10.5

1   A submarine cable, as shown on the chart, extends NE from Les Rosaires (48°34′N 2°45′W).

Marine farms
10.6

1   Marine farms, in the form of marine culture exploitation areas and shellfish beds, are situated throughout the waters of this chapter; most are charted and should be avoided. Some areas are subject to local regulations. Farms in proximity to shipping routes are generally marked by buoys. Other farms are marked by beacons (X topmark) and some are fitted with radar reflectors. Lights, when fitted, show flashing yellow. See 1.29.

Local magnetic anomalies.
10.7

1   Local magnetic anomalies were reported in 1978 between Plateau des Roches Douvres and Grand Léjon, 22 miles SSE.

Regulations concerning vessels carrying dangerous and polluting goods
10.8

1   For regulations concerning vessels carrying dangerous and polluting goods navigating in the approaches to the N and W coasts of France, see 1.68 to 1.76.

LES HÉAUX DE BRÉHAT TO BAIE DE SAINT-BRIEUC

General information

Charts 3670, 3674, 2669
Route
10.9

1   From a position N of Les Héaux de Bréhat (48°55′N 3°05′W) the passage to the approaches to Baie de Saint-Brieuc leads generally SE, about 20 miles, passing between Plateau de Barnouic (49°02′N 2°48′W) and the mainland.

Topography
10.10

1   Between Les Héaux de Bréhat and Pointe de Minard, 11½ miles SE, the coast is moderately high; it is bordered by rocks, islands and shoals which extend 4 miles N and NE, and 7 miles E from Île de Bréhat (48°51′N 3°00′W). Several channels lead through these dangers to Le Trieux (10.22) and Anse de Paimpol (10.40).
2   Île de Bréhat is the centre of a group of islands and rocks to which it is joined at LW by drying mudflats; at HW it appears as two islands connected by a short bridge. Île de Bréhat is low lying and difficult of access and the sea breaks heavily on its outskirts during bad weather from between W and NE.

Temporary explosives dumping ground
10.11

1   A temporary explosives dumping ground, for occasional use, is situated 9 miles ENE of Paimpol (48°47′N 3°03′W), for details see 1.7 and Appendix V.

Marine farms
10.12

1   Marine farms, in the form of marine culture exploitation areas and shellfish beds lie close to the shore between Les Héaux de Bréhat and Baie de Saint-Brieuc. Anchoring, and taking the bottom are prohibited in these areas.

Pilotage
10.13

1   **Station.** The pilot station for Paimpol-Pontrieux has no regular appointed pilots but relies on part-time pilots who are fishermen; one is for Le Trieux up to Pontrieux (10.34) and the other is for the port of Paimpol (10.52).

   ETA required. Send ETA off Paimpol or Île de Bréhat 48 hours in advance.

   For further details see *Admiralty List of Radio Signals Volume 6(1).*

2   **Boarding places.** The pilot for Le Trieux boards in Grand Chenal (10.28) close to Les Sirlots Buoy (starboard hand) (48°53′·0N 2°59′·5W).

   In good weather the pilot for the port of Paimpol boards in Anse de Bréhec anchorage (48°43′N 2°56′W) (10.72) or on the line joining L'Ost Pic (48°47′N 2°56′W) to Grand Léjon, 11 miles E, equidistant from the two lights. In bad weather mariners, whatever their destination, should anchor in the anchorages off l'Île à Bois (48°50′N 3°04′W) (10.32).

Rescue
10.14

1   **Inshore lifeboat** is stationed at Loguivy-de-la-Mar (48°49′N 3°04′W) (10.39).

   Signal station (Sémaphore) (48°51′N 3°00′W) (10.16) is situated on Île de Bréhat.

   For details regarding lifeboats, see 1.117 and for signal stations, 1.95 and 1.110.

2   **VHF Direction-finding station,** for emergency use only, operates from Île de Bréhat, for details see *Admiralty List of Radio Signals Volume 2.*

Tidal streams
10.15

1   **Tidal streams** are strong in the whole area between Plateau de Barnouic, Plateau de la Horaine (48°54′N 2°55′W) and Plateau des Penn Azen (48°52′N 2°59′W) causing severe overfalls when opposed to the direction of the wind, especially where the bottom is uneven.

2   Outside Plateau des Penn Azen the E-going stream sets SE towards Plateau de la Horaine; the W-going stream sets NW towards Roch ar Bel (48°55′N 3°00′W). Near Plateau de la Horaine they begin as follows:

Interval from HW Brest	Direction
−0335	ESE
+0235	WNW

3   The maximum spring rate is 4 kn and 3¾ kn on the E and W-going streams, respectively.

   See also *Admiralty Tidal Atlas for the Channel Islands and adjacent coasts of France.*

Directions
(continued from 9.131)

Principal marks
10.16

1   **Landmarks:**
   Roches Douvres Lighthouse (pink tower with green roof on dwelling, 65 m in height) (49°06′N 2°49′W) situated on the largest rock of the plateau.
   Le Paon Lighthouse (white tower, 12 m in height) (48°52′N 2°59′W) standing on a rock of the same name.

Le Paon Lighthouse from NE (10.16)

(Original dated 2000-02)

(Photograph – Jean Guichard)

2   Rosédo Lighthouse (white tower and green lantern, 13 m in height) (48°52′N 3°00′W).
   Signal Station (grey square tower, white dwelling and mast) (48°51′·3N 3°00′·3W) on Île de Bréhat.
   La Horaine Lighted Beacon Tower (grey octagonal tower on black hut, 23 m in height) (48°54′N 2°55′W).

3   Tower (white) (48°49′·1N 3°00′·6W) on Pointe de L'Arcouest.
   Water tower (48°48′·4N 3°01′·9W)
   Church Spire (48°48′·1N 3°02′·0W).
   L'Ost-Pic Light (two white towers red tops, 15 m in height) (48°47′N 2°56′W).
   Water tower (123 m) (48°45′·2N 2°59′·1W).

Major lights:
Les Héaux de Bréhat Light (48°55′N 3°05′W) (9.130).
Roches Douvres Light (49°06′N 2°49′W) — as above.
Rosédo Light — as above.

Charts 3670, 2669
Les Héaux de Bréhat to Grand Léjon
10.17
1 From a position N of Les Héaux de Bréhat (48°55′N 3°05′W) the route leads generally SE passing (with positions given from Pointe de Paon (48°52′N 2°59′W)):
NE of Roc'h ar Bel (3½ miles N) and the shoaler Karreg Mingi lying 4 cables SW and farther from the track, the outermost dangers on the N side of the approach to Grand Chenal (10.28), passing clear of Basse Maurice (6 miles NNE); and:
2 SW of Roche Gautier (49°01′N 2°49′W), marked by a light buoy (W cardinal) of the same name moored 3½ miles WNW, on the W side of Plateau de Barnouic (11.17) from where a light is exhibited. The plateau is covered by the red sector (227°–247°) of Les Héaux de Bréhat Light, noting however that the plateau itself lies outside of the nominal range of this light. Thence:
3 NE of Basses du Nord (3½ miles NE), situated at the N end of Plateau de la Horaine, marked on their N side by Nord Horaine Buoy (N cardinal). La Horaine Lighted Beacon Tower (10.16) stands on the SW part of the plateau. Great care should be exercised when approaching this plateau in thick weather as the rising stream sets strongly onto it. Thence:
4 NE of Plateau de Men Marc'h marked on its NE side by Men-Marc'h Buoy (E cardinal) (5 miles ENE), noting a wreck with a safe clearance over it of 4 m (position approximate), 1 mile ESE of the buoy; thence:
Along the NE side of Bancs de Sable (6 miles ESE), which extend about 5 miles SSE from the E end of Plateau de Men Marc'h, to a position N of Grand Léjon (48°45′N 2°40′W) from where a light (10.68) is exhibited.

10.18
1 **Clearing marks:**
The alignment (219°) of La Horaine Lighted Beacon Tower (3 miles NE) with Ploubazlanec Belfry (spire) (4½ miles SW), the most conspicuous church in the vicinity, clears SE of Plateau de Barnouic (11.17).
2 **Clearing bearing:**
The line of bearing 196° of Le Paon Light (48°52′N 2°59′W) (10.16) changing from red to white clears W of Plateau de Roches Douvres (49°06′N 2°46′W) (11.17) and Plateau de Barnouic.
(Directions continue for Baie de Saint-Brieuc at 10.68, for the approaches to Saint-Malo at 10.130 and for Guernsey W coast at 11.189)

Side channels

Charts 3673, 3670
Chenal de Bréhat
10.19
1 **General information.** Chenal de Bréhat, the N approach to Anse de Paimpol (10.40), passes E of Île de Bréhat (48°51′N 3°00′W) and has a least depth of 8·9 m as far as its junction with Chenal du Denou (10.48).
Tidal streams between the parallels of latitude of the N end of Île de Bréhat and Men Garo (48°50′·8N) begin as follows:

Interval from HW Brest	Direction
–0405	SSE
+0205	NNW

The maximum spring rate is 4 kn and 3¾ kn on the S and N streams, respectively; see also 10.45.
10.20
1 **Directions — leading marks:**
Front mark. La Cormorandière (rock surmounted by a white pyramid beacon) (48°48′·3N 2°56′·4W).
Rear mark. Pors Moguer Beacon (white tower) (6¼ miles SSE of the front mark) (chart 2669).
The alignment (167½°) of these marks leads in the channel passing (with positions given from Pointe du Paon (48°52′N 2°59′W)):
2 Between Plateau des Penn Azen (5 cables NNE) (10.28) and Penn ar Bre or Pain de Bray (1¾ miles NE) marked on its NW side by Les Échaudés Buoy (port hand), the NW-most danger on Plateau des Échaudés which consists of numerous rocks, some of which dry; thence:
3 WSW of Beg en Biz (1 mile ENE), the W-most danger on Plateau des Échaudés; thence:
Between Men Goarin (1 mile ESE), marked on its E side by Roche Guarine Buoy (E cardinal), and Roc'h Steuda (1¼ miles ESE), noting the shoaler Roc'h Gouban which lies 2 cables SE and farther from the track.
4 The track then continues 168° passing close ENE of Mein Garz (1½ miles SE) to join Chenal du Denou (10.48), the N approach to Paimpol, or SE through Chenal ar C'hign Bras (10.21).
Useful marks:
Île-ar-Morbic (48°51′·6N 2°58′·8W).
Roc'h Louet (white pyramid) (48°51′·4N 2°58′·8W).
Raguénès Meur (48°50′·9N 2°58′·7W).

Chenal ar C'hign Bras
10.21
1 **General information.** Chenal ar C'hign Bras leads from Chenal de Bréhat SE into Baie de Saint-Brieuc (10.58).
Leading line — by day. From a position NE of Men Garo Beacon Tower (E cardinal) (48°50′·8N 2°58′·0W), at the S end of Chenal de Bréhat, the line of bearing, 302½°, astern, of Les Héaux de Bréhat Light (48°55′N 3°05′W) (9.130) just open NE of Pointe du Paon, 4¾ miles SE, leads in the channel passing (with positions given from Pointe du Paon):
2 NE of Mein Garz (1½ miles SE); thence:
SW of Kein Fall (2¼ miles ESE), the shoalest depth on the SW side of Plateau de Men Marc'h (10.17); thence:
NE of Kein ar Mons (2½ miles SE), marked on its NW side by Cain Ar Monse Buoy (N cardinal); thence:
3 Dependent upon draught, over Basses de Pierre Lefranc (48°50′·1N 2°54′·7W) which lie close S of Plateau ar C'hign Bras; thence:

Between Basses Promoriou (48°49'·6N 2°53'·8W) and
Petit Promoriou which lies 3 cables NE; thence:

4   NE of Basse Petite Bon (48°48'·7N 2°52'·8W); and:
SE of Bancs de Sable (48°50'N 2°50'W) (10.17) to
Baie de Saint-Brieuc.

Alternative route. The line of bearing 312°, astern, of
Le Paon Light (48°52'N 2°59'W) or at night in its white
sector (307°–316°) leads in the channel, in lesser depths,
passing over Basse de la Dorade (48°49'·1N 2°54'·0W), the
shoalest depth in the white sector.

5   The white sector (269°–272°), astern, of Pointe de
Porz-Don Light (48°48'N 3°01'W) then leads in the
channel towards Baie de Saint-Brieuc.

Le Trieux and approaches

General information
10.22

1   **Description.** Le Trieux (48°50'N 3°04'W), or Rivière de
Pontrieux, contains many sheltered anchorages and leads to
Lézardrieux (48°47'N 3°06'W) (10.33), a small commercial
port with a marina which lies on the W bank of Le Trieux.
Pontrieux (10.34), a smaller port, lies 6 miles above
Lézardrieux.

10.23

1   **Route.** Le Trieux is approached from S of Plateau de
Barnouic (49°02'N 2°48'W) (11.17) and entered through
Grand Chenal (10.28), the principal channel leading into
the river, which lies between the NW side of Île de Bréhat
(48°51'N 3°00'W) (10.10) and the mainland; it is indicated
by leading lights and is well marked and can be used by
day or night.

2   The river can also be approached through Chenal de la
Moisie (48°53'N 3°02'W) (10.29) or through Le Ferlas
(48°50'N 3°00'W) (10.30), two secondary channels.

All these channels are bordered by dangerous rocks and
shoals.

10.24

1   **Controlling depths.** Grand Chenal has a least depth of
6 m as far as Pointe de Coatmer (48°48'N 3°06'W) and
3·2 m as far as Lézardrieux, 1 mile farther up river. About
1 mile above Lézardrieux the river dries.

Vertical clearance, 17 m under a suspension bridge
spanning the river about 5 cables above Lézardrieux; a tide
gauge on the E bank indicates the clearance.

2   **Tidal levels** at Lézardrieux, see information in *Admiralty
Tide Tables.* Mean spring range about 9·2 m; mean neap
range about 4·2 m.

Maximum size of vessel. Lézardrieux is accessible to
vessels of 80 m LOA, 20 m beam with a draught of up to
8 m at springs and 6 m at neaps and Pontrieux by vessels
of 60 m LOA, 11 m beam with a draught of up to 4·5 m at
springs and 3·0 m at neaps.

10.25

1   **Marine farms.** There are numerous oyster beds in deep
water in the entrance and in the river and floating fish
cages, which in places reduces the width of the channel,
are established in the river on both sides of the channel;
their positions are best seen from the chart. Fishing is
restricted to line fishing only in an area of shellfish beds
indicated on the chart NE of Plateau de la Horaine (10.17).

2   **Dredging area.** A charted dredging area 1 mile in length
and 2¼ cables in width is situated between La Croix Light
(10.28) and Rerv ar Vein (10.28).

10.26

1   **Pilotage.** The river between Lézardrieux and Pontrieux
should not be attempted without a pilot; for details see
10.13.

Local knowledge. All the channels are bordered by
dangerous rocks and shoals. Local knowledge is required
for Chenal de la Moisie and Le Ferlas, the two secondary
channels.

10.27

1   **Tidal streams.** In Grand Chenal between Plateau des
Penn Azen (48°52'N 2°59'W) and Gosrod Beacon Tower,
1½ miles SW, the E-going stream runs S towards Île de
Bréhat, and the W-going stream runs N towards Plateau
des Sirlots; they begin as follows:

Interval from HW Brest	Direction
–0405	Inward
+0205	Outward

2   The maximum spring rate in each direction is 3¾n. The
spring rates of the streams S of Gosrod Beacon Tower are
about 1 kn less than these rates.

See also information on the chart.

Directions
10.28

1   **Grand Chenal — leading lights:**
Front light. La Croix (two grey round towers joined,
white on the NE side, red tops, 23 m in height)
(48°50'N 3°03'W).
Rear light. Bodic Light (white house with green
gable, 23 m in height) (2 miles SW of the front
mark).

2   From a position S of Plateau de Barnouic (49°02'N
2°48'W) the alignment (224¾°) of these lights, which are
intensified near their alignment, leads in Grand Chenal
passing (with positions given from Pointe du Paon
(48°52'N 2°59'W):

3   NW of Basses du Nord (48°54'N 2°55'W) (10.17),
marked on their N side by Nord Horaine Buoy (N
cardinal); thence:
NW of Plateau des Échaudés (10.20), marked on their
NW side by Les Échaudés Buoy (port hand)
(2 miles NE); and:

4   SE of Basse Plate (2 miles NNW) on the SE end of
Plateau Men ar C'hastreg. Karreg Don, a shoal at
the NE end of the plateau, is often marked by
violent overfalls. Thence:

5   Between Plateau des Sirlots, marked on its E side by
Les Sirlots Buoy (starboard hand) (1 mile NNW),
and Plateau des Penn Azen, marked on its NW
side by Petite Pen Azen W Buoy (port hand)
(5 cables NNW). Petite Penn Azen Beacon Tower
(N cardinal, 7 m in height) stands near the N edge
of the plateau; thence:

6   SE of Vieille du Tréou (1¼ miles W) marked by a
beacon tower (starboard hand); thence:
SE of Ar Rodellou Beacon (starboard hand)
(1½ miles W); thence:
NW of Gosrod (1½ miles WSW) marked by a beacon
tower (port hand); thence:

7   SE of Min-Guen (2 miles WSW) marked by a beacon
tower (starboard hand); thence:
Dependent upon draught, over Men ar C'hanod
(2 miles WSW), a rocky patch; thence:
NW of Rerv ar Vein (2¼ miles WSW) a rock awash;
thence.

The alignment (234¾°) of Moguedhier Beacon (48°50'·4N 3°03'·4W) with a white house, which is difficult to make out, on L'Île à Bois, 1 mile SW, then leads in the fairway for about 6 cables passing:.

8   NW of a rock which covers and uncovers 0·4 m (2½ miles WSW) close N of Les Frères (48°50'·6N 3°02'·5W), a group of drying rocks.

9   Should the previously described alignment be difficult to see then an alternative alignment may be used when SE of Min-Guen (see above). The alignment (063°) astern of Gosrod Beacon Tower (see above) with Le Chandelier islet (5 cables ENE of Gosrod Beacon Tower) leads WSW for about 5½ cables.

Caution. Marine farms may be encountered in the vicinity.

10   **Coatmer Leading Lights:**

Front light (white gable, 11 m in height) (48°48'·3N 3°05'· 8W) situated on Pointe de Coatmer on the W bank of the river.

Rear light (white gable, 8 m in height) (3½ cables SW of the front light).

11   The alignment (218¾°) of these lights then leads in the fairway between La Croix Lighted Beacon Tower and Plateau de Moguedhier, marked on its SE side by Moguedhier Beacon (starboard hand) (1½ cables NW), passing across the W end of Le Ferlas (10.30), until Bodic Light (48°48'·7N 3°05'·5W) bears 270°.

12   Thence, keep in mid-channel passing E of Les Perdrix Lighted Beacon Tower (starboard hand) (48°47'·8N 3°05'·7W) on the W bank of the river, distant about 60 m, and the same distance W of Roc'h Donan on the E side of the river, avoiding the drying bank which extends close SW of the latter. Once clear S of Roc'h Donan there is direct approach to the marina and berth at Lézardrieux (10.33). Two wrecks with depths of 4·8 and 5·1 m over them, the positions of which can be seen from the chart, lie close E of mid-channel between Pointe de Coatmer and Les Perdrix.

13   **Caution.** There is an N-going eddy during the rising stream S of Roc'h Donan.

Side channels
10.29

1   **Chenal de la Moisie** (48°53'N 3°02'W), a secondary channel practicable only by day, joins Grand Chenal from N and leads through the shoals on the NW side of Grand Chenal along the E edge of the reefs which extend E from Sillon de Talber (9.148).

2   **Tidal streams** begin as follows:

Interval from HW Brest	*Direction*
At N entrance to the channel:	
–0450	SE
+0120	NW
S of La Moisie (48°54'N 3°02'W):	
–0450	S
+0120	N

The maximum spring rate in each direction is 3¾ kn.

3   **Directions — leading marks:**

Front mark. Amer du Rosédo (white tower) (48°51'·5N 3°00'·7W).

Rear mark. Saint-Michel Chapelle (red roof and belfry) (6 cables SSE of the front mark).

4   From a position about 1¾ miles E of Les Héaux de Bréhat Light the alignment (159½°) of these marks leads in

Chenal de la Moisie in depths of less than 2 m passing (with positions given from the front mark):

5   Close ENE of La Moisie (2½ miles NNW) marked by a beacon tower (E cardinal); thence:

Close ENE of An Ogejou Bihan Beacon (E cardinal) (2 miles NNW); thence:

Close ENE of an isolated 0·1 m drying patch (48°53'·0N 3°01'·8W) situated on the W side of Ar Gazeg bank, thence:

Close ENE of a rock which covers lying 2 cables NE of Pen ar Rest (1 mile NNW); thence:

Close ENE of Vieille du Tréou (10.28) (6 cables NNW), marked by a beacon tower (starboard hand), to join Grand Chenal.

6   **Caution.** Beg ar C'hog (48°54'·2N 3°02'·1W), a drying rock, lies at the entrance to the channel ENE of the leading line; there are numerous other unmarked dangers ENE of the leading line, their positions can best be seen from the chart.

10.30

1   **Le Ferlas — by day** (48°50'N 3°00'W), a secondary channel between the S side of Île de Bréhat and the mainland, is approached from E passing SW of Bancs de Sable (10.17), or from N through Chenal du Bréhat (10.19).

2   Tidal streams begin as follows:

Interval from HW Brest	*Direction*
–0405	E
+0205	W

The maximum spring rate in each direction is 3¾ kn.

3   **Directions.** From a position in Chenal ar C'hign Bras (10.21) the line of bearing 277° of La Croix Light (48°50'N 3°03'W) (10.28) just open S of Île Raguénès, 1¼ miles E, leads in the approach passing (with positions given from the S extremity of Île Raguénès):

4   N of Banc de la Comorandière (48°50'N 2°56'W); thence:

S of Kein ar Mons (3 miles E) (10.21); thence:

S of Karreg Minguy (2¾ miles E); thence:

S of Al Lean Sonn (2¼ miles E); thence:

5   Between Lell ar Skrev, marked on its S side by Lel ar Serive Buoy (S cardinal) (1¾ miles E), and Cadenenou Buoy (N cardinal) (1½ miles ESE) which marks the S side of the entrance to Le Ferlas; thence:

6   S of La Chambre, a drying rock (1 mile E) (10.37) marked by a beacon (S cardinal); thence:

N of Les Piliers (9 cables ESE), marked by a beacon tower (N cardinal).

Leading marks:

Front mark. Rompa Beacon Tower (isolated danger) (1¼ miles WSW).

7   Rear mark. N extremity of Roc'h Levret (8 cables WSW of the front mark).

The alignment (259°) of these marks leads in the channel passing:

Between Vif Argent (4½ cables E) and Roc'h Ourmelek (7 cables SE), marked by beacons (S and N cardinal, respectively); thence:

8   S of Roud al Linenn (2 cables SSE) marked by a beacon (S cardinal) to a position about 4½ cables WSW of the same beacon.

The alignment (071°), astern, of Roud al Linenn Beacon with Vif Argent Beacon then leads in the channel in depths of less than 2 m for about 5½ cables passing:

9   SSE of Receveur Bihan (6 cables WSW), marked by a beacon (S cardinal); thence:

Between Trebeyou, on which stands a beacon tower (S cardinal) (7 cables WSW), and Roc'h ar C'hroueier (9 cables SW). There are several shallow patches in this vicinity and care should be taken particularly at LW.

10   The line of bearing 275° of Vieille de Loguivy Beacon Tower (W cardinal) (1¾ miles WSW) open S of Roc'h Kranked, close E, then leads in the fairway for about 3 cables passing S of Rompa Beacon Tower.

The alignment (084°) astern, of Rompa Beacon Tower with Les Piliers Beacon Tower, 1¾ miles E of the front mark, then leads in the fairway passing:

11   Between Roc'h Kranked and the beacon (starboard hand) standing on the drying flat extending N from Roc'h Quinonec (1¾ miles WSW) (10.31); thence:

Between Vieille de Loguivy Beacon Tower and Roc'h Levret to Grand Chenal (10.28).

10.31

1   **Le Ferlas — by night** keep in the white sector (279°–283°) of Men Joliguet Lighted Beacon Tower (W cardinal, 8 m in height) (48°50′N 3°00′W) passing between Lel ar Serive Buoy (S cardinal) and Cadenenou Buoy (N cardinal).

The line of bearing 257¼° of the narrow white sector of Roc'h Quinonec Direction Light (grey turret, 6 m in height) (48°49′N 3°04′W) then leads in the channel passing between Roc'h ar C'hroueier and Trebeyou Beacon Tower.

2   The line of bearing 271° of the centre of the white sector (270°–272°) of Kermouster Direction Light (white structure, 2 m in height) (48°50′N 3°05′W) then leads in the channel from S of Rompa Beacon Tower passing between Roc'h Kranked and Roc'h Quinonec to Grand Chenal (10.28).

Anchorages
10.32

1   **Mouillage de La Traverse** (48°50′·9N 3°02′·5W) lies NW of Grand Chenal between Min-Guen Beacon Tower (starboard hand) and Plateau de Moguedhier, 1¼ miles SW (10.28). The anchorage is sheltered from all except NE winds which cause a choppy sea during the out-going stream. The anchorage lies on the alignment of Coatmer Leading Lights (10.28) in depths of 11 to 15 m, sand, shells and rocks with moderately good holding ground and out of the strong tidal streams; there is swinging room with a diameter of about 3 cables in depths of more than 10 m as shown on the chart. The anchorage lies within a dredging area as shown on the chart.

2   **Rade de Pommelin** (48°50′·5N 3°03′·7W), NW of Plateau de Moguedhier as shown on the chart, affords better shelter in depths of 6 to 9 m but there is less swinging room between the drying banks.

3   **Mouillage de Coatmer** lies between Lostmor Beacon Tower (48°48′·4N 3°05′·5W) (starboard hand), situated close NE of Pointe de Coatmer, and Les Perdrix Lighted Beacon Tower, 5 cables S. Mariners can anchor in depths of 8 to 12 m, sand and shells with good holding ground clear of the white sector of Les Perdrix Lighted Beacon Tower. There are chains laid on the W side parallel to the river bank.

Arrival. Mariners are recommended to arrive at the above anchorages at HW or soon after.

4   **Rade de Bréhat** (48°50′N 3°00′W) lies off the SE side of Île de Bréhat and is sheltered from all except E winds; the latter raise a heavy sea during the E-going stream.

There is anchorage in depths of 5 to 7 m, mud and clay, good holding ground; a recommended berth is shown on the chart. The anchorage is approached through Le Ferlas (10.30). Submarine cables and pipelines cross Le Ferlas W of Pointe de l'Arcouest (48°49′N 3°00′W) (10.16); anchoring and fishing are prohibited in their vicinity in an area shown on the chart.

Chart 3673 plan of Port de Lézardrieux Le Trieux
Ports
10.33

1   **Lézardrieux.** The commercial port (48°47′·3N 3°05′·9W) accepts coastal traffic of up to 80 m in length and 20 m in width at a quay which dries between 0·6 and 2 m.

Tidal streams above Lézardrieux run in the direction of the channel at a rate of up to 2½ kn, but under the bridge they may attain a rate of 3½ kn in both directions.

Chart 2675
10.34

1   **Pontrieux** (48°42′·5N 3°09′·2W), a port mainly used by leisure craft, consists of a wet dock, about 1 mile in length, which is formed by the river, and which is entered through a lock with a usable length of 65 m, width 12 m and depth over the outer sill of 2.9 m and over the inner sill of 4.8 m above chart datum. The lock is used when the height of tide is less than 10 m; when it exceeds this, entrance is made direct. The level of the water in the wet dock is maintained by a weir, usually at a depth of 3·9 m.

2   Access to the port may be made throughout 24 hours between 2¼ hours before and 1¾ hours after HW from June to September and between 2 hours before and 1¼ hours after HW from October to May.

Port radio station, with limited hours, operates from the port, for details see *Admiralty List of Radio Signals Volume 6(1)*.

3   **Facilities** available at both ports: fuel, small quantities of marine diesel and petrol; fresh water; provisions. Hospital at Lézardrieux.

Chart 3673
Minor harbours and anchorages
10.35

1   **Port de la Corderie** (48°51′N 3°00′W), on the NW side of Île de Bréhat, provides sheltered anchorage with good drying out berths. Anchoring is controlled due to frequent congestion. It is approached from Grand Chenal between Amer du Rosédo (48°51′·5N 3°00′·7W) and Gosrod Beacon Tower, 3 cables WSW, thence through a channel marked by beacons.

2   **Tidal streams**, very strong, flow through Le Kerpont, a narrow channel which is navigable by mariners in small craft at HW and leads S from the entrance to Port de la Corderie between Île de Bréhat and Îles Biniguet and Raguénès, two islets situated about 3 cables W, and set across the entrance to Port de La Corderie rendering access to that port difficult.

3   **Submarine power cable** is laid across the entrance to the harbour, as shown on the chart.
10.36

1   **Port Clos** (48°50′·4N 3°00′·2W), an inlet on the S side of Île de Bréhat, is entered W of Men Joliguet Lighted Beacon Tower (W cardinal). The best drying out berths lie on the W side of the inlet. A channel, marked by beacons, which dries 5·4 m leads to a landing slip at the head of the inlet. When there is insufficient water to reach this landing slip mariners can go alongside a jetty, the end of which is marked by a beacon (port hand), situated on the W side of

the inlet. At or near LW mariners can go alongside a jetty which projects from Point Gwéréva, the W entrance point of the inlet.

10.37

1   **La Chambre** (48°50′·4N 2°59′·7W), between the SE side of Île de Bréhat and Île Logodec, 1½ cables E, provides sheltered anchorage with good drying out berths; it is approached from Rade de Bréhat through a channel marked by beacons. Anchorage is prohibited between the N part of Île Logodec and Île de Bréhat, as shown on the chart. Access and anchoring are controlled by the Île de Bréhat authorities.

10.38

1   **Pointe de l'Arcouest.** A jetty which covers at HW, mid-tide, is situated 3 cables NW of Pointe de l'Arcouest (48°49′N 3°00′W) (10.16) and is used as a ferry landing linking Île de Bréhat.

10.39

1   **Loguivy** (48°49′N 3°04′W), a small harbour at the W end of Le Ferlas which dries up to 5 m to a bottom of mud, is protected by a breakwater and is used by the pilot boats and by a large number of coastal fishing boats.

2   **Anchorage:** 3 cables NE of the entrance on the alignment of Rompa and Les Piliers Beacon Towers (10.30), as shown on the chart, in depths of 5 to 7 m, sand and shells, moderately good holding ground.

    Berths: quay on the E side of the harbour for fishing boats; three slips.

    Supplies: water; provisions.

    Rescue, see 10.14.

Anse de Paimpol

Charts 3673, 3670

General information

10.40

1   **Description.** Anse de Paimpol, a wide bay, is entered between Pointe de la Trinité (48°48′N 3°00′W) and Pointe de Bilfot (Plouézec), 2¾ miles SE; the head of the bay is dominated by the church (10.47) at Paimpol. The bay dries through most of its extent and vessels can lie aground on the large areas of mudbanks. The approach to the bay is obstructed with rocks and dangerous shoals; the port of Paimpol (10.52) lies at its W end.

10.41

1   **Approach channels.** Chenal de la Jument (10.47) leads from E to the anchorage in Rade de Paimpol and is the principal channel into Anse de Paimpol; Chenal du Denou (10.48), a continuation of Chenal de Bréhat (10.19), forms the N approach. There are other minor channels but none should be attempted without local knowledge.

10.42

1   **Controlling depths:**
    Chenal de la Jument (10.47); least depth 1·1 m.
    Chenal du Denou (10.48); least depth 3·2 m.

10.43

1   **Marine farms.** There are numerous marine culture exploitation areas in the bay, their positions are best seen from the chart.

10.44

1   **Pilotage** is compulsory for the port of Paimpol, for details see 10.13.

    In good weather mariners awaiting the pilot can anchor in Anse de Bréhec (48°43′N 2°56′W) (10.72) or as given at 10.13.

10.45

1   **Tidal streams.** The in-going stream enters Anse de Paimpol from Le Ferlas (10.30) and Chenal de Bréhat; it runs at first SSE and as the banks cover it turns S and finally SW. An eddy then runs NW along the coast from Pointe de Minard (48°45′N 2°56′W) to Pointe de l'Arcouest, running strongly through Chenal de la Trinité (48°49′·7N 2°59′·7W), a minor channel. The out-going stream from Anse de Paimpol follows on after this NW-going eddy and runs towards Île de Bréhat while the banks are covered, and as they gradually uncover it tends to run in the direction of the channels. One part of the out-going stream runs W through Le Ferlas, and N through Le Kerpont (10.35), and NW through Ar Vinkre (48°50′·0N 3°03′·5W) where it joins the out-going stream from Le Trieux; the other part runs N through Chenal du Denou, passing E of Île de Bréhat.

2   In Chenal de la Jument tidal streams at the positions indicated begin as shown in the following table:

Interval from HW Brest	Position	Direction
−0405	At the E entrance to the channel	SSE
+0120		NNW

3   The maximum S-going and N-going spring rates are 2¾ and 2½ kn, respectively.

−0405	Between La Jument and Le Denou Beacon Towers	SSE
+0120		NNW

    The maximum spring rate in each direction is 3½ kn.

4   Tidal streams at the N end of Chenal du Denou begin as follows:

Interval from HW Brest	Direction
−0420	SE
+0135	NW

    The maximum spring rate in each direction is 2¾kn.

5   In the anchorages (10.50 to 10.51) tidal streams begin as shown in the following table:

Interval from HW Brest	Position	Direction
−0405	Rade de Paimpol	SE
+0105		NW
−0435	Mouillage de la Croix-Chenal:	SW
+0105		NE

    The maximum spring rates in each anchorage and in each direction are 2 kn.

6   Tidal streams at the head of the bay begin as follows:

Interval from HW Brest	Direction
−0400	W
+0100	E

    The maximum spring rate in each direction is 1½ kn. The W-going stream corresponds to the E-going stream in the English Channel.

7   At the entrance to the port a S-going eddy runs towards Jetée de Kernoa at a rate of ½ kn during the rising (W-going stream) but ceases when the tide reaches a height of 10 m.

Directions

10.46

1   **Landmarks:**

Ploubazlanec Belfry (spire) (48°48'·1N 3°02'·0W), the most conspicuous church in the vicinity.

Mast (48°47'·9N 3°03'·0W).

Tower (48°47'·5N 3°02'·0W).

10.47

1   **Chenal de la Jument — leading marks:**

Front mark. Pointe Brividic Summit (48°47'·0N 3°01'·7W).

Rear mark. Paimpol Belfry (spire) (9 cables WSW of the front mark).

By day the alignment (260°) of these marks leads through Chenal de la Jument passing (with positions given from L'Ost Pic Light (48°47'N 2°56'W)):

2   Between Les Barbottes (1¼ miles NE) and Ar Charretourien Bras (1 mile NE); the shoaler Ar Charretourien Bihan lies 2½ cables SE and farther from the track; thence:

S of Les Charpentiers (1¼ miles NNE), rocks marked by a beacon tower (E cardinal); thence:

Along the S side of Roches du Roho, a rocky reef extending 1 mile W from Les Charpentiers; and:

3   N of Roc'h Gouayan (5 cables NNW), marked by a beacon tower (port hand), and Roc'h Gueule (8 cables NW) marked on its N side by La Gueule Buoy (port hand); thence:

N of La Jument Beacon Tower (port hand) (1¼ miles WNW) to the anchorages (10.50 to 10.51) or harbour (10.52) as required.

4   **At night** approach in the white sector (269°–272°) of Pointe de Porz-Don Light (white house, 8 m in height) (48°48'N 3°01'W) to the anchorage passing, dependent upon draught, over Ar Charretourien Bihan (1 mile NE), noting that La Gueule Buoy (9 cables NNW) also lies in this white sector.

10.48

1   **Chenal du Denou** is a continuation of Chenal de Bréhat (10.19); the leading marks must be very closely followed as the channel passes close to drying rocks.

Leading marks:

Front mark. Roc'h Denou Beacon Tower (white) (48°47'·9N 2°58'·0W). Do not mistake this beacon tower for La Cormorandière Beacon (10.20) which is much taller and lies 1 mile ENE.

2   Rear mark. Plouëzec Belfry (spire) (3 miles SSW of the front mark).

From a position in the vicinity of Basse du Chenal (48°50'N 2°57'W) the alignment (193°) of these marks leads in the channel passing (with positions given from the front mark):

Over, depending on draught, Basse du Chenal with a minimum depth of 3·6 m, thence:

3   WNW of Kein ar Mons (2¼ miles NNE) (10.21); thence:

Between Karreg Minguy (2 miles NNE) and Al Lean Sonn (2 miles N); thence:

Between Basse Misère (1¼ miles NNE) and Basse Bon Krenv (1¼ miles N); thence:

4   Between a rock drying 1 m (6 cables N) which lies close E of Roc'h Denou Vihan, marked by a beacon (starboard hand), and Roc'ho an Tier, a drying reef marked at its N end by La Petite Moise Beacon (port hand) (7½ cables NNE), passing 50 m E of the drying rock.

5   The track then continues generally SSW passing between the 0·6 m patch close W of Roc'h Denou Beacon Tower and a rocky patch drying 4·7 m (1 cable W) before rejoining the leading line to join Chenal de la Jument at Rade de Paimpol (10.50).

10.49

1   **Useful marks:**

Île Saint-Rion (two pointed summits) (48°48'N 2°59'W), the largest of a number of islands and islets in the vicinity.

Le Grand Mez de Goëlo (48°47'N 2°57'W) covered with verdure, the largest and most prominent of the islands at the S entrance point of the bay.

Anchorages

10.50

1   **Mouillage de la Rade de Paimpol,** also known as Mouillage de la Fosse SE, (48°47'·3N 2°58'·2W) affords anchorage sheltered from most winds, in depths of 6 to 8 m, sand and gravel, W of La Jument Beacon Tower.

At night mariners can anchor in depths of 4 to 5 m in the red sector (272°–279°) of Porz-Don Light when L'Ost Pic Light changes from red to white bearing 116°, as shown on the chart.

10.51

1   **Mouillage de la Croix-Chenal** lies in a channel about 1 cable wide between mudbanks on either side, as shown on the chart, situated 5 cables SW of Île Saint-Rion (48°48'N 2°59'W); it has depths of up to 7 m and is well sheltered from all winds.

Chart 3673 plan of Port de Paimpol

Paimpol

10.52

1   **General information.** Port de Paimpol (48°47'N 3°02'W) lies at the head of Anse de Paimpol and is used by coasters, fishing vessels and yachts. The harbour is entered from Rade de Paimpol by a channel which dries, marked by light buoys, buoys and beacons as shown on the chart; the channel is indicated by leading lights.

2   **Port radio** station, with limited hours, operates from the port; for details see *Admiralty List of Radio Signals Volume 6(1)*.

10.53

1   **Limiting conditions — controlling depth:** approach channel 30 m wide which dries 5·5 m.

Tidal levels, see information in *Admiralty Tide Tables*. Mean spring range about 9·5 m; mean neap range about 4·5 m.

Maximum size of vessel handled: up to 80 m in length if both lock gates are open, or 58 m in length when using the lock, with 11·5 m beam and draughts of up to 4·6 m at springs or 3·0 m at neaps.

10.54

1   **Directions.** From the anchorage at Rade de Paimpol continue on the alignment of the leading marks for Chenal de la Jument (10.47) until N of Roc'h ar Zel (48°47'·1N 2°59'·3W), marked by a beacon (isolated danger). The track then continues generally WNW to join the alignment (262¼°) of the following leading lights which lead to the buoyed channel. The turn into the port round the head of Jetée de Kernoa is very sharp and difficult with a cross wind; vessels with a large turning circle should run a hawser to the end of the jetty to assist the turn.

2   Front light. Kernoa Light (white and red hut, 4 m in height) (48°47'·1N 3°02'·4W) at the head of Jetée de Kernoa.

Rear light. Kerpalud Light (white pylon red top, 10 m, in height) (2 cables W of the front mark).

10.55

1   **Basins and berths.** The port consists of an Avant-port, which dries between 4 and 7 m, and two wet basins which are entered through a lock. Avant-port lies between Jetée de Kernoa on its E side, Cale de Bréhat, a sloping quay, on its W side and a further quay fronting Terre-plein de Kerplaud, an area of reclaimed land, marked by a light (starboard hand) at its SE extremity on the N side. The channel leading to the lock lies parallel with, and close to, Jetée de Kernoa, and dries 4·0 m. Jetée de Kernoa dries up to 5·5 m on its W side to a bottom of mud.

2   The wet basin is entered from Avant-port through a lock 60 m long and 12 m wide, the outer and inner sills of which are 3·3 and 5·0 m, respectively, above chart datum; the lock leads into No 2 Basin. The lock gates are opened for 2½ hours on either side of HW. The level of the water in the wet basins is usually maintained at a depth of 4·5 m.

3   Exceptions can be made to these times provided a sufficient level of water can be maintained in the basins; mariners in yachts and pleasure craft can usually be locked in or out 1 hour either side of HW.

When both lock gates are open a fairly strong stream of up to 2 kn sometimes runs through the lock during the rising stream.

4   No 2 Basin is equipped with floating pontoons and is reserved for pleasure craft, with the exception of Quai du Platier at its NE end which is used by commercial and fishing vessels.

No 1 Basin is entered from No 2 Basin through a passage 45 m long and 11·9 m wide; it is used principally by commercial and fishing vessels and by yachts.

Facilities: repairs; fuel, marine diesel and petrol; freshwater; provisions; hospital.

Anchorage and landing
10.56

1   **Mouillage de Porz Even**, in a small bay 4 cables SW of Pointe de la Trinité (48°48′N 3°00′W), provides good drying out berths for mariners in small craft, sheltered by a jetty and quay for fishing vessels which extend S from the E entrance point of the bay. Numerous moorings and several rocky areas are reported (1994) in the vicinity of the anchorage, shown on the chart. The approach to the bay is marked by beacons. Local knowledge is required.

10.57

1   **Port Lazo.** A jetty marked by a beacon (special) is situated at Port Lazo situated 6 cables SW of Pointe de Bilfot (48°46′N 2°57′W); the approach to the jetty is marked by beacons.

BAIE DE SAINT-BRIEUC AND APPROACHES

General information

Charts 3674, 2669
Description
10.58

1   Baie de Saint-Brieuc is entered between Pointe de Minard (48°45′N 2°56′W) and Cap Fréhel, about 25 miles ESE. Its shores are formed by cliffs broken by sandy beaches and the bay is obstructed by large rocky flats.

2   Anse d'Yffiniac, a wide inlet which dries completely at the head of the bay, is entered between Pointe du Roselier

(48°33′N 2°43′W) and Pointe du Grouin, 1¾ miles SE. Rivière Le Gouet, leading to Le Légué (10.74), flows into the W side of Anse d'Yffiniac between Pointe à l'Aigle (48°32′N 2°43′W) and Pointe de Cesson, 3 cables S (10.78).

Route
10.59

1   A channel, 3 miles wide, between Plateau du Rohein (48°39′N 2°38′W) and Roches de Saint Quay (10.70) on the W side of the bay, gives access to the head of the bay.

Topography
10.60

1   From Pointe de Minard to Pointe du Roselier, a bluff point 15 miles SE, the coast is cliffy and bordered by sandy beaches; from SE of Pointe de Saint Quay (48°39′N 2°50′W) the beaches dry up to 8 cables offshore.

2   At Pointe du Roselier the coast recedes to form a wide inlet giving access to Le Légué. Thence ENE the coast is cliffy, interspersed with sandy beaches and some small harbours. One of the most prominent features on this side of the bay is Bois de Bienassis (48°35′N 2°30′W), a wooded hill the SW side of which is sheer, situated about 1 mile inland.

Marine farms
10.61

1   Numerous shellfish beds lie in the bay, their positions are best seen from the chart. Touching bottom and anchoring are prohibited in these areas.

Temporary explosives dumping grounds
10.62

1   Temporary explosives dumping grounds are situated SE of Grand Léjon (48°45′N 2°40′W), for Saint Quay-Portrieux, E of Rohein (48°39′N 2°38′W), for Le Légué and Erquy, and for Cap Fréhel, WSW of Cap Fréhel (48°41′N 2°19′W).

For details see 1.7 and Appendix V.

Pilotage
10.63

1   **Compulsory pilotage area limits** for Le Légué-Saint-Brieuc are bounded by the following:
 The parallel through Pointe du Bec de Vir (48°40′·6N 2°51′·5W).
 A line bearing 312° joining Le Verdelet (48°36′·3N 2°33′·4W) and Rohein Lighted Beacon Tower, 3¾ miles NW.

2   The station also provides pilotage in the interior of a line joining La Mauvre (48°42′·2N 2°52′·7W), Grand Léjon (48°45′·0N 2°39′·8W) and Cap d'Erquy (48°38′·8N 2°29′·2W).

3   **Pilotage** is compulsory for all vessels over 45 m LOA.

Boarding places. The pilot boards vessels in the vicinity of Le Légué Light Buoy (safe water) (48°34′·3N 2°41′·2W). Should conditions prevent the use of this position, then vessels will be requested to make for the entrance to the buoyed channel until the pilot is able to board.

4   **Notification** for a pilot should be sent 24 hours in advance, confirming at 12 and 4 hours. In case of any difficulty mariners should communicate with their agents or with the Bureau du Port de Légué, for details see *Admiralty List of Radio Signals Volume 6(1)*.

5   **Waiting anchorages** Owing to shallow water in the channel the pilot vessel is unable to put to sea until about 2½ hours before HW. For Le Légué the pilot boards vessels

anchored within the pilotage area awaiting entry when the height of water permits entry to the outer port.

6   Mariners awaiting a pilot should anchor in accordance with instructions given by Baie de Saint-Brieuc signal station. The usual positions available for anchoring are:

For Le Légué, as indicated at 10.76.

7   For Saint Quay-Portrieux (10.81) and Binic (10.92) in the roads off these ports.

For Dahouet (10.99) and Erquy (10.106) about 2 miles S of Rohein.

Pilot boats are motor fishing vessels painted black with white upperworks; at night they flash the letter "H" of the Morse code at intervals.

Traffic regulations
10.64

1   **Approach channel**, about 1 mile wide, leads into Baie de Saint-Brieuc round the W side of Grand Léjon from a position 7 miles N to a position 5 miles S of Grand Léjon Light. The use of the channel is compulsory for vessels over 1600 gt laden with hydrocarbons or carrying dangerous and polluting goods. For regulations see 1.68 to 1.76.

2   Mariners in vessels of over 1600 gt carrying dangerous substances should establish contact on entering the charted approach channel and should maintain a continuous watch on VHF; mariners in any other vessels intending to enter this channel should first establish listening watch on VHF. Saint Quay Signal Station (48°39′N 2°50′W) is designated for communication between vessels using the channel and the port authorities.

3   Mariners at anchor or in transit in Baie de Saint-Brieuc should make contact with Saint Quay-Portrieux Signal Station (48°39′N 2°50′W).

For details see *Admiralty List of Radio Signals Volume 6(1)*.

Rescue
10.65

1   **Inshore lifeboats** are stationed at:

Saint Quay-Portrieux (48°39′N 2°49′W) (10.81).

Erquy (48°38′N 2°29′W) (10.106).

Signal station (Vigie) is situated at Pointe de Saint Quay (48°39′N 2°50′W).

For details regarding lifeboats see 1.117 and for signal stations 1.95 and 1.110.

2   **VHF Direction-finding station,** for emergency use only, operates from Saint Quay-Portrieux, for details see *Admiralty List of Radio Signals Volume 2*.

Natural conditions
10.66

1   **Local magnetic anomalies** are reported to exist in the area between Grand Léjon (48°45′N 2°40′W) and Rohein, 6 miles SSE. See also 10.7.

10.67

1   **Tidal streams** midway between Pointe de Minard (48°45′N 2°56′W) and Pointe de Saint Quay, 7 miles SE, begin as follows:

Interval from HW Saint Helier	*Direction*
−0600	SSE
−0010	NNW

The maximum spring rate in each direction is 3 kn.

2   Off the entrance to Baie de Saint-Brieuc the tidal streams attain a maximum spring rate of 3 kn; the in-going

stream runs E and then SE for a shorter period than the out-going stream but it is slightly stronger.

3   Off Grand Léjon the streams begin as follows:

Interval from HW Saint Helier	*Direction*
−0600	SE
+0020	NW

The maximum spring rate in each direction is 3¾ kn. Off Petit Léjon (48°42′N 2°37′W) they run similarly but begin about ¼ hour earlier.

4   In the bay tidal streams begin as follows:

Interval from HW Saint Helier	*Direction*
Off Rohein and Les Comtesses:	
−0600	ESE
−0010	NW
Off Les Landas (48°41′N 2°31′W):	
−0545	E
+0050	W

The maximum spring rate in each direction 3½ kn.

5   For details see information on the charts and *Admiralty Tidal Atlas for the Channel Islands and adjacent coasts of France*.

Directions
(continued from 10.18)

Principal marks
10.68

1   **Landmarks:**

Grand Léjon Lighthouse (red truncated conical tower white bands, 25 m in height) (48°45′N 2°40′W).

Saint Quay Church (spire) (48°39′·2N 2°50′·0W) standing 4 cables W of Pointe de Saint Quay; a signal station stands on the point.

Church (spire shaped like a helmet) (48°37′·7N 2°50′·1W) at Étables sur Mer.

2   Pordic Church (spire) (48°34′·3N 2°49′·0W).

Church (pointed spire) (48°35′·1N 2°32′·1W) at Pléneuf-Val-André.

Water tower (96 m) (48°37′·7N 2°25′·8W).

Cap Fréhel (sheer cliff) (48°41′N 2°19′W) with Cap Fréhel Lighthouse (grey square tower green lantern, 33 m in height) and an old disused lighthouse standing 3 cables S of the cape; a fog signal hut stands on the extremity of the cape.

3   **Major lights:**

Roches Douvres Light (49°06′N 2°49′W) (10.16).

Rosédo Light (48°52′N 3°00′W) (10.16)

Grand Léjon Light — as above.

Cap Fréhel Light — as above.

Approach channel
10.69

1   From a position N of Grand Léjon (48°45′N 2°40′W), from where a light (10.68) is exhibited, the track leads initially SSW through the approach channel (10.64) shown on the chart passing (with positions given from Rohein (48°39′N 2°38′W)):

2   Between Grand Léjon (6 miles NNW), a rocky shoal with a number of above water rocks, and Bancs de Sable (48°50′N 2°50′W) (10.17) to a position NW of Grand Léjon when the approach channel then leads SSE. A dangerous wreck (position doubtful) (48°45′N 2°45′W) is charted W of the approach channel. Thence:

3   WSW of Basses du Sud-Est (5½ miles NNW); thence:

WSW of a dangerous wreck (3 miles N) which lies 5 cables W of Petit Léjon, a rocky shoal marked on its W side by a buoy (W cardinal), to the waiting anchorage (10.76) or pilot boarding place (10.63) for Le Légué as required.

4   **Clearing marks:**

Front mark. Pors Moguer Daymark (white tower) (48°42′·0N 2°54′·3W).

Rear mark. Plouha Belfry (spire) (1¾ miles SW of the front mark).

The alignment (213°) of these marks clears SE of Bancs de Sable.

5   **Useful marks:**

L'Ost Pic Light (two white towers, red tops, 15 m in height) (48°47′N 2°56′W).

Rohein Light (48°39′N 2°38′W) (10.70).

Île Harbour (48°40′N 2°48′W), the largest rock on Roches de Saint Quay; a light (white tower and dwelling red top, 13 m in height) is exhibited from the rock.

6   Light (white tower green lantern, 12 m in height) (48°36′N 2°49′W) exhibited from the head of Binic N Mole.

South end of approach channel to Le Légué
10.70

1   From a position at the S end of the approach channel NW of Rohein (48°39′N 2°38′W) the track leads generally S, or at night in the white sector (350°–015°) of Grand Léjon Light, astern, passing (with positions given from Rohein):

2   E of Plateau des Hors (4½ miles W), a large rocky flat which extends E from Roches de Saint Quay, marked on its NE side by Les Hors Buoy (E cardinal). Roches de Saint Quay (48°40′N 2°45′W), a plateau of above-water and drying rocks, extends about 5 miles offshore parallel to the coast fronting the ports of Saint Quay-Portrieux (10.81) and Binic (10.92). Between the plateau and the coast there is a narrow channel which gives access to these ports. And:

3   W of Rohein, the largest rock at the SW end of a rocky plateau; a lighted beacon tower (W cardinal, 15 m in height) stands on the rock. Thence:

E of Caffa (3¾ miles WSW) marked on its E side by a light buoy (E cardinal); thence:

To the vicinity of Le Légué Light Buoy (safe water) (5 miles SSW).

4   **Useful marks:**

La Longue Beacon Tower (S cardinal) (48°38′·0N 2°44′·6W).

Rocher Martin (whitened rock surmounted by a cross) (48°33′·7N 2°43′·2W).

Le Légué Light (white tower green top, 14 m in height) (48°32′N 2°43′W) on Pointe de l'Aigle.

5   Saint-Michel Church (two square towers) (48°31′·0N 2°45′·3W) at Saint-Brieuc.

Beacon Tower (N cardinal) (48°33′·4N 2°38′·4W) at the E end of Roches Tra-Hillion.

La Petite Muette Lighted Beacon Tower (48°35′N 2°34′W) (10.103).

Le Verdelet (conical rock) (48°36′·3N 2°33′·4W).

Erquy Molehead Light (48°38′N 2°29′W) (10.110).

10.71

1   **Clearing bearings:**

The line of bearing 350° of Grand Léjon Light changing from red to white clears W of Basse du Sud-Est, Petite Léjon and Rohein.

The line of bearing 180° of Rohein Light changing from green to white clears W of Petit Léjon, but not clear of the dangerous wreck lying 5 cables W. *(Directions for Le Légué are given at 10.78)*

Anchorages

Charts 3673, 3674
Anse de Bréhec
10.72

1   **General information.** Anse de Bréhec (48°43′N 2°56′W) is entered between Beg Min Rouz and Pointe de la Tour, 7 cables SSE, and affords the best anchorage during W winds. A harbour suitable only for small craft is situated in the NW corner of the bay.

2   **Tidal streams** in the anchorage begin as follows:

Interval from HW Saint Helier	Direction
+0600	SSE
–0115	NNW

The maximum spring rate is 2 and 2½ kn on the S and N-going streams respectively.

3   **Approach.** A dangerous offshore wreck (position doubtful) is charted 3¾ miles ENE of Pointe de la Tour. Le Taureau Beacon Tower (isolated danger) stands on a rocky shoal in the approach to the bay 5 cables NE of the same point; it can be passed on either side but a 3·2 m rocky shoal lies about 1½ cables W of the beacon tower.

4   **Anchorage:** West or NW of Le Taureau in depths of 6 m, sand and mud, good holding ground. A recommended berth is shown on the chart.

Landing. In the NW corner of the bay there is a jetty which dries 5 m; the submerged end is marked by a beacon (starboard hand). There are no facilities.

Waiting anchorages
10.73

1   For details of anchorages for mariners waiting to enter Le Légué, see 10.76.

Saint-Brieuc-Le Légué

Chart 3674
General information
10.74

1   **Position and function.** The outer port of Saint-Brieuc-Le Légué (48°32′N 2°44′W) lies at the entrance to Rivière Le Gouet. The inner port lies about 1 mile upstream and is accessible via a lock. The port is used by coasters of up to 5 000 dwt, fishing vessels, sand dredgers and pleasure craft.

Approach and entry. The port is approached through Anse d'Yffiniac (10.58) and entered through a drying channel which leads to Rivière Le Gouet.

Traffic. In 2006 the port was used by 171 vessels totalling 373 390 dwt.

Limiting conditions
10.75

1   **Controlling depth.** The channel dries about 5 m; it has depths of 5·8 m at MHWS and of 3·0 m at MHWN.

Tidal levels; see information in *Admiralty Tide Tables.* Mean spring range about 10·0 m; mean neap range about 4·8 m.

Le Légué from WSW (10.74)

(Original dated 1997)

(Photograph - Service Hydrographique et Océanographique de la Marine)

Maximum size of vessel handled: 120 m length; 15 m beam; 5 m draught at springs and 3·5 m at neaps.

A vessel of 82·5 m LOA, 12·8 m beam and 4·8 m draught has used the port via the lock system. Maximum permitted draught (2008) for vessels leaving the lock inbound is 4·0 m.

Arrival information
10.76

1   **Port radio** station, with limited hours, operates from the port.

Notice of ETA required: 24, 12 and 4 hours in advance stating draught and overall dimensions.

For details see *Admiralty List of Radio Signals Volume 6(1)*.

2   **Outer anchorages.** Mariners waiting to enter Le Légué can anchor in the following positions about 2¼ miles ENE of Pointe du Roselier (48°33′N 2°43′W):

Position A, 48°35′·0N 2°41′·0W.
Position B, 48°35′·0N 2°40′·0W.
Position C, 48°34′·4N 2°40′·0W

Baie de Saint-Brieuc signal station will instruct vessels which anchorage to use.

With strong NE winds mariners are recommended to anchor S of Rohein (48°39′N 2°38′W); a recommended berth is shown on the chart.

3   With strong NW winds mariners are recommended to anchor in Mouillage de Binic (10.94), 4 miles NW of Pointe du Roselier.

Pilotage, see 10.63.

Regulations concerning entry. Priority is given to coasting vessels because of their draught; the Harbour Master and Pilot order the sequence of entry.

Harbour
10.77

1   **General layout.** The port consists of an Avant-port, which dries, and two wet basins entered through a lock.

Signals. The approach channel to the harbour entrance is maintained by sluicing periodically and when this is being done a blue flag is displayed at the lock and at Pointe à l'Aigle.

2   **Tidal streams** at the entrance to Anse d'Yffiniac begin as follows:

Interval from HW Saint Helier	*Direction*
−0600	S
HW	N

The height of the tide is influenced by the wind and can vary by as much as 0·7 m.

Directions for entering harbour
10.78

1   From the vicinity of Le Légué Light Buoy (safe water) (48°34′N 2°41′W) the track leads SSW, about 2 miles, to a position between Nos 1 and 2 Light Buoys (lateral), which mark the entrance to the approach channel to the harbour. The channel, which is marked by light buoys (lateral), contains some bends and is dredged to 5 m above chart datum.

2   On the S side of the channel an area of reclaimed land enclosed by a dyke extends 4 cables ENE from Pointe de Cesson (48°31′·9N 2°43′·0W) and a breakwater extends 2¼ cables NW from the NE extremity of the dyke. A light is exhibited at the NW extremity of the breakwater.

3   Le Légué Light Tower (white column green top, 9 m in height) (48°32′·0N 2°43′·4W) is situated on Jetée de la Douane, which covers at HW. The head of the jetty is not perpendicular and should thus be given a wide berth. Thence continue between the channel buoys to the lock entrance.

Basins and berths
10.79

1   **Avant-port.** Quais Sebert, three berths over a continuous length of 250 m and capable of accepting vessels of 120 m LOA, maximum draught 5 m, situated on the S side of the channel immediately W of the root of Jettée de Cesson, the outer breakwater. The approaches to these berths dredged to 2 m (2004).

2   Quai de la Ville Gilette, 1½ cables ENE of the lock, 120 m in length and capable of accepting vessels of 90 m LOA, maximum draught 5 m dependent on tidal conditions.

A waiting berth is situated on the S side of the channel immediately below the lock; it can accommodate vessels up to 65 m in length and dries 5·5 m. A drying out berth, 120 m in length, is situated on the N side of the channel below the lock; the berth dries to 6·9 m.

3   **Lock.** The lock to the wet basins, with a sill 5·1 m above chart datum, will accept a vessel of maximum size 82·5 m LOA, breadth 12·8 m and draught 4·0 m.

There are two tide-gauges at the lock entrance; that on the N side indicates the depth above the sill, and that on the S side the depth above chart datum.

4 The opening times of the lock depend on the height of the tide and are as follows:

Height of tide at Saint-Malo	Opening hours
9 to 10 m	1 hour before to 1 hour after HW
10 to 11 m	1¼ hours before to 1¼ hours after HW
11 to 11·5 m	1½ hours before to 1½ hours after HW
Above 11·5 m	2 hours before to 1½ hours after HW

5 **No 1 Basin** immediately within the lock has 605 m of quay space and accepts vessels with a maximum draught of 4·0 m

6 **No 2 Basin** communicates with No 1 Basin through a passage 80 m long spanned by a swing bridge, which when open, gives access through a passage with a width of 11 m. The basin has a total quay space of 1337 m with a mean width of 28 m and depths alongside from 3·2 to 4·2 m; twenty vessels of 45 m LOA can be berthed. Vessels of up to 52 m in length can be turned in a swinging basin near the centre of the S side of the basin. A stone bridge crosses the W end of the basin.

7 **Water level.** The level of water in the wet basins is kept constant, except possibly in periods of drought, by a weir on the N side of No 1 Basin.

Port services
10.80
1 **Repairs** can be carried out afloat. Hoist and shore facilities for vessels up to 350 dwt.

Supplies: fuel oil, marine diesel and petrol; fresh water; provisions.

Communications: local airport at Saint-Brieuc, distant 5 km.

Saint Quay-Portrieux and approaches

Charts 3672 plan of Saint-Quay-Portrieux, 3674
General information
10.81
1 **Position and function.** Saint Quay-Portrieux (48°39′N 2°49′W) comprises two harbours, an old harbour which dries and a new fishing harbour and marina, accessible at all states of the tide, NE of, and outside the old drying harbour.

Approach. The port is approached through a narrow channel between Roches de Saint Quay (10.70) and the coast.

Limiting conditions
10.82
1 **Controlling depths and draught.** The controlling depth in the fishing harbour is 3 m.

The old drying harbour is accessible to vessels up to 700 gt with a length of 47 m and draughts of up to 3·5 m at springs and 2·5 m at neaps.

2 **Least charted depth.** Depths of less than 2 m are charted in the S approach about 1¾ miles SE of the entrance.

Tidal levels, see information in *Admiralty Tide Tables.* Mean spring range about 9·8 m; mean neap range about 4·6 m.

Arrival information
10.83
1 **Port radio** station operates from the port, for details see *Admiralty List of Radio Signals Volume 6(1).*

Outer anchorage. Anchorage can be obtained in Rade de Saint Quay-Portrieux, about 6 cables E of the entrance to the old harbour on the alignment (228°) of Le Four Beacon Tower (white) (48°38′·4N 2°48′·8W) with Notre-Dame de l'Espérance Church (belfry), 5 cables SW, in depths of 3 to 4 m, sand and mud with good holding ground. The anchorage is exposed to N and E winds when Roches de Saint Quay are covered. Tidal streams in the anchorage attain a maximum rate of about 2 kn.

2 This anchorage is difficult to approach; mariners in larger vessels should anchor off Binic (10.94).

Pilotage, for details see 10.63.

Local knowledge is necessary as the channel between Roches de Saint Quay and the coast is obstructed with dangers. The S approach to the harbour or anchorage at Saint Quay-Portrieux presents less difficulty.

Harbour
10.84
1 **General layout.** The old drying harbour is protected by a stone jetty which extends SSE from Pointe de Portrieux, on its N side, and by a mole of rough stone which extends N from its S side. The new fishing harbour and marina is protected on the N and E sides by a breakwater extending E and SE from Pointe de Portrieux and on the S and SE sides by a breakwater extending E and NE from the head of the stone jetty protecting the E side of the old harbour.

2 **Tidal streams** in the channel at the positions indicated begin as shown in the following table:

Interval from HW Saint Helier	Position	Direction
+0600	Channel W of Roches de Saint Quay	SSE
−0015		NNW

The maximum S and N-going spring rates are 2¼ and 2 kn, respectively.

3 −0545	Off Plateau des Hors:	ESE
+0005		NW

The maximum spring rate in each direction is 3½ kn.

Directions for entering harbour
10.85
1 **Approach from south-east:**

From a position SE of Saint Quay-Portrieux the line of bearing 318° of Le Pommier (48°42′·1N 2°53′·2W), an islet with whitened summit, leads in the channel passing (with positions given from Île Harbour Light (48°40′N 2°48′W)):

2 Between Basse Gouin (3¾ miles SSE) and Basse du Sud (3½ miles SE), the S-most danger on Roches de Saint Quay; thence:

Close NE of a stranded wreck (position doubtful) (3 miles SSE); thence:

SW of La Roselière (3 miles SSE), marked on its S side by La Roselière Light Buoy (S cardinal); thence:

3 Close SW of a 0·3 m rock (2¼ miles SSE), noting a 1·9 m patch 2½ cables SSE; thence:

Between Basse Méridionale de la Rade (2 miles SSE) and a stranded wreck (2¼ miles SSE), marked by a buoy (E cardinal), to anchorage or harbour as required.

4 **At night:**

The white sector (316°–320½°) of Saint Quay-Portrieux Direction Light (concrete tower, 12 m in height) (48°39′N 2°49′W) exhibited from the elbow of Saint Quay-Portrieux Mole leads in the fairway passing close SW of the 0·3 m rock (2¼ miles SSE) but over the 1·9 m patch (2½ miles SSE).

10.86

1 **From north.** The anchorage and harbour can also be approached from N passing between Roches de Saint Quay (10.70) and the coast, see 10.83.

10.87

1 **Fishing harbour and marina** are entered from SE passing between the breakwater heads; lights (towers, 6 m in height) are exhibited from each breakwater head and a direction light (10.85) is exhibited from the elbow of the NE breakwater. A channel and turning area, dredged to 3 m, leads from the entrance to the fishing harbour.

Caution. A 1·5 m rock, marked by a buoy (starboard hand) lies in the NE part of the turning area.

10.88

1 **Drying harbour.** A light (white and green octagonal metal tower, 12 m in height) is exhibited from the head of the jetty on the N side of the entrance and a light (white mast red top, 6 m in height) is exhibited from the head of the mole on the S side. The head of the mole is not perpendicular and extends beyond its crown; it must therefore be given a wide berth.

10.89

1 **Useful marks:**

La Mauvre (48°42′·2N 2°52′·7W), an above-water rock.

Madeux Beacon Tower (W cardinal) (48°40′·5N 2°48′·7W).

Grandes Moulières de Saint Quay Beacon (N cardinal) (48°39′·8N 2°49′·8W) standing at the N end of Moulières de Saint Quay.

2 Moulières de Portrieux Beacon Tower (E cardinal) (48°39′·3N 2°49′·1W).

Herflux Directional Lighted Beacon Tower (48°39′·1N 2°47′·9W).

La Ronde Beacon Tower (W cardinal) (48°37′·9N 2°46′·4W).

L'Ours Seul Beacon (isolated danger) (48°37′·3N 2°48′·3W).

Berths

10.90

1 **Fishing harbour:** quay, 120 m long, and three pontoons in the NW part of the harbour reserved for fishing vessels with berths for 100 vessels in depths of 3 m. A further quay, 138 m long extending E from Quai de Pêche, has berthing on both sides for fishing vessels and separates the fishing harbour from the marina.

2 **Drying harbour:** flat wharf at the N end of the jetty drying 3 to 6·5 m; landing slip in the S part of the harbour reserved for fishing vessels, W of the S mole; quay, 85 m long backed by a wide flat wharf with a launching slip for pleasure craft at the W end of the quay; the berths in the S part dry up to 4 m.

Port services

10.91

1 **Facilities:** small repairs; fuel; fresh water; provisions.

Rescue, see 10.65.

Binic

Chart 3674

General information

10.92

1 **Position and function.** Binic (48°36′N 2°49′W), a small port consisting of an Avant-port, which dries, and a wet basin, is used mainly by yachts and fishing vessels.

10.93

1 **Limiting conditions — tidal levels,** see information in *Admiralty Tide Tables.* Mean spring range about 10·0 m; mean neap range about 5·0 m.

Local weather. Avant-port is sheltered from all except E winds which, when strong, make access difficult.

10.94

1 **Arrival information — port radio** station, with limited hours, operates from the port, for details see *Admiralty List of Radio Signals Volume 6(1).*

2 **Anchorage** can be obtained about 2 miles ENE of the harbour entrance in Mouillage de Binic, clear of the shellfish beds, as shown on the chart 5 cables SSE of La Roselière Light Buoy, in depths of 5 to 6 m, mud and clay, midway between Basse Gouin and La Roselière (10.85). At night anchorage can be obtained on the intersection of the line of bearing 072° of Rohein Light (48°39′N 2°38′W), changing from red to white, with the line of bearing 312° of Saint Quay-Portrieux Direction Light.

Pilotage, see 10.63.

10.95

1 **Harbour.** The Avant-port, or Port de Penthièvre, is protected on its NE side by Môle de Penthièvre and on its S side by Quai des Corsaires, the outer part of Môle du Pordic; it has good drying-out berths.

The wet basin is entered from the Avant-port through a dock gate 10 m wide with a depth over the sill of 5·5 m above chart datum; the gate is usually opened in working hours from when the height of the tide is 8·5 m or more until HW.

2 **Eddy.** Between –0230 and –0130 HW Saint Helier an eddy runs E along the S jetty and across the harbour entrance at a rate not exceeding 1 kn.

Directions for entering harbour

10.96

1 With the exception of Basse Gouin, which lies about 1½ miles ENE of the entrance, the approach is clear of dangers. A light is exhibited from the head of Môle Penthièvre. The best times for entering harbour are either at half-tide or at HW.

Berths

10.97

1 **Avant-port:** 200 m of waiting berths along Quay de Penthièvre and Quai des Corsaires; the harbour dries 4 m at the entrance and up to 6 m within; mooring buoys for 180 craft up to 7·5 m in length.

Wet basin: moorings on the W side and pontoon berths on the S side in depths of 1·5 to 3 m.

Port services

10.98

1 **Facilities:** fuel; fresh water; slip.

Port de Dahouet and approaches

General information

10.99

1 **Position and function.** Port de Dahouet (48°35′N 2°34′W), a small port which dries, lies in a gap in the

cliffs about 1 mile SW of Pointe de Pléneuf. The port is used by fishing vessels and pleasure craft.

2   **Topography.** From Pointe du Grouin (48°32′N 2°41′W) to Pointe de Pléneuf, a rocky point 6½ miles NE, the coast is bordered by a long sandy beach which dries up to about 1 mile offshore at its SW end. The beach for about 1 mile SW of Pointe de Pléneuf is fronted by the seaside resort of Le Val André.

10.100

1   **Limiting conditions — tidal levels,** see information in *Admiralty Tide Tables.* Mean spring range about 10·0 m; mean neap range about 4·6 m.

   Local weather. With strong NW winds the sea breaks up to 2 cables offshore rendering access to the harbour very difficult.

10.101

1   **Arrival information — port radio** station, with limited hours, operates from the port, for details see *Admiralty List of Radio Signals Volume 6(1).*

   Pilot is recommended, for details see 10.63.

   Outer anchorage, see 10.76.

10.102

1   **Harbour.** The port comprises a drying harbour, at the N side of the entrance, and a fishing port and marina in the S part of the port enclosed by a sill.

2   **Tidal streams** off Plateau des Jaunes (48°37′N 2°34′W) begin as follows:

Interval from HW Saint Helier	Direction
−0600	ESE
−0010	W

The maximum spring rates are 3 kn and 2½ on the E and W-going streams, respectively.

Directions for entering harbour
10.103

1   From a position in clear water NW of the port the track leads SE with La Petite Muette Lighted Beacon Tower (triangle point up on green and white tower, 17 m in height) (48°35′N 2°34′W) as a headmark, or at night in its white sector (114°–146°), which leads in the approach passing (with positions given from La Petite Muette Beacon Tower):

2   SW of Basse Godiche (2 miles NNW), the SW-most danger off Plateau des Jaunes (10.110). The plateau is covered by the red sector (146°–196°) of La Petite Muette Light. Thence:

3   NW of Le Dahouët (8 cables WNW) a rock which covers and uncovers, marked on its N side by Le Dahouët Buoy (N cardinal). The numerous drying rocks and shoal patches within 1½ miles of the coast between Le Dahouet and Roches Tra–Hillion (10.70), 2½ miles SW, are covered by the green sector (055°–114°) of La Petite Muette Light.

4   The entrance channel, which dries 4·5 m, lies on either side of La Petite Muette; the N channel is the usual passage, which should be used at night. Local knowledge is required for the S channel.

   Useful mark:

   Light Beacon (green metal pylon, 6 m in height) (48°34′·8N 2°34′·2W) on the S entrance point to the harbour.

Berths
10.104

1   **Drying harbour:** 400 m long and 60 m wide with outer quay drying 5·5 m reserved for fishing vessels. Tide gauges

on the outer quay indicate the depth of water in the harbour.

Port services
10.105

1   **Facilities:** slipway; boat park; careenage area; water; provisions.

Erquy and approaches

Charts 3672 plan of Erquy, 3674

General information
10.106

1   **Position and function.** Erquy (48°38′N 2°29′W), a small port which dries, is situated 7½ cables SE of Cap d'Erquy and is used by small vessels.

2   **Topography.** Between Pointe de Pléneuf (48°36′N 2°33′W) and Cap d'Erquy, about 4 miles NE, the coast is fronted by a prominent stretch of sand nearly 4 miles long and is bordered by rocky ledges which extend up to 1 mile offshore. The cliffs between Cap d'Erquy and Cap Fréhel (10.68), 7 miles ENE, are rent by reddish fissures; they are interspersed by sandy beaches of which Grève de Minieu (10.117), the largest, lies fronting the seaside resort of Sables-d'Or-les-Pins situated midway between these two points.

3   Rohinet, 1¾ miles N of Cap d'Erquy, is a white rock which lies near the centre of an extensive rocky flat and is its highest feature. Le Grand Pourier, 5 cables NW of Rohinet, is a large mass of rock with a flat top which only covers at very high spring tides.

4   **Approach.** Erquy can be approached from W between Rohein (48°39′N 2°38′W) and Plateau des Jaunes, 2½ miles SE, from N between Petit-Léjon (48°42′N 2°37′W) and Les Landas, 4 miles E, or from E through Chenal d'Erquy (48°40′N 2°28′W) (10.112).

   The approach from W is the best approach to Erquy at night.

Limiting conditions
10.107

1   **Tidal levels,** see information in *Admiralty Tide Tables.* Mean spring range about 10·1 m; mean neap range about 4·6 m.

   Maximum size of vessel handled. The harbour is accessible to vessels with a draught of up to 2·5 m.

Arrival information
10.108

1   **Outer anchorage.** Anchorage can be obtained in Rade d'Erquy, about 8 cables S of Cap d'Erquy (48°39′N 2°29′W), in depths of between 5 and 10 m, sand and mud, with good holding ground. It is the best anchorage on this part of the coast in E winds, but should only be used in fine weather or with offshore winds. A recommended berth is shown on the chart.

   Pilotage, see 10.63.

Harbour
10.109

1   **General layout.** A mole of rough stone, 250 m in length, projects S from the coast 2½ cables ESE of Pointe des Trois Pierres (48°38′·4N 2°29′·0W) protecting the new harbour. Two cables E of the mole an inner jetty projects S protecting the old inner harbour.

   Swell. With W winds there is a heavy swell off the entrance to the harbour.

2   **Tidal streams.** At the entrance to the port the in-going stream runs ESE at a rate of about 1 kn until mid-way

between local LW and HW. At –0200 Saint Malo a counter current runs W towards the end of the jetty attaining a rate of 2 kn at HW; care should thus be exercised when approaching the jetty between these times.

Directions for entering harbour
10.110

1   **From west.** From a position S of Rohein (48°39′N 2°38′W) (10.70) the line of bearing 087½° of Erquy Molehead Light (white tower red top, 10 m in height) (48°38′N 2°29′W), or at night in its white sector (081°–094°), leads in the approach passing (with positions given from Erquy Molehead Light):

2   Between Les Comtesses (4 miles WNW) and Plateau des Jaunes (4 miles WSW), an extensive rocky plateau parts of which dry; Petit Bignon at the W edge of the plateau is marked by a beacon (W cardinal). Thence:

S of Plateau des Portes d'Erquy (2 miles W) (10.111); thence:

3   N of Les Écarets (1½ miles WSW) to the anchorage (10.108) or harbour as required.

Caution. Drying ledges extend 1½ cables W of the high yellow cliffs of Pointe des Trois Pierres (4 cables NW); their extremity is marked by a buoy (port hand).

10.111

1   **From north.** Approaching from N pass between Petit Léjon (48°42′N 2°37′W) (10.69) and Les Landas, 4 miles E, a group of rocks marked on their NW side by a light buoy (N cardinal). La Pierre du Banc is 1 mile NW and closer to the track.

The line of bearing 115½° of Erquy Molehead Light (48°38′N 2°29′W) (10.110), or at night in its white sector (111°–120°), then leads in the approach passing (with positions given from Erquy Molehead Light):

2   NNE of Basse des Comtesses (4¼ miles WNW); thence:

Between Plateau des Portes d'Erquy (2 miles W) and Cap d'Erquy (8 cables NW). L'Evette Beacon Tower (N cardinal) stands near the N end of the plateau which is covered by the green sector (094°–111°) of Erquy Molehead Light. Basse à Brouard with a least depth of 7 m over it, which lies midway between, is the controlling depth for the passage.

10.112

1   **Chenal d'Erquy** lies N of the rocks bordering the coast between Cap d'Erquy (48°39′N 2°29′W) and Îlot Saint-Michel, 2½ miles ENE, and S of the buoys marking the SE side of the extensive rocky flat (10.106) which lies SW of Plateau des Justières (48°41′N 2°27′W). The channel is suitable for navigation by day and has its least depth over a rock, with a depth of less than 4 m over it, lying 1 mile NE of Cap d'Erquy.

2   A dredging area, buoyed and shown on the charts, lies centred 2¼ miles NE of Cap d'Erquy.

Tidal streams in Chenal d'Erquy begin as follows:

Interval from HW Saint Helier	*Direction*
–0540	ENE
HW	WSW

The maximum E-going and W-going spring rates are 3 and 2½ kn, respectively.

3   **Route.** From a position N of Cap Fréhel (48°41′N 2°19′W) (10.68), clear of a wreck (10.134) which is charted 1 mile NNE of the cape, the line of bearing 243°

of Cap d'Erquy (48°39′N 2°29′W) leads in the channel passing (with positions given from Cap d'Erquy):

NNW of Amas du Cap (6¾ miles ENE), a large wedge-shaped above-water rock; thence:

4   Between La Petite Livière (4½ miles NE) and La Mouillée (4¼ miles ENE).

Leading marks:

Front mark. S edge of Amas du Cap (6¾ miles ENE). Rear mark. N extremity of Cap Fréhel, 5 cables ENE of the front mark.

5   The alignment (077°), astern, of these marks then leads in the channel passing:

NNW of Basse Saint-Michel (3¼ miles ENE); thence: Between Les Justières Light Buoy (S cardinal) (2½ miles NE), which is moored off the E side of Plateau des Justières, and the rocks bordering the coast W of Îlot Saint-Michel (2½ miles ENE) on which stands a chapel.

6   From a position on the alignment (224°) of the NW edge of Les Chatelets (close NE), two large above-water rocks, with Pointe de Pléneuf (10.99), 4 miles SW of the front mark, the track then leads SW through Chenal d'Erquy passing:

Over a 3·5 m rocky patch (1 mile NE), the controlling depth for Chenal d'Erquy; thence:

7   Between Basses du Courant (6 cables N), marked on their S side by a light buoy (S cardinal), and Les Chatelets (close NE), noting a buoy (special) moored 1 cable NE; thence:

Between Cap d'Erquy, distant about 2 cables, and a 3·4 m rocky patch (3½ cables NW).

10.113

1   **Useful marks:**

Light (red and white tower, 10 m in height) on the inner jetty head.

Church Belfry (spire) (48°37′·7N 2°24′·2W) at Plurien.

Berths
10.114

1   **New harbour:** small quay at the head of the mole reserved for fishing vessels; open quay perpendicular to the root of the mole; mooring area drying to 1 m with bottom of sand and mud. Depths alongside the E side of the mole drying 0·3 to 2·5 m.

Old harbour: jetty with good drying out berths which dry 4 to 5 m; quay perpendicular to the jetty with berths drying to 6·7 m.

The W part of each harbour is reserved for fishing vessels.

Port services
10.115

1   **Facilities:** slipways, largest 80 m in length; fuel in limited quantities; fresh water; provisions.

Rescue, see 10.65.

Minor bays

Chart 3674
Gwin Zégal
10.116

1   **General information.** A drying anchorage for about 30 small craft sheltered by Île Gwin Zégal (48°42′·2N 2°53′·7W), an islet with whitened summit, is situated W of the isle.

Landing can be obtained between two jetties SE of the anchorage.

Grève de Minieu
10.117

1   **General information.** Les Bouches d'Erquy (48°39′N 2°25′W), a small haven which dries, lies S of Pointe du Champ du Port at the W end of Grève de Minieu where several small streams flow into the sea. A jetty, not suitable for berthing, gives some protection from N and NE. The bottom, consisting of fine sand, dries 5 m but there are rocks in the vicinity. More to the N drying anchorage berths are available in Mouillage des Hôsitaux situated SSE of Îlot Saint-Michel.

2   Port Barrier, at the E end of Grève de Minieu, is used for the working of Fréhel quarries; navigation is restricted, and anchoring and fishing prohibited, in the vicinity except to vessels using the quarries.

   Approach between Roche Plate Saint-Michel (48°39′·6N 2°24′·9W) and Rocher Bénard, a dark conical above-water rock 8 cables ESE, avoiding a dangerous rock lying 3 cables SW of Rocher Bénard.

APPROACHES TO SAINT-MALO

General information

Charts 2700, 3659, 2669
Route
10.118

1   From a position N of Baie de Saint-Brieuc (10.58) the route leads generally SE, about 30 miles, to the port of Saint-Malo (10.159).

   Channels. An approach channel (10.131), 1 mile wide, leads towards Saint-Malo from a position 7¾ miles NNW of Cap Fréhel (48°41′N 2°19′W) to a position 1 mile N of Le Vieux Banc (10.131). Chenal de la Petite Porte (10.132), the NW approach and continuation of the approach channel, and Chenal de la Grande Porte (10.135), the W approach, are the two principal entrance channels and can be used by day or night; they are indicated by leading lights.

2   The other side channels (10.140 to 10.143) are only practicable by day with a rising tide, and then only with local knowledge.

Topography
10.119

1   From Cap Fréhel (48°41′N 2°19′W) (10.68) to Pointe du Grouin, 19 miles E, the coast is formed by many bays with sandy beaches, and by inlets separated by rocky headlands. Nearly midway between these points the coast recedes to form Baie de Saint-Malo (10.159). Between Cap Fréhel and Pointe du Décollé, 8½ miles ESE, the coast is deeply indented by several bays which dry.

2   Between Pointe du Décollé and Pointe de Dinard (48°38′N 2°03′W) the coast consists of sandy beaches, separated by rocky points, fronting the seaside resorts of Saint-Lunaire, Saint-Enogat and Dinard (10.182). Fronting this part of the coast is a large plateau, extending about 1½ miles offshore, containing numerous above-water rocks and dangers.

3   The town of Saint-Malo is surrounded by ramparts and dominated by its conspicuous cathedral (10.130). It is fronted by a drying reef, extending 5 cables offshore, on which stand several useful marks.

Between Pointe du Meinga (48°42′N 1°56′W), consisting of a steep cliff on which stands a water tower, and Pointe du Grouin, 3½ miles ENE, the coast is high, rocky and interspersed with sandy beaches.

Controlling depths
10.120

1   **Chenal de la Petite Porte:** 10·5 m.
   Chenal de la Grande Porte: 6·2 m.

High speed craft
10.121

1   Mariners are advised to maintain a good lookout for these craft, see 1.7.

Temporary explosives dumping grounds
10.122

1   Temporary explosives dumping grounds (Zones de Dépôts d'Explosifs) for Saint-Jacut and Saint-Cast (10.153) are situated N of Saint-Cast Signal Station (48°38′N 2°15′W) and for Saint-Malo, SW of Rochefort Beacon Tower (48°43′N 1°58′W).

   For details see 1.7 and Appendix V.

Pilotage
10.123

1   **Compulsory pilotage area.** Saint-Malo compulsory pilotage area limits are bounded by the following:

     West limit. A line joining Cap d'Erquy (48°39′N 2°29′W) to Grand Léjon, 9 miles NW.

     North limit. The parallel of Basse Grune (48°45′N).

     East limit. The meridian of Mont Doll (1°46′W).

2   Pilots for Le Guildo (10.146), Dinard (10.182), La Rance (10.183) and Cancale (10.205) can also be obtained from the pilot station at Saint-Malo.

   Pilotage is compulsory in the above area for vessels over 45 m LOA and all vessels carrying dangerous and polluting substances.

3   **Pilot boarding place.** Pilot boards in position 48°42′N 2°07′W, about 1 mile N of Atterrage Saint-Malo Light Buoy, as shown on the chart. Mariners are recommended to arrive at the light buoy ½ hour before local HW if bound for Saint-Malo; a waiting area is established E of the boarding point.

   In bad weather, particulary during N gales when boarding is impracticable, the pilot vessel will lead mariners into port, communicating with them by VHF.

4   **Availability.** Pilots are available throughout the locking times.

   Notification. Send ETA and draught 6 hours in advance, confirming ETA 2 hours before arrival.

   Pilot vessel: black hull, white upperworks with lettering PILOTE SM.

   For further details see *Admiralty List of Radio Signals Volume 6(1)*.

Local knowledge
10.124

1   The approaches to Saint-Malo are well marked by lights, buoys and beacons, but they are obstructed with numerous islets and dangers extending up to 3 miles offshore. Apart from Chenal de la Grande Porte and Chenal de la Petite Port, the two principal entrance channels which can be used by day or night, the other channels are only practicable by day with a rising tide; local knowledge is required for their use.

Traffic regulations
10.125

1   **Approach channel** (10.131), shown on the chart, leads to Saint-Malo from a position 7¾ miles NNW of Cap Frehel (48°41′N 2°19′W). The use of the approach channel is compulsory for vessels over 1600 gt laden with hydrocarbons or with dangerous substances, for details see 1.68.

   From the SE end of the approach channel mariners in these vessels must follow Chenal de la Petite Porte (10.132) and thereafter as instructed by the pilot and if required to wait are advised to use the charted waiting area.

2   Saint-Cast Signal Station (48°39′N 2°15′W) is designated for communication between mariners using the approach channel and the Port Authorities. Mariners in vessels over 1600 gt laden with dangerous and polluting goods should inform the port of their entry into the approach channel, maintain a continuous watch on VHF and contact Saint-Cast Signal Station.

3   For details see *Admiralty List of Radio Signals Volume 6(1)*.

10.126

1   **Prohibited areas.** Due to the existence of underwater explosives, traffic and anchoring are prohibited within an area of 100 m around Île de Cézembre (48°41′N 2°04′W) (10.139) extending from the HW mark, except for the access channel to the jetty, the E and W limits of which are marked by the transits of beacons on the island and shown on the chart.

2   Anchoring, fishing and stopping are prohibited in the pilot waiting area and in the main approach channels to, and in, Rade de Saint-Malo and Rade de Dinard, as shown on the chart.

3   Diving is prohibited on the wreck (10.134) 1 mile NNE of Cap Frehel (48°41′N 2°19′W).

Rescue
10.127

1   **All-weather lifeboat,** see 10.181.

   Inshore lifeboats are stationed at:

      Saint-Cast (48°38′N 2°15′W) (10.153).

      Lancieux (48°37′N 2°09′W) (10.155).

      Saint-Briac-sur-Mer (48°37′N 2°08′W) (10.156).

2   **Signal station** (Sémaphore) is situated on Pointe de Saint-Cast (48°39′N 2°15′W).

   For details regarding lifeboats see 1.117 and for signal stations 1.95 and 1.110.

   VHF Direction-finding service, for emergency use only, operates from the signal station on Pointe de Saint-Cast, for details see *Admiralty List of Radio Signals Volume 2*.

Natural conditions
10.128

1   **Tidal streams — west approaches.** Between Cap Frehel (48°41′N 2°19′W) and Pointe du Décollé, 8½ miles ESE, the tidal streams begin as follows:

Interval from HW Saint Helier	Direction
Near Le Catis (48°43′N 2°15′W):	
−0515	ESE
+0045	WNW

2   The maximum E-going and W-going spring rates are 2½ and 2¼ kn, respectively.

Interval from HW Saint Helier	Direction
Near Banchenou (48°40′N 2°11′W):	
−0555	ESE
−0015	NW

   The maximum spring rate in each direction is 2½ kn.

   About 1½ miles N of Cap Frehel:

−0525	ESE
−0030	WNW

   The maximum spring rate in each direction is 3¾ kn.

3   In the bays, and along the coast generally between Cap Frehel and Pointe du Décollé, W-going eddies, which do not extend far offshore, run during the greater part of the E-going stream. The direction of the E-going stream depends on the trend of the coast and its duration is very variable.

4   **Channels.** In Chenal de la Grande Porte tidal streams in the outer part of the channel as far as Le Grand Jardin (48°40′N 2°05′W) follow the direction of the channel, but in the inner part, between Le Grand Jardin and Le Buron, 1¼ miles SE, they set across the channel; SE of Le Buron they gradually change to the direction of the channel. They begin as follows:

Interval from HW Saint Helier	Direction
−0510	E
+0030	W

   The maximum spring rate in each direction is 3¾ kn.

5   In Chenal de la Petite Porte the tidal streams set obliquely across the channel attaining a maximum spring rate of about 3 kn; they begin as follows in the vicinity of Le Vieux Banc (48°42′N 2°10′W).

Interval from HW Saint Helier	Direction
−0510	E
+0030	W

   The maximum spring rate in each direction is 3 kn.

6   **Rade de Saint-Malo.** Tidal streams begin as follows:

Interval from HW Saint Helier	Direction
−0525	SSE
HW	NNW

   The maximum in-going and out-going spring rates are 2½ and 2¼ kn, respectively.

7   **Rade de Dinard.** The in-going stream runs at first towards Pointe de la Vicomté, the S entrance point to Baie du Prieuré, but later as the sands in the bay cover, it runs clockwise round the bay.

   The direction and rates are greatly influenced by the operation of the turbines or sluices of the hydro-electric power station in the barrage of La Rance (10.183).

8   See also *Admiralty Tidal Stream Atlas for the Channel Islands and the adjacent coasts of France* and information on the chart.

10.129

1   **Local weather.** The approach to Baie de Saint-Malo is obstructed with numerous islets, rocks and shoals, between which there are several passages which are well marked by lights, beacons and buoys, and indicated by leading marks. The approach, however, is dangerous in low visibility.

Le Grand Jardin Lighthouse from WSW (10.130)

(Original dated 2003)

(Photograph - Captain H. Townsend)

Directions
(continued from 10.18)

Principal marks
10.130

1   **Landmarks:**
     Cap Fréhel (48°41′N 2°19′W) (10.68).
     Fort (tower) (48°40′N 2°17′W) on Pointe de la Latte.
     Le Grand Jardin Lighthouse (grey truncated conical tower red top, 38 m in height) (48°40′N 2°05′W).
     Rochebonne Lighthouse (grey square tower W face white, red top, 20 m in height) (48°40′N 1°59′W).

2   Saint-Malo Cathedral (spire) (48°39′·0N 2°01′·5W).
     Les Bas-Sablons Lighthouse (white square tower black top, 19 m in height) (48°38′N 2°01′W)
     La Balue Lighthouse (grey square tower, 37 m in height) (48°38′N 2°00′W).
     Radio Mast (48°40′N 1°58′W).
     Water Tower (48°38′N 1°55′W).
     Water Tower (48°41′N 1°52′W).

3   Pointe du Grouin (48°43′N 1°51′W) (10.194).
   Major lights:
     Cap Fréhel Light (48°41′N 2°19′W) (10.68).
     Le Grand Jardin Light — as above.
     Rochebonne Light — as above.
     Les Bas-Sablons Light — as above.
     La Balue Light — as above.

Charts 3659, 2669
Approach channel
10.131

1   From a position N of Grand Léjon (48°45′N 2°40′W) (10.69) the track leads ESE passing (with positions given from Cap Fréhel (48°41′N 2°19′W)):

SSW of a light buoy (special) (13½ miles NNW) (11.190); thence:

SSW of Brisants du Sud (14 miles N), the SW-most dangers on Plateau des Minquiers (11.243); SW Minquiers Light Buoy (W cardinal) is moored 1¾ miles SW.

2   The track then enters the approach channel to Saint-Malo, as shown on the chart, about 7¾ miles NNW of Cap Fréhel and continues ESE in the approach channel passing:

Between Basse des Sauvages (6 miles NE) and La Catis (3 miles ENE); thence:

3   NNE of Le Vieux Banc (6 miles E), a rocky ledge marked on its SW side by a light buoy (W cardinal). Basse NE du Vieux Banc lies on the NE part of the ledge and is marked on its NE side by a light buoy (N cardinal). Thence:

To the pilot boarding place (10.123).
(Directions for Granville continue at 10.194)

Charts 2700, 3659
Chenal de la Petite Porte
10.132

1   **Leading lights:**
     Front. Le Grand Jardin Light (48°40′N 2°05′W) (10.130).
     Rear. La Balue Light (4 miles SE of the front light) (10.130).

From a position about 7 cables SW of the pilot boarding place (10.123) the alignment (129¾°) of these lights, as shown on the chart, leads in the channel passing (with positions given from the front light):

2   Close NE of Atterrage Saint-Malo Light Buoy (safe water) (2 miles NW); thence:

Between La Grande Hupée (9 cables NW) and Rat des Courtis (9 cables WNW); the shoaler La Nouvelle Découverte lies 1 cable SW and farther from the track. Thence:

Close NE of Basse NE des Portes (5 cables WNW); Les Courtis Lighted Beacon Tower (starboard hand, 21 m in height) stands 1 cable WSW. Thence:

3   NE of Basses à Louise (4½ cables WNW).

When Le Grand Jardin Light bears 129¾°, distant about 4 cables, the track leads 158¼° for about 1½ cables as shown on the chart, or at night, on the line of bearing 092° of Rochebonne Light (4¼ miles E) (10.130) open S of Île de Cézembre (4 cables NE), or alternatively, when E of Les Courtis Lighted Beacon Tower (6 cables WNW), the track leads generally SE, to join the inner part (10.138) of Chenal de la Grande Porte.

Chenal du Bunel
10.133
1   Chenal de la Petite Porte can be approached from N, using Chenal du Bunel, and joined NW of Le Grand Jardin. From position 48°42'·3N 2°06'·5W, 5 cables ESE of the pilot boarding position, the route leads SSE for 2 miles.
Leading lights.
Front light Saint-Énogat Light (white metal mast, 4 m in height) (48°38'·4N 2°04'·0W).
2   Rear light Dinard Water Tower (white tower, 35 m in height) (1½ miles SSE of front light).

The alignment (158¼°) of these lights leads through Chenal du Bunel passing (positions given from Le Bunel (48°40'·8N 2°05'·1W)):
ENE of La Petite Hupée (4 cables WNW):
3   WSW of Le Bunel, marked on its NW side by a light buoy (W cardinal):
ENE of Basse NE des Portes (10.132), where the route joins Chenal de la Petite Porte (10.132).

Charts 3659, 2669
Approaching from west
10.134
1   Approaching from W pass at least 2 miles N of Cap Fréhel (48°41'N 2°19'W) (10.68) clear of a wreck (position approximate) with a depth of 20·7 m over it, charted 1 mile NNE of the cape, N of Le Catis (48°42'·5N 2°14'·7W) and thence between Le Vieux Banc (48°42'N 2°10'W) (10.131) and Banchenou, 2 miles SSW, a rocky patch marked on its N side by a light buoy (N cardinal), noting a dangerous wreck (existence doubtful) charted 1 mile NNW, and a dangerous wreck (position approximate) 4 cables W, of Banchenou, to Chenal de la Grande Porte (10.135).
2   **Clearing bearing:**
The line of bearing 276° of Le Grand Léjon Light (48°45'N 2°40'W) (10.68), astern, clears N of Cap Fréhel and associated dangers.

Charts 2700, 3659
Chenal de la Grande Porte — outer part
10.135
1   **Leading lights:**
Front. Le Grand Jardin Light (48°40'N 2°05'W) (10.130).
Rear. Rochebonne Light (4¼ miles E of the front light) (10.130).
From a position SE of Banchenou (48°40'N 2°11'W) (10.134) the alignment (089°) of these lights leads in the channel passing (with positions given from the front light):
2   N of La Folette (2½ miles W); thence:

S of Les Buharats (1½ miles W) marked on their S and SW sides, respectively, by Buharats Est No 4 Buoy (port hand) and Buharats Ouest No 2 Light Buoy (port hand); thence:
Very close N of 6·4 m rock (1¼ miles W) thence:
3   Between Les Couillons de la Porte (9½ cables W), noting Les Couillons de la Porte No 6 Buoy (port hand) moored nearly 2 cables E of the shoal, and Basse à Colas (9½ cables W); thence:
N of Basse du Boujaron (7 cables W) marked on its N side by No 1 Light Buoy (starboard hand). Le Boujaron Beacon Tower (starboard hand) stands on a drying reef ¾ cable SW of the shoal. Thence:
4   S of Les Pierres des Portes (7 cables WNW) marked by a beacon tower (port hand); thence:
Between Fontaines des Portes (5½ cables WNW) and a 1·7 m rock (5 cables W); thence:
N of a 5·5 m wreck (3 cables WSW) marked on its NE side by Le Sou Light Buoy (E cardinal). Le Sou a drying rock lies 1 cable SE of the wreck.
5   When Le Grand Jardin Light bears 089°, distant about 2¾ cables, the track then alters gradually SE after Le Buron Lighted Beacon Tower (1¼ miles SE) is open SW of La Balue Light (48°38'N 2°00'W) (10.130) passing between Le Grand Jardin, marked on its SW side by a beacon (port hand), and a 6·1 m rocky patch at the NW end of Banc de la Traversaine (1¼ cables SW) to join the inner part (10.138) of the channel on the alignment (128½°) of Les Bas-Sablons and La Balue Leading Lights.
10.136
1   **Alternative leading marks — by day:**
Front mark. Les Cheminées (rock) (48°39'·7N 2°06'·0W).
Rear mark. Saint-Malo Cathedral (3 miles ESE of the front mark) (10.130).
From a position between Banchenou (48°40'N 2°11'W) and a dangerous wreck (10.134), charted 1 mile NNW, the alignment (104½°) of these marks leads in the outer approach to join the alignment (089°) of Le Grand Jardin and Rochebonne Leading Lights NNE of La Folette (48°40'N 2°09'W).

Approaching from east
10.137
1   **General information.** Approaching from E pass at least 4 miles N of the coast W of Pointe du Grouin (48°43'N 1°50'W) (10.194) passing N of Basse Grune, which lies 3 miles NW of the point, to the pilot boarding place (10.123). Numerous dangers extend 2 miles NE from Pointe du Grouin terminating at La Fille (10.195).
2   **Clearing marks:**
Front mark. Rochefort Beacon Tower (W cardinal, 8 m in height) (48°42'·9N 1°58'·2W).
Rear mark. Pierre de Herpin Lighted Beacon Tower (6¼ miles E of the front mark) (10.194).
The alignment (082°) of these marks clears N of the offlying dangers between Pointe du Meinga (48°42'N 1°56'W) and Pointe de la Varde, 2½ miles SW, apart from Basse Rault which lies 1½ miles N of Pointe du Meinga.

Chart 2700
Chenal de la Grande Porte — inner part
10.138
1   **Leading lights:**
Front. Les Bas-Sablons Direction Light (48°38'N 2°01'W) (10.130).
Rear. La Balue Direction Light (9 cables SE of the front light) (10.130).

2 From a position between Le Grand Jardin (48°40'N 2°05'W) and a 6·1 m rocky patch, 1¼ cables SW, the alignment (128½°) of these lights, which are intensified near their alignment and shown throughout 24 hours, leads in the inner part of the channel passing (with positions given from Le Petit Bé (48°39'N 2°02'W)):

NE of Banc de la Traversaine (2 miles WNW); thence:

3 SW of Les Pierres Garnier (1¾ miles WNW), marked on their S side by No 8 Buoy (port hand); thence:

NE of Les Patouillets (1½ miles WNW), marked on their E side by a light buoy (starboard hand); thence:

SW of Les Clefs d'Aval (1¼ miles WNW), marked on their SW side by No 10 Buoy (port hand); thence:

4 SW of La Chevalière (9 cables WNW); thence:

Between Basse du Buron (8 cables WNW), marked on its W side by No 12 Light Buoy (port hand), and Le Buron Lighted Beacon Tower (starboard hand, 23 m in height) (9 cables W); thence:

5 Between La Cointière (6 cables WNW) and La Couillemandière (8 cables W); thence:

SW of Les Grelots, marked on the SW side by Les Grelots Light Buoy (S cardinal); thence:

To Rade de Saint-Malo or the harbour (10.177) as required.

Charts 2700, 3659

Useful marks

10.139

1 **Approach channel:**

Grand Léjon Light (48°45'N 2°40'W) (10.68).

Grande Île Light (48°52'N 1°49'W) (10.194).

La Plate Lighted Beacon Tower (N cardinal 22 m in height) (48°41'N 2°02'W).

Chenal de la Petite Porte:

Île de Cézembre (two rounded summits) (48°40'·7N 2°04'·2W).

2 **Chenal de la Grande Porte:**

Saint-Cast Molehead Light (green and white structure, 9 m in height) (48°38'·5N 2°14'·5W).

Île Argot (wedge-shaped and grass covered, sheer on its SW side) (48°38'·4N 2°09'·5W).

Chenal de la Grande Porte — inner part:

Île de Harbour (fort ruins) (48°39'·2N 2°04'·1W).

3 Le Petit Bé (islet with fort surmounted by a house) (48°39'·2N 2°02'·2W).

Le Grand Bé (islet) (48°39'·2N 2°01'·9W).

Le Fort National (48°39'·4N 2°01'·3W).

Light (48°38'·6N 2°01'·8W) (10.177) at the head of Môle des Noires.

(Directions continue at 10.177)

Side channels

Chenal du Décollé

10.140

1 **General information.** Chenal du Décollé, a W approach which leads close N of Pointe du Décollé (48°39'N 2°07'W) (10.119), is bordered by numerous dangers and can only be used by day and with a rising tide. The channel lies close inshore passing between Pointe de Dinard (48°38'N 2°03'W) and Banc des Pourceaux, close N, and leads into Rade de Dinard (10.144); it is obstructed by a bank, drying 3·9 m, N of Pointe de Dinard.

2 **Local knowledge** is required, see 10.124.

Tidal streams run similarly to those in Chenal de La Grande Porte (10.128).

Leading marks. From a position NE of Nerput (48°39'·2N 2°08'·0W), a drying rock marked by a beacon tower (E cardinal) near the outer edge of the dangers extending N from Pointe de la Garde Guérin, the alignment (133°) of the following marks leads in the outer part of the channel:

3 Front mark. Le Grand Genillet Beacon Tower (white) (48°38'·7N 2°05'·8W).

Rear mark. La Roche Pélée Beacon Tower (white) (7 cables SE of the front mark).

Chenal de la Grande Conchée

10.141

1 **General information.** Chenal de la Grande Conchée (48°41'N 2°02'W), the N approach, should only be used by day and with a rising tide.

Local knowledge is required, see 10.124.

Tidal streams run similarly to those in Chenal des Petits Pointus (10.142).

2 **Leading marks.** From a position about 2½ miles W of Rochefort Beacon Tower (48°42'·9N 1°58'·2W) (10.137) the alignment (181½°) of the following marks leads through the channel to a position close E of Roches aux Anglais Light Buoy (starboard hand), 5 cables N of Le Petit Bé.

Front mark. East side of Le Petit Bé (48°39'·2N 2°02'·2W) (10.139).

Rear mark. Villa Brisemoulin (1½ miles S of the front mark).

3 **Useful marks:**

La Grande Conchée (48°41'·1N 2°02'·6W) on which stands a square fort in ruins.

La Plate (48°40'·9N 2°01'·8W), a drying reef upon which stands a lighted beacon tower (10.139).

Chenal des Petits Pointus

10.142

1 **General information.** Chenal des Petits Pointus (48°41'N 2°01'W), the NNE approach, should only be used by day with a rising tide and in very good visibility.

Local knowledge is required, see 10.124.

Tidal streams set obliquely across the channel, beginning as follows:

Interval from HW Saint Helier	*Direction*
–0540	E
HW	WSW

2 The maximum E-going and WSW-going spring rates are 2½ and 1½ kn, respectively.

Directions. From a position about 1¼ miles W of Rochefort Beacon Tower (48°42'·9N 1°58'·2W) (10.137) the line of bearing 203° of Dinard Church (spire) (48°37'·7N 2°03'·3W) open to the right of Le Petit Bé, 1¾ miles NNE, leads through the channel to its junction with Chenal de la Bigne (10.143) about 7 cables NNE of Le Petit Bé.

3 **Useful marks:**

Les Grands Pointus (48°42'·0N 1°59'·6W).

La Plate Lighted Beacon Tower (48°40'·9N 2°01'·8W) (10.139).

Chenal de la Bigne

10.143

1 **General information.** Chenal de la Bigne (48°41'N 1°59'W), the NE approach, has depths less than 5 m and should only be used by day with a rising tide and good visibility.

Local knowledge is required, see 10.124.

Tidal streams run approximately in the direction of the channel, beginning as follows:

Interval from HW Saint Helier	Direction
–0540	ENE
HW	SW

2 The maximum ENE-going and SW-going spring rates are 2¾ and 1½ kn, respectively.

Leading marks:

Front mark. La Crolante Beacon Tower (white) (48°41′·1N 1°59′·4W) standing close W of Pointe de la Varde, a low point which rises to a cliff at its extremity.

Rear mark. NW part of Le Grand Bé (2½ miles SW of the front mark (10.139).

3 From a position W of Basse Grune (48°45′N 1°54′W) the alignment (222°) of these marks leads in the approach for a distance of about 5 miles passing clear of a number of offshore shoals; thence:

Between La Petite Bigne (48°41′·7N 1°58′·7W), marked by a beacon (starboard hand), and the rocky drying area extending NNW from Le Bénétin, 4 cables SE, passing close SE of the former danger, to a position about 2 cables S of La Bigne, a conical rock standing about 1½ cables W of La Petite Bigne.

4 **Leading marks:**

Front mark. Le Buron Lighted Beacon Tower (48°39′·4N 2°03′·6W) (10.138).

Rear mark. SE corner of Villa Lonick (1¾ miles SW of the front mark) on Pointe Bellefard.

The alignment (236°) of these marks then leads in the channel for a distance of 2½ miles to join Chenal de la Grand Conchée, 8 cables S of La Plate (48°40′·8N 2°01′·9W) passing (with positions given from Le Petit Bé (48°39′·2N 2°02′·2W)):

5 Between Les Létruns (48°40′·8N 2°00′·5W), drying rocks marked on their SE side by a buoy (starboard hand), and La Cornée, a 0·8 m rock; thence:

NW of Grand Dodehal (9 cables NE), marked by a beacon (port hand); thence:

NW, and subsequently W, of Petit Dodehal (6 cables NNE).

6 When La Plate Lighted Beacon Tower (10.139) bears 194° the track follows the alignment (181½°) of the leading marks for Chenal de la Conchée (10.141) to a position close E of Roches aux Anglais Light Buoy (10.141).

The line of bearing 221° of Saint-Énogat Church (cupola-shaped belfry) (48°38′·2N 2°04′·1W) then leads in the channel passing:

7 SE of Les Roches aux Anglais (5 cables N), marked on their SE side by a light buoy (starboard hand); thence:

Close NW of Les Crapauds du Bé (2 cables NNW), marked on their NW side by a buoy (port hand); thence:

SE of Les Grelots (5 cables WNW) to Rade de Saint-Malo or the harbour (10.177) as required.

8 **Useful marks:**

Rochefort Beacon Tower (48°42′·9N 1°58′·2W) (10.137).

Grand Chevreuil (rock with rounded summit surmounted by a turret) (48°41′·9N 1°57′·2W).

Anchorages and moorings

Rade de Dinard
10.144

There are four mooring buoys for large vessels in Rade de Dinard (48°38′N 2°02′W).

Rade de Solidor
10.145

1 **General information.** Rade de Solidor between Anse de Solidor (48°38′N 2°01′W) and Banc de Solidor is reserved in principle for the use of small vessels of the French Navy. There are some naval moorings at the N end of the anchorage which may be occasionally released temporarily for use by other vessels.

2 Anse de Solidor, which dries, contains several yacht moorings.

An area used occasionally for fish farms is situated on Banc de Solidor as shown on the chart.

Le Guildo and approaches

Charts 3659, 2669
General information
10.146

1 **Position and function.** Le Guildo (48°35′N 2°13′W), a small tidal harbour used occasionally by coasters, lies within the mouth of Rivière de l'Arguenon which flows into the head of Baie de l'Arguenon.

2 **Topography.** Between Pointe de Saint-Cast (48°39′N 2°15′W), a high steep headland on the summit of which stands a signal station consisting of a white house and mast, and Pointe de la Haye, 3¾ miles ESE, the coast is deeply indented by two large bays which are separated by the peninsula of Saint Jacut de la Mer which terminates at its N end in Pointe du Chevet (48°37′N 2°12′W). Île des Hébihens (10.155) lies about 5 cables N of Pointe du Chevet, with numerous dangers between it and the point. La Nellière, an islet, and L'Arganon and Les Oitellières, two drying reefs each marked by a beacon (W cardinal), lie near the NW and W extremities of the drying reef extending W from Île des Hébihens.

3 Baie de l'Arguenon, the W bay, is entered between Pointe du Bay (48°36′·7N 2°13′·7W) and Pointe du Chevet, 1¼ miles E; the bay dries completely within these points. Anse de Saint-Cast (10.153) lies S of Pointe de Saint-Cast.

4 Between Pointe du Chevet and Pointe de la Haye, 2¼ miles NE, the coast is indented deeply by Baie de Lancieux (10.155), the E bay, and by the estuary of Rivière Le Frémur (10.156), the approach to both of which is obstructed by several rocks and shoals; they are suitable only for small craft.

Limiting conditions
10.147

1 **Controlling depth.** The channel leading to the port is about 1 cable wide and dries 7·0 m; the harbour is about 1 cable wide at HW.

Tidal levels, see information in *Admiralty Tide Tables.* Mean spring range for Saint-Cast (48°38′N 2°15′W) about 10·6 m; mean neap range about 5·0 m.

2 **Maximum size of vessel handled.** Le Guildo is accessible at spring tides by vessels of 4·5 m draught with a LOA of less than 55 m.

Arrival information
10.148

1 **Pilotage** for Le Guildo is compulsory for vessels over 45 m in length. Pilots are embarked off Saint-Malo, for details see 10.123. Mariners must give at least 12 hours notice of their ETA in order to arrange pilotage.

Local knowledge is required.

Harbour
10.149

1 **Shellfish beds** extend across the entrance to the bay.

Tidal streams in the approach begin as follows:

Interval from HW Saint Helier	*Direction*
Off Pointe de Saint-Cast:	
−0540	SSE
−0515	NNW
Off Les Bourdinots:	
−0540	SE
−0045	NW

The maximum spring rate in each direction is 2 kn off Pointe de Saint-Cast and 2¾ kn off Les Bourdinots (48°39′N 2°13′W).

2 Off Pointe de Saint-Cast, although the SE-going stream begins at the same time as off Les Bourdinots, it runs for about ½ hour only, and the NW-going stream begins about 4½ hours earlier than that off Les Bourdinots.

In Baie de l'Arguenon, when the passage between Île des Hébihens and the land is covered, the stream runs continuously SW.

Directions for entering harbour
10.150

1 Baie de l'Arguenon is entered from seaward keeping W of the drying reef to the W of Île des Hébihens (48°37′·5N 2°11′·3W) and W of L'Arganon (48°37′·2N 2°12′·7W) a drying rock with a ruined beacon standing on it, and marked close SSW by L'Arganon Light Buoy (W cardinal), thence through the channel between the mussel beds until W of a beacon (isolated danger) standing 2 miles SSW of Pointe du Chevet. The channel is subject to frequent changes.

2 **Useful marks:**
La Grande Roche (48°36′·8N 2°12′·4W), an islet with two summits connected by a saddle, 13 m in height (charted 10 m).
La Petite Roche (48°35′·6N 2°12′·0W).

Berths
10.151

1 **General information.** Quay on the W bank dries up to 6 m to a bottom of mud.

Port services
10.152

1 **Supplies:** fuel oil and marine diesel oil; fresh water.

Anse de Saint-Cast
10.153

1 **Anse de Saint-Cast** is entered between Pointe de Saint-Cast (48°39′N 2°15′W) and Pointe de la Garde, 1 mile SSE. The bay is shallow and dries out to a sandy bottom up to 3 cables offshore. It is exposed to NE winds and affords poor anchorage.

Tidal streams in the bay are predominately N-going attaining a spring rate of about 2 kn.

2 **Harbour.** Saint-Cast Harbour, protected by a mole 160 m in length, lies 2½ cables S of Pointe de Saint-Cast and has depths of from 1 m to drying 2·5 m; a light (10.139) is exhibited from the head of the mole. Les Bourdinots (48°39′N 2°13′W) which are marked on their NE side by a buoy (E cardinal) and covered by the green sector (217°–233°) of Saint-Cast Molehead Light lie in the approaches to the harbour. Off the entrance there are two rocks; Bec Rond (whitened summit), marked off its NE side by a beacon (port hand), lies 2 cables SSW of the molehead and Le Feuillade, marked by a beacon (isolated danger), lies midway between it and the jetty. There are 37 anchorage berths reserved for fishing vessels.

3 **Port services:** landing slip which dries; fuel; fresh water; provisions.

Rescue, see 10.127.

Minor bays and harbours

Chart 3659
Baie de la Fresnaye
10.154

1 **General information.** Baie de la Fresnaye, the greater part of which dries to a sandy bottom, is entered between Pointe de la Latte (48°40′N 2°17′W) (10.130) and Pointe de Saint-Cast, 2¼ miles ESE (10.146). Banc Chelin, a gravel bank, lies 5 cables NNW of Pointe de Saint-Cast; in the vicinity of this point drying rocks extend up to 2 cables offshore.

2 **Tidal streams** in the bay are predominately N-going, attaining a maximum spring rate of about 3 kn. In Anse des Sévignés, close W, the streams begin as follows:

Interval from HW Saint Helier	*Direction*
−0540	SE
−0445	NW

The maximum spring rate in each direction is 1 kn.

3 Between Basses de la Latte, 3 cables N of Pointe de la Latte, and the coast the streams attain a rate of 2¾ kn in each direction; the NW-going stream begins about 2¼ hours later.

Shellfish beds extend across the bay abreast Pointe de la Touche, 1¼ miles SSW of Pointe de la Latte; mussel beds, in the centre of the bay, are marked by buoys.

4 **Anchorage,** sheltered from W winds, can be obtained close S of Pointe de la Latte in good holding ground of sand and mud. A 7·5 m wreck, marked by Laplace Buoy (isolated danger) lies 6 cables SE of the point.

Landing can be made at a slip on the S side of Pointe de la Touche; the end of the slip dries 3·5 m.

Harbour. Port Nieux (48°37′·8N 2°19′·1W), a small port on the NW shore of the bay, is sheltered from E by Pointe du Muret. It has a quay and a small jetty which dry 7·8 m to a bottom of muddy sand.

Baie de Lancieux
10.155

1 **General information.** Baie de Lancieux is entered between Pointe du Chevet (48°37′N 2°12′W) and Pointe de Lancieux, 1¼ miles E; it dries completely.

Rescue, see 10.127.

2 **Tidal streams** run regularly into and out of Baie de Lancieux beginning as follows:

Interval from HW Saint Helier	*Direction*
−0540	S
HW	N

The maximum in-going and out-going spring rates are 2¾ kn.

There is no eddy E of Île des Hébihens

3   **Approach:** between Île des Hébihens (tower on summit) (48°37'·5N 2°11'·3W), from which Les Haches, a chain of above-water and drying rocks terminating in Portes des Hébihens, extend 5 cables N, and Les Platus, rock which dries 5·5 m, marked on its W side by Les Platus Buoy (W cardinal), 5 cables ENE, keeping clear of the several isolated rocks, marked by beacons.

4   **Submarine cable** is laid between the S end of Île des Hébihens and the NE side of the peninsula of Saint-Jacut-de-la-Mer; anchoring, dredging and trawling is prohibited within 100 m of the cable, as shown on the chart.

5   **Harbours.** La Houle-Causseul (48°36'·3N 2°11'·1W), a small port which dries and is only suitable for small craft, lies on the NE side of the peninsula of Saint-Jacut-de-la-Mer. There is a short slip which dries 5·8 m at its head and 11 m at its root.

Port du Châtelet (48°36'·0N 2°11'·0W) lies about 4 cables S of La Houle-Causseul. It is protected from E by a jetty which dries 8 m at its head.

Chart 2700
Saint-Briac-sur-Mer
10.156

1   **General information.** Saint-Briac-sur-Mer (48°37'N 2°08'W), a small port which dries to a sandy bottom, lies on the E bank of Rivière Le Frémur near its mouth, and has several drying-out places.

Tidal streams between Île Agot (48°38'N 2°10'W) and the mainland begin as follows:

Interval from HW Saint Helier	Direction
–0540	NNE
–0300	SW

The maximum in-going and out-going spring rates are 2¾ kn.

2   **Approach.** From a position about 2 cables N of Portes des Hébihens (10.155) the line of bearing 125° of the centre of the white sector (124½°–125½°) of Embouchure du Frémur Direction Light (white mast on hut, 6 m in height) (48°37'N 2°08'W) at Saint-Briac leads in the approach passing between Les Herplux and La Moulière, each marked by a beacon (port hand and N cardinal, respectively) lying 1¾ and 1½ miles NW, respectively, of the direction light, thence in the channel to the port. A bridge with a vertical clearance of 8 m spans the river close S of the direction light.

3   **Anchorage,** sheltered except with winds from NW to NE, can be obtained S of Île Argot (10.139) and W of Île du Perron in depths of 7 to 8 m sand. A number of drying anchorages for small craft exist in the approaches to the port for which the chart is the best guide.

Drying-out places. There are three drying out places with a total of 1000 berths; Le Petit-Porte, nearest the village, has a landing slip which dries from 8 to 9 m.

Rescue, see 10.127.

Chart 2700
Île de Cézembre
10.157

1   For details of a prohibited area around Île de Cézembre (48°41'N 2°04'W), see 10.126.

Chart 3659
Havre de Rothéneuf
10.158

1   **General information.** Havre de Rothéneuf (48°41'N 1°57'W), a small haven which is well sheltered but dries completely, is entered between Pointe de Rothéneuf and Île Besnard, 1½ cables NE, on the summit of which stands the white house of a disused signal station.

2   **Approach.** From Chenal de la Bigne (10.143) the line of bearing 163° of a disused mill (white tower) standing about 1 mile SSE of Île Besnard leads close E of Le Roger, a drying rock lying 6 cables NNW of Île Besnard. The line of bearing 161° of the disused mill then leads between Île Besnard and a rock, marked by a beacon (starboard hand) lying ½ cable W.

SAINT-MALO

General information

Chart 2700
Position
10.159

1   The port of Saint-Malo (48°39'N 2°01'W) lies at the head of Baie de Saint-Malo, entered between Pointe du Décollé (48°39'N 2°07'W) and Pointe du Meinga, 8 miles NE (10.119).

Function
10.160

1   The port has an important import trade and is a major fishing port; ferry services operate from the port to Channel Islands and to the United Kingdom mainland.

Port limits
10.161

1   The outer port limits extend generally NNW from the head of Môle des Noires (48°38'·5N 2°01'·9W) to the vicinity of Le Petit Bé, 7 cables NNW; thence generally W to the vicinity of Île de Harbour; thence generally SE to Pointe de la Vicomté, as shown on the chart.

Approach and entry
10.162

1   The port is entered on crossing the port limits E of Le Buron Lighted Beacon Tower (48°39'N 2°04'W). The harbour is approached from Rade de Saint-Malo and entered between the head of Môle des Noires and the ferry terminal, 1 cable SE.

Traffic
10.163

1   In 2006, apart from ferries, 374 vessels used the port totalling 1 290 680 dwt.

Port Authority
10.164

1   Département Ille-et-Vilaine, Arrondissement Territorial et Maritime de Saint-Malo, 1 Rue de la Crosse, PO Box 9, F–35402, Saint-Malo.

Limiting conditions

Controlling depths
10.165

1   **Approach channel to Ferry Terminal:** 3·8 m.
    Approach channel to Écluse du Naye: less than 3 m.

Deepest and longest berths
10.166
1   **Avant-port:** Car Ferry Terminal (10.178).
    Wet basins: Quai des Corsaires in Bassin Vauban (10.179).

Tidal levels
10.167
1   Mean spring range about 11·0 m; mean neap range about 5·1 m. For further information see *Admiralty Tide Tables.*

Density of water
10.168
1   **Density:** average 1·022 g/cm³.

Maximum size of vessel handled
10.169
1   The maximum size of vessel which can be accommodated in the lock is 150 m LOA, 21 m beam and 9 m draught.
    Maximum size of vessel handled: 15 000 dwt.

Arrival information

Port radio
10.170
1   Port radio stations operate from Saint-Malo, for details see *Admiralty List of Radio Signals Volume 6(1).*

Notice of ETA required
10.171
1   Send ETA and draught 6 hours in advance, confirming ETA 2 hours before arrival; for details see *Admiralty List of Radio Signals Volume 6(1).*

Pilotage and tugs
10.172
1   **Pilotage,** see 10.123.
    Tugs. Tugs are taken after passing Le Buron Lighted Beacon Tower (48°39′N 2°04′W) and are compulsory in accordance with the following table:

Vessel LOA	No dangerous and polluting goods	Dangerous and polluting goods
Below 100 m	None	1
100 to 120 m	1	1
Over 120 m	2	2

2   Exemptions are available for vessels fitted with bow thrusters.

Traffic regulations
10.173
1   **Speed limits:** 5 kn in Avant-port; 3 kn in the wet basins.

Harbour

General layout
10.174
1   **Main berthing areas.** The port of Saint-Malo consists of a tidal Avant-port, mainly for passenger vessels, partially protected by Môle des Noires, which extends 2½ cables SW from the SW corner of the town, with RoRo and Jetfoil berths and a marina at Anse des Bas-Sablons. Four wet basins are entered through Écluse du Naye, the entrance lock. The water in the wet basins can be maintained at the required level by a pumping station. The basins are interconnected.

Traffic signals
10.175
1   International port traffic signals regulating the movement of vessels entering and leaving the harbour are displayed by day and night near the lock entrance. For details see 1.93 and *The Mariner's Handbook.*

Tidal streams
10.176
1   **Port.** At the entrance to the port the in-going stream sets towards Fort de la Cité (48°38′N 2°02′W) and then N towards the entrance channel and SW along Môle des Noires. The out-going stream runs WSW from the lock along the approach channel to join the out-going stream from La Rance.
    See also *Admiralty Tidal Stream Atlas for the Channel Islands and the adjacent coasts of France* and information on the chart.

Directions for entering harbour
(continued from 10.139)

Lock
10.177
1   **Écluse du Naye Leading Lights:**
        Front Light (white round daymark purple border, 4 m in height) (48°38′·6N 2°01′·4W) one at each end of the lock near the inner and outer lock gates exhibited alternatively depending on the position of the lock gates.
        Rear Light (white round daymark red border on white column, 23 m in height) (6 cables ENE of the front light).

2   From a position about 2 cables WSW of the head of Môle des Noires the alignment (070½°) of these lights leads in the channel to the lock passing SSE of the head of Môle des Noires, on which stands a light (white tower red top, 10 m in height). The channel is 150 m wide and has depths of 4 to 2 m below chart datum. The S edge of the channel is indicated by the alignment (071°) of white square daymarks with red stripes, and at night by violet lights, situated ½ cable S of Écluse du Naye.

3   The lock is 154 m long, 24 m wide, with a depth of 1·7 m over the sill; it is normally worked from 2½ hours before until 2½ hours after HW. The times of lock openings vary according to the time and range of the tide and the volume of traffic expected. Times are promulgated by the Harbour Master only a few days beforehand. Mariners in inward bound vessels are recommended to arrive at the lock not later than 1 hour after HW.

4   **Caution.** At the lock entrance shortly before HW during spring tides there is a strong N-going stream which becomes very weak at HW and ceases about ½ hour later. When the sluices of the barrage across La Rance (10.183) are open, or when the turbines are operating in the direction from sea to river, a strong N-going set is generated across the lock entrance.

Basins and berths

Avant-port
10.178
1   Avant-port, the N part of which dries except for the approach channel to Écluse du Naye (48°38′·6N 2°01′·4W) (10.177) which is dredged to 4·0 m, and Anse de la Bourse, which is dredged to 1 m, is partially protected by Môle des Noires. The jetfoil service to Channel Islands

Saint-Malo from WSW (10.177)

(Original dated 1997)

(Photograph – Service Hydrographique et Océanographique de la Marine)

operates from two piers, approached through Anse de la Bourse, on the N side of the entrance to the lock. A RoRo ferry terminal extends 2 cables SW from the lock entrance.

2   Anse des Bas-Sablons lies in the S part of Avant-port and contains a yacht harbour.

Deepest and longest berth: RoRo Ferry Terminal dredged to a depth of 7·0 m.

Wet basins
10.179

1   **Bassin Vauban,** is entered from Écluse du Naye and has depths or from 2·1 to 7 m. Quai des Corsaires, on the E side of the basin, is 385 m long with a RoRo ramp in the N part of the quay and berths for petroleum, liquid and phosphate cargoes. There is a marina at the N end of the basin.

2   **Bassin Duguay-Trouin** is entered from the N end of Bassin Vauban through Pertuis de Saint-Malo, a passage 17·5 m wide with a depth of 7·0 m. The maximum size of vessel admitted is 120 m in length, 16·5 m beam and 6 m draught. The depths in the basin are irregular but there are several berths with depths alongside of from 4·6 to 6·6 m.

3   **Bassin Bouvet** is entered from the S end of Bassin Vauban through Pertuis de Saint-Servan a passage 16·5 m wide with a depth of +4·6 m on the sill. The maximum size of vessel admitted is 120 m in length, 16 m beam and 6 m draught. Depths in the basin are from 4·4 to 7·7 m. The N and W quays are used by commercial vessels, the S quays are used for fishing industry activities. There is a slipway at the E end of the basin.

4   **Bassin Jacques Cartier,** with depths of from 1·4 to 2·0 m, is entered from the SE end of Bassin Vauban by Pertuis des Corsaires, 30 m wide; a turning area marked by buoys (special) is situated in the basin. The maximum size of vessel admitted is 150 m in length, 21 m beam and 9 m

draught. Quai Chateaubriand, 285 m in length, lies on the W side of the basin.

Movement between basins
10.180

1   The passages between the basins can be used during normal locking times. They are spanned by bridges and mariners requiring these to be opened should make the appropriate signals, details of which are given in *The Mariner's Handbook.*

Port services
10.181

1   **Repairs** of all kinds can be carried out.

Dry dock entered from Bassin Vauban: useful length 126 m; breadth 15 m for vessels up to 120 m LOA.

Slipway in Bassin Bouvet: useful length 22·5 m; breadth 9·4 m; lifting capacity 350 tonnes; for vessels up to 30 m length, 8 m beam and 4·5 m draught.

2   **Other facilities.** Compass adjustment; ship sanitation control exemption certificates issued; hospitals.

Supplies. Fuel by road tanker, 48 hours notice required; fresh water; fresh provisions.

Communications. International airport at Dinard-Pleurtuit, 15 km from the port.

Canal. There is connection by canal with Rennes and Nantes, for details see 10.186.

3   **Rescue.** Saint-Malo all-weather lifeboat is stationed at Saint-Servan close E of Pointe Béchard (48°38′N 2°02′W) and inshore lifeboats are stationed at Saint-Malo and Dinard (10.182), see 1.117.

Landings
10.182

1   **Baie du Prieuré** (48°38′N 2°03′W), a large bay on the W side of the mouth of La Rance (10.183), is entered between Pointe de Dinard and Pointe de la Vicomté, 1 mile

SE, the bay dries out completely to a line between its entrance points. There is a marina with dredged channel in the N part of bay.

Marine farms, charted as occasional, lie in the N part of the bay E and S of Pointe de Dinard.

Landing can be obtained at Cale de Dinard, on the SE side of Pointe de Dinard.

2   **Quai de Dinan** (48°38′·8N 2°01′·6W) on the N side of the Avant-port of Saint-Malo is approached through Anse de la Bourse (10.178).

Cale de Solidor (48°38′·1N 2°01′·5W) gives access to Saint-Servan and dries; it is primarily for the use of the Saint-Servan-Dinard ferry which has priority of use.

The landing places are usable at all states of the tide.

La Rance

Charts 2700, 3659, 2669
General information
10.183

1   **Barrage.** The estuary of La Rance is crossed by a barrage about 1½ miles S of Écluse du Naye (48°39′N 2°01′W), between Pointe de la Brebis, on the W bank, and Pointe de la Briantais, on the E bank. In the centre of the barrage there is a hydro-electric power station operated by the tides; between it and the E end of the barrage are the sluices from which the station derives its power.

2   **Lock.** A lock at the W end of the barrage gives access to the river; the lock is 65 m long, 13 m wide, with a depth over the sill of 2 m above chart datum. Approach channels on each side of the lock are dredged to a depth of 2 m above chart datum. La Jument Lighted Beacon Tower (starboard hand, 15 m in height) stands on Pointe de la Jument, 3½ cables N of the W end of the barrage and marks the W side of the N approach channel; the E side is marked by Z1 12 Light Buoy (port hand), ¾ cable ENE. Dolphins, marked by a light (red pylon), are situated NE and SE of the lock; mariners may secure to them while awaiting entry to the lock. The NW and SW walls of the lock entrance are each marked by a light (green pylon).

3   The lock normally operates by day and by night provided the height of the tide on each side of the lock is 4 m or more above chart datum; it is opened at the exact hour for 15 minutes. Mariners should arrive 20 minutes before the hour and inform the lock keeper of their draught and masthead height.

4   **Traffic signals** (Diagram 10.182.1) regulate entry to the locks. If both signals are displayed it signifies that entry from both directions is prohibited.

Day	Night	Meaning
●	● (orange)	Entry from N prohibited
▼	● (green)	Entry from S prohibited

La Rance - lock traffic signals (10.183.1)

5   **Prohibited area.** In order to avoid the danger of being drawn towards the sluices in the barrage, navigation is prohibited within an area extending 6 cables N and 4 cables S from the barrage; the limits of the area are marked by Z1

buoys, light buoys and beacons. In addition there is a safety device on the seaward side of the barrage consisting of a number of buoys (red and orange) joined together by a nylon line moored between Pointe de l'Aiguille (48°37′·7N 2°01′·1W), a position 2 cables S of Bizeux an islet in mid-channel, and the dolphin NE of the lock.

6   **Water level.** The water level at each half-hour at Saint-Suliac (48°34′N 1°59′W) together with the times of operation of the power station, are announced at least 24 hours in advance at the harbour office at Saint-Malo, at the lock in the barrage, and at Écluse du Châtelier at Dinan. This information can also be obtained from an automatically recorded telephone message.

7   **Signals.** A signal station near the centre of the barrage indicates the direction of flow of the current as shown in Diagram 10.182.2. Another signal station, situated over the sluices, uses similar signals to indicate the direction of the stream resulting from the opening of the sluice gates. The absence of any signal indicates slack water.

Day	Night	Meaning
△ ▲	● (green) ○	In-going stream
▼ ▽	○ ● (green)	Out-going stream

La Rance - current flow signals (10.183.2)

8   **Tidal streams.** At about the times of HW and LW the turbines can be operated to complete the filling or emptying of the basin which can produce a stream at slack water. Normally the streams thus produced are no greater than those of the natural tidal streams, but in exceptional circumstances, the former can attain twice the natural rate; in such circumstances the following signals are displayed:

9   Five red isophase lights in the form of a Saint-Andrew's cross exhibited from the slipway at Mordreaux, about 7 miles above the barrage.

Two fixed red lights exhibited on each side of the bridge near Écluse du Châtelier.

La Rance — above the barrage
10.184

1   **General information.** Navigation in the river above Pointe de Cancaval, on the W bank 8 cables above the barrage, should not be attempted without a pilot. Above Saint-Suliac, on the E bank 3½ miles above the barrage, the channel is marked during the summer months by buoys (port hand).

2   **Vertical clearances.** A suspension bridge, with a vertical clearance of 20 m, spans the river at Port Saint-Hubert, 2 miles above Saint-Suliac. De Lessard Viaduct, with a vertical clearance of 18·9 m, spans the river 2½ miles farther up-stream.

Seaplanes may be encountered in the area between Pointe de Cancaval and Saint-Suliac. Anchoring is prohibited in this area.

3   **Anchorages.** There are several anchorages in the river which are used by coasting vessels, notably at Saint-Suliac; the holding ground is good.

Shellfish beds lie in the river above the barrage.

Submarine telephone cables cross the river at Pointe de Cancaval; anchoring, fishing or dredging within 2 cables on either side of the point is prohibited.

4   **Submarine pipeline** crosses the river between Anse de la Gauthier and Anse de Saint Hélier; anchoring within 100 m either side of the pipeline is prohibited.

Dinan
10.185
1   **General information.** Écluse du Châtelier, a lock giving access to the small port of Dinan and Canal d'Ille et Rance lies about 5 miles above Saint-Suliac. It is 39 m long, 7·9 m wide, with a sill 6·3 m above chart datum. For water levels, see 10.183.

2   Dinan, a small port on the lowest reach of Canal d'Ille et Rance, lies about 10 miles above the barrage and is frequented by ferries and pleasure craft. The port is about 3½ cables in length on the left bank of the canal and about 1 cable in length on the right bank, with a width of from 25 to 40 m; each bank has a walled quay. There are 130 berths, including some for visitors, in a depth of 1·5 m.

A stone bridge at Dinan is the head of navigation for masted craft.

10.186
1   **Canal d'Ille et Rance** leads from La Rance to Rennes, a distance of 85 km; there are 47 locks. The locks can be used by vessels not exceeding the following dimensions: length 25·8 m; beam 4·5 m; draught 1·3 m; height 2·5 m.

2   At Rennes the canal joins Rivière Vilaine which flows into Bay of Biscay at Pointe du Halguen (see *Bay of Biscay Pilot*), a distance of 140 km. There are 13 locks; the mean river level is 1·5 m at which state the minimum vertical clearance of the bridges is 3·2 m.

There is access to Canal de Nantes à Brest at Redon, 89 km below Rennes.

SAINT-MALO TO GRANVILLE

General information

Charts 3659, 2669
Route
10.187
1   It is usual to approach the port of Granville (48°50′N 1°36′W) from W, see 10.2. From a position N of Atterrage Saint-Malo Light Buoy (48°41′N 2°07′W) the route runs generally E, about 21 miles, to Granville (10.207) passing S of Plateau des Minquiers (48°58′N 2°04′W) and Îles Chausey (48°53′N 1°49′W).

Topography
10.188
1   Plateau des Minquiers (11.243), consisting of numerous rocks and shoals lying on a plateau of about 130 square miles the centre of which is situated about 18 miles N of Saint-Malo, and Îles Chausey (10.216), a group of islets rocks and shoals lying on an extensive plateau farther E, lie on the N side of the route.

On the S side of the route Baie du Mont Saint-Michel (10.199), obstructed with drying sandbanks, is entered E of Pointe du Grouin (48°43′N 1°51′W) (10.194).

2   Le Roc, the peninsula which protects Granville from N, terminates in Pointe du Roc (48°50′N 1°37′W) a steep cliff. A light (10.194) and a signal station, consisting of a

wooden structure on top of a blockhouse, stand on the point.

A coastal bank on which there are some drying patches fringes the coast extending in places 4½ miles offshore between Pointe du Roc and Pointe de Champeaux (10.199), about 5 miles S.

Hazards
10.189
1   **Dredging area.** Vessels engaged in dredging for aggregates may be encountered in the vicinity of position 48° 48′N 1° 56′W.

High speed craft. Mariners are advised to maintain a good lookout for these craft, see 1.7.

Traffic regulations
10.190
1   **Control of navigation.** For vessels over 1600 gt carrying dangerous and polluting goods approaching or leaving Granville should comply with the regulations (1.68 to 1.76).

Mariners in such vessels should contact Pointe du Roc Signal Station; for details see *Admiralty List of Radio Signals Volume 6(1)*.

Rescue
10.191
1   **Lifeboats.** An inshore lifeboat is stationed at Cancale (48°40′N 1°51′W) (10.205) and an all-weather lifeboat at Granville (48°50′N 1°36′W) (10.207).

Signal station is situated on Pointe du Roc (Sémaphore) (48°50′N 1°37′W).

For details regarding lifeboats, see 1.117 and for signal stations 1.95 and 1.110.

VHF Direction-finding station, for emergency use only, operates from Pointe du Grouin for details see *Admiralty List of Radio Signals Volume 2*.

Temporary explosives dumping grounds
10.192
1   Temporary explosives dumping grounds (Zones de Dépôts d'Explosifs) are situated SE of Pierre de Herpin (48°44′N 1°49′W) for Cancale and SSW of Pointe du Roc (48°50′N 1°37′W) for Granville.

For details see 1.7 and Appendix V.

Tidal streams
10.193
1   For details of tidal streams see *Admiralty Tidal Atlas for the Channel Islands and adjacent coasts of France* and information on the chart.

Directions
(continued from 10.131)

Principal marks
10.194
1   **Landmarks:**
> For landmarks at Saint-Malo, see 10.130.
> Pointe du Grouin (48°43′N 1°51′W), dominated by a white signal station (disused).
> Water Tower (domed top) (48°50′N 1°35′W); when viewed from seaward is the highest mark near the built up area of Granville.

2   **Major lights:**
> Cap Fréhel Light (48°41′N 2°19′W) (10.68).
> La Pierre de Herpin Light (white tower black top and base, 28 m in height) (48°44′N 1°49′W).

Grande Île Light (grey square tower, 19 m in height) (48°52′N 1°49′W) on Îles Chausey.

Pointe du Roc Light (grey tower red top, 16 m in height) (48°50′N 1°37′W).

Approaches to Saint-Malo to Granville
10.195

1   From a position N of Atterrage Saint-Malo Light Buoy (safe water) (48°41′N 2°07′W) the track leads generally E passing (with positions given from Pointe du Roc (48°50′N 1°37′W)):

S of Le Four (48°54′N 2°09′W) and La Souarde, 2½ miles E, the S-most dangers off the S side of Plateau des Minquiers (11.243). South Minquiers Light Buoy (S cardinal) is moored 1 mile SSW of Le Four. Thence:

2   Clear of Basse Trouvée (48°49′N 2°05′W), noting two dangerous wrecks which are charted 3¼ miles NE (position approximate) and 2½ miles SE, of the shoal; thence:

S of Les Sauvages (48°54′N 2°00′W), a detached rocky shoal marked on its SE side by SE Minquiers Light Buoy (E cardinal). A dangerous wreck (position doubtful) is charted 4 cables ENE of the light buoy. Thence:

3   N of Basse Grune (48°45′N 1°54′W) noting an obstruction 1¼ miles N; thence:

Between Grande Île (48°52′N 1°49′W), the largest of the islands and islets on Îles Chausey (10.216), and La Fille (48°44′N 1°48′W), marked on its N side by a buoy (N cardinal), the outermost danger off Pointe du Grouin. A light (10.194) is exhibited from Grande Île. Thence:

4   Clear of a 7·5 m patch (6 miles W); thence:

N of Basse Parisienne (5½ miles WSW); thence:

Between Le Videcoq (3¼ miles W), marked by a light buoy (W cardinal), the outermost danger on the edge of the coastal bank extending W from Pointe du Roc, and Banc Rondehaie (4¼ miles SW). Thence:

To the pilot boarding place (10.210) which is close SE of Le Videcoq.

10.196

1   **Clearing marks:**

Front mark. La Corbière (rock) (48°52′·5N 1°51′·8W) on the SE extremity of Plateau de la Corbière.

Rear mark. Grande Île Light (1½ miles E of the front mark) (10.194).

The alignment (097°) of these marks clears S of Les Sauvages.

2   **Useful marks:**

Maîtresse Île (48°58′N 2°04′W) (11.243).

Le Pignon Lighted Beacon Tower (black tower, white band, 20 m in height) (48°53′·5N 1°43′·3W).

See also useful marks for Granville at 10.213.

Entrée de la Déroute

Chart 3656
General information
10.197

1   **Description.** Entrée de la Déroute (48°54′N 1°55′W), a side channel from 3½ to 5 miles wide subject to strong and erratic tidal streams, separates Îles Chausey (10.216) from

Plateau des Minquiers (11.243) and Les Ardentes (10.198) and leads into Passage de la Déroute (11.290).

2   **Tidal streams.** From early data which should consequently be used with caution, the tidal streams close around Îles Chausey begin as follows:

Interval from HW Saint Helier	*Direction*
1 mile N and S:	
−0555	E
−0015	W
1 mile E and W:	
−0310	N
+0230	S

Spring rates of about 3¾ kn in both directions have been reported.

Directions
10.198

1   From a position SE of Les Sauvages (48°54′N 2°00′W) (10.195) the route leads NE passing (with positions given from Grande Île Light (48°52′N 1°49′W)):

Over Banc de la Corbière (5½ miles WNW) which extends NW from the W side of Îles Chausey; thence:

2   NW of Les Rondes de l'Ouest (2½ miles WNW) the W-most dangers on Îles Chausey; thence:

NW of La Déchirée (2¾ miles NW), the outermost of a group of drying reefs forming the NW extremity of Îles Chausey; thence:

3   SE of Les Ardentes (6 miles NNW), a group of rocks which form the E extremity of Plateau des Minquiers; Les Ardentes Light Buoy (E cardinal) is moored close SE of the E-most rocks. Thence:

To the alignment (126°) of L'Etat Beacon Tower (white, black top, 9 m in height) (3¼ miles NE) with Pointe du Roc Light (7¾ miles SE of the front mark) (10.194), when the track then leads N into Passage de la Déroute (11.290) or NE into Déroute de Terre (11.289).

4   **Caution.** The dangers on the W and N sides of Îles Chausey should not be approached within a distance of 3 cables.

Useful marks:

Disused Signal Station (white building black flagstaff) (48°52′·7N 1°50′·1W) on the N end of Grande Île.

L'Enseigne Beacon Tower (48°53′·7N 1°50′·3W) (10.219).

La Sellière (above-water rock) (48°54′·6N 1°48′·3W).

Baie du Mont Saint-Michel

Charts 3659, 2669
General information
10.199

1   **Description.** Baie du Mont Saint-Michel is entered between Pointe du Grouin (48°43′N 1°51′W) (10.194) and Pointe de Champeaux, a rocky point 11 miles E, which when viewed from N or W slopes regularly at an angle of 45°. The bay is encumbered with drying sandbanks which extend up to 7 miles from its head. Le Mont Saint-Michel (48°38′N 1°31′W), dominated by the spire of the abbey, lies in the SE part of the bay about 1 mile off the low-lying shore.

2   **Pilotage,** see 10.123. Saint-Malo pilots conduct vessels into Grande Rade de Cancale (10.200), La Houle-sous-Cancale (10.205) and Le Vivier-sur-Mer (10.206); the pilot boats resemble local fishing vessels.

3   **Tidal streams** in Baie du Mont Saint-Michel begin as follows:

Interval from HW Saint Helier	*Direction*
In the middle of the bay:	
−0505	SE
+0035	NW
Off Pointe de Champeaux:	
−0340	N
+0155	S

4   The maximum spring rate in each direction is 2¾ kn in the middle of the bay and 2 kn off Pointe de Champeaux. In the SW part of the bay a current runs W and N round the coast when the sands are covered.

5   Near La Fille (48°44′N 1°48′W) the tidal streams begin as follows:

Interval from HW Saint Helier	*Direction*
−0555	SE
HW	NW

The maximum spring rate in each direction is 4¾ kn.

6   **Marine farms** in the form of oyster and mussel beds, marked by buoys, are established to the S and SE of Banc des Corbières (48°41′N 1°49′W). Mussel beds, marked by beacons, and fishing grounds are established over a wide area of the foreshore in the S part of Baie du Saint-Michel. Mariners are forbidden to anchor or take the ground on these beds which are shown on the chart.

Anchorages
10.200
1   **Grande Rade de Cancale** (48°42′N 1°49′W) is bounded on its E side by Les Banchets, a group of gravel shoals which lie 1 mile E of Pointe du Grouin, and by Banc des Corbières which lies about 1 mile farther S, and on its W side by Banc de Chatry which extends 1¼ miles N from Pointe de la Chaîne (48°41′N 1°50′W).

Numerous dangers extend 2 miles NE from Pointe du Grouin, terminating at La Fille (10.195).

2   **Anchorage.** The anchorage in Grande Rade de Cancale is about 5 cables wide with depths of 10 to 13 m, rock overlaid with muddy clay less than 1 m thick. The anchorage is sheltered from W winds but the tidal streams are strong. A recommended anchorage is shown on the chart.

10.201
1   **Mouillage de Chatry** (48°42′N 1°50′W) affords anchorage between Banc de Chatry and the coast in depths of 7 to 9 m, rock covered with a thin layer of mud; the holding ground is poor and mariners should only anchor there at neaps as the tidal streams are strong; a recommended anchorage is shown on the chart.

10.202
1   **Île des Rimains.** Mariners in small vessels can anchor SE of Île des Rimains (48°40′·9N 1°49′·6W), on which stands an old fort, in depths of 3 to 5 m, mud, with good holding ground and well sheltered from W winds.

10.203
1   **Tidal streams** in the anchorages begin as follows:

Interval from HW Saint Helier	*Direction*
Grande Rade:	
+0600	S
−0115	N
Mouillage de Chatry:	
−0610	S
−0245	N

The maximum spring rate in each direction is 2 kn in Grande Rade and 3 kn and 1½ kn on the N-going and S-going stream, respectively, in Mouillage de Chatry.

2   In the anchorage SE of Île des Rimains the S-going stream begins at about the time of local LW but only lasts for about 1¾ hours after which it is N-going; the spring rates in each direction are about 2 kn.

Side channels
10.204
1   **Le Grand Ruet,** a passage 3½ cables wide with a least depth of 11 m in the fairway, lies between Roche Herpin (48°43′·3N 1°49′·8W) and Basse du Milieu, about 4½ cables NNE. The tidal streams run strongly through the passage and there are numerous overfalls. Depths of 9·3 m and 4·1 m lie on the N side of the passage, 3¼ cables N and 7 cables ENE, respectively, of Roche Herpin.

2   **Chenal de la Vieille Rivière,** a passage ½ cable wide with depths of about 6 m, lies between Île des Landes (48°42′·7N 1°50′·3W), a long narrow island with a rocky crest, and the mainland. A buoy (N cardinal) marking the N side of Grande Bunouze and Ruet Buoy (W cardinal) are moored in the N approach to the channel, 4½ cables NNW and 8 cables NNE, respectively, of Pointe du Grouin. Depths of 3·4 m and 3·1 m lie on either side of the channel 3 cables NNW and 4½ cables NNE, respectively, of the same point.

Minor harbours
10.205
1   **Cancale** (48°40′N 1°51′W) stands on the cliffs between Pointe de la Chaîne and Pointe des Crolles, 1 mile SW; it contains a small tidal harbour at La Houle-sous-Cancale on the S side of the town. Rocher de Cancale, an islet, and Le Châtellier a high conical rock lie within 5 cables E of Pointe de la Chaîne. Oyster beds, marked by buoys and shown on the chart, are established within 1 mile E of the port.

2   **Harbour,** which dries from 6 to 10 m to a bottom of mud, is protected from E by Môle de la Fenêtre and from the W by Môle de l'Épi. A light (white pylon green top green hut, 11 m in height) (48°40′N 1°51′W) is exhibited from the head of Môle de la Fenêtre.

3   **Berths:** quay between the two moles. Vessels secure to a transverse chain, laid on the bottom parallel with the quay and about ½ cable from it, with stern to shore.

Facilities for the support of fishing vessels are available.
Rescue, see 10.191.

10.206
1   **Le Vivier-sur-Mer** (48°36′N 1°46′W), a small harbour where craft can lie aground, lies on the coast at the mouth of Rivière Guioult. It is approached through a narrow buoyed channel, barely 6 m wide, which dries 7 m.

Granville and Hérel from S (10.207)

(Original dated 1997)

(Photograph - Service Hydrographique et Océanographique de la Marine)

Granville and approaches

Charts 3672 plan of Granville, 3659
General information
10.207
1   **Position and function.** Port de Granville (48°50′N 1°36′W) is a commercial and fishing port of local importance, and a summer resort.

Traffic. In 2006 the port was used by 67 vessels totalling 142 034 dwt.

Port Authority. Capitainerie du Port, Terre-Plein de l'Ecluse, 50400, Granville.

Limiting conditions
10.208
1   **Controlling depths.** The harbour can only be approached towards HW. Mariners in vessels over 4·6 m draught should consult the Port Authority before arrival.

Deepest and longest berths: Bassin à Flot (10.214).

Tidal levels, see information in *Admiralty Tide Tables.* The port is noted for its exceptional range of tides; the mean spring range is about 11·3 m and the mean neap range about 5·3 m. At equinoctial springs the range may exceed 13 m.

2   **Maximum size of vessel handled:** length 120 m; beam 19 m; draught 4 m rising to 7·0 m depending on tidal height.

A vessel of 122 m LOA; 7·2 m draught has used the port.

Local weather. With fresh W and NW winds there is a choppy sea at the entrance to Avant-port and mariners wishing to enter should have a draught of 0·8 m less than the depths in the channel.

Arrival information
10.209
1   **Port radio** station, with limited hours, operates from Granville, for details see *Admiralty List of Radio Signals Volume 6(1).*

Notice of ETA required. Send request for pilotage and ETA 18 hours in advance, or on departure from the previous port if the period time of the voyage is less, for details see *Admiralty List of Radio Signals Volume 6(1).*

2   **Outer anchorages.** Mariners waiting to enter the port may anchor S of Le Videcoq Light Buoy (48°50′N 1°42′W) in a depth of about 7 m.

During W gales mariners will find shelter in Grande Rade de Cancale (10.200), 9 miles SW; in N gales they should anchor under the lee of Îles Chausey (10.217), 4 miles NW.

10.210
1   **Pilotage.** The compulsory pilotage area limits are bounded by the following:

West limit. A line through Pierre du Herpin (48°44′N 1°49′W) and Grande Île Light, 8½ miles N.

North limit. A line through Grande Île Light and Le Pignon Tower (48°53′·5N 1°43′·3W).

Pilotage is compulsory for vessels over 45 m in length.

2   **Boarding place.** When a vessel is expected the pilot boat cruises in the vicinity of Le Videcoq Light Buoy (48°50′N 1°42′W) as shown on the chart. In bad weather, if draught permits, mariners may close the harbour 2 hours before HW to about 5 cables off Le Loup Lighted Beacon Tower (48°50′N 1°36′W), where the pilot will board.

3   For details see *Admiralty List of Radio Signals Volume 6(1).*

Tugs are not available.

Requirement for local knowledge. The harbour is difficult of access and local knowledge is necessary.

Harbour
10.211

1　**General layout.** The commercial port of Granville consists of Avant-port, entered between W and E jetties, and a wet basin situated to the NE of Avant-port and communicating with it through a single gate. Port de Hérel, a marina, is situated close E of the commercial port.

　Channel. A dredged channel which dries (10.214), leads from the entrance to Avant-port to the wet basin entrance.

2　**Signals.** Depth signals and signals regulating departure and entry are displayed by day and at night from a mast on the W side of the entrance to the wet basin. For details of depth signals see, 1.96 and for International Port Traffic Signals, see *The Mariner's Handbook.*

3　**Tidal streams** run into Avant-port in the middle of the channel and along the E jetty from –0255 to –0035 HW Saint Helier at a spring rate of about 2 kn; during this period an eddy runs outwards along the W jetty. After –0005 HW Saint Helier the eddy widens out and runs N along the outer side of W jetty towards Pointe du Roc. In 1996 it was reported that the construction of the yacht marina to the E had augmented the strength of the tidal streams in the entrance to Avant-port by about 2 kn by refraction from the marina breakwater.

Directions for entering harbour
10.212

1　**General information.** The best time to enter Port de Granville is ½ hour before HW. Theoretically the entrance gate is open from 1½ hours before until 1½ hours after HW; in practice the duration of the opening of the entrance gate varies with the height of HW which is affected by the winds. Fresh W winds cause the tides to rise higher, while E winds lower the level; the differences can amount to over 0·6 m.

2　When signals signifying that the entrance gate is open are displayed, commercial vessels have priority over other craft between Le Loup Lighted Beacon Tower and the entrance to the wet basin.

10.213

1　**Approach.** After passing S of Le Loup Lighted Beacon Tower (isolated danger, 24 m in height) (48°49′·6N 1°36′·1W) make for the harbour entrance passing as close as possible to the E jetty as an eddy always sets towards the W jetty. Once the vessel enters the shelter of the E jetty the thrust of this eddy on her stern assists her in turning E towards the entrance gate.

2　**Useful marks:**
　　La Fourchie Beacon Tower (W cardinal) (48°50′·2N 1°36′·9W).
　　Light (red pylon, 9 m in height) (48°49′·9N 1°36′·2W) on Jetée Ouest head at Granville.
　　Light (white pylon green top on hut, 8 m in height) (48°50′·0N 1°36′·1W) on Jetée Est head at Granville.
　　Light (white round tower red top, 9 m in height) (48°49′·9N 1°35′·8W) at the head of Port de Hérel S breakwater.

Basins and berths
10.214

1　**Avant-port.** A dredged channel from the entrance of Avant-port to the entrance to the wet basin dries 3·8 m; a mudbank across the entrance dries to the same height as the sill of the entrance gate. Elsewhere in Avant-port the

bottom, composed of a layer of mud on rock and encumbered with obstructions, dries from 4·9 to 7 m. The N part of Avant-port is quayed.

2　**Berths:** three ferry terminals in the SE part of Avant-port for vessels up to 50 m in length and 6 m beam.

　Wet basin. The entrance to the wet basin, through a single gate, has a width of 19·8 m and its sill is 3·9 m above chart datum.

　Berths: five quays with depths ranging from 4·5 to 5·0 m.

Port services
10.215

1　**Repairs.** Small repairs can be effected.

　Supplies: fuel, in limited quantities; fresh water.

　Other facilities: hospital.

　Rescue, see 10.191.

Îles Chausey
Chart 3656
General information
10.216

1　**Description.** Îles Chausey (48°53′N 1°49′W), which belong to France, consist of a group of islets, rocks and shoals lying on an extensive plateau situated nearly midway between Plateau des Minquiers (48°58′N 2°04′W) (11.243) and the French coast about 6 miles farther E. Grande Île, the largest and only populated island, lies in the SW part of the group. The islet, indented with sandy bays and bordered on its E side by Sound de Chausey (10.218), has a small population who live principally by fishing, but in the summer months it attracts many yachts and visitors from the mainland.

2　The passage between Îles Chausey and the French coast is obstructed with numerous banks of hard sand and should not be attempted without local knowledge or the use of a pilot. For details of this passage, see 11.289.

3　**Caution.** Owing to the immense range of the tide the appearance of Îles Chausey is continually changing; it would not be prudent to place reliance on positions fixed by bearings of the various islets and rocks in the group as only pilots and local mariners can identify them with certainty at all states of the tide.

4　**Nature reserve.** Access is prohibited from 1st April to 30th June in the area E of a line joining Grande Île light (48°52′N 1°49′W) (10.194), and L'Enseigne Beacon Tower (48°53′·7N 1°50′·3W) (10.219), except Aneret (48°52′·7N 1°47′·7W). Anchoring is prohibited between 1st April to 30th July in the area centred on (48°53′·7N 1°48′·8W).

5　**Marine farms** in the form of shellfish beds, marked by perches, are to be found on the plateau of Îles Chausey clear of the navigable channels; their positions are shown on the chart.

6　**Crustacean reserved fishing area** lies N and E of Grande Île (48°52′·3N 1°49′·8W); within the area only hand-held line fishing is authorized.

　Local knowledge is required for the navigable channels through the islets and rocks which lie on the plateau.

　Clearance. Mariners arriving from outside the European Union are not permitted to visit Îles Chausey, except in the case of necessity, without first obtaining clearance at Granville or some other French port.

Anchorage off Îles Chausey
10.217

1　**Anchorage** can be obtained off the SE side of Îles Chausey between Grande Île (48°52′N 1°49′W) and Le Founet, a detached rock (which covers and uncovers),

5 miles ENE,, marked close E by Le Founet Light Buoy (E cardinal). Within this area there is shelter from winds between NW and W. The bottom is sand and shells and the holding ground is good.

2   **Caution.** The islets and rocks which lie on the S side of Îles Chausey should not be approached within a distance of 5 cables.

    Useful marks:
> Basses du Fis-Cous Beacon Tower (S cardinal) (48°52′·1N 1°47′·3W).
> Beacon Tower (white, black top) (48°52′·5N 1°46′·0W) on the NE-most islet of Les Huguenans.

3 > La Conchée (48°52′·5N 1°45′·1W), the largest of a small group of above-water rocks at the SE extremity of Îles Chausey.
> La Haute Foraine Beacon Tower (E cardinal) (48°53′·0N 1°43′·6W).

Sound de Chausey
10.218
1   **General information.** Sound de Chausey, which is the principal channel through the islands, is marked by beacons and dries out for its greater part. The channel leads from open water SE of Îles Chausey through a clearly defined channel along the NE side of Grande Île (49°52′N 1°49′W) and then crosses an area of drying sands and rocks before emerging on the NW side of the islands at La Grande Entrée (48°54′·5N 1°50′·2W).

2   **Tidal streams** in Sound de Chausey run as follows:

Interval from HW Saint Helier	Direction
−0525	NW
+0335	SE

The maximum N-going and S-going spring rates are 2¾ and 2 kn, respectively.

For details of tidal streams close around Îles Chausey, see 10.197.

10.219
1   **Leading marks — south-south-east approach:**
> Front mark. La Crabière-Est Light Beacon (10 m in height) (48°52′·5N 1°49′·4W).
> Rear mark. L'Enseigne Beacon Tower (black and white, 15 m in height) (1¼ miles NNW of the front mark). Near LW and from a low height of eye, L'Enseigne Beacon Tower is hidden by an islet situated close N of La Crabière-Est.

2   From a position between Basse du Château (48°51′·8N 1°49′·5W) and Basse de Longue Île, 9¼ cables E, the alignment (332°) of these marks, or at night in the white sector (329°–335°) of the light beacon, leads in the SSE approach to the sound passing between a light buoy (starboard hand), marking the E side of the entrance, and the rocks extending about 1½ cables SE from Pointe de la Tour, the SE extremity of Grande Île, which are marked by

three beacons (E cardinal). Inside the entrance and ENE of Grande Île Light the leading line crosses the edge of a drying sandbank extending E from Grande Île. Depths from 1·5 to 2·5 m have been reported over this bank at about 1 hour after MLWS; there is plenty of water over the bank at neap tides.
10.220
1   **Leading marks — north-west approach:**
> Front mark. L'Enseigne Beacon Tower (48°53′·7N 1°50′·4W) (10.219).
> Rear mark. Grande Île Light (1½ miles SSE of the front mark) (10.194).

The alignment (156°) of these marks leads into the N entrance; thence follow the recommended track shown on the chart.

Chenal des Roquettes à l'Homme
10.221
1   **General information.** Chenal des Roquettes à l'Homme, which is entered on the N side of Îles Chausey close W of the beacon (W cardinal) marking La Petite Entrée (48°54′·5N 1°49′·6W), runs SE and S entering open water on the S side of Îles Chausey through Chenal Beauchamp to the W of Les Huguenans (10.217), or alternatively through Passe de la Conchée to the E of Les Huguenans; the channel is marked by buoys (special) and beacons (cardinal).

    Caution. A dangerous wreck (position approximate) lies 2½ cables NNW of La Petite Entrée.

2   **Tidal streams** in the N part of the channel run as follows:

Interval from HW Saint Helier	Remarks
−0530	Sets NW for about 9 hours at rates of up to 3 kn
+0330	Sets SE for only about 3½ hours

There are several smaller channels connected with the two main channels.

Berths and anchorages
10.222
1   **Moorings.** Numerous yacht moorings, the majority of which are private, are to be found in the channel to the NW of La Crabière-Est Light-beacon (48°52′·5N 1°49′·4W).

2   **Anchorage** may be found in these reaches clear of the moorings but room is limited at spring tides; the anchorage is uncomfortable in strong NW and SE winds when the stream is against the wind. During W winds, anchorage may be found under the lee of Grande Île in the channel S of La Crabière-Est Light-beacon, but the water is relatively deep and the tidal streams strong.

3   **Landing** at Grande Île may be effected at a slipway situated 3 cables NNW of the light, depending on the height of the tide.

Chapter 11 - Channel Islands and adjacent coast of France

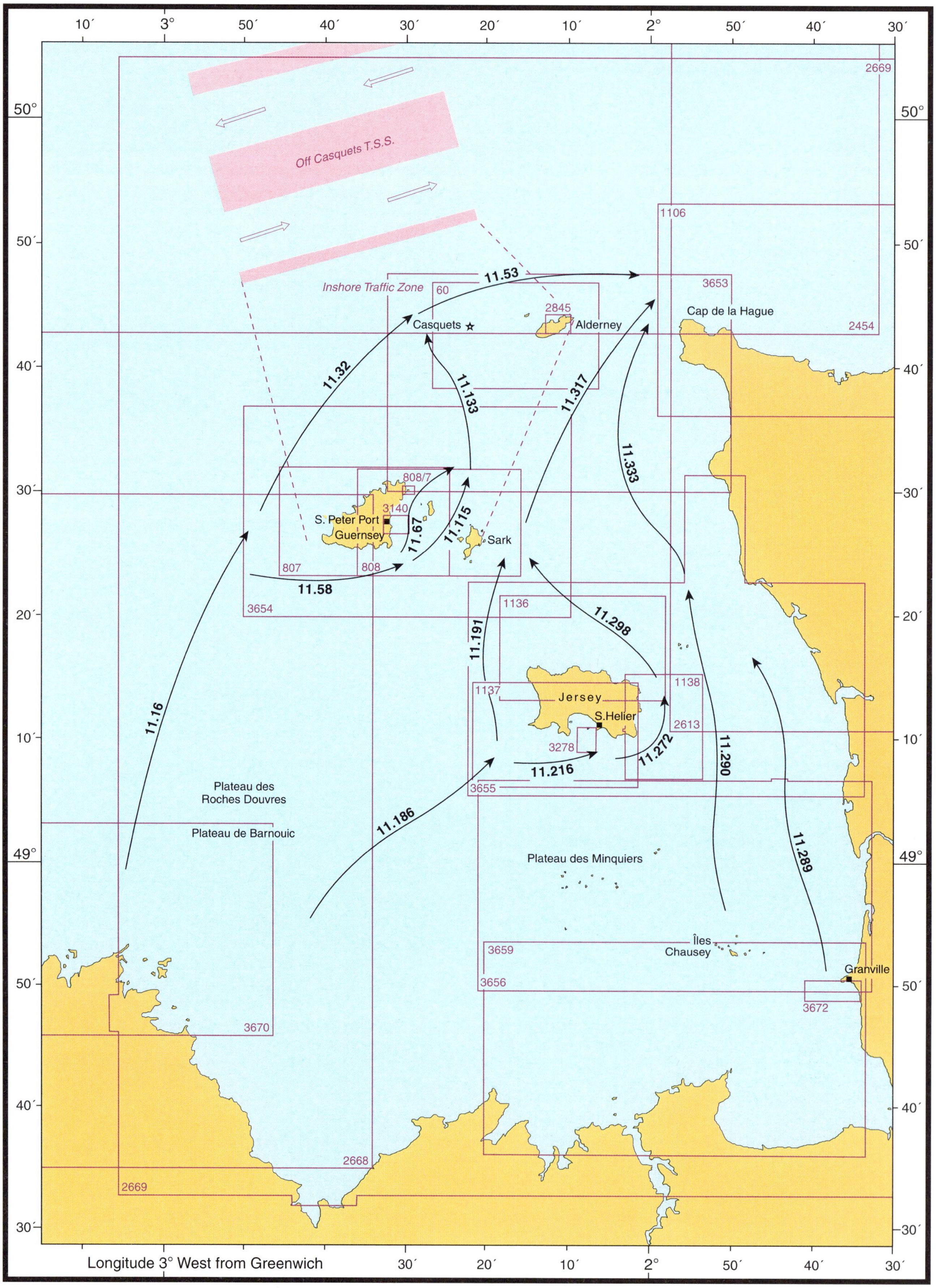

50°

10′ 3° 50′ 40′ 30′ 20′ 10′ 2° 50′ 40′ 30′

2669

1106

Off Casquets T.S.S.

3653

Cap de la Hague

2454

Inshore Traffic Zone

60

11.53

2845

Casquets ☆

Alderney

11.32

11.133

11.317

11.333

808/7

3140

S. Peter Port
Guernsey

11.67

11.115

Sark

807

808

11.58

3654

1136

11.298

11.191

11.16

1137

Jersey

1138

S.Helier

2613

3278

11.272

11.216

11.290

3655

Plateau des
Roches Douvres

Plateau de Barnouic

11.186

Plateau des Minquiers

11.289

3659

Îles
Chausey

3656

Granville

3670

3672

2668

2669

Longitude 3° West from Greenwich

30′ 20′ 10′ 2° 50′ 40′ 30′

030408

CHAPTER 11

CHANNEL ISLANDS AND ADJACENT COAST OF FRANCE

GENERAL INFORMATION

Chart 2669
Scope of the chapter
11.1
1   This chapter covers the Channel Islands and the adjacent coast of France from Granville (48°50′N 1°36′W) to Cap de la Hague, about 56 miles N.

Exercise areas
11.2
1   Detailed information concerning these areas, which are found in the waters of this chapter, may be found on Practice Exercise Area (PEXA) charts. Such areas are also shown on all new, and new edition navigation charts. For further details see 1.30 and *Annual Summary of Admiralty Notices to Mariners Nos 5 and 8.*

Marine farms
11.3
1   Marine farms are situated throughout the waters of this chapter and should be avoided. Farms in proximity to shipping routes are generally marked by buoys. Other farms are marked by beacons (X topmark) and some are fitted with radar reflectors. Lights, when fitted, show flashing yellow. See 1.29.

Description
11.4
1   **Channel Islands**, with outlying islands and rocks, occupy a large portion of the bight between Île de Bréhat (48°51′N 3°00′W) and Cap de la Hague, nearly 70 miles NE. Casquets, Burhou and Alderney, lie to the N and form a chain of islands separated from the coast of France by Race of Alderney; Guernsey, with the off-lying islands of Herm and Sark, lie to the NW of the bight; Jersey and Plateau des Minquiers, an extensive reef, are situated in the middle. For further information, see 1.127.

2   The Channel Islands are encompassed by numerous rocks and shoals rendered doubly formidable by the great rise and fall of the tides and the great rates attained by the tidal streams.
     Gales from between SW and NW send in the heaviest seas amongst the islands and this is accentuated by the strength of the tidal streams, particularly between 3 hours before and 3 hours after HW, by the shore.
11.5
1   **French coast.** The W coast of the Cotentin Peninsula between Granville and Cap de la Hague is most inhospitable; it is bordered by dangers which extend towards Îles Chausey (48°53′N 1°49′W), Plateau des Minquiers (48°58′N 2°04′W) and Jersey (49°13′N 2°08′W), and landmarks are few. The coast is exposed to winds from W and N, and fog, although not very frequent, may occur in any season; the tidal streams are strong.

Routes
11.6
1   **Recommended routes** to be followed when making the Channel Islands are outlined in the following paragraphs.
     Approaching from south-west and passing W of Guernsey and Casquets, the NW coast of Guernsey should not be approached within a distance of 3½ miles owing to the numerous off-lying shoals. To ensure being clear of the heavy swell prevalent off this coast, mariners should keep at least 5 miles offshore.
2   **Approaching from south,** pass well to the W of the buoys marking the W edge of Plateau des Minquiers (48°58′N 2°04′W) as the sea breaks on the edge of this plateau.
3   **Approaching from north through Race of Alderney** (49°44′N 2°05′W) and bound for Saint Helier, Jersey, pass 5 miles E of Sark, close W of Banc Desormes (49°19′N 2°17′W) and clear of the W coast of Jersey until the W approach to St Helier may be made.
4   The E coast of Jersey can be approached between Pierres de Lecq (49°17′N 2°12′W) and Les Dirouilles, about 5 miles E, thence through Le Ruau (49°16′N 2°03′W), but owing to the strength and erratic direction of the tidal streams, mariners usually prefer to proceed via the W coast of the island.
5   **Approaching from north through Race of Alderney** and bound for Saint Peter Port, Guernsey, shape course for either Little Russel, the channel between Guernsey and Herm, or Big Russel the channel between Herm and Sark.
6   **Approaching from north or north-west, passing W of Casquets** (49°43′N 2°22′W) and bound for Saint Peter Port, shape course for either Little Russel or Big Russel taking care to avoid Casquets SW Bank (49°39′N 2°25′W). The approach to Little Russel in poor visibility can be dangerous and there is much to be said for passing round the SW of Guernsey and making Saint Peter Port from S.
7   **Book order.** Detailed directions for the above routes are included in the relevant waterways and are described, in book order, from S to N.

Topography
11.7
1   As Channel Islands are approached from W, the slope down of the land from S to N of Guernsey, as contrasted with the slope down from N to S of Jersey, should prevent the possibility of either island being mistaken for the other.

Traffic regulations
11.8
1   **Traffic Separation Scheme.** Off Casquets TSS (49°43′N 2°22′W), shown on the chart, is IMO adopted and Rule 10 of *International Regulations for Preventing Collisions at Sea (1972)* applies.
2   **Inshore Traffic Zone.** Casquets Inshore Traffic Zone, shown on the chart, is designated as the area between the S boundary of the TSS and Channel Islands bounded by lines drawn from the SW corner of the scheme to Les Hanois Light, at the SW end of Guernsey, from Saint Martin's Point Light, at the SE end of Guernsey, to the S extremity

of Sark, from the E extremity of Sark to Quénard Point, at the NE extremity of Alderney, and from Quénard Point to the SE corner of the scheme.

3   For details regarding TSS and Inshore Traffic Zones see 1.8 to 1.14.

11.9

IMO recommendation. Race of Alderney is not recommended for use by ships other than those proceeding to and from ports in Channel Islands, ports located on the French coast between Cherbourg and Île d'Ouessant, or inshore routes at Île d'Ouessant.

11.10

1   **Regulations concerning vessels carrying dangerous and polluting goods,** see 1.68 to 1.76.

   Ship Movement Reporting System (MANCHEREP). See 1.14.

Natural conditions

11.11

1   **Tidal streams.** The range of the tide in the bight formed by the N coast of Brittany and the W coast of Normandy is large and consequently, as the water flows in and out of Baie du Mont Saint-Michel (10.199), the tidal streams attain great rates round the islands and in the wider channels; they run particularly strongly in Race of Alderney. Channel Islands lie mainly across the direction of the strongest streams and both direction and rate are affected by their presence.

2   The streams are generally rotatory in an anti-clockwise direction, the E-going stream being of shorter duration and greater strength than the W-going stream; this is particularly noticeable in the S part of the area.

3   In the approaches to Channel Islands tidal streams begin as follows:

Interval from HW Saint Helier	*Direction*
In the English Channel, N of Channel Islands:	
−0220	E
+0405	W
W of Channel Islands, well clear of the land:	
−0430	E
+0140	W
SW of Channel Islands, near Plateau de la Horaine (48°54′N 2°55′W):	
−0555	E
+0015	W

4   On the W coast of Cotentin Peninsula tidal streams generally run in the direction of the coast, N during the greater part of the E-going stream and S during the greater part of the W-going stream, in the English Channel. The streams begin as follows at the localities indicated:

Interval from HW Saint Helier	*Direction*
Off Regnéville (49°00′N 1°35′W)	
−0210	N
+0340	S

The maximum spring rate in each direction is 3¾ kn.

5   Off Pirou (49°11′N 1°35′W)

−0145	N
+0400	S

The maximum spring rate in each direction is 2¾ kn.

Interval from HW Saint Helier	*Direction*

6   Off Havre de Carteret (49°21′N 1°49′W)

−0105	NW
+0445	SE

The maximum spring rate in each direction is 3¾ kn.

7   5 miles NW of Cap de Carteret

−0205	N
+0350	S

The maximum spring rate in each direction is 3¾ kn. In this position the stream is nearly rotatory anti-clockwise; the times given in the table are those at which the stream begins to run generally in the direction given.

8   Anchorage off Diélette (49°33′N 1°53′W)

−0325	NE
+0220	SW

The maximum spring rate in each direction is 1¾ kn.

9   Middle of Anse de Vauville (49°36′N 1°55′W)

−0220	N
+0320	S

The maximum spring rate in each direction is 2¾ kn.

10   Between Les Huquets de Jobourg (49°39′N 1°56′W) and the mainland

−0200	WNW
+0430	ESE

The maximum spring rate in each direction is 3¾ kn.

11   Off Basse du Rhin (49°41′N 1°58′W) chart 3653

−0235	N
+0400	S

The maximum spring rate in each direction is 3¾ kn.

12   1 mile W of La Foraine Buoy (49°43′N 1°59′W)

−0220	NNW
+0430	S

The maximum spring rate is 9¾ kn in the NNW direction and 6½ kn in the S direction.

13   Off Gros du Raz (49°44′N 1°58′W)

−0220	NE
+0430	SW

The maximum spring rate is 4¾ kn in the NE direction and 6½ kn in the SW direction.

   For details of the tidal streams in the vicinity of Channel Islands and outlying banks and shoals and off Cotentin Peninsula, see information on the charts and *Admiralty Tidal Stream Atlas for the Channel Islands and adjacent coasts of France.*

14   **Overfalls and ripples** form over submerged rocks and outlying banks in the vicinity of Channel Islands when the tidal stream is running strongly; in poor visibility such indications can be used to advantage.

15   **Sea level.** Meteorological effects on sea level are probably greater in Channel Islands than in localities on the N coast of France; for example, at Saint Helier (49°11′N 2°07′W) the height of the sea level appears to be increased by as much as 0·6 m during strong and long continued W

winds, and to be correspondingly decreased during similar NE winds.

16   **Refraction.** Considerable variations in refraction caused by atmospheric conditions have been observed in the vicinity of Channel Islands.

Cautions
11.12

1   **Appearance.** Owing to the great range of the tide, rocks and islets have a marked difference in appearance at HW and LW. Dependence should not be placed on identifying the distant marks for outlying dangers, many of which can only be distinguished in clear weather and by those with local knowledge.

2   **Soundings.** When approaching the islands, the necessity for taking soundings at night and in thick weather cannot be overstressed. Although the islands and reefs are generally steep-to and soundings may give little warning, it is possible for a mariner to be set inside their boundaries without seeing them and the knowledge of the depth may enable him to steer clear or anchor to avert stranding.

Harbours and anchorages
11.13

1   **Channel Islands.** The principal harbours in the Channel Islands are at Saint Peter Port (11.102), Guernsey, Alderney Harbour (11.169), Alderney and at Saint Helier (11.246), Jersey.

Anchorages in Channel Islands are described in the appropriate text.

2   **French coast.** Granville (48°50′N 1°36′W) (10.207), the only harbour on Cotentin Peninsula which possesses a wet dock, is only accessible during certain times of the day. There are no safe anchorages on this coast but a few small harbours are accessible to mariners prepared to take the ground.

High speed craft
11.14

1   Mariners are advised to maintain a good lookout for these craft, see 1.7.

Dumping grounds
11.15

1   There are two disused dumping grounds for explosives 8 miles and 5¼ miles NW of Alderney; there is a further disused ammunition dumping ground about 8 miles SW of Guernsey. Their limits are shown on the charts.

Roches Douvres Lighthouse (11.19)

(Original dated 2000-02)

(Photograph - Jean Guichard)

LES HÉAUX DE BRÉHAT TO GUERNSEY WEST COAST

General information

Chart 2669
Route
11.16

1   From a position N of Les Héaux de Bréhat (48°55′N 3°05′W) the passage to the W coast of Guernsey, passing WNW of Plateau des Roches Douvres, leads generally NNE, a distance of about 25 miles.

Description
11.17

1   Plateau des Roches Douvres, the outermost of the dangers fronting this part of the coast, lies about 17 miles offshore. It is composed of above-water, drying and below-water rocks and is divided into two parts. A light (49°06′N 2°49′W) (11.19) is exhibited from the largest rock near the E side of the N part of the plateau; the S part of the plateau, which is detached, lies 1 mile S of the light.

2   Plateau de Barnouic lies S of Plateau des Roches Douvres from which it is separated by a navigable passage 2 miles wide. The plateau consists of a number of above-water rocks separated from one another by comparatively deep water. Barnouic Lighted Beacon Tower (E cardinal, octagonal tower on white base, 19 m in height) (49°02′N 2°48′W) stands on a drying rock in the E part of the plateau.

Natural conditions
11.18

1   **Tidal streams.** In a position 2½ miles WSW of Plateau des Roches Douvres the tidal stream reaches a rate of 4½ kn at springs; for details see information on the chart.
  Magnetic anomalies, see 10.7

Directions
(continued from 9.131)

Principal marks
11.19

1   **Landmark:**
      Roches Douvres Lighthouse (tower with green roof on dwelling, 65 m in height) (49°06′N 2°49′W) situated on the largest rock of the plateau.
  Major lights:
      Les Héaux de Bréhat Light (48°55′N 3°05′W) (9.130).
      Roches Douvres Light — as above.

Rosédo Light (48°52′N 3°00′W) (10.16).
Les Hanois Light (49°26′N 2°42′W) (11.36).

Les Héaux de Bréhat to Les Hanois
11.20

1   From a position N of Les Héaux de Bréhat (48°55′N 3°05′W) (9.131) the passage leads generally NNE passing:
      WNW of Plateau de Barnouic (49°02′N 2°48′W) (11.17); the dangers on this plateau rise abruptly from depths of about 40 to 50 m and, as soundings give no indication of their proximity, it is therefore advisable to give them a wide berth in low visibility. Roche Gautier Light Buoy (W cardinal) (10.17) is moored WSW of the plateau, in position 49°02′·0N 2°54′·8W. Thence:
2   WNW of Plateau des Roches Douvres (49°06′N 2°49′W) (11.17) to a position W of Les Hanois (49°26′N 2°42′W) (11.39).
For general directions for approaching Guernsey from W, see 11.38.
11.21

1   **Clearing bearing:**
      The line of bearing 196° of Le Paon Light (48°52′N 2°59′W) (10.16) changing from red to white clears WNW of Plateau des Roches Douvres and Plateau de Barnouic.
      (Directions continue at 11.36
      and for Guernsey S coast at 11.60)

GUERNSEY, HERM AND SARK

GENERAL INFORMATION

Charts 3654, 2669
Description
11.22

1   **Guernsey,** the second largest of Channel Islands, is highest along its S coast where a ridge rises steeply and attains a height of over 70 m at its W extremity above Pleinmont Point (49°26′N 2°40′W) and over 90 m towards its E end. The S side of this ridge is covered with scrub and stunted trees and is indented by many short ravines. To the N the ground slopes down gradually and there are long deep valleys running towards the NW coast where they broaden out and the land in some places is little above sea level. The interior is divided into small fields interspersed with numerous glasshouses used for the intensive cultivation of tomatoes, flowers and grapes. For further information, see 1.127.
11.23

1   **Herm and Jethou,** two islands situated 2 miles off the E coast of Guernsey, belong to the States of Guernsey and attract many visitors in the summer months. These two islands, together with the rocks extending about 3¼ miles NE from Herm and those extending about 1½ miles SSW from Jethou, divide Big Russel (11.115) from Little Russel (11.67).
11.24

1   **Sark** (49°26′N 2°22′W), with the small island of Brecqhou close off its W extremity, lies 6 miles E of Guernsey. Little Sark, its S part, is almost separated from the main part of the island by La Coupée, a narrow high isthmus. From the rocky coastline, which is indented by many small bays and coves, some with sand and shingle

beaches, the ground rises steeply, and in many places precipitously, to a plateau which is divided into many small, highly cultivated fields; the few trees are confined to low depressions, mainly near the coast. Houses are spread over the island, the main hamlet being La Collinette which lies on the plateau above La Maseline and Creux Harbour, the principal landing places, both at the E extremity of the island. Sark constitutes a royal fief or manor, held directly from the Crown; the head of the island is the Seigneur. The main occupations are agriculture, fishing and tourism.
2   **Approach.** A close approach to Sark on all but the NW coast of the island is difficult, not only from the numerous rocks which encompass it, but also from the rate and irregularities of the tidal streams. These difficulties, however, may be overcome if attention is paid to the leading marks and direction of the tidal streams. The island affords good shelter from offshore winds.

Routes
11.25

1   The usual approach to Saint Peter Port from N and NW is through Little Russel (49°30′N 2°28′W), the entrance to which lies between Platte Fougère (11.79), off the NE extremity of Guernsey, and Platte Boue (11.79) off the N end of Herm. This approach can be exceedingly dangerous owing to the strong tidal streams which set across the entrance of the channel and of the numerous drying and submerged rocks in the vicinity. In poor visibility there is much in favour for passing W of Guernsey and making Saint Peter Port from the S.
2   Big Russel is the E and deep-water channel to Saint Peter Port and although the tidal streams are strong and there are overfalls, it is easy of access.

The NW coast of Guernsey should not be approached within a distance of 3½ miles owing to the numerous offshore dangers. To ensure being clear of the heavy swell prevalent off this coast, particulary in winter, mariners should keep at least 5 miles offshore.

Topography
11.26

1 Approaching from N, the higher contours of Sark and Herm are frequently sighted before the island of Guernsey.

Harbours and anchorages
11.27

1 **Harbours.** Saint Peter Port (11.102) is the principal town and harbour on the island of Guernsey, there is also a small harbour which dries out at Saint Sampson (11.88); both of these ports lie on the E coast.

2 **Anchorages.** The only anchorage for large vessels is E of Saint Peter Port (11.86). There are several bays where mariners in small craft may anchor, such as Icart Bay (11.65) and Moulin Huet Bay (11.66) on the S coast, Rocquaine Bay (11.48) on the W coast, and Grand Havre (11.54) on the NW coast.

Natural conditions
11.28

1 Tidal streams round Guernsey, Herm and Sark are mainly rotatory, more so in open waters and in the wider channels between the islands, less so near the land and in the narrower channels. In general, the direction of the streams constantly progresses in an anti-clockwise direction as follows:

Interval from HW Saint Helier	Direction
HW	NE
+0300	NW
+0600	SW
−0400	SE

2 For details, see information on the charts and *Admiralty Tidal Stream Atlas for the Channel Islands and adjacent coasts of France.*

Eddies. There may be eddies close inshore which sometimes run contrary to the main stream; on occasions two opposing streams may be separated only by a narrow band of water.

Climate information. See 1.195 and 13.244

Regulations
11.29

1 **Customs and immigration.** Masters of all vessels arriving in Guernsey must complete, within 2 hours of arrival, the customs and immigration declaration form which is handed to them by the Harbour Authorities.

2 **Speed limit** of 6 kn is in force in most bays on the coast of Guernsey and in the approaches to Herm and Jethou. There is also a speed limit of 6 kn off most of the bathing beaches in Herm and off Rosière Steps (49°28′N 2°27′W).

Pilotage
11.30

1 Pilotage is compulsory except for those vessels exempted by law.

Pilotage zone is an area bounded by the following: Saint Martin's Point (49°25′N 2°32′W); Lower Heads Light Buoy (49°26′N 2°28′W); SE coast of Herm; Grande Amfroque (49°31′N 2°25′W); Grandes Brayes (49°31′N 2°30′W) and Fort le Plomb (49°31′N 2°31′W).

2 **Notice of ETA.** Mariners should confirm their ETA at least 4 hours in advance, to Saint Peter Port Coast Radio Station and call Port Control when approaching the pilotage zone. If difficulty is experienced contacting Port Control on VHF, messages may be sent via Saint Peter Port Coast Radio Station.

3 **Boarding place.** Pilot boards in the following positions:
49°25′·0N 2°29′·3W.
49°30′·8N 2°27′·7W.

If the pilot is unable to board because of rough weather, the pilot boat will act as lead-in guide.

4 **Pilot boats** are stationed at Saint Peter Port and Saint Sampson Harbour.

For further details, see *Admiralty List of Radio Signals Volume 6(1).*

Rescue
11.31

1 **All-weather lifeboat.** Guernsey all-weather lifeboat is stationed at Saint Peter Port (49°27′·5N 2°32′·0W) (11.102), for details, see 1.113.

VHF Direction-finding service, for emergency use only, operates from a position (49°26′N 2°36′W) on Guernsey. For details see *Admiralty List of Radio Signals Volume 2.*

GUERNSEY WEST COAST TO CASQUETS

General information

Charts 3654, 2669
Route
11.32

1 From a position off the SW point of Guernsey the route leads generally NNE passing along the W coast of the island to W of Casquets, a distance of about 17 miles.

Topography
11.33

1 The W coast of Guernsey between Pleinmont Point (49°26′N 2°40′W) (11.59) and Lihou Island (11.36), 2 miles N, is fringed with precipitous rocks, many of which are detached and lie as much as 2 miles offshore.

Between Lihou Island and Fort Doyle which stands on the NE extremity of Guernsey, 7 miles ENE, the coast is low and consists mainly of a succession of small bays which are sandy and flanked by drying rocky ledges.

Off-lying dangers
11.34

1 There are numerous rocks on the coastal bank between Pleinmont Point and Fort Doyle which extends up to 2 miles offshore; the coast is also fringed by a chain of detached shoals on which the sea breaks heavily, situated about 1 mile farther offshore.

Traffic regulations
11.35

1 For details of an Inshore Traffic Zone N of Casquets and Off Casquets TSS, see 11.8.

Hanois Lighthouse from SW (11.36)

(Original dated 2001)

(Photograph - Air Images)

Directions

(continued from 11.21)

Principal marks
11.36

1   **Landmarks:**

Hanois Lighthouse (grey round granite tower black lantern, 33 m in height) (49°26′N 2°42′W).

Lihou Island (conspicuous island with its summit at its W end and Saddle Rock and a ruin in its central part) (49°28′N 2°40′W) (chart 807).

Fort Saumarez (conspicuous disused lookout tower) (49°27′·5N 2°39′·4W) on a hillock on L'Erée Point.

2   **Major lights:**

Alderney Light (49°44′N 2°10′W) (11.151).

Hanois Light — as above.

Platte Fougère Light (49°31′N 2°29′W) (11.74).

Casquets Light (49°43′N 2°23′W) (11.151).

Channel Light Float (49°54′N 2°54′W) (2.40).

Roches Douvres Light (49°06′N 2°49′W) (11.19).

Other aids to navigation
11.37

1   **Racons:**

Casquets Light (49°43′N 2°23′W).

Channel Light Float (49°54′N 2°54′W).

Platte Fougère Light (49°31′N 2°29′W)

For details see *Admiralty List of Radio Signals Volume 2.*

General directions
11.38

1   Bound for Guernsey from W, mariners should not approach the island in thick weather within a depth of 70 m unless certain of their position. Careful allowance

should be made for the tidal stream setting in towards the island.

Approaching from S and W and passing W of Guernsey, at night, Hanois Light should not be brought to bear more than 164° until Casquets Light bears more than 050°, in order to keep W of all dangers lying off the coast.

2   Many of the dangers off-lying Rocquaine Bay and the NW coast, lie very close to the coastal shelf and soundings give very little warning of their proximity; caution is required.

Les Hanois to Casquets
11.39

1   From a position W of Les Hanois (49°26′N 2°42′W), an extensive group of above, drying and below-water rocks from where a light (11.36) is exhibited from the S part and which lie 1¼ miles WNW of Pleinmont Point, the route leads generally NNE passing (with positions given from Lihou Island summit (49°28′N 2°40′W)):

2   WNW of Banc des Hanois (1½ miles WSW); thence:

WNW of Les Trois Pères, three black rocks lying near the SW end of a drying reef; La Pendante (9 cables WSW) (chart 807), the W rock, is the largest of the group. Thence:

3   WNW of a line of detached shoals, on which the sea breaks heavily, which runs parallel to the NW coast of Guernsey and about 3 miles offshore consisting of Boue Blondel (2¼ miles NNW), La Platte Pierre (2½ miles N), Les Roques aux Bois (3½ miles NNE) and Les Frettes (5 miles NNE); thence:

4   WNW of Casquet SW Bank (49°40′N 2°25′W), a thin bank which runs about 3 miles N to S; there are strong overfalls on this bank. Thence:

To a position W of Eight Fathom Ledge (49°43′N 2°24′W), a small rocky ledge which lies 8½ cables W of Casquets Light. The ledge causes violent eddies and during fresh winds the sea breaks on it.

(Directions continue at 11.151)

Vazon Bay and approaches

Chart 807
General information
11.40

1   **Description.** Between L'Erée Point (49°28′N 2°39′W) (11.36) and the point on which Fort Richmond stands, 1¼ miles ENE, the coastal reef, which mostly dries, extends about 9 cables offshore. La Conchée, together with Cone Rock, stand on the drying part of this reef 7 cables NW of Fort Richmond.

2   Vazon Bay (49°28′N 2°37′W) is entered between the rocky point situated 2 cables NE of Fort Richmond and the point on which Fort Hommet, stands 7 cables farther NE. Gros Pont and La Jaune Pont are rocks standing on the coastal reef which extends from the W entrance point of the bay.

3   **Local knowledge.** A bank, which should not be approached within a distance of 2 miles without local knowledge, extends 2 miles from the shore between Lihou Island (49°28′N 2°40′W) (11.36) and Grande Rocque, 3½ miles NE. Numerous detached rocks and reefs, some of which dry, lie on this bank, the outermost of which are (with positions given from Lihou Island summit): Grande Étacre (5 cables NW); Boue Sarre (7 cables NNW); Soufleuresse (1¼ miles NNE); Le Boin (1½ miles NNE); Les Grunes de Nord-Ouest (3 miles NNE).

Directions
11.41

1   **Approaching from west — leading marks:**
   Front mark. S edge of Fort Hommet (49°28′·5N 2°36′·7W).
   Rear mark. Saint Matthew Church (belfry) (7½ cables ESE of the front mark).
The alignment (102°) of these marks leads in the approach passing (with positions given from the front mark):

2   Between Soufleuresse (2 miles WNW) (11.40) and Flabet (2¼ miles W); thence:
   Between Messelettes (1¼ miles WNW) and the dangers extending N from La Conchée (1¼ miles W) (11.40); thence:
   Between Boue Vazon (6½ cables WNW) and the dangers extending NW from Les Fourquies (6 cables WNW), from where the track then leads generally SE to the head of the bay.

11.42

1   **Approaching from north-west,** from a position NE of La Platte Pierre (49°30′N 2°40′W) (11.39) the line of bearing 130° of Fort Hommet (49°28′·5N 2°36′·7W) leads in the approach passing (with positions given from Fort Hommet):
   Between Le Boin and associated dangers (2 miles WNW) (11.40) and the rock awash (2 miles NW) lying 2 cables SW of Les Grunes de Nord-Ouest (11.40); thence:

2   Midway between the dangers off-lying Boue Aubert (1½ miles WNW) and a 2·5 m patch (1 mile NW) lying 2 cables WSW of Boue de Jardin; thence:

NE of Boue Vazon (6½ cables WNW) to the alignment (194°) of Fort Richmond (1 mile SW) with Torteval Church (spire), 2 miles farther SSW, when the track leads SSE to the anchorage passing:

3   Between Petit État and associated danger (3 cables NW) and Les Fourquies (6 cables WNW).
Clearing bearing:
   The line of bearing 201° of Hanois Light (49°26′N 2°42′W) (11.36) open W of La Pendante, 1¼ miles NNE (11.39), clears WNW of Grande Étacre, Boue Sarre and Le Boin.

11.43

1   **Approaching from north — leading marks:**
   Front mark. Fort Richmond (49°27′·9N 2°37′·8W).
   Rear mark. Torteval Church (spire) (2 miles SSW of the front mark).
   From a position SE of Les Frettes (49°32′N 2°37′W) (11.39) the alignment (194°) of the these marks leads in the approach passing (with positions given from Fort Hommet (49°28′·5N 2°36′·7W)):

2   ESE of Suzanne (1¾ miles NNW), Les Grunettes (1½ miles NNW) and Boue De Jardin (1 mile NNW); and:
   WNW of Boue Saint Saviour (1 mile N) and Moulière (6 cables NNW) to a position E of Boue Vazon (6½ cables WNW) when the track leads generally SSE to the head of the bay as given above.

3   **Clearing bearings.**
   The line of bearing 108° of Martello Tower No 11 standing on Rousse Point (49°30′N 2°33′W) seen midway between Vale Church (heavy prominent spire) and Vale Mill Tower (6½ cables and 1½ miles ESE, respectively) (11.74) clears NNE of Les Grunes de Nord-Ouest and Suzanne.

4   The alignment (204°) of Fort Hommet with Torteval Church (3 miles SSW) and open WNW of Grand Saut Rocher (1¾ miles NNE) (11.51) clears WNW of Hoffets (3 miles NNE) (11.50).

Anchorage
11.44

1   A good anchorage is afforded in Vazon Bay during E winds in depths of 4 to 9 m, sand. With W winds there is usually a heavy swell rendering it dangerous to approach the bay.

Landing
11.45

1   **Vazon Bay.** A seawall borders the E and W shores of Vazon Bay; a slip is situated 3 cables SE of Fort Hommet.

Minor bays and anchorages

Rocquaine Bay
11.46

1   **Description.** Rocquaine Bay indents the coast between Pezeries Point (49°26′N 2°40′W) and L'Erée Point, 1½ miles NNE (11.36). The coastal bank consisting of sand and shingle is broken by many outcrops of rock and dries up to 6 cables offshore.

2   Lihou Island (11.36) lies on a drying reef 3½ cables NW of L'Erée Point to which it is connected by a causeway; several rocks and islets extend 2 cables W of the island. Île Lissroy is joined to the SE corner of Lihou Island by a shingle ridge. Fort Grey (white tower) stands in the S part of the bay, 6 cables ENE of Pezeries Point.

Local knowledge is required.

11.47

1 **Approaches.** The S entrance is between La Grosse Rock, lying 2 cables WSW of Pezeries Point, and Hayes Rock situated 4 cables W. The NW entrance is between the rocks SW of Lihou Island and the reef 3 cables SW. The alignments for approaching the bay and anchorages are shown on the chart.

11.48

1 **Anchorage:** 4 cables SSW of Fort Saumarez (11.36) in depths of about 4 m, gravel and sand covered with grass and weed, as shown on the chart. The holding ground is not good and W winds send in a heavy sea, especially from 3 hours before to 3 hours after HW.

Anchorage can also be obtained 1½ cables N and 3¾ cables NE of Pezeries Point, as shown on the chart, approaching through the S entrance.

Landing: pier, marked at its outer end by a beacon, in the SW corner of the bay 4 cables SW of Fort Grey.

Perelle Bay

11.49

1 **Description.** Perelle Bay (49°28′N 2°38′W) is entered between Cone Rock (11.40) and the drying reef which forms the SW side of the bay. About 3½ cables from the head of the bay there is a channel between the reefs, about ½ cable wide, which leads to the beach; the W entrance point is marked by a beacon (black staff).

2 **Local knowledge** is required.

Approach on the alignment (102°) of Fort Hommet and Saint Matthew Church (11.41) to a position W of Soufleuresse when the line of bearing 128° of the Cement Mill leads into the bay passing very close SW of Colombelle situated in the approaches to the bay.

3 **Anchorages.** Perelle Bay affords good shelter to mariners in small craft in offshore winds at LW; it is not safe in W winds.

Anchorage can also be obtained under the shelter of Lihou Island, as shown on the chart, distant about 3¾ cables N of L'Erée Point.

Dangerous bank

11.50

1 A bank extends out to about 1¼ miles from the coast between Grande Rocque (49°29′N 2°35′W) (11.40) and Fort Pembroke, 2½ miles NE (11.55). Numerous reefs and detached rocks, many of which dry, lie on this bank; the outermost are (with positions given from Grande Rocque): Grand Saut Rocher (8 cables N) (11.51); L'Etacq (1 mile N); Petite Saut Rocher (9 cables NNE); Moulière (1¾ miles NNE); Hoffets (2 miles NNE); Fruquiers (2¼ miles NNE); Boues de la Fosse (2½ miles NE); Fosse de Faye (3¼ miles NE).

2 **Local knowledge** is required for the channels S and E of this bank.

Clearing bearing:

The line of bearing 108° of Cul de L'Autel (49°30′·4N 2°25′·5W) (11.116) open NNE of Grandes Brayes, 3 miles WNW, (11.68) (chart 3654) clears NNE of Fosse de Faye but not the dangerous wreck (position approximate) charted 9 cables WNW of Fosse de Faye.

Grand Saut Rocher

11.51

1 **Anchorage,** sheltered from E winds, can be found inside Grand Saut Rocher (49°30′N 2°35′W).

Local knowledge is required.

Grand Havre and approaches

11.52

1 **Description.** Between Grande Rocque (49°29′N 2°35′W) (11.40) and Rousse Point, 1½ miles ENE, the coast is indented by four small bays all of which dry out; they are sandy but their entrances are narrowed by drying rocky ledges extending in places 6 cables offshore. Knife Rock stands on one of these ledges, 4¾ cables WNW of Rousse Point.

2 Grand Havre (49°30′N 2°33′W) is entered between Rousse Point and a point 4 cables NNE; there is a martello tower on each of the entrance points. The bay consists mainly of sand broken by several large outcrops of rock; it dries over 4 cables from its head and about 2 cables from its E shore.

Local knowledge is required, see 11.50.

11.53

1 **Approach.** From N the alignment (171°) of the E extremity of Rousse Point with Victoria Tower (11.74), 2½ miles S, leads in the approach passing between La Main and Rousse de Mer, which lie 1¼ miles N and 1 mile NNW, respectively, of Rousse Point and within ¼ cable of a 1·4 m patch lying 7½ cables N of the same point.

11.54

1 **Anchorages and berth.** Anchorage can be obtained in Grand Havre in depths of 3 to 4 m, sand and weed, with good shelter from S and E winds; NW winds send in a heavy swell, particularly from 3 hours before to 3 hours after local HW.

2 A recommended anchorage, shown on the chart, is situated 2¼ cables SW of the martello tower on the E entrance point but clear of the drying rocks in the entrance of the bay; mariners in smaller craft may anchor in a depth of 2 m about 1 cable SE of this berth.

3 A pier, marked at its head by a beacon (black pole) extends ENE from Rousse Point; a drying rock marked by a beacon (pole) lies close SE of the pierhead. There is a safe berth for craft capable of taking the ground on the SE side of Rousse Point.

Baie de la Jaonneuse

11.55

1 **Description.** Baie de la Jaonneuse is situated between Crève Coeur (49°30′·6N 2°32′·1W) and Fort Pembroke, 2 cables E. The bay is small and rocky; a narrow sandy gully dries at the head of the bay where there is a ramp and a martello tower.

L'Ancresse Bay

11.56

1 **Description.** L'Ancresse Bay (49°30′·5N 2°31′·5W) is entered between the rocky points on which stand Fort Pembroke and Fort Le Plomb, 5 cables E, and affords shelter to mariners in small craft during winds between SE and WSW. Martello towers stand at intervals close to the shore around the bay but the central one, No 6, is not easily distinguished from seaward. A rock which dries 2·8 m is situated about 1½ cables ESE of Fort Pembroke.

2 **Firing danger area,** see 11.85.

Local knowledge is required, see 11.50.

Anchorage can be obtained in depths from 4 to 9 m, muddy sand, clear of the submarine cables which are landed in the S part of the bay; the E cable is disused. The holding ground is good.

Side channel
11.57

1 **Passage between Grand Havre and Fort Pembroke** (49°30′·9N 2°32′·4W); a channel ½ cable wide leads between a chain of submerged reefs, parts of which dry, lying within 7½ cables of the coast between Grand Havre (49°30′N 2°33′W) (11.52) and Fort Pembroke, 7½ cables E.
Local knowledge is required.

2 The line of bearing 092° of Platte Fougère Light (49°31′N 2°29′W) (11.74), with Grande Amfroque (11.116) (3 miles E) open S, leads through the passage passing about ¼ cable S of two rocks which dry 1·0 and 1·2 m.

GUERNSEY SOUTH COAST

General information

Charts 807, 808, 3654
Route
11.58

1 From a position off the SW point of Guernsey the route leads generally ESE along the S side of the island to S of Saint Martin's Point (49°25′N 2°32′W), a distance of about 12 miles.

Topography
11.59

1 The S coast of Guernsey between Pleinmont Point (49°26′N 2°40′W) and Saint Martin's Point, 6 miles E, is high and cliffy; the whole coast is clear of dangers at 8 cables from the shore.

Between Pleinmont Point and Pointe de la Moye, 3¼ miles E, the S coast is steep and rocky and indented with small coves. La Corbière (49°25′N 2°37′W), a headland, lies 8 cables W of Pointe de la Moye.

Directions
(continued from 11.21)

Principal marks
11.60

1 **Landmarks:**
   Hanois Lighthouse (grey round granite tower black lantern, 33 m in height) (49°26′N 2°42′W).
   Lattice Mast (red lights) (49°26′N 2°40′W) on Pleinmont Point.
   Lookout Tower (disused) (49°25′·5N 2°39′·4W).
   Lookout Tower (disused) (49°25′·3N 2°37′·0W).

2 Saint Martin's Point Lighthouse (flat-roofed white concrete building, 5 m in height) (49°25′·3N 2°31′·7W) standing on a rocky spur below the point.
   Doyle's Column (square granite tower) (49°25′·6N 2°32′·0W) standing on high ground above Saint Martin's Point.

3 **Major lights:**
   Hanois Light (49°26′N 2°42′W) (see above).
   Roches Douvres Light (tower with green roof on dwelling, 65 m in height) (49°06′N 2°49′W).
   Grosnez Point Light (white concrete hut) (49°16′N 2°15′W).

Saint Martin's Point and Light from SE (11.60)
(Original dated 2001)

(Photograph - Air Images)

General directions
11.61

1 For general directions for approaching Guernsey from W, see 11.38.

Les Hanois to Saint Martin's Point
11.62

1 From a position W of Les Hanois (49°26′N 2°42′W) (11.39) the route leads generally ESE passing (with positions given from La Corbière (49°25′N 2°37′W)):

> SSW of South Boue (3½ miles WNW) the S-most danger off Les Hanois; thence:
> SSW of Baissière (2½ miles W); thence:

2
> SSW of Boue Phillips (1¾ miles WSW); the shallower Boue Baker lies 2 cables NNW. Thence:
> SSW of Boues des Kaines (1 mile WSW), a shoal lying 4 cables SSE of Les Kaines d'Amont, a rocky patch with drying rocks; thence:

3
> SSW of Les Lieuses (4 cables SSW), the outermost dangers off La Corbière (11.59). At night all dangers W of Les Lieuses, except Boues des Kaines, are avoided by keeping in the red sector (011°–081°) of Saint Martin's Light (49°25′N 2°32′W). Thence:
> SSW of Rousse de Moye (8 cables ESE), the outermost danger off Pointe de la Moye; thence:

4
> SSW of Baleine Rock (1¾ miles ESE), the SW-most danger off Icart Point; thence:
> SSW of Grune de Jerbourg (3 miles E), a group of rocks extending SSE from Jerbourg Point; they are covered by the red sector (011°–081°) of Saint Martin's Point Light. Thence:
> To a position S of Saint Martins' Point (3¼ miles E) (11.60).

11.63

1 **Clearing bearings:**

> The line of bearing 097° of La Corbière (49°25′N 2°37′W) (11.59) just open S of Tas de Pois d'Aval, 2 miles WNW, clears S of South Boue, distant 2½ cables.
> The line of bearing 298° of Hanois Light (49°26′N 2°42′W) (11.36) open twice the width of Tas de Pois d'Aval, 1¾ miles ESE, clears SSW of Les Kaines d'Amont and Les Lieuses.

2
> The line of bearing 294° of Hanois Light (49°26′N 2°42′W) and open SW of the land in the vicinity of Pleinmont Point, 1 mile ESE, clears SSW of Les Lieuses and all dangers E of them. The light is obscured by the S edge of Pleinmont Point N of the 294° bearing.

3
> The line of bearing 026° of Brehon Light Tower (49°28′N 2°29′W) (11.74) open ESE of Longue Pierre Beacon, 3¼ miles SSW (11.76), clears ESE of Grunes de Jerbourg and Fourquie de Jerbourg. This transit, and the transit "V's" of La Corbière in line with Pointe de la Moye 276° shown on the chart, pass very close to Grunes de Jerbourg and Fourquie de Jerbourg. Mariners in small craft using these transits should take particular care to avoid being set on to these dangers.

> *(Directions continue for the approaches to Saint Peter Port at 11.74 and for Big Russel at 11.119)*

Icart and Moulin Huet Bays
Charts 807, 808
General information
11.64

1 **Description.** Icart Bay and Moulin Huet Bay, separated by Icart Point (49°25′N 2°34′W), are situated between Pointe de la Moye and Jerbourg Point, 2 miles E; both bays afford a good anchorage during E and N winds, but Moulin Huet Bay, being easier of access, is preferable.

11.65

1 **Icart Bay.** The shores of Icart Bay, lying to the W of Icart Point, are rocky; Petit Bôt Bay, a small cove with a martello tower at its head, lies in the NW corner of the bay.

Anchorage can be obtained in Icart Bay, as shown on the chart, 2 cables NW of Fourquie de la Moye, a drying rock situated in the middle of the bay, in depths of 12 m fine sand.

Landing: stony beach in Petit Bôt Bay; care should be taken to avoid the rocks which front it.

11.66

1 **Moulin Huet Bay.** Two coves, Petit Port and Moulin Huet lie on the N shore of the bay. Saints Bay, with a martello tower at its head, lies on the W shore.

The W shore of Moulin Huet Bay is bordered by drying rocks extending in places nearly 2 cables offshore.

2 **Leading marks.** The alignment (291°) of the following marks leads from ESE towards Moulin Huet Bay passing SSW of the dangers off Jerbourg Point (49°25′N 2°32′W) (11.62):

> Front mark. Icart Point (49°25′N 2°34′W).
> Rear mark. White House on the W side of Icart Bay (1 mile WNW of the front mark).

3 When the rocky bluff on the E shore of the bay, about 3 cables N of Jerbourg Point, bears NE, the track then leads NE towards the anchorage.

From SW the rocky bluff on the E shore of the bay can be used as a headmark bearing NE which leads into the bay passing between Banc du Petit Port, lying 3 cables SW of Jerbourg Point, and the rocks on the W side of the bay.

4 **Anchorage** can be obtained 1 cable S of Mouillière, a drying rock situated in the middle of the bay about 4 cables NW of Jerbourg Point, in depths of about 8 m, fine sand, or in lesser depths of about 5 m about 1½ cables NE of the same rock. In 1992 it was reported that the drying rock charted 2 cables NNE of Mouillière does not cover and has a height of about 3 m.

A submarine cable runs SE from Saints Bay to Jersey. Disused submarine cables run across the entrance to the bay.

5 **Landing** can be effected in both Petit Port and Moulin Huet although there is often an awkward swell even in offshore winds. There is a rough slipway on the W side of Saints Bay.

APPROACHES TO SAINT PETER PORT

General information

Charts 807, 808, 3654
Routes
11.67

1 From S of Saint Martin's Point (49°25′N 2°32′W), the SE point of Guernsey, the route to Saint Peter Port (11.102) leads generally N passing between The Great Bank (11.76) and the E coast of the island, or alternatively, between The

Great Bank and the dangers extending W from Jethou (11.23).

2   Saint Peter Port can also be approached from N through Little Russel (49°30′N 2°28′W), the channel between Guernsey and Herm, which is much constricted by the reefs and dangers extending from, and lying off, the coasts of these islands, passing either NE or SW of Roustel (49°29′N 2°29′W). See also 11.25.

Topography
11.68

1   **Guernsey east coast.** The N half of the E coast of Guernsey is mainly low-lying with a few small hills, but close N of Saint Peter Port (49°27′·5N 2°32′·0W) the ground rises to the high ridge which borders the S coast, terminating at Saint Martin's Point, about 2½ miles S.

    Between Saint Martin's Point and Les Terres Point, 1½ miles N, the coast is steep and rocky except at Fermain Bay midway between these two points. This part of the coast is fronted by several dangers.

2   The coast between Saint Peter Port and Saint Sampson Harbour (11.88), 1½ miles NNE, consists mainly of sand broken by extensive rocky outcrops fringed by detached rocks and shoal patches. There are a number of prominent oil storage tanks on the coast to the S of Saint Sampson Harbour. Between Bordeaux Harbour (11.97), which lies 5 cables NE of Saint Sampson Harbour, and Fort Doyle, 1 mile farther N, the coast is bordered by drying rocks extending up to 3 cables offshore. Homptole and Houmet Paradis are two islets connected to the shore at LW situated 4 and 7 cables SSE, respectively, of Fort Doyle. Grandes Brayes (49°31′N 2°30′W), a reef which dries in most parts and on which stand above-water rocks, is situated nearly 1 mile N of Fort Doyle.

11.69

1   **Herm and Jethou.** Herm (49°28′N 2°27′·7W) (11.23), 1¼ miles long and 5 cables wide, has a rocky coast with wide sandy bays. There is a small harbour and a group of buildings, including an hotel, on the W side of the island. The N coast of the island is bordered by a sandy beach close off which stands Mouisonnière (11.100).

2   Jethou (49°27′·5N 2°27′·7W) is separated from Herm by Percée Passage (11.95). The rocky islets of Crevichon and Grande Fauconnière are connected with Jethou at LW; the former lies close NW and the latter close SE of the island. A beacon (white conical stone) stands on the summit of each of these islets.

Controlling depths
11.70

1   There are depths of 45 m in both entrances to Little Russel, but in the narrowest part of the channel there are a number of rocky shoals with depths considerably less than 10 m over them. The most significant of these rocky shoals is probably Grune au Rouge (49°28′·5N 2°29′·8W), two rocks with a least charted depth of 4·0 m over them (reported 1994 as 3·8 m), which lie in mid-channel only ½ cable NW of the principal leading line by day through Little Russel.

2   Using the S approach, W of The Great Bank, depths of about 20 m can be maintained as far as the anchorage (11.87) W of Herm.

Pilotage
11.71

1   For details of pilotage, see 11.30.
    Local knowledge, see 11.77.

Submarine cables
11.72

1   A submarine cable and a submarine power cable extends ESE thence generally S from the E coast of Guernsey at position 49°27′N 2°32′W in Havelet Bay (11.96) to the N coast of Jersey.

Tidal streams
11.73

1   In the narrowest part of Little Russel the streams are rectilinear attaining a spring rate of 5¼ kn in both directions. For details see information on the chart and *Admiralty Tidal Stream Atlas for the Channel Islands and adjacent coasts of France.*

Directions
(continued from 11.63)

Principal marks
11.74

1   **Landmarks:**
        Doyle's Column (49°25′·6N 2°32′·0W) (square granite tower).
        Castle Cornet (castle with flagstaff, SE bastion painted white) (49°27′·2N 2°31′·6W) on the S side of Saint Peter Port harbour.
        Castle Breakwater Lighthouse (dark round granite tower white on NE side, 12 m in height) (49°27′·3N 2°31′·5W) exhibited from the breakwater head.

2   Victoria Tower (49°27′·5N 2°32′·6W) standing on high ground overlooking Saint Peter Port.
        Brehon Light Tower (beacon on round tower) (49°28′·3N 2°29′·3W) standing on a rock of the same name situated in the middle of a reef.

Brehon Light Tower from SW (11.74)
(Original dated 1997)

(Photograph - A T Reynolds)

3   Three Chimneys (red obstruction lights) (49°29′·1N 2°31′·0W) standing N of Saint Sampson Harbour.
        Vale Mill Tower (conspicuous round concrete lookout tower) (49°29′·5N 2°30′·9W), the tallest object on the NE part of Guernsey.
        Platte Fougère Lighthouse (white octagonal tower black band, 25 m in height) (49°31′N 2°29′W).

4   **Major lights:**
        Castle Breakwater Light — as above.
        Platte Fougère Light — as above.

Other aids to navigation
11.75

1   **Racon:** transmits from Platte Fougère Light (49°31′N 2°29′W).
    For details see *Admiralty List of Radio Signals Volume 2.*

Approach from south passing west of The Great Bank
11.76

1   **Leading marks:**
        Rear mark. Vale Mill Tower (conspicuous round concrete lookout tower) (49°29′·5N 2°30′·9W).

Platte Fougère Lighthouse from NE (11.74)

(Original dated 2001)

(Photograph - Air Images)

Front mark (largest oil storage tank S of Saint
Sampson) (8 cables S of the rear mark) often
difficult to identify in conditions of moderate or
poor visibility.

2   From a position S of Saint Martin's Point (49°25′N
2°32′W) (11.60), from where a light is exhibited, the
alignment (004°) of these marks leads in the channel
passing (with positions given from Castle Cornet
(49°27′N 2°32′W)):

3   Along the W side of The Great Bank with its
shallowest part (1¼ miles SE) lying about 1 mile
offshore. The bank runs nearly parallel to the
coastline between Saint Martin's Point and Saint
Peter Port. And:
E of Longue Pierre (1¾ miles S), marked by a
beacon (yellow post, topmark letters "LP"); thence:

4   E of Gabrielle Rock (1¼ miles S); thence:
E of Piette (8 cables S), a patch lying 1 cable SE of
Anfré, a drying rock marked by a beacon (yellow
pole, red letter "A" topmark); thence:
E of Forein (2½ cables E) to the anchorage (11.86) or
Saint Peter Port harbour (11.102) as required.

5   **Useful mark:**
Pepperpot Beacon (white conical stone beacon)
(49°26′·2N 2°32′·1W) standing among trees above
Fermain Point.

11.77

1   **At night** the line of bearing 353° of Castle Breakwater
Light (49°27′N 2°31′W) (11.74) leads in the channel to a
position SE of Piette. The line of bearing 198°, astern, of
Saint Martin's Point Light (49°25′N 2°32′W) (11.60) then
leads in the channel passing between Anfré and The Great
Bank to the alignment (308°) of Castle Breakwater Light
and White Rock Pier Light, 1¼ cables NW, when the track

then leads as required to the anchorage (11.86) or Saint
Peter Port harbour (11.102).

2   Apart from Longue Pierre, the other dangers lying off
the SE coast are covered by the red sector (185°–191°) of
Saint Martin's Point Light.

Caution. The existence of numerous unlit fishing marker
floats, particuly in the S part, make it unadvisable to
attempt this passage by night without local knowledge.

Alternative approach from south passing east of The Great Bank
11.78

1   **Leading line.** The line of bearing 017° of Roustel Light
(49°29′N 2°29′W) (11.79) open ESE of Brehon Light
Tower, 1 mile SSW (11.74), leads in the channel passing
(with positions given from Castle Cornet (49°27′N
2°32′W)):

2   ESE of The Great Bank (1¼ miles SE) (11.76); and:
WNW of Lower Heads (2¼ miles SE) with Sardrière
lying 2 cables farther ESE, the S-most dangers off
Jethou, marked on their S side by Lower Heads
Light Buoy (S cardinal); thence:
WNW of Musé (2 miles ESE), a drying rock lying
1 cable WSW of Demie Ferrière, which is marked
by a beacon (yellow pole orange letter "M"
topmark); thence:

3   WNW of the chain of reefs, some of which dry and
on which stand a number of above-water rocks,
which lie between Demie Ferrière and Jethou
(2½ miles E). Les Barbées (2 miles ESE), a reef
with two above-water rocks on it, the N of which
is marked by a beacon (yellow pole, black cylinder
topmark) is situated near the centre of this chain.
Thence:
To anchorage (11.86) or Saint Peter Port harbour
(11.102) as required.

4   **Clearing bearing:**
The line of bearing 315° of White Rock Pier Light
(49°27′·4N 2°31′·5W) (11.112) open SW of Castle
Breakwater Light (11.74), 1¼ cables SE, clears SW
of Lower Heads.
Useful mark:
Alligande Light Beacon (orange "A" on black mast)
(49°27′·9N 2°28′·7W).

Little Russel — passing south-east of Roustel and Grune au Rouge
11.79

1   **Leading lights:**
Front mark. Brehon Light Tower (49°28′N 2°29′W)
(11.74).
Rear mark. Saint Martin's Point Light (3¼ miles SSW
of the front mark) (11.60). No other leading marks
are so prominent or show so quickly an alteration
of the mariner's position, but Saint Martin's Point
Light being lower than Brehon Tower may be
obscured when they are in transit.

2   From a position NE of Guernsey the alignment (208°) of
these lights leads in the channel passing (with positions
given from Castle Cornet (49°27′N 2°32′W)):
WNW of Platte Boue (49°31′N 2°25′W), the N-most
danger off Herm; thence:

3   Between Pensionnaire (49°30′N 2°27′W), a patch
lying 4½ cables W of Tautenay, a reef which dries
in parts marked by a light beacon (black and white
beacon) near its N end, and Platte Fougère
(49°31′N 2°29′W) a reef which dries, steep-to on

its E side. A light (11.74) is exhibited from the N end of the reef.

4   Thence to a position NE of Roustel (2¾ miles NNE) distant 3 cables.

Caution. Patches of considerably less than 10 m, the positions of which can best be seen from the chart, lie in the vicinity of Roustel on both sides of the leading line.

Leading marks:

Front mark (white patch on SE bastion of Castle Cornet) (11.74).

5   Rear mark. Belvedere House (large white building) (4 cables SW of the front mark).

The alignment (223°) of these marks then leads in the channel SE of Roustel passing:

NW of Cavale (3 miles NE) (11.100); thence:

6   Between Roustel, a reef which dries, on the S end of which stands a light beacon (white metal framework column, 8 m in height), and Rousse (2¾ miles NE, respectively), marked by a beacon (yellow iron cross with anchor fluke at each point); thence:

7   NW of Boues Genneté (2¼ miles NE), the outermost of the shoals extending NW from Corbette de la Mare, a drying rock marked by a beacon (yellow pole, orange disc topmark); thence:

NW of both Boue Petite and Brehonnet, two rocks which dry, the NW and W-most dangers off Brehon (1¾ miles NE) (11.74); and:

8   About ½ cable SE of Grune au Rouge (1¾ miles NE) (11.70). On approaching Grune au Rouge keep the N end of Belvedere House in line with the S edge of the white patch on Castle Cornet to ensure passing well clear SE of this rock. Thence:

NW of Boue de la Rade (1¼ miles NE); and:

SE of both Trois Grunes (1¼ miles NE) and Boue Agenor (1 mile NE) (11.81) to anchorage (11.86) or Saint Peter Port harbour (11.102) as required.

11.80

1   **Clearing bearings:**

The alignment (231°) of Platte Light (49°29′N 2°29′W) (11.81) with Victoria Tower, 2½ miles SW (11.74), and the alignment (221°) of Tautenay Light (49°30′N 2°27′W) (11.79) with Brehon Light Tower, 2½ miles SW (11.74), clears NW of Platte Boue by 1¼ and ½ cable, respectively.

2   **Positioning marks:**

The alignment (152°) of the two beacons on Grande Amfroque (49°31′N 2°25′W) (11.116) indicate the position of Platte Boue.

Little Russel — passing north-west of Roustel and Grune au Rouge

11.81

1   **Leading marks:**

Front mark. Roustel Light Beacon (49°29′·3N 2°28′·7W) (11.79).

Rear mark. Brehon Tower (1 mile SSW of the front mark) (11.74).

From a position NE of Guernsey the alignment (198°) of these marks leads in the approach passing (with positions given from Castle Cornet (49°27′N 2°32′W)):

2   ESE of Platte Fougère (4 miles NNE) (11.79); thence:

ESE of Grande Canupe and Petite Canupe, the principal rocks of a group of drying and below-water rocks. Petite Canupe (3½ miles NNE). The S rock is marked by a light beacon (S cardinal). Thence:

Passage NW of Roustel - Leading Marks from NNE (11.81)

(Original dated 1997)

(Photograph - Capt F A Lawrence MRIN, Navitrom Limited)

3   ESE of Tasse (3 miles NNE) a rock which dries lying about 1½ cables E of Corbette d'Amont, which is marked by a beacon tower (yellow conical, yellow staff with framework globe topmark), to a position about 3 cables NNE of Roustel.

4   **Leading marks:**

Front mark. Castle Breakwater Light (2 cables NE) (11.74).

Rear mark. Belvedere Light (white square daymark on white tower, 4 m in height) (4 cables SW).

Belvedere House   Belvedere Light

Castle Breakwater Light

Passage NW of Roustel - Leading Marks 220° (11.81)

(Original dated 2003)

(Photograph - D. Acland)

5   The alignment (220°) of these marks, which are often difficult to distinguish in the afternoon light or if it is hazy, then leads in the fairway NW of Roustel passing:

Between Roustel (2¾ miles NE) (11.79) and Le Gant (2¾ miles NNE); thence:

6   Between the patches lying close NE and E of Platte (2¼ miles NNE), a drying rock from where a light (green conical stone tower, 9 m in height) is

exhibited, and Boues Genneté (2¼ miles NE) (11.79); thence:

> Between Grune au Rouge (1¾ miles NE) (11.70) and Fosse Torode (1¾ miles NE) and Mervilliere (1½ miles NE), two shoals, the outermost dangers E and SE of Torode (11.92).

7   On the line of bearing 337° of Vale Mill Tower (2½ miles N) (11.74) open W of Vale Castle (ruins) (2 miles NNE) Belvedere Light should be opened a little SE of Castle Breakwater Light to pass clear SE of both Trois Grunes (1¼ miles NE) and Boue Agenor (1 mile NE) with its associated shallower 2·1 m patch close SW, and NW of Boue de la Rade (1¼ miles NE) to anchorage (11.86) or Saint Peter Port harbour (11.102) as required.

Caution, see 11.79.

11.82

1   **Clearing bearings:**

> The alignment (149°) of La Pointe du Gentilhomme (49°29′N 2°27′W), the low NE point of Herm, with the SW extremity of Little Sark, 5 miles SSE, clears ENE of all dangers between Grandes Brayes (11.68) and Petite Canupe.

Little Russel — at night
11.83

1   **Approach** in the white sector of Platte Fougère Light (49°31′N 2°29′W) (11.74) between the bearings of 176°–243° to a position NE, distant 2 miles, from that light. The track then follows the alignment (198°) (11.81) of Roustel and Brehon lights to a position NNE, distant 3 cables, from Roustel. The track then follows the alignment (220°) (11.81) of Castle Breakwater and Belvedere Lights passing NW of Roustel.

2   This latter alignment leads close to Trois Grunes, Boue Agenor and over its associated shoal patch close SW of it (11.81), but these dangers can be avoided by opening the leading lights after passing Grune au Rouge and keeping in the white sector of Platte Light (49°29′N 2°29′W) (11.81), which changes from red to white on the line of bearing 024°, astern, until clear, noting Boue de la Rade which lies in the channel 2 cables E of Trois Grunes.

> *(Directions for Saint Peter Port continue at 11.111,*
> *for W of Casquets at 11.135*
> *and for Race of Alderney at 11.327)*

Side channels

Musé Passage
11.84

1   **General information.** Musé, the S-most of the passages S of Herm and Jethou, leads between Lower Heads (49°26′N 2°29′W) (11.78) and Musé, 5 cables N.

Leading marks:

> The alignment (291°) of the N end of Castle Cornet (49°27′N 2°32′W) with Victoria Tower, 7 cables WNW, leads through the passage.

2   **Caution.** Les Têtes Enragées and Les Audames, two shoal patches, lie on the S side of the passage 1¾ cables N and 4 cables NNW, respectively, of Lower Heads.

Doyle Passage
11.85

1   **General information.** Doyle Passage, a side channel which leads into Little Russel from NW, lies between Fort Doyle (49°30′N 2°30′W) (11.33) and the dangers lying to the NE of it.

Local knowledge is required.

2   **Firing danger area.** Firing practices are carried out from a rifle-range situated on the headland S of Fort Le Plomb (49°31′N 2°31′W) (11.56). The danger area, as shown on the chart, extends about 1¼ miles N and 1½ miles NE of Fort Le Plomb. Red flags are displayed from Fort Le Plomb, No 4 Martello Tower and occasionally from a flagstaff standing 2 cables S of No 4 Martello Tower, ½ hour before firing begins and when practices are in progress. Mariners should keep clear of the danger area when the red flags are displayed, see also 1.30.

3   **Approaching** from NW the line of bearing 146° of Corbette d'Amont Beacon Tower (49°29′·6N 2°29′·4W) (11.81) seen midway between Herm and Jethou, about 2¼ miles SE, leads into Doyle Passage passing 1 cable NE of Fort Doyle.

Anchorages

Charts 3140, 807, 808
Great Road
11.86

1   **General information.** Great Road fronts the harbour of Saint Peter Port (49°27′·5N 2°32′·0W) (11.102) and affords good shelter from winds from SSW through W to N; the holding ground is good. Winds from between SE and SSW send in a considerable sea and swell, especially with a falling tide, rendering the anchorage untenable; conditions are also uncomfortable with strong winds from between NNE and SE.

2   **Tidal streams.** In Great Road there may be eddies close inshore; thus off Saint Peter Port about 1½ cables ENE of White Rock Pier (11.109), the N-going stream begins 1¾ hours earlier and the S-going stream ¾ hour earlier than the streams farther offshore. For details see information on the chart and *Admiralty Tidal Stream Atlas for the Channel Islands and adjacent coasts of France.*

3   **Anchorage.** The best anchorage for mariners in larger vessels is found 5 cables E of the harbour entrance, as shown on the chart. Recommended anchorages for smaller vessels are situated 4 cables and 6½ cables NE, respectively, of the head of Castle Breakwater, as shown on the chart.

4   **Mooring buoy.** A lighted mooring buoy (yellow casing, orange light) is moored in position 49°27′·9N 2°31′·0W, close SE of the recommended anchorage position 6½ cables NE of the harbour entrance.

Caution. Demie Flieroque (49°28′·1N 2°31′·4W) marked by a beacon (yellow, orange letter "F" topmark) and Fourquies of Belle Grève, 2½ cables ESE, two groups of rocks which dry, lie in the N part of the anchorage.

5   **Sewer outfall** runs between Demie Flieroque and Boue Agenor, 5 cables ESE.

Restricted anchorage. Mariners should not anchor within the circular area, shown on the charts, off the entrance to Saint Peter Port; this area should be kept clear for vessels entering or leaving the port.

Useful marks:

> Sardrette Beacon (yellow, orange letter "S" topmark) (49°27′·6N 2°31′·5W).

Charts 807, 808
West of Herm
11.87

1   **Anchorage.** Shelter from E winds can be found under the lee provided by Herm and Jethou anchoring on the alignment (018°) of Brehon Light Tower (49°28′N 2°29′W) and Roustel Light Beacon, 1 mile NNE, distant 7 cables or

more from Brehon Tower. A recommended berth is shown on the chart.

When the wind is between SE and SSW, smoother conditions will be found NE of Herm.

2   **Caution.** Boue Marquand and Les Guepés, two patches, lie in the anchorage area 5 cables SSW and 7½ cables S, respectively, of Brehon Light Tower.

Saint Sampson Harbour

General information
11.88

1   **Position and function.** Saint Sampson Harbour (49°29′N 2°31′W), a minor port, is situated about 1½ miles NNE of Saint Peter Port and is suitable for small coasting vessels and pleasure craft.

Approach and entry. The harbour is approached from Little Russel and entered between the heads of North Pier and South Arm.

Limiting conditions
11.89

1   **Controlling depth.** The harbour, and its approaches for over 1 cable outside the entrance, dries to a sandy bottom. The entrance is 36 m wide and has depths of 7·3 m at MHWS and from 4·9 to 5·2 m at MHWN.

Maximum size of vessel handled. The harbour is suitable for small coasting vessels with a draught of about 4·6 m and up to 76 m in length.

2   A vessel of 76·2 m in length and 6·1 m draught has used the port.

Tidal streams set across the entrance to the harbour making the approach difficult.

Arrival information
11.90

1   **Port radio.** All communication is through Saint Peter Port (Port Control), for details see 11.108.

Pilotage and ETA requirements, see 11.30.

Harbour
11.91

1   **General layout.** The harbour, which dries, is entered between New North Pier and South Arm and is divided into an inner and outer harbour by Crocq Pier which extends N from the S side of the harbour. On the S side of the entrance a breakwater extends about 1 cable ENE from Mont Crevelt and is continued ESE for a further cable by the N sea wall of the Longue Hougue basin.

2   There is a non-tidal marina in the inner harbour.

Traffic signals are exhibited by day and at night from Crocq Pier; when a red light is displayed mariners are prohibited from entering or leaving harbour. A flashing orange light on South Arm indicates that the commercial berths will be occupied over the next tide and should not be utilised for layby.

Directions for entering harbour
11.92

1   **Leading lights:**
     Front mark. Light (post, 2 m in height) (49°28′·9N 2°30′·7W) on the head of South Arm.
     Rear mark. Light (clock tower, 12 m in height) (2 cables WNW of the front mark).
   From a position about 4 cables S of Platte (49°29′N 2°29′W) (11.81) the alignment (286°) of these lights leads into the harbour passing (with positions given from the front mark):

2   Between SW Platte (5 cables E), a reef which dries in parts, and Torode (4 cables ESE) the highest of a number of drying rocks on a shoal on the S side of the entrance; thence:
   Between Crabière (2 cables E) and the NE corner of the sea wall of the Longue Hougue basin (2 cables ESE) on which chevron boards, floodlit at night, are established, to the harbour entrance.

3   **Useful marks:**
     Vivian (drying reef) (49°28′·5N 2°30′·7W) marked near its E end by a beacon tower (black and white bands).
     Light (post, 2 m in height) (49°28′·9N 2°30′·7W) on the head of North Pier.
     Light (red column, 6 m in height) (49°28′·9N 2°30′·7W) on the head of Crocq Pier.

Port services
11.93

1   **Repairs.** Patent slip with an extreme length of 60 m, extreme breadth of 10 m and a lifting capacity of 400 tonnes.

Passages south of Herm and Jethou
11.94

1   **General information.** Musé, Parfonde and Tobars Passages lead through the dangers S of Jethou and Herm. Apart from Musé Passage (11.84), the other passages should only be attempted with local knowledge.

The marks and alignments for these passages are shown on the chart.

Passages between Herm and Jethou
11.95

1   **General information.** Corbette, Percée and Alligande Passages, which lie between Herm and Jethou, should only be attempted with local knowledge. Alligande Passage should not be used near LW and in 1994 Percée Passage was reported to be silting up.

The marks and the alignments for the various passages are shown on the chart.

2   **Tidal streams.** No information regarding the tidal streams round Herm is available, except for that given below, but there must be strong eddies round and between the islets and rocks extending NE from the island. In Percée Passage the tidal streams begin as follows:

Interval from HW Saint Helier	Direction
−0530	SE and runs for 9 hours
+0330	NW and runs for 3½ hours

The NW-going stream is weaker than the SE-going stream.

Charts 807, 808, 3140
Harbours and anchorages — Guernsey east side
11.96

1   **Havelet Bay** (49°27′·1N 2°31′·7W) is entered between Castle Pier (11.109) and Les Terres Point, 5 cables S; the bay is sandy in the middle with many rocky patches extending from its shore.

2   **Approach:** between Moulinet (49°27′·0N 2°31′·5W) and Oyster Rock, 1½ cables NNE, two drying rocks marked by beacons (yellow poles, letter "M" and "O" topmarks, respectively) through an entrance fairway marked by can buoys (port and starboard hand) the outer pair of which are lighted in summer only.

3   **Anchorage,** sheltered from WSW through W to N, is available in the bay in depths of 1 to 2 m, clear of private moorings situated in the N part of bay. Care should be

taken not to anchor near the submarine cable and submarine power cable (11.72).

11.97

1   **Bordeaux Harbour** (49°29′·4N 2°30′·4W), about 2¼ miles N of Saint Peter Port, is suitable only for small craft; it has a bottom of sand and stones and dries out at about half tide.

Local knowledge is required.

Harbours and anchorages — Herm west side
11.98

1   **Rosière Anchorage** situated W of Point Sauzebourge (49°27′·8N 2°27′·1W), the S extremity of Herm, provides shelter to mariners in small craft except for winds from SW through S to ESE.

Percée, a rock marked by Gate Rock Light Beacon (W cardinal), lies 3 cables NW of Point Sauzebourge with Mouette a second rock 1 cable farther NE; these rocks lie close to the S edge of the drying bank extending W from Herm.

Local knowledge is required.

2   **Anchorage:** about 1 cable W of Point Sauzebourge, as shown on the chart. At spring tides the SE-going stream is strong and renders the anchorage uncomfortable until the bank to the N dries. Mariners in smaller craft can anchor closer inshore off Rosière Steps, 2 cables NNW of the same point, but the holding ground is not good.

Approach. The best approach is from Big Russel (11.115).

Landing: at Rosière Steps.

11.99

1   **Herm Harbour** (49°28′·2N 2°27′·2W), which dries, lies 2 cables N of Rosière Steps and is formed by a short pier extending NNW from the shore, from the head of which a light is exhibited. It is used extensively in the holiday season by excursion boats from Guernsey.

Several above-water rocks lie on the bank extending from the W side of Herm; Vermerette, a rock at the SW extremity of this bank, is marked by a light beacon (orange "V" on beacon).

2   **Shellfish beds,** as shown on the chart, are established on the bank between Hermetier, 2 cables NW of Herm Harbour, and Oyster Point, the NW point of the island, and also N of La Pointe du Gentilhomme, the N point of the island.

11.100

1   **Anchorage east of Cavale.** Cavale, a rock which dries, lies 3 cables E of Roustel (49°29′N 2°29′W) (11.79). Horse Rock and Boues Arees, drying rocks about 4 cables ENE of Cavale, lie on the NW extremity of a coastal bank extending 7 cables NW from the N coast of Herm.

2   Anchorage can be obtained ESE of Cavale on the alignment (117°) of Mouisonnière (49°29′·9N 2°27′·3W), a remarkable pointed rock, with Pierre au Rats (stone obelisk), 1½ cables ESE, on the line of bearing 224° of Brehon Tower (11.74), distant 1·2 miles, seen midway between Rousse (11.79) and Blanche, in depths of 7 to 8 m.

11.101

1   **Anchorages south of Tautenay.** Anchorage can be found 4 cables SSW and 4½ cables SW, respectively of Tautenay Light Beacon (49°30′N 2°27′W) (11.79), as shown on the chart, out of the strength of the tidal streams in depths of about 14 m, sand.

For passages between the N point of Herm and Grande Amfroque, see 11.131.

SAINT PETER PORT

General information
Chart 3140
Position
11.102

1   Saint Peter Port (49°27′·5N 2°32′·0W) is situated on the E coast of Guernsey and provides facilities for the island's thriving tourist trade.

Function
11.103

1   Saint Peter Port is the only deep-water harbour on the island and is a commercial port which handles the cargo produce of the island and various passenger services. It is also a popular port of call for yachts in the summer months.

Approach and entry
11.104

1   Saint Peter Port is approached from S passing between the E coast of the island and The Great Bank (11.76) about 7½ cables E, or alternatively E of The Great Bank. The port can also be approached from N through Little Russel (11.67), see also 11.6.

The port is entered between the heads of Castle Breakwater and White Rock Pier.

Traffic
11.105

1   Channel Island figures given at 11.249.

Port Authority
11.106

1   States of Guernsey, Board of Adminstration, States Harbours, Harbour Office, St Julian's Emplacement, Saint Peter Port, Guernsey, GY1 2LW.

Limiting conditions
11.107

1   **Controlling depth.** Least charted depth in the fairway 4·1 m in the entrance close N of the leading line, as shown on the chart.

Deepest and longest berths are at New Jetty (11.113).

Tidal levels. For information regarding tidal levels see information in *Admiralty Tide Tables.* Mean spring range about 7·9 m; mean neap range about 3·4 m.

2   **Maximum size of vessel handled.** Vessels up to 130 m in length with a draught of 8·9 m at MHWS or 6·7 m at MHWN can use the port.

A vessel of 11 000 dwt, 5·5 m draught and 130 m in length has used the port.

Arrival information
11.108

1   **Radio stations.** A coast radio station and a port radio station operate from the port and an information service is maintained throughout 24 hours, for details see *Admiralty Lists of Radio Signals Volume 1(1) and Volume 6(1)* respectively.

Pilotage. For details of pilotage and ETA requirements, see 11.30.

2   **Tugs** are not available at Saint Peter Port but can be obtained from Jersey.

Outer anchorages. For details of anchorage outside the harbour in Great Road or W of Herm, see 11.86 and 11.87.

Prohibited anchorage. Anchoring in the harbour is prohibited without the States Harbour Master's permission.

Albert Marina   Victoria Marina   North Esplanade   Queen Elizabeth II Marina

Albert Dock   Castle Cornet   Castle Breakwater

Saint Peter Port from SE (11.102)

(Original dated 2001)

(Photograph – Air Images)

Speed limit of 6 kn between the harbour entrance and New Jetty and 4 kn W of New Jetty is in force.

Harbour

General layout
11.109

1   The harbour at Saint Peter Port is formed on the N side by Saint Julian's Pier and White Rock Pier, and on the S side by Castle Pier and Castle Breakwater, which extends

1 cable to seaward of Castle Cornet (11.74). New Jetty extends SE from near the outer end of Saint Julian's Pier. The main commercial berths are on the N side of The Pool, immediately within the harbour entrance, in the vicinity of New Jetty and White Rock Pier.

2   The head of the harbour is bordered by a bank which dries out to a distance of 1¼ cables. Saint Julian's Emplacement extends S from Saint Julian's Pier, W of New Jetty. Victoria Marina, Albert Marina and Albert Dock are

Saint Joseph's
Church Spire

Elizabeth College
Tower

Castle Breakwater
Light

Harbour
Leading Lights

Port Control
Signal station

Saint Peter Port Harbour Entrance from E (11.109)

(Original dated 1998)

(Photograph – Capt F A Lawrence MRIN, Navitrom Limited)

situated in the SW part of the harbour with Fish Quay at the entrance to Albert Dock.

Queen Elizabeth II Marina is situated outside the harbour on the N side of Saint Julian's Pier.

Signals
11.110

1 **Traffic signals** are exhibited by day and at night from the signal station on the head of White Rock Pier. When a red light is exhibited mariners are prohibited from entering or leaving harbour.

A supplementary red light is exhibited towards the land from the SW corner of a building on New Jetty for the benefit of mariners berthed W of this jetty. When this light is exhibited mariners may not leave their berths or moorings.

2 The States Harbour Master may, at his discretion, permit a particular vessel to enter harbour, or to leave its berth or mooring, notwithstanding that such lights are exhibited.

Mariners may not enter or leave Saint Peter Port or shift berth without obtaining permission from port control through port radio. Mariners in vessels under 15 m in length, except those under sail, are exempt.

Directions for entering harbour
(continued from 11.83)

Principal marks
11.111

1 **Landmarks,** in addition to those given at 11.74:
    Elizabeth College (tower four spires) (49°27′·4N 2°32′·4W).
    Saint Joseph's Church (copper spire 95 m) (49°27′·3N 2°32′·7W) the church with the highest elevation of numerous other conspicuous churches in the vicinity of the port; the positions of these other conspicuous churches may best be seen from the chart.

2 **Major light:**
    Castle Breakwater Light (49°27′·3N 2°31′·4W) (11.74).

Saint Peter Port
11.112

1 **Saint Peter Port Harbour Leading Lights:**
    Front mark. Victoria Marina South Pier Light (white framework tower red lantern, 7 m in height) (49°27′·3N 2°32′·0W).
    Rear light (160 m W of the front light) on top of the tall square white building, only visible between 260°–270°.

2 From a position in Great Road the alignment (265°) of these lights leads into the harbour passing between Castle Breakwater and White Rock Pier into The Pool. A conspicuous lighthouse (11.74) stands on Castle Breakwater head and a light (round stone tower, 10 m in height) is exhibited from the head of White Rock Pier.

3 **Caution.** A supporting ledge with a least depth of 2·1 m extends out to 3 m from the W side of the outer spur of White Rock Pier. Care must be exercised when manoeuvring in the vicinity.

Berths

Alongside berths
11.113

1 **Deepest and longest berth.** New Jetty (49°27′·5N 2°31′·8W) No 1 Berth: maintained depth 5 m.

St Peter's Church Spire   St Joseph's Church Spire   Victoria Marina Entrance

South Pier   Leading Lights   North Pier

St.Peter Port – Leading Lights 265° (11.112)

(Photograph - D. Acland)   *(Original dated 2003)*

There are terminals for RoRo, container, car ferries and hydrofoils on and near the root of New Jetty.

No 2 RoRo berth can accept ferries up to 11 000 dwt, wave-piercing catamarans and hydrofoils.

Port services

Facilities
11.114

1   **Repairs:** slipways, largest 15·4 m long with cradle length of 64 m, width 12·2 m, grid of similar dimensions with light displacement of 700 tonnes; minor repair facilities.

Customs office in Saint Peter Port.

Divers are available.

2   **Rescue,** see 11.31.

Supplies: fuel by road tanker; fresh water; provisions; stores.

Hospitals are available.

Communications: airport 6 km from the port with connecting flights to major international airports.

BIG RUSSEL

General information

Charts 808, 3654
Description
11.115

1   Big Russel (49°27′N 2°25′W) is bounded NW by Herm, Jethou and offlying rocks, and on the SE side by the islands of Sark and Brecqhou; it is about 2 miles wide and easy of access.

Topography
11.116

1   **Herm and Jethou — east coast.** Grande Fauconnière (49°27′·4N 2°27′·5W) (11.69), a rocky islet, lies close SE of Jethou with Goubinière, an above-water rock, 4 cables farther SSE.

Between Point Sauzebourge, the S extremity of Herm, and Caquorobert, an islet 7 cables NE on the S side of Belvoir Bay, the coast is steep and rocky. Putrainez, a prominent rock protruding from the shore, and Selle Roque, both of similar height, lie 1½ and 3½ cables, respectively, S of Caquorobert.

2   The E coast of Herm has fewer dangers than the N coast but detached rocks lie as much as 1 mile offshore. Shell Beach, which is low and sandy and bordered by several drying ledges, extends about 4 cables S from the N point of the island. Belvoir Bay is separated from Shell Beach by Moulière, an above-water rock. Cul de L'Autel, a flat-topped rock, lies near the extremity of a chain of drying reefs on which there are many above-water rocks, extending nearly 1¾ miles NE from the N point of Herm.

3   Grande Amfroque (49°30′·5N 2°24′·6W) lying nearly 2¼ miles NE of the N extremity of Herm is the outermost above-water rock; it has two peaks and is surrounded by drying and below-water rocks. On the W part of the rock there are two beacon towers, the N tower (white cage topmark, 6 m in height) and the S tower (black and white bands, cross topmark, 11 m in height).

For general description of Herm and Jethou, see 11.23.
11.117

1   **Sark — west coast.** The W coast of Sark is indented by two large bays, La Grande Grève (11.123) and Banquette

Bay (11.127), which are joined by Gouliot Passage (11.126).

Bec du Nez (49°27′·2N 2°22′·2W) is the outermost and smallest of three rocky islets lying on a reef extending from the N extremity of Sark.

For general description of Sark, see 11.24.

Natural conditions
11.118

1   **Tidal streams.** The NE going tidal stream slackens ½ hour earlier on the SE side of Big Russel close to Sark than in the middle of the channel.

2   The times at which the tidal streams in the close vicinity of Sark change direction differ materially from those in Big Russel and in the waters to the E of the island. It is said that these streams can be avoided by keeping outside a line joining: a position 3 to 4 cables S of L'Étac (49°24′N 2°22′W); La Grune Noire; a position about 2 miles NE of Point Robert (49°26′N 2°21′W); Bec du Nez (49°27′N 2°22′W); La Givaude (49°26′N 2°24′W); and the starting point.

3   The streams begin as follows at the localities indicated:

Interval from HW Saint Helier	Direction	Remarks
In Baleine Bay and off the SE coast:		
−0445	NE	
+0245	SW	Very weak
The NE coast, near the land:		
−0130	SE	
−0515	NW	Very weak
Off Bec de Nez:		
+0500	NE	
−0100	SW	
In Gouliot Passage:		
−0250	N	
+0330	S	
In La Grande Grève and off SW coast where the stream is rotatory:		
−0610	SW	
−0510	S and E	
HW	NE	
+0100	N and W	

4   See also information on the chart and *Admiralty Tidal Stream Atlas for the Channel Islands and adjacent coasts of France.*

Eddy. There is an eddy or slack water off the NE coast of Sark during the whole period of the NE-going stream in Big Russel. This eddy extends about 2 miles offshore but not right up to it, and decreases in width as the distance from the coast increases. The Sark eddy is used by mariners in low powered vessels crossing from Sark to Guernsey when the main stream is NE; they proceed from Bec du Nez down close to Brecqhou before crossing in order to reduce the effect of the NE set.

5   **Overfalls.** There are numerous overfalls in Great Russel which extend across the channel at its SW end, along the NW side of the channel and in places off Sark and Brecqhou. There are also numerous overfalls off the S and E coasts of Sark some of which can be dangerous to small

craft, especially near spring tides; their positions are marked on the chart.

6   Information regarding the rates of the streams and eddies round Sark is scant but they are probably strong and erratic in places particularly off salient points and where the coast changes direction.

Directions
(continued from 11.63)

Principal marks
11.119
1   **Landmarks:**
Barracks Block (49°24'·7N 2°22'·3W) on Little Sark.
Pilcher Monument (49°25'·7N 2°22'·4W) on the N side of Longue Point.
Castle (49°26'·0N 2°23'·5W) on the W part of Brecqhou.

2   Tower (49°26'·9N 2°22'·0W) at the N end of Sark.
Major lights:
Castle Breakwater Light (49°27'N 2°31'W) (11.74).
Platte Fougère Light (49°31'N 2°29'W) (11.74).
Point Robert Light (49°26'N 2°21'W) (11.196)

Other aids to navigation
11.120
1   **Racon:** Platte Fougère Light (49°31'N 2°29'W), for details see *Admiralty List of Radio Signals Volume 2.*

From south
11.121
1   From a position S of Saint Martin's Point (49°25'N 2°32'W) (11.60), from where a light is exhibited, the route through Big Russel leads generally NE passing (with positions given from Noire Pute (49°28'N 2°25'W)):
SE of Sardrière (3 miles SW) (11.78); thence:
SE of a 5·2 m patch (2¼ miles SW) which lies close SE of Banc des Anons; and:

2   NW of Les Hautes Boues (3½ miles SSE), an extensive group of drying rocks the W-most dangers off Little Sark (11.24). Grode Bank (2½ miles S) is one of several banks which lie across the S entrance to Big Russel between La Givaude (2½ miles SSE) and the dangers S of Jethou. The rate of the tidal streams through Big Russel cause heavy overfalls on these banks and in bad weather the seas can be very dangerous to small craft. Thence:

3   Between Fourquies of Big Russel (1½ miles SW), marked on their NE side by a light buoy (N cardinal), and La Givaude (2½ miles SSE) which, with La Neste close N, are the W-most dangers off Brecqhou (11.24). The falling tidal stream runs very strongly over Fourquies of Big Russel. Thence:

4   SE of Les Grands Bouillons (8½ cables WSW; thence:
SE of Noire Pute, a large black rock from where a light is exhibited. A chain of drying rocks extends nearly 1½ cables NNE from the rock. Thence:
NW of Bec du Nez (2 miles ESE) (11.117); a light (white wooden structure, 1 m in height) is exhibited from Corbée du Nez, a rock lying close S; thence:

5   SE of Tête Quipet (1½ miles NNE) which, with Longue Gripe, 3 cables farther NE, are the outermost of several rocky patches and shoals

lying out to 1 mile E and S of Grande Amfroque (11.116); thence:
SE of Bonne Grune (3 miles NNE), marked by overfalls, the NE-most danger off Herm.
11.122
1   **Clearing bearings:**
The alignment (355°) of the W side of La Givaude (49°26'N 2°24'W) with the middle of Grande Amfroque, 4¾ miles N, clears close W of Les Hautes Boues.
The alignment (182°) of the E bluff of Brecqhou (49°26'N 2°23'W) with the W edge of Little Sark, 1 mile S, clears E of Bonne Grune and the other dangers NE of Herm; the former by only 1½ cables.

*(Directions for the passage
W of Casquets continue at 11.135
and for the Race of Alderney at 11.327)*

Anchorages

La Grande Grève
11.123
1   **General information.** La Grande Grève is entered between Brecqhou (49°26'N 2°23'W) (11.24) and the W extremity of Little Sark, 1 mile S. It provides good shelter from winds between N and SSE but winds from between SW and W bring in a heavy swell making the anchorages untenable.

2   Pierre Norman, a drying rock, is the outermost of a chain of drying rocks extending 1½ cables W from Longue Pointe in the N part of the bay. Between Longue Pointe and La Pointe de la Joue, 4½ cables S, are situated the sandy beach of Port és Saies and a small bay which lies below the high isthmus of La Coupée (11.24). From La Pointe de la Joue to the W point of Little Sark, 5 cables SW, the coast is rocky.
11.124
1   **Directions.** The alignment (070°)of Pilcher Monument (49°25'·7N 2°22'·4W) (11.119) with Sark Mill (disused) (5 cables ENE) leads in the approach passing (with positions given from Pilcher Monument):
Between Les Dents (8 cables W) and the shallow patches in the middle of the bay of which a 3·2 m patch (4 cables WSW) is the N-most.

2   On the line of bearing 007° of the W side of Moie Saint Pierre (3 cables WNW) (11.126) the track leads SE with La Pointe de la Joue (5 cables S) as a headmark to the anchorage.
Alternative approach. The alignment (090°) of La Pointe de la Joue (5 cables S) with the bluff at the S end of La Coupée (6 cables SE) leads in the approach passing:

3   Between Boue de la Baie (5½ cables SW) and a 2·6 m shoal (6½ cables SSW) lying 1 cable NNE of La Baveuse.
When the W extremity of Moie Saint Pierre (3 cables NNW) bears 000° the track then leads NE to the anchorage.
11.125
1   **Anchorage:** 2 cables NNW of La Pointe de la Joue as shown on the chart; small craft may anchor 1 cable N of the point.
11.126
1   **Landing** can be obtained on a stony beach in a narrow cove 1 cable NE of the W extremity of Little Sark as shown on the chart.

2   **Havre Gosselin,** a small inlet, the head of which is stony and dries out about ½ cable, lies NE of Longue Pointe. Anchorage, as shown on the chart, can be obtained in offshore winds in the entrance and there are landing steps on the S side of the mouth of the inlet.

3   **Gouliot Passage,** which joins La Grande Grève with Banquette Bay (11.127), lies between Brecqhou and Moie Saint Pierre, a large above-water rock close off the W extremity of Sark; the passage is 65 m wide with a least depth of 2·6 m and the tidal streams run through it at a great rate. From S the line of bearing 020° of Bec du Nez seen in the middle of the pass leads through the pass close WNW of a rocky shoal extending ½ cable from the SW corner of Moie Saint Pierre. From N the alignment (169°) of the W side of Moie Saint Pierre with the Old Mill (ruins), 1 mile S on Little Sark, clears E of Boue de Grune Gouliot, the NE-most danger off Brecqhou.

Banquette Bay
11.127

1   **General information.** Banquette Bay (49°27′N 2°23′W) on the NW coast of Sark is entered between the W extremity of Brecqhou and Bec du Nez, 1½ miles NE (11.117); its shores are indented by coves and bordered by rocks. The NW coast of the island may be approached to a distance of about 5 cables without danger as there are no rocks at a greater distance than 3½ cables offshore between Brecqhou and Bec du Nez.

   The bay affords shelter in offshore winds but the anchorages are very uncomfortable in W weather.

11.128

1   **Anchorages.** The best deep water anchorage is to be found 4½ cables N of Brecqhou on the alignment (223½°) of Moie Batard, a square rock of whitish colour lying close off the NW extremity of Brecqhou, with La Givaude, 3 cables SW, in depths of about 16 m, as shown on the chart.

   Anchorages closer inshore may be found about 1½ cables N of Moie du Mouton (49°26′·1N 2°22′·5W), as shown on the chart.

2   **Caution.** Épisseresses, below-water rocks, lie about 9 cables NE of Moie Batard. Petite Banquette, a narrow shoal of fine sand with a sharp ridged apex, lies 2 cables S of Épisseresses; it is reported that in strong gales this shoal can shift 1 cable or more in one tide.

11.129

1   **Port à la Jument,** a narrow rock-strewn shingle beach, lies at the head of a small bay of which Moie du Mouton is its S entrance point.

   Port du Moulin, 2½ cables NE of Port à la Jument, is a small cove with a shingle beach which is rocky at LW. Platte Rock, a drying rock, lies 1 cable offshore in the entrance to the cove.

   Saignie Bay, rocky and about 1¼ cables wide, is situated 7 cables S of Bec du Nez.

Sark — west side
11.130

1   **Port Gorey** (49°24′·7N 2°22′·6W), a small inlet with a rocky beach at its head, is situated on the SW side of Little Sark; the ruins of abandoned mines overlook this inlet.

   From south when the head of Port Gorey opens N of Grande Bretagne, an islet lying 1 cable SW of the S entrance point to the inlet, the track leads NE passing between this islet and Boue Tirlipois, 2 cables W.

2   **Useful marks:**
   Sercul (49°24′·3N 2°22′·9W) a rock on a drying reef on the SE side of the approach.
   Moie de la Bretagne (49°24′·8N 2°23′·1W).
   Moie de la Fontaine (49°24′·9N 2°23′·0W).

Herm — east side
11.131

1   **Channels.** Gran Hayes Channel, Le Boursée and Usurie Passage are channels which run through the reefs which lie between the N point of Herm and Grande Amfroque (49°30′·6N 2°24′·6W) (11.116).

   Local knowledge is essential for these passages as they are extremely intricate and are rendered dangerous by the great rate and varying direction of the tidal streams.
11.132

1   **Anchorages.** Belvoir Bay (49°28′·5N 2°26′·5W) (11.116) affords a good anchorage to mariners in small craft at neap tides, a similar anchorage, sheltered from NW winds, can be found close SE of Putrainez situated 3 cables SSE of the bay. The anchorages are shown on the chart.

NORTH EAST OF HERM OR SARK TO WEST OF CASQUETS

General information

Charts 3653, 3654, 2669
Route
11.133

1   From a position NE of the N entrances to Big or Little Russel, or from E of Sark, the passage to W of Casquets leads NW.

Traffic regulations
11.134

1   For details of an Inshore Traffic Zone N of Casquets and Off Casquets Traffic Separation Scheme, see 11.8.

Directions
(continued from 11.83, 11.122, 11.199 and 11.306)

Major lights
11.135

1   Sorel Point Light (49°16′N 2°09′W) (11.302).
   Grosnez Point Light (49°15′N 2°15′W) (11.196).
   Platte Fougère Light (49°31′N 2°29′W) (11.74).
   Hanois, Les Light (49°26′N 2°42′W) (11.36).
   Casquets Light (49°43′N 2°23′W) (11.151).
   Channel Light Float (49°54′N 2°54′W) (2.40).

Other aids to navigation
11.136

1   **Racons:**
   Platte Fougère Light (49°31′N 2°29′W).
   Casquets Light (49°43′N 2°23′W).
   Channel Light Float (49°54′N 2°54′W).
   For details see *Admiralty List of Radio Signals Volume 2.*

North entrances to Big and Little Russel, or east of Sark, to west of Casquets
11.137

1   From a position at the N entrances of Big or Little Russel, or E of Sark, the passage to W of Casquets leads generally NW passing:

If coming from E of Sark, between an area of sandwaves with a least depth of 9·4 m over them (49°28′N 2°19′W), which lie 1¾ miles NE of Sark, and Banc de la Schôle (49°35′N 2°13′W) (11.329); thence:

NE of Bonne Grune (49°31′N 2°23′W) (11.121); thence:

2   NE of Barsier de Braye (49°31′N 2°30′W), the outermost danger NE of Grandes Brayes (11.68). These dangers are covered by the red sector (085°–155°) of Platte Fougère Light. Thence:

SW of Casquet SW Bank (49°40′N 2°25′W) (11.39); thence:

3   To a position W of Casquets, W of Eight Fathom Ledge (49°43′N 2°24′W) (11.39), when passage

may be made to English ports.

For instructions to mariners in vessels crossing the recommended direction of traffic flow in Off Casquets TSS, see 1.10.

11.138

1   **Useful marks:**
         Noire Pute Light (49°28′N 2°25′W) (11.121).
         Tautenay Light (49°30′N 2°27′W) (11.79).

Anchorage

Casquet SSE Bank
11.139

1   For details of an anchorage on Casquet SSE Bank (49°40′N 2°20′W), see 11.168.

CASQUETS, BURHOU AND ALDERNEY

General information

Charts 60, 3653
Description
11.140

1   **Casquets**, (49°43′N 2°22′W) a prominent group of islets, are situated 5½ miles W of Alderney; a light (11.151) is exhibited from the largest and highest islet of the group. Between the largest islet and Point Colotte, a rock 2¾ cables E, lie six detached rocks separated by narrow gullies through which the tidal streams run very strongly. The S side of the group is steep-to but there are two drying rocks close off the N side. L'Auquière (11.179) lies ¾ cable W of the main islet.

11.141

1   **Burhou** (49°44′N 2°15′W) lies about 5 miles E of Casquets Light, for details see 11.161.

11.142

1   **Alderney** is the third largest of Channel Islands being 3¼ miles long and about 1¼ miles wide; Le Rond Bût (49°43′N 2°12′W), the highest part of the island, lies on a plateau near the S coast. The S and W coasts of the island consist of high precipitous cliffs, broken by narrow valleys and fronted by outlying rocks, of which the most prominent are Coque Lihou and The Noires Putes (11.319) off the S coast and Les Étacs and Clonque Rock (11.161) off the W coast. On the N and E coasts, low hills slope down to a series of sandy bays separated by rocky points, the majority of which are almost inaccessible on account of outlying rocks. The heights along the S and W coasts are covered with heath and furze but the interior is generally cultivated. There are but few trees and these only grow in the valleys N of Saint Anne, the town of Alderney, which lies near the centre of the island; Alderney Harbour (11.169), with the village of Braye at its head, is situated about midway along the N coast and is the only harbour.

2   The constitution of Alderney, reformed in 1949, provides for its own popular elected President and States and its own court. The principal activities of the island are tourism, the shell fish industry and finance.

Routes

11.143

1   Alderney and the dangers to the W of it, form a chain extending from Cap de la Hague (49°44′N 1°56′W) on

Cherbourg Peninsula, to the prominent group of islets known as Casquets, 18 miles W.

The usual routes for mariners coming from Guernsey, Jersey and the N Brittany coast and making N, is either to the W of Casquets or through Race of Alderney (11.318) between Cap de la Hague and Alderney.

2   The Swinge (11.160), a side channel between Alderney and the island of Burhou (49°44′N 2°15′W), can also be used in clear weather and favourable conditions.

Ortac Channel (11.156), another side channel to the W of Burhou, is used less frequently.

Topography

11.144

1   **Alderney north coast.** The coast between Château à L'Étoc Point (49°44′N 2°11′W), on which stands a fort and a light, and the islets of Les Homeaux Florains, 1 mile E, on the largest of which stands the ruins of a fort, is indented by three sandy bays flanked by drying rocks.

Quénard Point, on which stands a fort, is the NE point of Alderney and is situated 1¼ cables SE of Les Homeaux Florains; Alderney Light (11.151) stands on the coast 1¾ cables W of the point.

2   **Cherbourg Peninsula.** After passing N of Alderney, the high land S of Cap de la Hague which terminates SW at Nez de Jobourg (49°40′N 1°56′W) (11.320) will be the first land sighted on the French mainland.

Historic wrecks

11.145

1   **Restricted areas.** A restricted area, 1¼ miles radius, centred on position 49°43′·3N 2°22′·4W, about 1¾ cables E of Casquets Light, and a second restricted area (49°44′·3N 2°09′·9W), radius 200 m, about 5 cables ENE of Château à L'Étoc Point, contain the remains of historic wrecks; the former historic wreck is that of *HMS Dragon*.

For details regarding restrictions, see 1.89.

Traffic regulations

11.146

1   For details of an Inshore Traffic Zone N of Casquets and Off Casquets TSS, see 11.8.

Natural conditions
11.147

1   **Tidal streams.** For details of tidal streams, see the information on the chart and also *Admiralty Tidal Stream Atlas for the Channel Islands and adjacent coasts of France*.

11.148

1   **Eddies** extend SW from Casquets during the SW-going stream and NE from the islets during the NE-going stream, as follows:

Interval from HW Saint Helier	Direction of main stream	Remarks
+0355 to –0530	SW	A strong eddy of considerable width extends about 2 miles SW from Casquets; its direction, which is unknown, is probably variable.
–0530 to –0330		Eddy extends farther SW and dies away as the main stream turns to NE.
–0230 to +0355	NE	An eddy extends NE from Casquets but no information regarding its duration, direction or rate is available.

2   Eddies of considerable extent are found off the N coast of Alderney as follows:

Interval from HW Saint Helier	Remarks
–0005	A W-going stream, about 100 m wide, starts to run along W side of Alderney Harbour Breakwater at about 4 kn; outside it, separated by a narrow band of deadwater, an E-going stream of about 4 kn also runs.
+0025	Off Sauquet Rock (49°44′N 2°09′W), a W-going stream begins as a thread extending to entrance of Alderney Harbour. E-going stream in the offing is at its strongest.
+0045	E-going stream ceases; W-going stream established along N coast and seaward to a line running from Sauquet Rock to a position about 1 mile N of the breakwater end, thence W, SW and S to Corbet Rock (49°43′N 2°14′W).
+0300	NE-going stream in The Swinge slackening and W-going eddy extends across the N part of The Swinge towards Nannels (49°44′N 2°15′W).
+0430	Main SW-going stream in The Swinge established.
–0215	E-going stream begins along N coast.

11.149

1   **Overfalls.** Owing to the unevenness of the bottom and the great rate of the tidal streams, heavy overfalls, which can be dangerous, occur in both Race of Alderney and The Swinge.

   Caution. The approach to Alderney on every side except from NE is dangerous owing to numerous rocks and navigation is made more difficult by the rate of the tidal streams.

Rescue
11.150

1   **Lifeboats.** Alderney all-weather lifeboat and an inshore lifeboat are stationed in Alderney Harbour (11.169), for details see 1.113.

Directions
(continued from 11.39)

Principal marks
11.151

1   **Landmarks:**
   Water Tower (49°42′·9N 2°12′·5W).
   Saint Anne's Church (spire) (49°42′·9N 2°12′·3W).
   Tower (framework tower red obstruction light, 100 m) (49°42′·8N 2°12′·1W).

2   Television Tower (framework tower red obstruction light, 91 m) (49°43′·1N 2°11′·3W).
   Blockhouse (concrete) (49°43′·6N 2°10′·1W) standing on a hill at the NE extremity of the island above Alderney Light.
   For landmarks on Cherbourg Peninsula, see 11.327.

3   **Major lights:**
   Channel Light Float (49°54′N 2°54′W) (2.40).
   Casquets Light (white tower with two red bands and red lantern, the highest and NW of three towers, 23 m in height) (49°43′N 2°23′W).
   Alderney Light (white round tower black band, 32 m in height) (49°44′N 2°10′W).
   Cap de la Hague Light (49°43′N 1°57′W) (12.9).

Alderney Lighthouse from NE (11.151)

(Original dated 2001)

(Photograph - Air Images)

Other aids to navigation
11.152

1   **Racons:**
   Channel Light Float (49°54′N 2°54′W).
   Casquets Light (49°43′N 2°23′W).
   For details see *Admiralty List of Radio Signals Volume 2*.

Inshore Traffic Zone north of Casquets
11.153

1   From a position W of Casquets (49°43′N 2°22′W) (11.140) the route leads generally ENE passing (with positions given from Ortac (49°43′N 2°17′W)):

NNW of Casquets from where a light (3½ miles W) (11.151) is exhibited; thence:

2   NNW of Pommier Banks (2 miles WNW), two groups of below-water rocks divided by a channel 3½ cables wide which border the W side of Ortac Channel (11.156); thence:

NNW of Verte-Tête Reef (8 cables NNE) (11.157) on which stand three high rocks. Speedy Rock (11.159) lies 5 cables N of the reef and closer to the track. Thence:

3   NNW of L'Emproué (2 miles ENE), the outermost of several reefs which extend up to 3 cables N of Great Nannel (11.166). The sea breaks heavily in this area during fresh NW winds. Thence:

To a position N of Alderney Harbour (11.169) or N of Cap de la Hague (12.9) as required.

11.154

1   **Clearing bearings:**

Front mark. Alderney Harbour Breakwater Head (black and white stripes) (49°43′·8N 2°11′·7W). A light is exhibited on the highest point of the outer end of the breakwater.

Rear mark. NE Bastion of Fort Albert (5 cables ESE of the front mark).

The alignment (115½°) of these marks clears NNE of the dangers N of Great Nannel.

(Directions continue at 12.14)

Channel between Casquets and Pommier Banks

Chart 60
General information
11.155

1   **Description.** The channel between the bank with depths of 10·1 m over it, 3 cables E of L'Équet (49°43′N 2°21′W) (11.159) and Danger Rocks, 1 mile NE, is safe in good weather but should not be attempted in bad weather especially at spring tides. At such times, neither this nor any of the channels between Casquets and Ortac, 3 miles E, should be used as the area may be covered by dangerous overfalls.

2   **Leading marks.** From a position N of Casquets the alignment (098°) of Ortac (49°43′N 2°17′W) (11.157) with Saint Anne's Church Alderney, 3¾ miles E (11.151), leads through this channel.

Ortac Channel

General information
11.156

1   **Description.** Ortac Channel (49°44′N 2°18′W), a side channel, is bounded on the W by L'Équet, Danger Rocks and Pommier Banks, and on the E by the rocks extending W from Burhou and Ortac. The depths in this channel are fairly regular although the bottom is rocky and foul, and anchoring should be avoided. Dasher Rock, which lies in the middle of the channel, may be passed on either side although the channel E of it is preferred and for which directions (11.159) are given.

11.157

1   **Topography.** Ortac (49°43′N 2°17′W), a prominent rock, lies 3½ miles E of Casquets Light and marks the S end of Ortac Channel; it is nearly inaccessible and is a nesting place of gannets. Verte-Tête, with two heads, stands on the main part of Verte-Tête Reef 8 cables NNE of Ortac, the S and higher of these heads is flat-topped, the N and smaller is pointed. Cone Rock lies towards the W extremity of the reef. Renonquet, an islet situated 3 cables ESE of Verte-Tête, stands on a reef of below and above-water rocks; detached reefs extend 5 cables NE and 3½ cables SW from this islet.

11.158

1   **Tidal streams.** In Ortac Channel, spring rates of 7 kn have been reported.

An eddy extends several miles SW of Renonquet and Burhou during the first 4 hours of the SW-going stream; the stream in this eddy is irregular, both in direction and rate, at times setting strongly on to Ortac from the S. During the last 2 hours of the SW-going stream, the stream becomes more regular and runs W towards Casquets. See also information on the chart.

Overfalls, see 11.159.

Directions
11.159

1   Casquet SSE Bank (49°41′N 2°20′W) (11.168) straddles the S approach to Ortac Channel.

Clearing bearings:

The alignment (035°) of the E side of Ortac (49°43′N 2°17′W) with the W side of Renonquet, 8 cables NE, clears NW of the shallowest part of Casquets SSE Bank.

2   The alignment (017°) of the E side of Ortac with Verte-Tête, 9 cables NNE, clears ESE of the shallowest part of Casquet SSE Bank.

From a position S of Ortac Channel the recommended route, shown on the chart, leads 009° passing (with positions given from Ortac (49°43′N 2°17′W)):

3   E of L'Équet (2¼ miles W), a group of drying rocks near the E edge of a bank of pebbles, rocks and sand which extends nearly 1¼ miles E of Casquets. It is not safe to approach the E side of L'Équet within 5 cables owing to the whirling eddies caused by the tidal streams setting over the rugged bottom in the vicinity. Thence:

4   W of a 3·4 m patch which lies 1¾ cables W of Ortac; thence:

E of Danger Rocks (1½ miles WNW); these rocks may have less depth over them than charted and should be approached with caution, passing E of Dasher Rock (1 mile WNW) (11.156).

5   From a position on the alignment (088°) of Verte-Tête (8 cables N) with Great Nannel, 1½ miles farther E, the line of bearing 155° of Ortac, astern, then leads in the channel passing:

Between the E group of Pommier Banks (1½ miles NW) (11.153) and Speedy Rock (1¼ miles N), which marks the N extremity of the E side of Ortac Channel.

The Swinge

General information
11.160

1   **Description.** The Swinge is a channel which leads between Burhou (49°44′N 2°15′W) and the NW coast of Alderney, about 1¼ miles SE.

11.161

1   **Topography.** Burhou, a mainly grass covered islet with rocky shores, has its summit near its W end; it is the home of many seabirds during the breeding season. A refuge hut stands, with a prominent rock close W of it, on the S coast. Little Burhou, an islet, and several above-water rocks stand at the NE end of Burhou Reef which extends SW from Burhou.

2   Les Étacs (49°42′·3N 2°14′·3W), a group of several rocks, of which the W is the largest, lie on a rocky bank extending 5 cables W from the W extremity of Alderney. Between the W extremity of Alderney and a point 1 mile NE on which Roque Tourgis Fort stands, the coast is cliffy and fringed by a coastal ledge. Fort Clonque (49°43′N 2°14′W) with Clonque Rock, 10 m high, close NW lies on this coastal ledge which here extends 3¼ cables offshore; a causeway, covered at HW, connects the fort to the shore. Numerous rocks, most of which dry, extend out to 5½ cables offshore between Les Étacs and Grosse, a prominent large above-water rock situated 7 cables NNE of Fort Clonque.

   Local knowledge is required.

11.162

1   **Natural conditions — tidal streams.** For details of the tidal streams in The Swinge see information on the chart. A rate of about 7 to 8 kn in both directions is stated to be attained at spring tides.

   Overfalls. There are several dangerous rocks in The Swinge, marked by overfalls even in the calmest weather. Overfalls, which become more dangerous in bad weather, also form in the main channel. Their position varies with the tidal stream.

2   During E winds and on the NE-going stream, overfalls extend nearly across the channel from Burhou to the end of Alderney Harbour Breakwater. With W winds and a SW-going stream, overfalls extend from Ortac to Les Étacs.

   Eddies. There are strong eddies on both sides of The Swinge close to the rocks, and these can be used to advantage by mariners with local knowledge when proceeding through this channel against the main stream.

   For details of eddies in the N part of The Swinge and along the N coast of Alderney, see 11.148.

3   **Local weather.** In W gales and in the strength of the SW-going stream, The Swinge is covered with broken water and is dangerous. It is recommended that at such times mariners, bound S through The Swinge, should anchor in Alderney Harbour (11.169) and await favourable conditions.

Recommended routes for vessels bound south through The Swinge

11.163

1   Bound S from NE on the first of the SW-going stream at about +0400 Saint Helier, proceed along the SE side of The Swinge passing Les Étacs (11.161) and E of Pierre au Vraic (49°41′·6N 2°16′·9W).

   Bound S from NE during the strength of the SW-going stream from +0440 Saint Helier to about –0330 Saint Helier, keep towards the NW side of The Swinge avoiding North Rock and Boues des Kaines.

2   In W gales, endeavour to pass through The Swinge directly the NE-going stream begins to slacken at about +0300 Saint Helier, as the sea will then be comparatively smooth. At this time, advantage can be taken of an eddy

which runs SW along the outside of Alderney Harbour Breakwater, for details of this eddy see 11.148.

   See also recommendation to mariners at 11.162.

Directions

11.164

1   **General information.** In thick weather allowance for tidal streams should be made as accurately as possible for mariners may find themselves in the vicinity of Pierre au Vraic (49°41′·6N 2°16′·9W), a dangerous isolated rock which dries and which lies in the fairway of the SW approaches to The Swinge, before the leading marks can be identified. If there is a swell running the sea breaks on this rock even when it is well covered by the tide.

11.165

1   **From south-west passing north-north-west of Pierre au Vraic.** From a position SW of The Swinge the route leads generally ENE passing (with positions given from Fort Clonque (49°43′N 2°14′W)):

   NNW of Pierre au Vraic (2¼ miles WSW) (11.164); thence:

   SSE of Ortac (2¼ miles WNW) (11.157); thence:

2   SSE of Boues des Kaines (1½ miles WNW) lying 2¾ cables S of the SW extremity of Burhou Reef (11.161); thence:

   NNW of South Rock (6 cables WNW); thence:

   SSE of North Rock (1 mile NW) passing clear of a 9·4 m rocky patch (7 cables NW); thence:

   NNW of Corbet Rock (5 cables N), the NW-most danger off the NW coast of Alderney; thence:

3   SSE of Nannels (1½ miles NNW) (11.166); thence:

   NNW of Alderney Harbour breakwater (1¾ miles NE).

   If making for Alderney Harbour bear in mind that the outer part of the breakwater has been destroyed and the remains extend a further 3 cables NE, for details see 11.173.

4   **Clearing bearings:**

   The alignment (063°) of the NW side of Fort Clonque with Tourgis Beacon (white cone) (6 cables ENE) clears NNW of Pierre au Vraic.

   The alignment (080°) of the N end of Alderney Harbour breakwater (1¾ miles NW) with the N side of Château à L'Étoc (2½ miles ENE) clears N of all dangers between Corbet Rock and the breakwater.

5   The line of bearing 259° of Ortac (2¼ miles WNW) seen between Burhou and Noir Houmet (1¼ miles NW) clears N of the submerged end of Alderney Harbour breakwater.

11.166

1   **From south-south-west passing south-east of Pierre au Vraic — leading marks:**

   Front mark. W extremity of the largest of Les Étacs (49°42′·3N 2°14′·5W) (11.161).

   Rear mark. Fort Clonque (6 cables NNE of the front mark).

2   From a position SSW of The Swinge the alignment (032°) of these marks leads in the approach passing (with positions given from Fort Clonque (49°43′N 2°14′W)):

   ESE of Richards Rock (2 miles SW) to a position on the line of bearing 074° of S Coque Lihou (1¼ miles SE) (11.319) open a little N of the highest of the Noires Putes (1¼ miles S) (11.319).

3   **Leading marks:**

   Front mark. E side of Burhou (1¼ miles NNW).

Old Harbour   Little Crabby Harbour   Grosnez Point

Admiralty Breakwater

Alderney Harbour from E (11.169)

(Original dated 2001)

(Photograph – Air Images)

Rear mark. Great Nannel (1½ miles NNW), a steep-sided rock the largest of several above–water rocks standing on Nannels Reef.

The alignment (009°) of these marks then leads in the channel passing:

4   W of Les Étacs Bank (1 mile WSW); thence:

Between Hope Rock (6 cables W) and a 9·7 m rocky patch (8 cables W); thence:

W of South Rock (6 cables WNW) to a position NNW of the same rock when the track then leads generally ENE joining the route (11.165) which passed NNW of Pierre au Vraic.

5   **Clearing bearings.** The alignment (057°) of the SE side of Fort Clonque with Tourgis Beacon (6 cables ENE) (11.165) clears SE of Pierre au Vraic.

Anchorages

The Swinge north side
11.167

1   Anchorage during the SW-going stream, sheltered from winds between NNW and NE, can be obtained from 1 to 2½ cables S of Little Burhou (49°43′·8N 2°15′·6W) (11.161), as shown on the chart, in depths of 9 to 15 m.

Casquet SSE Bank
11.168

1   **General information.** Casquet SSE Bank (49°40′N 2°20′W), with Casquet SSW Bank about 2 miles W, are two steep sided banks of sand which lie in the SW approach to Ortac Channel (11.156); there are strong overfalls over the middle of the latter bank.

Good anchorage, in moderate weather, can be obtained on Casquet SSE bank.

Clearing bearings, see 11.159.

Alderney Harbour

Charts 2845, 60
General information
11.169

1   **Position and function.** Alderney Harbour (49°43′N 2°12′W) is situated about midway along the N coast of the island.

Topography. The coast between Bibette Head, the E entrance point of the harbour, and Roselle Point, 2 cables SW is rocky. Fort Albert, which is prominent, stands on the crest of a hill behind Roselle Point. Braye Bay, sandy with rocky ledges, lies at the head of Alderney Harbour between Roselle Point and Braye Jetty, 5 cables WSW. The town of Saint Anne is situated at the top of a steep hill, about 5 cables from Braye Jetty.

2   **Approach and entry.** The harbour is approached from NE and entered between the submerged portion of Admiralty Breakwater and Aiguillons, 2 cables E.

Traffic. Channel Island figures given at 11.249.

Harbour Authority. Alderney Harbour Authority, Harbour Office, Alderney, Channel Islands.

Limiting conditions
11.170

1   **Controlling depth.** The controlling depth for Alderney Harbour is 4·3 m, the least depth in the fairway.

Tidal levels, see information in *Admiralty Tide Tables.* Mean spring range about 5·3 m; mean neap range about 2·2 m.

Maximum size of vessel handled. A vessel of 85 m in length, depending on draught and weather limitations, can berth on the W side of Braye Jetty.

2   **Local weather.** The value of Alderney Harbour as an anchorage is impaired by the partial destruction of the breakwater but it is sheltered from all but N and NE winds. There is often an uncomfortable swell in the harbour especially during W gales.

Arrival information
11.171

1 **Port radio** station, with limited hours, operates from Alderney Harbour. A VTS is available when the Harbour Office is open.

Pilotage. Pilotage is compulsory for commercial vessels over 60 gt. Send ETA not less than 24 hours in advance, for details see *Admiralty List of Radio Signals Volume 6(1)*.

2 Pilot boards about 3 miles NE of the breakwater head as shown on the chart, or for small vessels, about 1 mile NE of the breakwater head.

Tugs are not available but the pilot boat is available to assist vessels berthing.

Local knowledge is recommended for night entry on account of the rates of the tidal streams across the entrance.

Harbour
11.172

1 **General layout.** Alderney Harbour (49°44′N 2°12′W) is formed by Admiralty Breakwater which extends 5 cables NE from Grosnez Point. The submerged remains of the outer part of the breakwater, which has been destroyed, extend about 3 cables farther NE.

Braye Jetty, in the SW corner of the harbour, has facilities for commercial vessels. Little Crabby Harbour, a small craft harbour, lies close SW of the root of Braye Jetty.

Directions for entering harbour
11.173

1 **General information.** Particular attention is drawn to the fact that the present visible end of Admiralty Breakwater terminates so abruptly as to resemble the original finished end. Mariners rounding it without paying attention to the marks and directions given, run the risk of grounding on the submerged portion of the breakwater.

2 The W-going stream, especially at spring tides, sets strongly across the harbour entrance and on to the submerged end of the breakwater for about 9½ hours. Great caution, particularly at night, is necessary in entering and mariners should always be ready to anchor in case of necessity.

11.174

1 **Approaching from north-east of the island.** The tidal streams must be carefully considered in this approach especially during the SW-going stream which sets strongly over Sauquet Rock (49°44′N 2°09′W) and the other dangers (11.331) lying off the NE coast of the island.

2 **Clearing bearings.** The line of bearing 262° of Casquets Light (49°43′N 2°23′W) (11.151) open N of Burhou, 5 miles E (11.161), or alternatively, the alignment (257°) of the S extremity of Burhou with Ortac, 1½ miles W (11.157), clears these dangers to the N and also ensures being in The Swinge or Channel stream for approaching the harbour entrance.

3 **Braye Leading Marks:**
Front mark (white conical beacon) (49°43′·4N 2°11′·9W) at the head of Old Harbour Pier.
Rear mark. Saint Anne's Church (5½ cables SW of the front mark) (11.151).

These leading marks are frequently difficult to identify especially in the afternoon light when the village of Braye lies in the shadow of the hill behind.

4 **Braye Leading Lights:**
Front light (orange triangular daymark point upwards, 2 m in height) (49°43′·4N 2°11′·9W) on the elbow of Old Harbour Pier.

Rear light (orange triangular daymark point upwards, 5 m in height) (1¾ cables SW of the front mark).

5 From NE of the harbour the alignment (210½°) of the leading marks by day, or at night on the alignment (215°) of the leading lights, leads into the harbour passing (with positions given from Homet des Pies (49°43′·9N 2°10′·9W):

6 NW of The Grois Rocks (3 cables NE), drying rocks lying near the middle of a rocky bank which extends nearly 3 cables N of Château à l'Étoc Point. Outer Grois, the highest rock of this group, is pointed. Boues Briées, a group of rocks, lie near the NE edge of this bank. The tidal streams attain considerable rates over these rocks and there are overfalls, particularly on the W-going stream. Thence:

7 Between the submerged portion of Admiralty Breakwater (3 cables NW), which forms a reef with numerous isolated heads, and Aiguillons (¾ cable NW), a group of rocks situated about 1½ cables N of Bibette Head (11.169), noting that the alignment of the leading marks passes close SE of the submerged portion of the breakwater; thence:

8 Between the breakwater head (4½ cables W) from where a light is exhibited and Roselle Point (5 cables SW) (11.169).

11.175

1 **From west and north-west — leading marks.** Approaching from W and NW and when the E-going stream is running the alignment (142°) of the following marks leads in the approach until the harbour leading marks come into line. When the W-going stream is running the line of bearing more than 143° of the rear leading mark, and well open E of the front mark, should be followed to allow for the set of the tidal stream.

2 Front mark. Beacon (white, white globe topmark) (49°43′·9N 2°11′·0W) on the N extremity of Homet des Pies.
Rear mark. Beacon (black, black triangle topmark) (4 cables SE of the front mark).

Clearing marks:
Front mark. Château à L'Étoc Point Light (49°43′·9N 2°10′·6W) (11.144).
Rear mark. Alderney Light (5½ cables ESE of the front mark) (11.151).

The alignment (111°) of these marks clears NNE of Nannels Reef (49°44′N 2°15′W) and the submerged outer part of Admiralty Breakwater. Mariners should keep a prudent distance NE of this alignment.

3 **At night** from NW keep NE of the alignment of the clearing marks and in the white sector (111°–151°) of Château à L'Étoc Point Light. The submerged outer portion of Admiralty Breakwater is covered by the red sector (111°–071°) of this light.

11.176

1 **Fairway.** An approach fairway for commercial vessels runs parallel to Admiralty Breakwater and adjacent to the breakwater small craft mooring area. It extends 3 cables SW from No 1 Light Buoy (starboard hand) (49°43′·7N 2°11′·7W) into the inner harbour. The fairway is about 100 m wide and has isolated patches with depths of less than 5 m near its edges.

Berths
11.177

1 **Alongside berths:** Braye Jetty (49°43′·5N 2°12′·0W) has three berths only two of which, Nos 1 and 2, are suitable for commercial shipping. No 2 Berth, which is on the W side of the jetty, lies N–S and is 56 m in length, with alongside depths of up to 4·0 m. No 1 Berth, which is S of No 2 Berth and lies NE–SW, is 61 m in length and has alongside depths of about 1·2 m.

Attention is drawn to the fact that the jetty wall is not vertical and certain vessels should therefore maintain separation off the wall especially in high wind and swell conditions when the ship may be moving on the berth.

2 **Anchorage.** Mariners can anchor anywhere in the harbour clear of the yacht moorings, the fairway to the commercial berth and the turning area. In NE winds the least uncomfortable anchor berths will be found under the lee of the land in the E part of Braye Bay, S of Toulouse Rock in depths of 2 to 3 m.

Anchorage can also be found in Saye Baye (49°43′·8N 2°10′·9W).

Port services
11.178

1 **Facilities:** divers; hospital.

Supplies: diesel fuel; fresh water; fresh provisions; stores.

Rescue, see 11.150.

Harbour regulation. Landing is not permitted on the breakwater.

Minor passages and anchorages

Chart 60
Casquets and adjacent rocks
11.179

1 **Caution.** The great rates attained by the tidal streams in the vicinity of Casquets (49°43′N 2°22′W) (11.140) renders approach in thick weather hazardous; mariners should never approach proceeding with the tidal stream.

2 **Channels.** L'Auquière lies ¾ cable W of the main islet of Casquets and is surrounded by drying rocks out to about ½ cable. There is a boat passage between this rock and the main islet but it is narrow with a drying ledge in the middle and should only be used with local knowledge. Noire Roque, craggy and unapproachable, lies 1¾ cables SW of L'Auquière, and The Ledge, the position of which is generally indicated by a strong ripple or breaking sea, lies 1 cable WNW of Noire Roque. A rock with a depth of 1·2 m over it lies midway between Noire Roque and L'Auquière and mariners should not attempt to pass between them.

3 There is no safe channel between Fourquie (49°43′·3N 2°21′·7W), a drying rock situated 6 cables E of Casquets Light, and L'Équêt, 5 cables E (11.159). However, the streams set fairly through the channel between Fourquie and Point Colotte, 3 cables W (11.140).

4 **Anchorage.** A safe anchorage in fair weather and sheltered from the tidal stream can be found, during the SW-going stream only, 2 cables SE of Casquets Light, as shown on the chart, in depths of about 27 m, fine sand.

Landings. Little Casquet, a rock lying close S of Casquet Light, affords shelter to a landing place for boats in Petit Havre inlet. There is another landing place on the NE side of Little Casquet and a third in a small rocky inlet on the N side of the main islet.

Little Swinge and Passes de la Maure and de la Frette
11.180

1 **General information.** Little Swinge lies off the N coast of Burhou (49°44′N 2°15′W) (11.161) and is about 2 cables wide at its E end between Burhou and Nannels where L'Équêt divides it into two parts; the deeper channel lies to the N. Passe de la Maure is a channel at the W end of Little Swinge between Burhou Reef and the reefs surrounding and to the E of Renonquet (11.157) but it is only ½ cable wide and the rocks are difficult to distinguish except at MLWS. There is a relatively deep-water channel between Burhou Reef and the rocks extending E and N from Ortac.

L'Auquiere

Lighthouse   Casquets from SE (11.179)   *Point Colotte*

(Original dated 2001)

(Photograph - Air Images)

2   Passe de la Frette, a narrow channel between Renonquet and Verte-Tête, is encumbered with drying rocks. There is no safe passage between the rocks extending E from Verte-Tête to Les Maquereaux, situated 7 cables ENE of Renonquet.

3   **Local knowledge.** Owing to the very great strength of the tidal streams which often set directly on to and across the numerous reefs and drying rocks, passage through these channels is extremely dangerous; local knowledge is essential.

4   **Temporary anchorage** can be obtained in Little Swinge

about 1¼ cables N of the NW extremity of Burhou in depths of about 12 m, sand over rock. This anchorage is best approached from N on the line of bearing 164° of the W and largest rock of Les Étacs (49°42′·3N 2°14′·3W) (11.161) well open E of the W peak of Burhou, 1½ miles NNW, until Les Maquereaux have been passed.

   Landing on Burhou is best made on the N side of a gully, the N end of which lies close S of the Refuge Hut. Landing is prohibited during the bird breeding season from 15th March to 15th July.

JERSEY, PLATEAU DES MINQUIERS AND ADJACENT COAST OF FRANCE

GENERAL INFORMATION

Chart 2669
Description
11.181

1   **Jersey** (49°13′N 2°08′W), the largest and most S of Channel Islands, rises to a height of more than 120 m in the N from whence the land slopes gradually to the coast in the S. The interior is fertile and intensively cultivated in small fields; thick scrub covers the headlands and ravines of the N and SW coasts. Trees are scattered sparsely except in some valleys which are deep and wooded.

Harbours
11.182

1   Jersey possesses several good bays and roadsteads in addition to its artificial harbours. The best anchorages are in Gorey Roads (11.285) on the E coast and Saint Aubin's Bay (11.239) on the S coast.

   The principal town and port is Saint Helier (11.246) on the S coast. There are small harbours, which dry, at Saint Aubin, Gorey and Rozel also at Bouley Bay, Bonne Nuit and La Rocque.

Traffic regulations
11.183

1   **Vessel Traffic Service** is in operation for vessels over 50 gt proceeding along the S and E coasts of Jersey and entering Saint Helier (49°11′N 2°07′W) and Gorey (49°12′N 2°01′W). Positions of radio reporting points are shown on the chart. For further details see *Admiralty List of Radio Signals Volume 6(1).*

2   **Reporting.** Mariners in all vessels, including small craft, arriving at Jersey must first call and complete an arrivals form at either the port of Saint Helier or Gorey before proceeding to other harbours or anchorages on the island where it is intended to land.

Rescue
11.184

1   **All-weather lifeboat.** Jersey all-weather lifeboat is stationed in Saint Helier Harbour (49°11′N 2°07′W) (11.246), for details see 1.113.

   For details of inshore lifeboats, see 11.275.

   VHF direction-finding service, for emergency use only, operates from a position (49°11′N 2°14′W) on Jersey. For details see *Admiralty List of Radio Signals Volume 2.*

Natural conditions
11.185

1   **Tidal streams.** Along the N and S coasts of Jersey the E-going stream runs during the rising tide for about

5¾ hours and the W-going stream for nearly 6¾ hours; consequently the rate of the E-going stream is rather greater than the W-going stream.

   Slack water occurs nearly at HW and LW on the N and S coasts and near half tide on the E and W coasts.

2   **Eddies and overfalls.** There are eddies, and possibly overfalls, off the extreme points of the island at times other than at HW and LW and at half tide.

   Further details of local tidal streams round the coasts of Jersey are included under the area concerned later in this chapter. See also information on the charts and *Admiralty Tidal Stream Atlas for the Channel Islands and adjacent coasts of France.*

   Climate information. See 1.195 and 13.243

BAIE DE SAINT-BRIEUC TO JERSEY WEST COAST

General information

Charts 3655, 2669
Route
11.186

1   From N of Baie de Saint-Brieuc (48°40′N 2°40′W) the route to Jersey W coast leads generally NNE, about 24 miles if transiting the W coast, or generally NE about 22 miles, if bound to Saint Helier, passing between Plateau des Minquiers (48°58′N 2°04′W), to the E, and Plateau de Barnouic and Plateau des Roches Douvres, about 20 miles W.

Charted positions
11.187

1   For charted positions of Plateau de Barnouic and Plateau des Roches Douvres, see information on the chart.

Magnetic anomalies
11.188

1   For details of magnetic anomalies, see 10.7.

Directions
(continued from 10.18)

Major lights
11.189

1   Cap Fréhel Light (48°41′N 2°19′W) (10.68).
   Roches Douvres Light (49°06′N 2°49′W) (11.19).
   La Corbière Light (49°11′N 2°15′W) (11.196).

North of Grand Léjon to Point Corbière
11.190

1   From a position N of Grand Léjon (48°45′N 2°40′W), from where a light (10.68) is exhibited, the route leads generally NNE or NE passing (with positions given from Roches Douvres Light (49°06′N 2°49′W):

    Between Plateau de Barnouic (5 miles S) (11.17), from where a light is exhibited, and a light buoy (special; current meter) (19½ miles SE); thence:

2   Between Plateau des Roches Douvres (11.17) and Brisants du Nord-Ouest (48°59′N 2°18′W), the NW-most dangers on Plateau des Minquiers (11.243). NW Minquiers Light Buoy (N cardinal) is moored 1¾ miles W of these dangers. Mariners should pass well clear to the W of NW Minquiers Light Buoy and SW Minquiers Light Buoy (10.131), moored 5 miles farther S, as the sea breaks on the edge of the plateau on the line joining these two light buoys. Thence:

3   WNW or NW of a light buoy (special; wave recorder) (49°05′N 2°13′W), to a position W or SW of Point Corbière (49°11′N 2°15′W) (11.193) the SW extremity of Jersey.

Caution.

    A dangerous wreck (position approximate) is charted in the middle of the channel 9¼ miles ENE of Roches Douvres Light.

11.191

1   **Clearing marks:**

    The alignment (219°) of La Horaine Lighted Beacon Tower (48°54′N 2°55′W) (10.16) with Ploubazlanec Belfry (spire) the most conspicuous church in this vicinity, 7 miles SW, clears SE of Plateau de Barnouic.

(Directions for the W coast of Jersey continue at 11.196 and for the approaches to Saint Helier at 11.222)

JERSEY WEST COAST TO SARK EAST COAST

General information

Charts 3655, 3654, 2669

Route

11.192

1   From SW of Point Corbière (49°11′N 2°15′W), the SW extremity of Jersey, the route to Sark E coast leads generally N a distance of about 18 miles.

Topography

11.193

1   **Jersey — west coast.** Point Corbière (49°11′N 2°15′W), a low bluff, is the SW extremity of Jersey; it is connected by a causeway to La Corbière (11.196), a prominent rock from where light is exhibited, 2 cables WSW. Close within the point the land rises steeply to the high tableland of La Moye. At night the position of the airport (49°12′·4N 2°11′·8W) is very noticeable on account of the numerous coloured lights marking the runways.

2   The coast between Petit Étaquerel (49°14′N 2°15′W), on which stands a prominent tower, and Grosnez Point, the NW point of Jersey about 1 mile N (11.196), is high and rugged. Pinnacle Rock, situated about 5 cables NNW of Petit Étaquerel, is also prominent.

11.194

1   **Sark — east coast.** L'Étac (49°24′N 2°22′W), a prominent islet, lies 4 cables SE of Little Sark (11.24); it is steep-to on its E side. Between the SE point of Little Sark

and Derrible Point, 1 mile NE, the coast is indented by Baleine Bay (11.204).

    From Derrible Point to Point Robert, 8½ cables N, the coast is rocky and precipitous. Les Burons, a group of rugged rocks with drying rocky ledges extending NNE and S from it, are situated about 4¾ cables SSE of Point Robert and 1 cable off the E extremity of Sark.

2   Between Point Robert and Point Banquette, 6 cables NNW the coast is indented by La Grève de la Ville (11.207). A number of drying and below-water rocks lie up to 3 cables offshore between Point Banquette and Bec du Nez (11.117) at the N extremity of Sark.

Tidal streams

11.195

1   Tidal streams off the W coast of Jersey attain a spring rate of about 4 kn in both directions beginning as follows:

Interval from HW Saint Helier	*Direction*
−0230	N
+0330	S

Directions
(continued from 11.191)

Principal marks

11.196

1   **Landmarks — Jersey:**

    For landmarks on the S coast of Jersey, including those close E of La Corbière, see 11.222.

    La Corbière Lighthouse (round stone tower, 19 m in height) (49°11′N 2°15′W) stands on from La Corbière, a prominent rock on the SW point of the island.

    La Rocco Tower (49°12′N 2°14′W), on a rocky reef in the S part of Saint Ouen Bay.

La Rocco Tower (11.196)

(Original dated 1998)

(Photograph - Capt. F. A. Lawrence, MRIN, Navitron Limited)

    Radar tower at Jersey Airport (49°12′·2N 2°12′·2W).

2   Building (white) (49°12′·9N 2°13′·5W) on the foreshore in the centre of Saint Ouen Bay.

    Lookout Tower (49°15′·1N 2°15′·2W) on the NW part of the island.

    Grosnez Point (49°16′N 2°15′W), the NW point of Jersey, a precipitous bluff on which stands the ruins of Grosnez Castle. Grosnez Point Light (see below) is exhibited from the point.

3   **Landmark — Sark,** in addition to those given at 11.119:

    Point Robert Lighthouse (white octagonal tower, 17 m in height) (49°26′N 2°21′W) on Point Robert.

    Major lights:

    La Corbière Light — as above.

    Grosnez Point Light (white concrete hut) (49°16′N 2°15′W); the hut is small and difficult to identify.

    Point Robert Light — as above.

Fixed red light

Hotel   *Lookout Tower*

La Corbière Light from SW (11.196)

(Original dated 2000)

(Photograph – Capt. F. A. Lawrence, MRIN, Navitron Limited)

Grosnez Point Light (11.196)

(Original dated 1998)

(Photograph – Capt. F. A. Lawrence, MRIN, Navitron Limited)

Point Corbière to Grosnez Point
11.197

1   **East of West Rock.** From a position SW of Point Corbière (49°11′N 2°15′W) (11.193) the route leads initially N passing (with positions given from Grosnez Point (49°16′N 2°15′W)):

2   W of Green Rock (4¾ miles SSW), the outermost danger W of La Corbière. La Frouquie (4¼ miles S), one of the NW dangers off La Corbière is marked by a seasonal buoy (W cardinal, Mar–Oct). A safe distance off the outlying dangers can be maintained by keeping the lantern of La Corbière Light in line or below the top of the high land behind it. During NW gales, especially between HW and three-quarter ebb by the shore, keep at least 1½ miles off La Corbière to avoid breaking seas. Thence:

3   W of Great Bank (4¼ miles SSW) (11.203).
La Corbière Light (4¾ miles S) (11.196), astern, between the bearings of 140° to 145°, or at night in its white sector between the same bearings, then leads NW passing:

Through the channel, which is wide and clear of dangers, between West Rock (3¾ miles WSW) and Rigdon Bank (2 miles WSW) to a position W of Grosnez Point, distant about 3½ miles.

4   **West of West Rock.** The passage to the W of West Rock is free of dangers and the chart is the best guide.
Clearing bearing. The line of bearing 148° of La Corbière Light changing from red to white clears SW of Rigdon Bank.

Grosnez Point to Point Robert
11.198

1   From a position W of Grosnez Point (49°16′N 2°15′W) the passage to the E coast of Sark leads initially N passing:

W of Banc Desormes of which North West Head (49°19′N 2°17′W) is its shallowest part. Desormes Light Buoy (W cardinal) is moored 6 cables W of North West Head.

2   The route then leads generally NNE passing:

ESE of Blanchard (49°25′N 2°18′W), the E-most danger off Sark; a light buoy (E cardinal) is moored about 4½ cables ESE of it. Thence:

To a position E of Point Robert (49°26′N 2°21′W) (11.196), from where a light is exhibited, distant about 5 miles.

11.199

1   **Useful mark:**
Corbée du Nez Light (49°27′N 2°22′W) (11.121).
Clearing bearing:
The line of bearing 299° of Bec du Nez (49°27′N 2°22′W) (11.117) just open NNE of Petite Moie, 1¼ miles ESE, clears NNE of Blanchard.

(Directions for the passage W of Casquets continue at 11.135 and for the Race of Alderney at 11.327)

Side channels

Charts 1136, 3655
Swashway Channel
11.200

1   **General information.** Swashway Channel (49°14′·5N 2°16′·5W), 3 cables wide with a least depth of 7 m in the fairway, lies between the coastal reef which extends nearly 7½ cables W from Petit Étaquerel (11.193) and Rigdon Bank (11.197).

2   **Leading bearing.** The line of bearing 045° of Great Rock (49°17′·5N 2°11′·9W), the highest head of Pierres de Lecq (11.299), just open NW of Grosnez Point, 2¾ miles SW, leads through this channel passing between North East Rock and Mouillière Rock, situated 1½ miles WSW and 1¼ miles SW, respectively, of Grosnez Point, passing close NW of the latter rock.

Channel between Banc Desormes and Pierres de Lecq
11.201

1   **Leading line.** The line of bearing 177° of La Corbière Light (49°11′N 2°15′W) (11.196) just open W of Pinnacle Rock, 4 miles N (11.193), leads through the channel between Banc Desormes (49°19′N 2°17′W) (11.198) and Pierres de Lecq (11.299) of which North West Reef, 2¾ miles ESE, is the W-most danger.

Chart 808
Channels east of Sark
11.202

1   **General information.** Several rocky patches, among which Grune du Nord, Grand Huart, Ecrillais and Platte Grune are the shallowest, lie between Blanchard (49°25′N 2°18′W) (11.198) and the rocks lying close off the E coast of Sark. There are navigable channels between these shoals but owing to the impetuous whirl of the tidal streams in the area they are seldom used by any but mariners in small craft.

Local knowledge is required.

Anchorages

Charts 1137, 3655
Saint Ouen's Bay
11.203

1   **Description.** Saint Ouen's Bay (49°13′N 2°15′W), on the SW coast of Jersey between Point Corbière and Petit Étaquerel, 3½ miles N, is a low sandy bay backed by a seawall from which the land rises steeply to a plateau. It is fringed by drying rocky ledges and detached below-water rocks extending up to 1 mile offshore. Great Bank, which forms the S part of Saint Ouen's Bay, extends 1¾ miles NW from La Corbière Light. The bay affords good shelter in offshore winds but should not be used during W weather.

2   **Submarine cable,** shown on the chart, is laid generally W from a position on the coast E of La Rocco Tower.

Charts 808, 3654
Baleine Bay
11.204

1   **Description.** Baleine Bay (49°25′N 2°21′W), on the SE coast of Sark, lies between the SE point of Little Sark (11.24) and Derrible Point, 1 mile NE, and affords anchorage in offshore winds.

2   **Topography.** La Conchée, 1½ cables ESE of Derrible Point, is a square rock whitened on top, standing on a reef which dries in places. Point Château (49°25′·4N 2°21′·3W),

situated 2½ cables W of Derrible Point, separates Derrible Bay from Dixcart Bay; in both these smaller bays a bank of sand which is stony at its W end dries out nearly 1 cable. Convache Chasm, lies towards the centre of the shore bordering the bay and close E of the isthmus of La Coupée separating Sark from Little Sark. Baleine, a rock standing on a reef, lies 2 cables offshore 3 cables SSE of Convache Chasm.
11.205

1   **Approach from south-east.** From position 49°24′·0N 2°20′·4W, 1½ miles SSE of Point Château (49°25′·4N 2°21′·3W) the route leads NNW on the line of bearing (337°) of Sark Mill open W of Point Chateau passing (with positions given from Point Château):

2   Between Les Vingt Clos (1 mile S), a shoal consisting of sand and shingle interspersed with rocks, and Les Têtes de la Conchée (8 cables SE). The sand and shingle on this former shoal shift continually under the action of the tidal streams and wind. Thence:
        Between Demie de Balmée (5 cables S) and Gripe (5 cables SE) to the anchorage.

3   **Approach from east** with Point Château well open S of La Conchée (4 cables E) passing clear of a 7 m shoal (2 miles E). The line of bearing 275° of Convache Chasm (3 cables WSW) leads in the approach passing:

4   S of Platte Grune (9 cables E); thence:
        Between Gripe (5 cables SE) and Boue de la Craque (3 cables E) which lies 1¼ cables WSW of La Conchée, when the track then leads generally SW to the anchorage. There are extensive overfalls E and S of La Conchée.

5   **Caution.** Point Robert Light is obscured bearing more than 353° over the dangers lying off Baleine Bay.
    Clearing bearings:
        The alignment (277°) of La Conchée (49°25′·4N 2°20′·6W) (11.204) with Point Château, 4 cables W, clears S of Blanchard.

6   **Approach from south.** From S the alignment (007°) of Baleine (49°24′·9N 2°21′·7W) with the W point of Dixcart Bay, 4 cables N, leads between L'Étac (11.194) and Les Vingt Clos.
        Mariners rounding the S extremity of Sark can pass between the rocks extending 2 cables NNW from L'Étac and Pierre du Cours, 1 cable farther NW, or between Pierre du Cours and Little Sark, 1½ cables NW.
    Local knowledge is required.
11.206

1   **Anchorage:** about 2 cables SSE of Point Château, as shown on the chart, in depths from 6 to 10 m.
        There are other anchorages for mariners in small craft in Baleine Bay, closer inshore and out of the strength of the tidal streams, the positions of which can best be seen from the chart.

La Grève de la Ville
11.207

1   **Description.** La Grève de la Ville, on the NE coast of Sark, is entered between Point Robert (49°26′N 2°21′W) (11.196) and Point Banquette, 6 cables NNW.

    Topography. Grande Moie, a precipitous grass-capped islet, lies 1½ cables ENE of Point Robert. Petite Moie, a grass-capped islet, and La Gorge, a prominent rock lying close S, are situated off the middle of La Grève de la Ville.
11.208

1   **Leading line.** The line of bearing 153° of Noire Pierre (49°26′·7N 2°20′·9W), a small square steep-to rock, seen

between Grande Moie and Les Burons, 5 and 9 cables SSE, respectively, leads in the approach passing (with positions given from Noire Pierre):

2   ENE of Sardrière (8 cables NW). Jolicot, a drying rock, lies close S and farther from the track. Thence:

    ENE of La Grande Boue (5 cables NW), the outermost of the group of rocks lying to the E of Bec du Nez (11.117), to the anchorages.

11.209

1   **Anchorages,** as shown on the chart, can be obtained between La Grande Boue and Pavlaison, an isolated rock 5 cables ESE, and also 2¾ cables ESE of Pavlaison, in depths of about 25 m, fine sand and gravel. These anchorages, however, can only be used in good weather and with winds from between WSW and S.

2   The best anchorage for mariners in small craft is about 1½ cables N of La Chapelle a prominent hollow rock situated on the S shore of the bay, as shown on the chart, with the E edge of Les Burons just open of Point Robert, in depths of about 12 m sand and mud; outside this line the tidal streams run strongly. The anchorage can be approached passing either side of Noire Pierre.

Landings. There are two landing places, shown on the chart, in La Grève de la Ville.

Sark east coast — inshore channels
11.210

1   **Goulet Passage,** a narrow passage with a charted depth of 1·2 m lies between Les Burons (49°25'·8N 2°20'·3W) (11.194) and Sark. Pinnacle, an above-water rock, is situated on the W side of Goulet and is joined to the shore by rocks which dry. A rock lies very close SE of Pinnacle and it is reported that when it is awash there is about 3 m in the channel. Navigation southbound is forbidden for commercial vessels through this passage unless permission is obtained from the harbour authroity.

2   **Tidal streams** attain great rates through this passage in both directions especially at about 3 hours before local HW when the N-going stream sets strongly on to Founiais (11.214).

Local knowledge is required.

11.211

1   **Passage.** Grande Moie (49°26'·3N 2°20'·5W) (11.207) is separated from Point Robert by a passage with a least depth of 3·6 m and barely ½ cable wide, being restricted by drying rocks situated close W of Grande Moie. Point Robert itself is steep-to but drying ledges extend about ½ cable from the shore, ¾ and 1¼ cables WNW of the point. The E side of Grande Moie is dangerous to approach owing to rocky shoals extending out to 2½ cables NE.

2   **Local knowledge** is essential as the tidal streams run through this passage with great strength.

11.212

1   **Channel.** There is a channel, about 1 cable wide, between Jolicot (11.208) and Moulinet situated nearly 2 cables and ½ cable, respectively, E of Bec du Nez (49°27'·2N 2°22'·2W) (11.117) the N point of Sark.

Local knowledge is required.

Sark east coast — harbours and landings
11.213

1   **Creux Harbour** which dries out at MLWS is situated 4 cables S of Point Robert (49°26'N 2°21'W). The harbour is protected by stone piers and is used by local craft and also by ferries and excursion boats when the jetty at La Maseline (11.214) is untenable through weather.

Approach. The coast between Les Laches, an above-water rock 1½ cables S of the harbour, and Derrible Point, 4 cables SW, is bordered by rocky ledges and foul ground and should not be approached within 1 cable. The alignment (344°) of Point Robert Light with Creux tunnel, 4 cables SSE, leads in the approach to the harbour.

2   **Anchorages.** In offshore winds and settled weather anchorage is available close N and E of the harbour clear of the tidal stream through Goulet Passage; anchorage W of a line S from the harbour is prohibited.

There is an anchorage 2½ cables NNE of La Conchée (49°25'·3N 2°20'·7W) (11.204), as shown on the chart, in a depth of about 22 m sand; a temporary anchorage can be found ¾ cable farther N in depths of 9 m where the tidal streams are not so strong.

3   **Landings:** at steps on the inner side of the N and longer of the two piers; on a stony beach 1 cable S of the harbour.

Supplies. Limited quantities of provisions and fuel from the village which is connected by road to a tunnel leading to the harbour.

11.214

1   **La Maseline.** The harbour of La Maseline, 2 cables S of Point Robert (49°26'N 2°21'W), is separated from Creux Harbour by a steep rugged bluff, and is the principal landing place in Sark; it is connected by a tunnel to the road which leads up the steep valley to the village.

2   **Leading marks.** The alignment (211°) of the following marks leads in the approach to the harbour from NE passing between Grande Moie and Grune du Nord, situated 5 cables NNW and NE, respectively, of the front mark, to a position E of Founiais, a drying rock marked by a beacon (yellow pole, orange letter "F" topmark) which lies 1½ cables NE of the jetty; a 0·3 m patch lies about 1 cable ENE and a 1·6 m patch lies nearly midway between Founiais and the jetty:

3   Front mark. NW side of Les Burons (49°25'·8N 2°20'·4W) (11.194).

    Rear mark. E edge of L'Étac (2 miles SSW of the front mark) (11.194).

There are no leads directly to the anchorage or jetty but Founiais is always above water except at HW.

4   **Berth:** jetty extending 45 m N from the shore at the S end of the harbour with depths of from 5·1 to 0·2 m in an inshore direction on its W side.

11.215

1   **Landing** can be obtained at Éperquerie a small cove on the NW side of a low point situated 4 cables SE of Bec du Nez (49°27'·2N 2°22'·2W) (11.117). Between this low point and Point Banquette, nearly 4 cables ESE, lies Les Fontaines, a bay in the centre of which lies a small group of drying rocks.

APPROACHES TO SAINT HELIER INCLUDING PLATEAU DES MINQUIERS

General information

Charts 1137, 3655, 2669
Routes
11.216

1   Saint Helier (49°11'N 2°07'W) (11.246) is approached through any of the several passages leading through the reefs off the S coast of Jersey. These reefs lie up to 1½ miles offshore, between Saint Brelade's Bay (11.237) and Noirmont Point (49°10'N 2°10'W) and extend across the entrance to Saint Aubin's Bay (11.239); recommended tracks through these reefs are shown on the chart.

Topography
11.217

1 The coast between Point Corbière (49°11′N 2°15′W) (11.193), the SW extremity of Jersey, and Noirmont Point, 3 miles E (11.222), consists of high cliffs with reefs and detached rocks extending up to 3 cables offshore. Between Noirmont Point and La Collette, 2¼ miles ENE, the coast is indented by Saint Aubin's Bay (11.239).

2 The coast E of Saint Helier, between La Collette (49°10′·4N 2°06′·5W) and Point Le Croc, 1½ miles SE, is low and sandy forming the beaches of Hâvres des Pas and La Grève d'Azette. Between Point Le Croc and La Rocque Point (11.273), the SE extremity of Jersey, lies Saint Clement's Bay; there is a seawall along much of the coastline of this bay.

Controlling depths
11.218

1 **Least charted depth** in North West Passage (11.225), the most frequented and usual route between English ports, Guernsey and Saint Helier, is 4·3 m (49°09′·9N 2°08′·1W) on La Grève d'Azette Leading Lights (11.226).

Pilotage
11.219

1 **Pilotage** is compulsory for vessels of 50 gt and over, except those exempt by law, and is available throughout 24 hours.

Boarding places. Pilot boards about 1 mile W of Noirmont Point (49°10′N 2°10′W) for mariners approaching from W, as shown on the chart, or 5 cables S of Demie de Pas Light (49°09′N 2°06′W) for mariners approaching from SE.

An optional boarding point for vessels unfamiliar with the port, tankers and cruise liners is located 1 mile S of Corbière Lighthouse and can be arranged with the pilots.

2 **Notice of ETA required.** Send ETA and draught to Jersey Harbour Master at least 1 hour before arrival.

For details see *Admiralty Lists of Radio Signals Volume 6(1)*.

Yacht racing marker buoys
11.220

1 South Pier Marine Light Buoy (special) is moored in position 49°09′·1N 2°06′·3W and Hettich Light Buoy (special) is moored in position 49°08′·1N 2°09′·0W. Both buoys may become seasonal in due course.

Natural conditions
11.221

1 **Tidal streams** along the S coast between Point Corbière and La Rocque Point, about 8 miles E, attain a spring rate of about 4 kn in both directions, beginning as follows:

Interval from HW Saint Helier	Direction
−0530	E
+0015	W

Slack water occurs nearly at HW and LW.

For details, see information on the chart and *Admiralty Tidal Stream Atlas for the Channel Islands and adjacent coasts of France*.

2 **Race.** A race forms off Noirmont Point with the first of the W-going stream, is at its strongest at half tide and eases by LW slack. It can be violent and dangerous to small craft especially during W gales near spring tides. A race may, on occasions, form off Noirmont Point during the last half of the E-going stream.

3 **Sea state.** In strong W gales the whole area between the outlying rocks off Noirmont Point is a confused mass of breakers; marks at sea level may be obscured by driving spray.

Directions
(continued from 11.191)

Principal marks
11.222

1 For details of principal marks on Jersey W coast and at Saint Helier, see 11.196 and 11.267.

Landmarks:
Jument Rock (conspicuous white patch) (49°10′·6N 2°14′·5W).

Jument Rock and Weather Radar Station from W (11.222)
(Original dated 1998)

(Photograph - Capt. F. A. Lawrence, MRIN, Navitron Limited)

Lookout Tower (Jersey Radio) (49°10′·8N 2°14′·4W).
Hotel (49°10′·9N 2°14′·3W).

Lookout Tower and Hotel from S (11.222)
(Original dated 1997)

(Photograph - A T Reynolds)

2   Weather radar station (tower 22 m in height surmounted by a white golfball aerial cover) (49°10′·6N 2°13′·5W).

Weather Radar Station from SW (11.222)

(Original dated 1997)

(Photograph – A T Reynolds)

Noirmont Point Light Tower (black tower white band, 10 m in height) (49°09′·9N 2°10′·1W) at the foot of Noirmont Point. A conspicuous lookout tower is situated on the higher ground above the light tower.

Noirmont Point Light-tower (11.222)

(Original dated 1998)

(Photograph – Capt. F. A. Lawrence, MRIN, Navitron Limited)

3   Chimney (118 m) (red lights) (49°12′·0N 2°07′·3W).
Le Marais Flats (49°10′·1N 2°04′·7W) four blocks of flats on Point Le Croc.
Icho Tower (round stone tower with its upper half whitewashed, 14 m in height) (49°08′·9N 2°02′·9W) standing on a rock.
Major light:
La Corbière Light (49°11′N 2°15′W) (11.196).

Icho Tower from S (11.222)

(Original dated 1997)

(Photograph – HMSML Gleaner)

Other aid to navigation
11.223
1   **Racon:** Demie de Pas Light (49°09′N 2°06′W).
For details see *Admiralty List of Radio Signals Volume 2.*

General information
11.224
1   **Channels.** When navigating the passages leading through the reefs particular attention should be paid to the following: the height of tide, as some of the recommended tracks pass close to or over shallow patches; the strong set of the tidal streams across the reefs in an E and W direction; the difficulty in identifying some leading marks in poor visibility and without local knowledge.
2   Approaching Saint Helier and Saint Aubin's Bay, between half flood and HW, proceed according to the draught of the vessel, for at half tide there is a depth of at least 4 m over all the rocks in the offing with the exception of Sillette (49°09′N 2°10′W), Hinguette (49°09′N 2°08′W), Pignonet (49°10′N 2°10′W) and the drying rock 1½ cables WSW of Pignonet. At half tide depths in all charted passages are greater than 6 m.

North West Passage
11.225
1   **Description.** North West Passage is the most frequented and the usual sea route between English ports, Guernsey and Saint Helier; it is 2½ cables wide at its narrowest part off Point Le Fret (49°10′N 2°11′W). The inner part of the fairway is indicated by leading lights.
11.226
1   **Route.** From a position SW of La Corbière Light (49°11′N 2°15′W) (11.196) the line of bearing 095° of Noirmont Point Light Tower (49°10′N 2°10′W) (11.222) leads in the channel passing (with positions given from Noirmont Point):
        S of Noirmontaise Reef (3½ miles WNW) the SW-most danger off La Corbière; thence:
2   S of Jument Rock (3 miles WNW) (11.222); thence:
        Between Les Kaines (1¾ miles WNW) and Banc de Saint Brelade (1½ miles W).
    The line of bearing 290°, astern, of La Corbière Light (3¼ miles WNW) just open S of Point La Moye (2¼ miles WNW) then leads in the channel passing:
        Between Point Le Fret (8 cables WNW) and Banc Le Fret (8 cables W); thence:
        SSW of Portelet Ledge (4½ cables W).
3   **La Grève d'Azette Leading Lights:**
        Front light. La Grève d'Azette Light (red rectangular daymark on white metal framework tower, 20 m in height) (3¼ miles E).

Rear light. Mont Ubé Light (white metal framework tower, 14 m in height) (1 mile ENE of the front light).

4 The alignment (082°) of these lights with Dog's Nest Rock Beacon (white concrete pillar, black band, globe topmark), which stands on the same alignment 1¼ miles WSW of the front mark, leads in the inner part of the fairway passing:

> Between Noirmont Point (11.222) and Grand Four (5 cables S), marked on its N side by Les Fours Light Buoy (N cardinal); thence:

5 > Between Pignonet (2½ cables E), marked by a beacon (S cardinal), and Noirs Hommes (5 cables SE); thence:

> N of Ruaudière Rock (1 mile ESE), marked on its NW side by a light buoy (starboard hand); thence:

6 > N of West La Cloche (1¾ miles E) (11.232) to a position S of Breakwater End (1¾ miles ENE) (11.267), SSW of the harbour entrance, or to the anchorages in Saint Aubin's Bay (11.239).

Useful mark:

> Grosse Tête (prominent square rock) (49°10′·5N 2°12′·6W).

Western Passage
11.227

1 **Description.** Western Passage lies between Passage Rock (49°09′·5N 2°12′·2W) and Banc de Saint Brelade, 6 cables NW, and is 1¼ cables wide at its narrowest. It is the simplest route from W but as the marks are difficult to identify in poor visibility North West Passage (11.225) is the best and safest both by day and night.

La Grève d'Azette Leading Lights

Dog's Nest Rock Beacon
Western Passage alignment (082°) (11.227)

(Original dated 1998)

(Photograph – Capt. F. A. Lawrence, MRIN, Navitron Limited)

11.228

1 **Route.** From a position SW of La Corbière Light (49°11′N 2°15′W) (11.196) the alignment (082°) of La Grève d'Azette Leading Lights (49°10′N 2°05′W) and Dog's Nest Rock Beacon (11.226) leads in the approach.

2 Alter course as required to leave this alignment and pass N of Passage Rock, marked on its NW side by a light buoy (N cardinal), and close N of Petite Grune, 4 cables E, then regain the alignment and pass N of Grand Four (49°09′·5N 2°10′·2W) (11.226) and thence as directed for the inner part of North West Passage (11.226).

Caution: A dangerous wreck lies ½ cable S of the alignment in position (49°09′·3N 2°13′·3W).

Danger Rock Passage
11.229

1 **Description.** Danger Rock Passage is the most direct route to Saint Helier from SW.

Local knowledge is required.

Danger Rock Passage Leading Marks in line 044° (11.229)

(Original dated 1998)

(Photograph – Capt. F. A. Lawrence, MRIN, Navitron Limited)

11.230

1 **Leading marks:**

> Front mark. Breakwater End (49°10′·2N 2°07′·4W) (11.267).

> Rear mark. Fort Regent Signal Mast (1 mile NE of the front mark) (11.267).

From a position SW of Saint Helier the alignment (044°) of these marks leads in the channel passing (with positions given from Elizabeth Castle (49°11′N 2°08′W)):

2 > SE of Frouquie des Vrachères (3½ miles SW) the SSW-most danger off Point Le Fret; thence:

> SE of Les Grunes Vaudin, of which South West Rock (2½ miles SW) and Les Poches à Suie (2¼ miles SW) are the SE and NE-most dangers; thence:

> NW of Hettich Light Buoy (special) (2½ miles SSW) (11.220), thence:

3 > Between Grunes aux Dardes (1¾ miles SW) with Frouquie, a patch close NE, and a 3·4 m patch which lies close SE of the leading line 1½ cables NW of Danger Rock (1¾ miles SSW); thence:

> NW of Grunes Saint Michel (1¼ miles SSW) to the anchorages in Saint Aubin's Bay (11.239) or harbour (11.246) as directed, for the inner part of North West Passage (11.226) as required.

Sillette Passage
11.231

1 **General information.** Sillette Passage leads from S of Saint Aubin's Bay (11.239) between Sillette (49°09′·2N 2°09′·7W), a drying reef, and Grunes aux Dardes, 3 cables E (11.230), to join the alignment (082°) of La Grève d'Azette Leading Lights and Dog's Nest Rock Beacon (11.226) about 5 cables ESE of Noirmont Point, or into Saint Aubin's Bay, as required.

It is reported (2003) that the transit 000° of Platte Rock beacon with Martello Tower No 2 (see photograph) is difficult to discern from the vicinity of Sillette Passage.

Local knowledge is required.

Red and Green Passage
11.232

1 **Description.** Red and Green Passage is an extension seaward of the leading line which leads into Small Road.

Sillette Passage Leading Marks in line 000° (11.231)

(Original dated 1998)

(Photograph - Capt. F. A. Lawrence, MRIN, Navitron Limited)

Red and Green Passage Leading Lights in line 22¾° (11.232)

(Original dated 1998)

(Photograph - Capt. F. A. Lawrence, MRIN, Navitron Limited)

Local knowledge. It is inadvisable to use this channel below half tide; local knowledge is required.

2 **Leading lights:**

Front light (red rectangle on metal framework tower on dolphin) (49°10'·6N 2°06'·9W) (11.269) close SE of the head of Elizabeth Harbour East Pier.

Rear light (red rectangle on metal framework tower, 15 m in height) (1¼ cables NNE of the front mark) (11.269) standing at the elbow of Albert Pier.

3 From a position SSW of Saint Helier Harbour the alignment (022¾°) of these marks leads in the channel passing (with positions given from Elizabeth Castle (49°11'N 2°08'W)):

ESE of Hettich Light Buoy (special) (2½ miles SSW) (11.220), thence:

Dependent upon draught over Fairway Rock (1½ miles S); thence:

4 Between Grunes Saint Michel (1¼ miles SSW) and Hinguette (1¼ miles S) (11.234) to the harbour (11.246) passing between West La Cloche (7 cables S) and East La Cloche (7 cables SSE), two rocks 1¼ cables apart off the entrance to Saint Helier Harbour about 3½ cables S of Breakwater End, or to the anchorages in Saint Aubin's Bay (11.239) as required.

Middle Passage
11.233

1 **Leading marks:**

Front mark. Saint Aubin's Fort (49°11'·1N 2°09'·7W) (11.239).

Rear mark. Mon Plaisir House (7 cables NNW of the front mark).

Middle Passage Leading Marks in line 339° (11.233)

(Original dated 1998)

(Photograph - Capt. F. A. Lawrence, MRIN, Navitron Limited)

From a position S of Saint Aubin's Bay the alignment (339°) of these marks leads through Middle Passage in a least depth of 9·5 m as far as Ruaudière Rock, 1½ miles SSE of the front mark, passing (with positions give from the front mark):

ENE of Hettich Light Buoy (special) (2½ miles SSW) (11.220), thence:

2 ENE of Danger Rock (2¼ miles SSE) and Frouquie (1¾ miles SSE) (11.230); and:

WSW of the shoals SW of Grunes Saint Michel (2 miles SE); thence:

WSW of Ruaudière Rock (1½ miles SSE) (11.226) to the anchorages in Saint Aubin's Bay (11.239), or to the harbour (11.246) as directed, for the inner part of North West Passage (11.226) as required.

South Passage
11.234

1 **Leading marks:**

Front mark. Gros du Château (rock with twin heads) (49°10'·6N 2°07'·8W).

Rear mark. Conspicuous Mark (black and white) (1¼ miles NNW of the front mark) on the sea wall at the head of Saint Aubin's Bay.

South Passage Leading Marks in line 341° (11.234)

(Original dated 1998)

(Photograph - Capt. F. A. Lawrence, MRIN, Navitron Limited)

2   From a position SSE of Saint Helier the alignment (341°) of these marks leads in South Passage passing (with positions given from Elizabeth Castle (49°11′N 2°08′W)):

Between Les Têtards (1¾ miles S) and the shoals SW of Demie de Pas (1¾ miles SE) (11.235); thence:

3   ENE of Hinguette (1¼ miles S), groups of rocks marked on their E side by a light buoy (port hand); thence:

Between West La Cloche (7 cables S) (11.232) and East La Cloche (7 cables SSE) (11.232) where the route joins Red and Green Passage (11.232).

Eastern Passage
11.235

1   **Route.** From a position S of Icho Tower (49°09′N 2°03′W) (11.222) the line of bearing 290° of La Corbière Light (49°11′N 2°15′W) (11.196) open close SSW of Point La Moye, 1 mile ESE, leads in the approach passing (with positions given from Elizabeth Castle (49°11′N 2°08′W)):

2   Between the S side of Violet Bank (11.278), which is the general name applied to the reefs which lie off the SE coast of Jersey, and Icho Bank (4 miles SSE) to a position SSW of La Frouquie (2¼ miles SE), an above-water rock.

3   From a position on the alignment (332°) of Demie de Pas Light Beacon (S cardinal, black tower yellow top, 13 m in height) (1¾ miles SE) with Dog's Nest Rock Beacon (7 cables SE) (11.226) the line of bearing 314° of Saint Aubin's Fort (1½ miles WNW) then leads through Eastern Passage passing:

Demie de Pas Light-beacon from S (11.235)

(Original dated 1997)

(Photograph - HMSML Gleaner)

4   Between Demie de Pas (1¾ miles SE), a drying rock at the SE extremity of Violet Bank, and a 2·7 m patch (1½ miles SSE), noting South Pier Marine Light Buoy (special) (1¾ miles SSE) (11.220). When passing Demie de Pas, keep the E side of Hermitage Breakwater, which extends SSE from Elizabeth Castle, open, to ensure clearing the 2·7 m patch. Thence:

Between Trois Grunes (1¼ miles SSE) and Hinguette (1¼ miles S) (11.234) where the route joins South Passage (11.234).

(Directions continue, for Saint Helier at 11.267 and for Jersey E coast at 11.277)

Anchorages

Chart 1137
Outer anchorages
11.236

1   **Caution.** There is no safe anchorage for vessels of deep draught off the S coast of Jersey.

In fine weather mariners may anchor 1 mile SSW of Demie de Pas (49°09′N 2°06′W) (11.235) on the alignment (031°) of the beacon tower with La Grève d'Azette Light (11.226), 1¼ miles NNE, in depths of about 14 m. Temporary anchorage may be found in a depth of 14·6 m, rock and shells, about 6 cables S of Demie de Pas Light Beacon in the vicinity of the pilot boarding position.

Saint Brelade's Bay
11.237

1   **Description.** Saint Brelade's Bay (49°10′·5N 2°12′·1W), with a white sandy beach at its head, is entered between Grosse Tête (11.226) and Pointe Le Fret, 1 mile ESE. The bay is inferior to Saint Aubin's Bay (11.239), 2 miles E, as an anchorage and is more exposed to S gales. Fournier Rock and Fourché, drying rocks, lie in the entrance and there are numerous drying reefs in the bay. Frouquie and Rousse Rock are small islets lying on the E side of the entrance to the bay.

11.238

1   **Anchorage** can be obtained, in fine weather, outside the bay 6½ cables W of Pointe Le Fret as shown on the chart, however, see caution at 11.236.

Anchorages for mariners in small craft can be obtained off Bouilly Port, on the W side of the bay, where the holding ground is good, but the best anchorage lies 1½ cables NE of Fournier Rock in depths of about 7 m, sand; it is seldom used.

Saint Aubin's Bay
11.239

1   **Description.** Saint Aubin's Bay lies between Noirmont Point (49°10′N 2°10′W) (11.222) and La Collette, 2½ miles ENE, and affords good shelter from offshore winds and there is sufficient room for several vessels to lie at single anchor, however, see caution at 11.236.

2   **Topography.** From Noirmont Point to Point de Bût, 6 cables NNE, the coast is rocky; from thence the shores of Saint Aubin's Bay consist of sand, except at its SW and SE ends where there are a number of drying rocks some of which are marked by beacons. A seawall runs round the head of the bay from which several ramps lead to the beach. Saint Aubin's Fort (tower) stands on a rock, 2½ cables offshore, abreast the town of Saint Aubin with its small craft harbour (11.241) which is situated on the W shore of the bay; the town and harbour of Saint Helier (11.246) lies on the E shore of the bay protected by Elizabeth Castle and Hermitage Breakwater about 2 cables offshore.

3   **Tidal streams.** The first of the E-going stream runs strongly across the rocks close E of Noirmont Point and into Saint Aubin's Bay; after running for about 3 hours, it forms an eddy in the direction of Elizabeth Castle thence W and S round the bay and out past Noirmont Point. The W-going stream runs NW into Saint Aubin's Bay, along the W shore and out past Noirmont Point.

11.240

1   **Anchorages.** The best berths lie to the NW and N of Diamond Rock (49°10′·2N 2°08′·7W), which lies in the middle of the entrance to the bay and is marked on its SSE side by a light buoy (port hand), in depths of about 4 to

5 m where mariners may ride out S gales in safety being out of the strength of the tidal stream and where the sea and swell are broken by the outlying reefs; the N berth, with depths of about 4 m, is shown on the chart.

2 A berth nearer to Saint Helier may be found 3½ cables E of Ruaudière Rock (49°09′·7N 2°08′·6W) (11.226) in a depth of about 5 m. A further berth may be found about 3 cables N of the same rock; the berths are shown on the chart.

3 **Caution.** Les Grunes du Port, a group of rocks, one of which dries, marked by a buoy (port hand) close SE, lie on the W side of the entrance to the bay, 5 cables ENE of Noirmont Point. Baleine, a rocky patch marked by a buoy (starboard hand) 1¼ miles ENE of the same point, is the SW-most of several rocky patches which extend out to about 5 cables W and SW from Elizabeth Castle on the E side of the bay.

11.241

1 **Saint Aubin Harbour** (49°11′·2N 2°10′·1W) lies on the W side of Saint Aubin's Bay and is formed by two piers; the entrance faces NE.

2 **Approach.** Pass E of several rocks which dry which lie to the SE and S of Saint Aubin's Fort (49°11′·1N 2°09′·7W); a light is exhibited from the pier which extends ½ cable N from the fort. The line of bearing 254° of the centre of the white sector (253°–255°) of Saint Aubin Direction Light (metal column) situated on the N pierhead leads through a buoyed channel (seasonal) clear of yacht moorings to the harbour. The entrance between the pierheads is about 25 m wide; the pierheads are marked with a white mark, and a rock groyne, marked by a beacon (S cardinal), extends SE from the S pierhead.

3 **Berths.** The harbour pierheads dry 6·2 m and the area within is largely occupied by small boat moorings.At half tide there is a depth of 2·4 m inside Saint Aubin's Fort pier.

Portelet Bay

General information
11.242

1 Portelet Bay, on the S coast of Jersey, lies between Point Le Fret (49°10′·2N 2°11′·2W) and Noirmont Point, about 8 cables E. Portelet Ledge, awash, lies in the middle of the entrance to the bay; the bay is encumbered with rocks.

2 **Tidal streams** run strongly, except at HW and LW, across the entrance to the bay rendering the bay dangerous of approach.

Anchorage is not recommended, but in case of necessity, the best berth is about 1 cable NNW of Portelet Ledge, in a depth of about 8 m, sand.

Plateau des Minquiers

Charts 3656, 2669
General information
11.243

1 **Description.** Plateau des Minquiers, which forms part of Channel Islands, consists of numerous rocks and shoals lying on a plateau of about 130 square miles, the centre of which is situated 12 miles S of Jersey.

2 Maîtresse Île (48°58′N 2°04′W), the highest rock, is situated near the middle of the plateau. There are several stone cottages on the isle, several of which are habitable. At the N end, the highest part of the isle, a flagstaff (black and white bands on its lower half) stands near to a helicopter emergency landing pad. Puffin Beacon Tower (black and white stripes) stands on drying rocks 1 cable to the NE of the isle. There is a slipway on the SE side and the States of Jersey maintain a mooring buoy ½ cable offshore.

3 Caux des Minquiers (49°00′N 2°00′W), a large group of drying and below-water rocks form the NE part of the plateau. Basse NE des Caux, the NE-most of these dangers, is marked close ENE by NE Minquiers Light Buoy (E cardinal). La Nuisible, the NW-most danger, is marked by N Minquiers Light Buoy (N cardinal) moored about 3 cables N of the shoal.

4 **Tidal streams** are rotary anti-clockwise in the waters around Plateau des Minquiers; for details see information on the chart and *Admiralty Tidal Stream Atlas for the Channel Islands and adjacent coasts of France.*

Near Maîtresse Île the streams run in a NNW and SSE direction.

11.244

1 **Directions.** The best approach to Plateau des Minquiers is from N to Demie de Vascelin Buoy (starboard hand) (49°00′·8N 2°05′·2W) moored on the N edge of the plateau 2¾ miles NNW of Maîtresse Île. The recommended track for crossing the plateau is shown on the chart and passes close WSW of Maîtresse Île. The E extent of the drying sandbank close ENE of Grune Tar Beacon varies from year to year and may extend across the leading line.

Local knowledge is required.

2 **Useful marks,** with positions given from Maîtresse Île:
Grand Vascelin (2¾ miles NW), an above-water rock on which stands a beacon tower (white cone topmark, black and white bands, white base).
Jetée des Fontaines de Bas (8 cables NNW) marked by a beacon (red and white).

3 Rocher du Sud Bas (7 cables SSW) on which stand two leading beacons.
Pipette Rocks (black beacon with steel refuge cage, 5 m in height) (4½ miles WNW).
Les Maisons (4½ miles W), three remarkable steep above-water rocks on one of which stands a concrete beacon tower.

11.245

1 **Anchorages.** There is an anchorage which almost dries out at MLWS close S of Maîtresse Île; there is a further anchorage 5 cables W of Le Coq a detached drying rock which lies 1½ miles ESE of the isle and is marked by a beacon (red and white, cylinder topmark). Both these anchorages are exposed towards HW and should not be attempted without local knowledge.

2 The anchorage S of Maîtresse Île can be approached, with sufficient height of tide, by crossing the bank extending from Demies, marked by a beacon, which lies about 2½ cables SW of the isle.

SAINT HELIER

General information

Charts 3278, 1137
Position and function
11.246

1 Saint Helier (49°11′N 2°07′W), on the E shore of Saint Aubin's Bay (11.239), is the capital town and principal port of Jersey. The port handles cargo and a considerable volume of passenger traffic particularly in summer months when the tourist trade is at its height. The port accomodates an inshore fishing fleet and has three yacht marinas.

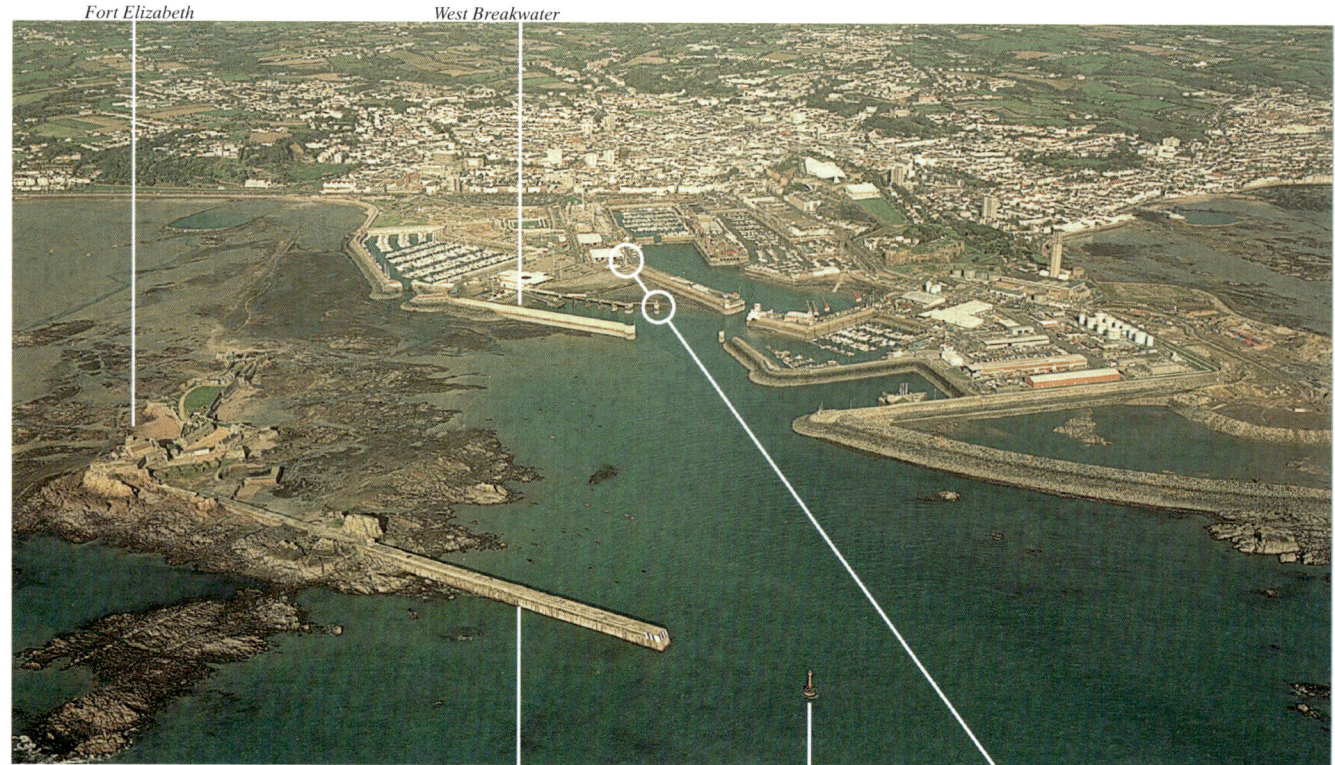

Fort Elizabeth   West Breakwater

Hermitage Breakwater   Platte Rock Beacon   Leading Lights 022¾°

Saint Helier from SW (11.246)

(Original dated 2001)

(Photograph – Air Images)

Topography
11.247

1   For a description of Saint Aubin's Bay, see 11.239.

Elizabeth Castle (49°11′N 2°08′W) (11.267) stands on the rocks fronting the harbour and is connected with Hermitage Rock by Hermitage Breakwater and extends 1¾ cables farther SSE to Breakwater End, providing shelter to the harbour entrance. A causeway, which covers about half tide extends NNE from the castle to the shore.

Approach and entry
11.248

1   Saint Helier is approached through any of the several passages through the reefs, which lie up to 1½ miles offshore between Saint Brelade's Bay and Noirmont Point (49°10′N 2°10′W), and extend across the entrance to Saint Aubin's Bay; for directions see 11.224 to 11.235.

The port is entered between Hermitage Breakwater and Crapaud of the Mangeuse (a drying reef) 2 cables E of Hermitage Breakwater End.

Traffic
11.249

1   In 2006, 703 vessels totalling 1 541 372 dwt visited the ports of Saint Helier, St Peter Port (11.105) and Alderney Harbour (11.169).

Port Authority
11.250

1   Jersey Harbours, Maritime House, La Route du Port Elizabeth, Saint Helier, Jersey, JE1 1HB.

Limiting conditions

Controlling depth
11.251

1   The least charted depth is 2·4 m on the leading line through Small Road abreast La Collette .

Deepest and longest berths
11.252

1   The deepest and longest berths are as follows:
For RoRo vessels at Elizabeth Harbour (11.270).
For container vessels at North Quay (11.270).
For tankers at La Collette Harbour (11.270).

Tidal levels
11.253

1   For information on tidal levels, see *Admiralty Tide Tables* and information on the chart.

Mean spring range about 9·6 m; mean neap range about 4·1 m.

Maximum size of vessel handled
11.254

1   A vessel of 127 m LOA and 5·2 m draught uses Elizabeth Harbour on a daily service. Tankers up to 95 m LOA and 6·1 m draught use La Collette tanker terminal. Other vessels up to 80 m LOA and 5 m draught are handled, without special arrangements, at New North Quay.

Local weather
11.255

1   In strong winds, mariners in large vessels are advised to wait until after HW before entering harbour.

Arrival information

Port operations
11.256

1   **Vessel Traffic Service.** Operated from Port Control. For details see *Admiralty List of Radio Signals Volume 6(1)*.
    Reporting regulations, see 11.183.

Saint Helier Port Control from NE (11.256)
(Original dated 2002)

(Photograph - Jersey Harbours)

Port radio
11.257

1   **Coast radio** station operates from Jersey, for details see *Admiralty List of Radio Signals Volume 1(1)*.
    Port radio station, with a limited VHF range, operates from Saint Helier, for details see *Admiralty List of Radio Signals Volume 6(1)*.

Notice of ETA required
11.258

1   For details, see 11.219.

Outer anchorages
11.259

1   For details of anchorages on the S coast of Jersey, see 11.236 to 11.240.
    Prohibited anchorages. Mariners are not permitted to anchor in Small Road, the fairway, between Albert Pier and London Berth or in any place other than indicated by the Harbour Master.

Pilotage and tugs
11.260

1   **Pilotage,** see 11.219.
    Tug is available.

Local knowledge
11.261

1   Local knowledge is required for entry into Small Road near LW at night.

Traffic regulations
11.262

1   **Precautionary area.** A circular precautionary area with radius 3 cables is centred on position 49°09′·9N 2°07′·4W at the entrance to the fairway into harbour. The area is further extended NNE to encompass Small Road. Mariners navigating in the precautionary area should do so with extreme caution. Vessels with limited manoeuvrability may be encountered and traffic may converge from all directions.

2   Within the precautionary area all vessels should abide by Rule 6 of *International Regulations for the Prevention of Collisions at Sea (1972)*. In addition, vessels of less than 20 m in length and sailing vessels must abide by Rule 9(b) of these rules.
    Breakwater End Channel. The harbour entrance channel between Hermitage Breakwater and Platte and Oyster Rocks is prohibited to all commercial traffic.

Traffic regulation
11.263

    Movement. Mariners in vessels of over 25 m in length must contact Port Control before entering, leaving or shifting berth.

1   **Speed limit** of vessels within Small Road and the harbour must not exceed 5 kn and wash must not cause damage to other vessels and structures.

Harbour

General layout
11.264

1   The port of Saint Helier is protected to the W by West Breakwater, to the S and SW by Hermitage Breakwater (11.247).
    Saint Helier Harbour (11.270), entered between Albert Pier and Victoria Pier, completely encloses Old Harbour, which lies on the E side of Saint Helier Harbour.

2   Elizabeth Harbour (11.270) has RoRo facilities and a passenger terminal. A fishing vessel basin and La Collette yacht basin lie S of of Albert Pier and farther S is La Collette Harbour (11.270) with facilities for petroleum products.
    There are marinas to the N of Saint Helier Harbour and Elizabeth Harbour.
    Reclamation is taking place (2008) to the S of La Collette Harbour (11.270)

Traffic signals
11.265

1   International Port Traffic Signals are exhibited from the Port Control tower on Victoria Pierhead and at the entrances to Saint Helier and Elizabeth Marinas to control the movement of non-commercial vessels when a commercial vessel is manoeuvering in the port area.

2   Exemption signals (Oc.Y), when exhibited, means power driven vessels less than 25 m in length may enter or leave harbour contrary to the main light signals. Such vessels must keep to the starboard side when passing between the pier heads.
    For further details see *The Mariners Handbook*.

Storm signals
11.266

1 Weather warning signals are exhibited from the signal mast at Fort Regent (11.267); see Diagram 11.266.

Day	Night	Meaning
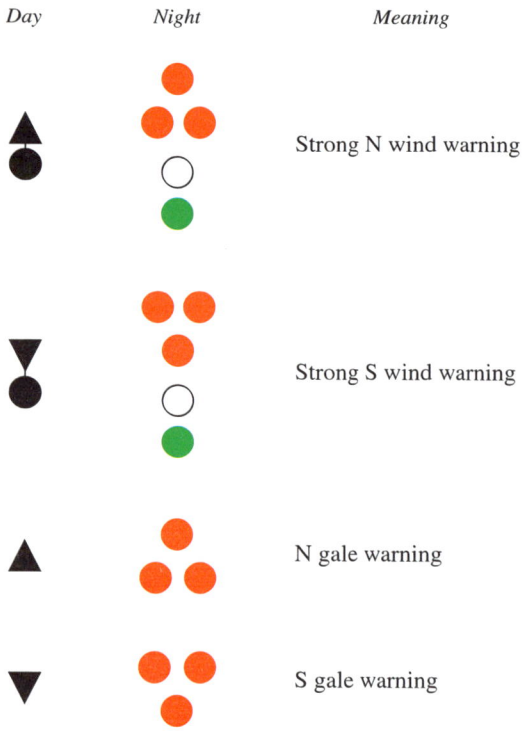		Strong N wind warning
		Strong S wind warning
		N gale warning
		S gale warning

Saint Helier – weather warning signals (11.266)

Directions for entering harbour
(continued from 11.235)

Landmarks
11.267

1 Landmarks, in addition to those on the S coast given at 11.222:

Elizabeth Castle (49°10′·6N 2°07′·6W) with Breakwater End (black and white stripes) 3½ cables SSE.

2 Fort Regent (white dome and a signal mast on N bastion) (49°10′·9N 2°06′·3W).

Swimming Pool (concave roof) (49°10′·8N 2°06′·4W) conspicuous on the skyline.

Chimney (95 m) (floodlit at night) (49°10′·5N 2°06′·5W) of La Collette Power Station.

Other aids to navigation
11.268

1 **Racon:** Demie de Pas Light (49°09′N 2°06′W).

For details see *Admiralty List of Radio Signals Volume 2.*

Small Road
11.269

1 **Leading lights:**

Front light. Dolphin (red rectangular daymark on metal framework tower on dolphin) (49°10′·7N 2°06′·9W) standing close SE of the head of Elizabeth Harbour East Pier.

Rear light (red rectangular daymark on metal framework tower, 15 m in height) (1¼ cables NNE of the front mark) standing at the elbow of Albert Pier.

2 From a position S of Breakwater End the alignment (022¾°) of these lights leads in the fairway through Small Road passing (with positions given from Elizabeth Castle (49°10′·6N 2°07′·5W)):

3 Between West Rock (5½ cables S), which lies close SE of Oyster Rocks marked by a beacon (red and white bands letter "O" topmark), and East Rock (6¼ cables SSE), marked on its SW side by a light buoy (starboard hand); thence:

Between Platte Rock and associated dangers (4½ cables SSE), marked by a light beacon (port hand), and Sharp Rock (5 cables SE); thence:

4 Between Crapaud of the Castle (2¾ cables SE), marked on its SE side by No 2 Light Buoy (port hand), and the head of reclaimed land to the S of La Collette Harbour(4 cables ESE), to the required berth.

5 **Caution.** During the E-going tidal stream when approaching from W care should be taken when altering course from the alignment of the Grève d'Azette Leading Lights (11.226) to the alignment of the leading lights for Small Road as there is a danger of being set towards the reefs on the E side of the passage.

6 **Saint Helier Harbour leading lights.** The alignment (078°) of leading lights (white columns) (6 cables E) exhibited near the S end of Old Harbour leads through the entrance to Saint Helier Harbour.

Saint Helier Harbour Leading Lights in line 078° (11.269)

(Original dated 1998)

(Photograph – Capt. F. A. Lawrence, MRIN, Navitron Limited)

Basins and berths

Alongside berths
11.270

1 **Elizabeth Harbour:** East Berth and West Berth, two linkspan RoRo berths each 130 m in length with a maintained depth alongside of 6·0 m.

La Collette Harbour: La Collette tanker berth, on the S side of the basin, is 57 m in length, and can accept vessels up to 95 m LOA; it has a maintained depth of 5·5 m.

Saint Helier Harbour: New North Quay berths 6 and 7, for container and bulk traffic, with a total length of 153 m and maintained depth alongside of 5·2 m. Other container berths are available at Victoria Pier.

2 **Old Harbour,** which is completely enclosed by Saint Helier Harbour, is entered between North Quay and South Pier, and is used by fishing vessels and pleasure craft. The entrance is dredged but the harbour dries 4·0 m close within the entrance and in excess of 6 m at its N and S ends.

3 **Marinas.** There are two marinas and one yacht basin at Saint Helier.

Port services

11.271

1   **Repairs.** Minor repair facilities and divers are available.
Other facilities: Ship sanitation control exemption certificates issued; hospital; limited oily waste reception facilities.
  Supplies: fuel, by road tanker; fresh water; stores.

JERSEY EAST COAST AND ADJACENT COAST OF FRANCE

General information

Charts 1138, 3655, 2669
Routes
11.272

1   From the SE end of Jersey the route leads generally NE through Violet Channel (11.278) or Anquette Channel (11.282) thence generally N along the E coast of the island passing either inside or outside of Banc du Château (49°12′N 1°59′W) to the NE end of the island, a total distance of about 12 miles.

2   Two inshore secondary channels, Passage de la Déroute (11.290) and Déroute de Terre (11.289) lead closer to the French coast from Pointe du Roc (49°50′N 1°37′W) to Cap de Carteret, about 33 miles NNW.

Topography
11.273

1   **Jersey — east coast.** is entered between La Rocque Point (49°10′N 2°02′W) and the bluff, 2 miles N, on which Mont Orgueil Castle (11.277) stands; its shores are composed of white sand backed by a seawall which runs the length of the bay. A coastal sandbank, the S half of which is broken by numerous rocky outcrops, dries up to 1¼ miles offshore E of La Rocque Point and up to 7 cables offshore in the middle of the bay. Gorey Harbour (11.291) lies at the N end of the bay.

2   Anne Port, a small bay encumbered with rocks, with a ramp at its head, lies between Mont Orgueil Castle and La Crête Point, 5 cables NNW.
  Between La Crête Point and La Coupe Point, 1½ miles N, the coast is indented by (11.292) and Fliquet Bay (11.293).
  French coast, see 11.288.

Prohibited anchorage
11.274

1   Submarine power cables (11.286) (11.292) (11.296) have been laid from a position on the N shore of Havre de Surville (49°17′N 1°41′W) to Saint Catherine's Bay (49°13′N 2°01′W). Anchoring and fishing are prohibited in the vicinity of these cables, as shown on the chart.

Rescue
11.275

1   **Inshore lifeboats** are stationed at:
    Saint Catherine's Bay (49°13′N 2°01′W) (11.292), see 1.113.
    Havre de Carteret (49°23′N 1°47′W) (11.297), see 1.117.
  Signal station (Sémaphore) (49°22′N 1°48′W) is situated at Carteret on the French coast, for details see 1.110.

2   **VHF Direction-finding station,** for emergency use only, operates from Carteret Signal Station for details see *Admiralty List of Radio Signals Volume 2.*
  Refuge Beacon. A refuge beacon (lattice pyramid; height of structure 7·5 m) stands on Violet Bank (11.278) in position 49°09′·9N 2°01′·1W.

Tidal streams
11.276

1   When navigating Violet Channel particular attention should be paid to the set of the tidal streams which change direction by the hour.
  Tidal streams off the coast between La Rocque Point and La Coupe Point attain a spring rate of about 4 kn in both directions, beginning as follows:

Interval from HW Saint Helier	*Direction*
−0230	NW
+0330	SE

2   Slack water occurs near half tide.
  For details, see information on the chart and *Admiralty Tidal Stream Atlas for the Channel Islands and adjacent coasts of France.*

Directions
(continued from 11.235)

Principal marks
11.277

1   **Landmarks — Jersey east coast:**
    Seymour Tower (stone tower E, S and W sides white, 16 m in height) (49°09′·5N 2°00′·4W) completely isolated at HW.

Seymour Tower from ENE (11.277)

(Original dated 1998)

(Photograph - Capt. F. A. Lawrence, MRIN, Navitron Limited)

    Mont Orgueil Castle (49°12′N 2°01′W) standing on a rocky promontory to the E of Gorey.

2   Archirondel Tower (red and white bands) (49°12′·7N 2°01′·4W).
    La Coupe Turret (small white stone tower with white round topmark) (49°14′·0N 2°01′·6W) on La Coupe Point.
  For landmarks at Saint Helier and the S coast of Jersey, see 11.267 and 11.222.

3   **Landmarks — French coast:**
    Lessay Loran Mast (pylon, 213 m in height, two flashing white lights at night) (49°08′·5N 1°30′·2W) (uncharted).
    House (49°13′·6N 1°38′·7W) on the W entrance point of Havre de Lessay (Havre de Saint-Germain).
    Water Tower (49°19′·9N 1°43′·4W) W of Portbail.
    Building (white with grey roof) (49°22′·1N 1°46′·3W) on the shore at Barnville-Plage.

Archirondel Tower bearing 327½° (11.277)

(Original dated 1998)

(Photograph – Capt. F. A. Lawrence, MRIN, Navitron Limited)

4   Cap de Carteret (49°22'·4N 1°48'·6W), a dark
headland which terminates in a rocky cliff and on
which stands a light (see below) and a signal
station. A conspicuous house stands 7 cables E of
the cape.

Major lights:

Cap de Carteret Light (grey tower green top, 18 m in
height) (49°22'·4N 1°48'·4W).

Pointe du Roc Light (48°50'N 1°37'W) (10.194).

Grande Île Light (48°52'N 1°49'W) (10.194).

Violet Channel

11.278

1   **Description.** Violet Channel (49°08'N 1°58'W) lies
between the SE extremity of Violet Bank and the reefs
which lie SE and S of it.

2   Violet Bank is the general name applied to the reefs
which lie off the SE coast of Jersey. This bank dries as far
as La Conchière (49°08'N 2°00'W), a rock situated 2 miles
SE of La Rocque Point, the SE extremity of Jersey. The
bank, which consists of shingle and sand interspersed with
drying rocky ledges, fringes the coast and extends out to
1½ miles offshore; the greater part of this bank covers at
half tide. The S side of the E extremity of Violet Bank is
bordered by Taxe Rock, West Rock and La Route en Ville,
a chain of drying and below-water rocks extending from
7 cables to 1¼ miles E of La Conchière. A bank with
numerous rocks lying on it, extends 1 mile NE from La
Route en Ville to Petite Four and forms the NW side of
Violet Channel.

3   Plateau de la Frouquie, consisting of numerous rocks,
some of which dry, borders the SW side of Violet Channel.
Petite Anquette (11.283) and Seal Rocks, which both dry,
and La Maraine Reef lie 7 cables E of the E edge of Violet
Bank and form the NE side of Violet Channel.

11.279

1   **Route.** From a position on the alignment (021°) of Icho
Tower (49°09'N 2°03'W) (11.222) with Mont Orgueil
Castle, 3¼ miles NNE (11.277), seen over La Rocque
Point, the track leads parallel with the outer edge of Violet
Bank (11.278) passing (with positions given from Seymour
Tower (49°10'N 2°00'W)):

2   Midway between La Conchière (1¼ miles S), a rock
marked by a beacon (iron pole disc topmark, 5 m
in height) at the SE end of the drying part of
Violet Bank, and Canger Rock (2½ miles S)
which, together with La Goubinière close S, lie at
the W end of Plateau de la Frouquie (11.278).
Canger Rock Light Buoy (W cardinal) is moored

about 4½ cables WNW of these two drying rocks.
Thence:

3   Between La Route en Ville (1¾ miles SE) (11.278)
and Plateau de la Frouquie (2¼ miles SSE)
(11.278).

Karamé Beacon from SSE (11.279)

(Original dated 1998)

(Photograph – Capt. F. A. Lawrence, MRIN, Navitron Limited)

From a position on the line of bearing 319° of Seymour
Tower just open NE of Karamé Beacon (concrete beacon
letter "K" topmark) (7 cables SE) standing on a rock of the
same name, the track then leads 026° through Violet
Channel. Alternatively, when La Rousse Platte (2¾ miles
SSE), a drying rock near the E end of Plateau de la
Frouquie, is uncovered, it may be kept astern on a bearing
of 204° passing:

Brett Beacon (11.279)

(Original dated 1998)

(Photograph – Capt. F. A. Lawrence, MRIN, Navitron Limited)

4   Between Middle Reef (1¾ miles SE) and a 5·3 m
patch (reported 1987) (2½ miles SE). Violet Light
Buoy (safe water) is moored 3 cables E of the
patch. Thence:

5   Parallel to the SE side of the bank (11.278), which
extends 1 mile NE from La Route en Ville to
Petite Four (2 miles ESE), to a position between
Petite Four and Seal Rocks (2½ miles ESE)
(11.278) on the alignment (279°) of Brett Beacon
(letter "B" topmark) (1¼ miles ESE), at the NW
end of Brett Rocks, with Karamé Beacon.

6   **Clearing bearing:**

From S, the line of bearing 351° of Mont Orgueil
Castle just open W of Seymour Tower and La
Conchière Beacon clears very close W of La
Goubinière and Canger Rock, but E of Canger
Rock Light Buoy.

Violet Channel to Gorey Outer Road
11.280

1   From a position at the N end of Violet Channel W of Seal Rocks (49°08'·7N 1°56'·5W) (11.278) the line of bearing 332° of La Coupe Turret (49°14'N 2°01'W) (11.277) seen over the root of Saint Catherine Breakwater and open E of Verclut Point, 5 cables SSE, leads in the fairway passing (with positions given from Seymour Tower (49°10'N 2°00'W)):

Breakwater House
La Coupe Turret bearing 332° (11.280)
(Original dated 1998)

(Photograph – Capt. F. A. Lawrence, MRIN, Navitron Limited)

2   WSW of Stony Banks (2½ miles E); thence:
    ENE of Le Cochon (1 mile ENE), marked on its NE side by a buoy (port hand); thence:
    ENE of La Noire (1 mile NE), marked by a beacon (E cardinal); thence:
    ENE of Le Giffard (1½ miles NE), a rock awash marked on its N side by a buoy (port hand); thence:
3   WSW of South Ridge (2 miles NE) at the SE extremity of Banc du Château; Middle Bank, near its centre is nearly awash. This bank composed of sand, gravel and shells, which extends about 2 miles NW from a position 2½ miles ENE of La Roque Point (1 mile NW), is much affected by the weather and action of the tidal streams. The shallower part is continually shifting and during W winds the sand ridges are about 1 m higher than with E winds. And:
4   ENE of Horn Rock (1½ miles NNE), marked by a beacon (port hand), the E-most rock of Les Frouquies de la Grève, to Outer Road (11.285).

Approach to Gorey Outer Road from north-east
11.281

1   **Leading marks:**
    Front mark. S side of Mont Orgueil Castle (49°12'N 2°01'W) (11.277).
    Rear mark. Grouville Mill (white top no sails) (1¾ miles SW of the front mark).
    From a position E of La Coupe Point (49°14'N 2°01'W) (11.277) the alignment (230°) of these marks leads in the channel passing (with positions given from Mont Orgueil Castle (49°12'N 2°01'W)):
2   Between the N end of Banc du Château (11.280), of which North Ridge (1 mile E) is the N-most danger, and Fara Ledge (1 mile NE). Le Fara (1 mile NNE), the most prominent drying rock on Saint Catherine's Bank (11.292), lies near the edge of the bank and is marked by a beacon (E cardinal).

3   The line of bearing 333°, astern, of La Coupe Turret (2 miles N) (11.277) just open E of Verclut Point (5 cables SSE) then leads in the channel along the W side of Banc du Château to Outer Road (11.285) passing:
4   ENE of Très Grunes (5 cables E) with its associated dangers Pacquet and Les Arch, the latter marked on their SE side by a beacon (black and white letter "A" topmark), the outermost dangers E of Mont Orgueil Castle, which border the W side of the passage to Outer Road from N. The alignment (327°) of Le Fara Beacon (E cardinal) (1 mile NNE) with La Coupe Turret is a good transit to use to make this sharp turn.
5   **Clearing bearings:**
    The alignment (183°) of Little Seymour Beacon (basket topmark) standing on a rock of the same name (2¼ miles S) in line with Seymour Tower (2½ miles S) clears ¾ cable E of Très Grunes and E of Pillon Rock (1½ miles NNE) (11.284).

Anquette Channel
11.282

1   **General information.** Anquette Channel (49°08'N 1°56'W) leads ENE from the S end of Violet Channel (11.278) thence NE between Petite Anquette and Grande Anquette.
    Mariners in vessels drawing more than 4·5 m should wait until the rising tide has fairly made before navigating Anquette Channel, and if there is a swell, until the first quarter of the rising tide.

11.283

1   **Route.** From a position at the S end of Violet Channel, N of La Rousse Platte (49°07'N 1°58'W) (11.279) the passage through Anquette Channel leads initially ENE passing (with positions given from Seymour Tower (49°10'N 2°00'W)):
    Clear of Violet Light Buoy (safe water) (2¾ miles SE) (11.279); thence:
2   NNW of Porpoise Rock (3½ miles ESE), the W-most danger on Plateau de l'Arconie on which lie numerous rocks, some of which dry, which extends from 5 cables to 1¾ miles S of Grande Anquette (3½ miles ESE), a drying rock on which stands a refuge beacon (iron conical, white and yellow, surmounted by a spherical refuge cage topmark).

Grande Anquette Beacon (11.283)
(Original dated 1998)

(Photograph – Capt. F. A. Lawrence, MRIN, Navitron Limited)

3   The passage then leads generally NE passing:
    Between Petite Anquette (3 miles ESE) marked by a beacon (yellow concrete, letters "PA" topmark) and Grande Anquette (3½ miles ESE) marked by a

beacon (yellow concrete cone surmounted by a spherical topmark); thence:

Between Grune Le Feuvre (3 miles E) and Anquette Patches (4 miles E) where the route continues NW (11.284) or N through Passage de la Déroute (11.290), a side channel.

Anquette Channel to La Coupe Point
11.284

1 **Leading marks:**

Front mark. Saint Catherine Light (white framework tower, 9 m in height) (49°13′N 2°01′W) standing at the head of Saint Catherine Breakwater.

Rear mark. La Coupe Turret (9 cables NW of the front mark) (11.277).

2 From a position at the NE end of Anquette Channel the alignment (315°) of these marks leads in the channel passing (with positions given from Mont Orgueil Castle (49°12′N 2°01′W)):

NE of Stony Banks (3½ miles SE); thence:

SW of East Tongue Sand (3½ miles E); thence:

3 Along the NE side of Banc du Château (11.280) passing clear of West Tongue Sand (2¾ miles ESE) (11.286).

The route then continues generally NNW crossing the approach (11.281) to Gorey Outer Road passing:

4 ENE of Pillon Rock (1½ miles NNE), lying 2 cables E of Saint Catherine Breakwater, to E of La Coupe Point (11.277), distant at least 5 cables, or anchorage (11.286) as required.

Clearing bearings, see 11.281.

Useful mark.

Saint Catherine Light (49°13′N 2°01′W) (11.284).

(Directions continue at 11.302)

Anchorages

Outer Road, Gorey
11.285

1 Outer Road (49°12′N 2°00′W), Gorey, lies close W of Banc du Château (11.280); it affords safe anchorage in depths from 9 to 15 m, gravel and mud. A recommended berth, about 1 mile ESE of Mont Orgueil Castle, is shown on the chart.

Mariners in small craft can anchor in Inner Road, Gorey (11.291).

North of West Tongue Sand
11.286

1 There is good anchorage for mariners in large vessels about 8 cables N of West Tongue Sand (49°11′N 1°57′W), as shown on the chart, in depths of about 18 m.

Submarine power cable (11.274) and disused submarine cables (11.293), shown on the chart, lie 1 mile and 6 cables N, respectively, of this anchorage.

Side channel — Jersey

Between Plateau de la Frouquie and Plateau de l'Arconie
11.287

1 **General information.** The passage between Plateau de la Frouquie (49°07′N 1°59′W) (11.278) and Plateau de l'Arconie (11.283), about 1½ miles E, is obstructed with numerous submerged rocks.

Local knowledge is required and mariners should not attempt this passage until after the first quarter of the rising tide.

Side channels — French coast

Charts 3655, 3656, 2669
General information
11.288

1 **Routes.** Passage de la Déroute (11.290), entered at its N end between Les Écrehou (49°17′N 1°56′W) and Basses de Taillepied, about 1¾ miles NE, and Déroute de Terre (11.289), entered at its N end between Basses de Portbail (49°19′N 1°45′W) and Bancs Félés, 1 mile SW, are two passages which lead from S of Plateau des Minquiers (48°58′N 2°04′W) (11.243) and Îles Chausey (48°53′N 1°49′W) (10.216) to Race of Alderney (11.318), passing E of Jersey; at night only Déroute de Terre is practicable.

2 These channels are little used because the tidal streams are strong and erratic and the marks difficult to identify. Bound for Race of Alderney from Granville or Saint-Malo, it is simpler to go W of Plateau des Minquiers and Jersey. However, provided the weather is clear, the passages between the reefs E of Jersey are not difficult to negotiate at HW owing to the great rise of tide. Passage de la Déroute is frequently used by ferries.

3 **Topography — French coast.** Between Pointe du Roc (48°50′N 1°37′W) and Le Sénéquet, about 15 miles N, the coast is fringed by a bank which dries up to 3½ miles offshore in places with foul ground extending 3½ miles farther to seaward. Between Le Sénéquet and the entrance to Havre de Portbail, 14 miles N, the coast is low and fringed with dunes; numerous dangers lie offshore.

Jersey — east coast, see 11.273.

Tidal streams, see 11.11.

4 **Fisheries.** Fishing buoys (special) are moored near the edge of the coastal bank between Pointe du Roc and Havre de Portbail, about 30 miles N.

Shellfish beds, marked by buoys and shown on the chart, extend up to 3 miles offshore between the latitude of Blainville (49°04′N) and that of Havre de Lessay (Havre de Saint-Germain) (49°13′·5N); fishing is prohibited in these areas except for the collection of shellfish and rod fishing.

5 **Controlling depths.** Passage de la Déroute has depths, near its S end, of less than 3 m close on each side of the channel between Southern Anquettes (49°05′N 1°51′W) and Basse Occidentale des Bœufs, 2 miles NNE, and least known depths of 4 m in the channel, near its N end, between Les Écrehou (49°17′N 1°56′W) and Basses de Taillepied, about 1¾ miles NE. Déroute de Terre has depths of 0·9 m at its S end.

Principal marks, see 11.277.

Directions
11.289

1 **Déroute de Terre.** This channel should only be attempted at or near the time of HW as depths of less than 1 m exist at its S end.

By day. From a position about 1 mile W of Pointe du Roc (48°50′N 1°37′W) (10.188) the track leads generally N passing (with positions given from Le Sénéquet Light (49°06′N 1°40′W)):

2 E of a dangerous wreck (48°53′N 1°41′W); thence:

E of a wreck (48°54′N 1°41′W) with a least depth of 1·6 m, marked by Anvers Buoy (W cardinal), and:

W of Roches de Bréhal (48°55′N 1°36′W); thence:

To a position on the alignment (251°) of Le Pignon Lighted Beacon Tower (48°54′N 1°43′W) (10.196) and Grande Île Light, 4 miles WSW (10.194).

3 The line of bearing 161°, astern, of Pointe de Champeaux (48°45′N 1°34′W) (10.199) just open W of Pointe du Roc then leads in the channel passing:

ENE of La Catheue (8 miles SSW) a rock marked by a light buoy (S cardinal) which lies towards the middle of Bancs de la Catheue, a chain of sandbanks extending between 5½ and 11½ miles NNW of Pointe du Roc; and:

4 WSW of Roches d'Agon an extensive group of above-water and drying rocks which lie with their SE part on the edge of the drying coastal bank W of Point d'Agon from where a light (white tower red top white dwelling, 12 m in height) (6¼ miles SSE) is exhibited. Le Ronquet, the highest rock of this group, is marked by a lighted beacon tower (isolated danger, no topmark) (5½ miles S). Basse Quesnel lies nearly 1¼ miles SW of Le Ronquet and closer to the track. Thence:

5 Between a 1·5 m patch (3 miles SSW) and a dangerous wreck (position doubtful) (charted 4¼ miles SW). Internationale F Buoy (special), which marks the outer limit of the local oyster fishery, is moored 6 cables E of the wreck.

6 The track then leads N passing:

W of Les Nattes (2¼ miles SSW), marked by a buoy (W cardinal); a 2·5 m patch lies 7 cables W of the group and closer to the track. Thence:

7 W of Le Sénéquet, a rock from where a light (white tower, 26 m in height) is exhibited, standing near the W extremity of a rocky ledge extending from the shore. Several rocks which dry lie within 1 mile W and NW of the light and closer to the track; the NW rock is marked by La Basse du Sénéquet Buoy (W cardinal). The whole area between Le Sénéquet and Les Nattes is encumbered with rocks on which the sea breaks with strong W winds. Thence:

8 E of Basse Jourdan (3½ miles WNW) at the E end of Chaussée des Bœufs (11.290), a light buoy (E cardinal) is moored 4 cables E of the shoal; thence:

To a position on the line of bearing 162°, astern, of Le Sénéquet Light, distant 6 miles.

9 The line of bearing 342° of Cap de Carteret Light (49°22′N 1°48′W) (11.277) or the line of bearing 162°, astern, of Le Sénéquet Light, then leads in the channel passing:

Between Basses de Portbail (49°19′N 1°45′W) and Bancs Félés, 1 mile SW.

The track then leads generally NW passing between Cap de Carteret and Plateau des Trois Grunes, 3½ miles W (11.290) to a position WNW of Cap de Carteret.

10 **At night.** From a position 1 mile W of Pointe du Roc the route leads generally N to the alignment (251°) of Le Pignon Lighted Beacon Tower with Grande Île Light.

The line of bearing 163° of Pointe du Roc Light (10.194), astern, then leads in the channel passing:

ENE of Bancs de la Catheue to the line of bearing 083½° of Le Sénéquet Light changing from white to red.

11 The line of bearing 196° of Grande Île Light, astern, then leads in the channel passing:

ESE of Basse Jourdan to a position NNW of Le Sénéquet Light.

The line of bearing 342° of Cap de Carteret Light, or the line of bearing 162° of Le Sénéquet Light, astern, then leads in the channel passing:

12 Between Bancs Félés and Basses de Portbail to the line of bearing 056° of Portbail Rear Leading Light (49°20′N 1°42′W) (11.296).

The track then leads generally NW passing:

Between Plateau des Trois Grunes and Cap de Carteret to a position on the line of bearing 355° of Cap de la Hague Light (49°43′N 1°57′W) (12.9) with Cap de Carteret Light bearing 123°, astern.

13 **Alternatively,** if proceeding from Saint-Malo via Entrée de la Déroute (10.197), from a position SE of Les Ardentes (48°58′N 1°52′W) (10.198) the line of bearing 040° of Le Sénéquet Light leads in the channel passing:

Between the N extremity of Bancs de la Catheue and Basse Le Marie, 3 miles NW (11.290).

The line of bearing 196° of Grande Île Light, astern, then leads in the channel to join the route from Pointe du Roc W of Le Sénéquet Light.

11.290

1 **Passage de la Déroute.** From a position SE of Les Ardentes (48°58′N 1°52′W) (10.198), at the N part of Entrée de la Déroute (10.197), the alignment (172°), astern, of L'Enseigne Beacon Tower (48°53′·7N 1°50′·4W) with the disused signal station, 1 mile S on Grande Île, leads in the channel for about 3 miles.

2 The line of bearing 025° of Le Bœuf Beacon Tower (49°06′·5N 1°17′·2W) then leads in the channel passing (with positions given from the beacon tower):

WNW of Basse Le Marié (4¾ miles S) marked by a light buoy (W cardinal). Internationale E Buoy (special), which marks the outer limit of the inshore fisheries, is moored 6 cables ENE of the ledge.

3 The alignment (312¾°) of Grande Anquette Beacon (5½ miles WNW) (11.283) with Saint Martin's Church spire, 7 miles farther NW on Jersey, then leads in the channel passing:

Between Chaussée des Bœufs, rocky ledges some of which dry; a beacon tower (N cardinal) stands on Le Bœuf the highest rock. Basse Occidentale des Bœufs (2 miles W) is the W-most danger. And:

4 Southern Anquettes (3¼ miles SW) consisting of a number of gravel ridges which extend 4 miles SE from the SW extremity of Plateau de l'Arconie (11.283). A dangerous wreck (position doubtful) is charted in the middle of the passage about 2½ miles SW of Le Bœuf Beacon Tower. Thence:

To a position 132°, distant about 2½ miles, from Grande Anquette.

5 The track then leads NNW passing:

ENE of Grune La Hauche (4½ miles W) and La Grand Arconie (4½ miles WNW), two patches which dry on the E side of Plateau de l'Arconie; and:

6 WSW of Basse NW des Bœufs (2 miles NW); thence:

To a position on the alignment (276°) of Grande Anquette Beacon (5½ miles WNW) with Icho Tower, 5 miles farther W (11.222), distant 1¼ miles from Grande Anquette.

7 The track then leads generally N passing off the E coast of Jersey to a position on the alignment (258°) of La Coupe Turret (49°14′·0N 2°01′·5W) (11.277) with Rozel Mill, 1 mile WSW, close E of Écrevière Light Buoy (S cardinal) (49°15′N 1°52′W) moored off the SE side of Écrevière Bank, which dries in parts and extends 2 miles

SSE from the SE edge of Les Écrehou (11.307). Tidal streams setting over this bank cause a confused sea in bad weather.

8   The route then leads generally NNW passing:

> Between Les Écrehou (49°17′N 1°56′W) and Basses de Taillepied (49°18′N 1°51′W); thence:
>
> WSW of Plateau des Trois Grunes (49°22′N 1°54′W). Les Trois Grunes Light Buoy (W cardinal) is moored close SW of the plateau. Thence:
>
> To a position 5½ miles W of Cap de Carteret (49°22′N 1°48′W) (11.277).

Minor bays and harbours

Chart 1138
Gorey Harbour
11.291

1   **General information.** Gorey Harbour (49°12′N 2°01′W), on the E coast of Jersey, lies at N end of Royal Bay of Grouville (11.273) and is formed by a pier extending SW from the foot of Mont Orgueil Castle. It is a popular port of call for mariners in yachts and pleasure craft and in summer months excursion boats run to Barneville-Carteret and Portbail on the French coast. The harbour and bank outside it dry out.

2   **Local knowledge** is required.

    Pilotage. The pilot boarding position is located 2 cables ESE of Fairway Light Buoy (starboard hand) in Gorey Roads as shown on the chart.

    Leading lights:

> Front light (white metal framework tower, 5 m in height) (49°11′·8N 2°01′·4W) on Gorey Harbour Pierhead.
>
> Rear light (white square orange sides on stone wall, 1 m in height) (3 cables WNW of the front mark).

Gorey Leading Lights in line 298° (11.291)
(Original dated 1998)

(Photograph - Capt. F. A. Lawrence, MRIN, Navitron Limited)

3   From a position in Outer Road (11.285) the alignment (298°) of these lights leads towards the harbour entrance passing SSW of Écureuil Rock, marked by a beacon (starboard hand), and clear of Azicot Rock, which may be passed on either side, lying 4 and 2 cables ESE, respectively, of the front mark. A beacon (E cardinal) standing about ½ cable NNW of the pierhead marks the extremity of a line of obstructions which extend SE from the NW shore of the harbour.

4   When entering Gorey Harbour between half flood and half ebb do not pass the pierhead too closely as there is a strong NE set across the entrance.

    Useful marks:

> Les Burons (49°11′·3N 2°00′·8W) marked by a beacon (red and white bands letter "B" topmark).
>
> Beacon (fishtail topmark) (49°11′·8N 2°00′·7W) on Équerrière Rock.

5   **Anchorage** is available in Inner Road between Road Rock (49°11′·3N 2°00′·2W) and Inner Road Rock, 3½ cables NW, as shown on the chart; Fairway Light Buoy (starboard hand) is moored in Inner Road about midway between the two rocks.

    In offshore winds and reasonably settled weather mariners can anchor, according to draught, E of Gorey Harbour Pierhead clear of the fairway, Écureuil Rock and small craft moorings.

6   **Berths:** mud and sand, drying from 3 to 5 m, in the harbour and alongside the pier. A landing stage just inside the pierhead is reserved for excursion boats.

    Repairs: slip; minor repair facilities.

    Supplies: fuel, diesel and petrol; fresh water; fresh provisions.

Saint Catherine's Bay
11.292

1   **General information.** Saint Catherine's Bay (49°13′N 2°01′W) lies between La Crête Point and Verclut Point, 9 cables N, and affords good shelter from offshore winds; near HW, E winds cause a short choppy sea which subsides as the tide falls.

2   Saint Catherine Breakwater, including a 15 m extension of protective rock armour, extends 3½ cables ESE from Verclut Point; a light (11.284) is exhibited from its head. A small breakwater extends 1 cable ENE from the shore 7½ cables S of the same point.

    Saint Catherine's Bank, consisting of mud interspersed with numerous rocks, some of which dry, extends in places up to 9 cables offshore from the central part of the bay.

3   **Submarine power cable** (11.274) from France is landed close N of the root of the small breakwater, as shown on the chart.

    Leading marks:

> Front mark. Saint Catherine Light (49°13′·3N 2°00′·7W) (11.284).
>
> Rear mark. La Coupe Turret (8 cables NW of the front mark) (11.277).

4   The alignment (315°) of these marks leads NE of all rocks on Saint Catherine's Bank, passing NE of La Grune du Nord, on the NE edge of Saint Catherine's Bank, and SW of a 5·3 m patch, Eureka and Pillon Rock (11.284), lying 4½ cables SE, 3 cables ESE and 2 cables E, respectively, of the light. When about 1 cable from the light alter course into the bay and anchor as convenient avoiding drying rocks extending S midway along the breakwater.

5   **Caution.** During spring tides the tidal streams attain a great rate over Saint Catherine's Bank both into the bay and round the end of Saint Catherine Breakwater; due allowance should be made for this when entering or leaving the bay.

6   **Anchorage:** close inside Saint Catherine Breakwater, as shown on the chart, in a depth of 8 m, sand and mud, avoiding a 1·9 m patch lying 2 cables SW of the light; the anchorage area is marked by small buoys (special).

    Mariners in smaller craft can anchor farther inshore, as shown on the chart, 3 cables S of Breakwater House;

attention is drawn to many small craft moorings in the area.

7 **Berths.** Vessels cannot lie alongside Saint Catherine Breakwater but there is a landing slip at the inshore end on the S side. The inner part of the bay is occupied by yacht moorings. Boats can use the small breakwater 7½ cables S of Verclut Point at HW; it is best approached from N.

8 **Ramp** at the head of the bay, close N of the Martello Tower (white), provides access to the coastal road; another ramp close S of the tower is used by the inshore lifeboat (11.275).

Fliquet Bay
11.293

1 **General information.** Fliquet Bay (49°14′N 2°01′W) is entered between Verclut Point and La Coupe Point; the bay affords a good anchorage in offshore winds.

Disused submarine cables, shown on the chart, lie in the middle of the bay.

Caution. Brayes Rocks, drying ledges, extend 2 cables NE from La Coupe Point and Coupe Rock lies 4 cables E of the same point.

Chart 3656
Regnéville
11.294

1 **General information.** Havre de Regnéville (49°00′N 1°34′W), which lies 10 miles N of Granville, is a small harbour situated within Point d'Agon, from where a light (11.289) is exhibited. The harbour dries out to sandy bottom and can accept small craft with a draught of 2 to 3 m at spring tides. A mole which covers extends SW from the E bank of the entrance 2 cables SE of Point d'Agon; it is marked at its seaward end by a buoy (starboard hand) and along its length by beacons (starboard hand).

2 **Local knowledge,** or the use of a local pilot is essential as the approach is encumbered with sandbanks through which there is only one channel whose position changes frequently; the channel is marked by buoys which are moved as necessary.

3 **Approach.** The line of bearing 028° of Regnéville Direction Light (house, 6 m in height) (49°00′·6N 1°33′·4W), or at night in its white sector (027°–029°) leads in the approach.

4 **Berths:** landing stage, used during summer months, at the E side of the entrance 2 cables SE of Pointe d'Agon; small pontoon at Regnéville-sur-Mer.

Chart 3655
Havre de Lessay (Saint-Germain-sur-Ay)
11.295

1 **General information.** Havre de Lessay (Havre de Saint-Germain) (49°13′N 1°37′W) is a sandy inlet, which dries out, situated nearly midway between Le Sénéquet and Portbail.

2 **Anchorage** is available about 3 miles S of Havre de Lessay in Mouillage de Pirou-Plage out of the full force of the tidal streams and clear of the disused submarine cables which lie close N of the anchorage, as shown on the chart, on drying sand. Le Robin Beacon (S cardinal) (49°09′·9N 1°36′·7W) marks the N limit of the channel to the anchorage.

Fishery, see 11.288.

Portbail
11.296

1 **General information.** Havre de Portbail (49°20′N 1°43′W) is a small harbour which dries and which provides

good shelter from all winds. Mariners in small craft with a draught up to 1 m can enter at HW spring tides; the entrance channel dries 8 m on the leading line about 2 cables SW of the entrance. A quay, the E end of which forms a slipway, is situated just inside the harbour entrance and is connected to the small town of Portbail by a causeway. A training wall extends to seaward from the W side of the quay; this wall covers at HW except at neap tides. A marina is situated on the E side of the causeway NE of the quay and is protected by a mole and breakwater.

2 **Local knowledge** is required and local advice should be sought before berthing.

Tidal streams set across the entrance channel.

Leading lights:
> Front light. La Caillourie Light Beacon (white pylon red top, 8 m in height) (49°19′·8N 1°42′·5W) on the N side of the entrance.

3 > Rear light. Portbail Church (belfry, 35 m in height) (5 cables NE of the front light). Do not mistake the belfry of Portbail church with that of Gouey Church close E.

From a position S of Bancs Félés (49°17′N 1°48′W) the alignment (042°) of these lights leads in the channel passing (with positions given from the front mark):

4 > SE of Landfall Buoy (safe water) (2 miles SW); thence:
> Through a channel marked by buoys along the SE side of the training wall, marked at its head by a light beacon (white mast red top, 7 m in height) (5 cables SW) and along its length by beacon poles, to the quay.

5 **Anchorage:** in the vicinity of Landfall Buoy in Fosse de la Bouguette in depths of 3 to 6 m, sand and rock.

Submarine power cables are laid from a position 2½ miles SSE of Portbail to Jersey. See (11.274).

6 **Berths:** alongside the SE side of the quay which dries out at about half tide.

Facilities: fresh water; provisions.

Barneville-Carteret
11.297

1 **General information.** Havre de Carteret (49°23′N 1°47′W) a small fishing port and a summer resort lies 1 mile E of Cap de Carteret (11.277); it is sheltered from winds from N to E but the approach is dangerous in strong S to SW winds. Mariners in small craft with draughts of less than 3 m can enter at HW spring tides.

2 **Local knowledge,** or the use of a local pilot, is required as the entrance is bordered by sandbanks which are liable to change, sometimes even between consecutive tides.

Tidal streams. During most of the period when it is practicable to enter the harbour, the tidal stream sets NW across the entrance channel at rates up to 4 kn. Inside the harbour the tidal stream runs strongly near HW on both rising and falling streams.

3 **Directions.** Entry is possible from 2 hours before to 2 hours after HW, but the best time of approach is about ½ hour before HW. The harbour is entered between the W jetty, on the extremity of which stands a light beacon (white metal post red top, 3 m in height) and a mole on the E side of the channel, giving a wide berth to the W jetty from which a sandbank extends. The mole covers at most high waters and is marked at its head by a light beacon (white mast green top).

4 From S the alignment (000°) of Carteret W jettyhead light with a water tower, 1 mile N (chart 2669), leads in the approach.

From W the conspicuous building (49°22′·1N 1°46′·3W) (11.277) should be used as a headmark until Carteret W jettyhead light is identified.

Anchorage: off the entrance to the port, in good weather and during offshore winds, in depths of 3 m, sand and rock.

5 **Berths:** quay at inner end of W jetty with berths drying 7 to 9 m. Further drying berths are available at Le Petit-port situated 4 cables upstream from the quay; these berths are only accessible at HW.

Facilities: fuel; fresh water; provisions in limited quantities.

Inshore lifeboat, see 11.275.

JERSEY NORTH COAST TO SARK EAST COAST

General information

Charts 1136, 3655, 2669
Route
11.298

1 From La Coupe Point (49°14′N 2°01′W), the NE extremity of Jersey, the route leads WNW through Le Ruau (11.299) to N of Sorel Point (49°16′N 2°09′W), thence N to E of Sark (49°26′N 2°22′W), a total distance of about 15 miles.

Topography
11.299

1 **Jersey — north coast.** The N coast of Jersey between La Coupe Point (49°14′N 2°01′W) and Grosnez Point, 9 miles W, consists of brown rocky cliffs indented with small bays backed by a high plateau. Tour de Rozel, a conical white-washed rock, is detached from the shore at HW and stands 1¼ miles WNW of La Coupe Point. Belle Hougue Point (49°15′N 2°06′W), the highest headland on the N coast, is fringed by rocks which extend up to 2½ cables offshore.

2 Les Dirouilles (49°18′N 2°02′W) (11.307), a group of rocks, are separated from the coast of Jersey by Le Ruau. Les Écrehou (11.307), consisting of reefs on which lie many rocks and islets, are situated close E of Les Dirouilles.

3 Pierres de Lecq or Paternosters (49°17′N 2°12′W), an extensive group of rocks, lies about 2½ miles NE of Grosnez Point. These rocks are separated from the N coast of Jersey by Plemont Deep (11.308). Great Rock and Sharp Rock, two above-water rocks, are situated near the centre of the bank. La Grune de Lecq, a detached drying rock, is separated from Great Rock by a channel 4 cables wide; patches with a least depth of 5·8 m extend 7½ cables NE from La Grune de Lecq.

Sark — east coast, see 11.194.

Depths
11.300

1 In the areas indicated on the chart along the N coast, the hydrographic data are incomplete. Uncharted shoals and rocks may exist and vessels should navigate with caution in the vicinity.

Tidal streams
11.301

1 Along the N coast of Jersey the tidal streams attain a spring rate of about 4 kn in both directions, beginning as follows:

Interval from HW Saint Helier	Direction
−0530	E
+0015	W

Slack water occurs nearly at HW and LW, for details see information on the chart and *Admiralty Tidal Stream Atlas for the Channel Islands and adjacent coasts of France.*

Directions
(continued from 11.284)

Principal marks
11.302

1 **Landmarks,** in addition to those on the E coast of Jersey given at 11.277:
    Building (grey stone with turret surmounted by green conical roof) (49°14′·4N 2°02′·7W) near the extremity of Nez du Guet.
    Hotel (49°14′·3N 2°04′·9W).
    House (49°15′N 2°06′W) on the W side of Bouley Bay.
    Television Mast (red obstruction lights) (49°15′·1N 2°07′·9W).
    Holiday Village (49°15′·4N 2°13′·5W) on Plemont Point.

2 **Major lights:**
    Sorel Point Light (black and white chequered round concrete tower, 3 m in height) (49°16′N 2°09′W) standing on Sorel Point.
    Grosnez Point Light (49°16′N 2°15′W) (11.196).
    Point Robert Light (49°26′N 2°21′W) (11.196).
    Cap de Carteret Light (49°22′N 1°48′W) (11.277).

La Coupe Point to Sorel Point
11.303

1 From a position E of La Coupe Point (49°14′N 2°01′W) (11.277) the route leads generally WNW through Le Ruau (11.299), keeping about 1 mile off the coast, passing (with positions given from Belle Hougue Point (49°15′N 2°06′W)):
    NNE of Brayes Rocks (3¼ miles ESE) (11.293); thence:
2   NNE of Tour de Rozel (2 miles ESE) (11.299); thence:
    NNE of a dangerous wreck (position approximate) (charted 1¼ miles E).

Leading marks:
    Front mark. La Coupe Point (3¼ miles ESE) (11.277).
3   Rear mark. Saint Catherine Breakwater Light, 9 cables farther SE, (11.284).
The alignment (138°), astern, of these marks then leads in the channel passing:
    Midway between Les Sambues (3½ cables E), the NE-most dangers off Belle Hougue Point, and La Hau (2½ miles NE) a detached rock which borders the SW edge of Les Dirouilles (11.307); thence:
4   NE of Shamrock Bank (1¼ miles WNW) which is covered by the red sector (230°–269°) of Sorel Point Light; thence:
    NE of Sorel Point (2½ miles W) on which stands a light (11.302); thence:
5   NE of a dangerous wreck (position approximate) (charted 3½ miles NW), the E-most danger off

Pierres de Lecq (11.299) which are covered by the red sector (188°–241°) of Grosnez Point Light and the red sector (112°–173°) of Sorel Point Light; thence:

To a position on the line of bearing 225° of Grosnez Point (49°16′N 2°15′W).

11.304

1 **Clearing bearings:**

The line of bearing 290° of Belle Hougue Point, open N of the N extremity of Tour de Rozel, 2 miles ESE (11.299), clears 2 cables NNE of Brayes Rocks.

The line of bearing 171° of Rozel Mill (49°13′·8N 2°03′·0W), just open W of Tour de Rozel, 9 cables N, clears W of all dangers on the W side of Les Dirouilles.

2 The alignment (078°) of Grande Rousse (49°17′·6N 1°58′·9W) (11.307) with La Vielle a rock situated in the N part of Les Écrehou, 2 miles ENE, clears 1 cable S of La Hau.

The alignment (124°) of the N part of Tour de Rozel (49°14′·7N 2°03′·0W) with La Coupe Turret, 1¼ miles SE, clears NE of Les Sambues and all other rocks NE of Belle Hougue Point and NE of Pierres de Lecq.

Useful mark:

Saint Catherine Light (49°13′N 2°01′W) (11.284).

11.305

1 **At night.** From a position in the vicinity of La Coupe Point the route leads generally WNW, keeping not less than 1 mile clear of the coast, to the line of bearing 269° of Sorel Point Light, changing from white to red. The line of bearing 138° of Saint Catherine Breakwater Light, astern, then leads in the channel until Grosnez Point Light bears 225°.

Sorel Point to Point Robert

11.306

1 From a position NE of Pierres de Lecq (49°17′N 2°12′W) (11.299), on the line of bearing 225° of Grosnez Point Light (49°16′N 2°15′W) (11.196), the line of bearing 187°, astern, of Sorel Point Light (49°16′N 2°09′W), or at night in its white sector (173°–230°) on the same bearing, leads in the channel to a position E of Sark (49°26′N 2°22′W) (11.24), distant about 8½ miles.

(Directions for Race of Alderney continue at 11.327 and for the passage to W of Casquets at 11.135)

Side channels

Charts 1136, 3655

Passe de l'Étoc

11.307

1 **General information.** Les Dirouilles, a group of rocks, lie between 3 and 5 miles N of La Coupe Point (49°14′N 2°01′W) and are separated from the coast of Jersey by Le Ruau (11.299). The group is composed of broken detached reefs with Les Burons (49°18′N 2°02′W), two conical rocks close together, situated near the centre; Frouquie, a smaller rock, lies 3 cables WSW. Between the E edge of Les Dirouilles and Les Écrehou, 1 mile E, lie a number of drying and below-water rocks of which the principal ones are (with positions given from Les Burons): La Platte and Frouquie (8 cables E) near the E end of Les Dirouilles; Grune de South West (1¼ miles SE); L'Étoc (1½ miles E);

Le Fierco (1¾ miles ENE); Grune de North West (1¾ miles NE).

2 Les Écrehou, consisting of reefs on which lie many rocks and islets, are situated close E of Les Dirouilles and form part of Channel Islands. Grande Rousse (49°17′·6N 1°58′·9W) stands on a reef situated near the W extremity of the bank. Le Ruquet and East Ruquet, both of which dry, lie at the NW edge of Les Écrehou. Maitre Île (49°17′·1N 1°55′·6W) surmounted by a beacon (pole, black barrel with white band topmark with a large pile of stones at its base) and Marmotier, a craggy islet capped by a cluster of buildings, 3½ cables N, together with other rocks and islets occupy the central part of the bank.

3 **Channels.** Passe de l'Étoc leads between Les Dirouilles and Les Écrehou; the channel E of L'Étoc (49°18′·1N 1°59′·6W) and Le Fierco, and W of Grande Rousse, is however the one generally used by fishermen wishing to pass between the two groups.

Local knowledge is required as the tidal streams set across these two channels for a considerable period.

Plemont Deep

11.308

1 **General information.** Plemont Deep separates Pierres de Lecq (49°17′N 2°12′W) (11.299), an extensive group of rocks lying about 2½ miles NE of Grosnez Point, from the N coast of Jersey. Grune de Becquet, a detached rocky patch situated 9 cables E of Plemont Point (49°15′·7N 2°13′·5W), is the N-most danger on the S side of the deep.

2 **Clearing marks:**

The alignment (111°) of Belle Hougue Point (49°15′N 2°06′W) (11.299), with Tour de Rozel (11.299), 2 miles ESE, clears SSW of Flat Rock and South West Grune, the S-most dangers on Pierres de Lecq, and SSW of La Grune de Lecq (11.299).

Anchorages and harbours

Chart 3655

South of Les Écrehou

11.309

1 **Tidal streams** in the vicinity of the anchorages in Les Écrehou (49°17′N 1°56′W) (11.307) attain a spring rate of about 3¾ kn in both directions, beginning as follows:

Interval from HW Saint Helier	Direction
–0225	NNW
+0415	S

For details of the tidal streams around Les Écrehou, see information on the chart.

11.310

1 **Anchorage:** 1¼ miles SSE of Maitre Île (49°17′·1N 1°55′·6W) (11.307) on the alignment (327°) of the E edge of Marmotier with Tas de Pois, a conical rock 5 cables NW, in depths of 14 m, gravel, as shown on the chart.

Mariners in small craft can anchor midway between Maitre Île and Petite Noire, as shown on the chart, with the houses on Marmotier bearing 337°.

2 **Caution.** Écrevière Bank (11.290), which extends 2 miles SSE from the SE edge of Les Écrehou, lies to the NE and Petite Noire and associated dangers lie to the NW of this anchorage.

Local knowledge is required as the tidal streams run strongly and their direction is erratic.

Chart 1136
Rozel Bay
11.311

1   **Description.** Rozel Bay is entered between Le Couperon (49°14′·1N 2°02′·1W) and Nez du Guet (11.302), 4 cables NW. Hiaux, a group of rocks which dry, extend 1½ cables from the E side of Nez du Guet.

    Temporary anchorage. The bay is sheltered from winds from SSE through S to W and affords temporary anchorage in depths of about 7 m.

2   **Rozel Harbour**, in the W part of the bay, is formed by a stone pier the head of which is painted white. The entrance to the harbour, which dries, is obstructed by a large flat rock which dries about 6 m, marked on its N edge by a beacon (red and white). North-west winds cause a scend in the harbour.

3   Approach on the line of bearing 245° of the centre of the white sector (244°–246°) of Rozel Direction Light (49°14′·2N 2°02′·8W) passing SE of Hiaux and through the entrance between the pierhead and the beacon. The approach may be marked by seasonal buoys (lateral).

    Berths: small drying jetty on the W side of the harbour.

Rozel Direction Light bearing 245° (11.311)

(Original dated 1998)

(Photograph - Capt. F. A. Lawrence, MRIN, Navitron Limited)

Bouley Bay
11.312

1   **General information.** Bouley Bay, entered between Tour de Rozel (49°14′·6N 2°03′·1W) (11.299) and Belle Hougue Point (11.299), 1¾ miles WNW, affords good shelter from offshore winds.

    L'Étaquerel, a rocky point on which stands an old fort, is situated 6½ cables SW of Tour de Rozel; Oyster Rocks extend 2 cables NE from the point.

2   **Anchorage,** as shown on the chart, can be obtained 5 cables NW of Les Troupeurs, a small rocky shoal lying 5½ cables WNW of Tour de Rozel, in depths of 15 m, gravel. Anchorage can also be obtained closer inshore, to the NE of the pier as shown on the chart, in depths of 7 to 9 m.

    Mariners should be prepared to weigh anchor if the wind begins to shift to the NW.

3   **Landing places:** pier 1 mile W of Tour de Rozel; sandy beach 1½ cables S of the pier. The shores of the bay elsewhere are rocky.

    Approaching from E the line of bearing 252° of the pier (white-washed head) (49°14′·5N 2°04′·8W) on the W side of the bay passes between Demie de la Tour, a drying rock which lies ¾ cable NNE of Tour de Rozel and onto which

the tidal streams set strongly, and Les Troupeurs. The approach to the pier may be marked by seasonal buoys (lateral).

Bonne Nuit Bay
11.313

1   **Description.** Between Belle Hougue Point (49°15′N 2°06′W) (11.299) and Fremont Point, a high bluff 8 cables W, the coast forms Giffard Bay and Bonne Nuit Bay separated by La Crête Point, on which stands an old fort. Demie Rock lies 2½ cables N of Fremont Point and is marked by a buoy (starboard hand) close N.

2   **Leading lights.** The alignment (223°) of the following lights leads from NE into Bonne Nuit Bay passing NW of Cheval Rock, a large black rock which dries with several drying rocks close N, situated in Bonne Nuit Bay 2 cables NW of the front light. Cheval rock is marked by a thin pole.

        Front light (white column) (49°15′·1N 2°07′·1W) situated on Bonne Nuit Bay Pierhead.

        Rear light (red daymark) (1 cable SW of the front light).

Bonne Nuit Bay Leading Lights in line 223° (11.313)

(Original dated 1998)

(Photograph - Capt. F. A. Lawrence, MRIN, Navitron Limited)

    The approach may be marked by seasonal buoys (lateral).

3   **Anchorages,** well sheltered from offshore winds, can be obtained 2½ cables N and 3 cables NW of La Crête Point in depths of 10 to 12 m, sand and gravel, as shown on the chart.

    Mariners in small craft can anchor between Fremont Point and Cheval Rock clear of the foul ground extending ½ cable from the E side of the point.

    Berth: short stone pier, with a depth of 6 m at HW at its head, on the W side of Bonne Nuit Bay.

Saint John's Bay
11.314

1   **General information.** Saint John's Bay is entered between Fremont Point (49°15′·3N 2°07′·3W) (11.313) and Ronez Point, 1¼ miles WNW; its shores are so fringed with rocks as to be almost inaccessible.

    Local knowledge is required.

    Clearing marks:

2   The alignment (269°) of Ronez Point with Plemont Point, 3 miles W, clears close S of Shamrock Bank (11.303), which lies 6 cables NNW of Fremont Point.

Berth. On the E side of Ronez Point there is a small wooden jetty which was used by mariners in coasting vessels to load granite from nearby quarries.

East of Grune de Douet
11.315

1 **Description.** Between Sorel Point (49°16′N 2°10′W), from where a light (11.302) is exhibited, and Plemont Point, 2½ miles W (11.302), the coast recedes to form a wide bay. The SE side of this bay is precipitous and bordered by drying and below-water rocks which extend up to 3 cables offshore; Plemont Point is bordered by drying ledges and foul ground.

2 The Demies, drying rocks, lie 2 cables N of the E entrance to Grève de Lecq, a small cove at the head of the bay, and are connected with the shore by a chain of below-water rocks.

3 **Anchorage,** as shown on the chart, can be obtained about 4 cables E of Grune de Douet (49°15′·4N 2°12′·3W), a detached patch, in depths of about 15 m; Grune de

Becquet (11.308), another detached patch, lies 3½ cables N.

Submarine cables are landed close to the pier in Grève de Lecq; their positions can best be seen from the chart.

Grève au Lancon
11.316

1 **General information.** Grève au Lancon (49°16′N 2°14′W), a small sandy bay, is entered between Plemont Point and Grosnez Point (11.196), 8 cables W.

Mariners in small coasting vessels rounding Grosnez Point bound S can, with advantage, anchor in this bay until the S-going tidal stream begins about 3 hours after HW at Saint Helier. Mariners bound E along the N coast of Jersey, can anchor until about LW when it will be possible to carry a fair tide as far as La Coupe Point.

2 **Anchorage** can be obtained off the middle of the bay on the line of bearing 249° of Grosnez Bluff; the holding ground is not good.

Cautions. A rock which dries 4·6 m lies 1 cable offshore on the W side of the bay. The bay contains many disused submarine cables as indicated on the chart.

SARK TO ALDERNEY AND ADJACENT COAST OF FRANCE

General information

Charts 60, 3653, 2669
Route
11.317

1 From E of Sark (49°26′N 2°22′W) the passage to Cap de la Hague leads generally N, about 18 miles, passing through the Race of Alderney.

Description
11.318

1 **Race of Alderney** or Raz Blanchard is the strait between Alderney and the coast of France in the vicinity of Cap de la Hague (49°44′N 1°56′W); it derives its name from the great rates attained by the tidal streams through it. The fairway of Race of Alderney is about 4 miles wide and lies between Race Rock (49°42′N 2°08′W) (11.329) and a rocky bank with a least depth of 15·6 m over it which lies about 3 miles WSW of Cap de la Hague.

Topography
11.319

1 **Alderney south-east side.** The coast between the SW extremity of Alderney and L'Étac de la Quoiré (49°42′·4N 2°11′·5W), a conical rock joined to the coast at LW by a bank of stones, nearly 1¾ miles E, consists of high cliffs. A beacon (white stone) is situated about halfway up the cliffs 1½ cables N of the rock. The remains of a jetty and stonework buildings are situated 1½ cables WNW of the rock.

2 Aiguillons, Coupé and Orbouée are three above-water rocks standing on a bank which lies between 5 and 9 cables SW of Old Telegraph Tower (49°42′·3N 2°13′·3W) (11.327).

3 The Noires Putes (49°41′·5N 2°13′·6W), the outermost group of rocks off the S coast of Alderney, consist of four rocks; the outer and W rock, 14 m high, is flat-topped. Coque Lihou, a group of three rocks the highest and largest of which is 35 m high, is situated 2½ cables offshore

6 cables ENE of The Noires Putes. Joyeux Rocks, a chain of rocks, extends 4 cables W from Coque Lihou.

4 La Roque Pendante, a remarkable overhanging rock which is visible from a considerable distance on a NE or SW bearing, stands about halfway up a bluff situated 7½ cables NE of L'Étac de la Quoiré. Rousset a pointed rock lies close to the shore below La Roque Pendante; Raz Island (11.338) lies 4 cables farther NE.

5 Houmet Herbé (49°43′·6N 2°09′·5W) lying 2 cables S of Quénard Point, the NE point of Alderney, is a rocky islet on which stands a fort and which is connected to the shore by drying rocks. Brinchetais Ledge, a group of rocks which dry, stands near the middle of a rocky bank which extends 4 cables SE from Houmet Herbé.

11.320

1 **French coast.** Between Cap de Carteret (49°22′N 1°48′W) (11.277) and Cap de Flamanville which terminates in a steep cliff, 9½ miles NNW, the coast is composed of dunes and sandy beaches separated by rocky points of which Pointe du Rozel, situated 6 miles NNW of Cap de Carteret, is prominent.

2 Between Cap de Flamanville (49°31′N 1°53′W) and Nez de Jobourg, which terminates in a steep cliff 9½ miles NNW, the coast is indented by Anse de Vauville (11.340). Thence between Nez de Jobourg and Cap de la Hague, 3 miles N, the coast is rocky and backed by high land. A coastal bank on which lie many above-water and drying rocks, extends in places 1½ miles offshore.

Incomplete surveys
11.321

1 The survey of the SE coast of Alderney is incomplete and uncharted shoals may exist.

Traffic regulations
11.322

1 **IMO recommendation.** For an IMO recommendation regarding Race of Alderney, see 11.8.

Regulations concerning vessels carrying dangerous and polluting goods, see 1.68 to 1.76.

Hazards
11.323

1 **Firing danger area.** For details of a firing danger area on the French coast NW of Cap de Flamanville, see 11.340.

High speed craft operate in the area covered by this section, see 1.7.

Rescue
11.324

1 **All-weather lifeboat.** Cap de la Hague all-weather lifeboat is stationed at Goury (49°43′N 1°57′W) (11.345), for details see 1.117.

Signal stations, see 11.275 and 12.12, 12.74.

VHF Direction-finding stations, for emergency use only, see 11.275 and 12.12, 12.74.

Natural conditions
11.325

1 **Local magnetic anomalies.** Abnormal magnetic variation may be experienced within an area bounded by lines joining Cap de Carteret (49°22′N 1°48′W), the island of Sark, 21 miles W, and Cap de Flamanville (49°31′N 1°53′W).

In the vicinity of Diélette (49°33′N 1°52′W) the normal magnetic variation can be exceeded by 2° and in the approach to Cap de la Hague by up to 1°.

11.326

1 **Tidal streams.** For details of the tidal streams in the Race of Alderney, see information on the chart and *Admiralty Tidal Stream Atlas for the Channel Islands and adjacent coasts of France.*

The times at which the streams begin to run in different parts of the Race do not appear to vary appreciably, but the rates are subject to considerable variation. The strongest streams are found on the E side of the Race; for example, 1 mile W of La Foraine Light Buoy (49°43′N 1°59′W) the spring rate of the N-going stream is 9¾ kn and that of the S-going stream, 6¾ kn. See also 11.11.

2 **Eddies** of considerable extent are found off the coasts of Alderney. Off the SE coast the E-going stream runs for about 9 hours at springs and 8 hours at neaps, the W-going stream runs for about 3 hours only.

3 In the area between the coast and about a line joining Orbouée, 5 cables SW of the SW extremity of Alderney, a position about 1 mile SE of The Noires Putes (49°42′N 2°14′W) and a position about 5 cables NE of Brinchetais Ledge (49°43′N 2°09′W), the E-going stream begins −0430 HW Saint Helier, spring rate about 3 kn, and the W-going stream begins +0255 HW Saint Helier, spring rate about 2½ kn.

4 For details of eddies in the N part of The Swinge and along the N coast of Alderney, see 11.148.

Overfalls. In heavy weather when the wind is blowing against the stream the sea breaks in all parts of Race of Alderney and there are heavy overfalls on the submerged rocks and banks. It is recommended at such times that mariners anchor in Alderney Harbour (11.169) and await favourable conditions.

Directions
(continued from 11.83, 11.122, 11.199 and 11.306)

Principal marks
11.327

1 **Landmarks — Alderney,** in addition to those given at 11.151.

Old Telegraph Tower (49°42′·3N 2°13′·3W) at the SW end of the island.

Landmarks — French coast:

Two Towers (Flamanville Nuclear Power Station) (49°32′·2N 1°52′·9W) situated about 1 mile N of Cap de Flamanville.

2 Chimney and buildings of the Atomic Energy Reprocessing Centre (49°40′·8N 1°52′·9W) (12.9).

Cap de la Hague Lighthouse (49°43′N 1°57′W) (12.9).

Major lights:

Point Robert Light (49°26′N 2°21′W) (11.196).

3 Platte Fougère Light (49°31′N 2°29′W) (11.74).

Casquets Light (49°43′N 2°23′W) (11.151).

Alderney Light (49°44′N 2°10′W) (11.151).

Cap de Carteret Light (49°22′N 1°48′W) (11.277).

Cap de la Hague Light (49°43′N 1°57′W) (12.9).

Other aids to navigation
11.328

1 **Racons:**

Platte Fougère Light (49°31′N 2°29′W).

Casquets Light (49°43′N 2°23′W).

For details see *Admiralty List of Radio Signals Volume 2.*

Big and Little Russel or east of Sark to Race of Alderney
11.329

1 From a position NE of Big or Little Russel, or from E of Sark, the route leads generally NE or N passing (with positions given from Quénard Point (49°44′N 2°10′W)):

2 Clear or E of Banc de la Schôle (49°35′N 2°13′W) with its least charted depth (2·7 m) on its W edge. Shoaler depths have been reported (1999). The bank extends about 3¾ miles S from a position 5½ miles S of the SW point of Alderney and lies nearly in the direct line and midway between Big Russel and Race of Alderney. The bank is steep-to on its S and W sides but the depths over its shallower parts are continually altering probably under the influence of weather and tidal streams. In heavy weather the sea breaks dangerously on all parts of the shoal. Thence:

3 SE of Alderney South Banks (3 miles SSW) (11.331); and:

Clear or E of Milieu (4¾ miles S). When the tidal stream is running strongly the position of this rock is marked by overfalls or breakers and there is at all times a ripple over it. Thence:

4 Between Race Rock (1¾ miles SE) and a rocky bank with a least depth of 15·8 m over it (4 miles ESE). This bank causes a strong overfall and it should be avoided as the sea occasionally breaks on it. Thence:

5 Between Blanchard Rock (7½ cables E) (11.331) and La Foraine (7½ miles E), the W-most of several rocks extending about 7 cables WSW from Gros du Raz (12.9). La Foraine Light Beacon (W cardinal) stands ¾ mile WSW of Gros du Raz. Thence:

As required into the English Channel.

11.330

1 **At night approaching from south-west** the line of bearing 064° of Cap de la Hague Light (49°43′N 1°57′W) (12.9) leads in the channel passing (with positions given from Quénard Point (49°44′N 2°10′W)):

NNW of Banc de la Schôle (49°35′N 2°13′W) (11.329); thence:

SSW of Alderney South Banks (3 miles SSW) (11.331); and:

NNW of Milieu (4¾ miles S) (11.329).

2   When Alderney Light (2 cables W) (11.151) bears 320° the track then leads NNE through Race of Alderney into the English Channel.

From south-west passing along the south-east coast of Alderney
11.331

1   **Leading marks:**
Front mark. Raz Island Fort (49°43′N 2°10′W) (11.338).
Rear mark. Grande Folie (4 cables NNE of the front mark), a prominent rocky outcrop on the hillside overlooking Baie du Grounard.

2   Approaching from SW from a position N of Banc de la Schôle (49°35′N 2°13′W) (11.329) the alignment (022°) of these marks leads in the approach passing (with positions given from Quénard Point (49°44′N 2°10′W)):

3   Close ESE of Alderney South Banks consisting of several small sandbanks, the shallowest of which (11 m) (3 miles SSW) lies 1¼ miles ESE of The Noires Putes (11.319). There are heavy overfalls on these banks on both E-going and W-going tidal streams. Thence:
ESE of Bonit (2¼ miles SW); thence:

4   The alignment (245°), astern, of the largest Coque Lihou (2¾ miles SW) (11.319) with the highest of The Noires Putes (19 m) (3½ miles SW), noting that the largest Coque Lihou is 16 m higher than the highest of The Noires Putes, then leads along the SE coast of Alderney passing:

5   Between Inner Race Rock (1¼ miles SE) and an 8·5 m patch (9 cables SE). An obstruction (position approximate, reported 1980) is charted 5 cables NE of Inner Race Rock.
When Château à l'Étoc Point (7 cables WNW) (11.144) bears 285° and open N of Quénard Point the track then leads as required into the English Channel.

6   If bound for Alderney Harbour (11.169) the track leads N until Château à l'Étoc Point is just open N of Les Homeaux Florains Fort (1½ cables NW) bearing 275°, or alternatively, the line of bearing 240° of the inner Coque Lihou (2¾ miles SW) open S of L'Étac de la Quoiré (1¾ miles SW) (11.319), when the track then leads NW passing:

7   NE of Blanchard Rock (8 cables E) on which there are overfalls and upon which the sea breaks heavily when the wind is against the tidal stream; thence:
NE of Sauquet Rock (3 cables N); thence:
NE of The Ledge (5 cables N).

8   On the line of bearing 262° of Casquets Light (49°43′N 2°23′W) (11.151) the track then leads generally W to Alderney Harbour as directed at 11.174.
Clearing bearings:
The line of bearing 323° of Verte-Tête (49°44′·2N 2°17′·0W) (11.157) open W of outer Noire Pute, 3½ miles SE, clears SW of the shallowest parts of Alderney South Banks.

9   The line of bearing 269° of Coupé (49°41′·8N 2°14′·1W) (11.319) seen between the two Coque Lihou islets, 1 mile E, clears S of Bonit.
The alignment (357°) of the E side of L'Étac de la Quoiré (49°42′·4N 2°11′·4W) (11.319) with the white beacon, 1½ cables N, clears very close E of Bonit.

10   The line of bearing 240° of the inner Coque Lihou open S of L'Étac de la Quoiré clears SSE of the rocky bank on which Brinchetais Ledge (49°43′·4N 2°09′·2W) (11.319) stands.
Useful mark:
Essex Castle (seaward wall painted white) (49°43′·1N 2°10′·5W).

From north
11.332

1   Approaching from N through Race of Alderney and bound for Guernsey, proceed through the fairway (11.318) and adjust track for either Big Russel (11.115) or Little Russel (11.67). After passing through the Race, due allowance should be made for the tidal streams which will then be running mainly across the track; care should be taken to avoid Milieu and Banc de la Schôle (11.329).

(Directions continue at 12.14)

Side channels

Charts 3653, 2669
Déroute de la Terre or Passage de la Déroute to Cap de la Hague
11.333

1   **General information.** For general information of Déroute de la Terre and Passage de la Déroute, see 11.288.
Topography, see 11.320.

Directions
11.334

1   **Déroute de la Terre to Cap de la Hague.** From a position WNW of Cap de Carteret (49°22′N 1°48′W), at the N entrance to Déroute de la Terre (11.289), the route leads generally N passing (with positions given from Cap de la Hague (49°44′N 1°56′W)):
W of Basse Bihard (49°26′N 1°53′W), distant about 1 mile, the outermost danger W of Banc de Surtainville; thence:

2   W of Cap de Flamanville (49°31′N 1°53′W) (11.320). A light buoy (W cardinal) moored about 1½ miles NNW of the cape marks the W limit of shoal water off Flamanville Nuclear Power Station. Thence:
W of Basses Saint-Gilles (4¼ miles SSW), the outermost shoal on Les Huquets de Jobourg (11.341), passing clear of a dangerous wreck (position approximate) (charted 5½ miles SSW); thence:

3   W of Basse du Rhin and Basses de la Dossière (2½ miles SSW), two shoals close together, the outermost dangers off Nez de Voidries (11.344), passing clear of a dangerous wreck (position doubtful) (charted 3 miles SW) and the 15·6 m bank (3½ miles WSW); thence:

4   W of the dangers which border Cap de la Hague, of which La Foraine (1¼ miles WSW) (11.329) is the outermost. Cap de la Hague can be rounded more closely than if passing through the main fairway (11.318) of the Race. Thence:
Clear of a wreck (position doubtful) (1½ miles WNW).

5   **Clearing bearing:**
The line of bearing 152° of Pointe du Rozel (49°28′N 1°51′W) well open WSW of Cap de Flamanville, 3½ miles NNW, clears WSW of Basses Saint-Gilles.

6   **At night.** From a position WNW of Cap de Carteret Light (49°22′N 1°48′W) (11.277) the line of bearing 355°

of Cap de la Hague Light leads in the channel passing W of Cap de Flamanville. With the green sector of Port de Diélette Light (49°33′N 1°52′W) (11.343) bearing 125°, astern, the track then leads 305° to SW of Basses Saint-Gilles, then generally N, passing W of Cap de la Hague Light, distant 4 miles.

11.335

1   **Passage de la Déroute to Cap de la Hague.** From a position 5½ miles W of Cap de Carteret (49°22′N 1°48′W) (11.277), and W of Plateau des Trois Grunes (11.290) at the N entrance to Passage de la Déroute, the route leads generally N to a position about 4 miles W of Cap de la Hague Light (49°43′N 1°57′W) (12.9).

Anchorages — Alderney south-east side

Chart 60
Fossée Malières
11.336

1   **General information.** An indifferent anchorage can be found off the SW part of Alderney in Fossée Malières (49°42′N 2°14′W), entered between Les Étacs (11.161) and Orbouée (11.319), about 2½ cables S of the former.
       Local knowledge is required.

La Tchue
11.337

1   **General information.** La Tchue, a rocky bay, lies close W of Rousset (49°42′·8N 2°10′·6W) (11.319). There are anchorages, as shown on the chart, between 1½ and 2½ cables off La Tchue in depths of 14 to 18 m, sheltered from winds between W and ENE, and less exposed to the tidal streams than the anchorages off Longy Bay (11.338).

Charts 2845, 60
Longy Bay
11.338

1   **General information.** Longy Bay, which dries and is sandy only at its head, is entered between Raz Island (49°43′·1N 2°10′·1W), lying across the entrance to the bay, and Queslingue, a pointed rock 2 cables SW; a rock which dries 0·6 m lies midway between the entrance points. The island is connected to the shore by drying rocks and a causeway which is covered at HW; a fort stands on the island. The bay affords shelter from offshore winds.

2   **Local knowledge** is required as the E-going stream runs across the entrance to the bay at a great rate.
       Anchorage, as shown on the chart, can be obtained off Longy Bay 2¼ cables S of Raz Island in depths of 21 m, gravel, sheltered from N and NW winds.

3   Mariners in small craft can obtain anchorage closer inshore in depths of 17 m on the alignment (020°) of the E side of Raz Island Fort with Grande Folie, 4 cables NNE (11.331), on the line of bearing 297° of Queslingue. There is also anchorage in Longy Bay 1¼ cables W of Raz Island in depths of less than 5 m.

Chart 60
Coque Lihou
11.339

1   **Anchorage.** A sandbank with a least depth of 2·7 m over it extends nearly 3 cables ENE of the highest Coque Lihou (49°41′·8N 2°12′·6W) (11.319). A convenient anchorage, for mariners in small craft and fishing vessels, can be obtained on this sandbank.

Anchorages and minor harbours —French coast

Chart 3653
Anse de Vauville
11.340

1   **General information.** Anse de Vauville is entered between Cap de Flamanville (49°31′N 1°53′W) and Nez de Jobourg, 9½ miles NNW (11.320). The S part of the bay consists of a sandy beach backed by rounded hills covered with vegetation; the N part of the bay is rocky. Dunes de Biville are situated about midway along the stretch of sandy beach.

2   **Firing danger area.** The outer limits of Vauville firing danger area, Secteur de Biville, extend 4 miles N from a position 4½ miles NW of Cap de Flamanville. Practice takes place in this area all year round except between 15th June to 15th September, for details see 1.31.
       Restricted area. An area to which entry is prohibited extends about 4 cables offshore from Flamanville Nuclear Power Station (49°32′·2N 1°53′·0W).

11.341

1   **Anchorages.** Anse de Vauville affords shelter in offshore winds in depths of 8 to 15 m, sand and gravel, but the holding ground is not good.
       Caution. Roches de Biville lie about 5½ miles N of Cap de Flamanville and about 1½ miles off the sandy beach. Les Huquets de Jobourg, an extensive rocky bank of drying and submerged rocks which are covered by the red sector (145°–180°) of Diélette Light (11.343), lie with their centre about 1½ miles S of Nez de Jobourg; tidal streams set strongly across this bank. Les Huquets de Vauville, a small detached group of rocks, lie about 7 cables E.

2   **Recommended anchorage,** sheltered from E winds, can be obtained 6 cables NW of Port de Diélette (49°33′N 1°52′W) on the alignment (125½°) of Diélette Light and a white house 2½ cables SE. The bottom is sand and rock and the holding ground is not good.
       Prohibited anchorage. Anchoring, fishing and diving are prohibited within an area, shown on the chart, extending about 2 miles S of Nez de Jobourg.

11.342

1   **Harbour.** A basin protected by breakwaters lies close W of Flamanville Nuclear Power Station; the entrance to the basin faces NW.

Port de Diélette
11.343

1   **General information.** Port de Diélette (49°33′N 1°52′W), a small harbour which partially dries out, is situated in the S part of Anse de Vauville. It consists of Avant Port, Bassin de Commerce et de Pêche, and Bassin de Plaisance. The harbour affords shelter from E winds to small craft, and is protected by Jetée Ouest and a breakwater extending W from the NE part of the harbour. Plateau du Cannichon, a drying ledge, lies N of the latter. Bassin de Plaisance is protected by an inner jetty. The bottom is very hard and the holding ground is poor.

2   **Local knowledge,** or the use of a local pilot, is required.
       Tidal streams. During the NE-going stream offshore (11.11) the stream in the harbour runs SE towards the inner jetty, spring rate about 1½ kn, and an eddy runs W along the inner jetty towards the N part of Jetée Ouest.

3   **Approach.** The line of bearing 140° of Diélette Light (white tower, green top, 11 m in height) (49°33′·2N 1°51′·8W), or at night in its white sector (135°–145°), leads in the approach to the harbour entrance.

4   **Caution.** The in-going stream sets NE across the entrance towards Plateau du Cannichon.

4   **Berths.** Avant Port has a drying berth on the W side of a short jetty projecting S from the N breakwater, and there are berths on buoys and on the inner side of Jetée Ouest in the S part of the harbour. Berths on Jetée Ouest dry from 4 to 5 m and afford shelter from winds between N and SE; winds from between S and NW raise such a swell in the harbour that vessels cannot lie there.

5   Bassin de Commerce et de Pêche, lying to the E of the Avant Port is used by commercial vessels; three pontoons provide berths for fishing vessels, passenger vessels, and waiting berths for yachts. It is dredged to 2 m.

Baie d'Écalgrain
11.344

1   **General information.** Baie d'Écalgrain lies between Nez de Voidries (49°40'·5N 1°56'·8W), which terminates in a steep cliff, and Pointe du Houpret, 1¼ miles N, and can be used by mariners awaiting a favourable tidal stream through Race of Alderney.

2   **Tidal streams.** In Baie d'Écalgrain, where the rate of the tidal stream does not exceed 1 kn, a S-going eddy begins at about the time of local HW when the N-going stream in Race of Alderney is decreasing. Similarly a N-going eddy has been observed in this bay when the S-going stream in the race is running at its maximum rate. See also 11.11.

3   **Temporary anchorage** can be obtained in Baie d'Écalgrain during offshore winds in depths of 5 to 9 m, sand and gravel.

    Caution. Rocks extend nearly 1 mile WNW from Nez de Voidries.

Chart 3653
Goury
11.345

1   **General information.** Goury (49°43'N 1°57'W), a small harbour situated among rocks about 7 cables SSW of Cap de la Hague, is formed by a breakwater at the head of which is a white patch. Inside the breakwater small craft can lie aground on muddy sand which dries up to 4·5 m. The surf in the harbour can be very heavy.

    Local knowledge, or the use of a local pilot is essential.

    Temporary anchorage: close W of the lifeboat slip in depths of about 3 m.

2   **Leading lights.** The alignment (065¼°) of leading lights situated in the harbour leads towards the entrance:

        Front light (red square on white square daymark on pier) (49°42'·9N 1°56'·8W).

        Rear light (white pylon on masonry hut) (116 m from the front mark).

    By day, the hexagonal roof of the lifeboat house (11.324) at the root of the breakwater is a useful mark.

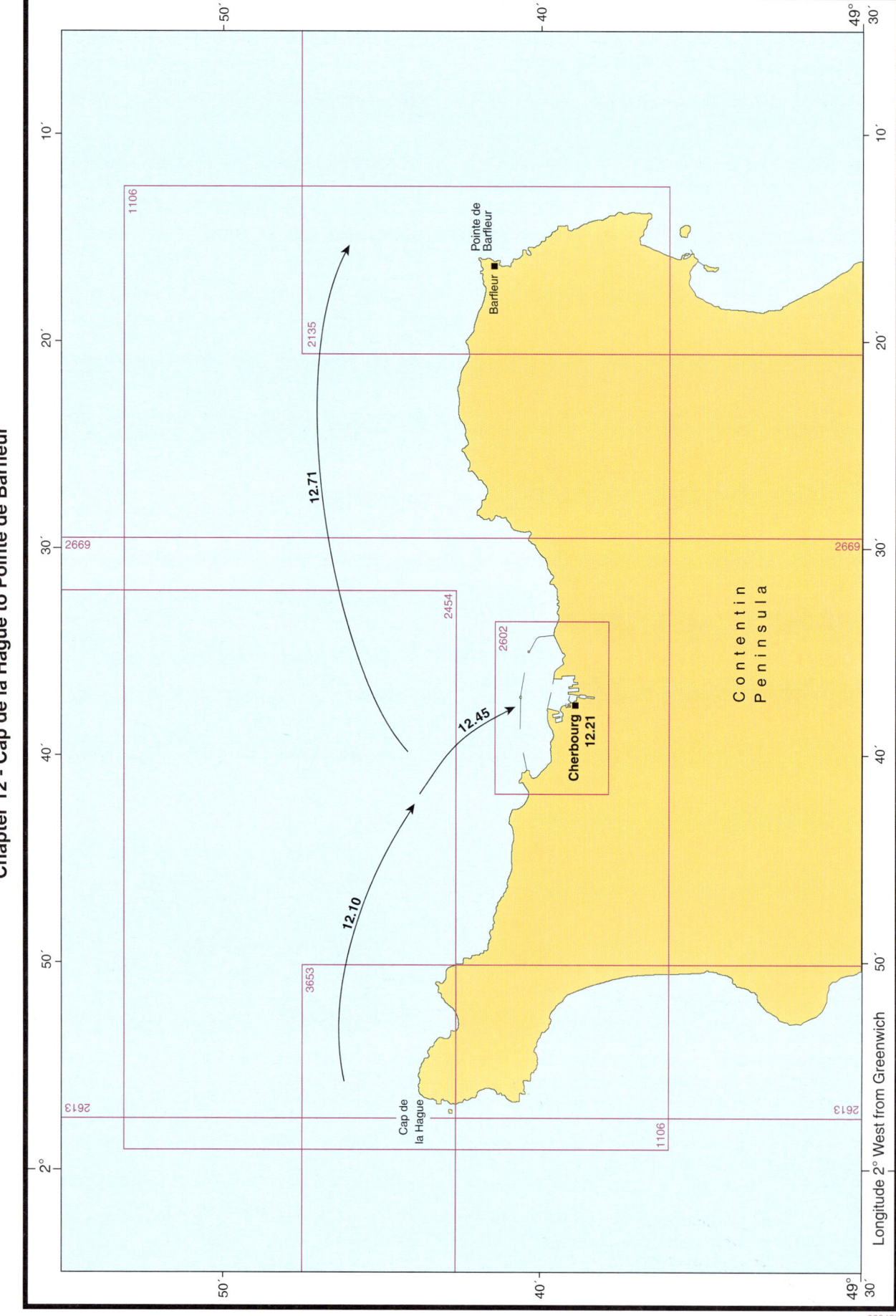

1106

2135

Pointe de
Barfleur

Barfleur

12.71

2669

2669

2454

2602

12.45

Cherbourg
12.21

Contentin
Peninsula

12.10

3653

Cap de
la Hague

2613

2613

1106

Longitude 2° West from Greenwich

030408

CHAPTER 12

NORTH COAST OF FRANCE — CAP DE LA HAGUE TO POINTE DE BARFLEUR

GENERAL INFORMATION

Chart 1106
Scope of the chapter
12.1

1   This chapter covers the N coast of France, on the N side of Cotentin Peninsula, from Cap de la Hague (49°44′N 1°56′W) to Pointe de Barfleur, 26 miles E.

Port. The port of Cherbourg (49°39′N 1°38′W) (12.21) is the only port of note covered by this chapter.

Topography
12.2

1   The N coast of Cotentin Peninsula (11.5) between Cap de La Hague and Pointe de Barfleur is low, backed by high land which rises to an elevation of about 180 m in the W, 170 m in the centre and to about 100 m in the E. On the summit of the high land, about 3½ miles SE of Cap de la Hague, stand the conspicuous buildings and tall chimney of the atomic energy reprocessing plant (12.9). Approaching from W, mariners will first sight the high land S of Cap de la Hague which terminates SW at Nez de Jobourg (11.320).

2   Cherbourg, an important naval and commercial port, lies approximately midway along this stretch of coast.

Dangerous rocks extend 1 mile from the coast between Cap de la Hague and Pointe Jardeheu, 3½ miles E, and up to 2½ miles from the coast between Cap Lévi (49°42′N 1°28′W) and Pointe de Barfleur.

Hazards
12.3

1   **Submarine exercise areas** have been established about 12 miles N 9 miles NNE and 16 miles NE of Cherbourg, as shown on the chart. Submarines exercise frequently, both surfaced and dived, in the areas indicated. A good lookout is to be kept for them when passing through these waters. See *Annual Notice to Mariners No 8*.

12.4

1   **Traffic schemes.** For details of an Inshore Traffic Zone N of Casquets, Off Casquets TSS and an IMO recommendation for Race of Alderney, see 11.8.

2   **Wrecks and obstructions.** Small unknown wrecks and obstructions, not detected by hydrographic surveys, may lie in the area covered by this chapter.

Temporary explosives dumping grounds
12.5

1   Temporary explosives dumping grounds (Zones de Dépôts d'Explosifs) for Cherbourg are situated 1¼ miles NNW of Fort Central on Digue Centrale (49°40′N 1°37′W), for heavy devices, and 4 cables S of the same fort, for light devices.

For details see 1.7 and Appendix V.

Marine farms
12.6

1   Marine farms are situated throughout the waters of this chapter and should be avoided. Farms in proximity to shipping routes are generally marked by buoys. Other farms are marked by beacons (X topmark) and some are fitted with radar reflectors. Lights, when fitted, show flashing yellow. See 1.29.

Tidal streams
12.7

1   Offshore tidal streams run with great strength, particulary off Cap de la Hague where they attain a rate of about 7 kn, and off Pointe de Barfleur where they attain a rate of about 5 kn, in each direction. Midway between these points they attain a rate of about 3 kn.

2   In general the streams off the N coast of Cotentin Peninsula are rectilinear, and with wind against the stream a heavy sea is raised.

For details see information on the chart and *Admiralty Tidal Stream Atlas of the Channel Islands and the adjacent coast of France* and *The English Channel.*

Regulations concerning vessels carrying dangerous and polluting goods
12.8

1   For regulations concerning vessels laden with dangerous and polluting goods navigating in the approaches to the N and W coasts of France, see 1.68 to 1.76.

Principal marks
12.9

1   **Landmarks:**

Chimney (red and white marked by obstruction lights) (49°41′N 1°53′W) and buildings of the atomic energy reprocessing plant on the summit of the high land S of Cap de la Hague. From W, the chimney is reported to be readily identified on the radar display before the surrounding land appears above the radar horizon.

2   Cap de la Hague Lighthouse (grey tower white top, 51 m in height) (49°43′N 1°57′W) standing on Gros du Raz, a rock situated 5 cables WSW of Cap de la Hague, a low point on which stands a blockhouse and signal station. Although a landmark in itself the lighthouse is not prominent against the background.

3   Pointe de Barfleur-Gatteville Lighthouse (grey tower black top, 75 m in height) (49°42′N 1°16′W) standing on an islet close off Pointe de Barfleur (12.77), to which it is joined by a mole. On first sighting the lighthouse appears as if rising from the sea. A signal station (grey tower and mast) stands close N of the light.

4   **Major lights:**

Cap de la Hague Light — as above.

Fort de l'Ouest Light (grey tower red top on fort, 9 m in height) (49°41′N 1°39′W) situated on the W end of Digue Centrale, Cherbourg.

Cap Lévi Light (grey square tower white top, 28 m in height) (49°42′N 1°28′W).

Pointe de Barfleur-Gatteville Light — as above.

CAP DE LA HAGUE TO CHERBOURG

General information

Chart 1106
Route
12.10

1   From a position N of Cap de la Hague Light (49°43′N 1°57′W) the route leads generally E, about 8 miles, to a position NW of Cherbourg CH1 Landfall Light Buoy (49°43′N 1°42′W).

Topography
12.11

1 The coast between Cap de la Hague (49°44′N 1°56′W) (12.9) and an unnamed point 2 miles ESE is bordered by drying rocks which extend up to 5 cables offshore. Pointe Jardeheu (49°43′N 1°51′W) can be identified by the prominent disused signal station which stands close within the point. Anse de Saint-Martin (12.19) is entered between the unnamed point and Pointe Jardeheu. Between Pointe Jardeheu and Omonville-la-Rogue (49°42′N 1°50′W) (12.20), 1 mile SE, rocks extend 5 cables offshore.

2 From a position about 2¾ miles ESE of Omonville-la-Rogue to the fort on Pointe de Querqueville, at the W end of Cherbourg harbour, the coast slopes gently to the sea. Pointe de Nacqueville (49°41′N 1°43′W), on which stands a beacon, lies midway between these positions. The point is fronted by drying rocks and on each side of the point there are sandy beaches; that on the W side is fronted by some drying rocks.

Rescue
12.12

1 **All-weather lifeboat**, see 11.324.
Signal stations are situated at:
La Hague (Sémaphore) (49°44′N 1°56′W).
Homet (Vigie) (49°39′N 1°38′W) (12.70), Cherbourg.
For details see 1.110.
VHF Direction-finding stations, for emergency use only, operate from:

2 Jobourg (49°41′N 1°55′W).
La Hague (49°44′N 1°56′W).
Homet (49°39′N 1°38′W).
For details see *Admiralty List of Radio Signals Volume 2.*

Tidal streams
12.13

1 Tidal streams in Anse de Saint-Martin (49°43′N 1°53′W) barely attain a rate of 1 kn and appear to have a constant E-going component.
Seaward of the bay a W-going eddy runs during the latter part of the E-going stream from 1 hour before to 1 hour after HW Cherbourg.

2 Tidal streams begin as follows:

Interval from HW Cherbourg	Direction
Off Basse Bréfort:	
−0330	ESE
+0100	WNW
Approximately 1½ miles NE of Pointe Jardeheu:	
−0215	ESE
+0120	WNW

3 The maximum E-going and W-going spring rates off Basse Bréfort (49°44′N 1°51′W) are 4 kn and 6 kn, and NE of Pointe Jardeheu, 3¾ kn and 5 kn, respectively.
An eddy runs W during the latter part of the offshore E-going stream, W of Pointe Jardeheu, from 1 hour before to 1 hour after HW Cherbourg.

4 Tidal streams off Le Mermistin (49°42′N 1°46′W) begin as follows:

Interval from HW Cherbourg	Direction
−0400	ESE
+0030	WNW

The maximum E-going and W-going spring rates are 2½ kn and 3¼ kn, respectively.

5 Nearer the shore the streams nearly always run more or less towards the coast.
Farther offshore they are more or less rectilinear, see information on the chart.
West-going eddies occur near the coast during the latter part of the E-going stream offshore, between 1 hour before and 1 hour after HW Cherbourg.
See also *Admiralty Tidal Stream Atlas of The English Channel.*

Directions
(continued from 11.154 and 11.332)

Principal marks
12.14

1 For details of landmarks and major lights, see 12.9.

Cap de la Hague to the approaches to Cherbourg
12.15

1 From a position N of Cap de la Hague Light (49°43′N 1°57′W) the route leads generally E passing (with positions given from Pointe Jardeheu (49°43′N 1°51′W)):

2 N of La Plate (3¼ miles WNW), marked by a lighted beacon tower (octagonal tower, N cardinal 19 m in height). La Grande Grune, La Petite Grune and La Ronde lying 9 and 4 cables WNW and close NE, respectively, of the beacon tower, and closer to the track, are the N-most dangers off Cap de la Hague (12.9); the two former dangers are covered by the red sector (115° through S to 272°) of La Plate Light. Fosse de la Hague, a deep with depths of up to 105 m, extends about 5 miles NE from a position 2 miles NW of Cap de la Hague; its S side is only 1 mile N of the outermost dangers in the vicinity of the cape. It is indicated by eddies on the surface. Depths of more than 80 m in this vicinity identify the deep. Thence:

3 N of Basse du Houffet (2 miles WNW) which is dangerous on account of the eddies and the high sea over it; it is covered by the red sector of La Plate Light; thence:
N of an unsurveyed wreck (1¾ miles NW) with a clearance depth of 11 m; thence:

4 N of Basse Bréfort (5 cables N), marked by a light buoy (N cardinal), the outermost of rocks and shoals which extend N from Pointe Jardeheu (12.11); thence:
N of Le Mermistin (3 miles ESE) a rocky bank; thence:

5 N of Raz de Bannes (4½ miles ESE), a chain of drying and below-water rocks the largest of which is marked by a beacon tower (N cardinal, 8 m in height) lying at the edge of a rocky coastal bank; dangerous rocks extend up to 5 cables WNW of this tower. Thece:
To a position NW of Cherbourg CH1 Landfall Light Buoy (safe water) (6 miles E).

12.16

1   **Clearing bearing.** Fort de l'Ouest (49°41′N 1°39′W) bearing more than 122°, and at night in the white sector (122°–355°) of the light, clears NE of all dangers E of Cap de la Hague.

From east
12.17

1   Mariners in larger vessels approaching from E should keep N of a line drawn 060° from Cherbourg CH1 Landfall Light Buoy (49°43′N 1°42′W) until E of the meridian of Cap Lévi (12.77).

Useful marks
12.18

1   **Lights:**
> Digue de Querqueville Light (white column green top, 7 m in height) (49°40′·3N 1°39′·7W).
> Fort de l'Est Light (white pylon green top, 9 m in height) (49°40′·3N 1°35′·9W).
> Fort d'Île Pelée Light (white and red pedestal on fort, 8 m in height) (49°40′·2N 1°35′·0W).
> *(Directions for Cherbourg continue at 12.45*
> *and for Pointe de Barfleur at 12.76)*

Anchorage

Anse de Saint-Martin
12.19

1   **General information.** Anse de Saint-Martin is entered between Pointe Jardeheu (49°43′N 1°51′W) (12.11) and an unnamed point, 1¾ miles W.

    Tidal streams, see 12.13.

    Directions. From N the line of bearing 187° of Pointe du Nez, a small low-lying point at the W end of the sandy beach at the head of the bay, leads between Basse du Fliart and La Parmentière and associated dangers, a rock awash in the middle of the entrance to the bay, which lie 9 cables N and 7 cables NNE, respectively, of Pointe du Nez.

2   **Anchorage** can be obtained in the bay in depths of 6 to 9 m, sand and mud, with good holding ground, but it is dangerous with winds from between NW and E.

    Caution. Extensive rocky ledges extend 5 cables from the E side of the bay terminating in Le Grun.

    Landing. Port Racine, on the W side of the bay, is formed by two jetties; it dries, and is only accessible to mariners in small craft.

Omonville-la-Rogue

General information
12.20

1   Omonville-la-Rogue (49°42′N 1°50′W) contains a small harbour, sheltered from W winds, and is useful for mariners in small craft awaiting suitable conditions for passage through Race of Alderney.

    Pilotage can be undertaken by local fishermen.

2   **Directions.** The alignment (255°) of the harbour light (white pylon red top) (49°42′·3N 1°50′·1W) with a church, 4 cables WSW, or at night in the white sector (252°–262°) of the light, leads into the harbour passing between L'Étonnard, marked by a beacon tower (starboard hand) at the end of a chain of drying and below-water rocks which extends 1 cable ESE from the head of the breakwater, and La Vallace, situated 2½ cables ENE and E, respectively, of

---

the harbour light. A buoy (special, X-topmark) is moored 6 cables E of the harbour light and S of the white sector.

3   Les Tataquets (49°42′·8N 1°49′·7W) with La Coque, 7 cables NW, are the outermost dangers fronting the coast between Pointe Jardeheu (12.11) and the harbour entrance, on the N side of the approach.

4   **Berth.** The harbour is protected from N by a breakwater which extends 1¼ cables ESE from the shore; a short spur projects S halfway along the breakwater. West of the spur, for a distance of 50 m, mariners can lie alongside the breakwater and take the ground which is sandy and dries 1 m. East of the spur the breakwater is bordered by rocks and cannot be used for berthing. There are several mooring buoys in the harbour.

CHERBOURG AND APPROACHES

General information

Charts 2602, 1106
Position
12.21

1   Cherbourg (49°39′N 1°38′W) lies on the N part of Cotentin Peninsula approximately midway between Cap de la Hague and Pointe de Barfleur.

Function
12.22

1   The port is an important naval, commercial and fishing port with a large deep-water anchorage and is accessible at all states of the tide.

Topography
12.23

1   The S part of Cherbourg is dominated by a high cliff, sheer on its W side and with some white quarries on its E side. On the summit stands Fort du Roule (49°38′N 1°37′W).

    The most conspicuous features, which will first be seen on the skyline when approaching from N, are a conspicuous water tower and a conspicuous Television Mast (12.45).

Port limits
12.24

1   The limits of Port Militaire, on the W side of the harbour, and of Port de Commerce, on the E, S and SSW sides, are shown on the chart.

Approach and entry
12.25

1   Cherbourg is approached direct from the English Channel and entered through Passe de l'Ouest (12.49), the deepest and most frequently used entrance, or through Passe de l'Est (12.50).

Traffic
12.26

1   In 2006 the port handled 295 vessels totalling 909 688 dwt.

Port Authority
12.27

1   **Military Authority:**
> Capitainerie du port, Terre-plein d'Écluse, Cherbourg, France.

Commercial Authority:

Chambre de Commerce et d'Industrie de Cherbourg Cotentin, Hotel Atlantique, Boulevard Felix Amiot, PO Box 839, F–50108, Cherbourg.

Limiting conditions
12.28

1   **Controlling depth** for the port is 11·5 m within the limits of the leading lines through Passe de l'Ouest.

Deepest and longest berths. The deepest berth is at Quai des Flamands (12.64), on the E side of Darse des Mielles, and the longest berth at Quai de France (12.64) in Darse Transatlantique.

2   **Tidal levels.** For information regarding tidal levels see information in *Admiralty Tide Tables*. Mean spring range about 5·3 m; mean neap range about 2·5 m.

Maximum size of vessel handled. A vessel of 350 000 dwt, 350 m length and 50 m beam, with a draught of 12 m, has used the port.

3   **Dumping ground.** A temporary explosives dumping ground lies in Grande Rade, centred on position 49°40'·0N 1°37'·0W; see Appendix V.

Arrival information

Port operations
SPARE 12.29

1   **Movements reporting system.** The system is compulsory for vessels over 1600 gt carrying dangerous and polluting goods; for details see *Admiralty List of Radio Signals Volume 6(1)*.

Vessel Traffic Service
12.30

1   **VTS** is operated from Vigie du Homet (49°39'·3N 1°37'·8W) and monitors all traffic for the military and commercial ports. In certain circumstances VTS may assume control of shipping and will authorize or prohibit vessel movements. For details see *Admiralty List of Radio Signals Volume 6(1)*.

Notice of ETA required
12.31

1   Send request for pilot 48 hours and 4 hours in advance, or on leaving previous port if later, stating ETA and draught.

Contact should be made with Vigie du Homet, Cherbourg Signal Station, 1 hour before arrival, for details see *Admiralty List of Radio Signals Volume 6(1)*.

For details of ETA and request for deep-sea pilots, see 12.34.

Outer anchorages
12.32

1   The only areas outside the breakwaters in which vessels are authorized to anchor are the waiting areas (12.36).

2   There are anchorage areas, sheltered from the prevailing weather, in the W part of Baie de Seine off Saint-Vaast-la-Hougue (49°35'N 1°16'W). These anchorages (13.31) are subject to the agreement of the local maritime authorities; permission for anchorage must be received through CROSS Jobourg or Barfleur Signal Station.

3   **Prohibited anchorage.** Anchorage is prohibited in the entrances to Grande Rade and their approaches, as shown on the chart.

Pilotage and tugs
12.33

1   **Pilotage** is compulsory for:

Vessels with an LOA of over 50 m.

Vessels towing where the overall length of the tow is greater than 50 m.

Compulsory pilotage applies within 7 miles of Fort de l'Ouest (49°41'N 1°39'W).

Boarding positions. Pilot boards in the South Waiting Area 2½ miles N of Fort de l'Ouest, as shown on the chart.

12.34

1   **Deep-sea pilots,** see 1.50. These pilots board in the North Waiting Area, centred 3½ miles N of Fort de l'Ouest, or, for laden tankers carrying hydrocarbons or other dangerous substances, 7 miles N of Fort de l'Ouest or at least 7 miles off the coast.

2   Deep-sea pilots board by launch or by helicopter, the helicopter rendezvous points, distance and bearing from Cap Lévi (49°42'N 1°28'W) are:

24 miles NW (chart 2675).

10 miles N.

5 miles N (not tankers).

32 miles N (disembarks pilots for W bound vessels) (chart 2675).

On request at any position within 100 miles of Cherbourg.

3   **Notice of ETA required.** Send request for deep-sea pilot 48 hours in advance with notice of ETA 24 hours and 4 hours in advance, for details see *Admiralty List of Radio Signals Volume 6(1)*.

4   **Tugs** are available.

Traffic regulations
SPARE 12.35

1   **Control of navigation.** Vessels exceeding 1600 gt laden with dangerous and polluting goods, approaching or leaving Cherbourg, must use the approach channel and waiting areas and should comply with regulations given at 1.68 to 1.76

12.36

1   **Waiting areas,** the limits of which are shown on the charts, have been established as follows:

North Waiting Area, centred 3 miles N of Fort de l'Ouest, is reserved for vessels with a draught of 10 m or more, or vessels with a gross tonnage of 3000 or more and for vessels that are not bound to or from the port of Cherbourg.

2   South Waiting Area, centred 1¾ miles NNE of Fort de l'Ouest, is reserved for vessels with a draught of less than 10 m or a gross tonnage of less than 3000 (600 for oil tankers), bound to or from the port of Cherbourg.

1   polluting goods. The following is a summary of French regulations concerning the above-mentioned vessels proceeding to embark a deep-sea pilot, or entering or leaving Cherbourg.

2   Vessels wishing to embark a deep-sea pilot must do so in a position 7 miles N of Fort de l'Ouest, and in all cases not less than 7 miles off the coast.

Vessels bound for Cherbourg must approach and leave the port within the sector 325° and 037° from Fort de l'Ouest to reach the South Waiting Area. When entering and leaving the port these vessels must have a pilot embarked when S of the South Waiting Area and use Passe de l'Ouest.

3   Vessels must contact VTS Cherbourg (12.30) giving 24 hours notice of their ETA and confirmation 6 hours in advance. On entering French territorial waters N of Cotentin Peninsula vessels must make VHF contact with VTS Cherbourg at Vigie du Homet and maintain the contact until alongside or clear of French territorial waters.

4   Vessels must report to VTS Cherbourg before entering French territorial waters any defects in their propulsion machinery, steering gear, anchoring gear or radar equipment. Should there be any defects the vessel must remain outside 7 nautical miles from the French coast unless expressly exempted by the Administrator of Marine Affairs Cherbourg who may require special measures to be taken by the vessel concerned.

12.38

1   **Speed limits,** for vessels over 500 gt, are in force as follows:

        In Grande Rade; 14 kn.
        In Petite Rade; 8 kn.

12.39

1   **Prohibited areas:**

        Anchoring, fishing and diving is prohibited in the circular area, radius 500 m, centred on position 49°45′·2N 1°32′·6W; a wreck with an estimated depth of 45 m over it lies in this position.

2   Anchoring, dredging and trawling are prohibited in the charted area 3¼ miles NE of Passe de l'Est.

        Entry to Port Militaire is prohibited without permission of the naval authorities.

3   Entry is prohibited on the S sides of Digue de Querqueville, Digue Centrale and Digue de l'Est, and to the N and W of Digue du Homet, as shown on the chart.

        A prohibited area extends about 250 m offshore in the vicinity of Fort de Querqueville (49°40′·4N 1°40′·8W).

12.40

1   **Diving prohibition.** Two circular areas, radii 900 m, within which diving is prohibited, are centred on positions 49°45′N 1°37′W and 49°45′N 1°42′W, respectively. Both areas contain historic wrecks.

Marine farm
12.41

1   A marine farm, marked by light buoys (cardinal and special), lies to the S of Digue Centrale between Fort del'Ouest and Fort Central; entry is prohibited.

Harbour

General layout
12.42

1   **Main berthing and anchorage areas.** The harbour consists of Grande Rade, a large deep-water anchorage protected by three outer breakwaters, within which there is Petite Rade, protected by two inner breakwaters, fronting the main port installations.

2   **Channels.** Passe de l'Ouest (12.49) between the head of Digue de Querqueville and Fort de l'Ouest is the deepest and most frequently used entrance. Its swept depth within the limits of the leading lines is the controlling depth for the port (12.28).

        Passe de l'Est (12.50), between Fort de l'Est and Fort de l'Île Pelée, is not recommended at night.

(12.28). Vessels exceeding 1600 gt laden with hydrocarbons or carrying dangerous substances must use this entrance.

        Passe de l'Est (12.50), between Fort de l'Est and Fort de l'Île Pelée, is not recommended at night.

Traffic signals
12.43

1   International Port Traffic Signals, as recommended by IALA, are in use for controlling movements into or out of Bassin du Commerce (12.64), a wet basin. For details see *The Mariner's Handbook.*

Tidal streams
12.44

1   **Tidal streams** about 3 miles N of Digue Centrale begin as follows:

Interval from HW Cherbourg	Direction
−0330	E
+0215	W

    The maximum spring rates are 3 kn in each direction.

2   As the breakwater is approached the streams begin earlier and their rates decrease.

    In Passe de l'Ouest slack water occurs at −0530, and from HW to +0100 Cherbourg, and in Passe de l'Est from +0500 to −0600 and at +0030 Cherbourg.

3   In the entrance channels and within Grande Rade the tidal streams run as follows:

Interval from HW Cherbourg	Direction and maximum spring rate
−0510	A weak stream sets in through Passe de l'Ouest, E through Grande Rade and out through Passe de l'Est
−0410	E-going stream continues with rates of ½ kn to 1 kn; clockwise eddy forms SE of Fort de Chavagnac
−0310	General E-going flow continues; rates increase to 2 kn near Passe de l'Ouest
−0210 to −0110	General E-going flow continues; anti-clockwise eddy develops S of W part of Digue Centrale. Rates of ½ to 2 kn
−0010	Main E-going flow slackens. The eddies SE of Fort de Chavagnac and S of Digue Centrale continue
+0045	Generally slack with two eddies expanding
+0145	W-going stream begins in Grande Rade setting in through Passe de l'Ouest; rates of ½ to 1 kn
+0245	W-going flow generally within Grande Rade; rates of ½ to 1 kn
+0345	W-going flow continues with slightly increased rates. Clockwise eddy begins to form S of E end of Digue Centrale
+0445	W-going flow continues. Eddy S of Digue Centrale expands
+0545	W-going stream slackens
−0610 (nearly LW)	Slack water

4   There is virtually no stream at the extreme W and E ends of Grande Rade, except in Passe Collignon (49°39′·7N 1°34′·2W) through which it attains a maximum E-going

rate of 3 kn at –0310 Cherbourg, and a maximum W-going rate of 3½ kn at +0345 Cherbourg.

There is no stream in Petite Rade.

See also information on the chart.

Directions for entering harbour
(continued from 12.18)

Principal marks
12.45

1   **Landmarks:**

Water Tower (radio antennae 137 m) (49°37′·5N 1°37′·3W).

La Glacerie (water tower) (49°37′·1N 1°35′·9W).

Television Mast (red lights) (49°37′·2N 1°32′·9W).

Major lights:

2   Fort de l'Ouest Light (49°41′N 1°39′W) (12.9).

Cap Lévi Light (49°42′N 1°28′W) (12.9).

Pointe de Barfleur-Gatteville Light (49°42′N 1°16′W) (12.9).

Cap de la Hague Light (49°43′N 1°57′W) (12.9).

General directions
12.46

1   Mariners will maintain depths of more than 10 m when N of the outer breakwaters at Cherbourg by keeping N of the alignment (090°) of Cap Lévi Light and Pointe de Barfleur-Gatteville Light.

Cherbourg Approach Channel
12.47

1   From a position NW of Cherbourg CH1 Light Buoy ght (safe water) (49°43′N 1°42′W) the route leads ads generally SE passing clear of the light buoy to the ing waiting areas (12.36).

Clearing bearing, see 12.16.   ous

ana ponuting goods must approach within the sector 325° and 037° from Fort de l'Ouest (49°41′N 1°39′W), for details see 12.37.

Clearing bearing, see 12.16.

Waiting areas to Passe de l'Ouest
12.48

1   **Cleared route.** A zone about 1000 m wide, extensively surveyed for obstacles (1979), orientated 177°-357° limited in the N by the position 49°43′·5N 1°40′·1W leads from the waiting areas to a position about 1 mile NW of Fort de l'Ouest (49°41′N 1°39′W) where the route then joins the 141¼° track (12.49) through Passe de l'Ouest.

Passe de l'Ouest and Grande Rade
12.49

1   **Leading lights:**

Front lights (white triangle point up, 4 m in height) (49°39′·6N 1°37′·9W) on a parapet at the root of Digue du Homet.

Rear light. Gare Maritime Light (white triangle point up on grey pylon, 35 m in height) (1 mile SE of the front lights) on the NE side of Gare Maritime at Cherbourg.

2   From a position about 1 mile NW of Fort de l'Ouest (49°41′N 1°39′W), E of Plateau de Nacqueville (49°41′N 1°42′W), the line of bearing 141¼° of the rear leading light seen midway between the two front lights leads through Passe de l'Ouest which is limited to the NE and SW by the alignments (142¼° and 140¼°, respectively) of

the common rear light on Gare Maritime with the two front lights on Digue Homet, passing (with positions given from Fort de l'Ouest (49°41′N 1°39′W)):

3   Very close NE of a 10·1 m obstruction (2½ cables NW) which lies close W of the W limit of the leading marks; thence:

Between Digue de Querqueville (6 cables WSW) and Fort de l'Ouest, passing about 1 cable SW of the fort. The extremity of below-water rocks, which extend from the W end of Digue Centrale, is marked by a light buoy (port hand) (½ cable SSW).

4   **Grande Rade leading lights:**

Front light (white support green top, 9 m in height) (49°39′·5N 1°36′·9W) on a blockhouse at the head of Digue du Homet.

Rear light (white column, black bands, white top, 15 m in height) (7½ cables ESE of the front light) situated on Terre-plein des Mielles.

5   The alignment (124¼°) of these lights then leads in Grande Rade to the anchorage (12.57). For vessels with a low height of eye the rear mark and its light may be obscured by vessels alongside, cranes or warehouses.

Thence, if required, the recommended track 112° shown on the chart leads to Petite Rade (12.61). A light buoy (port hand) (1¾ miles ESE) moored close NW of the head of Jetée des Flamands marks the limit of the slope of its foundations.

6   **Caution.** A charted depth of 10·6 m lies midway between the breakwaters at the entrance to Petite Rade.

Passe de l'Est
12.50

1   **From N by day — leading marks:**

Front mark. Prominent Building (white with two black stripes, 41 m in height) (49°38′·1N 1°35′·8W).

Rear mark. Water Tower (1 mile S of the front mark) (12.45).

2   **From N by night - leading lights:**

Front light (white metal pylon on hut, 8 m in height) (49°39′·3N 1′35′·9W) on E end of Jetée des Flamands.

Rear light (white column, black bands, white top, 15 m in height) (520 m S of front light) situated on Terre-plein des Mielles.

3   From a position N of Fort de l'Est (49°40′N 1°36′W) the alignment of the marks (183½°) by day, and the lights (189°) by night leads through Passe de l'Est passing (with positions given from Fort de l'Est):

E of a 9·6 m rocky bank (1 mile N) and over a rocky bank with a least depth of 8·9 m over it (8 cables NNE); thence:

W of Roches du Nord-Ouest (5 cables NE) marked on their NW side by Roches du Nord-Ouest Light Buoy (port hand); thence:

Close E of an obstruction (49°40′·4N 1°35′·8W) with a depth of 7·7 m over it; thence:

4   Between Fort de l'Est, from which below-water rocks extend to nearly ½ cable, and La Truite (3 cables ENE) marked on its W side by La Truite Light Buoy (port hand), the W-most danger at the edge of the bank extending W from Île Pelée, a drying rocky reef which extends nearly 5 cables seaward from the outer part of Digue de l'Est; thence:

In to Grande Rade (12.56).

12.51

1 **From north-north-east by day — leading marks:**
Front mark. Saint-Trinité Church (central belfry) (49°38′·6N 1°37′·3W).
Rear mark. Notre-Dame du Vœu Church (twin spires) (4 cables SSW of the front mark.

2 From a position NNE of Fort de l'Est the alignment (212°) of these marks leads through Passe de l'Est passing WNW of both Roches du Nord-Ouest and La Truite and ESE of Fort de l'Est (12.50).

12.52

1 **Useful marks:**
Tromet Beacon Tower (port hand, 9 m in height) (49°40′·5N 1°34′·9W).
Happetout Beacon Tower (E cardinal, 9 m in height) (49°40′·5N 1°34′·3W).

Passe Cabart-Danneville (Passe Collignon)

12.53

1 **General information.** Passe Cabart-Danneville (Passe Collignon) (49°39′·7N 1°34′·2W) is a passage, ½ cable wide, through the S part of Digue de l'Est for use by mariners in shallow-draught craft proceeding to or from Port du Becquet (12.79).

A light (white metal tank red top, 4 m in height) marks the S side of the passage.

Petite Rade

12.54

1 **Turning area.** There is a turning area in the centre of Petite Rade; the N, S and W limits of the area are marked by three sets of light transits which are shown on the chart.

12.55

1 **Port Militaire leading lights.** The alignment (257¼°) of leading lights exhibited on the W side of Bassin Napoléon III leads through the entrance of Avant-port Militaire. The avant-port, which gives access to the wet basins, is entered through a passage from Petite Rade. The sides of the passage are not perpendicular and small drying banks extend from them; the sides should be given a berth of at least 10 m in order to keep in depths of not less than 5 m.

2 Front light (orange triangle point up, black band, on mast, 4 m in height) (49°39′·2N 1°38′·3W).
Rear light (orange triangle point up, black band, on mast, 9 m in height) (255 m from the front light).

Basins and berths

Grande Rade

12.56

1 **Description.** Grande Rade is protected on its N side by three breakwaters. Digue de Querqueville, the W breakwater, extends about 7 cables ENE from Fort de Querqueville (49°40′·4N 1°40′·8W) with Fort de Chavagnac close within its head. Digue de l'Est, which covers at HW at its S end, extends SE and S from Fort de l'Île Pelée (49°40′·3N 1°35′·0W) to the shore at Pointe des Grèves, 1 mile SSE. Digue Centrale, a detached breakwater 2 miles long, on which stands Fort de l'Ouest, at its W end, Fort Central at its centre and Fort de l'Est at its E end, lies between the E and W breakwaters. Lights (12.9 and 12.18) are exhibited at the head of each breakwater.

2 It is bounded on its S side by Digue du Homet and Jetée des Flamands which extends NW and W from Fort des Flamands (49°39′·2N 1°35′·6W).

12.57

1 **Anchorage** for mariners in larger vessels can be obtained in the central part of Grande Rade in a depth of

11 m. The anchoring position is indicated by the intersection of the 124¼° leading lights (12.49), on Digue du Homet and Terre-plein des Mielles, with the alignment (192°) of the following lights:

2 Front light (white pylon) (49°39′·6N 1°38′·4W) situated 3 cables W of Fort du Homet.
Rear light (green pedestal on the roof of Rochambeau Barracks, 17 m in height) (3½ cables SSW of the front mark.

3 **Caution.** La Ténarde marked on its N side by La Ténarde Light Buoy (N cardinal) lies about 1 cable N of the root of Digue du Homet.

Numbered anchor positions, with defined swinging circles of radius 200 m lie S of Digue Centrale as follows (with positions from Fort Central (49°40′·5N 1°37′·1W)):

4 No 1 (1¾ cables S), depth about 8 m.
No 2 (3½ cables SE), depth about 7 m.
No 3 (6 cables ESE), depth about 6·5 m.
No 4 (4½ cables SSW), depth about 13 m.
No 5 (6 cables SE), depth about 8 m.

5 **Cautions.** Obstructions are charted in the SW part of No 3 anchorage position.

There is a temporary explosives dumping ground (12.28) in close proximity to anchorage positions Nos 1, 2, 4 and 5.

6 **Prohibited anchorage.** The limits of prohibited anchorage areas in the vicinity of the entrance channels, breakwaters and jetties are shown on the chart.

12.58

1 **Tanker berth** (49°40′·3N 1°40′·0W), under the jurisdiction of the French government, is situated on the S side of Digue de Querqueville, close W of Fort de Chavagnac, for vessels up to 180 m in length and 9 m draught. Vessels berth on floating pontoons, bows W with an anchor down, and stern secured to a buoy.

Grande Rade

12.59

1 **Port de Querqueville** (49°40′·2N 1°40′·7W) at the W end of Grande Rade in the NW corner of Baie de Sainte-Anne is a small port, which dries, used only by local fishing boats and is under the jurisdiction of the naval authorities.

Restricted and prohibited areas, as shown on the chart, front the approach to the port.

12.60

1 **Port des Flamands** (49°39′·2N 1°35′·1W), a small harbour with anchorage berths in the SE part of Grande Rade, is situated 3 cables E of Fort des Flamands; it is used by fishing boats and small craft.

Petite Rade

12.61

1 **Description.** Petite Rade lies within Digue du Homet and Jetée des Flamands. Port Militaire (12.63) lies on the W part of Petite Rade with Port de Commerce (12.64) on the S and E parts. Port de Chantereyne (12.64), a yacht harbour, is situated in its SSW part. Bassin du Commerce, a wet basin of secondary importance, is entered through Avant-port de Commerce S of Port de Chantereyne.

12.62

1 **Anchorages.** Anchorage in Port Militaire is reserved for naval vessels. Mariners in fishing vessels and yachts waiting to enter Port de Chantereyne or Avant-port de Commerce may anchor in an area, shown on the chart, situated in the S part of Port Militaire.

Prohibited anchorage. Anchorage is prohibited in an area shown on the chart from the entrance to Petite Rade to the entrance to Darse Transatlantique.

12.63

1   **Port Militaire.** The naval port and dockyard occupies the W part of Petite Rade as shown on the chart, and contains a number of mooring buoys for naval vessels.

The limits of Port Militaire within Petite Rade are indicated by BN1 and BN2 Light Buoys (special) moored in positions 49°39′·5N 1°36′·9W and 49°39′·0N 1°37′·1W

There are five berths along the S side of Digue du Homet for which catamarans can be provided if required. The centre berth, which is a fuelling berth, is formed by two dolphins 60 m apart. Forty-eight hours notice is required for the use of these berths.

Avant-port Militaire gives access to the wet basins.

2   Darse du Béton, a small basin in the S part of Port Militaire situated SE of the dockyard, is reserved for naval craft.

12.64

1   **Port de Commerce,** the commercial port, lies on the S and E sides of Petite Rade.

Darse Transatlantique, a tidal basin on the S side of Port de Commerce access to which is dredged to a depth of 11 m, contains Quai de France and Quai de Normandie. RoRo berths lie at the S end of Quai de France, at the S end of the basin, and at the N end of Quai de Normandie. The deepest and longest berths are:

2   Quai de France, on the W side adjacent to Gare Maritime, dredged to depths between 11 and 14 m with the deepest section at the N end.

        Quai de Normandie, on the E side dredged to a depth of 10 m over a 200 m length from N, and dredged to depths between 8 and 11 m over the remaining 290 m to the S.

3   No 1 RoRo Berth, in the S part of the basin, a spur 197 m in length with depths alongside of 6 to 9 m.

        No 4 RoRo Berth, at the N end of Quai de Normandie, connected to the quay by a footbridge and extends 250 m N; various pieces of debris are reported to be buried in the sandy bottom along the length of this berth.

4   **Darse des Mielles,** a tidal basin on the E and S sides of Port de Commerce, has berths on its E side, a RoRo berth on the W side and a launching slip, shiplift and a fitting out berth on the S side. The deepest and longest berths are:

5   Quai des Flamands, on the E side at the N end of Terre-plein des Mielles, has a length of 240 m and depths of 13 m. The quay has a container terminal adjacent and is for multi-purpose use.

        Quai des Mielles, at the S end of Terre-plein des Mielles, has a length of 400 m with two berths with depths of 4 to 5 m.

        No 2 RoRo Berth, on the W side, has a depth of 8 m for vessels up to 230 m in length.

6   **Port de Chantereyne,** a yacht harbour in the SW corner of Port de Commerce, is for pleasure craft.

Avant-port de Commerce, a tidal basin situated S of Port de Chantereyne, is approached through a narrow channel lying close to the W side of the W mole of Darse Transatlantique and gives access to Bassin du Commerce. There are charted depths between drying 3·5 and 2·5 m in the basin. The avant-port is used by fishing vessels, pleasure craft and by vessels of the port authorities. There is a quay 90 m long reserved for fishing vessels on the E side of Avant-port.

7   **Bassin du Commerce,** a wet basin with 1000 m of quayage is used by fishing vessels and small craft and is entered from Avant-port de Commerce through a dock gate. It can accommodate vessels of 110 m in length with a beam of less than 16 m; the dock gate is usually opened from 1 hour before to 1 hour after HW but an extension to these times can be requested from the Bureau de Port. The entrance to the basin is spanned by a swing bridge. Mariners requiring the swing bridge to be opened should make a request on VHF, or in the absence of same, sound one long blast followed by one short blast; the bridge is usually opened from 1 hour before to 1 hour after HW.

8   A stone ledge projects about 1·2 m from the quays from which vessels can be kept clear by the use of catamarans. The bottom of the basin consists of muddy sand with pieces of steel debris.

Port services

Repairs
12.65

1   **Dry docks.** There are several government dry docks, some of which can be used by commercial vessels. The largest which can be used by commercial vessels, No 5 Dock, has extreme dimensions of length 206·4 m, breadth 25·7 m.

All types of repairs to hull and machinery can be carried out.

Other facilities
12.66

1   **Ship sanitation control and ship sanitation control exemption certificates** issued at Cherbourg, see 1.140.

Hospitals, both civil and naval, are available.

Supplies
12.67

1   **Fuel:** fuel and diesel oil available.

Fresh water: available at all quays and by barge.

Communications
12.68

1   **Airport.** Cherbourg-Maupertus International Airport is situated 12 km E of Cherbourg.

Harbour regulations
12.69

1   The following are paraphrased extracts from the port anchorage regulations.

Naval vessels in the port or entering the port always have priority regarding choice of anchorage.

The maritime authorities may change the anchorage at any time of a passenger or merchant ship if they deem it necessary, without cost being incurred by the State.

2   The instruction to change anchorage may be made by signal, or brought by a State launch or Pilot's launch; it must be complied with immediately. The Pilot's launches are authorised to tow vessels from one anchorage to another; this is done at the vessels' Captains' own risk as they have the option to move themselves.

3   In order to allow quick and easy anchorage for large passenger ships, the Cherbourg pilots have the power, at the discretion of the maritime authorities, to themselves move any merchant ship which would hinder anchorage of a passenger ship or other large vessel.

4   As far as possible, in the case of vessels thus displaced, the preference of the Captain should be taken into account in the choice of a new anchorage; it is forbidden to anchor less than 150 m from the mooring buoys of large vessels.

Any ship which has anchored in the forbidden areas must slip its cable after having first attached a buoy rope and marker buoy.

5   Raising is undertaken either by the vessel itself, or by the Navy, according to the decision of the port authorities.

Any costs incurred, of whatever nature, as a result of this unauthorised anchorage, are the responsibility of the vessel.

Ships and tenders which do not belong to the State are forbidden to anchor or stop less than 100 m from Naval vessels anchored or moored in the roads.

Rescue
12.70

1 **Salvage tug** is based at Cherbourg.

Signal station. Homet Signal Station (Vigie) (white tower yellow flagstaff) (49°39′·5N 1°37′·9W), the Cherbourg signal station, is situated at the NW end of Petite Rade, for details see 1.95 and 1.110.

CHERBOURG TO POINTE DE BARFLEUR

General information

Chart 1106
Route
12.71

1 From NW of Cherbourg (49°39′N 1°38′W) the route to Pointe de Barfleur leads E, about 20 miles.

Topography
12.72

1 From Cap Lévi (49°42′N 1°28′W) (12.77) to Pointe de Barfleur, 8 miles E, the coast appears elevated in the W part and decreases in elevation towards Pointe de Barfleur; it is rocky and interspersed with sandy beaches.

Traffic regulations
12.73

1 **Prohibited anchoring and fishing area.** Mariners are prohibited from anchoring dredging and trawling within an area, situated 2 miles W of Cap Lévi, whose limits are shown on the chart.

Entry prohibited area. A circular area, radius 1½ miles, to which entry is prohibited, is centred on position 49°48′·6N 1°25′·8W.

2 **Explosives dumping ground.** An explosives dumping ground, whose limits are shown on the chart, lies centred about 7 miles NNE of Cap Lévi.

Prohibited diving areas. See 12.40

Rescue
12.74

1 **Signal station** is situated at:
Pointe de Barfleur (Vigie) (49°42′N 1°16′W) (12.9). For details, see 1.95 and 1.110.

VHF Direction-finding stations, for emergency use only, operate from:
Cap Lévi (49°42′N 1°28W).
Pointe de Barfleur (49°42′N 1°16′W).
For details see *Admiralty List of Radio Signals Volume 2.*

Natural conditions
12.75

1 **Tidal streams.** Off Port du Becquet (49°39′N 1°33′W) (12.79) the E-going tidal stream runs for about 3 hours only and the W-going stream for about 9½ hours, they begin as follows:

Interval from HW Cherbourg	Direction
−0600	E
−0300	W

The maximum E-going and W-going spring rates are 1 kn to 1½ kn, respectively.

2 About 2 miles W of Port du Cap Lévi (49°41′N 1°28′W) (12.80) the E-going stream runs for about 8 hours and the W-going stream runs for about 4½ hours only, beginning as follows:

Interval from HW Cherbourg	Direction
−0530	E
+0230	WSW

Off Port du Cap Lévi

+0315	N
HW	S

The maximum E-going and W-going spring rates are 1½ kn and 1 kn, respectively.

3 At La Pierre Noire Light Buoy N of Tête Septentrionale (49°43′·5N 1°28′·8W) tidal streams begin as follows:

Interval from HW Cherbourg	Direction
−0430	E
+0230	W

The maximum spring rate on the E-going stream is 5 kn and on the W-going stream 4 kn to 5 kn.

4 **Local weather.** Between Cap Lévi and Pointe de Barfleur the coast is bordered by dangerous rocky shoals which extend up to 2½ miles offshore. In bad weather, with wind against the tidal stream, the sea breaks heavily on these dangers.

Directions
(continued from 12.18)

Principal marks
12.76

1 For details of landmarks and major lights, see 12.9.

Cherbourg Approach Channel to Pointe de Barfleur
12.77

1 From a position NW of Cherbourg (49°39′N 1°38′W) the route leads generally E passing (with positions given from Cap Lévi (49°42′N 1°28′W)):

2 N of Tête Septentrionale (1¾ miles N), which together with a 9·3 m shoal close NE, lie near the N end of an area of uneven, shoal and rocky ground which extends about 2 miles N from Cap Lévi. It is steep-to and the sea breaks on it in rough weather and it is marked near its N end by La Pierre Noire Light Buoy (W cardinal). Raz du Cap Lévi, a dangerous race especially with wind against tidal stream, extends 2 miles N from Cap Lévi a low point which projects from the coast. A light (12.9) is exhibited from Cap Lévi and a disused signal station (white with white mast) stands on a hill 2 cables SE. Thence:

3 N of Tête du Nord-Ouest (3¼ miles NE) the outermost patch on Basses du Sen; thence:

N of Basses du Nord-Ouest (4¾ miles NE), marked on their NE side by Basse du Rénier Light Buoy (N cardinal), the outermost patch on Basses du Rénier; thence:

4 N of Haut-Fond des Équets (6½ miles ENE), marked on its N side by Les Équets Light Buoy (N cardinal), at the N end of Plateau des Équets; thence:

N of Banc de Saint-Pierre (49°43′N 1°17′W), an extensive shifting bank of sand and shells; thence:

5 To a position N of Pointe de Barfleur (49°42′N 1°16′W) from where a light is exhibited (12.9). Raz de Barfleur, a race in which the sea breaks heavily, especially at springs when wind is against the stream, extends 3 to 4 miles NE and E from Pointe de Barfleur. In consequence Pointe de Barfleur should be given a wide berth.

(Directions continue at 13.16)

Side channels

Inshore channels
12.78

1   **General information.** Chenal Hédouin and Chenal des Trois Pierres, where there is much less sea than farther offshore, lead inside the dangers bordering the coast between Cap Lévi (49°42′N 1°28′W) and Pointe de Barfleur, 8 miles E. These channels are only suitable for mariners in small coasting vessels proceeding between Cherbourg and Barfleur (13.19).

2   **Tidal streams** begin as follows at the positions indicated:

Interval from HW Cherbourg	Direction
Off Basses du Rénier: (49°44′N 1°22′W)	ESE
−0330	W
+0245	
In Chenal Hédouin: (49°42′N 1°15′W)	E
−0515	W
+0100	
Close N of Pointe de Barfleur:	ESE
−0400	NNW
+0100	

3   The maximum E-going and W-going spring rates off Basses du Rénier and in Chenal Hédouin are 5 kn and 4 kn, and close N of Pointe de Barfleur, 3¾ kn and 4 kn, respectively. See also information on the chart.

Local knowledge is essential, or the use of a pilot, as the tidal streams run strongly. See transit lines on the chart.

4   **Useful marks:**
Les Trois Pierres Beacon (S cardinal) (49°43′·0N 1°21′·7W).
Beacon (N cardinal) (49°42′·4N 1°19′·8W) at the N end of drying rocks extending N from Pointe de Néville.
La Jamette Beacon (E cardinal, 8 m in height) (49°41′·9N 1°15′·5W).

Minor harbours

Port du Becquet
12.79

1   **General information.** Port du Becquet (49°39′N 1°33′W) is a small harbour, 1 mile E of Cherbourg, used only by local fishing vessels and pleasure craft.

The harbour entrance, about ¼ cable wide, lies between La Tourelle Beacon Tower (port hand) marking the NW edge of a rocky ledge and the head of the N jetty which extends 1½ cables E from the coast. The S side of the harbour is quayed and there is a width of 48 m between it and the N jetty.

2   Fresh N and NE winds cause a heavy surf in the harbour.

Leading lights: The alignment (186½°) of the following lights leads in the approach to the harbour:

Front light (white octagonal tower, 6 m in height) (49°39′·3N 1°32′·8W).
Rear light (white octagonal tower red top, 10 m in height) (49 m S of the front mark).

3   A buoy (special), 2¼ miles N of the entrance, stands on this alignment which also leads close W of a buoy (special) moored 3¾ cables NNE of the entrance.

Berths. Good drying-out berths along the inner side of the N jetty which dries 1·4 to 3 m to a hard bottom covered with a thin layer of mud. The bottom alongside the S quay, which dries from 3 to 3·4 m, is unsuitable for taking the ground.

Port du Cap Lévi
12.80

1   **General information.** Port du Cap Lévi (49°41′N 1°28′W), a small drying harbour at the head of Anse du Cap Lévi, is used only by fishing boats and yachts.

The harbour is protected by two stone jetties, both of which dry; the heads of the jetties are painted white and the entrance between them is 76 m wide.

Winds from between SW and N cause a heavy surf in the harbour.

2   **Directions.** Approach within the white sector (083°–105°) of Port du Cap Lévi Light (white and grey hut white lantern, 6 m in height) (49°41′·3N 1°28′·2W) situated on the E side of the harbour passing clear of a buoy (special) moored 3½ cables W of the harbour entrance.

Caution. Les Grunes de Bretteville, a chain of below-water rocks which lie in the green sector of Port du Cap Lévi Light, extend 7 cables from the coast 2¼ miles SW of the light.

3   **Anchorage** off the port is only practicable with offshore winds.

Berths: quay 150 long on the E side of the harbour drying to a sandy bottom; good drying-out berths. Elsewhere the bottom is mainly rocky.

Anse de Vicq
12.81

1   **General information.** Anse de Vicq (49°42′N 1°24′W), a narrow inlet between drying rocks, lies 3 miles E of Cap Lévi.

The alignment (158°) of leading lights (red and white triangle point up on white pylon, red top, 5 m and 8 m in height) situated at the head of the inlet leads in the approach passing WSW of Basses du Sen (12.77).

Charts 1349 plan of Barfleur, 1106
Havre de Roubary
12.82

1   **General information.** Havre de Roubary (49°42′N 1°17′W), a narrow sandy cove, is a small port of refuge and lies 5 cables W of Pointe de Barfleur; it is well sheltered except from swells from NW and N. The harbour is used by fishing boats and local pleasure craft.

2   Roche Houmaizel, marked by a beacon (isolated danger) lies close off the entrance to the cove; the recommended approach passes E of the beacon. Access is difficult on account of the strong currents and numerous dangers in the entrance.

NOTES

423

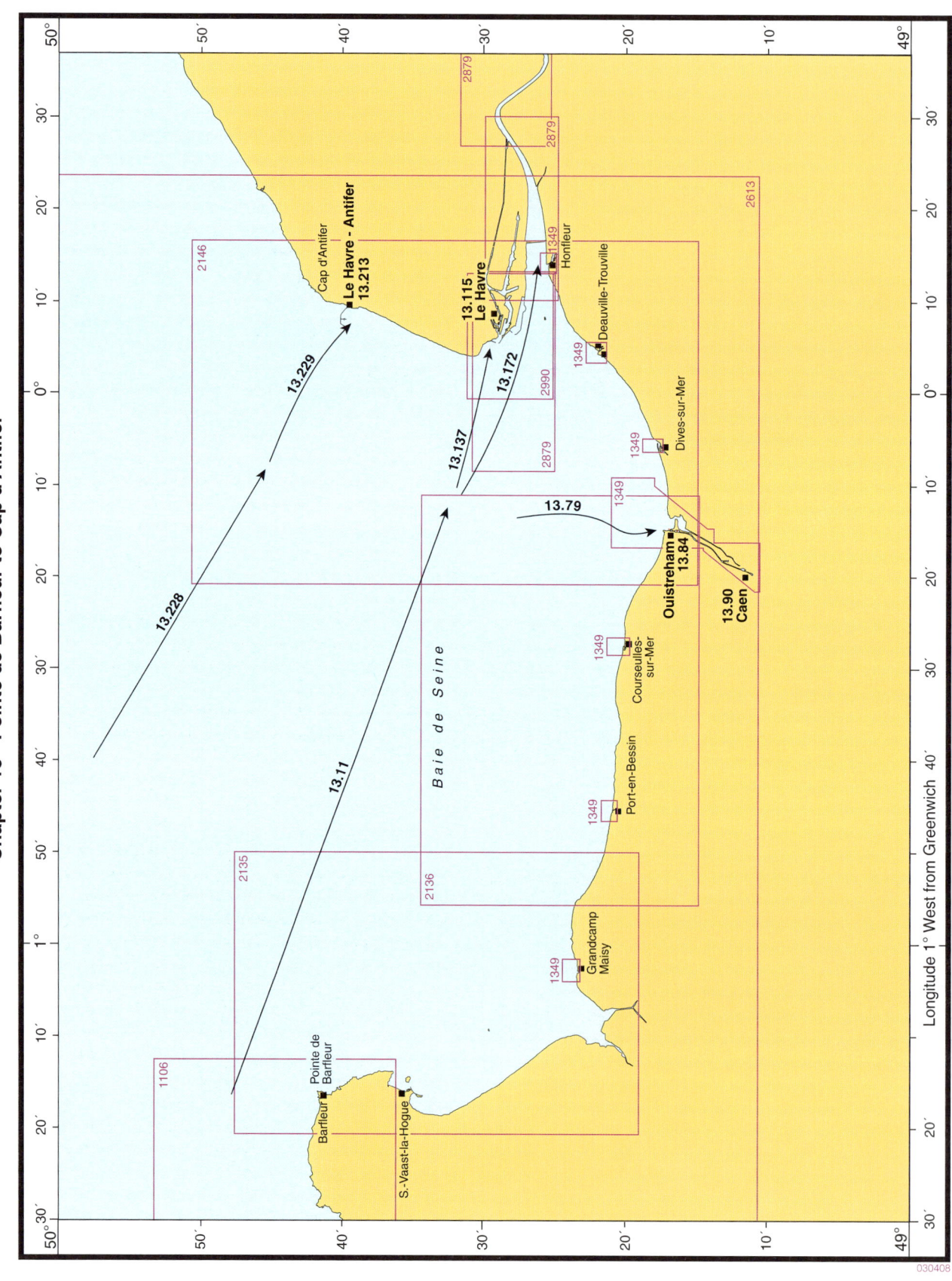

CHAPTER 13

NORTH COAST OF FRANCE — POINTE DE BARFLEUR TO CAP D'ANTIFER

GENERAL INFORMATION

Chart 2613
Scope of the chapter
13.1

1   This chapter covers Baie de Seine which is entered between Pointe de Barfleur (49°42′N 1°16′W) and Cap d'Antifer, 56 miles E.

Baie de Seine
13.2

1   **Description and ports.** The W side of Baie de Seine is formed by the E coast of Cotentin Peninsula (11.5) and contains some small harbours. In the N part of the peninsula the land is high, and the coast between Saint-Vaast-la-Hougue (49°35′N 1°16′W) and Grandcamp-Maisy, 15 miles SSE, is fronted by a line of banks, lying between 2½ and 5 miles offshore, in the centre of which are the low-lying Îles Saint-Marcouf.

2   The S side of the bay is fronted by the N coast of the Department of Calvados which is moderately high except in the vicinity of Ouistreham (49°17′N 0°15′W). The centre part of the coast is fronted by a rocky plateau which extends up to 2 miles offshore. Along this stretch of coast are the remains of the artificial harbours, built in 1944, which are now largely silted up; some of these installations have been removed or destroyed, but the remains constitute a hazard to navigation without providing any shelter. There are some small harbours, but the only port of any importance is that at Caen (13.90) which is connected by a canal to the sea at Ouistreham (13.84).

3   The E side of the bay comprises the estuary of Rivière La Seine which is obstructed with sandbanks through which there are well marked channels leading to Le Havre (49°29′N 0°07′E) (13.115), a major commercial and oil port, and into La Seine Maritime (13.158) giving access to the port at Rouen (49°27′N 1°05′E) (13.193) (chart 2994) and thence by a system of locks to the port at Paris and to the inland waterways of France. The smaller ports of Deauville-Trouville (49°22′N 0°04′E) (13.173) and Honfleur (49°25′N 0°14′E) (13.182) lie on the S bank of La Seine near its mouth.

4   **Deep-water route** (13.228) entered 35 miles WNW of Cap d'Antifer (49°41′N 0°10′E) leads to Port du Havre-Antifer (49°40′N 0°08′E) (13.213), a deep-water port for VLCCs, which lies 10 miles N of Le Havre.

   Anchorages. Off the E coast of Cotentin Peninsula, Rade de Saint-Vaast (49°34′N 1°14′W) (13.31) and Rade de la Capelle (49°26′N 1°05′W) (13.27) afford anchorage sheltered from W winds.

5   In the approaches to Le Havre there are anchorages in the waiting areas (13.108) and, for mariners in very deep-draught vessels proceeding to Port du Havre-Antifer, there are anchorages (13.221) about 20 miles WNW of Cap d'Antifer but these are exposed to N and W winds.

   There are no anchorages sheltered from N winds off the N coast of the Department of Calvados.

Depths
13.3

1   The greater part of Baie de Seine has depths of less than 30 m but Le Parfond, a comparatively deep bight, with depths from 20 to 36 m, penetrates the middle of the bay in an ESE direction towards the mouth of La Seine.

Hazards
13.4

1   **Cargo transhipment area.** Transfer of cargo operations take place in an area in the W part of Baie de Seine defined by the following positions as shown on the chart:

   49°42′·0N 1°04′·7W.
   49°42′·0N 0°56′·6W.
   49°37′·0N 1°02′·6W.
   49°37′·0N 0°54′·1W.

2   **Regulations.** The area is under the control of the French maritime authority, see 1.7. The following is a summary of the relevant regulations:

   The approach to the area should be made from E on a course between 200° and 270°.

   Should circumstances require, the authority may prohibit or, if in progress, terminate the operation.

3   At least 12 hours notice of transhipment must be given by the owner or master of the vessel to The Regional Operational Centre of Surveillance and Rescue, CROSS JOBOURG, at Jobourg, giving: name, flag, last port of call and destination of vessel to be lightened; name, flag and destination of vessel to be loaded; day, hour and position of transhipment and quantity to be transhipped. CROSS JOBOURG will inform authorities concerned.

4   Throughout the operation, and while in the area, vessels concerned are to maintain watch on VHF channel 16 and 2182 kHz.

   When visibility falls below 3 miles a warning will be broadcast, for details see *Admiralty List of Radio Signals Volume 3(1)*.

5   During transhipment vessels must display the shapes or exhibit the lights prescribed in *International Regulations for Preventing Collisions at Sea (1972)* and by *The International Code of Signals* for vessels engaged in special operations but not underway.

13.5

1   **Firing danger area.** A firing danger area, divided into E and W zones, in the S part of Baie de Seine, lies within the following overall limits:

   N limit — 49°55′N.
   E limit — meridian of 0°02′W.
   S limit — parallel of 49°32′N.
   W limit — meridian of 0°56′W.

2   Times when firings are to take place are promulgated in French notices to mariners and broadcast by Avurnav; for details see 1.31 and *Admiralty List of Radio Signals Volume 3(1)*.

13.6

1   **Wrecks and obstructions.** There are numerous charted wrecks and obstructions within 20 miles of the coast, the more important of which are marked by buoys. There are also wrecks of consequence to mariners in deep-draught vessels in the approach to Port du Havre-Antifer, for details of a deep-water route to this port, see 13.228.

Small unknown wrecks and obstructions, not detected by hydrographic surveys, may lie in the area covered by this chapter.

13.7

1   **Routeing.** For details of an IMO adopted TSS and a recommended direction of traffic flow N of Pointe de Barfleur, see 2.39.

Marine farms
13.8

1   Marine farms may be encountered in the waters of this chapter and should be avoided. Farms in proximity to shipping routes are generally marked by buoys. Other farms are marked by beacons (X topmark) and some are fitted with radar reflectors. Lights, when fitted, show flashing yellow. See 1.29.

Tidal streams
13.9

1   The tides in Baie de Seine, especially those at Le Havre and in La Seine Maritime, are remarkable for their stand at HW.

From outside a line joining Pointe de Barfleur and Cap d'Antifer the E-going and W-going streams of the English Channel bend slightly inwards towards Baie de Seine; off the W side of the bay the E-going stream runs more S'ly and off the E side of the bay more N'ly than in mid-channel, and similarly the W-going stream tends to run in the opposite direction.

2   In the bay itself and near the coast along the S shore the streams are more of less rectilinear; within 2 or 3 miles of the S shore they do not exceed 1½ kn in each direction but farther seaward, notably in the middle of the bay, they can attain or even exceed 2 kn.

The times at which the streams begin become later from E to W, and later from S to N.

3   Off the E side of Cotentin Peninsula the S-going stream is weaker and of shorter duration than the stream in the opposite direction.

For details see information on the chart and *Admiralty Tidal Stream Atlas for The English Channel.*

Regulations concerning vessels carrying dangerous and polluting goods
13.10

1   For regulations concerning vessels laden with dangerous and polluting goods navigating in the approaches to the N and W coasts of France, see 1.68 to 1.76.

POINTE DE BARFLEUR TO LA SEINE

General information

Chart 2613
Route
13.11

1   From a position N of Pointe de Barfleur (49°42′N 1°16′W) the passage to Le Havre approaches leads generally ESE, about 45 miles.

Topography
13.12

1   The coast between Pointe de Barfleur and Pointe de Saire, 5½ miles SSE, is bordered by rocks and shoals, some of which dry, extending in places up to 1¼ miles offshore. The coast is backed by wooded hills in the vicinity of La Pernelle (13.16), 3 miles W of Pointe de Saire. The high land of La Butte de Montaigu with a prominent summit (49°33′N 1°25′W) forms a prominent mark in the hinterland.

2   The coast from Saint-Vaast-la-Hougue (49°35′N 1°16′W) to Banc de la Madeleine (49°25′N 1°10′W) (13.39), 11 miles SSE, is low and fringed with wooded dunes; the coastal bank of sand and rocky ledges extends in places 1½ miles offshore. On the coast above Banc de la Madeleine stands a monument commemorating the Allied invasion landings of World War II in June 1944 on Utah Beach which extends to the NW of the bank. The remains of an artificial harbour lie off this beach.

3   The coast of the Département du Calvados from Grandcamp-Maisy (49°23′N 1°03′W) to the mouth of Rivière L'Orne, 32 miles E, is about 30 to 60 m high. From Grandcamp-Maisy the coast gradually rises to Pointe de la Percée (49°24′N 0°55′W) (13.53), 5 miles E, from whence it is composed of grey cliffs as far as Port-en-Bessin (49°21′N 0°45′W). The United States War Cemetery situated on a hill dominating the coast in the vicinity of Saint-Laurent-sur-Mer, about 3 miles ESE of Pointe de la Percée, is a prominent mark.

4   Between Arromanches-les-Bains (49°20′N 0°37′W) and Ouistreham, 15 miles ESE, the coast is bordered by the rocky Plateau du Calvados (13.60) which extends in places over 2 miles offshore. This coast affords no shelter during winds from W through N to E.

Temporary explosives dumping grounds
13.13

1   Temporary explosives dumping grounds (Zones de Dépôts d'Explosifs) are situated:

> SE of the entrance to Saint-Vaast-la-Hougue (49°35′N 1°16′W), for Barfleur and Saint-Vaast-la-Hougue.
>
> N of Grandcamp-Maisy (49°23′N 1°03′W).

2
> NNW of the entrance to Port-en-Bessin (49°21′N 0°45′W).
>
> NNE of the entrance to Courseulles-sur-Mer (49°20′N 0°27′W).
>
> NE of the entrance to Ouistreham (49°17′N 0°15′W) for Ouistreham and Dives-sur-Mer (49°18′N 0°05′W).

For details see 1.7 and Appendix V.

Rescue
13.14

1   **All-weather lifeboats** are stationed at:
> Barfleur (49°40′N 1°15′W) (13.19).
> Ouistreham (49°17′N 0°15′W) (13.67).

Inshore lifeboats are maintained at:
> Saint-Vaast-la-Hougue (49°35′N 1°16′W) (13.28).
> Grandcamp-Maisy (49°23′N 1°03′W) (13.47).
> Port-en-Bessin (49°21′N 0°45′W) (13.53).

2
> Courseulles-sur-Mer (49°20′N 0°27′W) (13.60).
> Cabourg-Dives-sur-Mer (49°18′N 0°05′W) (13.93).

For details of lifeboats, see 1.117.

Signal station (Vigie) (49°21′N 0°46′W) (13.16) is situated at Port-en-Bessin, for details see 1.95 and 1.110.

3   **VHF Direction-finding stations,** for emergency use only, operate from:

Barfleur (49°42′N 1°16′W).
Saint-Vaast-la-Hougue (49°35′N 1°16′W).
Port-en-Bessin (49°21′N 0°46′W).
For details see *Admiralty List of Radio Signals Volume 2.*

Tidal streams
13.15

1   In a position 2 miles offshore between Pointe de Barfleur and Pointe de Saire (49°36′N 1°14′W) the tidal streams begin as follows:

Interval from HW Le Havre	Direction
+0540	SSE
−0205	NNW

The maximum spring rates are 2¾ kn.

Directions
(continued from 12.77)

Principal marks
13.16

1   **Landmarks:**

Belfrey of La Pernelle Church (49°37′N 1°18′W) standing on the E slopes of the wooded hills of La Pernelle which slope gently N.

Broad Tower (turret on one side) (49°35′N 1°14′W) on the S extremity of Île de Tatihou, the low Fort de l'Îlet stands close S.

2   Water Tower (49°31′N 1°21′W) standing 1¾ miles W of Quinéville church (pointed belfry).

Church (spire) (49°23′N 1°03′W) on the higher land behind Grandcamp-Maisy.

3   Water Tower (49°22′N 0°56′W) standing 1 mile WSW of Vierville-sur-Mer church.

Pylon (red obstruction lights) (49°20′N 0°49′W) standing 1 mile ESE of Colleville-sur-Mer Church.

4   Signal Station (49°21′N 0°46′W) situated 5 cables W of Port-en-Bessin.

Water Tower (49°20′N 0°43′W) standing 1¾ miles ESE of Port-en-Bessin.

Statue (49°20′N 0°37′W) standing on the crest of a hill 2 cables E of Arromanches-les-Bains.

Ver Lighthouse (white tower grey top, 16 m in height) (49°20′N 0°31′W) situated amid trees on a hill.

5   **Major lights:**

Pointe de Barfleur-Gatteville Light (49°42′N 1°16′W) (12.9).

Ver Light — as above.

Ouistreham Main Light (49°17′N 0°15′W) (13.79).

Cap de la Hève Light (49°31′N 0°04′E) (13.114).

Cap d'Antifer Light (49°41′N 0°10′E) (13.211).

Other aids to navigation
13.17

Racons:

LHA Light Buoy (49°31′N 0°10′W).
Antifer A5 Light Buoy (49°46′N 0°17′W).
No2 Light Buoy (port hand) (49°27′·5N 0°01′·4E).
For details see *Admiralty List of Radio Signals Volume 2.*

Charts 1106, 2146, 2613

Pointe de Barfleur to the approaches to Le Havre
13.18

1   From a position N of Pointe de Barfleur (49°42′N 1°16′W) (12.77) the route leads generally ESE across Baie de Seine (13.2) passing:

NNE of Pointe de Barfleur, giving the point a wide berth; thence:

NNE of an obstruction (position doubtful) (49°33′·4N 0°48′·5W.); thence:

NNE of a 14·3 m wreck (49°30′N 0°43′W) marked on its W side by Cussy Light Buoy (W cardinal); thence:

2   Clear of a dangerous wreck (49°35′N 0°22′W) to the vicinity of LHA Light Buoy (49°31′N 0°10′W) (13.137). A wreck with a depth of 11·2 m over it (49°30′N 0°14′W) lies 3 miles WSW of the lanby. Dangerous wrecks (positions doubtful) are charted 2 miles WSW and S of the 11·2 m wreck.

3   **Useful marks:**

Le Havre Leading Lights (49°29′N 0°07′E) (13.138).

(Directions continue, for Le Havre at 13.135 and for La Seine Maritime at 13.170)

Barfleur and approaches

Charts 1106, 2135, 2613

General information
13.19

1   **Position and function.** Port de Barfleur (49°40′N 1°15′W), a small drying harbour situated about 1½ miles SSE of Pointe de Barfleur, is used by fishing and small craft.

2   **Topography.** Barfleur Church (square belfry tower) (49°40′·4N 1°15′·6W) and the entrance moles are easily identified in the approach. Pointe du Moulard (49°39′N 1°14′W) from which the coastal bank extends nearly 1 mile offshore is situated 1¼ miles SE of Barfleur. A beacon (E cardinal) marks the outer edge of the drying rocks off Pointe du Moulard and a white tower stands on the rocks about midway between the beacon and the shore.

3   **Approach and entry.** The harbour is approached from Baie de Seine through a channel which is bordered on both sides by rocky shoals, several of which dry, and is entered between two moles.

Limiting conditions
13.20

1   **Controlling depths.** The harbour, which is protected by two moles, completely dries out.

Tidal levels, see information in *Admiralty Tide Tables.* Mean spring range about 5·4 m; mean neap range about 2·8 m.

Maximum size of vessel handled. The harbour can accept fishing and leisure vessels up to 4 m draught.

Local weather. Fresh winds from between NE and E cause a heavy scend in the harbour.

Arrival information
13.21

1   **Outer anchorage.** Anchorage can be obtained in the approach channel in depths of 8 to 10 m, sand and mud; the holding ground is indifferent. Mariners in small craft can obtain anchorage, sheltered from all directions except E and NE, in the bay situated 3 cables NW of the harbour entrance.

Pilotage. Local fishermen are available for use as pilots.

Harbour
13.22

1 **General layout.** The port comprises a small drying harbour protected by two moles.

Tidal streams. About 1 mile NE of the harbour the duration of the E-going stream (direction S) is about 3½ hours only, the streams begins as follows:

Interval from HW Le Havre	Direction
+0520	S
–0220	N

The maximum spring rates are 2 kn.

Directions for entering harbour
13.23

1 **Approaching Barfleur from north and east** mariners should avoid Raz de Barfleur (12.77).

Approaching from north-east. The high land of La Pernelle (49°37′N 1°18′W) (13.16) will be seen dropping sharply towards the E and separated from the high land extending W by Coupée du Vast, a prominent cleft, bearing 217° from Pointe de Barfleur (49°42′N 1°16′W).

2 **From east** mariners will first sight the high land of La Butte de Montaigu (49°33′N 1°25′W) (13.12).

In low visibility it is advisable not to attempt to make Pointe de Barfleur because of the dangers which extend from it.

Leading lights:
> Front light (white square tower, 7 m in height) (49°40′·2N 1°15′·6W) situated within the harbour on the S side.

3 > Rear light (grey and white square tower green top, 13 m in height) (1½ cables SW of the front light). The leading marks are not very conspicuous and mariners should not mistake the low light-structure on Jetée Est (white hut red top, 4 m in height) standing at the head, which is painted white, of the E mole, for the front leading light which is within the harbour.

4 From a position NE of Barfleur the alignment (219½°) of these lights leads in the approach to the harbour passing (with positions given from Barfleur Church (49°40′N 1°16′W)):
> SE of Riden des Dents (1 mile NE), the outermost danger on the NW side of the channel; thence:

5 > SE of La Grotte (9 cables NNE), marked on its SE side by La Grotte Buoy (starboard hand); thence:

> Between Roche des Anglais (6 cables NE), marked on its E side by Roche-a-l'Anglais Buoy (starboard hand), and Le Hintar (5 cables ENE), a drying rock, marked on its N side by Le Hintar Buoy (port hand) on the N side of Plateau des Antiquaires; thence:

6 > SE of Roche Vimberge (3½ cables NE), marked on its S side by La Vimberge Buoy (starboard hand); and:

> NW of La Raie (3 cables ENE), marked on its N side by a beacon (port hand), and La Grosse Haie (2 cables E) marked on its N extremity by a beacon tower (port hand), both part of a drying reef extending NE from the S entrance of the harbour.

7 When within two or three cables of the harbour entrance, depending upon height of tide, the leading marks will be obscured by the E mole and the track should be adjusted to enter harbour passing between Rocher Rond (¾ cable E), marked by a beacon (starboard hand) and the head of the E mole; the width between the rock and the head of the mole is about 40 m.

8 **Useful marks:**
> Jetée Ouest Light (white pylon green top, 7 m in height) (49°40′·4N 1°15′·6W) standing over a white patch at the head of the W mole.
> Montfarville Church (belfry) (49°39′·3N 1°16′·2W) standing 1 mile SW of Barfleur.

Berths
13.24

1 The N and W sides of the harbour are quayed and vessels and yachts can lie alongside on a bottom of muddy sand and gravel; the N side dries from 2 to 2·8 m, and the W side from 2·8 to 4 m. The S side is encumbered with rocks extending ½ cable offshore.

Port services
13.25

1 **Facilities:** fuel; water; provisions.

Rescue. A lifeboat house (13.14) and slip are situated on the NE side of the W mole.

Anchorages

Chart 2135
Rade de Saint-Vaast
13.26

1 For details of the anchorages at Rade de Saint-Vaast (49°34′N 1°14′W), see 13.31.

Channel between Îles Saint-Marcouf and the coast of France
13.27

1 **General information.** The channel between the coast of France and the banks extending NW and SE from Îles Saint-Marcouf (49°30′N 1°09′W), two low-lying islands, affords good anchorage in moderate weather and with offshore winds. In the area W and SW of Îles Saint-Marcouf the bottom is rocky almost the whole way across the channel and is not recommended for anchorage.

2 **Îles Saint-Marcouf** (49°30′N 1°09′W), situated 6½ miles SE of Fort de la Hougue and 4 miles offshore, consist of Île du Large, from which a light (13.36) is exhibited, and Île de Terre, 3 cables SW; both of these islands are low. A small boat harbour is situated on the W side of Île du Large and Île de Terre is a bird sanctuary; landing is prohibited on this latter isle.

3 **Anchorage.** There is temporary anchorage for mariners in small craft, by day and in good weather, SW of Île du Large in depths of about 5 m close ESE of a beacon (S cardinal) which stands on drying rocks about 1 cable WSW of the harbour. Temporary anchorage is also available SE of Île de Terre. A submarine cable is laid SW from Îles Saint-Marcouf to the coast.

4 There is an anchorage, with good holding ground, sheltered from winds between S and SW in Rade de la Capelle (49°26′N 1°05′W) which lies between Banc du Cardonnet, extending 6 miles SE from Îles Saint-Marcouf, and Baie du Grand Vey (13.39) in depths of about 12 m, sand and mud; a recommended berth is shown on the chart. Est du Cardonnet Light Buoy (E cardinal) (49°27′N 1°01′W) is moored off the SE extremity of the bank and a wreck, marked on its NE side by Norfolk Light Buoy (E cardinal), lies on the N side of the bank 3½ miles ESE of Île du Large. CI Light Buoy (safe water) (49°26′N 1°07′W) (13.42), on the SW side of the anchorage, is moored 3 miles NW of Pointe de Maisy.

5   **Caution.** Numerous wrecks, the positions and types of which can best be seen from the chart, lie on and in the vicinity of Banc du Cardonnet and the roadstead.

Saint-Vaast-la-Hougue and approaches

Chart 2135
General information
13.28
1   **Position and function.** The port of Saint-Vaast-la-Hougue (49°35′N 1°16′W) is situated about 5 miles S of Barfleur, and is used by fishing vessels and pleasure craft.

Rade de Saint-Vaast (13.31), comprising two well sheltered anchorages, is situated SSE of the harbour.

2   **Topography.** Between Pointe de Saire (49°36′N 1°14′W) and the point on which stands the small town of Saint-Vaast-la-Hougue, 1¾ miles SW, the coast forms a bay at the head of which Rivière Saire flows into the sea. Drying sands, on which there are rocky ledges, fill the whole of this bay and extend SE of it. Le Pont de Saire, with depths of less than 5 m over it, extends nearly 8 cables SE from Pointe de Saire; during the NE-going stream onshore winds cause a heavy sea on Le Pont de Saire. A rock which covers and uncovers (position approximate) lies 5½ cables SSE of Pointe de Saire.

3   Fort de la Hougue (high tower surmounted by a turret), joined to the coast by a breakwater, lies near the SSW end of a bank of drying sands and rocks which extends nearly 1 mile SSW and 5 cables E from the coast in the vicinity of Saint-Vaast-la-Hougue. Îles Saint-Marcouf (49°30′N 1°09′W), two low-lying islands, are situated 6½ miles SE of Fort de la Hougue.

4   **Approach and entry.** The port is approached from Baie de Seine from E through Passe du Nord, or from S from W of Îles Saint-Marcouf, and entered between Île de Tatihou and a mole extending ENE from the E extremity of the town.

Limiting conditions
13.29
1   **Controlling depths.** The harbour consists of Avant-port, which dries, leading to an inner wet basin.

Tidal levels, see information in *Admiralty Tide Tables.* Mean spring range about 5·7 m; mean neap range about 3·0 m.

Maximum size of vessel handled. The inner wet basin is accessible to vessels up to 2·2 m draught.

Local weather. Fresh winds from between NE and SE cause a heavy scend in Avant-port near HW.

Arrival information
13.30
1   **Port radio** station, with limited hours, operates from Saint-Vaast-la-Hougue Marina, for details see *Admiralty List of Radio Signals Volume 6(1).*

Local knowledge is required.

Traffic regulations. Vessels entering the port have priority. There is a speed limit of 4 kn in the port.

Prohibited anchorage. Anchoring or touching bottom is prohibited to the N of Avant-port owing to shellfish beds, see information on the chart.

Harbour
13.31
1   **General layout.** Rade de Saint-Vaast (49°34′N 1°14′W), which is sheltered from W winds and the prevailing

weather, consists of the anchorages of Grande Rade and Petite Rade (13.35). These anchorages are subject to the agreement of the local maritime authority; permission for anchorage must be received through CROSS JOBOURG or Barfleur Signal Station.

2   The port consists of an Avant-port, which dries, protected from S by a jetty extending 2¼ cables ENE from the E extremity of the town. A short spur projects NNE from near the root of Avant-port jetty.

An inner wet basin, which is entered through lock gates and sheltered from N and E by a breakwater, is situated NW of Avant-port.
13.32
1   **Tidal streams.** In Grande Rade the stream begins as follows:

Interval from HW Le Havre	Direction
−0545	SW to W
−0035	NNE

The maximum spring rates are ¾ to 1 kn.

The stream runs N towards the land for a short period when changing direction clockwise from W to NNE and again when changing direction anti-clockwise from NNE to SW.

2   In Petite Rade an eddy runs N during the period the stream is running to the SW and W in Grande Rade, the streams begin as follows:

Interval from HW Le Havre	Direction
+0605	N
−0120	NE

The maximum spring rates are 1¾ kn.

3   **Eddy.** During the whole of the N-going tidal stream in Petite Rade a W-going eddy runs N of Avant-port jetty and across the entrance to the wet basin.

Directions for entering harbour
13.33
1   **Approaching Rade de Saint-Vaast from east through Passe du Nord — leading lights.** From a position E of Île de Tatihou (49°35′N 1°14′W) (13.16) the alignment (267°) of the following lights leads through Passe du Nord passing S of Basse de la Pernelle (49°36′N 1°11′W) to a position N of Banc de la Rade (13.37).

2   Front mark. La Hougue Light (white pylon green top, 7 m in height) (49°34′·3N 1°16′·4W) situated on the S end of Fort de la Hougue.

Rear mark. Morsalines Light (white octagonal tower green top, 13 m in height) (1¾ miles W of the front mark).

If proceeding to Petite Rade, and draught permitting, continue on the 267° alignment passing close S of Plateau du Ouest-Drix (13.37).

3   **If proceeding to Grande Rade,** on the alignment (345½°) of Pointe de Saire Light (white tower green top, 10 m in height) (49°36′N 1°14′W) with Barfleur-Gatteville Light, 5½ miles NNW (12.9), or alternatively, on the line of bearing 311° of La Pernelle Church (49°37′N 1°18′W) open NE of Île de Tatihou Tower, 3 miles SE (13.16), the recommended track leads 228°, as shown on the chart, to anchorage in Grande Rade (13.37).

4   **Side passage.** A passage with a depth of 7·7 m lies between Plateau du Ouest-Drix and La Dent Buoy (S cardinal) moored S of Le Gavendest and La Dent (13.37) which leads into Petite Rade.

13.34

1   **Approaching Rade de Saint-Vaast from south — leading marks:**

> Front mark. Île de Tatihou pierhead (49°35′·4N 1°14′·9W) on the W extremity of the island.
>
> Rear mark. Réville Church (spire) (2 miles N of the front mark).

2   From a position W of Ouest Saint-Marcouf Light Buoy (W cardinal) (49°30′N 1°12′W) marking the W side of the extremity of the dangers off Banc de Saint-Marcouf, on which the sea breaks heavily during fresh winds from between N and NE and which extends about 2½ miles NW from Îles Saint-Marcouf, the alignment (349°) of these marks leads through Passe du Sud passing (with positions given from Île de Tatihou tower):

3
> E of Roches Saint-Floxel (5 miles S) marked by a buoy (E cardinal) moored 1 mile ENE; thence:
>
> Along the W side of Banc de la Rade (13.37); Quinéville Light Buoy (W cardinal) (3¾ miles SSE) is moored near the S end of this bank. Thence:
>
> To Rade de Saint-Vaast (13.31) or harbour (13.35) as required.

13.35

1   **Harbour.** From a position in Petite Rade, clear of Plateau du Ouest-Drix, the white sector (310°–350°) of Saint-Vaast-la-Hougue jetty light (white octagonal metal tower red top, 11 m in height) (49°35′·2N 1°15′·3W) standing over a white patch at the head of the jetty leads towards the harbour. The entrance, about 30 m wide, lies between the head of Avant-port jetty spur, on the S side, and the head of the breakwater, on the N side; lights (white hut red top, 6 m in height) and (white tank, green top, 6 m in height) are exhibited over white patches on either side of this entrance.

13.36

1   **Useful marks:**

> Dranguet Beacon Tower (E cardinal, 18 m in height) (49°36′·8N 1°13′·0W) marking the E extremity of Roches Dranguet.
>
> Le Vitéquet Beacon (S cardinal, 11 m in height) (49°36′·1N 1°13′·4W) standing at the S extremity of the drying part of Roches de Saire.
>
> Île du Large Light (square grey tower green top, 17 m in height) (49°30′N 1°09′W).

Basins and berths

13.37

1   **Grande Rade.** There is anchorage available in Grande Rade situated between Banc de la Rade, a bank of shifting sand extending about 2 miles SSE from a position 2¼ miles ESE of Fort de la Hougue, and the coast in depths of 14 m, sand, mud and clay. The holding ground is good but onshore winds cause a heavy sea. A recommended anchorage is shown on the chart.

2   **Petite Rade,** situated N of Grande Rade, between the bank extending E from Fort de la Hougue and Plateau du Ouest-Drix, 1 mile E, affords anchorage sheltered during winds from S, through W, to NE, in depths of 2 to 6 m, mud; the holding ground is good. The extremities of the bank are marked by Le Creux de Bas Beacon (E cardinal), on the N, Le Bout du Roc Buoy (E cardinal) and Le Manquet Buoy (E cardinal) on the E and by Les Molquants Beacon (special), on the S, which stands close off the SW extremity of the fort. La Dent and Le Gavendest, drying rocks, are the outermost of a chain of rocks extending about 6 cables SSE from Fort de l'Îlet (13.16) on the E

side of the anchorage; these dangers are marked on their S sides by a buoy (S cardinal). Recommended anchorages are shown on the chart.

3   **Avant-port** dries completely. Drying berths, mud are available on the N side of Avant-port jetty.

Wet basin. Lock gates 16 m wide, with a depth over the sill of 1·7 m above chart datum, permit access to the wet basin, which has a least depth of 2·3 m, from 2¼ hours before to 3 hours after HW. Two quays on the S and SW side of the basin are reserved for fishing vessels.

Port services

13.38

1   **Repairs.** Hard between Avant-port spur and the Wet Basin with a slip for yachts and fishing craft. Small repairs can be undertaken. A 45 tonne boat hoist is available.

Supplies: fuel; fresh water; stores and provisions.

Rescue, see 13.14.

Baie du Grand Vey

Chart 2135

General information

13.39

1   **Description.** Baie du Grand Vey is entered between Pointe de Maisy (49°23′N 1°05′W), in the E, and Banc de la Madeleine fronting the coast of Cotentin Peninsula, in the W. Two buoyed channels, Passe de Carentan and Passe d'Isigny, lead through the bay between drying sandbanks, on which it is very dangerous to strand, to the minor ports of Carentan (13.41) and Isigny-sur-Mer (13.44).

2   The coast in the vicinity of Pointe de Maisy and the port of Grandcamp-Maisy (13.47), about 1½ miles E, is bordered by Roches de Grandcamp which dry and extend in places over 1 mile offshore; they are marked on their seaward side by No 1, No 3 and No 5 Buoys (N cardinal).

3   **Limiting conditions.** There is a high sea in the bay during onshore winds and mariners bound for Carentan and Isigny-sur-Mer should not attempt to reach these ports except in fine weather and at HW.

Local knowledge, or the use of a pilot, is required for Passes de Carentan and d'Isigny.

13.40

1   **Tidal streams.** In Passe d'Isigny the tidal streams begin as follows:

Interval from HW Le Havre	*Direction*
–0615	S
–0015	NNE

The maximum spring rates are 2¼ kn.

Carentan

13.41

1   **General information.** The port of Carentan (49°18′N 1°14′W) is situated 4½ miles inland from the head of Baie du Grand Vey, 1 mile SW of the confluence of Rivière Taute and Rivière Douve, both of which flow into the sea through Passe de Carentan.

13.42

1   **Directions.** Passe de Carentan, which dries 3·4 m, leads to the SW part of Baie du Grand Vey. Its outer part is marked by light buoys and buoys which are moved as necessary to meet changes in the depths. The inner part is contained between breakwaters which are submerged near HW; the breakwaters are marked by lighted beacons at the seaward end.

2   From a position in the vicinity of C-I Landfall Light Buoy (safe water) (49°26′N 1°07′W), which marks the entrance to Passe de Carentan and the approach to Passe d'Isigny, moored 3 miles NW of Pointe de Maisy, the alignment (209½°) of the following lights leads through that part of Passe de Carentan between the breakwaters:

3   Front light (white post red top, 6 m in height) (49°20′·5N 1°11′·2W) a direction light intensified between the bearings 208¼°–210¾° standing at the root of the E breakwater.

Rear light (white gantry green top, 15 m in height) (4 cables SSW of the front light.

Caution. Tidal streams make entry very difficult during W winds.

13.43

1   **Berths.** A wet basin about 8 cables long and 60 m wide extends NE from the town of Carentan to the head of Passe de Carentan where the two rivers meet. The water in the wet basin is retained by lock gates which are opened from 2 hours before to 3 hours after HW. The basin is dredged to 3·4 m and has a quay for larger vessels.

Facilities: slipways; fuel; fresh water; provisions.

Isigny-sur-Mer
13.44

1   **General information.** The port of Isigny-sur-Mer (49°19′N 1°06′W), a small fishing port which is also used by small coasting vessels, is situated on Rivière Aure about 1½ miles inland. The port is entered through Passe d'Isigny and dries, but can accommodate vessels of 55 m in length, 12 m beam and draughts of 4·2 m at spring tides and 2·2 m at neap tides.

Entry from the open sea is not recommended at night, or in bad weather from the NW or NE.

13.45

1   **Directions.** Passe d'Isigny, is marked by buoys which are frequently moved to meet changes in the depths. The embanked channel, marked by beacons and about 85 m wide, extends for 1¾ miles S from Pointe du Grouin (49°22′N 1°07′W) to the confluence of Rivière L'Aure and Rivière La Vire. IS Buoy (N cardinal) which marks the entrance to Passe d'Isigny is moored about 3 miles N of

Pointe du Grouin. There are oyster beds on Banc de Rouelle on the E side of the channel and a beacon (starboard hand) stands in the channel, 5 cables NNW of Pointe du Grouin.

2   From a position in the vicinity of Pointe du Grouin the alignment (172½°) of the following lights, which are direction lights and intensified between the bearings 170½°–174½°, leads through the embanked channel:

Front light (white post, 7 m in height) (49°19′·6N 1°06′·8W) situated on the point of confluence of the two rivers.

Rear light (white pylon black top, 23 m in height) (3¼ cables S of the front mark).

13.46

1   **Berths.** New Quay, about 200 m long with soft mud berths alongside drying 4 m and pontoon berths for yachts, is situated on the SW bank of the river in the lower part of the harbour. Upstream of this quay there is turning room on average tides for vessels up to 45 m in length and at spring tides for vessels up to 55 m in length.

2   The upper part of the harbour near the road bridge is 25 m wide and is quayed for about 340 m on both sides, the berths dry from 3 to 3·5 m.

Port services: careening slip at the end of the quay on the NE side of the river; fuel; fresh water; provisions.

Grandcamp-Maisy and approaches

Chart 1349 Plan of Grancamp-Maisy, 2135

General information
13.47

1   **Position and function.** The port of Grandcamp-Maisy (49°23′N 1°03′W), a small fishing and leisure port with a wet basin, is situated at the W end of the town of that name.

Limiting conditions
13.48

1   **Controlling depths.** The access channel dries 2 m.

Port de Grandcamp-Maisy from SE (13.47)

(Original dated 2002)

(Photograph - Service Hydrographique et Océanographique de la Marine)

Harbour

13.49

1   **General layout.** The port comprises a wet basin, with a lock gate, entered through an entrance channel.

Directions for entering harbour

13.50

1   **Leading lights:**

Front light (platform on white metal tube red top, 7 m in height) (49°23′·4N 1°02′·9W) standing near the root of the E mole.

Rear light (white mast red daymark, 11 m in height) (102 m SE of the front mark) standing close E of the entrance.

2   From a position in Rade de la Capelle (49°26′N 1°05′W) (13.27) the alignment (146°) of these lights, which are direction lights and exhibited 1½° on each side of the leading line, leads over Roches de Grandcamp (13.39) between No 3 and No 5 Buoys (N cardinal) (49°25′N 1°04′W) to the harbour entrance channel which is protected by two diverging jetties with a least width of 18 m between them at their roots and each prolonged by a rock extension which covers at HW. A light (white column red top, 8 m in height) and (white column green top, 14 m in height) is exhibited from the head of the E and W rock extensions, respectively.

3   **Useful marks:**

Perré Light (green pylon on white hut, 7 m in height) (49°23′·3N 1°02′·5W) standing on the coast about 2½ cables E of the entrance.

La Maresquerie Light (white post, 12 m in height) (49°23′·2N 1°02′·8W) standing in the town about 1½ cables SE of the wet basin.

Wet basin

13.51

1   The wet basin, with depths of 2·5 m above chart datum, is entered through a passage fitted with a lock gate at its S end; the passage is 14·3 m wide and the sill dries 2·3 m. The lock gate is opened from 2½ hours before to 2½ hours after local HW. Sluicing of the channel takes place at springs and is signalled 24 hours in advance by a blue flag hoisted at the lock gate.

2   **Berths.** Quays on the E and S sides of the basin are reserved for fishing vessels.

Port services

13.52

1   **Repairs:** marine railway and slips.
Supplies: fuel; fresh water; provisions.
Rescue, see 13.14.

Port-en-Bessin and approaches

Chart 1349 Plan of Port-en-Bassin, 2136

General information

13.53

1   **Position and function.** Port-en-Bessin (49°21′N 0°45′W), a drying fishing port with limited facilites for leisure craft, is situated on the coast about 5 miles NNW of Bayeux. The depression in the cliffs in which the harbour lies and inland the spires of Bayeux Cathedral, 5 miles SSE, aid identification.

Approach and entry. The port is approached from Baie de Seine on leading lights and entered between two moles.

2   **Offshore dangers.** Between Pointe de la Percée (49°24′N 0°55′W) and Port-en-Bessin the coast is bordered by a bank on which lie some rocky ledges extending in

places 1 mile offshore. Raz de la Percée, a tidal race, is formed off Pointe de la Percée when the wind is against the tidal stream. A dangerous area, extending from 1 to 3½ miles ESE from Pointe de la Percée and about 1 mile offshore, exists due to the remains of blockships and other obstructions which formed the artificial harbour off Omaha Beach during the Allied invasion landings of World War II in June 1944. This dangerous area is marked to seaward by three buoys (N cardinal) and is covered by the green sector (065°–114½°) of the light on the W mole of Port-en-Bessin harbour. A 2·4 m wreck (49°25′·3N 0°53′·2W), marked on its NE side by Broadsword Light Buoy (E cardinal), and a dangerous wreck (position doubtful) 1¾ miles NNW of the light buoy are the outermost dangers off this area.

Limiting conditions

13.54

1   **Controlling depths.** The entrance channel dries 2 m. The best time to enter the port is at the stand of tide at local HW.

Limiting draughts in the wet basins are 4·2 m at spring tides and 2·6 m at neap tides.

2   **Tidal levels,** see information in *Admiralty Tide Tables.* Mean spring range about 6·1 m; mean neap range about 3·3 m.

Local weather and sea state. The use of the port is not recommended during strong winds from between NW and NE when a very dangerous surf is caused in the outer Avant-port.

Arrival information

13.55

1   **Outer anchorage.** Mariners awaiting the tide to enter Port-en- Bessin can anchor off the entrance in depths of 3 m,, where the holding ground is good.

Prohibited anchorage. Anchoring and fishing are prohibited 1 cable either side of the leading line approach to the port, as shown on the chart.

Harbour

13.56

1   **General layout.** The port consists of an outer and inner Avant-port and two long narrow wet basins separated by two short spurs.

Traffic signals from the simplified code (1.93) are in use. A signal station (13.16) is situated about 7 cables W of the harbour entrance.

2   **Tidal streams** run parallel to the coast off Port-en-Bessin, for details see information on the chart.

At the extremity of the E mole, a local eddy which does not exceed 1 kn, runs W during the E-going stream.

Directions for entering harbour

13.57

1   **Leading lights:**

The alignment (204°) of the following lights leads into Avant-port passing through the entrance channel, 100 m wide, which lies between two moles the heads of which are painted white. A light (red pylon and green pylon, 10 and 9 m in height) is exhibited from the head of the E and W moles, respectively.

2   Front light (white pylon green top, 8 m in height) (49°21′·0N 0°45′·5W) situated on the cliff near the W edge of the town.

Rear light (white and grey house, 12 m in height) (93 m SSW of the front mark).

Caution. Dangerous wrecks (positions doubtful) lie 6¼ cables N and 2 miles NNE of the entrance.

Basins and berths
13.58

1 **Avant-port** is divided into an outer and inner part by two spurs, Épi Ouest and Épi Est, which extend from the S side of Avant-port and the middle of Jetée de l'Est, the E mole. A rock breakwater, which covers, extends 100 m NW from Épi Est; its NW extremity is marked by a beacon (port hand). Avant-port dries about 2·5 m except on the E side of the inner part where it dries 3 m. The channel through it dries 2 m and is maintained by periodical sluicing which is signalled 24 hours in advance by a blue flag hoisted at the lock gates.

2 In good weather vessels can berth in the inner part of Avant-port at Épi Est and at Épi Ouest, known as Épi de la Poissonnerie.

Wet basins. Access to the wet basins is through a long passage, 10·5 m wide, with a swing bridge at its outer end and a lock gate at its inner end; the sill of the passage dries 2 m. The lock gate is opened by day and night from 2 hours before to 2 hours after HW. The outer basin is quayed on its W side and the inner basin, access to which is through an opening 10 m wide, is quayed on both sides.

Port services
13.59

1 **Repairs:** gridiron, two slips, the largest for vessels up to 26 m in length, 8 m breadth and 200 tonnes deadweight; limited repair facilities.

Supplies: fuel; fresh water; provisions.

Rescue, see 13.14.

Courseulles-sur-Mer and approaches

Charts 1349 Plan of Courselle-sur-Mer, 2136
General information
13.60

1 **Position and function.** Courseulles-sur-Mer (49°20′N 0°27′W), a small fishing and leisure port is situated at the mouth of Rivière La Seulles which flows into the sea through shifting sandbanks, is also a popular yacht harbour with two marinas.

2 **Offshore features.** A dangerous area extending about 2 miles E from Cap Manvieux (49°21′N 0°39′W) and about 8 cables offshore contains the remains of Port Winston, used for the Allied invasion landings on Gold Beach during World War II in 1944. A passage between the blockships is marked by a pair of buoys; access to the blockships is prohibited. Plateau du Calvados, with depths of less than 9 m over it, extends about 2 miles offshore between Cap Manvieux and Langrune-sur-Mer, about 4 miles ESE of Courseulles-sur-Mer. Rochers du Calvados forms the W part of this plateau. Les Roches de Ver lie on the centre part of this plateau and consist of rocks which dry or are awash, extending about 8 cables offshore.

Limiting conditions
13.61

1 **Controlling depths.** The access channel to the harbour dries 2·7 m.

Tidal levels, see information in *Admiralty Tide Tables.* Mean spring range about 6·3 m; mean neap range about 3·4 m.

Maximum size of vessel handled. Vessels up to 3·5 m draught can be accommodated at spring tides.

2 **Local weather and sea state.** The approach to the harbour is dangerous during onshore winds; the best time for entry is at the HW stand which lasts for 1½ hours.

Arrival information
13.62

1 **Outer anchorages.** Anchorage can be obtained about 2 cables NNW of Roche de la Marguerite (49°21′·1N 0°27′·5W), in the vicinity of Courseulles Light Buoy (safe water) (13.64) in depths of about 6 m. Anchorage can also be obtained about 2 cables ESE of Roche de la Marguerite in L'Anneau de la Marguerite, a deep situated about 8 cables N of the entrance, in depths of 3 to 4 m, mudas shown on the chart. A patch drying 0·1 m lies about 3½ cables E of Roche de la Marguerite.

2 An indifferent anchorage outside port limits, normally used only by local fishing boats during offshore winds, may be found in Fosse d'Espagne (49°21′N 0°37′W), as shown on the chart, inside the remains of the artificial harbour (13.60) but clear of an obstruction marked by four white buoys.

Pilotage and local knowledge. There are no pilots; local knowledge is recommended.

Harbour
13.63

1 **General layout.** The port consists of an Avant-port leading to a wet-dock, and a tidal basin, reserved for yachts, NW of Avant-port with minimum depths maintained by a sill.

Tidal streams at a position 1 mile N of the harbour do not exceed 1 to 1½ kn; the direction is variable.

Directions for entering harbour
13.64

1 **Leading marks:**

From W the alignment (133½°) of the following marks leads in the approach passing NE of Les Roches de Ver (13.60) and Roche de la Marguerite situated 1½ miles NW and 8 cables N, respectively, of the entrance, passing clear of Courseulles Light Buoy (safe water) moored 2½ cables NNW of the rock.

2 Front mark. Bernières-sur-Mer Church (tower) (49°19′·9N 0°25′·4W).

Rear mark. Douvres-la-Déliverande Church (twin spires) (2¾ miles SE of the front mark).

3 The line of bearing 198° of the harbour entrance then leads to the entrance to Avant-port which lies between a jetty on the E side and a spur on the W side and has a least width of about 27 m; training walls which cover at HW, marked by beacons, extend N from both the jetty and the spur. A light (brown pylon red top, 12 m in height) is exhibited from the jetty head and a light (brown pylon on dolphin green top, 14 m in height) is exhibited at the extremity of the W training wall.

4 **Caution.** The approach is difficult because of the offlying dangers and the difficulty of mariners in small craft, with low height of eye, of recognising the leading marks which are screened by large trees. The spur on the W side is bordered by a sandbank which partly encroaches into the channel. Mariners entering should keep close to the E side which is clear of dangers.

5 **Useful mark:**

Cross (9 m in height) (49°20′·3N 0°27′·4W) at the root of the W spur.

Basins and berths
13.65

1 **Avant-port.** On the E side there is a sloping wall with a number of dolphins alongside at which the berths dry 3 m. On the W side there is a stone and concrete slipway, 200 m long, where vessels may dry out.

2 **Wet basins.** Bassin Joinville lying to the SW of Avant-port and Nouveau Bassin lying on the S bank of Rivière La Seulles are marinas.

3 **Tidal basin** is approached through Rivière La Seulles which flows into Avant-port on its W side S of the slipway, at which point there is a bridge across it, opened from 2 to 3 hours before to 2 to 3 hours after HW depending on the height of tide. The tidal basin dries about 3 m.

Port services
13.66

1 **Repair facilities** are available.
Supplies: fuel; fresh water; provisions.
Rescue, see 13.14.

Caen-Ouistreham and approaches

Charts 1349 Plans of Ouistreham and Caen, 2136, 2146, 2613
General information
13.67

1 **Position.** The port of Caen-Ouistreham (49°17′N 0°15′W) comprises the harbour installations at Ouistreham, Ranville, Blainville-sur-Orne and at Caen; the latter three harbours are approached through Canal de Caen a la Mer.
13.68

1 **Topography.** The valley of Arromanches-les-Bains (49°20′N 0°37′W) to the W of the port is a useful mark and the built-up seaside resort of Riva-Bella, on the W side of the entrance, is prominent in the approach.

2 A coastal bank on which lie Les Essarts de Langrune and Roches de Lion, both of which dry, borders the coast on the W side of the entrance between Courseulles-sur-Mer (49°20′N 0°27′W) (13.60) and Ouistreham, nearly 9 miles ESE. The bank extends in places 2¼ miles offshore and Pointe des Essarts (49°22′N 0°22′W), its N extremity, is marked by Essarts de Langrune Buoy (N cardinal) moored 8½ cables NNE. The remains of a line of blockships, some of which are dangerous, are situated to the SW of Rade de Caen (13.74) about 1 mile offshore; the centre of this line is marked by buoy (49°19′N 0°17′W) (E cardinal). Pointe des Essarts and the dangers S of it are covered by the red sector (115°–151°) of Ouistreham Main Light (13.79). Two stranded wrecks, lying nearly 3 miles offshore, are marked by Lion and Luc buoys (E cardinal).

3 On the E side of the entrance, Bancs de Merville dry out 1½ miles to seaward of the entrance and are extended NE by a spoil ground used by the canal dredgers, as shown on the chart.
13.69

1 **Outer port limits** of the port of Caen-Ouistreham are defined by the following:
    N limit the parallel of 49°18′·1N.
    E limit the meridian of 0°13′·1W.
    W limit the meridian of 0°15′·1W.
13.70

1 **Approach and entry.** The port of Ouistreham (13.84) is approached from Baie de Seine through an approach channel leading to Rade de Caen (13.74) and entered through an entrance channel contained between two training walls which cover at HW.
    Canal de Caen a la Mer (13.85) is entered through one of two locks at the S end of Ouistreham Avant-port.
    Port de Caen (13.90) is situated at the end of Canal de Caen a la Mer, about 7½ miles SW of Ouistreham.

13.71

1 **Traffic.** In 2006 Caen-Ouistreham was used by 225 vessels totalling 1 713 129 dwt.
13.72

1 **Port Authority:** Capitainerie du Port, Terre-plein des écluses, 14150, Ouistreham. The port office is situated on the quay between the two locks.
    Website: www.caen.port.fr

Limiting conditions
13.73

1 **Controlling depths.** The entrance channel to Ouistreham dredged to a depth of 8·0 m is the controlling depth for Ouistreham ferry berths; it is subject to siltation.
    The approach channel through Ouistreham Avant-port to Canal de Caen à la Mer locks, dredged to a depth of 3·2 m, is the controlling depth for entering the canal.
    For limiting conditions in Canal de Caen, see 13.86.

2 **Tidal levels.** See information in *Admiralty Tide Tables.* Mean spring range about 6·7 m; mean neap range about 3·7 m.
    Maximum size of vessel handled: 205 m LOA, 23·5 m breadth and 8·9 m draught.

Arrival information
13.74

1 **Vessel traffic service.** Caen-Ouistreham VTS operates from the entrance locks and covers shipping movments within port limits. For details of a compulsory VTS system within the SE part of Baie de Seine, including Caen-Ouistreham access areas and anchorages, see 13.104.
    Port radio stations operate from Caen-Ouistreham and a port information service is in operation. For further details see *Admiralty List of Radio Signals Volume 6(1).*

2 **Notice of ETA required.** ETA 24 hours in advance to the Ouistreham Harbour Master or Caen Pilot Office, or on departure from the previous port if the period is less, and confirm ETA 2 hours in advance, stating draught and height of vessel above water level.
    For details see *Admiralty List of Radio Signals Volume 6(1).*

3 **Outer anchorages.** Rade de Caen, which affords shelter during winds between SW and SE, is normally only used by vessels waiting for the tide to enter Ouistreham or Canal de Caen a la Mer. Anchorage may be obtained in depths from 7 to 12 m, sand and shells, good holding ground.
    There are several dangerous wrecks in the approaches to Rade de Caen, the positions of which can be seen from the chart.

4 **Waiting area.** There is a waiting area (49°20′N 0°12′W), part of the Ouistreham Approach Channel (13.80) shown on the chart, for use of vessels carrying dangerous cargoes, SE of the SW leg of the approach channel.
    Recommended waiting anchorage, for other vessels, is situated 6 cables NW of Nos 1 and 2 entrance channel buoys (49°19′·2N 0°14′·5W). W-SRCO Buoy (white and blue) is moored in the anchorage, 4 cables WNW of No 1 entrance channel light buoy; obstructions, shown on the chart, lie in this anchorage.

5 **Prohibited anchorage.** Anchorage is prohibited in the approach channel and on the leading line to the harbour entrance.
    Pilotage. Caen-Ouistreham Compulsory Pilotage Area limits are bounded by the following:
    W limit, the meridian passing through Essarts de Langrune Buoy (49°22′·7N 0°21′·3W).

6 E limit, the meridian passing through Dives-sur-Mer Light 0°05'·2W.

N limit, the parallel passing through Essarts de Langrune Light Buoy.

S limit, the coast between the E and W limits and the Canal de Caen a la Mer to Bassin Saint-Pierre.

The pilot station is part of La Seine pilot station, Rouen.

7 **Pilotage** is compulsory for the following:

All vessels carrying dangerous and polluting goods.

All vessels over 50 m in length when entering and departing the port ofCaen-Ouistreham.

8 Vessels not equipped with VHF.

Pilotage is not compulsory for vessels excluded by law.

Boarding place. Pilot boards in position 49°20'·0N 0°14'·8W, about 7½ cables N of No 1 Channel Light Buoy, or in the waiting area SE of the compulsory Ouistreham Approach Channel for vessels carrying dangerous cargoes.

9 **Availability.** Pilots are available from 2½ hours before to 3 hours after HW. Pilotage may not be available in strong onshore winds when the approach channel can be impracticable or dangerous. In this event, mariners are advised to seek shelter off Le Havre and await an improvement in the weather.

10 For details see *Admiralty List of Radio Signals Volume 6(1)*.

Tugs are available. Vessels over 17 m beam are advised to use two tugs.

13.75

1 **Regulations concerning entry.** The use of the Ouistreham Approach Channel and Waiting Area is compulsory for vessels over 1600 gt laden with dangerous and polluting goods, for details see 1.68 to 1.76.

2 Entry of these vessels into the approach channel is forbidden until authorised by the Port Authorities. Vessels in the above categories anchored in the waiting area must be at 15 minutes' notice to sail; it is forbidden for them to remain in the waiting area during periods of bad weather from NW to NE, when they should wait in Rouen Waiting Area No2 (13.109) or remain at sea more than 7 miles from the French coast. Vessels in the above categories are deemed to be "vessels restricted in their ability to manoeuvre" and must show the appropriate shapes or lights when within the channel; pilotage is compulsory for them from Ouistreham Light Buoy.

3 All navigation in the access channel is forbidden during entry or exit of car ferries.

For regulations concerning Canal de Caen à la Mer, see 13.87.

Harbour
13.76

1 **General layout.** Ouistreham (49°17'N 0°15'W), consisting of a turning basin with berths for RoRo ferries, an Avant-port with wharves for fishing vessels and a yacht harbour close inside the canal, is entered through an entrance channel, the inner part of which is contained between two stone training walls which are covered at HW and extend about 1 mile offshore, and gives access, through locks, to Canal de Caen (13.85).

2 Two further training walls which cover, and are marked by beacons, are situated SE of the turning basin and contain Rivière L'Orne which flows out to sea through the entrance channel.

13.77

1 **Traffic signals.** Light panels on the lock building lit by day and night control access to the port, International Port Traffic Signals system are in use, for details see *The Mariner's Handbook*.

A fixed white light E or W of the main message (green, green, green) permits fishing vessels and pleasure craft to enter one or other of the locks.

Ouistreham from SSW (13.76)
(Original dated 1993)

(Photograph - Service Hydrographique et Océeanographique de la Marine)

13.78

1   **Natural conditions — tidal streams.** In Rade de Caen the tidal streams begin as follows:

Interval from HW Le Havre	Direction
−0445	ESE
+0115	WNW

The maximum E-going and W-going spring rates are 1½ and 1 kn, respectively, for details see information on the chart.

2   **Flow.** When the lock gates are opened, due to the salinity gradient between the fresh water of the canal and the sea water, when entering the canal there is a noticeable current into the locks. On exiting the canal, the effects are even more significant with a large outflow of water from the locks dramatically effecting ship handling.

Directions for entering harbour
13.79

1   **Landmarks:**

Ouistreham Main Lighthouse (white round tower red top, 38 m in height) (49°17′N 0°15′W) situated on the E side of the entrance to the locks into Canal de Caen.

Church spire (49°16′·6N 0°15′·5W) at Ouistreham.

2   Water Tower (49°16′·3N 0°15′·9W) standing 4½ cables SW of Ouistreham church.

Major light:

Ouistreham Main Light — as above.

3   **General information.** Mariners, except those required to use the approach channel, waiting to enter harbour should lie to the NW of the approach channel keeping clear of the numerous wrecks in the vicinity particulary the 5 m wreck (49°20′·4N 0°14′·9W) marked by Ouistreham Light Buoy (E cardinal).

13.80

1   **Ouistreham Approach Channel,** in which navigation is controlled, is entered about 8½ miles NNE of Avant-port. The channel, 1 mile wide to begin with, leads S for 4½ miles, then SW to the beginning of the entrance channel to Ouistreham passing between Merville Light Buoy (N cardinal) (49°19′·7N 0°13′·4W) and a wreck (49°20′·4N 0°14′·9W) marked on its E side by Ouistreham Light Buoy (E cardinal).

13.81

1   **Entrance Channel — leading lights:**

Front light (white metal tube red top, 11 m in height) (49°17′·1N 0°14′·8W) at the head of the E jetty at the entrance to Avant-port.

Rear light (tripod, 25 m in height) (3 cables S of the front mark) situated close SE of Ouistreham Main Light.

2   The alignment (184½°) of these lights, which are directional lights and intensified 1½° on each side of the leading line, leads through the entrance channel as far as the entrance to Avant-port. The outer part of the entrance channel is marked by light buoys (lateral) and the section within the training walls by light beacons and beacons. No 1 and No 2 Light Buoys (starboard and port hand, respectively) are moored 2 miles N of the front leading light and just S of the entrance to the channel. The centre part of the channel has a width of 80 m.

3   In order to avoid the wrecks and other dangers in the approaches to Rade de Caen, mariners in vessels not required to use the approach channel, should bring the leading lights in line when about 4½ miles from the coast.

13.82

1   **Turning basin and Avant-port.** From the inner end of the entrance channel the line of bearing of the axis of the W lock leads through the turning basin and Avant-port.

13.83

1   **Useful marks:**

Saint-Médard Light (white pylon red top, 17 m in height) (49°18′·0N 0°14′·6W) at the head of the E training wall.

Barnabé Light (white pylon green top, 17 m in height) (49°18′·0N 0°14′·8W) standing on Banc de L'Île near the head of the W training wall.

2   Light (platform on white column green top, 16 m in height) (49°17′·6N 0°14′·8W) at the head of the W jetty 4 cables N of the entrance to Avant-port.

Chart 1349 plan of Ouistreham
Basins and berths
13.84

1   **Ouistreham.** The port of Ouistreham comprises a turning basin with two berths for RoRo vessels situated on the W bank, an Avant-port, which communicates by two locks at its S end with Canal de Caen a la Mer, with a slip and wharves which dry for fishing vessels, and a marina close inside the canal on the E side.

Pontoons are available for leisure craft, waiting to enter the locks, on E side of Avant-port.

2   **Deepest and longest berth:**

No 2 RoRo Berth for vessels up to 180 m in length and 30 m beam with a turning area adjacent dredged to 8·0 m.

Canal de Caen a la Mer
13.85

1   **Description.** Canal de Caen a la Mer runs parallel with Rivière L'Orne and is about 7½ miles long between the locks at Ouistreham and Bassin Saint-Pierre at Caen.

13.86

1   **Limiting conditions.** The depth of water in Canal de Caen a la Mer, which is fresh water, is maintained at 9·8 m and the use of the canal is limited to vessels of the following dimensions:

	Length	Beam	Draught (in FW)
Ouistreham to Bassin d'Hérouville:			
By day	205 m	23·5 m	8·4 m
By night		20·0 m	8·0 m
Hérouville to Calix:			
By day	180 m	23·5 m	8·2 to 8·6 m
By night	150 m	20·0 m	8·0 m
In Nouveau Bassin:			
By day	145 m	20·0 m	3·8 to 7·0 m
By night	135 m	20·0 m	3·8 to 6·0 m

2   **Note.** Between Ouistreham and Bassin d'Hérouville variations in vessel dimensions apply dependent on draught. The port authorities should be consulted for exact requirements.

Caen - Pont de Benouville, (Pegasus Bridge) (13.86)

(Original dated 2004)

(Photograph - Crown Copyright)

Caen - Pont de Colombelles from SSW (13.86)

(Original dated 2004)

(Photograph - Crown Copyright)

3   The passage of tankers is dependent on their cargo, size, and destination.

Bridges. The canal is crossed by the following movable bridges:

Pont de Bénouville (km 9), known to British mariners as Pegasus Bridge, with a width clearance of 40 m.

Pont de Colombelles (km 4) with a width clearance of 30 m.

4   Pont de la Fonderie, at the entrance to Bassin Saint-Pierre (km 0), with a width clearance of 12 m.

The signal requesting the opening of the bridges is one long blast on the whistle.

5   **Vertical clearance:** for Nouveau Bassin and Bassin Saint-Pierre is 33 m over a navigable width of 21 m under

Pont de Calix (km 2); the limits are marked on the span of the bridge.

13.87

1   **Regulations governing the use of Canal de Caen a la Mer.** The following extracts are taken from the regulations governing the use of the canal:

Entry to the Access Channel for the locks is under the control of the Harbour Master.

The maximum speed allowed is 7 kn.

2   Vessels navigating the canal must keep VHF watch to indicate their position if necessary and to receive information of traffic in the canal.

All overtaking is forbidden save in the case of emergency. Passing is prohibited within 400 m of the lock gates and above Nouveau Bassin at Caen.

Caen – Pont de Calix and entry to Bassin de Calix (13.86)

(Original dated 2004)

(Photograph - Crown Copyright)

A distance of at least 400 m should be kept between vessels travelling in the same direction; 600 m if the first vessel does not have a tug secured aft. Anchoring is prohibited in the locks and in the cable areas.

3   The opening of the bridges is indicated by green lights; if these lights are not exhibited or are replaced by a red light vessels should stop no less than 400 m from the bridge and should not proceed until the green light is exhibited.

Yachts should keep close to the bank when commercial vessels signify their approach by a long blast on the whistle.

13.88

1   **Locks.** The channel to the W lock, the main lock with a length of 225 m, width 28·4 m and a depth on the sill of 3·25 m, is the controlling depth (13.73) to the canal and can accept vessels of 30 000 dwt. The channel to the E lock is dredged to chart datum over a width of 20 m; the lock has a length of 181 m, width 18 m and a depth on the sill of 0·2 m and can be divided into two parts, the outer of which is 70 m long and the inner part 90 m long.

2   The W lock is normally open for navigation for 7 hours, from 3 hours before to 4 hours after HW, when the height of tide is 4 m or above, and the E lock is normally open for 6 hours 30 minutes, from 3 hours 15 minutes before to 3 hours 15 minutes after HW.

13.89

1   **Berths:**

La Maresquier (km 11) a wharf on the W bank for tankers up to 120 m LOA.

Two berths at Ranville on the E bank (km 10) the largest and deepest 200 m long with a depth alongside of 6 m.

Port de Caen
13.90

1   **Description.** Port de Caen (49°11′N 0°21′W), an artificial harbour, is situated on the E side of Canal de Caen à la Mer about 7½ miles SW of Ouistreham; the depths in the harbour are maintained at a constant level.

13.91

1   **Berths.** There are five main docks in Port de Caen; approaching the port along Canal de Caen a la Mer these will be found as follows:

Quai de Blainville (km 7) on the E bank about 4 miles S of Ouistreham; 625 m long for vessels up to 9 m draught with facilities for container and RoRo vessels and for the handling of bulk cargoes.

2   Bassin d'Hérouville (km 3); largest berth Quai Président Delaunay 370 m long for vessels up to 8·9 m draught, ore and bulk cargo facilities available.

Bassin de Calix (km 2); longest berth Poste DPC 170 m long for vessels up to 8·6 m draught.

3   Nouveau Bassin (km 1) on the S bank; deepest and longest berth Quai Gaston Lamy, C3 to C5, 550 m long for vessels up to 7 m draught.

Port services
13.92

1   **Repairs** at Caen, which do not require a dry dock, to vessels and machinery can be carried out.

Ship sanitation control certificates issued at Caen.

Other facilities: hospital; deratting exemption certificates at Ouistreham.

Supplies: fuel by road tanker at Caen; fresh water at all quays at Caen and at Ouistreham; fresh provisions and stores at Caen.

Approaches to Ouistreham Lock from SSW (13.88)

(Original dated 2004)

(Photograph - Crown Copyright)

Caen – Quai Gaston Lamy from NW (13.91)

(Original dated 2004)

(Photograph - Crown Copyright)

Communications: Caen-Carpiquet local airport 10 km from the city with connecting flights to international airports.

Rescue, see 13.14.

Rivière Dives and approaches

Charts 1349 Plan of Dives-sur-Mer, 2146, 2613
General information
13.93

1   **Position and function.** Rivière Dives which flows out to sea between Pointe de Cabourg (49°18′N 0°05′W) and

Pointe de Beuzeval, 7 cables NE, contains a large marina at Port Guillaume and a quay at Dives-sur-Mer and is used by fishing vessels and pleasure craft.

Topography. Mont Dives (49°17′N 0°03′W), a black hill situated 1 mile SSE of the river mouth, dominates the plain.

Limiting conditions
13.94

1   **Controlling depths.** The banks at the mouth of Rivière Dives dry out for about 1 mile seaward. The entrance channel frequently alters and should only be attempted when the tidal stream is slack near HW.

Tidal levels. Mean spring range about 6.9 m; mean neap range about 3.8 m. For further information see *Admiralty Tide Tables*.

Maximum size of vessel handled. The port is only accessible to fishing vessels and shallow draught craft 2 hours either side of HW.

Arrival information
13.95
1 **Local knowledge** or the use of a local pilot is required.

Harbour
13.96
1 **General layout.** A quay for fishing vessels is situated at Dives-sur-Mer on the S side of the river at Houlgate. Port Guillaume, a yacht harbour, is situated on the S side of the river close SW of the quay.

2 **Tidal streams.** In Rivière Dives off Pointe de Cabourg and along the quay at Dives-sur-Mer the in-going stream attains a rate of 4 to 5 kn. The stream begins to slacken about −0210 Le Havre and is nearly slack by −0400 Le Havre. The out-going stream, spring rate about 2¾ kn, begins at +0025 Le Havre.

Directions for entering harbour
13.97
1 The white sector (157°–162°) of Dives-sur-Mer Light (red hut, 5 m in height) (49°18′N 0°05′W) situated close

within the entrance to the river leads in the channel passing between No 1 Buoy (starboard hand) and No 2 Buoy (port hand), which mark the W and E sides of the entrance channel, respectively. DI Light Buoy (safe water) is moored 1½ mile NNW of the light, seaward of the entrance to the buoyed channel, which is marked by buoys and beacons, some of which are lit. The channel frequently alters and the limits of the sector of the light and the channel markings are altered to meet changes in the channel.

2 **Useful mark:**
Casino (49°17′·7N 0°07′·0W) at Cabourg.

Berths
13.98
1 **Dives-sur-Mer.** There is a quay, 100 m long, extending along the S side of the river, S of Pointe de Cabourg; the quay is used by fishing vessels. The berths alongside dry 3·4 m, sand and course gravel; mariners should always secure here with their bows to seaward. A curving spur extending about 1¼ cables S and SE from Pointe de Cabourg partially shelters the jetty and the entrance to the marina.

Port services
13.99
1 **Repairs:** slips.
Supplies: fuel; fresh water; provisions.
Rescue, see 13.14.

ESTUAIRE DE LA SEINE

GENERAL INFORMATION

Chart 2146, 2613
Description
13.100
1 Estuaire de la Seine is entered between Pointe de Beuzeval (49°18′N 0°05′W) and Cap de la Hève, 13½ miles NNE.

Data gathering light buoys (special) are moored in the estuary for the purpose of taking current and wave measurements; their positions change frequently.

Off-lying features
13.101
1 Banc de Seine, with depths of less than 15 m over it, extends 15 miles W from Cap de la Hève (49°31′N 0°04′E). The tidal streams when opposed to the wind cause a heavy sea on this bank.
See also 13.2, 13.3 and 13.6.

Port limits
13.102
1 Port limits for Le Havre, including Port 2000 and Rouen are shown on the appropriate charts.

Pilotage
13.103
1 For details of pilotage for Le Havre and Port du Havre-Antifer see 13.128, and for La Seine Maritime and Rouen 13.163.

Vessel traffic service
13.104
1 **Identification Zone.** Radar stations at Cap de la Hève and in Le Havre maintain surveillance over the estuary and

its approaches. The system, compulsory for all commercial vessels, provides maritime traffic surveillance. The identification zone for vessels bound for or departing the ports of Caen-Ouistreham (13.67), Le Havre (13.115), Rouen (13.193) and Port du Havre-Antifer (13.213) is bounded by an arc of radius 22 miles centred on Cap de la Hève Light (49°31′N 0°04′E). The system covers the access areas, anchorage and waiting areas to the ports of Caen-Ouistreham, Le Havre, Rouen and Port du Havre-Antifer, Le Havre Waiting Areas Nos 1, 2 and 3, Rouen Waiting Areas Nos 1 and 2 and the port areas, including access to the ports of Honfleur (13.182) and Port Jérôme (13.192).

2 The Control Centre is located at Le Havre Harbour Master's office, and is in operation throughout 24 hours.

Mariners in vessels and tows over 50 m in length entering or within the zone, situated within French territorial waters or internal waters, bound to for from any of the ports in the areas above, a waiting area or anchorage should call Baie de Seine Traffic.

3 Mariners should contact the Control Centre 48 hours before arrival at LHA Light Buoy (49°31′N 0°10′W) or Port du Havre-Antifer A5 Light Buoy (49°46′N 0°17′W).

Information on tidal, meteorological, or navigational conditions and radar assistance can also be supplied on request; call Le Havre Port or Antifer Port.

For further details see *Admiralty List of Radio Signals Volume 6(1)*.

Tidal streams
13.105
1 For tidal streams in the approaches to LHA Light Buoy see information on the charts.

In Estuaire de la Seine see information and diagrams for the directions and rates in kn of the tidal streams in the approaches to Le Havre and entrance to La Seine at 13.134; the stand of the tide is very marked.

2   In the anchorages the rate of the streams is less than 2 kn.

Caution. Since the construction of Le Havre Port 2000 (2006) (13.131) some tidal streams and directions may have changed in the approaches to Le Havre and Chenal de Rouen.

Regulations in approaches to Le Havre
13.106

1   **Vessels bound for Le Havre** should enter the approach channel W of the entrance buoys.

Vessels not bound for Le Havre wishing to cross the approach channel must do so W of LH7 and LH8 Light Buoys (49°30′N 0°01′W), having obtained prior clearance from Le Havre VTS to do so and then only without impeding shipping in the approach channel; the latter have absolute priority.

2   **Exempted** from these two rules are fishing vessels and pleasure craft less than 19·8 m in length, certain local vessels, vessels with a pilot on board provided that the port authority is informed, and vessels experiencing difficulty in embarking or disembarking the pilot in the roads provided that the concurrence of the port authority is obtained; in these cases it is conditional that no inconvenience is caused to shipping in the approach channel.

3   **Vessels carrying dangerous and polluting goods** must display a red flag by day and a red light at the mast at night.

Vessels constrained by their draught should exhibit the shapes and lights laid down in *International Regulations for Preventing Collisions at Sea (1972)*.

Pleasure craft under way in the approaches to, or within the port, whether under sail or power, must give way to all other shipping.

Regulations for vessels carrying dangerous and polluting goods
13.107

1   The following is a summary of the essential parts of the French regulations concerning the above mentioned vessels bound to or sailing from Le Havre, Rouen and other La Seine ports.

1) **Before entering** French territorial waters or getting underway in French ports vessels described above must:

2   a) Establish radio contact with Havre–Port Radio or Rouen Pilot Radio as appropriate. Contact must then be maintained continuously until berthed or outside French territorial waters.

b) Report to Le Havre port or Rouen pilots as appropriate any defects to propulsion machinery, steering or anchor gear, mooring winches or radar equipment. The port authority will require the master of such a vessel to complete a questionnaire.

3   2) **Vessels bound for Le Havre** must:

a) Comply with instructions given by Le Havre port radio. If they have to wait they must proceed to the area appropriate to their draught and dimensions as follows:

Vessels less than 250 m length or drawing less than 11 m, proceed to Waiting Area No 1 situated S of the approach channel passing N of a line through

LHA Light Buoy (49°31′N 0°10′W) and HP Light Buoy, 4½ miles ESE.

4   Vessels over 250 m in length or drawing more than 11 m should proceed to Waiting Area No 2 if tonnage is less than 100 000 dwt, or to Waiting Area No 3.

b) Have a Le Havre pilot on board while under way within 7 miles of the French coast except that vessels having a length of less than 250 m or drawing less than 11 m may proceed without a pilot to Waiting Area No 1. To facilitate the embarking and disembarking of pilots, vessels bound to or from Le Havre are permitted to manoeuvre in the Le Havre Access Area which lies close NNE of Waiting Area No 1.

5   3) **Vessels bound for La Seine ports:**

a) Vessels more than 250 m in length or drawing more than 12 m must wait for the pilot at a distance of more than 7 miles from the coast and S of a line passing through LHA Light Buoy and HP Light Buoy.

6   b) Vessels less than 250 m in length or drawing less than 12 m may proceed without a pilot to the Rade de la Carosse Access Area (49°28′N 0°02′E) keeping S of LHA Light Buoy and Le Havre Waiting Area No 1.

c) Vessels may not leave the waiting area in 3(a) above or Rade de la Carosse for La Seine without a Rouen pilot onboard.

7   4) During movements between Le Havre and La Seine a Le Havre pilot and Rouen pilot must be onboard.

5) Contravention of the regulations will render masters liable to prosecution.

For information on waiting areas, see 13.108.

For general regulations concerning vessels carrying dangerous and polluting goods navigating in the approaches to the N and W coasts of France, see 1.68 to 1.76.

Waiting areas
13.108

1   **Caution.** Mariners should note that the designated waiting areas for Le Havre and Rouen contain charted wrecks, obstuctions and foul areas which should be avoided.

2   **Le Havre Waiting Areas,** shown on the charts, are:

No 3 Waiting Area, approximately 3 miles square with depths from 20 to 25 m, centred about 13½ miles WNW of Cap de la Hève (49°31′N 0°04′E), is authorised for use by any vessels.

No 2 Waiting Area, approximately 2 miles square with depths of 17 to 22 m, centred about 9 miles WNW of Cap de la Hève, is authorised for use by vessels under 100 000 dwt only.

3   No 1 Waiting Area, with good holding in depths of 12 m, sand and shells, centred about 4¾ miles WSW of Cap de la Hève. This area, situated S of the approach channel and parallel with a line joining LH3 to LH7 Light Buoys, is authorised for use by vessels of less than 11 m draught and less than 250 m length.

Caution. An 11·8 m wreck, marked on its NW side by HP Light Buoy (special) lies in position 49°29′·6N 0°03′·7W. Two obstructions of unknown depth lie 1½ cables ENE and ½ cable S of HP Light Buoy.

4   There is a slight risk of anchors fouling disused submarine cables in these anchorages and also elsewhere in the estuary.

For anchorages for very deep-draught vessels bound for Port du Havre-Antifer, see 13.221.

13.109

1   **Rouen Waiting Areas.** Mariners bound for Rouen or La Seine Maritime can anchor while awaiting the pilot or the tide in the following areas, the limits of which are shown on the chart:

Rouen Waiting Area No 1. About 3½ miles WSW of Cap de la Hève; depths 12 to 13 m. RP Light Buoy (isolated danger) (49°28′·6N 0°01′·2W), marking a wreck close S with 9·7 m over it, is moored 4 miles SW of Cap de la Hève, in the SW of the area. Nord du Mouillage Light Buoy (special) is moored about 1 mile farther E at its NE corner. The area is for coasters and other small vessels expecting a wait of short duration, and only in fair weather conditions.

2   Rouen Waiting Area No 2. About 6¾ miles WSW of Cap de la Hève; depths 11 to 12 m. RNA Light Buoy (safe water) (49°28′·5N 0°04′·3W) is moored 5¾ miles WSW of Cap de la Hève at the NE corner of the area. An obstruction with a minimum depth of 10 m is charted close W of the E limit in position 49°28′·0N 0°04′·8W. The area is for vessels of 190 m LOA or less or with a draught of 9 m or less.

3   Rouen waiting Area No 3. About 8¼ miles WSW of Cap de la Hève; depths 12 to 14 m. The area is for vessels of more than 190 m LOA or with a draught of more than 9 m, and vessels of more than 150 m LOA or with a draught of more than 9 m carrying dangerous and polluting goods.

13.110

1   **Restricted areas.** Except in an emergency vessels are prohibited from anchoring, fishing or stopping in the following areas:

In the charted and partly buoyed approach channel to Le Havre, and within 100 m N or S of the channel.

2   In the charted and buoyed approach channel to Le Havre: Port 2000, and within 100 m N or S of the channel.

In the charted and buoyed approach channel to Rouen seaward of Honfleur and within 200 m either side of the channel.

3   In the charted North Disengagement Channel bound on its E side by a line joining LH10 Light Buoy (port hand) (49°30′·2N 0°00′·8E) and Octeville W Light-buoy (S cardinal) 1½ miles NNE, and on its W side by LH8 Light Buoy (port hand) (49°30′·5N 0°00′·8W), Grande Rade Sud Light Buoy (E cardinal) and Général Metzinger Light Buoy (N cardinal) lying 7 cables NNE and 2½ miles NNW, respectively. These latter two buoys mark the E and N sides of a foul area, in which there are several wrecks, which lies between 3 and 5 miles W of Cap de la Hève.

4   In an area reserved as either an exit or access channel lying W of the foul area and bound on its E side by Général Metzinger Light Buoy and LH4 Light Buoy (port hand), 2 miles SW, and on its W side by a line joining positions 49°34′·0N 0°02′·0W and 49°31′·5N 0°05′·4W.

5   Mariners are also prohibited from anchoring, dredging and trawling in an area, indicated on the charts, extending S from Cap de la Hève, W to the meridian of Greenwich and N along the coast for 3½ miles. A spoil ground, marked towards its E side by a light buoy (special) lies in this area 2¾ miles NNW of Cap de la Hève. Anchoring and dredging is prohibited in this area.

Dredgers

13.111

1   Suction dredgers carry the lights and shapes described in Rule 27 of *International Regulations for Preventing Collisions at Sea (1972)*. Whilst working in the channel they also display the signals shown in Diagram 13.111.

Day	Night	Side of channel dredger working	Side of channel vessel must pass
▲	●	starboard	port
■	●	port	starboard

Estuaire de La Seine - dredger signals (13.111)

Temporary explosives dumping grounds

13.112

1   Temporary explosives dumping grounds (Zones de Dépôts d'Explosifs) are situated:

NW of the entrance to Deauville-Trouville (49°22′N 0°04′E) for Deauville-Trouville and Honfleur (49°25′N 0°14′E).

WSW of the entrance to Le Havre (49°29′N 0°07′E).

For details see 1.7 and Appendix V.

Rescue

13.113

1   **All-weather lifeboat** is stationed at Honfleur (49°26′N 0°14′E) (13.182).

Inshore lifeboats are maintained at:

Le Havre (49°29′N 0°07′E) (13.115).

Deauville-Trouville (49°22′N 0°04′E) (13.173).

For details of lifeboats, see 1.117.

2   **Signal stations** are situated at:

Villerville (Sémaphore) (49°23′N 0°06′E) (13.179).

Cap de la Hève (Vigie) (49°31′N 0°04′E), 2 cables SSE of the lighthouse.

Le Havre (Vigie) (49°29′N 0°06′E) (13.140).

For details, see 1.95 and 1.110.

3   **VHF Direction-finding stations,** for emergency use only, operate from:

Villerville (49°23′N 0°06′E).

Cap de la Hève (49°31′N 0°04′E).

For details see *Admiralty List of Radio Signals Volume 2.*

Directions

13.114

1   **Principal marks:**

Two tall Chimneys (red and white tops, red obstruction lights) (49°29′N 0°09′E).

Saint-Joseph Church (tower) (49°30′N 0°06′E).

Television Tower (red lights) (49°30′N 0°11′E) at Graville.

2   Cap de la Hève Lighthouse (white octagonal tower red top, 32 m in height) (49°31′N 0°04′E) standing on Cap de la Hève. The cliffs of the cape are white and reddish in colour and easily seen when the sun shines on them. A radar tower (red lights) and two lattice towers (red lights) stand close SSW and 2 cables SSE, respectively of the light.

3 **Major lights:**
> Digue Nord Light (white tower red top, 15 m in height) (49°29′N 0°05′E) shown from the N breakwater head.
> Cap de la Hève Light — as above.
> Cap d'Antifer Light (49°41′N 0°10′E) (13.211).

4 **Other aids to navigation.** Racons transmit from:
> LHA Light Buoy (49°31′N 0°10′W).
> Antifer A5 Light Buoy (49°46′N 0°17′W).
> No2 Light Buoy (port hand) (49°27′·4N 0°01′·3E).
> For details see *Admiralty List of Radio Signals Volume 2*.

5 **Radar assistance.** In poor visibility and on request, Le Havre Control Centre will supply radar information to mariners relative to their position. The area of radar coverage is a circular zone 12½ miles radius centred on approximate position 49°39′N 0°08′E.

For details see 13.104 and *Admiralty List of Radio Signals Volume 6(1)*.

6 Mariners bound for Le Havre and La Seine Maritime (13.158) should make for LHA Light Buoy (safe water) (49°31′N 0°10′W) (13.137) and thence as directed at 13.135 for Le Havre, and at 13.170 for La Seine Maritime.

7 In poor visibility sounding in the vicinity of Le Parfond (13.3) can also assist in establishing an approximate position. Unless a mariner has verified his position he should not proceed within depths of less than 15 m since this depth contour passes close to dangers bordering the coast.

Mariners should avoid impeding the navigation of deep-draught vessels which are frequently encountered in the estuary.

LE HAVRE AND APPROACHES

General information

Charts 2990, 2146, 2613, 2879
Position
13.115

1 Port du Havre or Le Havre (49°29′N 0°07′E), at the mouth of the Seine, is situated to the S and SE of the city of the same name.

Function
13.116

1 The port is one of the most important French commercial and oil ports and the leading French container port.

Port limits
13.117

1 As shown on the appropriate charts.

Approach and entry
13.118

1 The port is approached from Baie de Seine on leading lights through Le Havre Approach Channel and entered between Digue Nord and Digue Sud, two breakwaters at the end of the approach channel.

Access to Port 2000 is common with Le Havre until within 9 cables of Le Havre entrance, when the approach channel to Port 2000 leads SE.

Traffic
13.119

1 In 2006 the port was used by 5412 vessels totalling 184 046 997 dwt.

Port Authority
13.120

1 Port Autonome du Havre, Terre-plein de la Barre, BP 1413, 76067, Le Havre.
> Website: www.havre-port.fr
> Email: capitanerie@havre-port.fr

Limiting conditions

Controlling depths
13.121

1 **Approach channel:** maintained depth 15·0 m; owing to siltation the designated depth cannot always be maintained.

Avant-port and tidal basins: 14·5 m at LW when on the centreline of the channel marked by the white sector of the Direction light (13.141); lesser depths are charted close to the centreline.

2 **Port 2000:** maintained depth of 15·0 m in the approach channel and tidal basin.

3 **Wet docks and constant level basins.** Depths in the constant level basins are given in relation to the chart datum; to obtain the depth of water in these basins a value between 6·8 and 7·4 m should be added. The Port Authority does not provide exact figures for draughts permitted alongside the quays. The actual depths may be less due to the basins silting up between dredging programmes.

The Port Authority should be consulted for the actual depths in the wet docks and constant level basins.

Maximum draught
13.122

1 A quarterly timetable published by the Port Authority gives, for each tide, the maximum admissible draught for large vessels calling at the port.

Deepest and longest berths
13.123

1 The deepest and longest berths are situated at Port 2000 (13.143). Other deep specialist berths are found in Bassin Théophile Ducrocq, Bassin René Coty (13.145) and Grand Canal du Havre (13.148).

Tidal levels
13.124

1 Mean spring range about 6·7 m; mean neap range about 3·8 m. For further information see *Admiralty Tide Tables*.

Maximum size of vessels handled
13.125

1 Tankers with a length of 392 m and approximate draught of 20 m, subject to tide, use the port; the maximum draught recorded is 20·73 m. Loaded tankers up to 280 000 dwt can use the port.

Vessels up to 17 m draught and 150 000 deadweight tonnes can use Grand Canal du Havre.

For the maximum size of vessel which has used Port du Havre-Antifer, see 13.217.

Arrival information

Port radio
13.126

1 **Port radio** stations operate from Le Havre, for details see *Admiralty List of Radio Signals Volume 6(1)*.

For details of a movements reporting system and notice of ETA required, see 13.104.

Outer anchorages
13.127

1 **Waiting areas,** see 13.108.

La Petite Rade du Havre, between Banc de l'Éclat (49°30′N 0°03′E) (13.138) and the coast, but S of the prohibited anchorage (13.110), affords anchorage to mariners in small vessels in depths from 6 to 7 m.

Caution. Two wrecks with a depth of 2 m over them lie in the SE part of this anchorage.

Pilotage and tugs
13.128

2 **Pilotage** is compulsory for the following:
Vessels of 70 m in length or over.
Vessels carrying dangerous and polluting goods.
Vessels not equipped with VHF.

Area. The Compulsory Pilotage Area Limits, including Port du Havre-Antifer (13.213), are bounded by the following:

3 North-east limit; a line joining Cap d'Antifer Light (49°41′N 0°10′E) to position 49°46′N 0°01′E.
North limit; the 49°46′N parallel.
West limit; the meridian passing through LHA Light Buoy (49°31′N 0°10′W).
South limit; the 49°27′N parallel.
East limit; the E-most extremity of Le Havre port including Canal du Havre á Tancarville upstream to Tancarville lock gates.

4 **Availability.** Pilots are available 24 hours. Send request for a pilot, together with arrival draught, to Havre-Port Radio 24 hours and 3 hours in advance for both Le Havre or Port du Havre-Antifer (13.213), for details see *Admiralty List of Radio Signals Volume 6(1)*.

5 **Boarding places — Le Havre.** Mariners should request a pilot before approaching the boarding positions below:
Vessels of 12 m draught in position 49°31′·6N 0°05′·9W.
Vessels of 16 m draught in position 49°33′·0N 0°09′·9W.
Vessels of 18 m draught in position 49°34′·4N 0°14′·1W.
Vessels with a draught between those specified above, pilot boards in a position between the specified pilot boarding positions.

6 **Boarding place — Port du Havre-Antifer:** 1 mile N of A5 Light Buoy (49°46′N 0°17′W).

Boarding method. Pilot boards by pilot boat, which has an orange hull and a white superstructure carrying the inscription "Pilote Le Havre" in black letters, or by helicopter; the method of pilot boarding will be specified to the vessel.

7 **Tugs** up to 4800 hp are available, of which two have fire-fighting capabilities.

Regulations concerning entry
13.129

1 For regulations in the approaches to Le Havre, see 13.106.

For regulations concerning vessels carrying dangerous and polluting goods, see 13.107.

Marine nature reserve
13.130

1 A marine nature reserve, as shown on the chart, is situated between Port 2000 (13.143) and Digue Basse du Nord (13.172).

Harbour

General layout
13.131

1 Le Havre comprises an Avant-port, tidal basins, constant level basins, wet docks reached through locks and the tidal Port 2000.

Avant-port, entered between Digue Nord and Digue Sud, with Petite-Port, a yacht harbour on its N side, is situated at the E end of the approach channel.

2 Bassin Théophile Ducrocq, situated SE of Avant-port, and Bassin René Coty (13.145) form one continuous tidal basin nearly 3 miles in length. They contain berths for the largest tankers and chemical carriers and for large passenger vessels, RoRo berths, berths for vessels carrying bulk cargoes, and repair berths. The E end of this complex consists mainly of container terminals and is known as Port Rapide. Écluse François Premier (13.147), at the E end of Bassin René Coty, is a large lock which gives access to the constant level basins and Grand Canal du Havre (13.148), which is joined to Canal du Havre á Tancarville (13.149) by Canal Bossière.

3 Bassin de La Manche (13.144), at the E end of Avant-port, gives access to the wet docks through Écluse Sas Quinette-de-Rochemont and Écluse de la Citadelle (13.150).

Canal du Havre á Tancarville, a constant level basin reached through Sas Vétillart (49°28′·9N 0°08′·4E), a lock at the E end of the wet docks, joins Le Havre with La Seine through two locks at Tancarville.

4 Port 2000, a tidal basin lies about 2 miles SE of Avant-port and provides deep-water berths for the largest container vessels.

Development
13.132

1 The first phase of Le Havre Port 2000 is complete (2006); the access channel, tidal basin and four berths are now in use. For details see 13.139 and 13.143. Works continue (2006) to construct additional berths within the Port 2000 complex.

Signals
13.133

1 **Visual traffic signals** are shown from masts at the head of Digue Nord, in the vicinity of the Port Control Tower, on the S side of the entrance to Bassin Théophile Ducrocq, at Quinette-de-Rochemont, François Premier and Citadelle Locks, as well as at various other passages through which mariners have to pass.

The signals employed are the International Port Traffic Signals, for details see *The Mariner's Handbook*.

Natural conditions
13.134

1 **Tidal streams** at Le Havre are characterised by a marked stand of the tide at HW, known locally as the "tenue de plein". This begins approximately 4 hours after LW and lasts for about 3 hours, during which time there is little variation, a maximum of 0·3 m, in the tide level. In contrast there is practically no stand at LW, the time of which is more definable than that of HW.

2 Diagrams on the following five pages show the direction and rates at springs and neaps in the approaches to Le Havre and the entrance to La Seine at hourly intervals; it should be noted that the tidal streams set across the approaches.

In Avant-port the rising stream may attain a rate of 1½ kn; it sets more strongly towards the tidal basins than towards Bassin de La Manche. Eddies may be experienced at the entrance to the wet basins, but there is little stream within the basins themselves.

3   In Bassin de La Manche the rising stream is weak, but there may be eddies off the W end of the quay on its S side, however for a short period after the opening of the locks at the E end of Bassin de La Manche a strong current is induced by the refilling of the wet basins and passage through the locks should not be attempted at this time.

See also information on the charts.

4   **Eddies** occur close outside the harbour entrance where there may be a line of ripples especially when the rising stream is running strongly.

Current. At about –0100 Le Havre, when the rising stream into the river has almost ceased, a current, known as Le Verhaule, becomes quickly established and sets NW across the approach channel until about +0100 Le Havre; farther W the direction of this current becomes N then NE.

5   **Local weather.** Strong W winds can increase the height of the tide by up to 0·7 m, and strong E winds, especially with high barometric pressure, can lower the height by up to 0·5 m. These variations can affect the time of HW by as much as 1 hour.

Climate information. See 1.195 and 13.245.

Directions for entering harbour
(continued from 13.16)

Principal marks
13.135
1   For details of principal marks, see 13.114.

Other aids to navigation
13.136
1   **Radar assistance.** In poor visibility and on request, four radar stations installed at Cap de La Hève, the Port Control Tower, the mole separating Oil Basins No 1 and No 2 and Écluse François Premier central control terminal, supply information on tidal, meteorological, or navigational conditions; radar assistance in the harbour can also be supplied.

See also 13.104 and 13.114

Le Havre Approach Channel
13.137
1   **General information.** For certain loaded vessels of little manoeuvrability the best time to enter the harbour is between 2 hours before HW Le Havre, and HW; the actual time of entry is determined by the pilot in consultation with Havre-port radio. Mariners in very large tankers bound for Le Havre should arrive off LHA Light Buoy (safe water) (49°31′N 0°10′W), moored 9 miles W of Cap de la Hève and seaward of all coastal dangers, about 3 hours before HW in order to berth on a daylight tide. For a limitation on tankers entering at night, see 13.129.

13.138
1   **Leading lights:**
Front light (grey tower green top, 35 m in height) (49°28′·9N 0°06′·5E) standing on Quai Roger Meunier 7½ cables ESE of the harbour entrance.
Rear light (grey tower green top, 77 m in height) (7½ cables ESE of the front mark) standing on Quai Joannès Couvert.
2   From a position about 7 cables N of LHA Light Buoy the alignment (106¾°) of these lights, which are shown throughout 24 hours and intensified 1° on each side of their

alignment, leads in the approach channel, the outer part of which is unmarked, entered about 7 cables NNE of LHA Light buoy, passing:

3   Between LH4 Light Buoy and LH3 Light Buoy (port and starboard hand) (49°31′N 0°04′W) marking the seaward end of the N and S sides, respectively, of the buoyed part of the channel. The channel is straight and 300 m wide. Thence:
Between pairs of light buoys (port and starboard hand) numbered LH6 and LH5 to LH8 and LH7, moored respectively between 6 and 5 miles WNW, of the front leading light; thence:
4   SSW of LH10 Light Buoy (port hand) (49°30′·2N 0°00′·8E); thence:
Between LH12 Light Buoy (W cardinal) and LH11 Light Buoy (starboard hand) moored 2¾ miles WNW of the front leading light; thence:
5   To a position between LH13 and LH16 Light Buoys, where for Le Havre harbour entrance and Avant-port, the route leads ESE passing between Digue Nord and Digue Sud. A light (13.114) and a tall signal mast stand at the head of Digue Nord and a light (white tower green top, 14 m in height) (49°29′·1N 0°05′·4E) stands at the head of Digue Sud; the entrance is 250 m wide. The E part of Digue Sud is known as Digue Ouest.

6   **Caution.** The channel is bordered on its N side by the foul area (13.110) between LH4 and LH8 Light Buoys (port hand) and by Banc de l'Éclat (49°30′N 0°03′E) between LH12 Light Buoy (W cardinal) and LH14 Light Buoy (port hand). Additionally, an obstruction of unknown depth lies 6 cables NW of LH12 Light Buoy. On the S side lies Les Hauts de la Rade (49°29′N 0°03′E) between LH11 and LH13 Light Buoys (starboard hand). These buoys are moored on the edge of the banks and should not be passed too closely.

Le Havre: Port 2000 Approach Channel
13.139
1   **Leading lights:**
Front: LH21 Light Beacon (N cardinal) (49°27′·6N 0°07′·0E.
Rear: Directional light standing on Digue François Le Chevalier (white tower, black band with radar scanner) (2¾ cables SE of front light).
2   The alignment (133°) of these lights, or at night in the white sector (132½°–133¼°) of the rear light, leads in the Port 2000 approach channel, passing:
Between LH2000 Light Buoy (W cardinal) and LH15 Light Buoy (starboard hand), thence:
3   Between LH18 and LH17 Light Beacons (port and starboard hand), 1¾ miles NW of the rear light, thence:
Between LH20 and LH19 Light Buoys (port and starboard hand), 1¼ miles NW from the rear light, thence:
4   To the Port 2000 entrance which leads into Bassin Hubert Raoul-Duval, passing between Digue Port 2000 on the head of which a light (red square on white tower, red top) (49°28′·0N 0°06′·5E) is exhibited, and the head of Digue François Le Chevalier on which a light (green triangle apex uppermost on white tower, green top) (8 cables NW of the rear light) is exhibited.

DIRECTIONS AND RATES IN KNOTS OF THE TIDAL STREAMS IN THE APPROACHES TO LE HAVRE AND ENTRANCE TO LA SEINE

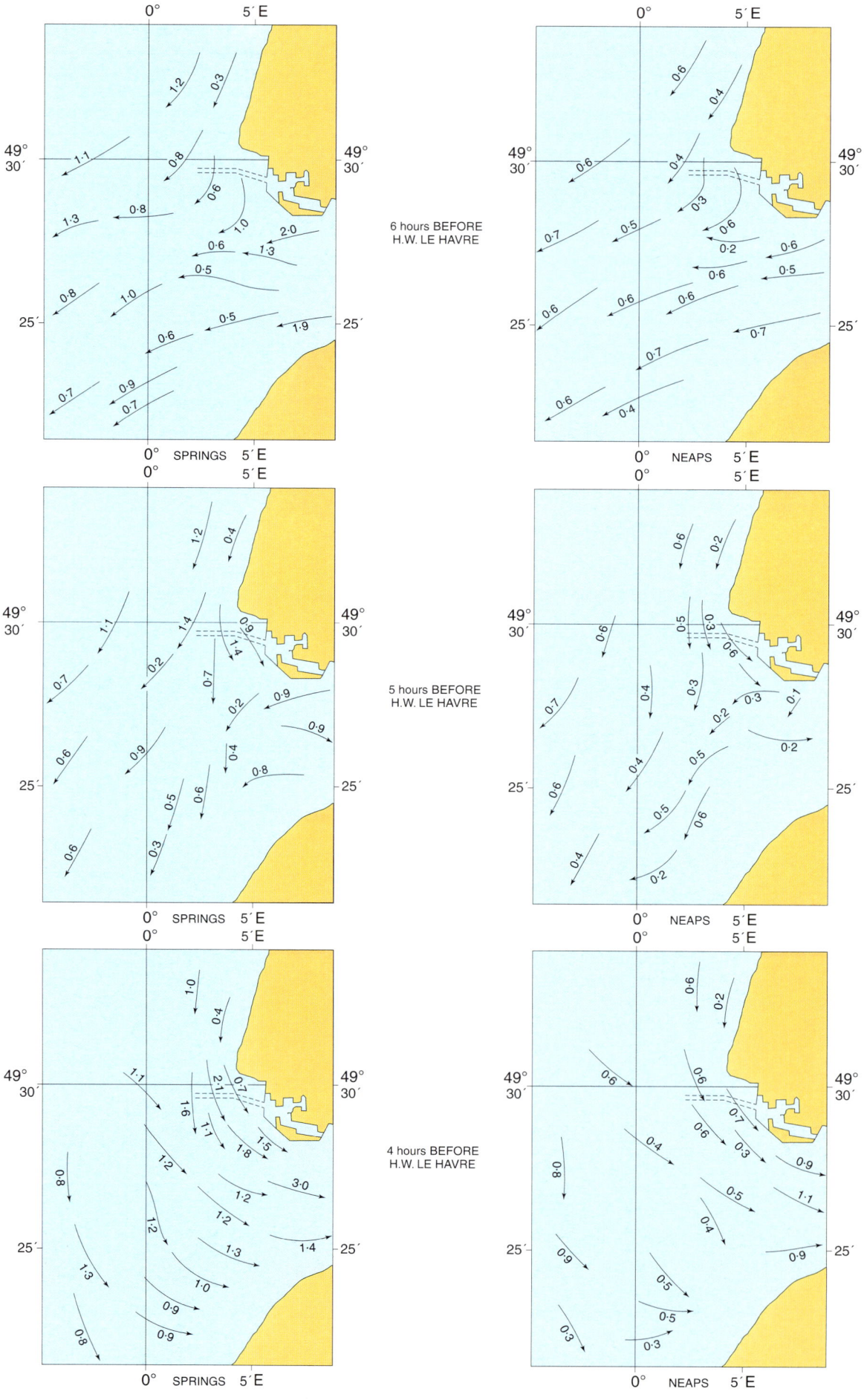

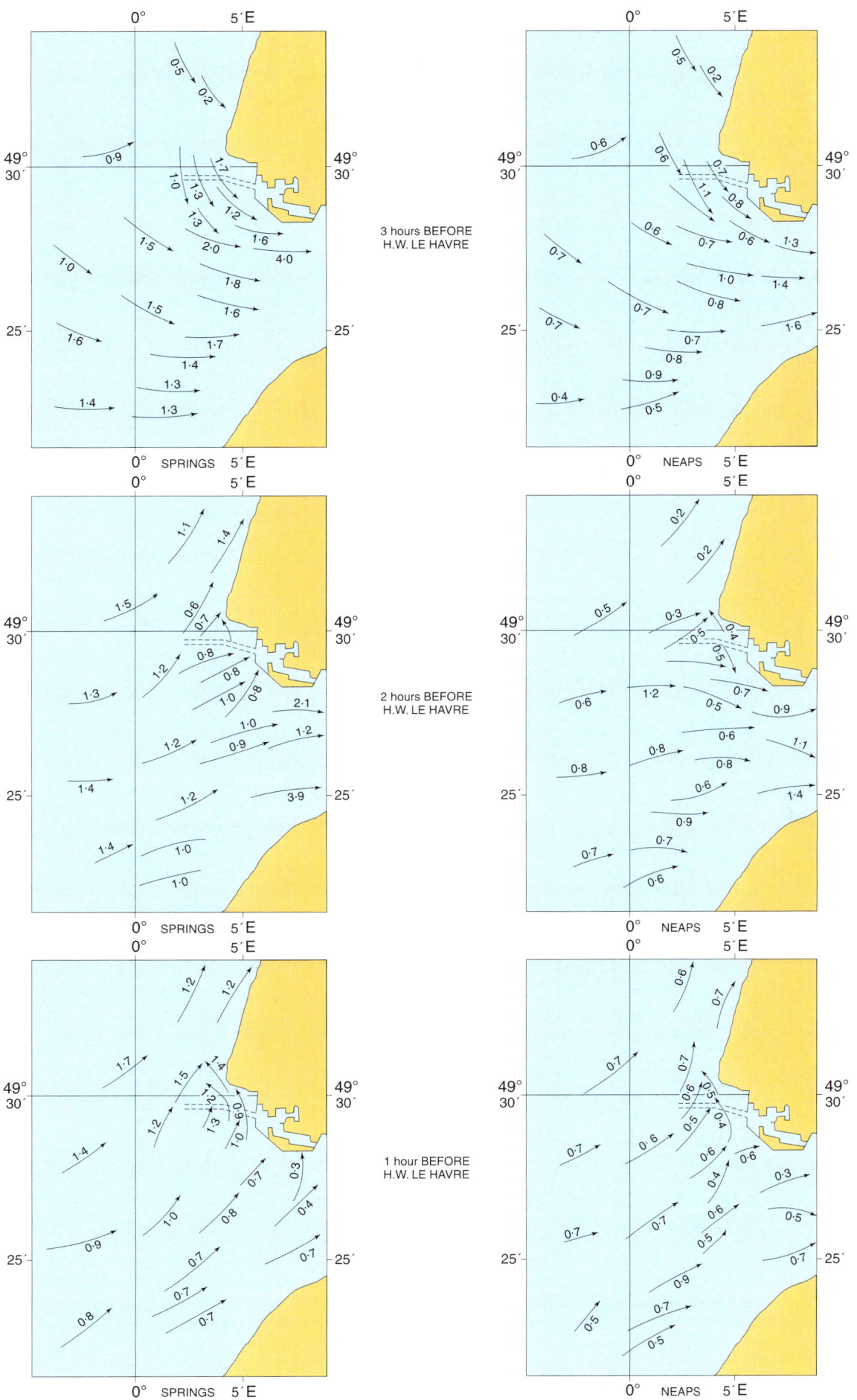

3 hours BEFORE
H.W. LE HAVRE

2 hours BEFORE
H.W. LE HAVRE

1 hour BEFORE
H.W. LE HAVRE

447

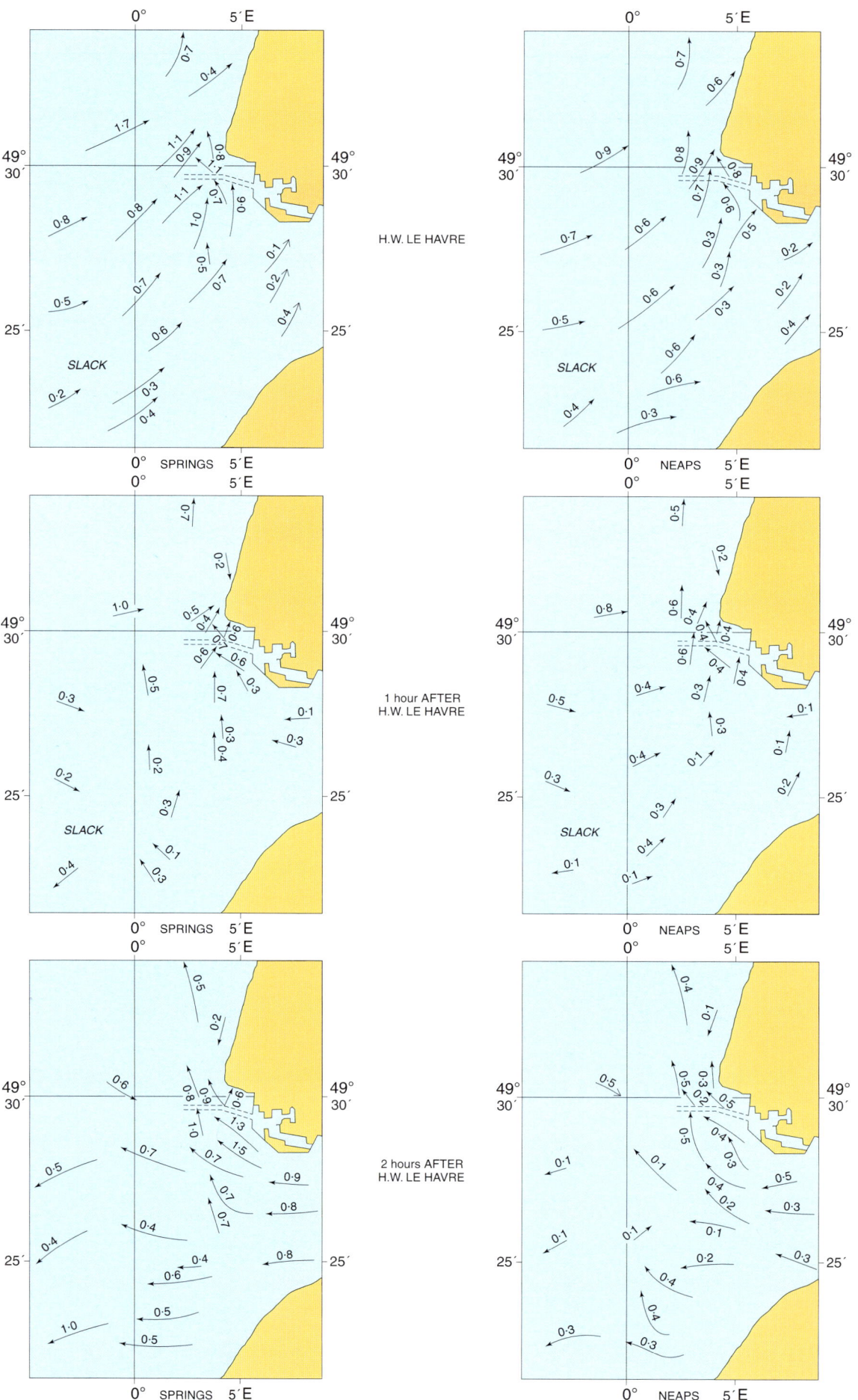

HW. LE HAVRE

1 hour AFTER
H.W. LE HAVRE

2 hours AFTER
H.W. LE HAVRE

448

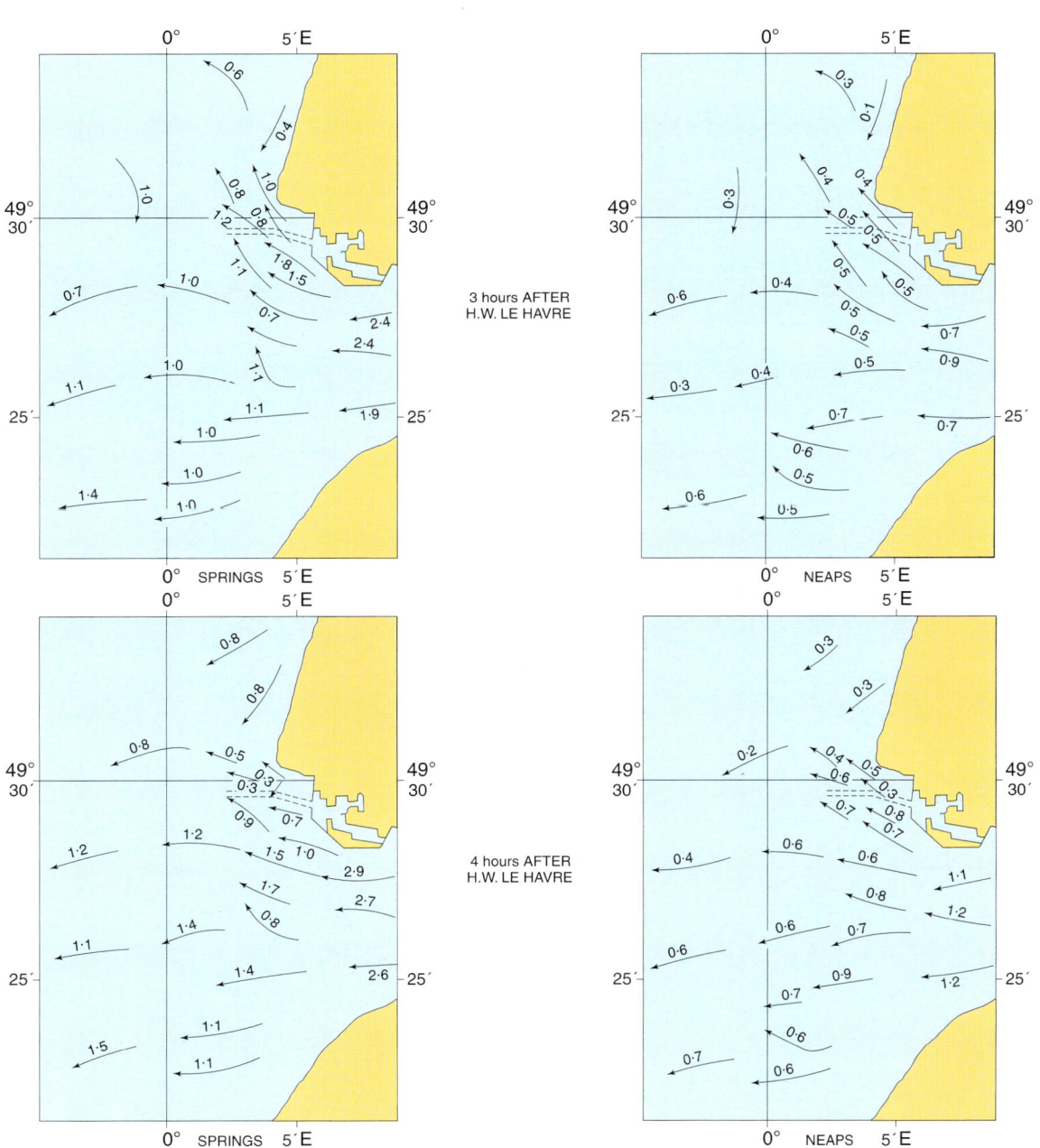

3 hours AFTER
H.W. LE HAVRE

4 hours AFTER
H.W. LE HAVRE

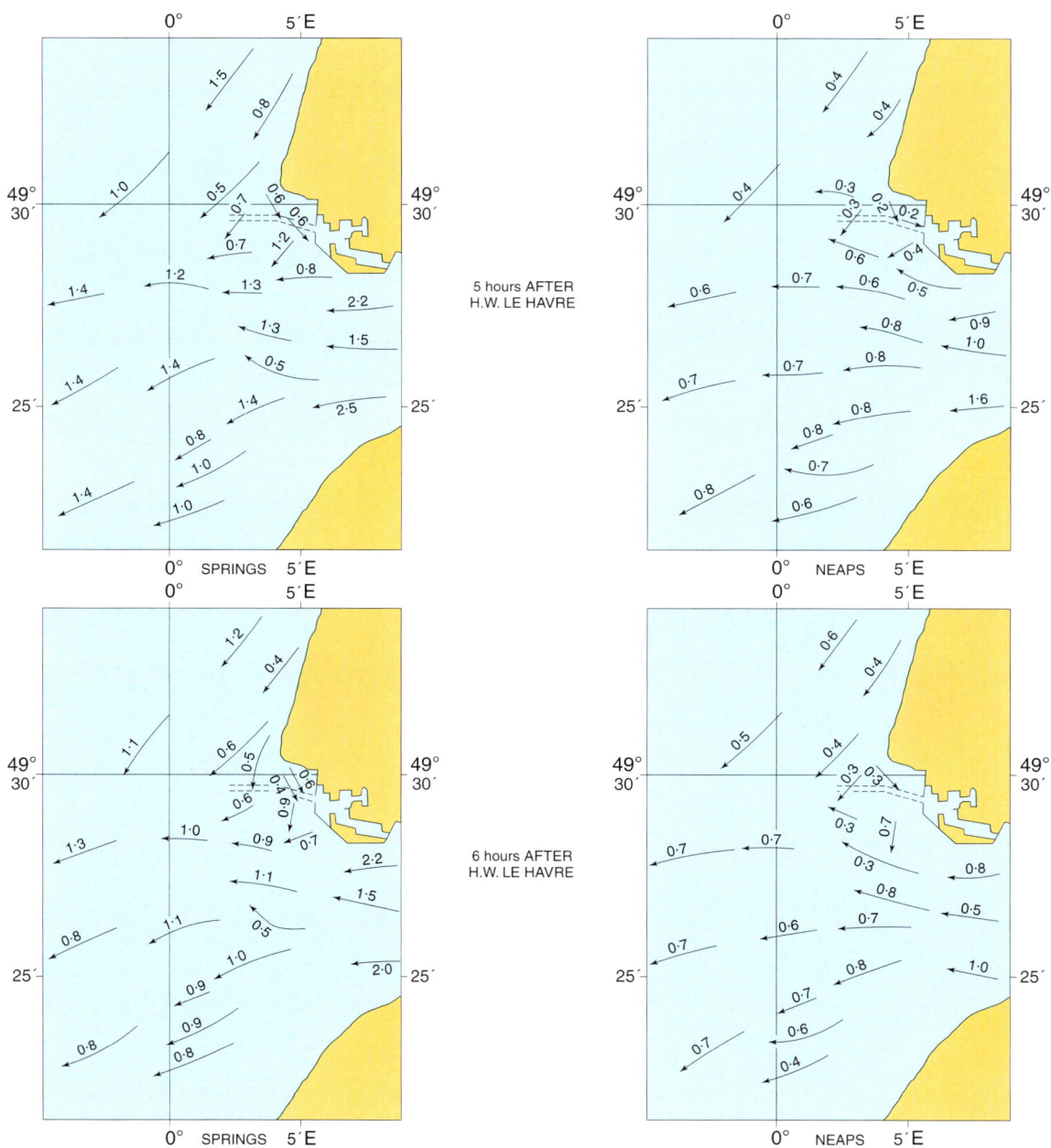

5 hours AFTER
H.W. LE HAVRE

6 hours AFTER
H.W. LE HAVRE

13.140

1   **Useful marks:**

Direction lights for the old approach channel which consist of a front light (white tower red top, 18 m in height) (49°29′·5N 0°05′·8E) and a rear light (red lantern square base on house, 41 m in height) (4 cables E of the front light) are normally unlit but can be exhibited in exceptional circumstances for short periods; in line they bear 090°.

2   Signal Station (port control tower) (49°29′·0N 0°06′·1E) situated on top of the Harbour Master's office on Quai des Abeilles.

Light (green lantern, 3 m in height) (49°28′·9N 0°06′·4E) (not shown on chart 2879), a powerful white light and close W of the approach channel front leading light, standing on the W corner of Quai Roger Meunier; exhibited occasionally in thick fog.

Le Havre tidal basins
13.141

1   **Direction light.** The white sector (119°–120°) of a direction light (lantern on white pyramidal tower green top, 6 m in height (49°28′·1N 0°08′·3E), shown throughout 24 hours lcads in Bassin Théophile Ducrocq.

Other leading lights, the positions and alignments of which are shown on the chart, indicate the approach to the oil basins on the S side, and to the repair berths at the E end, of Bassin Théophile Ducrocq, and to Bassin du Pacifique at the W end of Bassin René Coty.

2   **Turning areas.** A turning area of 600 m diameter is situated in Bassin Théophile Ducrocq, N of the oil basins and W of Môle Central. Another turning area, of the same diameter, is situated in Bassin René Coty; the alignment (067¼°) of two lights (white tower red top) (49°28′·6N 0°10′·4E) situated NW of Écluse François Premier, and lights in line (white round metal towers, red tops) (335¾°) situated at the E end of Terminal d'Atlantique, assist mariners when turning.

Port 2000 tidal basin
13.142

1   **Leading lights:**

Front (49°27′·2N 0°10′·7E).

Rear (2¼ cables ESE of front light).

From a position close N of LH21 Light Beacon (N cardinal) the alignment (102°) of these lights leads in Bassin Hubert Raoul-Duval to the berths at Quai du Havre and through the turning area (see below). Additional light buoys (lateral) mark the route.

2   **Turning area** about 700 m in diameter is situated in Bassin Hubert Raoul-Duval 1 mile WNW of the front leading light. A sectored light (white tower) (49°27′·1N 0°09′·2E) to assist turning vessels, is exhibited from Digue François Le Chevalier due S of, and on, the N/S axis of the turning area.

Basins and berths

Port 2000
13.143

1   **Description.** Port 2000 (49°27′·5N 0°08′·5E), a tidal basin situated S of the existing port, constructed for the container trades.

Berths. Quai du Havre, a single continuous line of berths, 4 200 m total length. Currently (2006) four berths are open at the E end of Quai du Havre; each berth 350 m

in length with depths of 14·5 m. Works in progress (2006) to create additional berths with depths between 14·5 and 17 m.

Bassin de la Manche
13.144

1   **Description.** Bassin de la Manche (49°29′·0N 0°06′·5E), a tidal basin situated E of Avant-port used by car ferries, general cargo and fishing vessels, port and national craft, gives access to the wet docks through Sas Quinette-de-Rochemont and La Citadelle (13.150), at the E end of the basin, and to Bassin Notre-Dame, Bassin du Roy and Bassin du Commerce, through dock gates at the N end of the basin; these latter basins are used by pleasure craft.

2   **Berths:** the largest and deepest berths are:

Terminal de Grande Bretagne, on the N side, two RoRo berths for vessels up to 160 m in length with depths of 5 m alongside.

Quai Roger-Meunier, on the S side, 500 m in length with depths of 8·5 m alongside. With strong NW winds a swell may be felt at this quay.

Bassin Théophile Ducrocq and Bassin René Coty
13.145

1   **Bassin Théophile Ducrocq** is entered from Avant-port through a passage 1 cable wide between Môle Nord and Môle Sud.

On the N side of the basin, Quai Pierre Callet and Quai Joannès-Couvert are used by general cargo vessels, passenger vessels and grain carriers; there are also facilities for handling containers.

2   The E side of the basin comprises a floating dock, graving dock and repair yards, with two RoRo berths on dolphins for vehicle ferries up to 160 m in length. Môle Central divides the E end of the basin into two parts; on the N side two berths for vessels under repair afloat, and on the S side a tanker and mineral berths.

The S side of the basin comprises an oil port, which is continued E into Bassin René Coty, with berths for vessels up to 280 000 dwt.

3   **Berths:** the longest and deepest berths in each complex are:

Quai Joannès-Couvert total length 1500 m with depths alongside between 11 and 12 m.A floating dock (13.153) is moored close S of Quai Joannès-Couvert at berths 5 and 6.

Quai Mazeline, disused since 2005, a floating repair berth, 428 m in length with a depth alongside of 10 m for vessels up to 300 000 dwt and 550 m in length

4   Môle Central Berth No 6, a mineral berth, 240 m in length with a depth alongside of 16 m for vessels up to 170 000 dwt.

Oil Basin No 1, a methane terminal, for vessels up to 230 m in length and 10 m draught carrying liquefied gas.

Oil Port Berth No 8, with a theoretical depth of 17 m and a working depth of 15 m alongside, for tankers up to 220 000 dwt.

13.146

1   **Bassin René Coty** continues ENE from Bassin Théophile Ducrocq for about 1 mile. There are container terminals, Terminal de l'Atlantique and Europe Atlantique Terminal, on the N side, and Terminal de Normandie on the S side of the basin. Bassin du Pacific, in the SE corner of the basin, E of Terminal de Normandie, is 225 m wide.

2 **Berths:** the longest and deepest berths in each complex are:

Oil Port Berth No 10, with a theoretical depth of 21 m and a working depth of 19 m alongside, for tankers up to 280 000 dwt.

Quai de l'Atlantique 800 m in length with a maximum depth of 12 m alongside.

3 Quai des Amériques 500 m in length with a maximum charted depth of 13·4 m alongside.

Quai de l'Asie 620 m in length with a charted depth of 13·1 m alongside.

Quai d'Osaka 450 m in length with a depth of about 13·5 m alongside.

Charts 2879, 2990
Constant level basins and berths
13.147

1 **Locks.** There are two principal locks leading to the constant level basins and Canal du Havre á Tancarville (13.149):

Écluse François Premier (49°28'·5N 0°10'·3E), 400 m long, 67 m wide with a depth over the sill of 14·5 m, is designed for vessels of 250 000 tons and leads from Bassin René Coty into Grand Canal du Havre (13.148).

2 Sas Vétillart (49°28'·9N 0°08'·4E), 175 m long, 27 m wide, with a least depth over the sills of 2 m, leads from Bassin Bellot (13.151) into Bassin Vétillart (13.149) and thence into Canal du Havre á Tancarville.

13.148

1 **Grand Canal du Havre,** entered from Bassin René Coty through Écluse François Premier, or from Canal de du Havre á Tancarville through Canal Bossière, leads E; it is straight and almost parallel with Canal du Havre á Tancarville. The canal is about 6 miles long and is marked by buoys on each side and can accept vessels with draughts up to 17 m; there are several large industrial complexes with adjacent berths on each side of the canal and a RoRo terminal on the S side near its W end.

2 Canal Bossière, about 7 cables long, leads NE from Grand Canal du Havre into Canal du Havre á Tancarville; it is spanned about mid-length by Pont Rouge, a bridge. Terminal de l'Europe, a large 4-berth container terminal, occupies the SW bank of the canal; there are tanker berths on the SE bank opposite the terminal.

3 Darse de l'Océan is entered from Grand Canal du Havre SE of Écluse François Premier; Terminal de l'Océan, a 5-berth container terminal, is situated on the E side of Darse de l'Océan.

The longest and deepest berths are:

Berths 1 to 3 Quai de l'Europe, about 910 m long, at the SW end of Terminal de l'Europe; also equipped to handle RoRo traffic.

4 Quai Bougainville, Berths 1 to 5 in Darse de l'Océan, 1625 m long for vessels up to 13 m draught; there is a floating link span for RoRo vessels on the quay.

RoRo Terminal, on the S side of Grand Canal du Havre about 5 cables E of the entrance, with a maximum depth at Berth No 2.

5 Sogestrol Berths, on the N side of Grand Canal du Havre about 8 cables E of the entrance, accommodates liquid gas and chemical carriers 200 m in length.

Multivrac Bulk Centre, on the S side of Grand Canal du Havre about 3 miles E of the entrance, accommodates bulk carriers up to 150 000 tons.

For depths in Grande Canal du Havre, see 13.121.

13.149

1 **Canal du Havre á Tancarville** leads E for about 12 miles, from the non-tidal and constant level basins to Tancarville where it connects with La Seine Maritime through Tancarville Locks (km 339). Sas Vétillart (49°28'·9N 0°08'·3E) (13.147), a lock at the E end of Bassin Bellot (13.151) the largest non-tidal basin, gives access to the constant level basins.

2 Bassin Vétillart, at the W end of Canal du Havre á Tancarville, is 975 m long and is used for handling fruit and by river barges. Quai de la Garonne, on the S side, is the longest berth. Bassin Fluvial leads W from Bassin Vétillart through a passage 15·8 m wide.

Garage de Graville, used as a turning basin, is entered from Bassin Vétillart through a passage with a width of 30 m spanned by Bridge No 5.

3 Bridge No 6, with a width of 30 m, spans the canal 3 cables E of Garage de Graville where the canal then widens to form Bassin Marcel Despujols, a turning basin. Quai du Rhin lies on the N side and Quai de la Moselle, for vessels carrying chemical products, lies on the S side of the basin. Bridge No 7 spans Canal du Havre á Tancarville at the E end of the basin.

4 Bassin de Lancement lies E of Bridge No 7; there are slipways on its N side and two berths for handling liquefied gas on its S side. Canal Bossière (13.148) joins Bassin de Lancement in the SW part of the basin. Bridge No 7b, with a vertical clearance of 7 m when closed, and Bridge No 8 span the canal at the E end of the basin, where a small canal branches N to the small port at Harfleur (49°30'N 0°12'E).

5 Gonfreville L'Orcher, on Canal du Havre á Tancarville 2 miles E of Bassin de Lancement, has berths for coasting vessels, small tankers and liquid gas carriers up to a length of 100 m. Between Gonfreville L'Orcher and the locks at Tancarville the maximum permitted draught of vessels is 3·5 m. The canal is spanned by Pont Du Hode, a bridge with a vertical clearance of 7 m when closed, and by a transporter bridge at km 10·3 with a vertical clearance of 17 m when closed.

For depths in Canal du Havre á Tancarville, see 13.121.

6 **Tancarville Locks** giving access to La Seine have the following dimensions:

North lock: 177 m long, 28 m wide with a depth of 0·4 m below chart datum.

South lock: 200 m long, 23·8 m wide with a depth of 3 m below chart datum.

The times of opening are broadcast monthly. A signal station which displays signals for Tancarville Locks is situated on the S side of the locks.

Charts 2879, 2990
Wet basins and berths
13.150

1 **Locks.** Two locks give access from the E end of Bassin de la Manche (49°29'·0N 0°06'·5E) (13.144) to the principal wet basins:

Sas Quinette-de-Rochemont, 232 m long, 30 m wide, with a depth over the sill of 4·5 m, leads into Bassin de l'Eure and Bassin Bellot; it is limited to vessels with a maximum beam of 26 m.

2   Citadelle Lock, 75 m long, 16 m wide, with a depth over the sill of 1·65 m leads into Bassin de la Citadelle.

The locks can be used at all times. The gates are normally open from 2 hours before to 1 hour after HW; the wind and barometric pressure have an appreciable effect on these times.

13.151

1   **Berths.** Bassin Bellot, the largest non-tidal basin, is equipped for handling grain and refrigerated cargoes; Sas Vétillart (13.147), a lock at the E end of the basin, gives access to the constant level basins. Quai Hermann du Pasquier, the deepest and longest berth on the S side of the basin, is 1524 m in length.

2   Bassin de l'Eure, on the NW side of Bassin Bellot, gives access to three dry docks and repair quays; it communicates on the N with Bassin Vauban and on the E with Bassin Paul Vatine. Quai de la Guinée, 377 m long, on the W side of the basin is the deepest and longest berth.

Bassin Vauban, entered from the N end of Bassin de l'Eure through a passage 16 m wide, gives access at its W end to Bassin de la Barre through a passage 12 m wide; both basins are used by port auxiliary and fishing vessels.

3   Bassin de la Citadelle is reserved for port auxiliary and fishing vessels; it is accessible only through Citadelle Lock. There is access at its NW end to Bassin de la Barre through a passage. Quai Delavigne, 360 m long, on the N side of the basin is the longest quay.

For depths in the wet basins, see 13.121.

Opening of movable bridges
13.152

1   Movable bridges which cross dock gates and span passages between basins, and those spanning Canal du Havre á Tancarville operate as follows:

2   Pont Paul Dennis, Pont Notre-Dame and Pont de Lamblardie, which gives access to Bassin du Commerce, open on demand between 0600 and 2100 from 2 hours before to ½ hour after HW.

Pont de l'Eure operates continuously with daily interruptions of short duration.

3   Bridges No 5 and No 6, between Bassins Vétillart and Marcel Despujols operate continuously.

Bridge No 7, Pont Rouge, Bridge No 7bis, Bridge No 8, between Bassin Marcel Despujols, Canal Bossière and Canal du Havre á Tancarville, operate permanently with daily interruptions of short duration.

4   Pont de Hode, request to be made before 1600.

Transporter Bridge requires 72 hours notice.

For signals, see 13.133.

Port services

Repairs
13.153

1   Repairs of all kinds can be carried out; there are several repair berths for vessels up to 90 000 dwt and two floating repair berths for vessels up to 300 000 dwt. There are several dry docks, the largest No 7 in Bassin Théophile Ducrocq has a length of 313 m and breadth of 38 m. There is a floating dock of length 310 m, breadth 53 m with a lifting capacity of 50 000 tonnes for vessels up to 220 000 tonnes deadweight and 9·7 m draught at Quai Joannès Couvert.

Other facilities
13.154

1   **Ship sanitation control and ship sanitation control exemption certificates** are issued at Le Havre. See 1.140.

Hospital. Good hospital and medical services are available.

Gas-freeing and tank cleaning facilities are available.

Supplies
13.155

1   **Fuel oil:** all grades can be supplied at the quays or by barge.

Fresh water is laid on to the quays.

Provisions and stores of all kinds are available.

Communications
13.156

1   **Airport:** Havre-Octeville International Airport 6 km from the port.

Rescue
13.157

1   **Lifeboat,** see 13.113.

LA SEINE MARITIME

General information

Charts 2990, 2879, 2146
Description
13.158

1   La Seine Maritime is that part of the river navigable by sea-going ships from just below Berville-sur-Mer (49°26′N 0°22′E) (km 48), situated 5 miles E of Honfleur, to Jeanne d'Arc Bridge at Rouen, a distance of about 57 nautical miles (105 km); see Diagram 13.189.

Above Rouen, La Seine is navigable to Paris, where there is an inland port at Gennevilliers, and whence there is access to inland waterways.

2   The river is marked at each kilometre, indicating distance from Paris.

Navigation in the river is governed closely by the tides. Vessels ascend with the in-going tide as soon as there is sufficient water for them to enter the channel. The passage up river to Rouen takes about 6 hours and can be done on a single tide.

Topography
13.159

1   **Estuaire de la Seine — south side of entrance.** The coast from Pointe de Beuzeval (49°18′N 0°05′W), the S entrance point to Estuaire de la Seine, to Trouville-sur-Mer, 7 miles NE, is backed by dark rounded hills with cliffs between the point and Villers-sur-Mer, a seaside town, 3 miles NE. Mont Canisy (49°20′N 0°02′E), with a flat summit, lies close to the coast between the valleys of Villers-sur-Mer and Rivière La Touques.

2   **North side of entrance.** The city of Le Havre (13.115) and its port installations lie to the S and E of Cap de la Hève (49°31′N 0°04′E), the N entrance point to the estuary.

Dimensions of vessels
13.160

1   For vessels proceeding to Rouen (km 245), Port-Jérôme (km 332) and Miroline Oil Wharf (km 353) the maximum length is 280 m. Some restrictions may be applied on certain night tides; the pilotage service should be consulted for details.

2   The maximum draughts for proceeding up or down river, as authorised by the pilotage service, are published monthly and amended by notices. The draughts given for vessels proceeding up river refer to the draught in salt water; for vessels proceeding down river they refer to the draught in fresh water. The maximum draughts given assume normal meteorological conditions; they may be increased or decreased at the moment of a vessel's arrival or departure if the water level differs considerably from that predicted. Port Authorities may impose draught restrictions for certain specific areas. Further restrictions may also be imposed, particulary at night, on vessels whose handling qualities, radio or radar equipment are considered to be deficient.

3   Masters are advised to obtain details of the maximum authorised draught from the pilotage service in borderline cases; in any event they are required to sign a document stating their vessel's draught and speed.

Controlling depths
13.161

1   **Normal maximum draughts.** The normal maximum draughts lie between 9·8 m and 11·8 m depending on berth and tidal conditions. The pilot office calculates maximum draughts on a daily basis and should always be consulted for the most recent information.:

2   Proceeding down river from Rouen a draught of 10·15 m for vessels capable of 12 kn and under normal conditions but variable depending on the vessel's speed, the range of the tide and the rate of the tidal stream. The permissible draught may be increased by making a short stop at Radicatel Quay (km 336).

3   Deep-draught vessels can proceed down river in two stages, either mooring at buoys at Villequier (km 314) or at dolphins at Vatteville-la-Rue (km 318), with the aid of two tugs. Under these circumstances a greater draught than normal is permitted (up to 10·6 m) on certain tides. Vessels can also proceed in three stages mooring at the buoys or dolphins, and at Radicatel Quay, when draughts similar to those vessels proceeding up river, up to a maximum of 10·6 m on certain tides, can be carried. This programmed descent of the river is not authorised for tankers which are not gas-free.

4   **Variations of depths** in the channel can be caused by natural phenomena; these are greatest in the stretch between Honfleur (km 356) and Tancarville (km 338) where it can be as much as 0·3 m in a week. Daily soundings of the channel are carried out and dredgers are permanently operating to maintain and improve depths.

Density. The river water is salty as far as Vieux-Port (km 325) but this may vary with natural conditions.

Hazards
13.162

1   **Fog** is the principal danger to navigation. It forms at dusk in the autumn and winter, and at dawn in the spring and summer, but normally clears during the morning. It is however exceptional for navigation to be interrupted. It occurs, on average, on about 29 days per year, on four of which it may last all day. Fog detectors are installed at various points in the river. The state of visibility is broadcast from Rouen Port Radio on request; for details see *Admiralty List of Radio Signals Volume 6(1)*.

2   **Ferries** cross the river at several points which are indicated by an inscription "BAC" on a notice board and a fixed violet light at night. In addition to the usual lights at night ferries exhibit lights shown in Diagram 13.162.1.

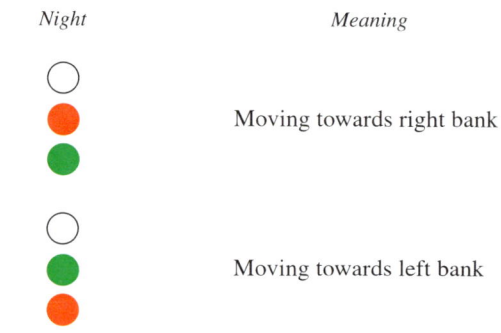

La Seine Maritime - ferry siginals (13.162.1)

3   **Dredgers** are permanently operating in the channel; they exhibit signals shown in Diagram 13.162.2.

La Seine Maritime - dredger siginals (13.162.2)

Pilotage
13.163

1   **Pilotage is compulsory** for vessels of more than 45 m in length.

Availability: 24 hours.

Boarding place. Pilot boards in position 49°28′·6N 0°02′·7W, about 4¾ miles WSW of Cap de la Hève Light.

Pilot boats have a black hull and an orange superstructure carrying the inscription "Pilote-Rouen" in black.

2   **Notice of ETA required.** At least 5 hours before arrival at Rouen Pilots. Advise changes 3 hours before arrival.

La Seine pilotage station also provides pilots for Caen-Ouistreham (13.67) and Deauville-Trouville (13.173).

For details see *Admiralty List of Radio Signals Volume 6(1)*.

Traffic regulations
13.164

1   **Baie de Seine Reporting Area**. The area covered is contained within a circle, 22 miles radius centred on Cap de la Hève Lighthouse (49°31′N 0°04′E), bordered to the S by the coast and to the N by the meridan of Cap d'Antifer Lighthouse (49′41′N 0°10′E). All vessels of 50 m length or

more bound for, or originating from, the waiting areas for Havre-Antifer, Le Havre and Rouen or the port of Caen-Ouistreham must report to Baie de Seine Traffic and maintain a listening watch whilst in the reporting area.

2 **Movement reporting system.** Two radar stations are located respectively E of Honfleur and on the north bank of the river at Radicatel, both stations are operated from Honfleur. The system is compulsory for all commercial vessels and ensures control of marine traffic from the estuary of the Seine to the port of Rouen. The system covers the working area of the Honfleur radar (49°26′N 0°14′E) at a range of 20 miles and along the Upper Seine to Pont Jeanne d'Arc at Rouen.

3 The Control Centre is located at the Harbour Master's Office, Rouen, and is in operation throughout 24 hours; mariners should contact the Control Centre 48 hours before arrival in Rade de la Carosse.

Information on visibility in the estuary up to Rouen, tidal conditions, meteorological and navigational conditions can be supplied on request; call Rouen Port or Radar Honfleur, see also 13.171.

4 For mariners in vessels carrying hydrocarbons or dangerous substances, see 13.107.

For further details see *Admiralty List of Radio Signals Volume 6(1).*

13.165

1 **Overtaking.** This is permitted provided there is clear visibility and no ship can be seen approaching from the opposite direction. Sound signals indicating this manoeuvre are:

By overtaking vessel	Two long blasts followed by two short blasts indicates overtaking to port. Two long blasts followed by one short blast indicates overtaking to starboard
By vessel being overtaken	One long blast, one short blast, one long blast, one short blast indicates overtaking is accepted. A series of five short blasts indicates overtaking is refused.

13.166

1 **Speed limit** in the river between Tancarville and Rouen is 15 kn, but vessels must not cause excessive wash.

Vessels of less than 20 m in length must not hinder other vessels and must comply with certain other regulations; pleasure craft are forbidden to navigate at night.

Marine nature reserve
13.167

1 A marine nature reserve is situated S of Chenal de Rouen (13.172) in an area of varying width, running from position 49°26′·0N 0°04′·2E to position 49°25′·7N 0°12′·3E

Rescue
13.168

1 For details of rescue facilities, see 13.113.

Tidal streams
13.169

1 The tidal streams in the river are complex and further complicated by a double HW which occurs at springs below Duclair (km 277) and which are separated by an average of 2½ hours at each point in the river. At neaps these HWs merge together and are indefinable. At springs the first HW becomes of less and less importance as the

river is ascended. At Rouen there is only one HW, but the rise of tide is very rapid in the first hour after LW.

2 The range of the tide at springs is:
   At Honfleur 7 m.
   At Caudebec (km 310) 4·5 m.
   At Rouen 3 m.
   Above Caudebec LW neaps are lower than LW springs.

3 See diagrams, Rivière Seine — Mean Spring and Mean Neap Curves, and Rivière Seine — Mean Spring and Mean Neap Tidal Stream Rates.

In periods of drought or in certain meteorological conditions the level of water can be lowered by as much as 0·8 m.

4 Tide gauges, some of which are illuminated at night, are situated at various points in the estuary and in the river; they give the height of tide above the datum of the charts at Le Havre. In addition the height of tide above this datum is broadcast every 10 minutes, and on request, from Honfleur Radar Station, on VHF from 2 hours before to 3 hours after the beginning of the HW stand at Le Havre.

5 **Times of tidal streams.** The following table gives the differences to be added to the time of LW Le Havre to find the time at which the in-going stream begins at various points in the river:

	Height of HW at Le Havre		
Place	*8 m*	*7 m*	*6 m*
Épi de La Roque (km 342)	0210	0200	0215
Quillebeuf sur Seine (km 332)	0230	0240	0250
Villequier Amont(km 313)	0325	0320	0320
Caudebec (km 311)	0330	0330	0330
La Mailleraye sur Seine (km 303)	0350	0350	0400
Duclair (km 278)	0440	0445	0500
La Bouille (km 257)	0510	0520	0550
Rouen	0540	0550	0615

6 The times at which the out-going streams begin are influenced by natural conditions; they usually begin at about the following periods after the beginning of the HW stand at Le Havre:

Berville-sur-Mer (km 346)	0215
Quillebeuf sur Seine	0315
Villequier Amont	0400
Duclair	0430
Rouen	0530

7 **Rates of the streams** decrease as the river is ascended; the maximum rates at springs are:
   Tancarville, in-going stream 6 kn, out-going stream 4 kn.
   Above La Mailleraye sur Seine, 2 to 3 kn in both directions.

8 **Bore.** A bore, called Mascaret, occurs in the river at springs, but because of the improvements to the channel its effect is only felt above Villequiers Amont, especially in the bends above this point; it ceases at Rouen but the arrival of the bore can be felt in the lower part of this port when the height of tide at Le Havre exceeds 7·6 m.

9 A bore detector at La Bouille registers the arrival of the bore; this information can be obtained from Rouen Port Radio on request by day or night.

The bore presents little inconvenience to navigation but ships at anchor or moorings should take special precautions to avoid parting their cables since they may be swung to the falling stream on its arrival; the pilots can give useful advice. Mariners in small craft can minimise the effect of the bore by keeping in mid-stream.

Directions
(continued from 13.16)

Principal marks
13.170

1   For details of principal marks in the approach, see 13.114.

Other aids to navigation
13.171

1   For details of other aids to navigation, see 13.114.

     Radar assistance. In poor visibility, and on request, Radar Honfleur (49°25′·7N 0°14′·0E) will provide navigational information on VHF. The area of radar coverage extends to 20 miles W of Radar Honfleur up to km 325. See also 13.164 and *Admiralty List of Radio Signals Volume 6(1).*

Chenal de Rouen
13.172

1   Mariners bound for ports on La Seine Maritime should make for LHA Light Buoy (safe water) (49°31′N 0°10′W) (13.137) and thence to a position W of RP Light Buoy (isolated danger) (49°28′·6N 0°01′·2W), moored at the W end of Rouen Waiting Area No 1 (13.109), to embark, or await, the pilot.

     Caution. An obstruction (position doubtful) lies 8¾ cables W of RP Light Buoy and another obstruction lies 1¾ miles W of the same buoy.

2   From the pilot boarding position make for the entrance to Chenal de Rouen, the channel which lies between Banc d'Amfard, a drying bank, on its N side, and Banc du Ratier on its S side, and forms the access to La Seine Maritime. Digue du Ratier, a training wall which covers, extends 4½ miles W from the entrance to Honfleur, flanking the S side of the channel. The height of the wall varies from 5 to 2 m above chart datum and it is marked by beacons lettered from A to G from seaward; a light is exhibited from A Light Beacon (N cardinal on black column, 10 m in height) (49°25′·9N 0°06′·6E) at the head of the training wall. Digue Basse du Nord, a training wall which covers, lies about 5 cables N of Digue du Ratier; the height of the wall varies from 3 to 6 m above chart datum and it is marked by beacons.

3   The channel is entered from Rade de la Carosse (49°28′·2N 0°01′·4E) between No 4 Light Buoy (port hand) (49°27′·0N 0°02′·6E) and Ratier NW Light Buoy (starboard hand), 1¾ cables SSW. Thence the channel narrows and is marked by pairs of light buoys (port and starboard hand) moored at intervals of about 1500 m, with a width between them of about 200 m, as far as Berville-sur-Mer (Km 346).

4   **Useful mark:**

         Falaise des Fonds Light (white tower green top, 18 m in height) (49°25′·5N 0°12′·9E) standing on the coast about 7 cables W of the entrance to Honfleur.

Deauville-Trouville and approaches

Charts 1349 Plan of Deauville-Trouville, 2146
General information
13.173

1   **Position and function.** The port of Deauville-Trouville (49°22′N 0°04′E), two neighbouring towns, is situated on each side of the entrance to Rivière La Touques and is used by fishing vessels and pleasure craft.

Trouville from SSE (13.173)

(Original dated 1993)

(Photograph - Service Hydrographique et Océanographique de la Marine)

     Port Authority:

         Municipal port of Deauville-Trouville, Maine de Deauville, Rue Fosserier, 14800 Deauville.

         Direction du port de Port-Deauville, Quai des Marchands, Deauville.

Limiting conditions
13.174

1   **Controlling depth.** The entrance channel dries 1·2 m at its N end. Depths less than charted (2007) exist in the entrance channel centred on position 49°22′·1N 0°04′·4E.

     Tidal levels, see information in *Admiralty Tide Tables.* Mean spring range about 7·0 m; mean neap range about 3·8 m.

2   **Maximum size of vessel handled:** length 55 m; beam 13 m; draught 3·5 m.

     Local weather. Entrance is difficult with fresh onshore winds when the sea breaks in the channel.

Arrival information
13.175

1   **Port radio** stations, with limited hours, operate from Deauville-Trouville, for details see *Admiralty List of Radio Signals Volume 6(1).*

2   **Notice of ETA required.** 48 hours and 5 hours in advance, stating length and draught.

     For details see *Admiralty List of Radio Signals Volume 6(1).*

RIVIÈRE SEINE
MEAN SPRING AND MEAN NEAP TIDAL STREAM RATES

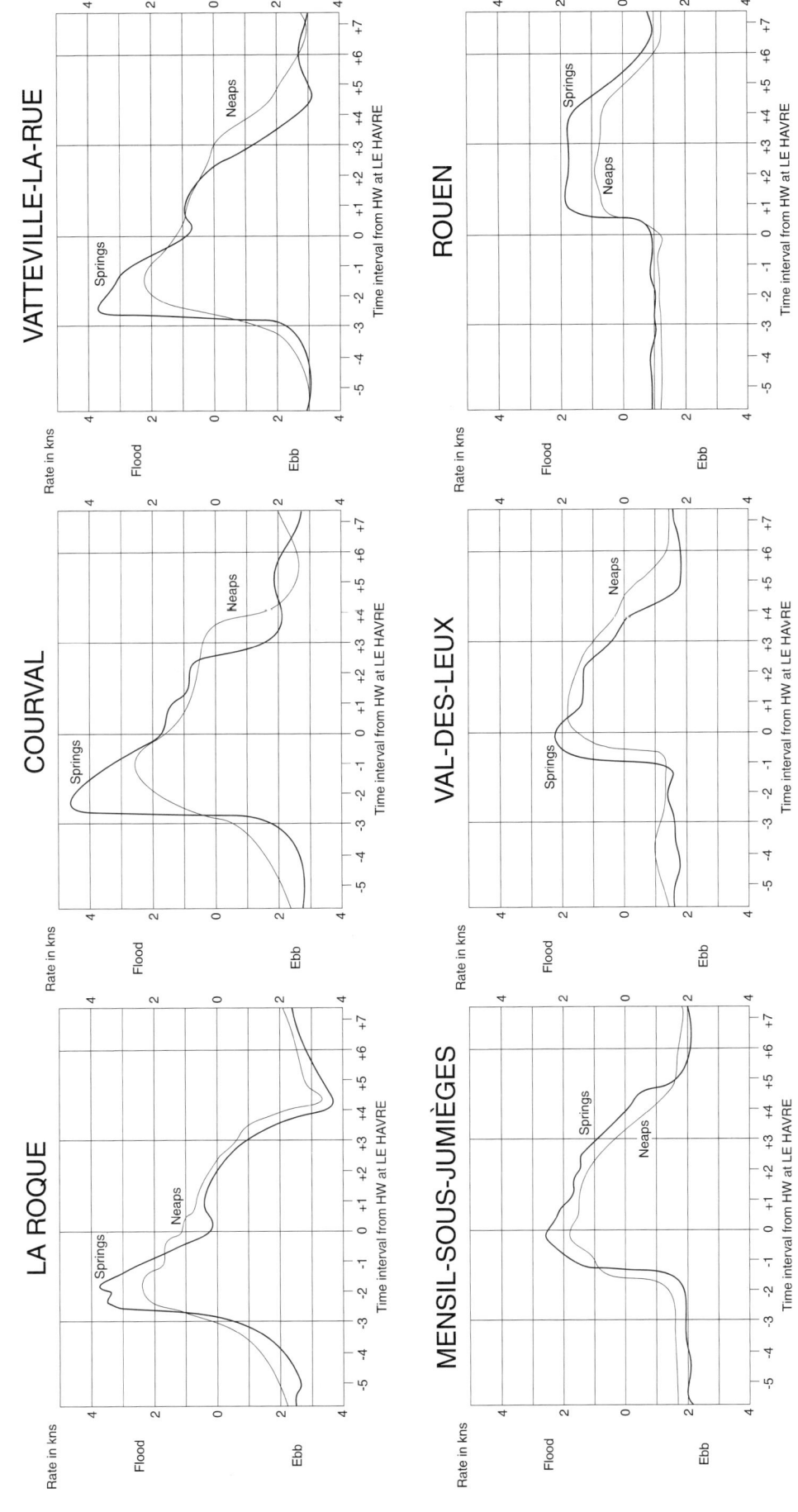

13.176

1   **Outer anchorages.** Mariners awaiting the pilot anchor in Rouen Waiting Areas, for details see 13.109.

Anchorage is available 2½ miles WNW of Pointe de la Cahotte (49°22′N 0°05′E) in depths of 4 m, as shown on the chart.

2   Mariners in small craft can anchor off the entrance to the port in an area SW of Banc de Trouville, and SE of Semoy Light Buoy (E cardinal) moored 2½ miles NNW of the entrance, and E of Trouville SW Light Buoy (W cardinal) moored 1 mile WNW of the entrance; there are depths of 2 to 3 m, sand and mud, NE of the alignment of the leading lights, and sand and shell SW of that line.

The anchorages off the port are untenable in strong onshore winds.

3   **Caution.** Between Jetée Roches Noires, a ruined jetty covered at HW and marked off its extremity by a buoy (port hand) situated 7 cables NE of Trouville-sur-Mer, and Pointe de Villerville (49°24′N 0°08′E) the coast is bordered by a drying rocky flat terminating in Les Perques de Villerville which extend 5 cables offshore almost as far as Banc de Trouville. Mariners are advised not to proceed E of a line joining Trouville-sur-Mer and Les Ratelets (13.179), 3½ miles N, unless certain of their position and proceeding solely to the anchorage NE of the alignment of the leading lights as described above.

4   **Clearing bearing.** Banc de Trouville and the greater part of Les Ratelets are covered by the red sector of Trouville Est Light (white pylon red top, 15 m in height) (49°22′·2N 0°04′·3E) at the head of the E training wall at Trouville bearing more than 175°.

13.177

1   **Pilotage** There is no official pilotage service for Deauville-Trouville. However, vessels may request asssitance from the port authorities.

Harbour
13.178

1   **General layout.** The harbour comprises an Avant-port, a drying harbour and wet basins. To the SW, Avant-port leads to Port-Deauville, a large yacht harbour on the W side of the entrance, and to the SE, between a breakwater and a jetty which run parallel to one another, to Bassins des Yachts and Morny and to a drying harbour formed by quays bordering Rivière La Touques; this latter complex is known as Vieux-Port.

2   **Dredgers.** A suction dredger, with spoil pipes attached, may be encountered in the approaches to the port and dredgers are frequently at work in the channel.

The channel is also frequently maintained by sluicing, except in mid-summer; when this is being done a blue flag is hoisted 24 hours in advance at the entrance to the wet basins.

3   **Traffic signals.** International Port Traffic Signals are exhibited at the W side of the locks at Port Deauville and Bassin des Yachts, for details see *The Mariner's Handbook*.

Tidal streams off Trouville begin as follows:

Interval from HW Le Havre	*Direction*
−0540	ENE
−0055	WSW

4   The maximum spring rates in each direction are 3 kn.

In the entrance channel the in-going and out-going streams begin at the same times and attain rates of 2¾ kn and 1¾ kn, respectively.

Slack water lasts from ¼ hour before to ¼ hour after local HW.

5   **Eddies.** There are eddies off the entrance to Bassin des Yachts about 1 hour before local HW

Directions for entering harbour
13.179

1   The best time for entering harbour is HW slack; see above.

Leading lights:

Front light (white metal tower red top, 11 m in height) (49°22′·0N 0°04′·5E) exhibited from the head of Jetée Est, the E breakwater.

2   Rear light (white pylon red top, 15 m in height) (1 cable SSE of the front light) exhibited from the root of the same breakwater at Pointe de la Cahotte.

From a position NNW of the port the alignment (148°) of these lights leads to the entrance channel passing (with positions given from Trouville Est Light (13.176)):

3   WSW of Les Ratelets (about 3 miles N) which form the W end of Banc du Ratier (13.172). Ratelets Light Buoy (W cardinal) is moored about 1 mile W of the drying part of Les Ratelets; a dangerous wreck (position approximate) is charted 1¼ miles NNW of the light-buoy. In 2004 it was reported that there was less water than charted in the vicinity of Les Ratelets Light Buoy. Thence:

4   ENE of a 1·7 m wreck (2½ miles NNW) marked by Semoy Light Buoy (E cardinal); thence:

ENE of Trouville SW Light Buoy (W cardinal) (1¼ miles WNW); thence:

Close ENE of an obstruction (position doubtful) (2½ cables NW); thence:

5   To the harbour entrance which is protected by rubble training walls which cover at HW. The W wall extends NNW from the outer end of the angled breakwater which protects the yacht harbour at Port Deauville, and the E wall, parallel but shorter, extends from the E breakwater. A light (black pylon green top, 16 m in height) is exhibited from the head of the W training wall and Trouville Est Light (13.176), is exhibited from a dolphin at the head of the E training wall. The walls are both marked at intervals by beacons; those on the W wall are green and those on the E wall are red. A light (green mast, 7 m in height) is exhibited from the head of the W breakwater protecting Port Deauville. The channel leading into the harbour, or Vieux Port, is bordered on its E side by a breakwater and on its W side by a jetty; the deepest water lies near the W jetty. A light (white metal tower green top, 10 m in height) is exhibited from the W jetty.

6   **Useful mark:**

Villerville Signal Station (red brick tower and house) (49°23′·2N 0°06′·6E) standing 1¾ miles NE of Trouville-sur-Mer.

Basins and berths
13.180

1   **Drying harbour.** The E bank of the river is quayed from Pointe de la Cahotte to Pont des Belges, about 6 cables within the entrance; a sandbank extends about 15 m from the N end of this quay. There are good drying-out berths alongside the quay which dries from 3 to 4 m, mud, except between the first landing steps and the ferry slipway where there are large pebbles; there are no berths alongside the W bank of the river. Mariners should not proceed above the last landing steps at Quai Fernand-Moureaux.

Port services
13.181

1   **Repairs** to small vessels can be carried out. There are several slipways on the river, the largest 25 m long and 6 m wide with a lifting capacity of 150 tonnes.

Supplies: fuel; fresh water; provisions.

Communications: Deauville-Saint-Gatien Airport 7 km E of the port with connecting International flights.

Rescue, see 13.113.

Honfleur

Chart 1349 Plan of Honfleur, 2879, 2146
General information
13.182

1   **Position.** Honfleur (49°25′N 0°14′E) is situated on the left bank of the estuary of La Seine.

Approach and entry. The port is approached from Chenal du Rouen, at the E end of Digue du Ratier (13.172), and entered through a large lock in the middle of an entrance channel between two high jetties.

2   **Traffic:** in 2006 the port handled 134 vessels totalling 654 843 dwt.

Port Authority: Bureau du Port, PO Box 45, F–14603, Honfleur; the port is administered by the port of Rouen (13.196).

Limiting conditions
13.183

1   **Tidal levels.** Mean spring range about 6·5 m; mean neap range about 3·8 m. A double HW occurs at Honfleur, see information in *Admiralty Tide Tables*.

Maximum size of vessel handled: 100 m length, 15·5 m beam; draughts vary depending on depths available between dredging programmes The port is subject to silting and frequent dredging takes place.

Arrival information
13.184

1   **Port radio** station, with limited hours, operates from Honfleur, for details see *Admiralty List of Radio Signals Volume 6(1)*.

For details of a Movement Reporting System, see 13.164.

Pilotage is compulsory; the port lies within the pilotage district of La Seine Maritime, for details see 13.163.

Tugs are available from Le Havre.

Harbour
13.185

1   **General layout.** The port comprises an Avant-port, a wet basin entered through a large lock in the entrance channel, leading to inner locks and wet basins. Bassin des Chasses, at the root of the E jetty, holds water which is used to sluice the entrance channel; sluicing does not take place when the entrance lock is in use.

2   **Traffic signals.** International Port Traffic Signals are exhibited by day and night from the mast at Honfleur Radar situated on level ground E of the entrance lock, for details see *The Mariner's Handbook*.

A simplified signalling system for the inner locks is shown on the S side of the entrance to Bassin de l'Est, for details see 1.93.

Directions for entering harbour
13.186

1   A channel, 100 m wide between two high jetties, leads to the entrance lock. A light (green pylon, 8 m in height) is exhibited from the head of the W jetty and another light (pylon N cardinal, 8 m in height) is exhibited from the head of the E jetty; Honfleur Radar stands close to the head of this latter jetty. The lock, which is about 40 m long and 23 m wide, permits passage of vessels of less than 36 m in length; vessels of more than 36 m in length must wait for HW slack to enter with both gates open. The lock operates throughout 24 hours except when sluicing is taking place; entrance takes place on the hour and departure on the half hour.

Honfleur Lock from NNW (13.186)

(Original dated 2004)

(Photograph - Drew Given, MV Doulos)

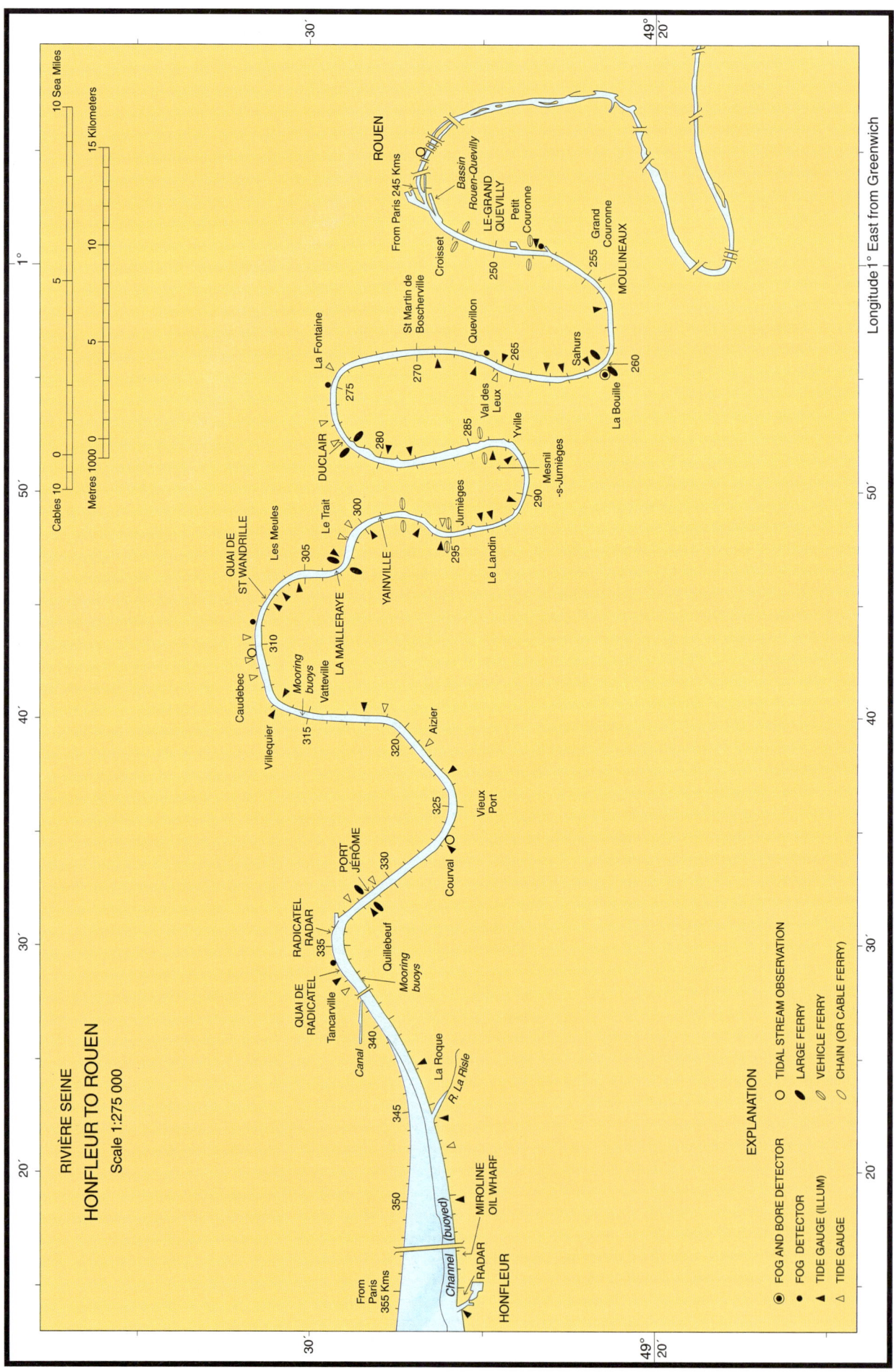

RIVIÈRE SEINE
HONFLEUR TO ROUEN
Scale 1:275 000

ROUEN

From Paris 245 Kms

Bassin
Rouen-Quevilly
LE-GRAND
QUEVILLY
Petit
Couronne
Grand
Couronne
MOULINEAUX

Croisset

St Martin de
Boscherville

Quevillon

La Fontaine

Val des
Leux

Sahurs

La Bouille

Yville

DUCLAIR

Mesnil
-s-Jumièges

QUAI DE
ST WANDRILLE

Les Meules

Le Trait

YAINVILLE

Jumièges

Le Landin

Caudebec

Mooring
buoys

Vatteville

LA MAILLERAYE

Villequier

Aizier

Vieux
Port

PORT
JÉRÔME

Courval

RADICATEL
RADAR

QUAI DE
RADICATEL

Tancarville

Quillebeuf

Mooring
buoys

Canal

La Roque

R. La Risle

From Paris
355 Kms

MIROLINE
OIL WHARF

Channel (buoyed)

RADAR

HONFLEUR

10 Sea Miles
15 Kilometers

Cables 10
Metres 1000 0

EXPLANATION

⦿ FOG AND BORE DETECTOR   ○ TIDAL STREAM OBSERVATION
● FOG DETECTOR   ⬤ LARGE FERRY
▲ TIDE GAUGE (ILLUM)   ⌀ VEHICLE FERRY
△ TIDE GAUGE   ⌀ CHAIN (OR CABLE FERRY)

Longitude 1° East from Greenwich

30′
49° 20′

1°

49° 30′

49° 20′

250
255
260
265
270
275
280
285
290
295
300
305
310
315
320
325
330
335
340
345
350

Basins and berths
13.187

1   **Avant-port,** a wet basin, gives access to the inner locks and wet basins; Avant-port is reserved for fishing vessels and for yachts waiting to enter Vieux Bassin. Vessels over 90 m in length must leave the port stern first.

2   **Vieux Bassin,** is entered from Avant-port through the W lock which is 10·5 m wide. The basin is 128 m long, 77 m wide with depths of 2·8 m; it is used by yachts.

3   **Bassin de l'Est** is entered from Avant-port through the E lock which is 16·5 m wide. The basin is 295 m long, 71 m wide with depths of 4 m. The basin is used by commercial traffic, with the exception of the S part of the basin which is reserved for fishing vessels. Vessels up to 70 m can be swung in the basin.

4   **Bassin Carnot** is entered from Bassin de l'Est through a passage 12·6 m wide and is limited to vessels with a maximum beam of 12·5 m and a maximum length of 90 m; it is used by commercial traffic. The basin is 788 m long, 108 m wide with depths of 4 m. Vessels up to 90 m can be swung in the basin.

    Inner locks. The locks to Vieux Bassin and Bassin de l'Est are open throughout 24 hours.

Port services
13.188

1   **Repairs.** Major repairs can be carried out to vessels afloat provided there is space available in the harbour.

    Oily waste disposal facilities are available.

    Supplies: fuel by road tankers; fresh water at quays in Bassin de l'Est and Bassin Carnot; provisions.

    Communications: local airport at Deauville-Saint-Gatien, 11 km distant.

    Rescue. All-weather lifeboat, see 13.113.

Honfleur to Rouen

Chart 2879
General information
13.189

1   **Description.** Chenal de Rouen (13.172) continues almost as far as the mouth of Rivière La Risle (km 345·7), about 5½ miles E of Honfleur (49°25′N 0°14′E). Thence as far as Rouen embankments confine the river to a permanent channel. See Diagram 13.189.

2   **Port radio** stations operate from Tancarville and Port Jérome; for details see *Admiralty List of Radio Signal Volume 6(1)*.

Bridges and overhead power cables
13.190

1   **Bridges.** Pont de Normandie (km 353), a bridge with a vertical clearance of 52 m, spans the river about 1¾ miles E of Honfleur; the supports of the bridge are situated on each bank.

    Pont de Tancarville (km 338), a suspension bridge with a minimum vertical clearance of 50 m, spans the river immediately above Tancarville Locks, where Canal du Havre á Tancarville (13.149) joins the river.

2   Pont de Brotonne (km 308), a bridge with a minimum vertical clearance of 52 m, spans the river immediately below Saint-Wandrille quays.

    A lifting bridge (km 244) with a minimum vertical clearance of 11 m when closed and 56 m when open, spans the river between Quai de Lessseps on the N side and Quai de la presqu'Île Rollet on the S side.

    Mariners in large vessels are unable to proceed above Pont Guillaume-le-Conquérant (km 243), at Rouen, which has a vertical clearance of 8 m.

La Seíne - Pont de Normandie from W (13.190)
(Original dated 2004)

(Photograph - Drew Given, MV Doulos)

La Seíne - Pont de Tancarville from SW (13.190)

(Original dated 2004)

(Photograph - Drew Given, MV Doulos)

Quai de Moisguilbert   *Quai de Béthencourt*

Rouen - Pont Guillaume le Conquérant from WNW (13.190)

(Original dated 2004)

(Photograph - Drew Given, MV Doulos)

13.191

1   **Power cables** span the river at Radicatel (km 336), Le Trait Amont (S of km 300), La Fontaine (km 275) and Caumont (km 262). The minimum safe vertical clearance is 49 m at Port-Jérôme (km 331). The positions and safe overhead clearances of the other cables can be seen from the chart.

River berths
13.192

1   The principal river berths are as listed below:

    Quais extérieurs de Honfleur (km 355), on the south bank E of the entrance to Honfleur, two quays 122 m in length. At LW springs vessels up to 220 m in length with 7 m draught can be accommodated. A third quay 136 m in length, 2½ cables E of Honfleur entrance can accommodate vessels up to 240 m in length and 7 m draught at LW springs.

2   Miroline Oil Wharf (km 353), on the south bank, a dolphin berth for tankers up to 60 000 tonnes displacement is subject to rapid siltation. Masters of vessels intending to use this berth should ascertain the current depth from their local agent in advance. All vessels using this jetty berth bows W.

3   Grain Wharf (km 352) on the S bank, dolphin berth for bulk aggregates and grain.

4   Quai de Radicatel (km 336) on the north bank, a quay 411 m long with a depth of 10·6 m alongside,

Honfleur – Quais extérieurs de Honfleur (Km355) from WNW (13.192)

(Original dated 2004)

(Photograph – Drew Given, MV Doulos)

La Seíne – Quai de Radicatel (13.192)

(Original dated 2004)

(Photograph – Drew Given, MV Doulos)

which can accommodate vessels of 45 000 tons, laden. There is a container terminal at Radicatel and a RoRo berth for vessels up to 180 m in length.

5   Port Jérôme (km 331·5), on the north bank, comprising six berths of which two can accommodate vessels up to 10·5 m draught; these berths can accommodate fully loaded vessels of 30 000 and 53 000 tonnes respectively. Vessels loading can go down river with the same draught as that authorized for ascending the river. The berths serve the adjacent petroleum installations.

6   Quai de Saint-Wandrille (km 307·4), on the north bank, with 645 m of quayage which can at all times accommodate vessels of 10·2 m draught.

La Mailleraye (km 303·3) which has private berths on both banks of the river and berths for river vessels on the south bank.

Quai du Trait (km 300), on the south bank, a quay 210 m long which can accommodate vessels of 7·5 m draught.

7   Berths at Caudebec (km 310), Yainville (km 299) and Duclair (km 278) are annexed to the port of Rouen and provide berths for coasters and lighters, as well as berths at dolphins for river vessels. The berth at Yainville serves the electricity power station.

ROUEN

General information

Chart 2879
Position and function
13.193

1   Rouen (49°27′N 1°04′E) is a large maritime and river port about 62 miles above Honfleur for import, export and transit traffic.

Port limits
13.194

1   The Maritime Port of Rouen, which is used by ocean going traffic, extends from La Bouille (km 260) to Pont Jeanne-d'Arc (km 242). The port is divided into two sections; the Maritime Port and the River Section which lies above Pont Jeanne-d'Arc.

Traffic
13.195

1   In 2006 the port was used by 2066 vessels totalling 26 281 690 dwt.

Port Authority
13.196

1   Port Autonome de Rouen, 34 Boulevard de Boisguilbert, BP 4075, 76022 Rouen Cedex 3.
      Website: www.rouen.port.fr
      Email: cpr@rouen.port.fr

Limiting conditions
13.197

1   **Controlling depths**: see 13.161.
      Vertical clearances, see 13.190.

2   **Navigable width.** In Maritime Port the river has an average width of 200 m and vessels always berth bows downstream. There are turning areas situated off the entrance to Bassin de Rouen-Quevilly (km 246) where the river is about 300 m wide and N off the E end of Quai de

Grand-Couronne (km 256). There is also a smaller turning area off Bassin Jupiter (km 253).

Tidal levels. Mean spring range about 2·9 m; mean neap range about 2·1 m. For further information see *Admiralty Tide Tables* and information on chart 2879.

Maximum size of vessel handled. See 13.160. The port is accessible to vessels of 45 000 dwt fully laden and 110 000 dwt partly laden; vessels over 280 m length have used the port.

Arrival information
13.198

1   **Port radio** station operates from Rouen port. Within the limits of the port, all vessels of 20 m in length and over must be able to communicate by VHF. Vessels transiting the area must maintain a listening watch on VHF, for details see *Admiralty List of Radio Signals Volume 6(1)*.
      Pilotage, see 13.163.

2   **Tugs** are permanently available in the port of Rouen. Tug assistance in La Seine is available on request.
      Traffic regulations: see 13.164. Speed limit of 7½ kn within the port.

Harbour

General layout
13.199

1   **Maritime Port,** which is used by ocean going traffic, extends from La Bouille (km 260) to Pont Jeanne-d'Arc. There are quays on each side of the river with a total berthing length of 13 km. There are also five tidal basins lying nearly parallel to the river with direct river access and entrances facing downstream. There are dolphin berths for vessels awaiting quay berths.

2   **River Section** lies above Pont Jeanne-d'Arc, extending to km 225. It is used by small coasters, which can lower their masts, by barge traffic and by yachts.

Basins and berths

Maritime Port
13.200

1   On the north bank lies Bassins Saint-Gervais (km 245), on the south bank upstream and downstream lie Bassin aux Bois, Bassin de Rouen-Quevilly, Darse des Docks and Bassin Jupiter de Petit-Couronne. Down stream of Bassin de Rouen-Quevilly as far as La Bouille there are numerous specialist berths serving the industries on the south bank; the more important of these basins and berths, in book order, are:

2   Quai de Grand-Couronne (km 256·6), on the south bank, has a berth 900 m long with a minimum charted depth of 5·5 m alongside for containers and general cargo.

Quai Sogama (km 254·5), a bulk commodities terminal on the south bank, has a berth 360 m long for vessels up to 10·7 m draught.

3   Bassin Jupiter (km 253), on the south bank, contains two berths for tankers up to 200 m in length and 10·5 m draught and one berth for gas carriers up to 160 m in length and 8 m draught, as well as several berths for oil barges; a flexible barrier can be laid across the entrance to the basin. Immediately below the basin there is a river berth for tankers up to 270 m in length with a draught of up to 10·5 m.

4   Quay (km 252·2), on the south bank, downstream of Quai de Petit-Couronne, has a berth with a stern

Rouen – Bassin Jupiter from SW (13.200)

(Original dated 2004)

(Photograph – Drew Given, MV Doulos)

La Seíne – Quai de Petit-Couronne from S (13.200)

(Original dated 2004)

(Photograph – Drew Given, MV Doulos)

ramp 18 m wide and load capacity of 400 tonnes for RoRo vessels.

Quai de Petit-Couronne (km 252), on the south bank, for RoRo vessels with stern or side-loading arrangements, can accommodate vessels up to 10 m draught; the berth can also handle containers.

Darse des Docks (km 251) lies on the south bank; it is used mainly for repairs.

Bassin de Rouen-Quevilly (km 246), on the south bank, has berths for unloading cereals on its N side with depths of between 3 and 5 m alongside and a quay 1630 m long on its S side for container ships and RoRo vessels with draughts up to 10 m.

Bassins Saint-Gervais (km 245), on the north bank opposite Bassin de Rouen-Quevilly, has an entrance about 140 m wide. Quai de l'Ouest, on

Docks Amont Light Beacon

Rouen – Darse des Docks from SSW (13.200)

(Original dated 2004)

(Photograph – Drew Given, MV Doulos)

Bassins Saint-Gervais   *Presqu'île Elie*   *Bassin de Rouen Quevilly*

Rouen – Approaches to Rouen Docks from WSW (13.200)

(Original dated 2004)

(Photograph – Drew Given, MV Doulos)

Rouen – Entrance to Bassins Saint–Gervais from SSW (13.200)

(Original dated 2004)

(Photograph - Drew Given, MV Doulos)

Rouen – Bassin aux Bois from WNW (13.200)

(Original dated 2004)

(Photograph - Drew Given, MV Doulos)

the NW side of the basin is about 700 m in length and specialises in container and general cargo traffic. The E end of the basin contains two smaller basins, Darse Barrillon to the N and Darse Babin to the S. In Darse Babin, on its S side, there is a berth for RoRo vessels up to 180 m in length with ramps for bow and stern loading and a floating dock on its N side.

7   Bassin aux Bois (km 245), on the south bank, has depths of between 3 and 6 m alongside the S side and handles paper, woodpulp and sugar.

Port services

Repairs
13.201

1   Repairs of all kinds can be carried out. There are several repair berths in the port, and a floating dock in Bassin Saint-Gervais with extreme dimensions of length 180 m, breadth 25·6 m with a lifting capacity of 14 000 tonnes.
Divers are available.

Other facilities
13.202

1   **Ship sanitation control exemption certificates** are issued at Rouen; see 1.140.
Oily waste disposal facilities are available in Bassin Jupiter.
Medical facilities are available.

Supplies
13.203

1   **Fuel,** of all grades, is available at some quays or can be supplied by road tanker or oil barge.
Fresh water is laid on the quays and can also be supplied by barge.
Stores and provisions are available.

Communications
13.204

1   **Waterways.** There is connection by waterways to Paris and thence to the inland waterway system, see 13.207.
Airports. International airports are available at Le Havre, distant 80 km, and Paris, distant 130 km. The nearest airport Rouen-Boos, distant 11 km, has connecting flights to international airports.

ROUEN TO PARIS

General information
13.205

1   **Description.** Between Rouen and Paris, a distance of approximately 133 miles (243 km) the river is much used by traffic consisting of pusher-barge convoys, totalling 3000 to 4000 tons, and other vessels some of which are specially constructed for river navigation.

2   **Limiting conditions.** The dimensions of vessels are limited by the dimensions of locks and bridges, and the depth of water as shown in the following table. There are eight locks between Poses (km 202) and Paris with a usable length of 180 m and usable width of 15·5 m. Send ETA by VHF 30 minutes in advance to the lock-keepers. In certain conditions the river level is such that some locks are left open. During the summer months the locks operate from 0700 to 1900. A red and green "Traffic Lights" system is also employed.

Section	LOA	Breadth	Draught
Rouen to Amfreville *	120 m	15·5 m	3·5 m
Amfreville to junction of l'Oise	120 m	15·5 m	3·5 m
L'Oise to Gennevilliers	120 m	15·5 m	3·5 m

3   **Speed limit* in the river is 5½ kn (10 km per hour). Information concerning navigation in this part of the river can be obtained from Service de la Navigation de la Seine, 4th Section, Centre de la Batellerie, 71 Avenue J Chastellain, Île Lacroix, Rouen.

Gennevilliers
13.206

1   **General information.** Gennevilliers, an island port situated about 5 miles NW of the centre of the city of Paris, lies on the south bank of the river (km 35) and is used by vessels proceeding up river from the sea with a draught of about 3·5 m thus avoiding the necessity of transhipment at Rouen.

2   **Maximum dimensions** of vessels using the port and carrying up to 3000 tons of cargo is: length 120 m; breadth 15·5 m; draught 3·5 m; air draught 7·7 m.
Harbour. The port comprises a series of six basins, dredged to a depth of about 4·7 m, the entrance to which is 65 m wide with a depth of 3·2 m and slants obliquely downstream.

3   No 1 Basin is about 564 m long and 90 m wide; No 2 Basin is about 800 m long and 700 m wide.
The W part of the port handles general cargo and the E part is equipped for handling petroleum products; there is a container and a RoRo terminal in the port.

4   There are also port facilities at:
Limay, 50 km downstream from Paris.
Conflans, at the junction of the Oise and Seine.
Saint-Ouen-L'Aumône, 30 km NW of Paris.
Bruyeres-sur-Oise, 40 km N of Paris.
Bonneuil, 10 km SE of Paris.

Inland waterways
13.207

1   **General information.** Inland waterways extend from Paris to Rivers Scheldt, Meuse and Rhine, and to River Rhône and thence to Marseilles on the Mediterranean coast.
They can be used by vessels not exceeding the following dimensions: length 38·5 m; beam 5·0 m; draught 1·8 m; height 3·5 m.

2   The quickest route from the Channel to the Mediterranean is up the Seine from Le Havre to Paris and Saint Mammes, then through canals du Loing, de Baire, Lateral à le Loire, du Centre and then down the Saône and Rhône.
Speed limit in the canals is 3¼ kn (6 km per hour).

CAP DE LA HÈVE TO CAP D'ANTIFER

GENERAL INFORMATION

Charts 2146, 2613
Topography
13.208

1   From Cap de la Hève (49°31′N 0°04′E) (13.114) to Cap d'Antifer (13.211), about 11 miles NNE, the coast consists of chalk cliffs, about 100 m high, which become reddish in colour except near their N end where they are white and easily seen when the sun shines on them. A water tower, 7 cables SSW of Cauville (49°36′N 0°08′E), is the most prominent object on this stretch of the coast.

Prohibited area
13.209

1   A prohibited area, shown on the chart, in which anchoring, dredging and trawling are not permitted extends W from Cap de la Hève, for details see 13.110.

Tidal streams
13.210

1   Information regarding tidal streams within 2 miles of this stretch of the coast is given on the chart.

Principal marks
13.211

1   **Landmark,** in addition to those given at 13.114:
   Cap d'Antifer Lighthouse (grey octagonal tower green top, 38 m in height) (49°41′N 0°10′E) standing on top of the high sheer cliffs at Cap d'Antifer.
   Major lights, in addition to those given at 13.114:
   Cap d'Antifer Light — as above.
   Jetée Nord Light (49°46′N 0°22′E) at Fécamp, see *Dover Strait Pilot.*

Other aids to navigation
13.212

   Racon: Antifer Approach A5 Light Buoy (49°46′N 0°17′W).
   For details see *Admiralty List of Radio Signals Volume 2.*
   Radar assistance, see 13.114.

PORT DU HAVRE-ANTIFER AND APPROACHES

General information

Position and function
13.213

1   Port du Havre-Antifer (49°40′N 0°08′E), an oil terminal for the largest VLCCs, is situated 1½ miles S of Cap d'Antifer.

Port limits
13.214

1   The port lies within Le Havre port limits, for details see 13.102.

Approach and entry
13.215

1   The port is approached from the English Channel through a Deep-water route, an approach channel and an access channel which lead generally ESE from a position 36 miles WNW of Cap d'Antifer and entered S of an angled breakwater which protects the harbour.

Port Authority
13.216

1   The Port Authority is the same as that for Le Havre, for details see 13.120.

Limiting conditions
13.217

1   **Controlling depth** for the port is the depth in the entrance channel which is maintained at 24 to 25 m.
   Deepest and longest berth is the W berth of the terminal (13.231).
   Tidal levels. Mean spring range about 6·8 m; mean neap range about 3·8 m. For further information see *Admiralty Tide Tables.*

2   **Maximum size of vessel handled.** The port can handle vessels up to 550 000 dwt at a draught of 28·5 m. A vessel of 414 m length, 79 m beam, 28·85 m draught and 555 031 dwt has used the port.

Arrival information

Port operations
13.218

1   **Movement reporting system,** for details see 13.104.

Radio stations
13.219

1   For details of radio stations, see 13.126.

Notice of ETA required
13.220

1   For details of notice of ETA required, see 13.104.

Outer anchorages
13.221

1   **Waiting areas.** Two anchorages for vessels waiting to enter the port, the limits of which are shown on the chart, are established S of the Deep Water Route to Port du Havre-Antifer as follows:
   An area centred about 20 miles WNW of Cap d'Antifer for vessels over 25 m draught. A wreck with a depth of 32 m over it lies in the NE part of this anchorage.

2   An area centred about 17 miles WNW of Cap d'Antifer for vessels of up to 25 m draught.
   The anchorages are exposed but good holding ground has been reported. A5 Light Buoy (W cardinal) (49°46′N 0°17′W) is moored close E of the dividing line between the two anchorages and close NE of a 27 m wreck.

Pilotage and tugs
13.222

1   **Pilotage.** Pilot boards about 1 mile N of A5 Light Buoy (49°46′N 0°17′W), as shown on the chart, for details see 13.128.

2   **Tugs** are available at the port. Additional tugs for berthing are available from Le Havre. When proceeding to the berths tugs are usually made fast before passing the breakwater end.

Regulations concerning entry
13.223

1   For regulations concerning vessels carrying dangerous and polluting goods navigating in the approaches to the N and W coasts of France, see 1.66 to 1.76.

2   The following is a summary of the essential parts of the French regulations affecting vessels laden with hydrocarbons and vessels constrained by their draught bound to and from Port du Havre-Antifer:

Radio contact must be established with Le Havre port radio before entering and, except when alongside, maintained continuously while within French territorial waters.

Significant defects to propulsion machinery, steering or anchor gear, mooring winches or radar equipment must be reported before entering territorial waters to the Port Authority who will require the Master of the vessel to complete a questionnaire.

3   Vessels bound for Port du Havre-Antifer must have a Le Havre pilot onboard while within 7 miles of the French coast.

Vessels laden with hydrocarbons and vessels constrained by their draught must enter the port by the approach and entrance channels. They may enter or leave the channel only W of A7 and A8 Light Buoys (49°45′N 0°07′W).

4   Inward bound vessels constrained by their draught may not turn or leave the channel once they have entered it at A7/A8 Light Buoys.

Outward bound vessels, except harbour craft, should keep in the entrance channel or safety area. When W of A19/A20 Light Buoys (49°41′N 0°03′E) vessels not constrained by their draught may leave the disengagement area, if navigational conditions allow, provided that they have a pilot onboard and they are in touch with movement control by radio.

5   Anchoring, fishing or, except when justified by special circumstances, stopping is prohibited within 200 m of the charted approach and entrance channels and associated controlled areas.

Vessels not bound for Port du Havre-Antifer may cross the approach channel W of A17/A18 Light Buoys (49°42′N 0°02′E) with prior permission from Port du Havre-Antifer. Such a crossing should be made as quickly as possible at right-angles to the channel and well clear of any shipping in the approach channel.

6   Vessels constrained by their draught and vessels carrying hydrocarbons or dangerous and polluting goods not bound for Port du Havre-Antifer may cross the approach channel W of A16 Light Buoy (49°43′N 0°01′W). Prior permission from Port du Havre-Antifer must be obtained.

7   Vessels constrained by their draught should exhibit the shapes or lights as laid down in *International Regulations for Preventing Collisions at Sea (1972)*. For the purpose of Rule 9 of the *Regulations* the approach and entrance channels are deemed to be narrow channels or fairways.

Harbour

General layout
13.224

1   An angled breakwater extends 1550 m NW from the coast about 1½ miles S of Cap d'Antifer thence 1000 m W and thence 950 m SW. Two berths for VLCCs are situated, one on each side of an arm, extending S from the central portion of the breakwater.

A small harbour, for port auxiliary vessels, lies 7 cables S of the root of the breakwater and is protected on its W side by a breakwater lying parallel with the coast.

Natural conditions
13.225

1   **Tidal streams** run generally parallel with the coast, attaining a maximum spring rate of about 3 kn, see information on the chart. They are very little affected by the streams in the estuary of La Seine. The HW stand is of the order of 20 minutes.

Local weather. The port is exposed to winds and swell between S and W; special regulations are in force to prevent incidents due to bad weather.

Directions for entering harbour
(continued from 2.43)

Principal marks
13.226

1   For details of principal marks, see 13.211.

Le Havre-Antifer from W (13.224)

(Original dated 1993)

(Photograph - Service Hydrographique et Océanographique de la Marine)

Other aids to navigation
13.227

1 Sylédis (1.56), a radio navigation aid, which provides information on a vessel's position and movement, is established at the port; the special receiver is brought on board by the pilot.

For details of other aids to navigation, see 13.212.

Deep-water route
13.228

1 From a position about 36 miles WNW of Cap d'Antifer (49°41′N 0°10′E) (13.211) a deep-water route, shown on the chart, leads ESE about 18 miles to the waiting areas (13.221) or about 25 miles to the approach channel (13.229) for Port du Havre-Antifer; the entrance to this route is not buoyed. Mariners in vessels constrained by their draught should display the appropriate signal on entering the deep water route, see 13.223. A wreck (position doubtful) with a least depth of 20 m over it lies in position 49°47′·5N 0°18′·1W.

2 The SE end of the deep water route, where it funnels into the approach channel, is a precautionary area.

Antifer Approach Channel
13.229

1 An approach channel, 5 cables wide and orientated 118½°-298½°, marked at its outer end (49°45′N 0°07′W) by A7 and A8 Light Buoys (N cardinal and port hand, respectively), moored 11½ miles WNW of Cap d'Antifer, leads ESE about 7 miles towards the entrance channel; the approach channel is marked by light buoys (port and starboard hand). Banc des Ridens, extending ENE from A14 Light Buoy (port hand) (49°43′·8N 0°03′·0W), lies close to the N side of the channel.

2 A disengagement area about 1 mile wide, which is to enable mariners in deep-draught vessels to turn, if necessary, and return to the anchorage area, is situated SW of the approach and entrance channels from which it is separated by A17 and A19 Light Buoys (starboard hand). A wreck (49°41′·2N 0°01′·7E) with a depth of 22·5 m over it, marked on its S side by DA Light Buoy (isolated danger), lies in the centre of this area.

Entrance channel and harbour
13.230

1 **Leading lights:**
  Front light (white pylon green top, 7 m in height) (49°38′·3N 0°09′·1E).
  Rear light (white pylon green top, 13 m in height) (2½ cables SE of the front light).

2 The alignment (127½°) of these lights, which are direction lights and visible 1° on each side of leading line, by day, and ½° at night, leads through the entrance channel, 3 cables wide and marked at its outer end by A19 and A20 Light Buoys (starboard and port hand, respectively) moored 4¾ miles NW of the front light, to the terminal passing between light buoys (port and starboard hand).

3 A safety area, about 4 cables wide, is situated on the SW side of the entrance channel, from which it is separated by A21, A23 and A25 Light Buoys (starboard hand). This area is for the use of mariners in outward bound vessels in circumstances which require them to keep clear of the entrance channel.

4 **Turning area,** 1450 m in diameter with a depth of 24·7 m, lies S of the breakwater; the S and E limits are marked by A27 and A29 Light Buoys (starboard hand). A wreck (49°39′·1N 0°08′·0E) with a depth of 22 m over it lies in the S part of the turning area 1 cable NE of A27 Light Buoy. Three direction lights are exhibited, two from the breakwater and one from the E side of the harbour, to assist mariners in turning and berthing. Vessels are swung to starboard within the turning area and backed into the berth.

5 **Berths.** Each berth is equipped with light-panels indicating the distance from the berth to the stem or stern of the vessel and the speed of approach to, or departure from, the berth in centimetres per second. The maximum impact velocity should not exceed 10 cm/sec parallel to the fendering of the berth, which will accept a maximum berthing angle of 8°.

6 **Useful mark:**
  Light (white beacon red bands, 17 m in height) (49°39′·8N 0°07′·1E) at the extremity of the breakwater; lights (white pylon purple top, 8 m in height) at the NW and NE corners.

Berths

Terminal
13.231

1 **Deepest berth:**
  West berth dredged to a depth of 28 m (charted 27·5 m) for vessels up to 550 000 tonnes, length 400 m, beam 65 m with draughts up to 28·5 m.

The terminal is exposed to winds and swell from S to W; the E berth is the more exposed. In winds of force 8 or more vessels at this berth require the assistance of tugs.

Port services

Supplies
13.232

1 Fuel is supplied by pipeline to the berths, fresh water is laid on to the berths.

Stores and provisions are available.

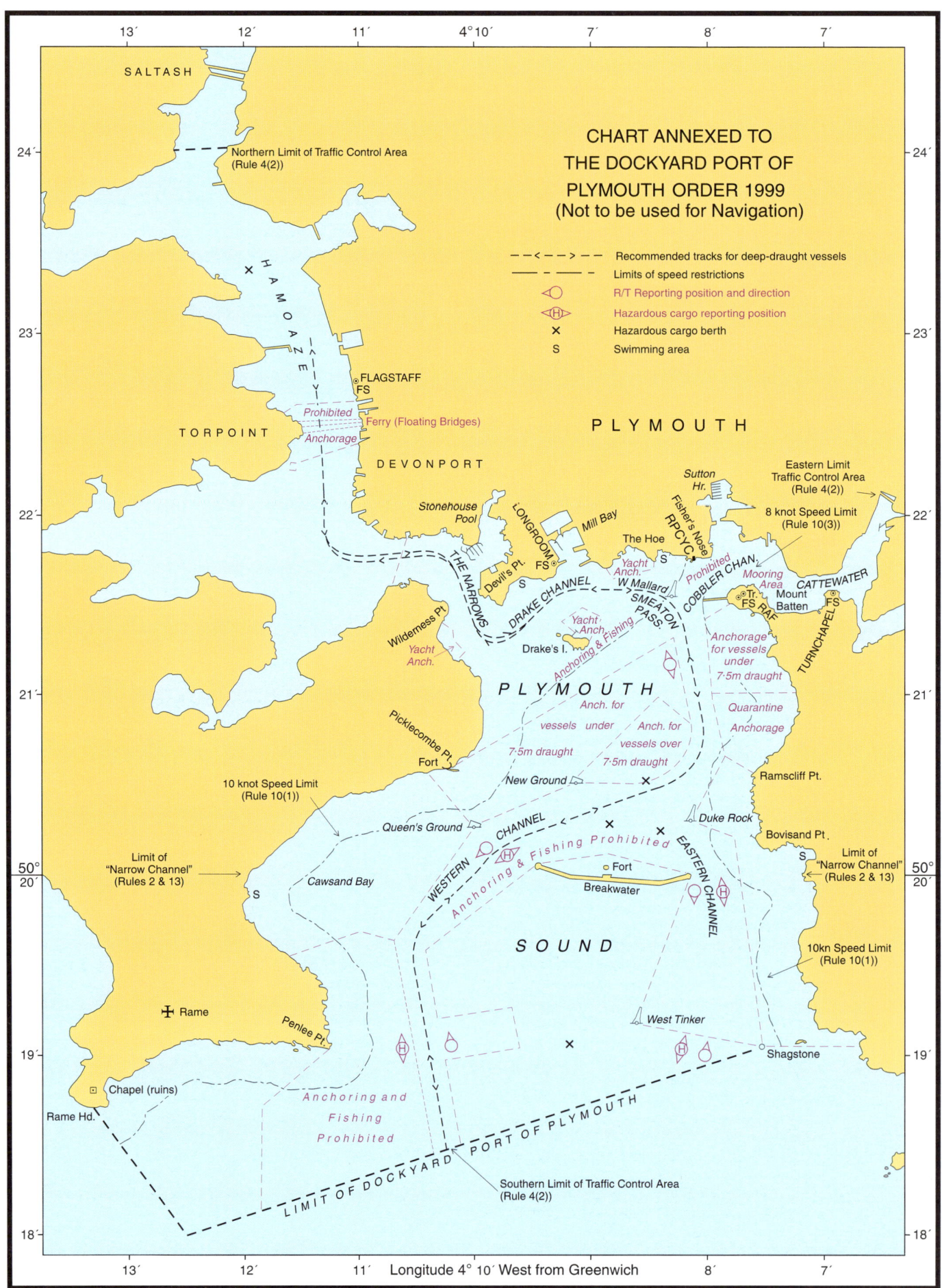

CHART ANNEXED TO
THE DOCKYARD PORT OF
PLYMOUTH ORDER 1999
(Not to be used for Navigation)

— — < — — > — — Recommended tracks for deep-draught vessels
— — — · — — — Limits of speed restrictions
◁○ R/T Reporting position and direction
◁H Hazardous cargo reporting position
× Hazardous cargo berth
S Swimming area

SALTASH

Northern Limit of Traffic Control Area
(Rule 4(2))

HAMOAZE

TORPOINT

FLAGSTAFF
FS

Prohibited

Ferry (Floating Bridges)

Anchorage

DEVONPORT

PLYMOUTH

Sutton
Hr.

Eastern Limit
Traffic Control Area
(Rule 4(2))

8 knot Speed Limit
(Rule 10(3))

Stonehouse
Pool

LONGROOM

Mill Bay

The Hoe

RPCYC

Fisher's Nose

Prohibited

Mooring
Area

CATTEWATER

THE NARROWS

Devil's Pt.

FS

S

DRAKE CHANNEL

Yacht
Anch.

W Mallard

SMEATON
PASS.

COBBLER CHAN.

FS RAF

Tr.

Mount
Batten

TURNCHAPEL

FS

Wilderness Pt.

Yacht
Anch.

Yacht
Anch.

Drake's I.

Anchoring & Fishing

PLYMOUTH

Anch. for
vessels under
7·5m draught

Anch. for
vessels over
7·5m draught

Anchorage
for vessels
under
7·5m draught

Quarantine
Anchorage

Ramscliff Pt.

Picklecombe Pt.
Fort

New Ground

×

Duke Rock

Bovisand Pt.

10 knot Speed Limit
(Rule 10(1))

Queen's Ground

WESTERN

CHANNEL

×

×

EASTERN CHANNEL

Limit of
"Narrow Channel"
(Rules 2 & 13)

Limit of
"Narrow Channel"
(Rules 2 & 13)

S

Cawsand Bay

○
H

Anchoring & Fishing Prohibited

Fort

Breakwater

S

10kn Speed Limit
(Rule 10(1))

SOUND

West Tinker

×

Rame

Penlee Pt.

H

○

H ○

Shagstone

Chapel (ruins)

Rame Hd.

Anchoring and
Fishing
Prohibited

LIMIT OF DOCKYARD PORT OF PLYMOUTH

Southern Limit of Traffic Control Area
(Rule 4(2))

Longitude 4° 10′ West from Greenwich

APPENDIX I
DOCKYARD PORT ORDERS
Statutory Instruments
1999 No 2029
HARBOURS, DOCKS, PIERS AND FERRIES
The Dockyard Port of Plymouth Order 1999

Made . . . . *21st July 1999*

Laid before Parliament . . . . *29th July 1999*

Coming into Force . . . . *31st August 1999*

At the Court at Buckingham Palace, the 21st day of July 1999
Present,
The Queen's Most Excellent Majesty in Council

Her Majesty, in pursuance of sections 3, 5, 6 and 7 of the Dockyard Ports Regulation Act 1865(**a**) and, in so far as section 7 of the Act is concerned, on the joint recommendation of the Secretary of State for Defence and the Secretary of State for Environment Transport and the Regions, is pleased, by and with the advice of Her Privy Council, to order, and it is hereby ordered, as follows:

Citation and commencement

1. The Order may be cited as the Dockyard Port of Plymouth Order 1999 and shall come into force on 31st August 1999.

Interpretation

2. In this Order unless the context otherwise requires:

"the Act" means the Dockyard Ports Regulation Act 1865;

"aircraft" means any fixed or rotary wing, powered, or unpowered, vehicle capable of flight or any parachute, canopy, balloon or airship;

"auxiliary" means a government vessel operating in support of naval and military forces;

"BCH Code" means the 1990 edition of IMO code for the Construction and Equipment of Ships Carrying Dangerous Chemicals in Bulk;

"bell" means any vessel's bell complying with Annex III of the Collision Regulations;

"Collision Regulations" means the regulations for the time being in force made pursuant to sections 85 and 86 of the Merchant Shipping Act 1995(**b**);

"Crown Establishment" shall mean any land or property which is owned or occupied by the Crown;

"channel"- all references to deep water channel, main channel and channel for deep draught vessels shall be as shown on current Admiralty charts

"Dockyard Port" means the Dockyard Port of Plymouth as it is described in Article 3 hereof;

"flashing light" means, except in Rule 4(4) of Schedule 2 to this Order a light flashing at regular intervals at a frequency of 120 flashes or more per minute;

"Foreign warship" means a vessel authorised to fly the naval ensign of a foreign state;

"IBC Code" means the 1994 Edition on the International Bulk Chemical Code published by the IMO;

"IMDG Code" means the 1994 edition of the International Maritime Dangerous Goods Code published by the IMO;

"IMO" means the International Maritime Organisation;

"International Gas Carrier Code" means the 1983 edition of the Code for the Construction and Equipment of Ships Carrying Liquified Gases in Bulk, as amended, published by the IMO;

"International Gas Carrier Code for Existing Ships" means the 1976 edition of Code for Existing ships carrying Liquified Gases in Bulk, as amended, published by the IMO;

"local Harbour or Docks Authority" means those Authorities for the time being empowered and having responsibility for the Cattewater Harbour, the Sutton Harbour and the Millbay Docks, being at the time of the making of this Order, the Cattewater Commissioners, the Sutton Harbour Improvement Company, and the Associated British Ports Board respectively;

"master" means the person having command or charge of a vessel for the time being;

"Naval Base" means the land occupied by Her Majesty's Navy and their operator lessees and known from time to time as HM Naval Base Devonport (including the buildings from time to time erected thereon, the basins, quays and docks therein and the Operator Leased and Licensed Areas);

"navigating within the Dockyard Port" excludes navigating within non-tidal basins;

"parascending" means an activity whereby a parachute is towed by cable in such a manner as to cause it to ascend until it is airborne;

"power-driven vessel" includes any vessel propelled by machinery;

"prolonged blast" means a blast of from four to six seconds duration;

"Queen's Harbour Master" means the person for the time being appointed under the Act to be Queen's Harbour Master for the Dockyard Port and any person having authority to act as Queen's Harbour Master;

(**a**) 1865c. 125; Section 6 was amended by Schedule 3 to the Criminal Justice Act 1967 (c. 80) and sections 40 and 46 of the Criminal Justice Act 1982 (c. 48) and part I of Schedule I to the Statute Law (repeals) Act 1993 (c. 50): Section 7 was amended by Part XIII of Schedule I to the Statute Law (repeals) Act 1986 (c. 12).

(b) 1995 c. 21; sections 85 and 86 were amended by the Merchant Shipping and Maritime Security Act 1997 (c. 28), sections 8(1)-(6), 29 (2) and Schedule 7.

"Radioactive substance" means any substance of Class 7 of the 1994 edition of the International Maritime Dangerous Goods Code published by the IMO;

"1987 Regulations" means the Dangerous Substances in Harbour Areas Regulations 1987 **(a)**

"short blast" means a blast of about one second's duration;

"under way" in relation to a vessel means a vessel not at anchor or made fast to the shore or seabed or aground;

"vessel" includes every description of water craft, seaplanes, or floating structure including all non-displacement craft, personal water craft, sailboards, used or capable of being used as a means of transportation on water; towed targets and other floating targets; and any of Her Majesty's vessels and vessels in the charge of Her Majesty's officers except where otherwise provided;

"whistle" means any vessel's whistle or siren complying with Annex III of the Collision Regulations.

Description of limits

3. For the purposes of the Act and of this Order the limits of the Dockyard Port of Plymouth shall be the waters including all the bays, creeks, lakes, pools and rivers, so far as the tide flows, to the northward of a line starting at a point on the shore due south (true) of the ruined chapel on Rame Head and proceeding in a south-easterly direction to a point 175° (true) 1·25 nautical miles from Rame Church, thence in a north-easterly direction to the Shag Stone and thence due East (true) to the shore.

Delineation of limits

4. The limits of the Dockyard Port are drawn on the Chart annexed to this Order.

Regulations and Rules

5. The Regulations contained in Schedule I hereto and the Rules contained in Schedule 2 hereto shall have effect within the limits (as described in Article 3 hereof) of the Dockyard Port, and if any inconsistency shall arise between the said Rules and the Collision Regulations the said Rules shall prevail.

Penalties

6. (1) The Master of every merchant or private vessel shall observe and cause to be observed the Regulations contained in Schedule I hereto, so far as they relate to his vessel, and any such master or other person who-

    (a) infringes any provision of those Regulations,

    (b) fails to cause the same to be observed,

    (c) fails to observe any direction given under those Regulations,

    (d) fails to comply with any condition or direction attached to a licence or permission granted under those Regulations; or,

    (e) fails to comply with any notice issued under those Regulations

        is guilty of an offence and shall for every such offence be liable to a fine not exceeding level 3 on the standard scale.

(2) The master of every merchant or private vessel shall comply with the Rules contained in Schedule 2 hereto and any such master, who by his wilful default infringes any of the said Rules shall in respect of each offence be liable to the same penalties as if the offence had been an infringement of the Collision Regulations.

Revocation

7. The Dockyard Port of Plymouth Order 1984**(b)** is hereby revoked.

A. K. Galloway,

Clerk of the Privy Council.

(a) SI 1987/37. amended by SI 1988/712, 1990/2605, 1990/2487, 1992/743, 1993/1746, 1994/669, 1994/241, 1994/3247, 1996/2092, 1997/2791, 1996/2095, 1997/2367 and 1998/2885.

(b) SI 1984/1148.

SCHEDULE I

PART I
REGULATIONS OF GENERAL APPLICATION

General

1. (1) The master of every merchant or private vessel or any other person within the limits of the Dockyard Port shall comply with any directions given by the Queen's Harbour Master for the purposes of the proper protection of the Port, Her Majesty's vessels, dockyards or property, or for the requirements of Her Majesty's Naval Service.

(2) The master of every merchant or private vessel or any other person within the limits of the Dockyard Port to whom any licence or permission has been granted by the Queen's Harbour Master in accordance with the provisions of the Act, these Regulations or the rules contained in Schedule 2, shall comply with any directions or conditions attached thereto.

(3) The Queen's Harbour Master may attach such conditions or directions to any such licence or permission as he considers necessary.

Control of movements within the Dockyard Port

2. (1) The Queen's Harbour Master shall, in the discharge of the provisions of Schedules 1 and 2 of this Order in relation to commercial shipping traffic, and subject to any operational requirement connected with national defence, have regard to the functions and responsibilities of the local Harbour or Docks Authority.

(2) The Queen's Harbour Master may, as necessary, require the owner, master or agent of any vessel of and above 20 metres in length to notify him of the times of prospective arrivals and departures of such a vessel within the Dockyard Port over a specified period, including any subsequent amendments thereto.

(3) Vessels of more than 20 metres overall length shall enter or leave the Dockyard Port under the direction of the Queen's Harbour Master.

(4) The master of any vessel shall comply with any requirements of the Queen's Harbour Master to change the time of arrival or sailing of a vessel in order to ensure the safe navigation of that or other vessels within the Dockyard Port.

Shipkeepers

3. No merchant or other private vessel of above ten metres in length, compelled or allowed to anchor in or near any of the navigable channels of the Dockyard Port, shall be left at any time without a shipkeeper.

Special navigation regulations

4. No merchant or other private vessel shall navigate–
    (a) within 50 metres of the walls, slipways and boundaries of HM Naval Base and Crown Establishments;
    (b) within 50 metres of any of Her Majesty's vessels (save for submarines) or foreign warships or auxiliaries; or
    (c) within 100 metres of submarines berthed alongside HM Naval Base.

Fishing

5. (1) Any person fishing in the Dockyard Port shall comply with any directions given to him by the Queen's Harbour Master.

(2) No fishing from any vessel or by persons swimming under the water shall be carried out either within–
    (a) 100 metres of the walls, slipways or boundaries of Her Majesty's Dockyard or other Crown Establishments; or
    (b) 150 metres of any of Her Majesty's vessels, save with the licence in writing of the Queen's Harbour Master.

(3) No fishing shall at any time be carried either–
    (a) within 125 metres of either side of the recommended tracks for vessels leading through Plymouth Sound to the Hamoaze as shown on current Admiralty Charts; or
    (b) on the line of any electric cable or pipe as described in Regulation 19.

(4) In any area in which anchorage is prohibited under Regulation 22 there shall be no–
    (a) trawling or fishing by any nets, long lines or rods;
    (b) laying, movement or lifting of lobster or crab pots, marked or unmarked; or
    (c) installing of equipment in connection with fish farming carried out from vessels in the said area.

(5) All lines used in connection with lobster or crab pots or similar devices shall be non-buoyant, and where any line of pots is less than 100 metres in length, only one end need be clearly marked, such mark indicating the identity of the owner of the said pots.

(6) In the navigable channels of the Rivers Plym, Tamar, Tavy and Lynher and of Millbrook and St Johns Lakes netting of fish may take place only if–
    (a) the nets are tended by boat throughout;
    (b) sufficient navigable water is left for other craft to navigate the channel;
    (c) anchored vessels are not impeded.

Diving

6. No person who is wearing or equipped with clothing or apparatus designed or adapted for swimming under water or diving shall swim under water or dive within-

    (a) 100 metres of the walls, slipways, or boundaries of Her Majesty's Dockyards or other Crown Establishments;

    (b) 150 metres of any of Her Majesty's vessels;

    (c) 125 metres of either side of the recommended tracks for vessels leading through Plymouth Sound to the Hamoaze as shown on current Admiralty Charts;

    (d) the fairway of the Dockyard Port; or

    (e) any area where anchorage is prohibited under regulation 22 save with the permission of the Queen's Harbour Master.

Swimming

7 No person shall swim on the surface or underwater within-

    (a) 100 metres of the walls, slipways, or boundaries of Her Majesty's Dockyards or other Crown Establishments;

    (b) 150 metres of any of Her Majesty's vessels;

    (c) any area where anchorage is prohibited under regulation 22 save with the permission of the Queen's Harbour Master.

Parascending and similar activities

8 No person shall engage or take part in parascending or other activity involving the towing of a kite or other thing, from a vehicle on land or water, in such a manner as to cause it to ascend until it is airborne in any part of the Dockyard Port save with the permission of the Queen's Harbour Master.

Firearms, weapons and explosives

9 (1) Save as provided by paragraph (3) below, no firearm, air-gun or explosive shall be discharged from any merchant or other private vessel within the limits of the Dockyard Port.

    (2) No ship's gun on board any merchant or other private vessel lying within the limits of the Dockyard Port shall be loaded, except in so far as may be necessary from time to time for training personnel in the loading and unloading of the equipment or for testing its mechanism, nor shall any such gun be discharged except as a signal of distress.

    (3) Race starting pistols, cannons and guns may be discharged for the sole purpose of controlling water based racing activities provided that blank ammunition rounds only are fired.

Dumping of rubbish, etc

10 Save with the licence in writing of the Queen's Harbour Master no person shall unload, cast or allow to fall into the water of the Dockyard Port, or on the shore of the Dockyard Port where the same may be able to fall into or to be washed into the said waters, any ballast, stones, earth, clay, refuse, or any other substance or object.

Reserved and recreational areas

11.(1) The Secretary of State or the Queen's Harbour Master may, where he considers it necessary to reserve any area for mining ,gunnery or dredging operations or experiments, other naval purposes, or to ensure the safe navigation of other vessels both naval and civilian, issue a general or local notice, which shall continue in force until 31 December of the year in which it was issued, unless revoked earlier, prohibiting any person from-

    (a) causing or permitting a vessel to enter or remain in that area, unless compelled to do so by stress of weather or to avoid accident;

    (b) entering into or remaining in that area, or from causing or permitting any vessel , animal or thing to enter into or remain in that area, except with the permission of the Queen's Harbour Master or the officer in charge of such operation, experiments or purposes: or

    (c) taking part in any recreational activities specified in the notice in such parts of that area as may be so specified, save or the purpose of avoiding danger or accident.

Use of whistle

12. A whistle shall not be used within the limits of the Dockyard Port except-

    (a) in accordance with the Rules contained in Schedule 2 to this Order;

    (b) as a signal of distress;

    (c) to prevent collision;

    (d) in any condition affecting visibility;

    (e) to test the whistle, provided that permission to do so has first been obtained from the Queen's Harbour Master.

Anchoring and mooring
General

13. Without prejudice to Regulation 1, all anchoring and mooring shall be subject to any directions of the Queen's Harbour Master.

Moorings for Her Majesty's vessels, etc

14. Moorings for Her Majesty's vessels, buoys, lights, marks, mark buoys and other aids to navigation, and such other buoys as may be required for any purpose in connection with naval, military or air force operations, may be placed by the Queen's Harbour Master in such positions as may be considered necessary for the requirements of Her Majesty's Service.

Private moorings

15.-(1) This Regulation shall apply to:

    (a) areas outside the jurisdiction of local Harbour or Docks authority;

    (b) any area designated by the Queen's Harbour Master in a local or general Notice to Mariners.

    (2) No person shall in an area to which this Regulation applies lay moorings for merchant or other private vessels, hulks, rafts, pontoons, bathing stages, racing marks, house boats, timber or any floating structures in the Dockyard Port, save with the licence in writing of the Queen's Harbour Master, and all such moorings shall be in such positions as the Queen's Harbour Master shall deem fit.

16. Any moorings anywhere within the Dockyard Port shall be removed forthwith on the Order of the Queen's Harbour Master.

17. The local Harbour or Docks Authority shall inform the Queen's Harbour Master of any proposals for altering the mooring arrangements in those areas within its jurisdiction.

Clearing Anchors and Moorings

18. If at any time the anchor of any merchant or other private vessel hooks any Crown moorings, or any electric cable, or moorings of buoys, or any pipe, the master of such vessel shall immediately give notice thereof to the Queen's Harbour Master and shall, if it is safe and practical, await his instructions before proceeding to clear the same.

19. No merchant or other private vessel shall anchor on the line of any electric cable or pipe laid down in the Dockyard Port when such a line is indicated by posts or other discernible marks on shore or is shown in current Admiralty Charts.

20. No merchant or other private vessel-

    (a) make fast to, or lie at, any of the buoys or beacons placed by the Queen's Harbour Master to mark channels or shoals in the Dockyard Port; or

    (b) be moored or fastened to any of Her Majesty's, Naval moorings, buoys, breakwaters, boom defences, dolphins, jetties, piles or vessels in the Dockyard Port, save with the licence in writing of the Queen's Harbour Master.

    (c) be moored or anchored within 100 metres of any of Her Majesty's Naval jetties, dolphins, vessels, hulks, installations or armament depots, or within 150 metres of the centre of any Naval moorings, save with the licence in writing of the Queen's Harbour Master;

    (d) be moored, anchored or placed in the Dockyard Port, so as to give a foul berth to any vessels already at anchor or at moorings or to obstruct passage within or entrance into Plymouth Sound or any other part of the Dockyard Port.

Anchorage in Plymouth Sound

21. (1) The anchorage in Plymouth Sound for vessels over 7·5 metres draught shall be the area so indicated on current Admiralty Charts east-north-eastward of New Grounds Buoy, the position at the time of making this Order being shown on the Chart annexed to this Order, and this anchorage shall be reserved for the use of Her Majesty's deep-draught naval vessels, and those commercial vessels with a draught of over 7·5 metres.

    (2) Vessels of under 7·5 metres draught shall anchor in the area south-eastward of a straight line joining Fort Picklecombe and Mount Batten Tower, save in the prohibited anchorage covering the approach to Smeaton Pass.

    (3) The anchorage for vessels in quarantine shall be the southern part of Jennycliff Bay south of 50° 21′ North and eastward of the deep water channel.

22. Unless otherwise notified by the Queen's Harbour Master in a general or local Notice to Mariners no merchant or other private vessel shall anchor in-

    (1) any area within the Dockyard Port shown as a prohibited anchorage on current Admiralty Charts:

    (2) any of the following areas shown on current Admiralty Charts-

        (a) the Western Channel and Eastern Channel entrances to Plymouth Sound, the approach therefrom to Smeaton Pass, and the water north of a straight line joining Fort Picklecombe and Mount Batten Tower, including Smeaton Pass, Drake Channel, and The Narrows together with Cobbler Channel and the Cattewater; but this prohibited area shall not include the Yacht Anchorage off the Hoe nor the Yacht Anchorage north of Drake's Island nor the Yacht Anchorage in Barn Pool;

        (b) the prohibited anchorage north and south of the track of the Torpoint Ferry;

        (c) the controlled mooring area adjacent to Mount Batten northwards;

        (d) the prohibited anchorage off Penlee Point;

        (e) the prohibited anchorage of the Shag Stone.

23. (1) No vessels carrying explosives, save for those exempted by Regulation 33(2)(a) to (g) of the 1987 Regulations, shall anchor or moor within the Dockyard Port except in the following locations shown on current Admiralty charts:

(a) Number 2 and 22 anchorages in Plymouth Sound;
(b) "C", "D" and "E" mooring buoys in Plymouth Sound;
(c) "Capital Ship Trot 1", "Capital Ship Trot 2", "N9", "N10" and "N11" moorings in the River Tamar;
(d) Ernesettle Jetty;
(e) North, South and West Tamar Trots;
(f) Such other positions as the Queen's Harbour Master shall promulgate as a general and local Notice to Mariners.

(2) No merchant or other private vessel-

(a) carrying hazardous, dangerous or noxious substances (as defined in Regulation 8 of the 1987 Regulations), as cargo; or
(b) which is in ballast having previously carried any such substances as cargo, but which has not been gas-freed, shall anchor or moor or secure alongside within the limits of the Dockyard Port save at a berth specified by the Queen's Harbour Master.

24. Where one of Her Majesty's vessels is anchored or moored in the Dockyard Port and displaying the signals described in Rule 3(2) of Schedule 2-

(a) no merchant or other private vessel shall moor or anchor within 700 metres of any such of Her Majesty's vessels without the prior permission on the Queen's Harbour Master;
(b) no merchant or other private vessel-
(i) carrying hazardous, dangerous or noxious substances (as defined in Regulation 8 of the 1987 Regulations) as cargo; or
(ii) which is in ballast having previously carried any such substances as cargo, but which has not been gas-freed,
shall anchor or moor within 1,000 metres of any such of Her Majesty's vessels without the prior permission on the Queen's Harbour Master.

Anchoring Within the Port
25. If in an emergency a vessel is obliged to anchor otherwise than in accordance with this Regulation, the Master of such vessel shall as soon as practicable thereafter inform the Queen's Harbour Master.

Navigational Marks, etc
26. No person shall trespass on, damage or without authority interfere with any light, beacon, sea-mark, tideboard, tidegauge, buoy, sign or notice of any description in the Dockyard Port.

Dredging for Lost Objects
27. Save with the licence in writing of the Queen's Harbour Master, no person shall dredge in the Dockyard Port with drags, hooks, nets or other apparatus for property dropped or thrown therein.

Landing on Plymouth Breakwater
28. Save with the licence in writing of the Queen's Harbour Master, no person or aircraft may at any time land upon Plymouth Breakwater.

PART II

REGULATIONS NORMALLY APPLICABLE TO VESSELS OVER 25 METRES

General

29. Regulations 29 to 39 shall apply only to vessels over 25 metres in length provided that the Queen's Harbour Master may by notice published as a general or local Notice to Mariners extend the provisions therein where applicable to cover all shipping traffic when necessary for operational requirements connected with national defence.

Notification of arrival of inward bound vessels

30. (1) The Master of every vessel shall so far as practicable, at least 24 hours prior to arrival or on leaving the last port, whichever is the later, advise the Queen's Harbour Master of his estimated time of arrival at the line joining Penlee Point to the Shag Stone.

(2) The Master of every vessel shall report by radio to the Queen's Harbour Master on passing each and either of the following reporting points–
  (a) the line joining Penlee Point to the Shag Stone;
  (b) Plymouth Breakwater.

(3) The master of every vessel shall, within 30 minutes after the vessel has completed mooring, or come to anchor, inform the Queen's Harbour Master of that fact.

Notification of departure of outward bound or shifting vessels

31. (1) The Master of every vessel which is berthed or anchored within the Dockyard Port and proposes to navigate within the Dockyard Port for the purpose of either leaving the Dockyard Port or shifting berths within the Dockyard Port shall–
  (a) so far as is practicable give prior notice to the Queen's Harbour Master of his intention–
    (i) not less than 60 minutes before he proposes to begin the navigation, and again
    (ii) within 10 minutes of the time when he proposes to begin the navigation, and
  (b) inform the Queen's Harbour Master on completion of the navigation or when passing Plymouth Breakwater outbound.

(2) In the event of it proving impractical to give the notice required in sub-paragraph (1)(a) above, the master or agent shall as soon as practicable advise the Queen's Harbour Master of the proposed navigation.

(3) the master shall notify the Queen's Harbour Master as soon as practicable of any change to any notice given under sub-paragraph (1)(a) above.

Anchoring within the Dockyard Port

32. No vessel over 25 metres in length shall anchor within the Dockyard Port north of the line joining Penlee Point to the Shag Stone without the prior permission of the Queen's Harbour Master.

Tows inwards or outwards

33. (1) Without prejudice to Regulation 30(1), the Master of every vessel other than a tug when employed in assisting the berthing of a powered vessel, towing another vessel within the Dockyard Port shall give prior notice to the Queen's Harbour Master of not less than 60 minutes prior to commencement of the tow

(2) Where notice is given pursuant to paragraph (1) the notice shall be accompanied by any of the following details:
  (a) whether the tow involves a dead ship, abnormal tow, partially disabled ship, is unstable or has an excessive list or trim, is leaking bunkers or oil, chemical or gas cargo;
  (b) or has any other defect which may cause the tow to be a hazard within the Dockyard Port.

Vessels with Mechanical, Equipment or Structural Defects

34. (1) No vessel shall be navigated within the Dockyard Port except with the permission of the Queen's Harbour Master and in accordance with any conditions attached thereto if the vessel has any of the following defects:
  (a) defects to main engines, steering gear or other auxiliary machinery which may affect the manoeuvring of the vessel;
  (b) inoperable equipment which may affect the safe navigation of the vessel including but without limitation to Very High Frequency radiotelephony equipment, radar, compass, whistle or siren, or rudder indicator;
  (c) inoperable capstans, winches, mooring winches, or anchors that are not cleared and ready for use;
  (d) a list of over five degrees or is excessively out of trim;
  (e) any cargo, or any hull or machinery damage which may affect the safety of the vessel or the containment or safety of the cargo or bunkers.
  (f) is unseaworthy in any respect;

(2) The Master of every vessel shall make a declaration to the Queen's Harbour Master that his vessel does not have any of the defects specified in paragraph (1) above at the same time as he advises or is required by Regulations 30 to 32 to advise the Queen's Harbour Master of his intention to navigate within the Dockyard Port.

Vessels carrying hazardous, dangerous, noxious or polluting substances as cargo

35. (1) This Regulation applies to any vessel which is carrying :

(a) Any articles or substances falling within Class I in the IMDG Code other than:

(i) explosives assigned to Hazard Division 1.4 and Compatibility Group S as defined by the IMDG Code;

(ii) distress signals assigned either to Hazard Division 1.2, 1.3 or 1.4 as defined by the IMDG Code;

(iii) fireworks assigned to Hazard Division 1.4 (Fireworks Type D) as defined by the IMDG Code;

(b) any liquefied gas in bulk listed in the International Gas Carrier Code for existing ships or in the International Gas Carrier Code for new ships;

(c) any hazardous liquid chemical cargo in bulk listed in IBC Code;

(d) Any hazardous liquid chemical cargo in packages (Classes 2, 3, 4, 5, 6, 8 or 9 of the Codes referred to in sub–paragraph (b) and (c) above).

(e) Radioactive Substances.

(2) The master of any vessel to which this Regulation applies hall-

(a) give notice to the Queen's Harbour Master not less than 24 hours in advance, or within one hour before expected time of departure from the last port of call, whichever is the later, of–

(i) his intention to navigate within the Dockyard Port and of the nature of the cargo, and

(ii) if the vessel is in ballast but not gas–freed after a previous cargo, the nature of that cargo, in accordance with the Merchant Shipping (Reporting Requirements for Ships Carrying Dangerous or Polluting Goods) Regulations 1995(**a**); and

(b) on giving notice under paragraph (a) above of leaving the Dockyard Port or shifting berth, inform the Queen's Harbour Master of the nature of the vessel, its cargo and that the vessel is in possession of a valid Certificate of Fitness to carry such hazardous cargo or has the prior permission of Queen's Harbour Master.

(3) No vessel to which this Regulation applies, but which is not in possession of a valid Certificate of Fitness to carry such hazardous cargo shall navigate within the Dockyard Port except with the prior permission of Queen's Harbour Master and in accordance with any conditions attached thereto .

(4) Any vessel to which this Regulation applies shall only anchor in such a position as directed by the Queen's Harbour Master and while at anchor shall remain at immediate notice to get underway.

Carriage of very high frequency radiotelephony equipment

36. (1) All vessels wishing to navigate within the Dockyard Port are required to carry fixed or portable Very High Frequency radiotelephony equipment, which shall comply with the Merchant Shipping (Radio Installation) Regulations 1992 (**b**).

(2) Every vessel shall maintain a listening watch in the wheelhouse on the frequency of 156·8 Megahertz (Channel 16), or any other frequency that the Queen's Harbour Master from time to time may order, when it is within the Dockyard Port..

(3) Vessels not carrying Very High Frequency radiotelephony equipment in accordance with paragraph (1) above shall not navigate in the Dockyard Port except with the prior permission of the Queen's Harbour Master.

Vessels Grounded, on Fire or which have been in Collision within the Dockyard Port

37. Where any vessel has grounded, is on fire or has been in collision within the Dockyard Port the master of that vessel shall-

(a) give immediate notice to the Queen's Harbour Master of the position of the vessel, known damage, confirmation of cargo or any other information required by the Queen's Harbour Master; and

(b) not navigate the vessel other than for the safety of the vessel except with the prior permission of the Queen's Harbour Master and in accordance with his directions.

Vessels which have been Grounded, had a Fire, been in Collision or Sustained Heavy Weather Damage Outside the Dockyard Port

38. (1) This Regulation shall apply to every vessel which is outside the Dockyard Port and intended to be navigated within the Dockyard Port and which has-

(a) been grounded, had a fire, or been in collision; or

(b) sustained damage to its structure, equipment or machinery; or

(c) sustained movement or instability of cargo has led to a list or likelihood of a list.

(2) The master of a vessel to which this Regulation applies shall give notice to the Queen's Harbour Master on the condition of his vessel and of its cargo, such notice is to be given at least 24 hours prior to the vessel's estimated time of arrival at the straight line joining Penlee Point to the Shag Stone or as soon as possible after the incident whichever is later.

(3) A vessel to which this Regulation applies shall only navigate within the Dockyard Port with the prior permission of the Queen's Harbour Master.

Use of Automatic Pilot Steering Devices

39. The Master of every vessel when navigating within the Dockyard Port shall ensure that in the event of use being made of an automatic pilot steering device a competent helmsman other than the Master or a pilot is in attendance at a steering position to steer the vessel manually immediately circumstances so require.

Vessels Wishing to Adjust Compasses Within the Dockyard Port

40. The Master of every vessel shall give the Queen's Harbour Master at least 24 hours prior notice of the intent to adjust the compass of the vessel and confirm the intention to adjust compasses immediately prior to commencing to do so.

(**a**) SI 1995/2498.
(**b**) SI 1992/3.

SCHEDULE 2
RULES

Collision Regulations

1. All vessels when within the limits of the Dockyard Port shall, except as is otherwise provided in Rules 3, and 9(2) below, carry such lights, flags or shapes prescribed by the Collision Regulations and all vessels shall observe the steering and sailing rules set forth in such Regulations except in so far as they are inconsistent with the Rules hereinafter contained.

Narrow Channels

2. For the purposes of the Collision Regulations and Rule 13 of this Schedule all the navigable water of the Dockyard Port north of latitude 50° 20'·00 North, that is to say the line passing through Plymouth Breakwater in an east-west direction, shall be deemed to be a "narrow channel".

Anchor and Other Lights and Signals (Exemptions, etc)

3. (1) Unmanned vessels and vessels with only shipkeepers onboard, where secured to moorings out of the fairway, may be exempted by the Queen's Harbour Master from the necessity of carrying anchor lights.

(2) Vessels carrying cargoes of hazardous, dangerous or noxious substances as defined in Regulation 8 of the 1987 Regulations when anchored, moored, or secured alongside within the Dockyard Port shall in addition to the lights and shapes prescribed in Rule 30 of the Collision Regulations, display the following lights or signals:

(a) between sunset and sunrise, a red all round light visible 2 miles situated above any other light being displayed by the vessel;

(c) between sunrise and sunset, a red swallow-tailed flag (International Flag Bravo) at the masthead which shall also be displayed when the vessel is underway.

(3) Submarines secured to buoys within the Dockyard Port shall, without prejudice to any requirement prescribed by Rule 30 of the Collision Regulations, display between sunset and sunrise an all round amber light, flashing at a frequency of between 90 and 105 flashes per minute.

4. (1) The Queen's Harbour Master may on any occasion when it is necessary to facilitate or ensure a clear passage for any vessel or for any other purpose, direct the Plymouth Port Control traffic light signals to he displayed.

(2) All vessels within the area bounded on the north by latitude 50° 24'·0 north and on the south by the southern limit of the Dockyard Port, are to observe the restrictions appropriate to that signal as specified below, for so long as the signal is displayed.

(3) Light signals displayed over Plymouth Sound located for the time being on Drake's Island shall govern the movement of vessels to seaward of a line drawn due south from Mutton Cove to Cremyll. Light signals displayed at Flag Port Control Station shall govern the movement of vessels north and west of a line drawn due south from Mutton Cove to Cremyll.

(4) The light signals will be disposed vertically and shall have the following meanings-

Unlit:	No restrictions unless a contrary intention is given on Very High Frequency radiotelephony Channel 13, 14 or 16
3 red flashing lights:	Serious emergency. All traffic movements suspended throughout the Dockyard Port except as specifically directed by Flag or Longroom Control Station.
1 red occulting light over 2 green occulting lights:	Outgoing traffic only may proceed along the channel for deep draught vessels. Vessels requiring to cross that channel are to seek Port Control Station approval. Vessels navigating in the Hamoaze are to ensure a clear passage for any vessel required to be given clear passage in accordance with paragraph (6)(a) of this rule proceeding southward in the main channel.
2 green occulting lights over 1 red occulting light:	Incoming traffic only may proceed along the channel for deep draught vessels. Vessels requiring to cross that channel are to seek Port Control Station approval. Vessels navigating in the Hamoaze are to ensure a clear passage for any vessel required to be given clear passage in accordance with paragraph (6)(a) of this rule proceeding northward in the main channel.
2 green occulting lights over 1 white occulting light:	Traffic may proceed in either direction but shall give a wide berth to any vessel designated in paragraph (6)(a) of this Rule proceeding along the channel for deep draught vessels or navigating in the Hamoaze.
3 green fixed lights:	Entrance to the Dockyard Port permitted.
3 fixed lights; red over green over red:	Movement of shipping within the Dockyard Port permitted.

(5) (a) Subject to paragraph 5(b) below, when any of the light signals specified in paragraph (4) of this Rule are displayed–

    (i)   no vessel shall enter the main channel so governed except in the direction indicated by the light signals;

    (ii) vessels already in the said channel and proceeding in a contrary direction shall clear the said channel;

    (iii) Notwithstanding any light signal displayed under paragraph (4) (other than the serious emergency signal) vessels of less than 20 metres in length may proceed in the contrary direction, so long as they navigate with caution and do not impede the passage of any vessel or vessels for which the light signal is being displayed.

    (b) When the serious emergency signal as specified in paragraph (4) above is displayed, all vessels are to remain alongside or at anchor until movement is approved by the Queen's Harbour Master. Vessels already underway shall either return to their point of departure or proceed to their destination (whichever is closer) or act as directed by either port control station.

(6) (a) Vessels which are to be given a clear passage, or the tug or tugs in attendance on such vessels shall display the international Code Pennant superior to Pennant Zero by day (no signal being displayed by night), while underway in the area specified in paragraph (2) of this Rule.

    (b) Any master if in any doubt as to which vessel is favoured by the traffic lights should call the appropriate port control station by any means to seek the answer.

5. When within the limits of the Dockyard Port the signals, lights and shapes prescribed in the Collision Regulations for a vessel not under command, or constrained by her draught, or restricted in her ability to manoeuvre are exhibited:

    (a) by any of Her Majesty's vessels, by any vessel in the charge of Her Majesty's officers or any other deep draught vessel; or

    (b) by any tug or tugs attending such vessels;

then all other vessels underway shall keep clear of such vessel, tug or tugs, provided always that nothing in this Rule shall relieve the restricted vessel or any attendant tug of the duty to navigate with care and at safe speed.

Low visibility

6. When visibility is less than 500 metres the Queen's Harbour Master may suspend all traffic and control individual movements.

Vessels Entering or Leaving Her Majesty's Naval Base

7. When any of Her Majesty's vessels in the charge of Her Majesty's Officers is turning in, entering or leaving Her Majesty's Naval Base at Devonport, every other vessel of whatever size under way in the vicinity of the said Naval Base shall then keep clear of that vessel and of tugs which may be in attendance upon her.

Pilotage

8. Save where the Queen's Harbour Master directs otherwise pilotage of vessels by qualified Admiralty pilots is mandatory for–

    (a) any of Her Majesty's vessels, entering, leaving or otherwise navigating within the Dockyard Port;

    (b) any government owned vessels or auxiliaries, or any foreign warships or auxiliaries navigating within the Dockyard Port for the purpose of taking up or leaving a Ministry of Defence owned berth, dock or mooring;

    (c) any vessel, including government chartered vessels, proceeding between Plymouth Sound and a Ministry of Defence owned berth, dock or mooring within the Dockyard Port.

Harbour Ferries

9. (1) Any harbour ferry vessel or floating bridge plying in the Dockyard Port shall give way to any other vessel which can only navigate in a narrow channel or fairway

    (2) Yachts and other recreational vessels shall be handled in such a way that interference with the timely operation of floating bridges on fixed tracks is reduced to the minimum.

    (3) Instead of the lights directed to be carried by the Collision Regulations, any floating bridge which is confined to a fixed track shall, shall display the following lights–

    (a) carry four lights, one at each corner, showing white ahead and astern in the direction of the ferry track and red on the beam or athwart the ferry track;

    (b) when such floating bridge is in progress an amber flashing light at the masthead at the leading end in the direction of progress;

    (c) where such floating bridge is being used by the emergency services a blue flashing light shall be displayed below the said amber flashing light indicating direction of progress.

    (4) Any light referred to under paragraph (3) above must be visible for at least two nautical miles.

    (5) Where visibility is less than 300 metres, any floating bridge in progress or stopped temporarily along a ferry track shall ring a bell rapidly for between 4 and 6 seconds duration at intervals of not more than 30 seconds.

Speed Limits in Certain Areas

10.(1) Except as provided for in paragraph (2) below no vessel shall exceed a speed of 10 knots through the water north of 50° 20'.0 North (the latitude of Plymouth Breakwater) or any waters of the Dockyard Port within 400 metres of the shore, save with a licence in writing signed by the Queen's Harbour Master.

    (2) Vessel;s under 15 metres in length overall may exceed the speed limit specified in paragraph (1) above in the following areas:

    (a) Such waters of the Dockyard Port that are outside 400 metres from the shore and in the access lane for water skiers and jet-skiers which is bounded to the east by the line joining Fisher's Nose to the western extremity of Mount Batten Breakwater, and bounded to the west by the line joining the western extremity of the Royal Plymouth Corinthian Yacht Club to the West Mallard Buoy;

(b) water skiing Areas shown on current Admiralty charts;

(c) Such other areas of the Dockyard Port as the Queen's Harbour Master shall from time to time determine and publish as a local Notices to Mariners.

(3) No vessel within the Dockyard Port shall exceed a speed of 8 knots through the water to the east of a line drawn from Fishers Nose to the western end of Mount Batten Breakwater, save with a licence in writing signed by the Queen's Harbour Master and where authorised in accordance with paragraph (2) (b) above.

(4) No vessel within the Dockyard Port shall exceed a speed of 4 knots through the water in the approaches to Sutton Harbour north of a line drawn due east from Fishers Nose save with a licence in writing signed by the Queen's Harbour Master.

(5) No vessel shall exceed a speed of 4 knots through the water in designated Bathing Areas shown on current Admiralty charts.

(6) No vessel shall exceed a speed of 4 knots through the water in designated Diving Areas shown on current Admiralty charts.

Vessels to be navigated with care and caution

11. The master of a vessel navigating within the Dockyard Port shall navigate the vessel with care and caution and in such a manner as shall not cause annoyance to the occupants of any other vessel or cause damage or danger to any other vessel or to any moorings or other property.

Conduct within the Dockyard Port

12.   The master of a vessel shall not navigate within the Dockyard Port when unfit by reason of drink or drugs to do so.

Vessels Passing Within the Narrow Channels of the Dockyard Port

13.   Notwithstanding Rule 4, when two power-driven vessels proceeding in opposite directions are about to meet one another in any narrow channel of the Dockyard Port, the power-driven vessel navigating against the tidal stream shall give priority of passage through such narrow channel to the vessel navigating with the tidal stream by easing her engines and waiting until the vessel navigating with the tidal stream shall have passed clear.

Vessel Turning Round

14.   Within the limits of the Dockyard Port, a power-driven vessel under way which is about to turn round shall sound five short blasts of the whistle in rapid succession, followed after a short interval by-

(a) one short blast if turning with her head to starboard;

(b) two short blasts if with her head to port.

Signal directing vessels and boats to keep out of the way

15.   If any power-driven vessel underway within the limits of the Dockyard Port is at risk of colliding with any other vessel, she shall sound one prolonged blast followed by two short blasts on the whistle, and all other vessels shall take all reasonable steps to keep out of the way.

Special Sound Signals for Vessels leaving Millbay Docks

16.   All vessels over 60 metres in length, shall when leaving Millbay Docks and prior to entering the main channel, sound one prolonged blast, in accordance with Rule 34*(e)* of the Collision Regulations.

Marking of Wrecks and Submerged Obstructions

17.   Should a vessel sink, be stranded, or become a wreck in any part of the Dockyard Port so that an obstruction is caused, or is likely to be caused, the master or owner of such vessel shall immediately notify the Queen's Harbour Master.

Diving Signals

18. (1) If the size or construction of a craft or vessel engaged in diving operations makes it impracticable to exhibit the shapes prescribed in Rule 27 (d) of the Collision Regulations, a rigid replica of the International Code flag "A" not less than 600 millimetres in height shall be exhibited and measures taken to ensure all-round visibility, such replica to be illuminated between sunset and sunrise on the approach of other vessels.

(2) Free swimming divers are to be marked by short-scope orange marker buoys, such buoys to be lit between sunset and sunrise with a white or amber light.

Blue flashing lights

19. (1) Vessels of the following organisations are authorised to exhibit a blue flashing light in the course of their duties:

Queen's Harbour Master Plymouth

Ministry of Defence Police

Her Majesty's Customs and Excise

Her Majesty's Coastguard

Devon and Cornwall Constabulary-Marine Police Unit

Devon Fire and Rescue Service-Plymstock Fire boat

The Torpoint Ferry

(2) Save with the licence in writing by the Queen's Harbour Master no other vessel is to exhibit a blue flashing light (of any frequency) on the waters of the Dockyard Port of Portsmouth.

(3) All vessels shall be ready to respond to instructions and requests for assistance from vessels displaying blue flashing lights.

EXPLANATORY NOTE

(This Note is not a part of the Order)

1. This Order is made under the Dockyard Ports Regulations Act 1865, which provides for the defining of the limits of a Dockyard Port, the appointment of a Queen's Harbour Master, the making of regulations to govern the mooring or anchoring of vessels and the making of rules concerning the lights or signals to be carried or used and the steps for avoiding collision by vessels navigating within the Dockyard Port.

2. This Order supersedes the Dockyard Port of Plymouth Order 1984 which it revokes. It provides for–
- (a) an increase in areas in which fishing is prohibited;
- (b) controls on the use of firearms, weapons and explosives;
- (c) revision to arrangements for notification to the Queen's Harbour Master of intentions regarding the arrival and departure of vessels;
- (d) revision to light signals used to control vessel movements;
- (e) pilotage of vessels by qualified Admiralty pilots;
- (f) revision to signals displayed by floating bridges;
- (g) reductions in speed limits in certain areas;
- (h) rules governing personal conduct of masters of vessels;
- (i) controls on swimming;
- (j) rules regarding the use of blue flashing lights.

3. Admiralty charts relating to the Dockyard Port area can be bought from authorised suppliers; details of these suppliers can be obtained from the Hydrographic Office, Taunton.

NOTES

485

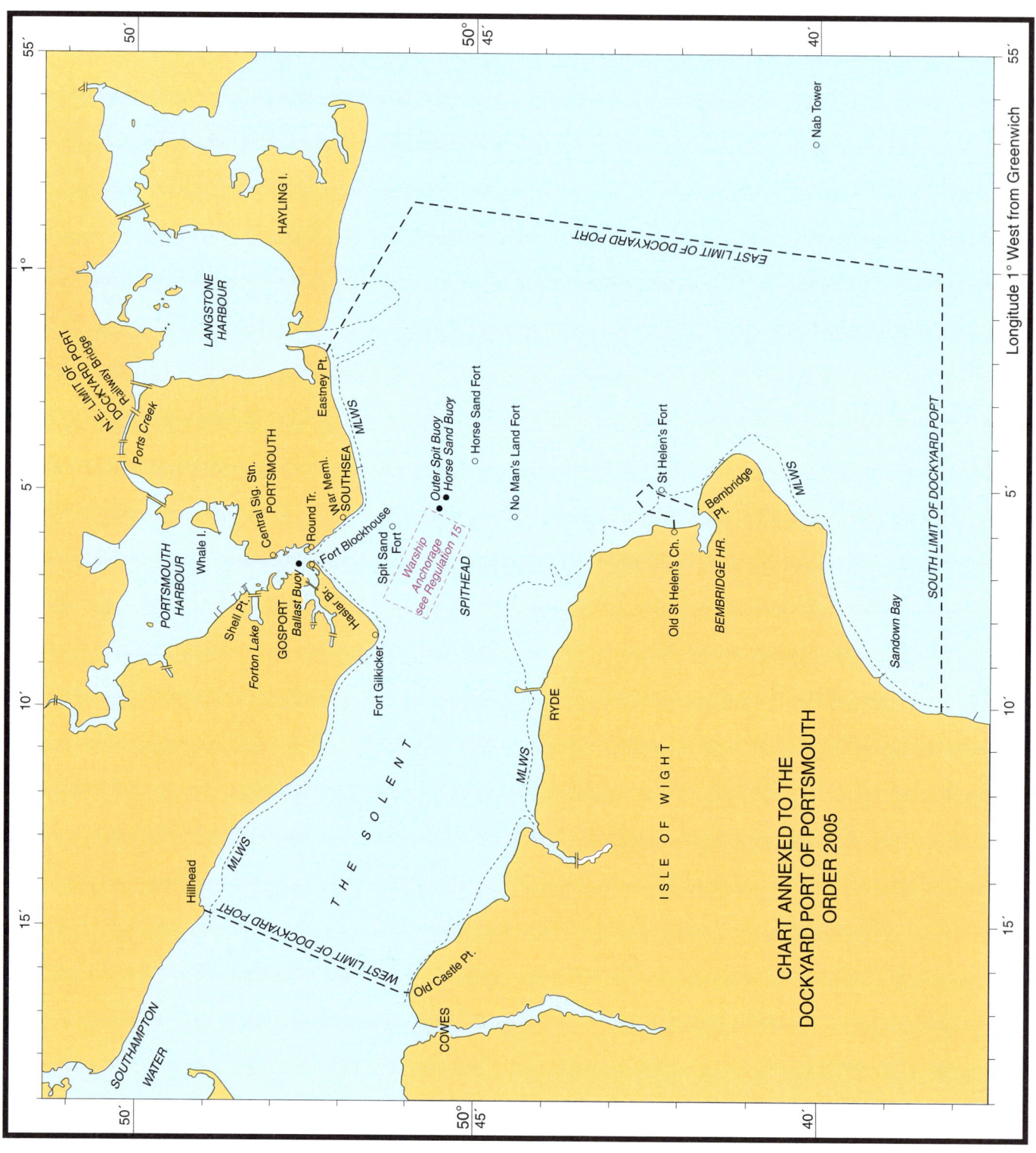

CHART ANNEXED TO THE
DOCKYARD PORT OF PORTSMOUTH
ORDER 2005

Longitude 1° West from Greenwich

EAST LIMIT OF DOCKYARD PORT

SOUTH LIMIT OF DOCKYARD PORT

WEST LIMIT OF DOCKYARD PORT

N.E. LIMIT OF DOCKYARD PORT

Nab Tower

HAYLING I.

LANGSTONE HARBOUR

Ports Creek

Railway Bridge

Eastney Pt.

MLWS

PORTSMOUTH HARBOUR

Whale I.

PORTSMOUTH

Central Sig. Stn.

Round Tr.

War Meml.

SOUTHSEA

Fort Blockhouse

Spit Sand Fort

Horse Sand Fort

No Man's Land Fort

Outer Spit Buoy

Horse Sand Buoy

St Helen's Fort

Old St Helen's Ch.

Bembridge Pt.

BEMBRIDGE HR.

MLWS

Shell Pt.

Forton Lake

GOSPORT

Ballast Buoy

Haslar Br.

Fort Gilkicker

Warship
Anchorage
see Regulation 15

SPITHEAD

THE SOLENT

RYDE

MLWS

ISLE OF WIGHT

Sandown Bay

Hillhead

MLWS

Old Castle Pt.

COWES

SOUTHAMPTON WATER

486

The Dockyard Port of Portsmouth Order, 2005

(extracts only)

Delineation of Limits
4. The limits of the Dockyard Port of Portsmouth are drawn on the chart annexed to this Order.

Regulations and Rules
5. The Regulations contained in Schedule 1 and the Rules contained in Schedule 2 shall operate within the limits (as described in Article 3) of the Dockyard Port and if any inconsistency shall arise between the said Rules and the Collision Regulations, the said Rules shall prevail.

SCHEDULE 1
REGULATIONS

General
1. (1) The Master of every vessel and every other person within the limits of the Dockyard Port shall comply with any specific or general direction given by the Queen's Harbour Master for the purposes of the proper protection of the Dockyard Port, Her Majesty's vessels, dockyards or property, or for the requirements of Her Majesty's Naval service.

(2) The Master of every vessel and every other person within the limits of the Dockyard Port to whom any licence or permission has been granted by the Queens's Harbour Master in accordance with the provisions of the Act, these Regulations or the Rules contained in Schedule 2, shall comply with any directions or conditions attached to them.

(3) The Queens's Harbour Master may attach such directions or conditions to any such licence or permission as he considers necessary.

Moorings for Her Majesty's Ships, etc.
2. Moorings for Her Majesty's vessels, buoys, lights, marks, marker buoys, and other aids to navigation, and such other buoys as may be required for any purpose in connection with naval, military or air force operations, may be placed by the Queen's Harbour Master in such positions as may be considered necessary for the requirements of Her Majesty's service.

Merchant or Private Moorings
3. (1) No person shall lay moorings for any merchant or private vessel, hulk, raft, pontoon, bathing stage, house boat, timber or any floating structure in the Dockyard Port, save with the permission of the the Queen's Harbour Master.

(2) All such moorings shall be in such positions as the Queen's Harbour Master shall deem fit.

(3) Any such moorings anywhere in the Dockyard Port shall be removed forthwith on the specific direction of the Queen's Harbour Master.

Clearing Anchors and Moorings
4. If at any time the anchor of any vessel hooks any Crown moorings, or any under-sea cable, or moorings of buoys, or any pipe, the Master of such vessel shall forthwith give notice thereof to the Queen's Harbour Master and shall, if it is safe and practicable, await his direction before proceeding to clear the same.

Anchoring and Mooring — General

5. No vessel shall anchor on the line of any under-sea cable or pipe laid down in the Dockyard Port when such a line is indicated by posts or other discernible marks on shore or is shown for the time being on Admiralty charts as an area in which anchorage is prohibited except with the permission of the Queen's Harbour Master.

6. No vessel, or barge, hulk, raft, pontoon or other floating structure shall:
(a) make fast to, or lie at, any of the buoys or beacons placed by the Queen's Harbour Master to mark channels or shoals in the Dockyard Port;
(b) be moored or fastened to any of Her Majesty's naval moorings, buoys, breakwaters, boom defences, dolphins, jetties, piles or vessels in the Dockyard Port, save with the permission of the Queen's Harbour Master;
(c) be moored or except in an emergency anchored within 100 metres of any of Her Majesty's naval jetties, floating docks, dolphins, vessels, hulks, installations or armaments depots, or within 150 metres of the centre of any naval moorings, save with the permission of the Queen's Harbour Master;
(d) lie or be moored so as to impede the free approach to any pier in the Dockyard Port used for the purposes of regular passenger traffic, or when buoys are placed by the Queen's Harbour Master to mark an approach to such pier, lie within the space so marked;
(e) lie or be moored, anchored, grounded, deposited or run on shore in the fairways of the channels of the Harbour, the main navigable channels or the approach channel; or
(f) except in an emergency drop anchor in water of greater than 10 metres in depth save with permission of the Queen's Harbour Master.

Vessels at anchor
7. No vessel of an overall length of 20 metres or more, compelled or allowed to anchor in or near any of the navigable channels of the Dockyard Port, shall be left at any time without a person having command or charge of it.

Fishing

8. (1) Any person fishing in the Dockyard Port is required to comply with any directions given to him by the Queen's Harbour Master.
   (2) No fishing from any vessel or by persons swimming under water shall be carried on within the limits of the Dockyard Port either within:
       (a) 100 metres of the walls, slipways or boundaries of any Crown Establishment;
       (b) 150 metres of any of Her Majesty's vessels, save with the licence in writing of the Queen's Harbour Master.
   (3) No fishing shall at any time be carried out either within:
       (a) the approach channel; or
       (b) the main navigable channels.
   (4) The us of any form of static fishing gear is prohibited in:
       (a) Fareham Creek, as far as Town Quay;
       (b) Portchester Lake;
       (c) the Approaches to Port Solent;
       (d) Tipner Lake;
       (e) Haslar Creek;
       (f) Weevil Lake;
       (g) Brick Kiln Lake; and
       (h) Wootton Creek.
   (5) South of the Harbour entrance in any area not shown on Admiralty Charts as an area within which fishing is prohibited, unattended fishing gear in respect of which a surface mark is employed must show a dan buoy or container with flag, which must be fitted with a radar reflector and have the identity of the laying vessel clearly displayed.
   (6) All lines used in connection with lobster, whelk or crab pots or similar devises shall be non-buoyant.
   (7) No fishing of any description shall be carried on in any area for the time being shown on Admiralty charts as an area within which fishing is prohibited.
   (8) No person shall store live fish or shellfish within the waters of the Dockyard Port save with the licence in writing of the Queen's Harbour Master.

Underwater Swimming and Diving

9. Save with the permission of the Queen's Harbour Master, no person who is wearing or equipped with clothing or apparatus designed or adapted for swimming underwater or diving shall swim underwater or dive or fish:
       (a) within the Harbour or in any of the creeks or lakes adjoining the Harbour; or
       (b) elsewhere in the Dockyard Port:
           (i) within 100 metres of the walls, slipways, or boundaries of a Crown Establishment;
           (ii) within 150 metres of any of Her Majesty's vessels; or
           (iii) where anchorage is prohibited.

Swimming

10. Save with the permission of the Queen's Harbour Master or, in the case of paragraph (c), in an area from time to time designated for such activity by him, no person shall swim on the surface or underwater within:
        (a) 100 metres of the walls, slipways, or boundaries of a Crown Establishment;
        (b) 150 metres of any of Her Majesty's vessels;
        (c) any area where anchorage is prohibited.

Water-skiing, etc.

11. (1) Save with the licence in writing of the Queen's Harbour Master no water-skiing, jet-skiing or windsurfing is permitted within the harbour.
    (2) No water-skiing or jet-skiing is permitted within the Dockyard Port outside the Harbour except:
        (a) with licence in writing of the Queen's Harbour Master;
        (b) beyond 0·5 of a nautical mile from the line of mean low-water springs; or
        (c) within 0·5 of a nautical mile of the line of mean low-water springs in any area which may be designated for such activity from time to time by the Queen's Harbour Master and marked with buoys.

Parascending and Similar Activities

12. Save with the permission of the Queen's Harbour Master, or in areas designated for such activity from time to time by him and marked with buoys, no person shall engage or take part in parascending or other activity involving the towing of a kite or other thing, from land or water, in such a manner as to cause it to become airborne in any part of the Dockyard Port.

Dumping of Rubbish, etc.

13. No person shall unload, cast or allow to fall:
        (a) into the waters of the Dockyard Port, or
        (b) upon the banks or any portion of the shores of the Dockyard Port where the same may be able to be washed into the waters by rain, tide or otherwise,
any ballast, stones, earth, clay, refuse or any other substance or object which is or might become a hazard to navigation.

Reserved and Recreational Areas.

14. The Secretary of State or the Queen's Harbour Master may, where he considers it necessary to reserve any area for mining, gunnery or dredging operations or experiments, or other naval purposes, or to ensure the safe navigation of vessels both naval and civilian, direct by notice published as a general or local notice to mariners, which shall continue in force until 31 December of the year in which it was issued, unless revoked earlier, that no person shall:

(a)   cause or permit a vessel to enter into or remain in that area, unless compelled to do so by stress of weather or to avoid accident

(b)   enter into or remain in that area, or cause or permit any vessel, animal or thing to enter into or remain in that area, except with the permission of the Queen's Harbour Master or the officer in charge of such operations, experiments or purposes; or

(c)   take part in any recreational activites specified in the notice in such parts of that area as may be so specified, save for the purpose of avoiding danger or accident.

Warship Anchorage

15. (1) No merchant or private vessel shall anchor within the area reserved for warships save with the permission of the Queen's Harbour Master.

(2) The area reserved for warships is bounded by lines joining the following four points designated by bearing and distance from Spit Sand Fort Light:

(a)   276° (true) 1·04 nautical miles,

(b)   154° (true) 0·55 nautical miles,

(c)   182° (true) 1·11 nautical miles,

(d)   249° (true) 1·40 nautical miles.

Firearms, Weapons and Explosives

16. (1) Subject to the exceptions in paragraph (2), within the limits of the Dockyard Port, no gun or explosive shall be carried on board any merchant or private vessel.

(2) The exceptions referred to in paragraph (1) are where:

(a)   the Queen's Harbour Master has given his licence in writing;

(b)   the sole design of the gun or explosive is for the purpose of giving an internationally recognised signal of distress; or

(c)   the sole purpose of the gun is to control water based racing activities and only blank ammunition rounds are fired.

(3) No gun or explosive shall be discharged from any such vessel or from shore over the waters of the Harbour except:

(a)   with the licence in writing of the Queen's Harbour Master;

(b)   as a signal of distress; or

(c)   as a signal in connection with the conduct of such racing activities.

Navigational Marks

17. No person shall trespass on, damage or without authority interfere with any radar head, light, beacon, sea-mark, tideboard, tide gauge, buoy, sign or notice of any description in the Dockyard Port.

Dredging for Lost Objects

18. Save with the licence of the Queen's Harbour Master, no person shall dredge in the Dockyard Port with drags, hooks, nets or other apparatus for property dropped or thrown therein.

SCHEDULE 2
RULES

Port Radio Telephone Communication
1. (1) Save with the permission of the Queen's Harbour Master, all vessels of an overall length of 20 metres or more, and, when engaged in any type of commercial activity, small boats navigating within the Dockyard Port shall carry fixed or portable VHF radiotelephony equipment.

(2) The Queen's Harbour Master from time to time may by notice published as a general or local notice to mariners direct that the provisions of Rule 1(1) be extended to small boats when necessary for safety within the Dockyard Port.

(3) Port radio telephone communications shall be conducted in accordance with any direction issued by the Queen's Harbour Master from time to time.

Vessels not to approach Vessels carrying Royal or other Standard at Masthead
2. No vessel when underway in the waters of the Dockyard Port outside the Harbour, shall unnecessarily approach within 400 metres of any vessel carrying the Royal or any other Standard at the Masthead.

Vessels constrained by their draught
3. (1) Subject to paragraph (2), within the limits of the Dockyard Port vessels constrained by their draught (as defined in the Collision Regulations) shall show the signals laid down for such vessels in the Collision Regulations .

(2) A submarine navigating on the surface within the Dockyard Port shall be deemed to be a vessel constrained by its draught but shall not be required to show such signals.

Shipping Movement Control
4. (1) Vessels restricted in their ability to manoeuvre and vessels constrained by their draught, as defined within the meaning of the Collision Regulations shall not operate in the Dockyard Port without the permission of the Queen's Harbour Master.

(2) Vessels of 20 metres or more in overall length shall:
(a) enter or leave the Harbour only under the direction of the Queen's Harbour Master.
(b) obtain permission from the Queen's Harbour Master to sail or move within the Harbour before leaving their mooring or berth or weighing anchor; and
(c) when inward bound obtain permission from the Queen's Harbour Master to enter the Harbour before passing the Saddle Buoy or entering the Swashway across Spit sand.

(3) No vessel shall, without the permission of the Queen's Harbour Master, navigate:
(a) save as provided for in sub-paragraph (c) below, within 50 metres of any of Her Majesty's vessels or foreign warships or auxiliaries alongside any Crown Establishment or which is at anchor, a buoy or a mooring within the Dockyard Port;
(b) within 50 metres of the walls, slipways and boundaries of any Crown Establishment; or
(c) within 100 metres of any submarine alongside in any Crown Establishment or which is at anchor, a buoy or a mooring within the Dockyard Port.

Exclusion Zones
5. (1) The Queen's Harbour Master, on any occasion when it is necessary to facilitate or ensure a clear passage for any of Her Majesty's vessels or vessels under the charge of Her Majesty's Officers in the Dockyard Port may direct immediately before and once she becomes underway that there be an exclusion zone of up to 250 metres radius in the water around the vessel,

(2) The vessel which is to be given clear passage shall display:
(a) (by day) two diamond shapes vertically disposed where best seen; or
(b) (by night) two flashing red lights at the masthead horizontally disposed.

(3) Where a direction specified in paragraph (1) above has been given and whilst the shapes or light signals specified in paragraph (2) above are displayed:
(a) no vessel underway in the Dockyard Port, save any vessel authorised to escort the vessel to be given clear passage, shall enter the exclusion zone; and
(b) vessels alongside, at anchor, at a buoy or at a mooring within the exclusion zone shall remain in such a position whilst the exclusion zone remains in force.

(4) The exclusion zone shall remain in force until either:
(a) the vessel which is to be given clear pasage leaves the limits of the Dockyard Port; or
(b) the The Queen's Harbour Master countermands the direction which promulgated the zone.

(5) A direction shall be given and countermanded using VHF Channel 11 or 13 and where practicable by the movements signal.

Temporary restrictions on movements within the Dockyard Port
6. (1) The Queen's Harbour Master shall when necessary make arrangements for the safe passage of vessels in accordance with the following subsections of this Rule.

(2) Such arrangements may include a Harbour closure (which may include closure of an area of the Harbour specified by the Queen's Harbour Master) or a channel closure.

(3) A closure will be promulgated using VHF Radio Channel 11 or 13 and where practicable by the movements signal.

(4) When a harbour closure is in force no vessel of any description may move in or enter the Harbour or area of the Harbour specified by the the Queen's Harbour Master save under direction given by the Queen's Harbour Master.

(5) A channel closure may be promulgated by the Queen's Harbour Master in respect of the approach channel and the main navigable channels in relation to a vessel which the Queen's Harbour Master determines requires a clear passage.

(6) Each of the following channel closures promulgated for a vessel movement shall have the effect ascribed to it:

(a) Channel closure for inbound and outbound vessels.	No vessel other than one in whose favour the channel is closed shall enter the approach channel or the main navigable channels of the Harbour.
(b) Channel closure for inbound vessels.	No vessel other than the one in whose favour the channel is closed shall enter the approach channel or the main navigable channels of the Harbour from seaward, but outgoing vessels from Portsmouth may proceed.
(c) Channel closure for outbound vessels.	No vessel other than the one in whose favour the channel is closed shall leave the Harbour but incoming vessels may use the approach channel or the main navigable channels of the Harbour in order to enter the harbour.

(7) The vessel which is to be given a clear passage and any tugs in attendance on such vessel shall display the International Code Pennant superior to Pennant ZERO by day (no signal being displayed at night) while underway in the area.

(8) Notwithstanding a channel closure being in force, small boats may continue to operate provided they do so with caution and that they do not impede the safe passage of the vessel for which the channel closure is implemented.

Small Boats in the Harbour

7. Power-driven small boats and all cross harbour ferries shall, when inside the Harbour, keep out of the way of all seagoing vessels, Isle of Wight car and passenger ferries and tugs conducting towing operations.

Speed of Vessels navigating the Dockyard Port

8. (1) All vessels shall comply with any direction which the Queen's Harbour Master may issue for speed limits from time to time and which may be published in a general or local notice to mariners.

(2) Subject to paragraph (1) above, no vessel, when navigating within the Harbour or (except for water-skiiers and jet-skiiers in an area for the time being designated by the the Queen's Harbour Master and marked by buoys) when within 0·5 nautical miles. of the line of mean low-water springs in any part of the Dockyard Port outside the Harbour shall proceed at a greater speed than 10 knots through the water save for the purpose and subject to the conditions specified in a licence in writing given by the Queen's Harbour Master.

Vessels to be navigated with care and caution

9. The master of a vessel navigating the Dockyard Port shall navigate the vessel with care and caution and in such a manner as shall not cause annoyance to the occupants of any other vessel or cause damage or danger to any other vessel or to any moorings or other property.

Navigation in the Harbour Entrance and Small Boat Channel

10. (1) Small boats flying official flags or discs which are pilot boats, police launches, HM Customs and Excise craft, Her Majesty's vessels or Royal Maritime Auxiliary Service craft, and tugs engaged in towing operations or escorting a vessel under instruction from a pilot, may use the approach channel and the main navigable channels of the Harbour when the exercise of their duties requires it.

(2) Subject to paragraph (1), small boats must:

(a) use the designated Small Boat Channel when entering or leaving the Harbour;

(b) if fitted with an engine, use it when in the Small Boat Channel and when crossing between Ballast and Gunwharf Quays or the Town Camber;

(c) not loiter in the Small Boat Channel;

(d) obey any directions in respect of traffic separation which the Queen's Harbour Master may from time to time issue by local or general notice to mariners in respect of the entrance to the Swashway and Inner Swashway; and

(e) not, without permission of the Queen's Harbour Master, cross the harbour between Ballast and Gunwharf Quays or the Town Camber.

Movements of Vessels in the Harbour and its approach channel during poor visibility

11. (1) At any time when the visibility in the Harbour or approach channel is less than 0·25 of a nautical mile the Queen's Harbour Master may declare fog routine to be in force. Whilst the routine is in force no vessel of an overall length of more than 20 metres shall enter the Harbour or approach channel or leave her berth or mooring therein or weigh anchor, except with the permission of the Queen's Harbour Master.

(2) Small boats may proceed at the Master's discretion with caution and must keep clear of the main navigable channels and the approach channel.

(3) The Queen's Harbour Master will direct that the routine is in force and when it has ended by broadcasts on VHF radio Channels 11 or 13.

[a] 1865 (c. 125); section 6 was amended by Schedule 3 to the Criminal Justice Act 1967 (c. 80) and sections 40 and 46 of the Criminal Justice Act 1982 (c. 48) and Part 1 of Schedule 1 to the Statute Law (Repeals) Act 1993 (c 50); section 7 was amended by sections 1(1)(a),1(2),3(2) and 3(6) of the Defence (Transfer of functions) Act 1964 (c 15) and Part XIII of Schedule 1 to the Statute Law (Repeals) Act 1986 (c 12).

[b] The function under the said section 7 of the Board of Trade is now vested in the Secretary of State for Transport by virtue of section 2(1) (repealed) of the Ministry of Transport Act 1919 (c 50), S.R. & O. 1919/1440, S.I. 1965/145, S.I. 1970/1537, S.I. 1974/692, S.I. 1983/1127, S.I. 1997/2971, S.I. 2001/2568, and S.I. 2002/2626.

[c] S.I. 1996/75, amended by S.I. 2004/302.

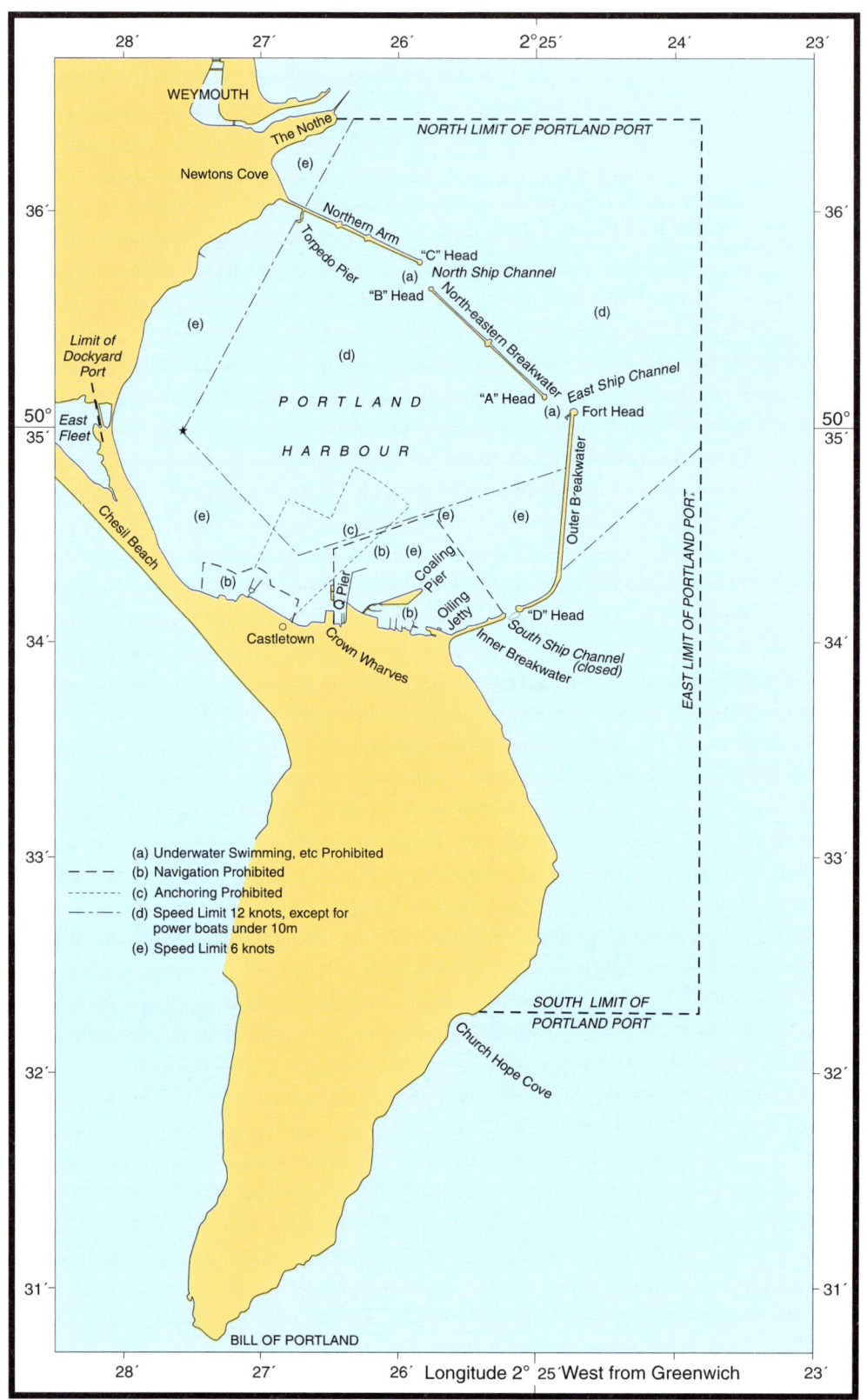

28′ 27′ 26′ 2°25′ 24′ 23′

WEYMOUTH

The Nothe

NORTH LIMIT OF PORTLAND PORT

(e)

Newtons Cove

36′

Northern Arm

"C" Head

North Ship Channel

Torpedo Pier

(a)

(d)

"B" Head

North-eastern Breakwater

(e)

(d)

East Ship Channel

Limit of
Dockyard
Port

"A" Head

(a) Fort Head

50°
35′

East
Fleet

P O R T L A N D

H A R B O U R

Outer Breakwater

50°
35′

EAST LIMIT OF PORTLAND PORT

(e)

(e)

(e)

Chesil Beach

(c)

(b) (e)

Coaling
Pier

(b)

Q Pier

Oiling
Jetty

(b)

"D" Head

Castletown

Crown Wharves

Inner Breakwater

*South Ship Channel
(closed)*

34′

34′

33′

(a) Underwater Swimming, etc Prohibited
(b) Navigation Prohibited
(c) Anchoring Prohibited
(d) Speed Limit 12 knots, except for
     power boats under 10m
(e) Speed Limit 6 knots

33′

*SOUTH LIMIT OF
PORTLAND PORT*

32′

Church Hope Cove

32′

31′

31′

BILL OF PORTLAND

28′ 27′ 26′ Longitude 2° 25′West from Greenwich 23′

APPENDIX II
The Portland Harbour Revision Order 1997
(extracts only)
PART I
PRELIMINARY

Interpretation
    2.   (1) In this Order:-
"the harbour" means so much of the sea to the South of Weymouth Bay below the level of high water as is within the following imaginary straight lines:-

    (a) a line drawn east (true) from a point at Latitude 50° 36'·42N, Longitude 02° 26'·50W (the Nothe Point, Weymouth) to a point at Latitude 50° 36'·42N, Longitude 02° 23'·84W, being coterminous with the southern limit of Weymouth Harbour;

    (b) a line drawn south (true) from that point to a point at Latitude 50° 32'·28N, Longitude 02° 23'·84W;

    (c) a line drawn west (true) from that point to a point at Latitude 50° 32'·28N, Longitude 02° 25'·45W (the north point of Church Ope Cove); and

    (d) a line drawn across New Channel at its entrance to East Fleet coterminous with the western side of Ferry Bridge;

"the inner harbour" means that part of the harbour which is enclosed by the breakwaters, and includes the breakwaters;

"the main fairways" means-

    (a) a fairway known as the North Ship Channel, being an area seaward from the entrance to the inner harbour between two lines of true bearing 036° from "C" Head Light and 090° from "B" Head Light to a distance of 600 metres and inward from the entrance to the inner harbour between two lines of true bearing 260° from "C" Head Light and 210° from "B" Head Light to a distance of 600 metres; and

    (b) a fairway known as the East Ship Channel, being an area seaward from the entrance to the inner harbour between two lines of true bearing 015° from "A" Head Light and 090° from Fort Head Light to a distance of 600 metres and inward from the entrance to the inner harbour between a line of true bearing 270° from "A" Head Light and the Outer Breakwater to a distance of 600 metres.

SCHEDULE 1 Article 15
REGULATION OF THE HARBOUR AND THE HARBOUR PREMISES

(extracts only)
PART I: PRELIMINARY
Interpretation

1. In this Schedule—
"Beacon E" means the point on the Outer Breakwater at Latitude 50° 34'·8N, Longitude 002° 24'·8W;
"the Collision Regulations" means regulations for the prevention of collisions made under sections 85 and 86 of the Merchant Shipping Act 1995;
"the controlled area" means the area of water within the inner harbour bounded by the following imaginary line—

    (a) drawn 325° (true) for 1,050 metres from the eastern extremity of the Inner Breakwater;

    (b) then drawn 251° (true) for 900 metres;

    (c) then drawn 180° (true) to the north-east corner of the Phoenix Pier;

    (d) then drawn from the south-east corner of the Phoenix Pier 150° (true) for 280 metres to the western dolphin off Castletown Slipway;

    (e) then drawn to the western edge of Castletown Slipway at the level of high water;

"fairway" means either of the main fairways or any other area designated as a fairway by the Company in a general direction;
"power-driven vessel" includes any vessel propelled by machinery.

PART II: NAVIGATION

Vessel movements

3. The master of a vessel other than a small vessel shall give prior notice to the harbour master or his agent of the vessel's arrival at, departure from or movement within, the harbour.

Declaration of particulars of vessel

4. The master of a vessel arriving at the harbour shall, if required by the harbour master, furnish to him a declaration in the form to be obtained from him containing a correct statement of the tonnage and draught of the vessel, its last port of call, name and address of owner, destination, and particulars of any cargo and passengers.

Vessels to be navigated with care and caution

5. The master of a vessel navigating in the harbour shall navigate the vessel with such care and caution and at such speed and in such manner as not to endanger the lives of, or cause injury to, persons or damage to property and as not to obstruct or prejudice the navigation, manoeuvring, loading or discharging of vessels or cause unnecessary damage to moorings, the banks of the harbour or other property.

Speed of vessels

6. (1) Subject to sub-paragraph (2) below, the master of a power-driven vessel other than a power boat shall not, except and in accordance with the prior permission in writing of the harbour master, cause or permit the vessel to proceed at a speed greater than 12 knots through the water when navigating—
   (a) within the inner harbour; and
   (b) in the approaches thereto north of a line drawn 048° (true) from "D" Head.
   (2) The master of a power-driven vessel shall not, except and in accordance with the prior permission in writing of the harbour master, cause or permit the vessel to proceed at a speed greater than 6 knots through the water in the following areas—
   (a) in Newton's Cove, west of a line drawn 026° (true) from Torpedo Pier Light to the northern limit of the harbour;
   (b) within 150 metres of the breakwaters, except as required to pass through the main fairways;
   (c) in the inner harbour—
      (i) west of a line drawn 026° (true) from the light structure (New Channel Beacon) situated at Latitude 50° 34'·87N, Longitude 002° 27'·61W to Torpedo Pier Light;
      (ii) south of a line drawn 119° (true) from New Channel Beacon to the light on the northern corner of Queen's Pier, and
      (iii) south of a line drawn 251° (true) from Beacon E on the Outer Breakwater.
   (3) For the purposes of sub-paragraph (1) above "power boat" means a power-driven vessel of less than 10 metres in length.
   (4) This paragraph is without prejudice to paragraph 5 above and the Collision Regulations.

Small vessels

7. (1) The master of a small vessel which is not confined to a fairway shall not make use of the fairway so as to cause obstruction to other vessels which can navigate only within the fairway; and when navigating across a fairway or through an entrance to the inner harbour, he shall do so by the shortest possible route that will avoid such obstruction.
   (2) The master of a small vessel shall not hamper the safe passage of any vessel greater than 20 metres in length which is in, entering or leaving a fairway or which is under way within the inner harbour.

Outgoing vessels to have priority

8. Subject to paragraph 7(2) above, outgoing vessels shall have priority of passage in the main fairways over incoming vessels, and no vessel proceeding inward shall enter either of the main fairways until any vessel proceeding outwards through that fairway has passed out.

Prohibition on navigation

13. Except with the prior permission of the harbour master, no vessel shall enter, or navigate within, the controlled area.

Anchorage

15. (1) No vessel shall anchor—
   (a) within 100 metres of the line of any cable or pipe laid down in the harbour, when such line is indicated by posts or other discernible marks on shore, in a general direction or on the Admiralty Charts; or
   (b) within 150 metres of any breakwater.
   (2) Without prejudice to sub-paragraph (1) above, if at any time the anchor of any vessel hooks any moorings, electric cable, moorings of buoys, or any pipe, the master of the vessel shall forthwith give notice thereof to the harbour master and shall, if it is safe and practicable, await his instruction before proceeding to clear the same.

Obstruction of main fairways

16. Except with the permission of the harbour master, no vessel shall lie or be moored, anchored, grounded, deposited or run ashore in the main fairways.

PART V: GENERAL

Fishing

43. (1) Any person fishing in the harbour shall comply with directions given to him by the harbour master.

(2) Subject to sub-paragraphs (4) and (5) below, no person shall fish—

   (a) in the main fairways;

   (b) in the controlled area;

   (c) within 150 metres of the harbour premises;

   (d) by trawl, nets or dredges within 100 metres of the line of any cable or pipe laid down in the harbour; and

   (e) with surface nets in the inner harbour, except with the written permission of the harbour master.

(3) No person shall fish in Newton's Cove—

   (a) by trawl or dredges, west of a line drawn due north from "C" Head to the northern limit of the harbour; or

   (b) by nets west of a line drawn 026° (true) from Torpedo Pier Light to the northern limit of the harbour.

Diving and underwater swimming

49. (1) Subject to sub-paragraph (2) below, no person, other than a duly authorised employee, contractor or agent of the Company, shall swim underwater or dive in the areas specified in paragraph 43(2)(a), (b) and (c) above.

(2) With the written permission of the Company a person may dive and swim underwater -

   (a) seawards from the seaward side of the Inner Breakwater (including the South Ship Channel entrance);

   (b) seawards from the seaward side of the Outer Breakwater but remaining clear of the main fairway concerned;

   (c) within 50 metres of the landward side of the Outer Breakwater but remaining clear of the main fairway concerned for the purpose of diving on the wreck adjacent to Beacon E, commonly known as the "Enecuri" or "Spaniard"; and

   (d) on the wrecks along the landward side of the Outer Breakwater between Beacon E and "D" Head.

SCHEDULE 2 Article 6
PROTECTIVE PROVISIONS
PART I: DEFENCE EVALUATION AND RESEARCH AGENCY
(SEA SYSTEMS SECTOR)

Interpretation

1. In this Part of this Schedule—

   (a) "the Acoustic Range Building" means the building located on the seaward side of the Northern Arm at Latitude 50° 35'·97N, Longitude 002° 26'·6W (150 metres north-west of the Vernon Building);

   (b) "the Distant Range Building" is the building on and co-located with the Torpedo Firing Point on the North-eastern Breakwater at Latitude 50° 35'·39N, Longitude 002° 25'·36W;

   (c) "the Short Range Building" is the building situated on Torpedo Pier on the Northern Arm;

   (d) "the Vernon Building" (formerly the Admiralty Magnetic and Calibration Station) means that building located on the Northern Arm at Latitude 50° 35'·93N, Longitude 002° 26'·48W;

   (e) "the Vernon Building Jetty" means the jetty on the seaward side of the Northern Arm adjacent to the Vernon Building; and

   (f) "the Vernon Landing Stage" means the landing Stage on the landward side of the Northern Arm adjacent to the Vernon Building.

Fishing, anchoring and mooring

2. (1) Subject to sub-paragraph (2) below, no person shall fish, anchor or moor within—

   (a) 350 metres of the landward side of the Northern Arm between the Vernon Landing Stage and Torpedo Pier;

   (b) 250 metres of that side of the Northern Arm between Torpedo Pier and the level of high water at the Northern Arm's landward end;

   (c) 150 metres to seaward of the Vernon Building Jetty;

   (d) the acoustic range area, being a rectangular area extending 25 metres each side of the Acoustic Range Building and extending 150 metres to seaward of the Northern Arm; and

   (e) 150 metres of the Distant Range Building.

Diving and underwater swimming

3. (1) Subject to sub-paragraph (2) below, no person shall swim underwater or dive within—

   (a) 150 metres of the North-eastern Breakwater;

   (b) 150 metres of the seaward side of the Northern Arm;

   (c) 150 metres of the landward side of the Northern Arm between "C" Head and the Vernon Landing Stage; and

   (d) the areas specified in sub-paragraphs 1 (a) and I (b) of paragraph 2 above.

(2) With the permission of the Company (which shall not be given without the written consent of the Secretary of State for Defence) a person may dive and swim underwater—

   (a) from either side of the North-eastern Breakwater but remaining clear of the main fairways and not within 150 metres of the Distant Range Building; and

   (b) from either side of the Northern Arm from "C" Head to a point 150 metres south-east of the Vernon Building, but remaining clear of the main fairway concerned.

PART II: DEFENCE EVALUATION AND RESEARCH AGENCY

(TEST AND EVALUATION RANGES SECTOR)

Interpretation

4. In this Part of this Schedule—
    (a) "the Grove Point Building" means the building co-located with the Coastguard Building located at Latitude 50° 32'·9N, Longitude 002° 25'·1W; and
    (b) "the Vernon Building" has the same meaning as in Part I of this Schedule.

Fishing, anchoring and mooring

5. (1) Subject to sub-paragraph (5) below, no person shall fish, anchor or moor—
    (a) within that part of an imaginary rectangle constructed 150 metres from the centre of the outer buoys marking the fixed degaussing range situated at or near a point at Latitude 50° 36'·3N, Longitude 002° 26'·12W as lies inside the harbour, and within a similar rectangle from the centre of the outer buoys marking the mobile degaussing range that may from time to time be situated at or near a point at Latitude 50° 36'·28N, Longitude 002° 24'·8W;
    (b) within the area used as a noise range bounded by the points at—
        (i) Latitude 50° 34' N, Longitude 002° 24'·4W;
        (ii) Latitude 50° 34' N, Longitude 002° 24'·0W;
        (iii) Latitude 50° 33'·6N, Longitude 002° 24'·0W; and
        (iv) Latitude 50° 33'·6N, Longitude 002° 24'·4W;
    (c) within 100 metres of any cables serving the ranges specified in this sub-paragraph; and
    (d) in any part of the harbour when it would obstruct vessels exhibiting International Code "PP" at the yardarm when making degaussing or noise range runs over the ranges and areas specified in this sub-paragraph.
    (2) No person shall fish by nets, anchor or moor in Newton's Cove west of a line drawn due north from "C" Head to the northern limit of the harbour when the fixed degaussing range specified in sub-paragraph (1)(a) above is in use, as indicated by an orange flag flying from the Vernon Building.
    (3) Subject to sub-paragraph (5) below, no person shall fish by trawl, nets or dredges, anchor or moor within the area of water bounded by the following imaginary lines—
    (a) a line drawn from a point at Latitude 50° 36'·42N, Longitude 002° 25'·2W, to a point at Latitude 50° 36'·42N, Longitude 002° 24'·5W ("point A");
    (b) a line drawn from point A to a point at Latitude 50° 36'·00N, Longitude 002° 24'·5W ("point B"); and
    (c) a line drawn from point B to a point at Latitude 50° 36'·00N, Longitude 002° 25'·2W, when the mobile degaussing range specified in sub-paragraph (1)(a) above is being established or is in use, as indicated by an orange flag flying from the Vernon Building.
    (4) No person shall fish, anchor or moor in the area of water bounded by the seaward side of the Outer Breakwater and the Inner Breakwater, the level of high water on the eastern side of the Isle of Portland, and the following imaginary lines—
    (a) a line drawn from Fort Head to a point at Latitude 50° 35'·08N, Longitude 002° 23'·84W (the eastern limit of the harbour);
    (b) a line drawn from that point to a point at Latitude 50° 32'·6N, Longitude 002° 23'·84W; and
    (c) a line drawn from that point to a point on the shore (Durdle Pier) at Latitude 50° 32'·62N, Longitude 002° 24'·97W when the noise range specified in sub-paragraph (1)(b) above is in use, which shall be indicated by an orange flag flying from the Grove Point Building.
    (5) Sub-paragraph (3) above, and the provisions of sub-paragraph (1)(a) above relating to the mobile degaussing range, shall only apply after 24 hours' notice of the establishment of that range has been given by the Company in a general direction.

Diving and underwater swimming

6. (1) Subject to sub-paragraph (2) below, no person shall swim underwater or dive in the ranges and areas specified in paragraph 5(1) above or within 100 metres of any buoys or cables associated with those ranges and areas.
    (2) Sub-paragraph (1) above shall only apply in relation to the mobile degaussing range after notice of the establishment thereof has been given by the Company in accordance with paragraph 5(5) above.

APPENDIX III

THE TERRITORIAL WATERS ORDER IN COUNCIL 1964

AT THE COURT AT BUCKINGHAM PALACE

The 25th day of September 1964

Present,

THE QUEEN'S MOST EXCELLENT MAJESTY IN COUNCIL

Her Majesty, by virtue and in exercise of all the powers enabling Her in that behalf, is pleased, by and with the advice of Her Privy Council, to order, and it is hereby ordered, as follows:

1. This Order may be cited as the Territorial Waters Order in Council 1964 and shall come into operation on 30th September 1964.

2. (1) Except as otherwise provided in Articles 3 and 4 of this Order, the baseline from which the breadth of the territorial sea adjacent to the United Kingdom, the Channel Islands and the Isle of Man is measured shall be low-water line along the coast, including the coast of all islands comprised in those territories.

(2) For the purpose of this Article a low-tide elevation which lies wholly or partly within the breadth of sea which would be territorial sea if all low-tide elevations were disregarded for the purpose of the measurement of the breadth thereof and if Article 3 of this Order were omitted shall be treated as an island.

3. (1) The baseline from which the breadth of the territorial sea is measured between Cape Wrath and the Mull of Kintyre shall consist of the series of straight lines drawn so as to join successively, in the order in which they are there set out, the points identified by the co-ordinates of latitude and longitude in the first column of the Schedule to this Order, each being a point situate on low-water line and on or adjacent to the feature, if any, named in the second column of that Schedule opposite to the co-ordinates of latitude and longitude of the point in the first column.

(2) The provisions of paragraph (1) of this Article shall be without prejudice to the operation of Article 2 of this Order in relation to any island or low-tide elevation which for the purpose of that Article is treated as if it were an island, being an island or low-tide elevation which lies to seaward of the baseline specified in paragraph (1) of this Article.

4. In the case of the sea adjacent to a bay, the baseline from which the breadth of the territorial sea is measured shall, subject to the provisions of Article 3 of this Order-

(a) if the bay has only one mouth and the distance between the low-water lines of the natural entrance points of the bay does not exceed 24 miles, be a straight line joining the said low-water lines;

(b) if, because of the presence of islands, the bay has more than one mouth and the distances between the low-water lines of the natural entrance points of each mouth added together do not exceed 24 miles, be a series of straight lines across each of the mouths drawn so as to join the said low-water lines;

(c) If neither paragraph (a) nor (b) of this Article applies, be a straight line 24 miles in length drawn from low-water line to low-water line within the bay in such a manner as to enclose the maximum area of water that is possible with a line of that length.

5. (1) In this Order-

the expression "bay" means an indentation of the coast such that its area is not less than that of the semi-circle whose diameter is a line drawn across the mouth of the indentation, and for the purposes of this definition the area of an indentation shall be taken to be the area bounded by low-water line around the shore of the indentation and the straight line joining the low-water lines of its natural entrance points, and where, because of the presence of islands, an indentation has more than one mouth the length of the diameter of the semi-circle referred to shall be the sum of the lengths of the straight lines drawn across each of the mouths, and in calculating the area of an indentation the area of any islands lying within it shall be treated as part of the area of the indentation; the expression "island" means a naturally formed area of land surrounded by water which is above water at mean high-water spring tides; and the expression "low-tide elevation" means a naturally formed area of drying land surrounded by water which is below water at mean high-water spring tides,

(2) For the purpose of this Order, permanent harbour works which form an integral part of a harbour system shall be treated as forming part of the coast.

(3) The Interpretation Act 1889(a) shall apply to the interpretation of this Order as it applies to the interpretation of an Act of Parliament.

6. This Order shall be published in the *London Gazette*, the *Edinburgh Gazette* and the *Belfast Gazette*.

W.G. AGNEW

(a) 52 & 53 Vict.c.63.

EXPLANATORY NOTE

(This note is not part of the Order, but is intended to indicate its general purport)

This Order establishes the baseline from which the breadth of the territorial sea adjacent to the United Kingdom, the Channel Islands and the Isle of Man is measured. This, generally, is low-water line round the coast, including the coast of all islands, but between Cape Wrath and the Mull of Kintyre a series of straight lines joining specified points lying generally on the seaward side of the islands lying off the coast are used, and where there are well defined bays elsewhere lines not exceeding 24 miles in length drawn across the bays are used.

TERRITORIAL SEA ACT 1987

Be it enacted by the Queen's Most Excellent Majesty, by and with the advice and consent of the Lords Spiritual and Temporal, and Commons, in this present Parliament assembled, and by the authority of the same, as follows:

1. (1) Subject to the provisions of this Act-
    (a) the breadth of the territorial sea adjacent to the United Kingdom shall for all purposes be 12 nautical miles; and
    (b) the baselines from which the breadth of that territorial sea is to be measured shall for all purposes be those established by Her Majesty by Order in Council.
  (2) Her Majesty may, for the purpose of implementing any international agreement or otherwise, by Order in Council provide that any part of the territorial sea adjacent to the United Kingdom shall extend to such line other than that provided for by subsection (1) above as may be specified in the Order.
  (3) In any legal proceedings a certificate issued by or under the authority of the Secretary of State stating the location of any baseline established under subsection (1) above shall be conclusive of what is stated in the certificate.
  (4) As from the coming into force of this section the Territorial Waters Order in Council 1964 and the Territorial Waters (Amendment) Order in Council 1979 shall have effect for all purposes as if they were Orders in Council made by virtue of subsection (1)(b) above: and subsection (5) below shall apply to those Orders as it applies to any other instrument.
  (5) Subject to the provisions of this Act, any enactment or instrument which (whether passed or made before or after the coming into force of this section) contains a reference (however worded) to the territorial sea adjacent to, or to any part of, the United Kingdom shall be construed in accordance with this section and with any provision made, or having effect as if made, under this section.
  (6) Without prejudice to the operation of subsection (5) above in relation to a reference to the baselines from which the breadth of the territorial sea adjacent to the United Kingdom is measured, nothing in that subsection shall require any reference in any enactment or instrument to a specified distance to be construed as a reference to a distance equal to the breadth of that territorial sea.
  (7) In this section "nautical miles" means international nautical miles of 1,852 metres.

2. (1) Except in so far as Her Majesty may by Order of Council otherwise provide, nothing in section 1 above shall affect the operation of any enactment contained in a local Act passed before the date on which that section comes into force.
  (2) Nothing in section 1 above, or in any Order in Council under that section or subsection (1) above, shall affect the operation of so much of any enactment passed or instrument made before the date on which that section comes into force as for the time being settles the limits within which any harbour authority or port health authority has jurisdiction or is able to exercise any power.
  (3) Where any area which is not part of the territorial sea adjacent to the United Kingdom becomes part of that sea by virtue of section 1 above or an Order in Council under that section, subsection (2) of section 1 of the Continental Shelf Act 1964 (vesting and exercise of rights with respect to coal) shall continue, on and after the date on which section 1 above of that Order comes into force, to have effect with respect to coal in that area as if the area were not part of the territorial sea.
  (4) Nothing in section 1 above, or in any Order in Council under that section, shall affect-
    (a) any regulations made under section 6 of the Petroleum (Production) Act 1934 before the date on which that section or Order comes into force; or
    (b) any licences granted under the said Act of 1934 before that date or granted on or after that date in pursuance of regulations made under that section before that date.
  (5) In this section-
  "coal" has the same meaning as in the Coal Industry Nationalisation Act 1946;
  "harbour authority" means a harbour authority within the meaning of the Harbours Act 1964 or the Harbours Act (Northern Ireland) 1970; and
  "port health authority" means a port health authority for the purposes of the Public Health (Control of Disease) Act 1984.

3. (1) The enactments mentioned in Schedule 1 to this Act shall have effect with the amendments there specified (being minor amendments and amendments consequential on the provisions of this Act).
  (2) Her Majesty may by Order in Council-
    (a) make, in relation to any enactment passed or instrument made before the date on which section 1 above comes into force, any amendment corresponding to any of those made by Schedule 1 to this Act;

(b) amend subsection (1) of section 36 of the Wildlife and Countryside Act 1981 (marine nature reserves) so as to include such other parts of the territorial sea adjacent to Great Britain as may be specified in the Order in the waters and parts of the sea which, by virtue of paragraph 6 of Schedule 1 to this Act, may be designated under that section;

(c) amend paragraph 1 of Article 20 of the Nature Conservation and Amenity Lands (North Ireland) Order 1985 (marine nature reserves) so as to include such other parts of the territorial sea adjacent to Northern Ireland as may be specified in the Order in the waters and parts of the sea which, by virtue of paragraph 9 of Schedule 1 to this Act, may be designated under that Article.

(3) Her Majesty may by Order in Council make such modifications of the effect of any Order in Council under section 1(7) of the Continental Shelf Act 1964 (designated areas) as appear to Her to be necessary or expedient in consequence of any provision made by or under this Act.

(4) The enactments mentioned in Schedule 2 to this Act are hereby repealed to the extent specified in the third column of that Schedule.

4. (1) This Act may be cited as the Territorial Sea Act 1987.

(2) This Act shall come into force on such day as Her Majesty may by Order in Council appoint, and different days may be so appointed for different provisions and for different purposes.

(3) This Act extends to Northern Ireland.

(4) Her Majesty may by Order in Council direct that any of the provisions of this Act shall extend, with such exceptions, adaptations and modifications (if any) as may be specified in the Order, to any of the Channel Islands or to the Isle of Man.

TERRITORIAL SEA (AMENDMENT) ORDER 1998

For the schedule to the Territorial Waters Order in Council 1964 (**a**) there shall be substituted the schedule set out below:

SCHEDULE

POINTS BETWEEN CAPE WRATH AND LAGGAN JOINED BY GEODESICS TO FORM BASELINES

	Co-ordinates of latitude and longitude of point						Name of feature
	Latitude N			Longitude W			
	°	′	″	°	′	″	
1.	58	37	40	5	00	13	Cape Wrath
2.	58	31	12	6	15	41	Lith Sgeir
3.	58	30	44	6	16	55	Gealltuing
4.	58	29	09	6	20	17	Dell Rock
5.	58	18	28	6	47	45	Tiumpan Head
6.	58	17	36	6	52	43	Màs Sgeir
7.	58	17	09	6	55	20	Old Hill
8.	58	14	30	7	02	06	Gallan Head
9.	58	14	01	7	02	57	Islet SW of Gallen Head
10.	58	10	39	7	06	54	Eilean Molach
11.	57	59	08	7	17	42	Gasker
12.	57	41	19	7	43	13	Haskeir Eagach
13.	57	32	22	7	43	58	Huskeiran
14.	57	14	33	7	27	44	Rubha Ardvule
15.	57	00	50	7	31	42	Greuab Head
16.	56	58	07	7	33	24	Doirlinn Head
17.	56	56	57	7	34	17	Aird a' Chaolais
18.	56	56	05	7	34	55	Biruaslum
19.	56	49	21	7	39	32	Guarsay Mór
20.	56	48	00	7	39	57	Sròn an Dùin
21.	56	47	07	7	39	36	Skate Point
22.	56	19	17	7	07	02	Skerryvore
23.	56	07	58	6	38	00	Dubh Artach
24.	55	41	36	6	32	02	Frenchman's Rocks
25.	55	40	24	6	30	59	Orsay Island
26.	55	35	24	6	20	18	Mull of Oa
27.	55	17	57	5	47	54	Mull of Kintyre
28.	54	58	29	5	11	07	Laggan

The positions of points 1 to 28 are defined by co-ordinates of latitude and longitude on the Ordnance Survey of Great Britain (1936) Datum (OSGB 36).

The Territorial Waters (Amendment) Order 1996 (**b**) is hereby revoked.

N. H. Nicholls
Clerk of the Privy Council

EXPLANATORY NOTE

(This note is not part of the Order)

The Order amends the Schedule to the Territorial Waters Order in Council 1964 by adding a new baseline between Mull of Kintyre and Laggan, as well as making minor changes to points 5, 9 and 22, which result from the publication of a new, larger scale chart of the area.

(a) 1965 III, p.6452A; revised Schedules were substituted by the Territorial Waters (Amendment) Order in Council 1979 and the Territorial Sea (Amendment) Order 1996.

(b) SI 1996/1628

APPENDIX IV

FORMER MINED AREA

An area in which a danger due to mines laid during the war of 1939–1945 still exists. Due to the lapse of time the risk from mines to surface navigation in these areas is considered to be no more than the ordinary hazards of navigation; but a real risk still exists with regard to anchoring, fishing or any form of submarine or seabed activity.

Chart 3668
Approach to Corréjou and Port de Tréssény
An area bounded by the coast, the parallel of 48°40′ N, and the meridians of 4°23′ W and 4°32′ W.

APPENDIX V

TEMPORARY EXPLOSIVES DUMPING GROUNDS IN FRENCH WATERS

Temporary explosives dumping grounds in French waters (Zones de Dépôt d'Explosifs).
Steps to be taken in case of the discovery of suspicious devices:
1. Make all efforts to mark it.
2. Inform the nearest CROSS station or, if this is not possible, the authorities at the nearest harbour.
3. Any vessel having a suspicious device on board, in its nets or in tow, must report as in paragraph 2, must not enter harbour without authorisation of the port authority and must keep clear of other vessels and of the shore.
4. Make all efforts to stand into one of the deposit zones (temporary) listed below. The position in which the device is dumped must be carefully marked, and if this procedure is considered to be dangerous then the vessel must remain in the area until the arrival of the intervention team.

Locality	Area radius	Centred on (approx)
Audierne	200 m	47°59'·0N 4°32'·0W
Île de Sein	200 m	48°03'·0N 4°50'·2W
Morgat/Douarnenez	200 m	48°11'·0N 4°21'·0W
Anse de Dinan	200 m	48°14'·5N 4°35'·4W

Camaret	A rectangular area 1000 m in length and 500 m in width centred on position 48°18'·7N 4°35'·0W off the W coast of Presqu'île de Quelern.

Locality	Area radius	Centred on (approx)
Brest	200 m	48°21'·2N 4°27'·7W
Le Conquet	200 m	48°22'·6N 4°47'·7W
Île Molène	200 m	48°24'·3N 4°55'·8W
Portsall	200 m	48°33'·6N 4°45'·7W
L'Aber Benoit	200 m	48°35'·4N 4°40'·7W
L'Aber Wrac'h	200 m	48°38'·2N 4°36'·9W
Kerlouan	200 m	48°40'·8N 4°26'·4W
Île de Batz	200 m	48°45'·3N 4°03'·3W
Morlaix/Carantec/Roscoff	200 m	48°44'·0N 3°55'·0W
Lannion	200 m	48°45'·0N 3°37'·2W
Perros–Guirec	200 m	48°51'·3N 3°24'·0W
Tréguier	200 m	48°54'·2N 3°08'·9W
Paimpol	200 m	48°50'·0N 2°50'·0W
Saint–Quay–Portrieux	200 m	48°43'·7N 2°38'·5W
Erquy/Saint–Brieuc	200 m	48°38'·8N 2°36'·0W
Cap Fréhel	200 m	48°39'·8N 2°24'·5W
Saint–Jacut/Saint–Cast	200 m	48°40'·5N 2°14'·9W
Saint–Malo	200 m	48°42'·5N 1° 58'·8W
Cancale	200 m	48°42'·9N 1°48'·0W
Granville	200 m	48°48'·9N 1°37'·2W
Cherbourg (heavy devices)	200 m	49°41'·6N 1°38'·2W
Cherbourg (light devices)	200 m	49°40'·0N 1°37'·0W
Barfleur/Saint–Vaast–la–Hougue	200 m	49°34'·1N 1°12'·8W

Locality	Area radius	Centred on (approx)
Grandcamp–Maisy	200 m	49°25'·3N 1°02'·7W
Port-en-Bessin	200 m	49°22'·8N 0°45'·9W
Courseulles-sur-Mer	200 m	49°22'·3N 0°27'·0W
Dives-sur-Mer/Ouistreham	200 m	49°20'·7N 0°09'·4W
Trouville-Deauville	200 m	49°24'·0N 0°01'·1E

Honfleur	Use Trouville-Deauville or Le Havre zone

Le Havre	200 m	49°28'·7N 0°01'·9E

INDEX

Names without a paragraph number are for gazetteer purposes only

NOTES

NOTES

NOTES

NOTES

PUBLICATIONS OF THE
UNITED KINGDOM HYDROGRAPHIC OFFICE

A complete list of Sailing Directions, Charts and other works published by the United Kingdom Hydrographic Office, together with a list of Agents for their sale, is contained in *Catalogue of Admiralty Charts and Publications*, published annually. The list of Admiralty Distributors is also on the UKHO website (www.ukho.gov.uk), or it can be obtained from:

The United Kingdom Hydrographic Office,
Admiralty Way,
Taunton, Somerset
TA1 2DN

Produced in the United Kingdom
by UKHO